DATE DUE

			PRINTED IN U.S.A.

CLASSICAL AND MEDIEVAL LITERATURE CRITICISM

Guide to Gale Literary Criticism Series

For criticism on	Consult these Gale series
Authors now living or who died after December 31, 1959	*CONTEMPORARY LITERARY CRITICISM (CLC)*
Authors who died between 1900 and 1959	*TWENTIETH-CENTURY LITERARY CRITICISM (TCLC)*
Authors who died between 1800 and 1899	*NINETEENTH-CENTURY LITERATURE CRITICISM (NCLC)*
Authors who died between 1400 and 1799	*LITERATURE CRITICISM FROM 1400 TO 1800 (LC)* *SHAKESPEAREAN CRITICISM (SC)*
Authors who died before 1400	*CLASSICAL AND MEDIEVAL LITERATURE CRITICISM (CMLC)*
Black writers of the past two hundred years	*BLACK LITERATURE CRITICISM (BLC)*
Authors of books for children and young adults	*CHILDREN'S LITERATURE REVIEW (CLR)*
Dramatists	*DRAMA CRITICISM (DC)*
Hispanic writers of the late nineteenth and twentieth centuries	*HISPANIC LITERATURE CRITICISM (HLC)*
Native North American writers and orators of the eighteenth, nineteenth, and twentieth centuries	*NATIVE NORTH AMERICAN LITERATURE (NNAL)*
Poets	*POETRY CRITICISM (PC)*
Short story writers	*SHORT STORY CRITICISM (SSC)*
Major authors from the Renaissance to the present	*WORLD LITERATURE CRITICISM, 1500 TO THE PRESENT (WLC)*

ISSN 0896-0011

Volume 16

CLASSICAL

AND MEDIEVAL

LITERATURE

CRITICISM

Excerpts from Criticism of the Works of World
Authors from Classical Antiquity through the
Fourteenth Century, from the First Appraisals
to Current Evaluations

Jelena O. Krstović
Editor

Gale Research

An ITP Information/Reference Group Company

I(T)P
Changing the Way the World Learns

NEW YORK • LONDON • BONN • BOSTON • DETROIT
MADRID • MELBOURNE • MEXICO CITY • PARIS
SINGAPORE • TOKYO • TORONTO • WASHINGTON
ALBANY NY • BELMONT CA • CINCINNATI OH

Contents

Preface   vii

Acknowledgments   xi

Albert the Great 1
  German scientist, philosopher, and theologian

Avicenna 132
  Arabic philosopher

Odyssey 182
  Greek poem

Razón de amor 336
  Spanish poem

Literary Criticism Series Cumulative Author Index   379

Literary Criticism Series Cumulative Topic Index   453

CMLC Cumulative Nationality Index   459

CMLC Cumulative Title Index   461

CMLC Cumulative Critic Index   479

Preface

Since its inception in 1988, *Classical and Medieval Literature Criticism* has been a valuable resource for students and librarians seeking critical commentary on the writers and works of these periods in world history. Major reviewing sources have assessed *CMLC* as "useful" and "extremely convenient," noting that it "adds to our understanding of the rich legacy left by the ancient period and the Middle Ages," and praising its "general excellence in the presentation of an inherently interesting subject." No other single reference source has surveyed the critical reaction to classical and medieval literature as thoroughly as *CMLC*.

Scope of the Series

CMLC is designed to serve as an introduction for students and advanced readers of the works and authors of antiquity through the fourteenth century. The great poets, prose writers, dramatists, and philosophers of this period form the basis of most humanities curricula, so that virtually every student will encounter many of these works during the course of a high school and college education. By organizing and reprinting an enormous amount of commentary written on classical and medieval authors and works, *CMLC* helps students develop valuable insight into literary history, promotes a better understanding of the texts, and sparks ideas for papers and assignments. Each entry in *CMLC* presents a comprehensive survey of an author's career, an individual work of literature, or a literary topic, and provides the user with a multiplicity of interpretations and assessments. Such variety allows students to pursue their own interests; furthermore, it fosters an awareness that literature is dynamic and responsive to many different opinions.

CMLC continues the survey of criticism of world literature begun by Gale's *Contemporary Literary Criticism (CLC)*, *Twentieth-Century Literary Criticism (TCLC)*, *Nineteenth-Century Literature Criticism (NCLC)*, *Literature Criticism from 1400 to 1800 (LC)*, and *Shakespearean Criticism (SC)*. For additional information about these and Gale's other criticism series, users should consult the Guide to Gale Literary Criticism Series preceding the title page in this volume.

Coverage

Each volume of *CMLC* is carefully compiled to present:

- criticism of authors and works which represent a variety of genres, time periods, and nationalities

- both major and lesser-known writers and works of the period (such as non-Western authors and literature, increasingly read by today's students)

- 4-6 authors or works per volume

- individual entries that survey the critical response to each author, work, or topic, including early criticism, later criticism (to represent any rise or decline in the author's reputation), and current retrospective analyses. The length of each author or work entry also indicates relative importance, reflecting the amount of critical attention the author, work, or topic has received from critics writing in English, and from foreign criticism in translation.

An author may appear more than once in the series if his or her writings have been the subject of a substantial amount of criticism; in these instances, specific works or groups of works by the author will be covered in separate entries. For example, Homer will be represented by three entries, one devoted to the *Iliad,* one to the *Odyssey,* and one to the Homeric Hymns.

Starting with Volume 10, *CMLC* will also occasionally include entries devoted to literary topics. For example, *CMLC*-10 focuses on Arthurian Legend and includes general criticism on that subject as well as individual entries on writers or works central to that topic—Chrétien de Troyes, Gottfried von Strassburg, Layamon, and the Alliterative *Morte Arthure.*

Organization of the Book

An author entry consists of the following elements: author heading, biographical and critical introduction, principal English translations or editions, excerpts of criticism (each preceded by a bibliographic citation and an annotation), and a bibliography of further reading.

- The **Author Heading** consists of the author's most commonly used name, followed by birth and death dates. If the entry is devoted to a work, the heading will consist of the most common form of the title in English translation (if applicable), and the original date of composition. Located at the beginning of the introduction are any name or title variations.

- A **Portrait** of the author is included when available. Many entries also feature illustrations of materials pertinent to the author or work, including manuscript pages, book illustrations, and representations of people, places, and events important to a study of the author or work.

- The **Biographical and Critical Introduction** contains background information that concisely introduces the reader to the author, work, or topic.

- The list of **Principal Works** and **English Translations** or **Editions** is chronological by date of first publication and is included as an aid to the student seeking translated versions or editions of these works for study. The list will focus primarily on twentieth-century translations, selecting those works most commonly considered the best by critics.

- **Criticism** is arranged chronologically in each entry to provide a useful perspective on changes in critical evaluation over the years. All titles by the author featured in the critical entry are printed in boldface type to enable the user to ascertain without difficulty the works being discussed. Also for purposes of easier identification, the critic's name and the publication date of the essay are given at the beginning of each piece of criticism. Anonymous criticism is preceded by the title of the journal in which it appeared. Publication information (such as publisher names and book prices) and parenthetical numerical references (such as footnotes or page and line references to specific editions of works) have been deleted at the editors' discretion to provide smoother reading of the text. Many critical entries in *CMLC* also contain translations to aid the users.

- A complete **Bibliographic Citation** designed to facilitate the location of the original essay or book precedes each piece of criticism.

- Critical excerpts are also prefaced by **Annotations** providing the reader with information about both the critic and the criticism, the scope of the excerpt, the growth of critical controversy, or changes in critical trends regarding an author or work. In some cases, these notes include cross-references to excerpts by critics who discuss each other's commentary. Dates in parentheses within the annotation refer to a book publication date when they follow a book title, and to an essay date when they follow a critic's name.

■ An annotated bibliography of **Further Reading** appears at the end of each entry and lists additional secondary sources on the author or work. In some cases it includes essays for which the editors could not obtain reprint rights. When applicable, the Further Reading is followed by references to additional entries on the author in other literary reference series published by Gale.

Topic Entries are subdivided into several thematic rubrics in which criticism appears in order of descending scope.

Cumulative Indexes

Each volume of *CMLC* includes a cumulative **author index** listing all authors who have appeared in Gale's Literary Criticism Series, along with cross references to such biographical series as *Contemporary Authors* and *Dictionary of Literary Biography*. For readers' convenience, a complete list of Gale titles included appears on the page prior to the author index. Useful for locating an author within the various series, this index is particularly valuable for those authors who are identified with a certain period but who, because of their death date, are placed in another, or for those authors whose careers span two periods. For example, Geoffrey Chaucer, who is usually considered a medieval author, is found in *Literature Criticism from 1400 to 1800* because he died after 1399.

Beginning with the tenth volume, *CMLC* includes a cumulative index listing all topic entries that have appeared in the Gale Literary Criticism Series *Classical and Medieval Literature Criticism, Contemporary Literary Criticism, Literature Criticism from 1400 to 1800, Nineteenth-Century Literature Criticism,* and *Twentieth-Century Literary Criticism.*

Beginning with the second volume, *CMLC* also includes a cumulative nationality index. Authors and/or works are grouped by nationality, and the volume in which criticism on them may be found is indicated.

Title Index

Each volume of *CMLC* also includes an index listing the titles of all literary works discussed in the series. Foreign language titles that have been translated are followed by the titles of the translations—for example, *Slovo o polku Igorove (The Song of Igor's Campaign)*. Page numbers following these translated titles refer to all pages on which any form of the title, either foreign language or translated, appears. Titles of novels, dramas, nonfiction books, and poetry, short story, or essay collections are printed in italics, while those of all individual poems, short stories, and essays are printed in roman type within quotation marks. In cases where the same title is used by different authors, the author's name or surname is given in parentheses after the title, e.g. *Collected Poems* (Horace) and *Collected Poems* (Sappho).

Critic Index

An index to critics, which cumulates with the second volume, is another useful feature of *CMLC*. Under each critic's name are listed the authors and/or works on whom the critic has written and the volume and page number where criticism may be found.

A Note to the Reader

When writing papers, students who quote directly from any volume in the Literary Criticism Series may use the following general forms to footnote reprinted criticism. The first example pertains to material drawn from a periodical, the second to material reprinted from books.

Rollo May, "The Therapist and the Journey into Hell," *Michigan Quarterly Review,* XXV, No. 4 (Fall 1986), 629-41; excerpted and reprinted in *Classical and Medieval Literature Criticism,* Vol. 3, ed. Jelena O. Krstović (Detroit: Gale Research, 1989), pp. 154-58.

Dana Ferrin Sutton, *Self and Society in Aristophanes* (University of Press of America, 1980); excerpted and reprinted in *Classical and Medieval Literature Criticism,* Vol. 4, ed. Jelena O. Krstović (Detroit: Gale Research, 1990), pp. 162-69.

Suggestions Are Welcome

Readers who wish to make suggestions for future volumes, or who have other comments regarding the series, are cordially invited to write or call the editors.

Acknowledgments

The editors wish to thank the copyright holders of the excerpted criticism included in this volume and the permissions managers of many book and magazine publishing companies for assisting us in securing reprint rights. We are also grateful to the staffs of the Detroit Public Library, the Library of Congress, the University of Detroit Mercy Library, Wayne State University Purdy/Kresge Library Complex, and the University of Michigan Libraries for making their resources available to us. Following is a list of the copyright holders who have granted us permission to reprint material in this volume of *CMLC*. Every effort has been made to trace copyright, but if omissions have been made, please let us know.

COPYRIGHTED EXCERPTS IN *CMLC*, VOLUME 16, WERE REPRINTED FROM THE FOLLOWING PERIODICALS:

The Journal of Hellenic Studies, v. CXI, 1991. Reprinted by permission of the publisher.—*Journal of Hispanic Philology,* v. I, Autumn, 1976. Copyright © 1976 The Journal of Hispanic Philology, Inc. Reprinted by permission of the publisher.—*Journal of the History of Ideas,* v. XXVIII, October-December, 1967. Copyright 1967, Journal of the History of Ideas, Inc. Reprinted by permission of the Johns Hopkins University Press.—*The Journal of Philosophy,* v. LXXVII, October, 1980. © copyright 1980 by the Journal of Philosophy, Inc. Reprinted by permission of the publisher.—*The Journal of Religious Ethics,* v. 11, Fall, 1983. Reprinted by permission of the publisher.—*Kentucky Romance Quarterly,* v. 31, 1984. Copyright © 1984 Helen Dwight Reid Educational Foundation. Reprinted with permission of the Helen Dwight Reid Educational Foundation, published by Heldref Publications, 1319 18th Street, NW, Washington, DC 20036-1802.—*The Monist,* v. 69, June, 1986. Copyright © 1986, The Monist, LaSalle, IL 61301. Reprinted by permission of the publisher.—*Nature,* v. 129, February 20, 1932. Copyright 1932 Macmillan Magazines Ltd. Reprinted by permission of the publisher.—*Revista de Estudios Hispánicos,* v. XX, May, 1986. Reprinted by permission of The University of Alabama Press.—*Romance Philology,* v. XXXII, August, 1978. © 1978 by the Regents of the University of California. Reprinted by permission of the publisher.—*Vivarium,* v. VII, 1969. Reprinted by permission of the publisher.

COPYRIGHTED EXCERPTS IN *CMLC*, VOLUME 16, WERE REPRINTED FROM THE FOLLOWING BOOKS:

Albert, S. M. From *Albert The Great.* Blackfriars Publications, 1948.—Auerbach, Erich. From *Mimesis: The Representation of Reality in Western Literature.* Translated by Willard R. Trask. Princeton University Press, 1953. Copyright 1953, renewed 1981 by Princeton University Press. Reprinted by permission of the publisher.—Bowra, C. M. From *Homer.* Gerald Duckworth & Company, 1972. © 1972 The Estate of C. M. Bowra. All rights reserved. Reprinted by permission of Gerald Duckworth and Co., Ltd.—Clarke, Howard W. From *The Art of the Odyssey.* Prentice-Hall, Inc., 1967. Copyright © 1967 by Prentice-Hall, Inc. All rights reserved. Used by permission of the author.—Davidson, Herbert A. From "Avicenna's Proof of the Existence of God as a Necessarily Existent Being" in *Islamic Philosophical Theology.* Edited by Parviz Morewedge. State University of New York Press, 1979. © 1979 State University of New York. All rights reserved. Reprinted by permission of publisher.—Ducharme, Léonard. From "The Individual Human Being in Saint Albert's Earlier Writings" in *Albert the Great: Commemorative Essays.* Edited by Francis J. Kovach and Robert W. Shahan. University of Oklahoma Press, 1980. Copyright © 1980 by the University of Oklahoma Press. Reprinted by permission of the publisher.—Felson-Rubin, Nancy. From *Regarding Penelope: From Character to Poetics.* Princeton University Press, 1994. Copyright © 1994 by Princeton University Press. All rights reserved. Reprinted by permission of the publisher.—Griffin, Jasper. From *Homer on Life and Death.* Oxford at the Clarendon Press, 1980. © Jasper Griffin 1980. Reprinted by permission of Oxford University Press.—Jaeger, Werner. From *Paideia: The Ideals of Greek Culture, Archaic Greece, the Mind of Athens, Vol. I.* Translated by Gilbert Highet. Blackwell, 1939. Copyright 1939, renewed 1967 by Basil

PHOTOGRAPHS AND ILLUSTRATIONS APPEARING IN *CMLC*, VOLUME 16, WERE RECEIVED FROM THE FOLLOWING SOURCES:

Odysseus and Circe. Foto Marburg/Art Resource, New York: **p. 284.** Giraudon. Photograph of Greek vase: **p. 214.**

Albert the Great

c. 1193/1206-1280

German scientist, theologian, and philosopher.

INTRODUCTION

Albert the Great (also known as Albertus Magnus and St. Albert) is considered among the most prominent of the Scholastics (a group of Medieval thinkers whose interest in theology, philosophy, science, and logic was awakened by the reemergence of classical Greek, Hebrew, and Islamic learning in the Christian West). A prolific writer, he was the first Christian thinker to undertake an analysis of the entire canon of Aristotelian writings and to record his observations in vast commentaries on each of the Stagirite's works. Known as *Doctor universalis* (universal doctor) for the versatility of his knowledge Albert also wrote treatises on nearly every mode of scientific thought available in the Middle Ages, including works on naturalism, biology, astronomy, and alchemy; all his works emphasize the importance of experimentation and critical evaluation instead of an appeal to authority. Although primarily remembered for these copious and original writings on science, Albert, like his famous student Thomas Aquinas, placed the study of theology at the top of the hierarchy of learning. Among his works in this field are many commentares on the *Bible,* theological speculations about Pseudo-Dionysis, and books on ethics, morality, and divine epistemology.

Biographical Information

While the facts of Albert's birth and childhood are somewhat sketchy, he appears to have been born sometime between the years of 1193 and 1206 near the small town of Lauingen on the Danube river. He was sent by his father, a wealthy German knight, to the University of Padua, but abandoned his study of the liberal arts in 1223 and, against the wishes of his family, sought admission to the Dominican order of mendicant friars. Albert studied, and later taught, theology for the next two decades at universities in Italy and Germany, eventually completing his education at the Dominican convent of Saint-Jacques, located in the University of Paris. He graduated as a master of theology in 1245, and while in Paris came into contact with Latin translations of Aristotle's works brought to western Europe through the commentaries of the great Arabic scholars Averroës, Avicenna, and others. Albert's scholarly pursuits of the next twenty years were devoted to the study of ancient Greek, Arabic, and Christian knowledge, and culminated in his commentaries on the *Bible,* Peter Lombard's *Sentences,* and the works of Aristotle. It is primarily because of the latter that he became esteemed among European intellectuals, prompting his renowned contemporary, Roger Bacon, to declare him "the most noted of Christian scholars." In 1248 Albert was sent to head a new *studium general* (general house of studies) in Cologne, which became his home for the rest of his life. Named prior of Teutonia (a province that stretched from eastern France in the west, to what are the modern nations of Switzerland and Austria in the south and the Baltic states of Latvia and Lithuania in the east) in 1254, Albert spent the next three years attending to administrative duties, while continuing to work on his scholarly projects. In 1256 Pope Alexander IV sent him back to the University of Paris to defend the rights of the Franciscan and the Dominican orders to teach. Successful in this endeavor, he was appointed Bishop of Regensburg in 1259, though he returned to teaching in Cologne after less than two years. He subsequently served as a papal legate in Germany and Bohemia from 1263 to 1264, but soon withdrew from active ecclesiastical life in order to teach. Beatified by Gregory XV in 1622, nearly three and a half decades after his death (the delay was likely due to charges of sorcery that can be traced to his dabbling in the alchemical sciences throughout his career), and canonized in 1931, Albert was named patron saint of natural scientists in 1941 by Pope Pius XII.

Major Works

The breadth of Albert's learning embraced the full spectrum of natural science, philosophy, and theology, and his ideas are said to encapsulate the state of human knowledge as it existed in thirteenth-century Europe. Among his earliest works are a group of biblical commentaries and other theological works such as his *Super sententiarum* (c. 1246-49), an exegesis of Peter Lombard's *Sentences,* and several books devoted to the Neoplatonic thought of Pseudo-Dionysius. *De bono* (c. 1246-48), another of Albert's early writings, focuses on ethics and is a synthesis of his thoughts on natural moral doctrine. At the request of his fellow Dominican friars he sought to render the thought of Aristotle in a form "intelligible to all Latins." His *Physica* (c. 1251), the first of these works undertaken, is, like the rest of his Aristotelian commentaries, a sustained reading of the text coupled with personal and critical reflections on the work and on the thoughts of past commentators, as well as digressions (often of considerable length) designed to bridge any gaps in the original and to elucidate particularly difficult passages. Albert also wrote several completely original works, the most well-known being his *Mineralia* (c. 1252-62; *Book of Minerals*), intended to alleviate the lack of information on geological matters in the Aristotelian corpus. Typical of Albert's many scientific writings (including works on physics, alchemy, botany, zoology, psychology, meterology, geography, astronomy, and astrology), *Mineralia* attests to his wide but personal experience of nature and his skepticism regarding knowledge that is derived solely from logic or past authority. Albert's scientific writings evince along with his forward-looking belief in experimentation, his deeply Christian worldview—a quality that is infused in all of his works. For him God is the prime mover and first cause of nature whose will is observable in all natural phenomena. Albert's goal, in keeping with his role as a Scholastic, was to create a synthesis of learning within the context of theology, which he saw as the highest form of human knowledge. Thus, Albert's writings, consistently address the metaphysical questions of being, unity, and the good and maintain that no contradiction exists between knowledge gained by faith or by reason, since both spring from the divine.

Critical Reception

Albert received the epithet "the Great" in his own lifetime, and his writings continued to have a powerful effect on the intellectual life of Europe for centuries after his death. In science his stated goal was to provide "a complete account of all nature," and critics have since noted his influence on later scientists in terms of the acquisition of knowledge through experimentation and observation. In addition, Albert's name has long been associated with the medieval science of alchemy. The authorship of several alchemical texts of questionable authenticity has often been ascribed to him: these include *De secretis naturae, Speculum astronomia,* and *Libellus de alchimia,* all of which were included in the Borgnet editions of his works (1890-99) and correspond with the rise in his popular reputation as a magician soon after his death. In terms of philosophy, critics have observed that Albert's renown was quickly superseded by the insights of his former pupil and disciple, Thomas Aquinas. Most commentators, however, have acknowledged that Albert paved the way for the theological synthesis of Aquinas and the growth of the scientific method in the late Middle Ages and the Renaissance. Recent critical assessments of Albert have emphasized several flaws in his thought, and some scholars have cited multiple examples of inconsistency and imprecision in his writings, but further evaluations await the completion of the modern Cologne editions (1951-) of his works. Likewise, future appraisals require the translation of Albert's corpus into English—only a small portion of which has been undertaken, primarily by Lynn Thorndike, Dorothy Wyckoff, and Simon Tugwell—for the present leaving many of the Albert's writings unexplored.

PRINCIPAL WORKS

De natura boni (treatise) c. 1243-44
Principium biblicum (treatise) 1245
Super Isaiam (treatise) c. 1245-50
De homine (treatise) c. 1246
De incarnatione (treatise) c. 1246
De quatuor coaequaevis (treatise) c. 1246
De resurrectione (treatise) c. 1246
De sacramentis (treatise) c. 1246
De bono (treatise) c. 1246-48
Super sententiarum (treatise) c. 1246-49
Super Dionysium de caelesti hierarchia (treatise) c. 1247
Quaestiones theologiae (treatise) c. 1247-48
Sermones parisiensis (treatise) c. 1247-48
De forma resultante in speculo (treatise) c. 1248
Super Dionysium de ecclesiastica hierarchia (treatise) c. 1249
Super Dionysium de divinis nominibus (treatise) c. 1250

Super Dionysium de mystica theologia (treatise) c. 1250
Super epistulas Dionysii (treatise) c. 1250
Super ethica, commentum et quaestiones (treatise) c. 1250-52
De caelo et mundo (treatise) c. 1251
Physica (treatise) c. 1251
De lineis indivisibilibus (treatise) c. 1251-52
De causis proprietatum elementorum (treatise) c. 1251-53
De generatione et corruptione (treatise) c. 1251-53
De natura loci (treatise) c. 1251-53
Meteora (treatise) c. 1252-54
Mineralia [Book of Minerals] (treatise) c. 1252-62
Analytica priora (treatise) c. 1252-71
De divisione (treatise) c. 1252-71
De praedicamentis (treatise) c. 1252-71
De sex principiis (treatise) c. 1252-71
De sophisticis elenchis (treatise) c. 1252-71
Peri herimeneias (treatise) c. 1252-71
Super Porphyrium de v universalis (treatise) c. 1252-71
Topica (treatise) c. 1252-71
De anima (treatise) c. 1254
De intellectu et intelligibili (treatise) c. 1254-57
De iuventute et senectute (treatise) c. 1254-57
De memoria et reminiscentia (treatise) c. 1254-57
De morte et vita (treatise) c. 1254-57
De motibus animalium (treatise) c. 1254-57
De nutrimento et nutribili (treatise) c. 1254-57
De sensu et sensato (treatise) c. 1254-57
De somno et virgilia (treatise) c. 1254-57
De spiritu et respiratione (treatise) c. 1254-57
De fato (treatise) c. 1256
Super Iohannem (treatise) c. 1256
Super Marcum (treatise) c. 1257-60
Super Matthaeum (treatise) c. 1257-64
Epistula de ungelt (treatise) c. 1258
Quaestiones super de animalibus (treatise) 1258
Sermones (treatise) c. 1258
De animalibus (treatise) c. 1258-62
De vegetabilibus (treatise) c. 1260
Ethica (treatise) c. 1261
Super Lucam (treatise) c. 1261-62
Metaphysica (treatise) c. 1262-63
De natura et origine animae (treatise) c. 1262-64
De principiis motus processivi (treatise) c. 1262-64
De unitate intellectus (treatise) c. 1263
Summa theologiae sive de mirabili scientia dei (treatise) c. 1263-74
Politica (treatise) c. 1264-74
De causis et processu universitatis a prima causa (treatise) c. 1267-71
De corpore domini (treatise) c. 1270
De mysterio missae (treatise) c. 1270
De XV problematibus (treatise) c. 1270
Problemata determinata (treatise) c. 1271
Super Iob (treatise) c. 1272-74
*Super Baruch (treatise)
*Super Danielem (treatise)

*Super Ezechielem (treatise)
*Super Ieremiam (treatise)
*Super prophetas minores (treatise)
*Super Threnos (treatise)

*The dates for these works are unknown.

PRINCIPAL ENGLISH TRANSLATIONS

Book of Minerals (translated by Dorothy Wyckoff) 1967
Albert and Thomas: Selected Writings (translated by Simon Tugwell) 1988

CRITICISM

Joachim Sighart (essay date 1876)

SOURCE: "Philosophical and Theological Works Written by Albert at This Period," in *Albert the Great, of the Order of Friar-Preachers: His Life and Scholastic Labours,* translated by T. A. Dixon, 1876. Reprint by Wm G. Brown Reprint Library, pp. 101-19.

[*In the following excerpt, Sighart surveys the writings Albert produced while he resided and taught in Paris and Cologne.*]

Contemplation, prayer, and preaching were to [Albert] but the accessories of the greatest activity, the adornment, the joy of his life, a sweet recreation and an interior refreshment amid his more serious studies. The principal work to which he felt himself called was, besides teaching, his labours as a writer, especially as a philosophical writer. It is in this capacity that he truly merits a glory which nothing can tarnish. On this rock of science his greatness as an educator of the human race rests. And it was precisely during the years of his first professorship at Paris and Cologne that he brought to light the most important of his works on these matters. We have proof of this, not only in divers passages of his writings, but in a host of contemporary witnesses besides.

We shall give, in a brief analysis, a list of the works which may date from this period. We must first observe that all these writings of Albert are not entirely his own compositions on philosophical subjects: they are, on the contrary, for the most part paraphrases, that is to say enlarged translations of the writings of Aristotle. Albert completed, corrected, and Christianised this philosophy. It is true that in the preceding ages the Christian Apologists, such as Origen, Clement, the great Bishop of Hippo, and later Scotus Erigena, Anselm, as well as the School of St. Victor, set forth in their writings the true meaning, the beauty, and magnificence of the Christian Faith. Some had recourse to scholastic reasoning; others were content with a mystical exposition of the sweet and superabundant fruits which this same Faith germinates in souls. Yet this was done only in detail and very imperfectly, inasmuch as they were wanting in that clearness of form which is requisite in order to explain Christian dogma. To render the harmony which exists between religious faith and natural science obvious—to completely unlock the treasures of revelation, impressed with unity and admirable beauty, and containing nothing contrary to the requirements of human reason, it needed a system of natural science which might serve as a body to generate truth, in order to compare it with Christian truth and serve as a basis. Aristotle's Philosophy appeared suited to supply this want. It embraced, in effect, the whole range of the natural sciences; it presented great ingenuity of conception, an admirable clearness of exposition, and conclusions common to revelation. It was difficult, then, not to view Aristotle as the representative of natural science, and to adopt his forms and doctrines so as to render Christian truth as intelligible as possible. Hence the reason why the Schoolmen attached themselves to Aristotle, studied, commented on, and adopted his doctrines with such incredible ardour. This was especially the case with the new Orders called to the defence of the Church. But Albert the Great was the first who ventured to tread in this difficult path with full consciousness of his success, and of the immense labour which it would entail. He then offered to the Church of the West the doctrine of Aristotle and a complete exposition of it.

But in order to attain this end it was necessary to know the harmony and the references of all the the works of the Philosopher; it needed careful study to discover their meaning, to interpret and correct them. The Schools possessed only the Latin translations of the detached writings of the Stagirite, his works on *Logic,* according to Boethius, to which were afterwards added his *Ethics, Rhetoric,* and some others on *Physics.* But long before this period Aristotle became the object of veneration in Spain, where, under the Mussulman Empire, the sciences took a new flight. Won by the splendour of natural knowledge which filled these works, the distinguished *savants,* of Arabian origin, and for the most part belonging to the medical profession, acquired them in the East. They brought them into Spain, translated them into their own language, and made them the object of personal research and of extensive education.

The names of Avicenna (Ibn Badsches), Avenpace (Ibn Poschd), and Sercal are known as the most renowned translators and interpreters of the works of Aristotle. After these come the learned Jews, who also in Spain rose to great eminence in the culture of science. Finally, masters and Christian princes themselves flocked to the fountains of Mussulman knowledge, whence they procured Arabian manuscripts of Aristotle's works. They had them translated into Latin, in order to render their circulation more general, and forthwith adopted them as the subject of indefatigable study. It was especially the privilege of the members of the new Orders to introduce into their monasteries these treasures and precious helps to scientific progress. Hence it was that during Albert's residence in Paris there already existed a considerable number of Latin translations of Aristotle, which he doubtless procured or caused to be transcribed by the pen of copyists. He would with equal facility acquire translations of the same Philosopher from the Greek, which was at that time well known. He purposed to compose out of these materials a system of Aristotelian Philosophy. It was fitting therefore, above all, that he should reproduce the text, by adopting, among the numerous manuscripts at his service, those which appeared to him the most suitable. But he did not confine himself to this first effort; he was desirous to elucidate the obscure passages of these works, to supply what was wanting in them, by turning modern research as well as his own personal studies to profit, to correct the errors, and finally to connect and harmonise them as a whole.

Thus did the philosophical works of Albert receive their birth. They embody the Philosophy of Aristotle under a popular, detailed, and Christianised form; they represent to us the Prince of ancient Philosophy as a pillar of natural science, with the marvellous harmony which exists between the latter and Christian truth.

Such was the sublime task which was offered to the minds of the *elite* in Albert's day, and which he himself was able to accomplish, in great part, at this period of his life which we are now studying: an overwhelming task, the fulfilment of which was possible only to his own gigantic mind, his penetration, his unwearied application, his vast and profound erudition, and doubtless also to the robust health with which Divine Providence endowed him. We can hardly conceive how a man was capable of executing in so short a space of time a work which claims in our day the longest existence.

We shall content ourselves here with quoting Albert's books on philosophical subjects, and which date from this period.

We first meet with his **Logical Treatises,** which were no doubt his first composition, inasmuch as he ever regarded logic as a preparation and introduction to the other sciences. He leaves us here the different works of Aristotle in a translation in paraphrastic form, to which he adds, after reviewing them, the logical researches of former philosophers.

Then follow the numerous treatises on natural science, which are entitled, **Physics.** In his Preface Albert explains the motive which led to the production of this masterpiece, saying,

> Our intention, in treating these questions of natural science, is to oblige as far as we can the brethren of our Order. For many years past they have asked us to write a book on the phenomena of nature which may supply them with a complete course of the natural sciences, and afford them suitable helps in studying the works of Aristotle. Although sensible of our incapacity for such an enterprise, we could not resist their entreaties. Overcome by the solicitations of some of them, we accepted this task. We have undertaken it above all for the glory of the Omnipotent God, the Source of wisdom, the Creator, Preserver, and king of nature, and also for the benefit of the brethren and of all who shall read this book and be desirous of acquiring the natural sciences.

Who can fail to recognise in these words the modest and truly Christian teacher, on whom the love of his neighbour imposes so laborious an undertaking, and who seeks in all things God's honour and the salvation of souls? It is thus that, walking daily in the footsteps of Aristotle, but perfecting him by his own additions, he cultivates thoroughly on a vast scale every branch of natural science.

By the side of these works stand the thirteen books of Aristotle's *Metaphysics,* which treat of the Immutable and Eternal, as physics treat of matters which are subject to change. As these researches are immediately connected with those on physics (in Aristotle they form but one and the same whole), and as they denote a work altogether similar, we may suppose that Albert published them also at this the most glorious period of his teaching. Here again Albert seeks to solve the most profound and difficult problems, by developing and analysing all anterior scientific researches. Had our indefatigable Professor but produced in this period of from ten to fifteen years these philosophical works (comprising five folios), we should admire his extraordinary zeal, his astonishing application, his fruitful and marvellous aptitude for science. But what we mention does not embrace all that he did as a writer at this period. He was, moreover, a Professor of Theology, and we observe that in treating the sublime mysteries of Divine science his pen is not less fruitful. It is well known that Albert, during Thomas of Aquin's first residence at Cologne, explained the books of Denis the Areopagite. These lectures, transcribed by his own hand, or dictated by him to a copyist are still extant.

As this work is of high importance by its relation to Albert's general acts, seeing that it becomes us to admire him here as a mystic, while elsewhere he passes as the representative of the Schoolmen, and as there is an ancient tradition attached to it, we cannot omit giving here some interesting details.

These works of Denis, which may be traced to the fifth century, were attributed, in the Middle Ages, to the famous Areopagite who was converted by the preaching of the Apostle St. Paul; they were, as such, the object of universal esteem and of deep study. They embodied the sublimest Mysteries of Faith blooming as so many beautiful flowers in this mass of doctrines sprung from Neoplatonism. It cannot be denied that they contained rich ideas, stamped with the impress of Christian orthodoxy. They moreover afforded food for devotion and meditation in a style that was racy and full of imagery. But they also frequently overshot the mark in matters of strict Catholic doctrine, inasmuch as they presented unbecoming ideas, arbitrary interpretations, and affirmations bordering upon error. The belief in the Apostolic origin of these writings strongly recommended in medieval times the doctrines which they set forth, and, despite the very obscurity and mystery that surrounded them, they had a secret charm for all. They were regarded as a sort of compliment to Biblical revelation, glimpses into God's kingdom in heaven and His image on earth.

It need not then surprise us to see the masterminds of that period imposing on themselves the task of penetrating, expounding, and translating these mystical writings. Albert, after the celebrated Hugo of St. Victor, the successor of Scotus Erigena, who had previously offered to the public a translation in paraphrastic form, wrote a vast commentary on these books, so universally esteemed, and discovered in them admirable thoughts in relation to the kingdom of God.

There is an ancient tradition connected with this work of the great master which we cannot pass over in silence. Rodolph speaks as follows:

> When the Master was expounding the works of Denis, and had completed the book on the Divine Hierarchy, his courage failed him at the sight of the difficulties which the rest of the work contained. He resolved, as St. Jerome before him did in regard to the book of Daniel, to put aside the work, and leave it unfinished, when the faithful Master, Who permits not the labourers of His vineyard to be tried beyond their strength, sent to him, in his sleep, the Apostle St. Paul, who encouraged him to renewed ardour. The manner in which the preacher of the Gentiles appeared to Albert is thus related. A Religious, renowned for his learning and eminent virtues, whom many suppose to have been Thomas of Aquin, one day found a document in Albert's handwriting in which the following occurred: 'When I had completed with much toil the book on the Celestial Hierarchy, I began to explain the Hierarchy of the Church. I got through the first chapter, on the Sacrament of Baptism, with much difficulty. But when I entered on the second my courage failed me, and I despaired of being able to pursue it, when after Matins I had a vision. I found myself in a church where St. Paul was celebrating Mass.

Consoled beyond measure, I hoped that he would enlighten me as to the meaning of Denis the Areopagite. When the Apostle had said the *Agnus Dei,* a multitude of people entered the church; the Apostle calmly saluted them and inquired what it was they wanted. "Behold," they all exclaimed, "we have brought to you one who is possessed, whom we implore you to cure by freeing him from the devil." Having cast out Satan, St. Paul communicated this man with a particle of the consecrated Host. I offered my services at the ablution of the fingers, and, with fear, said, "Sir, I have long wished to be instructed in the mysterious subjects contained in the book of St. Denis, but especially on the grace of true sanctity." He answered me, with much kindness of manner, "Come with me after Mass to the house of the Priest Aaron, which is on the other side of the river." I then followed the Apostle after Mass. When we reached the banks of the river, he without difficulty passed over. But it was otherwise with me, for I had scarce touched the water when it began to rise to such a degree as to render the passage impossible. The Apostle entered the house of Aaron, which he had pointed out to me; and while anxious as to how I should follow him, I suddenly woke. On reflection, I discovered the meaning of the dream. The first chapter explained by me treats, in effect, of the expulsion of Satan from the body of man by baptism, then his participation in the Sacrament of the Holy Eucharist. The following chapter leads him who receives the holy unction to the house of Aaron, for it treats of the chrism with which bishops are consecrated. The deep waters increasing so suddenly arrested my pen; but the Apostle, through God's grace, rendered the passage easy to me. I then commenced to write again, and accomplished, with God's help, what to my personal feebleness appeared impossible.'

From this we gather that it was in consequence of a dream that Albert was at length enabled to surmount the difficulties of this obscure book; what had for long days been the subject of his meditations, thoughts, and reading comes to him in sleep, in the form of a vision, and at the same time offers him a key to the solution. When awake, the powers of the soul often resemble dispersed troops; but in the depth of sleep they are collected together like a compact army, and are oftentimes capable of doing in that state what would have been impossible when awake. We can, then, view this dream as a natural phenomenon, seeing that it affords no direct proof of its being a Divine illumination. This is rendered all the more probable by the fact that other portions of the dream are reproduced in the same chapter on the Ecclesiastical Hierarchy: such as the walking towards the abode of the high-priest Aaron, and the difficulties that oppose him on the way. It is not for us to question whether Albert regarded this dream as a heavenly favour or not; for all that is good comes from on high, from the Father of lights, and every natural appearance should, in a general sense, be recognised as a message from and a providence of God, the Author of nature.

A second work, not less important, which Albert must have composed at this period, is his *Commentary on the Sentences of Peter Lombard.* Peter, born at Novara, a theological professor, then Bishop of Paris in 1164, provided by this work for an urgent want of the times. He wrote a book which contains a pithy outline of the whole of the dogmatic and moral teaching of the Church, based upon Scripture and the Fathers, and in which he sets forth and solves every possible objection. The most illustrious theologians made it the groundwork of their lectures, and enriched it with commentaries and expositions. It was in this way that Albert occupied himself when teaching at the Convent of St. James in Paris, and this was doubtless the origin of his splendid *Commentary on the Book of the Sentences,* which embraces three folios, and suprasses all other works of its kind in breadth and penetration. It is curious to see how unity appears under his pen in a work which is generally void of it. Witness the text on which this important work is grounded: "I came out of the mouth of the Most High, the First-born before all creatures: I made that in the heavens there should rise light that never faileth, and as a cloud I covered all the earth" (Eccles. xxiv. 5, 6). These words, according to our author, contain the different subjects of the work. *I came out of the mouth of the Most High:* here we have the first book on God Three in One. The passage, *Before all creatures,* represents all the creatures to whom reference is made in the second book. The words, *I made that in the heavens there should rise light,* indicate the subject-matter of the third book, where it treats of the justice of Christ, of grace, and precept. These words, *As a cloud I covered all the earth,* signify the Sacraments which are explained in the fourth book. It would be difficult, indeed, to imagine a more charming connection between the different portions of the *Book of Sentences.* What is still more worthy of note, is that Albert, in the fourth part of this work, deals with the faults against the holy virtue of chastity with a breadth and minuteness which was only surpassed, long afterwards, by the expositions of Suarez.

He treats especially of the conjugal life and endeavours, by turning to account the rich treasures of natural and medical knowledge, to distinguish between what is conformable to nature and is permissible, and that which is an abuse of nature, and which becomes matter of sin. One cannot deny the justice of his observations when speaking of these inquiries. "It is true," he observes, "we ought never to raise, and much less discuss these immoral questions, which we can scarce mention without shame. But the monstrous sins which are now-a-days brought to the holy tribunal unhappily too often oblige us to speak of them. They who seek to excuse their faults by saying that such acts are conformable to nature should be taught that they are, on the contrary, opposed to it." The great man, as we perceive, is not placed on such delicate ground, but that he can afford, in his charity and zeal for souls, to supply Confessors with excellent rules to be followed in the painful duty of directing consciences.

All these data should convince us that Albert during this period of his life was not only a Professor and a man of prayer, but that in his character of a writer he was like to a large and noble tree laden with fair and delicious fruit.

Lynn Thorndike (essay date 1929)

SOURCE: "Albertus Magnus," in *A History of Magic and Experimental Science during the First Thirteen Centuries of Our Era, Vol. II,* The Macmillan Company, 1929, pp. 517-92.

[*In the following excerpt, Thorndike examines Albert's representative thoughts on magic and natural science, his influence on his students, and his reputation among various critics and biographers.*]

It may be well at the start to indicate the scope and character of Albert's works in the field of science. In general they follow the plan of the natural philosophy of Aristotle and parallel the titles of the works then attributed, in some cases incorrectly, to Aristotle. We have eight books of physics, psychological treatises such as the *De an'ima* and *De somno et vigilia,* both in three books, and works dealing with celestial phenomena, such as the *De meteoris* and *De coelo et mundo* in four books each, and with the universe and life in general, such as the *De causis et procreatione un'iversi, De causis et proprietatibus elementorum et planetarum,* and the *De generatione et corruptione.* Geography is represented by the *De natura locorum,* zoology by the twentysix books on animals, botany by the seven books on vegetables and plants, and mineralogy by the five books on minerals. Björnbo called attention to a work on mirrors or catoptric ascribed to "Albert the Preacher" in several manuscripts but which is not included in the editions of Albert's works and which has never been printed. I do not know if this is the same treatise as a treatise on Perspective attributed to Albertus Magnus in a manuscript which Björnbo did not mention. A work on the planting of trees and preserving of wine is sometimes ascribed to Albert in the manuscripts, but is probably rather by Petrus de Crescentiis or Galfridus de Vino Salvo. I think that I have encountered only once in the manuscripts the attribution to Albert of an epitome of the *Almagest* of Ptolemy and of a *Summa astrologiae.* Fairly frequently one meets with some brief compendium of all natural philosophy ascribed to Albert, of which perhaps the most common is the *Philosophia pauperum* or "Introduction to the books of Aristotle on physics, sky and universe, generation and corruption, meteorology, and the soul." These are either spurious, or, if based on Albert's writings, add nothing of importance to them.

Finally we may note a group of works lying on the border of natural and occult science and which have been regarded as spurious: treatises on alchemy and chiromancy, the *Speculum astronomiae,* the *De secretis mulierum,* the *Liber aggregationis,* and the *De mirabilibus mundi.* . . .

The order in which Albert's numerous works were written is a matter difficult to determine but of some interest, although not of very great importance, for our investigation. The statement of Peter of Prussia that the translation of Aristotle "which we now use in the schools" was made by Thomas of Cantimpré at the suggestion of Aquinas, "for in Albert's time all commonly used the old translation," would, if true, suggest that Albert wrote his Aristotelian treatises early in life, since he actually outlived Aquinas. But not much reliance is to be placed in this statement of Peter, since it is reasonably certain that Thomas of Cantimpré at least did not translate Aristotle. I have been impressed by differing and almost inconsistent attitudes in different treatises by Albert, for instance in his attitude towards magic, which seem to hint that his opinions changed with the years, although it may be attributable, as in some other authors, to the fact that in different works he reflects the attitude of different authorities, or approaches different subjects with a different view-point, writing of theology as a theologian, but of Aristotle as a philosopher. However, [Clemens Baeumker, in *Die Stellung des Alfred von Sareshel,* and Arthor Schneider, in *Die Psychologie Alberts des Grossen,* 1906], pursuing in connection with Albert's writings a different line of investigation from mine, have been struck with the same thing and have concluded that Albert underwent a gradual intellectual development. They note that in his **Commentaries on the Sentences** he is still glued to the Augustinian tradition, while in his **Summa** he is strongly influenced by Aristotle and working for a synthesis of Aristotle and Augustine. Finally, in his philosophical and scientific works, related to the genuine and spurious works of Aristotle, "he goes very far with this Arabian-trimmed Neo-Platonism, often so far that he finally feels compelled to explain such exposition as mere citation, and in the strife of conflicting masses of thought surging within him refers for his own personal interpretation to his theological writings." From this it would seem that most of Albert's theological treatises were written before his scientific works, based upon Aristotle and spurious Arabic and other additions. But we have seen that many of his Aristotelian treatises were completed before the *Speculum naturale* of Vincent of Beauvais, whereas his *Sentences* name 1246 and 1249 as current dates.

But while Albert may sometimes refer to his theological works for his own personal views, he does not do so in those passages which will especially concern us, and it is in his works on natural science that he seems to the modern reader more original. Indeed Jessen declared that repeated perusal of Albert's many writings in the field of natural history had convinced him that he was "original everywhere, even where he seems to copy." Jessen, indeed, held that Albert would have been even more original and outspoken than he is, but for fear of the charge of heresy; but in my opinion there is little to support such a view. Be that as it may, in his works on natural science Albert does not merely repeat past ideas whether of Aristotle or others, but adds chapters of his own drawn in large measure from his own observation, experience, and classification. It is in his scientific works that he is as superior to Aquinas as the latter is generally considered to surpass him in the purely metaphysical and theological field. Since writing the foregoing sentences I have found that Peter of Prussia expressed much the same view in his life of Albert written toward the close of the fifteenth century. Peter says, "Moreover, this should be understood, that after Aristotle faith is to be put in Albert above all who have written in philosophy, because he has himself illuminated the writings of almost all philosophers and has seen wherein they spoke truly or falsely, nay more, since he himself was experienced above all others in natural phenomena. It may be that some, relying on their metaphysics or logic, can impugn him by certain arguments, but I think that no matter of great concern, since Albert himself says that faith is to be put in anyone who is expert in his art."

Albert's scientific fame perhaps reached its zenith shortly before the publication of Darwin's *Origin of Species* in 1859. In 1836 and 1837 Ernst Meyer published in *Linnaea* his "Albertus Magnus, ein Beitrag zur Geschichte der Botanik im XIII Jahrhundert," and later in his *History of Botany* ranked Albert as the greatest botanist during the long period between Aristotle and Theophrastus on the one hand and Andrea Cesalpini on the other. "Yes, more than that. From Aristotle, the creator of scientific botany, until his time this science sank deeper and deeper with time. With him it arose like the Phoenix from its ashes. That, I think, is praise enough, and this crown shall no one snatch away from him." In the meantime, at Paris in 1853, Pouchet had published his *History of the Natural Sciences in the Middle Ages* with the sub-title, *Or Albertus Magnus and his age considered as the point of departure of the experimental school.* But the extreme praise of Albert had occurred a little earlier in lectures on the history of science delivered by De Blainville at the Sorbonne in 1839-1841 and published a few years later. De Blainville too centered his discussion of medieval science about Albert, to whom alone he devoted some ninety pages, extolling him for affirming the permanence of species and for "broadening" Aristotle to fit the requirements of theology. In ten theses in which De Blainville undertook to sum up briefly the chief legacies of Albert to science, he held that he completed and terminated the circle of human

knowledge, adding to Aristotle the scientific demonstration of the relations of man with God; that he extended the scope of observation to every scientific field except anatomy; that he created the description of natural bodies, a thing unknown to the ancients; and that in filling in the gaps in Aristotle's writings he was the first to embrace all the natural sciences in a complete plan, logical and perfectly followed. "In accepting therefore with the Christian Aristotle," concluded De Blainville, "the first verse of *Genesis,* 'In the beginning God created heaven and earth,' and the consequences which follow it, we have, in my opinion, reached the *apogée* of the encyclopedia of human knowledge, which can now only extend itself in respect to the number and the deeper knowledge of material objects."

This passage from De Blainville, who seems to have been a Roman Catholic, is very interesting as showing how the progress of modern science in his own time and the centuries just preceding could be almost completely miscomprehended by a professed historian of science. We must not, however, suppose that such misconceptions of the progress of science were universal or even general in the first half of the nineteenth century. The article on Albertus Magnus in the *Histoire Littéraire de la France,* which was published in 1838, recognizes that Albert did not extend the bounds of the sciences as much as had been supposed, and that progress had been made since the sixteenth century which rendered that part of his works "almost useless." The passage from De Blainville is interesting also as showing the same intimate connection presupposed between Christian theology, natural science, and Aristotelianism as in the days of the great Dominicans themselves. Again, it reveals the extent to which natural science, since the appearance of *The Origin of Species,* has tended to the opposite extreme.

As for historians of science, they have been rather scarcer of late than in the earlier years of the nineteenth century, when the subject seems to have had a great vogue in France. Or at least the historians of science have been less sympathetic with the distant past. Perhaps the inclination has been to go almost as far toward the other pole of neglect as De Blainville went toward that of extollation. But the modern eulogies of the scientific attainments of Roger Bacon, supposed to be a thorn in the side of the medieval church and falsely regarded as its victim, and as the one lone scientific spirit of the middle ages, have been rather more absurd than the earlier praises of Albert, who was represented both as a strong pillar in the church and the backbone of medieval and Christian science. Indeed, the *Histoire Littéraire,* in the same passage which we a moment ago quoted against De Blainville, also states with probable justification that Albert did "more than any other doctor of his day" to introduce the natural sciences into the course of public and private studies, and that it was his taste for those subjects which won him his popular renown and the homage of scholars until the end of the seventeenth century. At no period, however, has Albert been entirely without defenders. Jessen in 1867 regarded him as an original natural scientist. Stadler in 1906 recognized that "he made many independent observations, perhaps even carried out experiments," and showed great interest in biology.

Coming back from the opinions of others concerning Albert to his own attitude towards natural science, it is to be noted that, while he may make all sorts of mistakes judged by modern standards, he does show unmistakable signs of the scientific spirit. This will become more apparent as we proceed, but for the present we may cite two examples of it, and these from a work based upon a pseudo-Aristotelian treatise and one which at first sight might seem quite superstitious and unscientific to the modern reader, since it is full of astrology, the *De causis et proprietatibus elementorum et planetarum*. In the first passage Albert repeats the justification of natural science against a narrow religious attitude which we heard from the lips of William of Conches in the previous century. When Albert finds that some men attribute the deluge simply to the divine will and believe that no other cause for it should be sought, he replies that he too ascribes it ultimately to the divine will, but that he believes that God acts through natural causes in the case of natural phenomena, and that, while he would not presume to search the causes of the divine will, he does feel free to investigate those natural causes which were the divine instruments. A little further on in the same chapter Albert declares that "it is not enough to know in terms of universals, but we seek to know each object's own peculiar characteristics, for this is the best and perfect kind of science."

This desire for concrete, specific, detailed, accurate knowledge concerning everything in nature is felt by Albert in other of his writings to be scarcely in the spirit of the Aristotelian natural philosophy which he follows and sets forth in his parallel treatises. In his work on animals a cleavage may be observed between those parts where Albert discusses the general natures and common characteristics of animals and seems to follow Aristotle rather closely, and those books where he lists and describes particular animals with numerous allusions to recent experience and considerable criticism of past authorities. At the beginning of his twenty-second book he apologizes for listing particular animals in alphabetical order, which is "not appropriate to philosophy," by saying that "we know we are debtors both to the wise and to the unlearned, and those things which are told in particular terms better instruct a rustic intelligence." But while this desire to describe particular objects precisely is felt by Albert to be not in accord with traditional philosophic methods

of presentation, it is a desire which many of his contemporaries share with him. At the beginning of his sixth book on vegetables and plants, where particular herbs and trees are listed, he explains, "In this sixth book of vegetables we satisfy the curiosity of our students rather than philosophy, for philosophy cannot deal with particulars."

This healthy interest in nature and commendable curiosity concerning real things was not confined to Albert's students nor to "rustic intelligences." One has only to examine the sculpture of the great thirteenth century cathedrals to see that the craftsmen of the towns were close observers of the world of nature and that every artist was a naturalist too. In the foliage that twines about the capitals of the columns in French Gothic cathedrals it is easy to recognize, says M. Mâle, a large number of plants: "the plantain, arum, ranunculus, fern, clover, coladine, hepatica, columbine, cress, parsley, strawberry-plant, ivy, snapdragon, the flower of the broom and the leaf of the oak, a typically French collection of flowers loved from childhood." *Mutatis mutandis,* the same statement could be made concerning the carved vegetation that runs riot in Lincoln cathedral. "The thirteenth century sculptors sang their *chant de mai.* All the spring delights of the Middle Ages live again in their work—the exhilaration of Palm Sunday, the garlands of flowers, the bouquets fastened on the doors, the strewing of fresh herbs in the chapels, the magical flowers of the feast of Saint John—all the fleeting charm of those old-time springs and summers. The Middle Ages, so often said to have little love for nature, in point of fact gazed at every blade of grass with reverence." But it is not merely love of nature but scientific interest and accuracy that we see revealed in the sculptures of the cathedrals and in the note-book of the thirteenth century architect, Villard de Honnecourt, with its sketches of insect as well as animal life, of a lobster, two parroquets on a perch, the spirals of a snail's shell, a fly, a dragonfly, and a grasshopper, as well as a bear and a lion from life, and more familiar animals such as the cat and swan. The sculptors of gargoyles and chimeras were not content to reproduce existing animals but showed their command of animal anatomy by creating strange compound and hybrid monsters—one might almost say, evolving new species—which nevertheless have all the verisimilitude of copies from living forms. It was these breeders in stone, these Burbanks of the pencil, these Darwins with the chisel, who knew nature and had studied botany and zoology in a way superior to the scholar who simply pored over the works of Aristotle and Pliny. No wonder that Albert's students were curious about particular things.

But one is inclined to wonder whether the passage from the *De causis et proprietatibus elementorum et planetarum,* which we quoted first, may not have been written after the passages which we have quoted from his works on plants and animals, and whether Albert had come, thanks possibly to that same stimulating scientific curiosity of his students, to cease to apologize for the detailed description of particular objects as unphilosophical and to praise it as "the best and perfect kind of science." At any rate it is those portions of his works on animals, plants, and minerals which he devotes to such description of particular objects which possess most independent value, and it is perhaps also worth noting that Ptolemy of Lucca in looking back upon Albert's work seems not only to distinguish his writings on logic and theology from those on nature, but also to imply a distinction between Aristotle's natural philosophy and his "very well-known and most excellent contribution to the experimental knowledge of things of nature." Ptolemy seems to say Aristotle's contribution, but the credit really belongs largely to Albert and his students.

Pouchet was therefore not without justification in his sub-title, "Or Albertus Magnus and his Period Considered as the Beginning of the Experimental School." His distinguishing, however, three stages of scientific progress in the history of civilization—the first, Greek, characterized by observation, and represented especially by Aristotle; the second, Roman, marked by erudition and typified by Pliny; the third, medieval, distinguished by experimentation, and having Albertus Magnus and Roger Bacon as its two great representatives;—was rather too general and sweeping. Galen, for instance, was a great experimenter and the ancient Empirics put little trust in anything except experience. Albert himself, in discussing "the serious problem" whether life is possible in the Antipodes or southern hemisphere, states that "the most powerful kings and the most accomplished philosophers have labored over it from antiquity, the kings forsooth by experiment and the philosophers by rational inquiry." Moreover, neither Roger Bacon nor Albert can be shown to have done much experimenting of the sort, carefully planned and regulated, which is carried on in modern laboratories. Meyer in his *History of Botany,* although Albert was a great favorite with him, felt constrained to renounce the credit for purposive experimentation which Pouchet had given him. "How gladly would I see this crown also placed deservedly upon my favorite's head! . . . But I do not know of his undertaking an experiment in order to solve a physiological or physical problem in which he had a clearly defined purpose and the suitable materials at hand for carrying it out; his books on plants certainly do not contain a single one."

Albert's work on plants does contain, however, many passages in which he recognizes experience as a criterion of truth or gives the results of his personal observations. Such passages occur especially in the sixth book where he tries to satisfy his students' curiosity, but we may first note an earlier passage where he recommends "making conjectures and experiments" in order to learn the nature of trees in general and of each variety of tree, herb, fruit, and fungus in particular. Since, however, one can scarcely have personal experience of them all, it is also advisable to read the books which the experts (*experti*) of antiquity have written on such matters. But a mistrust of the assertions of others often accompanies Albert's reliance upon personal observation and experience. Like Galen in his work on medicinal simples, he explains in opening his sixth book that merely to list the names of plants found in existing books would fill a volume, and that he will limit his discussion to those native varieties "better known among us." Of some of these he has had personal experience; for the others he follows authors whom he has found unready to state anything unless it was proved by experience. For experience alone is reliable concerning particular natures. He cautions in regard to a tree which is said to save doves from serpents, "But this has not been sufficiently proved by certain experience, like the other facts which are written here, but is found in the writings of the ancients." Of another assertion he remarks, "But this is proved by no experience"; and of a third he says, "As some affirm, but I have not tested this myself."

Personal observation and experience are equally, if not more, noticeable in Albert's work on animals. He proposes to tell "what he knows by reason and what he sees by experience of the natures of animals"; he adds that science cannot be attained in all matters by demonstration, in some cases one must resort to conjecture. After listing various remedies for the infirmities of falcons from the work on falconry of the Emperor Frederick, he concludes, "Such are the medicines which one finds given for falcons and the experience of wise men, but the wise falconer will with time add to or subtract from them according to his own experience of what is beneficial to the state of health of the birds. For experience is the best teacher in all matters of this sort."

In the treatise on animals as in that on plants Albert's allusions to experience occur mainly in the last few books where he describes particular animals. Here he often says, "I have tested this," or "I and my associates have experienced," or "I have not experienced this," or "I have proved that this is not true." Like Alexander of Neckam he rejects the story that the beaver castrates itself in order to escape with its life from its hunters; Albert says that experience near his home has often disproved this. In discussing whales he restricts himself entirely to the results of his own observation, saying, "We pass over what the Ancients have written on this topic because their statements do not agree with experience." According to Pouchet Albert gives even more detailed information concerning whales than do the Norse sagas, and also includes animals of the north unknown to classical writers. He occasionally reveals his nationality by giving the German as well as the

Latin names of animals, and he displays an acquaintance with the fauna of surrounding countries such as Norway, Sweden, Bohemia, and Carinthia. He asserts that there are no eels in the Danube and its tributaries, but that they abound in the other rivers of Germany. He tells of observing the habits of eagles in Livonia, or supports the account in Solinus of a monstrous beast with fore legs like human arms and hind legs like human legs by stating that he has seen both male and female of the species captured in the forests of Russia (*Sclaviae*). Of his wide travels and observation of natural phenomena we shall meet other examples as we proceed.

Albert has not only observed animal life widely, he has also performed experiments with animals as he apparently did not do with plants. He and his associates, for instance, have proved by experiment that a cicada goes on singing in its breast for a long time after its head has been cut off. He also proved to his satisfaction that the turtle, although a marine animal, would not drink sea water, unless possibly fresh water which flowed into the sea, by experimenting with a turtle in a vessel of water. He has heard it said that the ostrich eats and digests iron, but the many ostriches to whom he has offered the metal have consistently declined it, although they would devour with avidity stones and bones cut into small bits. Crude experiments these may be, but they are at least purposive.

Albert also often expresses doubt as to certain statements concerning animals on the ground that they have not been tested by experience, even if he has had no opportunity to disprove them. And he draws a sharp distinction between authors who state what they themselves have seen and tested and those who appear simply to repeat rumor or folk-lore. That there are any such birds as gryphons or griffins, he believes is affirmed in story-books (*historiae*) rather than supported by the experiments of philosophers or arguments of philosophy. The story found in the *Physiologus* of the pelican's restoring its young with its own blood he also considers as "read in story-books rather than proved philosophically by experience,"—a criticism which shows how mistaken those modern scholars have been who have declared the Physiologus and Bestiaries representative of the thirteenth century attitude towards nature. The accounts of harpies which one reads are also according to Albert "not based upon experience, but are the assertions of men of no great authority." They are said to be rapacious birds with crooked nails and human faces, and when a harpy meets a man in the desert it is said to kill him, but afterwards, when it sees by its reflection in the water that its own face is human, it grieves all the rest of its life for the man whom it has slain. "But these statements," says Albert, "have not been experienced and seem fabulous. Such tales are told especially by a certain Adelinus" (perhaps the Anglo-Saxon Aldhelm) "and Solinus and Jo-

rach." Albert is particularly chary of accepting the assertions of these last two authors, assuring us, anent their statement that certain birds can fly unharmed through flames, "These philosophers tell many lies and I think that this is one of their lies." In yet other passages Albert calls one or the other of them a liar. He also sometimes rejects statements of Pliny, once classing him with Solinus among those who rehearse popular hearsay rather than disclose scientific experience.

Albert thus displays considerable independence in dealing with past authorities. Yet at times statements in earlier writers which seem absurd to us pass him unchallenged. He is far, for example, from rejecting all of Pliny's marvelous assertions. He still believes that the little fish *eschinus* can stop "a ship two hundred feet or more" in length by clinging to its keel, so that neither wind nor art nor violence can move it. And he adds something to Pliny's tale of hunters who make good their escape to their ship with the tiger's cubs by throwing them one at a time to the pursuing tigress, who takes each whelp back to her lair before returning to the pursuit of the hunters. Albert's emendation is that the hunters provide themselves with glass spheres which they roll one at a time towards the pursuing tigress. Seeing her own reflection on a small scale in the glass ball, she thinks it one of her cubs until she has vainly tried to give it milk, when she discovers the fraud and bounds after the hunters again. But a second and a third glass ball deceive her temporarily as before, and so the hunters reach their ship without having had to surrender any of the real cubs. This imputation of singular stupidity to the tigress should be kept in mind to set against other passages in medieval writers where almost human sagacity is ascribed to animals. Although in two or three preceding passages Albert has refuted the doctrine of spontaneous generation of animal life, he attributes the following passage to Pliny without adverse criticism. "There is a worm shaped like a star, as Pliny says, which shines like a star at night; but it never appears except when after great clouds it predicts clear weather. He says that there is so much rigid cold in this worm that it extinguishes fire like ice. And if a man's flesh is touched with its slime, all the hair falls off and what it touches decays. And he says that they beget nothing, nor is there male or female among them. Therefore they are generated from decaying matter." Albert also accepts the story of the poisoned maiden sent to Alexander the Great.

Albert also is unduly credulous of utterances about animals supposed to be based upon experience, although he cannot be called a mere empiricist, since he tries to test particular statements by the general laws concerning living beings which he has read in Aristotle or derived from his own experience and reflection. He denies, for example, Pliny's statement that other animals are attracted by the pleasant smell which the panther emits as it sleeps after overeating, on the ground that man is the only animal who is pleased or displeased by odors. But it would seem that some of the fishermen, fowlers, and hunters from whom he gleaned bits of zoological information were not so trustworthy as he imagined. He says that "a trustworthy person" told him that he saw in an eagle's nest three hundred ducks, over a hundred geese, about forty hares, and many large fish, all of which were required to satisfy the appetites of the young eagles. He also "heard from trustworthy persons" that a serpent with the virgin countenance of a beardless man "was slain in an island of Germany and there displayed in our times to all who wished to see it until the flesh putrefied." Such reports of mermaids and sea-serpents have still, however, a certain currency. Experienced hunters said that worms could be killed in any beast by suspending from its neck a strip of citron (*sticados citrinum*) immediately after it had been dried. German artificers of Albert's day told him that the hyena bore a gem in its eyes, or more truly in its forehead. Albert sometimes has a tall story of his own to tell. At Cologne in the presence of himself and many associates a little girl of perhaps three years was exhibited who, as soon as she was released from her mother's hands, ran to the corners of the room searching for spiders, "and ate them all large and small, and flourished on this diet and greatly preferred it to all other food." Albert also learned by personal experience that moles gladly eat frogs and toads. For once he saw a mole who held by the foot a big toad which "cried loudly because of the mole's bite." He also found by experience that both frogs and toads would eat a dead mole. In affirming that the custom of killing off the old men is still prevalent within the borders of Saxony and Poland, Albert says, "As I have seen with my own eyes"; but really all that he has seen is the graves of their fathers which the sons have shown to him.

Albert's general attitude towards past authorities and present experience remains the same in his treatise on minerals. He will give the names of the important gems and state their virtues as known from authorities and experience, but he will not repeat everything that has been said about precious stones because it is not profitable for science. "For natural science is not simply receiving what one is told, but the investigation of causes in natural phenomena." Concerning metals, too, he intends to state "rationally either what has been handed down by the philosophers or what I myself have experienced." He adds that once he wandered far in exile to places rich in mines in order that he might test the natures of metals. "And for this same reason I investigated the transmutation of metals among the alchemists, in order that I might observe something of the nature and charactcristics of the metals." In a later chapter he alludes to workers in copper "in our parts, namely, Paris and Cologne, and in other places where

I have been and seen things tested by experience." *Fui et vidi experiri*, such is Albert the Great's peaceful paraphrase, probably unintentional, for warring Caesar's *Veni, vidi, vici.*

Again, also, in the treatise on minerals, reliance upon experience proves to be no sure guarantee against incorrect notions, credulity, and unquestioning trust in authority. Albert still repeats the old notion that "adamant," hard as it is, is softened and dissolved by the blood and flesh of a goat, especially if the goat for some time before has been fed on a diet of certain herbs and wine. He adds that this property of goat's blood makes it beneficial for sufferers from stone in the bladder. Albert repeats with a qualifying "It is said" the statement that the emerald comes from the nests of gryphons or griffins, but he does not stop to deny the existence of those birds, as we have heard him do elsewhere. He adds, however, as to the source of the emerald that "a truthful and curious experimenter coming from Greece" had said that it was produced in rocks under the sea. This expression, "curious experimenter" (*curiosus experimentator*), or perhaps better "inquisitive observer," Albert also applied to one of his associates who saw Frederick II's peculiar magnet. In the present discussion of the emerald he adds that experience in his own time has proved that this stone, "if good and true," cannot endure sexual intercourse, so that the reigning king of Hungary, who was wearing an emerald upon his finger when he went in to his wife, broke it into three pieces. "And that is probably why they say that this stone inclines its wearer to chastity."

Albert, however, had told as a personal experience a stranger tale than this of an emerald in his work on vegetables and plants in order to illustrate "the many effects of stones and plants which are known by experience and by which wonders are worked." But as a matter of fact, the incident is concerned not with an emerald and a plant, but an emerald and a toad, an animal which one would infer was in Albert's day often the subject of experiment.

"An emerald was recently seen among us, small in size but marvelous in beauty. When its virtue was to be tested, someone stepped forth and said that, if a circle was made about a toad with the emerald and then the stone was set before the toad's eyes, one of two things would happen. Either the stone, if of weak virtue, would be broken by the gaze of the toad; or the toad would burst, if the stone was possessed of full natural vigor. Without delay things were arranged as he bade; and after a short lapse of time, during which the toad kept its eye unswervingly upon the gem, the latter began to crack like a nut and a portion of it flew from the ring. Then the toad, which had stood immovable hitherto, withdrew as if it had been freed from the influence of the gem."

In the incident just narrated Albert was perhaps tricked by some traveling magician. But let us conclude our discussion of his general scientific method by some more rational instances of personal observation and experience. In his treatise on meteorology his discussion of the rainbow, which occupies some twenty-four pages of Borgnet's text, is especially based upon experience and full of allusions to it—a very interesting fact in view of the large space which the discussion of the rainbow occupies in Roger Bacon's better known eulogy of experimental science. Albert recounts his own observations when sailing over great waves or when looking down from the top of a castle built upon a high mountain, "and the time when this was seen was in the morning after a rainy night, and it was in the autumn with the sun in the sign of Virgo." Albert takes exception to Aristotle's assertion that rainbows caused by the moon at night appear only twice in fifty years. He and many others have seen a bow at night, and "truthful experimenters have found by experience" (*veridici experimentatores experti sunt*) that a rainbow has appeared twice at night in the same year. Nor can Albert conceive of any astronomical reason why it should appear only twice in fifty years. "And so I think that Aristotle stated this from the opinions of others and not from the truth of demonstration or experience, while those facts which have been adduced against his statement have been experienced beyond a doubt by myself and by other reliable investigators associated with me." The very chapter headings of this portion of Albert's treatise suggest an antithesis between the ancient authorities and recent experimental investigation, for instance: "Of the Iris of the Moon and what Ancients have said of it and what Moderns have tested by experience," and "A Digression stating Seneca's views concerning *virgae* and experiments with certain arcs seen in modern times." Thus while Albert of course believes that the statements of many of his authorities are based upon experience, he seems to feel that he and his associates have founded an important modern school for the investigation of nature at first hand. We may choose to regard it as a mere school of observation, but he dignifies its members by the title of *experimentatores*. Again therefore we may admit that Pouchet was not unjustified in associating Albert with the modern experimental school.

. . . . .

At the close of his story of the toad and the emerald Albert adds that there are many other such virtues of stones and plants which are learned by experience, and that magicians investigate the same and work wonders by them. It is therefore quite appropriate for us to turn directly from his attitude to experimental method to his conception of magic. Like William of Auvergne he hints at an association between the two. His pupil and contemporary, Ulrich Engelbert of Strasburg, actually called him "expert in magic."

In his *Life of Albert* Peter of Prussia not only is evidently concerned to make him out a saint as well as a scientist, telling of his devotion to the Eucharist and the Virgin Mary and the wood of the Holy Cross and of the miraculous visions which he had from childhood, in which the Virgin and the Apostle Paul appeared to him, and how he advanced more in knowledge by prayer than by study and labor, and that he read the Psalter through daily. He also devotes a number of chapters to a defense of Albert against the charge of having indulged in occult sciences, and of having been "too curious concerning natural phenomena." Peter explains that many superstitions were rife in Albert's time and that necromancers were fascinating the people by their false miracles, and pretending that their sorcery was worked by the sciences of astronomy, mathematics, and alchemy. It was therefore essential that some man who was equally learned and devout should thoroughly examine these sciences, proving what was good in them and rejecting what was bad. Peter is inclined to be disingenuous in stating Albert's attitude toward some of the occult sciences, especially the engraving of stones with images according to the aspects of the stars, which he misrepresents Albert as prohibiting, whereas Albert really calls it a good doctrine, as we shall show later. Peter however states "how useful it is to know natural and occult phenomena in the nature of things, and that those who write about such things are to be praised for it." Also "that it is useful and necessary to know the facts of nature even if they are indecent." Later on, towards the close of his book, Peter denies various feats of magic that by his time had come to be popularly recounted of Albert, and then does his best to make up for the subtracted marvels by himself inventing many pious miracles in which he would have us believe Albert was concerned.

The learned Trithemius (1462-1516), abbot of Sponheim, in a letter to John Westenburgh in which he defends himself against the charge of magic, admits that he "cannot say that he is entirely ignorant of natural magic," a form of wisdom which he regards very highly; and adduces in his justification the example of "Albertus Magnus, that most learned man and among the saints truly most saintly, of the profoundest intellect, worthy of eternal memory, who scrutinized the depths of natural philosophy, and learned to know marvels unheard of by others." Even to this day, continues Trithemius, he is unjustly regarded by the unlearned as a magician and devotee of superstition. For he was not ignorant of the magic of nature, and he had innocently read and mastered a great number of superstitious books by depraved men. For not the knowledge but the practice of evil is evil. Trithemius admits that he himself has read many books of superstitious and even diabolical magic, but contends that this is necessary, if one is to learn to distinguish natural from illicit magic.

The brief but sane estimate of Albertus Magnus published eighty years ago in the *Histoire Littéraire de la France,* from which we have already had occasion to quote regarding his importance in the history of natural science, mentions the efforts of Trithemius and Naudé to defend him from the charge of magic, but adds that even his panegyrists have called him "great in magic, greater in philosophy, greatest in theology," and agrees that he frequently shows a leaning towards the occult sciences. "He is an alchemist, he is an astrologer, he believes in enchantments; he delights like most savants of his age in explaining all phenomena that surprise him by supernatural causes." This rough characterization contains much truth, although it is hardly true that Albert gave supernatural explanations for strange natural phenomena. Rather he believed in occult forces and marvels in nature which we no longer credit. We also have already stated it as our opinion that he was really much greater as a natural scientist than as a theologian. But we have now to examine what grounds there are for calling him *magnus in magia,* and *in magicis expertus*.

Magic is often mentioned by Albert, both in his Biblical and Aristotelian commentaries, both in his theological writings and his works on natural science. Some references to magic arts, occurring chiefly in the Biblical commentaries, are too brief, incidental, and perfunctory to afford any particular information. The other passages seem scarcely consistent with one another and will require separate treatment. We shall first consider those in which Albert more or less adheres to the traditional Christian attitude of condemnation of magic as criminal and dealing with demons, of recognition of its marvels but jealous differentiation of them from divine miracle. It should be observed that all such passages occur in his theological writings and that in them he does little more than rehearse opinions which we have already encountered in the writings of the early Christian fathers with a few additional citations from books of necromancy or from Arabic works on natural science such as those of Algazel and Avicenna.

Albert has no doubt either in his scientific or religious writings that marvels can be worked by magic. It is true that one of its departments, *praestigia,* has to do with illusions and juggleries in which things are made to appear to exist which have no reality. But it also performs actual transformations. But even the actual performances of magic are deceptive in that demons by their means lead human souls astray, which is far worse than merely to deceive the eye.

Albert affirms in his theological **Summa** that it is the consensus of opinion that magic is due to demons. "For the saints expressly say so, and it is the common opinion of all persons, and it is taught in that part of necromancy which deals with images and rings and mirrors of Venus and seals of demons by Achot Grae-cus and Grema of Babylon and Hermes of Egypt, and invocations for this purpose are described in the book of Hermogenes and Philetus, the necromancers, and in the book called the Almandel of Solomon." In his **Commentary on the Sentences** Albert declares that to make use of "magic virtues" is evil and apostasy from the Faith, whether one openly resorts to "invocations, conjurations, sacrifices, suffumigations, and adorations," or to some simple operation which none the less requires demon aid for its performance. One must beware even of "mathematical virtues," that is, of astrological forces, especially in "images, rings, mirrors, and characters," lest the practice of idolatry be introduced. In commenting upon the passage in the gospel where the Pharisees accuse Christ of casting out demons through the prince of demons, Albert admits that necromancers are able to cast out demons and to restrain them from doing external damage, but holds that they cannot like Christ restrain the evil spirits from inciting inward sin.

Albert will not admit, however, that the marvels of magic compare with divine miracles. For one thing, feats of magic do not even happen as instantaneously as miracles, although they occur much more rapidly than the ordinary processes of nature. But except for this difference in speed the works of magic can usually be explained as the product of natural forces, and by the fact that the demons are aided in their operations by the influence of the stars. To change rods into snakes, for instance, as Pharaoh's magicians did, is simply hastening the process by which worms generate in decaying trees. Indeed, Albert is inclined to believe that the demons "produce no permanent substantial form that would not easily be produced by putrefaction." The magic power of fascination is after all only analogous to the virtue of the sapphire in curing ulcers or of the emerald in restraining sexual passion. Albert adds the comforting thought that neither fascination nor the magic art can harm anyone who has firm faith in God, but for us the most important thing to note is that even in his theological writings he has associated magic with natural forces and the stars as well as with demons. In this he resembles William of Auvergne rather than the early Christian fathers.

Like some other Christian commentators, Albert exempts the Magi of the gospel story, who followed the star to Bethlehem, from the category of magicians in the evil sense that we have just heard him define magic. In his commentary upon the gospel by Matthew he asserts that "the Magi are not sorcerers (*malefici*) as some wrongly think." He also affirms that there is a difference between a Magus and a *mathematicus* or an enchanter or necromancer or *ariolus* or *aruspex* or diviner. Like Isidore Albert adopts the incorrect etymology of connecting Magus and *magnus*. But for him the Magi are not so called on account of the magnitude of their sins. "Etymologically the Magi are great men" whose knowledge of, or conjecture from, the inevitable processes of cause and effect in nature often enables them to predict or produce marvels of nature. In his commentary on the Book of Daniel Albert quotes Jerome's similar description of them as "masters who philosophize about the universe; moreover, the Magi are more particularly called astronomers who search the future in the stars." It is interesting to note that this view of the Magi still persists among Roman Catholics; the recent Catholic Encyclopedia still insists concerning the wise men who came to Bethlehem, "Neither were they magicians: the good meaning of *mágoi,* though found nowhere else in the Bible, is demanded by the context of the second chapter of Matthew." But here is a still more interesting point to note: Albertus Magnus does not deny that the Magi were magicians. To contend that Magi were not *magi* was a contradiction of terms that was probably too much for his common sense. All that he tries to do is to exculpate them from the practice of those particular evil, superstitious, and diabolical occult arts which Isidore and others had included in their definitions of magic. From evil witchcraft and necromancy and fatalistic astrology, from augury and liver divination, from the arts of *sortilegi* and *pythones,* of enchanters "who by means of certain incantations perform certain feats with beasts or herbs or stones or images," or of diviners who employ geomancy or "the chance of fire" or hydromancy or aerimancy: from all such practices he acquits them. "They were not devoted to any of these arts, but only to magic as it has been described. And this is praiseworthy." Thus Albert not merely defends the Magi, he praises magic; and we begin to see the fitness of the epithet, *Magnus in magia,* as applied to him.

But how does this praiseworthy magic differ from the magic which he condemned in his **Summa** and commentary on the Sentences? Presumably in that its objects are good not evil, and that it does not make any use of demons. It would seem to resemble closely the natural magic of William of Auvergne. It is like evil magic in that both employ the forces of nature and the influences of the stars, but it is unlike it in that it employs them exclusively and is free from any resort to demons and also apparently from the use of incantations or the superstitious devices of geomancers and other diviners.

If in his theological writings Albert thus distinguishes two varieties of magic, one good and one evil, one demoniacal and one natural, we need not be surprised if in his scientific treatises, where he is influenced mainly by Arabian astrology, the pseudo-Aristotelian treatises, the Hermetic literature, and other such writings rather than by patristic literature, he introduces yet a third conception of magic, which scarcely agrees with either of the others and yet has features in common with both. He nowhere in his commentaries on Aristotle or other works of natural science really stops and discusses magic at any length. But there are a number of brief and incidental allusions to it which imply that it is a distinct and definite branch of knowledge of which, although he himself does not treat, he gives no sign of disapproval. He also cites even enchanters and necromancers without offering any apology, and now seems to regard as sub-divisions of magic those occult arts from which we have just heard him exculpate the Magi.

In his treatise on animals Albert states that anointing a sleeper's temples with the blood of a hoopoe makes him see terrible dreams, and that enchanters value highly the brain, tongue, and heart of this bird. He adds, "But we shall not discuss this matter here, for the investigation of it belongs to another science,"—presumably to magic. In his treatise on plants he says that certain herbs seem to have "divine effects" which those who study magic follow up further. Examples are the betony, said to confer the power of divination, the verbena, used as a love charm, and the herb *meropis,* supposed to open closed seas, and many other such plants listed in the books of incantations of Hermes the philosopher and of Costa ben Luca the philosopher and in the books of physical ligatures. "Enchanter" (*Incantator*), apparently the author or title of a book, is cited more than once for the virtues of herbs, and what enchanters in general say is also mentioned. "According to the testimony of the *praestigia* of the magi" the juice of a certain herb drunk in water makes a person do or say whatever the magician says or does. Students of magic believe that the seed of another herb extinguishes lust. Necromancers avow that betony indicates the future when plucked with an adjuration of Aesculapius, and students of necromancy say that a man invoking demons should have a character painted on him with the herb Jusquiam, and that gods invoked by characters and seals and sacrifices present themselves more readily if frankincense is offered them. Such passages seem to indicate that Albert regarded occult virtues as largely the concern of magic, but that at least in necromancy the invocation of gods and demons also enters.

Many allusions to magic occur in Albert's treatise on minerals, as the especially marvelous powers attributed to gems in antiquity might well lead us to expect. The magi, he tells us, make much use of the stone *diacodos,* which is said to excite phantasms but loses its virtue if it touches a corpse. But such things do not come within Albert's present scope; he refers the reader for further information to the books of magic of Hermes, Ptolemy, and Thebith ben Chorath. The stone magnet is also stated in the magic books to have a marvelous power of producing phantasms, especially if consecrated with an adjuration and a character.

Albert twice assures us that the "prodigious and marvelous" powers of stones, and more particularly of images and seals engraved on stones, cannot be really understood without a knowledge of the three other sciences of magic, necromancy, and astrology. He therefore will not in this treatise on minerals discuss the subject as fully as he might, "since those powers cannot be proved by physical laws (*principiis physicis*), but require a knowledge of astronomy and magic and the necromantic sciences, which should be considered in other treatises." For the reason why gems were first so engraved he refers his readers to "the science of the *magi* which Magor Graecus and Germa of Babylon and Hermes the Egyptian were among the first to perfect, and in which later wise Ptolemy was a marvelous light and Geber of Spain; Tebith, too, handed down a full treatment of the art." And in this science it is a fundamental principle that all things produced by nature or art are influenced by celestial virtues. Thus we comprehend the close connection of astrology and magic. As for necromancy, the third "science" involved, Albert's associates are curious to know the doctrine of images even if it is necromancy, and Albert does not hesitate to assure them that it is a good doctrine in any case. Yet in his theological writings he not only condemned necromancy, but declared the art of images to be evil "because it inclines to idolatry by imputing divinity to the stars, and . . . is employed for idle or evil ends."

Albert again refers to magic in his discussion of alchemy in the treatise on minerals, where he not only cites Hermes a great deal but refers to writings by Avicenna on magic and alchemy. Albert holds that it is not the business of a physical or natural scientist (*physicus*) to determine concerning the transmutation of metals; that is the affair of the art of alchemy, which thus seems to lie outside the field of natural science upon the borders of magic. Similarly the problem in what places and mountains and by what signs metals are discovered falls partly within the sphere of natural science and partly belongs to that magical science which has to do with finding hidden treasure. Albert perhaps has the employment of the divining rod in mind.

The occult virtue of the human mind is another matter which Albert seems inclined to place within the field of magic. In the treatise on minerals he remarks that whether fascination is true or not is a question for magic to settle, and in his *On Sleep and Waking* he cites Avicenna and Algazel as adducing "fascination and magic virtues" as examples of occult influence exerted by one man over another. It will be remembered that he cited the same authors anent fascination in his *Commentary on the Sentences,* but there denied that fascination or magic could harm anyone who had firm faith in God, although he illustrated the possibility of potent human occult virtue exercised at will by the marvelous virtues exerted constantly by the sapphire and emerald. Peter of Prussia gives us to understand that Albert's belief was that fascination did not

operate naturally but by the aid of demons; nevertheless certain men are generated at rare intervals who work marvels like the twins in Germany in Albert's time at whose approach bolts would open.

Albert also regards the interpretation of dreams as especially the affair of magic. In one passage of *On Sleep and Waking* he grants that probably the art of interpreting dreams cannot be acquired without a knowledge of magic and "astronomy." In a second passage he speaks of the magicians as teaching the interpretation of dreams and the "astronomers" as talking of signs of prophecies, but not the sort of prophecy accepted among theologians. In a third passage he defines the kind of dreams "which wise men interpret and for which was invented the art of interpretation in the magical sciences." Albert seems to have no particular objection, either moral or religious, to the interpretation of dreams, even if it is a branch of magic. Rather he censures Aristotle and other philosophers for not having investigated this side of the subject further, and he thinks that by physical science alone one can at least determine what sort of dreams are of value for purposes of divination and are susceptible to interpretation. Magicians make great use not only of dreams but also of visions seen when one is awake but with the senses distracted. The magicians indeed specialize in potions which clog and stupefy the senses, and thereby produce apparitions by means of which they predict the future.

In this same treatise *On Sleep and Waking* Albert lists together "the astronomer and augur and magician and interpreter of dreams and visions and every such diviner." He admits that almost all men of this type delight in deception and are poorly educated and confuse what is contingent with what is necessary, but he insists that "the defect is not in the science but in those who abuse it." Thus magic and divination in general are closely associated.

This last passage, like the connecting of enchanters and necromancers with magic which we have noted in a previous paragraph, is hard to reconcile with the passage in his commentary upon the Gospel of Matthew where Albert separated the Magi and magic from diviners, enchanters, necromancers, and their arts. So far as mere classification is concerned, Albert's references to magic in his scientific writings are in closer accord with his discussion of magic in the *Summa* and *Sentences,* where too he associated magic with the stars, with occult virtues, with fascination, and with images. But the emphasis which he there laid upon the evil character of magic and its connection with demons is now almost entirely lacking. Our attention is rather being continually called to how closely magic, or at least some parts of it, border upon natural science and astronomy. And yet we are also always being reminded that magic, although itself a "science," is essentially different in methods and results from natural science or at least from what Albert calls "physical science." Overlapping both these fields, apparently, and yet rather distinct from both in Albert's thought, is the great subject of "astronomy" which includes both the genuine natural science and the various vagaries of astrology. It is all like some map of a feudal area where certain fiefs owe varying degrees of fealty to, or are claimed by, several lords and where the frontiers are loose, fluctuating, and uncertain. Perhaps the rule of the stars can be made to account for almost everything in natural science or in magic, but Albert seems inclined to leave room for the independent action of divine power, the demons, and the human mind and will. . . . [In conclusion] let us make the one further observation that while Albert describes magic differently and even inconsistently in different passages, it is evident enough that he is trying to describe the same thing all the time.

Thomas Greenwood (essay date 1932)

SOURCE: "Albertus Magnus: His Scientific Views," in *Nature,* Vol. 129, No. 3251, February 20, 1932, pp. 266-68.

[*In the following essay, Greenwood comments on Albert's scientific writings "as they represent the state of scientific knowledge in the Middle Ages."*]

"Everything there was to be known, he knew." Thus is the genius of Albert the Great characterised by the Pope in the remarkable Bull "In Thesauris Sapientiæ" declaring the blessed Bishop of Regensburg a saint and a doctor of the Church. In this "Decretal Letter", dated Dec. 16, 1931, but published on Jan. 14, 1932, Pope Pius XI. points out that Albert the Great (1206-1280) was not only a lover of God, a pastor of souls, and a master of the sacred sciences, but also a pioneer in secular knowledge. He wrote about astronomy, physics, mechanics, chemistry, mineralogy, anthropology, zoology, botany, architecture, and the applied arts; and the modern edition of his writings makes thirty-eight thick quarto volumes. Indeed, Albert the Great broke the chains that kept natural science in the hands of unbelievers, and vindicated it against the more timid pious persons of his time who were afraid of it for fear of its abuse. For, says the Pope, "no real theologian is afraid of any damage from the operations of nature or of natural reason rightly investigated, for these very things bear upon them the light of the Creator himself".

We do not propose here to give any account of the edifying and active life of St. Albert the Great, or to report on the various causes which led to his canonisation by the Church. Nor do we intend to give an outline of the theological and philosophical views of a master mind who is now honoured as one of the twen-

ty-eight doctors of the Church, together with Gregory, Basil, Ambrose, Augustine, Jerome, Thomas Aquinas, Anselm, Bernard, Beda, Ephraem, John of the Cross, and Bellarmine. We shall endeavour, however, to give a short sketch of the scientific views of Albert the Great, which are of the greatest interest for the history of science, especially as they represent the state of scientific knowledge in the Middle Ages.

Though Albert seems to be less original and forceful as a scientific thinker than his contemporary Roger Bacon, yet he was far more influential on the age in which he lived. The peculiarity of his encyclopædic teaching was that it was based entirely on the writings of Aristotle. This was remarkable because the Aristotelian principles were resisted by the Church at the time; the provincial council at Siena in 1210 going so far as to forbid the use of Aristotle's books on natural philosophy. But though no professor was permitted to lecture on them, and in spite of the fact that in 1215 the *Physics* and the *Metaphysics* were banned by the statutes of the University of Paris, Albert the Great was actively promoting the new philosophy, probably with the connivance of the Church authorities, who allowed a responsible theologian to sift the true from the false the while they acted as the stern guardians of orthodoxy. He soon joined hands with his pupil Thomas Aquinas, who, if he surpassed his master in the theological and philosophical interpretations of the Stagyrite's system, does not, however, compare favourably with Albert in his scientific studies.

The astronomical beliefs of Albert, though partly inspired by Aristotle, differ widely on many important points from the views of the Stagyrite. Albert taught that the heavens move from east to west carrying along with them their particular stars which move from west to east, "something like the motion of an ant on a wheel rotating in a contrary direction". The whole world is like a huge machine moved by God according to secret principles which the human intellect, however, can partly discover. Each star, in turn, is moved by a pure intellect, each having its own heavens with its particular motion; so that the circles of the stars are not concentric, as Aristotle on the authority of Eudoxus taught, but eccentric as in Ptolemy's system. Yet the earth is at the centre of the world, the heavens of the Moon, Venus, Mercury, the Sun, Mars, Jupiter, Saturn, the fixed stars, the aqueous, the crystalline and the empyreal heavens, coming in succession, the last-named being the dwelling-place of the blessed. It is this system which must have inspired Dante's cosmology; and we find in the *Paradiso* this reference to Albert the Great:

> Questi, che m' è a destra più vicino
> Frate e maestro fummi, ed esso Alberto
> È di Cologna.

Albert was not entirely satisfied with his cosmological theories, which are sometimes very difficult to follow. He knew that his opinion could not be final when he wrote that "celestial phenomena are so far away from anything we know that we have no means of understanding them perfectly. All we know for certain is that the heavenly bodies are moved by a soul, that is, by a separate substance, an intellectual mover, a unit of intellectual life" (*De Coelo et Mundo*).

The belief in the existence of a pure intellect in each heavenly body led Albert to share the current opinion of his time about the influence of the stars on human beings, each intellect having a direct influence over the one immediately following it in the hierarchy of spirits. At the top of the scale, the omniscient and omnipotent mind of God controls the whole of the world, right down to the elements, the compound and the simple bodies. Parallel with this hierarchy of creatures there is a hierarchy of light and a hierarchy of weight: the four traditional elements, earth, water, air, and fire, are thus drawn up in echelons from the heaviest, earth, which is at the bottom or in the middle of things, to water, then air, and finally fire which rejoins the celestial bodies— a conception which reminds one of Anaximander's cosmogony. These considerations on the order in the realm of matter have their equivalent in the realm of spirit: the simplest intellect gives the most perfect motion to the star to which it is attached; and again, the simplest and most perfect intellect has the most adequate knowledge of things, the intrinsic and epistemological power of the various creatures being thus echeloned from the Highest God to the humblest of His creatures. The detailed development of this powerful vision of the nature of reality allows Albert the Great to state and explain his views about the various provinces of our knowledge: the part played by each natural or spiritual being is thus accounted for according to its place in the hierarchy of God's creatures.

Details about the particular sciences are interesting. In alchemy, for example, Albert himself tried several reactions, describing accurately enough the preparation of nitric acid or, as he called it, 'prime water' or philosophical water to the first degree of perfection, and giving at the same time its principal properties, such as the oxidation of metals and the separation of gold from silver. By combining three parts of prime water with one part of sal ammoniac he obtained the secondary water; the tertiary water is obtained by treating mercury with the secondary water, and the fourth water is the result of the distillation of the tertiary water after it has been left for four days in a vessel covered with manure. This fourth water was very popular among the alchemists of the time, who called it 'philosophers' vinegar', 'mineral water', and 'celestial dew'.

Albert distinguished four 'metallic spirits', mercury, sulphur, orpiment, and sal ammoniac, which could all be used to stain metals in gold or silver. But he warned us that the gold or the silver of the alchemists is not pure gold or silver. In fact, though the theory of a 'materia prima' and the conception of transmutation made chiefly an intellectual and philosophical appeal to him, Albert did not believe in the actuality of transmutation. Thus he wrote in *De Mineralibus* (Bk. 3, 9): "Alchemy cannot change metals, but can only imitate them. I have tested alchemistic gold; but after six or seven heatings, it is burned and reduced to ashes." He was the first to use the word "affinitas", in his treatise *De Rebus Metallicis,* which was no doubt suggested to him by the views of ancient Greek philosophers current at the time, that chemical reaction is due to a similarity or kinship between the reacting substances, or, as maintained by Hippocrates, that like unites only with like. Thus, said Albert, "sulphur blackens silver and generally burns all metals, because of its natural affinity with them" (propter affinitatem naturæ metalla adurit). It seems also that Albert was the first to call sulphate of iron "vitreolum". His small treatise *De Alchimia* gives a vivid picture of the state of alchemy and alchemists in the Middle Ages, a picture which has been confirmed since by the descriptions of Paracelsus.

In his biological works Albert follows very closely Aristotle's text, given a sentence or two of the Stagyrite and adding his own remarks by way of commentary; in sifting what is Aristotle's from Albert's additions, it has been found that the remarks of the Dominican monk contain a considerable amount of personal observations which prove that he was a naturalist of great ability. In his *Short History of Biology,* Prof. Charles Singer quotes a long passage of Albert's treatise *De Animalibus* in which there are some striking remarks about embryos of birds and of fishes; while he considers Albert's book *De Plantis* as the best work on natural history produced during the Middle Ages. Albert seems to be at a loss, however, in his attempt to draw up any general account of plants, since he reaches no satisfactory basis of classification, and is equally ignorant both of their minute structure and their true mode of reproduction. Yet his descriptions are fairly accurate, and show that he had a remarkable gift of observation.

These general remarks illustrate the range of Albert's knowledge and scientific interests. He probably wrote also on mathematics, as he often refers to his mathematical works, especially the 15th and 16th books of his geometry; but these works have not reached us. We know, however, that Albert placed mathematics between metaphysics and natural science, the object of mathematics being defined as the motion and material extension of natural objects independently of their essence and their fundamental causes. The mathematician studies the straight line, for example, as it is materially illustrated in Nature, but he does not consider the cause of the straight line or the particular matter which illustrates it. Such considerations were possible, of course, at a time when Euclidean geometry was the only known system in terms of which Nature could be interpreted.

Today these and the other scientific views of Albert the Great could scarcely bear the strain of a searching criticism. It would be unfair, however, to dismiss Albert's claims to consideration because they do not correspond to the extraordinary developments of modern science. Should one ignore Aristotle or Plato because his biology or his cosmology is behind the present state of science? Every system of philosophy has to give some account of Nature, with reference to the scientific beliefs of the time. None of the great thinkers of the past could have possibly established his doctrines in terms of the science of the future; nevertheless, one studies them as they are and often uses them in the interpretation of modern scientific conceptions. The scientific doctrines of Albert the Great are entitled to a similar consideration; and the historian who devotes his patient efforts to the study of the "doctor universalis" will be repaid to the full by the discovery of the valuable indications contained in his writings.

Thomas M. Schwertner (essay date 1932)

SOURCE: "All-Seeing Naturalist" and "Theologian," in *St. Albert the Great,* The Bruce Publishing Company, 1932, pp. 210-29, 270-95.

[*In the following excerpt, Schwertner describes the breadth and depth of Albert's erudition both as a scientist and a theologian.*]

ALL SEEING NATURALIST

One of the inevitable results of the assiduous cultivation of the history of the various natural sciences, so characteristic of all scientific research today, is the rehabilitation of Albert's good name as a scientist. Scholars in goodly numbers are again thinking it worth their while to seek to evaluate his original contributions to the various sciences and to insist upon his towering position in the story of their development. While it is true that for centuries Albert did occupy a leading rank among the makers of science, it is also well known that he was ruthlessly pushed aside when the sciences had freed themselves from the influence of the Church and churchmen. An age which sought to establish a frank enmity between science and religion could not be expected to treat gently a man who was first and foremost a churchman to his finger tips without on that account feeling himself called upon or compelled to foreswear scientific research. And it was an easy matter to besmirch and belittle the scientific

achievements of Albert because of the legends which a bedazzled age had attached to his name, in wonderment over his advanced ideas and novel experiments, as also because of the inevitable handicaps under which he worked and the prejudices against which he had to battle in order to accomplish as much as he did. If the first three centuries following Albert's death exaggerated most extravagantly his scientific attainments and achievements, then the next three hundred years unduly belittled them. Only since 1853 have scholars made a serious attempt to be fair and just to him. This is primarily due to F. A. Pouchet who turned the tide by his *Histoire des sciences naturelles au moyen age, ou Albert le Grand et son epoque considéré comme point de depart de l'ecole experimentalle.* While this important work has in the course of time been corrected in many respects and amplified with new historical data, while many of its secondary positions have been shown to be untenable the unassailable fact remains that its main contentions have not been set aside, even by so chronically prejudiced an authority as the anonymous author of the article on Albert in the *Histoire Litteraire de la France.* This writer had evidently been incensed by the extravagant claims of M. H. de Blainville, in his *Histoire des sciences de l'organization,* published from his notes, with additions, by F. L. M. Maupied. Subsequent scholars like Balss, Stadler, Wimmer, Jessen have supplemented and corroborated the main contentions of Pouchet. At the eightieth convention of the Society of German Naturalists and Physicians at Cologne, on September 31, 1908, Herman Stadler held up Albert to modern investigators as a model of what a true and conscientious scholar should be. Father Eric Wassmann, S.J., whose name will be remembered forever in the history of entymology for his epoch-making discoveries in ant life, remarked that this was the first time on record to his knowledge that a medieval churchman had been proposed as a model scientist to modern savants of any and every or of no shade of religious thought and belief. Naturally, this tardy rehabilitation of a medieval monk and scientist aroused the vehement anger of men like White and Draper who, in challenging the claims put forward for Albert and other churchmen, only succeeded in betraying their own woeful lack of historical knowledge, erudition, and fair-mindedness.

It is worthy of remark in this connection that of all the scholars who in the past seventy-five years have studied the scientific attainments of Albert, Catholic students have been the most cautious, reserved, and modest in their claims and conclusions. They have taken nothing for granted. With laudable wisdom they have abstained from making panegyrics on Albert's character and from turning to apologetic uses his great achievements in the realm of medieval science. They have acted on the assumption that Albert is his own best justification and that, with all his scientific short-

St. Albert; detail of the predella of the great passion, by Fra Angelico.

comings, he was sufficiently in advance of his age to merit respectful consideration from all subsequent times. This admirable historical attitude is probably due in great measure to George von Hertling who, in his *Albertus Magnus. Ein Beitrag zu seiner Würdigung,* laid down historical norms to be followed in dealing with Albert's scientific labors which are a model of their kind for exacting criticism and rigorous scholarship. And the several scholars who have studied the philosophical and theological aspects of Albert's many-sided activity have been ensouled with the principles which von Hertling demanded of all those who essayed to delve in this field where exaggeration seems almost inevitable. Much of the same fine critical spirit—despite occasional betrayals of ignorance of Catholic dogma and regrettable lapses into anti-Romanist terminology—pervades the latest and most erudite study on *A Comprehensive History of Experimental Sciences* by George Sarton, of the Carnegie Institute, where Albert appears with laudable and well-merited frequency in the large section devoted to medieval experimentation.

It must suffice to point out briefly, rapidly, and summarily, under special rubrics, the outstanding achievements of Albert in the various sciences he touched, and to indicate those points in which he outran his day and anticipated our own. In quoting the approving words of modern historical investigators we shall give the preference to those who, not being members of the Catholic Church, cannot be suspected of any undue sympathy for her attitude on the relations of science and faith and for Albert himself, who vindicated that attitude so magnificently.

BOTANY

In his *De Vegetalibus* Albert followed what he thought was a genuine work of Aristotle, but which, in 1857, was allocated to Nicholas of Damascus by Ernest Meyer. After following the pseudo-Aristotelian text for eight chapters Albert abandoned it because, as he said, he found it untrustworthy. Albert's first book, in six chapters, deals with the question of plant souls. The second book has to do with a classification of plants in which he comes very near modern times in the norms he lays down for distinguishing one plant from another. The third book discusses seeds and fruits. The fourth book follows the pseudo-Aristotelian text very closely. The fifth treats of the medicinal properties and effects of plants. The sixth describes trees in alphabetical order. The last book is a treatise on agriculture. Albert is the first European to mention and describe spinach, the relation of grapes to the vines and leaves, the distinction between buds and flowers, the influence of heat and sunlight on the bark of trees. He anticipates Knight by centuries in holding that sap is odorless in the root but fragrant in the trunk and branches. He is the first man to refer scientifically to the rarity of duplicate leaves. He established the difference between thorns and thistles. He had clear ideas on grafting—his remarks on the subject anticipate Luther Burbank. Ellison Hawks says [in *Pioneers of Plant Study,* 1928]: "His description of the apple, its three coats, the five-chambered core, the floral receptacle above the seed with testa and two hemispheral cotyledons is far superior to anything in any earlier writer." Ernest Meyer, as early as 1836 [in *Leschicte der Bontanik*], said: "We do not find a botanist before Albert's time who can be compared to him with the exception of Theophrastus whom he did not know; after his time no one investigated the nature of plants more intelligently and fully until Conrad Gessner and Cisalpin." Carl Jessen remarks [in *De Vegetalibus*]: "Albert was the first man to describe German flora in a scientific way." Remembering the ignorance about botanical studies in the Middle Ages, Hawks declares that "there was one man—Albertus Magnus—who did something to arrive at a scientific study of plants as living things. This had practically been at a standstill since the days of Aristotle."

ZOÖLOGY

George Sarton writes: "The best parts of Albert's works are the botanical and zoölogical books. The zoölogy was based on Michal Scot. It is divided into twenty-six books, of which the first nineteen are a paraphrase of Aristotle's treatises. Books twenty to twenty-six contain new matter, partly derived from personal observation or from direct information. Books twenty and twenty-one deal with generalities; book twenty with the nature of animals' bodies, their structure and forces; book twenty-one with perfect and imperfect animals and the causes of their perfection or imperfection (this is a kind of comparative psychology); books twenty-two and twenty-six are devoted to the description of individual animals, these being introduced in each chapter in the alphabetical order of their Latin names. These books were a sort of appendix to the *De Natura Rerum* of Thomas of Cantimpre, who had sat at his feet in Cologne. Book twenty-two, *gressabilia* (i.e., quadruples; our mammals, excepting bats, whales, and seals); book twenty-three, *volatilia* (i.e., birds and bats); book twenty-four, *aquatica* or *natalilia* (i.e., fishes, whales, seals, cephalopods, shellfishes, water snails, and other aquatic animals); book twenty-five, serpents (i.e., snakes, lizards, salamanders) including the varieties of snakes discussed in Ibn Sina's *Quantum;* book twenty-six, *vermes* (i.e., worms, insects, toads, frogs and snails). Many of the animals were here described for the first time."

In the introduction to the critical edition of the *De Animalibus,* Stadler pointed out that Albert knew and described one hundred and thirteen kinds of quadrupeds, one hundred and fourteen birds, one hundred and thirty-nine aquatic animals, sixty-one serpents and forty-nine worms. He was the first man to mention the weasel, two kinds of martens, and the arctic bear. He was also the first to give the German names to the chamois, the ermine, and the fitchen or polecat. He has the distinction of first insinuating that the peculiarities of cats are due in great part to climatic conditions. He discovered the similarity between the teeth and claws of cats and lions. His brief treatise on falcons was an improvement on the classic work on the same subject by Frederic II. His veterinary erudition was remarkable for the age, so much so, indeed, that several anonymous writers on the same subject, by appropriating Albert's name, obtained instant success for their books. Thus many of the chap-books on "the white and black art of man and beast," circulating to this day under the name of Albert, while not due to his pen are an outcome of the authority he enjoyed among simple hostlers and veterinary doctors. He set the fashion of departing from the custom of the "bestiaries" where moral reflections are made *apropos* the habits and peculiarities of animals. He was one of the first founders of the science of animal anatomy and animal psychology. Lynn Thorndike says [in *A History of Magic and Experimental Science,* 1923]: "Albert has not only observed animal life widely, he has also performed experiments with animals as he apparently did not do with plants. . . . Crude experiments these may be, but they are at least purposive." Stadler points out that from Albert's treatises one could reinhabit German forests with animals found therein. And Wassmann and Balss prove that his name cannot be overlooked in the history of evolution. Balss also insists that in his remarks about the various kinds of squirrels in various countries which he had visited, the foundations of comparative zoölogy were laid. George Sarton remarks:

"He had had and improved many opportunities of observing things in the course of his long travels as provincial of his Order (the Dominican rule obliged him to travel afoot). He observed animals in the Danube region, in the vicinity of Cologne, Augsburg, Worms, Treves in Friesland, Holland, Brabant, Italy. . . . He also collected information from the many people of all classes he came across in the course of his missions."

ENTYMOLOGY

Stadler remarks [in *Albert von Cöln als Naturforscher,* 1909] that "Albert showed an especially keen interest in insects," and this can be adequately proved from a study of his works, especially what he had to say about ants, spiders, and bees. No medieval man described so minutely and intelligently the life of these insects. What Fabre's classic descriptions are to our days, that Albert's pictures of insect life were to Europe for three hundred years. He studied the anatomy of bees as none of his predecessors had. Jessen declares that he was the first to point out the belly marrow and structure of their feet and proboscis. In his botanical works he added supplementary data on these points as also keen observations regarding crabs and scorpions. Stadler insists that Albert's researches into the life and habits of ants was the finest achievement in this field during the entire Middle Ages.

ICHTHYOLOGY

From his experience in Dominican refectories, where fish fare was almost perpetual, Albert could not remain indifferent about fish. From his youth he had been fascinated by their idiosyncrasies. He was the first to designate and describe the spolke; to call attention to the teeth of the carp; to reject the myths about griffins; to laugh at the common belief that pelicans feed their young with their own blood; to disprove the beaver's self-castration, the incombustibility of salamanders, and the birth of barnacle geese from trees. He was far ahead of his age in his knowledge of oysters and, probably, one of the first to suggest oyster beds, as we know them today. He knew the habitat of various kinds of fish, especially eels and salmon. No medieval man wrote more extensively on this point. He was one of the first men to point out the distinction between fish and amphibians and how to establish it from the peculiarities of their anatomical structure. No preceding writer had as much to say, nor said it so engagingly, on whales and whale hunting. He was the first to describe accurately the Greenland whale. From what he saw in Friesland, where he participated in a whale hunt, he knew the properties and uses of blubber. Even as a bishop in momentary retirement at his villa, Donaustauff, Albert did not lose interest in the denizens of the deep. Despite his many intellectual pursuits and social cares he found time to reveal himself a premature Isaak Walton.

ORNITHOLOGY

Since in Albert's time Germany was rather sparsley settled and since, as a consequence, the many large forests were alive with birds, we need not be surprised that he devoted much time to their study and to a description, in alphabetical enumeration, of their habits and peculiarities. Stadler says: "Now I could enumerate the entire German feathery kingdom which Albert knew: three (or rather four) species of swallows, five species of finches, three kinds of woodpeckers, besides the black, gray and green mocking birds, and two kinds of sparrows." But this enumeration is obviously incomplete, for he knew and described at least six species of eagles, three kinds of peacocks, five kinds of wild geese and three of wild ducks, four kinds of gold finches, two kinds of falcons besides three pure and three mixed species. It must be borne in mind that these are only the birds with whose habits Albert was familiar. Since, for some inexplicable reason, legends of a moralizing or symbolical purport have attached to birds more numerously than to any other category of the animal kingdom—for which reason, no doubt, birds are at home in the decorations of Gothic cathedrals, as the sketches in the notebook of Villard de Honnecort, the greatest medieval architect, bear witness—Albert, with his sharp eye for their characteristics and his critical sense, puts himself to great pains to reject the statements of the Ancients, especially Pliny. He rejects the fable of the one-eyed peacock, the peacock with one web foot, the peacock which weeps tears of blood. He will not admit that ostriches eat iron. He is the first German to mention the black stork, the best beloved of German birds. He discovered that swans sing in pain and not for the purpose of driving off pursuers. He knew more than any of his predecessors about eagles and none of his contemporaries were so uniformly correct in describing their habits. He loathes buzzards—probably he learned their rapacious ways on the hunt. With his love for the hunt he is a veritable mine of information on wild geese, ducks, and partridges. He sniggers at Hermes for holding that a rooster lays one egg before dying, from which the sun hatches a serpent, though this supposed prerogative of the rooster was stoutly maintained at Paris up to the late sixteenth century. He almost grows lyrical over the nightingale, which even then played a large part in the folk song along the Rhine. Albert's love of birds must have been generally known, for some of the earliest representations of him—even in Paris where birds have been proverbially rare—show him surrounded, like another *Poverello* of Assisi, with the most varied specimens of these songsters. He was familiar with the anatomical peculiarities of birds, from personal experimentation, as Vassalius suggested centuries later. Franz Strunz points out that Albert was the first to speak intelligently, with understanding wisdom and childlike simplicity, about the sex life of birds. And Balss suggests that what Albert says about the life of a brood of birdlings in the nest is one of the most incomparably beautiful pieces of writing of that epoch. There are echoes of Albert in so late a book as Thompson's *Ten Commandments Amongst Animals.* Emile Male, in his superb book, *The Religious Art of the Thirteenth Century,* does not forget to suggest how much the ornithological teachings of Albert contributed to the dazzling splendor of the medieval Cathedrals, while Louis Gillet, in his *L'Art Religieuse et les Ordres Mendiants,* gives even higher praise to the bird lore of Albert.

COSMOGRAPHY

The average medieval man knew intimately his own little patch of ground. He entertained the most fantastic ideas about the far-off lands, concerning which the returned crusader or warrior spoke freely and extravagantly on every street corner or in every wine shop. In answering the many questions about these unknown parts of the world and exploding the tales about the wonders to be found in them, Albert was not only meeting a very urgent need of his day but also keeping alive an interest in exploration. He adopted Aristotle's teaching, with many reservations, in his **De Coelo et Mundo** and **De Natura Locorum,** where are to be found jumbled together elements of physical geography, mineralogy, metallurgy, astronomy, and in fact of all the sciences that had to do with the earth and the sky. He accepts Aristotle's theory about the rotundity of the earth, adding a mathematical argument of his own which is stronger and more convincing than any alleged by the Greek. He also invoked the argument from gravitation for, he says, since all parts of the earth converge to the center, there can be no doubt about the world's sphericity. Contrary to the opinions of Lactantius and St. Augustine he holds that there is an inhabited, or at least an inhabitable, land at the antipodes. Answering those cocksure writers who flippantly said that, if such a continent existed, the position, motion, and action of the sun must necessarily be inverted, Albert boldly proclaimed that right and left, upper and lower, Orient and Occident, are relative terms and that, therefore, the order of the heavenly motion on the supposed continent would be identical with that in Europe. In answer to the second facile argument that, since there is four times more water than land, more than half of this continent would be submerged in water, Albert insisted upon the many causes which might diminish the volume of water or the facility with which the water can transform itself, as for instance, by evaporation. In reply to the third stock objection that the supposed continent would be useless, since no one could go to it or across over to Europe from it, Albert shrewdly parried that it would be illogical to hold that no one lives there or might possibly live in that torrid zone. "I believe," he says, "that it is difficult to cross to those regions but not impossible. The difficulty about the entire matter arises from the large sandy wastes bleached by the sun. It is for this reason that there is so little communication between men south of this region and ourselves who are in the north." This cosmographical teaching was traditional in Dominican schools for centuries and scarcely any other-where. Hence it comes that Albert's theories were taught to Dante by his Dominican professor, Fra Remigio de Girolami, and that they appear prominently in the tenth canto of the tenth *Paradiso*. This also accounts for the reverential mention of Albert by the great Florentine poet.

[Albert] accepts Aristotle's theory about the rotundity of the earth, adding a mathematical argument of his own which is stronger and more convincing than any alleged by the Greek.

—Thomas M. Schwertner

So, too, the man whose name was attached to the western hemisphere, Amerigo Vespucci, got his cosmographical ideals at San Marco, Florence, from his uncle, the Dominican George Anthony Vespucci. That these ideas were in the air when Columbus was seeking support for an expedition to the Indies is plain from the poem *La Sfera* of Leonardo Dati, which reproduced faithfully the teaching of Toscanelli, the friend and correspondent of Columbus. No wonder Diego Deza, the Dominican confessor of Isabella, faithful to the Albertinian tradition in the Dominican schools, took up the case of Columbus with the queen, about the year 1485. No wonder that Columbus whose set of Albert's works, annotated in his own handwriting, is still preserved in Seville, found a hearing, sympathy and shelter at St. Stephen's Convent, Salamanca, where the question of an expedition to the Indies was once more agitated after having been shelved for the seven years following the first junta of learned men at Santa Fe in Spain. And only a few months before his death the discoverer wrote to his son Ferdinand begging him to convey to the gracious queen the information that, but for the goodly offices, interest, and learning of Diego Deza, she would not have been able to add the jewel of the Indies to her crown. Mandonnet, who has written an exhaustive study on the subject, remarks with justice: "Thus it is a true title of glory for the two men who dowered the Middle Ages with the most solid speculations and the most positive teaching, that they were the first and most powerful patrons of those cosmographical ideals which conspired in preparing the *milieu* in which the genius of Columbus developed and in which would emerge the project of the discovery of the Indies." And, later on, repeating what Humboldt

had suggested earlier in his *Cosmos,* he says: "Nearly everything true and fluid which fifteenth-century science possessed came from antiquity by passing through the Middle Ages by way of Albert the Great above all others, who was the first man to introduce the Latin world to the scientific riches of the Arabs. The Dominican school, faithful to peripatetic philosophy, preserved the traditional teaching without difficulty and at the time of the discovery of the Indies it had denied nothing elementary in its teaching." Perhaps there is something reminiscent of all this in the words of Pope Clement VIII who, in canonizing St. Rose of Lima, the first American saint, remarked that the Dominican Order seems to have received from God "the mission of watching over the two continents of the western hemisphere and the Phillippines."

Albert's curiosity about the physical constitution and conformation of this world extended in all directions and we find him speaking with originality on all phases of cosmography. In establishing the rotundity of the world he speaks in the plainest terms of the Suez Canal as it was built in our own age. Emil Michael sees in his cosmographical doctrine a very clear adumbration of Laplace's theory. As regards the movement of planets, he suggested theories that were put forth later on as practicable and workable. It is no wonder that Albert's influence on Copernicus has often been pointed out. There is still preserved a well-worn set of Albert's works, filled with original notes by that indomitable investigator. His influence on Keppler cannot be denied, and the researches of these two together cleared the way for Newton and his immortal laws. Nor is it unlikely that Newton harked back to Albert, for there are points of view and modes of expression in the great Englishman which sound like echoes of the medieval scientist. If another Englishman, Locke, spoke about the *tabula rasa* and primary and secondary qualities of things, it has been shown that this terminology had first been used with a fixed philosophical meaning and connotation by Albert.

Alexander Humboldt called attention to the fact that Albert had sketched a workable theory of zones in connection with, and growing out of, his treatise on climatology. Better than most of his contemporaries Albert indicated the effects of temperature on flowers, beast, and men. He was far in advance of his age in explaining rain, dew, and snow. His acquaintances, Konungo Skuggsja or Peter of Dacia, the Dominican, and Matthew Paris, for all their remarkable work which shows the influence of Albert, were resigned to follow him when speaking of winds, currents, tides and floods, and earthquakes. He stands alone in his day for his vivid and accurate description of volcanic eruptions.

CHEMISTRY

Though the knowledge of chemistry was very rudimentary in the Middle Ages and hampered by the most grotesque experiments, Albert was familiar with many chemical processes and their operations such as distillation and sublimation, purification of gold and silver by cementation and the use of lead. He knew that mercury may be successfully distilled without loss of weight. He recognized that wine, when heated, gives off a substance "supernatant" and "inflammable." He taught that cinnabar is produced by the union of mercury and sulphur; that sulphur attacks all metals but gold; that pure arsenic is produced by heating two parts of soap with one part of orpiment (arsenic trisulphide); that the nature of arsenic is metallic; that nut galls are a source of tannic acid; that the compounds which he called *marchasita* include iron, zinc and copper pyrites and other sulphides of metallic luster. According to Professor Florian Cajorie, of the University of California, he knew as early as 1250 that gunpowder could be prepared from sulphur, saltpeter, and charcoal. He introduced the term *vitroleum* to designate sulphate of iron. In a recent issue of *The Laboratory,* published by the Fischer Chemical Company, of Pittsburgh, it was shown that Albert knew the color reaction between gall nuts and vitriol.

Professor John M. Stillman, of Stanford University, writes in *The Story of Early Chemistry:* "Of the great value of the work of Albertus Magnus in helping to spread the knowledge of chemistry of his time there can be no doubt. . . . He presents this knowledge with a clearness and directness that characterizes him as one of the ablest thinkers of his century—this very clarity of expression—free from intentional secrecy or mystification—must have given his works an important value in helping to lay the foundations for sane and sensible points of view, in a time when, according to the writers of the times, fraud, charlatanry and imposture in alchemy were very prevalent."

In order to show the style used by Albert in his descriptions and also to furnish examples of his general attitude to the subject of chemistry and to alchemy as well, we are quoting directly from Stillman's translations: "Those who operate much in copper in our region, namely in Paris or Cologne and in other places where I have seen them at work, convert copper into brass by powder of a stone called *calamina.* And when this stone evaporates there still remains a dark brilliancy turning slightly to the appearance of gold. But that it be rendered paler and thus more like the yellowness of gold, they mix with it a little tin by reason of which the brass loses much of the ductility of the copper. And those who wish to deceive and to produce a brilliancy like gold retain the stone (*calamina*) so that it remains longer in the brass in the fire (or furnace) not quickly vaporizing from the brass. It is thus retained by *oleum vitri* (liquefied glass), for fragments of glass are powdered and sprinkled in the pot (*testa*) upon the brass after *calamina* is introduced, and then the glass so added swims upon the brass and does not allow the

stone and its virtue to evaporate, but turns the vapor of the stone back into the brass, and thus the brass is long and strongly purged and the feculent matters in it are burned away. Finally, the *oleum vitri* vaporizes the virtue of the stone, but the brass is made much more brilliant than it would be without it. He who desires to simulate gold still more completely repeats these operations of heating (*optesim*) and purging of the melted glass frequently and mixes with the brass, silver instead of tin, and thus it is made so red and yellow that many believe it to be gold itself when, in truth, it is still a kind of bronze (or brass, *aes*)."

"Besides we have never found an alchemist so-called, operating generally (*in toto*) but that he colors with a yellow elixir into an appearance of gold and with the white elixir colors to the resemblance of silver, seeking that the color may remain while in the fire and may penetrate the whole metal, just as the manner of working it is possible to produce a yellow color, the substance of the metal remaining. And here again it is not to be maintained that several kinds of metals are contained in one another. It is from this and similar things, that is demolished the dictum of those who say that any kind of metal you please is contained in another."

Albert's description of nitrum, which in his time, as also in that of the ancients, meant carbonate of sodium or potassium as contained in plant ash is here described by him: "Nitrum is thus called from the island of Nitrea where it was first found. The Arabs call it baurac. It is a kind of salt less known than *sal gemma* (rock salt) transparent but in thin plates. It is roasted in the fire, and then, all superfluous aqueous substance being given off, it is burned to a high degree of dryness (*'efficiter siccum magis combustum'*) and the salt itself is rendered sharper. The varieties are distinguished according to the localities where it is formed."

Tuchia, a name applied to a more or less impure sublimate of zinc oxide is described by Albert in the following paragraph: "Tuchia, which has frequent use in the transmutation of metals, is an artificial and not a natural mixture, for tuchia is made from the smoke which rises and is solidified by adhering to hard bodies, when brass is purified from stones (minerals) and tin which are in it. But the best kind is that which is sublimed from that (that is, re-sublimed) and then that which in such sublimation remains at the bottom is *climia,* which is called by some *succudus.* There are many kinds of tuchia, as it occurs white, yellow, and turning red. When tuchia is washed, there remains at the bottom a sort of black sediment of tuchia. This is sometimes called *Tuchia Irida.* But the difference between succudus and tuchia is as we stated, namely because tuchia is sublimed and succudus is what remains at the bottom unsublimed. The best is volatile and white, then the yellow, then the red; the fresh is considered better than the old. All tuchia is cold and dry and that which is washed is considered better in those operations (that is, in above mentioned transmutation of metals)."

J. W. Mellor, in *A Comprehensive Treatise on Inorganic and Theoretical Chemistry,* accentuates not only the original contributions of Albert to chemistry but his undoubted influence on St. Thomas Aquinas.

"Albertus Magnus especially studied the union of sulphur and the metals; and like the Arabian Rhases, he considered the metals themselves to be compounds of different proportions of the three principles or elements: arsenic, mercury, and sulphur. Sulphur, said he, 'blackens silver and burns the metal on account of the *affinity* which it has for these substances.' The term affinity was thus used for the first time to designate the unknown cause of chemical action. Silver was supposed to be the metal most closely allied to gold, so that he considered the transmutation of silver into gold would be the easiest to realize. Albertus Magnus knew how to separate the noble from the base metals by fire, and how to separate gold from silver by *aqua regia*. Some suppose the treatise ascribed to Albertus Magnus to be spurious. The canonized scholar, Thomas Aquinas (1225-1274), was a pupil of Albertus Magnus. It has been said that while the master was a student of nature and philosophy, the pupil was a student of man and society. Both are considered to have excelled as exponents of theology rather than as students of natural science. From the little knowledge that is available concerning the alchemical labors of Thomas Aquinas he would appear to have been particularly attracted by the action of mercury on the metals—tin, lead, etc.— and he applied the term *amalgam* to the liquid or paste which is formed when these metals are opened up with mercury."

But not only on Thomas Aquinas did the powerful influence of Albert react. Besides Dietrich of Freiburg and Ulrich of Strasburg, who could not deny their dependence on Albert, there were John Glogan, Joachim de Gostnum, Michael of Breslau, and Stanislaus Rozycki, who gave Poland the best scientific books in their day, all filled with the audacious spirit of Albert and his suggestive and inventive temper. But before them there appeared in Germany Albert of Orlamund, whose *Philosophia Pauperum* was a favorite textbook with a frank bias for physical sciences; Conrad Summerhard, for whose book on science Wimpheling wrote some of his bombastic verses to serve as an introduction; Conrad of Halberstadt, an authority on gems and metallurgy; John Weiss, the best scientist of his day, and Konrad von Meyerberg, whose scientific attainments were the wonder of his age. These and scores of lesser students were outspoken advocates of Albert's scientific methods and devotion to the natural sciences.

By a strange paradox, when men began tiring of natural philosophy and sought peace of mind in the study of theology, it was John of Dambach who, in his *Consolatio Theologiae,* gave birth to a big literature known as the *Trostbücher*. And his favorite author was Albert, not Thomas Aquinas. In these books of consolation intended for wornout, jaded, or disappointed students and scholars, the last flickerings of Albert's scientific influence upon the ages must be sought. And just as in Albert's work there was always a preoccupation to lift man's mind to God through the natural sciences, so in these *Trostbücher* the knowledge of created things is made to subserve the purposes of theology. Albert could not have desired a finer consummation for his own study of nature nor the impetus he gave to the study of the natural sciences.

. . . . .

THEOLOGIAN

In proposing to himself to assimilate the wisdom of pagan antiquity to the wisdom of the Christian world and in leaving no stone unturned to achieve this colossal task, Albert was following the only course open to him as an honest thinker, a conscientious educator, and a loyal Christian. As an honest thinker he was obliged to select a system of philosophy which seemed to him best suited to satisfy the curiosity of his mind; as a conscientious educator he was bound to instruct in the best ways of thinking those disciples who would be called upon in the future to solve the difficulties which were agitating the world; as a loyal Christian he could not forswear his faith. Deliberately he chose Aristotle as his guide in the labyrinthine ways of thought. But in adopting the Stagirite Albert was painfully conscious of his false and truncated teaching on the question of the creation of the world, the origin and immortality of the soul, the creation of particular objects from no preëxisting matter, and the ordination of man to a supernatural destiny.

Would he follow the Averroistic school of Aristotelian interpreters by adhering to Aristotle despite the Church's positive teaching on these fundamental truths? Would he like them, pervert the minds of his students, and through their teaching subsequently muddy the stream of Catholic tradition, by advocating the eternity of the world; by denying the immortality of the soul, the providence of God, human liberty and responsibility; by championing a crude pantheistic monopsychism according to which there was a world-soul of which the souls of individual men were but parts or emanations? There were goodly numbers of Christian professors—and their ranks were growing apace every day— who in their exaggerated loyalty to what they considered genuine Aristotelianism, and in their desire to avoid breaking with the Church, elaborated the monstrous theory of a double category of truths, self-identical and independent, but in an open and irreconcilable opposition to one another. The conclusions of philosophy and theology could be true in their respective domains and a man owed loyalty to the body of truth he was investigating at the moment. Reason and faith, they held, were in conflict and their respective findings might be and frequently were in opposition, because both envisaged different objects, proceeded from different starting points, employed divergent principles, and operated by different methods. The academic world was threatened with intellectual anarchy, and there were many who, ensnared by the slippery sophisms of the Averroists, espoused a system which did violence not only to the psychological laws of man's being but entailed forfeiture of the Catholic tradition. As a keen philosopher Albert felt outraged to be called upon to subscribe to such an awkward system; as an educator he recoiled from polluting the minds of the intellectual leaders growing up around him; as a Christian he abhorred such a subtle assault upon and chronic injustice to the teaching prerogative of the Church and the educative value of her dogmas. He could not remain oblivious of the fact that though Aristotle stretched the reasoning powers of man further than any other philosopher he, without any fault of his own, had not been able to make them answer questions which pure reason alone, even at its best, could not supply. But he knew that as a Christian he had at his disposition unerring helps which solved the difficulties Aristotle could not explain, helps whose use and exercise would not invalidate Aristotle's arguments or processes of reasoning. To be a philosopher man needed not disregard theology or take refuge in the dishonest subterfuges of the doctrine of the dual truth.

In proposing to himself to assimilate the wisdom of pagan antiquity to the wisdom of the Christian world and in leaving no stone unturned to achieve this colossal task, Albert was following the only course open to him as an honest thinker, a conscientious educator, and a loyal Christian.

—*Thomas M. Schwertner*

Now Albert taught that philosophy and theology did really differ by reason of the different objects they were respectively minded to explore: philosophy was concerned about the problem of *ens,* or being, whereas theology focussed all its attention on God. They differed, too, by reason of the principles upon which they respectively proceeded: philosophy depended upon metaphysical or self-evident truths whereas theology relied upon the dogmas of the faith which, because

they came into the possession of man by revelation, could obviously not be discovered by man's unaided reason alone. Both sciences had truth for their object, and inasmuch as they discovered truth they afforded revelations of the author of truth, the Primal Truth, God, though in different spheres. Hence, there could not be an irreconciliable opposition or contradiction between the two sciences, as there could not be ultimately any question about truth which must essentially be one and immutable. Each science in its own sphere vouchsafed man a revelation of God. But it did not follow that there was a harmony of identity or coördination between both sciences. The only possible union must necessarily be one of subordination since the higher presupposes the existence of a lower. Theology was undoubtedly the higher by reason of its object and the light of revelation in which it walked. Philosophy operating freely and in its own right needed not blush to take a secondary or subsidiary station, since it was not called upon to investigate problems which did not belong to its sphere of investigation. Hence, theology was not arrogant in claiming the right to utilize the findings of philosophy. Philosophy itself was really scientific only when it confined its operations to its own problems. It might rightfully look to theology for an answer to questions which only a science endowed with a superior light and assistance could presume and dare to resolve with anything like finality. In this wise Albert describes the nature, rights and functions of Christian philosophy, which walked arm in arm with theology without the blush of degradation or the suspicion of complete absorption. He vindicated for the *philosophia perennis* which he created the privilege of using the arguments excogitated and employed by the Fathers of the Church in their efforts to make faith a reasonable service. The philosophical uses to which the Fathers of the Church might be put in Christian philosophy were clearly demonstrated by Albert in his **Commentary on the Sentences of Peter Lombard,** in his **Summa de Creaturis,** and in his **Summa Theologica.**

In Albert's delimitation of the respective provinces of these two sciences theology utilized philosophy without being called upon to make excuses or apologies, while philosophy looked to theology without blush or fear. It was the first really successful wedlock of the two sciences. Since the days of the great Archbishop of Canterbury, St. Anselm of Aosta, thinkers had been trying to elaborate a verification of the definition of theology as *fides quaerens intellectum:* faith invoking reason in order to save reason from running amuck in regions where the light of revelation was needed to find the way. The many skeletons of heresies along the Roman Road of Dogma proved conclusively that men of the best intentions and the greatest intellectual powers were doomed if they forgot or disregarded the postulates and imperatives of each of the two sciences. In theology, man walked on dizzy heights, using the light of faith all the time, without on that account spurning the light of reason. Albert's success in assigning both sciences their respective fields, without allowing them to sink into the bogs of misunderstanding as to their proper functions and mutual helpfulness, was the most remarkable conciliation between the two sciences which had so far been effected. Thomas Aquinas would soon seal the pact definitively.

Now, Albert with his deeply mystic nature had a teleological preoccupation before his mind in all his diversified intellectual labor. He admitted it in the preface of practically every work he wrote. He was seeking the footprints of God's passage in nature as in the invisible fields of the mind. It is this search for God everywhere which made William Arendt write complainingly [in *Die Staats- und Gesellschaftslehre Alberts des Grossen,* 1929] that in all his scientific researches "Albert always speaks as a theologian." Balss and the *Realenziklopädie für Protestantische Theologie* concur in the same criticism. That Albert, however, did not permit his theological bias to run away with him is plain from the complaint of Henry of Ghent who said that Albert obfuscated theology by giving too much prominence in his work to philosophy and by Gerson who, in revamping the theology of St. Bonaventure, remarked that Albert's preferences for philosophy brought hurt to theological science. The genius of Albert was so all-inclusive that it is true to say that knowledge of all and every kind was precious in his sight. It has been said that by temperament he was a naturalist and scientist, by deliberate choice a philosopher, by mood a theologian. He seemed to verify in himself the full significance and implication of the Anselmian axiom: *Credo ut intelligam.* His piety and native theological bent or sense made him look upon the faith not as an imposing dumb sphinx but as a living voice giving luminous explanations of the manifold mysteries around him on all sides which, given his intellectual curiosity, aroused his passion for knowledge. In the light of dogma the mysteries of nature resolved themselves into concrete exhibitions of God's loving kindness which men were meant to explore for the purpose of extracting thence a deeper appreciation of God's goodness and beauty. The mysterious nature and processes of thought served but to allure him to a deeper investigation of the Primal Truth which cannot ever be fully grasped here below. Hence it came that Albert made a greater effort to understand St. Anselm's doctrine than most scholars of that epoch, that he treated him with more consideration and utilized him with greater finesse than any of his contemporaries. It is this intellectual sympathy for and affinity with the spirit of St. Anselm which prompted Joseph Schwane to write [in *Dogmengeschicte,* 1882] that "Albert rather than Anselm is the father of scholasticism if by that name we understand theological science impregnated with Aristotelianism."

We are prepared therefore, to find Albert interchanging arguments from philosophers and theologians in order to elucidate the dogmas of the faith. He does so consciously and consistently. Consciously: because he was always aware of the nature of the argumentation he was invoking at the moment and never in any doubt as to what was its validity and its compelling force; hence, he tried conscientiously to observe the distinction he had drawn between philosophical and theological reasoning. Consistently: because he never tried to make one set of arguments do service for the other—thus, for instance, when in philosophy he quoted the Fathers of the Church, it was not because of the authority their names carried in the eyes of believers but because of the validity of their arguments. Realizing that theology had run perilously near stereotyping into a cold formalism, by reason of the overobtrusion of the argument drawn from authority, he was at pains to introduce into the study of the sacred sciences the reasoning methods of Aristotle and the Peripatetics. Finding that Aristotle's natural theology was substantially conformable to the propositions of the faith on the nature and existence of God and the ways by which man could arrive at a knowledge of the First Cause, he did not hesitate to say that it would be possible to construct a true natural theology from the doctrines of the Stagirite without recourse to revelation but not in conflict with it. Yet he did not hesitate to reject Aristotle when he found him out of step with Catholic dogma, insisting that in such a case Augustine was to be preferred. And he made his position clear by maintaining that, though the soul had an impress of the Trinity, Aristotle could never help man to arrive at a knowledge of that august mystery. And it is worthy of note that precisely on the doctrine of the Most Blessed Trinity Albert wrote better than any man before him and was not surpassed subsequently even by St. Thomas. To forget this fact might lead scholars into looking upon Albert as a lop-sided theologian deserving the criticisms of Henry of Ghent and John Gerson.

Had Albert not been dowered with a markedly sharp theological sense he would never have succeeded so well in distinguishing between faith and reason, between theology and philosophy; he would never have formulated so clearly their separate domains; hence, he would never have been the first to consider theology a separate and distinct science. And it does not militate against this claim to find that Albert differed from Aquinas in describing the nature of theology and its end. However, his treatment and concept of theology as a sacred and supernatural science, using argumentation in the Aristotelian way, coincided with Thomas. Had Albert been less a philosopher, it is safe to assume that he would not have excelled in theology. If he cultivated philosophy so assiduously it was in the shrewd conviction that it would sharpen his theological sense. Certainly he did not Christianize Aristotle for mere intellectual pleasure or pastime. It was meant to develop his own appreciation of theology about whose superior claims and rights he discourses so lucidly and eloquently in the first part of the third treatise of his *Summa Theologica*. But in that same eulogy on the eminent rôle of theology he does not forget to write a bill of guarantees for philosophy, saying: "Whatever is known by two ways instead of one, is better grasped; hence what is known by faith and reason is better understood than that which is known only by faith." For all his love of the faith and its dogmas Albert could not be induced to prove traitor to reason.

Now Albert's merits as also his shortcomings as a philosopher determine to a greater degree than has generally been admitted his standing as a theologian. If he excelled in explaining so well the dogmas of religion it was because, aside from his erudition, he employed more generously and expertly than his predecessors every bit of philosophical data which would make faith a reasonable service.

The chief merits of Albert's philosophical labors are his critical evaluation of various past systems of thought, his astounding erudition, his critical utilization of the most disparate elements of knowledge, and his originality and geniality of outlook on many occasions. These characteristics of his philosophical contributions to the sum of knowledge in his day appear strikingly in what he added to the study and advancement of theological science.

It must be borne in mind, first, that theology in the Middle Ages was not as clearly divided up as in our own day. Hence, we cannot expect to find in Albert's works a systematic presentation and treatment of dogmatic, moral, pastoral, and ascetical theology in separate tracts, treatises, or courses. Since the medieval man looked upon the salvation of his own soul as his chief business in life, moral reflections were attached not only to dogmatic disquisitions but practically to every form of mental productivity whether in philosophy or the sciences. Knowledge in those ages of faith was looked upon as a rule of right living and not as an intellectual plaything, curio, or treasure. Secondly, since theology was rightfully considered the queen of all the sciences the remaining branches of learning were glad to recognize their dependence on it and, in case of a recalcitrant mood, were violently whipped into line. Modern science, without the logical justification of medieval theology, asserts as great a hegemony and dictatorship for itself without such favorable immediate results. Hence, we must be prepared to find a great deal of straining in the arguments of medieval theologians, especially when there is question of adducing reasons for their arguments and positions, or of compelling other branches of learning to do service for their peculiar form of argumentation. Hence, too, there is in most medieval theologians on occasion a sharpness of tone amounting sometimes to invective, a di-

rectness of dialectical argument which argues at least for the honesty of their convictions and their love of truth. In several instances Albert was a match for the most vitriolic of his contemporaries.

With these two preliminary observations constantly in mind it will appear from a study of Albert's theological labors that he was more critical in his attitude toward, and treatment and utilization of, the corpus of theological literature at his command than any of his predecessors. First, as regards the texts, whether of Aristotle and his commentators or the theologians whom he quoted, Albert displayed an unwonted and keenly incisive spirit and attitude of reserve. We know from his own words that he compared variant texts of the Stagirite in order to get at a correct reading; that he revealed in the commentators false ascriptions of authorities; that he rejected parts of Aristotle's text because of internal criticism of the text itself. In his *Commentary on the Divine Names* he used the translation of John Saracenus, abandoning it on occasion for one by John Scotus whom he went out of his way to compliment for his fine rendering of the original. It is true to say that, with the possible exception of Robert Grosseteste, no medieval scholar manipulated textual criticism so largely, easily, and with such amazing and happy results. If he did not always succeed in discovering the true author of a text, as in the case of the pseudo-Dionysius, it is well to remember the condition of criticism in that uncritical age.

In the next place, Albert discovered a really fine critical sense in evaluating the authentic thought of the authors he read and quoted. It is safe to say that with his sharp powers of perception he understood without much difficulty or long application everything he read. It is well known how benignly he interpreted St. Augustine when he seemed out of tune with the theological thought of the medieval world. On occasion he gave very ingenious reasons for his emendation of another's thought. Hence it comes that in recapitulating the thoughts of writers he is very fresh and concise. He selects with sure instinct the skeleton thought and cuts away ruthlessly the literary flesh. Hence, too, it follows that his books are not a mosaic of quotations which do not touch intimately the truth he is trying to establish. Albert quoted an unusually large number of authorities but he did not quote one authority profusely or exclusively. His quotations are always as brief as the thought demanded. And in this respect he was unique among medieval scholars.

Finally, he did not quote the disassociated thought of an author, separated from the context, but evaluated his entire process of argumentation or even his system. One feels in reading Albert that he knows the authors he is utilizing. He dissects systems mercilessly but fairly. He worked so rapidly that he did not always take the time or pains to give a minute criticism. But one feels that there was never any doubt in his mind as to what judgment should be passed eventually on a body of thought. One or two decisive blows sufficed him to dispatch a theory or point of view. In this summary adjudication—pointed, direct, sometimes violent—Albert differed from Thomas Aquinas, who worked more slowly and systematically. Albert overturned, Thomas demolished; Albert smothered, Thomas strangled; Albert tore up false theories by the root, Thomas tore the ground from the root so that there was no chance of life for the suspect doctrine. This, perhaps, is one reason why Albert's theology soon became outmoded, was soon superseded.

The second characteristic of Albert's philosophical spirit reflected in his theological work is the large part played by erudition. Albert was more widely conversant with theological literature than any of his contemporaries. He knew intimately the Fathers of the Church, ecclesiastical writers, pagan and recent authors as no other scholar of the epoch. He was not so much concerned about names but solely about ideas, as he himself avows. Hence it comes that he has more than one title to be looked upon as the first historian of dogma in the modern sense. He knew the heresiarchs, who seem to come to life in his pages. The errors they made in treating of the dogmas of the faith were a matter of such vital and personal concern to Albert that he writes as if they were still in the flesh, going about their unholy and nefarious business of poisoning the minds of the unwary and ignorant. This tone of actuality and immediacy saves his writings from becoming a dusty gallery of dead men's dead opinions. He often traces an error to its last lair and frequently establishes a hoary paternity for opinions which were looked upon in his day as up-to-date. This is particularly the case with the false Trinitarian doctrines he refuted and those, also, having reference to the existence of God. The historico-critical temper is highly developed in all of Albert's theological writings and, as heresy has a way of coming to life in successive ages under new names, his treatment of suspect doctrine gives a note of continuity to his discussions. In his **Commentary on the Divine Names** he returns no less than seventy times to the pantheism of Scotus Erigena which, from the consideration it received from a coterie of newfangled professors, he looked upon as highly insidious and menacing. He even grapples with anonymous authors, as when in his **Mystical Theology** he combats the semiagnosticism of a writer who has been identified as Thomas Gallus (d. 1246).

It is not to be wondered at, therefore, that in his Scripturistic works Albert gathered together elements and laid down norms for what centuries later came to be spoken of as the history of dogma or the evolution of belief. He makes it plain in scores of passages how the ages witnessed a fuller and more explicit uncovering of the meaning, content, significance, and beauty of individual points of faith. A treatise on ecclesiology has been pieced together from scattered passages in Albert's works and it has a distinctly modern ring. His **Valiant Woman,** which would have been impossible without a wide and intimate acquaintance with the theological thought of the past, presents astounding and highly suggestive elements of the new apologetic which deals with Catholicism as a whole and not as a loosely joined assemblage of parts, as a living thing and not as a system. Because the difficulties urged against the Church in the past were looked upon by Albert as a whole body of teaching he is not forced, by the very manner of his dealing with them, to take the roundabout way of dealing with individual doctrines. Because the Church is a living entity in Albert's conception he sees more in her wonderful life than can be said by logic-choppers about her orderly operation in the world. This kind of apologetic, so much in accord with the universalist temper of Albert, was entirely new in that age. If the hint he dropped in his manner of approach to his conception of the vital life of the Church as a living organism was not taken up by defenders of the Church for ages to come, it was due in great measure to the fact that Albert was inexplicably indifferent to ecclesiastical history—an indifference all the more strange in a man who lived at a time when the papacy was at its apogee of secular power and influence, when the inner life of the Church was not cribbed and confined by her exterior and secular activity, and when the successors upon the Fisherman's Throne seemed endowed with prophetic vision in laying down norms for the Church's dealings with the newly born democratic spirit which was testy and cocksure, if it was anything at all.

Had Albert kept history more consciously and consistently in the foreground in drawing up his map of the theological background of his apologetic, he undoubtedly would have achieved modernity in the best sense of the word. This does not mean that he was out of touch with his times or indifferent about the currents of thought which, filtering down from the professors, affected mightily the unthinking masses. He did give extended consideration to the lucubrations of recently deceased thinkers—thus from his elaborate refutation of David of Dinant's *De Tomis*. Father Thery has been able to reconstruct the essential body of this pernicious teaching. He did flay the social abuses of his age in many places, but especially in his **Commentary on St. Luke,** and from what he says we can gather how the secular affluence of the Church was planting stumbling stones for the feet of the simple faithful. But in the big and large Albert did not call into requisition the historical data with which he must have been familiar from his wide reading of the records of the past. And it is worthy of note that, of the large body of writers who have essayed to treat of various aspects of his universal interests, not a single scholar so far has deemed it worth his while to envisage this phase of his work. The reason for this may probably be that there is so little positive data to show that he exercised in historical erudition practically the same sound and sharp critical sense and instinct which he showed in dealing with the historical aspect of philosophical and theological doctrines.

The third merit of Albert's philosophical work, reappearing on the surface of his theological productiveness, is his successful utilization of elements of learning which no preceding theologian had dreamed of laying under contribution. First, it need not be insisted upon that Albert pilfered the pagan teachers freely. He performed the miracle of almost making a Father of the Church out of Aristotle. He knew and utilized Jewish and Muslim learning better than any medieval scholar. He did not forget or overlook his findings in the natural sciences when writing theology or preaching to the people. Thus when analyzing the act of contemplation he has an open eye to the effects of physical health, the condition of the blood, the state of digestion upon the mental processes. He is familiar with the idea and effects of what are called today dreads and tacks. He anticipates the moderns by insisting upon the need of taking into account the physical and psychical conditions of a man when trying to banish scruples or when seeking to get at the root cause of crime and repeated acts of abnormal practices, or when setting out to resolve cases of conscience. This is a very attractive side of his intellectual activity and one deserving of the fullest study. He was not the man to multiply sins by utterly disregarding the influence of the body on the soul, in many cases lessening the real gravity of delinquency. He was one of the first, if not the very first, to introduce medical and physical considerations in dealing with questions of moral theology. As a consequence of this sane and measured utilization of data of a scientific kind, which he had come by through personal experimentation or the conscientious reports of trustworthy witnesses, he gave an entirely new tone to the discussion of many moral problems—a direction which was to blossom forth in a most genial way in the *Summa Confessorum* of his pupil John of Freiburg. This aspect of his theological thought opens up a wide field for the most fascinating and fruitful investigation, especially if the study be pursued in the light of his teaching on phrenology in which he was a forerunner of Gall, on physiognomy in which he anticipated Lavater, and on the *amore quodam voluntatis,* "the certain love in the will," which is nothing else than a metaphysical adumbration of the modern superconscious.

Finally, Albert's exhibitions of originality in philosophical speculation are duplicated in the domain of theological research. For it appears from Albert's general tone of enthusiasm in lecturing on theological questions that he felt himself engaged on thoroughly congenial and supremely delightful work. Even in his declining years, when he was hopelessly broken in body, he was thrilled so deeply in speaking of the things of God that he undertook the composition of an elaborate **Summa Theologica,** intended for professors and experts, in which he gathered, as in a choice nosegay, what he considered best in the theological investigations and speculations of a lifetime. In all his formal theological writings his language is uncommonly rich and elastic, colorful, pulsing with life and feeling, bulging with figures of speech and comparisons drawn from all domains of knowledge and experience. He seems to have set himself the aim of divesting speculation of its coldness, remoteness, formalism. Herbert Doms has pointed out [in *Der. sel. Albertus Magnus,* 1930] that in some passages, where the sublimity of the subject swept him off his feet he seems to be thinking aloud, in German modes of thought, which surrendered themselves only haltingly and awkwardly to the fixed and precise literary forms of Latin. One needs little imagination to picture what an electrical effect such impassioned and inspired outbursts must have had upon the German, if not the foreign, youths gathered around his chair. This exuberance, this virtuosity, this immediacy of language, combined with his adept use of Aristotelian methods, helped to make Albert the idol of his pupils.

To his credit it must be said that this literary finesse was never employed by him for mere display or empty effect. It was but the vibration of a mind and heart stretching themselves consciously Godwards. This perfervid tone came naturally to Albert, for he was by bent a mystic and the mystical element was never far removed from his most rigid and coldest speculation. He was not only a professor of mystical theology, being the only man of the medieval period to write a commentary on the entire pseudo-Dionysian corpus, but he was a mystical professor of theology who did not hesitate to add the fire of divine charity to his most formal lectures, as anyone would be inclined to expect from a man who defined theology as the science which serves the purposes of piety: *scientia quae secundum pietatem est.* Without the least trace of egotism Albert introduced the recital of personal experiences in his theological writings in order to elucidate a point. And even where he does not directly speak of himself the sharp eye can discover in countless passages veiled references to what had transpired in his inner life or in his secret dealings with men.

He is original above all medieval authors in the literary form he gave his thoughts, in the personal touches and turns of thought, in the frankly direct, almost brusque, method of his approach to the core question of the subject he treated of. He was a poet, though we have scarcely anything in rime or meter from his pen. He sang because he loved and he loved because he insisted that theology helped man to a fuller vision of God, and the fuller the knowledge the deeper the love. Hence arose his unique power of giving fresh and suggestive outlooks, intimations, explanations, descriptions, and interpretations of theological questions and moods of which other theologians seemed not to have had an inkling. It explains why he marks a distinct advance and an almost unapproachable eminence in treating of the Most Blessed Trinity and, especially, the procession of the Holy Ghost from the Father and Son through love; why he treated of the gifts of the Holy Spirit, especially the gift of Wisdom, as none of his predecessors; why his explanation of the progressive stages of union with God through contemplation made room for psychological data of which no theologian so far had stopped to take cognizance; why he wrote at greater length and with more feeling of the Most Blessed Sacrament than any earlier writer; why his treatment of all phases of Marian doctrine impelled Rudolf of Nijmegen to call him "the secretary of Mary" and Peter Labbe, S.J., *Albertus Deiparae Philosophus:* Albert, the philosopher of the Mother of God. On occasion he paused to draw pictures of inner experiences which are counted among the finest which a Christian pen has ever achieved, as, for instance, when he describes the banquet of the soul with the Godhead in the mansions of the blessed or when, again, he explains the powers of the Precious Blood to cleanse the human soul.

Pope Pius XI, in his encyclical *Studiorum Ducem* (June 29, 1923), suggested that by providential disposition Thomas Aquinas was carefully shielded and screened from contact with the world so that, in the company of his own pure thoughts, he might be formed to become the Angelic Doctor with a sharp eye for an understanding of the mysteries of faith and the secrets of the soul united to God. Perhaps the same Providence was at work when Albert's ways were cast in the busy marts of men. For being by nature so strongly inclined to mysticism he was hindered, by the very circumstances of his life, from devoting himself exclusively to mystical subjects. As a professor Albert was called upon to discourse on the various questions of dogmatic theology without having an opportunity, ordinarily, to convert this knowledge to the uses of devotion. How difficult he must have felt this academic inhibition can be seen from his conduct in turning the propositions of Peter Lombard's *Sentences* into fervent prayers. As a citizen of the world, a prince of the Empire, and a bishop of souls, he was brought into active touch with the everyday life of men and communities of men. Now the ordinary life of the average man is frayed and seamy. Hence, this eager listener to the subdued whispers of the Divine Lover on the mountain peak of meditation must, perforce, attune his ear to the sad stories of human failure, frailty, and frustration. The mystic theologian is almost bested by the moral theologian; the moral theologian almost outstrips the dogmatic theologian. It is one more instance of that paradox in the history of mystical thought when we find the seer forced to turn sewer of the robes of conscience

which sin had torn apart; when the dreamer becomes the doer; when the contemplative must needs act as chaplain of souls in crowded centers and adviser of the commercial-minded and practical man of affairs. With the exception of St. Theresa of Avila, Albert best exemplifies the practicality of the professional student and mystic.

He may justly be looked upon as an innovator in the method of teaching moral theology, not indeed as an independent ecclesiastical science, but as a department of clerical knowledge which could give a rational account of its own measures and prescriptions. For the space of forty years he touched upon most of the aspects, implications, and applications of three fundamental questions of moral theology: the reason and psychology of the human act; reason and the norms of morality; reason and the acquired moral virtues. These questions had scarcely been touched upon before Albert's day with the fullness, consistency, and consecutiveness which they deserved and demanded. The primary reason for the neglect and oversight of these basic problems in moral theology was due to the very nature of the method of teaching sacred science at the time. The Lombard's pupil, Peter of Poitiers, had provided a casuistic textbook which satisfied the professional needs of the clergy during a period when the theological schools were languishing and when learning was difficult to acquire except in university centers. Robert de Courcon, Stephen Langton, and Godefroid of Poitiers, following the lead of Peter the Chanter and Master Martin, produced casuistic works in which the canonical element was given a preponderating rôle and importance, largely as a result of the revival of interest in Canon Law at the University of Bologna, following upon the work of Gratian, a revival which reached its apogee in the codification of Canon Law by St. Raymond Penyafort at the command of Pope Gregory X. In the second place Albert's immediate predecessors, almost to a man, were in a high state of reaction against the philosophical element introduced into the study of moral questions by Abelard and his school, especially Gilbert de la Poirree. Thus the fundamental questions of natural ethics were scarcely ever touched upon in the schools when Albert appeared on the scene. With the exception of William of Auxerre, who wrote the first treatise on natural law, about 1220, no professor discussed the moral but only the theological virtues. Albert began in good earnest to treat of these neglected questions of moral theology in his **Tractatus de Natura Boni** (1235-1240), prosecuted his study with a clarification of his doctrine in the second part of his **Summa de Creaturis,** in the **Summa de Homine,** in the third part of his still unedited **Summa de Bono,** in his **Commentary on the Sentences** (1245-1248), in his unedited course on the *Nicomachaean Ethics* written down and edited by Thomas Aquinas, in the printed course on the *Nicomachaean Ethics,* and, finally, in his **Summa Theologica,** written after 1275.

In espousing Aristotle as a guide in the study of theology Albert was necessarily obliged from the very beginning of his scholastic career to treat of the basic questions of natural ethics which theologians had not treated of, with the exception of that metaphysical professor who hid his identity (was it in fear or shame?) under the name of Philip. Aristotle helped Albert in no small measure in analyzing the questions on the faculties of the soul, liberty and the analysis of the human act under the impulsion of the will as the efficient cause, and under the dictation of the reason as the formal cause. He almost created the idea of synderesis in moral theology, but not so completely or clearly that the finishing touches of Aquinas could be dispensed with. He was far in advance of his predecessors in his treatment of conscience, habits, the virtues (especially prudence), the distinction between mortal and venial sins. Though his fellow religious and friends, Roland of Cremona and Hugh of St. Cher, had essayed to place the study of moral theology on a rational basis, the chief merit for having done so belongs to Albert. That he did not neglect the tedious task of descending to particular and specific cases is clear from the fact that the great medieval Franciscan preacher, Berthold of Ratisbon, submitted cases of conscience to him for solution, especially in the matter of money lending; that he was called upon to quiet the fears or scruples of persons in high and low station; that he flayed the evils of the time in his sermons and commentaries on Scripture, especially on the Gospels of St. Luke and St. John, not as a professional reformer or chronic critic but as an adviser who had a definite program of social reform and an unfailing method for the betterment of individuals. Arendt has shown that Albert's political doctrine was not divorced from his moral teaching. No man wrote more sanely on scandal and the sins of the flesh, and in dealing with the latter he betrayed an instinctive modesty, reserve, and restraint which were remarkable in that age of plain, often uncouth, speaking. His frequent dealings with nuns enabled him to treat of simple and solemn vows of religion in an epoch-making way. His development of the Church's teaching on the duty and blessedness of almsgiving is a genial presentation of a subject which in all ages lends itself easily to exaggeration. His important and clean-cut teaching on usury, or interest taking, should prove especially illuminating in an age of economic problems like our own. It is abundantly plain that Albert not only opened the way but cleared it notably for the superb treatment of most of the questions of moral theology by Thomas Aquinas. It is not without significance that we possess Thomas's autograph of Albert's notes on Aristotle's Ethics—a sure proof of the eagerness with which the young Neapolitan gathered up the wisdom of his Suabian master. And the concern of Albert to have his thought accurately preserved is evidenced by the fact that he looked through the notes carefully—a trial to his eyes if not his patience on account of Thomas's miserable scrawl and intricate system of shorthand, second only to the craziness of Albert's own handwriting.

There are many other merits and excellencies in Albert's enormous mass of theological writing waiting to be discovered and brought out in all their brilliance by careful and conscientious scholars.

—Thomas M. Schwertner

There are many other merits and excellencies in Albert's enormous mass of theological writing waiting to be discovered and brought out in all their brilliance by careful and conscientious scholars. Students of our own and coming ages, if only to refute the silly charges that the Church has been the implacable foe of intellectual and scientific progress, have the obligation—which is none the less a privilege—of making ever clearer Albert's prodigious industry, unrivaled erudition, adept utilization of the most disparate elements of learning. They can let in a breath of fresh air on the critical study of the sources of medieval theological tradition by accentuating Albert's personal note in many of his most abstract reasoning processes, his original method of approach to difficult problems and his expert handling of them, his frequent fresh outlook, his deep psychological insight into the workings of the human mind and heart, and his sage understanding of the variability of the social consciousness, of the half articulate masses of his age. They must show, often in contrast with other writers of that period, Albert's consistent sweet sanity and persistent reasonableness, his keen appreciation of the kind of teaching needed by his age and desiderated by its most farseeing educators. We are agreed today—though past ages have long since admitted it—that no single medieval theologian, with the exception of Thomas Aquinas, soared higher and nearer to God on the strong winds of scholastic philosophy and theology than Albert the Great, that none in his upward sweep remembered so lovingly the poor struggling thinkers on this planet who were trying painfully and laboriously but as best they could to fit together the wondrous patterns of God's oceanic love for humankind.

Lest students of Albert's theological labors be charged with blind enthusiasm when insisting upon his eminent gifts and achievements, they have been among the first to admit that, as in everything human, so, too, in Albert's work there are discoverable its own imperfections, such as the lack of a perfectly operating architectonic spirit, which might have succeeded in welding a bewildering mass of data into a tightly knit system and synthesis; that there is in him at times a bit of confusion when assigning things to their proper places and in their right proportions; that there is a sudden inexplicable hesitation to grasp the first implications and draw the last conclusions of an elaborate body of argumentation; that sometimes his divisions are not clear; that on occasion he divides up his matter too nicely thus losing sight of the central theme, the core question, the main contention; that at infrequent intervals his arguments get in another's way thus producing vagueness and confusion; that he does not always reject outright theories which fit ill into the general synthesis he was aiming at; that occasionally he fails to press out of a proposition all its rich savor. But these are the defects of a great man conscious every waking moment of his life that in the short span of a lifetime he had a gigantic task to perform in the face of great odds. For his tireless energy in collecting data he has been compared to Origen, and his stupendous work shows the minor blemishes of the great Alexandrine doctor without his major shortcomings. For having subjugated to Christian uses the proud, stubborn, and vagrant wisdom of the Greek and Jew and Moslem he has been compared to Godfrey de Bouillon—and like Godfrey's Kingdom of Jerusalem, Albert's hegemony in the schools did not long survive.

Had Albert been an isolated student or research worker, a selfish bookworm, shielded from the distractions of a busy and beneficent life in the mad swirl of the medieval world, perhaps he would have found time to eliminate these small blemishes from his written works. For these shortcomings are the inevitable result of the rapidity with which he perforce had to work in order to dispatch the many tasks which somehow found their way to his cell's door. They arise naturally out of the eagerness with which he followed up any new avenue of knowledge, made known to him by the discovery of a new manuscript, or by the appearance on the scene of a new teacher, that so, in his apostolic zeal, he might shield his students or the academic world against the danger of infection or pollution; out of the multiplicity of interests which solicited his mighty brain, that saw in every manifestation of life or activity a theater for the conquest of souls or an arena to maintain their possession; out of distractions incidental to the offices of trust he filled and the importunities of his friends and pupils which he in his big-heartedness always tried to satisfy in a regal fashion; and lastly out of the mystical bent of his heart which induced him often to stop in the very midst of an argument to paint engaging pictures of a devotional kind for the spiritual edification and benefit of his auditors. If our experience proves the truth of the poet's words that we love our friends mostly for their faults and foibles, then the very slight blemishes in Albert's theological writings, which show him to have been the willing victim of his own magnificent, magnanimous, and munificent nature, cannot but increase our admiration for a man who,

despite his undeniable greatness, did not seek to disguise his inherited trends nor cover over his acquired outlooks; who did not blush to reveal his moods and methods, his prejudices and preferences; who did not disown his native loyalties, nor deny his congenital antipathies. His consistent striving to be a saint without ceasing on that account to be a man makes him one of those lovable men from whom we do not shrink to take advice because we sense that he has the understanding heart of charity. As the twenty-eighth Doctor of the Church he has been deemed big enough in heart and mind to take his place in that select and resplendent gallery of heaven where he stands with Augustine, from whom he was not afraid to differ for all his love of him, with Ambrose, from whom he borrowed his own understanding Romano-legal spirit; with Anselm, from whom he learned the utilities of psychology in explaining the mysteries going on within a human heart that is keeping high festival with its Guest and Lord. In a word, Albert the theologian has well merited the words which Dante, the theological master poet, has put into the mouth of the prince of theologians:

> *Questi che m'è a destro più vicino*
> *frate e maestro fumni, ed esso Alberto*
> *fu di Colonia, ed io Thomas d'Aquino.*
> (*Paradiso*, X, viv.)

S. M. Albert (essay date 1948)

SOURCE: "Doctor Universalis," in *Albert the Great,* Blackfriars Publications, 1948, pp. 59-88.

[*In the following essay, Albert discusses the accomplishments of Albert the Great as a scientist, philosopher, and theologian, stressing "the universality of his genius" and his vocation as a teacher.*]

In one of his books Ulrich von Strassburg, who is usually described as St Albert's favourite pupil, says of his master that "he was the wonder and miracle of his age"; and Pius II in his dogmatic letter to the Turks 1464, hails him as one "who was ignorant of nothing, and knew all that was knowable." In his preface—in verse after the fashion of the times—to the first printed edition of the works of the saint, published in 1651, Peter Jammy, the editor, wrote the following lines:

> *Cunctis luxisti*
> *Scriptis praeclarus fuisti;*
> *Mundo luxisti*
> *Quia totum scibile scisti.*

[You enlightened all men, you were made illustrious by your writings: you illumined the whole world because you knew everything that could be known].

In our own day Pope Pius XI has declared:

> Historians and those who have written about him
> have rightly singled out for special praise the
> extraordinary universality of his mind; for he was
> occupied not only with divine things and the truths
> of philosophy, but also with all other human
> sciences. Bartholomew of Lucca, a contemporary,
> declared that in his knowledge of all the sciences
> and in his method of teaching, he excelled all the
> learned doctors of his day.

It was the universality of St Albert's genius which,
above all else, gained him the admiration of his contemporaries.

Others had been deeper thinkers; though no one could
call his thought superficial. Others had been more original thinkers; though many of the theories which he
enunciated or to which he pointed have been hailed by
those who followed him as the great discoveries of
their age. Others have been more polished, more finished in their style; but no one has shown such a combination of depth, originality and versatility of thought
as did Albert the Great.

> He would seem to have gathered up in himself the
> very different temperaments of a metaphysician, a
> mystic and a scientist . . . It is [not easy] to find
> people who, to the study of a wide range of subjects,
> unite true depth, and severe scientific precision . . .
> In the history of these great minds we have to jump
> from Aristotle to Albert the Great.

Before examining more closely the extent of the saint's
learning it is well to bear in mind that both his knowledge and his ignorance were conditioned by the circumstances of his age. In the intellectual sphere Western Europe had received two great legacies from antiquity, the Christian Faith and the treasures of the Grae-
co-Roman civilisation embodied in its philosophical
and scientific works. In the Dark Ages political and
social conditions were such that only ecclesiastics had
the leisure and opportunity for study and the pursuit of
education. Therefore the curriculum was determined
by their requirements—theology, Holy Scripture, canon and civil law. Theology dominated everything, and
from the inheritance from antiquity only those things
were taken which would best serve towards the understanding and development of that science. "Science"
in the modern sense was unknown, and natural objects
were only used to illustrate the supernatural. What might
be called the text-book of the natural science of the
day was the *Physiologus* (c. A.D. 300), a collection of
fairy stories, fables and myths about beasts and the
things of nature and their influence for good or ill, and
from this book was drawn the rich symbolism which
found expression in the architecture of the middle ages.
The works of Isidore of Seville (c. A.D. 600), though

less popular, were regarded as the best authorities and
St Thomas often quotes them.

By A.D. 1200 and therefore during Albert's early years
the situation was rather different. A good deal of the
Greek learning, till then almost unknown to Western
Europeans, had become available through translations
from the Greek and Arabic, e.g. in the medical writing
of the School of Salerno and the works of Adelard of
Bath (c. A.D. 1115). Some alchemical and astronomical
as well as medical works had been translated. The court
of the Emperor Frederick II was the great centre of
European science, and it seems almost certain that all
scientific men of the thirteenth century received their
stimulus from Sicily, Southern Italy and Spain, where
Latin, Greek, Moslem and Jewish cultures met on equal
terms.

Even in theology books were few and consisted principally of the Bible and commentaries thereon, and of
the *Sentences* of Peter Lombard, which was the nearest
approach to the text-book of theology in the modern
sense. Philosophy was more or less proscribed in the
schools, but at the time of St Albert it was insinuating
itself through the writings of the Arabian and Jewish
philosophers who were disciples of Aristotle. Such in
outline is the intellectual background against which St
Albert's achievement must be judged—not according
to the standards of our own day.

THE SCIENTIST

Albert was a student before he was a religious, for he
was at the University of Padua when he entered the
Order of Preachers. Padua was the centre of the study
of the liberal arts, just as Paris was the metropolis of
theological learning and Bologna that of law. From
this one may assume that Albert's tastes naturally tended in the direction of what we now call science, but
which in those days usually went under the name of
philosophy. Philosophy in the modern sense and theology were later developments; yet from the outset there
seems to have been present a tendency, springing from
grace, to see all things from a theological point of
view, i.e. as coming from God, leading to him, and
having him as their first cause and final end. Such an
attitude of mind shows the workings of the gifts of
wisdom and knowledge which, together with the gift
of prudence, "the executive of wisdom," are perhaps
the most characteristic traits of the saint's spiritual
physiognomy. He was a scientist by nature, but a saint
by grace, and the natural was always seen, loved, and
taught, in its relation to the supernatural.

We have said that Albert was a scientist from the start,
and a scientist he always remained. He merited the
title in a twofold sense; firstly because he investigated
and treated of the various branches of knowledge which
can be classed under the general head of the natural

sciences; and secondly and with even more justice, because he possessed the true scientific temperament which bases all its researches on observation, takes over the results of others only when morally certain of their validity and never seeks to prove from the data it possesses more than can be legitimately deduced therefrom. In all this he was the first scientist of our Western culture and the greatest biologist since Aristotle whom, however, he corrected on many points; and he was the forerunner of the modern researchers.

> Albert was endowed with a singular gift for the investigation of nature; a keen eye well adapted to the observation and determination of the slightest variation; a calm judgment capable of excluding any but sure results; above all a sensitive heart which embraced in its love the whole of nature down to its smallest elements.

As a boy he was not too carried away by the excitement of the chase to notice the behaviour of the wild falcons which came to receive their reward and then flew off; and we can picture him as a youth in Italy standing watching the workmen who were sawing up marble blocks and questioning them about the head of a bearded man, crowned with a royal crown, which he saw in one of them.

> The countenance [he says] had no other defect, save that the forehead was too high and ascending towards the top of the head. All of us who examined were satisfied that it was the work of nature. And I [he was still a youth, note] being questioned as to the cause of the disproportion of the forehead, replied that this stone had been coagulated by the work of vapour, and that by means of a more powerful heat, the vapour had risen without order or measure. (*De Mineralibus*)

Or again in Padua pushing his way to the front of a crowd which was watching the opening of a well and waiting about anxiously for the recovery of the man who lay unconscious for two hours, asphyxiated by the fumes which had killed his two companions. This interest which dates back even to his childhood persisted throughout his life, for we know from the observations which he records in his writings and which refer to what he had seen in different parts of Europe that, unlike our holy Father, St Dominic, who kept his eyes cast down while travelling, St Albert kept his very wide open and missed nothing that was worth seeing. The fishes in the Danube, the squirrels in the forest, the cattle, the deer, the birds, insects, plants, all came under Albert's scrutinising gaze so that he was able to give descriptions such as have not been improved upon even by modern scientists with all the instruments they have at their disposal. The description of the spider must have been the result of hours of patient watching and one wonders whether this was in his cell, and if

so, whether it was the model of cleanliness and order that is oftentimes considered the necessary outward expression of a saintly and orderly mind! The accounts of the habits of ants and bees must have required long periods of observation out of doors, perhaps in the garden whither the saint used to betake himself to sing hymns when wearied by prayer and study. Once he found three handfuls of honey in a nest of wild bees; but he remarks: "It was unfinished, inferior honey."

His description of the ant-lion may be quoted not only for its interest but because it illustrates Albert's carefulness to distinguish between what he had seen and what he had been told—a rare trait in those days.

> The formicaleon (the *lish* of Job iv, 11) is called the ant-lion, which is also called murmicaleon. To begin with this animal is not an ant as some say. For I have a great deal of experience of it and have shown my colleagues that this animal has very much the shape of the tick, and it hides itself in the sand, digging in it a hemispherical cup, at the bottom of which is the ant-lion's mouth; and when the ants, bent on gain, cross the pit, it seizes and devours them. This we have very often watched. In the winter also it is said to rob the ants of their food, for it gathers nothing for itself in the summer. (*De Animalibus*, xxvi, 20)

History tells us how Albert's friend and pupil St Thomas Aquinas was so abstracted at table that he even forgot that he was dining with the King of France, so that one may reasonably assume that he did not take much interest in the food set before him; while we are told that St Dominic partook only of one dish and that sparingly, and then went to sleep while the brethren finished their meal. This does not appear to have been the case with St Albert. As early as 1245 he had come to be known as an authority on fishes and when he was then in Paris the son of the King of Castile presented him with a curious mussel shell, on which were engraved numerous tiny serpents. His biographer concludes that it would be during dinner, at which fish would usually be served, that the saint had leisure to examine in detail the different specimens which were set before him. A similar explanation is given for the perfection of his description of an apple from the rind to the core, which has never been surpassed. Albert also remarks that once when eating oysters he found ten pearls at one meal, which leads one to think that his appetite must have been such as is usually associated with men of his race. These details, which incidentally afford a charming insight into the human side of the saint, show that the scientific instinct was always on the alert and that always and in all places he was observing the objects which lay around him, not as a mere onlooker but with the eye of a true scientist, and one who was versed first of all in the science of the saints—"investigating natural causes which are the instruments through which the divine will is manifested" (St Albert).

St Albert also showed his true scientific spirit in the manner in which he used the works of Aristotle, who was the only person who had so far produced any really comprehensive treatises on the natural sciences. However, these writings of the Greek philosopher were available only in very imperfect and defective texts; and they were in many places obscure, and often inaccurate; so that the saint's task was, to paraphrase his own words, to provide a natural history which would make Aristotle intelligible; and this he did by following the arrangement of the Greek's book, but now giving a commentary or a paraphrase, now simply reproducing the original text, but frequently making additions, corrections, supplying deficiencies and missing portions, and whenever possible substituting examples from his own observations, which, as they related to the northern countries which were familiar to his readers, would be more helpful than those in the original. Very often he disposed of the many myths concerning flora and fauna which had been prevalent in the ancient world and still persisted in his own day; but because he did not free himself from all he has been long regarded by most scientists as a romancer and the slavish and uncritical follower of Aristotle, and it is only within the last seventy or seventy-five years that his true position as a scientist has begun to be recognised. But "whosoever believes that Aristotle was a god, must also believe that he never erred. But if one believes that he was a man, then doubtless he was liable to error just as we are." So Albert wrote in his *Physicorum.* And again in *Meteororum:* "And therefore I think that Aristotle must have spoken from the opinions of his predecessors and not from the truth of demonstration or experiment." In his *Summa Theologica,* there is a whole section entitled "The Errors of Aristotle." This could hardly have come from a "slavish follower of Aristotle"!

The reputation of romancer, too, is probably partly due to the books which were attributed to Albert but which he did not write, and partly to the ignorance of critics who did not understand the background of his knowledge. It is very remarkable how often he does reject marvellous tales, and how he distinguishes what he has read or been told from what he has seen. His recent nomination by the Holy Father as Patron of all the Natural Sciences shows that the Church has now realised his greatness in this sphere of knowledge; but he has yet to come into his own among scientific circles in general.

That he will do so eventually, when reliable critical editions of his various writings are produced, is almost certain. He treated, among other things, of astronomy, meteorology, climatology, mineralogy, alchemy, chemistry, physics, mechanics, anthropology, zoology, psychology, weaving, navigation, architecture, botany. In almost every subject he anticipated by several centuries some of the major discoveries of modern times.

Speaking of St Albert's botanical writings a nineteenth-century investigator said, "To the man who was complete master of all the learning of his day and definitely advanced it, who for three centuries was never equalled let alone surpassed, the finest laurels are rightly due." The *De Vegetabilibus,* a masterpiece of its kind, owes its perfection to four main considerations; the independence with which the subject is treated; the acuteness and range of the observations, many of which were quite new; the clarity and precision of the description of original plants; and the attempt at a systematic classification to separate the essential from the non-essential, and to group together all plants with essential characteristics in common. In this section he made the celebrated division of flowers into the bird or wing-shaped, the bell-shaped, and the star-shaped. In many cases the natural science of to-day has completed the work which Albert began but never had time to pursue seriously; and a famous botanist has declared, "The defects in this book are the fault of his age; its merits belong to him alone."

He was the first to mention spinach in western literature, the first to point out the difference between tree buds enveloped by scaly coverings and the buds of plants which are without them, the first to notice the influence of light and temperature on the growth of trees as affecting their height and spread, the first to establish that the sap in the root is tasteless, becoming more flavoured as it ascends—a phenomenon noted again by the English naturalist Knight, at the beginning of the nineteenth century.

Similarly, in his zoological treatise *De Animalibus* which is based on Aristotle and Avicenna, St Albert made many new observations and gave detailed descriptions of all the fishes, birds, animals and insects which he had encountered on his journeyings on foot through Germany, France and Italy. He is said to have been the first to describe the weasel, the rat, the dormouse and the martens, also the spook-fish. He rejected many of the popular medieval myths, such as that of the pelican opening its breast to feed its young, or that the cock in its old age lays an egg from which a serpent is hatched. But because he included fabulous creatures in his list of animals his zoological knowledge has been underestimated and his contributions to this science insufficiently appreciated.

The dog seems to have interested him especially, likewise the whale and the bee, but one of his most charming and characteristic descriptions is that of the squirrel (*De Animalibus*):

> The pirolus is an extremely lively little animal; it nests in the tops of trees, has a long bushy tail, and swings itself from tree to tree, in doing so using its tail as a rudder. When on the move it drags its tail behind it, but when sitting it carries it erect up its

back. When taking food it holds it as do the other rodents in its hands, so to speak, and places it in its mouth. Its food consists of nuts and fruit and suchlike things. Its flesh is sweet and palatable. In Germany its colour is black when young, and later reddish, in old age it is even partly grey. In Poland it is reddish grey and in parts of Russia quite grey.

Among the characteristics of the cat he includes modesty—not the true modesty which belongs to man, but something remotely resembling it—love of beauty, and a habit of biting. Of the nightingale he remarks:

> In the case of the nightingale I have observed how it flew up to good singers, to whose song it quietly listened, and then, as if to challenge them, started up its own song. In this way two nightingales mutually provoke one another to song. (*De Animalibus*)

The description of the capture of a small lizard by a spider is very graphic.

> When the little creature had got itself entangled the spider at once came down and spun a web round its mouth so that she might not be injured in that way. Then she settled down to the creature and bit and stabbed it until it was dead or quite helpless. Then she went to the net where she stored her provisions and drew her prey after her by a web. This I saw myself with my own eyes and marvelled at the ingenuity of the spider. (*De Animalibus*)

To his acute observation Albert seems to have united great dexterity in the use of the scalpel as is shown by his dissections of plants and insects.

Thus it should be noted that although *De Animalibus* is not quite so free from the myths of the age as is the *De Vegetabilibus,* the recent appearance of a reliable critical edition has proved that it is invaluable to the zoologist. Critical editions of his other works in the category of the natural sciences have not yet been produced, but sufficient research has been undertaken to make it evident that here too Albert occupies a leading rank among scientific thinkers and investigators.

In an age when all save the learned believed the earth to be flat and inhabited only in the north he asserted that it was a sphere, proving his thesis as Aristotle had done before him by arguments from the force of gravity (in which some critics have seen a foreshadowing of Laplace's theory), which, he said, would also enable the southern zone to be inhabited. He even believed that the greater part of the earth was not only habitable but actually inhabited, except at the poles where he imagines the cold to be excessive. If there are any animals there, he says, "they must have very thick skins to defend them from the rigour of the cli-

mate, and they are probably of a white colour." Did he here anticipate the theory of protective coloration?

His treatise on climate and the various branches of geography foreshadows many modern theories. The formation of the earth's crust is due to a slow cooling of a central fire; mountain ranges are the result of upheaval, and he correctly traces the chief mountain chains of Europe, with rivers that take their source in each, mentioning sections of the coast which have been submerged by the sea's action in later times, and islands which have been formed by volcanic action; treating too of the effect of latitude and longitude and other factors in influencing local climate. His description of Germany surpasses, and in several places corrects, that of Tacitus whose *Germania* has always been considered a classic on the subject. The explorations of the fifteenth century are said to have been inspired, at least indirectly, by the saint's geographical writings. In his description of the British Isles he speaks of the island of Tile or Thule, not yet visited by man, and probably uninhabitable by reason of its frightful climate. He several times refers to his own maps, none of which have come down to us.

In Physics some of his explanations could well have been taken from a modern text-book. Sound, he says, is caused by the impact of two hard bodies, and this vibration is propagated in the form of a sphere whose centre is the point of percussion. Light is converted into heat, he declares, on being absorbed by a body. He speaks of the refraction of the solar ray, of the laws of the refraction of light, and remarks that none of the ancients and few of the moderns were acquainted with the properties of mirrors. He was familiar with the properties of magnets.

He seems to have undertaken experiments in alchemy, and is sometimes said to have been the first to isolate the element of arsenic. He compiled a list of over one hundred minerals, giving a description of each, and in the course of this book he remarks, "At one time when I was away from home I wandered far and wide to places where metals were to be found that I might discover their nature and properties" (*De Mineralibus*); and again: "I saw and studied how they worked in copper in our parts, namely Paris and Cologne and other places where I was."

Although he had no telescope he decided that the Milky Way must be composed of myriads of stars, and he says that the dark spots on the moon are not due to the earth's shadow, as the ancients believed, but to configurations on her own surface. He corrects Aristotle's assertion that a lunar rainbow occurs only twice in fifty years. "I myself have observed two in a single year," he says.

In anatomy he takes the vertebral column as the basis of the structure, whereas in his day and for long afterwards most anatomists began with the skull. In this sphere again he takes Aristotle to task. The Greek had held that man had eight ribs on either side. Albert declares, "Man has seven true ribs and five false ribs on either side."

Mathematics, anthropology, biology—every branch of science offers examples of Albert's anticipation of modern theories and discoveries, and it has been said that if his principles had been followed science might have been spared a detour of three centuries.

But he did not confine himself to theories. His researches must have involved many experiments, and one wonders how he managed to find time for them amidst all his other activities. He is known to have invented some sort of hydraulic machine; he possessed apparatus for registering the phenomena of an earthquake; he is said to have invented the first greenhouse. He made figures move by means of mercury, and in the nineteenth century a cup was still preserved in the museum of Cologne with which he was supposed to have cured every disease. Such was his interest in architecture that he is said to have drawn up the plans for the new cathedral of Strassburg which was then under construction. This seems likely, and it is certain that he produced those for the Dominican churches of Cologne and Louvain (St Dominic's Priory in London is modelled upon the latter). His influence on the growth of gothic architecture in Germany was so great that in ancient manuals the original style is called "the Albertine science." He was evidently something of a musician and a poet too, but all his songs are lost and most of his verses. Rudolph of Nymegen says that he composed many proses and sequences in honour of our Blessed Lady—no doubt those which he used to sing in the garden—offices of St Joseph and the Crown of Thorns, and the sequence in honour of the Blessed Trinity beginning "Profitentes Unitatem," which was in the old Dominican *Graduale*.

On this basis of fact many legends grew up. St Albert was thought to have a cure for every disease—he had written on medicine, Rudolph says—and so the goblet he had made was regarded as miraculous. He invented so many things that the common people believed he could produce something to satisfy every need. Despite his own condemnation of magic and astrology the legend grew up that he was something of a magician. So there is the story of the talking woman which St Thomas is supposed to have found behind a curtain and to have smashed up, crying out, "Get thee behind me Satan," thinking he was faced by a diabolical illusion. Whereupon St Albert is said to have entered the room and asked, "What have you done? You have destroyed the labours of thirty years!" This story does not ring true to what we know of the character of either saint, and legend has credited Roger Bacon also with the invention of a talking head. But it does give

some idea of what people could believe about Albert. The reputed production of a summer's day in the priory garden in honour of the visit of the Emperor William of Holland may also be a magical illusion, but it may refer to his hothouse if the tradition that he invented this is true.

In the order of the miraculous Albert is said to have had a vision of our Blessed Lady and the Four Crowned Martyrs, Patrons of architects, while the plans for Cologne Cathedral were under discussion. At a word from the Mother of God and under her direction the saints drew the plans for a most wonderful edifice. Then the dream faded, but Albert remembered and reproduced the design, which was the one chosen.

Legends such as these have earned for the saint the reputation of magician as well as the contempt of scientists—at least until the process of his rehabilitation began in the past century. But enough has been said to show that Albert has every right to be regarded as one of the greatest scientists Europe has produced, and he has still a third claim to such a title, and one which, if it is recognised before it is too late, may yet be able to save both science and the world from the destruction towards which they seem to be heading.

For science, as we understand it today, seeks to know what can be quantitatively observed about the external—the shapes, sizes, movements, and changes of things—and then endeavours so to manipulate and arrange these things and circumstances that man's will shall be done. Its sphere is very limited, its conclusions can only be provisional, its laws are only probabilities. It can describe what a thing is, how it works in terms of matter and energy; it cannot, it is not meant to, explain the ultimate reason of things. That is the task of the philosopher, who can and should make use of the material provided by science. But that is what the science of today tries to do. Although it cannot see things as a whole, nor even for that matter see even the minutest thing as a whole, it limits reality to what it can observe in its test-tube and admits only one explanation of reality—the materialistic one from which the spiritual and God are *a priori* excluded. Thus it sets itself up as a "philosophy" in which neither natural philosophy nor theology can even make an appearance; rather than acknowledge its inferior position in the hierarchy of knowledge it refuses to recognise any form of wisdom other than its own, though in truth mere *scientia* is not wisdom at all.

St Albert was a true scientist, remarkably free from that confusion between science and philosophy, as we know them, which was so general in his day.

> There are some people who attribute all these things to divine order [he says], and say that we must not consider in them any other cause save the will of

God. This in part we can agree to . . . yet . . . we are not seeking a reason or explanation of the divine will but rather investigating natural causes which are as instruments through which God's will is manifested. It is not sufficient to know these things in a general sort of way; what we are looking for is the cause of each individual thing according to the nature belonging to it.

But he was an equally great philosopher and he pursued his scientific studies from a teleological standpoint, realising with St Paul that "the invisible things of him from the creation of the world are clearly seen, being understood by the things that are made" (Rom. i, 20), and that the ultimate answer to the problem of the origin and purpose of the universe which science itself can never solve is, in the words of St Thomas that God "has produced things into being in order that his goodness might be communicated to creatures and be represented by them" (***Summa Theologica***). The whole universe is the work of his hands, he guides it and directs it to its end. It came forth from him and to him it must return, and each thing is what it is because he so wills it, and because it thus best serves the purpose of the whole. He preserves it not from afar but from within and the true natural philosopher, such as Albert was, is conscious "not only that the beauty (of things) is a reflection of his infinite beauty, but that the invisible beauty is within them and about them, hallowing them."

Others had been deeper thinkers; though no one could call his thought superficial. . . . [But] no one has shown such a combination of depth, originality and versatility of thought as did Albert the Great.

—*S. M. Albert*

And when, like Albert, he is above all a theologian and a saint, he will recognise, in the things that are made, traces of that Triune Life of knowledge and love which is the being of the God of revelation. He who is present everywhere in his creation is Father, Son and Spirit of Love, and his love of his own goodness is the ultimate explanation of everything.

Science has suffered considerably for having disregarded Albert's principles of experience for nearly three centuries: it will suffer still more if it does not accept his teleological conception of science before it is too late; if it does not recognise that science of itself can never provide a philosophy of life, but at best can only supply the material on which others may build one.

That is why Pope Pius XI declared that

> the present moment would seem to be the time when the glorification of Albert the Great was most calculated to win souls to the sweet yoke of Christ. Albert is exactly the Saint whose example should inspire this modern age—so full of hope for its scientific discoveries . . . In him the rays of divine and human science meet to form a shining splendour . . . His life is a standing proof that there is no opposition, but rather the closest fellowship between science and faith . . . Like St Jerome, Albert, as it were with powerful voice, declares and proves in his wonderful writings that science worthy of the name, and faith, and a life lived according to the principles of faith, can, and indeed should, all flourish together in men because supernatural faith is the crown and perfection of science.

Albert was then first of all a scientist, endowed with the true scientific temperament and retaining all his life a deep interest in things scientific. His writings on scientific subjects embraced every branch of that form of learning and occupy a high place among such writings of any age. Because of them, because of his scientific spirit and because of the discoveries which he made and the principles which he laid down, he is rightly considered one of the first true scientists of our Western culture after Aristotle in order of time, he is given a place amongst the greatest scientists of all ages, and is undeniably the greatest Catholic scientist of any age. And yet in a life filled with teaching, preaching, writing, and apostolic work of every kind, his scientific interest took the place almost of a hobby. Natural science was an important part of the curriculum for the Faculty of Arts in which Aristotle's writings were read in the order in which they are commented on by St Albert, who may well have taught them in the schools of Arts in the Order. He certainly wrote his commentaries at the earnest request of the brethren, even though he also had a wider end in view. As he says himself in his commentary on Aristotle's *Physicorum:*

> Our object in these treatises on natural science is to meet as far as lies in our power, the wishes of the brethren of our Order, who now for several years have been begging us to compile such a book on the things of Nature, as would give them a complete natural history, by means of which they could arrive at a sufficient understanding of Aristotle's writings. Though we do not consider ourselves to be equal to such a work, we could not resist the wishes of the brethren.

But although the Arts, in which natural science occupied an increasingly large place, were important as preliminary studies, theology still remained the friars' chief preoccupation and to that Albert must have devoted the lion's share of his teaching and study. Yet his academic life itself was only one aspect of an existence which was crammed with activities of every sort, in the midst of which he found time to write and to collect the material for writing those treatises which give him a place among the leaders of science, and one wonders what he would have achieved had he devoted the whole of his time, energy and mighty intellect to this one congenial subject. Perhaps it is as a reward for the self-abnegation involved in this sacrifice that he is now honoured in the Church as Patron of all the Natural Sciences.

A biographer, Thomas of Chantimpré, reports this story which he declares he had often heard from the lips of the saint himself, to prove the supernatural nature of his vocation to cultivate the natural sciences:

> One day when Albert was seated at the table in his tiny cell ardently seeking the solution of some scientific problem, the evil spirit made his appearance under the guise of a Dominican religious. Feigning modesty and compassion he first spoke of his too great application to study, representing to him that he was overburdening both soul and body, taking no care of his health and wasting his energy on things which were foreign to his profession. Albert, supernaturally enlightened as to the designs of the evil one, was content to reply by making the sign of the Cross and the apparition disappeared.

THE PHILOSOPHER

The catalogue of St Albert's scientific writings which has already been given might almost of itself justify the title of Universal Doctor, and yet they form only a part of the total output of his works. The exact number of these is still unknown for many are unedited, many lost or hidden in libraries, and while some unauthentic works are attributed to him, others probably genuine may still go under the name of other authors. One thing is certain that great as was Albert's reputation as a scientist his fame as a philosopher was even greater, and it is in this sphere that he made his greatest contribution to learning.

He was described by Henry of Hereford as "the most resplendent son of the philosophers of Christendom," and he was called by his contemporaries *Maximus in philosophia* even before he received the general title of "the Great." As in natural science, his writings embrace every aspect of the subject—logic, metaphysics and moral philosophy, while he has separate treatises against the outstanding philosophical errors of the day. It is true that he did not create a perfectly finished philosophical system as did St Thomas; but St Thomas could never have produced his system without the preliminary labours of St Albert, and without Albert Thomas might never even have been a philosopher. Roger Bacon, Englishman who had no love for Dominicans, least of all for Albertus Magnus, tried to belittle and ridicule him when he wrote—"He had never

studied philosophy, nor did he attend lectures on the subject in the schools, he was also never in a *Studium Solemne* before he became a theologian; he could not have received any instruction in his Order, for he was the first Master of Philosophy in it."

Actually this gibe only serves to show the greatness of Albert as a philosopher. He found the philosophical works of Aristotle proscribed from the schools, and accessible only in defective translations, and in the commentaries of Arabs and Jews to whom they had come through African translations and writings which were greatly influenced by Neo-Platonist philosophy, so that their Aristotelianism was to a great extent mixed with Neo-Platonism. Without apparently any previous training, he set out as he himself said "to make all these parts [of Aristotle's writings] intelligible to Latins," and he succeeded so well that he produced commentaries which are still of value today, collected an immense range of material, secured for Aristotle an entrance into the schools, and prepared the way for the dedication of philosophy to the services of theology, a task which theologians had been attempting since the time of Augustine, and which Thomas was to bring to a happy conclusion.

In his commentaries Albert set out not to give his own views so much as to reproduce those of Aristotle, elucidating them by means of those Arabian and Jewish writers who he thought had understood him most clearly: for he like St Thomas—or perhaps it would be more correct to say that St Thomas like St Albert—believed in making use of truth no matter where it was found. He does, however, make it clear that in presenting the thought of Aristotle he does not necessarily make it his own, and that while agreeing with his system and method as a whole he disagrees very decidedly with some sections of it, and while following Aristotle in general he does from time to time in his own works adopt the theories and arguments of Plato.

Albert wrote in his commentary on Aristotle's *Politics:*

> It is not I who have said anything in this book; I have only set out what has been said and stated principles and causes. Similiarly in all the physical books I have never put forward my own opinions, but have rather expounded as faithfully as I could the views of the Peripatetics. This I only say on account of some lazy people who, seeking an excuse for their laziness, scrutinise the book for something they can find fault with.

Yet he did, in fact, in the course of his expositions set down some of his own views, if only in the way he pronounced for or against the views of others which he was reporting; but he never produced the coherent, finished synthesis of St Thomas, and in different writings he seems to sponsor now one view now another. This is one of the defects of his work, but a defect which springs from and is almost conditioned by its merits. He set out to render Aristotle intelligible to the West, and he certainly succeeded in that self-appointed task. William of Moerbeke's Latin translation from the original Greek, done at the request of St Thomas, had made available a reliable text, but the need for equally reliable commentaries was urgent.

These commentaries were Albert's own contribution, and to write them he made himself master of all the philosophical knowledge of his time, taking especial pains to assimilate the whole body of Arabian and Jewish knowledge with which he became more familiar than did any other Christian scholar of the day. The amount of information which he thereby collected was enormous and he had to sift, criticise and correct it before setting it out in his commentaries. Small wonder then that he did not attempt to give a decisive vote on every theory which he mentioned. That he left to minds less burdened with detail than his own. For a like reason, he did not produce a complete philosophical system, although he did conceive the idea of linking together all the truths found in the various philosophical systems, and he worked at this in his various monographs, thus founding a self-sufficient Christian philosophy, of which the superstructure, the general fundamentals and many details were taken direct from Aristotle. . . . [The] universality of Albert's genius embraced the whole philosophical knowledge of his day; and that it is in this sphere that his originality and genius, by initiating and making possible the formation of a Christian philosophy, the *philosophia perennis,* found their most perfect expression.

THE THEOLOGIAN

> Albert was by natural inclination a naturalist, by conscious effort a philosopher, and with his whole devout soul from the bottom of a heart which glowed with charity, a theologian.

So writes a biographer; and Pius XI, in the Bull from which we have quoted so often, declares:

> To him belongs this great honour, that (excepting St Thomas) there is scarcely another doctor of equal authority, whether in philosophy, theology or the interpretation of Scripture. Indeed it was to theology that the whole trend of his mind was inevitably directed. It would be an endless task to relate all that Albert has done for the increase of theological science. . . . He used philosophy and the scholastic method as a kind of implement for the explanation of theology. In fact he is regarded as the author of that method of theology which has come down in the Church to our own time as the safe and sound norm for clerical studies.

Yet while Albert takes a first rank among theologians the defects in his philosophical writings are reproduced here and he has always to take second place to St Thomas except perhaps in one or two sections. Yet here too Albert prepared the way for Thomas, and neither can be properly appreciated save in relation to the other.

When Albert began to write and to teach theology still meant primarily the study of Holy Scripture, so that it is not surprising to find that, according to his earliest biographer, he commented on the whole of the Bible. The only treatises extant today are the commentaries on the Psalms, the Prophets, the four Gospels, the Book of Job, the Canticle of Canticles, and one on the *Mulier Fortis,* whom he takes as a type of the Church and of the individual soul. The style of these different works varies. The commentary on the Psalms was written for the faithful with a view to bringing to memory the moral precepts and truths of the Faith, and so he follows the allegorical method which had traditionally been adopted by the Western Fathers. The commentary on the Prophets, on the other hand, was written to refute the Jews, and here Albert was at pains to establish the literal sense, showing the Prophets as the signposts to Christ, and only referring briefly to the allegorical meaning. The Gospel commentaries are of a different nature again, the allegorical character being almost entirely disregarded, so that the literal sense is thrown into the foreground and the significance of the books as the historical source of Christianity is brought out. These treatises show that Albert had a gift for historical writings, although we do not possess any such works from his pen. Among these commentaries that on St Luke's Gospel stands out so conspicuously that Peter of Prussia remarks that in the opinion of many the saint must have been very specially illuminated by the Holy Ghost in writing it. According to tradition this work was written, or at least completed, while Albert was bishop which may account for the more than usually severe denunciations of the failings and disorders of the times which it contains. One critic has said of this treatise:

> Here the current of Albert's own thought and his mystically inclined disposition find their freest expression, and at times in passages of great nobility and sublime genius, passages which must surely rank with the greatest and most profound in the religious literature of all times.

Albert's contribution to scriptural exegesis was threefold. He strongly insisted on the literal meaning, he led the way in introducing a systematic analysis of the text, and he traced the progressive development of revelation, a thought which was novel in his day. In all these things he pointed the way towards modern exegetical methods, so that although he does not occupy any position of special importance in biblical science—

since the auxiliary sciences at the disposal of the modern scholar were unknown to him—his position among medieval exegetes is one of outstanding importance, as it witnessed by the epithet applied to him in a 1473 Preface to his *Mariale*—"the most renowned interpreter of the Sacred Books."

In the sphere of moral philosophy, Albert's position is the same as that in philosophy and in theology as a whole; he prepared the way for St Thomas to whose works his own are inferior. It is interesting to note, however, that while the second part of the *Summa,* wherein the whole of moral theory is worked out in relation to the good, has long been considered the masterpiece of Thomas's method and exposition, a manuscript has lately been discovered containing the third part of Albert's *Summa de Creaturis* wherein he treats of ethics in relation to the good, thoroughly discussing the four cardinal virtues; and this was composed a good twenty years before St Thomas's *Summa.* Here as everywhere Aristotle is the basis, but St Augustine's ethical theories are also given prominence, and in an age which was essentially objective in its theological expositions Albert anticipates later times in giving consideration to the personal element.

> The great discerner of souls does not belie himself here. More than once his vast experience of life, his charity in judgment, his just and wise weighing of all the circumstances, manifest themselves. This is especially the case when Albert, as for instance in his teaching on anger, or on the spiritual works of mercy, descends to the particular and gives advice on the proper ordering of life, for then he reveals a unique greatness, a rare combination of high scientific training and a practical wisdom born of his own experience of life . . . We can then catch a glimpse of his own soul, as in moving speech his loving heart sings the canticle of God.

This introduction of the personal element . . . differs so much from Thomas. . . . Here it may be noted it follows from his whole conception of theology, which was not to him a dry impersonal abstract science, a theoretical knowledge of God, but a knowledge breathing forth love, intensely practical, in fact 'Mystical Theology' in Denis's sense, which is the knowledge of God flowing from the Gift of Wisdom. To quote once more from the Bull of canonisation:

> Albert's numerous theological works, and above all, his commentaries on the sacred Scriptures, bear the marks not only of an enlightened mind and a deep knowledge of Catholic training, but they are stamped with the spirit of piety and arouse in souls the desire to cleave to Christ. We readily discern therein the holy man discoursing of holy things . . . His mystical writings show that he was favoured by the Holy Ghost with the gift of infused contemplation.

In dogmatic theology Albert produced the usual commentary on the *Sentences* of Peter Lombard, which belongs to his early teaching days, and a **Summa** which was unfinished at the time of his death. Neither approaches the sublimity of St Thomas's *Summa* for which, however, all Albert's theological studies prepared the way. As in philosophy, he was usually content to set down the different opinions on a point, leaving it to others to decide which was the true one, so he gives the impression at times of himself wavering between different points of view. On some subjects—the nature of original sin, and the creation of Adam in a state of sanctifying grace—he adopted doctrines which were contrary to those usually held and which only became generally accepted when they had been further sponsored by St Thomas. His favourite subjects were our Blessed Lady and the Holy Eucharist. He wrote more on our Lady than did any other scholastic doctor—the **Mariale,** a treatise on her virginity, a commentary on the *Ave Maria,* and lengthy sections in the scriptural commentaries—and in them he displays a burning love and devotion towards the Queen of Heaven. Peter of Prussia points out that the saint never mentioned her name without adding some epithet in her praise. His most important contribution to Mariology is his teaching on her universal mediation which he developed from her position as bride and co-helper of Jesus.

The doctrine of the Holy Eucharist receives even more attention; the sermons on the Eucharist for a long time circulated under the name of St Thomas and were extremely popular: **De Eucharistico Sacramento** is a veritable *Summa* on the subject, while **De Sacrificio Missae** is an exposition of the prayer and ceremonies of the Mass which broke away from the arbitrary and artificial method then common and took a road which is followed even today. In these treatises as in those of our Blessed Lady the saint is obviously dealing with a subject dear to his heart, and the fervour of his devotion cannot be concealed. This is also the case when he deals with the theology of the Procession of the Holy Ghost to which he had obviously devoted much thought and study.

It is in the sphere of mystical theology, however, that Albert is at his best, nor was he surpassed even by Thomas. The popular *De adhaerendo Deo,* so long regarded as his masterpiece, is now considered to be either wholly or in part the work of another; but his other mystical works, especially the commentaries on Denis the Areopagite, are quite sufficient to give him a leading place among masters of the spiritual life. He alone of all the scholastics commented on all these books, and his commentaries are a masterpiece of interpretation. Moreover he showed how every word and every phrase can be given an interpretation comfortable to sacred Scriptures, although the author was actually tinged with Neo-Platonic and unorthodox ideas;

and he pointed out many errors into which mystics are liable to fall, especially the dangers of quietism. Rudolph of Nymegen records the following story apropos of the commentaries on Denis the Areopagite:

A religious renowned for his learning and virtue [whom most people believe to have been St Thomas] one day picked up a sheet of paper on which the following was written in Albert's hand. "When I had with much difficulty completed the book on the 'Celestial Hierarchy' I began the exposition of the 'Ecclesiastical Hierarchy.' With incredible difficulty I had got through the first chapter on Baptism, but when I started on the second my strength failed me. I despaired of being able to go any further when after Matins, this vision was vouchsafed to me. I found myself in a church where St Paul was saying Mass. Consoled beyond measure I felt sure that he himself would enlighten me on the meaning of Denis. When the Apostle had said the *Agnus Dei,* an enormous crowd entered the church, and the celebrant asked what they wanted. "We have brought you a demoniac," replied someone; "please deliver him." When Satan had been driven out, Paul gave Holy Communion to the happy Christian. I offered myself as server, and said with a certain fear, "For a long time I have desired to be instructed on the profound mysteries contained in the pages of the Areopagite, and especially on the nature of true holiness." Paul replied kindly; "After Mass come with me to the house of Aaron the High Priest, situated on the other bank of the river."

Accordingly when Mass was over I followed the Apostle. When we arrived at the water's edge the Doctor of the Nations crossed without difficulty. It was not so with me; for hardly had I touched the waves than they began to rise so as to make my crossing impossible. St Paul entered the house which he had pointed out to me; and I asked myself anxiously how I could possibly follow him, and then suddenly I awoke. After some reflection I believed I had found the explanation of the dream. The first chapter of Denis treats, in effect, of the expulsion of Satan from the human soul by Baptism. Then the new Christian participates in the sacrament of Holy Eucharist. The following chapter leads him who would receive the holy chrism to the house of Aaron, because here it is a question of the chrism with which bishops are anointed. The deep waters which so suddenly heaped up had terrified me, but by the grace of God the great Apostle had made my passage easy. I therefore betook myself once more to my writing, and I have completed, with help from on high, what my own feebleness had shown me was an impossibility.

As a mystical writer he had tremendous influence over the German School which followed him, and, as in the case of the natural sciences, if his example and teaching had been followed, a detour of several centuries would have been avoided. "In the field of mysticism

Albert not only achieved great things in individual problems, but also laid new foundations, and set up signposts for the further development of the subject."

This inadequate survey of Albert's writings may perhaps convey some idea of the universality of his genius. It may be added that he was always a "doctor" in the most literal sense of the word, i.e. a teacher. He studied and wrote not for love of so doing, and perhaps not even principally out of a love of truth but out of a love of God and of souls in God, which made him anxious to impart to others the knowledge which he had himself amassed, and to employ for the good of souls the talents which had been entrusted to him. That one of those was the gift of teaching, of imparting knowledge, is evident. No saint has taught for so long nor been so determined to return to the office of teaching when other works could be laid aside. That he was chosen as the first regent of studies of the *Studium Generale* at Cologne shows the esteem in which he was held by the authorities of his Order; and the crowds who flocked to his lectures proved that the students of Europe had a like opinion of his ability.

A prolific writer is not necessarily a good writer and to be endowed with an encyclopedic brain is not necessarily a sign of greatness, but in Albert these were manifestation of the essential greatness of his intellect, while his teaching ability depended perhaps most of all on the greatness of his soul. As Pius XI wrote, "All the works of Albert are of monumental value and of imperishable authority. With our predecessor Leo XIII we venture to say—'Although time will bring its increase to every kind of science, still Albert's teachings which served to form Thomas Aquinas and were regarded in his time as miraculous can never really grow old.'"

Stanley B. Cunningham (essay date 1967)

SOURCE: "Albertus Magnus on Natural Law," in *Journal of the History of Ideas,* Vol. XXVIII, No. 4, October-December, 1967, pp. 479-502.

[*In the following essay, Cunningham maintains that Albert's writings in his* De bono *constitute a significant development in the Medieval conception of natural law.*]

In the history of the concept of natural law and its development in the Middle Ages, a privileged authority is commanded by the writings of St. Thomas Aquinas. By comparison, only scant attention has been paid to speculations in the area of law and morals carried out by Thomas' teacher, Albert the Great (1206-1280), and still less to the extent of Thomas' dependency upon the latter. The full import of Albert's contributions, however, is appreciable when measured

St. Albert, from a painting by Joos van Gent.

against the background of moral theorizing in the XI-IIth century. For one thing, his own independent writings as well as two commentaries clearly establish him as the first Christian thinker in the Latin West to confront boldly and enthusiastically the theory of natural virtue contained in Aristotle's *Nicomachean Ethics*. Secondly, prior to Albertus Magnus there is a conspicuous paucity of systematic moral treatises; and, with the exception of brief studies made by the canon lawyers of the time and by one theologian, William of Auxerre, scarcely any interest had been shown in the concept of natural law and its relationship to the moral life in general. The inclusion, therefore, within one of

Albert's early moral treatises of a section on natural law stands out as a turning point in the history of the problem.

Two places in Albert's writings give a concentrated treatment of natural law. The earliest and most important of these belongs to a relatively youthful work, entitled *De bono,* composed during the period 1240-1244. The work is incomplete. What we have is the first part of an ambitiously conceived synthesis dealing with the natural moral virtues prior to a proposed but missing examination of supernaturally endowed perfections. The composition stands in noticeable contrast to the moral sections of his later *Scripta super Sententias* and his commentaries on the *Ethics* of Aristotle, where the order is not laid down by Albert himself but by the authors on whose works he is commenting. The extant text of the *De bono,* on the other hand, written in a format inspired by the medieval academic disputation and freely assembled according to principles of Albert's own formulation and choice, may be treated as an independently organized synthesis of Albert's own moral theories. Put more simply, it is our best source for an understanding of his moral philosophy in its organic outlines. The number of times in later works he refers his readers back to the *De bono* adds up to an obvious corroboration of the work's value as a lasting and faithful expression of the author's thought. As to its over-all structure, the *De bono* opens with a metaphysical disquisition upon the nature of goodness in general, then moves on to an examination of the natural and psychological causes of virtue before defining the notion of virtue in general. Each of the four long tractates which follow is a detailed analysis of one of the four cardinal virtues and its parts. At the beginning of the last tractate, devoted to justice, Albert has inserted two *quaestiones* divided into a total of seven articles which constitute a full-fledged treatise on natural law.

The second source of Albertinian natural-law theory is found in Book V, Chapter 9 of a hitherto unedited commentary on the *Nicomachean Ethics* composed around 1248-52. The material in question comprises eight *dubia* or problems, each of which is handled separately in article form in the manner once again of the medieval disputed question. Although this section does include a number of minor precisions not present in the earlier work, there does not appear to be any major development in doctrine. Even at a glance these eight brief articles quite obviously lack the scope and detail which characterize his earlier investigation. The *De bono,* therefore, contains the most thorough and definitive treatment of law in the entire collection of Albert's works and the one to which he does not hesitate to refer in later writings.

Pre-Albertinian Theorists

What relevancy does natural law have within the moral order? More specifically, what relationship did the medieval thinkers envisage between law and virtue? The question, to be sure, was seldom posed so explicitly; but even implicitly the problem manifested itself as a tension coloring the attitudes and conceptions of moralists in the late XIIth and early XIIIth century. The *De bono,* containing a metaphysics of morals, a theory of the virtues and an analysis of *ius* and *lex,* presents itself as an ideal witness to one man's thoughts on this question. Even more significantly, when studied against the background of earlier and contemporary compositions in the Middle Ages, Albert's treatise on law as well as its position within the *De bono* reveals a radical departure from the general tenor of moral speculation at this time in which the spirit of legalism was prevalent. Two conditions make such a comparative viewing possible even within the short compass of this [essay]: the late emergence of systematized moral writings; and the relative scarcity of expositions on law by philosophers and theologians. A representative view of the most commonly conceived connection between law and virtue can be had by consulting three major treatises, two of them written in Albert's own lifetime, in which this relationship is made evident: Alan of Lille's *De virtutibus et vitiis et de donis Spiritus Sancti;* William of Auxerre's *Summa aurea;* and Part Three of the *Summa fratris Alexandri,* the moral section of which is generally believed to have been written by the Franciscan John of Rupella.

Alan of Lille's work, composed around 1160, has been appraised as "greatly contributing to a more technical elaboration of the treatise on virtues" in the Middle Ages. It is of special interest in the historical evolution of the definition(s) of virtue because Alan is confronted by a seeming conflict between the theocentric-Augustinian conception of virtue of Peter the Lombard and the philosophical definitions proposed by Peter Abelard and his school. In addition to this, he is faced with more than one definition by the classical philosophers, for he reports that according to Aristotle virtues belong to the genus of "quality," while Cicero in the *De inventione* speaks of them as species of natural right (*species naturalis iuris*). By natural right, Alan continues, is meant everything in a thing bestowed upon it by nature. Virtue, then, falls into the genus of quality, and at the same time it is a species of natural right conferred upon the soul at creation. It would seem, then, that the coincidence of the terms "genus" and "species" fulfills the strict logical requirements of a definition. Yet Alan goes on to say that what is really conferred upon us at creation is not the full-fledged virtue, but merely a disposing quality. The virtues at the moment of their inception are "potencies." To become full-blown perfections, these qualitative potencies must be developed through our acts or "use." Essentially this implanted seminal potency is a quality, but since its subsequent growth and completion depends upon our use or performance, it is only accidental to it that it

becomes a virtue: *"accidentale est enim ei esse virtutem, sed substantiale est esse qualitatem."*

In order that this qualitative potency expand to the dimensions of virtue, two conditions must coincide in the use: attendance to obligation or duty (*debitum officium*) and to end (*debitus finis*). If our actions are not commensurate with both of these, then we cannot be said to possess virtue. The end which Alan has in mind is God. What is more relevant to our problem, however, is his notion of *officium.* "Since *officium,*" he writes, "is the act of any person conforming to the customs and laws of the country (*secundum mores et instituta patriae*), the *officium* of the Christian religion is the act of any person in conformity with the customs and laws of the Church. Moreover, the customs and laws of the Church are that a man's actions be directed to God and performed in a spirit of charity." It is immediately evident, of course, that Alan of Lille's conception of virtue, though starting with a philosophical definition, ends up in a decidedly theological perspective. What is more significant, however, is the relationship he draws between virtue and law. Our innate and potential proclivities towards perfection are not virtues in themselves; they become that only if we act in conformity with the laws of the Church. We have here a legalistic conception of morality in which conformity to law precedes the birth of virtue as its indispensable cause.

About sixty years later we find a similar priority of law to virtue attested to by William of Auxerre in his *Summa aurea* (1220-1225): "since natural law (*ius naturale*) is the origin and principle of all the virtues and their acts, it behooves us to treat first of natural law." Now it is true that, unlike Alan of Lille, William in the present text speaks of *natural* law and not the positive written law of the Church, but the difference is not really very great when we consider what William understands by natural law, and the historical influences at work in the shaping of his thought. When the decretists of the XIIth and XIIIth centuries came to treat of natural law, they did so with the traditional vocabulary and techniques proper to a study of positive or prescribed law. This very practice of clothing their theories of natural law in the vocabulary proper to civil and canon law was bound to produce misconceptions of the former. One of the dominant figures in this tradition of natural-law theory is the canonist Rufinus, in whose *Summa decretorum* (1157-1159) there is an attempt to codify in a broad manner the content of natural law into "commands," "prohibitions," and the remoter "demonstrations" deducible therefrom. Now William of Auxerre, as we have seen, proposes to add a treatise on natural law prior to his treatment of the virtues. Part and parcel of his doctrine is the Rufinian division of natural law into precepts, prohibitions, and demonstrations. These divisions are treated by William in terms of obligation: precepts and prohibitions oblige us absolutely, whereas the force of obligation in "demonstrations" depends upon circumstances. The obligational force of natural law is divisible as well into another range of categories: primary, secondary, and even tertiary necessity. To put it briefly, the main feature in terms of which William interprets natural law is the binding force of obligation and necessity. These precepts of natural law, he tells us, "are primarily and principally given to habilitate us towards the acquisition of political (i.e., cardinal) virtues." Moral wisdom *per se* rests upon the precepts of natural law which are inscribed in the heart of man. It must have seemed perfectly logical and consistent, then, to William that his theory of law should preface his disquisition upon the virtues. Hence, his conception of law as prior to and the source of virtue, reveals itself as the major architectonic principle of order in this moral section on the virtues.

This apparent spirit of legalism is even more pronounced in another part of his *Summa.* Well after the treatises on natural law and the virtues, William embarks upon a new section which is to be primarily moral:

> After theological questions we move on to moral questions in which we learn about external acts and particular cases. I say this for the most part, because among the following questions there are some as well which are theological. Now we divide these moral questions in two: that is, into precepts and sacraments or into questions concerning precepts and questions concerning the sacraments.

It was not uncommon for theologians at this time to formulate the major division in their theology in terms of "faith and morals" (*fides et mores*). This division reappears in the text above, for the implication reads all too clearly that the earlier questions of the *Summa aurea,* even those including William's theories on natural law and the cardinal virtues, belong not so much to moral science as to the theology of faith. Only now are we really embarking upon the elaboration of moral science (*mores*), an investigation, moreover, which reduces itself in large part to an examination of laws and particular cases.

Whereas both Alan of Lille and William of Auxerre accord a priority of law to virtue in their moral treatises, no real proof has yet been offered to justify this order of speculation. In John of Rupella there is an explicit defense given for this mode of procedure. In addition to the many scattered and unedited treatises attributed to him, it is now generally agreed that John is author of a moral section contained in Book III of the *Summa fratris Alexandri.* It was being written about the same time at which St. Albert was engaged in work on the *De bono,* that is around 1241-1245. For this reason the work supplies us with an immediate back-

ground of information concerning contemporary views on law, and in particular certain trends of thought in the Franciscan school.

In his treatise John of Rupella explicitly asks about the order obtaining between law and virtue: *"Iuxta hoc secundo quaeritur de ordine praeceptorum et virtutum, quod horum est prius."* In his own resolution to the question there is an unequivocal statement and defense of the NATURAL priority of law to virtue: *"lex sive praecepta legis naturaliter sunt priora virtutibus."* As proof he observes that God, the *summum bonum,* moves in two ways: as the beginning (*principium*) and end (*finis*) of creation. When God is viewed as the origin of creatures and their goodness, we find in the creatures a corresponding *debitum,* an obligation to conform to their principle. Law is to be placed in this context, that is, at the point where creatures issue from their maker. It is law which dictates the *debitum bonum* to these creatures and holds them to the good. Virtue is situated in the second context. It consists in the aptitude to pursue obediently the good already dictated to us. The essence of virtue, then, is obligation and obedience; it is submission to law. In point of fact this article provides the justification for the order of John's moral treatise: a disquisition on law precedes his treatment of the virtues.

This emphasis upon the centrality of law within the moral order is no less apparent in the Prologue to John's unedited *Summa de praeceptis.* In the passage in question, John proposes to cast the main principles of his moral doctrine into the framework of the four Aristotelian causes, and it is the particular designation given to the material cause which is so revealing. "The material cause of morals," he writes, "are the laws of God." It is these laws which constitute the moral order (*esse morum*).

This brief survey of three major treatises, written before the middle of the XIIIth century, shows that medieval thinkers generally conceived of virtue primarily in terms of law. In the case of William of Auxerre and John of Rupella, an alleged priority of law to virtue reveals itself as the architectonic principle determining the very structure and arrangement of material in their treatises. It might be rash to insist that *all* the moralists at this time shared this juristic conception of ethics; but taking into account the slow emergence of the systematic moral treatise and noting that in the history of this evolution these three works are major contributions, it seems evident that the general tenor of speculation was indeed legalistic. A quick glance at the outline of Albert the Great's *De bono* and the place in which law is discussed would be enough to indicate a departure from this traditional emphasis on law. The work opens with a metaphysics of the good in which no mention is made of law. A disquisition upon the causes of virtue, preceding the detailed analyses of the virtues themselves, grounds the origin of virtue not in law but in the human act seen in all of its dynamic complexity. The section on law is found towards the end of the extant text of the *De bono* in the last tractate. It is placed here, Albert remarks several times, because the notions of *ius* and *lex* serve as determinations in the definition of justice, and he has in mind statements made by Cicero and St. Augustine. His affirmations, however, read as mere statements from authority. Behind them is Albert's whole philosophy of law dictating such a move.

Natural Right: Innate or Acquired?

Before launching directly into this part of the *De bono,* the modern reader, lest he misconstrue the spirit of Albert's moral philosophy, should be forewarned about the use of the term "right" (*ius*). When Albert, or any of the medieval moralists for that matter, speaks of "natural right" (*ius naturae, ius naturale*) or "right of reason" (*ius rationis*), this must not be translated into the modern sense of "subjective right." In the XIIIth century, "right" means that which *is* objectively right. "Right of reason" does not mean personal right to which my opinions or individuality entitle me, but that which is objectively and universally right for rational nature. Prior to the *De bono,* the terms "right" and "law" are used interchangeably. Both in doctrine and procedure Albert distinguishes between these notions: Question One of the treatise deals with right; Question Two with law. The first article in Question One opens with a definition taken from Cicero's *De inventione:* "The law of nature is that which is not born of opinion, but implanted in us by a kind of innate instinct." A number of other definitions and descriptions of natural right alluded to by Albert in these articles, notably those of Isidore of Seville, Gratian, St. Augustine, and William of Auxerre, show that he was conversant with the statements of the most important authorities, both classical and medieval, in this area. Taking his start from the opinions and statements already worked out by earlier and contemporary thinkers, Albert moves on from there to present his own distinctive doctrine of natural law in the traditional terms already familiar to his readers.

Natural right, he points out, is a *habitus* concreated with, and innately impressed upon, the human rational soul. No one, unless he be wanting in reason, would ever seriously question that it is a *habitus,* that is to say, a unified ensemble of the first and most ultimate principles of human morals directing us in our human actions. Its content or nature is variously described by Albert in several places as embracing universal principles directing us in our actions (*universalia iuris illa dirigentia nos in opere; universalia morum*), first principles of right (*prima principia iuris*), first seeds (*prima semina*), or seeds of moral goodness (*seminaria boni pertinentis ad vitam*). The seminal character of these principles, it will be clear later, has a special significance in relation to written law. The more universal and indeterminate these principles are, the more truly they pertain to natural right. As examples he cites from St. Matthew (7, 12) the Golden Rule, "do unto others as you would have them do unto you," as well as the Ten Commandments set down in Exodus (20, 1-17). These universal principles, writes Albert, are all included within natural right, and inscribed in man by the very fact that he has reason.

It is precisely this relationship to reason which seems to interest Albert in Article One, and which he continues to develop in the following articles as well. He points out that in the theoretical or speculative intellect, prior to the operation of understanding or science, there is a twofold potency. There is first of all a potency with respect to knowledge of the instruments, and these in turn serve as the principles of our completed science or understanding. To illustrate this he cites the case of the child who does not yet know how to write. First of all, the child is in potency to a knowledge of the instruments involved: pen, ink, parchment. Subsequent to his knowledge of these, he is still in potency to a mastery of writing itself. This analogy serves to illustrate a corresponding situation in the moral order. In our practical intellect which directs us in our operations, there is implanted a "habit" which is a knowledge of right (*scientia iuris, scientia boni*). The innate wisdom, however, is only a "first potency," because it is still open to a more precise and determinate formulation of the universal principles indeterminately contained therein. In order that these principles be made explicit, we still require a knowledge of the terms in which the universal principles are formulated. Thus the knowledge that stealing and adultery are wrong is embedded in our natures as part of natural right, but that this knowledge be had as completed acts of understanding, i.e., "thou shalt not steal," "thou shalt not commit adultery," there must be added an acquired knowledge of the terms "stealing" and "adultery." Hence, Albert concludes, the knowledge of these principles is implanted absolutely by nature (*per naturam simpliciter*), but it is also gained in a qualified manner (*per accidens*) through an acquired knowledge of the terms involved. The human intellect, in itself a potency, is devoid of knowledge (*tabula rasa*) not with respect to this absolutely implanted habit, but only with respect to the acquired knowledge of terms.

Among pre-Albertinian thinkers there seems to have been complete unanimity in the belief in the innate character of natural right. When Albert insists that natural right is implanted in us "absolutely," he aligns himself with a tradition stretching back through the Middle Ages into classical antiquity. It was Cicero himself who had laid down this line of thought when he spoke of a "certain innate instinct" (*quaedam in natura innata vis*); and St. Paul (Romans 2, 14-15)— quoted by Albert in the opening lines of his solution—

speaks of a law inscribed in the hearts of men. Hence it became commonplace among the canonists and theologians alike to identify the insertion of this universal law with "nature," or, in the case of man, to equate the insertion and knowledge of these principles with "natural reason" (*ratio naturalis*). William of Auxerre in particular was at pains to emphasize the radical innatism of natural law. Taking his start from the writings of St. Augustine, William had argued that the human soul, created in the image of God, has a vision of the divine essence, and along with that a knowledge of the supreme goodness, true justice, in short a knowledge of the principles of natural right—all this without the benefit of any sense experience!

It seems quite clear, however, that Albert finds these previous accounts inadequate. Though adhering to a basic innatism of the "habit" of first principles, he nevertheless has attempted to supplement that theory with his own doctrine of the necessity for an acquired knowledge of the terms. That the inspiration behind this innovation is evidently Aristotelian can be seen in the startling relationship he draws between the Ciceronian "innate instinct" and the power of agent intellect. The *"vis innata"* or *"vis naturae,"* Albert insists, is nothing else than the light of our own agent intellect which makes known to us the terms of the principles, and subsequently a completed understanding of, and assent to, the innate moral principles themselves. In this way, the native power of the human intellect appears to be an active and indispensable contributor to the knowledge of those principles. This, as will be clear in greater detail, strictly limits natural right to the human species. At this point, then, Albert seems to have reached a position midway between the traditional doctrine of radical innatism and the philosophy of St. Thomas Aquinas, for whom natural law is not essentially an innate "habit" but rather a product of reason (*aliquid per rationem constitutum*) consisting in judgments.

Synderesis

The subject in which the principles of natural right are imbedded, according to Albert, is practical reason. More specifically, they inhere in an active power of reason called by some *"naturale iudicatorium,"* by the Greeks *"synderesis."* Armed with these principles, practical reason is directed and assisted in its practical judgments concerning what is to be done or what is to be avoided. Since very little is said about *synderesis* in the *De bono,* we may safely assume that Albert is still relying upon his treatment of this in an earlier work. In the *De homine* he has told us that *synderesis* is a special power (*vis*) of the soul in which are inscribed the universal principles of natural right. He exploits a certain parallel first suggested by William of Auxerre between the speculative or theoretical reason on the one hand, and practical reason on the other. Just as in

the theoretical intellect there are certain innately implanted first principles aiding man in the area of speculative truth, so too in the practical order of human moral acts there are certain universal directive principles through which the practical intellect is aided in its discrimination between moral good and evil, principles moreover which are not acquired by man, but which are simply the content of natural law inscribed upon the human mind. The subject or substratum of these is *synderesis*.

Albert the Great is certainly not the first of the medieval thinkers to speculate on the rôle of *synderesis* in the moral life. In his lengthy investigation into the theories of *synderesis* in the Middle Ages, Lottin has shown that prior to Philip the Chancellor (died about 1237) this notion and the problems related thereto appear a number of times in the writings of both the canonists and the theologians. Indeed, nearly seventy years before Albert had tackled these questions, that is around 1175, one of the decretists, Simon of Bisiniano, had already anticipated the Albertinian position by equating natural right with *synderesis*. These earlier thinkers, however, were mainly preoccupied with two problems: the indestructibility of *synderesis,* and its infallibility as a guardian of the moral order prompting man to goodness. Theologians and canonists alike looked to it as a stable and permanent element in man, an abiding source of rectitude in human nature which survived in spite of his sinful defections. There was not always the same unanimity, however, when it came to the question of the infallibility of this principle. Reason can and does err in its moral judgments, and so to some this meant that *synderesis* as well was not altogether immune to error. For our purposes it is not necessary to enter into this maze of questions. Suffice it to say that from the middle of the XIIth century, the occurrence of the term *synderesis* sparked a number of questions, but almost invariably these questions were concerned only with the properties, notably its inextinguishable and infallible character. What was almost totally neglected was an appreciation of *synderesis* within the general framework of the human psychology, and so an understanding of it in its very nature. Other than a more or less general agreement that it pertained to man's reason, and William of Auxerre's more specific equation between it and the Augustinian notion of "superior reason," the basic question "What is synderesis?" remained largely unanswered. Moreover, the questions devoted to an analysis of its properties had not yet grouped themselves into a full-fledged technical treatise. The merit for this impressive undertaking falls to Philip the Chancellor, in the light of whose theory the full significance of Albert's position becomes apparent.

The first question posed by Philip the Chancellor is a new and original attempt to arrive at some understanding of *synderesis* in its very nature, prior to a discussion of its properties. Is it a "power of the soul," he asks, or a connatural habit inhering in the soul from birth? A number of authorities and arguments have been assembled in defense of either position. These two seemingly disparate lines of thought, however, are not really in conflict: Philip answers by way of compromise that *synderesis* is an "habitual power." An habitual power, he tells us, is one which is more readily and easily disposed to its act because it is not impeded in the performance of its operation, unlike reason, for instance, which can experience difficulty in judgments. *Synderesis* is a motive power which moves man's power of free choice by dictating to it the good and restraining it from evil. In this exercise it moves not towards this or that particular good, but rather inclines us to the element of common goodness found therein. Its movement belongs simultaneously to the cognitive order, and to the affective or appetitive order, but primarily to the latter. In the same place Philip even goes so far as to assert that *synderesis* is identical in subject with the natural will. Yet even though it stands mainly on the side of will, he seems anxious to draw several qualifications which will avoid too complete an identity between these powers. The objects of both *synderesis* and our natural will are rationally determined moral goods. Natural will inclines towards these purely and simply as a mere power, but not as an "habitual power" free from impediments. Moreover, whereas *synderesis* inclines solely towards rational moral goods, the scope of the will's appetition is less determinate because it embraces goods both of the rational and the nonrational order. In other words, the much wider latitude of the will's inclination makes it relatively indeterminate in its movement towards moral goodness. *Synderesis* appears to be a superadded habituation or power coalescing with the will to insure in man a permanent and indefectible inclination in the direction of moral goodness.

Although William of Auxerre and some of the decretists had made *synderesis* the subject of natural right, Philip seems to ignore this line of reasoning altogether. As an affective or voluntaristic power, *synderesis* operates not so much on the side of reason, but rather as an efficient cause insuring the will's movement towards moral goodness. We might simply add that subsequent to Philip's doctrine there is a noticeable tendency among the Franciscan writers to perpetuate this voluntaristic interpretation of *synderesis*. It is especially evident in the writings of St. Bonaventure, who speaks of *synderesis* as a "certain kind of natural weight" (*naturale quoddam pondus*) residing in the will and infallibly steering it towards moral goodness.

Now in contrast to this current of voluntarism stemming from Philip the Chancellor, Albertus Magnus clearly situates *synderesis* on the side of reason, and along with it the principles of natural right. Statements in both the **De homine** and the **De bono** are in agree-

ment on this point, and further corroboration may be found in a fragment attributed to Albert entitled **De sinderesi**. These informing principles of natural right serve as formal determinations directing and assisting the practical intellect of man in its operations. As the immediate subject of these principles, *synderesis* is no less a dynamic principle than it was for Philip the Chancellor, but its force is now exercised not as an efficient cause propelling the will to goodness, but rather in the line of formal causality and in the cognitive order as well. More than any other thinker before him, then, Albert has attempted to delineate the close union between right and reason. Article Two of the first question is a logical continuation of that theme: it examines the nature and scope of natural right conceived as an integral element in rational nature. It is this close relationship to reason that results in a conception of natural right which sets Albert apart from the prevailing notions of natural law in the XIIth and early XIIIth centuries.

Albert versus the Canonists

The second article concerns itself with the number of ways in which we may speak of natural right. It opens with a verbatim quotation from the work of one of the decretists composed shortly after 1215, Johannes Teutonicus' *Glossa ordinaria* on the *Decretum* of Gratian, in which there are recorded five different meanings of the term *"natura."* Now the first two definitions speak simply of "nature," while the last three speak as well of "natural right." In point of fact all five definitions are interpretations of natural right which have already appeared in the works of other authors. According to Johannes Teutonicus, nature may first of all be taken to mean the innate procreative power by which things produce their like. This seems to extend to inanimate as well as animate nature. Secondly, nature may refer to the impulse or instinct of sensuality in animal nature terminating in the activities of desiring, procreation, and the rearing of the young. In this second sense, Albert comments, natural right would be that to which we are inclined by the natural concupiscence of our senses. Thirdly, nature signifies the natural instinct of reason (*instinctus naturae ex ratione proveniens*) which gives rise to the right known as equity. According to this natural right, all things are said to be common in time of dire necessity. In its fourth usage, natural right is seen to be an ensemble of natural precepts: e.g., "thou shalt not steal," "thou shalt not commit adultery." Fifthly, natural right is equated with divine right (*ius divinum*).

Now it is evident that the catalogue of Johannes Teutonicus reads as a kind of hierarchy in which we begin with nature in its broadest sense as a principle of generation common to animate as well as inanimate being. From this most common signification of nature, there is a progressive ascent to the higher grades of nature and right: to animal nature, rational nature and equity, precepts known to reason, and finally divine right. The hierarchy itself is probably Johannes' most influential contribution in this one area of natural-law theory because its impact will be clearly discernible in later theologians beginning with William of Auxerre. But the five definitions themselves do not originate with his *Glossa*. All of them have already appeared in canonical *summae* prior to Johannes in which it had been common practice to record any number of definitions. Four of them, for instance, appear after 1188 in the *Summa* of Huguccio. The *Summa Lipsiensis* (*ca.* 1186) records a total of six definitions without indicating any preference. Three definitions may be found in Sicard of Cremona (*ca.* 1180), four in the *Summa Monacensis* (1175-1178); five in the *Summa* of Stephen of Tournai (*ca.* 1160). This survey does not pretend to be complete, but it gives a picture of the tendency among the decretists to pile up a number of definitions without a corresponding increase of precision in their understanding of natural right. On the contrary, in the minds of many there prevailed a conception of natural right so wide as to encompass all of animal nature, and even inanimate nature.

At least two classical authorities known to the canonists could be said to have encouraged this kind of latitude in their thinking. The *Digesta* (known also as the *Pandectae*) of Justinian, compiled in 593 A.D., records a fragment of the Roman jurisconsult Ulpian (d. 228) in which natural right is extended to all animal nature in contrast to the "right of peoples" (*ius gentium*) which is restricted to mankind. The definition of natural law from this fragment became classical in the history of jurisprudence: *"Ius naturale est quod natura omnia animalia docuit."* Either this sentence or a formulation of the same doctrine closely approximating it appears in nearly every one of the major *summae* of canon law in the XIIth and XIIIth centuries. The same holds true for the expressions used to describe some of the actions determined by natural law: "the union of male and female," "procreation," and "training of the young" (*educatio*). This is not to say that in all cases Ulpian's definition was to prove entirely acceptable without any sort of qualification. Gratian in his *Decretum* (*ca.* 1140) chose to ignore it; Rufinus some fifteen years later explicitly limits natural right to the human species. Henceforth, a number of decretists, though continuing to report a series of definitions, will relegate the broad notion of Ulpian to a minor position, concentrating their exegeses instead upon those definitions which relate natural law to human reason, moral precepts and prohibitions, and to God. This is true of many, we say, but by no means of all. The anonymous author of the *Summa Monacensis,* for instance, sees no reason not to extend natural right to the whole order of creation, since the sun in its revolutions is ruled by the law of nature. In view of these ambiguities, the language in the passage from the *Glossa ordinaria* quoted by Albert may have been chosen with greater deliberation than might appear at first sight, since the first two definitions speak simply of "nature" while the last three specify "natural right." Albert, nevertheless, in the paragraph of commentary that follows, treats all of them as interpretations of natural right. The second authority occasioning widespread confusion in the classical and medieval conceptions of natural law is once again the Ciceronian formula which attributes natural right to a "certain innate instinct" (*quaedam in natura innata vis*). A number of theologians and canonists, pointing to Boethius or Aristotle as their authority, commonly equated the *innata vis* in question with *natura* conceived as a generative or procreative principle. Albert himself mentions that this is one opinion.

Up to this point we have dealt mainly with those interpretations of natural right found in the writings of canon lawyers. History dictates this selection since it was primarily the decretists, not the theologians, who showed an interest in the problem of natural law. William of Auxerre appears to have been the first of the theologians to break with this long tradition of silent indifference. Not only does he reiterate the classical definition of Ulpian, but in his own doctrine of natural law William incorporates as well that broadest of all conceptions found in the *Summa Monacensis*. The result is another hierarchy of natural laws, much like that of Johannes Teutonicus, corresponding to three levels of community in nature: *ius naturale speciale* is natural right taken in its strictest sense, and this is found only in those beings possessing reason; *ius naturale universalius* pertains to the whole realm of animal nature; finally, *ius naturale universalissimum* is nothing else than the law and harmony of all creation, inanimate as well as animate. The first two Dominican masters to hold chairs in Theology at Paris, Roland of Cremona (1229-1230) and Hugh of St. Cher (1230-1235), betray a noticeable dependence upon William's *Summa* for their doctrine of natural law. They literally repeat William's doctrine and vocabulary, and even the same authorities cited by William (i.e., Plato's *Timaeus,* and St. Augustine). These dates bring us up almost to the eve of the composition of St. Albert's **De bono**.

Albert's verbatim quotation from the *Glossa ordinaria,* his many allusions to Gratian throughout the treatise, and his obvious familiarity with the *Summa aurea,* offer ample evidence that he was conversant with the history of the problem of natural law. A statement in Article Two, written apropos of the passage from the *Glossa ordinaria,* sheds some light on his attitude towards these previous treatments:

> If perchance it should be said that this distinction is without art or reason, as is the custom among the decretists to posit distinctions, the question then remains in what sense nature is to be taken when we speak of natural right.

It is quite apparent that Albert is critical of these earlier attempts to define natural law. The distinctions posed by the decretists, and in particular the fivefold distinction of Johannes Teutonicus, lack "art and reason" because they fall short of a synthesis which shows skill and thought. In short, the decretists have not arrived at an understanding of natural right. This is something which Albert reserves to the theologian. Albert then substitutes definitions of nature taken from Boethius.

Albert's own doctrine, succinctly stated in the second sentence of his resolution, marks a departure from this "custom of the decretists to posit distinctions." Without a proliferation of definitions he states simply: *"Est enim ius naturale nihil aliud quam ius rationis sive debitum, secundum quod natura est ratio."* Natural right is nothing else than what is objectively right for rational nature. In calling it the *debitum* of reason Albert is using a term, borrowed from the jurists, which normally signifies legalistic obligation. In the present context, however, *debitum* has a more ultimate and metajuridical connotation: it signifies that which is proportionate to, and commensurate with, the nature of man. This becomes apparent from his analysis of the meaning of "nature."

The acceptance of nature as reason (*natura ut ratio*) may be viewed in three ways: where *ratio* is taken primarily as nature, or primarily as reason, or equally as nature and reason. If taken primarily as nature, then natural right is seen to operate as the principle of those actions pertaining to the welfare and preservation both of the individual (e.g., the acquisition of food, clothing, home and bed, and the enjoyment and protection of health) and the species (e.g., marriage, progeny, and the enjoyment and protection of both). But Albert is anxious to stipulate that even though the emphasis at this level of natural right is upon the natural impulse of nature, this by no means excludes reason, and even more precisely "right reason." Only a nature which is rational is the subject of natural right. Although training and nutrition and procreation are common to animal nature in general, they do not fall within the compass of natural right unless in some way they participate in reason and are morally virtuous acts. In the second level of natural right, the emphasis rests upon the rational element in man's nature, and to this pertain religion, justice, and the moral excellence of man (*honestas*) both in himself and in relation to others. Yet these forms of moral excellence involve not simply an element of pure reason, but other facets in man's nature as well. To natural right considered in this way belong the precepts of the Decalogue, according as they are taken generally and as indeterminate principles, and, in short, any kind of absolute goodness (*honestum*). In a third sense, where natural reason is considered as equally reason and nature, natural right encompasses all that which right reason determines to

man's benefit and use. Albert adds here that we are speaking of natural right as of seeds of goodness, not of an ensemble of particular cases and specific decrees.

Albert is concerned with showing how widely the influence of the right of reason extends itself to every level of human activity. But natural right in all cases is a right of *reason*. At least six times throughout the treatise on law he explicitly takes exception to the broader conceptions of natural law which stretch it beyond the range of reason. "We do not agree with that distinction posed by some," he writes, "namely that natural right may be spoken of in many ways, and that in one way it is common to us and the beasts." The fact that in the course of this treatise he insists repeatedly upon this precision gives us some idea of the importance he attaches to this conviction. His words are an unequivocal repudiation of a tradition we have witnessed dating back to Roman times. What he proposes in its stead is a humanism wherein natural right appears as an integral element proper to man's practical reason. Natural right is "human right." While it is true that some of the canonists, notably Rufinus, had partly anticipated the Albertinian reservation, Albert, through intimately linking the principles of natural right to human reason, has given a philosophical justification for his assertions.

In Article Three, Albert moves on to consider the very content of natural right. He begins with two quotations. In his classical definition of natural right in the *De inventione,* Cicero included as well an enumeration of its contents: religion (*religio*), duty (*pietas*), gratitude (*gratia*), revenge (*vindicatio*), reverence, (*observantia*), truth (*veritas*). Gratian, reporting on the words of Isidore of Seville, offers a longer classification, and in this passage the influence of Ulpian is still discernible:

> the union of man and woman, the succession of children, the education of boys, the common possession of all things and the same freedom for all; the acquisition of those things which are harvested from sky, earth and sea; likewise the restitution of a deposited item or entrusted money; the repelling of violence with force.

These are the only two major authorities mentioned by Albert. But the problem of ascertaining the content of natural law had been complicated for the medieval theologians by another division proposed shortly after Gratian's. Around 1149, Roland Bandinelli (later to become Pope Alexander III) spoke of all law as being comprised of precepts, prohibitions, permissions, and counsels. Ten years later, the decretist Rufinus was to echo much the same doctrine, but this time with specific reference to natural law:

Natural law is comprised of three things: namely, commands, prohibitions, demonstrations. For it commands that which is beneficial, such as "thou shalt love the Lord thy God." It forbids that which harms, such as "thou shalt not kill." It demonstrates that which is fitting, such as "all things should be had in common," "let there be the same freedom for all," and things of this sort.

Henceforth, nearly all the decretists, and William of Auxerre as well, adopt this division of natural law into commands, prohibitions, and demonstrations.

This kind of analysis, however, was to produce a curious effect. The reduction of natural law to a number of categories, the subsequent endeavor to multiply examples and to fit them into these categories, and the catalogue of functions envisaged by Gratian and others—all these divisions, we say, read as so many attempts to codify natural law in much the same way as these authors were teaching and studying a codified canon and civil law. From this custom of borrowing terms and techniques proper to a study of written positive law, there developed a tendency to speak of natural law *as if it were the same as written law*.

Albert's approach marks a departure from this tradition of juridified natural law. In the last article he simply defined natural right as that which is the objective right of rational nature. In the present article he neither divides natural right into a number of categories, nor does he attempt any enumeration of percepts. He simply points out that a diversification of natural right is effected through its objects:

> Following our earlier statements, we say that natural right resides only in the ultimate principles of human right and, as has been shown, it is those principles. For just as the speculative intellect does not have one principle by which it knows all knowables, so the practical intellect does not have one principle by which it knows all practicable objects. Rather, just as the principles of the speculative intellect are diversified through diverse objects, so too the principles of the practical intellect are diversified through diverse actions, and the conditions of those acting, and place and time.

There is no one principle guiding the practical intellect just as there is no single principle assisting the speculative intellect in its understanding. When Albert speaks of natural right as a "habitus" he simultaneously conceives of a nature with its own unity and economy. Nevertheless, that "habit" in its very unity embraces a potential diversity of ultimate universal principles and *is* those principles. The principles themselves do not accrue to the intellect as so many clearly formulated directives and prohibitions. On the contrary, their very multiplicity is effected by a diversity in the objects of the practical intellect and by a diversity of

circumstances and condition. Albert seems to have been the first to realize that the custom of classifying natural law not only destroys its unity by substituting for it a kind of mysterious "a priori" multiplicity but leaves unanswered as well the ultimate questions about the extent and causes of that very diversity.

In this same article, Albert proposes to distinguish three ways in which principles and acts fall within the compass of natural justice or right: essentially, suppositively, and particularly. Essentially belonging to and constituting natural right are those most universal and ultimate principles of which mention has been made in Article One: e.g., the Golden Rule, the Decalogue. Mention of these, however, is not intended to exhaust the content of natural right. Rather, by reason of their obvious goodness and relative indeterminacy they exemplify the kind of principle Albert has in mind when attempting to explain the nature of natural universal right. In the second way, "suppositively," there are natural acts determined by these first principles and presupposing them (*supposita communia illorum principiorum*). Such are the perfections and acts listed by Cicero and Isidore of Seville (and Gratian) in their divisions of natural right. They owe their origin to natural reason, but they are obviously of a more determinate or concrete nature than the first ultimate principles. Finally, those things pertain to natural right "particularly" which have been established by popular ordinance, the deliberations of the ruling body, and the pronouncements of the wise men. The suppositive and particular determinations, especially the latter, do not derive in their totality from natural reason, but entail as well a consideration of the concrete conditions and circumstances in which man finds himself.

Let there be no misunderstanding of Albert's purpose in presenting this threefold division. It is neither a division of natural right into three compartments, nor a hierarchy in the manner of those of Johannes Teutonicus and William of Auxerre. Rather, it is an attempt to view in its totality the scope and influx of natural right as seen through a series of progressive diversifications and specifications. Essentially, natural right *is* the most ultimate and universal principles of goodness and right. The other two manifestations of natural law are not absolute and essential, but rather participations. That is to say, they are prolongations or continuations of these ultimate principles into the less universal positive rights and specific operations of man. In these last two levels, right extends into the area of human, positive, and written laws, where a number of features other than natural reason intervene: e.g., the will of man, the consent and approval of peoples, covenants; diversifications through circumstances of time, place, events and affairs, and persons, etc. Especially at the third level we are dealing with "particular cases" which are reducible to natural right not simply and absolutely, but only "per accidents," as Albert says, precisely because of the addition of these other features. Opinion, not simply reason, is now at work in the formulation of written and positive right, since we now cope with things which in their very nature are variable and probable. This is not to say that, at this level, right rests upon doubt (arising from a confrontation of contradictories) and ambiguity (arising from confrontation of equal possibilities), but rather upon that which seems highly likely and right in the counsels of wise men because little or no reason militates against it. Moreover, even though these determinations of written and positive right do not derive in their entirety from reason, they nevertheless look to the rule of reason and bear its imprint. They are certainly not determinations contrary to reason. All right ultimately stems from nature and participates in natural right; if not, then it is not right, but injustice (*iniuria*).

Natural right is the metajuridical basis of all subsequent human rights and laws. Albert's constant emphasis upon the seminal character of these first principles now becomes clearer. The principles of natural right, he tells us, are "first seeds" which are inherently present in the public laws and decrees of the rulers and wise men as well as in the human and written laws which derive therefrom. They are intimately present as principles and directives assisting the work of prudential reason amidst a real network of conditions and circumstances. Even acts or rights which are seemingly antithetical, e.g., common possession and private possession of goods, can stem from one and the same natural law because different objects and conditions effect a difference in the principles. The *habitus* of natural right is one in its inclination towards goodness, but as refracted through different states and conditions this one force can pluralize itself in different manifestations.

Law

Question Two of the tractate on justice is devoted to a discussion of law (*lex*). The term, Albert admits, is an analogous one signifying four main laws: the law of nature, the law of Moses, the law of grace, and the law of sin. Of the three definitions of law in general, reported in Article One, the one imputed to Cicero, though not authentically Ciceronian, is favored by Albert in his magisterial resolution: "law is written right (*ius scriptum*) ordering the good (*honestum*) and prohibiting the contrary." Not above stretching a point, Albert argues that this is still a valid definition of natural law because the term "written" in this case may be taken in a much wider sense to mean "written by the finger of God and inserted in the heart of man." He then proceeds to tie the definition in with Aristotelian theory. In the *Nicomachean Ethics,* notes Albert, Aristotle had stated that it is the aim of every lawmaker to promote virtue in the citizens; and so political science includes laws as to what people shall do, and from

what things they shall refrain. The end of law is the same as that of political wisdom: it is the human good (*humanum bonum*). The pseudo-Ciceronian definition seems to coincide with this philosophy, since it gives as the end of law the acquisition of moral excellence (*honestum*) and the prohibition of evil. *Honestum* has been the term used throughout the **De bono** to designate the mode of goodness proper to virtue. The end of law, then, as envisaged by Albert is primarily the growth of virtue in people. Prohibitions against evil are only incidentally (*per accidens*) the end of law, and they are made only when there are impediments or obstacles to goodness. This emphasis upon the positive end of law opposes a tradition dating back to Rufinus and even earlier to St. Augustine, wherein prohibitions were made to be an essential ingredient of natural law.

One of the most significant passages in these two articles is one containing an explicit defense of Albert's distinction between *ius* and *lex:*

> To the second objection it must be said that law pertains more to obligation arising from the command of rational nature; and right pertains rather to the deliberations about practicable objects through rational nature; and thus the difference between natural law and natural right is clear. Hence, natural right adopts the good and prohibits the contrary through the manner of one judging. Natural law, however, effects these two through the manner of obligation and rule or precept. And thus the difference is clear.

In two sentences Albert has given us his doctrine of natural law in a nutshell. "Law" derives from the Latin word "to bind" (*ligare*). Its goal is moral excellence which it effects by means of obligation, command and precept. "Right," on the other hand, moves us to moral goodness through the work of judgment (*per modum iudicantis*). Its influence is felt in the deliberations of right reason concerning what man is to do (*cogitationes operabilium*). The notion of "right," then, is ontologically prior: it is the universal knowledge possessed by man of what is good, fitting, and proportionate to his rational nature. But this same *habitus* of first principles carries with it the force or instinct of a nature inclining man to goodness. Thus Albert speaks of natural law as an "inclining nature" (*inclinans natura*). That inclinational or instinctual movement *is* the obligation attached to natural law.

Natural law for St. Albert is scarcely something static; nor is it a defined code of precepts, prohibitions, and legislation covering a host of particular cases. Rather it is a dynamic operative habit of the practical intellect inclining man to human natural goodness through his understanding and judgments. In an age where natural law was commonly treated in terms of dictates, prohibitions, restriction, and obligation, and where as a result it came to be conceived as if it too were positive law, Albert has effected a noticeable change. The division of his treatise into a question on *ius* followed by another on *lex* both reflects and clarifies this move. The quitessence of natural law for Albert is not obligation and prohibition, but the innate wisdom of practical reason. Obligation, not in the sense of a formal static restriction, but rather in the sense of an inclination towards goodness, naturally and necessarily follows upon this. *Ius* and *lex,* therefore, though distinguishable, are not really two different things, but two facets of the one reality: the *debitum rationis*. The result is a flexible and analogical notion of law wherein a priority belongs to natural law because it is the meta-juridical basis of all subsequent human rights, laws, and obligations. In this way Albert reverses the traditional procedure of viewing natural law through the medium of positive law.

Conclusion

We are now in a position to view synoptically the place of law within the over-all framework of Albert's moral thought and, knowing this, to appreciate as well the differences in theory, spirit, and order which distinguish his science of ethics as found in the *De bono* from earlier and contemporary medieval speculations. Let there be no misunderstanding of the importance which Albert assigns to natural law. For him it is an infallible objective knowledge of "the right and the good," formally innate, but still open to clarification and specification through our own experience and acts of cognition. At one point he writes that "natural right is the light of morals (*lumen morum*) impressed on us according to the nature of reason." Not only has he made it the basis of all subsequent written positive laws, but its influence as a habit of directive principles is felt as well in the deliberations of practical reason in the area of particular cases and individual acts. As intimately present to the mind of man, it necessarily extends to every aspect and corner of the virtuous life. More proximately, the principles of natural right, without usurping the role of prudence, immediately guide the work of prudential reason in ascertaining the quality of goodness in all our moral acts and their objects. Now there is a world of difference between this viewpoint and the outright legalism of the moralists reviewed earlier. For Alan of Lille and John of Rupella the principal cause and source of virtue was conformity to prescribed law. The same is true of William of Auxerre who made natural law—conceived in terms of positive law—the "origin and principle" of virtue. The result in all three cases is a juridified ethic wherein law and obligation figure as pivotal notions. Consistent with this is the internal order of their treatises: law precedes the disquisition upon the virtues. For Albert the Great, on the other hand, there is a great deal more to the life of natural virtue than mere conformity to law. At least two major factors could be said to have contributed to his thinking in this regard: the influence of Aristotle's moral science known to him through fragments of the *Nicomachean Ethics,* as well as Albert's own distinctive and highly original conception of the nature and role of natural law. For Albert, the direct and immediate cause of natural virtue is not law, but the right human act seen in all of its dynamic complexity. That complexity of the human operation analyzed into its four Aristotelian causes precedes his detailed disquisition upon the virtues themselves. Natural law is treated toward the end of the extant text of the *De bono* within the context of general justice because it is an integral element in man's nature contributing to his general rectitude or *debitum generale*. It is, in short, not an exterior norm to which man *must* conform, but an interior perfection of reason guiding and inclining man to the just life from within.

Dorothy Wyckoff (essay date 1967)

SOURCE: An introduction to *Book of Minerals,* by Albertus Magnus, translated by Dorothy Wyckoff, Oxford at the Clarendon Press, 1967, pp. xiii-xlii.

[*In the following excerpt, Wyckoff presents an overview of Albert's life and discusses the nature of his scientific writings, specifically of his* Book of Minerals.]

LIFE OF ALBERT

Albert was a famous man even in his own time but, as so often with famous men of the Middle Ages, contemporary biographers omitted much that we should like to know about him. Modern scholars have had to piece together the sometimes contradictory statements in medieval chronicles and histories of the Dominican Order, local traditions, surviving documents of business transacted in many different places, and casual references to times and places in Albert's own writings. The most comprehensive reconstruction is that of H. C. Scheeben, on which this sketch is chiefly based.

Nothing is known about Albert's parentage or childhood. The chonicles say that he was born of a family of the official class (*ex militaribus*), but there is no record of his father's name. The claim that he was the son of a Count of Bollstadt does not appear until the late fifteenth century and seems to be unfounded. He was known as Albert of Cologne and Albert of Teutonia, and various laudatory epithets were attached to his name, but *Albertus Magnus,* 'Albert the Great', became common only in accounts of him written by the later scholastics. The earliest documents bearing his signature and seal show that he then called himself Albert of Lauingen, a little town on the Danube about half-way between Ulm and Regensburg. Henry of

Lauingen, who became prior of the Dominican house at Würzburg, is supposed to have been Albert's brother.

The year of his birth is unknown. Dates ranging from 1193 to 1206 or 1207 have been suggested, on the basis of conflicting statements as to his age when he died in 1280, or when he entered the Order of Preachers. The earlier date is rather more likely. Nor is anything known of his boyhood. An interest in natural history usually develops early, and some of the observations recorded in his scientific works, especially about animals, are certainly his own memories of a country life, but these cannot be dated with any accuracy.

Nevertheless, the earliest reliable date is given us by Albert himself, in describing as an eye-witness the earthquakes which in midwinter 1222-3 caused widespread destruction in Lombardy (*Meteora* III, ii, 9). What brought him to Italy and how long he remained there we do not know. Tradition mentions an uncle, whom he may have accompanied on some official mission. Or he may have been travelling by himself, for it was probably during this period of his youth that he visited mining districts in order to learn about metals, as he said in the ***Book of Minerals*** (III, i, 1). In the same work (II, iii, 1) he recalled a visit to Venice, when his companions asked him to explain a natural picture in a slab of marble—evidence that even as a young man he had a reputation for knowledge of such things. He was also in Padua (*Meteora* III, ii, 12), where he is said to have been an Arts student, though his familiarity with medical writings seems to point to some medical education as well. At that time, indeed, the medical curriculum was the nearest approach to a 'scientific' training, and therefore might have had a special attraction for a man of Albert's tastes. He did not, so far as is known, take any degree.

Whatever his plans may have been, he abandoned them to join the Order of Preachers, founded by the Spanish monk Dominic in 1216. After Dominic's death in 1221 Jordan of Saxony, the second Master General of the Order, devoted much effort to recruiting young men from the universities. Histories of the Order say (and the story probably came from Albert himself) that Albert first became acquainted with the Dominicans in Padua and was deeply moved by Jordan's preaching, but that his decision to enter the Order was not made quickly or easily: his uncle opposed it and persuaded him to delay for a while, and he himself seems to have hesitated before so total a commitment. Several years may have passed while he continued his studies or his travels, for it was probably not until 1229 that he was received and 'clad in the habit'.

The preaching friars were generally trained for service in their own countries, where they were familiar with the language and local customs. Since Albert came from the German-speaking part of Europe he was assigned to the *Teutonia* province; and thus began his long association with Cologne. The Dominicans had been established at Cologne since 1221 and already had an important school, where for the next few years Albert devoted himself to theology and moral philosophy, the course of study leading to ordination as a priest.

Every Dominican house had its *lector,* who read and explained the texts that were studied; but it was customary for the more advanced students to help the others, and no doubt Albert's gift for teaching was discovered before he had finished his training. He was then given the duties of *lector* and sent to teach in other Dominican houses, going first, perhaps, to the newly founded one at Hildesheim (opened in 1234), then to that at Freiburg-im-Breisgau (opened in 1235 or 1236). Later, having proved himself, he taught in older and more important schools in Regensburg and Strassburg, and still later returned to Cologne.

In 1238 he may have revisited Italy as one of the representatives of the Teutonia province at the General Chapter meeting in Bologna. Jordan of Saxony had died in a shipwreck off the coast of Syria, and a new Master General was to be chosen. Tradition says that on the first ballot the votes were evenly divided between Albert of Cologne and Hugo of St. Cher. Perhaps this reflects a rivalry between the German and French provinces; if so, a compromise was reached on the second ballot, when Raymond of Pennafort, a Spaniard, was elected. (Raymond, however, served only two years and was succeeded by John of Wildeshausen.)

Albert remained a *lector* for some years after 1238. He may have taught at other schools beside those mentioned above, for he recorded that he was in Saxony when he saw the great comet that appeared in 1240 (*Meteora* I, iii, 5); and he seems to have been in Cologne again for a time. About 1243 he was sent to the University of Paris, where the Dominicans had maintained a school for advanced studies since 1217. After taking the degree of Master of Theology (probably in 1245) he held a professorship there until 1248.

During this stay in Paris Albert, already learned in theology, turned to the broader aspects of philosophy, and was drawn into the scholastic movement centring on the revival of Aristotle, in which he was to be involved for many years. Greek philosophy and science were still in the process of being rediscovered, but already it was possible to read in Latin translations many works that were to become the foundations of later science—the medicine of Hippocrates and Galen, the geometry of Euclid, the astronomy of Ptolemy, and most of the Aristotelian *corpus,* as well as commentaries and original works on these subjects by Muslim writers. All this 'new' knowledge was exciting and disturbing—Aristotle perhaps most disturbing of all, with his marvellously complete and persuasive philosophical system, presenting novel ideas about the world of nature and doctrines quite at variance with the accepted teaching of the Church. The possible dangers of conflict between intellectual curiosity and religious faith were recognized in 1210, and again in 1215, when the teaching of Aristotle's metaphysics and science was forbidden at the University of Paris. How far this ban was, or could be, enforced is uncertain. But in 1231 Pope Gregory IX again forbade the use of Aristotle's books until they had been 'examined and purged of all suspicion of error'. Thus by the time Albert came to Paris many scholars must have been reading Aristotle, and his ideas were becoming more familiar, if not yet systematically taught.

Within a few more years, however, certainly by 1254, many of Aristotle's works were required reading for a degree—a change due in part at least to Albert and his pupil, Thomas Aquinas, who advocated not censorship and suppression but study and interpretation, with a view to reconciling Aristotle's teachings with those of the Church. Albert began this task at the request of members of his own Order (*Physica* I, i, 1), probably while he was still at Paris.

In 1248 the General Chapter, meeting in Paris, decided to establish a *studium generale*—a higher school, of university grade—in each of the four provinces of Lombardy, Provence, England, and Teutonia. Albert was appointed *lector*—a title in this case equivalent perhaps to Regent of Studies—at the school for the Teutonia province in Cologne. His return to Cologne must have more or less coincided with the beginning of the building of the present cathedral, though the pious legend that he was its architect can be rejected. Plans for enlarging the old cathedral must have been made while he was still in Paris; at an early stage in the work fire broke out and totally destroyed the church and many of its treasures. But Albert must have been in the city when the debris was being cleared away and new foundations were being dug, and it was probably then that he saw a Roman pavement discovered deep below the surface of the ground (*De Causis Proprietatum Elementorum* I, ii, 3).

The school at Cologne was already an excellent one, but Albert seems to have broadened the curriculum, himself lecturing on the theology of the pseudo-Dionysus and the *Ethics* of Aristotle. Among his students, three may be especially mentioned here, although there is some uncertainty about the dates of their attendance at Albert's courses. One was Thomas of Cantimpré, author of a well-known encyclopedia. Another was Ulrich of Strassburg, who became a lifelong friend of Albert. The third was Thomas Aquinas, the great

theologian, who had entered the Order very young and had been much harassed by the opposition of his family in Italy; perhaps it was for this reason that he was sent to Germany for his training. One of the legends says that he was a silent youth, nicknamed 'the dumb ox' by his fellow students, but that Albert quickly recognized his quality and predicted that his voice would be heard in the world; and apparently it was at Albert's instigation that he was sent to Paris in 1252, where he became a famous professor.

But Albert was not entirely immersed in academic affairs. The year 1252 also saw the beginning of another task that went on for many years—that of composing the turbulent quarrels of the citizens of Cologne with their archbishops. Cologne, the most important centre of manufacture and trade in the Rhineland, had in the preceding century gradually won most of the rights of a free city, with the citizens themselves in control of such matters as coinage of money, customs duties, and other trade regulations. When Archbishop Conrad von Hochstaden, an autocratic nobleman, attempted to curtail these rights, bloody fighting took place before both sides agreed to accept arbitration. The agreement drawn up by Albert, and signed before him and the Papal Legate, Hugo of St. Cher, in April 1252, put an end to the strife for a time, but Albert's intervention was to be invoked again and again in the future.

In 1254 the Provincial Chapter, meeting in Worms, elected Albert Prior Provincial of Teutonia, an office he held until 1257. These were years of heavy responsibility and arduous travel, for it was the duty of the Prior Provincial to visit as many as possible of the Dominican houses under his charge. The Teutonia province then included all Catholic Europe north of the Alps and east of France, with the exception of Scandinavia and the British Isles—that is, Alsace, Lorraine, Luxemburg and the Low Countries, Germany, Austria, Switzerland, Bohemia, and parts of Poland, Lithuania, and Latvia. There were about forty Dominican houses in 1254, and several more were founded in the next few years.

The course of Albert's journeys is a matter of conjecture, though some documents exist to show where he was at certain times. The Provincial Chapter generally met in late summer, and after leaving Worms in 1254 he seems to have returned to Cologne. In February 1255 he went to profess the first nuns at the Paradise Convent near Soest, and preached to them. He then went on into northern Teutonia, visiting Dominicans in Saxony and Brandenburg, perhaps going as far as Lübeck, or even Riga. The Provincial Chapter met that year in Regensburg, where Albert presided; after which he would presumably have made visits in south Germany and Austria. In January 1256 he was again in Cologne. He could have visited houses in Holland and

Belgium in the spring, before going on to the General Chapter at Whitsun in Paris. He returned to Teutonia in the summer for the Provincial Chapter at Erfurt; but by the end of September he was at the Papal Curia at Anagni.

Travel in medieval times was slow and toilsome. Moreover, the Dominicans were vowed to poverty—mendicant friars who had no money, begged for food and lodging except when entertained in the houses of their Order, and were forbidden to use wagons or horses except in direst emergency. Albert's long journeys on foot are an amazing achievement: he covered hundreds of miles and must have been on the road almost continuously for weeks on end. He can have had little opportunity for study or writing, but many things that he saw or heard on the way he remembered and later put into his scientific books.

The reason for his journey to Italy was probably the trouble that had been brewing for some years over the right of the mendicant friars—the Franciscans and Dominicans—to teach at the University of Paris. In 1254 William of St. Amour had published a violent attack on them, and the matter had been discussed at the General Chapter in the spring of 1256. It is almost certain that Albert was then selected, as a distinguished member of one of the embattled Orders, and a former professor at Paris, to go and testify before the Commission of Cardinals that was to meet at Anagni in the autumn. The case was finished in October, when the Pope, Alexander IV, condemned William's book; but Albert remained with the Papal Curia, which moved in December to Rome, and in May 1257 to Viterbo. During this winter he lectured at the Curia on the Gospel of St. John and the Epistles of St. Paul, and collected material for his tract (not finished until much later) *On the Unity of the Intellect: against Averroes*. In May, when the General Chapter met at Florence, he obtained release from his office as Prior Provincial; and in the summer he set off, by way of Bologna, on the long journey back to Cologne.

There he resumed his duties as *lector* and his studies of Aristotle. In 1259 he attended the General Chapter at Valenciennes, serving on a committee that included also Thomas Aquinas and Peter of Tarantaise (later Pope Innocent V), to consider revisions of the curriculum in the Dominican schools.

In Cologne his services as negotiator and peacemaker were again in demand. He took part in another attempt to resolve the conflict between the citizens of Cologne and Archbishop Conrad von Hochstaden. A settlement was signed in June 1258; and, as an aftermath of this, negotiations over the liability of Cologne for damage done in Deutz during the fighting went on until 1260. There was also a trade dispute between Cologne and Utrecht, settled in 1259.

Meanwhile events in Regensburg on the Danube were about to give Albert's life a new direction. The citizens were having trouble with their bishop, Count Albert von Peitengau, who was more soldier than priest, constantly involved in war, and had been paying little attention to his diocese. In 1259, after an appeal to the Papal Curia, he was forced to resign. The Cathedral Chapter elected in his place their Provost, Henry of Lerchenfeld, who (perhaps prudently) declined the honour. The naming of a bishop then became a matter for the Curia, who chose Albert of Cologne.

This seemed to many a surprising choice, though it may have been suggested by Hugo of St. Cher, who was then at the Curia; and of course Albert was personally known to the Pope from his stay in Italy three years earlier. But Albert was now in a somewhat difficult position: the regulations of the Order forbade any Dominican to accept such office in the Church without the permission of his superiors; and when the Master General, Humbert of Romans, heard the news, he wrote to Albert begging him, for the good of the Order, to decline. The notification of his election and Humbert's letter of remonstrance must have reached Cologne at about the same time, near the beginning of February 1260. Albert seems to have taken some weeks to make up his mind, but in the end he accepted. In mid March he was consecrated as a bishop (where and by whom is not known) and set out for Regensburg. He arrived on March 29, spent the night at the Dominicans' house of St. Blaise, and next day went in procession to the cathedral to be enthroned. On the same day he began to look into the affairs of the diocese.

These were in a sorry way, and a reformer is seldom popular. No doubt he met with opposition and even ridicule: Regensburg hardly knew what to make of a bishop who walked the streets in the crude sandals of a begging friar. Surviving documents tell something of his activities during the next year. In August he consecrated an altar at Lerchenfeld, and in September he attended a conference of bishops at Landau. He struggled with debts and financial reforms, seeing that tithes were collected and properly used, devising means for the support of parish priests and a hospital.

When spring came he seems to have felt that he had done what he was sent to do, and that it was time to give the diocese back to a locally chosen bishop. In May he set out for Italy to present his resignation to the Pope in person. He arrived at Viterbo just about the time of Alexander IV's death (25 May 1261); nothing could be done until after the election of a new Pope. Urban IV was elected in August, but it was not until the following May (1262) that he confirmed the election of Leo, former dean of the Cathedral Chapter at Regensburg, as Albert's successor.

Finally freed of his office, Albert might have been expected to return to the Dominican Order, but he did not do so, probably because the new Pope had other plans for him. In fact, there is no evidence as to his whereabouts during most of the years 1261 and 1262. It has been conjectured that he returned for a while to Regensburg, or that he travelled to southern Italy or even to Greece. What is most likely, perhaps, is that he remained at the Curia, where Urban IV gathered a group of scholars and theologians including Thomas Aquinas, summoned from Paris in 1261, and no doubt others whom Albert had known in 1256-7. There he could devote himself again to writing, and it is not improbable that it was there that he finished his commentary on St. Luke and perhaps some of his commentaries on Aristotle.

At the beginning of 1263 Urban IV appointed Albert Preacher of the Crusade in Germany and Bohemia, giving him the powers of a Papal Nuncio, and providing him with letters commanding all bishops to assist his mission. Once again the prospect of long journeys lay before him, and Albert was growing older. These journeys are much better documented than those of 1254-6, because at many places along the way he consecrated altars or churches, granted indulgences, or settled local disputes. He is thought to have been in Orvieto when Hugo of St. Cher died there on March 19, and to have remained to celebrate Easter on April 1. But he must have left soon afterwards and travelled by way of the Brenner Pass, for on May 5 he was at Polling in Upper Bavaria. He can then be traced to Augsburg (May 10), Donauwörth (May 13), Würzburg (May 27), Frankfurt-am-Main (June 5), and back again to Würzburg (June 28). He reached Cologne about the end of July.

Once again there was trouble in Cologne. Archbishop Conrad von Hochstaden had died in September 1261; but the new archbishop, Engelbert von Falkenberg, was no more able to get on with the citizens than his predecessor had been. On 25 August 1263 Albert witnessed another agreement; but in November, after he had left Cologne, fighting broke out again, and Engelbert was taken prisoner. There was talk in December, and again in the following May (1264), of getting Albert to come back. But he did not come back, and a new settlement was attempted by the Bishops of Liège and Münster.

From Cologne Albert probably travelled through Holland and north Germany. At the end of October he was in Brandenburg, where he carried out a special mission: the local clergy, unable to agree on the choice of a bishop, had appealed to the Pope, who had sent Albert to deal with the case. After this he may have continued eastwards to the Saxon-Polish frontier, but by the end of the year he was at Adelhausen, near Freiburg-im-Breisgau. On 20 February 1264 he was in Speyer, and on March 18 in Regensburg. There are no records for the next few months, but it is likely that he was then carrying out his mission in southern Germany and Bohemia. In late summer he was in Mainz, where a document of 20 August 1264 is the latest one known bearing his signature as *praedicator crucis*.

It is strange that we have no information about the actual preaching of the crusade; but this is perhaps because it was not very successful. The Age of Crusades was nearly over and men's minds were turning to other interests. Albert's commission came to a sudden end with the death of the Pope and the next Pope did not renew it.

Urban IV died on October 2, but it may have been some weeks before the news reached Albert. When it did, he seems to have gone at once to Würzburg, for by December 4 he was engaged in mediating a dispute there. One of the witnesses to the agreement was Albert's brother Henry, Prior of the Dominicans; and it was perhaps because his brother was there that Albert remained in Würzburg (so far as we know) until May 1267. Numerous documents show that he took part in the settlement of local cases, but there is little to tell of his private life and occupations.

He lived with the Dominicans, but his status is not entirely clear. During his years in the papal service he had been released from the rule of the Order—that is, he owed obedience not to the Master General but directly to the Pope; and the Pope had granted him some property or revenues for his support, which he still retained and finally disposed of by will, in contravention of the vow of poverty. It may also be noted that he never again held any office in the Order, and was perhaps free to choose his place of residence. Yet in other respects he certainly returned to the Order and was identified with it for the rest of his life.

In the early summer of 1267 Albert left Würzburg, probably visited Regensburg, and then went to the Rhineland. In July he consecrated an altar in Burtscheid, near Aachen, and in August and September was in Cologne. Later in the autumn he arrived in Strassburg, which was to be the centre of his activities for the next few years. The Dominican school had grown in importance since Albert had taught there many years before, and was now second only to Cologne in the Teutonia province; and the *lector* was Ulrich of Strassburg, a former pupil of Albert's. Whether Albert himself resumed any teaching at this time is unknown; he may have lectured occasionally, but he was often away. Again there are records of churches consecrated and indulgences granted in many places not very far from Strassburg, as well as in Strassburg itself, where on 7 April 1269 he ordained a large group of clergy.

He undertook one more long journey at the command of the Pope, Clement IV, probably in the summer of

1268, to settle a dispute in Mecklenburg over property which had been given to the Knights of St. John in 1229 and was later claimed and seized by other nobles and the Abbot of Colbaz. Albert was now an old man, and efforts seem to have been made to save his strength. He was accompanied by two assistants, John of Freiburg (a young Dominican, probably a pupil of Ulrich's) and Albert of Havelburg. He was also permitted to use a vehicle; but the springless carts of those days could hardly mitigate the badness of the roads or shorten by very much the time spent on the way. This must have been an exhausting journey, and Albert may well have felt that it was in vain, for after his return the agreement he had arranged was broken, and he had to excommunicate the Abbot of Colbaz and his party, who were again trying to dispossess the Knights of St. John.

Another claim on his services came from John of Vercelli, now Master General of the Order, who wrote asking him to go to Paris and teach again at the university. It was unusual to recall a man to a post he had already held, but the mendicant friars were once more under attack, this time by Gerhard of Abbeville and Siger of Brabant, and the Master General no doubt wanted the Order's most distinguished teacher in Paris just then. Albert, however, excused himself, saying that he felt unequal to the work and he had no assistant; and he may have suggested the recall of Thomas Aquinas, who returned to Paris early in 1269. All this can be inferred from a letter of John of Vercelli, apparently written in 1270, in which, after mentioning the earlier call to Paris, he urged Albert to go to Cologne. This time an assistant was provided, probably Gottfried of Duisburg, who remained with him to the end.

The political situation in Cologne had been going from bad to worse. When the Papal Nuncio, Bernard of Castaneto, had tried to intervene and failed in 1268 he had excommunicated all parties to the quarrel, and the citizens had appealed to the Pope in vain. The fighting did not stop, though Engelbert was still a prisoner; and in the summer of 1269 the severity of the interdict was increased. Another appeal was sent to Rome; but Pope Clement IV died in 1269 and there was a delay of almost two years before his successor was elected. We may surmise that a message was sent through the Cologne Dominicans to the Master General, or to Albert himself, begging him to help as he had helped in the past.

The exact date of Albert's return to Cologne is uncertain—presumably about the end of the year 1270. Nor is it known just how he opened negotiations. But by spring Engelbert had been released, and on 16 April 1271 he signed a document declaring his complete reconciliation with his enemies, and agreeing to submit any future points of dispute to an arbitration commission headed by 'Brother Albert of the Order of Preachers, formerly Bishop of Regensburg'. Peace was

at last restored, though the interdict of excommunication was not finally removed until after Engelbert's death and the election of his successor, Siegfried von Westerburg, in 1275.

For the remaining years of his life Albert lived with the Dominicans of Cologne. He contributed money for enlarging their church and is said to have laid the cornerstone of the choir in 1271, and to have given a large crucifix and some sacred relics. Very likely he still took an interest in the school, but he was no longer responsible for it, and he was busy finishing several theological works and revising earlier ones. His eyesight was beginning to trouble him, but he had his helper, Gottfried of Duisburg, to read to him or write at his dictation.

It would be a mistake, however, to imagine that Albert had now 'retired' from active life. His name appears on many documents, not only in Cologne and near-by places, but as far away as Utrecht and Nijmegen in Holland. And he still kept in touch with larger affairs. Ulrich of Strassburg was elected Prior Provincial of Teutonia in 1272, and records of his term of office show that he several times consulted Albert and went to see him. It was probably on one of these visits to Cologne that Ulrich and John of Vercelli, Master General of the Order, met Rudolph of Hapsburg 'in the Church of the Friars'. Rudolph was crowned at Aachen on 24 October 1273, and in November spent some time in Cologne. He may have known Ulrich and Albert in Strassburg, and very probably he would have wished to enlist the support of these eminent Dominicans. If so, he evidently succeeded, for a letter of Ulrich's mentions him with enthusiasm, and tradition says that Albert spoke in his favour at the Council of Lyons.

The spring of 1274 was saddened for Albert by news of the death of Thomas Aquinas in March at Fossanova, on his way to the Council of Lyons. As to Albert's attendance at the Council, the evidence is conflicting. The earliest chronicles of his life do not mention it, and his name does not appear in the records of the assembly, which opened on May 6. This however, might be explained by his late arrival, if he travelled with the German Dominicans who attended the General Chapter of the Order, also held in Lyons that year, and opening on May 13. The Council had many important matters to discuss and the election of Rudolph of Hapsburg was not taken up until June 6. On that occasion, at least according to a fifteenth-century account, Albert was present among the bishops, and spoke on the text 'Behold, I will send them a saviour and a defender, and he will deliver them'. If we may judge his sentiments from the text, Albert, like many of his contemporaries, saw in the Hapsburg prince the best hope of ending the long interregnum which, ever since the decline of the Hohenstauffens, had kept Germany in turmoil.

In August Albert was in Cologne and from there went to Fulda, on a commission from Pope Gregory X to look into the election of the Abbot of Fulda. In September 1276 he was in Antwerp, where he consecrated the Dominican church and attended the Provincial Chapter, at which Ulrich of Strassburg presided. This may have been his last meeting with Ulrich, who died in Paris a year or two later.

A legend of Thomas Aquinas relates that when, in 1277, some of his opinions were included in Bishop Tempier's condemnation of 219 theses ascribed to Siger of Brabant, Albert went to Paris and successfully defended them. This is extremely improbable. Albert was a remarkably vigorous old man—indeed he is not known to have suffered any illness during his whole life. But by 1277 he is said to have become very bent with age and to have begun to fail mentally.

For Albert himself there was no conflict between science and religion: his study of Aristotle's science was undertaken in order to understand Aristotle's philosophy as a whole and to reconcile it with the Christian faith.

—Dorothy Wyckoff

Yet in January 1279, when he made his will, he described himself as 'of sound mind and body' (*sanus et incolumen*). The will is known to us in a copy made 'word for word' in 1408 by a Dominican, Narzissus Pfister, at Cologne. It is of interest because Albert appears to have feared that some question of its validity might arise, since the rules of the Order did not permit the friars to own or bequeath property. He therefore stated at the beginning that he had been exempted from this rule by the Pope, and wished to record his wishes while still able, so that no doubt be felt after his death. He left everything to the Order: his books to the library; his bishop's vestments to the sacristry; bequests in money to three Dominican nunneries; the rest of his property to be used for completing the choir of the Dominican church, to which he had already contributed. As executors he named the Prior Provincial, the Priors of Cologne and Würzburg (the latter his 'dear brother Henry'), Gottfried 'the physician', and Gottfried of Duisburg. The will was witnessed by the Prior of Cologne and two laymen, respected citizens of Cologne.

In February of that year he was still well enough to take part in the ceremony of translating the relics of St. Cordula to the Chapel of the Knights of St. John in Cologne; and in the summer he authenticated two more documents; so his decline seems to have been gradual. The end finally came on 15 November 1280. He died peacefully in his own cell, and was deeply mourned by the Dominicans, who buried him three days later in the choir of their own church, which he himself had helped to build. The funeral mass was attended by a sorrowing crowd of clergy and citizens of Cologne.

Albert's memory was honoured for five centuries in the Dominican church. Many people came to visit his grave and he was soon regarded locally as a saint. In 1483 his remains were transferred to a reliquary and placed upon an altar. But after the French Revolution, when Alsace was invaded, the Dominicans were expelled and their buildings put to secular uses. The church was torn down in 1804, and the cloister, where the friars had lived, after serving as a barracks during the Prussian occupation, was later demolished. Albert's bones had already been removed to the near-by church of St. Andrew, where in the nineteenth century they were kept in an ornate gilded shrine. During the Second World War this church was severely damaged in the bombing of Cologne. When it was being restored, the ancient crypt beneath the choir, long ago filled in, was re-excavated and made into a simple white-walled chapel, and in 1954 Albert's relics were placed there in a plain stone sarcophagus that rests beneath the high altar.

Even during his lifetime legends had begun to gather around Albert's name and this process was accelerated after his death. On the one hand, it was told of him—as of his contemporaries Michael Scot and Roger Bacon—that he had been a great magician skilled in the black arts; and books on magic, astrology, and alchemy were falsely attributed to him. On the other hand, there were stories of a saint's miracles. A cult was already forming in the fourteenth century, and in 1484 Pope Innocent VIII gave permission to the Dominicans of Cologne to celebrate Albert's Feast each year on November 15. This permission, equivalent to beatification, was extended by later Popes, and in 1670, by a decree of Clement X, became world-wide. Albert was canonized in 1931, and in 1941 Pope Pius XII declared him the patron saint of scientists.

ALBERT'S SCIENTIFIC WRITINGS

Albert's works are so numerous and cover so wide a range of interests that we can only wonder how, even in a long life, he found time to write them all. The scientific treatises, taken all together, are but a small part of his complete works, which include also commentaries on many books of the Bible and on texts used in the schools, and original theological treatises. For Albert himself there was no conflict between science and religion: his study of Aristotle's science was undertaken in order to understand Aristotle's philosophy as a whole and to reconcile it with the Christian faith. He began his commentary on the *Physics* (I, i, 1) in these words:

> Our intention in natural science is to satisfy, to the best of our ability, the Brothers of our Order, who have been asking us, for several years now, to compose for them the kind of book on *Physics* that should give them a complete natural science and make them really competent to understand the books of Aristotle. Although we do not consider ourselves capable of this task, yet we cannot withstand the entreaties of the Brothers; and so at last we accept the task that we have often refused. Persuaded by their entreaties, we undertake it, first of all for the honour of Almighty God, the Fount of Wisdom and the Creator, Founder, and Ruler of nature; and also for the benefit of the Brothers, and of any others who read it with the desire of acquiring natural science.

Albert wrote commentaries on other works of Aristotle—on the logical works, the *Ethics, Politics,* and *Metaphysics.* But those on natural science form a special group, since Albert considered them as one closely related series, and listed them all together, rather elaborately classified in logical order, near the beginning of his **Physics** (I, i, 4). Here is his list:

* Physics (**Physica**)

* The Heavens (**De caelo et mundo**)

The Nature of Places (**De natura locorum**)

Properties of the Elements (**De causis proprietatum elementorum**)

* Generation and Corruption (**De generatione et corruptione**)

* Meteorology (**Meteora**)

The Book of Minerals (**Mineralia**)

* The Soul (**De anima**)

* Life and Death (**De morte et vita**)

* Youth and Age (**De iuventute et senectute**)

Nourishment (**De nutrimento et nutribili**)

* Sleep and Waking (**De somno et vigilia**)

* The Senses (**De sensu et sensato**)

* Memory and Recollection (**De memoria et reminiscentia**)

Movement of Animals (**De motibus animalium**)

* Breath and Breathing (**De spiritu et respiratione**)

The Intellect (**De intellectu et intelligibili**)

* Plants (**De vegetabilibus**)

* Animals (**De animalibus**)

Those marked with an asterisk (*) are directly based on corresponding works in the Aristotelian *corpus.* But we must remember that Albert never had a 'complete edition' of Aristotle. Various treatises or groups of treatises circulated in separate manuscripts: some were available in two or more different translations, and some were embedded in Arabic commentaries. Critical scholarship hardly existed, but an intelligent man like Albert could see that some of the works generally received as Aristotle's were not entirely satisfactory; and some that he had heard of could not be found.

The *Properties of the Elements* is now known to be a Muslim work; and Albert had to add a good deal to it to make it fit into his Aristotelian scheme. ***Nourishment*** and ***The Intellect*** probably correspond to the spurious *De alimentiis* and *De intelligentia* that appear in medieval lists of Aristotle's works; and Albert acknowledged that he had not seen Aristotle's own books on these subjects but only writings by his followers (*De intellectu,* I, i, 1). He was in the same difficulty when he wrote the ***Movement of Animals*** (***De motibus animalium***); he later referred to this as if it were largely his own composition (*ea quae ex ingenio proprio diximus*), and wrote a new commentary, ***De principiis motus processivi,*** after he found a manuscript of Aristotle's *Movement of Animals* in Italy. ***The Nature of Places*** and the ***Book of Minerals*** were put together by Albert himself, when he failed to find any Aristotelian treatises on geography and mineralogy.

In doing this he did not feel that he was taking unwarrantable liberties with his author; he did not think of himself as a scholar editing a text but as a teacher explaining new and difficult ideas. He justified this, too, in the Introduction to his **Physics** (I, i, 1):

> Our method in this work will be to follow the sequence of Aristotle's thought, and to say in explanation and demonstration of it whatever may seem necessary; but without any quotation of the text. And also we shall put in digressions, so as to clarify difficulties as they arise or to add whatever may make the Philosopher's thought clearer to anyone. And we shall divide the whole work by chapter headings: where the heading simply gives the contents of the chapter, this means that the chapter is one of those in Aristotle's own books; but wherever the heading indicates that there is a digression (*digressio*), there we have added something in the way of supplement or demonstration. By such a procedure, we shall make our books

correspond, in their numbering and titles, with those of Aristotle. And we shall make additions wherever books are incomplete, and wherever they have gaps in them, or are missing entirely—whether they were left unwritten by Aristotle or, if he did write them, they have not come down to us. But where this is done, the ensuing tractate will say so clearly.

Thus Albert's treatises are more original than the term 'commentary' might suggest. If there was a basic text, it was paraphrased and interwoven with his own contributions—sometimes exposition or refutation of the opinions of previous commentators, sometimes new illustrations, drawn from his own wide reading and experience, which reveal his lifelong interest in science and his quality as an observer. If there was no basic text, as for the **Book of Minerals,** the selection and arrangement of materials offered even more scope for the development of his own ideas. His aim was a complete account of all nature, and the titles of his treatises indicate the broad scope of the undertaking. But the individual treatises are not independent, they are all parts of one continuous and coherent 'natural history', and the reader is constantly reminded that points explained in the earlier books are necessary for understanding the later ones.

At the end of the **Animals** (which he expanded from nineteen to twenty-six books) Albert says that this is the end of the series on natural science. But he so often mentions astrology and alchemy that we may inquire whether or not he ever wrote anything on these subjects. Both lie outside the true 'Aristotelian' tradition (though the pseudo-Aristotelian **Properties of the Elements** contains some astrology), but they were an important part of medieval science.

Astrology was, of course, closely linked with astronomy; in fact the words *astrologia* and *astronomia* were used interchangeably by thirteenth-century writers. The two-fold character of the science of the stars is shown by the *Mirror of Astronomy,* or astrology (*Speculum astronomiae*). This was attributed to Albert as early as the fourteenth century, and has been printed in his collected works (Borgnet, Vol. X), although this attribution has been challenged. The author, if he was not Albert, certainly held views very similar to Albert's. He recognized the two aspects of *astronomia* and listed books dealing with both: first, the science that observes and describes the movements of the heavenly bodies; and second, the application of this knowledge to predicting the future or invoking celestial influences for various purposes. In the latter science he carefully distinguished licit from illicit practices; and this sort of distinction, together with some of his citations of authorities, we find also in Albert's discussion of astrological images (**Mineralia** II, iii).

Scientists of today who scorn astrology as mere superstition perhaps forget that at one time it included several subjects which have since become respectable fields for scientific research—weather and weather forecasting, the relation of climate to latitude, and the effects of climate on plants, animals, and men. But if all these things were influenced by 'the aspects of the heavens', medieval astrologers thought, the stars must surely affect men's lives in still other ways. Albert, for all his remarkable intelligence and his sturdy common sense, was, after all, a child of his time. He may well have written the *Mirror of Astronomy*. But other astrological works bearing his name are certainly spurious.

The same may be said of the alchemical treatises attributed to Albert, with the possible exception of the *Little Book on Alchemy* (*Libellus de alchimia*), also known as the *Straight Path* (*Semita recta*), which has been printed with his other works (Borgnet, Vol. XXXVII) and translated into English by Sister Virginia Heines (1958). It contains anachronistic references to Geber and Jean de Meung, but these may be later interpolations. The title *De alchimia* in a fourteenth-century list of Albert's writings has been taken to mean this work, but it may refer to a part of the **Book of Minerals.** *The Little Book on Alchemy* is a practical 'laboratory manual', giving good advice to the novice, and describing the apparatus, materials, and procedures of the art; and it is quite free of the obscurity and mystification common in alchemical books.

Whether or not Albert wrote this, he had, according to his own statement (**Mineralia** III, i, 1), investigated alchemy. But he could have studied alchemical texts, talked with alchemists, and even visited their laboratories, without being an adept himself. He certainly was much interested in alchemical theories, and, as the **Book of Minerals** makes clear, he realized that 'chemical' explanations were needed for many natural phenomena. But in my opinion his style and his expressed views on transmutations are unlike those of the author of the *Little Book on Alchemy.*

THE ARGUMENT OF THE **BOOK OF MINERALS**

The Aristotelian *corpus* contains almost nothing on mineralogy. The only discussion of the subject, some thirty lines at the end of *Meteora,* III sets forth a theory that there are underground two 'exhalations': one of these, a 'dry smoke', produces earths and stones, the other, a 'watery vapour', produces metals. The passage ends with the remark that each of these kinds of mineral must be taken up separately and in detail; and this seems to point to some work no longer extant. When Albert came to write the **Book of Minerals** he tried to find this missing work. He believed it existed, because he had heard of a *Lapidary* or *Book of Stones* by Aristotle, but he could obtain only a few excerpts from it (**Mineralia** I, i, 1; II, iii, 6; III, i, 1). He was therefore forced to draw up his own plan for dealing with minerals. The result is of unusual interest, in that it shows us not only the contemporary state of mineralogy, but also Albert's idea of what a *science* of mineralogy should be.

The **Book of Minerals** is a typical scholastic treatise, and since this form of presentation is rather unfamiliar today, a brief summary of its argument may be useful.

Albert's model is, of course, Aristotle, who says at the beginning of his *Physics* that data gained from direct observation of nature are of concrete particulars, but are often confused and difficult to understand. Science concerns itself with analysing the data, in order to arrive at general principles, to make things understandable by explaining their *causes*. For Albert, then, a *science* of mineralogy must be based on a discussion of the *causes* of minerals, that is, 'the four causes' distinguished by Aristotle as *material, efficient, formal,* and *final.*

First the *material cause,* the matter of which minerals are made: Albert's 'chemistry' is based on what is said of the *elements* (Fire, Air, Water, and Earth) in *The Heavens, Generation and Corruption,* and *Meteorology* (especially Book IV). And the *material cause* is the basis of his general classification of minerals into three groups—stones (Books I-II), metals (Books III-IV) and 'intermediates' (*media,* Book V). He treats stones first because they are 'simpler' than metals, being mixtures of Earth and Water; metals are made up of Sulphur and Quicksilver, which are themselves mixtures, Quicksilver containing Earth and Water, Sulphur something of all four elements. (The Sulphur-Quicksilver theory is not Aristotle's; Albert got it from Avicenna and other alchemists.) The 'intermediates' are neither stones nor metals, but have some characteristics of both.

Next, the *efficient cause,* the process by which minerals are made: here Albert adopts the two-exhalations theory of *Meteora* III and extends it, for metallic ore deposits, by equating the 'dry smoke' with Sulphur and the 'most vapour' with Quicksilver. These exhalations, confined within the earth, are converted into minerals by the direct action of heat and cold; but heat and cold are merely the 'instruments' of the real *efficient cause* which is a 'mineralizing power' (this concept also came from Avicenna). Just how this power acts Albert can explain only through an analogy drawn from Aristotle's biology (especially *Generation of Animals*): the female supplies only the matter of which the embryo is made (*material cause*), and the male semen is the *efficient cause* of its development. For minerals, too, the process of development must be started somehow, and the impulse, according to Albert, is the 'influence' of the heavenly bodies, though this may be modified by the nature of the material and the place where the minerals are forming.

Then, the *formal cause,* that which makes a thing what it is: here the biological analogy is pushed still further, for Aristotle said that the male also contributes the *form* of the offspring, its *species* (e.g. the offspring of a dog is a dog and not any other kind of animal). In the same way, Albert argues, the *forms* of minerals are due to a 'formative power' that descends from the heavens through the influence of the stars—and this is what determines the particular kind of mineral that will be formed at any particular time and place. (The best-known example of this belief is the supposed formation of the seven metals under the influences of the seven planets.)

Last, the *final cause,* that for the sake of which a thing exists: this is hardly mentioned, presumably because Albert agrees with Aristotle that inanimate things like minerals can hardly be said to have an 'end' or 'purpose' of their own.

This whole account is un-Aristotelian in its emphasis on astrology. Yet to some extent it had its roots in Aristotle's cosmology, as described in the *Physics, The Heavens, Generation and Corruption,* and *Meteorology:* a spherical universe, with the earth at the centre, and as it were the *focus,* of all the motions, transmitted inwards from one etherial sphere to another, that cause all the changes in the atmosphere, sea, and land, in the life of plants and animals, and even in the growth of minerals underground. But in the course of centuries this scheme had been elaborated and fused with the notions of neo-Platonists and astrologers, who assigned to each of the heavenly bodies more specific and more varied influences than Aristotle ever did. Albert believes in these 'powers', but he always maintains that they are subject to God's will.

Having thus dealt with the *essential* causes of stones (I, i) and metals (III, i), he next considers their 'accidental' properties, those features which, according to Aristotle (*Metaphysics,* VI, ii, 1026 a 33 ff.) are not really essential nor always present, but occur in some individuals and not in others. Again there are two parallel tractates: the one on stones (I, ii) deals with texture, colour, hardness, fissility or cleavage, density, structure, and fossils; the one on metals (III, ii) with fusibility, malleability, colour and lustre, taste and odour, and various chemical reactions. The systematic discussion of a list of physical and chemical properties seems to have been suggested by a similar list in *Meteora* IV, and much of the material is drawn from that work and from *Generation and Corruption;* the account of colours, tastes, and odours, from the treatment of senseperceptions in *The Soul* and *The Senses.* To all this Albert adds field observations of his own and, in the tractate on metals, information from alchemical sources.

These two tractates (I, ii and III, ii) make vivid to us the difficulties that hindered the development of modern chemistry and mineralogy. The Peripatetic doctrine of elements and qualities was, in fact, quite inadequate for developing any sort of chemical classification of minerals. With metals, particularly, it is plain that if we regard fusibility, malleability, colour, etc., as 'accidentals' (because these can be altered by alloying, bronzing, annealing, etc.), we are left asking: But then what is it that is *essential*—the *real* difference between one metal and another? It was this uncertainty that fostered the hope of transmutation, which Albert does not entirely reject although he knows that many alchemists' claims are fraudulent (III, i, 9). On the strength of Aristotle's account of the transmutation of the elements in *Generation and Corruption* he accepts the theoretical possibility, and reasons that something of the kind must occur in nature, in the formation of ore minerals (III, ii, 6). But he seems to be doubtful whether the natural processes can be imitated successfully in the laboratories of the alchemists.

Finally, in Books II, IV, and V, he carries out still further his plan for system and completeness, naming stones, metals, and 'intermediates', one by one, and describing each one, some of them in considerable detail. This kind of 'catalogue' is not found in Aristotle; but it was familiar in the popular medieval *herbals, bestiaries,* and *lapidaries.* The tradition goes back at least as far as Pliny and was still followed by the thirteenth-century encyclopedists.

In the tractate on stones (II, ii) Albert incorporates an alphabetical lapidary, which is similar to, and probably partly based on, those of Arnold of Saxony, Thomas of Cantimpré, and the 'Dyascorides' cited by Bartholomew of England. Such unacknowledged use of others' works was not in those days regarded as plagiarism: Albert similarly incorporates a bestiary in his book on **Animals** and a herbal in his **Plants**. Compilations of this type seem to have been regarded as common property, at the free disposal of anyone who had occasion to write on topics animal, vegetable, or mineral. Albert, in fact, was doing just about what anyone today might do in writing an elementary book on mineralogy—taking data from standard works familiar at the time.

The compilers of popular lapidaries transmitted some factual information; but their chief interest was the curative or magical powers of stones. Albert therefore prefaces his 'lapidary tractate' (II, ii) by another tractate (II, i) in which he endeavours to account for these wonderful powers. In order to understand his explanation, we must consider again the Aristotelian notion of *form.* To the mineralogist of today this term may suggest the 'crystal form' or 'habit' of a mineral; but to Aristotle, *form* was something more than shape or structure—it was the *essential being,* or identity of a thing; in living things, the 'life' or 'soul'.

This is why Albert (I, i, 6) engages in what seems to us a needless argument, denying that a stone has a soul (*anima*) or is in any sense 'alive'. But even an inanimate thing has *form,* that which makes it distinctively what it is and able to do whatever it does (e.g. the *form* of an axe is what makes it able to cut). In this sense, then, the *forms* of stones account for whatever effects they produce. An excellent example is the 'power' of magnetism, essential to our identification or definition of the mineral magnetite. And medieval lapidaries ascribed many other 'powers', medical or magical, to other stones—powers that Albert considers to be inherent in their *forms* and imparted to them by the *formal cause,* the 'formative power' of the heavens.

This theme is further developed in a third tractate in this book (II, iii) on the *sigils,* images, or markings, found in certain stones. Albert intends (II, iii, 1) to distinguish between those made 'by nature' (picture agates, mineralized fossils, casts and moulds of shells, etc.) and those made 'by art' (antique cameos and intaglios); but subsequent chapters show that he often confuses 'natural' and 'artificial' figures, and knows little about gemcutting. He recognizes the ancient practice of enhancing the powers of a stone by carving upon it some image or inscription, and gives his somewhat cautious approval by inserting here (II, iii, 5) another brief lapidary, of engraved gems bearing astrological figures.

The parallel book on metals (Book IV) is shorter and simpler than Book II, since less information was available about metals than about stones. The first two chapters describe sulphur and quicksilver, and the others take up all the other metals then known—lead, tin, silver, copper, gold, and iron (including steel). Since Aristotle had said little about metals, the material here is drawn partly from alchemical books and partly from Albert's own observations on visits to mines, smelters, or brass foundries.

Book V, on minerals intermediate between stones and metals, is a brief compilation, mostly from alchemical or medical sources: it includes salt, vitriol, alum, soda, etc.—the chief 'chemical reagents' of the alchemists' laboratories.

Taken as a whole, the **Book of Minerals** is an impressive attempt to organize a science of mineralogy. Despite its background of medieval thought, its many errors of fact or interpretation of fact, there is something here that we recognize: the introductory exposition of general principles (the origin, physical and chemical properties of minerals), followed by descriptions of individual minerals (appearance, mode and place of occurrence, uses, etc.). This general pattern is still to be seen in our own textbooks.

An excerpt from *Libellus de Alchimia* (13th century)

... [At] the beginning of my discourse I shall invoke the aid of Him Who is the Fount and Source of all good to deign, in His goodness and love, to fill up by grace of His Holy Spirit my small knowledge so that I may be able by my teaching to show forth the light which lies hidden in the darkness and to lead those who are in error to the pathway of truth. May He Who sitteth on High deign to grant this. Amen.

Though I have laboriously traveled to many regions and numerous provinces, likewise to cities and castles, in the interest of the science called Alchemy, though I have diligently consulted learned men and sages concerning this art in order to investigate it more fully, and though I took down their writings and toiled again and again over their works, I have not found in them what their books assert. Therefore, I examined books pro and con and I found them to be worthless, devoid of all profit and of usefulness. I found, moreover, many learned men of wealth, abbots, bishops, canons, natural philosophers, as well as unlettered men, who expended much money and great effort in the interest of this art, and yet failed because they were not capable of tracking it down.

Yet I have not despaired, but rather I have expended infinite labor and expense, ever going from place to place, observing, considering, as Avicenna says, "If this is so, How is it? If it is not, How is it not?" I persevered in studying, reflecting, laboring over works of this same subject until finally I found what I was seeking, not by my own knowledge, but by the grace of the Holy Spirit. Therefore, since I discerned and understood what was beyond nature, I began to watch more diligently in decoctions and sublimations, in solutions and distillations, in cerations and calcinations and coagulations of alchemy and in my other labors until I found possible the transmutation into Gold and Silver, which is better than the natural [metal] in every testing and malleation.

I, therefore, the least of the Philosophers, purpose to write for my associates and friends the true art, clear and free from error; however, in such a way that seeing they may not see, and hearing they may not understand. Therefore, I beg and I adjure you by the Creator of the world to hide this book from all the foolish. For to you I shall reveal the secret, but from the others I shall conceal the secret of secrets because of envy of this noble knowledge. Fools look down upon it because they cannot attain it; for this reason they consider it odious and believe it impossible; they are, therefore, envious of those who work in it and say that they are forgers. Beware, then of revealing to anyone our secrets in this work. A second time, I warn you to be cautious; persevere in your labors and do not become discouraged, knowing that great utility will follow your work.

Albertus Magnus, in Libellus de Alchimia, *translated by Virginia Heines, University of California Press, 1958.*

Stanley B. Cunningham (essay date 1969)

SOURCE: "Albertus Magnus and the Problem of Moral Virtue," in *Vivarium,* Vol. VII, 1969, pp. 81-119.

[In the following essay, Cunningham examines Albert's treatise on ethics, Do bono, *arguing that the work displays an innovative concern with "the purely natural and human elements of morality."]*

I. THE HISTORICAL SETTING

Within the intellectual upheaval that attended the appearance of Greek philosophical literature in the Latin West in the early thirteenth century, a special problem was put for Christian moralists when they were confronted by the theory of natural virtue contained in the *Nicomachean Ethics* of Aristotle. Not surprisingly, Christian thinkers had been primarily concerned with supernaturally endowed perfections through which man could hope to achieve beatitude. In this preoccupation, however, they tended to ignore the question and indeed the very possibility of virtue naturally acquired. Albert the Great (1206-1280) appears to have been one of the first to respond enthusiastically to the challenge of Aristotle's *Ethics;* and the originality of his venture can be gauged by the extent to which in his own theory he included the purely natural and human elements of morality. Now as it developed, the problem of natural virtue in many ways was allied to the question of what constitutes the moral character of an agent's actions. Earlier thinkers, to be sure, had come to see, though gradually, that a number of factors are involved; but there was both in their theories and in their written presentations a noticeable absence of cohesion and unity. Albert's awareness of these problems and his response to them are evident in one of his early works. His contribution was nothing less than a methodical treatment of a number of moral distinctions, inherited from his predecessors, culminating in a causal grounding of those natural virtues which, in the career of moral speculation before him, had been so conspicuously ignored.

The *De bono*

Albert's innovations show up most strikingly in a relatively early work entitled *De bono,* written about 1240-1244 during his residence in Paris. It is worth remarking that at this time he was conversant with only fragments of the *Nicomachean Ethics:* the *Ethica vetus,* comprising a Greek-Latin translation of Books II and III, the *Ethica nova* containing a Greek-Latin translation of Book I, and a few excerpts from Books VII and VIII. The *De bono,* therefore, reveals only a partial knowledge of Aristotle's ethics. It was also written early in Albert's career, nor is it his only or latest publication in this field. Yet by contrast to this other writings it enjoys a number of merits which make it a primary source for an appreciation of his own moral philosophy in its organic outlines.

Prior to the *De bono* Albert had undertaken to write the *Tractatus de natura boni* which remains unpublished to this day. The *Tractatus,* abandoned in considerable disorder far short of its projected aims, is an awkward and premature attempt to erect a comprehensive synthesis of the natural and supernatural perfections. His experiment in this direction was resumed with greater success in the *De bono*. The moral sections in Books II-IV of Albert's *Scripta super sententias* (written from 1245-1249), while admittedly providing a valuable source for this thought, stand as so many separated components of a comprehensive presentation of theology. In the *Scripta,* Albert is not concentrating exclusively upon morals alone, but rather composing a theological *summa* along lines laid down ninety years earlier by Peter the Lombard. Finally, Albert is the author of two full-fledged commentaries on the *Nicomachean Ethics*. In works of this nature, however, the arrangement of the material is not Albert's but Aristotle's. To put it in other words, neither of these commentaries necessarily reflects the controlling principles of organization according to which Albert would frame his own moral treatise.

By contrast, the *De bono* is neither a commentary nor part of a theological *summa*. Though it is incomplete, what we have is the first part of a projected synthesis of moral doctrine in which Albert devotes himself to an investigation of the natural principles of morality prior to an examination of the supernatural virtues. Since he wrote in a form inspired by the medieval academic disputation, Albert was free to assemble his material according to principles of his own formulation and choice. Indeed, in the early articles Albert carefully establishes a number of broad metaphysical principles which dictate both formal and material aspects of his theory of virtue. Being an independent and exclusively moral synthesis, the *De bono* is our best source for tracing his theory of natural virtue in its consecutive development.

Briefly, the work opens with a metaphysical disquisition on the 'good' (*bonum, bonitas*) and the physical good (*bonum naturae*). The implication, clearly stated in one of Albert's later commentaries, is that we cannot move into the area of moral goodness unless we first understand the notion of goodness. Metaphysics proper is followed by sections dealing respectively with the causes of virtue and the nature of virtue in general. The major and remaining part of the *De bono* is composed of four tractates each of which deals with one of the cardinal virtues (*virtutes cardinales, virtutes politicae*) in the following order: fortitude, temperance, prudence and justice. The final treatise on justice contains a revolutionary treatment of natural law theory.

Pre-Albertinian Theories

The full significance of Albert's theory of human virtue as elaborated in the *De bono* stands out against the background of his contemporary and earlier writers. That history, as Dom Odon Lottin did so much to demonstrate in his monumental *Psychologie et Morale aux XIIe et XIIIe siècles,* was a rich and highly variegated complexus of interlocking themes and tensions. For our purposes, two facets of that history are especially relevant. There was first of all a tendency among most writers to restrict extensively the moral worth of human acts to the level of supernatural virtue and merit. The second facet of this overall history concerns itself with the development in theories about the nature and number of factors contributing to the moral specificity of human acts.

A) *The problem of moral worth*

Apropos of the first problem, Lottin has remarked time and time again that prior to St. Thomas Aquinas there was a conspicuous tendency among medieval writers to confuse the moral goodness of acts with supernatural merit. Underlying this confusion was the implication that the only kind of moral perfection is that which derives from a divine infusion. That is, instead of merit being visualized as a property resulting from the morally good act, it was confusedly made the condition. Since these Christian moralists favoured an almost exclusively supernatural perspective, there resulted theories of moral neutrality, so to speak, at the natural level of human conduct. Now since the time of Peter Abelard in the early twelfth century, the moral specification of human acts was, in varying degrees, explained by the agent's intention. And as it developed, the only kind of good intention was one rooted in charity and directed by faith. One might not be surprised to discover this attitude running through a theological literature which was largely preoccupied with the principles contributing to man's salvation. But the result came to be that little if any value was laid upon *naturally* acquired virtues which, by themselves, would admittedly be insufficient to insure supernatural beatitude. Seen through the higher medium of theological virtues (faith, hope and charity), the natural cardinal virtues (fortitude, temperance, prudence, justice) appeared to be little else than essentially incomplete and imperfect qualities. In short, they were not *moral* virtues. In St. Albert's own time, this line of thought culminates in a theory held by some Franciscan theologians, notably John of Rupella and St. Bonaventure, who viewed the human act, taken at the level of nature, as being essentially *indifferent* even though it be a deliberated act. Lottin insists that this confusion between moral goodness and merit arose in large measure from faulty organization. "The principal cause of this in the twelfth century", he writes, "was the inclusion of treatments on virtue into a doctrine of grace."

The widespread confusion, diagnosed by Lottin, between natural and supernatural moral perfections stems largely from a manual of theology widely read at that time, the famed *Sentences* of Peter the Lombard. Published between the years 1153-1158, the work is a compilation of extracts gleaned from scriptural and patristic sources to which are adjoined Peter's own comments and explications. As to its architectonic structure, Peter follows a plan already adhered to in the works of some of his immediate predecessors, namely, the order of the Apostolic Creed. In two different places within this framework he has inserted moral treatises: in Book II within the context of sin, and in Book III following the treatise on Christ. Yet in either section no room is made for a treatment of the natural acquired virtues as such. True, in Book III following the chapter on charity and preceding those on the gifts of the Holy Spirit, Peter cursorily mentions the four cardinal virtues, but these are clearly conceived as divinely infused perfections. By the same token, he steers clear of any philosophical approach to moral virtue. Indeed, not only in reference to this particular matter, but throughout the entire work, it has often been remarked that there is a noticeable absence of the principles and precisions of philosophy. Symptomatic of this attitude is "a notion of virtue which is plainly theocentric and Augustinian". From passages in St. Augustine's *De libero arbitrio*, the Lombard culls a definition of virtue which is really Peter's own amalgam of St. Augustine's words and the Augustinian idea of the gratuitous nature of grace: *bona qualitas mentis, qua recte vivitur, et qua nullus male utitur, quam Deus solus in homine operatur*. The exclusively divine origin of virtue is even more apparent when one of the Lombard's disciples, Peter of Poitiers, supplies his own interpolation to the definition in order to stress the moral inefficacy of man: *Virtus igitur est qualitas mentis qua recte vivitur, qua nemo male utitur, quam Deus in homine* SINE HOMINE *operatur*.

Commenting on the Lombard's definition, Lottin once again has occasion to remind us of the subsequent tendency in the twelfth century to equate the goodness in human acts with supernatural merit. The result was either to ignore or to minimize the value of natural virtue, and to regard the Christian perfection of charity as the only genuine cause of goodness.

That Peter the Lombard's *Sentences* could be so influential in this respect becomes evident when we stop to consider that a major proportion of speculative theological literature in the next two centuries consisted of works which, in varying degrees, were modelled upon the *Sentences*. These writings, whether they be *Scripta* or the later and more independently wrought syntheses known as *Summae*, tended to perpetuate the original defect in Peter's *Sentences*. No one can deny, of course, that there was a progressive increase in the attention and space given to moral speculation. There were even

new materials inserted into the traditional Lombardian framework. But the bits and pieces of each man's moral theory generally remained scattered and disconnected. In the wake of Peter the Lombard, then, the emergence of moral treatises showing a logical consecutiveness and organization was slow to materialize. Moreover, in commenting upon this late appearance of systematized moral treatises, Lottin also indicated the scarcity of any such treatments until the third and fourth decades of the thirteenth century. As the earliest and most noteworthy experiments in this direction he cited the *Summa aurea* of William of Auxerre (written about 1220-1225) and Philip the Chancellor's *Summa de bono* (completed before 1236). Oddly enough he did not mention St. Albert's *De bono,* yet the dates and authors cited bring us almost to the eve of its composition. Up to this time, the continuity of the Lombardian framework as well as the privileged authority of the Augustinian definition of virtue tended to discourage any positive recognition of the natural dimension in morals.

B) *The multiplicity of moral elements*

In diagnosing the prevailing conception of moral worth prior to Albertus Magnus, we have seen the position given by medieval thinkers to their moral sections within the wider structure of their theological syntheses and the effect this had upon their theories of virtue. There is still another dimension to the historical context, this time involving attempts made both to identify and to correlate the elements which contribute to the moral specification of human acts. What factors, elements, or principles are necessary to constitute a morally good action? How many are there? Assuming that several are required, what are their inter-relationships and interdependencies?

With respect to the identification of these principles, there is a pertinent passage in St. Albert's *De bono* wherein he states that in a morally good act a plurality of elements is required. He enlists the authority of Pseudo-Dionysius who says:

> . . . in Chapter IV of *Concerning the Divine Names* that 'the good is constituted by a total and single cause, but that evil originates omnifariously'. By this it is understood that for the reality of virtue there are required all the circumstances together with the end harmonizing with the act as it is brought to bear upon its proportionate object. For evil and vice, however, the corruption of any one of these by itself is sufficient.

The same doctrine is reiterated in Book III of Albert's *Scripta super Sententias:*

> It must be said that good and evil in acts are not caused in only one manner, but that the good, as

Dionysius says, is caused by a total cause that is one. That is, in the constitution of the good act all the circumstances and the end and the agent's intention must coincide. It is caused only when all of these are simultaneously present in the manner of an integral whole which is made up of all its parts taken together at once. Evil, however, as Dionysius says, derives omnifariously, that is, from the corruption of any particular part, just as an integral whole is broken up when any one of its parts is destroyed. And so it is that there is no good act without a good intention, but it is not made good solely by the intention.

Throughout his lifetime, Albert seems to be quite consistent in this regard. Supported by a statement of the Neo-Platonic author, Pseudo-Dionysius, Albert insists that moral goodness, more specifically virtue, derives only from a total synthesis of all the elements involved, namely circumstances, the agent's intention, the end, and the act itself. The corruption of any one of these constituents vitiates the act. In the *Sentences,* Albert admits that intention plays a major rôle in the moral determination of acts, but it is not the sole feature.

We have briefly anticipated the Albertinian position merely to indicate one stand taken in the history of this problem. Prior to Albert's arrival in Paris, however, this particular problem had been vexing moralists for over a century. Albert's words are certainly a far cry from those written a century earlier by that intrepid figure of the twelfth century, Peter Abelard. In his relatively short treatise entitled *Ethics, or Know Thyself* written about 1135, Abelard distinguishes between an external human act (*opus*) and the intention which precedes it. The term 'intention' connotes a determination or consent of the will to perform an external action. That is, it is an internal act of the will distinguishable from other natural undeliberated tendencies. Now, external acts in themselves are morally neutral: their moral goodness or turpitude accrues to them *solely* from our interior act of consent which precedes them. As long as consent is withheld, a disposition to evil or weakness cannot be called evil. On the contrary, if weakness is conquered it serves as an occasion for merit. The pleasure accompanying a sinful act does not augment its turpitude. As for the physical act itself, it is morally indifferent. Killing a man may be committed accidentally, that is without consent, in which case it could scarcely be called evil. In short, the morality of external acts is a borrowed one, and identical with that of the intention. God does not weigh the things we do, but rather the spirit in which we perform them.

As if anticipating future indictments of propounding a radical moral subjectivism, Abelard attempts to place the morality of intention on a more objective footing. It is not enough, he says, that one's intention *seem* good; it must really be good by conforming to God's will. Otherwise, he observes, the acts of non-believers would be good like ours, since they too believed that their works were pleasing to God.

Even after the condemnation of his theories at the Council of Sens in 1140, Abelard still clung to his position. External acts are morally indifferent. He is prepared to admit that virtues and vices are essentially good and evil in themselves, but the relationship of these to the act itself is far from clear.

It is too easy to brand Peter Abelard as a radical moral subjectivist and to let it stand at that. What is often overlooked is that his position stems from a reaction to legalistic moral doctrine. In the penitential and canonical literature of the times, it was common practice to codify acts according to their conformity or opposition to law. In opposition to this excessive legalistic objectivism, Abelard had emphasized the rôle of individual intention, but to such a degree that he had seriously undermined all objective basis for morality.

In the next hundred years and more, the doctrine of intention ran a torturous course due in large measure to the initial imprecision of its vocabulary. Suffice it to say that with few exceptions later moralists were prepared to recognize the primacy of intention in the moral determination of human acts. The problem was not so much this, however, as to supplement Abelard's simplistic theory of intention with other moral principles which would ground the morality of acts upon a solid and objective footing. It was this search, originally sparked by the Abelardian crisis, which partly accounts for the growth of moral speculation in the next century and a half. Efforts were made to define morality in terms of certain rationally discernible features in the human act itself; and early overtures to a philosophical approach to virtue represent one facet of this doctrinal evolution. In addition to the discovery and enlistment of new principles, of course, there still remained the problem of integrating them into a logically consecutive and cohesive account.

A first significant step in the post-Abelardian movement is found in Peter the Lombard's *Sentences.* Peter enlists no less an authority than St. Augustine to confirm his thesis that certain acts are intrinsically bad and that no degree of good will or intention can erase their turpitude. This stand constitutes a positive reaction to the Abelardian thesis. End, or intention, is not the sole determinant of morality. Independently of it, some acts are evil in their very constitution (*per se mala, per se peccata*); that is, they are objectively evil. Intention, the Lombard admits, determines the other kinds of external acts. An act inherently good, for instance, may be vitiated by a bad intent.

Moreover, in speaking about acts, different levels or kinds of goodness are discernible. *All* actions are ontologically good in their very nature (*essentia sui*). Unlike Abelard, the Lombard feels that some acts may also be classified as objectively good. Feeding the hungry, for instance, in addition to possessing ontological goodness, is what he calls *'genere bonus'* because it belongs to that class or genus called works of mercy. This generic goodness, though somewhat broad and indeterminate, is independent of the intention; it is objective. Nevertheless, it is still inferior to the perfectly good act which, in addition to possessing the goodness of essence and its class, issues from a good intention and is directed to a good end.

The end which Peter the Lombard has in mind is supernatural, namely charity or God. On the other hand, rather than refuse all goodness to the actions of non-Christians who lack faith and charity, he allows for a goodness of intention at the purely natural level. The extension of the notion of the good will allow for this, he says. Without contradicting it, he refers, to one theory which says that operations aimed at the alleviation of natural wants and the welfare of one's relatives or neighbors are morally good. The statement, however, reads in a spirit of concession. To account for moral goodness in acts, Peter reasons mainly within a supernatural perspective.

By partially extending the notion of goodness beyond the rigid limits imposed on it by Abelard, the Lombard indicated certain lines along which subsequent theories of the morality of acts evolved. Henceforth, moral speculation was characterized by analyses of additional elements which, over and above intention, contribute to the moral specification of acts. In the writings of one of the Lombard's disciples, for instance, a new and important dimension was added. *Circumstances,* said Peter of Poitiers, in some way influence the character of our acts and must be taken into consideration. The point was only mentioned in passing; it received no further development. But the formula *"bonum ex circumstantia"* continued to reappear often in later writers even though its rôle was never clearly defined. One must wait until St. Albert's *De bono* for the first full-fledged treatise on circumstances.

By the early decades of the thirteenth century it was not uncommon for writers to discern several levels or moments of goodness in the human act. The following formulae appear with increasing frequency: *bonum naturae* or *bonum naturale* referring to the physical reality of the act; *bonum in genere, bonum ex circumstantia, bonum virtutis politicae,* and finally the goodness of supernatural grace—*bonum gratiae.* The formula *bonum in genere,* since the time of Peter the Lombard, generally signified the objective goodness of a class of actions. Albert's immediate predecessor, Philip the Chancellor, through an ingenious application of the hylomorphic theory, interpreted it to mean a natural fittingness between an act (say, feeding) and its object (a hungry man). Yet its status as a moral or non-moral feature was left ambiguous.

This evolving awareness of the multiplicity of elements involved in the morality of human actions may be taken as an index of the development in moral theory at this time. And yet, at the same time, this complexity in the data of the problem was scarcely attended by any kind of apparent cohesiveness. Amidst this plurality of factors, some kind of intelligible synthesis was wanting. This in turn would presuppose clearly defined relationships between the various elements involved. In short, there was need for systematic integration. Albert's *De bono* was written in response to this need.

II. Albert's metaphysics of the good

It would exceed the scope of this [essay] to attempt a thorough analysis of Albert's metaphysics of the good even as contained in the *De bono*. There are, however, three salient metaphysical themes which must be kept in mind since they determine his theory of virtue.

A) *Goodness and Appetition*

In the opening article of the *De bono* where in Albert reports three definitions of the good, he credits Avicenna with defining the good as the "undividedness of act from potency" (*indivisio actus a potentia*). Throughout these early articles, Albert identifies the notions of perfection and completion (*actus, complementum*) with that of the good. This is apparent in the definition imputed to Avicenna which is clearly an attempt to express the absolute without enlisting something yet more ultimate. Though seemingly negative, the definition affirms a positive reality, the nature of the good in itself, this being a unity between any kind of potency or avidity and its corresponding perfection (*actus*). The 'act' in question, however, does not stand simply for the operation performed by some being, nor for the fulfilment which is added to that same being by its substantial form. The notion of perfection here is rather one of fulfilment and completion which accrues to a thing from the attainment of its end. The allegedly Avicennian definition, then, truly expresses the proper nature (*propria ratio*) of goodness, namely, an identity with end (*indivisio finis*).

All things, from inanimate bodies to intellectual agents, desire the good at proportionate levels of appetite. On the one hand, there is 'perfect appetite' which is always accompanied by some form of cognition or apprehension. There is also 'natural appetite' which is universally present in all beings, and

> . . . which is nothing else than the aptitude and inclination of that which is in potency towards perfection. This is in all things, and by this is meant what is said, 'that the good is what all things desire',

St. Albert teaching: detail of the Altar, Chapel of St. Albert; Ratisbon, Germany.

just as the Philosopher at the end of Book I of the *Physics* says that matter desires form as the female the male and evil the good.

The desire for the good among some things may be no more than the inclination of the imperfect towards perfection, but this entitative willingness is rooted in all beings. At the heart of each and every nature is a desire for goodness. Correlatively, it is the very quintessence of the good to be desired, if not cognitively and actively, at least according to this innate propensity. *Only* goodness can be desired, or at least that which is apprehended as being good (*in ratione boni ut hunc*).

God is the *primum* or *summum bonum*. All created goods, even though standing as certain perfections in themselves, are nonetheless defective in comparison to God who is the source of all goodness. Their goodness owes its presence to an *influx* of perfection from the supreme good; and the universal desire inherent in all things is simply a desire for this influx of perfection. Or to put it another way—and this time Albert is consciously exploiting the Neo-Platonic doctrines of St. Augustine and Pseudo-Dionysius—all things are good by *participation* in the sense that the first good or exemplar is reflected (*relucet*) in created goods. Exemplarism tells us the mode of presence. Albert rejects any attempt to visualize this participation as a direct

sharing in the nature itself of the supreme good. Rather, participation is taken to mean that each thing, possessing as it does a certain finite and particular instance of goodness, is somehow reducible to the efficacy of the *primum bonum* as the cause of this goodness. As a particular instance (*ratio particularis*) of goodness, it only mirrors the supreme goodness. What is really possessed is created goodness (*ratio boni creati*), and this as particularized in individuals through their differences and matter.

B) *The analogical Nature of Goodness and Appetition*

In no way, then, can goodness as some sort of common nature be predicated univocally of an infinite God and the universe of finite creatures. On the contrary, to explain the unity in goodness between the *summum bonum* and creatures, as well as among created goods themselves, the principle of analogy is introduced by Albert, more precisely that type of analogy which is called a community of proportionality:

> To the fourth objection it must be said that that good which all things desire is not reducible to one species or to one genus, but to a community of proportionality in such wise that a distinction obtains between proportion and proportionality . . . And so we say that the proportionality and commensuration of all possibles in relation to a perfecting end is one, and the end of all things in this proportionality is one, and so too is the appetite which inclines to the end.

> It must be said that there is a community of proportionality, as was established earlier, which is reduced to the third mode of analogy. For although there is not one end which every good attains as its fulfilment, nevertheless there is one end beyond the order of creation to which every good inclines according to its power. And this end is the highest good. Other goods are not good unless they derive from it and tend back to it.

All creatures, in desiring their own particular perfections, are really moving towards a perfecting end which, by a community of proportionality, is one. This is the same as saying that every thing has some kind of natural inclination towards goodness. More than once, Albert points to the writings of Pseudo-Dionysius who has said that, corresponding to the different levels of nature and appetition discernible in the universe, there results a hierarchy of degrees in which perfection is shared by creatures. Intellectual and rational beings desire the good knowingly; sentient creatures reveal a desire for the good in their sensible appetites; other living things without sense, desire the good by their innate urge to live; and finally, inanimate creatures tend to the good in their mere inclination to participate in being. All this is to say that creatures, by a movement commensurately one, desire an end which is also proportionately one: goodness. Now, we have already seen that the absolute instance of goodness is God, the *summum bonum*. Even though all creatures do not actually attain to Him as their *complementum,* nevertheless He is the absolute end, beyond the order of creation, towards which all of creation is drawn according to diverse specific powers and natures. What creatures achieve on this natural level, of course, is not a part of God, but rather a certain instance of created goodness.

The principle of analogy and the doctrines of Pseudo-Dionysius coalesce in Albert's explanation of the relationship between creatures and God. The result is a universe conceived in Neo-Platonic fashion as a hierarchy of beings which derive from, and are tending back towards, an infinite good. Each thing desires and shares in goodness according to the level of its nature and powers. Our general concept of the good is broad enough to accommodate every instance of the good, both finite and infinite, since predication is made analogically in each case.

By enlisting the principle of analogy, Albert has bestowed upon the notion of goodness a flexibility and unity which hitherto was missing in pre-Albertinian thinkers. Application of the principle ensures the reduction of all the various degrees and kinds of goodness to a more overall intelligible unity. Moreover, what has been said of the good in general will be no less applicable to the elements of moral goodness proper: all these in some way will connote a perfection and an "undividedness of act from potency". Each of them, in view of this analogical similitude, has a certain intelligible setting within the more comprehensive notion of *bonum.*

The notion of the innate appetency for perfection in creatures dovetails with the Albertinian doctrine of being. Every created being in some way is a composition of potency and act. Hence, it is not entirely destitute of goodness, but only relatively so. Yet if each thing possesses a certain degree of perfection, it still remains susceptible to additional increments. Reiterating the conceptions of the *Liber de causis,* Albert says that stability in being (*fixio et permanentia*) accrues to created things through an influx of the good. When they have incorporated the desired perfection, beings are perfected in their very nature.

The terms 'influx', 'participation', and 'information' all convey the same idea. For Albert, goodness is scarcely a remote ideal or standard which creatures merely imitate. Rather, it is seen as a perfective element which has been incorporated and shared in by the creature. As an interiorized perfection, inhering intimately within the thing, it consummates a corresponding potency or need thereby fulfilling the created nature in its very being. This is why the Avicennian

definition of the good, "the undividedness of act from potency", most truly characterizes the quintessence of goodness.

C) *Causal Explanation of the Goodness of Creatures*

The problem of the relationship between created being and the good does not end here. In Article Seven of the first Question in the **De bono,** Albert boldly confronts the classic dilemma voiced by Boethius in his *De hebdomadibus.* In this tractate, Boethius had raised the question how natures or substances, from the very fact that they exist, are good, since they can scarcely be called absolute goods. If, as St. Albert has already done, we are prepared to admit that each and every being is not entirely devoid of goodness, but only relatively so, would this not lead us to equate the being of creatures (*esse*) with their goodness (*bonum esse*)? In this article Albert undertakes to clear up this dilemma.

Boethius had urged that the substantial being of creatures may be called good since it derives from and participates in the Prime Good in whom goodness and being are identical. The solution offered by Boethius, Albert admits, is 'imperfect and obscure'. To clarify Boethius' answer one must invoke a theory of causes. In a vocabulary highly redolent of Avicenna, Albert begins by observing that nothing can exist (*esse in effectu*) except by a cause since the effect owes its whole being to an antecedent cause. Now the four Aristotelian causes—form, matter, final cause or end, and efficient or agent cause—fall conveniently into two groupings or arrangements. Form and matter, which we may also designate as act and potency or *quo est* and *quod est* respectively, are intrinsic principles or constituent causes of a being. The end and efficient causes are its extrinsic causes. These combinations coincide in the production of being. The end or final cause exists in the agent cause as that which is intended (*per intentionem*); the form exists potentially in the matter (*per potentiam*). The final cause is the highest of all the causes; it is the 'cause of causes'. Though completely unmoved and immobile in itself, it nevertheless moves all the other causes. As that which is desired, it effects motion in the efficient cause, and this in turn induces the material principle or 'that which is' to receive the form. With this hierarchical arrangement of the causes, Albert feels prepared to interpret the relationship between the being of creatures and their goodness. The being is given them by the efficient cause which moves the matter to the reception of form. The goodness, on the other hand, derives from the end which moves the efficient cause as an object of desire and intention. According to their absolute and abstract consideration, the being and goodness of creatures, therefore, cannot be equated. They may be identified only through mutual inherence in one and the same subject or supposit. Goodness and being, or if you will, nature, are not identical although in reality they are inseparable.

It seems obvious, therefore, that for Albert any explanation of the good and its reference to being merely in terms of the traditional doctrine of participation does not suffice. All this does is to indicate the *kind* or *type* of presence. Over and above this, one must explain, why, and how, such a presence by participation is effected, i.e., a *causal* explanation and knowledge of the good is required. To account for the origin of goodness in creatures, then, one must ground his explanation on the four ultimate causes of Aristotle. This solution to the Boethian dilemma becomes a significant methodological principle. When Albert comes to treat of moral goodness, its various elements will be systematically integrated according to this hierarchy of Aristotelian causes.

III. The Causes of Moral Virtue

In the *Tractatus de natura boni,* Albert had commenced his moral disquisition proper by pointing out a certain disjunction between the order of nature and the human moral order. Some things are not caused by human beings such as the created things in this world; other things, however, are caused by us, namely our voluntary acts of which we are the masters. Now just as in nature there is one primary thing—matter—which serves as the subject for additional forms, so too in our moral voluntary actions there is a primary subject in potency to further moral specifications which is called *bonum in genere*. The *bonum in genere,* Albert adds, is simply the human act brought to bear upon its proportionate object: *actus solus super materiam debitam.* For instance, the act of feeding a hungry man, abstracting from those particular circumstances of time and place which surround the act, may be called *bonum in genere. Bonum in genere,* therefore, designates the first moment of goodness in the order of morality, and it is subject to further increments of moral perfection.

At the corresponding point in the *De bono,* that is, immediately after the short disquisition on *bonum naturale,* Albert commences his moral section by distinguishing between the two main orders of moral goodness: *bonum consuetudinis* and supernatural grace. 'Consuetudo' or 'consuetudinalis'—terms found in the *Ethica vetus*—were employed by mediaeval writers to designate moral virtues acquired at the level of nature. For Albert too they connote moral excellence won through the repetition of acts. In this treatise, *bonum consuetudinis* comprises three levels or types of moral perfection: *bonum in genere,* the moral determinations of circumstance (*bonum ex circumstantia*), and virtue (*bonum virtutis politicae*). These divisions are taken over by Albert. Earlier writers had coined these formulae, and tradition sanctioned them. There is no attempt

at this point to justify the classification by explicitly invoking a hierarchy of potencies and corresponding degrees of perfection such as Philip the Chancellor had done, but it is evident that this same scheme is operative here as well.

These first three degrees of perfection are natural, rationally discernible elements in the morality of acts whose investigation logically precedes the order of divinely infused goodness. A number of statements in the *De bono* clearly indicate that an elaborate study of the perfections of the supernatural order would follow as part of the *De bono.* The *De bono,* then, heralds a noticeable departure from the traditional procedure adhered to in mediaeval treatises: there is to be a treatment of natural virtue outside the context of grace and preceding a disquisition upon the supernatural virtues. This is possible because the *De bono* is a work patterned independently of the *Sentences* of Peter the Lombard. We may therefore anticipate a treatment of the acquired virtues more consonant with their natural status.

Indeed, all through this work Albert appears to be cognizant of the difference between the two moral orders. For instance, *bonum in genere,* he tells us, is still immediately susceptible to the more specific moral determinations of virtue. This latter superadded determination is still in potency to merit. Moral specificity, therefore, is already discernible on the natural level, and prior to the order of merit. Grace, in turn, the condition of merit, neither destroys nor dispenses with nature, but rather, as its 'most connatural' excellence, raises it to its highest state of perfection.

A) *The moral status of rational, voluntary actions*

Bonum in genere is clearly included into the moral order. Even though its status as a *moral* factor was not always clear among pre-Albertinian scholars, these same authors from the time of Peter the Lombard generally regarded it as the first consideration in any discussion of morality. Now, in Albert's treatise, the first article in the specifically moral section is devoted to an analysis of *bonum in genere.* In spite of this, however, Albert admits that the absolutely first consideration in moral speculation is not really the *bonum in genere,* but the voluntary act abstractly considered as such:

> The absolutely first thing in morals, however, is that which is susceptible to the condition of praise, which is virtue, or the condition of blame, which is vice, and this is the voluntary act brought to bear upon its object following choice and deliberation. For this act is susceptible to either of the contraries, and equally so. *Bonum in genere,* however, does not signify the absolutely first principle in morals, but rather something ordered to one of the contraries, that is, to the good of virtue.

Here we have a precision which seems to be absent from the earlier *Tractatus*. The voluntary act as such, a deliberated act bearing upon a definite object, is an abstraction distinguishable from the *bonum in genere*. It is the act seen as being *equally* susceptible to the conditions of good or evil. *Bonum in genere* is really the same act, but now as having a certain ordination or determination to subsequent moral goodness.

Does this mean that the voluntary act is morally indifferent? The question is explicitly raised in Article Seven of Question Two: "Whether in voluntary acts there is anything indifferent such that it be neither good nor evil *in genere* or concretely (*in specie*)?" This is indeed a perplexing problem in the moral philosophy of Albertus Magnus, and a certain imprecision in his writings makes it difficult for us to arrive at a definite solution. When he explicitly raises this question in Article Seven, he seems to have in mind the concrete individual act. In the last text quoted from Article Four, wherein the voluntary act is depicted as being equally susceptible to either good or evil, he was speaking of actions in a general and abstract manner. Abstractly conceived, the voluntary act could be viewed both as the absolutely first moment in the moral order, as well as morally indifferent in itself since it is equally open to good or evil.

The opening arguments of Article Seven preceding Albert's own magisterial resolution mention two possible kinds of morally indifferent acts: the vain or futile act (*vanum*), and the useless or idle act (*otiosum*). A definition of the vain act Albert takes from Aristotle's *Physics:* it is that which is a means to some end, but which falls short of that end. Now, that which is vain is condemned by Holy Scripture (Psalms 4, 3) wherein it is written "Why do you love vanity and seek after lying"; and so this kind of indifferent act ranks among those acts which are sinful. The definition of the idle act is taken from St. Gregory the Great's *Moralia:* "the idle is that which lacks the character of rightful necessity or dutiful service". It is also condemned as sinful in the Gospel of St. Matthew (12, 36) when Christ states "that of every idle word men speak, they shall give account on the day of judgment". On the basis of Holy Scripture, then, it would seem that these so-called morally indifferent acts in effect are evil acts.

Albert the Great does not seem entirely opposed to this line of reasoning. In his reply, he begins with a distinction between the theologian's position, and that of the moral philosopher. According to the Christian theologian, no deliberated voluntary act is morally indifferent because he knows that *all* our actions should issue from charity, that is, from a love of God. Charity, an infused perfection by which we incline to God, is a universal virtue (*virtus . . . generale movens*) moving us to the acts of all other virtues. The moral philosopher, on the other hand, philosophizing beyond the pale of faith and Scripture, is ignorant of any such universal virtue presiding over the economy of the moral life. He knows only of a specific number of acquired virtues, each of which has a defined and limited moral influence. At this level, then, it appears that indifferent natural acts are possible, indifferent because they lack the information of charity.

According to St. Albert, then, the testimony of Holy Scripture adds a new dimension to the morality of acts of which the philosopher is unmindful, and this is the reference which all human actions, external as well as internal, have to God. "Not everything futile", continues Albert, "is condemned by the moral philosopher, but everything futile is condemned by the theologian"; and so at one point, he classes the futile with the evil.

Critical of a univocally theocentric conception of moral worth, Albert attempted to enlarge the area of human moral efficacy by making man the responsible agent in the generation of his own natural excellences.

— *Stanley B. Cunningham*

The idle act, as defined by St. Gregory, is also an indifferent act, and it too is condemned by the Christian theologian. But in direct contrast to certain contemporary Franciscan authors, notably John of Rupella, Albert in Article Seven goes on to show what the *otiosum* is not. Now, as Lottin has pointed out, the Franciscan thinkers of this time regarded any act directed to a natural end as morally neutral. This is particularly evident in the writings of John of Rupella who had said that those acts which are aimed at the daily necessities of living, such as nourishing one's self, are neither good nor bad; they are indifferent. In opposition to this attitude, Albert goes on to state that any act directed to the alleviation of our own natural exigencies or the pressing needs of others does indeed have the "character of rightful necessity" (*ratio iustae necessitatis*), and so is not indifferent. These purely natural exigencies arise from the daily necessities of life and the toil of labor. Hence the activities of eating, drinking, sleeping, are not indifferent since they procede from natural necessities; they fall within the moral order. This applies also to the comforts of peace and rest, conversation, strolling, singing and play, which dispel the tedium and fatigue of labor. For support Albert appeals to a passage in the *Nicomachean Ethics* in which Aristotle treats of wittiness or urbanity (*eutrapelia*) as a virtue.

There is another very important dimension to this problem of the morality of acts. Every *deliberated* action is good or bad:

> . . . we say that many things are done without deliberation and these are neither indifferent, nor bad, nor good because they do not fall into the sphere of morality. Whatever things are done with deliberation, however, are good or bad, according as the futile act (*vanum*) is called evil.

Here Albert is pointing out the key principle of rational ethics: reason is the indispensable condition of morality, while a non-rational act is simply non-moral, that is, neither good, bad, nor indifferent. But as far as we can gather from his words, the futile action is still a deliberated or rational act. It is also an indifferent act whose full significance escapes the moral philosopher, but which the theologian recognizes and so classifies among evil acts. In the realm of natural ethics, then, it is possible to have a concrete deliberated, but indifferent, act. The principle that natural reason is that which essentially constitutes an act as moral is not accepted unconditionally by Albert. In the final analysis, the rôle of reason is found wanting; unlike the universal virtue of charity, it does not universally initiate the moral character of all our natural acts, and so must be supplemented by the data of the theologian.

Concerning the morality of acts, then, Albert's theory betrays not only a certain ambiguity, but also a qualified acceptance of the rôle of reason as an adequate determiner of moral specificity. At the same time, it is important to note that Albert is attempting to validate and emphasize, to a greater extent than any of his predecessors, the purely rational and natural factors in the morality of acts. Every *naturally* virtuous act is a morally good act. Every *rational* act is a moral act (with the added stipulation that futile or idle acts are evil). In relation to his predecessors and contemporaries, Albert's position represents an advance. At the same time, he falls short of St. Thomas for whom all rational acts are *ipso facto* moral. Lottin has aptly characterized St. Albert's position as a *"mi-chemin sur la voie d'une morale strictement naturelle"*.

B) *The material cause of virtue: bonum in genere*

Like the absolute consideration of the voluntary act, *bonum in genere* is also an abstraction. It signifies this same human act not as being in a state of absolute indetermination or equal liability to good or evil, but more positively as having an inclination or disposition to the good. Albert calls it a 'first potency' to the good. He also refers to *bonum in genere* as the 'matter' and the '*materia circa quam*' which, over and above the concept of matter, includes as well a certain reference to the end of the act. At the same time, it is the 'first subject' which receives and supports the added determinations of circumstance and virtue.

It seems obvious, then, that not unlike Philip the Chancellor, Albert is conceiving *bonum in genere* as the material cause of virtue.

To the standardized description of *bonum in genere—actus solus super debitam materiam*—Albert adds a new precision which is helpful to the modern reader who is apt to find the term '*debitum*' both strange and misleading. At this point in the thirteenth century, '*debitum*' had a strong juridified ring arising from its traditional associations with the notions of law, right (*ius*) and a legalistic conception of justice. Albert, however, under the influence of Philip the Chancellor's interpretation of *bonum in genere,* uses the term in a meta-juridical sense: and he warns us that in this context the notion of *debitum* is not to be taken in a specific sense as the *debitum iustitiae*. The main purpose of these early questions in the **De bono** is to render an intelligible account of the nature and genesis of moral virtue. Hence, if the *debitum* in question were the *debitum iuris* which derives from justice (as yet uninvestigated), we would be caught in a circular argument by trying to invoke a special virtue in order to account for virtue in general. No, the *debitum* here connotes a natural and right *proportion* between the act and its corresponding material object: for instance, feeding a hungry person, or teaching an ignorant person, or consoling a sorrowful person. It is a proportion between two natures, as it were. Hence, as the first degree of moral goodness founded on a proportion, *bonum in genere* appears as a true instance of the transcendental good which, we recall, analogically embraces all instances of goodness through a community of proportionality. Conversely, *malum in genere* signifies a privation of this proportion.

In the history previous to Albert, the formula *bonum in genere* is characterized by a certain ambivalence. Sometimes it was viewed as a positive perfection, the first in a series of moral perfections. On the other hand, it was given an almost entirely indifferent status in which it was regarded as equally liable to corruption by subsequent circumstances. Both themes are still discernible in the **De bono**. The *bonum in genere* is a first potency, matter and subject with respect to specific moral goodness. It is the act seen as having a disposition to goodness in the same way that matter has a disposition to form. Albert also admits that it can be specified and vitiated by circumstances. However, this possibility of change in the morality of an act by circumstances, from *bonum in genere* to *malum in specie*, does not constitute its essence: it is more of an accidental property. The true essence of *bonum in genere* is its inherent disposition or proclivity to goodness—*ad bonum magis quam ad malum*. The indifference is a by-product, so to speak, of the relatively indeterminate moral status of *bonum in genere*. What is essentially indifferent is the voluntary act abstractly conceived.

C) *The Formal Cause of Virtue: Circumstances.*

In the history of moral speculation in the Middle Ages, Albert's **Tractatus de natura boni** seems to have been the first known instance in which a distinctive treatment is given to the rôle of circumstances. Question three of *Tractatus* I in the **De bono** is devoted to the same analysis. The inclusion of these treatises within the **Tractatus** and the **De bono** is an innovation. No longer is *bonum ex circumstantia* just a formula mentioned in passing, one whose own status as a moral factor, and whose relationship to the other moral factors, remains in obscurity. On the contrary, Albert's recognition of their function as a necessary cause in the genesis of virtue has finally prompted the inclusion of a treatise on the circumstances within the wider scheme of a natural ethic.

In this section of the **De bono,** Albert relies heavily upon passages from Cicero's *De inventione* and the *De differentiis topicis* of Boethius. All the circumstances enumerated by Cicero, writes Albert, are reducible to seven main headings: agent or person (*quis*), the nature of the act, or what was done in the performance of the act (*quid*), intention, motive, or reason for the act (*cur*), the time (*quando*), the place (*ubi*), the manner of performance (*quomodo*), and finally the means or instruments involved (*quibus auxiliis*). This enumeration, in effect, is a convenient abbreviation of Cicero's long catalogue made by Boethius, and used and commented upon by Albert. The Universal Doctor, of course, would know the six major circumstances listed by Aristotle in Book III of the *Nicomachean Ethics* which partially coincide with the seven headings just listed; but in the present section, Albert seems to prefer the testimony of Cicero and Boethius.

A better name for circumstances, Albert points out, is *'singularia'* because the moral philosopher is primarily concerned with concrete actions which are immersed in individuating conditions, and not simply with problematic or rhetorical questions. Indeed, Albert insists upon the difference between circumstances and 'singulars'. Strictly speaking, circumstances are universal or general considerations which are extrinsic to the act, and which give rise to the rhetorical syllogism and question. 'Singulars', on the other hand, are numerically particularized differences which characterize, and attach to, each and any act. One is universal and extrinsic to the act; the other is real and, as we shall now see, intrinsic to the act's morality. Nevertheless, in deference to tradition and for the sake of convenience, Albert continues to use the term 'circumstances' when what he really means is 'singulars'.

Circumstances inform our acts with the being of moral goodness (*honestum*) or evil (*vituperabile*). They do not constitute the ontological nature of the act as such, but they do confer upon it a moral being. Hence, although extrinsic to the act as such, they are nevertheless intrinsic components of its morality:

> To the first argument, therefore, we say that these qualifying principles (*talia*) do not give being to the act inasmuch as it is an act, but rather they give it being inasmuch as it is good or evil. And for this reason, although they are extrinsic to the act, they are not, however, extrinsic to moral goodness or evil.

> . . . circumstances . . . give being to virtue and they are intrinsic to virtue . . .

It is clear that St. Albert draws a line between the act conceived as a psychological entity, and its moral accidents, so to speak. Morality is something superimposed, a quality tacked on to the nature of an external act. It does not permeate the act as in St. Thomas for whom the 'human act' is through and through a 'moral act'. At this crucial point, then, Albert, not unlike many earlier and contemporary thinkers, seems to regard the physical and substantial core of a human act as being essentially infra-moral. The point is worthy of note if only to indicate one more instance in the enduring history of the fact-value distinction.

The 'circumstance' *quid,* however, raises some difficulty. Inasmuch as it designates the kind or nature of the act performed (e.g., adultery, homicide), then surely it must connote the very 'substance of the act'? In his replies to this objection, Albert does not altogether deny that this one circumstance connotes the essence or physical subtrate of an act. But this connotation is secondary and minimal. He emphasizes the fact that what *quid* really designates is the *moral species* of the act, that is, the act (together with its material object) as enveloped in, and specified by, circumstances. It primarily points up the moral character of an act which is constituted by circumstances. Albert appears unwilling to allow *quid* any more than an oblique signification of the physical act itself.

Good and evil, therefore, accrue to the agent and to his behaviour not so much from the act as such, but from the manner in which the act is performed. Circumstances are *modes* or ways of acting which inform the act with its moral character:

> The being of moral goodness, moreover, derives from the manner (in which the act is performed) rather than from the act itself in such a way that all the circumstances may be called 'the manner'. And this is made clear by Aristotle in Book II of the *Ethics* where he says that 'we are not just and

temperate because we perform just and temperate acts, but because we act *as* just and temperate persons do (*ut iusti et casti*)'.

Albert cites Aristotle who says that it is not simply the performance of just and temperate acts which make us to be so, but rather our acting in the manner of those who are just and temperate. The *ut* of *ut iusti et casti* in this text signifies the mode of circumstance, and not the *habitus* of virtue itself. Obviously, I do not act already with the virtues of justice and temperance since it is precisely these which we are in the process of trying to account for. Virtues, at this point, are not the conditions of good acts, but the result of morally good acts.

Circumstances, then, inform our actions with moral specificity when they actualize the potency towards goodness (i.e., the *bonum in genere*) which is in these acts. Indeed, it becomes apparent that Albert envisages circumstances in the rôle of formal causes of an act's morality. This formula has actually been suggested in the opening arguments of Article One: " . . . it does not seem that these should be called circumstances, but rather forms of the act . . . Therefore, it seems that circumstances constitute the act as a formal cause". Albert does not dismiss this proposal. His only rejoinder is that these circumstances are not the intrinsic causes of the physical act as such, but of its moral character. That is, they are the formal and intrinsic causes of natural virtue.

In describing circumstances as the 'modes' or 'forms' of our acts, Albert has followed out a line of reasoning suggested by the vocabulary of Philip the Chancellor. Moreover, for Albert, the element of *cur,* the agent's intention, is included within the catalogue of circumstances. It is that for the sake of which the deed is performed, and so a cause of that operation. Now, in the *De bono,* Albert really raises the problem of intention only once; this is in the answer to an objection, and so the treatment is very brief and incomplete. He mentions two kinds of intention. First, there is a 'simple intention' which sets up an end, but which does not take into account the quality of the means, or of the end itself, or the proportion between the means and the end. This, Albert says, is a 'foolish intention' (*intentio stulta*). The other kind of intention is one informed and directed by faith. This is the theological notion of intention prevalent in Albert's time, and whose inspiration was Scriptural. The objection itself refers to a passage from St. Matthew's Gospel (12, 35): "The good man from his good treasure brings forth good things". The treasure of a man's heart, continues the objection, is his intention, and it is this which determines the moral quality of acts, and which God will judge. Albert, moreover, must certainly have had in mind the divinely orientated intention of which St. Paul speaks (*Romans,* 14, 23): "for all that is not from faith is sin".

Is no other kind of intention conceivable? The issue at stake once again, of course, is the reality and degree of *natural* moral goodness in the moral philosophy of Albertus Magnus. Does Albert admit to an intention which, though not informed by faith, is nevertheless able to assess the value of some end and the relationship of the means to the end? Surely the fact that thinkers of antiquity recognized and used this circumstance *cur,* which Albert himself has equated with the term 'intention', would suggest that in spite of an absence of positive recognition by Albert of a purely natural intention in the present passage, he does not in his own mind exclude the possibility. Yet, with special reference to this passage, Lottin believes this is absent from Albert's thought.

The brevity of this particular passage would seem to reflect hesitancy on the part of Albert himself. Nevertheless, this same brevity is significant in its implications. For a complete analysis of his theory of intention, Albert refers us to another work, namely to Book II of his **Scripta super Sententias**. This would seem to indicate that in his mind the theological notion of intention, one informed by charity and faith, is out of place in the present discussion. The circumstances are formal causes of virtue. To invoke an intention informed by faith and charity would nullify the purpose at hand: namely, to render an account of the genesis of natural virtue. Then too, in a later section of the **De bono,** he makes the statement that the natural virtues may be distinguished from the theological perfections on the basis of naturally and supernaturally orientated intentions. It seems clear, then, that some understanding of a natural intention is operative in the moral philosophy of St. Albert, a natural intention expressed by the term *cur.*

Must all the circumstances coincide in the formation of virtue, or does one suffice without the others? In answer to this problem, Albert leaves no doubt that *all* the circumstances are involved, although one or more of them may play a prediminant rôle. At this point he credits Aristotle and Pseudo-Dionysius with the following doctrine: *"virtus est ex una tota et sola causa, vitium autem omnifariam"*. Virtue results from a total convergence of all the elements or causes involved, whereas the corruption of any one of these suffices to account for evil. The wording of this statement is not only a curious amalgam of statements by two different authors; there is also a distortion in vocabulary. Dionysius had said that the good (*bonum*) is characterized by a wholeness or completeness with respect to its causes. This is consonant with Albert's own general conception of the good as a virtual whole. In the present context he ties it down to virtue which is a specific kind of goodness. In Albert's mind, then, virtue presupposes a convergence of all the circumstances.

Up to this point, Albert has analyzed the intrinsic causes of virtue; and the account is structured in terms of the principles enunciated in the preliminary metaphysical discourse. Both circumstances and *bonum in genere* are analogical varieties of goodness. *Bonum in genere,* resulting from a fusing of two relatively indeterminate principles, namely, an action and its proportionate object, is a natural instance of the good. In their real and concrete setting, circumstances inhere in the *bonum in genere* as in their subject. The same kind of affinity which generally unites act to its correlative potency obtains here as well. As formal or modal elements proportioned to the potency of the act, circumstances endow it with moral specificity. The goodness which results from this 'indivision' is the specific goodness of virtue.

At the same time, we should not forget that these two factors have been treated as *abstractions*. Since they are distinguishable aspects of the moral act, we are justified in abstracting them from their proper concrete setting in order to give each a separate and distinct consideration. In reality, however, they exist only as integrated components of the individual act.

D) *The 'Matter' of Virtue*

In his general metaphysics of the good, Albert had made it clear that any account of the genesis of goodness must also include efficient and final causation. The final cause, as an object of desire, moves the efficient cause which, in turn, moves the matter to a reception of forms. Question Four of *Tractatus* I which is devoted to an analysis of the efficient causes of virtue shows clearly that Albert is faithfully adhering to this principle. Article One of this same question, however, contains a discussion of what is called the *'materia virtutis'*. Having already treated of the *bonum in genere* which is described in terms of 'matter', one might be surprised to see the same term and problems cropping up again. As it turns out, however, the formula *'materia virtutis'* in its present context is a far more comprehensive notion than that used to describe *bonum in genere*. Furthermore, this article has been prompted by certain statements in the *Ethics* of Aristotle in which it is said that acquired virtue has to do with pleasure (*voluptas, delectationes*) and pain (*tristitia*). If such is the case, then virtue should be situated and studied in reference to these connatural passions. But since they are really the proper domain (*materia*) of fortitude and temperance, this would seem to limit the definition of moral virtue to only these two, thereby excluding at one blow prudence and justice from the moral order. Some sort of clarification is wanting.

In the formula *'materia virtutis'*, not one, but several distinguishable factors are welded together. Some understanding of the complexities involved is given by those texts in the **De bono** which most significantly contain some allusion to the term *'materia'*. It is found to embrace (a) the *materia debita,* better still, the act

itself taken at the level of *bonum in genere*. Yet over and above this, it also includes reference to (b) the agent's intention and the end, and (c) man's appetitive powers together with their concomitant feelings of pleasure and pain. At the same time, *materia virtutis* is really something completely individualized: the concrete act immersed in, and clothed by, all its moral circumstances, factors, and concomitants, and brought to bear upon a proportionate object. The formula *'materia circa quam'* is employed as an equivalent.

In the solution to Article One, Albert explains that all acts and powers of the soul are differentiated by their corresponding objects. This is no less true of virtuous actions. The proximate object of the moral act is its moving cause or terminus (*movens, finis*), and what this does is to specify the indeterminate movement of the will pervading any particular act. The element of finality—the most decisive feature in morality—prevails over this entire network. Necessarily, bare matter without reference to an end would fail to adequately differentiate human acts and their proportionate qualities. In this way, the terms *'obiectum'*, *'finis'*, *'opus'*, *'materia'*, and *'materia circa quam'* are all intended to convey the same function of determination and specification. In most cases, the end or terminus is simply the operation itself as virtuous; in the case of justice, it is a result (*operatum*) distinct from the operation. Regardless of the type, it belongs to the very nature of these objective ends to essentially determine the kind of virtue in each concrete act.

Now, our external acts are performed through bodily organs, and at the same time they are accompanied by affections or feelings (*passiones*) of pleasure and pain. These acts and their concomitant sensations issue directly from the sensible soul, that is, from the irascible and concupiscible powers of man's soul. Hence, Albert agrees that virtue may be situated *'circa passiones'* and *'circa delectationes et tristitias'*. But at the same time, such statements taken simply as they stand would not adequately define the province of virtue since they ignore the other factors involved, and especially a reference to the primary factor of the final cause. Over and above the mere notion of passion, as we have seen, one must take into account the end or object of these appetitive powers, and indeed the entire complexus, as signified by the term *'materia'*. Hence, because the specification of natural moral virtues is not arrived at merely by their reference to the passions, then by speaking analogically (*differenter*) we may say that prudence and justice are also referable to them.

'Matter of virtue', therefore, is a comprehensive formula intended to circumscribe virtue in its real and concrete setting. It is, to put it simply, a comprehensive view of the virtuous act in all its moral relations. Instead of connoting merely one aspect or facet of the moral act, it signifies rather a totality of factors or complexus. Now, it is from its nature as an integrated whole or complexus, and not from this or that particular element, that the human act receives its moral specification, i.e., virtue. In this way virtue reflects the condition of totality which characterizes the Pseudo-Dionysian theory of the good:

> . . . and blessed Dionysius agrees in Chapter Four of *Concerning the Divine Names* in saying that 'the good is constituted by a total and single cause, but evil originates omnifariously'. By this it is understood that for the reality of virtue there are required all the circumstances together with the end harmonizing with the act as it is brought to bear upon its proportionate object. For evil and vice, however, there suffices the corruption of any one of these by itself.

The formation of virtue entails all the circumstances and the end which are proportioned to the act. This is consonant with the statement of Pseudo-Dionysius, and so falls perfectly in line with the Albertinian vision of the good as something whole and complete.

E) *The Efficient Causes of Virtue*

By situating the virtuous act in a much wider context, Article One has shown that the formation of moral goodness rests upon a plurality of converging elements: the act itself, end, circumstances, the powers of man's soul, and the accompanying affections of pleasure and pain. The account of the genesis of virtue up to this point, however, has dealt only with two intrinsic causes. A complete examination must also include the active or efficient causes of morality, and the final cause. The following seven articles of Question Four are devoted to an analysis of the efficient causes of virtue. In dealing with this problem as well as the notions of free choice, voluntariness, and deliberation, Albert relies heavily upon the *Ethics* of Aristotle. The integration of this material worked out at this particular point in the **De bono** is really an innovation. In the traditional Augustinian conception of virtue with its emphasis upon the exclusively divine origin of virtue, no such causal explanation was really called for. St. Albert, however, is concerned with virtue acquired through our own natural acts, and so the inclusion of these considerations within his general doctrine of virtue is both necessary and consistent.

Five positions are suggested in Article Two which would call for a direct supernatural intervention to explain the cause of natural virtue. In his answer to the question raised, however, Albert outlines the natural setting and origin of moral virtue. It is directly and immediately caused by the exercise of human acts (*ab opere*). Within our nature lies an innate power or ability to develop these perfections. The *capacity* is innate, not the full-fledged virtue itself which must be cultivated by a repetition of acts. In the solution to Article Two, he goes on to say that this purely natural ability to generate virtue cannot be conceived as something purely material and passive. Over and above this, one must distinguish its active and immaterial components: right choice (*eligentia recta*) which is combination of right reason (*recta ratio*) and will. Right reason, Albert tells us, consists in the correct discernment of the mean to be observed in our operations. In other words, our inherent capability to perform virtuous acts ultimately stems from our faculties of reason and will. Hence, he concludes, nature is not only a material or passive cause, but in some way it is also the efficient cause of virtue.

Albert goes on to say that the efficient cause of virtue is the operation seen in its dynamic activity (*in agere*) and not simply in its physical being (*in esse*) since this substratum is really outside the moral order. A helpful analogy is that of manual labourers who develop those special limbs they use in their work to greater and stronger proportions than other men. So too in the case of virtue; its most efficacious cause (*potissima causa*) will be that immediate power of the soul which is called into play. Operations by their very nature issue in virtue. On the other hand, the bare performance of actions without a conscious attendance to the particular conditions or circumstances involved would not really be an immediate efficient cause of virtue. At most it could only be called a remote cause. As we shall see, such actions would, to a certain extent, be involuntary by reason of this ignorance. Hence, just as the formal cause of virtue requires and presupposes the material cause, so too the operation as the efficient cause of virtue, if it is to be an adequate and direct cause of the virtuous act, entails the formal cause of circumstances.

Virtue is described as being a 'potential whole'. Now, in any such whole no one part completely constitutes the whole. Rather, the first part or component is necessarily presupposed by a second, and so on. It is, as Albert says, in potency to subsequent augmentation: *semper prior materialis ad sequentem*. Hence, in the generation of virtue many distinct acts are required. From the first operation a certain disposition accrues to the soul and likewise this disposition is in potency to the superimposition of a second, and so on. In itself, a disposition lacks the stability and permanence of a virtuous habit. It is easily displaced (*facile mobile*). But by a process of moral metamorphosis, so to speak, many successive dispositions are welded into a habit. No definite and exact number of operations can be assigned to this cumulative development.

So much for the proximate efficient cause of virtue. In Albert's attempt to circumscribe this notion of efficient cause operative in the moral order, the next step is to ascertain the *remote* efficient causes. Such causes are remote because, as in the case of voluntariness or deliberation, they precede the exercise of the final human operation which itself immediately issues in the formation of virtue. In his introductory preface to this section, Albert observes that, since human operations are voluntary, then it behooves us to analyze this notion of voluntariness. This can be thrown into relief by starting with negative considerations, that is, by contrasting it to that which is involuntary. Articles Three and Four, therefore, deal with the involuntary; Article Five establishes the positive nature of voluntariness.

In the ensuing discussion, Albert relies heavily upon the doctrine of Aristotle. There are two kinds of involuntariness. Some acts are involuntary by reason of an external violence or compulsion worked upon the agent. Other acts are involuntary through ignorance. The ignorance in question is of the circumstances conditioning the act. This may also be called 'ignorance of the fact' (*ignorantia facti*) according as the deed (*factum*) is taken in its real and concrete setting, and as including the particular circumstances in which it is immersed. Once again, then, knowledge of all the circumstances is an indispensable condition of the voluntary act.

By this contrast to the kinds of involuntariness, Albert is now able to establish positively the nature of a voluntary act. Two conditions are involved: first, the moving principle of the act must be within the agent himself, and in this way it escapes the impediments of the act which is exteriorly coerced. Secondly, the agent must be aware of the particular circumstances of the action, and in this way it is opposed to involuntariness through ignorance.

The second section given over to a study of the remote causes of virtue, includes another three articles in which special consideration is devoted to the nature of choice (*prohaeresis, eligentia*), deliberation (*consilium*), and the difference between these and will. Since we are primarily concerned with virtue which is a species of the good, considerations about will and voluntariness in general are insufficient. We must know more in detail about the catenation, as it were, of the individual acts which precede the formation of virtue. Voluntary goodness (*bonum voluntarium*), which is the object of the will, lacks determination; it is the good as such, the good absolutely conceived abstracting from any particular type or instance. The particular acts of deliberation and choice which immediately issue in virtuous operations also have this good ultimately as their end, but not as their immediate and proper object. Rather, they are directly ordered to particular instances of the good, i.e., the means to the end. Moreover, in the case of deliberation, we cannot say just any means, but rather those means whose usefulness are open to question. Still, we cannot even say all debatable means, but more precisely those which we discern by reason as being helpful in the attainment of the end. We then desire what has been ascertained as useful.

Choice, then, is not simply a power belonging exclusively to the will. Just as the will compenetrates with reason, so too the element of reason or intellect is indispensable to choice.

A final and necessary characteristic of choice is that we be the masters of these actions: '*actus quorum nos domini sumus*'. In all our moral acts we are sufficient agents. In this respect, however, one must distinguish between acts and their resultant habits. Aristotle, writes Albert, has said that we are the masters of our individual operations from the beginning of the act to its completion. As to the habit or virtue generated by these acts, however, the same is not entirely true. We are the masters of habits at their inception. But since it is impossible for us to ascertain just how much of a contribution each operation makes to the formation of a habit, then we are to a certain extent 'involuntary' in their possession.

F) *The Final Cause of Virtue: Happiness*

Hitherto, Albert has discussed the material, formal and efficient causes of virtue. Even though there are indications that a treatment of the final cause of virtue was to be included in the **De bono,** no distinct question or treatise dealing with this mode of causality is to be found. The notion of *finis,* however, appears often enough in this moral treatise, and so we are able to arrive at some understanding of the meanings which Albert gives to this term.

In his preliminary metaphysics of the good, Albert had argued that the good analytically includes a reference to end: of its very nature, the good is that which is desired. The notion of end, therefore, is necessarily analogical or, if you will, as flexible and relative a notion as the good itself. Within any particular order or perspective, it always connotes that which is ultimately willed or desired. In general, writes Albert, one can distinguish two kinds of final causes: a proximate or immediate end which is intended in one act, and the remote or ultimate end intended in all, or in a series of acts. This is true both of the order of nature as well as of the moral order. In the latter, the proximate end or object would be that complexus known as the 'matter of virtue' or *materia circa quam,* the human act seen in all its dynamic complexity, which specifies and differentiates the various virtues and vices. The remote end, which is not intended merely in one act or in one virtue, is man's final end: happiness or beatitude.

Another distinction, partially overlapping the first, is that of 'end of the act' (*finis operis*) and 'end of the agent' (*finis operatis*). 'End of the act' signifies the immediate object of a particular action. In the case of *bonum in genere,* it would be the proportionate object (*debita materia*) of the act in question. In some cases, such as adultery, an act is *malum in genere,* and regardless of the agent's intention or other circumstances it can never be made good because the 'end of the act' is itself something evil. 'End of the agent', on the other hand, obviously designates the agent's motive or intention. In contrast to 'end of the act', it usually connotes a more ultimate goal. Virtue, according to Albert, may be regarded either as the 'end of the act' or the 'end of the agent' depending upon which way we choose to look at it.

Since there is no question or section in the **De bono** devoted to man's last end, it is difficult to reconstruct adequately Albert's thought on this point. Like the earlier **Tractatus de natura boni,** the **De bono** was to include such a treatment. The Preface to Question Four clearly proposes this move: after a detailed analysis of the natural virtues, we are to expect a disquisition upon "the end and perfection of virtue which is happiness." Both works, however, were abandoned in an incomplete state and so fall short of this proposed endeavor. Consequently, in the **De bono** we are left with only a few scattered and cursory remarks about this.

Whether we choose to call it happiness (*felicitas*) or something else, Albert says in one text, is not our present concern. Apparently precisions in doctrine and terminology were to be made later on. Inasmuch as it is the end, it is the absolute good (*bonum honestum*), and so something desired for its own sake. There are several statements, however, in which Albert distinguishes between happiness (*felicitas*) as that to which the virtues are essentially ordered, and 'eternal beatitude'—man's supernatural destiny—which is not possible without grace and meritorious works. *Felicitas viae,* on the other hand, is another phrase used by Albert which seems to connote that kind of happiness known or experienced by non-Christian thinkers (*philosophi*) who philosophized without the benefit of faith, and who lacked grace.

There are additional texts in the **De bono** which point to a fundamental relationship obtaining between the virtues and this concept of happiness. Happiness, we read, is a perfection but a dynamic perfection (*actus*) of the soul which is consequent upon the possession of all the perfected virtues. The presence of one complete and perfected virtue does not suffice, but rather the possession of each and every natural virtue is required in the attainment of happiness. In this respect, prudence plays an important rôle. With reference to happiness, Albert says that it enjoys a 'more excellent act' because it guides us to the *primum bonum,* God, wherein the greatest happiness is found. Nevertheless, not just prudence, but all the virtues, are essentially ordered to, and consummated in, happiness. Happiness, then, is truly the end and perfection of natural virtues in relation to which they stand as so many necessary steps or means.

The texts seem to show that Albert understood quite well the Aristotelian idea of *eudaimonia* through and in the virtuous life; but for all this, the **De bono** gives only a sketchy idea about the final end of man. In spite of this reticence, however, a significant feature of Albert's thought comes to light. It concerns his method of procedure. Happiness is that in which the virtues culminate. As so many necessary steps or means in the acquisition of happiness, their treatment would seem logically enough to precede the analysis of happiness.

IV. CONCLUSION

At this point Albert's account of the genesis of natural moral virtue terminates. The next question, Question V of *Tractatus* I, rounds out general moral considerations with an enquiry into the essence of virtue in general. The preceding articles, beginning with *bonum in genere* and ending with the passages on choice and deliberation, are clearly an attempt to render an intelligible account of the origin of the humanly acquired virtues. This undertaking is an innovation. The Augustinian definition of virtue which attributed all moral excellence to a divine infusion made such an enquiry seem superfluous. St. Albert, however, distinguishes between the order of acquired perfections and those which are divinely infused; and since the former accrue to man through his own agency, an investigation into their origin is in order.

In his account, Albert draws upon an established vocabulary; and yet his concern for methodological rigor can be seen in his program to interpret and to integrate these inherited distinctions in terms of principles enunciated in his preliminary metaphysics of the good. Thus, *bonum in genere* is a first instance of goodness grounded in the natural proportion between an act and its object. Viewed in this light, it enjoys a certain unity, but it still remains in potency to further completion and actualization through the formal determinations of circumstances. The resulting goodness is that of virtue which, as Albert demonstrates in later sections of the **De bono,** manifests itself in various modalities. In this way, *bonum in genere,* circumstances and, of course, virtue, are established as genuine though analogical varieties of goodness.

The enquiry, moreover, is *causal,* and in this way conforms to the principle established earlier by Albert that any enquiry into goodness must be framed in terms of the four Aristotelian causes. Elements traditionally included in moral treatises fall into this framework. *Bonum in genere* and circumstances emerge as the intrinsic causes of virtue. Incomplete expressions of this doctrine, to be sure, are found in Philip the Chancellor, but the consecutive and unified elaboration of this theory originates with Albert himself. For the first time too, room is made for a brief but distinctive treatment of the rôle of circumstances. A new treatise is also devoted to the efficient cause of virtue. Here the inspiration is quite evidently Aristotelian, and Albert relies heavily upon the doctrine and vocabulary of the fragmentary versions of the *Nichomachean Ethics*. The incompletion of the *De bono* robs us of a more thorough treatment of the final cause of virtue.

This whole section, indeed, exemplifies the naturalist and humanist strains in Albert's ethical theory. Critical of a univocally theocentric conception of moral worth, Albert attempted to enlarge the area of human moral efficacy by making man the responsible agent in the generation of his own natural excellences. Though a certain unresolved gap is noticeable in his conception of the physical structure of the human act in relation to its moral determinations, it is still true to say that for Albert nature, through its human potentialities, becomes a real and significant cause of moral values.

James R. Shaw (essay date 1979)

SOURCE: "Albertus Magnus and the Rise of an Empirical Approach in Medieval Philosophy and Science," in *By Things Seen: Reference and Recognition in Medieval Thought,* edited by David L. Jeffrey, University of Ottawa Press, 1979, pp. 175-85.

[*In the following excerpt, Shaw argues that Albert's works were among the first to emphasize experimentation in the biological sciences.*]

I

Insofar as it is possible to generalize meaningfully about such things, it is true that at the beginning of the thirteenth century Plato was the establishment philosopher, but at the end of the same century he was not so firmly established. At the end of the century, though Aristotle was not yet recognized as a Christian, he was not completely ostracized from the Church, and he was certainly at home in the Continental universities. This radical change was due, in part, to the efforts of Albertus Magnus.

When Albert began his commentaries on Aristotle (sometime in the 1240s) Aristotle had already been the subject of several ecclesiastical condemnations, not only papal, but also provincial and episcopal. Of course, the logical works of Aristotle were not the subject of the condemnations. The ecclesiastical authorities had long since learned to live with the parts of the *Organon* which had been known to the early Middle Ages. The *Categories* especially were used in the early cathedral schools, but the *Categories* can easily be read—and were so read—in the light of the more favored Platonic and Neoplatonic philosophy. One can still read the *Categories* as a rather analytical elaboration of the Platonic theory of Ideas.

It was this theory of ideas which from the beginning of Christianity had favorably disposed educated pagan converts to Plato. Since they only had a bit of the Platonic corpus they could not know that the theory, especially as interpreted by some Neoplatonists, plays a very small part in Plato's own thought. Nevertheless, some of the most influential Church fathers read Plato, particularly in the *Timæus*, as promoting a belief in subsistent ideas which the Fathers saw as eternal exemplars of things existing in the mind of God. Accompanying the belief in the reality of these eternal exemplars was the corresponding view that this world was but a shadow of the Real world. Platonism was also compatible with the Fathers' interpretation of Christianity. Thus the eternal χώρα of the *Timæus* was thought to be the created chaos of *Genesis* out of which God the Father had made the world. Other dialogues known either completely or in part in the early Middle Ages, such as the *Phædo, Meno,* and *Alcibiades* I, show the influences of Pythagorean mystical beliefs, and were easily appropriated to the Christianity of many early Church Fathers. Doctrines such as the complete separation of soul and body, the definition of man as a soul who uses a body, the need for purification, the eternity of the soul, were associated with Platonic philosophy and made possible the very early baptism of Plato into the faith. As Plato's philosophical views were honored, so his rather meager scientific views came to be accepted by churchmen. The views expounded in the *Timæus* about the macrocosm and the microcosm, i.e., about the universe and about man, were carefully repeated and finely elaborated upon in the hexameral literature. These treatises or homilies were commentaries on the two accounts of creation found in the Scripture. The scientific education of many people in the early Middle Ages was founded on this hexameral literature, and while the intelligentsia concentrated on many of the physical details, several of the major themes were generally adopted. In addition to the Platonic views already mentioned, another belief that emerges very clearly in the hexameral literature is the belief in the geometrical or mathematical construction of the macrocosm and the microcosm. Though for many this came down to an interest in what we might be tempted to call mystical numerology, for others, such as early astronomers or astrologers, it meant that a paradigm for true science was a kind of geometry of celestial spaces. In this kind of science empirical observations played little if any part. Such non-empirical science was easily compatible with what they knew of Plato and the little Aristotle that they possessed.

When an integral Aristotelian corpus began to be translated in Latin, however, it was seen that many of the major Platonic doctrines were repudiated by Aristotle. When, for example, the biological works were made available in the mid-thirteenth century, the schoolmen were startled to see someone who claimed, as Aristotle does in the *Generation of Animals*, that "credence must be given to observation rather than to theory, and to theory only insofar as it agrees with what is observed," or that his own earlier astronomy (which was largely an *a priori* construction) was a "conjecture" (*Parts of Animals*) and not based on observed facts. Though many of the schoolmen were startled, others were shocked and there began the long series of ecclesiastical condemnations of Aristotle.... This is something pointed out by all the histories of medieval philosophy and science. What is not generally pointed out is that most of the early condemnations, such as those of 1210, 1215, and 1231, were aimed specifically at the books of so-called natural philosophy and that the books of Aristotle with a specifically biological content were sometimes mentioned by name. It is in these books that we find the strongest statements of Aristotle's demand for empirical observations in the natural sciences, as well as the complete absence of any sort of mathematical or deductivist explanations. This is an absence which is especially noticeable when one looks at other—earlier—works of Aristotle as well as the Platonism that they knew. Though these two views, (1) the stress on the need for empirical observations in the biological sciences and (2) the implied rejection of mathematical accounts in biological investigations, were certainly not the sole reason for the many condemnations of Aristotle's works in the natural sciences, these views were inimical to the house-Platonism of the time, and yet constitute an approach which is quite typical of much of the writing of Albert the Great on the natural sciences.

II

Albert's exact date of birth is unknown, but he died in 1280 when he was more than eighty years old. Though there is uncertainty about the date of his birth and his family background, quite a bit is known about his later life and travels, since Albert himself—unlike most other scholastics—records many autobiographical details in his voluminous writings. From his birthplace in a small town on the Danube, Lauingen, between Regensberg and Ulm, he traveled to Padua for his university education. There he studied the usual arts curriculum, as well as medicine. It was not until he was over thirty years old that he joined the Dominican Order and was sent back to his native country to study in the houses of the Order there. This education consisted almost entirely of the study of Scriptures and the more famous commentaries on them. Soon after he completed his own education he became a lector himself and began a long career in his Order as an educator and administrator. Though he spent a considerable amount of the rest of his life in Germany, his duties involved much traveling, almost always on foot. These journeys were the opportunity for many observations which he minutely recorded in one work or another. In 1243 he walked to Paris from Cologne, a distance of over 300 miles, the first of many times. At the University of

Paris he took an advanced degree in theology and taught there for a short while. It was here that he first met up with something like an integral Aristotle. For, despite the many prohibitions, the Dominican library at Paris had a comparatively good collection of Aristotelian works. Albert, as he tells us explicitly in the beginning of his commentary on the *Physics,* decided that he would read and write commentaries on the entire Aristotelian corpus, because he said that it is important to make Aristotle's works "intelligible to the Latins." The entire project took Albert about twenty years and is an amazing achievement. It seems even more amazing when one realizes that the commentaries on Aristotle form only seventeen of the forty volumes in the Cologne critical edition of Albert's own work, that the actual writing had to be squeezed into a very busy schedule, and that there was great opposition to the entire project. There was some temporary opposition from within his own Order, and the early chronicles contain stories of the devil appearing to his fellow Dominicans and warning them of the dangerous project Brother Albert was about. However, the external opposition from the secular clergy and the Franciscans proved more continuous. Albert was aware of the opposition to his project and apparently thought that those opposed to it should at least read his work before they condemned it. If they did not do that much, he cared little for their opinions.

The commentaries themselves were by Albert's own design intended to be paraphrases with brief explanatory notes. However, many of the explanatory notes are not very brief and Albert adds what he calls 'digressions'. A single digression in the work *On Animals* is over three hundred pages long in the edition which was published in 1920.

The work *On Animals* was probably written over a four-year period and the actual writing of it did not begin until around 1258. There is absolutely no doubt about its authenticity and since the autograph still exists it provides a unique opportunity for examining Albert at work. The Stadler edition of it which was published 1917-1920 runs to 1598 pages of text. It was, of course, intended to be a commentary on Aristotle's biological treatises. The text shows that Albert had access to the translation of these works which was prepared by a friend and fellow Dominican, William of Moerbeke, sometime in the middle 1260s. Another earlier edition, that of Michael Scot, was also used by Albert, as was a Greek text. This work is the first of its kind, and remained a reputable, acknowledged authority for almost five hundred years. Like all pioneers, Albert left a trail of mistakes behind him; but in the period between Aristotle and the sixteenth century there is no other work which even comes close to Albert's in its attempts to provide a descriptive and experimental approach to biological phenomena.

Of course, one has to be very careful when one sees in Albert (or any other medieval author, for that matter) references to "experience" and "experiment" as well as claims about having observed some particular phenomena. In Albert's case some of the repeated statements about the need for observation should, I think, be thought of as part of his polemic against those (e.g., the "Plato" whom Albert knew) who denied the essential role of observations. Nevertheless, it is quite easy to make a case for the claim that Albert's general approach is empirical in a sense of that word which is contemporary.

To support this claim I would like to mention three aspects of Albert's writings: (1) his theoretical defense of an empirical approach against those who claimed that the divine will was a sufficient explanation of natural events; (2) his repeated references to empirical criteria in his own works on natural science; (3) his comments on sexual anatomy.

One of the strongest criticisms of an observational approach to nature was the claim that such an approach led to a denial of divine causality. In Albert's work *On the Causes and Properties of the Elements and of the Planets,* Albert raises this question in the beginning. Albert says that some men attribute the Biblical flood to God's will; he answers that he too believes that ultimately God was the cause of the flood. However, this does not mean that to attribute it to God's causality explains the phenomenon. God acts through natural causes, and it is important to seek out the *natural* causes of *natural* phenomena. And the way to do this is to make observations of particular phenomena. He ends the discussion of the question with the following comment: "It is not enough to know in terms of universals, but we seek to know each object's own peculiar characteristics, for this is the best and perfect kind of science." Though Albert thought that one must deal with the general principles of natural sciences, he stresses the necessity for including the details. This demand for concrete, specific, detailed, accurate knowledge of discrete particulars is a complete about-face from the contemporary interpretations of Plato and from much that is also in Aristotle's earlier works. It amounts to a rejection—at least for the natural sciences—of any practical interest in the subsistent ideas of Plato.

In addition to this theoretical defense of the need for observation in the natural sciences, the work *On Animals* contains many references to empirical criteria to justify a claim. This can be made clear by examining Albert's attitude to some of the ancient authorities and by noticing the phrases he uses to describe animals and their behavior. Though Albert used Pliny as a source for his work, he is doubtful of Pliny's accuracy and even observes that Pliny says many things which are quite false. Others come in for equally strong condemnation. Even Aristotle is occasionally questioned, though always diffidently.

The usual grounds on which Albert corrects some authority, and the customary verification of some claim is that he has "tested" it. "Expertus sum" or some variation on it appears over and over, especially toward the end of the work *On Animals*. Sometimes he says that he has tested it by observing some particular animal behavior, other times that he not only tested it himself but showed it to his associates, or that he has observed it many times. He many times indicates that he has himself not observed some phenomena, but is relying on the reports of others. Among those who make reports he attempts to distinguish between those who are believable and those who are not. Thus he says an associate who is trustworthy (unus de nostris sociis fide dignus) told him that large lizards, as large as the shinbone of a man, can be observed in Spain. Other times he says that a common belief is not proved, or something just has not been proved, or that it has not been proved "per experimentum." Occasionally he simply reports ("dicitur") some claim without commenting, or simply comments that he is uncertain ("an verum sit ignoratur").

Not only does Albert use expressions indicating that he has "tested" the truth of certain claims through observations, he also reports some crude experiments which he conducted in order to verify or falsify certain empirical claims. The kind of experiments were, of course, simple and crude by our standards. Thus he says that he and his associates discovered that if cicadas have their heads cut off, they will continue to make their distinctive noise. ("Experti sumus ego et mei socii quod capite amputando aliquando diu cantat in pectore sonans sicut fecit antea.") He dismissed the view that ostriches eat iron, and suggests a possible source for this erroneous belief, when he reports his own attempts to feed different bits of things to these birds. ("De hac ave dicitur quod ferrum comedat et digerat: sed ego non sum hoc expertus quia ferrum sæpius a me pluribus strutionibus obiectum comedere noluerunt. Sed ossa magna ad breves partes truncata et arida et lapides avide comederunt.") He talks about the dissection which he and his associates have done on bees and grasshoppers, and the behavior of scorpions which he submerged in olive oil. Though these are not experiments devised to test a sophisticated modern hypothesis, they are controlled attempts to empirically verify or falsify some observational claim. Thus, in addition to Albert's theoretical defense of the need for observation of particulars (against those who claimed that such interests were irreligious and inclined one to deny Divine causality) Albert's own practice of making many empirical observations shows, at the very least, his commitment to an empirical approach.

This commitment can be made even more apparent by paying close attention to what Albert has to say about sexual anatomy and physiology. There are, of course, many mistakes in Albert's treatment of these topics.

However, I think we should remind ourselves that of all areas of human structure and function, the sexual seems to be most incapable of throwing off mistaken and often quite superstitious beliefs. Even our own day (which is supposed to be one of sexual enlightenment) holds onto some absurd beliefs. Thus as recently as 1969, the coaches of the Superbowl warned the players not to have intercourse the night before the game since intercourse debilitates the body. And William Ogle, M.D., in what is an extremely well done and accurate commentary on Aristotle's *Parts of Animals,* notes that some Negroes have bones in their penises. If supposedly educated people in the 20th Century hold such beliefs, we cannot expect a 13th-Century Dominican priest to be entirely free of error on these matters. That he is comparatively free of the kind of errors that can be found, for example, in his early contemporary Constantine the African, is, I believe, a tribute to Albert's reliance on observation.

Albert's major comments on sexual anatomy and physiology are in Books 1, 15 and 22 of his work on animals; there are also many other references to sexual structure and function in the other twenty-three books of this work. The sections in Books 1 and 15 are attempted periphrastic restatements of Aristotle's views in the *Parts of Animals* and the *Generation of Animals* with the frequent digressions spoken of earlier. By Book 22, Albert has long since given up the paraphrasing-with-additions and presents a synthetic treatment of various topics with occasional references to authorities, both ancient and modern, especially to Avicenna.

Albert's treatment differs from his chief ancient authority, namely Aristotle, by the addition of empirical observations not found in Aristotle, by stressing homologies—that is, the parallels—between male and female structures and functions and by adding a "psychology of sexual arousal" not found in Aristotle. Albert differs from his early contemporary, Constantine the African, in several ways: Albert has much more detailed and accurate description of anatomy; Albert's treatment of physiology is not nearly so dependent on the four-humor theory and Galenic physiology; Albert devotes about equal space to his description of male and female—whereas in Constantine's treatise, references to the female are quite incidental; finally, Albert leaves out all mention of Constantine's dubious pharmaceutical remedies for impotence and for prolonging intercourse. I think that this omission is significant and an indication of Albert's more empirical approach, since Albert quotes Constantine by name and explicitly refers to the work *On Intercourse.* Albert also refers to the problems of sterility and impotence. He apparently even repeated a putative test for sterility which Aristotle mentions in the *Generation of Animals.* Albert claims that the sperm of a fertile male will briefly float on the surface of water and then gradually sink to the bottom in sort of viscous globs. On the other hand, the sperm of an infertile man—especially an older male—lacks the viscous, globular texture and will therefore be diffused on the surface of the water. This "test"—which, given certain qualification, happens to be the case—shows that Albert was interested in problems of sterility and the several passages where he discusses them provided the opportunity to analyze Constantine's views. However, he never mentions them; and in one place, where he refers to pharmaceutical preparations connected with sterility, he says, "All these kinds of things seem absurd to us," though Albert does say that he must study the causes of sterility since "medicine must cure them." Having noticed these passages from Albert, it seems at least probable that he left out the preparations mentioned by Constantine because he thought that they, too, were "absurd". It is well known that Albert and other 13th-century scholastics generally did not mention by name their immediate predecessors and contemporaries when they were in serious disagreement with them. Of course, it is not too difficult to show that Albert's work, from a scientific standpoint, is quite superior to that of Constantine, even though Constantine's works were required texts in the medical curriculum until long after Albert's time.

However, I think that Albert's work compares favorably with Aristotle's. Though Albert did not do the extensive dissections that Aristotle did, when the opportunity presents itself, he adds observations of his own and points out homologies that Aristotle either denied or did not mention. From a technical viewpoint, Albert is wrong about some of his homologies, but he is convinced that there are structural parallels between the male and female sexual organs. An indication of Albert's conviction about the homologies between male and female is that he uses one word for penis and clitoris (usually *virga*). He several times refers to various homologies such as when he talks about the vagina as a sort of invaginated scrotum, and about the two testicles in the male and two testicles in the female. These parallels are not stressed in Aristotle, who says, in the *History of Animals,* that the vagina is proper only to the female and the penis is proper only to the male, and the "privy parts of the female" (to use the rather Victorian phrase in the Oxford English Aristotle) are the opposite of the male's. In another place Albert notes carefully what the differences are between the structures which he parallels in these passages. For example, he says that the testicles of the male are exterior to the body and larger than those of the female which are interior.

Albert also sees a parallel in the physiology of intercourse. Albert apparently thought that Aristotle's explanation of engorgement is too simple, and Albert speaks of a special substance, *ventositas,* which he sometimes refers to as a gas and other times as a liquid. He thinks of it as a special modification of body heat, which modification is only found in the genital region. By means of this ventosity, the heat "enlarges the genital organs (of both sexes); and since there is some difference between the sexes, the male organs swell out and harden while the female organs open up and become engorged, though less so than the male organs." I should point out that his reference to "some difference" occurs after he has stressed that the differences between the sexes are mainly differences of shapes of the breasts and genital organs. Albert thinks of the differences between the sexes as "modal" and not "real".

Another interesting difference between the Aristotelian text and Albert's commentary are the additional comments he makes to verify some things Aristotle has said by referring to some observation or "experiment" Albert has made. I have already referred to Albert's description of the action of male sperm in a container of water. Albert similarly elaborates when he says that not only is the hymen broken during the first intercourse, it can also be broken by sticking one's finger through it. He adds to Aristotle's account of the ejaculation of sperm that one can produce a substance in both the male and female, which is intermediate between sperm and sweat, by slight sexual stimulation. He says that this substance is not an ejaculation but is produced in a man, for example, by the touch of a woman with whom he would like to have intercourse. According to Albert, one can also show that women have sperm. He says that the way to do this is by moving rapidly the end of the clitoris with the hand. Albert adds that thus she will feel the delight of intercourse and have an orgasm. Parenthetically, mention should be made of the fact that in Book 22, after Albert has given up paraphrasing Aristotle, he says that "Generation among men is through intercourse in which there is a mixture of the powers of the two sexes; from the male sperm which acts as the mover and from the female sperm or rather the female clear fluid as well as the menstrual blood which is the material." This passage seems to indicate that though Albert has apparently adhered to the male and female sperm view of Aristotle as well as assigning to each a different kind of causality, he believes that the two are by no means the same liquid.

Albert does not offer a "proof" that males have sperm, but he does say that the way we know that the source of the male sperm is in the testicles is that during coitus at the time of orgasm, the testicles are drawn up and hug the pecten or pubic bone so that the sperm may be expelled. This localization of the sperm apparently was a problem for Albert. In the same section as the above comment, he says that one should not be surprised if a bull is fertile right after castration: it may be the case that sperm is already in the canals of the penis itself.

I think that all of these comments—and others could be cited to the same purpose—show that Albert was committed to serious, scientific observation of things some might think are not the proper business of a 13th-century friar. As mentioned before, there were those who thought that the study of Aristotle and the adoption of an empirical outlook would lead to irreligion. Some apparently found in Albert's work the incarnation of their worst fears. The Franciscan, Roger Bacon, thought that Albert's reputation for learning had seduced the Latins and that Albert's learning was a disgrace. However, Albert's championing of Aristotle's later empirical approach caught on in some quarters. But lest these pages lead the reader to believe that Albert's empirical approach should have been in the eyes of his ecclesiastical colleagues entirely unobjectionable, let me close with one of his own summaries:

> So far we have spoken of the act of generation among animals in general. However in man, since his nature is nobler, the act of intercourse is more complex. One important difference is that humans enjoy sex more than other animals. In the human animal at the time for intercourse consciousness of a sexual form exists: thus in the male with the image of a lovable woman before the eyes of his heart, and in the female with the image of a desired man before the eyes of her heart, there arises a fierce longing for intercourse. These interior images are like the first movers toward those things which lead up to intercourse.

There follows a short passage in which Albert explains briefly how body heat is changed into the "ventosity" mentioned above, and his text continues

> . . . and when the ventosity is firm and plentiful the penis becomes almost bone-like; the penis becomes so hard that sometimes the canal through which the sperm should be ejaculated is closed off with ventosity and the sperm cannot shoot out until a moment later when the ventosity is given off.

How Albertus got his information we can only guess. But his observations clearly manifest a growing interest in the empirical.

Léonard Ducharme (essay date 1980)

SOURCE: "The Individual Human Being in Saint Albert's Earlier Writings," in *Albert the Great: Commemorative Essays,* edited by Francis J. Kovach and Robert W. Shahan, University of Oklahoma Press, 1980, pp. 131-60.

[*In the following essay, Ducharme analyzes Albert's "ambiguous and puzzling" metaphysics of individual being and dicusses in detail his borrowings from Christian faith, Aristotle, the Doctors of the Church, and Neoplatonism..*]

The self-standing value of individual beings often appears as holding little interest for philosophers and metaphysicians. Since they are mainly preoccupied with the universal and the necessary, they grant scant recognition to the singular and the contingent and often seem to explain it away. Yet uneasiness pervades many of their theories. Our thinking and our language maintain uncanny links with the modest individual things, and philosophy has never succeeded in ignoring those links for a very long period without giving rise to a reaction. In the twelfth century, the outcry shared by all opponents of "exaggerated realism" was: *Nihil est praeter individuum.* None of the lofty universals, "man," "animal," enjoys the undisputed resilience of the humble individual thing, a result of the unchallengeable fact of its being here and now, and no trick of scientific legerdemain can really obliterate that unique privilege, even in the eyes of philosophy.

Medieval authors had extra reasons to pay attention to individual material beings, and particularly to individual human persons. Because of their religious belief, they had to see every singular thing as the result of God's creation, and various accommodations of the theory of participation could not satisfy many of them, when they attempted to account for the authenticity of the individual. Still more, they had to find a way of saying how every individual human soul is immortal and how every individual human body is to resurrect. Moreover, they needed clear notions of "person" and of "individual," in order to express two dogmas of their faith, namely the Trinity of Persons in God and the union of the human and divine natures in one individual being, Christ. They also had to outline an unequivocal distinction between God's unique identity and the unquestionable identity of individual men and Angels. One can discover a medieval's vision of the individual being within those various theological contexts or within outwardly philosophical contexts (e.g. Is matter simple?), where those theological preoccupations are present.

The present essay will try to do just that, about Albert's earlier writings, his **Summa de Creaturis,** and his **Commentary on the Sentences.**

Terminology and General Description

A general presentation of the individual being is given twice in the **Commentary,** first, when Albert deals with Trinity and, second, when he considers Christ. In both instances the immediate subject of interest is found in the quest for a precise vocabulary that could be used in theology. Without being repetitious, both texts have practically the same content, and they will be summed up together.

About earthly things (*in inferioribus*) we use different words when speaking of an individual being. We say "natural thing" (*res naturae, res naturalis*), and that expression designates the individual as a well-identified thing in nature (*hoc aliquid*); first intended by nature in generation, it is also the ultimate fruit of that generation. That natural thing is a composite of matter and form, or of *quod est* and *quo est*. The word "supposit" (*suppositum*) adds to that original meaning, since it says that a natural thing stands under (*supponitur*) a common nature as incommunicable (while the common nature is communicable). Further, the natural thing, a complete being in itself, provides the accidents with the support they need to be; it is a "subject" (*subjectum*). As such it is called "substance" (*substantia*), or, in Greek, *hypostasis*. On the other hand, a given sum total of accidents can be found together only in one natural thing and identifies it among all others. So recognizable, the natural thing is called "individual" (*individuum*). Ultimately, the human individual being is called "person" (*persona*), in order to stress the fact of its absolute incommunicability; it is permeable only to the "composition" of the intellect in an affirmative proposition. There is more in that enumeration than a mere multiplicity of words; it reveals the many facets on the individual being. Albert sees an order among those terms: "natural thing" is first, and the others "add" to its meaning.

The natural thing is described as a composite of matter and form, or of *quod est* and *quo est*. The analysis of those two compositions will lead us to the comprehension of Albert's doctrine about the individual being. But two previous points must be noted. First, only the composite is truly a "something" (*hoc aliquid*); the human soul is not. The nature, common to many individuals, is not either, even if it can be called a "substance," in a secondary sense of that word; only the "natural thing" is a "first substance." Second, Albert, with many others, considered that God alone is absolutely simple, that absolute simplicity being the guaranty of his uniqueness. All created beings consist of a plurality, at least of a duality.

The compositions of matter and form and of *quod est* and *quo est* are compared with each other in a text dealing with universal hylemorphism. "Is there one matter for all creatures?" Albert says that some do admit such a common matter, and he explains how their position can be understood. Then he proceeds to propose what is evidently his personal opinion:

> If one would rather speak differently, one would say that there is not one matter for all substances, just what is said in the text quoted from Aristotle; and, according to that view, substances' composition is twofold; in some substances there is a composition of matter and form, as is the case in substances subject to generation and corruption, in which neither [matter nor form] is predicated of the composed substance. The composite, indeed, is

neither matter nor form; therefore, in such [substances], the universal which is predicated of the composite is not found in the form of the matter, but in the form of the united whole (*forma totius conjuncti*). In some [substances], on the other hand, there is no such composition, but [a composition] of *quo est* and *quod est* as Boethius says; and the *quo est* is the form of the whole, *quod est* signifies the very whole, whose form the *forma totius* is. That composition is found in substances not subject to generation and corruption, and, in them, the *formatotius* does not differ from the form of the matter, since such [substance] does not have matter. Therefore, the very whole, which is expressed by *quod est,* is not made distinct [individually] by matter, because of the same reason [viz., it does not have matter]. And, this is true mainly of spiritual substances, in which one is not to admit any other composition than that of the supposit and of the nature whose supposit it is.

The text is self-explanatory. Two preoccupations are present all through Albert's writings: to ensure that all created things are composed, God alone being simple, and, second, to maintain the possibility of universal predication. The hylemorphic composition, proper to earthly substances, answers both preoccupations, thanks to the addition of the *forma totius* to the couple matter and form. The composition of *quod est* and *quo est,* found principally (*praecipue*) in spiritual substances, performs the same functions. (The heavenly bodies, while ungenerated and incorruptible, are in a special situation.) As is often the case with medieval writers, the opposition between the two compositions, given here as radical, does not indicate that they cannot be found together in the same being, and Albert superimposes them in some of his texts; that is suggested by the "principally." Little, if anything, will be added, in the following pages, to that vision of the individual being. It is a composite, and it contains an element which makes universal predication possible. Nevertheless, the separate analysis of both compositions should help toward a better understanding of that basic idea.

Matter and Form

According to Albert's doctrine concerning the distinction between various sciences, the consideration of matter belongs to the natural philosopher, at least when matter is seen as the principle of motion. But the metaphysician is also interested in matter; metaphysics considers the first predicaments of being, and mainly the very first, substance; it will, therefore, consider matter and form as parts of substance, and of being.

Albert's version of hylemorphism is rather standard Aristotelianism, at least in the expression of its major pronouncements. Yet some elements of it sound somewhat foreign to what is still largely considered as authentic "Aristotelian" tradition. Reasons for that are

well known. Aristotle had just been discovered; he had come to the School together with commentaries and texts using him in a Neoplatonic context, and he had met with a trend of thought which was strongly influenced by Augustine, and by the Pseudo-Denis. Accommodations were unavoidable, which would, at times, modify the Philosopher's very inspiration. Aristotle's thought had its own difficulties. Some of them resulted from the extension of hylemorphism to man. Aristotle himself had changed his view of intellectual knowledge, and of the personal immortality of the human soul, after he had made that extension. While the medievals were unaware of that evolution, some of them were ill at ease with the idea of a spiritual soul being the form of a material body. The controversies about the unity or plurality of forms, about the unity of the human intellect, and about the personal immortality of the soul were looming on the horizon. On the other hand, Augustine's idea of the soul being a spiritual substance in itself, governing a body, was widely admitted, and the soul thus appeared as the true reality of man. Adopting Aristotle's vocabulary, and calling that soul the substantial form of a body did not immediately alter the "traditional" understanding of man. Since many of Albert's general affirmations about form are found in contexts where he deals immediately with the human soul, accommodations were again unavoidable, even if he affirms that the soul is not a completely independent substance.

Another difficulty arises from the fact that Albert has adopted, from Avicenna by his own recognition, a distinction between *forma partis* and *forma totius,* between the form of matter, a part of the composite with matter itself, and the form of the whole as such.

Albert's doctrine about matter has been found wanting by some historians, in comparison with what was considered as "stock Aristotelianism." For instance, the fact that he does not see matter as "pure potency" but as an incipient form, has been judged as a weakness of his hylemorphic theory. That could be true, but texts supporting that vision of matter, when explained, seem natural within Albert's general way of thinking. God alone is absolutely simple, and a matter that would be pure potency could hardly be seen as a composite. Along the same line of thinking, Albert would not say that matter, in its very substance, is totally relative to form. The only entities that have no other reality besides their very referral to another are the divine persons within Trinity, and no such entirely relative entity can be found among created things. But, Albert hastens to assure, that matter is united to form immediately, without the intervention of an intermediary link. When the theological inspiration of those accommodations is recognized, one might still be right in seeing them as "weaknesses," in reference to another approach, but Albert's conception, as a whole, is coherent and reasonably faithful to "Aristotelianism." Standard affirmations to that effect are numerous. Thus matter is not intelligible in itself, but it can be known only through its very reference to form. If one would attempt to know it as not actually united with form, one would then see it as "privation," that is, in relation to a form of which it would appear deprived. Since forms are acquired through change, matter is given as the basic substratum of the primary type of change: generation and corruption. The subject, constituted by the union of matter and form, will be the substratum of all other changes, but because of its matter. Matter is the "principle of individuation" of material beings. Other elements of Albert's idea of matter belong to natural philosophy rather than to metaphysics.

In his description of the earthly substances Albert mentioned two forms: the form of the matter (*forma partis*) and the form of the whole (*Forma totius*). The form of the matter is the source of all the perfections that are present in the matter and in the composite, giving them their *esse*. It gives them *esse* and *rationem*. Still more, the form is said to "be" the *ratio* of the common nature. *Ratio* cannot be translated; it can, at best, be explained. In this context, and in others similar to it, *ratio* can be understood as meaning the ultimate core of the reality of whatever it is said to be the *ratio,* not as isolated in itself, that would be its *esse,* but as the mind's interlocutor, mostly but not exclusively, in the epistemic dialogue; the *ratio* is the mind's objective partner, in the exchange medievals understood knowledge, and science, to be. The form gives the composite to be of a distinct nature (*esse*), and within the composite, it confers, upon matter and upon the composite itself, the capacity it possesses of its own, to be the objective associates of the mind in the knowledge undertaking (*ratio*). That interpretation seems to account for the texts where Albert says that form "gives" *esse* and *rationem*. It may appear to be wanting in reference to affirmations where form is said to "be" the *ratio* of the common nature. Those texts could be understood as stating that form, alone and by itself, provides all that is worth knowing in a thing, at least when scientific knowledge is concerned. Such an interpretation would probably be too narrow, particularly when reading Albert, not always a master of precision in his use of words. Descriptions of the manner in which form gives *esse* might provide a better insight into his vision. Form is the giver of *esse* by "producing" itself in the whole (*facit se in formato*) and, still better, its "giving" is a diffusion of itself in the whole (*suum dare est diffusio sui in formato*). Form is certainly the main element of the reality (*esse*), and of the knowability (*ratio*), but it radiates both over matter and over the composite, by the very diffusion of itself within the whole. It "is" the *ratio* of the common nature, just by being itself within the composite. One last character of the form is rather standard: it is the act of matter, and the first act of the whole.

Another affirmation needs more explaining. It has been said above that Albert considers matter to be the "principle of individuation" of the common nature, among material individual beings. According to him, form also has an influence on that distinction.

> Strictly speaking, diversity opposes identity, and identity has no other source but a substantial element, therefore, no diversity can be found anywhere but where there is a distinction (*divisio*) according to substantial forms, distinct [from one another] according to *esse* [i.e., actual conditions of realization]; division (*divisio*) occurs through matter's separation.

> In earthly things, there is the substantial form of each thing, whose act is to bound the thing to itself, and to separate it from others in which there is not actually the same numerical form; the act of that form therefore, which is to bound and separate from others, makes the thing one in itself, and is its unity.

Albert is faithful to himself. Form is the source of all perfections in a thing. Self-identity and unity are perfections, even at the level of numerically multiple beings, united under a common species; therefore, form must, in some way, be their source. In earthly substances forms are multiplied numerically because of the separation of matter into distinct portions, but, within an individual being, form is the principle of unity and cohesion, of identity, and it gives the being to be what it is, sealing in perfection, so to speak, a separation which, of itself, it would not have produced. The distinction (*divisio*) is a result of matter, but the diversity (*diversitas*) of distinct identities is attributed to form. Earthly individual beings are true beings, and their diversity is not a screen which would hide a more basic identity. Their diversity and their unity have a substantial source, their form, which is part of them and gives them unity, just as it gives them *esse* and ratio. The metaphysical authenticity of the individual earthly "natural thing" is unquestionable, and its root is found in the substantial form. Even if that form is submitted to the laws of matter; it assumes them and elevates them to perfection. Nothing is, but the individual, and it truly is, thanks to its form. With this said, and well said, the problem of the "universals" remains untouched. Albert will solve it through his theory of abstraction.

Here is a text that gives the essentials of Albert's theory of abstraction. It is the *solutio* of an article dealing with the intelligibility of the "intelligible species":

> All that is intelligible, according to its being intelligible, has that simplicity which is produced through disentanglement (*resolutionem*) from matter, and from matter's sequels (*appendicitiis*). But matter is twofold (*duplex*), viz, subject to movement, and

standing under the universal (*substans universali*). Matter which is subject to movement is not what the thing is, and it is in potency to a form which is a part of the thing and is not its whole, and, because of that, such a form is not predicated of the thing. Matter, on the other hand, which is standing under the universal, is what the thing is, because it is that particular being which is pointed to (*hoc aliquid*), and its form is the form of the whole (*forma totius*), and not the form of a part [of the same whole] (*forma partis*), and, because of that, such a form is predicated of the thing in its totality. Sequels of that [second] matter are properties and accidents, restricting and individualizing the form which is universal, [molding] that form on matter, which is particular. And, when it is said that the intellect abstracts from matter, it is understood about matter that is particular. That is evident: the intellect does not indeed abstract "man" but from this and that man, and it does not abstract "man" from the [initial] semen, nor from the [complete] body. And, in like manner, the intellect abstracts "angel" from this and that Angel, and "soul" from this and that soul, and likewise for others.

The immediate meaning of the text is simple. Abstraction has one purpose: to reach a universal content of knowledge that can be predicated of things. The substantial form, as a part of the whole, cannot be that predicable universal, even if it is a human spiritual soul; since it is individual, isolating it from its body would not result in universality. Universality is found in another form, the *forma totius,* disengaged from all individual restrictions. (Even the universal "angel" is reached through a similar process. Angels are purely spiritual beings, devoid of all matter, yet "angel" must abstract from this and that Angel, who do appear as some "second matter".) That understanding is rather common among various proponents of abstraction. What is less common is the distinction between two matters and two forms, even if Albert says that he borrowed the distinction between *forma partis* and *forma totius* from Avicenna; and is sure that it is present in Averroes, and even if, according to him, Aristotle "seems" to mention it. Those two levels of signification, in the use of the hylemorphic vocabulary, are not unrelated in Albert's mind. The matter which is part of the whole is the principle of individuation for the whole; it is easy to understand that the individual subject should be called "matter," precisely when it is considered as individual. Albert also says that the subject owes its potentiality, an attribute of materiality, to its matter.

The meaning of the distinction between the *forma partis* and the *forma totius* is less apparent and demands more explanation. Approaching the question "is *the* soul *a* substance?" Albert meets with an objection saying that if *the* soul is *a* substance, the human soul will fall under the subdivision of "incorporeal substance," while man would come under "corporeal substance." Now species coming under a subalternate genus are further

apart than species coming under a proximate genus; therefore, there would be a greater distance between a man and his soul than between a man and a donkey. The context is evidently logical, and "substance" is primarily used as a genus, with species under it. Here is Albert's answer:

> When "substance" is divided into corporeal and incorporeal, *the* soul is not considered in any way as constituted by a "difference" that would be "incorporeal," because it would then be considered as a species; but, rather, when "body" is divided into "besouled" and "unbesouled," "soul" is used as the "difference" within that division of "body," and *the* soul [of a living being] differs from that difference only in that, that under the word "soul," it is given as a natural form, which is the form of a part, namely matter, a form which is not predicated either of that part or of the whole, while, under "besouled," it is understood as a form which can be predicated of the whole; nevertheless, that form which is "difference" is abstracted from the whole, according to the potency which is in one of its parts, that is in *the* soul.

Albert adds that those considerations are logical, but he finally draws from them a conclusion that is no longer logical and brings us back to the problem of the two forms. In "besouled," a species, the difference "soul" determines the genus "body," as any specific difference does, but Albert adds that it so appears as a *forma totius*. We must then understand that a *forma totius* is the expression of a species according to its difference, and that, when predicated, it signifies the species. We must also understand that the difference "soul" is abstracted from the whole, "according to the potency that is in one of its parts, that is in the soul." The *forma partis* is the source of the *forma totius*. The soul is consistently given as an act by Albert; here, he describes it as "potency"; that is an extension. Since matter is together the source of individuation and of potentiality, whatever is individual can be called a "potency," even a form; being individual, it is not actually intelligible, and must undergo abstraction.

While the question "Is *the* soul *a* substance?" was general, the objection was raised in reference to the human soul. Here is another text where the problem of the two forms reappears about the human being. In it Albert compares the "composition" of the human and divine natures in Christ, which he calls an "improper composition," with another "composition," which he considers as first, and properly called "composition":

> The first composition, properly called composition, is that of soul and body, soul which I say to be the act of an organic physical body, having life in potency. And to that composition follows the *forma totius,* which is "man", or "humanity", if one may speak about it abstractedly; and that form is the

species in this particular individual. Indeed, form is twofold [or: there are two forms (*est duplex forma*)], namely the form of the matter, or form of a part, or of potency, and that form is the end of generation in nature, and it is a part of the thing, and such a form, the soul, is in man. There is another form, which is the *ratio* of the thing, and its whole *esse* according to the *ratio* (*secundum rationem*); and that form follows the composition of the natural form and of the natural potency, which is matter. And the Lord Jesus did have that consecutive form, because of the natural composition thanks to which he is a true man, and one *suppositum* in the human species.

The first composition of natural matter, or potency, and of natural form gives a being to be of a definite specific nature, and makes it a supposit in a species. We know that the giver is the form, radiating itself within the composite. Another form follows (*sequitur*) that first composition, the *forma totius*. That second form is "the species in this particular individual" (*species in hoc individuo particulari*), it is its *ratio* and "its whole *esse* according to [for the?] the ratio" (*secundum rationem*). The first *ratio* means again "the core of the reality of the thing." The second, in *secundum rationem,* is more intricate. It could have the same meaning and only stress the fact that what gives *esse* gives *rationem* also; but it could explicitate that the *forma totius* stands out as the whole meaning of a thing, when that thing confronts the knowing power, the reason. One thing though is clear, the *forma totius* is "the species in this particular individual" (*species in hoc individuo particulari*). The formula recalls Avicenna's distinction between nature in (of) itself (*natura secundum se*), universal nature (*natura ut universalis*), and nature as found in individuals (*natura ut in individuis*). Albert has not adopted Avicenna's theories about the "absolute essence" (*essentia absoluta*), but something of it can be found in his writings. "Species in this particular individual" is an example of that. The *forma totius* follows the first composition, because of the form of the matter, and it gives *esse* and *ratio* both to the matter and to the composite; that *esse* is called, at times, the *esse* of the essence (*esse essentiae*). Since Christ is composed of a body and of a human soul, he is a true man and a supposit in the human species; that was Albert's immediate preoccupation. But we must find in the whole text an account of Albert's vision of the individual being: it is a supposit to the specific nature. Within a particular individual, the specific nature is evidently not in a situation of universality, and abstraction will have to bring it to the state of simplicity which is proper to intelligibles, so that its latent universality be unveiled. But, following the coming of the *forma partis,* the *forma totius,* the species is present within the individual.

Two more questions deserve attention about that theory. One refers to the better wording to be used, when speaking of the *forma totius;* should one say "man" or "humanity"? In this text Albert hesitates about "humanity": "if one may talk about it abstractedly" (*si licet*). Another can arise about the relationship between the two forms. Here Albert says only that the *forma totius* "follows" the first composition of matter and form. Both questions reappear in another text, the second more explicitly.

Albert wants to establish that a resurrected man is numerically identical with the man he was before he died. One of the objections against that identity reads as follows:

> Those whose substantial form is not numerically identical are not numerically identical; but, the substantial form of a dying man, and the substantial form of that man when he resurrects are not numerically one. [. . .] The substantial form is "humanity" which perishes with death, since a dead man is no man, and a form that disappears into nothingness does not return numerically identical; as the Philosopher says, "morning's health is not evening's health."

Here is Albert's answer:

> There are two ways in which this can be answered. If we say with Avicenna that the *forma totius* is other than (*alia quam*) the *forma partis* which is the soul, since the *forma totius* is predicable, like "man" and "animal" of this and that man, then that form is signified abstractedly, even if improperly, when I say "humanity," and that form does not remain otherwise than potentially after death, in the elements of the whole, whose form it is. And, because of that form (*ratione illius formae*), the individual does not have numerical identity, but only the species [remains identical], which [species] is indifferent toward numerical identity or diversity. But from that soul completing that matter, and from that matter, it does possess numerical identity. Therefore, it does not follow that, not having the same *forma totius,* be that form the form of species, genus or *esse,* it is not numerically identical. Furthermore, it is the same species, even if its *esse* is not identical in that given individual, before and after death. [The resurrected man] is therefore numerically identical in the species with the first man, and the species is not destroyed by death but accidentally, according to the *esse* it has, following its situation in this individual.

> But if we think, with Averroes and Aristotle, that the *forma totius* is the form of the matter, distinct from it *ratione* (*ratione tamen differens*), as he [Aristotle] seems to admit it, in the seventh [book] of the First Philosophy, then it is clear that a resurrected man is numerically identical [with the previously living man] and that the form is not destroyed, [neither] in itself nor according to its *esse,* but only according to the *ratio* of its predication of the composite, since that composite is dissolved.

It is easy to understand why Albert prefers the concrete "man" over the abstract "humanity," as an expression of the *forma totius*. The *forma totius* must be predicable, and "man" predicates easily; "humanity" does not. Albert accepts "humanity" from the objection, but he considers that the expression is not proper.

The wording of the text does not help seeing Albert's position about the relationship between the two forms. The *forma totius* is given as being possibly the form of a species, of a genus, and even of *esse*. In almost all other texts it is the simple equivalent of species; here it appears as if any predicable universal can be considered as a *forma totius,* e.g., genus; the *forma totius* of *esse* could then be *ens,* which is predicable. But even in this text, out of that unique sentence, the *forma totius* is always the species; and *esse,* in all its other appearances, means the concrete manner in which the specific nature is realized: before death, after death, after resurrection. *Ratio* is given a very weak meaning in "according to the *ratio* of its predication" (*quoad rationem praedicationis de composito*), and could be translated by "point of view." The only change that befalls the *forma totius* after death is that it can no longer be predicated of the composite, since the composite is dissolved. In *"ratione illius formae," ratione* means because, but that "because" is strong, it is the very *ratio* of the form that makes the consequence necessary.

It would be useless to analyze the reasoning through which Albert shows how the resurrected man is identical with the man who had died; it does not belong to our purpose. But the two opinions about the relationships between the two forms will hold our attention. According to Albert, Avicenna says that the *forma totius* is "other" than the *forma partis,* while Averroes and Aristotle say that it is the *forma partis,* differing from it *ratione.* He could seem to lean toward that second view, for motives of theological expediency, since it offers an easier solution for his immediate problem. But, most of the time, he admits readily that he has borrowed the distinction between the two forms from Avicenna, and even here he manages to salvage the numerical identity of the resurrected man, while thinking within the Avicennian context. It would be a mistake to find in our text an opposition between a "real distinction" and a "distinction of reason," if one is to consider Albert's own position, and even Avicenna's position as Albert understands it. That this could be the immediate meaning of our text might provide the subject of a spirited debate, spirited and useless. It will be more profitable to forgo that chance and read the text together with all the others that deal with the two forms. The *forma totius* is reached by abstraction from the individualizing conditions, in which the species is found in a natural thing, and abstraction finds it in the form of the matter, seen as "potency." The two forms are "others," just as the universal is "other" than the

singular, while giving it its *esse* and its *ratio.* Anybody is free to argue that such a difference is "real" or "of reason," Albert may have done it, even if this is not the way I read the text, but little benefit would derive from that argument. There is more here than an academic discussion about the difference between the two forms, with an explanation of universal knowledge as its background, together with the solution of a theological problem. Albert is dealing with immortality and resurrection, and the form he has in mind is a spiritual human soul. That a spiritual soul is the substantial form of a body does raise very special problems no other forms would evoke. Final resurrection is an object of faith; immortality is not necessarily; but, because of Albert's view of the theological expression of faith, a whole philosophy of man is involved here, with its own difficulties. That philosophy is important in our present study. Another text will bring us back to the heart of that philosophy, since it deals directly with the conditions of an embodied spiritual soul. Again, the immediate question is theological: "Is Christ's soul submitted to suffering in its totality?"

I say that the soul is completely subject to suffering in the body. [. . .] But one must understand that two [points] are to be considered about the soul, namely that it is the nature of man, and [that it is] the principle of human activities. From the first point of view, it is considered in three ways. Some [characteristics] belong to it as substantial form, some as soul, some as it is the nature of man, precisely as man. According to its being a substantial form, it is itself the perfection of the human body. [Albert then explains that the balance (*temperamentum*) it produces in the human body between the various "elements" is superior to the balance obtained in other bodies because of their forms. Because of that, as a substantial form, it resembles the forms of heavenly bodies]. Therefore, the *ratio* of form and act in it is the highest of all (*nobilissima*). As soul, it is the act of a body, which is not only the fruit of such a balanced composition, but also having life; that is found in all organic [things], and thus it belongs to the soul to radiate various energies (*vires*) in various parts of the body. That again, the human soul possesses in the highest way. [To Albert, this is evident because of the superior beauty of human bodies, as compared with other living bodies]. Third, [the soul is considered] according to its being the nature of man as man (*ut homo est*), nature, I say, giving a man the *esse* and *rationem* of man (according to what the Philosopher says in II *De Anima,* that the soul is substance according to the *rationem,* because it gives *esse* and *rationem* to the besouled body). And so, the rational soul, considered as [the] nature [of man], must necessarily have something more than a [mere] form, and more than a [mere] soul. And that is what a certain philosopher says: that it must have, flowing from it, some energies that are linked to organs, because it is a form giving *esse* as a nature [does], and other [energies] that are not linked [to organs];

these [last energies] are related to energies that are linked [to organs], inasmuch as they receive their species from them, and they are related to separate substances, inasmuch as they participate of their light. And that is what the Philosopher says: the noble soul has three operations, viz., divine, animal, and intellectual. So considered, the whole of a soul united [to a body] shares into the sufferings [of its body]. Soul is also to be considered as being the principle of human activities, and seen as such, it is not necessary that it shares in its totality, the [body's] suffering, because some of its energies may be [occupied] in the contemplation of eternals, and some others submitted to passivities proper to bodies.

The immediate question is theological, and it touches the reality of Incarnation. Is Christ a true man, and, during his Passion, did he suffer as completely as any other human being would have? The question was debated, and, at the beginning of his *solutio,* Albert recalls that a certain abbot had said, in a sermon, that Christ's soul had not suffered in its "superior part"; but the Parisian university of Masters had condemned him as heretical. Albert's argumentation comes to this: Christ has suffered, just like any other man would have. But, in all men, the human soul is capable of a "divine" activity, the contemplations of "eternals"; that contemplation is not hampered, even if the soul shares completely in the body's torture, and the beatitude that follows that contemplation does not oppose total human suffering. That idea of the soul owes nothing to faith, since it is found in Aristotle.

In order to establish that, Albert sums up his whole philosophy of the human soul. That soul is a true substantial form; it is even superior to all other forms; it is also an authentic soul, the act of a body; again, it is superior to all other souls. But it is also the "nature" of man as man; it gives a man the *esse* and the *ratio* of man; and, so considered, it appears as man's very "substance." Now, since it is rational, it is more than a mere form, and more than a mere soul. Albert, quoting an unnamed philosopher, goes on to say that, while some of that soul's resources of activity are linked to an organic support, others are not. The latter are indeed related to the former, since they receive their "species" from them, but they are also akin to separate substances and share some of the light which is proper to them. And so, the human soul, in most of its activities, is entirely involved with its body, but, its "divine" activity, the contemplation of eternals, is not impeded because of that involvement: its species may come from functions that are bound to a bodily organ, but its "light" is of a different order.

All that leads to the conclusion that Albert sees the human soul as enjoying a certain degree of freedom toward its body. The human soul does perform all its functions as a form and as a soul; it even does it better than other forms and other souls, but it is more than a mere form or soul. In his answer to an objection, Albert uses the vocabulary of the argument and calls the soul an "intelligence," an obvious reference to the "intelligences" of Neoplatonism; as an "intelligence," it is very close to separate substances, and its "divine" activity is not engulfed in its body.

That immediate solution of a theological problem concurs with Albert's general philosophy of man. A rigid application of the hylemorphic theory to man raises serious difficulties, and not only for a Christian believer. Aristotle had changed his mind about the immortality of the soul, and about intellectual knowledge, after he had extended that theory to human beings. Albert went the other way, and softened the hylemorphic theory, by introducing into it, with Avicenna, elements of Neoplatonism. He does see the soul as a form, but the idea of "perfection" attracts him, and comparing the soul to a "pilot" appears as appropriate: the soul is a perfection in itself, besides, and even before, being the form of a body. By some of its "parts," the two intellects, which are not attached to organic parts of the body, it is one of the "intelligences," the separate substances. And again, those accommodations are not to be attributed exclusively to Albert's theological preoccupations, even if those preoccupations should not be disregarded. Albert really sees man in this manner. It is then natural that he should consider the soul as the "substance," the "nature" of man.

Within that general perspective some points of Albert's doctrine find a very natural meaning. For instance, the human soul is a true *forma partis,* but it possesses some of the attributes of the *forma totius,* or better, the *forma totius* owes all that it is to the soul. Being just a part, the soul cannot be predicated of the whole, and, as such, it is "other" than the predicable *forma totius.* But abstraction will reach the *forma totius* just by disengaging the human soul, the "nature," the "substance" of man, from the individuating conditions it would not have caused by itself, even if it consecrates them in perfection and unity. Individualized or universal, the *ratio* of man is always the same, and ultimately, the soul "is" the *ratio* of the common nature, of the "species in this particular individual," it gives it its *esse.* While analyzing the texts, one after the other, discretion seemed to be imperative on that matter. The overall impression that remains, after they have all been read, is clear. The human soul "is" the *ratio* of the human nature.

Yet Albert tries to maintain a balance between two extremes. The soul is the *ratio* of the human nature in the individual man, but Albert is very consistent in his affirmations about it being only a part of the living composite. The human soul is independent from its body, it will subsist after its dissolution in death, but that independence is not total, and Albert refuses to see the soul as a concrete being, a *hoc aliquid.* "In its very nature (*secundum naturam*) it depends on its body, even if it could be without it. But I do well concede that its [the soul's] perfection is not altogether (*omino*) complete without its body." Even Albert's most fervent admirers must admit that his philosophy of man is ambiguous.

His philosophy of the individual being is also puzzling. The individual being is extolled: it alone is a "natural thing," a "something," a "substance" in the complete sense of the word; the soul is not, and the common nature is not either. But the individual being is declared unintelligible. Intelligibility is reached together with simplicity, and abstraction will have to disengage a universal *forma totius* from the complexity of individuating elements in order to reach intelligibility. So that the unique individual being appears as the "Great Unknown" in Albert's philosophy. The *forma totius* is the "species in that particular individual," and Albert often repeats: "The species is the whole *esse* of individual things" (*species est totum esse individuorum*). The individual thing is the Great Unknown, because, in its very individuality, it is uninteresting; its whole meaningful reality is found in the species present in it, as in a container.

The manner in which Albert's philosophy of the individual being is both ambiguous and puzzling, is typically medieval; the fact that it be both is not.

Quod Est-Quo Est (Esse)

The first description we have read of the "natural thing" said that it is composed of matter and form, or of *quod est* and *quo est,* the latter composition being found principally in spiritual substances. Throughout Albert's earlier writings that is the first meaning of that composition. (It does happen, though, that the material subject, composed of matter and form, is called a *quod est* while the *forma totius* is given as a *quo est.*) Albert did not admit universal hylemorphism. In the text from the **Summa,** where the description of the individual being is found, he first presents the opinion of those who do admit it and gives the reasons why they do. He then adds: "If one would rather speak differently," and offers what is evidently his own opinion. The **Commentary** is more affirmative.

> that there is matter, unless "matter" is given a very broad and improper meaning.

His main reason is that "philosophers do not speak of matter, unless they refer to the subject of a privation." Further in the text he repeats that, according to Boethius and "all philosophers," the *ratio* of potency is not identical in the potential element present in spiritual substances, and in matter. But there is potency in spiritual substances, and that explains "unless 'matter' is

given a very broad and improper meaning." Besides potency, created substances also have other common characteristics, e.g., to stand under a form and to support it. It is necessary, therefore, to find a "substance" common to all of them. But that "substance" should be called *fundamentum* rather than matter, since, because of the *ratio* of potency, "matter" would be said equivocally of them all. Albert might be more lenient toward "material." In the **Summa,** already facing the fact that there is potentiality in spiritual substances, he would concede that their potency could be called "material," since "material" says less (*minus dicit*) than "matter." Potency, in spiritual substances, has some of the properties found in matter: it "receives," it "does not reduce itself to act, but is reduced to act by another"; that potency, in spiritual substances, has its source in the *quod est.* He adds: "therefore in matter," a concession he will reject in the **Commentary.** I do not believe that this is sufficient to admit an evolution about that question. Matter is often given as the prototype of all "potencies," and that is enough to explain what looks like a concession, in the answer to an objection, particularly in an article whose *solutio* begins with a presentation of the opinion held by the supporters of universal hylemorphism. Albert did understand their stand, but we may accept as an expression of his true mind, even in the **Summa,** the affirmation of the **Commentary:** "It has always been my opinion that Angels are composed of essential parts, but not of matter and form." Albert's leniency in the **Summa,** as compared with his more uncompromising stand in the **Commentary,** may have come from a different understanding of the "philosophers." In the **Commentary** he simply rejects the word "matter" when he speaks about Angels, because Boethius and all philosophers do not speak of matter unless they want to explain "privation," and the *ratio* of potency is different in spiritual substances from what it is in material beings. While writing the **Summa,** he had read them differently:

> Philosophers give "matter" and "form" a broad meaning. And that is apparent in the 3rd [book] of the *De Anima,* where the Philosopher says: Because, as in any nature, other is the matter in each genus, which is potency in all of them, and other is the cause, the efficient [agent] [. . .].

Albert then explains that this is the reason why philosophers do admit a passive and an active potencies in spiritual beings. But he adds that, even if some philosophers use the hylemorphic vocabulary, strictly speaking (*proprie*), *quod est* and *esse* are better than "matter" and "form."

Albert had inherited the vocabulary of *quod est* and *quo est* from Boethius, as he acknowledges it himself. Boethius said *esse* rather than *quo est,* and Albert does the same at times, as in the text just quoted above, but, very often, he says *quo est,* a practice widely followed by *Doctores,* according to him. The origin of that vocabulary is well known. *Quod est* had long been the only available Latin translation for the Greek *to on,* before the Latins, reluctantly indeed, coined and accepted *ens. Esse* translated *einai,* and, in Boethius, it had all the nuances of Aristotle's *einai.* That vocabulary was to be used, later on, within the context of the controversy about the distinction between essence and existence. Albert himself was to yield to that usage in the **Summa theologiae.** No texts from the **Summa de Creaturis** or from the **Commentary** can be understood as referring to that controversy; Albert does not yet even think about it. He follows Boethius. Later on, under Avicenna's influence, he will change his views, and modify the meaning of his vocabulary.

The general meaning of *quod est* is presented early in the **Summa.** Albert, in order to justify one of Aristotle's definitions of matter, explains some elements of the Philosopher's vocabulary. Here is how he understood *quod est,* as he had probably found it where *quod est* translated *to on:*

> By *hoc quod est,* he [Aristotle] understands the *ratio* of subsistence (*rationem subsistentiae*) a composed substance has from the composition of matter and form. Thus, *quod est* is identical with "what is being now" (*quod nunc est*) in nature.

Quod est means "what is being now," the actual, individual being. Albert himself explains the "ratio of subsistence." It is the *ratio* of actual presence in nature a substance has, from the composition of matter and form: *quod est* is the equivalent of "what is now in nature," a being, being now.

That general meaning has been given a more specific use in the duality of *quod est* and *quo est,* in order to explain how created spiritual substances are composed, even if they do not consist of matter and form. In that specific usage, *quod est* is the concrete subject, and *quo est* is the equivalent of the *forma totius* of the material substances. But the original general meaning is not entirely lost, and Albert often writes "in the thing that is [now]" (*in eo quod est*). That general meaning of the duality of *quod est* and *quo est* is known to us, and we have already read it in the text where the "natural thing" was described. Here is another text where it is further explained. Albert uses the *quod est* and *quo est* duality more frequently when he speaks of Angels. He also advocates it when he wants to establish that the human soul is not simple. That is the question here: "Is the soul composed in its substance (*secundum substantiam*)?"

> I agree—that the soul is essentially composed, but not [that it is composed] of matter and form.

He then repeats the reasons why he does not admit universal hylemorphism. He goes on:

But Doctors say that it is composed of *quod est* and *quo est;* and, then, *quod est* differs from matter, like a supposit from its potency to the form under which it is (*cui supponitur*). That *quod est* is a "something" that can be predicated of the thing that is (*de eo quod est*). *Quo est,* on the other hand, is not found in our Author, Boethius says *esse.* That is the essence, according to the act it has in the thing that is (*in eo quod est*), that is in "this something" (*hoc aliquid*), or in this "supposit." So that, in such [substances], the individuation of *esse* comes from the properties following the *quod est* itself, inasmuch as it is something revealing itself here and now to the intellect. I say that the soul is composed of those [two elements], and so are Angels.

Because of that, *quo est* differs from *a* form, since *a* form is separable, and it is the form of a part (*forma partis*) which is matter; but *quo est* or *esse* is not separated from what is (*eo quod est*), and it is a *forma totius,* that says the whole *esse* of the *quod est,* by way of a formal *esse,* the *esse* of the species in this individual, in conformity with what Boethius says: the species is the whole *esse* of individuals. Whatever is after the species is part of the individuating [elements].

The general meaning of the text is clear, even if it is intricately woven. Doctors who do not admit universal hylemorphism follow Boethius and substitute *quod est* and *quo est* (*esse*) to matter and form, in order to explain the soul's composition. But that substitution is not to be understood as a mere duplication; it is a parallel, and just that. All that can be said of matter cannot be repeated about the *quod est,* nor what is said of the form, be said of the *quo est.*

The *quod est* differs from matter as does the subject from its potentiality to its form. The "like" is to be understood as denoting a parallel, not a similarity. In material things the subject owes its potentiality to its matter, and it is different from that matter, which in turn differs from its potentiality. Not having matter, the spiritual supposits owe to themselves a potentiality from which they differ. The *quod est* can be predicated of the very thing that is; matter cannot. (Another text will help make this clearer.)

The *quo est,* the *esse* is the essence, according to the act it has in the *quod est.* Essence appears here openly as "beingness," giving *esse,* being, to the thing that is.

Spiritual substances, having no matter (Albert thinks of the Angels he is about to mention, not of the human souls he is presently discussing), must be individuated by themselves. Human souls are individually multiplied under the human species, because of their bodies. Angels are distinct from one another, as subsisting species under a genus; each of them is a personal being.

Here Albert admits ignorance: the differences causing that multiplicity are hidden from us.

The duality of *quod est* and *quo est* fulfils one primary function. It expresses that all created substances are composed, even spiritual substances devoid of matter. God only is absolutely simple. Albert presents that composition in a comparison with the composition of matter and form but insists that this comparison expresses a parallelism, not an absolute identity. Such is the unvarying meaning of the composition of *quod est* and *quo est* throughout his earlier writings. Piling up more texts where that view is repeated, even with minor variations, would be no more than a very scholarly exercise in futility.

Some particular points may be of interest. The parallel between the two compositions helps understand the distinction between the soul's two "parts," the active and the passive intellects:

> The active intellect is a part of the soul. We have said above that the diversity of properties and potencies of the soul flow from the diversity of the principles entering the composition of the soul, which are *quod est* and *quo est,* or act and potency if those [last two] terms are understood in a broadened way. And, because of that, we say that the active intellect is a part of the soul, flowing from that through which [the soul] is (*quo est*), or act, the passive intellect is a part of the soul, flowing from what the soul is (*quod est*), or potency.

Albert takes advantage of the grammatical flexibility of the expressions *quod est* and *quo est,* and, doing this, he reveals the ultimate meaning of that "composition," the composition of an individual subject with its common nature. His *quod est* must, very often, be translated by "the" *quod est,* and his *quo est* by "the" *quo est,* since they are given as two parts of a composition. *Quod est* really means "something that is" [what it is], thanks to the *esse* giving it to be [what it is]. That *esse* is primarily formal, essential. But since matter and form, the matter and the substantial form of earthly beings, are the first instances of "act" and "potency," Albert finds it necessary to guard against too close a comparison, and he points out that the meaning of the two words must be broadened, when they are used to describe the *quo est* and the *quod est* as parts of a spiritual substance.

There is another point which it is important to remember: the parallel between the two compositions is to be understood just as that, a parallel. Matter is not predicable of the supposit; *quod est* is:

> If one asks how that [composition] must be "worded" (*significari*), it is to be said, following what Aristotle says in the first [book] of the *De coelo et mundo:* "When I say 'this heaven,' I say matter, when I say

'heaven,' I say form." Similarly, when I say "this Angel" or "that soul," I say the supposit, when I say "Angel" or "soul," I say the nature whose [that Angel or that soul] is the supposit. And, therefore, in these, and *quod est* and *quo est* are predicated of the supposit.

Again Albert refers primarily to the immediate meaning of *quod est* in *id quod est;* that is why I have omitted "the" before *quod est* and *quo est. Id quod est* means "what it is." Albert just wants to salvage predicative propositions like "Sortes is what he is," and "Raphael is what he is" (*est id quod est*). What is truly predicable is the expression *id quod est,* not "the" *quod est,* the individual supposit. We know that, as far as predication is concerned, the *quo est* and the *forma partis* are in the same situation. They are predicable, provided one uses a concrete term, such as "man," rather than an abstract term, such as "humanity."

One last text will hold our attention. It sums up most of what we have read about the *quod est-quo est* duality, and it will bring us back to the conclusion we had reached, after studying the hylemorphic composition of the individual being. The question is: "Is truth (*veritas*) simple, and unchangeable (*incommutabilis*)"?

> Truth is a form that is first in its genus, just as goodness, unity and entity, even though there is an order among those as has already been said, and, therefore, I do not believe that any of those [first forms] are composed of *quod est* and *quo est,* inasmuch as *quod est* expresses something being in itself (*aliquid ens in se*), in which *esse* is diffused, which [*esse*] is the act of the essence. But I do well concede that truth contains in itself many elements of intellection (*plures intellectus*), because it contains indirectly (*oblique*) the understanding of essence (*intellectum essentiae*), as [the understanding] of that to which a form belongs (*ut cujus est*), and [besides that] it has its own proper understanding (*intellectum*). And therefore, it does not equal God's simplicity. And, I believe similarly, that the same must be said about any form that is first in its genus.

Whenever the problem of simplicity arises, Albert's first preoccupation is to ensure that anything, even a notion, is seen as consisting of a duality, God alone being absolutely simple. So he finds a duality of understanding within the meaning of "truth," which, later on, he will list among the "first notions" (*primae intentiones*). Those first notions are no equals; there is an order among them: "essence" is first, and it stands as an exception. When it is used as meaning the pure and simple understanding of being, it signifies "simple essence," and *Qui est,* as a name, is proper to God. "Truth" is not absolutely simple in its significative content; it means "essence," adding to it its own proper "form." Within that complex signification "essence" appears as some sort of a "subject" having the quality expressed by "truth" (*ut cujus est*). But Albert does not believe (*non credo*) that that duality can be considered as one of *quod est* and *quo est,* because of the meaning of *quod est.* A *quod est* is a subject, and a true subject is a "something that is." "Essence" may appear as the subject of the form signified in "truth," but "essence" is an abstract term; it designates a form, not a something." The "understanding of essence" (*intellectus essentiae*) is found, as designating a subject, in "being" (*ens*), a concrete term, and not in the abstract "essence" (*essentia*).

Later on in the same article Albert refuses to accept one of Augustine's affirmations, according to which one could say: "truth is true"—"goodness is good," etc. The detailed argumentation is rather intricate, and would add nothing to what we already know about the duality of *quod est* and *quo est.* It comes to this: Albert does not admit, even at the level of the first notions, that a concrete predicate can be attributed to an abstract subject (*concretum ponitur de abstracto*). Even as an adjective "true" means "something having truth," and "truth," not signifying "something," cannot be said to be "having truth." Augustine's authority notwithstanding, "oneness" (*unitas*) does not signify a "something" but a form, a form giving a subject to be one, to have unity. Albert prefers the concrete "man" over the abstract "humanity" as an expression of the *forma totius,* because it can be predicated of the concrete subject. But only because of that reason. Strictly speaking, "truth is true" means nothing more than "truth is truth." Brought down to its basic meaning, the concrete term means only the form expressed by the abstract word.

And here we find the ultimate meaning of Albert's frequent affirmation: "The species is the whole reality of individuals" (*Species est totum esse individuorum*). That meaning is absolute. The concrete term "man" may well be a more suitable predicate than the abstract "humanity," but, even if it designates a concrete subject more appropriately than its equivalent abstract "humanity," it does not mean more than the species, which is signified directly by "humanity"; individual characters are left unsaid by the concrete, just as completely as they are by the abstract term. This is why "truth is true" means nothing more than the tautological "truth is truth." "Truth" is a form, and it is the form that gives something having it, being its subject, to be true, and to be knowable as "true." "Essence" is a form; "humanity" is a form. It is the form that gives *esse* and *rationem,* because the form (*forma totius, quo est*) is the "species in the individual," and the species is the whole reality of individuals. Albert prefers the concrete terms for the sake of sound predication, not because they would reveal the secrets of individuality more completely than the abstract words.

Conclusion, Historical and Philosophical

From a historian's point of view, Albert's philosophy of the individual human being appears as thoroughly medieval. It evolves within the boundaries set by the Christian faith; it borrows from Aristotle, from Doctors of the Church, and from Neoplatonism. It stands on guard for God's simplicity, it compares individual human beings and human souls with Angels and with celestial bodies, in the perspectives created by the simultaneous admission of hylemorphism and of the hierarchy of "separate intelligences." It is also typical of the first part of the thirteenth century, when it had become apparent that official prohibitions, even backed up by threats of excommunication, would not stop Aristotle's invasion of the School, not only at the Faculty of Arts, but also at the Faculty of Theology. Albert belonged to the group of Masters who were aware not only that Aristotle would not be avoided but also that he was offering theologians an admirable philosophical instrument. As Gilson has demonstrated, Albert did not see clearly that Avicenna's Aristotelianism was quite different from Aristotle's doctrine. He read the Philosopher with Avicenna's eyes, but he wanted to make the Philosopher readable for all. But, at the end of this essay, I feel very free to say that one must be interested in medieval thought to read a detailed presentation of Albert's philosophy of the individual being.

Yet all historians and all philosophers must learn a lesson from Albert. Philosophical thinking had developed and flourished within very concrete historical conditions before Albert, it did the same in Albert's time, and it has continued to do the same since the thirteenth century. That period had characteristics of its own; they have disappeared. Other periods have offered philosophy other resources, and they have also tried to keep it within their own frontiers. Historians must record it, and philosophers should be aware of it and fear any orthodoxy. Philosophers cannot be foreign to their times, but they must try to keep philosophy reasonably free from incidental restrictions that would become too stringent. Some of the philosophical "dogmas" of the thirteenth century were legacies from pagan antiquity, they have been handed down to philosophers of following ages, and they have remained "dogmas" long after religious dogmas lost their dominion over philosophy.

Saving God's simplicity is not our main preoccupation any longer; we leave Angels to theologians, and space science has mercifully relieved us of any concern about "celestial bodies." Individual human beings are still a part of our lot, and I think that they should constitute the main part of it. We should pay more than tepid lip service to them. Albert had adopted the very ancient idea that philosophy, being a science, had to deal with the universal, the species, in individuals, of course, but mainly in itself. Philosophers all through the ages have cherished that view of philosophy as the most precious gem of their collective heritage. The history of philosophy knows of many blazing holocausts offered before the altar of universality. Philosophy must salvage its universal scientific character with the same obstinacy Albert displayed in his defense of God's simplicity and of the personal immortality of human souls. What cannot be universal and necessary we should forget, or entrust to belief. Philosophy can be a science only if it is universal and deals in necessity, and philosophy will be a science, or it will be no longer.

Seldom, in long whiles, timid efforts were made in order to recognize the unique value of individual beings, and to say it philosophically. The Middle Ages have witnessed some of those efforts, other periods have, and our own does too. But, very often, those undertakings come to the same conclusion: the individual being is unique and admirable, but it is philosophically unexpressible. Confronted with that dead end, philosophy either turns back to the more manageable universals or it admits its defeat, and philosophers have written thousands of admirable pages lamenting the tragically heroic fate of philosophy, the sighing, sobbing, "impossible science."

We might possibly do better. We could leave "science" to the specialists of various sciences, and while listening to them, since we are far away from Albert's four elements, philosophize, trying to lend the voice of reason to human beings and to the unexpressible individual human being. Reason is not necessarily "scientific." Our philosophical congresses would never attract half the attention the media keep for terrorist attacks, wars, sex scandals, or sports events. But they might be more lively, and human beings might listen to us, if we, as philosophers, would speak in defense of the innocent individual victims of senseless violence, in defense of the individual human beings, distorted into zombies in our sex shows and in our boxing rings. The shortcomings in Albert's philosophy of the individual human being do not set him apart among philosophers; having read about them might help us recognize our own shortcomings and loathe them.

Pearl Kibre (essay date 1980)

SOURCE: "Albertus Magnus on Alchemy," in *Albertus Magnus and the Sciences: Commemorative Essays 1980,* edited by James A. Weisheipl, Pontifical Institute of Mediaeval Studies, 1980, pp. 187-202.

[In the following essay, Kibre focuses on Albert's association with the Medieval science of alchemy and on several apocryphal alchemical texts sometimes attributed to him.]

Albert's interest in alchemy, the art, in his words, that best imitates nature, is revealed in the references to the subject in his authentic writings, particularly the **Book of Minerals (*Liber mineralium*)**, his **Commentary on Aristotle's Meteorology,** and other tracts. He had investigated and made a careful study of the subject in the course of his inquiry into the nature of metals, for guidance in which he had sought in vain for the treatise by Aristotle. Without that guide, he was, as he reported, obliged to follow his own devices and to set down what he had learned from philosophers or from his own observations. He had thus at one time become a wanderer, journeying to mining districts to "learn by observation the nature of metals." "And," he stated, "for the same reason I have inquired into the transmutations of metals in alchemy, so as to learn from this, too, something of their nature and accidental properties." Among the names of the philosophers to whom Albert had turned were some of the principal authorities on alchemy, current in the twelfth and thirteenth centuries in Latin translation from the Arabic, comprising chiefly Hermes, Callisthenes (that is Khālid ibn Yazīd), Democritus, Gigil, and Avicenna. Of these Albert relied principally upon Avicenna (Abū 'Alī Sīnā, 980-1037), utilizing both the apocryphal and authentic tracts appearing under his name. Albert thus cited a section of the supposititious Avicenna tract *On the Soul in the Art of Alchemy (De anima in arte alchemiae)*, one of the most influential of the alchemical tracts upholding the possibility of the transmutation of metals. Naming the work, "The Physical [Stone]," Albert referred only to the final section, the "Exposition of the physical stone by Avicenna to his son Aboali (Abū 'Alī)," which circulated as a separate tract. In addition, Albert utilized the so-called "Letter of Avicenna to King Hasen (or Hazen), the philosopher," in which is set forth the view commonly held in the thirteenth century, that quick-silver (mercury or *argentum vivum*) and sulphur are the materials of all metals and hence basic to the alchemical process. This so-called newer theory of the components of metals, Albert contrasted with the older view expressed by Aristotle, that metals are formed from a subtle fatty moisture (*humidum unctuosm subtile*) combined with a subtle earthy tincture.

In addition, in his search for "immediate efficient causes existing in the material and transmuting it," Albert continued his critical evaluation of so-called authorities and the operations of alchemy. He characterized as erroneous the opinions of Hermes, Empedocles, Democritus, "and some of those in our own time who are practitioners of alchemy," and who are concerned with the generation of stones. These authorities mistakenly suggested, he reported, that all stones are produced by accident without a specific cause for their production, whereas the true or productive cause, Albert asserted, is a "mineralizing power." The making of stones, he concluded, by the operations of the alchemists is even more difficult than the making of metals. Albert had earlier noted that just as metals are formed from water congealed by intense cold and dryness, just so is the work of the alchemists performed, that is by separating and sublimating the humidity of iron. Moreover, in the operations of alchemy, he noted that mercury (*argentum vivum* or quicksilver) that is dried by much burning and mixture with sulphur will be coagulated by heating in a furnace with green wood.

Albert next went on to draw attention to the discussions unfavorable to the transmutation of metals which he attributed also to Avicenna, wrongly citing the "Letter to King Hasen" as the source rather than Avicenna's tract on minerals, *De congelatione et conglutinatione lapidum*. In this treatise which has been shown to be an excerpt from the authentic book *Book of the Healing of the Soul* (Kitāb al-shifā'), Avicenna disparaged the "claims of the alchemists" whose "power to bring about any true change of metallic species," he denied with the words, "Let practitioners of alchemy know that they cannot transmute one form of metal into another, but only make something similar. . . . As to the rest, that is that specific differences between metals may be removed by some clever method, I [Avicenna] do not believe . . . possible." Albert went on also to paraphrase Avicenna's further statement (in the "Letter to King Hasen on Alchemy") that he had examined the books of those upholding "the art of transmutation" and had found them devoid of the reasoning that belongs to every art. He had found most of their content nonsensical. Moreover, an examination of the books of those who opposed the art of transmutation revealed that their arguments and reasoning were too feeble and trivial to destroy belief in the art. Hence it appeared prudent to add that "specific forms are not transmuted, unless perhaps they are first reduced to prime matter (*materia prima*) . . . and then, with the help of art, developed into the specific form of the metal" desired. Albert then added to Avicenna's stricture his own criticism of the alchemical literature: "I have examined many alchemical books, and I have found them lacking in [evidence] and proof." They merely rely "on authorities," and conceal "their meaning in metaphorical language, which has never been the custom in philosophy. Avicenna is the only one who seems to approach a rational [attempt], though a meagre one, towards the solution of the above question, enlightening us a little."

Albert, moreover, was critical of opinions expressed by alchemists which did not coincide with those of Aristotle or Avicenna. He cited the undeniable but nonspecific statement that metals are made up of all the elements, expounded in the *Book of Alchemy,* by Hermes, the mythical or legendary founder of alchemy, who was probably of Greek origin but was known to the west through Latin translations from the Arabic. Albert also characterized as "the strangest and most ridiculous of all opinions, the one that held that '*calx* (quicklime) and *lixivium* (lye) are the material of all metals'," an opinion he attributed to Democritus. Albert asserted that this statement about the material of metals does not fit the fact, and is incorrect. He further referred to the opinion "that alchemy is the science that confers upon inferior metals the nobility of the superior ones," expressed by Callisthenes; and to the attempt "to prove that fused ash is the material of metals," reported in the book of *Secrets* by "Gigil of Moorish Seville," which Albert noted, "has now been returned to the Spaniards." Albert went on to characterize Gigil's arguments in defense of his assertion as "unconvincing and stupid," and "Gigil himself" as "a mechanic and not a philosopher" who relied too greatly upon "the mechanical operations of alchemy" and was guilty of making incorrect assertions regarding natural science.

Albert next drew attention to the procedures and objectives of the alchemists. "The experience of the alchemists," he asserted, "confronts us with two grave doubts. For they seem to say that the specific form of gold is the sole form of metals and that every other metal is incomplete—that is, it is on the way toward the specific form of gold, just as anything incomplete is on the way toward perfection." Thus metals lacking the form of gold in their material "must be diseased." Hence to cure or remove these diseases the alchemists endeavor "to find a medicine which they call the *elixir,* by means of which they may remove the diseases of metals . . ." and bring "out the specific form of gold." Continuing further with the use of the *elixir* and the transmutation of metals, Albert asserted that since "it is found by experience that by means of the *elixir* copper turns to silver, and lead to gold, and iron likewise to silver," the alchemists erroneously conclude "that the specific form of all metals is one and the same, but the diseases of the material are many," an opinion with which Albert would not concur. He went on rather to discuss the means, that is the use by the alchemists of "calcination, sublimation, distillation, and other operations," to induce the *elixir* to penetrate into the material of metals, and hence possibly "to destroy the specific forms of metals that originally were in the material. The material that remains can then with the help of the alchemical art be reduced to another specific form, just as seeds are helped by ploughing and sowing or [as] nature is helped by the efforts of the physician." This explanation, Albert noted, was not acceptable to "Hermes and Gigil, and Empedocles and almost all that group of alchemists," who appeared to defend the "stranger" principle "that in any metal whatever there are several specific forms and natures, including one that is occult and one that is manifest." Albert himself had earlier expressed his opinion that in the case of the "experiments which the alchemists bring forward," to establish the validity of their conclusions, they do not offer enough proof.

Albert then went on further to compare the procedure of the skillful alchemists with that of the skillful physicians, and also to enlarge upon his theory of nature's role. The skillful physicians, he asserted, "by means of cleansing remedies clear out the corrupt or easily corruptible matter that is preventing good health—the end which physicians have in mind. In doing so, they strengthen and aid the power of nature, directing it to bringing about natural health. [Good] health will [thus] be produced by nature, as the efficient cause; and also by art as the means and instrument." The skillful alchemists also proceed similarly in transmuting metals. They first cleanse thoroughly the mercury or quicksilver and sulphur, the constituents of metals; then, when this is done, "they strengthen the elemental and celestial powers in the material, according to the proportions of the mixture in the metal that they intend to produce." Thus "nature itself performs the work, and not art, except as the instrument, aiding and hastening the process." "The alchemists appear, in this manner, to produce and make real gold and real silver, since the elemental and celestial powers can produce in artificial vessels, if they are formed like those in nature, whatever they produce in natural vessels. Hence "whatever nature produces by the heat of the sun and stars, art also produces by the heat of fire, provided the fire is tempered so as not to be stronger than the self-moving formative power in the metals." The inclusion of the "stars" as an agency influencing chemical operations is further exemplified in Albert's assertion in his *De causis elementorum* that "when skilled alchemists work during the waxing of the moon, they produce purer metals and stones." Albert also referred to the introduction by Hermes of the association of the seven planets with the seven metals so that the substitution of the names of the planets for the metals, such as *sol* for gold, *luna* for silver, and so on, became common practice. In general, Albert noted, "of all the operations of alchemy, the best is that which begins in the same way as nature," that is "with the cleansing of sulphur by boiling and sublimation, and the cleansing of quicksilver, and the thorough mixing of these with the material of metal; for in these by their powers, the specific form of every metal is induced." Moreover, the alchemist proceeds by destroying "one substance by removing its specific form, and with the help of what is in the material producing the specific form of another [substance]."

Although Albert recognized in the above directions the theoretical validity of the alchemical process he was obliged to admit that he had never seen it successfully carried to completion. He thus stated that "we have rarely or never found an alchemist, as we have said, who [could] perform the whole [process]." It is true that "One of them may indeed produce with the yellow *elixir* the color of gold," and with "the white *elixir*, a color similar to silver"; and "may endeavor to make the color remain fast when it is placed in the fire and

has penetrated the entire metal just as a spiritual substance is put into the material of a medicine." He may by this operation induce a yellow color, while at the same time "leaving the substance of the metal unchanged." Such operators Albert denounced as "deceivers." Without doubt they are deceivers . . . since they do not make real gold and real silver." And yet most alchemists follow this practice in whole or in part. "For this reason I have had tests made on some alchemical gold, and likewise silver, that came into my possession, and it endured six or seven firings, but then, all at once, on further firing, it was consumed and lost and reduced to a sort of dross."

In accord, moreover, with his view that the aim of a natural scientist is not merely to accept the statements of others, but rather to make an effort to observe the phenomena at first hand, Albert supplemented the knowledge of alchemy that he had derived from past authorities in his reading of books on medicine and alchemy, with the results of his own observations and experiences. From his visits to mining districts, metal workshops, and alchemical laboratories, he had acquired a practical acquaintance with the nature of metals by a direct observation of processes in nature. "I have learned," he explained, "by what I have seen with my own eyes, that a vein flowing from a single source was in one part pure gold, and in another silver. . . ." And "[from what] miners and smeltermen have told me . . . [that] what artisans have learned by experience is also the practice of alchemists who, if they work with nature, transform the specific form of one metal into another." Furthermore, from visits to laboratories, in all probability in Cologne and Paris, Albert reported on the results of his inquiries into "the transmutation of metals in the art called alchemy" which he had directed to contemporary workers in the field, that is the "alchemists of our time," whose names he does not reveal. He referred to alchemical experiments which showed that watery moisture is easily converted into vapour, and to the use of the alembic. He noted that minerals that seem to be intermediate between stones and metals are important reagents in alchemy since they may be influenced by laboratory treatment. And he added, "On these substances depends most of the science of those who endeavor to convert one [metal] into another." He had further reported on operations similar to those of the alchemists, such as drying of mercury by frequent burning and mixture with sulphur or when placed in a hot furnace with green wood," or of the forming of metals "from water congealed by intense coldness and dryness." And he also went on to note in his exposition of the alchemical art, which as earlier noted he had termed the best imitator of nature, that of the two major constituents, sulphur is known as the father and quicksilver as the mother, "as the writers on alchemy metaphorically" suggest. Moreover, he drew attention to the fact that since in alchemy there is no better way of proceeding than with the yellow *elixir* made with sulphur, the alchemists have observed that there is an unctuousness in sulphur so intensely active in burning that it burns all metals, and in burning blackens everything on which it is cast. Hence, the alchemists recommend that the sulphur be washed in acid solutions and that it be cooked until no more yellow liquid comes forth. These solutions may then be sublimed until all the unctuousness capable of burning has been removed, and there remains only as much subtle unctuousness as can endure the fire without being reduced to ash. This is, Albert added, "expressly stated by the authorities, Avicenna, Hermes and many others, who are men of great experience in the nature of metals." Albert had also noted unskilled alchemists at work in the digestion or boiling by moist heat of the earthiness in the moisture in metals.

The foregoing details regarding Albert's concern with alchemy provide convincing evidence of his interest in the subject. They also demonstrate Albert's belief in the possibility of the transmutation of metals, although he judged the process to be very difficult and beset with the errors and imitations of imposters. "For [as quoted by Partington] alchemical gold does not gladden the heart like the real gold, and is more [easily] consumed by fire, yet transformation may really be produced by exspoliation of properties by alchemical operations, as Avicenna teaches." Albert's desire to explore the entire matter of the possible transmutation of metals as thoroughly as possible is further exemplified by his study of the principal authorities and direct observation of alchemical procedures in laboratories as well as by association with contemporary alchemists whose names he does not provide. However, there appears to be a dearth of contemporary evidence to attest that Albert himself was considered an adept alchemist or that he engaged in or performed the alchemical processes he describes. He appears rather to have been an acute observer, an onlooker, but not an active participant in the laboratory experiments.

Despite the lack of contemporary and specific evidence of Albert's direct participation in alchemical laboratory procedures, his fame and repute as a skilled alchemist became manifest not long after his death. By the mid-fourteenth century he is mentioned in catalogues as author of an alchemical tract and is credited with having had as a disciple in this art, Roger Bacon, the English schoolman. Nor did this repute diminish in the fifteenth and sixteenth centuries. In a collection of Stowe manuscripts, Hugh of England named Albert as one of the several authorities in the field. This fame, whether deserved or not, appears to have motivated the attachment to Albert's name of some twenty-eight or more tracts on alchemy. They appear in manuscripts dating from the close of the thirteenth century with the major number in the late fourteenth or fifteenth century. How much of this literary output can be attributed to the common practice in the Middle Ages of attaching to such treatises the names of prominent churchmen in order to give them respectability and insure their acceptance cannot be determined. Nor does the explanation that Albert was confused with a chemist who lived at Cologne, provided by Naudé in his "Apology for all Great Personages Who Have Been Falsely Suspected of Magic," seem adequate. What does appear clear is the fact that for the most part the alchemical tracts bearing Albert's name as author reflect, in keeping with Albert's authentic writings, an active interest in not only the philosophical bases of the alchemical art but also in its practical and experimental aspects.

The individual alchemical treatises that appeared under Albert's name have elsewhere been enumerated and analyzed briefly together with the manuscripts and printed editions in which they are found. Hence it will perhaps suffice here merely to draw attention first to some general characteristics of the tracts and second, to choose some examples for more specific comparison with the information contained in Albert's authentic works. In general the treatises are free from the mystifying and allegorical features upon which Albert himself in the *Book of Minerals* had cast aspersion as characteristic of alchemical tracts. In this respect the imprint of Albert's didactic method, noteworthy for clarity of expression and systematic arrangement, was strong enough to influence those who professed to write under his name. As in Albert's exposition to his confreres of the Aristotelian scientific corpus, the professed purpose of the authors of the alchemical tracts, in the majority of cases, was to explain to their readers in as simplified a fashion as was necessary for their understanding, the art of alchemy, its theory and practice.

The above features are exemplified specifically in the *Little Book of Alchemy* (*Libellus de alchimia* or *Semita recta*), the tract most consistently attributed to Albert and extant in manuscripts dating from the close of the thirteenth century. The clear, concise, and well ordered account of alchemy contained in this tract resembles Albert's treatment of other topics of natural science in his authentic works. It also provides an excellent introduction to the alchemical art of the late thirteenth and fourteenth centuries. The author is particularly concerned with making known to his confreres, the aims, accoutrements and processes of alchemists and the alchemical art. His instructions are detailed and even repetitious in character. They are, moreover, together with the frequent cautions and admonitions, largely practical in nature. Yet, true to the professed author's ecclesiastical calling, the work opens with the phrase from Ecclesiasticus: "All wisdom is from the Lord God." However, despite the fact that the suggestions contained in the tract are largely practical in nature and might perhaps have emanated from Albert, the author's style, beginning with the introduction, differs pointedly from that of Albert in his authentic works.

For example, the introductory phrases contain the author's stated conviction that he has found what he was seeking; not, however, (in his words) "by my own knowledge, but by the grace of the Holy Spirit. Therefore, since I discerned and understood what was *beyond nature,* I began to watch more diligently in decoctions and sublimations, in solutions and distillations, in cerations and calcinations and coagulations of alchemy and in many other labors until I found possible the transmutation into gold and silver, which is better than the natural [metal] in every testing and malleation." This does not coincide with Albert's view in the ***Book of Minerals***. There he had expressed his belief that while the transmutation of baser metals into gold was theoretically possible, it had not so far been accomplished by the alchemists; also that while the alchemists were able to produce a metal similar to gold, their product was inferior to natural gold or silver and did not stand the accepted test for gold. Moreover, while the author of the *Little Book of Alchemy* looked "beyond nature," Albert had repeatedly stipulated that the observation of nature and natural processes provided the best guide.

Yet despite these essential differences it appears evident that the author of the *Little Book of Alchemy* was acquainted with Albert's work, or at least utilized similar sources. He repeated from Avicenna's *Congelatio* the phrase which he mistakenly attributed to Aristotle, "Let the masters of alchemy know that the species of things cannot be changed," and the accompanying statement, here also attributed to Aristotle, "I do not believe that metals can be transmuted unless they are reduced to prime matter, that is purified of their own corruption by roasting in the fire." Only then is transmutation possible.

The treatise itself also has some interesting features. Among these are the enumeration of possible errors and the list of specific precepts to guide those undertaking the enterprise. For example, attention is drawn to the fact that some were incapable of carrying out certain sublimations "because they failed to grasp the fundamentals"; "others because they used porous vessels." Also, in the precepts, the first provided that "the worker in this art must be silent and secretive and reveal his secret to no one"; and the eighth "that no one should begin operations without plenty of funds . . . for if he should . . . lack funds for expenses then he will lose the material and everything." Contributing further to the practical nature of the tract are the descriptions of the various utensils, furnaces, ovens, and flasks; then the spirits: quicksilver, sulphur, orpiment, and sal ammoniac; and finally the *elixir* or *fermentum,* the medicine or philosophers' stone capable of transmuting baser metals into gold and silver.

Another even more practical tract, the *Alkimia minor,* is attributed in the manuscripts to "Brother Albert of Cologne of the Order of Preaching Friars." Best described, perhaps, as a laboratory manual, it has directions for the preparation of chemical substances, for the dyeing of metals red or white, that is the transmutation into gold or silver, and for the preparation of the *elixir* or medicine, the transmuting agent. Like the *Little Book of Alchemy* or *Semita recta,* of which it seems to include abstracts, the *Alkimia minor* appears to have been in circulation by the mid-fourteenth century, although no manuscripts of the text earlier than the fifteenth century have been located so far. However, the tract is listed with the same opening words among the books contained in a collection of alchemical treatises of the early fourteenth century. The text itself gives no indication of the date of composition, although the chemical knowledge coincides with that of similar writings of the thirteenth and fourteenth centuries. The tract provides details of laboratory procedure and of apparatus and utensils. The directions are simple and straightforward with no attempt to mystify. Yet, the work does conform to the common practice of assigning names of planets to the minerals, and it also makes use of the term medicine as a synonym for *elixir,* the transmuting agent. Similarly, the use of "to redden" (*ad rubeum*) or "to whiten" (*ad album*) for the gold or silver making recipes can be found. An explanation for the use of these terms is given in the ***Book of Minerals***. Many of the chemical substances utilized were already described in such works as the ***Book of Minerals*** and the *Little Book of Alchemy.* In general, the *Alkimia minor* is characterized by a total lack of attention to theory; the emphasis is on actual procedure and practice. Many of the processes listed, such as sublimation and distillation, for example, are common to pharmacy as well; and there is great variety in the laboratory apparatus. Included were furnaces, the baker's oven (*furnus panis*), and the furnace of reverberation, the dung bath, marble slab, alembics, aludel, recipient (*ampulla*), and various kinds of jars, flasks, and vessels; earthen, copper, and glass, closed or open; a descensory, that is a vessel or retort used in distillation by descent, and pestles of iron or wood, as well as a mallet or hammer.

A further tract attributed to Albertus Magnus for which there are no fourteenth-century manuscripts extant but which is named in the same fourteenth-century alchemical miscellany as the *Alkimia minor,* is that entitled "On the hidden things of Nature" (*De occultis naturae*). This treatise provides a survey of the various alchemical doctrines set forth by alchemical authorities chiefly of Arabic origin. The work bears only a slight resemblance to the other alchemical tracts ascribed to Albertus Magnus. It professes to have been written in response to a request by a reverend father, addressed in the course of the work. Unlike either the *Semita recta* or the *Alkimia minor,* with which it is frequently found in the manuscripts, the *De occultis naturae* relates more to the theoretical side of alchemy than to the practical although both aspects are covered. The author has utilized a large number of writers with the intention, he informs us, of making it unnecessary for the reader to consult them further since their principal doctrines will have been transferred in briefer form to the present compendium. In general the treatise appears to resemble more the alchemical writings of the fourteenth rather than those of the thirteenth century in its predilection for alchemical jargon, allegorical devices, and mystical phraseology.

Of the remaining alchemical treatises appearing under Albert's name, it may suffice to note here two further examples. The tract *On Alchemy* (*De alchimia*) which appears not to have been available before the fifteenth century, bears a close relationship with the **Book of Minerals** in several of the arguments presented and in the discussion regarding alchemy. It is distinguishable from the *Little Book on Alchemy* (*Libellus de alchimia* or *Semita recta*) by the opening words: "Callisthenes one of the earlier founders of our art after Hermes. . . ." In addition to Callisthenes, the author names other authorities similar to those included in Albert's discussion in the **Book of Minerals,** such as Hermes, and Avicenna. In addition he names Geber Hispanus instead of Gigil and attributes to him the statement with some verbal changes, that Albert expresses as his own, in the **Book of Minerals,** namely that he has examined certain alchemical books and has found them to be without distinction and with their intention hidden under the guise of allegory. The author here also follows the current practice of using the names of the seven planets as synonyms for the metals, a practice that Albert attributed to Hermes. But he fails to repeat here the references to the influence of the heavens in the alchemical process found in the **Book of Minerals**. On the other hand he follows Albert's emphasis upon the principle that alchemy imitates nature and hence that it is necessary to observe carefully and closely natural processes.

The other tract attributed to Albert that we would note here, namely the *Compound of Compounds* (*Compositum de compositis*) attracted attention in the fifteenth to seventeenth centuries when it was translated into French and English. However, the text in the late manuscripts resembles closely that found without Albert's name as author in a fourteenth-century manuscript at Edinburgh. In that text the work is said to have been collected and promulgated by masters at Paris in the year 1331. However, in the later manuscripts at Paris and the Vatican it is clearly attributed to Albertus Magnus. In the course of the work reference is made to "our *Book on Minerals*" which is suggestive of Albert. There are included in the tract discussions on the theory of alchemy along with practical recipes for the preparation of vermillion and of white sublimate.

St. Albert writing; from an etching of the Nazarene School.

Of the remaining alchemical treatises appearing under Albert's name, none, with the exception of those that are also ascribed to other authors as well, appeared before the fifteenth century. Although the relation of these alchemical texts to Albert is tenuous to say the least, they do attest to his repute as an adept alchemist in the decades and centuries following his death.

Nicholas H. Steneck (essay date 1980)

SOURCE: "Albert on the Psychology of Sense Perception," in *Albertus Magnus and the Sciences: Commemorative Essays 1980*, edited by James A. Weisheipl, Pontifical Institute of Mediaeval Studies, 1980, pp. 263-90.

[*In the following essay, Steneck explores Albert's theory of sense perception, arguing that it typifies the general level of scientific understanding in the field at the time.*]

By the mid-fourteenth century, when the anonymous *Tractatus ad libros Aristotelis . . .* was copied, most Latin writers in the scholastic tradition held in common a conceptualization of sense perception that served well the needs of natural philosophers, theologians, and physicians alike. While there was debate about the fine details of this conceptualization, its basic outline was clearly understood by all involved. Two centuries earlier, when Adelard of Bath wrote his well-known *Quaestiones naturales,* the situation was quite the reverse. Numerous ancient teachings on sense perception were known in part, but no single theory was available to tie these teachings together and provide a common ground upon which further debate could take place. In the events that transpired between these two stages in the history of psychology one figure that stands out above all others as playing a major role is undoubtedly Albert the Great.

The development of the psychology of sense perception between the twelfth and fourteenth centuries is evident in a comparison of the writings of Adelard with the assumptions that are implicit . . . in the *Tractatus ad libros Aristotelis.* Adelard clearly was working within the general framework of the ancient tradition of sense perception when he wrote:

> whatever operation of this sort the mind performs in the body, it performs with a certain amount of assistance from the body and this is done one way in the brain in another in the heart and in yet another in the other members [i.e., in the senses].

But Adelard was not aware of most of the details of the ancient theories that lay behind this framework. The highly organized, almost mechanistic view of the body that was so familiar to the author of the *Tractatus,* the view that tied the five external senses to the brain by connecting nerves and then localized a number of internal senses (usually four or five) in the cells of the brain, had yet to find its way into the Latin West through the writings of Aristotle and his commentators. Since Albert played an important role in bringing these works to the attention of his contemporaries, it should come as no surprise that by virtue of this role he became an important figure in the history of the psychology of sense perception.

That Albert did play an important role in the development of the scholastic theory of sense perception was widely recognized by fourteenth-century contemporaries of the anonymous author of the *Tractatus.* In their discussions of the actions and localization of the senses, Albert's name is the only contemporary one (post 1200) mentioned with any frequency and with an authority equal to that of the ancients. Even though he

may not have been the first writer to sort through the newly translated works of Aristotle, Avicenna, Averroës, and others with an eye toward elucidating and systematizing their thoughts, he was clearly the author quoted (and presumably read) when a weighty opinion was needed to settle a dispute among these authorities. The reason for this is not difficult to understand. The comprehensiveness of Albert's discussion of sense perception in the *Summa de creaturis* and later works far exceeded that of other thirteenth-century writers and made them an ideal introduction to the topic at hand. For our purposes they provide as well an entry into the scientific thought of this important scholastic.

The hundreds of folios that Albert devoted to the problem of sense perception make the task of summarizing his thoughts on this subject a difficult one. However, over the course of his lifetime his psychology of sense perception seems to have changed very little; the basic description set out early in his career in the *Summa de creaturis* is followed fairly closely in his commentary on *De anima* and the *Parva naturalia* and is implicit in *De animalibus* and miscellaneous references to the senses in works not devoted strictly to science. As a result, his earliest major treatment of sense perception in the *Summa* is in general a good guide to this aspect of his thought, and it will be focused upon first. Thereafter, the later works will be drawn upon to help round out Albert's views on sense perception and place them very briefly into an overall epistemological and methodological framework. This latter discussion is designed to explain in part how Albert, and other scholastics, could spend so much time discussing how the senses functioned while still falling far short of developing a rigorous psychology of sense perception.

A. *Summa de creaturis*

For Albert, as indeed for most scholastics, the topic of sense perception was most commonly broached within discussions of the soul and its powers. The soul, which is one in substance and the active form of the body, moves the body in many ways. It does so not because it consists of several individual souls or a number of substances—one soul is not responsible for sense perception and another for reason—but because the one soul of the body exerts its actions in different ways (called powers of the soul) in the many parts of the body. Or conversely, the parts of the body can be said to pervert or corrupt the activities of the soul in different ways, thereby accounting for its many powers. Just as an old man who receives (*accipiat*) the eye of a young man will see like a young man (*sicut juvenis*), so too the remaining senses and even the rational soul will act differently depending on the organs of their activity.

Given this general definition of the soul and its powers, the investigation of sense perception very rapidly came to focus on four basic issues: the precise definition of the sense (power of the soul) under consideration, its organ, its mode of action, and the medium or media that are responsible for initiating its activity. Definition clearly established which of the powers of the soul was being discussed; the question of organ established a proper part of the body for each power to act through; the discussion of actions explained how each power actually acts through its organ; and the discussion of medium tied the actions of the senses to external stimuli. Except for a few general questions, Albert's discussion of these issues, which proceeds sense by sense, comprises the psychological portions of the *Summa*.

i. The Definitions of the Senses

Albert's classification of the senses has led to a great deal of controversy among modern scholars regarding his consistency. I have dealt with this issue elsewhere and endeavored to show that the apparent inconsistencies that previous scholars have pointed to in his works involve differences in his use of terms and not in his overall conceptualization of sense perception. Throughout his writings Albert remains faithful to his particular understanding of the Greco-Islamic tradition he received, as described initially in the *Summa*. According to this tradition the actions or powers of the sensitive soul can be divided into two major subgroupings, the external and the internal senses, with the former including the five proper senses—vision, hearing, smell, taste, and touch—and the latter three, four, or five internal powers, depending on the authority followed. (Albert discusses five such powers in the *Summa:* common sense, imagination, phantasy, estimation, and memory.) The distinction being pointed to here is the distinction between those senses (the external senses) that have the capacity to sense only that which is proper to them alone (their proper sensibles) and those (the internal senses) that respond in one way or another to information received from many senses.

The fact that each of the five external senses was assumed to have a proper object or objects that it alone can perceive and that each was assumed to reside in a proper organ provided sufficient information to establish suitable definitions for them. Thus Albert at one point defines vision as the power that has its seat of activity in the eye (*visus sit vis ordinata in oculo*), taste the power that is limited to the nerve that covers the surface of the tongue (*diffinitus a nervo expanso in superficie linguae*), and so on for the other senses. Similarly, vision can be defined as the sense that perceives color, hearing the sense that perceives sound, smell the sense that perceives odor, and so on for taste and touch. This much was fairly evident. Few commentators who dealt with the external senses had trouble defining each of the five commonly assumed ones.

However, the fact that suitable definitions could be established for five of the external senses did not end the problem of definition. If other organs or sensibles exist, beyond those associated with vision, hearing, smell, taste, and touch, then it might be possible to argue that there are other senses that need to be defined. Albert resolves this issue by demonstrating that animals need only five external senses and therefore there are no additional ones. The senses serve two functions: they preserve the being of the living creature (*ad esse*), and they allow it to survive in some semblance of comfort (*ad bene esse*). For preserving the being alone the living creature needs to grow (*ad esse constituendo*), which requires touch, or simply to survive (*ad esse conservando*), which requires taste. To preserve well-being, sense is needed either to regulate eating (*secundum regimen in cibo*), which requires smell, or to pursue progressive motion (*secundum regimen in motu processivo*). The latter encompasses both direct and circular motion, which require vision and hearing respectively. Since these are the only senses that are necessary and since nature provides only that which is necessary, it can safely be argued (*posset probare*) that there are only five external senses.

Having established that there are five and only five external senses Albert turned next to a related problem, their order. When faced with several entities in a single larger grouping, the scholastic mind frequently attempted to arrange these entities in a hierarchy, to establish a first sense and a last sense among the external senses. Since, according to Albert, this order can be established in at least two ways, the first and last among the senses differs. If the senses are judged on the basis of their capacity to contribute to one of the most fundamental properties of an animal, its power to sense, then touch is of primary importance. Touch is the only sense that animals cannot live without. Since "in the destruction of touch the animal is destroyed and this is not so for the other senses, namely for hearing, vision, smell, and taste," touch constitutes the foundation (*fundamentum*) of the other senses. If, however, the senses are ordered not in terms of what actually makes an animal an animal (*in constituendo animal*) but in terms of the primary function of the sensitive soul, cognition (*secundum . . . rationem cognitionis*), then vision is first and touch last. We receive more information through vision than the other senses, followed by hearing, smell, taste, and touch. How the senses are ordered depends, therefore, on the criteria that are used for ordering.

The internal senses, like the external senses, were sometimes defined by reference to either the object or organ of their activity. However, since the internal senses all reside in one organ, the brain, and seem not to receive distinct stimuli, definition via object and organ did not produce a very precise understanding of their division.

For example, on the basis of the object of perception Albert notes that one internal sense (internal by virtue of the fact that it resides within the brain), the common sense, apprehends through things that are external to the brain (*apprehensiva deforis*), while the remaining four senses (imagination, estimation, phantasy, and memory) apprehend through things that are within the brain (*apprehensiva deintus*). But this distinction does not do justice to the many senses that reside within the brain. As a consequence, Albert tends initially to accept the fivefold classification of Avicenna (common sense, imagination, phantasy, estimation, and memory) and waits to distinguish them more precisely from one another on the basis of their actions, as will be discussed in the next section.

ii. The Acts of the Senses

Since sense perception, within the framework of an Aristotelian epistemology, must of necessity be initiated by the actions of external objects, the senses, as recipients of these actions, were commonly understood to be passive powers. "It must be said, in accordance with the pronouncements of all the philosophers, that 'sense' is a passive power and that it is said to be acted upon." However, as passive powers the senses do not undergo physical, form-matter transformations. If they did, the action of the form of light on the eye would change it to light, which clearly does not happen. In sense perception, "there is no physical alteration in the soul" (*in anima nulla est alteratio physica*). Therefore, the act of sensing can be described as the senses being acted upon but not being acted upon by the forms of objects *per se*. Instead, the senses are acted upon by the represeresentatives of the objects, called sensible species, which convey the active intention of the object and not the form of the object itself to the senses. When this happens the senses, as passive powers, receive (*accipit*) these intentions and perception takes place.

Although there is no physical alternation of the senses during perception, sense perception is a physical process. Moreover, it is only when the soul and body are in proper harmony with their sensible species that sense perception takes place. Such harmony is established through three successive activities: first, the power of the soul is joined with its organ; thereafter, its disposition is established through the activity of the animal spirit and the natural heat and harmony of the organ (*dispositio fit per spiritum animalem et calorem naturalem et harmoniam organi*); and finally, the sensible *species* are received (*quando vero habet speciem sensibilem*). At this last stage, the passive power of the soul apprehends its proper object and the act of perception is completed (*tunc est potentia completa per actum*).

The grounding of the passive action of each of the senses in one organ not only establishes the mecha-

nism through which sense perception takes place but also the object that each of the senses is able to perceive. Unlike the intellect, which is able to receive all intelligibles (*potest recipere omnia intelligibilia*) because it does not operate through an organ, the senses, whose organs are not made to receive all sensibles (*organum suum non est fabricatum ad naturam omnium sensibilium*), receive only those sensibles that are proper to them, their proper sensibles. This is why the eye receives only color and not sound or smell or some other sensible, and so on for the other senses. In sum, it is the nature of a sense, as determined by the soul acting through and being influenced by the potency of its organs, that determines its actions. The nature of the eye is to perceive color, and vision, which is the proper action that the sensitive soul exerts through the eye, is the action of the eye.

The coincidence of sense and proper sensible serves one additional function besides confining particular pieces of information to particular senses. The coincidence of sense and proper sensible provides the assurance in the chain of cognition from object to intellect that the information that is perceived by the senses is correct. A sense acting in accordance with its proper sensible does not err (*non contingit errare*). It may err with regard to information that is not within the bounds of its proper sensible, such as when the sense of vision attempts to determine the composition of a particular color (*circa compositionem colorum*), but it does not err when it perceives the information that pertains strictly to its proper sensible—that the colored body is red or green and so on. To this extent, sense cognition can be said to be true and accurate.

Having set out this general framework for understanding the acts of the senses, the specific details that Albert relates for each one, particularly for the external senses, are fairly straightforward. The act of vision is to receive the sensible species of color, the act of hearing to receive the sensible species of sound, and so on for taste, smell, and touch. Nonetheless, there is always room for subsequent debate and questioning.

In his discussion of vision Albert launches into a lengthy recapitulation of past opinions, particularly those of al-Farābī (Averroës) in **De sensu et sensato** and Avicenna in **De anima,** which discussion prompts him to append a detailed analysis of a problem that had long currency in discussions of vision, the problem of extra- versus intromission theories of vision.

A full assessment of the act of hearing rests on an understanding of the exact location of its organ, as will be discussed in the next section. As to the object of hearing, sound, Albert queries whether or not it comes to the ear very rapidly (*subito*), as does light. He concludes that it does only if that which produces the sound is very close, thus making the time of transmission imperceptibly small. Otherwise, hearing requires time (*percipitur tempore*).

Clarifying the act of smell leads Albert to question whether or not different animals can smell the same odor differently. Since odors initiate the act of smell, it would seem that the same odor would produce the same act in all animals. This obvious inconsistency—some animals can smell better than others—is resolved by pointing out that since the organ of smell is closely associated with the brain and since the brains of animals differ in their dispositions, animals smell differently. The sensible species of smell are able to act upon the dry brain of some animals much more easily than the wet, cold brain of humans, and consequently these animals have better senses of smell.

Finally, the definition of the acts of taste and touch depends upon resolution of the problem of whether they comprise one sense or two. It was sometimes suggested that they do not comprise two separate senses since they seem to have the same objects (hot, cold, wet, and dry) and are at times in the same organ—we both feel and taste with our tongue. However, since the act of taste is to judge flavors (*judicium saporum*) and the act of touch to judge that which can be felt (*tangibilium judicium*), they are, Albert concludes, two separate senses.

The simple data received directly from proper sensibles accounts for only a small portion of the information that is eventually known about an object. Moreover, since each of the senses apprehends only its own proper sensible, none is able to compound this information with information received in other senses and form a composite image of an object: that a particular tree is green, has the smell of pine, and so on. Consequently, Aristotle and most of his commentators argued in favor of the existence of a common sense to receive species from the external senses and form them into a composite image of the object. Having formed this composite image, common sense then has the capacity to compare the composite image of one object with that of another and reach comparative judgments about two objects: that one object is sweeter or whiter than another object. Thereafter the sensibles species received from the five external senses are passed from the common sense to the imagination, the second internal sense, where they are stored for future reference or further transmitted to phantasy, estimation, and memory, the three remaining internal senses.

The fact that imagination stores the images of things in their absence means that an entirely new type of sensitive action begins, the internally apprehensive action. From this point on in the cognitive process, additional sense data can be derived even in the absence of any material object simply by reflecting upon (imagining) the images that are stored in the imagination or the memory. But imagination does more than store images. It also prepares them (*praeparat imaginationes quadrupliciter aliis virtutibus operantibus in ipsa*) for the future actions that will follow (1) in phantasy and estimation, (2) in memory, (3) in the intellect, or (4), by a reflowing action, in common sense. In this way, Albert is able to incorporate into this power the comprehensive actions assigned to imagination by John Damascene, Gregory of Nyssa, and Augustine.

The need for additional internal powers, besides common sense and imagination, stems from the fact that animals and humans apprehend certain things that are not sensed by the external senses. The most common example given in support of the contention was a sheep apprehending the hostility of a wolf and fleeing even though it has never seen a wolf before. Obviously some internal power, in this case "estimation," is called for to evaluate the suitableness or unsuitableness of the intent (*intentio*) of an object by a special apprehension and thereupon motivate the apprehending creature to approach or flee from the object (*sit determinare de fugiendo et imitando per apprehensionem convenientis et inconvenientis*). Since this additional information is of great importance in directing the actions of animals, a fourth internal power, phantasy, was added, which has the capacity to compose and divide intentions with the less complex information that is received in the common sense and stored in the imagination. Phantasy also has the power in humans to act under the influence of the intellect, thereby making it in some ways a cogitative power (*vis cogitativa*). And then ultimately all of this information is stored in the memory where it can be recalled by the simple action of the senses (true memory) or by the intervention of reason (reminiscence), thereby completing the acts of the internal senses.

iii. The Organs of the Senses

Interest in the organs of the senses arose to large extent after the time of Aristotle. To be sure, there were numerous references to sense organs scattered through his writings, but the systematic localization of the senses, particularly the internal organs, in specific parts of the body had to wait for the anatomical writings of Galen to be fused with the Aristotelian corpus by later commentators. Few Latin writers in the thirteenth and fourteenth centuries paid more than routine attention to this aspect of sense perception. Writers such as Thomas Aquinas mention the organs of the senses, but seldom in any detail or with an eye toward actual organic placement. Albert does not share this common disinterest. Throughout his writings it is clear that he is localizing the senses in an anatomically real body and not simply repeating descriptions handed down from an earlier tradition. This is especially true of the discussion of the senses in *De animalibus* (as noted below), but also to a lesser degree is the conclusion reached from a careful reading of the **Summa de creaturis**.

Of all the sense organs, Albert pays the most attention by far to the organ of vision. Here he is following a long tradition that extended from the writings of Aristotle through those of Avicenna and Averroës (his principal sources) to the works of his own contemporaries. In reviewing this tradition, Albert attempts to steer a middle course between Gregory of Nyssa, who held that vision resides in the forepart of the brain, and Avicenna, who assigned vision to the optic nerve and crystalline humor, by outlining three stages through which the act of vision proceeds. Vision begins in the sensitive portion of the eye (the crystalline humor), where the sensible species of color is received, is advanced toward greater perfection in the optic nerve, where it is mixed with the sensitive spirit, and is perfected (finally and completely perceived) in the anterior part of the brain. Thus to a certain extent the eye, the optic nerve, and the brain can each be considered to be the origin of vision, depending on the definition of the act of perception being considered.

The appearance of the auditory nerve, as described by Aristotle and his followers, led to some confusion regarding the act of hearing. According to this description the auditory nerve is hollow and contains within it, as it extends from the brain to the tympanum of the ear (*apparet versus tympanum auris*), air that is similar to the air outside the ear (*claudat in se partem connaturalem aeris*). It would seem, accordingly, that the ear and its nerve are capable of receiving sound as it exists materially in the air (*esse soni secundum materiam*), thereby obviating the need for sensible species. However, since apprehensive powers can only perceive immaterial species (*speciem sine materia ejus*), clearly this is not how hearing takes place. Albert concludes, therefore, that air is in contact with the auditory nerve only at its beginning (*aer tangit nervum in principio sui*). Beyond this point, in the spirit that flows outward from the brain to the tympanum, only sensible *species* are impressed (*non imprimitur nisi species soni*). Thereafter, if hearing follows the same path as vision, these species would be carried to the brain where the act of hearing would be completed.

After passing briefly over the organs of smell and taste, which one assumes begin in the nose and tongue respectively, are perfected in the connecting nerves, and completed in the brain, Albert turns to the difficult problem of touch. At first glance touch appears not to have a single organ but to be diffused throughout the body and to perceive objects in and of themselves without the intervention of an external medium. Albert agrees that in one way this is true. As the first of the senses, touch is the form and perfection of the animate body (*est forma et perfectio animati corporis*) and therefore has the entire body as its organ (*pro organo*)

and senses without a medium. Its capacity to sense in this instance depends on the degree to which a particular part of the body is influenced by the sensible spirit (*participant spiritum sensibilem*). Those parts that are influenced the most, such as nerves, flesh, and skin, sense better than those that are influenced the least, such as bones, brain, and hair. The latter, Albert suggests, sense

> insofar as they are surrounded by membranous nerves, in the breakdown of which, such as around the brain and around the bones, pain is sensed.

As the last of the senses, touch is simply the sense that receives tangibles, and in this case it acts like the other senses; it is completed in the brain, perfected in the sensible spirits that flow out from the brain through the nerves of the body, and begun in the flesh. In this latter way touch senses those qualities that have opposites and are active toward touch (*prout habent contrarietatem et motum ad ipsum*), such as hot, cold, wet, and dry. In the first way, touch senses those things that are harmful and beneficial to life (*quod est dissolvens continuationem talis corporis, et . . . conservans*), such as the pain of a flogging or the pleasure of intercourse.

Since Albert most commonly holds to a fivefold classification of the internal senses, his need with regard to their localization is to find five loci for them within the three Galenic cells of the brain. Avicenna, Albert's primary source for localization, had accomplished this by assigning two powers to the anterior cell (common sense and imagination), two to the middle cell (phantasy and estimation), and memory to the posterior cell. Albert agrees with this description, but adds one qualification. The two-two-one arrangement, Albert argues, applies to the senses of animals. The internal senses of animals are not, however, entirely analogous to those of humans. In humans the internal senses are in one crucial way decidedly different, and that is insofar as they act as a cogitative power that is influenced by the intellect. Albert assigns this cogitative activity to the middle portion of the brain and to accommodate it moves phantasy and estimation in humans toward the anterior cell. This displacement prompts him to present the unconventional conclusion that in humans the anterior cell of the brain has four powers: common sense, imagination, phantasy, and estimation.

B. Later Works

i. De anima

The years that passed between the writing of the **Summa de creaturis** and the commentary on *De anima* undoubtedly afforded Albert the opportunity to read more widely and reflect more deeply on, among other issues, the problem of sense perception. Certainly this is the impression that is received on turning to the commentary on that portion of *De anima* that begins the treatment of the senses (II, tr.3). The clear delineation of problems and the structured presentation of the opinions of previous authorities give every indication that Albert's thoughts on this subject are now firmly established and that he is himself fully in control of the material being presented. Although his basic psychology of sense perception seems to have changed very little in the dozen or so years that separate the two works, his confidence in and mastery of this psychology seems to have grown and matured greatly.

Albert's increased mastery of the problem of sense perception is evident in more than his style of presentation. By the time he commented on *De anima* he had clearly thought through and was prepared to make explicit a suggested metaphysical unity to sense perception that is implicit but never clearly articulated in the **Summa**. His thoughts on this subject are presented early in the sections on the senses as "a digression explaining the degrees and manner of abstraction" (*digressio declarans gradus abstractionis et modum*). In this digression Albert looks beyond the common element that had informed his discussion in the **Summa,** the common element of the senses as powers of the sensitive soul, and seeks to uncover the unity of the metaphysical process that underlies all perception. He presents this unity in the form of an explanation of the way in which the senses can be arranged hierarchically through a consideration of their relationship to the objects of perception.

Building on the same basic definition of perception set out in the **Summa,** "to apprehend is to accept the form of that which is apprehended" (*apprehendere est accipere formam apprehensi*), Albert notes that that which is accepted, the representative of the object (*intentio ipsius et species*), is received in four distinct ways.

The first and least abstract way is when the representative of the object is accepted in abstraction "from its matter but not from its presence or its appendices" (*a materia, sed non ab eius praesentia nec ab eius appendiciis*). This is the abstractive level of the externally apprehensive power (*vis apprehensiva deforis*), which, Albert notes, is sense (*quae est sensus*). By sense there can be little doubt that he is including, as he had in the **Summa,** the five external senses and the common sense.

The second level of abstraction contains imagination, which apprehends the form of the object apart from both its presence and matter but not in abstraction from the conditions or appendices of matter (*sed non ab appendiciis materiae sive condicionibus*). By "conditions" Albert is referring to the attributes of the form as it exists or existed in a particular subject.

At the third level of abstraction the intentions (*intentiones*) of the form are known by estimation and the compounding action of, one assumes, phantasy and estimation (*et numquam est sine aestimatione et collatione*).

And lastly, the form is known simply and separated from all the prior conditions. This is the cognition that is achieved solely in the intellect.

Translating this description into more concrete terms and adding to it the initial advances toward the complete perception of proper sensibles that take place between the senses and the brain, Albert would describe the process of apprehending an object, such as a particular person, as follows. When that person is present before us, its species, or representative is accepted by the organs of the external senses, where perception begins. The species received in the external senses are then transmitted by the sensitive spirits that flow in the connecting nerves to the brain, where a composite image of the object is formed. These steps take place only in the presence of the object. Thereafter, the form of the object is transmitted to the imagination and at the same time abstracted from the presence of the matter. We now know the form of the person even if that person should leave, but we know this form only as it existed in that person and not as it could have existed in another person (*in uno individuo unius speciei, quod non sunt in alio*). That is to say, we as yet do not apprehend the form of *"homo"* apart from a specific set of attributes—a particular placement of limbs, facial color, age, and so on—belonging to the person originally perceived. At the third level of abstraction, certain tangential information, called "intentions" (*intentiones*), is apprehended by phantasy and estimation, such as the potential friendly or unfriendly nature of the person in question. This is information that is received along with the sensible species but not impressed in the senses (*cum sensibilibus accipimus, et tamen eorum nullum sensibus imprimitur*). Finally, at the level of the intellect the form *"homo"* is known as a universal concept, now in abstraction from all specific limiting features associated with the existence of that form in a particular subject.

Having established the physiological background for dealing with sense perception, Albert then continues his discussion of the external senses along the same general lines followed in the **Summa.** Under sight he once again focuses on the proper sensible of vision and the manner in which it is transmitted to the eye. His discussions of hearing, smell, and taste entail detailed considerations of the nature of sounds, odors, and flavors and the manner in which they are transmitted from object to sense organ. In fact, the only major difference between these two works, from the point of view of this study, is their corresponding treatments of the organs of perception. In line with Aristotle's own discussion of the senses *De anima* and unlike his earlier interests expressed in the **Summa,** Albert for the most part ignores the problem of localization in *De anima*. The only exception to this generalization is found in his discussion of touch. The lack of any obvious sense organ for touch had prompted Aristotle to discuss its localization in some detail, thus providing Albert with an opportunity to consider at least this one organ in *De anima*.

The reason given for a detailed consideration of the organ of touch is the apparent disagreement between Alexander of Aphrodisias, Themistius, and Avicenna on the one hand and Aristotle on the other over the role of flesh in touch. Aristotle clearly states that flesh is the medium and not the organ of touch, whereas the other three authorities argue that the flesh that is imbued with nerves (*carnem nervosam*) is the organ of touch. Albert's compromise, which is similar to one set out in the *Summa* but now discussed in more detail, rests on an understanding of the types of flesh that exist. True flesh (*id quod vere caro est*) seems to be what Aristotle has in mind by flesh and as such Albert does not object to calling it the medium of sense perception. However, flesh that has sensitive nerves mingled with it or that is situated in the vicinity of other senses does perceive what touches the body and as such can be considered the organ of touch. The manner in which flesh senses in the latter way is explained through mention of two apparent anomalies: flesh-like organs that do not sense and nonflesh-like organs that do sense.

It is clear, Albert argues, that the sensitive power of nerve-imbued flesh extends to parts of the body that are not flesh-like in appearance, such as teeth. Teeth obviously feel pain. The cause of this, Albert conjectures, is the vivifying influence of the surrounding flesh that is carried to the teeth along with the nutriments they receive. That teeth do receive nutriments from the surrounding flesh is evident from the fact that they sometimes regrow after being extracted (*dentes extractos recrescere*) or that they increase in size when a facing tooth is removed (*dentes superiores vel inferiores habet extractos . . . dentes illis oppositos super alios prolongari*). This would only happen if the teeth were influenced by the nutriments of the body and explains how they can participate in sense perception. But not all nerve-imbued flesh senses, to turn to the second anomaly. The brain and liver, for example, were believed by Albert to have no sense capacity of their own. The reason for this is that the brain and liver are more influenced by their own qualities than by the surrounding flesh (*quorum complexio ad medietatem carnis non accedit*) and hence do not sense. If we feel pain in these organs it is due to the nerves that surround them (*hec est in panniculis, qui sunt circa substantias eorum*) and not the organs themselves, as was noted above. The same would be true of the nerves of ligaments and sinews (*funes sive ligamentum*) that attach to bones and likewise do not sense. Ultimately,

then, whether or not a particular part of the body can be said to be the medium or organ of touch depends on the vivifying and sensitive spirits that are active within it and the degree to which they are active.

Following his discussion of the external senses, Albert goes on to question whether or not they are five in number, as had Aristotle, and then orders the remainder of his discussion of sense perception with "a digression clarifying the five interior powers of the sensitive soul" (*digressio declarans quinque vires animae sensibilis interiores*). These powers are clearly delineated as common sense, imagination, phantasy, estimation, and memory, and localized within the three ventricles of the brain in accordance with the teachings of "the Peripatetics" (*Peripatetici*), in this case, Avicenna. Thereafter, the action of each is explained in turn and various problems discussed, such as an error of the ancients that maintained "that to know and to sense would be the same" (*quod intelligere et sentire essent idem*). A great deal of this material simply repeats the discussion of the senses in the *Summa,* although in *De anima* its organization is more straightforward and easier to follow. Throughout, Albert's initial psychology of sense perception remains essentially that of the earlier work. If his views in *De anima* differ at all from those of the *Summa* it is in emphasis and not in content.

ii. Parva naturalia

The *Parva naturalia* turn from thinking about the soul in and of itself (*secundum seipsam considerata*) to a consideration of the soul as it acts through the bodies of animals, which means ultimately to a consideration of the natures of animals, (*considerationem de animalium naturis*). Since one aspect of the nature of animals is their capacity to sense, sense perception appears as an important topic for discussion throughout these shorter works, with the major treatment being found in the two treatises devoted specifically to sensation, *De sensu et sensato* and *De memoria et reminiscentia,* and in a treatise that dealt with an unusual form of sense perception, dreaming, as discussed in *De somno et vigilia*. The latter work adds an important dimension to an understanding of Albert's psychology of sense perception, the role of the heart in sensing, and therefore needs to be considered briefly at this point.

Confusion over the heart's role in sense perception stemmed from yet another apparent disagreement between Aristotle and his commentators; Aristotle specifically states at several points that sense perception begins in the heart whereas most of the commentaries on his works tend to stress the importance of the brain in sensing. Albert's solution to this problem, which becomes standard in later works, eliminates this disagreement by explaining how the heart functions in perception. Just as the sun is the source of all things that are generated in the macrocosm, so too the heart is the source of all vital actions in the body, and like the sun, which is active through light, the heart too has its vehicle, which is called spirit. The spirit that arises in the heart, from its heat, flows and reflows through the body, changing in subtlety in the process and motivating the vital actions of the body, such as sense perception. In the brain, spirit "perfects the animal powers, which are to sense, to imagine, and to understand" (*perficit in cerebo virtutes animales, quae sunt sentire, imaginare, et cogitare*). From here they flow to the organs of the external senses, where seeing, hearing, and the like are carried out. Accordingly, both opinions are in a way correct; the spirit that activates sense perception arises in the heart but is perfected in the brain.

Given this general description of the origin of perception, the reason for the senses ceasing to be active in sleep follows with little difficulty. During sleep the spirit that activates the senses and causes them to sense is withdrawn (*somnus autem est retractio spiritus ab exterioribus organis*). This withdrawal renders the senses ineffective (*impotentia earum ad agendum*), thus explaining why in sleep we are not aware of external stimuli. However, when the animal spirit is withdrawn from the external senses a different type of perception occurs, the sense perception of dreams.

Dreams arise from the mixing and mingling of the images stored in the brain through the action of the vapors that arise during sleep. Such mixing does not take place during the day because the images received from the external senses tend to dominate any internal mixing that may take place. But when these external images are no longer present, due to the withdrawal of the animal spirit during sleep, the internal mixing of forms takes over and produces the images that we see in sleep. Exactly how this happens and the causes of various types of dreams are topics that were of great interest to Albert, as is clear from the discussion in *De somno* and even more in the lengthy treatment of this subject in the *Summa*. This sidelight to sense perception forms an interesting chapter in the history of medieval psychology that is well worth a detailed study, especially in relation to developments in physiology and anatomy. Unfortunately, to date very little has been written along these lines.

iii. De animalibus

The physiological and anatomical background to Albert's theory of dreams as well as to his entire psychology of sense perception is treated most fully in *De animalibus*. In this mammoth work, which ranges broadly over human and animal anatomy and physiology, he broaches the issue of sense perception on numerous occasions. Most frequently the resulting dis-

cussions focus on anatomy and provide descriptions, sometimes in very careful detail, of a particular sense or some aspect of the sensitive process. Less frequently he engaged in speculations on the relative role or placement of the senses in humans and animals or on some other comparative topic. In sum these discussions add very little to an understanding of Albert's psychology of sense perception. Very seldom does he attempt in *De animalibus* to explain the origin of any but the most obvious apprehensive processes. His goal in this work is not to explain *what* the senses know but rather *how* they know.

The anatomy and physiology of sense perception set out in *De animalibus* clearly reaffirms Albert's belief that sensation begins in the heart. The nerves of the body, which some physicians (*secundum multos medicos*) suggest come from the brain, have their place of origin in the heart and are only divided at the brain and base of the neck (*a corde oriantur, et a cerebro et a nucha dividantur*). Even the brain's location is dependent on the heart; since the heart is in the front of the body, the brain, which requires blood for perception, is also located in the front part of the body (*cor . . . est in anteriori corporis, et ideo etiam cerebrum*). Therefore, it can be argued that sensation begins when the warm vapors and animal spirit of the heart rise, like water vapors in the macrocosm, to the brain where they enliven the sensitive process (*spiritus enim venit corde ad cerebrum, et digeritur ibi ad operationes animales*) and are cooled. (Cooling at this point is not simply an adventitious action, it is a necessary one. If the warmth of the heart were never overcome, animals would never sleep and, of perhaps even greater consequence, the constant flow of heat from the heart into the external senses would eventually destroy them [*fluerent ex ipso humores calidi in oculos et aures et olfactum, et destruerentur operationes organorum*].) In brief, then, sense perception rests on the same basic heating, cooling, moistening, drying, and enlivening actions that the physicians of this period, working in the Galenic tradition, used to account for the rest of the body's actions.

The loci within which this array of physiological activities are carried out comprise the organs of sense perception. Once at the brain, the spirit that arises in the heart passes through the complex cerebral, neural, and sense anatomy of the body to those places where perception actually takes place. Ultimately, then, it is in the organs of sense perception that body and soul join together and render those who possess the attributes of animals capable of receiving and responding to external stimuli. It is in the organs of perception that the universal principles that lie behind sense perception, the principles of animal soul and animal spirit, are shaped and formed by the substance of the body into the various forms of sense cognition that are classified under the activities of the external and internal senses. As a consequence, at this most basic level, sense perception falls squarely within the Aristotelian metaphysics of form-matter composition and Albert's task, as a medieval psychologist, has been to determine how the form of the animal soul is active through the body. This in essence, and as was stated at the beginning of this [essay], comprises the psychology of sense perception in the Middle Ages.

C. MISCELLANEOUS REFERENCES AND CONCLUSIONS

Having placed Albert's psychology of sense perception squarely into its Aristotelian framework, it should be pointed out that it is not, in my opinion, this framework as such that separates his science from its modern counterpart. The assumption is too often made by historians of science who are not familiar with medieval science that Aristotelian science is synonymous with a preoccupation with final causes and that it is only when this "incorrect" focus is overturned that modern science emerges. A moment's reflection on Albert's psychology of sense perception quickly indicates the fallacy of this assumption. Throughout his writings on the senses Albert is concerned primarily with material and efficient causality. It could not be otherwise within a psychology of the senses that stresses the role of the body in shaping and directing the activities of the soul. Albert's scientific explanations do not rest on final causes. At the most he could be accused of allowing too many issues to be explained in terms of formal causes, but even this criticism misses the point. The search for formal causes, in Aristotelian science, means the search for the most fundamental characteristics of things—their propensity or nature to act in certain ways—which is akin to, although certainly not in any way as sophisticated as, the modern search for the fundamental properties of matter. As a consequence, it is incorrect to look to the Aristotelian framework of Albert's psychology of sense perception *per se* as the ingredient that sets him apart from today's thinking on the same subject. Rather, it is the values that he holds as a scientist that are so alien to our present way of thinking, values that are apparent if one turns to Albert's views on sense perception advanced outside the context of his strictly scientific works.

Albert's fascination with sense perception clearly extended beyond the technical context of his commentaries and *summae*. Just as mention of the ten men in Zacharia provided a ready excuse to once again remind his audience that ten is also the number of the senses, so too mention of the ten maidens in Matthew 25:1 prompted a similar enumeration, this time with a more detailed description of some of their actions:

> The philosophers assume that there are five internal senses: common sense, which compounds that which is sensed; imagination, which retains and brings back an image in the absence of its object; estimation, which draws forth friendliness and hostility, compatibility and incompatibility to itself from the sensibles; phantasy, which composes and divides that which is drawn forth [by estimation]; and memory, which preserves everything, as in a repository.

Similar partial listings can be found in the commentaries on the *Sentences* and on Dionysius' *De coelesti hierarchia*. There can be little doubt that Albert's world view contained as part of its working vocabulary the psychology of sense perception set out in the **Summa** and elaborated in his many later works.

Within the context of such digressions in works not directly on natural philosophy Albert continued to explain and clarify the more subtle points associated with sense perception. Confusion over Augustine's use of the term memory in *De trinitate,* which use seemed to contradict Avicenna's and Algazel's distinction of memory from imagination, prompts Albert to comment that Augustine was speaking only generally when he noted that memory retains corporeal images and that he did not intend to address himself to a more subtle distinction of powers. In the *Liber topicorum,* judgment regarding truth and error (*rectitudo et peccatum*) is assigned to the common sense, "which composes and divides designated particulars, and by composing and dividing it judges concerning them through the mingling action of the estimative power. Mention of the doubt of the Apostle Thomas in John 24:25 prompts Albert to suggest that Thomas was seeking first the simple verification of vision, then, since vision can deceive, the reassurance of information gained through the touch of a finger, and finally, to reassure himself that the touch of this single finger was not deceived, the infalliable experience (*simul infallibile nuntient tactus experimentum*) of all the fingers. Again, the conclusion is reached that his Aristotelian understanding of sense perception formed a working part of his world view.

However, as important as this understanding was to Albert and despite the amount of time he spent discussing sense perception, his scientific sensitivities in this area of investigation fall far short of being in any way equivalent or even preparatory to later and more modern developments in psychology. To a certain extent this is perhaps obvious. The simplified description of the senses that he received from his predecessors missed the mark on so many points that it is difficult to imagine how it could ever have evolved into our modern description. But it is not at this level that I would set Albert apart nor would I agree that his basic approach to the study of sense perception is particularly "unscientific." Certainly wherever possible he resorts to experience and he is profoundly interested in the physical processes that underlie cognition.

Accordingly, it is not his science of sense perception that is so alien to us as moderns as it is the importance he assigns to this science and the fruits he would expect to derive from an exhaustive study of how the senses function.

Albert believes, in harmony with the Aristotelian tradition of his day, that knowledge begins with the senses. It is objects that lie outside the soul that lead to *scientia* (*res extra animam existentes sint causa nostrae scientiae*). But just because the senses are necessary to the intellect it does not follow that the senses themselves attain much knowledge nor is there much pleasure to be gained through the senses alone. In fact, just the opposite is true. Since the purity of a sense, and hence its capacity to give pleasure, is directly proportional to its remoteness from matter (*purior . . . sensus est remotior a materia*) and since in the order of abstraction the external senses are the most closely joined to matter, followed by the internal senses, and then the mind, which is the most remote from matter, it follows that there is much more pleasure to be gained from the activities of the mind than from the activities of the senses. Moreover, it is only insofar as the senses are directed by the mind that Albert finds any real dignity in their actions. When faced with the problem of the frailty of the senses in humans, he makes no effort to defend their strength as senses *per se,* vis-à-vis animals. Since the quality of a sense depends on its organ, if animals have better sense organs they can sense better; dogs have superior senses of smell, wolves and wild boar better hearing, geese better vision. For Albert, the only essential superiority found in the senses of human beings as such is derived from their immediate and proper ordination to reason (*secundum quod coniungitur rationi, et in illa excedit*). Just as matter is ordained to form as to its final cause, so man's senses are ordered to reason, and thereby derive all their nobility and perfection.

Katharine Park (essay date 1980)

SOURCE: "Albert's Influence on Late Medieval Psychology," in *Albertus Magnus and the Sciences: Commemorative Essays 1980,* edited by James A. Weisheipl, Pontifical Institute of Mediaeval Studies, 1980, pp. 501-35.

[*In the following excerpt, Park discusses Albert's theory of the soul and its importance to Medieval psychological theory, including that of his student Thomas Aquinas.*]

Albert wrote four major works on the soul: a commentary on *De anima;* **Summa de homine** (Book II of his **Summa de creaturis**); **De natura et origine animae;** and **De intellectu et intelligibili.** The first two were the most important for later psychology. In these, as in Albert's other writings on the subject, the most frequently cited philosopher, apart from Aristotle, was Avicenna, whose *De anima seu Sextus de naturalibus* was Albert's principal source. Albert depends on Avicenna for many of his particular doctrines and for much of his method.

Concerning his method, Albert distinguishes two approaches to the study of the soul.

> On this subject, Avicenna says in *Sextus de naturalibus* that there are two ways of defining a sailor: in one he is considered in himself and is called a worker governing a boat by skill; in the other he executes his functions through the instruments of the boat, namely the yard, mast, sail, and oars. In the same way, the soul has two definitions: one according to which it performs the operations of life in the body and its organs. The other is given of the soul in itself and as it is separable from the body.

Thus, says Albert, one may study the soul *a priori,* in itself, or *a posteriori,* as it performs its various operations in and through the body. Considered in the first sense, the human soul is in its essence a separable spiritual substance which differs from the angels only in its affinity for the human body. Because it is, in principle, independent of matter, it should be thought of as the body's motor, perfection, or act, not as its form. It is joined to the body only incidentally by the lower functions of nutrition and sensation.

From this point of view, the human soul is not simple: it contains a lower part which performs the corporeal functions, and a higher which performs these and the intellectual ones as well. The two enter the foetus at different times and in different ways. The lower vegetative and sensitive faculties are drawn out from the matter of the embryo by the formative power (*virtus formativa*) in the seed of the parents. They remain incomplete, however, until God, the First Cause, illuminates the composite by infusing into it from outside the higher part, individually created. As soon as this happens, the "intrinsic" lower parts are transformed by their association with the "extrinsic" higher ones, and the product is a substantial whole—entirely human, rather than vegetable or animal, in nature. In more technical terms, "the powers are faculties which follow the constitutive species." For example, although the faculty of vision is the same in a man and an ass with respect to object and operation, nonetheless in the man it belongs to a different species—the human— because it is completed and "denominated" by the intellectual soul.

As a result, the intellectual soul becomes united to the body, depending on the lower parts, such as sensation, for all its operations. This is why, in Aristotle's maxim, "the soul never thinks without an image." Despite its association with the body, however, the intellectual soul remains fundamentally separable from it and closely allied with the other spiritual substances: with the angels and God himself. Therefore, while relying on sense images for its initial stimulation, the intellect may proceed beyond them to contemplate first itself, then the celestial intelligences, and finally God. Albert calls this intellectual state "assimilative":

> the assimilative intellect is that in which man, as much as is possible or permitted, springs up analogically toward the divine intellect, which is the light and cause of all things. . . . Therefore from the light of its own agent intellect, it reaches the light of the intelligence, and from that extends itself toward the intellect of God.

Thus the soul ascends to virtue, wisdom, and prophetic powers.

In his *a priori* discussion of the soul as substance, Albert depends heavily, as many scholars have shown, on the neoplatonic elements in Avicenna's version of Aristotle; using them, he can integrate Aristotle's psychology into the Augustinian tradition of the separable and immortal soul. In his *a posteriori* inquiry into the soul as revealed through its various operations, he takes as the center of his analysis Avicenna's transformation of the Aristotelian notion of faculty.

Aristotle considered the faculties as potentialities of the soul for different kinds of action and used them mainly as convenient categories to classify different levels of living things. Albert, following Avicenna, visualizes them as really existing and distinct powers which possess, in some sense, continuous actuality. For all practical purposes, the study of the soul *a posteriori* reduces to the study of the faculties as powers of the soul. In Albert's image, the soul is divided into diverse powers as a potestative whole. Like the organs of the body, the faculties are separate from each other, but mutually dependent and arranged in a hierarchy of nobility and command which resembles the chain of authority in a well-ordered monarchy.

The element of order is central for Albert. He takes the division of the soul into faculties as the organizing principle of his psychological works. In *De anima* and *Summa de homine,* after introductory sections which define the soul, each tractate or question is devoted to a different power or group of powers. These are of great importance in the history of medieval psychology. At the time Albert wrote the *Summa de homine,* his first extended discussion of the soul, Latin psychological theory was in chaos. The powers were acknowledged as central to any account of the soul, but there was no consensus as to what they were and how they should be divided, since the various Greek, Arabic, and Christian authorities had all proposed different models. Most earlier Latin writers, like Jean de la Rochelle, were content to give several different classifications without attempting to reconcile them.

Albert transforms the situation with his *Summa de homine.* He replaces the chaos of authorities and opinions with a coherent system based on Avicenna and incorporates elements from earlier Latin writers. In the first place, he rationalizes the enumeration of the powers of the soul by establishing a single system derived from Avicenna's interpretation of Aristotle and by relegating the faculties according to Augustine and Lombard to an appendix as motive powers "according to the Platonists and theologians." The result is a complex but coherent scheme of faculties divided into four main groups—vegetative, sensitive, motive, and intellectual. These correspond to three types of soul: vegetative, sensitive (or animal), and intellectual (or human). Albert's divisions and subdivisions, with minor variations, remain standard in Latin psychological theory through the end of the fifteenth century, and they persist in many authors well past 1600.

In the second place, Albert establishes the general philosophical terms in which the powers will be discussed throughout the later Middle Ages. As actual operative principles, the powers demanded a much more rigorous and systematic discussion than was found either in earlier literature or in Aristotle himself. Albert is the first adequately to provide such a discussion, and he does so by drawing on both Avicenna and earlier Latin sources, notably Boethius. Applying Aristotelian logical and philosophical principles, he develops a coherent explanation of the faculties which addresses the issue of their ontological status.

For Albert, the central questions are the following: In what sense can the soul be said to be composed of parts? What are the logical and ontological relations between the soul as a single substance and its multiple powers and sub-powers? He takes his answer, as he takes his image of the soul as hierarchy of authority, from Boethius' *De divisione.* Although physical objects may be divided into essential or integral parts, a spiritual entity like the soul has only "potestative" parts—natural powers—which flow from it; it must be considered as a whole composed of powers, or what Boethius and Albert call a "potential whole" (*totum potestativum, potentiale,* or *virtuale*). If the faculties of the soul are natural powers, then they lie, according to Aristotle's *Categories,* in the category of quality.

Albert uses Boethius not only to establish the logical status of the faculties, but also to answer a question which had plagued psychological theory for more than a century: Is the soul identical with its faculties? The Augustinian tradition, dominant through the end of the twelfth century, had argued that the distinction between the powers was only verbal; the different powers were in fact various names given to the soul as it performed various actions, but in essence identical to the soul. With the new translations, it became clear that both Avicenna and Averroës accepted a real distinction between the soul and its powers and that Latin psychologists would have somehow to accommodate this position. Albert is the first to do so in a satisfactory manner. Rejecting the strained compromises of his earlier contemporaries, he demonstrates that, if the soul is truly a *totum potestativum,* it is a substance, while the powers are qualities which function as its powers. Logic thus demands a real distinction between them.

Albert's significance for the history of medieval Latin psychology mirrors his significance for medieval science in general. His influence extended beyond that of a generalized Aristotelianism, however; many specific aspects of his thought on the soul entered the tradition of medieval psychology. He took over two particular strains of Avicenna's theory: the Platonic strain which emphasized that nature of the soul as a separable substance—the "perfection" rather than the form of the body—and the scholastic strain which manifested itself in the elaborate hierarchical subdivisions of the faculties. Using concepts from the logical writings of Aristotle and Boethius, he developed a clear and reasonably consistent explanation of the way in which the faculties could be really distinct from the soul and from each other, but still of the same essence and substance. Later Latin writers often reject or alter Albert's conclusion, but they remain interested in Albert's questions, asked in his own terms.

The psychological theory of Thomas Aquinas, once a student of Albert, is both an index and a vehicle of his master's influence on late medieval psychology. Thomas' principal philosophical concerns are different from Albert's: for him metaphysics and theology replace natural philosophy and physiology as the center of attention. Nonetheless, his thought on the soul and its faculties clearly reflects that of his early teacher. On the one hand, he is very similar to Albert in his account of the faculties. He describes them as composing a hierarchy of authority like that in a monarchy, and his list of them in the *Summa theologiae* follows Albert's quite closely. The soul is a virtual whole and its powers are its natural properties—accidents flowing from its essence—and therefore really different from the soul itself. Thomas elaborates on Albert's conclusions by noting that the faculties, as natural powers, must lie in the second species of quality.

On the other hand, Thomas explicitly rejects the *a priori* discussion of the soul as separable substance that Albert took over from Avicenna and other Arabic sources. For Thomas, the soul is first and foremost the substantial form of the body. This leads him to reject a number of Albert's other claims. In the first place, he denies that the developing foetus derives its vegetative and sensitive powers from the formative power of the semen and is only later perfected by the infusion of a rational soul. This would mean, he argues, that

> the substantial form would be continuously perfected. It would further follow that the substantial form would be drawn not all at once, but progressively from potency into act, and further that generation would be a continuous motion, like alteration. All of these things are naturally impossible.

What really happens, according to Thomas, is that the embryo receives a succession of increasingly perfect forms: it is first animated by a purely vegetative soul. At a certain point, this is wholly corrupted and replaced by a sensitive soul and, later, through God's direct creation, by a rational soul.

By the same token, Thomas rejects Albert's apparent contention that in this life the human intellect, as a separable spiritual substance, can know itself directly or the other separable substances—God and the celestial intelligences. As the substantial form of the body, the human soul is bound inextricably to corporeal modes of cognition. To know immaterial reality it must rely on what it can abstract from sense images, and as a result may understand this reality only reflectively and by analogy. Albert's "assimilative" intellect does not exist: "according to the state of present life, neither by the possible nor by the agent intellect can we understand the separate immaterial substances in themselves."

While in actual fact both Albert and Thomas insist that the proper object of the human intellect is the essence of material things and that everything above man can be known only *by analogy* to what is proper to man, Albert seems to stress the self-sufficiency of the human intellect in self-knowledge more than does Thomas. But even Thomas admitted with Albert that the human intellect can through discourse know itself as an intellectual substance.

These differences were later exaggerated by opposing camps of Albertists and Thomists, and they became central to the debates over Albert's authority in fifteenth-century discussions of the soul.

Simon Tugwell (essay date 1988)

SOURCE: An introduction in *Albert and Thomas: Selected Writings,* edited and translated by Simon Tugwell, Paulist Press, 1988, pp. 3-129.

[*In the following excerpt, Tugwell investigates Albert's theological writings on epistemology, especially those that concern human knowledge of God.*]

In 1241 William of Auvergne, by now bishop of Paris, together with the Masters of the University, issued a formal condemnation of several propositions, of which the first is that "the divine essence will not be seen in itself either by any human being or by any angel." The ninth proposition is that "whoever has better natural endowments will of necessity have more grace and glory," which almost certainly reflects a Neoplatonist doctrine of hierarchy, apportioning divine illumination strictly according to ontological status. The other condemned propositions do not directly concern us here but, as M. D. Chenu has shown [in *Mélanges Auguste Pelzer,* 1947], they all seem to derive from an essentially oriental theology.

Exactly who was the author of the condemned propositions is not known for certain, but they are presented in some sources as emanating from mendicant circles, and it is clear that the Dominicans were immediately affected. Successive Dominican chapters insisted on the books of the brethren being corrected to eliminate the condemned doctrines, and the manuscripts of Hugh of St. Cher show various attempts to implement this ruling. Guerric of St. Quentin, who had previously maintained that God's essence, as such, is not known to the blessed, made a sort of public retraction by presiding over a new disputation on the subject and pronouncing the opposite conclusion.

The condemnation of 1241 represented a victory for those who were disillusioned with the attempt to accommodate the Christian hope of the beatific vision to a general, philosophical epistemology. The conviction that we can have a real knowledge of God was taken to be a primary datum; if philosophical epistemology could not cope with it, so much the worse for epistemology. Before the condemnation William of Auvergne denounced the "Aristotelian" doctrine that there can be no true knowledge of individuals on the grounds that "this error prevents and altogether denies the glory of human souls, which is the most complete and clear vision of the Creator," since, in William's view, the Creator is "very individual" (*singularissimus*). Some years later, probably in the mid-1250s, St. Bonaventure alludes to the epistemological problem posed by the lack of proportion between God and the soul and, instead of trying to deal with it, he simply dismisses it, on the grounds that "if proportionality were necessary for knowledge, the soul would never reach the knowledge of God . . . by nature, by grace or by glory." This is tantamount to saying that it *must* be possible for us to know God, even if there is no way that we *can* know God. . . .

When Albert came to Paris in the 1240s, the issue of "Eastern" theology was a live and delicate one in Dominican circles. The attempt to provide a viable epistemological account of how we know God had apparently reached an impasse and had, in the process, brought negative theology into a certain disrepute; the only form of negative theology that was quite unaffected was one which posited a non-intellectual way of knowing God by love, which by-passed rather than settled the epistemological problem.

Albert, it is quite clear, was not prepared simply to abandon the attempt to interpret Christian claims to present or future knowledge of God in terms of some coherent epistemology, and it is precisely on the subject of epistemology that he found himself most seriously at odds with the Latin tradition. On just the issue that had provoked the "anti-oriental" backlash, he aggressively opted for a frankly "oriental" view. For a full statement of his doctrine of how the intellect functions and how it comes to the knowledge of God—and it is evident that his position is Aristotelian with a strong dose of Neoplatonism, both Dionysian and Islamic—we have to wait for books written after the completion of the Dionysian commentaries. But at least in germ the same doctrine is already contained in the commentary on the first book of the *Sentences* and in the Dionysian commentaries themselves, so there does not seem to have been any essential change in his attitude.

At the beginning of the section of his **De anima** devoted to the intellect Albert announces emphatically that "in settling these questions we utterly abhor what the Latin doctors say." His objection to the Latins is that they follow Plato too much and suppose that the mind somehow contains within itself all that is needed for knowledge, with its own private supply of universals. Albert makes fun of these private universals, which could never be the basis for any objective knowledge of reality as it exists outside the soul and which would mean that no two individuals could ever be said to have the same knowledge. And against the idea of knowledge being somehow innate he affirms the Peripatetic doctrine that the mind acquires knowledge from things, not from itself.

One of the main points of controversy arising out of this concerns the soul's self-knowledge. The Augustinian tradition maintained that the soul has, in principle, a direct, immediate knowledge of itself and all that is in itself, including God. This theory is mentioned in the commentary on the *Mystical Theology,* and Albert opposes it firmly. He insists, with Aristotle, that we acquire knowledge of our own minds in the same way that we acquire knowledge of anything else. What we are is not intrinsically luminous to us, it has to *become* an object of understanding to us.

On certain crucial points, then, Albert is a loyal Peripatetic. But this is far from being the whole of his epistemology, as we see in his fascinating treatment of Augustine's recantation of the claim that "any truth that is known is inspired by the Holy Spirit":

Four things are needed in the soul if it is to receive any knowledge of truth: the possible intellect, which is ready to receive it; secondly the agent intellect, by whose light the abstraction occurs of the forms in which the truth or the particular truth resides; thirdly the reality (*res*) which is present as an object either through an image of itself or in its own right—this is what the truth is about; and fourthly the principles and axioms which are as it were the instruments which arrange in due proportion the possible, impossible and necessary connections and separations, on the basis of which the particular truth is received. Of these four the first is purely receptive, the second is simply a source of light, the third is what receives light from the agent intellect and gives to the possible intellect the light of a specific truth, and the fourth is moved as an instrument and in turn moves the conceptual connections and separations with regard to the matter in which truth is known or sought. Some philosophers have concluded that these four things suffice for the knowledge of any truth which is subject to our reason. But we must rather say that the light of the agent intellect is not sufficient by itself without being directed by the light of the uncreated intellect. . . . This can happen in two ways, depending on whether there is simply a twofold light or whether there is a threefold light. The light is twofold if the mind is joined to the light of the uncreated intellect, and that light is the "interior teacher." But sometimes the mind is joined to an angelic intellect as well as to the divine. . . . This is what Dionysius calls the leading back of our hierarchy through the hierarchy of the angels. Augustine says this happens in many ways. And this is what some philosophers call the "link-up of intellects," because they too said that nothing is seen except by way of the first light.

So, to return to the question whether a new grace is needed, we must say that if any gift freely given by God is called "grace," then no knowledge comes about without grace. Indeed one philosopher has said that even if we have a habitual knowledge of something, that knowledge will not become actual unless the mind turns to the light of the uncreated intellect.

Even without identifying all the sources of this remarkable passage, we can see at once that its doctrine is essentially Neoplatonist, though Albert himself may have been unaware of this; and Albert seems to have remained faithful to it throughout his life.

The combination of this Neoplatonist illuminationism and the Aristotelian denial of any immediate and primitive intellectual self-knowledge gives Albert a philosophical basis for a very rich and profound Christian intellectualism, such as we find in several passages in the *De Intellectu et Intelligibili,* in which we are surely entitled to recognize his own convictions, not just his interpretations of what he took to be Peripatetic doctrine:

Our intellect is more closely joined to imagination and the senses than it is to the first agent intellect, and so it is dark and, with regard to things which are in principle thoroughly separate from matter, it is like the eye of a bat with regard to sunlight. For this reason it has to be imbued with physics first, and then with mathematics, so that once it has been strengthened in this way by many lights coming from many intelligibles it can rise to the understanding of the things of God. And in all these intelligibles, when it becomes an effective understanding of any of them, it discovers both itself and the agent intellect. . . . But though it is closer to physics and mathematics because of its connection to the body, it is really more akin by nature to the things of God, and so it discovers more of itself in the intelligibles which pertain to God than it does in those which belong to mathematics and physics.

Furthermore it seems true to say that, since anything which is only potentially a knower actually knows nothing at all, the intellect knows nothing at all unless it becomes effective. And from this it follows that anyone who does not study philosophy knows nothing at all, neither himself nor anything other than himself. . . . As long as the intellect remains potential and in no way effective, it is impossible to know anything other than oneself or oneself or even to know that one does not know. . . . So Hermes reproached the uneducated in antiquity, saying that such people paid no attention to anything human in their lives, but spent their days like pigs. . . .

The possible intellect is potentially everything that can be understood. So it is not actually received except in as much as what is potentially understood becomes effectively understood, and it is completely obtained and received when it attains to the effective realisation of all the intelligibles which it potentially is. This is how human beings take possession of their own intellect.

Plato accordingly said that the truest definition of philosophy is "knowledge of oneself," and Alfarabi said that the soul is placed in the body in order to discover and know itself, and he claims that Aristotle said this, but I have not found where he said it. . . . The reason for all this is that the first image of the light of the first cause to be joined to space and time is the human intellect, and so it must be a kind of likeness of everything that comes into being through the light of the first cause, it must enfold all these things, being a receptacle of some in as much as it is an image of the first cause and of others in as much as it is joined to space and time; in both it has to take possession of itself. . . .

This makes it evident that the contemplation of wonderful truths is the highest delight and the most natural occupation, in which people's whole human nature, precisely as such, blossoms, particularly in the contemplation of the things of God, because it is particularly in these that the intellect discovers itself in its proper nature, because human beings, precisely as human, are essentially intellect. . . . This reveals how it is by study that the intellect takes possession of itself.

Now let us talk about the understanding which some of the oldest philosophers call "assimilative" or "assimilating," and in doing so let us also clarify the soul's perfection, which arises from all the kinds of understanding alluded to. "Assimilative understanding" is that in which human beings rise to the divine intellect, which is the light and cause of everything, insofar as it is possible and lawful and in a way which is proportionate to them. This comes about when the intellect has become fully actual and has taken possession of itself and of the light of the agent intellect and, on the basis of the lights received from everything and of its self-knowledge, it reaches out in the lights belonging to the intelligences and so gradually ascends to the simplicity of the divine intellect. From the light of its own agent intellect it passes to the light of intelligence and from there it reaches out to the intellect of God. . . .

Strengthened in that light (of intelligence) the intellect rises to the divine light, which has no name and is unutterable, because it is known by no name of its own, becoming known only as it is received. And it is received first in intelligence, which is the first effect to be caused, and when it is uttered it is uttered with the name of intelligence, which is the effect it causes, not with any name of its own. So Hermes said that the God of Gods is improperly grasped by a name which is not properly his own. . . . So the human intellect is joined to its final goal and its light and united with that light it shares in somewhat of his Godhead. . . .

Notice that in all these kinds of understanding the possible intellect is as it were primary and the foundation. The light of the agent intellect is a disposition in it and a kind of basis for the understanding of principles, and the understanding of principles is the basis for effective understanding, and effective understanding is the basis for taking possession of the intellect, because here particularly the soul acquires knowledge of itself; and possession of one's own intellect is the basis for the assimilative intellect, which rises step by step from lower light to higher light up to the light of the divine intellect, and there is stops as having reached its destination. Since everyone naturally desires knowledge, the goal of everyone's desire is to come to rest in the divine intellect.

There is a similar message in the commentary on the *Metaphysics:*

Since all human beings naturally desire knowledge and desire is not unlimited, it must be possible to bring this desire to an end in some form of knowing. And this can be nothing other than the knowledge of that which is the cause and light of all beings and all objects of knowledge, and this is no other than the divine intellect. . . . This is why Averroes says in his comment on book XI of the *Metaphysics* of Aristotle that the question of the divine intellect is the one which all human beings desire to know.

The human intellect becomes aware of itself by understanding other things, and by an "analysis" (*resolution*) of its own light (once it has discovered this through coming to understand things) it comes to the "first, pure intellect." "This is what is most pleasant and most desirable in contemplation (*theoria*), this is what every being that has an intellect naturally desires to have actual knowledge of and to contemplate." The "first, pure intellect" is, of course, God.

In these writings Albert is not expressly developing his own views, and he objected to people supposing that he endorsed all that he said in his expositions of what he took to be Peripatetic philosophy. But so much of the same doctrine of the intellect recurs in his other works, and his comments are sometimes so enthusiastic, that it is difficult to believe that he would really insist on disowning it.

The highest thing that the soul can have while it is in the body is at least sometimes to reach the pure intellect in its mind. And if, once it is freed from the body, what it sometimes fleetingly attains in the body becomes continuous, that will be supreme joy and the kingdom of heaven.

The intellectual nature of beatitude is affirmed already in the early work **De Resurrectione** with the same quotation from Averroes that we find in the Metaphysics commentary, and it is reaffirmed in the commentary on Dionysius' *Divine Names,* again with the same text from Averroes.

The hypostatized "intelligence" that is the *primum causatum,* mentioned in the text cited from **De Intellectu et Intelligibili,** is easily identified with suprahuman intellectual beings, that is, the angels, . . . Albert is quite willing to ascribe an important role to the angels in the illumination of the human mind, so the passage through the light of "intelligence" to the divine light needs little comment, if any, to make it acceptable to him.

Above all, Albert's illuminationist doctrine of the intellect allows him to develop a theory of how we come to know God. In the early **De Resurrectione** he was content to say, like William of Auxerre, that God "is in the intellect in his own right, that is, substantially, because he is in every essence. So for him to be seen all that is needed is the removal of any obstacle that is in the way. And there are two such obstacles: the imperfection that goes with this present wretchedness and our being turned in another direction. Since both of these are removed by beatitude, in beatitude we shall see him as he is."

In the commentary on the *Divine Names* Albert gives us a much more precise account of how God is in the soul, and it presupposes already the doctrine later expounded in *De Intellectu et Intelligibili:* "God is essentially present in the soul, not as any kind of nature of the soul, but as a certain light of the intellect, and this is sufficient for him to be known by the intellect; indeed because of his being in the soul like this he is known under the appearance of anything that is understood, as the philosophers say about the agent intellect. In the same way we know of God 'that' he is by way of our knowledge of any creature."

We know God through his works, then, essentially because he is implicitly present in our actual *knowing* of creatures. The divine being of God is the principle of all knowledge, because it is the "first light"; our intellect receives him as a "principle," and if we could know him perfectly (which we cannot) we should be able to derive a knowledge of everything from our knowledge of him. All knowledge derives from God's own knowing, the light which is the causal principle of all knowing; but actual knowledge is received by different creatures in different ways, and our human way is laborious and circuitous.

The divine intellect is the "cause and light of all beings," the "intellect which is the mover in all of nature," and for Albert this does not just mean some remote Aristotelian deity moving all things simply by attracting them, without in any way being concerned for them, nor does it mean a remote Platonist principle acting in all things, but not deigning to be cognizant of individuals or particulars: it means the creator God whose knowledge is the source of the whole reality of all things in all their particularity.

God is the source of the existence of all things, and at the same time, as the primordial Intellect, he is the source of the intelligibility of all things, and it is this latter which most interests Albert. Our minds approach God by way of the intelligibility of his creatures, discovering themselves and the light that is in them in the process. Bit by bit, as they exercise their own intellectual powers, they move toward an ever simpler, more comprehensive view of things, in which the light, which comes from God and enlightens angelic and (in a more diffuse and obscure way) human intellects, is apprehended more clearly.

The Aristotelian principle that it is only in understanding other things that the mind takes possession of itself is, of course, an admirable justification for Albert's own wide-ranging interests. He evidently took seriously and found congenial the belief that the intellect takes full possession of itself only when it realizes to the full its capacity to understand all that can be understood. But this is not simply a justification of curiosity; it is an application of the Dionysian principle that God, who is not adequately named by any name, must be given *all* names. Any narrowing of our intellectual interests would in fact shut out ways in which we are meant to be led to God. Precisely because the light of God is discovered only indirectly through the intelligibility of his works theology cannot profitably be undertaken as a narrow specialization. The link between negative and affirmative theology is fully restored in all its amplitude.

Albert's view of how we ascend to the knowledge of God leaves no room for any kind of shortcut. Nor does it leave room for any kind of specialized faculty for union with God, such as Gallus posited. And the idea that there might be some kind of non-intellectual knowledge of God receives very short shrift from Albert: if we cannot know God by the intellect, "it is clear that we cannot know him in any other way." And if we are to know God by the intellect, it must be by the whole, ordinary process of intellection, beginning with the "possible intellect." (Albert cannot really accommodate the popular distinction between a "higher" intellectual power directed toward God and a "lower" power directed toward creatures.)

If all intellectual activity depends on an illumination that comes from God, it is obvious that there can be no radical division between natural knowledge and faith. The proper object of faith is the First Truth, which is the source of all knowledge, not just knowledge of the truths of faith, so the distinction between faith and natural knowledge is a distinction within an essentially coherent illumination from God: "Without a light to enlighten the intellect our possible intellect cannot receive any knowledge; it is by this light that the possible intellect becomes an eye to see with. This light is natural with regard to our receiving knowledge of natural things, it is freely given (*gratuitum*) with regard to our receiving the objects of belief, and it is glory with regard to our receiving what beatifies us." And the illumination of faith functions in the same way as any other illumination: light enables us to see but does not determine what we see, and the light of the agent intellect enables us to know but does not determine any particular object of knowledge; in the same way the light of faith enables us to believe, but does not of itself specify any object of belief. The actual content of faith comes to us, like any other kind of knowledge, through the senses—through hearing sermons, reading the bible and so on. This is why, as Albert says in the **Mystical Theology,** there is need both for the inward teaching of God and for an "external teacher."

The salient characteristic of faith, as distinct from ordinary knowledge, is that by it we believe certain things to be true that are not susceptible of rational proof, though it is important to note that they are not susceptible of rational refutation either: if they could be refuted, we should have to believe the refutation as well as the refuted article of faith, so two contradictories would have to be true at the same time, which is impossible. Natural knowledge is limited in its scope, but it is not, in Albert's view, unnatural for the mind to be carried beyond the limit of its own resources. The abandonment of intellectual activity recommended in the *Mystical Theology* is interpreted by Albert to mean only the abandonment of the intellectual activity which is "connatural" to the intellect, that is to say, the activity which is sustained by the powers with which the human mind is born. But it is precisely the *intellect* that is carried beyond its innate capacity by the higher illumination it receives from God, and this does not involve any essential change in its nature. It is, as Albert makes clear in his commentary on the *Mystical Theology,* an *intellectual* union with God that is our final goal.

The light of faith is not an alternative to, let alone a negation of, the mind's natural way of functioning, it is precisely a strengthening of the mind, enabling it to do better and more surely the very thing that it is naturally designed to do.

> The bodily vision of some creatures, like the bat, is totally shattered by the light of the sun, but the vision of other creatures, like human beings, is capable to some extent of looking at the sun, but because it is weak it cannot do so without the eyes trembling; other creatures, like the golden eagle, have their vision so strengthened that they can see the sun in the round. In the same way the mental vision of people who are held down by earthly affections and bodily images is material and is totally rebuffed by the divine radiance, but if their vision draws away from these things into intellectual speculation then it becomes immaterial, but it is still trembling, because it looks upon the things of God from afar, as it were, with the principles of reason. But if it is strengthened by the light of faith it ceases to tremble."

There is a fine passage in the commentary on the *Divine Names* that develops a similar point:

> "This reason" (divine reason) "is the simple truth of what exists, which itself exists . . . and divine faith is about it" (it is the proper object of the faith we have about God). "It is pure," by contrast with the truth there is in other sciences, inasmuch as some impurity overflows into them from the things on which they are based; "it is not erroneous," as against the truth which is derived from reasoning, which is often liable to error because of the way things shift around. "It is knowledge of all things,"

in that it pours out knowability on all things, which is the situation of the first truth.

Next he defines faith, of which this truth is the object. First he gives the definition and comments on it, then he explains why he said, "If knowledge unites those who know. . . ."

So first he says that "faith is an abiding" and firm "establishment of believers," and this is interpreted in two ways: it "establishes" believers "in the truth" through their assent to it and it establishes the truth in them, placing it in their minds, in the minds, that is, of "believers who have a simple knowledge of the truth" in the first truth, "in unalterable steadfastness," inasmuch, that is, as someone remains unalterably in the one faith which also unites all the faithful. And the cause of this unchangeable steadfastness is indicated next: it is of the nature of knowledge to be "unitive," and this is understood in two ways: of the object of knowledge, because perfect knowledge makes us stand firm in the one, simple "whatness" of something, and also of the act of knowing, because at first the act of knowing is unsteady and wanders round various ideas, but once it gets a probable idea of something it sticks to one idea, but is nervous there because it is afraid of its opposite; but when it has perfect knowledge and enters into the proper and essential cause of something, then it stands firmly in one place, and this is the reason why all those who know something are at one in a single knowledge of the truth.

Neither Dionysius nor Albert would actually want to claim that faith gives us "perfect knowledge" in this life, but it is clearly implied that faith does give us the same kind of solidity as perfect knowledge. Whereas opinion is always unsettled because of its "fear of the opposite," both faith and knowledge give us a kind of certainty, and faith has at least some advantages over any other kind of knowledge, because of its direct reliance on the "first truth." And Albert seems to have no hesitation in treating faith as a kind of knowledge: although faith and reason differ in us, "they belong to the same genus, namely *natura cognoscitiva.*"

Faith, however, cannot be regarded simply as a "given," allowing us to rest on our laurels. It shares with the investigation of truth the responsibility for bringing our reason to perfection, presumably by sharing in its own way the task of reason, which is to explore reality so that the general principles known by our intellect are applied and we come to a real understanding of things. By faith we have access to more material, which we can explore; and theology is the exploration of it. In his commentary on St. John, Albert says he likes the "ancient" view of faith, found in St. Gregory, which differentiates between two facets of faith: "believing is thinking together with assent" (*cogitare cum assensu*). As assent, it is simply a given, a "changeless foundation"; but as "thinking" it is clearly open to all kinds of development. "In faith . . . we first assent to the first truth for its own sake, then we look for reasons, so that we can to some extent understand what we believe."

The wonderful humane and intellectual perspective opened out to us by faith is indicated by St. Albert in his comment on John 8:31-2, "Jesus said to the Jews who believed in him, 'If you abide in my word, you will truly be my disciples and you will know the truth and the truth will set you free.'":

> "Jesus said to those who believed in him." They were already beginning to be free, in that they had been called to faith. "You have been called into freedom, brethren, only do not make freedom an occasion for the flesh" (Gal. 5:13). Faith is the beginning of freedom because it makes people know what freedom there is in grace. Therefore he speaks to these believers as to people who already understand freedom. "Let people with understanding speak to me, let a wise man hear me" (Job 34:34). "If you abide" with perseverance, intelligence and obedience "in my word." With perseverance, so that you meditate on it by study; with intelligence, so that you understand the mystery of the Holy Spirit in it; with obedience, so that you fulfill it by practicing it in what you do. On the first of these it says, "Persevere in discipline; God offers himself to you as to his children" (Heb. 12:7), and God's children are free. On the intelligibility of the words it says, "Understand what I say, for the Lord will give you understanding in everything" (2 Tim. 2:7), and "I will give you understanding" (Ps. 31:8). On obedience, "Cursed is anyone who does not abide in the words of this law and who does not accomplish them in practice" (Deut. 27:26), and "If you hear the voice of the Lord your God in order to do and to keep all his precepts, which are my command to you today, the Lord your God will make you higher than all the peoples who live on the earth" (Deut. 28:1), than those who live in earthly desires, that is, because you will be free and will be master of them. See how it is the beginning of true freedom thus to abide in the Lord's word.

> "You will truly be my disciples." A true disciple is one who is truly imbued, without any error, with the teachings of his master. And this is how freedom grows. As the philosopher says, we call people free if they are their own cause. And as it says in book ten of the *Ethics,* a human being is just intellect— all the rest that is in us is not human but animal. And the intellect is perfected in the study of the things of God, not in anything else. "If you are outside the instruction of which all have been made partakers, then you are bastards and not children" (Heb. 12:8), as if to say, "You were not born of free stock, but of a bastard, servile stock." "The Lord God opened my ear and I do not contradict, I have not gone away" (Is. 50:5). "In this everyone will know that you are my disciples, if you have love for one another" (John 13:35), because it is love

which makes you hold to my instruction. "If anyone loves me, he will keep my word" (John 14:23). A true disciple is one who holds to the instruction he received, just as it was imparted by his master. "Learn from me, for I am meek and humble of heart" (Matt. 11:29).

> "And you will know the truth." This brings true liberty to perfection. Knowledge of the truth is the knowledge of that by which things truly are what they are, and this is no other than the divine art and wisdom which is proposed to us in the words of God. It is by God's art and wisdom that things truly are what they are. Because of certain other principles things fall from the truth of their being, inasmuch as they are material and mutable and inclined to sag away from what is true. "Sanctify them in truth; your word is truth" (John 17:17). And it says of the Word in John 1:14, "Full of grace and truth." "I am the way and the truth and the life" (John 14:6). "Truth abides and is strong for ever" (3 Esdras 4:38). "Truth prevails over everything" (ibid. 3:12). And so it frees us from the futility of changeability and is the principle which makes freedom itself perfect.

> There follows, "And the truth will set you free." And this is the completion of true liberty. "Creation itself will be set free from enslavement to corruption into the freedom of the glory of the children of God" (Rom. 8:21). "The Jerusalem which is above is free, and that is our mother" (Gal. 4:26). So the word of the Lord, as being the truth, frees us from the coercion and constraint of futility. As the word of grace, it frees us from enslavement to guilt and sin. As the word of almighty God, it frees us from enslavement to wretchedness. First it gives us the freedom of nature, then it gives us the freedom of grace and thirdly it gives us the freedom of glory.

If the study of the liberal arts already gives us a certain freedom, faith leads us into a far greater freedom, because it gives us access to the word of God, the study of which, if undertaken perseveringly and obediently, will eventually bring us to the complete fulfilment of our intellectual nature and to complete moral freedom. The theological study, which alone is fully satisfying to our minds, cannot be isolated from the study of the arts though. At the end of his life Albert is still insisting on this. "Theology in itself is the first of all sciences, but it comes last in the order of our study and investigation. This is why Alfarabi says that it is in the study of theology that the philosophers have ended their lives."

It is rather surprising, at first sight, that Albert was not prepared to regard theology as essentially and simply a speculative science, for all his intellectualism. Both in the early commentary on the *Sentences* and in the late **Summa Theologiae** he cites Titus 1:1-2 to identify theological truth as being *secundum pietatem,* inseparable therefore from the practice of the Christian life and the hope of salvation and everlasting bliss. In the *Summa* he concludes that theology is a practical science, in the commentary on the *Sentences* that it is neither speculative nor practical, it is an "affective science," bringing both mind and heart to their proper perfection. This does not mean that theology is not a genuine science; it is a science, an organized body of knowledge with its own proper consistency. And even in the commentary on the *Sentences* it is indubitably correct to say that Albert's view of beatitude is an intellectual one: the "truth which beatifies" beatifies precisely by being the truth which fully satisfies the intellect. What Albert is concerned to deny is surely the tendency we have noticed in the twelfth century for theology to become just another specialization which could, in principle, be mastered by anyone who was competent, without its engaging and shaping a whole human and Christian life. In calling theology an "affective science" Albert is by no means proposing to subject theology to the control of that affective piety that was already beginning to define itself against learning and intellectualism. On the contrary, he is refusing to concede that there is any tension between piety and theology; he is locating piety in the heart of the intellectual discipline of theology. . . .

One of the crucial problems involved in the attempt to determine the nature of theology was the very vexed question of the precise nature of faith. The traditional data made it difficult for early thirteenth-century scholastics to see faith precisely as a form of knowledge. St. Augustine had insisted on the voluntary nature of belief, which suggested that faith had to be located in the will. Faith had also to be interpreted as a virtue, and it was generally accepted that the object of all virtues was some practical *good,* whereas the object of knowledge was always some *truth*. In accordance with this problematic Albert locates faith, in the commentary on the *Sentences,* as not being a kind of *scientia,* because the knowledge (*cognitio*) it involves comes more from affection than from reason, from love in the will rather than from rational proof. Faith is situated in "affective" rather than speculative understanding. Knowledge may be the "matter" of faith, but it is affection that actually makes it faith and has the dominant role in faith. Faith is a kind of virtue, rather than a kind of *scientia*. If it is objected that faith's object is truth and that therefore it belongs to the domain of the speculative intellect (and could therefore not be a virtue unless we are prepared to say that *all* speculative achievements count as a virtue), Albert proposes in reply a distinction between the kind of truth that is the goal of speculation and the kind of truth that "beatifies the intellect." Speculative truth consists in "the complete account of something" and involves a "kind of movement from the thing to the intellect." Beatifying truth, by contrast, is outside the mind and is not an "account of something" but a "something" (*res*), "a light of eternal

happiness" that is the "goal of an understanding which is moved by love for this truth."

Albert is well aware of the awkwardness of this position. It seems to entail that the object of faith is not truth as such, but truth viewed as good (*secundum rationem boni*), and this was indeed the doctrine, for example, of Philip the Chancellor and of the first Dominican Master in Paris, Roland of Cremona. But in Albert's judgment this is "no solution," because the truth has to be valued in its own right, precisely as truth. Otherwise it is difficult to see how we can escape saying that we believe something to be true just because we find it attractive (or "helpful," as people say these days), which would be a disastrous concession to wishful thinking. But then it is hard to see how Albert has not already made such a concession in declaring that the light of faith "convinces the reason by a kind of love in the will."

In the Dionysian commentaries we find Albert telling a very different story. The essentially cognitive nature of faith is affirmed there, as we have seen. He can still allude, without comment, to the voluntary quality of faith as a virtue that informs our conscience rather than persuading us with arguments, so that we are not constrained to believe by any rational proofs. But there is no longer any question of our being "convinced by love" to go beyond what can be demonstrated by the principles of reason. The divine light is not a proposition, it is true, but "it is a reality (*res*) which convinces the intellect." It convinces the intellect directly, it seems, by its sheer actuality.

On one point, at least, the development of Albert's theory of the intellect enabled him to come to a clearer understanding of faith. In the commentary on the *Sentences* one of his concerns was to insist that faith directs us toward a reality outside our own minds, in which our hope of beatitude is vested, and he contrasts this with the "account of a thing" that is the goal of intellectual speculation. But when he turned his attention to the subject of the intellect, he acquired . . . a hearty distaste for the "Latin" theory, which made the whole intellectual process a purely private, internal affair going on within the individual mind. His own view gave the intellect itself more of an outward orientation. What makes our understanding an understanding of some specific reality is the reality itself which is being understood (*ipsa res*). On this view it is precisely as an intellectual virtue that faith directs us to something outside our own minds, and this is no doubt why Albert is now able to say that faith unites all believers, which he was earlier not prepared to say.

The orientation of the intellect toward that which is outside itself means that there is no essential contradiction between the "ecstatic" structure of its natural workings and the "ecstatic" nature of faith, on which the text of Dionysius obliges Albert to comment. Exploiting the ambiguity of the word *ekstasis* Dionysius remarks that many people will suppose the believer to be "beside himself" (to have suffered an "ecstasy"), not realizing that he has indeed undergone an "ecstasy" (in a good sense) in "stepping out" quite properly from error. Albert, willfully or otherwise, misconstrues the sentence and takes *extasis* in a stronger sense than was intended here by Dionysius: "The believer has undergone an ecstasy for truth, that is, he has been placed outside himself in divine truth." This is the *excessus* referred to in *Mystical Theology* 1, on which Albert comments that it means "not holding oneself back within reason's own principles"—it does not, as Albert explains at some length, necessarily involve *excessus* in the sense of rapture or ecstatic trance.

The insertion of faith into a more general account of the working of the intellect does not mean that Albert has lost interest in the affective component in our knowledge of God. Even apart from his lifelong conviction that knowledge of God is our highest and most satisfying joy, he still wishes to ascribe a certain role to our affections in the very process whereby we come to know God; but his more developed intellectual theory allows him to state more precisely what this role is. "There is a kind of science which is about things beyond the reach of reason, so the knowledge of these things has to be received from some higher nature by participating in its light. . . . Although science is the perfection of our understanding, yet it is by the perfection of our affectivity (*affectus*) that we draw near to God and participate in his light; this is how our understanding is brought to perfection with regard to things which cannot be had simply by human reason. There is no question of affectivity taking over the role of the intellect, but if we are to get beyond the limits of our own rationality we need a greater share in the divine light than is given to us in purely natural knowledge, and there are moral presuppositions for such a sharing. Purity of heart is what immediately disposes us to receive the vision of God.

There is also an affective coloring to any genuinely Christian knowledge of God. In a famous passage in the *Divine Names* Dionysius refers to Hierotheos as "not just learning about the things of God, but undergoing them. . . ." Albert comments on this: "'Also he was perhaps taught the things of God by a diviner inspiration,' diviner than teaching or study, that is, 'not only learning' from others 'but also undergoing divine things,' being moved in his affection about them, 'and by his very sympathy for them,' by his affection for the things of God . . . 'he was made perfect for union with them,' union with the things of God in heart and mind, 'and for faith,' that is, for the certain knowledge of spiritual things. . . . This is called a diviner way because thus the things of God are perceived, in a way, experientially, just as someone who is suffering

from a wound has a more certain knowledge of what a wound is than someone who only hears about it or sees it, and someone who tastes wine has a better knowledge of its pleasant flavor." A text like this does not contradict Albert's conviction that our union with God is fundamentally intellectual, it draws out one aspect of what intellectual union with God means: the certainty of faith is not like the certainty that a cogent rational argument produces, it is much more like the certainty which comes from a direct perception of something. What convinces the mind to assent to the first truth is not a proposition but a *reality,* and the reality of God cannot properly be apprehended dispassionately. In the commentary on the *Mystical Theology* Albert distinguishes between the ability to form propositions and *real* knowledge (*realis scientia*), that is, knowledge which actually touches in some way the *res,* the reality, of God, and this knowledge is "part of beatitude" and so cannot be divorced from its affective component. The idea that we could have a real knowledge of God that was not, to some extent, beatifying is simply incoherent.

So faith has a necessary affective component precisely because it is concerned with the reality of God, not just with words about him; but this very insistence on the reality of God means that the status of our talk about God has to be examined carefully. If, as several twelfth-century theologians maintained, the relationship between theological and non-theological use of words is one of equivocation, then theology will tell us nothing about the reality of God unless we can unscramble the equivocation and determine what the words actually mean when they are used theologically. And if we can do no more than say that they have "miraculous new meanings," then all we shall be able to achieve is the arrangement of more or less coherent verbal patterns, without having the remotest idea what we are actually talking *about*. If the only kind of bank that I am familiar with is the kind that deals in money, and have no acquaintance with the other kind "whereon the wild thyme blows" (and perhaps try to arrive at some idea of what "wild thyme" is by imagining a nightmarish world in which savage clocks chime irregular hours according to some scheme of chronometry untamed by arithmetic), then I shall quite strictly not have a notion what the bard is talking about, and shall not be any the wiser for being told that he is using words in miraculous new senses. Similarly if all theological language is metaphorical, theology will at most be a vaguely suggestive expression of people's religious aspirations; it will not have any capacity to tell me anything about what God really is. If none of our language properly applies to God and all we can do is transfer words to him without the "things" (*res*) they signify, then we can never be sure we are really saying anything about God at all. And it is no good appealing to some kind of direct experiential knowledge of God, which would render words superfluous, if it is true, as

Albert believed in common with most of his contemporaries, that in this life we never have a direct encounter with God unmediated by creatures. In Albert's view the *res* that convinces the mind to cleave to the first truth is the divine light itself, but this does not in itself present us with any specific *object*. It would be more correct to say that it is like the sheer fact of daylight than that it is like direct perception of any particular thing. You cannot argue with daylight (though you can draw the curtains and shut your eyes, if you want to); it "convinces the mind." But if we actually want to see something, there has to be something there for us to see. The light of faith enables us to believe, but it does not of itself give any content to belief, and the content comes largely from words (the words of the creeds, the words of the bible, and so on). So if faith does in some way confront us with the reality of God it must be, in this life, largely through the medium of words. And these must, then, be words that really do succeed, however inadequately, in putting us in touch with God himself.

Thirteenth-century theologians had learned from Aristotle at least one linguistic gambit they could use to escape from the twelfth-century dilemma. Instead of having to decide simply whether theological usage was univocal, metaphorical or equivocal, they could also consider the possibility that it might be analogical. Barclays and Chase manhattan are both banks in the same sense (univocally). The bank where I keep my overdraft and the bank where I keep my wild thyme are banks in two quite unrelated senses, apparently connected only because of a linguistic accident, so here "bank" is equivocal. As for yon Cassius' lean and hungry look, he may indeed have been dieting and he may be pining for his lunch, but his look is "hungry" with reference to a different appetite and can properly be regarded as metaphorically hungry, a use of language justified by the evident similarities between different kinds of appetite. But what about that shockingly fine specimen, the Earl of Blandings' brother? He has a healthy look, a healthy body and a healthy appetite. Here, according to medieval Aristotelianism, we have a case of analogy. The look and the appetite are certainly not healthy in the same way as the body, but they are called healthy with reference to the same health that makes us call the body healthy.

This notion of analogy suggests a promising way of upgrading theological language. If we say (in the manner of Alan of Lille) that words like "good" are applied to God causally (we call God "good" because he causes goodness), then it is not clear that they really tell us anything about God, though Alan evidently wanted them to do so. But in the Platonist perspective of an Augustine or a Dionysius any goodness in creatures is not just caused by God, it is a participation of some kind in God's goodness. We certainly cannot say that God is good in just the same way that a sausage is good. Sausages, unfortunately, can be bad, so being a sausage is not the same as being a good sausage, whereas for God to be God and for God to be good are exactly the same, in accordance with that most basic of medieval theological rules that God is whatever he has. But could it not be the case that there is some real common referent involved in both God's goodness and that of the sausage, like the common referent involved in the healthy appetite and the healthy body? Albert is not prepared to go so far as that. Full-fledged analogy requires that there be something in common, and there is nothing that is strictly common to God and creatures; it would never be proper to cite God and a creature as two instances of the same thing, even with all the refinements introduced by the notion of analogy. But there is a kind of halting analogy, after all: even if there is, strictly, nothing in common between God and creatures, creatures do, in their various ways, "imitate" God. We call a sausage good with reference to its being a sausage, not with reference to the divine nature; but a good sausage is still, in its own dim way, a reflection of the goodness of God. There is something in God that is responsible for there being a world in which things like sausages can attain to excellence. Creatures are obviously unlike God, but they are also, however palely, like the God who made them. Albert therefore concedes that there is an "analogy of imitation" between God and creatures, even if there is no full analogy.

On this basis we can now take a further step. Of course all our language is human language and, as such, is inadequate for talking about God. But does that mean that we are confined to transferring words to God without the reality which they signify? If in at least some cases the link between our talking about creatures and our talking about God is an "analogy of imitation," that suggests that in some cases God has a prior claim on certain words. Albert therefore makes a distinction between what words mean (the reality they signify) and the way in which we learn how to use them. It is from God the Father that all fatherhood is named, according to St. Paul (Eph. 3:15), but it is obviously from the fatherhood we encounter among creatures that we learn to talk about fathers. So the meaning of the word can be said to apply properly to God; what is inadequate is its *modus significandi,* the way it functions in our human language. This means, then, that we must distinguish between words that properly refer to creatures, which can only be used metaphorically of God, and words that really do indicate genuine attributes of God. And when negative theology bids us negate all that we say of God, we must distinguish between different kinds of inadequacy in our language: in some cases we are not denying that the reality indicated by the word belongs to God; we are just reminding ourselves that we cannot properly state what it means for it to belong to God.

Instead of a simple declaration, then, that all human language is inadequate, Albert gives us a rather more nuanced doctrine:

> Divine names are formed in two ways: (1) from things which in reality belong to God first and only secondarily to creatures, and these are the names which blessed Dionysius calls "mystical," such as "being," "life," "intellect," "wisdom," "goodness." "Mystical" in Greek is the same as "secret" in Latin, and a "mystical name" is so called because (owing to the character imparted to words by the way they are instituted) it signifies imperfectly and partially something that exists in God perfectly and totally, and sometimes it suggests that something is an accidental property which exists substantially in God and is the divine substance. Because of this the divine reality which it names remains hidden from us, because we know that the reality is higher than the name and that our tongues fall short of declaring it. . . . Affirmations are inadequate because the way that names function in our language (their *modus significandi*) is at odds with the divine reality, particularly in three ways: they present as complex a reality which is of infinite simplicity; they present imperfectly what is absolutely perfect; and they sometimes present as an accident something which is really substance. So Anselm says that "Father" and "Life" and so on actually come down to our level from God, but we are more at home with "father" meaning a human, fleshly father than we are with "Father" meaning God. (2) In the case of symbolic names God is designated by transferring some property that belongs to bodies to a spiritual sense. He is called "stone," for instance, because stone is solid and provides a solid basis for building on, so in a spiritual sense God's truth is solid and is the foundation for our whole spiritual edifice.

So only some names of God are metaphorical, and in their case negative theology has the simple task of reminding us that God is not really a stone or a lion, that he is not really angry or drunk. But some names of God are not metaphorical, they are "mystical" and apply primarily to God; in their case negative theology comes in to insist that they do really apply to God, and that therefore we cannot fully know what they mean. It is particularly with reference to these mystical names that the importance of holding together negative and affirmative theology is apparent: affirmative theology must not exaggerate its competence in talking about the reality of God, but negative theology must not degenerate into pure negation, its aim is to clarify how we *are* talking about God, not simply to stop us talking about God. The mystical names of God are, according to Albert, the subject of two books of the Dionysian corpus, the *Divine Names* and the *Mystical Theology,* corresponding to the two ways in which these names can be considered: "They can be viewed in terms of the flowing out from the cause of the effects it causes, which participate in a secondary way in the content of some name, and this is how they are dealt

with in the *Divine Names;* or they can be viewed in terms of the way in which an analysis of the caused effects traces them back to their cause and the meaning of the name, as it exists in the cause, is left unknown because of the transcendence of the cause, and this is how the names are dealt with in the *Mystical Theology*." These are obviously complementary approaches: one emphasizes that we are *talking* about God and explores the manifestation of God in the intelligible structure of creation, while the other emphasizes that we are talking about *God* and so leads us back from creation to the transcendent mystery that lies hidden within the whole process of revelation.

It is, incidentally, interesting to contrast Albert's interpretation of the distinciton between mystical and symbolic names with that of William of Auxerre. According to William, "Mystical theology, which is called 'mystical,' that is, 'hidden,' names God by means of what it hiddenly perceives about God through some intellectual vision or contemplation, as when it calls God 'sweet,' 'beloved,' and so on. In both symbolic and mystical theology God is named by means of creatures, but in symbolic theology he is named from external creatures, whereas in mystical theology he is named by way of inner, hidden and more worthy effects which the soul receives above itself from the contemplation of God, and the soul imposes such names through the gift of wisdom, to which it belongs especially and properly to know experientially what God is like (*qualis sit deus*)."

Albert's much more objective understanding of what the mystical names signify is patently facilitated by metaphysical considerations, but it would be wrong to see it as a purely philosophical doctrine. At the beginning of the *Divine Names,* as in the *Celestial Hierarchy,* Albert points out that the *habitus regens* in this science is faith, and specifically "the faith, as it is passed on to us in sacred scripture." And, following Dionysius, he interprets this strictly. "Our intellect might think that, though it has to be guided by the practice of sacred scripture in its exposition of the divine names, it could legitimately discover something about God by reason beyond what is in scripture. Dionysius excludes this and says that we must say and think nothing about God except what is passed on to us by sacred scripture, so that we reserve to God himself the knowledge of himself in anything which is not given to us in scripture." Every science has its own basic principles, and in the case of theology its "principles" consist of scripture. And it should not be forgotten that in this period any intellectual discipline was intimately associated, if not identified, with its "set books," so that the very word *scientia* could be used to refer to such authoritative writings. *Theologia* as a science is inseparable from *theologia* as the word of God in scripture. In the case of other disciplines it would be a sign of intellectual weakness to follow "authority" too uncritically. But in theology the "authority" in question is not just human authority; it rests on the infallible "reason" of God, and so it is rational for us to submit to it unhesitatingly, even if we do not always understand the reason for what is said. It is this submission to scripture that gives theology its special solidity and certainty.

Intellectual speculation has no right to try to supplement or to criticize the data of revelation. But scripture is meant "to enlighten our intellect," and this calls for sustained and intelligent study, and this is where we may benefit from the tools supplied by philosophy and other disciplines. A naive devotion to the mere text of scripture will lead only to "childish fancies." It may be true, as St. Gregory said, that "sacred scripture is a river in which sheep paddle and elephants swim," but this does not justify even the simple faithful in resting content with the mere symbols in which the scriptural message is often clothed, because even the literal meaning of the text should be located, not in the symbols themselves, but in what they signify.

Mystical theology, then, is located firmly within the enterprise of Christian reflection on the word of God, and it is an intellectual discipline, even if it requires a mind strengthened by a supernatural light so that it can go beyond its natural limits in the "ecstasy" of faith.

. . . . .

Albert's analysis of theological language leads him to a relatively optimistic view of our ability to say things that do really apply to God, to ascribe the substance, the *res,* of at least some of our words to him, and not just the words without their *res.* But at the same time he is keenly aware of how little we actually know God, and he is clearly far from unsympathetic to the "oriental" theology that provoked the condemnation of 1241.

The epistemological problem of how any created intellect can know God, which Bonaventure could dismiss so breezily in his *quaestio disputata,* was for Albert a very serious question.

In the **De Resurrectione** Albert makes a valiant, if not very successful, attempt to deal with the issues involved in the claim that we shall see God directly in heaven, a claim which the 1241 condemnation made it necessary to endorse, and in any case Albert seems to be persuaded that if we cannot ever attain to a genuine knowledge of God then our whole intellectual life (and therefore our whole life) will be eternally doomed to frustration. But there are problems. Only an infinite act of understanding could cope with an "infinite intelligible," and that is what God is; and our intellectual capacity is finite and so there seems to be an irremediable disproportion between it and God. We also need

to show that there is some procedure whereby our minds could know God without either actually being God (which would bring us back to the pantheism condemned in 1210) or needing some intelligible form of God, which would leave us with a knowledge of God by way of something which is not God, and that would be merely a "vision in theophanies," such as Hugh of St. Victor had reprobated and which some people believed to have been condemned as heretical in 1241. To evade the second kind of difficulty Albert falls back on an Augustinian notion of immediate knowledge of God by virtue of his real presence in the intellect, which we cannot see now because of the conditions of life in this world (particularly the flesh and sin) and because our attention is turned elsewhere, hindrances which will both be removed in the hereafter. Our immediate knowledge of God is thus to be understood on the model of our immediate knowledge of ourselves, and Albert even goes so far as to say "God will present himself to us without any medium, just as he sees himself without any medium."

To deal with the problem of disproportion and with the patristic authorities marshalled against the possibility of any direct vision of God, Albert resorts to distinctions in true scholastic vein. Taking up a phrase from 1 John 3:2 he distinguishes between seeing something "as it is" and seeing what something is, the latter meaning an exhaustive vision of all that something is. Clearly in this sense we cannot see what God is, and in this sense, as Damascene says, God is "incomprehensible and boundless, known by none, the sole contemplator of himself." But we can see God "as he is," Albert maintains, and seeing something "as it is" means "seeing its existence (*esse*) or being (*essentia*)." This rather underdeveloped distinction seems to rely heavily on the analogy of bodily vision: when the long-awaited visitors from Alpha Centauri eventually decide to land, we shall no doubt see many exotic pieces of equipment "as they are," without having the remotest idea what they are.

This still leaves the problem of disproportion. The only possibility of coping with something infinite, Albert suggests, is by finding some way in which it is finite. There is no chance of our intellect being able to delimit *what* God is, but it can handle God's attributes, and in reality any of God's attributes *is* God, so if our minds can reach any of them they will in fact be reaching God's essence. This also provides the answer to the problem raised by Chrysostom: if God's essence is simple, then all those who see it must be seeing the same thing, yet "one praises it as glory, another as majesty, another as holiness and another as wisdom." The answer is that "though any attribute, as it exists in God, is the divine essence, yet as perceived by the intellect the attributes are distinguished by what they connote. And that is why one praises God as glory, another as wisdom and another as majesty." What is "connoted" by the divine attributes is their derivatives in creation (their reality in God being what they denote), and if this is the source of their distinction it might be felt that Albert has not sufficiently established that knowledge of God by way of his attributes is any different from knowledge of him through creatures, and his implied suggestion that the attributes of God are somehow "finite," which must mean that we can "define" them in a way that is impossible with the question "what" God is, surely prompts us to wonder whether it is not at the level of their created counterparts that they are thus definable, rather than at the level of their existence in God. And if these anxieties are legitimate, we may further suspect that Albert has not sufficiently distinguished between the vision of God that we shall have in heaven and the knowledge of God we can have by faith here on earth.

In his account of the "mechanics" of the vision of God, at this stage, Albert is essentially at one with the Augustinian critics of "oriental" theology, but in his account of what we shall be able to see he stops a long way short of the utterly complete and clear vision of God to which William of Auvergne aspired, and he concedes a great deal to the Dionysian contention that "complete ignorance is the way to know him who is above all that is known": "'Complete ignorance' means 'ignorance of the complete,' that is, ignorance of what God is; the most perfect knowledge of God is the vision of him together with the recognition that we are powerless to reach 'what' he is. He is thus known to be above all knowledge and all mind. And this is what Job says, that all who see him look on him from afar" (cf. Job 36:25).

In the commentaries on the *Sentences* and on Dionysius' *Celestial Hierarchy* we can see that Albert's position has already matured considerably. He now repudiates the suggestion that the divine attributes might provide a way round the problem of God's infinity: God is "infinite in any one of his attributes." Precisely as infinite he cannot be known, except in the sense that we can know that he is infinite. But because he is simple and because we are not talking of any kind of infinite bulk, knowing God incompletely does not mean knowing just a "part" of God (as we might see just the tail of a mouse, which would not of itself tell us much about the rest of the animal). So there is no radical impossibility about our knowing God (who is infinite), even though we cannot know him precisely in his infinity—only God can have that kind of through knowledge of himself. God, according to a phrase inspired by Damascene, is "an infinite ocean of substance," entirely eluding any attempt to say what he is. So our minds are rather in the position of people gazing out to sea: they are definitely looking at the sea, but at the same time they are not looking at anything precisely defined.

The question of proportionality was largely sidestepped in *De Resurrectione* by means of the Augustinian doctrine of knowledge by presence in the intellect. If God is really there the whole time and it is only the nuisance of this present life that prevents us from seeing him, then clearly the soul just *is,* as Augustine claimed, capable of God (*capax Dei*). Our inability to see him is no more than a temporary, if tiresome, fact about us. In the commentary on the *Sentences* Albert becomes less and less happy with this scenario. In book I he is still essentially relying on the model of the intellect's awareness of itself: "The divine substance is seen by all the blessed; as to how it is seen, without wishing to preempt further discussion we say that it is seen unmediatedly by conjunction, in such a way that God offers himself to our intellect in his own substance, just as the intellect does to itself." But there is no longer any hint that this immediate vision of God was all along a possibility lurking within the soul. The lack of proportion between God and us has to be taken seriously, and Albert now maintains that naturally there really is no such proportion; it is only "by the help of God" that our minds can rise up to become capable of seeing God.

God is the source of the existence of all things, and at the same time, as the primordial Intellect, he is the source of the intelligibility of all things, and it is this latter which most interests Albert.

—Simon Tugwell

Once a more active role is ascribed to God in making it possible for us to see him, the question of "theophanies" begins to demand more attention. The use of this term was integral to the Eriugenist interpretation of the Dionysian hierarchical worldview, and had been interpreted to involve (a) that God is seen, even by the angels and the blessed, only indirectly by way of "images," and (b) that the vision of God is accorded to the angels and saints strictly in accordance with their position in the hierarchy of being, so that lower beings receive only the illumination that passes down to them through higher beings and therefore do not actually see God. Both conclusions were condemned in 1241 and "theophany" became a word to be avoided. But Albert is now no longer prepared to leave the word in the hands of its enemies, whom he accuses of "insulting holy books" and "presumption." His own maturing theory of the intellect makes possible an interpretation of theophanies that allows for a direct vision of God: in intellectual as in bodily vision there has to be some kind of light to make things visible (or intelligible), but there has also to be a specific visible (or intelligible) object, and it is this that determines what in particular is seen (or known). A created intellect needs to be reinforced by a light from on high if it is to see God, and this light may come either directly from God or through the mediation of higher created beings, but the role of intelligible object, which determines the content of the act of understanding, is God himself, God's own substance. So Albert distinguishes between purely symbolic theophanies, which have no place in the beatific vision, and theophanies that are perfectly compatible with the beatific vision: We may see an object which is truly God in a divine light that is not God (that is, a light which flows to us from God through created intermediaries, which fortifies the mind to see God himself). We may also see an object which is truly God in a divine light which is God: "God himself is in all the blessed as a kind of light, making them into a likeness of himself through their participation in him." In this way Albert is able to revive the Eriugenist doctrine that we see God by participating in God and to allow room even in heaven for a process of illumination that respects the structural interdependence of created intellects, without any denial of the immediacy of the vision of God. The spiritual solipsism which can, even if rather unfairly, be deduced from Plotinian or Augustinian doctrine, is thus shown to be unnecessary: the richly coherent cosmos of later Neoplatonism in which all beings are connected with each other in multiple ways does not exclude the possibility of direct intellectual union between any created mind and God.

In the commentary on the fourth book of the *Sentences* Albert formally and finally rejects the Augustinian knowledge by presence: substantial presence of something in the soul is not a sufficient basis for understanding. The mind understands itself in the same way that it understands anything else. Albert concedes this, but with an unexpected reservation: there is no other way of interpreting understanding, "provided we know what we are saying or understanding. But in heaven it will not be like this. There the unbounded light of the Godhead, which is God himself, is united with the agent intellect and poured out substantially over the whole soul and fills the soul, and in this way the soul will be full of God who is its bliss." It is by being united directly with God like this that the blessed soul will "understand" him, but it seems to be a rather odd kind of derstanding, if it excludes knowing what we are talking about or understanding. In fact Albert seems to be proposing to us a state of complete, but rather vague, luminosity, in which nothing in particular is understood.

In the later Dionysian commentaries Albert moves with much greater confidence toward a coherent and surprisingly Eriugenist doctrine, in which the notion of theophanies plays an important part. It is in terms of theophanies that Albert manages to do justice to both sides of the dispute that resulted in the 1241 condem-

nation, showing that it possible for a created intellect to have a direct vision of God's essence, that such a vision is not ineluctably confined to the natural capacity of any given being, and that in spite of the simplicity of the divine essence it can truly be seen directly by different intellects in different ways.

Let us look at some texts from the commentary on the *Divine Names:*

> "Seeing" means actually making contact with the thing seen. . . . It also means running your eye over something. As Euclid shows, anything that is seen is seen from the vantage point of the corner of a triangle, whose apex is in the eye and whose base is in the thing seen. . . . The thing is seen along a line dividing the triangle, and so it is not seen all at once, but by passing from one point to another. When we have run our eye over the whole thing, we can be said to have seen the whole thing. In this sense God cannot be seen by running our mind's eye over all that he is.

> . . . Although God is simple in his substance, he is multiple in his attributes, whose principle (*ratio*) exists truly in him without any real plurality. If we saw God by surveying his substance with the knowledge of "what" he is, then all who see him would see and praise him in the same way. But as it is he is seen only in the sense of an immediate contact with his substance, in whatever way he makes himself present (*se obiicit*). And since he makes himself present to one in one light (*secundum unam rationem*) and to another in another light, one sees what another does not see, although they are all seeing his substance, because knowledge and goodness and everything that can have a *ratio* [i.e., more or less, everything that can properly be predicated of God] is God's substance.

> . . . A created intellect has no proportionate capacity to know God by its own natural endowments, but it is made proportionate inasmuch as it is helped by enlightenments or theophanies coming down to it from God; even so it is not made capable of seeing "what" God is, but only of seeing him by a real contact with his substance, in accordance with whatever way he makes himself present in one or another light (*sub tali vel tali ratione*).

> The life of glory is a perfection above nature, in which nature without grace is incompetent; so since it is not granted in accordance with the power of nature, since it increases the capacity of nature, though without destroying nature, it can come about that a being whose nature is lower can be brought to the level of some being of a higher nature or even beyond it.

> The intellect, making contact with God's substance, knows him either in some image, as in this life in

which we know God in a mirror and enigmatically, or immediately, as in heaven. The intellect is not proportionate just by its nature to this contact, but it is made proportionate by the light of glory coming down to it and strengthening it and raising it above its nature; and this is what is meant by saying that God is seen by way of theophany and participation, inasmuch as different intellects are strengthened in different ways to see God.

Albert's whole scheme presupposes that no created intellect can see "what" God is, so that we are all entirely dependent on the various ways in which God strengthens our minds and the various lights in which he proposes himself to our thus strengthened minds. And Albert's doctrine is quite unambiguous on this point. Even the highest angels do not know "what" God is. All that is proportionate to our understanding is "that" God is (*quia est*). And even this is perhaps going too far: "A created intellect cannot perfectly reach God in such a way that no knowledge of him remains outside it; it is joined to him as to something transcending its capacity, indistinctly (*sub quadam confusione*) because there can be no knowledge 'what' he is, since he is unlimited, or of 'why' he is, since he has no cause, or even a distinct knowledge 'that' he is, since he has no remote cause or effect proportionate to him, so neither on earth nor in heaven can anything be seen of him except an indistinct 'that he is' (*quia confusum*), although God himself is seen more or less luminously according to different kinds of vision and different kinds of seer."

The knowledge "that" God is apparently "proportionate" to our minds, and this calls for a more precise statement of what is meant by saying that our minds do not naturally have any "proportion" or capacity for the knowledge of God. There was a tradition, going back to St. Paul, that some kind of knowledge of God is possible to us by way of his creatures, independent of the gift of faith. St. John Damascene specified that the knowledge "that" God is is implanted in us by nature, and Albert accepts this. Such a claim is entirely coherent with Albert's belief that God is present in us as a light in our minds, so that he is known, implicitly, in our knowledge of anything, as the ground of all intelligibility. But if knowledge "that" God is is natural to us, and knowledge "that" God is is all we shall have even in heaven, what becomes of the alleged "strengthening" of our intellect by some supernatural influx of light?

In response to a suggestion that our knowledge of God is perfected in heaven and must therefore move on from knowledge "that" to knowledge "what" or "why," Albert replies very firmly, "Our knowledge will not be perfected with a different kind of knowledge, either knowledge 'what' or knowledge 'why,' but with another way of knowing 'that': we shall have an unme-

diated vision 'that,' where now we have only a veiled and enigmatic vision in a mirror." The supernatural reinforcement of our minds does not enable them to do something quite different from what they could do naturally; it enables them to do more fully what they could already, to some extent, do. Albert is fully serious in his concern that the supernatural should not be envisaged in any way that jeopardizes the natural. However much a created intellect may be enhanced by grace or glory, its understanding will always be conditioned by its own nature. Albert does not believe that some miraculous change will overtake our intellectual or perceptual powers in heaven. The text in the pseudo-Augustinian *De Spiritu et Anima,* which suggests that in heaven our senses will be turned into reason and our reason into intellect and our intellect into understanding (*intelligentia*), is interpreted by Albert to mean only that the lower powers turn *to* the higher powers and receive a kind of overflow from them so that they too can share in their enjoyment; he explicitly denies that they are "drawn out of their own natures."

All that our minds are capable of, then, is an indistinct knowledge "that" God is, a knowledge which is, to start off with, simply implicit in the sheer fact that we can understand anything at all. This purely natural and indirect knowledge of God can be enhanced in various degrees, for instance, by the light of faith, that *res convincens intellectum,* the sheer fact of illumination contained in the fact that we find the articles of belief credible. Inasmuch as we are united with the light of God, we can come to know the unknown God more and more, but even in heaven, even with the light of glory, we cannot get beyond an indistinct knowledge "that" God is; he remains for us an "infinite ocean" of which we know more truly what it is not than what it is. What is new in heaven is that we shall meet this brute fact of light directly, instead of meeting it indirectly in its reflection in the intelligibility of God's works, whether of grace or of nature. But does this mean, then, that there is nothing for us to see except a vague, unbounded luminosity?

Vistas of infinite and indeterminate light no doubt appeal to some people, and if that is all that there is to be known about God, the comparative mysticists will have no difficulty in proving that all religions are really one and that the systems of doctrine that divide them are no more than hopeless attempts to formulate the ineffable. There have presumably always been people who prefer their religion to provide uplift and inspiration, without requiring them actually to believe anything in particular. In the Middle Ages Eriugena could perhaps be read (inaccurately, to be sure) as recommending a rather nebulous deity, when he announced that even God does not know what he himself is, because he does not have any particular "what" to know. This doctrine was duly passed on in Honorius

Augustodunesis. Avicenna also denied that God has an essence or quiddity.

William of Auvergne had little sympathy for any such imprecise divinity. In his view it is impossible to speak either about God or to God unless God is "intelligible and nameable as an individual (*singulariter*)," unless he can be clearly picked out and distinguished from everyone and everything else. Any philosophy that could not accommodate this clearly locatable individuality of God was automatically disqualified. If we cannot identify God as an individual, to whom shall we pray, whom shall we worship, how shall we know we are not worshipping the wrong God?

St. Albert is definitely not happy about calling God "individual." Apart from the problem that God is not "an individual" (he is three Persons), the term *individual* suggests only improperly the real uniqueness of God. In principle, wherever there is one individual there could conceivably be more than one; even if in fact we have only one sun in our sky, there is no absolute reason why we should not have half a dozen. To call God "an individual" (*singularis*) suggests that he might always turn out to be merely one God among several, and "God," according to St. Albert, properly has no plural. On this view William of Auvergne's anxiety is somewhat misconceived. The problem is not how we identify the right God, so that we do not worship the wrong one, but how we make sure we do not worship anything which is not God. And if this is the right way to formulate the problem, it is not really necessary to "pick out" God, so long as we remember not to worship anything that we can pick out. But this still leaves the other side of William's anxiety, which was mentioned earlier on, that if we cannot know God as an individual, our whole hope of beatitude collapses. Are we really looking forward only to an eternity of gazing out into (supernatural) space?

Albert certainly does not accept that God actually *is* indeterminate. The contention that God has no *quid est* is explicitly repudiated: God is "a kind of quiddity and essence"; there is something "intrinsically intelligible in God, by which he is distinguished from others." Although God "is infinite in every way, in his essence, in his power and in every other way that is conceivable in him," Albert does not want this to be understood as implying that God is fuzzy at the edges: "Though God is not measured or limited by anything created, he is measured by himself and so in a way he is finite to himself, though not to us."

The trouble is that God is "infinite" as far as we are concerned and "what" he is is therefore indeterminate in our minds. He is not properly to be thought of as an "object" to any created intellect. All the same, Albert is not prepared to leave us simply with a vast, unfocused luminosity to gaze at. In his commentary on

Dionysius' fifth epistle he formally raises the question: If it is God who enlightens us, then how can it also be God who perfects our intellect, since the perfection of the intellect requires that it should have some definite object to know? And it is not light that provides the mind with any definte object; the mind comes to intellectual fulfilment in the form of actual understanding because its intellectual light is particularized by the thing understood.

Albert answers that God brings the intellect to its fulfilment by acting in two ways. He enlightens the mind (this picks up the doctrine formulated in the commentary on the fourth book of the *Sentences* that God unites himself with our agent intellect), but he also "brings it to a particular knowledge, inasmuch as he is something particular (*quiddam determinatum*), particularized not by matter, but by his nature and the attributes of his nature and inasmuch as there are Persons with their own particular properties."

So God is not in any ordinary sense an "object" for the intellect, yet he takes the place of the things known. How are we to understand this? In the commentary on the fifth epistle Albert refers us back for the rest of his discussion of the vision of God to the commentary on the first epistle, where Dionysius makes the devastating comment, "If anyone who sees God understands what he has seen, then he has not seen God himself, but only something that is his. . . . Perfect ignorance in the best sense is how we know him who is above all that is known." Since understanding and mental vision are essentially the same thing, Albert takes Dionysius to be propounding the startling paradox that "anyone who sees God does not see God, but only something that is his," that is, something that derives from him, and he comments accordingly:

> When he says that anyone seeing God does not see him, this must be understood in terms of a vision of "what" God is or a distinct vision "that" he is, and God is not seen in either of these ways; all there is is an indistinct and inadequate vision "that" he is, and this is true both on earth and in heaven, as we have already said.

> When he says, "but only something that is his," this must be understood with reference to the starting-point of vision, because vision always begins with some effect of God's, either one in which the intellect sees, as in a mirror, or one by which it sees, as with light. But the intellect is fixed on God himself as the goal (*terminus*) of its vision, because the intellect receives God's effects and plunges itself in him and sees God himself. . . .

The "perfect ignorance" Dionysius recommends is taken to mean that "we know ourselves to be failing completely to comprehend God because of his excellence.

. . . And so it is clear that Dionysius does not mean that God is not seen in any way, but that he is seen precisely in our ignorance of him."

If we put these comments on the epistles together with the passages cited earlier from the *Divine Names,* it is reasonably clear what Albert's doctrine is. God unites himself with our minds as light; he also confronts us with himself, indirectly on earth and directly in heaven, but our minds cannot really take him in as an "object" because we can only attain to an indistinct knowledge "that" he is. But God presents himself to us, *obiicit se,* almost "objectifies himself" for us, "under this or that *ratio,"* as goodness or wisdom or whatever. These are surely the "somethings that are his" that we see and that are a way of reaching a real vision of God, which begins with some effect of his. It is through God's effects that we have a distinct grasp of his attributes (which in him are simply himself). And in as much as it is by participating in God that we know him, it is surely not least by discovering the effects of his attributes in ourselves that we see him in the light of them. Thus we do have a real and immediate vision of God in heaven, but simply as such it provides no specific content for our intellect. Inasmuch as God provides the content as well as the light for our intellect, it is in terms of his attributes, on which we can get some intellectual purchase because of their visibility in God's effects. Starting from these effects, we see through them to God who is presenting his substance to us (which is not really distinct from his attributes) precisely by knowing that we are not capable of comprehending what God is. It is quite literally in our ignorance, our not-knowing, that we actually see God in himself, because it is the not-knowing that takes us beyond the intelligible effect of God to the reality of the attribute of God that it manifests, and so to the essence of God, that sheer presence whose very transcendence delights the intellect supremely.

If this interpretation of Albert's doctrine is correct, then the position he has reached by the end of his Dionysian commentaries is, as I have suggested, surprisingly Eriugenist. Unlike Eriugena he does formally allow for an unmediated vision of God's esence, but as such this unmediated vision is unintelligible to us. What makes it intelligible is that God presents himself to us in the light of his attributes, which are distinct and intelligible to us because of their manifestation in creatures. So what actually gives intelligible shape to our vision of God is the vision of God's effects become entirely transparent to himself, and this is precisely what Eriugena believed. It is God who is seen, but he, as it were, nuances the vision of himself in different ways for different people, so that it is in terms of theophanies that the vision of God becomes, as it were, manageable to them. And this is just how Eriugena's twelfth-century follower, Honorius Augustodunensis, interprets the "many mansions" of John 14:2.

It is clear that any theory like this of how we see God requires the sort of theory we were looking at earlier of how we talk about God. If theophanies are to provide a real, direct vision of God, then it must be possible to ascribe real attributes to God which, in him, actually *are* his substance but which are at the same time real in their own right, so that the affirmation of them does genuinely succeed in saying something about God, even if, because of the inadequate *modus significandi* of all our language, the affirmation needs to be capped by a negation.

We can also see how important the *Mystical Theology* is in Albert's view of the Christian life. There is real continuity between the vision of God in heaven and our attempts to develop our faith into a theological science on earth. Even in heaven we have only an indistinct vision of God's essence, as such, and whatever distinctness there is comes from an increasingly perspicuous knowledge of how the attributes of God are manifested in his works. Thus there has to be a rich affirmative theology, culling signs and riddling disclosures of God from all his creatures and all his words. But if this elaborate and no doubt lengthy process is to debouch into a vision of God himself, every light has to be transcended. If it is "transcended" without first being affirmed, there will be no revelation, no theophany; but equally if it is affirmed without being transcended, then we shall stop short of the knowledge of God that is possible to us.

FURTHER READING

Coleman, Janet. "Albert the Great." In *Ancient and Medieval Memories: Studies in the Reconstruction of the Past,* pp. 416-21. Cambridge: Cambridge University Press, 1992.

> Discusses Albert's ideas about memory as they pertain to the development of the Scholastic theory on the subject.

Hawks, Ellison. "From Charlemagne to Albertus Magnus." In *Pioneers of Plant Study,* pp. 100-07. New York: Macmillan, 1928.

> General overview of Albert's botanical writings and their historical sources.

Heines, Virginia. Introduction to *Libellus de alchimia,* ascribed to Albertus Magnus, translated by Virginia Heines, pp. xv-xxii. Berkeley: University of California Press, 1958.

> Describes the "Little Book of Alchemy," a text attributed by some scholars to Albert.

Kennedy, Leonard A. "St. Albert the Great's Doctrine of Divine Illamination." *The Modern Schoolman* XL (November 1962-May 1963): 23-37.

Traces the development of Alfred's theory of knowledge, stressing his belief in illuminationism, or the idea that "the soul knows without dependence on the body."

Kibre, Pearl. "Alchemical Writings Ascribed to Albertus Magnus." *Speculum* 17 (October 1942): 499-518.

Offers "a preliminary survey of the manuscript literature" in an attempt to determine Albert's authentic writings on alchemy.

————. "Further Manuscripts Containing Alchemical Tracts Attributed to Albertus Magnus." *Speculum* XXXIV, No. 2 (April 1959): 235-47.

Follow-up to Kibre's 1942 article (see above).

Partington, J. R. "Albertus Magnus on Alchemy." *Ambix* 1, No. 1 (May 1937): 3-20.

Surveys Albert's writings on chemistry and alchemy as contained in *Mineralia* and several other works.

Steneck, Nicholas H. "Albert the Great on the Classification and Localization of the Internal Senses." *Isis* 65, No. 227 (June 1979): 193-211.

Seeks to present Albert's thoughts on the internal senses—common sense, imagination, estimation, fantasy, and memory—as a "unique and unified theory."

Thorndike, Lynn. "Further Consideration of the *Experimenta, Speculum astronomiae* and *De secretis mulierum* Ascribed to Albertus Magnus." *Speculum* XXX, No. 3 (July 1955): 412-43.

Asserts that *De secretis mulierum* was in part written by Albert and that the *Experimenta* was not.

Washell, Richard F. "Logic, Language, and Albert the Great." *Journal of the History of Ideas* XXXIV, No. 3 (July-Sept 1973): 445-50.

Examines Albert's definition of logic in relation to language and the methods of scientific inquiry.

Additional coverage of Albert the Great's life and career is contained in the following source published by Gale Research: *Dictionary of Literary Biography, Vol. 115: Medieval Philosophers.*

Avicenna

980-1037

(Full name Abū 'Alī al-Husayn ibn 'Abd-Allāh ibn Sīnā) Persian philosopher and physician.

INTRODUCTION

A Muslim religious philosopher and physician, Avicenna attempted to synthesize the ideas of Islam, Plato, and Aristotle. From his point of view of philosophical monotheism he thus developed the Aristotelianism (as interpreted by the neo-Platonists) that became the basis of most Muslim philosophy of that period and that helped transmit the teachings of Aristotle to the West. In addition, Avicenna's medical writings, especially his *Al Qānūn fī al-Tibb* (*Canon of Medicine*), collected the medical knowledge of Avicenna's predecessors and served as standard medical texts for several centuries.

Biographical Information

Abū 'Alī al-Husayn ibn 'Abd-Allāh ibn Sīnā, called Avicenna by his Latin translators, was born in 980 in Afshana, near Bukhārā, Persia. At an early age, Avicenna undertook both a secular and a traditional Islamic religious education: he learned grammar, dialectics, astronomy, geometry, and arithmetic, and he knew the *Qur'ān* by rote at the age of ten. Recognizing his son's precocity, Avicenna's father hired a tutor named al-Nātilī, who introduced Avicenna to logic, geometry, and astronomy; under his tutelage, Avicenna read Porphyry's *Isagoge* and the first propositions of Euclid. However, doubting his tutor's abilities, Avicenna began an intensive regimen of self-education. Aided by commentaries, he mastered logic, geometry, and the *Almagest* of Ptolemy. When al-Nātilī departed, Avicenna studied medicine, at which he excelled and which he soon began to teach. Then, when he was sixteen years old, he began an intensive study of logic and philosophy that lasted for one and a half years. Avicenna read constantly, and when he encountered a passage he did not comprehend, he went to a mosque and prayed for understanding. His studies were interrupted, however, when in 997 he was summoned with other physicians to attend the ruler Nūh ibn Mansūr, who was suffering from a dangerous illness. After helping him recover, Avicenna became court physician and was given access to the Sāmānid library, where he immersed himself in rare and unique books. There Avicenna completed his studies, and when his father

died in 999, he left the Sāmānids, whose realm was disintegrating. Avicenna travelled to various regions, serving as physician to several Persian princes, the most notable of which was Shams al-Dawla of Hamadhān. He served as vizier and physician to al-Dawla, himself a poet and a scholar, from 1015 to 1022. During this time, Avicenna lectured on logic and astronomy, wrote several treatises dedicated to his patron, and completed his *Canon of Medicine*. Political turmoil led to a four-month imprisonment, but Avicenna escaped to Esfahan, where he served as vizier to its ruler, Abū Ya'far 'Alā al-Dawla. Encouraged to pursue his scientific and philosophical investigations, Avicenna began to study literature and philology. However, his health began to decline, and, after taking harsh medicines for some time with little improvement, he resigned himself to dying. Avicenna freed his slaves, gave his wealth to the poor, and listened to readings from the *Qur'ān*. He died in 1037 while accompanying his patron on a military expedition against Hamadhān, where he is buried.

Major Works

About one hundred treatises have been attributed to Avicenna, some in Persian, but most in Arabic. Between 1012 and 1022 Avicenna wrote his major medical work, an encyclopedia of medical knowledge known to the West as the *Canon of Medicine*. Primarily comprised of the teachings of Hippocrates modified by Aristotle as heard through Galen, the *Canon* consists of five books covering physiology, pathology, hygiene, methods of treating disease, and pharmacology. Besides assembling the cumulative learning of his predecessors, Avicenna also introduced a number of herbs into medical use, and was aware of the antiseptic affects of alcohol and of the psychosomatic nature of some illnesses. Avicenna's philosophical magnum opus is the *Kitīb al-Shifā'* (*Book of Healing,* written between 1020 and 1027), an eighteen-volume encyclopedia with sections on logic, physics, mathematics, metaphysics, psychology, and natural history. As was the custom among Aristotelians at the time, Avicenna often paraphrased Aristotle's texts and interspersed them with many of his own original thoughts. In addition to his philosophical and medical works, Avicenna also wrote symbolic mystical narratives and Arabic verse, some of which was erroneously attributed to Omar Khayyám.

Textual History

Avicenna kept few of his own manuscripts, so that when he died they were scattered throughout collections in the Middle East. A Hebrew version of the *Canon* was published in Naples in 1491, as was an Arabic edition in Rome in 1593. About thirty editions in Latin appeared shortly afterward, all based on the original translation by Gerard of Cremona. Other medical works translated into Latin were *Medicamenta Cordialia, Canticum de Medicina,* and *Tractatus de Syrupo Acetoso.* Nearly complete manuscripts of the *Shifā* exist in the Bodleian library and elsewhere. Translated into Latin by Dominicus Gundissalinus (Gondisalvi) with the assistance of Avendeath ibn Daud, the *Shifā* sparked the revival of Aristotle at the end of the twelfth and beginning of the thirteenth century. Separately published sections—*De Anima, Logic, Metaphysics, Physics,* and *De Caelo*—were also printed several times, including a Pavian edition in 1490 and Venetian editions in 1493, 1495, and 1546.

Critical Reception

Avicenna's best-known work, and that to which he primarily owes his reputation as the "Prince of the Physicians," is the *Canon of Medicine,* which was widely read in the West and remained a standard medical textbook for several hundred years. The *Canon* elicited a great deal of commentary, especially in the fifteenth century, and was a guide for medical studies in Europe from the twelfth to the seventeenth centuries: it was still used at the universities of Louvain and Montpellier in France as late as 1650. Not until dissection was allowed in European universities were certain anatomical and physiological errors of Galen, passed on by Avicenna, discovered. In addition to his renown in medical studies, Avicenna's philosophical contributions earned him the title "Second Teacher" (after Aristotle) among Arabs and *Princeps Philosophorum*—"The Great Master"—among Western Scholastics. His *Shifā* exerted a strong influence on Muslims, Jews, and Christians alike and led to the revival of interest in Aristotle in the Middle Ages. Avicenna's attempt to fuse Aristotle's tenets and Islamic beliefs, however, eventually aroused the hostility of Islamic theologians. Al-Ghazālī's *Incoherence of the Philosophers* was directed primarily against Avicenna; overcome by the opposition of orthodox religious leaders, the popularity of Avicenna's philosophy quickly declined in the Middle East. Still, such Western Medieval philosophers as Roger Bacon and such theologians as Thomas Aquinas, Albertus Magnus, and John Duns Scotus were greatly influenced by Avicenna. His concept of God as the being in whom existence and essence are identical was widely accepted, especially by Aquinas and Maimonides. Although they point out that Avicenna's influence in the West has not been fully appreciated, critics agree that Avicenna's medical and philosophical works greatly contributed to learning in Medieval Europe and indelibly affected the history of mid-Eastern science and philosophy.

PRINCIPAL WORKS

Al Qānūn fī al-Tibb [*Canon of Medicine*] (nonfiction) 1012-22

Kitāb al-Shifā' [*Book of Healing*] (philosophy) 1020-27

Dāneshnāma-yi 'Alā'ī [*The Book of Science Dedicated to 'Al ' al-Dawla*] (philosophy) c. 1027

Kitāb al-Najāt [*Book of Salvation*] (philosophy) c. 1027

Kitāb al-Ishārāt wa al-Tanbihāt [*The Book of Remarks and Directives*] (philosophy) 1030

Fī Ithbāt al-Nubuwwat [*On the Proof of Prophecies*] (philosophy)

Al-Falsafa al-Mashriqīyya [*The Eastern Philosophy*] (philosophy)

Sirat al-Shaykh al-Ra'īs [*The Life of the Leading Master*] (autobiography)

*The date of composition for these works is unknown.

PRINCIPAL ENGLISH TRANSLATIONS

Avicennae De congelatione et conglutinatione lapidum, Being Sections of the "Kitāb al-Shifā'": *The Latin and Arabic Texts with an English Translation of the Latter and with Critical Notes* (translated by E. J. Holmyard and D. C. Mandeville) 1927

The General Principles of Avicenna's "Canon of Medicine" (translated by Mazhar H. Shah) 1966

The Metaphysics of Avicenna (Ibn Sina): A Critical Translation-Commentary and Analysis of the Fundamental Arguments in Avicenna's Metaphysics in the Danish "Nama-i 'Ala'i" (The Book of Scientific Knowledge) (translated by Parviz Morewedge) 1973

The Life of Ibn Sina (translated by William E. Gohlman) 1974

Remarks and Admonitions (translated by S. Inati) 1984

CRITICISM

Fazlur Rahman (essay date 1963)

SOURCE: "Ibn Sīna," in *A History of Muslim Philosophy, with Short Accounts of Other Disciplines and the Modern Renaissance in Muslim Lands, Vol. One,* edited by M. M. Sharif, Otto Harrassowitz, 1963, pp. 480-506.

[*In the following excerpt, Rahman surveys Avicenna's metaphysics, philosophy of mind, epistemology, and philosophy of religion, and briefly discusses Avicenna's influence in the East and West.*]

In the history of philosophical thought in the Medieval Ages, the figure of ibn Sīna (370/980-428/1037) is, in many respects, unique, while among the Muslim philosophers, it is not only unique but has been paramount right up to modern times. He is the only one among the great philosophers of Islam to build an elaborate and complete system of philosophy—a system which has been dominant in the philosophical tradition of Islam for centuries, in spite of the attacks of al-Ghazāli, Fakhr al-Dīn al-Rāzi, and others. This ascendancy has been possible, however, not merely because he had a system but because that system had features of remarkable originality displaying a type of genius-like spirit in discovering methods and arguments whereby he sought to reformulate the purely rational and intellectual tradition of Hellenism, to which he was an eminent heir, for and, to an extent, within the religious system of Islam. The exact terms of this reformulation and their relation to Islam we shall discuss presently . . . ; it is only to be noted at the outset that it was this

kind of originality which rendered him unique not only in Islam but also in the medieval West where the reformulations of the Roman Catholic theology at the hands of Albert the Great, and, especially, of Thomas Aquinas, were fundamentally influenced by him.

Since . . . we are mainly concerned with ibn Sīna's interpretation of Greek philosophical doctrines, we need not give an account of his sources in the Greek and Muslim philosophers. To be sure, the elements of his doctrines are Greek, and certain reformulations of Greek doctrines in his writings are also to be found in al-Fārābi (to whom ibn Sīna's debt is immense) in varying degrees of development; but our task here is to state, analyse, and appreciate ibn Sīna's teaching. And, indeed, ibn Sīna's system, taken as a whole, is such that it is *his,* bearing the unmistakable impress of his personality. This is proved by the fact that he states his cardinal doctrines over and over again in his different works and often gives cross references, which are unmistakable signs of systematic thinking and not of random borrowing from heterogeneous sources.

The most fundamental characteristic of ibn Sīna's thought is that of arriving at definitions by a severely rigorous method of division and distinction of concepts. This lends an extraordinary subtlety to his arguments. It can often give his philosophical reasoning a strongly scholastic complexity and intricacy of structure which can annoy the modern temperament, but it is doubtlessly true that it is also this method which has resulted in almost all the original doctrines of our philosopher. It has enabled him to formulate his most general and basic principle, viz., to every clear and distinct concept there must correspond a *distinctio in re,* a principle on which later Descartes also based his thesis of the mind-body dualism. The fecundity and importance of this principle of analysis in ibn Sīna's system are indeed striking: he announces it recurrently and at all levels, in his proof of the mind-body dualism, his doctrine of universals, his theory of essence and existence, etc. Examples of this principle are: "that which is affirmed and admitted is different from that which is not affirmed and admitted," and "a single conceptual (lit. specific) entity cannot be both known and unknown at the same time except with regard to different aspects."

This [essay] will deal mostly with those concepts and doctrines of ibn Sīna which are not only capital and bring out the nature of his system, but have also both been influential and originally elaborated by him to a greater or lesser extent. . . .

Ibn Sīna's doctrine of Being, like those of earlier Muslim philosophers, e.g., al-Fārābi, is emanationistic. From God, the Necessary Existent, flows the first intelligence alone, since from a single, absolutely simple entity, only one thing can emanate. But the nature of the first intelligence is no longer absolutely simple since, not being *necessary-by-itself,* it is only *possible,* and its possibility has been actualized by God. Thanks to this dual nature which henceforth pervades the entire creaturely world, the first intelligence gives rise to two entities: (i) the second intelligence by virtue of the higher aspect of its being, actuality, and (ii) the first and highest sphere by virtue of the lower aspect of its being, its natural possibility. This dual emanatory process continues until we reach the lower and tenth intelligence which governs the sublunary world and is called by the majority of the Muslim philosophers the Angel Gabriel. This name is applied to it because it bestows forms upon or "informs" the matter of this world, i.e., both physical matter and the human intellect. Hence it is also called the "Giver of Forms" (the *dator formarum* of the subsequent medieval Western scholastics). We shall return later to these intelligences and these spheres to examine more closely their nature and operations; meanwhile we must turn to the nature of Being.

The procession of the immaterial intelligence from the Supreme Being by way of emanation was intended to supplement, under the inspiration of the Neo-Platonic Theory of Emanation, the meagre and untenable view of God formulated by Aristotle according to whom there was no passage from God, the One, to the world, the many. According to Muslim philosophers, although God remained in Himself and high above the created world, there were, nevertheless, intermediary links between the absolute eternity and necessity of God and the world of downright contingency. And this theory, besides, came very close to satisfying the Muslim belief in angels. This is the first occasion to remark how Muslim philosophers, by a re-elaboration of the Greek tradition of philosophy, not only sought to build a rational system, but a rational system which sought to integrate the tradition of Islam. But what about the Theory of Emanation itself? Would it not destroy the necessary and all-important gulf between the Creator and the creation and lead to a downright pantheistic world-view—*tat tvam Asi*—against which Islam, like all higher religions, had warned so sternly? No doubt, this type of pantheism, being *dynamic,* is different from the absolutist and static forms of pantheism; yet it could lead to anthropomorphism, or, by a reverse process of ascent, to the re-absorption of the creature's being into the being of God. Now, the guarantee against any such danger shall be ibn Sīnā's doctrine of essence and existence. This celebrated theory again is designed to fulfil equally both religious and rational needs and, once again, to supplement Aristotle.

Early in this section we said that God and God alone is absolutely simple in His being; all other things have a dual nature. Being simple, *what* God is and the fact that He *exists* are not two elements in a single being but a single atomic element in a single being. What

God is, i.e., His essence, is identical with His existence. This is not the case with any other being, for in no other case is the existence identical with the essence, otherwise whenever, for example, an Eskimo who has never seen an elephant, conceives of one, he would *ipso facto* know *that* elephants exist. It follows that God's existence is necessary, the existence of other things is only possible and derived from God's, and that the supposition of God's non-existence involves a contradiction, whereas it is not so with any other existent. A cosmological argument, based on Aristotle's doctrine of the First Cause, would be superfluous in establishing God's existence. Ibn Sīna, however, has not chosen to construct a full-fledged ontological argument. His argument, which, as we shall see later, became the cardinal doctrine of the Roman Catholic dogmatic theology after Aquinas, is more like the Leibnizian proof of God as the *ground* of the world, i.e., given God, we can understand the existence of the world. Here cause and effect behave like premises and conclusion. Instead of working back from a supposed effect to its cause, we work forward from an indubitable premise to a conclusion. Indeed for ibn Sīna, God creates through a rational necessity. On the basis of this rational necessity, ibn Sīna also explains the divine pre-knowledge of all events, as we shall see in his account of God. The world, as a whole, is then contingent, but, given God, it becomes necessary, this necessity being derived from God. This is ibn Sīnā's principle of existence stated in brief; we shall now analyse it according to the complex materials which ibn Sīna has left us. It involves more than one point of view.

From the metaphysical point of view, the theory seeks to supplement the traditional Aristotelian analysis of an existent into two constituent elements, as it were, viz., form and matter. According to Aristotle, the form of a thing is the sum total of its essential and universalizable qualities constituting its definition; the matter in each thing is that which has the potentiality of receiving these qualities—the form—and by which the form becomes an individual existent. But there are two major difficulties in this conception from the point of view of the actual existence of a thing. The first is that the form is universal and, therefore, does not exist. Matter too, being pure potentiality, does not exist, since it is actualized only by the form. How then shall a thing come into existence by a non-existent form and an equally non-existent matter? The second difficulty arises from the fact that, although Aristotle generally holds that the definition or essence of a thing is its form, he nevertheless says in certain important passages that matter is also to be included in the essence of a thing, otherwise we shall have only a partial definition of it. If, then, we regard both form and matter as constitutive of definition, we can never arrive at the actual existence of a thing. This is the rock against which the whole scheme of Aristotle to explain Being threatens to break.

This is why ibn Sīna holds that from form and matter alone you would never get a concrete existent, but only the essential and accidental qualities. He has analysed at some length the relation of form and matter in *K. al-Shifā'*, where he concludes that both form and matter depend on God (or the active intellect) and, further, that the composite existent also cannot be caused by form and matter alone but there must be "something else." Finally, he tells us, "Everything except the One who is by His essence One and Existent acquires existence from something else. . . . In itself it deserves absolute non-existence. Now, it is not its matter alone without its form or its form alone without its matter which deserves non-existence but the totality (of matter and form)." This is why ibn Sīna substitutes a three-term analysis of the existent matérial objects instead of the traditional Greek dyadic formula. It must be noted that it is Aristotle's doctrine which is being developed here. Many scholars have held that ibn Sīna is here following a Neo-Platonic line instead of the Aristotelian one, but, from this point of view, the Neo-Platonic doctrine is the same as that of Aristotle, viz., the dyadic scheme of form and matter, except that, according to Plotinus, under the influence of Plato, the forms have a higher ontological status and exist in God's mind who then proceeds to make them existent in matter. It should also be borne in mind that existence is not really a constituent element of things besides matter and form; it is rather a relation to God: if you view a thing in relation to the divine existentializing agency, it exists, and it exists necessarily and, further, its existence is intelligible, but when out of relation with God, its existence loses its intelligibility and meaning. It is this relational aspect which ibn Sīna designates by the term "accident" and says that existence is an accident.

Ever since the criticism of ibn Sīnā's doctrine by ibn Rushd who, among other things, accused ibn Sīna of having violated the definition of substance as that which exists by itself, and of Aquinas who, although he adopts the distinction between essence and existence under the direct influence of ibn Sīna, nevertheless follows ibn Rushd in his criticism, the unanimous voice of the Western historians of medieval philosophy has been to the effect that existence, according to ibn Sīna, is just an accident among other accidents, e.g., round, black, etc. We have said that when ibn Sīna talks of existence as an accident *with relation to objects (as distinguished from essence)* he just means by it a relation to God; it is, therefore, not an ordinary accident. Further, if existence were an accident, one could think it away and still go on talking of the object just as one can do in the case of other accidents and, indeed, in that case ibn Sīna would have been forced to hold something like the Meinongian view held by many Muslim Mutakallims that non-existents must also "exist" in some peculiar sense of that word. But this is the very doctrine which ibn Sīna ridicules. . . . [ibn Sīna] criticizes the view of those who hold that a non-existent "thing" must, nevertheless, "exist" in some sense so that we can talk about it. He says, "Those people who entertain this opinion hold that among those things which we can know (i. e., be acquainted with) and talk about, are things to which, in the realm of non-being, non-existence belongs as an attribute. He who wants to know more about this should further consult the nonsense which they have talked and which does not merit consideration." Indeed, according to ibn Sīna, the ideas of existence and unity are the primary ideas with which we must start. These underived concepts are the bases of our application of other categories and attributes to things and, therefore, they defy definition since definition must involve other terms and concepts which are themselves derived.

It will be seen that this problem now is not a metaphysical one but has to do with logic. Ibn Sīna has attempted to give his own answer to the question: How is it possible that we can talk of non-existents and what do these latter mean? His answer is that we can do so because we give to these objects "some sort of existence in the mind." But, surely, our individual images cannot constitute the meanings of these entities for the obvious reason that when we talk, e.g., of a space-ship, it must have an objective meaning. It is, nevertheless, true that ibn Sīna has seen the basic difficulty of the logic of existence. And our modern logic itself, despite its superior techniques and some valuable distinctions, seems nowhere nearer the solution. It has tried hard to contend that whenever I talk of a space-ship, although none exists, I am not talking of a "thing," of an individual object, but only of a generic object or a conglomeration of properties. But is this really so? Is it absurd to say that the "individual space-ship I am talking of now has this and this property"? Besides, the crux is the phrase "conglomeration or set of properties"—what is it to which they belong and of which I profess to be talking?

Besides this meaning of "accident" as a peculiar and unique relation of an existent to God, the term "accident" in ibn Sīna has another unorthodox philosophic meaning. This concerns the relationship of a concrete existent to its essence or specific form, which ibn Sīna also calls accidental. This use of the term "accident" is quite pervasive in ibn Sīnā's philosophy and, without knowing its correct significance, one would be necessarily led to misinterpret some of his basic doctrines. Now, *whenever two concepts are clearly distinguishable from each other, they must refer to two different ontological entities,* as we said above, and, further, *whenever two such concepts come together in a thing, ibn Sīna describes their mutual relationship as being accidental,* i.e., they *happen* to come together, although each must be found to exist separately. This is the case, for example, between essence and existence, between universality and essence.

According to ibn Sīna, essences exist in God's mind (and in the mind of the active intelligences) prior to the individual existents exemplifying them in the external world and they also exist in our minds posterior to these individual existents. But these two levels of the existence of an essence are very different. And they differ not only in the sense that the one is creative, and the other imitative. In its true being, the essence is neither universal nor particular, but it is just an essence. Hence he holds that both particularity and universality are "accidents" which happen or occur to the essence. Universality occurs to it in our minds only, and ibn Sīna takes a strictly functional view of the universals: our mind abstracts universals or general concepts whereby it is enabled to treat the world of infinite diversity in a summary and scientific manner by relating an identical mental construction to a number of objects. In the external world the essence does not exist except in a kind of metaphorical sense, i.e., in the sense in which a number of objects allow themselves to be treated as being identical. Existents in the external world are the individual concrete objects, no two of which are exactly the same. He says, "It is impossible that a single essence should exist identically in many", and again, "It (i.e. absolute manness) is not the manness of 'Amr; it is different from it, thanks to the particular circumstances. These particular circumstances have a role in the individual person of Zaid *. . . and also a role in the 'man' or 'manness' inasmuch as it is related to him."* It is clear especially from this last statement that the "essence" virtually undergoes a change in each individual. That is why we must say that *if we regard essence as a universal,* that concrete determinate existence is something over and above the essence; it is something added to the essence, or it is an "accident" of the essence.

Two things must be specially noted here. First, that existence is something added not to the existent objects—this would be absurd—but to the essence. This is because everything whether it exists or not—indeed whether it is existable or not—in fact every concept is "something" of which assertions can be made, whether positive or negative. Indeed, even non-existence is "something," since one can talk about it. But a positive individual existent is more than just "something." (This distinction between "something" and an existent, treated by ibn Sīna which has confusedly returned in present-day logic, was originally made by the Stoics.) Hence ibn Sīna says that when existence is attributed to essences, this existence is equivalent to "is something" and, therefore, such statements are not "profitable." But statements about existents are informative and profitable, since they add to the essence something that is new. Secondly, we must note that although ibn Sīna speaks in several places of matter as the principle of multiplicity of forms or essences, he never says that matter is the principle of individual existence. The sole principle of individual existence is God—the Giver of

existence; matter is the occasional cause of existence, supplying external attributes of multiplicity.

We have given a considerable number of quotations from ibn Sīna in the treatment of this problem not only because it is of capital importance for ibn Sīnā's philosophy, but also because there has been such a great deal of fundamental confusion in the traditional treatment of the subject that a clarification of the terms "existence," "accident" in this relation, and "essence" is absolutely necessary. . . .

It may be said that ibn Sīna is a citizen of two intellectual-spiritual worlds; the Hellenic and the Islamic. In his own mind he has so intrinsically unified the two worlds that they are identical; the question of disloyalty to either, therefore, does not arise for him at all.

—Fazlur Rahman

With Aristotle, ibn Sīna stresses the intimate connection of mind and body; but whereas Aristotle's whole trend of thought rejects a two-substance view, ibn Sīna holds a form of radical dualism. How far these two aspects of his doctrine are mutually compatible is a different question: ibn Sīna certainly did not carry his dualism through to develop a parallelistic, occasionalistic account of mind-body relationship. His remarks, nevertheless, on either side are both interesting and profound. We shall first state his arguments for the two-substance view and then discuss their close interconnection. To prove that the human soul is a substance capable of existing independently of the body, our philosopher employs two different arguments. One appeals to direct self-consciousness, the other seeks to prove the immateriality of the intellect. We can postpone his teaching on the intellect till we discuss his theory of knowledge; here we shall state and discuss his first argument. Indeed, according to him, this is the more direct way of proving the incorporeal substantiality of the soul acting not as an argument but as an eye-opener.

The argument is stated by ibn Sīna in the first chapter of the psychological book of the **K. al-Shifā'** and then re-stated and discussed in the last but one chapter of the same book. Let us suppose, as he says, that a person is created in an adult state, but in such a condition that he is born in a void where his body cannot touch anything and where he cannot perceive anything of the external world. Let us also suppose that he cannot see his own body and that the organs of his body are prevented from touching one another, so that he has no sense-perception whatsoever. Such a person will not affirm anything of the external world or even the existence of his own body but will, nevertheless, affirm the existence of his self as a purely spiritual entity. Now, that which is affirmed is certainly not the same as that which is not affirmed. The mind is, therefore, a substance independent of the body. Our philosopher is here describing an imaginary case impossible of realization, but his real point, as of Descartes, is that we can think away our bodies and so doubt their existence, but we cannot think away our minds.

The affinity of ibn Sīnā's argument with that of Descartes' *cogito ergo sum* has been justly pointed out by historians of philosophy. Actually, this whole trend of thought is inspired by the argument of Plotinus for the separateness of the mind from the body. But there is an important difference between ibn Sīnā's and Descartes' formulations. With regard to Descartes, the question can be and has been raised: Is the existence of the self a matter of inference or an immediate datum of consciousness? Whatever the answer to this question may be, there is no doubt that consciousness or "I think" is constitutively and necessarily involved in Descartes' "I am." This is so much so that "I think" and "I am" have the same meaning in Descartes. This being the position, it is obvious that in this case the consciousness of the self and its existence cannot be logically disengaged from each other. In ibn Sīna, however, although the element of consciousness is present since one can "affirm one's own existence," it is nevertheless present only as a way of locating the self: it is a contingent fact and not a logical necessity. In fact, ibn Sīna presents a medial position between Descartes and Plotinus, for, according to the latter, consciousness, being a relation, signifies not utter self-identity but a kind of otherness; in complete self-identity, consciousness must cease altogether.

This argument, which seeks to establish dualism by doubting or denying the existence of the body, may be called the argument from abstraction in that it abstracts psychical functions from the total functions of the organism. Its fundamental weakness obviously is to insist that by thinking away the body, the body ceases to play a role in one's total consciousness. If the problem could be solved by a simple inspection of the self in this manner, nothing would be easier. Ibn Sīna seems to be aware that the position is liable to objections. He says: (If my self were identical with any bodily members) "say, the heart or the brain or a collection of such members and if it were their separate or total being of which I were conscious as being my self, then it would be necessary that my consciousness of my self should be my very consciousness of these members, for it is not possible that the same thing should be both cognized and uncognized in the same sense." He then goes on to say that "in fact I do not know by self-consciousness that I have a heart and a brain but I do so either by sense-perception (experience) or on authority." "I

mean by what I know to be my self that which I mean when I say: 'I perceived, I intellected, I acted,' and all these attributes belong to *me*." But, ibn Sīna pauses to consider the possible objection: if you are not aware of your self being a bodily member, you are neither directly aware that it is your soul or mind.

Ibn Sīnā's answer to this objection is: "Whenever I present bodily attributes to this something which is the source of my mental functions, I find that it cannot accept these attributes," and thus this incorporeal entity must be the soul. Here we clearly see that the argument has taken a new turn and the phenomenon of direct consciousness is being supplemented by a further consideration to the effect that the disparateness between the mental and physical qualities is such that both cannot belong to one substance. And this is the perennial argument for the two-substance theory, viz., that the mental and the physical attributes are of qualitatively disparate *genré*.

From the acceptance of the view, that the mind is a substance, the conclusion that the mind is a unity follows tautologically and ibn S na lays great stress on it. Indeed, once again, both doctrines, viz., the reality of faculties and the unitary nature of the soul, are stated with equal emphasis by him. The reality of mental faculties was established by Aristotle but was further pursued by his commentators, notably Alexander of Aphrodisias. Ibn Sīna has devoted a special chapter to the question where he bases the multiplicity of faculties on the qualitative differences among mental operations. Nevertheless, he repeatedly stresses the necessity of an integrative bond (*ribāt*) for the diverse operations. Indeed, he declares that even the vegetative and perceptual functions in man, for example, are specifically different from those in plants and animals, thanks to the rationality present in man which pervades and changes the character of all his functions. This integrative principle is the mind itself.

The soul in its real being is then an independent substance and is our transcendental self. We shall return to its transcendence when we discuss ibn Sīnā's theory of knowledge. . . . Here we shall note only that Ibn Sīnā's arguments for the immortality of the soul are based on the view that it is a substance and that it is not a form of the body to which it is attached intimately by some kind of mystical relation between the two. There is in the soul which emerges from the separate substance of the active intelligence simultaneously with the emergence of a body with a definite temperament, a definite inclination to attach itself to this body, to care for it, and direct it to the mutual benefit. Further, the soul, as being incorporeal, is a simple substance and this ensures for it indestructibility and survival, after its origination, even when its body is destroyed.

But if at the transcendental level the soul is a pure

spiritual entity and body does not enter into its definition even as a relational concept, at the phenomenal level the body must be included in its definition as a building enters into the definition of a (definite) builder. That is why ibn Sīna says that the study of the phenomenal aspect of the soul is in the field of natural science, while its transcendental being belongs to the study of metaphysics. Now, since at the phenomenal level there exists between each soul and body a *mystique* which renders them exclusively appropriate for each other—whether we understand this *mystique* or not—it follows that the transmigration of souls is impossible. (Transmigration is rejected by Aristotle who does not hold the two-substance view.) Indeed, this *mystique* is both the cause and the effect of the individuality of the self. Ibn Sīna, therefore, totally rejects the idea of the possible identity of two souls or of the ego becoming fused with the Divine Ego, and he emphasizes that the survival must be individual. It is a primary fact of experience that each individual is conscious of his self-identity which cannot be shaken by any kind of argument. Indeed, our philosopher is so keen to affirm the individuality of personality that he says that even the qualitative nature of the intellectual operations in different individuals may be different—a statement which would have shocked not only the Platonists and Neo-Platonists, but even perhaps Aristotle, since, according to the universal Greek doctrine, the intellect represents, at least, the qualitative identity of mankind, a doctrine which was later pushed to its logical extremes by ibn Rushd.

The relationship, then, between soul and body is so close that it may affect even the intellect. It goes without saying that all the other psycho-physical acts and states have both aspects—mental and physical. This was emphasized by Aristotle himself. But Aristotle's doctrine, even if it is not outright materialistic, is quasi-materialistic and, whereas it either emphasizes the double aspect of each state or operation, or tends strongly to point out the influence of the body on the mental phenomena, exactly the reverse is the case with ibn Sīna. Indeed, his insistent stress on the influence of the mind on the body constitutes an outstanding and one of the most original features of his philosophy. Whereas in Aristotle, life and mind give a new dimension to the material organism, in ibn Sīna, under the inspiration of the Neo-Platonic thought and the influence of his own metaphysically spiritual predilections, this no longer remains a mere dimension. The material side of nature is both pervaded and overshadowed by its mental and spiritual side, even though, as a medical man, he is keen to preserve the importance of the physical constitution, especially in the case of the character of the emotions and impulses. Indeed, as we shall see, his medical art helped him to gauge the extent of mental influence on apparently bodily states.

At the most common level, the influence of the mind on the body is visible in voluntary movement: whenever the mind wills to move the body, the body obeys. In his detailed account of animal motion, ibn Sīna has enumerated four stages instead of Aristotle's three. The three stages according to Aristotle are: (1) imagination or reason, (2) desire, and (3) movement of the muscles. Ibn Sīna has split up the second into (1) desire and (2) impulsion (*ijmā'*) for, he says, not every desire can move to action but only when it is impulsive, whether consciously or unconsciously. The second, and more important difference between ibn Sīna and the traditional view is that according to the latter the initiation of bodily movement must always lie in a cognitive state, whether it is imagination or reason. Ibn Sīna holds that, while in most cases the cognitive act precedes the affective and the conative ones, this is not true of all cases. We read: "All (the appetitive and conative) faculties also follow imaginative faculties. . . . But sometimes it happens, e.g., in cases of physical pain, that our natural impulse tries to remove the cause of pain and thus initiates the process of stirring up imagination. In this case, it is these (appetitive) faculties which drive the imagination to their own purpose, just as, in most cases, it is the imaginative faculty which drives the (appetitive and conative) faculties towards the object of imagination." Thus, according to ibn Sīna, the initiation of the animal motion can lie in the affections as well as in the cognitive states. Psychologically, this is of great significance and marks an advance over the purely and one-sidedly intellectual accounts of traditional philosophy.

Here we reach the second level of the influence of the mind on the body, viz., that of emotions and of the will. Ibn Sīna tells us from his medical experience that actually physically sick men, through sheer will-power, can become well and, equally, healthy men can become really ill under the influence of sickness-obsession. Similarly, he says, if a plank of wood is put across a well-trodden path, one can walk on it quite well, but if it is put as a bridge and down below is a chasm, one can hardly creep over it without an actual fall. "This is because he pictures to himself a (possible) fall so vividly that the natural power of his limbs accords with it." Indeed, strong emotions like fear can actually destroy the temperament of the organism and result in death, through influencing the vegetative functions: "This happens when a judgment takes place in the soul; the judgment, being pure belief, does not influence the body, but rather when this belief is followed by joy or grief." Joy and grief too are mental states, ibn Sīna goes on, but they affect the vegetative functions. Again, "We do not regard it as impossible that something should occur to the soul, in so far as it is embodied, and be then followed by affections peculiar to the body itself. Imagination, inasmuch as it is knowledge, is not in itself a physical affection, but it may happen that, as a result, certain bodily organs, sexual for example, should expand. . . . Indeed, when an idea becomes firmly established in the imagination, it necessitates a change in the temperament. . . ." Just as, we are told, the ideas of health present in the doctor's mind produce actual health in a patient, so the soul acts on the body; only the doctor produces cure through media and instruments, but the soul does it without any instruments.

If, indeed, the soul were strong enough, it could produce cure and illness even in another body without instruments. And here ibn Sīna produces evidence from the phenomena of hypnosis and suggestion (*al-wahm al-ʿāmil*). He uses these considerations in order to show the possibility of miracles which are a part of the discussion of the question of prophethood. Here we will recall what we said before that, according to ibn Sīna, a soul becomes exclusively attached to one body. Our newer consideration shows that it can transcend its own body to affect others. This would become possible only when the soul becomes akin to the universal soul, as it were.

It is on these grounds that ibn Sīna accepts the reality of such phenomena as the "evil eye" and magic in general. We may note that the influence of the emotions on the body was known and discussed in later Hellenism. Especially since the Stoic conception of the principle of "Sympathy" in nature and Plotinus' elaboration of that principle, the mind-body interaction was explained on these lines. What is scientifically new in ibn Sīna is that he also explains phenomena like magic, suggestion, and hypnosis, and, in general, the influence of one mind on other bodies and minds on these lines, i.e., by referring them to the properties of the influencing mind. In Hellenism, these phenomena were accepted, but were regarded as exceptionally occult. And in the mystery-mongering superstition of later Hellenism, "Sympathy" was given an occult twist. Magical properties were assigned to special objects: metals, animals, etc., through which the magician or the hypnotizer worked or pretended to work on the gods or spirits to *intervene* in the realm of nature and to produce occult effects. But the only principle which ibn Sīna will accept—and here he strikes a very modern note—is to refer efficacy to the special constitution of the mind itself. This rests on the premise that it is of the nature of mind to influence matter and it belongs to matter to obey the mind, and ibn Sīna will have no theurgic magic: "This is because the soul is (derived from) certain (higher) principles which clothe matter with forms contained in them, such that these forms actually constitute matter. . . . If these principles can bestow upon matter forms constitutive of natural species . . . it is not improbable that they can also bestow qualities, without there being any need of physical contact, action, or affection. . . . The form existing in the soul is the cause of what occurs in matter." The reason for this great change is that in later Hellenism the human soul had lost its dignity and

people relied more and more for the explanation of the "para-natural" phenomena on the intervention of the gods. . . .

In accordance with the universal Greek tradition, ibn Sīna describes all knowledge as some sort of abstraction on the part of the cognizant of the form of the thing known. His chief emphasis, elaborated most probably by himself, is on the degrees of this abstracting power in different cognitive faculties. Thus, sense-perception needs the very presence of matter for its cognitive act; imagination is free from the presence of actual matter but cannot cognize without material attachments and accidents which give to the image its particularity, whereas in intellect alone the pure form is cognized in its universality. It is very probable too that ibn Sīna elaborated this theory "of the grades of abstraction" to avoid the objection to which Aristotle's doctrine of cognition (according to which all cognition is the abstraction of form "without its matter") was liable, viz., if perception is the knowledge of form alone, how do we know that this form exists in matter? Or, indeed, how do we know that matter exists at all?

Ibn Sīnā's position on perception is generally that of naïve realism, like that of Aristotle and his commentators, holding a representational view of perception. But under criticism from scepticism and relativism which point out the relativity of perceived qualities, this representational view becomes seriously modified and ibn Sīna finally accepts a quasi-causal or, rather, relational view of perceptual qualities, i.e., objects, which have certain real qualities in themselves, appear as such-and-such under such-and-such circumstances and from such-and-such a position. This is responsible for several subjectivist statements in ibn Sīna, who comes to distinguish between "primary" and "secondary" perceptions: the "primary" perception being subjective or of the state of the percipient's own mind, the "secondary" perception being that of the external world. He did not clearly see, as we moderns do, the basic difficulties in this position. But his conception reappears in Western medieval philosophy as the distinction between the psychological or "intentional" object and the real object, a distinction which was much later developed by Locke into that of primary and secondary perceptual qualities.

But the great key-stone of ibn Sīnā's doctrine of perception is his distinction between internal and external perception. The external perception is the operation of the external five senses. Ibn Sīna also divides the internal perception formally into five faculties, although he shows a great deal of hesitation on the subject. His chief aim is to separate the different functions or operations on a qualitative basis, and, of course, we once again remember his principle that to every clear idea there must correspond a distinction in reality. Indeed, his doctrine of the internal senses has no precedent in the history of philosophy. The first internal sense is *sensus communis* which is the seat of all the senses. It integrates sense-data into percepts. This general sense must be internal because none of the external five senses is capable of this function. The second internal sense is the imaginative faculty in so far as it conserves the perceptual images. The third faculty is again imagination in so far as it acts upon these images, by combination and separation. In man this faculty is pervaded by reason so that human imagination can deliberate and is, therefore, the seat of the practical intellect. The fourth and the most important internal faculty is called *wahm* which passed into the West as *vis estimativa*: it perceives immaterial motions like usefulness and harmfulness, love and hate in material objects, and is, in fact, the basis of our character, whether influenced or uninfluenced by reason. The fifth internal sense conserves in memory those notions which are called by him "intentions" (*ma'āni*).

The doctrine of *wahm* is the most original element in ibn Sīnā's psychological teaching and comes very close to what some modern psychologists have described as the "nervous response" of the subject to a given object. In Aristotle, this function is performed by imagination or perception itself, but ibn Sīna contends that perception and imagination tell us only about the perceptual qualities of a thing, its size, colour, shape, etc.; they tell us nothing about its character or "meaning" for us, which must be read or discerned by an internal faculty of the organism. In the Stoics, again, we have the perceptual-moral theory of the *oikeiosis* or "appropriation," according to which whatever is perceived by the external senses is interpreted internally by the soul as the bearer of certain values. But the Stoics, in this doctrine, were primarily concerned with the development of a moral personality in man. Ibn Sīnā's doctrine of *wahm,* on the other hand, despite its moral significance, is primarily a purely psychological doctrine, explaining our instinctive and emotional response to the environment.

This "nervous response" operates at different levels. At one level it is purely instinctive as when a sheep perceives a wolf for the first time and flees from it, or as the mother instinctively feels love for her baby. This occurs without previous experience and hence through some kind of "natural inspiration" ingrained in the constitution of the organism. Secondly, it also operates at a "quasi-empirical" level. This occurs through association of ideas or images of memory. A dog which has suffered pain in the past from being beaten by a stick or a stone, associates the image of the object and the "intention" of pain and, when it sees the object again, at once runs away. This phenomenon of direct association can also become indirect and irrational. This happens in the case of animals and also in the case of less reasonable human beings. Some people who have irrationally associated the yellow

colour of honey with both the colour and the bitter taste of gall, do not eat honey and in fact at its sight exhibit symptoms of gall-like taste. This principle of association appeared later in Leibniz; and the principle of irrational or automatic association has appeared more thoroughly worked out in recent experimental psychology under the name of the "conditioned reflex." Since *wahm* makes perceptual predictions on the basis of association of ideas, for which, says ibn Sīna, there are innumerable causes (contiguity, similarity, etc.), its perceptual judgments may sometimes be false. Aristotle had noticed this failure of perception but could not explain it since he did not discern the influence of past experience on present perceptual judgments.

We come next to the doctrine of the intellect which ibn Sīna has elaborated in great detail. He has taken over in his doctrine the theory of the development of human intellect announced by Aristotle very briefly and rather obscurely and then elaborated by Alexander of Aphrodisias and later by al-Fārābi. But he has added quite new and original interpretations of his own. The doctrine, in brief, distinguishes between a potential intellect in man and an active intellect outside man, through the influence and guidance of which the former develops and matures. Basically, the problem is that of the origin of human cognition and it is explained on the assumption of a supra-human transcendent intellect which, when the human intellect is ready, bestows knowledge upon it.

As against Alexander, al-Fārābi, and probably Aristotle, ibn Sīna holds that the potential intellect in man is an indivisible, immaterial, and indestructible substance although it is generated at a definite time and as something personal to each individual. This has important religious consequences, for, whereas according to al-Fārābi only men of developed intellect survive and others perish for ever at death, ibn Sīna holds the immortality of all human souls. (According to Alexander of Aphrodisias, even the actualized intellect is perishable so that no soul is immortal.) The immateriality of the intellect is proved by ibn Sīna in an unprecedented, elaborate, and scholastic manner, the basic idea being that ideas or "forms," being indivisible, cannot be said to be localized in any material organ.

But it is in his account of the intellectual operation and the manner of the acquisition of knowledge that the most original aspect of his doctrine of the intellect lies. Whereas, according to the Peripatetic doctrine, accepted by al-Fārābi, the universal, which is the object of the intellective act, is abstracted from the particulars of sense-experience, for ibn Sīna it issues directly from the active intellect. The Peripatetic tradition has given the following account of the rise of the universal from perceptual experience: First, we perceive several similar individuals; these are stored up in memory and after this constant operation the light of the active intellect "shines" upon them so that the essential nature common to all the particulars emerges *from* them. This theory is neither nominalistic nor realistic: it does say that the universal is more than what the instances of experience have given to the mind, but it holds that the universal *lies* somehow in these instances. For ibn Sīna, the universal cannot emerge from the images of sense because it does not lie there. Further, as we have seen already, the essence, according to ibn Sīna, is not really a universal: it only *behaves* as such when it is in *our* minds. Besides, no amount of particular instances would actually suffice to produce the universal essence which is applicable to *infinite* instances. He, therefore, declares that the task of our minds is to "consider" and reflect upon the particulars of sense-experience. This activity prepares the mind for the reception of the (universal) essence from the active intellect by an act of direct intuition. The perception of the universal form, then, is a unique movement of the intellective soul, not reducible to our perceiving the particulars either singly or totally and finding the common essence among them, for if so, it would be only a spurious kind of universal.

There is, besides, another vital consideration which leads to this view. If the perception of the individual instances and the noting of their resemblance (which latter, indeed, itself presupposes the possession of the universal by the mind) were sufficient to cause the universal, then acquisition of knowledge would become mechanical and this mechanism would operate necessarily.

It is, however, in fact not true that cognition can be so mechanically and deterministically produced. The origin of knowledge is mysterious and involves intuition at every stage. Of all intellectual knowledge, more or less, it is not so much true to say "I know it" as to admit "It occurs to me." All seeking for knowledge, according to ibn Sīna (even the emergence of the conclusion from the premises), has this prayer-like quality: the effort is necessary on the part of man; the response is the act of God or the active intellect. We are, indeed, often not aware as to what it is we want to know, let alone go ahead and "know it." A theory of knowledge which fails to notice this fundamental truth is not only wrong but blasphemous.

All ideas or forms then come from outside. The precise sense of the "outside" we shall try to work out [later]. But in the meantime we should notice certain other important characteristics of our knowledge. The first is that it is piecemeal and discursive, not total: it is also mostly "receptive" in the sense noted just above. In our normal consciousness we are not fully aware of the whence and whither of our cognition. True, there are people who are receptive in the ordinary sense of the word in that they do not discover either anything, or much that is new and original: they only learn for the most part; while there are others who discover new

things. But even these latter are only "receptive" in the sense that, not being fully conscious of the whence and whither of their knowledge—not aware of the total context of reality—they do not know the full meaning of their discoveries. This is because, in the common run of thinkers ideas come and go in succession and, therefore, their grasp of reality is not total. Hence ibn Sīna rejects the general and especially later Greek doctrine of the absolute identity of subject and object in intellectual operation, for, he argues, in the case of normal consciousness, there being a succession of ideas, if the mind became identical with one object, how could it then become identical with another? In this connection he rebukes Porphyry for his "mystical and poetical statements." Why he should single out the pupil of Plotinus, is not quite clear, for the doctrine is both Peripatetic and Neo-Platonic, although there are, it must be admitted, moderate representatives like Alexander of Aphrodisias just as there are extremist champions of the doctrine like most Neo-Platonists.

Ideas in this detailed, discrete, and discursive form of knowledge, as we have said, come into the mind and go out of it. Ibn Sīna is insistent that when an idea is not actually being used in intellection, it does not remain in the mind, or, in other words, there is, properly speaking, no intellectual memory as there is a memory of sensible images. There is nothing in the mind which can conserve intelligibles just as there is a conservatory in the soul for sensibles, for the existence of an intelligible in the mind means nothing else than the fact that it is actually being intellected. Absolutely speaking, it should be remarked that the word memory, when applied to sensible objects and individual events of the past, is radically different from the memory of universals and universal propositions, for in the former case there is a reference to the past. Aristotle himself had indicated this doctrine in his *De Memoria et Reminiscentia* where he says that universals are remembered only *per accidens*. The ordinary human thinking mind, says ibn Sīna, is like a mirror upon which there is a succession of ideas reflected from the active intellect. This does not mean that a truth once acquired, because it "goes out of the mind," has to be *relearnt* all over again when it is remembered. By our initial acquisition we acquire a skill to contact the active intellect and in remembering we simply use that skill or power. Resuming the analogy of the mirror, ibn Sīna says that, before acquisition of knowledge, the mirror was rusty; when we re-think, the mirror is polished, and it only remains to direct it to the sun (i.e., the active intellect) so that it should readily reflect light.

Even so is the ordinary philosophic (or mystic) consciousness: it is mostly partial (in varying degrees) even when it is original and creative (again in varying degrees) and it is, therefore, obviously not in total contact with reality, or, as ibn Sīna puts it, "is not one with the active intellect." But even in our ordinary cognitive processes, there are serious pointers to the existence of a type of consciousness in which this partiality and discursiveness may be overcome and which may be wholly creative, with the pulse of the total reality in its grasp. These pointers are illustrated by ibn Sīna by the example of a man who is confronted suddenly with a questioner who asks him a question which he has never asked himself before and, therefore, to which he cannot give a detailed answer on the spot. He is sure, however, that he *can* answer it because the answer has just "occurred" to him and lies within him. He then proceeds to the details and formulates the answer. "The strange thing is," says ibn Sīna, "that when this man begins to teach the questioner the answer to his question, he is simultaneously teaching himself as well" the detailed and elaborated form of knowledge even though he previously possessed this knowledge in a simple manner. This simple, total insight is the creator of that detailed, discursive knowledge which ensues. Now, this simple, total insight (the *scientia simplex* of the medieval Latin scholastics comes from ibn Sīna) is the creative reason (or the active intellect); the formulated and elaborate form is the "psychic" knowledge, not the absolutely intellectual cognition. A person possessed of this simple creative agency, if such a one exists, may well be said to be one with the active intellect; and since he possesses a total grasp of reality, he is sure, absolutely sure, of the whence and whither of knowledge (ibn Sīna puts a great emphasis on this self-confidence, certainty, conviction, or faith); he alone is aware of the total context of truth and, therefore, in him alone there is the full awareness of the meaning of each term in the process of reality; and, therefore, finally, only such a person can enter (and must enter) most significantly into temporal history, moulding it and giving it a new meaning. This is the prophet; but how to ascertain his existence? . . .

The necessity of the phenomenon of prophethood and of divine revelation is something which ibn Sīna has sought to establish at four levels: the intellectual, the "imaginative," the miraculous, and the socio-political. The totality of the four levels gives us a clear indication of the religious motivation, character, and direction of his thinking. Indeed, from our description and partial interpretation of his central philosophical theses so far, his deeply religious spirit has emerged very clearly. His theory of "Being" has led to the dependence of every finite being on God; and his doctrines of mind-body relationship and of the genesis and nature of knowledge have both culminated in the religious conception of miracles in the one case, and of a creative revelatory knowledge in the other. And there is not the slightest suggestion that religiosity is something artificially grafted upon his purely rational thinking; on the contrary, it has organically grown out of a rigorous process of ratiocination, and goes down to the very kernel of his thought.

It may be said that ibn Sīna is a citizen of two intellectual-spiritual worlds; the Hellenic and the Islamic. In his own mind he has so intrinsically unified the two worlds that they are identical; the question of disloyalty to either, therefore, does not arise for him at all. Under this circumstance, both traditional Islam and the heritage of Hellenism were inevitably interpreted and modified to a greater or lesser extent. This is apparent in the whole of his philosophy which enters into the technically religious field, but is most palpably so in his doctrine of prophecy. In this doctrine, ibn Sīna drastically modifies the Muslim dogmatic theology by declaring that the Qur'ānic revelation is, by and large, if not all, symbolic of truth, not the literal truth, but that it must remain the literal truth for the masses (this does not mean that the Qur'ān is not the Word of God; indeed, as we shall see, it is in a sense *literally* the Word of God); further, that the Law, although it must be observed by everyone, is also partly symbolic and partly pedagogical and, therefore, an essentially lower discipline than philosophic pursuits. (This again does not mean that we can dispense with the Law at any stage of our individual or collective development, for to be social belongs to the essence of man.) The interpretation and modification of Hellenism in this doctrine is obvious: although most elements of the Muslim philosophic doctrine of prophethood exist in Hellenism, they nevertheless exist in a nebulous and sometimes in a crude form; further, they are scattered. Indeed, the Greeks had no conception of prophethood and prophetic revelation as the Muslims knew it. In fact, the Muslim conception of prophethood is new and unique in the history of religion. For the Muslim philosophers (especially ibn Sīna, for although al-Fārābi had pioneered the way, we do not find all the elements in him, notably, the intellectual and the miraculous), to have evolved out of these nebulous, crude, and disjointed elements an elaborate, comprehensive, and refined theory of prophecy to interpret the personality of Muhammad, is nothing short of the performance of a genius.

At the intellectual level, the necessity of the prophetic revelation is proved by an argument elaborated on the basis of a remark of Aristotle that some people can hit upon the middle term without forming a syllogism in their minds. Ibn Sīna constructs a whole theory of total intuitive experience on the basis of this scanty remark. Since, he tells us, people differ vastly with regard to their intuitive powers both in quality and quantity, and while some men are almost devoid of it, others possess it in a high degree, there must be a rarely and exceptionally endowed man who has a total contact with reality. This man, without much instruction from outside, can, by his very nature, become the depository of the truth, in contrast with the common run of thinkers who may have an intuitive experience with regard to a definite question or questions but whose cognitive touch with reality is always partial, never total. This comprehensive insight then translates itself into propositions about the nature of reality and about future history; it is simultaneously intellectual and moral-spiritual, hence the prophetic experience must satisfy both the philosophic and the moral criteria. It is on the basis of this creative insight that the true prophet creates new moral values and influences future history. A psychologico-moral concomitant of this insight is also the deep and unalterable self-assurance and faith of the prophet in his own capacity for true knowledge and accurate moral judgment: he must believe in himself so that he can make others believe in him and thus succeed in his mission to the world.

This insight, creative of knowledge and values, is termed by ibn Sīna the active intellect and identified with the angel of revelation. Now, the prophet *qua* prophet is identical with the active intellect; and in so far as this identity is concerned, the active intellect is called '*aql mustafād* (the acquired intellect). But the prophet *qua* human being is not identical with the active intellect. The giver of revelation is thus in one sense internal to the prophet, in another sense, i.e., in so far as the latter is a human being, external to him. Hence ibn Sīna says that the prophet, in so far as he is human, is "accidentally," not essentially, the active intellect (for the meaning of the term "accidental," see the first section of this essay). God can and, indeed, must come to man so that the latter may develop and evolve, but the meaning of God can at no stage be entirely exhausted in man.

But although the intellectual-spiritual insight is the highest gift the prophet possesses, he cannot creatively act in history merely on the strength of that insight. His office requires inherently that he should go forth to humanity with a message, influence them, and should actually succeed in his mission. This criterion leads the Muslim philosophers, although they admit the divineness of the leading Greek thinkers and reformers, to fix their minds upon Moses, Jesus, and, above all, Muhammad who, undoubtedly, possesses the requisite qualities of a prophet to the highest degree. These requisite qualities are that the prophet must possess a very strong and vivid imagination, that his psychic power be so great that he should influence not only other minds but also matter in general, and that he be capable of launching a socio-political system.

By the quality of an exceptionally strong imagination, the prophet's mind, by an impelling psychological necessity, transforms the purely intellectual truths and concepts into lifelike images and symbols so potent that one who hears or reads them not only comes to believe in them but is impelled to action. This symbolizing and vivifying function of the prophetic imagination is stressed both by al-Fārābi and ibn Sīna, by the

Part of a leaf from an eleventh-century Arabic translation of the works of Galen, with notations in Avicenna's handwriting.

latter in greater detail. It is of the nature of imagination to symbolize and give flesh and blood to our thoughts, our desires, and even our physiological inclinations. When we are hungry or thirsty, our imagination puts before us lively images of food and drink. Even when we have no actual sexual appetite but our physical condition is ready for this, imagination may come into play and by stirring up suitable vivid images may actually evoke this appetite by mere suggestion. This symbolization and suggestiveness, when it works upon the spirit and the intellect of the prophet, results in so strong and vivid images that what the prophet's spirit thinks and conceives, he actually comes to hear and see. That is why he "sees" the Angel and "hears" his voice. That is why also he necessarily comes to talk of a paradise and a hell which represent the purely spiritual states of bliss and torment. The revelations contained in the religious Scriptures are, for the most part, of the figurative order and must, therefore, be interpreted in order to elicit the higher, underlying, spiritual truth.

It is the technical revelation, then, which impels people to action and to be good, and not the purely intellectual insight and inspiration. No religion, therefore, can be based on pure intellect. However, the technical revelation, in order to obtain the necessary quality of potency, also inevitably suffers from the fact that it does not present the naked truth but truth in the garb of symbols. But to what action does it impel? Unless the prophet can express his moral insight into definite enough moral purposes, principles, and indeed into a socio-political structure, neither his insight nor the potency of his imaginative revelation will be of much use. The prophet, therefore, needs to be a Lawgiver and a statesman *par excellence*—indeed the real Lawgiver and statesman is only a prophet. This practical criterion throws into still bolder relief the personality of Muhammad in the philosopher's mind. The Law (*Sharī'ah*) must be such that it should be effective in making people socially good, should remind them of God at every step, and should also serve for them as a pedagogic measure in order to open their eyes beyond its own exterior, so that they may attain to a vision of the true spiritual purpose of the Lawgiver. The Law is not abrogated at any stage for anybody, but only the philosophic vision of the truth gives to the Law its real meaning; and when that vision is attained, the Law seems like a ladder which one has climbed but which it would still be unwise to discard. For those relatively unfortunate souls which cannot see through the Law its philosophic truth, the technical revelation and the letter of the Law must remain the literal truth. . . .

We have learnt [earlier] that God is unique in that He is the Necessary Being; everything else is contingent in itself and depends for its existence upon God. The Necessary Being must be numerically one. Even within this Being there can be no multiplicity of attributes—in fact, God has no other essence, no other attributes than the fact that He exists, and exists necessarily. This is expressed by ibn Sīna by saying that God's essence is identical with His necessary existence. Since God has no essence, He is absolutely simple and cannot be defined. But if He is without essence and attributes, how can He be related to the world in any way? For Aristotle, who held this conception of the Deity, the world presented itself as a veritable other—it was neither the object of God's creation, nor of care, not even of knowledge. His God led a blissful life of eternal self-contemplation and the world organized itself into a cosmos out of love and admiration for Him, to become like Him.

The Muslim philosophical tradition finds the solution under the influence of the Neo-Platonic example which combines God's absolute simplicity with the idea that, in knowing Himself, God also knows in an implicit, simple manner the essence of things. The system is worked out and systematized by ibn Sīna, who strives to derive God's attributes of knowledge, creation, pow-

er, will, etc., from His simple unchanging being, or, rather, to show that these attributes *are* nothing but the fact of His existence. This is done by an attempt to show that all the attributes are either relational or negative; they are, thus, identical with God's being and with one another. The Deity is, therefore, absolutely simple. That God is knowing, is shown by the fact that being pure from matter and pure spirit, He is pure intellect in which the subject and object are identical.

But God's self-knowledge is *ipso facto* knowledge of other things as well, since, knowing Himself, He also inevitably knows the rest of the existents which proceed from Him. Here ibn Sīna strikes an original note. According to the philosophical tradition of Hellenism, God, at best, can know only the essences (or universals) and not the particular existents, since these latter can be known only through sense-perception and, therefore, in time; but God, being supra-temporal and changeless and, further, incorporeal, cannot have perceptual knowledge. This doctrine of the philosophers was especially repugnant to Islam, for it not only made God's knowledge imperfect, but it made God Himself useless for those whose God He is to be. Ibn Sīna devises an argument to show that although God cannot have perceptual knowledge, He nevertheless knows all particulars "in a universal way," so that perceptual knowledge is superfluous for Him. Since God is the emanative cause of all existents, He knows both these existents and the relations subsisting between them. God knows, for example, that after such a series of events a solar eclipse would occur, and knowing all the antecedents and consequences of this eclipse, He knows in a determinate manner its qualities and properties; He knows, therefore, what this particular eclipse will be, and can differentiate it completely from all other events even of the same species, viz., eclipse in general. But when the particular eclipse actually occurs in time, God, not being subject to temporal change, cannot know it. But He also *need* not know it in this way, for He knows it already. Very ingenious though this theory is and, we think, successful in showing that sense-perception is not the only way to know the particulars, it is obvious that it cannot avoid the introduction of time factor, and, therefore, change in divine knowledge. Al-Ghazālī's criticism of the theory in the thirteenth discussion of his *Tahāfut al-Falāsifah* certainly finds the target at this point, although his view that according to ibn Sīna God cannot know individual men but only man in general, is obviously mistaken, for if God can know a particular sun-eclipse, why can He not know, in this manner, an individual person? Indeed ibn Sīna declares in the Qur'ānic language that "not a particle remains hidden from God in the heavens or on the earth."

As regards God's attributes of volition and creation, ibn Sīna's emanationist account renders them really pointless as al-Ghazālī has shown. In a thoroughly intellectualist-emanationist account of the Deity, will has no meaning. For ibn Sīna, God's will means nothing but the necessary procession of the world from Him and His self-satisfaction through this. Indeed, he defines it in purely negative terms, viz., that God is not unwilling that the world proceed from Him; this is very different from the positive attributes of choice and the execution of that choice.

Similarly, the creative activity of God, for ibn Sīna, means the eternal emanation or procession of the world, and since this emanation is grounded finally in the intellectual nature of God, it has the character of unalterable rational necessity. Even though al-Ghazālī's criticism which assimilates the divine activity of ibn Sīna to the automatic procession of light from the sun and, thus, rejects the appellation of "act" to God's behaviour, is not quite correct (since according to ibn Sīna, God is not only conscious of the procession of the world from Him, but is also satisfied with and "willing" to it), the term "creation" is nevertheless used only in a Pickwickian sense, and the term "act" (in the sense of voluntary action) is also seriously modified, since, as we have said, there is no question of real choice. Rationally determined, activity is, of course, compatible with will and choice and can also be said to be done with choice, but this choice has to be brought in as an *additional* element both initially and finally. For, suppose, a man chooses to think about a certain problem. Now, the initial choice is his own to think about this rather than that problem and then at any moment he can also choose or will to terminate this process of thinking. What goes on between the beginning and the end will be a rationally determined process of thought, and not a series of choices, though the process as a whole is also chosen and voluntary. But in the philosophical account of God there is just no room for this additional factor either at the end or at the beginning.

The world, then, exists eternally with God, for both matter and forms flow eternally from Him. But although this concept was abhorrent to Islamic orthodoxy, ibn Sīna's purpose in introducing it was to try to do justice both to the demands of religion and of reason and to avoid atheistic materialism. For the materialists, the world has existed eternally without God. For ibn Sīna, too, the world is an eternal existent, but since it is in itself contingent, in its entirely it needs God and is dependent upon Him eternally. We see here the double purpose of the doctrine of essence and existence. Unlike atheism, it requires God who should bestow being upon existents; and in order to avoid pantheism, it further requires that the being of God should be radically differentiated from the being of the world.

The chief crux of the eternity of the world, which has been stressed by the opponents of the doctrine throughout the history of thought, is that it involves an actual infinite series in the past. In answer, it has been said, ever since Kant, that it is not impossible at all to imagine an infinite in the past, just as it is not impossible to imagine it in the future, i.e., there is no absurdity involved in starting from any given moment backwards and traversing the past and at no point coming to the beginning of the past. The fallacy of this answer consists in assimilating the past to the future, for the past is something actual in the sense that it has happened and is, therefore, determinate once and for all. But the same fallacy, we think, is implied in the objection itself, and it seems that the application of the term "infinite" is inappropriately used for the past: the term "infinite" is used either for a series which is endless or which is both beginningless and endless. According to the thesis, the series is beginningless *in the past,* and endless in the future, whereas the objection seeks to put an end to the series at a given moment of time and then argues for an infinity in the past. Also, whereas beginning is a temporal concept, beginninglessness is a negation and need not be a temporal concept, but the objection obviously implies "infinity in the past" as a temporal concept. . . .

The influence of ibn Sīna's thought has been enormous. In the East, indeed, his system has dominated the Muslim philosophical tradition right down to the modern era when his place is being given to some modern Western thinkers by those who have been educated in modern universities. In the *madrasahs* run on traditional lines, ibn Sīna is still studied as the greatest philosopher of Islam. This is because no subsequent philosopher of equal originality and acuteness produced a system after him. Ibn Rushd, the last great philosophical name in the medieval tradition of Muslim philosophy, did not formulate his thought systematically, but chose to write commentaries on Aristotle's works. These commentaries, because of their superb scholarliness and acuteness, had a tremendous impact on the medieval West (which received Aristotle first through him) but were not only not influential in the Muslim East, but most of them are even lost in the original Arabic. His comparative lack of influence, of course, is chiefly due to the destruction of his works. For the rest, the subsequent philosophical activity was confined to the writing of commentaries on ibn Sīna or polemics against him. Rare exceptions, like Ṣadr al-Dīn al-Shīrāzi, who wrote works on systematic philosophy, became less philosophical and more mystical in their intellectual, if not spiritual, temper. Nevertheless, these commentaries and polemics against and for ibn Sīna and later systems have never yet been studied to any appreciable extent by modern students.

Now, let us determine more exactly the influence of ibn Sīna within the Islamic tradition. To say that he has dominated the philosophical tradition in Islam is certainly not to say that he has dominated the Islamic tradition itself. On the contrary, the influence of ibn

Sīna—which is equivalent to the influence of philosophy—within Islam suddenly and sharply dwindled after the polemics of al-Ghazāli and later on of al-Rāzi and then declined and became moribund. He continued to be read in the *madrasahs* merely as an intellectual training ground for theological students, not to philosophize anew but to refute or reject philosophy. The chief contributory factors to this situation were the formal rigidity of dogmatic theology and the fact that human reason itself became suspect due to the incompatibility of certain tenets of ibn Sīna with this theology (besides, of course, social, political, educational, and economic causes). Not only did the philosopher's concept of the eternity of the world give affront to orthodoxy but also to those doctrines of his own which were developed with an especial regard for Islam, like the doctrine of prophethood. But perhaps the greatest theological objection was to his rejection of the bodily resurrection. On this point, although he maintains in the **K. al-Najāt** (and the **Shifā'**) that the resurrection of the flesh, while not demonstrable by reason, ought to be believed on faith; in his expressly esoteric work called **Risālat al-Adwīyyah** he rejects it in totality and with vehemence.

Ibn Sīna's works were translated into Latin in Spain in the middle of the sixth/twelfth century. The influence of his thought in the West has been profound and far-reaching. We have, while discussing ibn Sīna's individual theories, alluded time and again to certain definite influences of his. But as it is impossible to do justice to this aspect fully within the space at our disposal, we shall be content with certain general remarks. Ibn Sīna's influence in the West started penetrating palpably since the time of Albert the Great, the famous saint and teacher of St. Thomas Aquinas. Aquinas' own metaphysics (and theology) will be unintelligible without an understanding of the debt he owes to ibn Sīna. No one can fail to observe ibn Sīna's influence even in Aquinas' later and bigger works like the *Summa Theologica* and the *Summa contra Gentiles*. But the influence of the Muslim philosopher in the earlier formative period of the Christian Saint is overwhelming; he is mentioned by the latter, e.g., on almost each page of his *De Ente et Essentia* which is, indeed, the foundation of Aquinas' metaphysics. No doubt, ibn Sīna is also frequently criticized by Aquinas and others, but even the amount of criticism itself shows in what esteem he was held in the West.

But the influence of ibn Sīna is not restricted to Aquinas, or, indeed, to the Dominican Order or even to the official theologians of the West. The translator of his *De Anima,* Gundisalvus, himself wrote a *De Anima* which is largely a wholesale transporation of ibn Sīna's doctrines. Similar is the case with the medieval philosophers and scientists, Robert Grosseteste and Roger Bacon. Duns Scotus and Count Zabarella, the finest of the late medieval commentators of Aristotle, also bear testimony to ibn Sīna's enduring influence. . . .

But it would be futile to go on giving a mere catalogue of individual authors. In fact, the historic influence of this rich personality is a phenomenon which is being realized only now in the West. . . .

Nizámí-i-'Arúdí, in the *Chahár Maqála* (written in the mid-twelfth century), compares Avicenna favorably to Aristotle:

For four thousand years the physicians of antiquity travailed in spirit and spent their very souls in order to reduce the science of Philosophy to some fixed order, yet could they not effect this; until after the lapse of this period that pure philosopher and most great thinker Aristotle weighed out this coin in the balance of Logic, assayed it with the touchstone of Definitions, and measured it with the measure of Analogy, so that all doubt and uncertainty departed from it, and it was established on a sure and critical basis. And during these fifteen centuries which have elapsed since his time, no philosopher has won to the inmost essence of his doctrine, nor travelled the high road of his preeminence save that most excellent of the moderns, the Philosopher of the East, the Proof of God to mankind, Abú 'Alí Husayn ibn 'Abdu'lláh ibn Síná [Avicenna]. Whosoever, therefore, finds fault with these two great men will have cast himself out from the fellowship of the wise, ranked himself with madmen, and revealed himself as fit company only for fools. May God by His Grace and Favour keep us from such stumblings and vain imaginings!

Quoted by Edward G. Browne in Arabian Medicine, *Cambridge University Press, 1921.*

Herbert A. Davidson (essay date 1979)

SOURCE: "Avicenna's Proof of the Existence of God as a Necessarily Existent Being," in *Islamic Philosophical Theology,* edited by Parviz Morewedge, State University of New York Press, 1979, pp. 165-87.

[*In the following essay, Davidson insists that, although Avicenna purports to prove God's existence based on the concept of a necessarily existent being, his ontological argument is rather a kind of cosmological proof.*]

1. The cosmological proof of the existence of God may be characterized as a proof that begins by recognizing the actual existence of something in the universe; then it employs the principle of causality to establish that that thing and the universe as a whole have a cause. The a priori or ontological proof, in contrast, operates in the realm of thought without as-

suming the actual existence of anything. It begins with a concept of the nature of God, such as "that than which nothing greater can be conceived"; the "best"; the "absolutely simple"; "most perfect being"; "immeasurably powerful being"; "inifinite being"; or "substance" par excellence. Then, as the proof is generally understood, merely by analysis the concept, it undertakes to demonstrate that such a being must exist. It does their either directly, by showing that actual existence can be logically deduced from the concept; or indirectly, by showing that a self-contradiction would result from assuming that the being in question does not exist.

The term *necessary being* echoes through much of the history of the ontological proof. This term is not defined by every writer using it, but it seems, in ontological proofs, to have been used in one of two senses: (a) *Necessary being* may be understood in the sense of a being whose existence is established as a necessary truth, in the way that necessary truth is defined by Leibniz. According to Leibniz: "When a truth is necessary, its reason can be found by analysis, resolving it into more simple ideas and truths until we come to those that are primary . . . Truths of reasoning are necessary and their opposite is impossible." (b) A necessary being may also be understood as that which exists "through itself" or "through its essence," as that "which has in its essence the sufficient reason of its existence."

There have been instances of ontological proofs employing the term *necessary being* in one sense or the other, as well as instances employing the term without specifying which sense is intended or whether both are. In fact, however, whether a given argument does happen to use the term *necessary being* in one sense or the other, every ontological proof should, it would seem, make both points. That is to say, every ontological proof attempts to show that the existence of God follows by logical necessity from an analysis of the concept of God's nature; such simply is what we mean by an ontological proof. And, it would further seem, an ontological proof can infer the existence of God from a concept of His nature only if the essence of God, as reflected in the concept, should somehow contain the "sufficient reason" of His existence. Thus the ontological proof assumes that the existence of God can (a) be proved by a priori, logical necessity; and by virtue of this assumption it further assumes that (b) God exists *through His essence,* that He has in His essence a *sufficient reason of His existence.*

Ontological proofs formulated with the aid of the term necessary being or necessary existence are known from the time of Descartes, and that term can appear in different stages of given argument. Descartes, in the course of elucidating his ontological proof, introduces *necessary existence* as a middle term, to justify passing from the concept of God as a perfect being to the actual existence of God: "Because actual existence is *necessarily* and at all times linked to God's other attributes, it follows certainly that God exists." In a number of philosophers, the thesis that God is necessarily existent is the conclusion of an ontological proof. Thus Spinoza, More, Leibniz, perhaps Christian Wolff, Baumgarten, and Moses Mendelssohn offer ontological proofs establishing the existence of a "necessary being," a "necessarily existent being," or a being that "necessarily exists." There also are at least two instances of proofs that start with necessary existence. That is to say, rather than beginning with a concept such as *perfect being* or *infinite being* or the like, they begin with the concept of *necessary being,* and then, by analyzing the concept, they establish that such a being does in fact exist. One of several formulations of the ontological argument in Leibniz consists in the following bare syllogism: "necessary being exists," which, Leibniz explains, is equivalent to saying that "being to whose essence existence belongs, exists; or being *per se* exists." This "is evident from the terms." "But God is such a being. . . . Therefore God exists," Mendelssohn reasoned, also as one of several formulations: "It is clear that necessary being . . . must possess all perfections in the highest degree. . . . The concept of the necessary must accordingly also include within itself the perfection of existence. Therefore the necessary must also actually exist."

In addition to its role in the ontological proof, which must undertake to establish the existence of God as a necessary being in both senses of the term distinguished earlier, necessary being also plays a role in the cosmological proof. Now whatever sense the term *necessary being* may have in a given cosmological argument, the first of the two senses distinguished earlier would presumably be excluded. A cosmological proof could hardly establish the existence of a necessary being in the sense of a being whose existence is established merely by analyzing concepts: for the characteristic of this proof is precisely that it does not restrict itself to the mere analysis of concepts. On the other hand, every cosmological proof, whether or not it happens to use the term *necessary being,* must explicitly or virtually establish that God exists as a necessary being in the second sense. For the cosmological proof undertakes to establish the existence of God as an uncaused cause, consequently as a being that exists through itself, a being that has a sufficient reason of its existence in itself. Thus the cosmological proof—whether or not a given instance of the argument happens to use the term *necessary being*—cannot establish the existence of God in the first sense of necessary being affirmed by the ontological proof; and it must undertake to establish the existence of God in the second sense.

Leibniz gave perhaps the best known instance of a cosmological argument using the term *necessary be-*

ing. By the side of his ontological argument, Leibniz offered another wherein he begins by considering the actual existence of objects in the external world. Then, employing the principle of sufficient reason, a form of the principle of causality, Leibniz establishes that "contingent things . . . can have their final or sufficient reason only in the necessary being," that is to say, in a being "which has the reason of its existence in itself"—the second sense of necessary being. Wolff, Baumgarten, and Mendelssohn all repeat, with minor variations, Leibniz's cosmological proof, concluding in the existence of a necessary being. Thus Leibniz, perhaps Wolff, Baumgarten, and Mendelssohn give parallel proofs, one ontological and the other cosmological, of the existence of a necessary being. The contention of these philosophers is that the ontological and cosmological proofs lead independently to the same result, the existence of a necessary being in some such sense as that which exists "through its essence."

The two proofs were not, however, always kept distinct. At least one philosopher, Samuel Clarke, intentionally or inadvertently combined the two into a single overall demonstration. Clarke presents a cosmological argument in the spirit of Leibniz, contending that the changeable and dependent beings in the universe must have their "ground or reason of existence" in an eternal being which is "self-existent, that is, necessarily existing." But the only meaning of "self-existent" recognized by Clarke is that whose "necessity . . . must be antecedent in the natural order of our ideas to our supposition of its being"; whose necessary existence "must *antecedently* force itself upon us whether we will or no, even when we are endeavoring to suppose that no such being exists"; "the supposition of whose non-existence is an express contradiction." That is to say, the cosmological argument, which begins with the actual existence of things in the external world, establishes a being which is *necessarily existent* in the sense that its existence can be discovered merely by examining its concept "antecedently" and without considering the existence of anything in the external world, a being such that assuming it not to exist gives rise to a self-contradiction. This, however, is the sense of necessary being that can be established only through an ontological argument. Thus Clarke has intentionally combined or inadvertently confused two arguments, following the reasoning of the cosmological, but giving the conclusion of the ontological.

Clarke is of particular interest because he inspired Section IX of Hume's *Dialogues Concerning Natural Religion.* In Section IX of the dialogue, Hume allows the conservative participant to have his say. This participant maintains that the most effective way of establishing the existence of God is the "simple and sublime argument *a priori.*" The argument, it turns out, has three steps, the first two of which correspond to the cosmological part of Clarke's demonstration. The third step then concludes that in order to explain the existence of the world "we must . . . have recourse to a necessarily existent being who carries the reason of his existence in himself; and who cannot be supposed not to exist without an express contradiction." That is to say, we must have recourse to a first "necessary" cause—a proper conclusion of the cosmological argument—whose concept is such that a self-contradiction results from assuming it not to exist—the conclusion of an ontological argument. If there should be any doubt, Hume's critique reveals that two arguments are in fact present here. The critique begins by showing that the existence of nothing at all can be established a priori, merely by examining its concept; that is a criticism appropriately directed against the ontological method. But then Hume goes on to argue that perhaps the universe as a whole has no cause, a criticism appropriate for refuting a cosmological argument.

Whereas Hume's critique blurs the distinction between the cosmological and ontological proofs of a necessarily existent being, Kant's critique, as is well known, clearly distinguishes the two, and then proceeds to establish an intrinsic connection between them. The cosmological proof, Kant argued, ultimately reduces itself to the ontological. Kant gives a concise statement of a cosmological argument establishing the existence of an "absolutely necessary being," and then contends: "What properties this being must have, the empirical premise cannot tell us." Consequently, human reason is led to "abandon experience altogether and endeavors to discover from mere concepts what properties an absolutely necessary being must have." The only means human reason can discover for pouring content into *absolutely necessary being* is to identify this being with *ens realissimum,* being possessing the fullness of perfection. But in order to show that *ens realissimum* is identical with the *necessary being* established by the cosmological argument, human reason must first analyze the concept of *ens realissimum* and derive *necessary existence* from it. Since *ens realissimum* is a necessarily existent being and in fact the only one, so human reason proceeds, it must be identical with the necessarily existent being established by the cosmological argument. Thus the absolutely *necessary being* whose existence is established through the cosmological argument acquires meaning only on the assumption that *necessary existence* can also be analyzed out of the concept of *ens realissimum*—which, according to Kant, amounts to the assumption that the concept of *ens realissimum* can serve as the basis for an ontological argument. Hence Kant concludes that the cosmological argument inevitably reduces itself to an ontological argument.

The foregoing survey shows that an ontological argument, whether it explicitly says so or not, must establish the existence of God as a necessary being in two senses: as a being whose existence can be established by a prior, logical necessity; and as a being that exists *through itself,* whose essence contains sufficient reason for its existence. Individual instances of the ontological proof have used the term *necessary being* at different stages of their argument. A cosmological argument, whether explicitly or not, should establish the existence of God in the second of the two senses of necessary being. And individual instances of the cosmological proof, it was seen, did undertake to prove the existence of God as a necessary being in this sense. In at least one instance, Clarke, a cosmological and an ontological argument were combined or confused: from a cosmological argument, Clarke concludes the existence of a necessary being in the sense that can be established only by the ontological proof. Of the two best known critiques of the cosmological argument, Hume's deals with the combined or confused version, and Kant's contends that the cosmological argument for a necessary being must inevitably reduce itself to an ontological argument.

The first philosopher known to use the concept of *necessary existence* in order to construct a proof of the existence of God was Avicenna. Avicenna's proof, it will appear, neither is, nor inevitably reduces itself to, an ontological proof. It is rather a certain kind of cosmological proof.

2. The concept of necessary existence is used by Avicenna to prove the existence of God in two works, at length in the *Najāt,* briefly and somewhat obscurely in the *Ishārāt.* The concept is also discussed fully in two other works, the *Shifā* and *Danesh Namesh,* but there Avicenna employs it only to define the nature of God, not, as far as I can see, to establish His existence.

Avicenna gave thought to the method of his proof. The proof, he explains, consists in "examining nothing but existence itself"; by "considering . . . the nature (*hāl*) of existence," the proof has "exitence *qua* existence testify to the first [cause]." This method pursued by Avicenna is contrasted by him with another whereby the existence of God is established not from a consideration of existence in general, but rather from a consideration of one segment of existence: God's "creation and effect." Although the latter method, which takes its departure from "creation and effect," is also recognized by Avicenna as legitimate, his own method, he claims, is "more certain and more exalted."

The difference between the two is stated here in language that is deliberately allusive, but easily deciphered. Metaphysics was defined in the Aristotelian tradition as the science that "examines the existent *qua* existent and what belongs to it by virtue of itself." Accordingly, when Avicenna claims to have constructed a proof exclusively by examining "existence itself" and by considering "existence *qua* existence," he means that he has constructed a proof using philosophic principles

drawn only from the science of metaphysics. This he contrasts with the proof that begins with God's "creation and effect" and reasons back from them to the existence of God as a first cause. Avicenna cannot mean that his proof uses absolutely no data drawn from God's "creation and effect." For, as we shall see, his proof does require at least one datum from the external world; and the parts of the world accessible to man are himself and physical nature, both of which belong to God's "creation and effect." Avicenna does mean that his proof considers no peculiar properties of God's creation, that is, no properties of physical nature, but instead considers the attributes belonging to physical nature or anything else solely insofar as it is existent. He is thus claiming to have constructed a metaphysical proof which is superior to proofs that do use principles drawn from physical science, such as—to take the most notable example—Aristotle's proof from motion does. Averroes was later to attack Avicenna for this presumption. At every possible opportunity, Averroes undertook to refute the claim that the existence of God can be established by nothing more than metaphysical principles; and in opposition he defended the position, represented as truly Aristotelian, that the proof of the existence of God is at least in part a subject for the science of physics.

It is easy to point out advantages Avicenna could have perceived in the metaphysical proof, rendering it "more certain and more exalted" than the physical proof. Aristotle's proof from motion rested on a set of physical principles: motion in place underlies all other kinds of change; everything moved has the cause of its motion outside itself; nothing can maintain itself in motion unless it is continuously moved by an agent, only circular motion is continuous; only an infinite force can maintain the heavens in motion for an infinite time. Using all these physical principles, Aristotle undertook to establish the existence of an unmoved incorporeal cause solely of the *motion* of the universe. Avicenna, although not rejecting Aristotle's physical principles, dispenses with them in his metaphysical proof. And yet, without them, he is confident that he can prove the existence of a cause not merely for the motion, but for the very existence of the universe. The metaphysical proof requires fewer premises and is thus "more certain." And it is "more exalted," for it establishes a cause of the very existence of the universe. With less fuel it travels, or attempts to travel, further.

Avicenna found two passages in Aristotle especially suggestive. One of them appears in Aristotle's *Metaphysics,* Book XII. There Aristotle gives a version of his proof from motion, then adds a postscript: Since the prime mover "can in no way be otherwise than as it is," it "is an existent . . . of necessity." Avicenna's proof, particularly the fuller version in the *Najāt,* can be understood as starting just where Aristotle left off. Avicenna sets aside all the physical arguments leading up to Aristotle's prime mover, which is an "existent . . . of necessity." He begins afresh by analyzing the concept "existent . . . of necessity" or, as he calls it, *necessarily existent,* working out everything contained in the concept. Then he undertakes to establish that something corresponding to the concept actually exists. He does this, however, without using the principles of physical motion employed by Aristotle, and also without relying exclusively on his analysis of the concept, as an ontological proof would.

The second Aristotelian passage underlying Avicenna's proof appears in another part of the *Metaphysics,* in Book V. *Metaphysics* V is a philosophic glossary that strikes a modern scholar as "evidently out of place" in the totality of the *Metaphysics.* Avicenna, however, read Aristotle differently. The subject matter of metaphysics was after all understood to be the existent *qua* existent and its attributes, and *Metaphysics* V consists precisely in an analysis of *existence* and of attributes of existence such as *unity, plurality, necessity, potentiality, actuality,* and the like. Book V can therefore be understood as a philosophic analysis of the subject matter lying at the heart of metaphysics. Avicenna must have read it that way, for he used Book V of Aristotle's *Metaphysics* as a cadre for a good half of his own *Metaphysics,* the subject of the remainder of his *Metaphysics* being the existence of God, His attributes, and the incorporeal realm.

Among the terms analyzed by Aristotle in the section in question is *necessary; necessary,* he explains, has three senses, of which the most fundamental is "what cannot be otherwise." Then, Aristotle observes: "For certain things, something else is a cause of their being necessary, but for some nothing is [a cause of their being necessary]; rather it is through them that others exist of necessity." That is to say, there is a class of things that are necessary without having a cause of their being necessary; and a second class of things that are necessary through a cause, this cause to be found in the former class. The Aristotelian distinction was to be mirrored in the painstaking distinction Avicenna drew between the necessarily existent by reason of itself and the necessarily existent by reason of another.

Avicenna for his part begins his analysis of metaphysical concepts by showing that primary concepts cannot truly be defined. Definitions in Aristotelian logic are framed by taking a wider and already known concept, the *genus,* and setting apart a segment of it through a *specific difference.* Accordingly, Avicenna writes, primary concepts such as *existent,* and *thing,* which are not "subsumed under anything better known," cannot be defined; they are rather "imprinted in the soul in a primary fashion." And among the concepts that cannot be "made known . . . in a true sense" are *necessary, possible,* and *impossible.*

Because *necessary, possible,* and *impossible* are not definable, ostensible definitions of them lead to a vicious circle. Avicenna considers two ostensible definitions of necessary: "That which can (*yumkin*) not be assumed [to be] absent (*ma'dūm*)"; "that which is such that an impossibility would result if it should be assumed to be other than it is." The first of the two definitions employs the term *possible* (*mumkin*)—"can (*yumkin*)"—and the second uses *impossible.* But, Avicenna observes, when we consider ostensible definitions of *possible* we find that they in their turn employ either *necessary* or *impossible;* possible is defined as "that which is not necessary" or as "that which is absent (*ma'dūm*), but is such that its existence is not *impossible* if it should be assumed to occur at any time in the future." Ostensible definitions of *impossible,* finally, include either *necessary* or *possible.* Thus attempts to define the triad chase one another in a circle. Yet, although primary concepts are not explicable by anything wider and better known and are thus inaccessible to true definition, there is, according to Avicenna, a way of explaining them to the man who for some reason does not have them imprinted in his soul. We may "direct attention" to the primary notions and "call them to mind" through a "term or an indication." On this basis, Avicenna ventures an explanation of *necessary:* "It signifies certainty of existence."

When Avicenna turns from *necessary* and *possible* to "necessarily existent being" and "possibly existent being," he offers the following explications: A necessarily existent being is a being that "perforce exists"; alternatively, it is "such that when it is assumed not to exist, an impossibility results." A "possibly existent being" is a being that "contains no necessity . . . for either its existence or nonexistence ('*adam*)"; alternatively it is "such that whether assumed not to exist or to exist, no impossibility results." These obviously are not definitions by Avicenna's standard, since they do not explain the concepts by anything wider and better known. They are in fact merely adaptations of the blatantly circular definitions of *possible* and *necessary* that Avicenna has just been seen to criticize.

The distinction between possibly existent being and necessarily existent being is supplemented by the distinction, originating in Aristotle's *Metaphysics* V, between two ways in which a thing can be necessary. Reflecting Aristotle's distinction, Avicenna writes that we can conceive of a being as necessarily existent either by reason of itself or by reason of something else. The former would be something "such that because of itself and not because of anything else whatsoever, an impossibility follows from assuming its nonexistence." The latter would be a being "such that should something other than itself be assumed [to exist], then it becomes necessarily existent." The illustrations Avicenna adduces for the latter category are "combustion," which is "necessarily existent . . . when contact is assumed to take place between fire and inflammable material," and "four," which is "necessarily existent . . . when we assume two plus two." If some thing is necessarily existent only by reason of something else, it must—since it will not exist by virtue of itself without that other thing—be possibly existent by reason of itself. Thus Avicenna distinguishes three categories: (a) the necessarily existent by reason of itself; (b) the necessarily existent by reason of another, but possibly existent by reason of itself; and (c) the possibly existent by reason of itself, which is not rendered necessarily existent by reason of another.

What Avicenna calls *necessarily existent by reason of itself* is the same as *necessary being* in the sense of that which exists "through itself" and "has in its essence the sufficient reason of its existence." What Avicenna calls *necessarily existent by reason of another* is the same as the category of things having, in the terminology of Leibniz, "physical or hypothetical necessity"; physical or hypothetical necessity" consists in "things, happening in the world just as they do" because "the nature of the world is such as it is." However, the necessity characterizing these two categories of necessarily existent being was already seen to be indefinable for Avicenna; it is a primary concept to be grasped by the human mind immediately. As a mere "indication" of its meaning, Avicenna wrote that necessity "signifies certainty of existence." The necessarily existent by reason of itself would accordingly be that which has certainty of existence by reason of itself; the necessarily existent by reason of another would be that which has certainty of existence by reason of another. And the impossibility involved in supposing such a being not to exist would consist in contradicting the certainty of its existence, the fact that it does exist. If no more than this can be said about the meaning of *necessarily existent,* it is difficult to see just how necessary existence differs from actual existence; not surprisingly, Ghazālī was later to accuse Avicenna of vagueness in his use of the term.

These remarks relate to the meaning of *necessity* and of *necessarily existent:* Avicenna rules out any definition of *necessarily existent* and we can only infer that its meaning amounts virtually to *actually existent.* When Avicenna subsequently comes to delimit the class of necessarily existent beings, that class turns out, in fact, to coincide exactly with the class of actually existent beings. For the two categories of necessarily existent being—that which is so by virtue of itself and that which is so by virtue of another—are, according to Avicenna, the only two conceivable categories of actual existence. To put this in another way, the possibly existent does not actually exist unless rendered necessary by something else; and conversely, everything actually existing, including whatever occurs in the physical world, such as combustion, is necessary in one sense or the other. To justify the point, Avicenna

reasons that as long as something is merely possible, nothing is present to "prefer" its existence over its nonexistence. The possibly existent can enter the realm of actual existence only if a factor distinct from itself should "select out" its existence. But whenever that factor is present, the existence of the possibly existent being is rendered necessary. The proper way of construing possible existence, according to Avicenna, is therefore to say that during the time the possible existent actually exists, its existence is necessary, and during the time it does not exist, its existence is impossible. but that necessity and that impossibility are both conditioned, due not to the thing itself, but only to the presence or absence of an external condition which necessitates its existence or nonexistence. Considered in itself, in isolation from the external conditions, the possibly existent at all times remains possible.

Actual existent is thus either: (a) Necessarily existent by reason of itself; this is something "such that if assumed not to exist an impossibility results," with the proviso that it has that character "by reason of itself." Or (b) necessarily-existent by reason of another, but possibly existent by reason of itself; this is something, again, such that if assumed not to exist, an impossibility results, with the proviso that it has that character only inasmuch as "something else is assumed" to exist. In distinguishing these categories, it must be stressed, Avicenna is operating exclusively in the realm of concepts, without committing himself to the actual existence of anything: He is saying that if something should be assumed to exist, then it has to be classified in one of the two categories of necessarily existent being.

3. Avicenna, it appears, rejects a true definition of (a) the necessarily existent by reason of itself, (b) the necessarily existent by reason of another but possibly existent by reason of itself, or (c) the possibly existent by reason of itself which is not rendered necessarily existent by anything else. Still, he writes, the "properties" of these three can be set forth. His proof of the existence of God consists in analyzing the concept of the *necessarily existent by reason of itself* and establishing its attributes; then analyzing the concept of the *possibly existent* and showing that if anything actually exists, something necessarily existent by reason of itself must also exist.

Avicenna's analysis of the *necessarily existent by reason of itself* was not original with him. Proclus had analyzed the concept of the "self-existent" (*qā'im bi-dhātihi*) and "self-sufficient (*mustaghnīyya bi-nafsihā*) first cause" and shown that it must be eternal, uncaused, and free of composition. Alfarabi subsequently applied the same type of analysis to the concept of the "First," as he called the Deity, arriving at a wider set of attributes than did Proclus. And the set of attributes deduced by Alfarabi from the concept of the "First" parallels the set Avicenna now derives from the concept of the *necessary by reason of itself*. Significantly, neither Proclus nor Alfarabi required the concept of *necessity* for their analysis. This supports the suggestion that the concept of *necessity* adds nothing to Avicenna's proof, and that his proof could have as well been based on an analysis of the *actually* existent by reason of itself instead of on an analysis of the *necessarily* existent by reason of itself.

Avicenna's analysis runs as follows: The necessarily existent by reason of itself clearly can "not have a cause." If it did have a "cause of its existence," its existence would be "by virtue of something" and therefore not solely by virtue of itself. Aristotelian philosophy distinguished no less than four senses of cause, including causes internal to the effect as well as those working on the effect from without, yet Avicenna does not specify which sense he is using here. However, the omission is apparently intentional, for Avicenna understands that the necessary by reason of itself is incompatible not only with an external cause—an agent upon which its existence depends—but also with internal causes—elements within itself making it what it is.

The denial of internal causes means that the necessarily existent by reason of itself can have no "principles which combine together and in which the necessarily existent consists." The full argument for this rests on a distinction between a given entity as a whole and the parts of which it is composed. Any composite entity, Avicenna contends, exists by virtue of its parts and not by virtue of itself as distinct from its parts. Accordingly, considered as a whole, it does not exist by virtue of what it is in itself but only by virtue of something else—by virtue of the components that constitute it. And it is therefore not necessarily existent by reason of itself. The implications of the thesis are far reaching. For if the necessarily existent by reason of itself can contain no parts whatsoever, it is simple in every conceivable way. It is incorporeal, inasmuch as it is not composed of matter and form. It is unextended and immaterial, inasmuch as it is free of quantitative parts. It is indefinable, inasmuch as it is not composed of genus and specific difference. And it is free of the distinction of essence and existence. The argument for simplicity also gives an implied answer to a much repeated object later to be directed against the proof of the existence of God as a necessary being. Perhaps, that objection runs, the physical world is itself the necessary being. Avicenna would by implication reply that the physical world cannot be conceived as necessarily existent by reason of itself, since the physical world cannot be assigned the attributes deducible from the concept of the necessarily existent by reason of itself: The physical world is not simple, unextended, and incorporeal.

There can, Avicenna further contends, be only one being necessarily existent by reason of itself. To prove this thesis, he argues basically that assuming two such beings amounts to assuming two beings that are sim-

Medieval woodcut of Avicenna.

ilar in one respect—their necessary existence—but different in another—the respect whereby they can be distinguished and called two. But that situation would be conceivable only if at least one of the two things should be composite, containing both the element in common with its counterpart and another element whereby it can be distinguished and by virtue of which two distinct beings can be enumerated. Thus at least one of the two would have to be composite, and consequently, as already seen, not necessarily existent by virtue of itself. It follows that not more than one being necessarily existent by reason of itself is conceivable.

Avicenna derives other attributes from the concept of *necessarily existent by reason of itself*. It must be pure *intellect,* for such is the nature of beings free of matter. It must be *true,* for truth consists in the highest grade of existence, and the necessarily existent by reason of itself would have the highest grade of existence. It must be *good,* for evil consists in privation, whereas the necessary by reason of itself has fullness of being and therefore suffers no privation. It must constitute the highest *beauty,* be the highest *object of desire,* be possessed of the greatest *pleasure,* and so forth. Avicenna's analysis of the concept of *necessarily existent by reason of itself* thus establishes that such a being must be uncaused, simple, incorporeal, one, pure intellect, true, good, beautiful, an object of desire, possessed of the greatest pleasure.

But is there anything in the external world corresponding to that concept? Does such a being actually exist? Its existence, Avicenna writes, is surely not self-evident. Nor can its existence be established through a syllogistic "demonstration" (*burhān*). For a demonstrative syllogism must be constructed with propositions that are "prior to," and the "causes" of the conclusion, whereas there is nothing prior to existence, and the cause of the presence of actual existence in the necessarily existent is accepted by reason of itself. What can be provided is an indirect "proof" (*dalīl*) of the existence of a being necessary by reason of itself, and that is what Avicenna undertakes.

To accomplish his proof, Avicenna leaves the conceptual realm for a single empirical datum: "There is no doubt that something exists (*anna hunā wujūdan*)." It makes no difference what it is that exists or what its peculiar properties might be; for the purpose of his proof Avicenna considers merely the "existent *qua* existent" and therefore all he needs is the fact that something does indeed exist. Applying the proposition that there are only two conceivable categories of actual existing beings, Avicenna proceeds: "Everything that exists is either necessary [by reason of itself] or possible [by reason of itself and necessary by reason of another]. On the first assumption, a necessarily existent [by reason of itself] has immediately been established, and that was the object of our demonstration. On the second assumption, we must show that the existence of the possible [by reason of itself but necessary by reason of another] ends at the necessarily existent [by reason of itself]." If the first alternative were accepted, the proof would be complete; the being conceded to be necessarily existent by reason of itself would simply be assigned all the attributes already shown to belong to such a being. But the real issue is of course posed by the second alternative, the assumption that the random existent object with which the proof started is necessarily existent only by reason of another, and possibly existent by reason of itself. The heart of the proof therefore lies in showing that anything possibly existent by reason of itself must ultimately depend for its actual existence upon something necessary by reason of itself.

Professor Wolfson has pointed out that two philosophic principles underlie Avicenna's proof, as well as other cosmological proofs of the existence of God in the Aristotelian tradition: (a) the principle of causality, and (b) the impossibility of an infinite regress of causes. Avicenna does not posit the two principles in their own right, but ingeniously derives them from his analysis of *necessarily existent by reason of itself* and *possibly existent by reason of itself.*

In formulating his version of the principle of causality, Avicenna employs a distinction between the cause of the "generation" (*hudūth*) of an object and the cause of its "maintenance" (*thabāt*). The cause of generation is more obvious since no one, Avicenna is certain, can doubt that whenever an object comes into existence, it does so by virtue of something else. But Avicenna's proof cannot pursue a first cause of the generation of every possibly existent being, both because Avicenna believed that some possible beings are eternal and not generated, and also because his proof requires causes that exist together with their effect, whereas the cause of generation may perish after the effect comes into existence. Therefore Avicenna gives his attention to the *maintaining* cause. If, he contends, we consider any object possible by reason of itself, irrespective of whether it is generated or eternal, we may legitimately ask what maintains it in existence. The factor maintaining the object in existence must be distinct from the object, for in itself the latter is only possible and does not exist by virtue of itself. And that factor must exist as long as the object exists; for even when the object is actual, it never ceases to be possible by reason of itself and dependent on something else for its existence. Thus the analysis of the concept *possibly existent by reason of itself*—or, to be more precise, merely asking what *possibly existent* means—establishes that if anything possibly existent should exist, it must at all times depend on a cause distinct from itself to maintain it in existence.

The second proposition required by Avicenna is formulated by him as the impossibility that "causes go to infinity"—the impossibility of an infinite regress of causes. In fact, unlike other philosophers, Avicenna does not argue that an infinite regress, specifically, is absurd. He rather argues for the more general principle that whether all actually existent possible beings are "finite or infinite," they must ultimately depend on a being necessarily existent by reason of itself; and from this more general principle he derives the impossibility of an infinite regress as a corolary.

Avicenna's reasoning here too is conducted solely through an analysis of concepts, in the present instance both the *necessarily existent* and the *possibly existent.* IIe is considering a situation wherein Z, for example, depends for its existence upon Y, which exists simulatneously with it; Y then depends upon X, which also exists simultaneously; ad infinitum. To show that such a situation is inconceivable, he mentally collects into a single group all possible beings actually existing at a single moment. Then he reasons as follows: The totality of possibly existent beings, considered as a whole, must be either (a) necessarily existent by reason of itself or (b) possibly existent by reason of itself. The former alternative would involve the absurdity that the "necessarily existent [by virtue of itself] is composed of possibly existent beings." Avicenna does not give any reason why that thesis is absurd. He presumably means that assuming the necessarily existent by reason of itself to be composed of possibly existent beings amounts to assuming that the necessarily existent is composite, whereas his earlier analysis showed that the necessary by reason of itself cannot be composite.

If the totality of possibly existent beings cannot (a) constitute a group that is necessarily existent by reason of itself, there remains (b) the second alternative, according to which the totality of possibly existent beings, taken collectively, is possible by reason of itself. On this alternative, Avicenna proceeds, "whether the group is finite or infinite," it stands in need of a factor that will continually "provide [it] with existence." That factor must be either (b-1) within the group or (b-2) outside of it. Assuming (b-1) that one [or more] of the members maintains the whole group is equivalent to assuming that the member in question is a cause of itself. For to be a cause of the existence of a group is "primarily" to be the cause of the individual members, and since the supposed cause is itself one of the members, it would be a cause of itself. Yet the supposed cause has already been assumed to be possibly existent, and the possibly existent is precisely what does not exist by virtue of itself. Therefore it could not be the cause of the collection of which it is one member.

If the totality of possibly existent beings cannot form a group that is necessarily existent by reason of itself, and if, further, that totality cannot be maintained by one of its own members, the sole remaining alternative is that what does maintain the totality of possibly existent beings in existence is (b-2) outside the group. Since, by hypothesis, all possibly existent beings were included inside, anything left outside is not possibly existent; it must accordingly be necessarily existent by reason of itself. Avicenna was able to reach this result, it should be observed, through the device of considering all possibly existent beings as a single group and then asking what maintains the group in existence; and the cogency of his argument depends upon the legitimacy of that procedure. Once he has established that the series of all possibly existent beings does depend on a necessarily existent being, Avicenna infers, as a sort of corollary, that the series must be finite; for the possibly existent beings must "meet" their necessarily existent cause and "terminate" there. Thus an infinite regress of causes would be impossible—a regress, however, of only one type, that wherein all the causes exist together.

Avicenna's complete proof now proceeds as follows: Something clearly exists, and it must be either necessary by reason of itself, or necessary by reason of another and possible by reason of itself. On the former assumption the proof is immediately complete: There is a being necessarily existent by reason of itself, which is to be assigned all the attributes of such a being. On the other assumption, the possible by reason of itself must be maintained in existence by something else, which exists as long as it exists. That other factor, in turn, must be either necessary by reason of itself or possible by reason of itself. If it is assumed to be necessary by reason of itself, the proof is again at once complete. If, on the other hand, it is assumed to be possible by reason of itself, it too must depend on a further factor distinct from it and existing as long as it exists. Once again, Avicenna asks whether the new factor is necessary by reason of itself or possible by reason of itself. It is inconceivable, he has contended, that the series of all possible beings existing simultaneously, whether finite or infinite, should be maintained in existence by part of itself or by itself as a whole. The series must be maintained in existence by something outside, something which can only be necessarily existent by reason of itself. The latter is to be assigned all the attributes shown to belong to the necessary by reason of itself, and it is the Deity in Avicenna's system.

4. Avicenna thus offers a proof of the existence of God that he characterizes as metaphysical since the proof considers the attributes of what exists solely insofar as it is existent and not insofar as it is a certain type of existent. The proof begins by distinguishing that which is *necessarily existent* from that which is *possibly existent,* and that which is necessarily existent *by reason of itself* from that which is necessarily existent *by reason of something else;* it analyzes those concepts; and it shows that the possibly existent can actually exist only if ultimately dependent on something necessarily existent by reason of itself. Necessarily existent, as far as I can see, means nothing more than actually existent for Avicenna, and the proof could be executed unchanged using the distinction between what is *actually* existent by reason of itself, and what is *possibly* existent by reason of itself but actually existent by reason of something else.

Avicenna has not given an ontological proof, for although his proof depends on an analysis of the concept *necessarily existent by reason of itself,* the analysis alone is not intended to show that anything exists in the external world corresponding to the concept. In deriving various attributes from the concept of necessary existence, Avicenna in fact follows a procedure later to be sanctioned explicitly by Kant, not for necessary existence, but for the concept of *God.* The proposition "God is omnipotent," Kant granted, is a "necessary judgment," inasmuch as "omnipotence cannot be rejected if we posit a deity, that is, an infinite being; for the two concepts are identical." Only the derivation of actual existence from a concept gives an ontological proof, subject to the several objections raised by critics of that proof. What Kant sanctions for the concept of *God* but rules out for the concept of *necessary being,* Avicenna does undertake with the concept *necessarily existent by reason of itself;* he derives a set of attributes from the concept, but does not pretend to derive actual existence from it.

Like other cosmological proofs of the Aristotelian type, Avicenna's proof employs the principles of causality and the impossibility of an infinite regress of causes. Avicenna's proof goes beyond Aristotle's, however, in establishing a first cause of the very existence of the universe rather than just a first cause of motion. His proof, further, is original in basing even the philosophical principles needed for the argument exclusively upon an analysis of concepts. Merely by analyzing the concept *possibly existent by reason of itself,* Avicenna establishes that if such a being actually exists, it must have a cause. And merely by analyzing the concepts *possibly existent by reason of itself* and *necessarily existent by reason of itself,* Avicenna shows that actual existence cannot consist solely in a series of possibly existent beings. Since Avicenna derives the philosophic principles used in the proof from an analysis of those concepts, the only proper way of refuting the proof would be to go back and question the analysis. In other words, the critic would have to go back and question Avicenna's dichotomy of what exists by virtue of itself and what exists by virtue of something else; and, more importantly, he would have to question whether what exists by virtue of another can indeed at no time in its career be self-sufficient, and whether what exists by virtue of itself cannot be composed of internal factors. Criticisms along these lines were directed against the proof by Ghāzālī, Averroes, and Hasdai Crescas.

Avicenna's proof was widely used, less as a whole than in parts or in adaptations. The methodological insistence that a proof of the existence of God is a subject for metaphysics, not physics, was, for example, taken up by the Latin writer Henry of Ghent, although the proof Henry gives is different from Avicenna's. The analysis of necessary and possible being on which the proof rests was employed by *Kalām* writers and there even appeared an adaptation of the proof as a proof of creation. A watered down version of the proof is given in *'Uyūn al-Masā'il,* and related works; these are works mistakenly attributed to Alfarabi but in fact dependent on Avicenna. The proof was reformulated by Maimonides, from whom it was copied by Thomas Aquinas. Another reformulation was offered by Crescas. Avicenna's analysis of necessary and possible existence enriched one of Spinoza's ontological arguments. The proof is central for Leibniz and his followers, who—although the historical filiation is unclear—reveal striking similarities with Avicenna. The two best known critiques of the cosmological proof are directed against versions of this proof as formulated by the followers of Leibniz. Despite the critiques, the proof is accepted by such widely-read twentieth century writers as Mohammed Abduh and F. Copleston.

Pickering on the impact of Avicenna:

Comparatively short as [Avicenna's] life was, it has left an indelible mark on the world. His Arabic redaction of Aristotle was for ages the main or only form in which the peripatetic science was available to the awakening mind of Europe. To study and to reproduce him was the life-long labour of Athelard of Bath, the first bright name in the annals of English thought. To confute and refute him and his school in the person of its most famous representatives, Ibn Rushd or Averroes of Cordova, was the aim of the great schoolmen from the Master of Sentences to Thomas of Aquino and Bonaventure. Dante meets him among the heretics in hell. . . . In the Vatican fresco of Raffaelle, a Moorish doctor is represented prostrate beneath the feet of Aquinas. The turbaned figure has been guessed at as Averroes, but may as well stand for Avicenna himself. The "twenty bookes clothed in blake and reed of Aristotil and of his philosophie," which formed so large a part of the library of Chaucer's "Clerke of Oxenforde," must have mainly consisted of Latin translations from Avicen. And it required the academical cataclysm of the Puritan revolution and the subsequent age of science to finally banish the spirit of the old Arabian master from the national schools of thought.

Charles J. Pickering, "The Persian Poetry of Avicenna," in The National Review, *Vol. XIV, 1889-90.*

A. I. Sabra (essay date 1980)

SOURCE: "Avicenna on the Subject Matter of Logic," in *The Journal of Philosophy,* Vol. LXXVII, No. 10, October, 1980, pp. 746-64.

[*Here, Sabra outlines Avicenna's influential conception of logic as a part of philosophy that can lead one to "knowledge of the unknown."*]

I think it is true to say that modern logicians have no great interest in the ancient debate about whether logic was a part or an instrument of philosophy. They are of the opinion that the debate, at least in the form it took in the ancient schools of Greek philosophy, raised a question the solution of which was largely a matter of convention. Avicenna would readily agree, and for the same reason; in one place at least he characterized the question as nothing more than a quibble about the meaning of words. But in both ancient and medieval discussions the question was often linked with another concerning the subject matter of logic. If, as the Platonists and the Stoics maintained, logic is a part of philosophy and the various parts of philosophy are studies of various portions or aspects of being, then what portion or aspect of being should be assigned to logic? *This* was not a verbal question. And since Avicenna decided to come down on the side of the Academy and not on the side of his "friends" the Peripatetics who maintained that logic was only an instrument, it is not surprising that he should take the trouble in his *Kitāb al-Shifā'* to expound his views on these two interrelated questions.

The dispute as to whether logic was a theory or an instrument has a further significance for the historian of Islamic thought: it became part of a continuing struggle of far-reaching consequences between the champions of Arabic and Islamic learning and the followers of an imported Hellenistic tradition. It should be remembered that in Islam the *trivium* was not an accepted category: logic and grammar stood on opposite sides of the fence, supported by rival groups. The word chosen by the translators of Aristotle for the art of logic, *mantiq* (speech), could naturally be used, and was sometimes used, as a title of works on grammer; and this alone was bound to impose the question as to which group, the grammarians or the logicians, was to be regarded as the true custodian of sound discourse. The ensuing controversies may have been motivated in part by religious or nationalistic impulses, but they were not devoid of philosophical interest—being ultimately concerned with the relation between language and thought. The documents that have survived from the early period of this debate appear to indicate that it was the grammarians who had the better of the argument. Logicians were content at first to claim that they were concerned with meanings whereas grammar was competent to deal only with words. This was too simple a view of the task that the grammarians had set for themselves. In the famous debate that took place in the tenth century between the logician Mattā ibn Yūnus and the grammarian Abū Saʿīd al-Sīrāfī, both recognized leaders in their respective disciplines, the case for logic appears to be vulnerable and lacking in sophistication. With regard to the logicians' view of grammar, Sīrāfī cites example after example of how subtle shades of meaning are reflected in linguistic features which it was the business of the grammarian to identify. It is true that Mattā—whose translations of Greek philosophical works into Arabic were done not directly from the Greek but from Syriac—is being repeatedly put on the defensive by being reminded of his ignorance of Greek, the original language of the logic he now claims to explicate in another language (Arabic) which he has not mastered. The audience is clearly unsympathetic to him, and he is rarely given the chance

to answer the questions put to him. But even with the admission that this was perhaps not a fair trial, one comes away from reading it with the clear impression that it was Sīrāfī who had a deeper appreciation than his adversary of the incongruences generated by the "creation of a language within a language," as he aptly described the logicians' enterprise.

Abū Nasr al-Fārābī, at one time a student of Mattā, was the first Arabic logician to take seriously the questions of the relation of logic to grammar and of language to thought. His *Enumeration of the Sciences* briefly formulates the idea of logic as universal grammar (grammar furnishes the rules proper to the utterances of a given language; logic furnishes the rules common to the utterances of all languages), and states some of the implications of the connection between "inner" and "outer" speech. His book on *The Utterances Employed in Logic* can be viewed as an attempt to face the problems of introducing an artificial mode of speaking into natural Arabic. In his so-called *Short Commentary on Aristotle's* Prior Analytics, he tried to convince other Muslims of the usefulness of Greek logic by illustrating Aristotelian forms of inference in terms taken from Islamic theology and jurisprudence. He thus preceded al-Ghazālī in formulating the kind of argument that finally succeeded in securing for Aristotelian logic a permanent place in Muslim education.

It is one of the paradoxes of Islamic intellectual life that the man most responsible for admitting Aristotelian logic into the scheme of traditional learning was an opponent of Greek philosophy who wrote a powerful book in its refutation. The great religious thinker Abū Hāmid al-Ghazālī (d. 1111) not only rejected the metaphysical doctrines of Peripateticism and Neoplatonism but also warned against the dangers of studying astronomy and mathematics. Nevertheless he wrote several books on Aristotelian logic and, what was more crucial for the history of logic in Islam, prefaced his influential work on Islamic jurisprudence (*al-Mustasfā*) with a lengthy introduction in which he went so far as to say that without logic one could not be sure of any part of knowledge (whether secular or religious, theoretical or practical). Al-Ghazālī was able to do this because he understood logic as a mere instrument, a kind of "balance" for weighing arguments which did not commit its user to any doctrine or belief.

Ghazālī's attitude was in great contrast to that of another religious thinker who lived some two hundred years after him. Ibn Taymiyya was a strict jurisconsult who had no use for mystical or speculative approaches to religion, let alone an unbridled habit of thought such as philosophy. He could not tolerate the fact that Greek logic had appeared to gain a firm foothold in the field of religious learning, and he singled it out for a concentrated and persistent attack. Unlike Ghazālī, Ibn Taymiyya believed that Aristotelian logic was committed to certain metaphysical doctrines from which it could not be detached. One could not adopt Aristotelian logic without being contaminated by its false presuppositions. One of these was a pervasive belief in universals or essences. According to Ibn Taymiyya, only individuals exist, and what is called "essence" is nothing but a conventional device for grouping individuals together for practical or theoretical purposes of our own. A universal term like 'man' does not refer to something shared by individuals, for no such thing exists. The inevitable conclusion was a total rejection of Aristotle's theories of definition and syllogism.

Ibn Taymiyya's criticisms, often acute and original, constituted the most radical critique of Aristotelian logic in the Arabic language. But they were not the work of a concerned logician; their aim was not to reform logic but to destroy it. They came too late in history to achieve that aim on a wide scale; the trend initiated by Ghazālī had taken root and was already well established. But the logic that Ghazālī had made acceptable was not a part of philosophical inquiry, a search for new truths, but an instrumental discipline consisting of a fairly fixed set of rules that one learned in order to apply them in other disciplines.

Avicenna, too, appreciated the instrumental character of logic, but his perspective differed from that of any of the thinkers I have mentioned. In broad terms he belonged to the same philosophical tradition to which al-Fārābī and al-Kindī before him also belonged. But he was more independent of mind than either of his two predecessors, and he spoke more often than they with an individual voice of his own. He was frequently critical or skeptical of the Aristotelianism he embraced and modified, and openly dissociated himself from the Peripatetic school of Baghdad, feeling himself the equal of the ancient commentators whom he read of course in translation. In matters of logic, as in other parts of his philosophy, he helped himself more freely than members of that school to Platonic (and Stoic) doctrines which had already been fused together in the late Greek writings that became the common heritage of Islamic philosophers. He did not always do this in the spirit of eclecticism, but often as the work of an independent thinker who felt able and obliged to make up his own mind.

Logic occupies a major part of *Kitāb al-Shifā'*, the huge philosophical *summa* which Avicenna completed just before he reached the age of forty. It is known from Avicenna's own account and from a supplementary account provided by his pupil al-Jūzjānī, that the book was composed in varying and sometimes difficult circumstances which had their effect on the character of its various parts. Al-Jūzjānī says, for example, that Avicenna dictated most of the Physics and the Metaphysics during a period of only twenty days without referring to other writings. When he came to write

the Logic, however, he was able to consult the books of others "whose order [of treatment] he followed and whose objectionable views he discussed"—a fact which the historian of Avicenna's logic must bear in mind. The logical part of the *Shifā'* is divided into sections corresponding generally to the parts of Aristotle's *Organon*. Only the first section, the Introduction paralleling Porphyry's *Isagoge*, was translated into Latin in the middle ages. It happens to be the section in which Avicenna directly addresses the question of the subject matter of logic. Avicenna's discussions thus continue a tradition that goes back to the Greek commentators, and his own treatment of these questions entered into the stream of philosophical thought in the West. In this [essay] I shall not in general be concerned to reconstruct the complex process of transmission of Greek ideas into Arabic, or follow Avicenna's discussions into the writings of medieval thinkers; my main object will be to identify and clarify Avicenna's views. I hope that the following remarks, despite their preliminary character, will not fail to show that Avicenna's style of thinking and writing does lend itself profitably to the kind of analytical approach attempted here.

To avoid confusion I shall refer to sections of Avicenna's Logic in the *Shifā'* by English titles, such as *"Introduction"* or *"Interpretation,"* reserving for Greek works their commonly used titles in Latin or Greek.

Chapter 2 of the *Introduction,* on the chief divisions of the sciences, ends with a longish passage giving Avicenna's first statement in the *Shifā'* on the nature of logic and its relation to the other sciences. The essences of things (*māhiyyāt al-ashyā'*—*māhiyya . . .*) may exist in the actual things (*a'yān al-ashyā'*) or in thought (*fīal-tasawwur*). Certain accidents (*a'rād*) attach themselves to the essences when these possess one or the other of the two modes of existence. We may therefore examine the essences in themselves, without reference to their existence in individuals or in thought, or our examination of them may involve those adventitious properties which accrue to them in consequence of their external or mental existence. Avicenna here gives some examples of the kind of accidents that may attach to essences as mental entities: being subject or predicate, universality or particularity of predication, essential or accidental predication. He explains his examples by briefly remarking that "in external things there is no essential or accidental predication, nor is a thing a subject or a predicate, a premiss or a syllogism or the like."

These opening sentences are misleading in that they give the impression that the accidents exemplified here come into being simply as a result of bringing the essences into one's mind. But Avicenna seems to be struggling to dispel this misunderstanding in the following words:

> If we wish to investigate things and gain knowledge of them we must conceive them; thus they necessarily acquire certain states (*ahwāl*) that come to be in conception: we must therefore consider those states which belong to them in conception, *especially as we seek by thought to arrive at things unknown from those that are known.* Now things can be unknown or known only in relation to a mind; and it is as concepts that they acquire what they do acquire in order that we move from what is known to what is unknown regarding them, without however losing what belongs to them in themselves; we ought, therefore, to have knowledge of these states and of their quantity and quality and of how they may be examined in this new circumstance (emphasis added).

I take this to mean that, although the properties of being a subject or a predicate or the like can attach only to concepts and not to external things, they do so only when the concepts are manipulated for the purpose of arriving at (or conveying) a piece of knowledge. Thus, in addition to the two varieties of investigation whose aim is to gain knowledge of external and mental things as such, there exists an inquiry whose aim is to be of use in carrying out the other two investigations. Such an inquiry is called "logic."

Avicenna is thus arguing that logic has its own subject matter which it does not share with any other science. But because of the very nature of this subject matter (properties acquired by concepts when organized for the purpose of attaining or transmitting knowledge), he maintains at the same time that the goal of logical investigation is to help in other investigations. He concludes this passage by saying that if philosophy is understood as the investigation of external and conceptual things as such, then logic is not a part of philosophy, but, as an aid in other investigations, it is an instrument of philosophy. If, however, the term 'philosophy' is applied to "all manner of theoretical investigation," then logic is a part of philosophy and a tool for the other parts. To Avicenna's mind, the question whether logic is a part or an instrument of philosophy is both false and futile—false because it presupposes a nonexistent contradiction between the two roles and futile because "to busy oneself with such matters serves no purpose." But this brief discussion at least allows him to offer something like a definition of logic: it is an inquiry into concepts, and into their properties, insofar as they can be made to lead to knowledge of the unknown.

In the *Introduction* Avicenna has no name for those concepts which, on account of certain properties that attach to them in the context of proof, he sets apart as the proper object of logic. He does, however, provide such a name in his **Metaphysics,** in a passage which

[William and Martha Kneale, in their *The Development of Logic*] believed to be "the origin of that discussion of first and second intentions which continued until the end of medieval logic":

> As you have known, the object of logic was the secondary intelligible concepts (*al-ma'ānī al-ma'gūla al-thāniya*)—those that depend upon (*tastanid ilā*) the primary intelligible concepts—insofar as they may be of use in arriving at the unknown from the known, and not insofar as they are thoughts (*ma'gūla*) having an intellectual existence that is not attached to matter at all or attached to non-corporeal matter.

As has been noted more than once, Avicenna's doctrine had a precursor in the Porphyrian distinction between terms in first position and terms in second position . . . , a distinction which we do find in Arabic writers before and contemporary with Avicenna. A look at some of these writers will show the wider scope of Avicenna's remarks, brief though they are.

Al-Fārābī's *Commentary on Aristotle's* De interpretatione makes the standard observation: 'name' and 'verb' are terms in second position, whereas, he implies, the categories are terms in first position. The notes (*ta'līqāt*) that Ibn Bājja (Avempace, d. 1138) wrote on Fārābī's account (?the same as the just-mentioned *Commentary* or rather a separate paraphrase of Aristotle's *De int.*) furnish a longer list of terms in second position including 'particle', 'definite' . . . , 'indefinite' . . . , 'straight' . . . , 'oblique' . . . , 'derivative' as well as 'name' and 'verb'.

Let us look next at the relevant sentences in the notes that a late tenth-century translator and commentator of Aristotle, the Syrian Christian al-Hasan ibn Suwār, has written on the *Categories*. He states first that Aristotle's aim in the *Categories* is to discuss those "single utterances in first position (*fīal-wad' al-awwal*) which signify the highest genera of things (*al-umūr*) by means of the affections (*āthār*) [produced] by them in the soul, and [to discuss] things insofar as they are signified by the utterance." In regard to the expression 'first position' al-Hasan explains:

> We say utterances in the first position in order to distinguish them from utterances in second position; for utterances in first position are those names and labels (?) that are first applied to things as signs (*simāt, 'alāmāt*) that signify them in a general way (*dalāla mujmala*), such as calling this "silver" and this "copper" and this "gold," while utterances in second position are those that signify what we have set apart as utterances in first position, such as calling ["name"] every utterance signifying something definite, without time, as "Zayd" and "'Amr," and calling "verb" everything that additionally signifies time, as "stood up" and "will

stand up." These are utterances in second position because we have posited them subsequent to the existence of the others.

Finally, here are two examples of what a leading logician and teacher of logic in eleventh-century Baghdad, Abū al-Faraj ibn al-Tayyib (d. 1043), had to say about the two expressions in question. In his *Commentary on Porphyry's* Isagoge, Abū al-Faraj wrote:

> . . . utterances are investigated in two ways, as utterances in first position and as utterances in second position. Utterances in first position are those that signify things (*al-umūr*), such as "Zayd," "'Amr," and "has struck." Utterances in second position are those that signify utterances in first position. . . . And [Porphyry's] concern here is with utterances in first position.

The only examples given by Abū al-Faraj of words in second position are 'name' and 'verb', which, as he also observes, are discussed at the beginning of Aristotle's *De interpretatione*.

What is lacking in all these examples is any statement to the effect that terms (or concepts) in second position constitute the specific subject matter of logic.

Al-Fārābī in his *Commentary* on Aristotle's *De interpretatione* does employ the phrase "secondary concepts" (*al-ma'qūlāt al-thawānī*), the very same expression which we encountered in Avicenna's **Metaphysics**. I shall here paraphrase Fārābī's text without attempting to do full justice to his rather difficult arguments, my aim being simply to indicate the context in which he introduces that phrase. The occasion is Aristotle's statement at 16^{b}19 ff which prompts Fārābī to speculate about the combinative function of "existential verbs" (is, exists). An existential verb, he says, indicates three things: a time, a combination or connection, and an unspecified subject. A question may arise as to how an existential verb, whether used existentially or copulatively, can perform the combination. The problem (as presented by Fārābī) is that a non-existential verb like 'walks' is analyzable into 'is walking', so that "man walks" is equivalent to "man is walking," where 'is' performs the combinative function. Should we then say that "man is (exists)" is also analyzable into "man is existing," where existence would occur twice—once as a connector and again as a predicate?

Fārābī answers that in the case of the existential 'is' ("when 'is' is predicated by itself") no absurdity would result from such a repetition. But no repetition would need to be involved in the case of the copulative 'is' (when the latter is "predicated for the sake of something else"). In this last case 'is' signifies only time, an (unspecified) subject, and "the notion of a copulative existence," the predicate (say, white) being something apart from that.

Fārābī then goes on to pose the unexpected question of whether the copulative 'is' did not itself require a connector which in turn required a connector and so on to infinity—to which question he gives the following enigmatic answer in terms of "secondary concepts":

> There would be nothing impossible or absurd in this consequence [of an infinite series of connectors], for the notion of connector is here one of the secondary concepts, and it is neither impossible nor absurd for secondary concepts to go on to infinity, as you have heard me say many times and as I have set down in writing.

He finally adds that repetition of one and the same secondary concept is not necessary, but does no harm if it occurs.

All this is rather baffling. But the character of Fārābī's arguments, the sudden but surprisingly brief appearance of the idea of an infinite chain of connectors regarded as secondary concepts, and the reference to his previous teachings and writings, all this is clear indication that we do not yet possess all we need to have to penetrate the thoughts of early Arabic logicians on the subject that has concerned us. Avicenna's remarks in the *Introduction* and in the **Metaphysics** thus remain the clearest and fullest statement on the topic of the subject matter of logic which has come down to us from the period between the translation of Aristotle's logical works into Arabic and the middle of the eleventh century. It is remarkable that they also seem to have become henceforward the standard doctrine to which later Arabic logicians turned for a ready answer to the question of what logic was about. To illustrate this last point I shall quote a passage [from 'Alā' ibn 'Alī al-Tahānawī's *Kashshāf istilāhāt al-funūn*] that describes the situation as it appeared to an erudit living in the eighteenth century:

> The authorities are of the opinion that the subject matter [of logic] comprises the secondary concepts (*al-ma'qūlāt al-thāniya*), not in respect of what they are in themselves, nor insofar as they exist in the mind (for this [inquiry] is a function of philosophy), but insofar as they lead or can be of use in leading to the unknown. Thus a universal concept in the mind, when compared to the particulars under it, will be considered essential or accidental to them according as it enters into or lies outside their essences, and it will be considered a species if it coincides with those essences. . . . Now for a universal concept to be essential, accidental or a species or the like, is not something external but something that arises in universal natures when they exist in the mind. It is so with a proposition's being predicative or conditional and with an argument's

being a syllogism, an induction or an example. . . .
The logician [also] investigates tertiary and higher-
level concepts, for these are essential attributes of
secondary concepts. "Proposition," for example, is
a secondary concept which may be investigated in
regard to its division, conversion, or conclusiveness
when combined with other propositions. Thus
"conversion," "conclusiveness," "division,"
"contradiction" are concepts on the third level of
thought; and if, in a logical inquiry, something is
judged to be one of the divided parts or
contradictories, then that thing will belong to the
fourth level of thought, and so on.

The gist of all this had already been said by Avicenna;
only the idea of a multi-level hierarchy of concepts is
lacking in Avicenna's writings. When and in what
context did that idea become articulated; and with what
consequences, if any? These are questions that must
await further search of the enormous bulk of logical
writings that relentlessly piled up in the centuries separating Avicenna from the author of the above passage.

**Avicenna's remarks in the *Introduction*
and in the *Metaphysics* . . . remain the
clearest and fullest statement on the
topic of the subject matter of logic
which has come down to us from the
period between the translation of
Aristotle's logical works into Arabic
and the middle of the eleventh century.**

—*A. I. Sabra*

Avicenna further develops his views in chapters 3 and
4 of the *Introduction,* on the utility and the subject
matter of logic, respectively. His discussion in chapter
3 begins with the famous distinction between *taṣawwur*
and *taṣdīq* which we find in almost every Arabic writer on logic after Avicenna. The same terms have been
found in the logical writings of al-Fārābī, but their
ultimate provenance remains somewhat uncertain. Paul
Kraus suggested [in *Recherches Philosophiques* V,
1935-36] in 1936 that they translated the Stoic terms
ρ α ν τ α σ ί α and σ υ γ κ α τ ά θ ε σ ι ς, and, on the basis
of this suggestion, M.-D. Chenu has argued [in "Un
Vestige du stoïcisme," *"Revue des Sciences
philosophiques et théologiques* XXVII (1938)] for a
Stoic infiltration of medieval Latin thought by way of
translating into Latin certain Arabic texts containing
the words *taṣawwur* and *taṣdīq*.

Literally, *taṣawwur* is the act of grasping or receiving
a form (*ṣūra* . . .) in the mind, and *taṣdīq* is the act
of taking or believing something to be true (*ṣādiq*).
Both are described by Arabic logicians as acts of knowledge (*'ilm*), but truth and falsity are said to have to do

only with the second. Often the two words are also
applied, respectively, to the form received or the proposition believed to be true. 'Concept' and 'conception'
usually do well as translations of *'taṣawwur'*, ('thought'
is also appropriate in some contexts); for rendering
"taṣdīq" one has to oscillate between a number of
words such as 'assertion', 'belief', 'judgment', 'proposition'. The medieval Latin translation of Avicenna's
Introduction has *intellectus* for *taṣawwur* and *credul-
itas* for *taṣdīq*.

Whatever the origin of these two terms, Stoic or otherwise, a similar distinction to what they are meant to
convey can be easily found in Aristotle, and it appears
that Avicenna at least conflated the two distinctions.
We read in Aristotle's *De interpretatione:*

> Just as some thoughts in the soul are neither true
> nor false while some are necessarily one or the other,
> so also with spoken sounds. For falsity and truth
> have to do with combination and separation. Thus
> names and verbs by themselves—for instance 'man'
> or 'white' when nothing further is added—are like
> the thoughts that are without combination and
> separation; for so far they are neither true nor false.

The ninth-century Arabic translation of this passage
(by Isḥāq ibn Hunayn) does not use the words *taṣawwur*
and *taṣdīq*. But in the corresponding chapter in Avicenna's *Interpretation* the plural *taṣawwurāt* is used
interchangeably with *āthār,* the equivalent in Isḥāq's
translation of Aristotle's π α θ ή μ α τ α; and in a passage of the same chapter that parallels the lines just
quoted from Aristotle, *ma'qūl* . . . and *i'tiqād* (belief)
are made to stand for *taṣawwur* and *taṣdīq*: a single
thought (*ma'qūl*), says Avicenna, is neither true nor
false; only the belief (*i'tiqād*) associated with relating
one thought to another affirmatively or negatively is
true or false. Now there is no term in Aristotle's text
that corresponds to Avicenna's *i'tiqād* (a word which
usually rendered the Greek π ί σ τ ι ς); only combination and separation of thoughts are said by Aristotle to
have truth or falsity. But Avicenna clearly understands
Aristotle's remarks in terms of a distinction between
acts of conceiving single thoughts and acts of belief
applied to the conceived relations between thoughts.
How Avicenna himself understood the distinction is
made abundantly clear in chapter 3 of the *Introduction:*

> . . . a thing is knowable in two ways: one of them
> is for the thing to be merely conceived (*yutaṣawwar:
> intelligatur*) so that when the name of the thing is
> uttered, its meaning (*ma'nā: intentio*) becomes
> present in the mind without there being truth or
> falsity, as when someone says 'man', or 'do this!'
> For when you understand the meaning of what has
> been said to you, you will have conceived it. The
> second is for the conception to be [accompanied]
> with belief (*taṣdīq: credulitas*), so that if someone

says to you, for example, "every whiteness is an accident," you do not only have a conception (*taṣawwur*) of the meaning of this statement, but [also] believe it (*ṣaddaqta*) to be so. If, however, you doubt whether it is so or not, then you have conceived what is said, for you cannot doubt what you do not conceive or understand, but what you have gained through conception in this [latter] case is that the form of this composition and what it is composed of, such as "whiteness" and "accident," have been produced in the mind. Assertion (*taṣdīq*), however, occurs when there takes place in the mind a relating (*nisba: comparatio*) of this form to the things themselves as being in accordance with them; denial (*takdhīb: mentiri*) is the opposite of that.

It is clear from this text that *taṣdīq* is *not* the relation between subject and predicate in a predicative proposition. Such a relation is here called "form of composition" which (as in the case of doubting) can be entertained in the mind without truth or falsity being applied to it; that is, it can be the subject of mere conception (although, of course, unlike the conception of a single thought, it is *capable* of being described as true or false). *Taṣdīq* is the attribution of this relation or form to the things themselves.

The role of belief or assertion is again emphasized by Avicenna in his *Interpretation,* in an account of what a predicative statement is made of. "A predicative proposition (*qaḍiyya ḥamliyya*), he says, consists of three things, a subject-concept, a predicate-concept, and a relation (*nisba*) between the two. Concepts (*maʿānī*) do not, however, become subjects and predicates by being gathered together in the mind; in addition to this mind must believe (*yaʿtaqid*) affirmatively or negatively the relation between the two concepts." He goes on to insist that mere concatenation (*tatālī*) of terms does not make up a statement. To be a complete expression of a predicative preposition a sentence must therefore contain, in addition to the terms indicating the subject and predicate, a sign that indicates the relation or connection between these. Such a sign is of course the copula (*rābita: connector*) which, he says, may take the form of a verb (as in Greek or Persian or, sometimes, Arabic), or a noun (the Arabic pronoun *huwa*), or a vowel change (modifying the predicate term or both subject and predicate terms). In any case, three linguistic elements are needed to correspond, one to one, with the three essential components of a predicative proposition.

But if assertion is something apart from the relation to which it is applied in predicative propositions, should not such propositions be analyzed into four, rather than three, components, and should not their complete verbal expressions contain four, rather than three, elements? As far as I can see, the question is nowhere broached by Avicenna himself, but it was raised by later Arabic logicians, no doubt led to do so by Avi-

cenna's own remarks. Some argued that since a "relation of judgment" (*nisba ḥukmiyya*) is found equally in the affirmation and negation of that relation, it must be clearly distinguished from both; four components must therefore be recognized in the make-up of a predicative proposition. Others maintained that the copula would not be able to perform its function as a connector unless it signified both the judgment relation and its affirmation or negation. The copula would thus give expression to both the assertion (*taṣdīq*) made and the concept (*taṣawwur*) to which the assertion is applied, and there would thus be no need for a separate assertion sign. This is not the occasion to pursue this discussion in the various writers, but it seems that it was the latter view that finally prevailed. It was also the latter view that very likely expressed Avicenna's own implicit opinion.

I have dwelt at some length on the distinction between *taṣawwur* and *taṣdīq* because it became the accepted doctrine of all Arabic logicians. As pointed out earlier, *taṣawwur* and *taṣdīq* divided between them the whole sphere of knowledge, the first being attainable by definition, the second by argument. Logic, being concerned with the appropriate means of acquiring knowledge, therefore divided into two parts: a theory of definition (*mabḥath al-taṣawwurāt*) and a theory of proof (*mabḥath al-taṣdīqāt*). The following passage succinctly expresses this pervasive doctrine. It comes from Avicenna's **Kitāb al-Najāh,** a summary account of **Kitāb al-Shifā':**

> Every knowledge is either conception (*taṣawwur*) or belief (*taṣdiq*). Conception is the prior knowledge (*al-ʿilm al-awwal*) and it is acquired by means of definition or the like. . . . Belief is acquired only by means of syllogism or the like. . . . Thus definition and syllogism are two instruments by means of which knowledge of unknown things is acquired through discursive thought (*al-rawiyya*). . . . Now every syllogism and every definition is made up by bringing intelligible notions (*maʿānī maʿqūla*) into a definite composition so that each would have a matter from which it is composed and by means of which the composition is effected. And just as a house or seat cannot properly be made from any chance matter or in any chance form, but rather every thing has its own matter and form which are proper to it, so also there belong to every object of knowledge (*maʿlūm*) which is knowable by means of discursive thought a proper matter and form by means of which that object may be grasped (*taḥaqquq*). And just as a house may be improperly built because of deficient matter or form or both, so also discursive thought may be vitiated (*fasād*) on account of its matter even if the form is valid (*ṣāliḥa*), or on account of the form even if the matter is appropriate (*ṣāliḥa*), or on account of both.

Fārābī had said in his *Enumeration of the Sciences* that the objects with which the rules of logic are concerned are "the thoughts (*ma'qūlāt*) in so far as they are indicated by the utterances, and the utterances in so far as they indicate the thoughts." We establish an opinion in ourselves by setting up in our minds those thoughts which are apt to verify it. This process is called by the ancients "inner speech" (*al-nuṭq al-dākhil*). To impart the truth of an opinion to someone else we employ the forms of speech (*aqāwīl*) suitable for achieving that purpose. This is called "outer speech" (*nuṭq khārij bi-al-ṣawt*). It is the function of logic to provide the rules (*qawānīn*) that guide us toward the proper conduct (called *"qiyās,"* reasoning) of both kinds of speech.

Avicenna seems to have had some such statements in mind when he wrote in chapter 3 of the *Introduction* (= chapter 4 in the Latin edition) that "there is no value in the doctrine of those who say that the subject of logic is to investigate utterances in so far as they indicate notions (*al-ma'ānī*)." It is noticeable that in the two previous chapters the question of language and its relation to logic is nowhere brought into the discussion. Now that Avicenna has put forward in those chapters his own view of the subject and use of logic, he feels he can settle that question without much belaboring of words. Unfortunately his remarks are much too brief. The logician, he says, would have been able to dispense with utterances only if it were possible to learn logic by means of "pure thought." But we are forced to use utterances,

> . . . especially as it is not possible (*muta'adhdhir: non potest*) for the reasoning faculty (*al-rawiyya: ratio*) to arrange notions (*al-ma'ānī: intellecta*) without imagining the utterances corresponding to them, reasoning being rather a dialogue with oneself by means of imagined utterances. It follows that utterances have various modes (*aḥwāl*) on account of which the modes of the notions corresponding to them in the soul vary so as to acquire qualifications (*aḥkām*) which would not have existed without the utterances [*seguitur ut verba habeant diversas dispositiones per guas differant dispositiones intentionum gue concomitantur esse in anima, ita quod fiant eis indicia gue non haberentur nisi per verba*]. It is for this reason that the art of logic must be concerned in part with investigating the modes of utterances. . . . But there is no value in the doctrine of those who say that the subject of logic is to investigate utterances in so far as they indicate notions . . . but rather the matter should be understood in the way we described.

The modes mentioned here are of course those secondary properties which concepts acquire when they constitute definitions and arguments. They are thoughts (*ma'qūlāt*) of a second order, twice removed from the things of the material world to which outward speech belongs. Avicenna now tells us that reasoning is impossible without utterances, whether spoken or imagined. By itself this is not a new thing to say. But the

consequence he draws from this statement is not the simple language-thought parallelism noted by the writers whose views he found inadequate. He clearly says that the conceptual modifications are *brought about* by modifications in the utterances. This means that the secondary concepts, the proper object of logic, not only are reflected in language but are generated by it. Is this so because logical concepts arise only in the context of a process, reasoning, which is dependent on language in a peculiar way? In any case, however one interprets his words, and I am not sure I quite understand them, he seems to be making a stronger claim for the role of utterance in logic than I have encountered in any writer before and up to his time. Avicenna is not just saying that utterances are important in the study of logic. Having already pointed out that logic was not a (psychological) inquiry concerned with mental entities as such, he is now telling us that it is an inquiry primarily concerned with language. The reason is, or seems to be, that the properties constituting the subject matter of logic would be inconceivable without the exercise of a particular function of language.

Avicenna returns to the question of the relation of logic to philosophy and the related question of the subject matter of logic in other parts of the Logic in *Kitāb al-Shifā'*. In the section on *Categories,* for example, he again asserts his independence from the Peripatetics (including Fārābī and Ibn al-Tayyib) by emphatically excluding the doctrine of categories from the proper domain of logic. This agrees with his understanding of logic as concerned with second-order concepts. And in the section of *Syllogism* he devotes a chapter to showing how the function of logic as an instrument is to be understood. His interesting views in these and in other places are, however, too detailed and too complex to be dealt with adequately here.

Charles E. Butterworth (essay date 1983)

SOURCE: "Ethics in Medieval Islamic Philosophy," in *The Journal of Religious Ethics,* Vol. 11, No. 2, Fall, 1983, pp. 224-39.

[*In the following excerpt, Butterworth discusses Avicenna's moral and political philosophy.*]

[Avicenna's] writing takes the form of essays about Aristotelian treatises and themes, essays which explore the subject of the treatise or the theme itself in such a manner that one learns far more about Avicenna's opinions than about what he thinks Aristotle was trying to explain. For example, in his multi-volume *Shifā* (or *Healing*)—a work divided into four major sections, somewhat along the lines of Aristotle's account of the sciences, and each section further divided into parts which frequently bear the names of Aristotelian treatises—Avicenna explains what he understands of these sciences or arts with nary a reference to Aristotle. Much of the rest of his writing presupposes the importance of the *Shifā* insofar as it summarizes or enumerates in abbreviated form the themes discussed there. And Avicenna indicates his differences from Aristotle in yet another way: whereas Aristotle presented his moral and political teaching as belonging to practical science and as independent of as well as distinct from theoretical science, Avicenna frequently blurs that distinction. Though he does admit that morals and politics belong to practical science, he elaborates upon them only in the course of his theoretical discussions, that is, either in his *On the Soul* of the *Shifā* (a treatise which takes up the theme and many of the discussions of Aristotle's *De Anima*) or in his *Metaphysics,* also a part of the *Shifā.*

It is in Book Ten of his *Metaphysics* that Avicenna provides his fullest account of moral virtue. He begins by explaining the superiority of the prophet to all other men, indicating thereby that both philosophy and politics are subordinate to religion. The prophet is the best of men because he has acquired the practical moral habits by which he can manage his own affairs as well as provide for those of the people for whom he sets down laws and establishes justice, and because he has developed his soul to the point that it has become a free intellect. Such an explanation tacitly suggests that the prophet completes the partial lives of the philosopher and the virtuous ruler—the philosopher having a fully developed intellect, but not the practical moral virtues whose mastery would allow him to rule people well, and the virtuous ruler having the latter but not the former.

Whereas the opinions and actions Farabi's virtuous first ruler set before the people were clearly such as to help them acquire the moral habits and dispositions which would allow them to live together harmoniously, and in such living to move towards ultimate happiness, Avicenna's prophet dwells more on beliefs which have no such immediate political relevance. Some even have an anti-political or ascetic bent, as though the highest goal towards which thoughtful humans should strive were to weaken the ties between their soul and their body in order to achieve separation from the body. In this sense, ultimate happiness is not acquired through political association, but through a turning away from political life and all other bodily concerns. Running throughout Avicenna's writings, this tension between the demands of political life and the demands of complete spiritual life derives from the subordination of philosophy and politics to religion, from the claim that the highest human achievement is the pure intellectual or spiritual perception proper to a disembodied soul which has gone beyond the concerns of the practical intellect. Unfortunately, Avicenna never explains what prompts the prophet to turn aside from this all-important goal of untrammeled spiritual perception in order

to legislate for a political community. Nor, in spite of his repeated insistence on the need to do away with or go beyond the practical intellect in order to develop fully the theoretical or spiritual intellect, does he ever make clear why the prophet's mastery of the practical moral virtues should constitute his superiority over the philosopher.

This tension or unclarity notwithstanding, Avicenna's prophet does set down laws for a political community, laws which provide for its administration and survival as well as for the moral and physical well-being of its citizens. Avicenna pictures human beings as first coming together in order to survive. Initially no more than a basic response to nature's inattentiveness, it leads, under the best of circumstances, to their spiritual betterment as well. Their immediate need for someone who will set down laws and thereby establish justice so that they might live together harmoniously points beyond mere physical concerns because justice, properly conceived, provides for all human good. Avicenna's reasoning is that justice is a balance or mean acquired by means of moral habits and character traits and sought either to break the hold of the passions so that the soul may be purified and liberated from the body or to use the passions with respect to the concerns of this world.

One way men should make use of the passions for what pertains to this world is to take pleasure in their natural appetites for things like food, clothing, and sex in order to preserve their bodies and to have children. Avicenna also suggests another way, namely, giving vent to those passions like anger, hate, and pride in order to be courageous enough to preserve the city. With respect to this proper use of the appetitive passions (or temperance) and of the irascible passions (or courage), Avicenna speaks of the need to observe a mean between vices of excess and deficiency. Though he does no more than hint at the consequences, he must have in mind that men can harm one another by pursuing the bodily pleasures to excess or by being rash and foolhardy; on the other hand, if they are so insensitive to pleasure that they do not eat adequately and fail to engage in sexual intercourse or shy away from protecting what is their own as do those who are overly fearful, the city will be harmed.

Avicenna says little here, or in the treatise which discusses these same issues—*On the Science of Moral Habits*—about practical wisdom. We are told that it is to be used for administrative affairs and is opposed to the vices of discernment, nothing more.

These three moral habits and character traits (temperance, courage, and practical wisdom—also referred to by Avicenna as moral virtues), by means of which justice is acquired, are for the well-being of human beings in this world. They can be pursued adequately

Illustration in a sixteenth-century manuscript of Mansūr's Anatomy *depicting Avicenna lecturing.*

without theoretical wisdom, even though it is superior to them. At the end of his account, Avicenna presents theoretical wisdom as being so important that one can attain happiness only by acquiring it as well as these three virtues, all of which add up to justice. Clearly, one cannot be happy—however virtuous one is—without having theoretical wisdom, but Avicenna says nothing about the converse. Instead he indicates that the only thing to be desired more than justice plus theoretical wisdom is "to win, in addition, the prophetic qualities" [1960: X, 455: 14-16].

The communal basis of Avicenna's ethical teaching can now be stated as follows. Adherence to the laws set down by the prophet will permit the citizens to acquire the moral virtues, which together are tantamount to justice, and thus to live harmoniously in this world. If the citizens also embrace the beliefs about

God and the life to come as set down by the prophet (the non-political beliefs alluded to above), they can aspire to happiness in the hereafter. Those able to acquire theoretical wisdom as well as justice may aspire to happiness in this life, but to a happiness inferior to that of the prophet—presumably because the prophet alone is able to purify his soul so that it becomes liberated from the body and thus achieves intellectual or spiritual perception. . . .

Michael Marmura (essay date 1986)

SOURCE: "Avicenna's 'Flying Man' in Context," in *The Monist,* Vol. 69, No. 3, July, 1986, pp. 383-95.

[*In the essay below, Marmura discusses the three instances of Avicenna's "Flying Man" scenario, which illustrates Avicenna's philosophy of mind.*]

The psychological writings of the Islamic philosopher Avicenna (Ibn Sīnā) (d. 1037) are noted for the hypothetical example he gives of the man suspended in space—the "Flying Man." This example, which left its impress on the Latin scholastics and has engaged the attention of modern scholars, occurs thrice in his writings in contexts that are closely related, but not identical. Its third occurrence, which represents a condensed version, conveys the general idea. It states, in effect, that if you imagine your "entity," "person," "self" (*dhātaka*) to be created at birth fully mature, sound in mind and body, but suspended in temperate air in such a manner that this "self" is totally unaware of its body and physical circumstances, "you will find that it will be unaware of everything except the 'fixedness' (*thubūt*) of its individual existence (*anniyyatihā*)."

What Avicenna intends to show by this hypothetical example is not as obvious as it might initially seem. For one thing, the roles the "Flying Man" plays in its three appearances, although closely related and complementary, are not identical. More to the point is the difficulty of Avicenna's texts, both in terms of language and thought. The "Flying Man" and the arguments it includes or relates to in the texts are problematic.

But whatever the difficulties it poses, the example remains an expression of its author's Neoplatonic soul-body dualism. Before attending to its three versions for a clearer idea of what they are all about, some remarks about its relation to other psychological theories—particularly in medieval Islam—may help place it in its historical setting. Similarities between it and the Cartesian *cogito* have been discussed by scholars. The notion that we have certain knowledge of our individual existence is one of the things inherent in the example. This notion, as will be seen, is part of Avicenna's paradoxical belief that we have constant, intimate knowledge of the existence of our individual selves, even if we do not know this. The primary concern here, however, is psychology, not metaphysics. Avicenna is not seeking in this example the certainty of his existence as a premise on which to build a philosophical system. His metaphysical starting point is not doubt. It is the certainty "that there is here existence."

That we have certain knowledge of our individual existence was also the prevalent view among the Islamic speculative theologians, the *mutakallimūn*. Both the Muᶜtazilite and the Ashᶜariate rival schools of speculative theology (*kalām*) held this. They included knowledge of the existence of ourselves among those cognitions that are "necessary" or "compulsory." Now Avicenna opposed the doctrine of the self held by these theologians, but not because they maintained that we have indubitable knowledge of the existence of ourselves. His disagreement with them was on the question of the nature of the self, or, as the issue was sometimes expressed, about the referent of the personal pronoun, 'I'. Is this the immaterial rational soul, as Avicenna held, or a material entity as the theologians and other Muslims maintained? Thus he begins [***Ahwāl al-Nafs***] as follows:

> We say: what is intended by "the soul" is that which each of us refers to by his saying, 'I.' Scholars have differed as to whether what is being referred to is this body, observed and experienced by the senses, or something else. As regards the first [alternative], most people and many of the speculative theologians (*almutakallim n*) have thought that the human being is this body and that everyone refers to it when saying, 'I.' This is a false belief as we shall show.

The vast majority of the *mutakallimūn,* it should be remarked, were atomists, upholding a materialist concept of the human soul. There were exceptions and variations, to be sure. The Muᶜtazilite al-Naẓẓām (d. 845), for example, rejected atomism. He maintained that the soul is a subtle material substance that is diffused throughout the body, rendering it animate. Another ninth century Muᶜtazilite, Muᶜammar (d. 835), did not reject atomism, but maintained that the human soul is immaterial, a spiritual atom. Most of the *mutakallimūn,* however, were atomists and materialists. They maintained either the doctrine that the soul is an individual material atom to which life, a transient accident, attaches, or else, the doctrine that the soul and the transient accident, life, that attaches to an organic body, are one and the same.

The more traditional Islamic doctrine of the soul accords with what the ninth century al-Naẓẓām held. Accordingly, life meant the conjunction of soul and body. The soul is a subtle substance that spreads throughout the body making it alive. Death is the separation of soul from body. The soul, though a material substance, is

immortal and rejoins the body at the resurrection. This traditional concept is summed up by the fourteenth century, Ibn Qayyim al-Jawziyya (d. 1350). He states that the human soul "differs in quiddity (*al-māhiyya*) from the sensible body, being a body that is luminous, elevated, light, alive and in motion. It penetrates the substance of the body organs, flowing therein as water flows in roses, oil in olives and fire in charcoal."

Avicenna is also opposed to this traditional doctrine of the soul. This concept of the soul as a subtle substance has a striking resemblance to what he conceived to be "spirit" (*al-rūh*), namely "the subtle body" that pervades the living body, acting as the substratum for the vegetative and animal soul. This spirit, however, is material and, for Avicenna, what is material (in the terrestrial realm) is corruptible. The rational soul, on the other hand, is immaterial and hence immortal. Avicenna's "Flying Man", as will be seen, is intended, among other things, to indicate the immateriality of this soul—by implication, its immortality.

The "Flying Man's" first version occurs at the end of ***Psychology,*** I, 1, an intricately argued chapter whose objective—as its heading proclaims—is to establish the existence of the soul and to define it "inasmuch as it is soul." This latter phrase suggests that Avicenna is referring to the soul's essence or quiddity. This, however, is not the case. He is only referring to its functional relation to the body, a relation, he repeatedly tells us, which is other than the quiddity and which does not indicate the category of existence, namely, substance, to which the soul belongs.

He states this, for example, at the beginning of the chapter where he argues in Aristotelian terms for the existence of the soul: The observed animate activities of organic bodies cannot be due to their sheer corporeality, but to principles within them. "Soul" is the name for "whatever is a principle for the issuance of activities that are not of the uniform pattern that negates volition." This, he goes on, "is the name of the thing, not inasmuch as it is substance, but by way of some relation it has." Again, in a lengthy discussion where he differentiates between entelechy and form ("every form is an entelechy but not every entelechy is a form") and where he maintains that "entelechy" rather than "form" is the more comprehensive term referring to the soul, he writes:

> If we have come to know that the soul is an entelechy, . . . we still do not know the soul and its quiddity, but have only known it inasmuch as it is soul. The term, "soul," does not apply to it by way of its substance, but by way of its being governor over bodies and in relation to them. . . . Indeed, we ought to set aside another investigation for knowing the essence of the soul.

After further discussion of "entelechy," leading to the

Aristotelian definition of the soul as the first entelechy of a living, acting natural organ, and a discussion of the difficulty of applying this definition univocally to both terrestrial and celestial souls, Avicenna gives a last reminder that this relational definition of the soul does not refer to the quiddity. It is with this reminder that the last part of the chapter devoted to the "Flying Man" is introduced:

> We have now known the meaning of the name that applies to the thing termed soul because of a relation it has. It thus behoves us to occupy ourselves with apprehending the quiddity of this thing which through the above consideration has become spoken of as soul.

Avicenna continues:

> We must indicate in this place a manner of establishing (*ithbāt*) the existence of the soul we have by way of alerting (*tanbih*) and reminding (*tadhkīr*), giving an indication (*ishāra*) that has a strong impact on someone who has the power of noticing (*mulāḥaẓa*) the truth himself, without the need of having to educate him, constantly prod him, and divert him from what causes sophistical errors.

The example of the "Flying Man" immediately follows this statement. But before turning to the example, we must pause to consider the above statement, which is quite basic for understanding the first (and most problematic) version of the example. The statement, though structurally complex (and difficult to translate), is quite clear in expressing its intention, namely, to indicate a way of establishing the soul's existence by means of "alerting" and "reminding."

But what does Avicenna mean by "alerting" and "reminding"? Some light is shed on his meaning by *Psychology*, V, 7, where he criticizes and rejects various psychological theories, two of which involve the concepts of "alerting" and "reminding." The first maintains that the human soul by its very nature knows all things: the activities of perceiving and reasoning simply "alert" it to the knowledge it already has but from which it has been distracted. The second theory also maintains that the soul has knowledge of all things, knowledge, however, which it has acquired "previously." Avicenna does not identify this theory. But the Platonic theory of reminiscence seems an obvious candidate. At any rate, knowledge is reminiscence, the activities of perceiving and reasoning acting as reminders of what is already known.

Avicenna's philosophical system can accommodate neither theory and he rejects them and their claim that the soul has within it, so to speak, knowledge of "all" things. But he does not reject the view that the soul by its very nature has self-knowledge. The main intention

of the third version of the "Flying Man," as will be seen, is to state and illustrate the soul's constant knowledge of itself. Another statement about "natural" self-knowledge occurs in **al-Taʿlīqāt,** comments Avicenna dictated to his student Bahmanyār:

> The human soul is [so constituted that] it is by nature aware of existents. It is aware of some of them naturally; with others, it gains the power to become aware of them by acquisition. That which is attained for it naturally is realized for it actually and always. Thus its awareness of itself is by nature, this being a constituent of it and hence belongs to it always and in actuality. Its awareness that it is aware of itself is by acquisition.

In this work, Avicenna does not elaborate: he does not explain how one is always aware of one's self and yet has to "acquire" awareness of this awareness. Elsewhere, he offers an answer to the related question of why should one seek after knowing one's self (and its immateriality) if one already has such knowledge. In *Psychology,* V, 7, he writes:

> It is not the case that if you are seeking the existence [of the self] and its being non-corporeal you are therefore ignorant of this in an absolute sense. Rather, you are oblivious of it. Many a time knowledge of a thing is near at hand, but one is oblivious of it. It becomes within the bound of the unknown and is sought after from a more distant place. Often knowing that it is near at hand is of the order of alerting (*al-tanbīh*).

To return to the statement immediately preceding the first version of the "Flying Man," it clearly states that the intention of what is to follow is to indicate "a manner of establishing the existence of the soul . . . by way of alerting and reminding, giving an indication that leaves a strong impact on someone who has the power of noticing the truth himself." This first version is as follows:

> We say: The one among us must imagine himself as though he is created all at once and created perfect (*kāmil*), but that his sight has been veiled from observing external things, and that he is created falling in the air or the void in a manner where he would not encounter air resistance, requiring him to feel, and that his limbs are separated from each other so that they neither meet nor touch. He must then reflect as to whether he will affirm the existence of his self (*dhātahu*).

> He will not doubt his affirming his self existing, but with this he will not affirm any limb from among his organs, no internal organ, whether heart or brain, and no external thing. Rather, he would be affirming his self without affirming for it length, breadth and depth. And if in this state he were able to imagine

a hand or some other organ, he would not imagine it as part of his self or a condition for its existence.

You know that what is affirmed is other than what is not affirmed and what is acknowledged (*al-muqarr bihi*) is other than what is not acknowledge. Hence the self whose existence he has affirmed has a special characteristic (*khāṣṣiyya*) of its being his very self, other than his body and organs that have not been affirmed.

Hence the one who affirms (*al-muthbit*) has a means (*lahu sabīl*) to be alerted (*yatannabah*) to the existence of the soul as something other than the body—indeed, other than body—and to his being directly acquainted (*ʿārif*) with [this existence] and aware of it. If he is oblivious to this, he would require educative prodding.

The last paragraph brings home the point that the process of imagination and contemplation Avicenna asks us to undertake alerts us ultimately to the experiential knowledge of our immaterial selves. More specifically, it states that the one who in the example affirms (*al-muthbit*) his existence without affirming the existence of his body "has a means" (*lahu sabīl*) "to be alerted" (*an yatanabbah*) to the existence of the self as immaterial and subsequently to the experiential knowledge of this immaterial existence. (The use of the term, *ʿārif*, the active participle of the verb *ʿarafa*, is very significant. In Avicenna's vocabulary (and that of the mystics of Islam) it means "to know" in the sense of having experiential, intimate knowledge, gnosis.) In other words, we discern here two stages of knowing. The first is knowing *that* the self is immaterial, leading to the second, the experiential knowledge of one's self as an immaterial entity.

When Avicenna speaks of the "means" for alerting the self to this knowledge, he is referring to the argument immediately preceding the final paragraph which can be summed up as follows: In the circumstances of the example where the self is totally unaware of the physical and the bodily, it is still aware of its existence, not doubting this. It thus affirms its existence without affirming the existence of the body. But since what is affirmed is other than what is not affirmed, the self whose existence is being affirmed is not the body.

This argument, however, so very central to the first version of the "Flying Man," is problematic. It operates within an imagined, hypothetical framework and hence one expects its conclusion to be hypothetical and tentative. But an unwarranted swerve from the hypothetical to the categorical seems to take place. For the language of its conclusion is categorical. That Avicenna intended this conclusion to be categorical is also indicated by the example's other two versions. In this connection, it should be noted that there are in-

stances in Avicenna's logical writings where he uses a similar hypothetical example for categorical ends. Thus, he tells us, if a person is created fully mature and rational, having, however, had no contact with other humans and human institutions, and is confronted with a commonly accepted moral dictum and a self-evident logical truth, he will be able to doubt the first, but not the second. The example here is used as a criterion for self-evidence. Again, he uses this example to define natural knowledge. This is the knowledge, he states, that a person born fully mature and rational but having had no human contact will have.

Moreover, the argument begs the question. This brings us to its assumptions which perhaps may help explain how Avicenna treats its conclusion in categorical terms. As indicated earlier, he holds that the self has natural, constant knowledge of itself. In the third version of the "Flying Man," as we shall see, he elaborates on this. Provided the self is able to "discern a thing correctly," then whatever the circumstances, it will have this constant knowledge of itself. Now Avicenna includes as one of these circumstances in which the self is still able "to discern a thing correctly" the state of its being totally unaware of the bodily and the physical, exemplified by the "Flying Man." But once he includes this, then he is already assuming the very thing to be proven—an immaterial self capable of self-awareness while totally oblivious of the body and anything physical.

Our concern, however, is not so much with the shortcomings of this argument as it is with the role it plays in the example. As already hinted at in passing, it really performs two tasks, not one. The first is to prove that the soul is immaterial; the second, by showing this, to awaken the self to the experiential knowledge of itself as an immaterial entity. Since the argument's conclusion that the self is immaterial is in agreement with the experiential knowledge it helps "trigger off," so to speak, the distinction between these two related tasks is easily blurred.

[The second version of Avicenna's "Flying Man"], which is very short, occurs in *Psychology,* V, 7. As mentioned earlier, this is a chapter in which Avicenna criticizes and rejects a number of psychological theories. One of these is the theory that the human soul cannot be one entity, that the vegetative, animal and rational souls are three numerically distinct souls. In rejecting this theory, he argues for two points: (1) that the different psychological faculties require something that binds and unifies them; (2) that this binding entity cannot be corporeal but must be the immaterial rational soul. In the course of arguing for the second point, the "Flying Man" reappears, playing a related but different role than the one it played in its first apperance.

Avicenna argues that there must be a binding entity for the psychological faculties, relating to them in the way the Aristotelian common sense relates to the various senses. For each faculty is restricted to its own kind of act. The sensory acts are other than the appetitive and irascible. Yet these faculties interact. It is thus that we can make such true statements as "when we perceived, we desired," and "when we saw such a thing, we were angered." We can say such true things because there is an entity that binds and links the various faculties. This entity, Avicenna concludes, "is the thing which each of us perceives to be his self."

To show that this binding entity is the immaterial rational soul, Avicenna advances three arguments. The first and shortest is that body qua body cannot be this binding entity. Otherwise every corporeal thing would be performing this task, which is clearly not the case. The second argument harkens back to an earlier chapter where Avicenna had given lengthy arguments to show that the faculty receptive of the abstract intelligibles must be immaterial. Thus at least one of the human psychological faculties is immaterial. Now the binding entity, he argues, is the one from which the power emanates on the rest of the psychological faculties. This entity cannot be material because matter is not the source of emanation, but the recipient of it. The third argument is the longest. It reintroduces the "Flying Man."

If one supposes the binding entity to be a body, then it would have to be either the whole of the body or only part of it. Avicenna then proceeds to show that it is neither, concluding that this binding entity is immaterial. The "Flying Man" is used as part of the refutation of the first alternative. This refutation begins with the argument that if the binding entity is the whole body, then if a part is missing, it follows that what we perceive to be our selves would not exist. But this is not the case:

> For, as we've mentioned in other places, I know that I am myself even if I do not know that I have a leg or one of the organs. Rather, I believe these things to be attachments to my self and believe that they are instruments of mine which I use for certain needs. Were it not for such needs, I would dispense with them. I will still be 'I', when they are not [existing].

The second version of the "Flying Man" follows immediately, giving further support to what has just been uttered:

> Let us repeat what we've said earlier. We say: If a human is created all at once, created with his limbs separated and he does not see them, and if it so happens that he does not touch them and they do not touch each other, and he hears no sound, he would be ignorant of the existence of the whole of his organs, but would know the existence of his

individual being (*anniyyatihi*) as one thing, while being ignorant of all the former things. What is itself the unknown is not the known.

This brief appearance of the "Flying Man" is followed by an elaboration on the idea that the bodily organs are mere attachments to the self, akin to garments:

> These organs belong to us in reality only as garments which due to constant adherence to us have become as parts of our selves. When we imagine our selves, we do not imagine ourselves unclothed, but imagine them possessing covering garments. The reason for this is constant adherence, with the difference that with [real] clothes we have become accustomed to taking them off and laying them aside—something we have not been accustomed to with the bodily organs. Thus our belief that the organs are parts of us is more emphatic than our belief that garments are parts of us.

Avicenna then gives a spirited argument to disprove the second alternative, namely that the binding psychological entity cannot be one organ or a combination of some organs. For if an organ (or a combination of some organs), then when one is aware of one's self, one must be aware of the particular organ or organs. This is not the case. For even our knowledge of the heart, if we suppose it to be the binding entity, comes through experiment. It is not the thing one perceives to be the self when one has self-awareness. This argument, as it appears in this chapter, stands on its two feet, quite independently of the hypothetical example. We meet it elsewhere in Avicenna's writings without any reference to the "Flying Man."

To return, then, to the brief second entry of the example, we notice that it is used conjointly in support of another independent argument for disproving an alternative statement in a larger argument. We also notice that its conclusion is categorical. Thus, once again, we encounter Avicenna's arriving at the categorical conclusion from hypothetical premises. This version re-echoes the first, but there is no indication here that it is intended to awaken the soul to its self-knowledge. Its task is quite limited—to help disprove an alternative statement in a larger argument.

Avicenna's third (and also very short) version of the "Flying Man" occurs in his *al-Ishārāt wa al-Tanbīhāt,* one of his late works that sums up his philosophy. In the title, the term *ishārāt* is the plural of *ishāra,* "indication," "hint," "directive," "sign," "signal"; *tanbīhāt,* the plural of *tanbīh,* "alerting," "awakening," "drawing attention to," or, as recently translated, "admonition." Avicenna presents his ideas in short paragraphs each bearing the heading of either *ishāra* or *tanbīh,* although other related terms are also sometimes used. The paragraph containing the "Flying Man" has the heading *tanbīh.* Each of the three subsequent paragraphs that constitute an argument for the soul's immateriality also bear this heading. As we have seen with the first version of the example, the term *tanbīh* is used in a special epistemological sense of arousing the self to the self-knowledge it already possesses. The heading, *tanb h,* for the third version of the "Flying Man" and the related paragraphs that follow suggests that the term is meant to convey the same idea.

The example appears as part of the first paragraph, a first *tanbīh,* introducing a chapter entitled, "On the Terrestrial and Celestial Soul." The paragraph is as follows:

> Return to your self and reflect whether, being whole, or even in another state, where, however, you discern a thing correctly, you would be oblivious to the existence of your self (*dhātaka*) and would not affirm your self (*nafsaka*)? To my mind, this does not happen to the perspecacious—so much so that the sleeper in his sleep and the person drunk in the state of his drunkenness will not miss knowledge of his self, even if his presentation of his self to himself does not remain in his memory.

> And if you imagine your self (*dhātaka*) to have been at its first creation mature and whole in mind and body and it is supposed to be in a generality of position and physical circumstance where it does not perceive its parts, where its limbs do not touch each other but are rather spread apart, and that this self is momentarily suspended in temperate air, you will find that it will be unaware of everything except the "fixedness" (*thubūt*) of its individual existence (*anniyyathihā*).

Thus, according to the opening statement of this *tanbīh,* introspection shows that as long as the self is able to "discern a thing correctly," then whatever other circumstance it happens to be in, it will have self-knowledge. Commenting on this *tanbīh* as a whole, the philosopher-scientist Naṣīr al-Dīn al-*Tūsī* (d. 1274) writes: "Hence the absolutely first and clearest apprehension is a human being's apprehension of his self. It is clear that this kind of apprehension can neither be acquired through definition (*hadd*) or description (*rasm*), nor established by argument (*hujja*) or demonstration (*burhān*)."

The main intention of this version of the "Flying Man" is not to prove or demonstrate. Rather, it is to point out and illustrate that self-knowledge is the most primary of human cognitions. Thus, as noted earlier, it states explicitly what is implicit in the first version. Unlike the latter, it does not contain the explicit argument that the self is immaterial. An argument for the immateriality of the self, different from the one encountered in the first version, however, comes immediately after. This argument, no less than the one in the first version,

is open to the criticism that it assumes the point at issue and that it makes a shift from the hypothetical to the categorical. For it uses the "Flying Man" as a premise. But this example, as we have tried to show, already assumes that the self is immaterial. Furthermore, it appeals to this hypothetical example as though it has established the factual. The argument, spread over three *tanbīhs,* is expressed in cryptic language. Its essentials can be paraphrased as follows:

In the first *tanbīh,* Avicenna argues that self-knowledge is direct, not mediated, on the basis that the example excludes awareness of anything other than the self. In the second *tanbīh,* he argues that the self cannot be the body since the body is apprehended by the external senses. Now, he continues, the body has apparent external parts seen and felt by our senses and internal organs known to us only through dissection. The external parts cannot be the self. This is because we can be "stripped" of these parts and because these parts undergo growth and change without our losing our identity. Moreover, in "the supposition" (*al-fard*), that is, the "Flying Man," the senses are not operative and the activities of dissection enabling us to have knowledge of our inner organs is likewise excluded. The self hence is not the body. In the third *tanbīh,* Avicenna raises the question of whether self-knowledge is mediated through one's action. This, he argues, is not the case because, once again, "the supposition" excludes any action. Moreover action is either general or specific. General action does not lead to the knowledge of the particular self. The action would have to be particular; for example, my own individual act. But when I state that I am performing an act, the "I" is prior to my act. My act presupposes the existence of my self; otherwise I would not refer to it as my act.

One notices in this argument, not only the appeal to the hypothetical example as though it has established what is factual, but two other things. The first is Avicenna's reference to it as "the supposition" (*al-fard*), a concrete indication that he is only too well aware of its hypothetical nature. The second is that there are parts of the argument, more specifically, in the second and third *tanbīhs,* that are quite independent of the "Flying Man." One must also recall that the second version of the example was introduced conjointly with an argument that is independent of it. To this one must add that in the *Psychology* he devotes a whole chapter in an attempt to give a rigorous demonstration for the immateriality of the rational soul, quite independently of the "Flying Man" and without once referring us back to this example. All these considerations raise the question: Was Avicenna using the "Flying Man" to prove in the rigorous sense of "to prove" the existence of the self as an immaterial entity?

The indications are that he was not. In introducing the first version, as we have seen, he makes it quite plain that he intends to indicate "a manner of establishing the existence of the soul we have by way of alerting and reminding" and that this way is effective only with those capable of seeing the truth themselves. Underlying this approach is not only the conviction that experiential knowledge of ourselves is the most basic of our cognitions, but that the real object of this knowledge is an immaterial entity, an 'I' that is totally other than the body. Some who have this proper knowledge are inattentive to it, distracted from it. A thought experiment, not intended, however, as a rigorous proof, will awaken them to this knowledge. Others, the *mutakallimūn* would be an example of this, have been so accustomed to associating the body with the 'I' that they believe that this primary self-knowledge we have is knowledge of the body. Such people require a rigorous rational argument to show them their error.

Turning to the condensed third version of the example, its appearance in the *Ishārāt wa al-Tanbīhāt* is itself significant. This is a very intimate, personal work, written at the end of Avicenna's life, that gives the quintessence of his philosophy. Its mood is meditative, its tone religious, climaxed in the moving chapter on the stations of the mystics. The work is intended for kindred spirits, its contents, as he tells us, not to be divulged to anyone. If we read Avicenna aright, the "Flying Man" reappears in this work intended once again for "someone who has the power to see the truth himself, without the need of having to educate him, constantly prod him, and divert him from what causes sophistical errors."

Russell on the importance of Arabic philosophy:

Arabic philosophy is not important as original thought. Men like Avicenna and Averroes are essentially commentators. Speaking generally, the views of the more scientific philosophers come from Aristotle and the Neoplatonists in logic and metaphysics, from Galen in medicine, from Greek and Indian sources in mathematics and astronomy, and among mystics religious philosophy has also an admixture of old Persian beliefs. Writers in Arabic showed some originality in mathematics and in chemistry—in the latter case, as an incidental result of alchemical researches. Mohammedan civilization in its great days was admirable in the arts and in many technical ways, but it showed no capacity for independent speculation in theoretical matters. Its importance, which must not be underrated, is as a transmitter.

Bertrand Russell, in A History of Western Philosophy, *Simon and Schuster, 1945.*

Nancy G. Siraisi (essay date 1987)

SOURCE: "The *Canon* of Avicenna," in *Avicenna in*

Renaissance Italy: The Canon *and Medical Teaching in Italian Universities after 1500,* Princeton University Press, 1987, pp. 19-40.

[*In the following essay, Siraisi outlines the main ideas of Avicenna's* Canon of Medicine, *focusing on the Latin translation by Gerard of Cremona, and comparing it with its Galenic sources.*]

The encyclopedic medical work written by Avicenna (d. 1037) is far too lengthy and, as the massiveness of the Latin commentaries on short sections of it testifies, far too complex to be adequately characterized in brief. The following comments are intended only to draw the reader's attention to certain features of the organization and content of the *Canon* that seem particularly relevant to its reception in the schools of the West and the emergence of a tradition of Latin commentary and, especially, to the adoption of *Canon* 1.1 as a textbook for the teaching of medical theory. Beginning with a brief overview of the *Canon* as a whole, I shall then pass to a somewhat more detailed, but still highly compressed, account of the physiological treatise in Book 1, Part 1. In the absence of full studies of Avicenna's relationship to his sources and of the relationship of the Latin to the Arabic text of the *Canon,* a summary of *Canon* 1.1 can only be, at best, sketchy and impressionistic. The immediate goal is, however, merely to indicate some of the main features of that treatise as its appears in its Latin form. A few comparisons with other ancient and medieval treatments of somewhat similar material illustrate the distinguishing characteristics of *Canon* 1.1.

The following description refers to the Latin translation of the *Canon* attributed by his pupils to Gerard of Cremona (d. 1187), since, although revisions of the Gerard translation and retranslations of parts of the work began to circulate in the sixteenth century, the twelfth-century Latin text was the original basis of Western understanding of Avicenna's book. Furthermore, as we shall see, various of the later revised Latin versions retained much of Gerard's work. Given the length, complexity, and technical nature of the *Canon,* the translation attributed to Gerard of Cremona is a remarkable accomplishment. Certainly the long history of the use of this version attests that by and large Gerard or his pupils managed to produce a generally understandable rendering of Avicenna's opus. Nonetheless, even though comprehensive studies of the translation have yet to appear, various scholars in the sixteenth century and the twentieth have pointed out that it is characterized by a high proportion of both errors and obscurely rendered passages. It also retains numerous transliterated Arabic words, especially for names of plants and minerals in the pharmacological sections and for anatomical terms. But whatever its merits or defects, the Gerard translation was the means whereby the *Canon* reached all its readers in western

European medical schools up until the early sixteenth century, and a good many of them thereafter.

Considered as an encyclopedia of Greco-Arabic medicine, the **Canon** is in many respects distinguished by comprehensiveness and good organization. Praise of Avicenna's work for these qualities became, indeed, a commonplace among Latin commentators. As G. B. Da Monte put it [in his 1554 commentary on the **Canon**], Avicenna was moved to write the **Canon** when he saw that "neither among the Greeks nor among the Arabs was there any single, complete, continuous book that taught the art of medicine," the Hippocratic writings being enigmatic and obscure, Galen extremely prolix, and Rasis confusing. [In his Preface to *Galeni opera ex sexta Juntarum editione,* 1586], the same author asserted that Avicenna "intended to reduce all the monuments of medical art scattered at large in various works of Galen into one, as it were, corpus. . . . Indeed, he collected much dispersed information into appropriate and defined places and arranged it in sequence." One may certainly agree that the **Canon** is comprehensive. Few aspects of traditional Greek and Arabic medicine are left untouched in its five books, which together amount to about a million words in length. However, the **Canon** is at least as much a collection of essentially separate and distinct manuals and reference works as it is an architectonic *summa* of medicine. Moreover, while individual sections are as a rule clearly organized and succinctly expressed, the overall arrangement is somewhat confusing and involves a certain amount of overlapping. The reader turns with gratitude to the lengthy analytic table of contents found in the early printed editions of Gerard's translation immediately after Avicenna's preface to the whole work and before each of its subsequent books.

Book 1 is divided into four main parts, or fen, to use the term adapted from the Arabic by the Latin translator. It opens with the statement of principles and handbook of physiology. The second fen of Book 1 classifies varieties, efficient causes, and symptoms of disease. Diseases are divided primarily into those caused by imbalance of the four elementary qualities of hot, wet, cold, and dry in the body, those caused by faulty composition, or conformation of bodily parts, and those caused by *solutio continuitatis* or *continui,* which may be rendered, more or less, as trauma. The efficient causes of disease are categorized as either connected with environment, regimen, and psychology (among them are included the factors embraced in the traditional scheme of the "non naturals"—air, food, and drink; repletion and inanition; motion and rest; sleep and waking; and passions of the soul) or as due to any of a wide range of individual physical events, some of which (for example, pain and swelling) the modern reader might be inclined to consider symptoms rather than causes. The section on symptomology both lists an array of individual signs of imbalance of complex-

ion, of *solutio continuitatis,* of obstruction, and so on, and reviews the standard means of diagnosis by pulse and urine. The third fen of Book 1 concerns the conservation of health: separate sections on pediatric, adult, and geriatric regimen are followed by regimes for the delicate and complexionally imbalanced, and for travelers. The fourth and final fen of Book 1 deals with principles of therapy and forms of treatment appropriate for different conditions. Therapies discussed include emetic, cathartic, sedative, and other medications, bleeding, cauterization, blistering, and enemas.

Book 2 is on the subject of medicinal simples; most of it is given over to a list—arranged more or less in Latin alphabetical order, presumably by the translator—of individual substances, their properties, and the conditions for which they are supposedly remedies. In his third book, Avicenna provided twenty-one fen on ailments peculiar to each major organ of the body— arranged from head to toe—and their treatment. Most of the sections are preceded by one or two chapters on the anatomy and aspects of the physiology of the organ in question. Book 4 suveys diseases and injuries that either affect the whole body or may occur in any part of it, and their treatment; of its seven fen, the most notable is probably the first, on fevers, which provided a famous and influential account of the subject. The remaining fen of Book 4 concern the concept of crisis or critical days in illness; tumors and pustules; *solutio continuitatis* in the form of wounds, bruises, sprains, and ulcers; dislocations and fractures; poisons of mineral, vegetable, and animal origins (including animal bites and stings); and skin conditions. The fifth and final book of the **Canon** is an *antidotarium,* or manual on the preparation of compound medicines.

If one wishes to use the **Canon** as a reference tool, the arrangement of material just summarized works well for some subjects, but a good deal less well for others. A reader who is primarily interested in disease, for example, finds a sequence of more or less self-contained treatises offering complementary information. He or she can begin with classification, efficient causes, and symptoms of disease in general in Book 1, Fen 2, and proceed to the survey arranged by varieties of treatment in Book 1, Fen 4. Then, moving from the general to the particular, there is the account of diseases affecting different parts of the body in Book 3 and of diseases affecting the body as a whole in Book 4. Yet the division of the material into separate sections, and the provision of the analytical table of contents, means that anyone who is interested only in one particular topic—*lepra,* say, or diseases of the eyes—can easily turn to a few chapters on that subject alone.

The results are also fairly satisfactory if one considers the material available to a reader primarily interested in therapy. There is a self-contained survey of treatment methods (1.4) and a dictionary of medicinal simples (2); much discussion of treatments appropriate for disease of particular bodily parts is found in Book 3, and of ills affecting the entire body in Book 4; Book 5 provides guidance for compounding medicines. The arrangement has the merit of making it possible to approach the subject of therapy from a variety of different standpoints. One can, for example, relatively easily find an answer to any of the following questions: When and in what conditions is bleeding an appropriate treatment? What are the medicinal powers of cinnamon? What treatments are recommended for deafness? For various kinds of fevers? How is theriac compounded? However, although no systematic survey has been attempted for present purposes, it is clear that consistency throughout the whole, whether in terms of therapeutic recommendations or of properties attributed to substances, is not always achieved.

Least satisfactory, in some respects, is the arrangement of the physiological and anatomical material. Principles of physiology and the anatomy of bones, muscles, nerves, veins, and arteries are discussed in the first fen of Book 1; but the accounts of the anatomy and some further discussion of the physiology of other major organs (brain, lungs, heart, digestive and reproductive organs, for example) are scattered through the opening chapters of the twenty-one fen of Book 3. This separation, which is the result both of Avicenna's division of medicine into theory and practice and of the classification of bodily parts that he adopted, was, as we shall see, further accentuated by the curricula and practices of medieval university faculties of medicine. But in order to understand both the basis for Avicenna's treatment of physiology and anatomy and the principles underlying the organization of the *Canon* as a whole, it is necessary to turn to the content of the first fen of Book 1.

The easiest way to describe *Canon* 1.1 is as a manual of Galenic physiology, although such a description is slightly misleading because the work also contains other elements of considerable importance. Furthermore, although the subject matter of the treatise is primarily physiological, the discipline with which it is concerned is not coterminous with even the loosest and most general modern definition of the science of physiology. Instead, Fen 1, along with other parts of Book 1, deals with the theoretical part of medicine, a subject that embraced the definition of medicine and of its place among the arts and sciences, and the fundamental principles of medical learning. *Canon* 1.1 is subdivided into six *doctrinae,* the last four of which are mainly physiological in content. The first two sections concern the definition, subdivisions, and subject of medicine and the theory of the elements, the last being considered to provide the basis in physical science for physiological theory.

The first section (*doctrina*) of Fen 1 opens with a definition of medicine: "Medicine is the science by which we learn the various states of the human body, when in health and when not in health, whereby health is conserved and whereby it is restored, after being lost." Medicine is thus presented from the outset as a science in the Aristotelian sense of a body of knowledge derived by demonstrative reasoning from true premises, but a science with a practical purpose. Implicit in the definition is the repudiation of any notion that medicine is merely a practical art, technology, or craft. Avicenna next asserts that medicine is divided into theory and practice, rebutting the counterclaim that any true science must of necessity be entirely theoretical with the example of philosophy, also, in his view, divided into theoretical and practical parts. Furthermore, it is not the theoretical part of medicine alone that is categorized as *scientia;* the practical part is also *scientia,* since it too involves formally organized knowledge, in this case the knowledge of how the tasks of healing should be carried out.

The subject of medical science, we learn in the following chapter, is the human body, insofar as it is subject to health and sickness. Since complete knowledge only comes with knowledge of causes, the physician must know the causes of health and sickness, these being classified in the Aristotelian manner into material, efficient, formal, and final causes. The subject of Fen 1 is announced to be the material, formal, and final causes of the human body as it is subject to health and sickness (efficient causes Avicenna identified with external factors affecting the body and discussed, as already noted, in Book 1, Fen 2). The *medicus,* who must also know regimen, symptoms, and medications, should investigate these causes by sense and anatomy, but he should take the fundamentals of physical science (for example, that the elements exist and are four in number) from natural philosophy without himself engaging in natural philosophical investigation.

The second *doctrina* of Fen 1, on the elements, is an admirable illustration of this last principle, since it provides a highly compressed account of those, and only those, parts of a mainly Aristotelian element theory necessary to establish the human body as an object in the physical world and to provide the foundations for an understanding of two central concepts of Greco-Arabic medical theory, namely humoral physiology and the idea of *complexio,* temperament, or *krasis* (that is, the balance of the elementary qualities of hot, wet, cold, and dry in living bodies). We read that the human body, like all other bodies, is compounded of the elements. The two heavy elements, earth and water, contribute chiefly to the formation of its members; and the two light elements, air and fire, contribute mostly to the generation of *spiritus* and motion of the members (although only the soul actually moves the members). In addition to learning the natural place and qualities of each element (earth in the center, cold and dry, and so on), the reader is also reminded that earth preserves shapes and forms; that water receives all shapes but does not preserve them, that air helps in rarefying and elevating substances; and fire assists in processes of maturation, mixing, and making subtle. When one recalls, for example, the notion frequently expressed by medieval authors that a good memory is due to the physical retention of images by relatively dry (that is, earthy) brain tissue, or the frequency with which the heating of mixtures plays a part in medical recipes, the medical and physiological relevance of the latter information becomes readily apparent.

The first two *doctrina* of Fen 1 thus constitute an important statement about the nature of medical learning. The definition of medicine is broad enough to include the study of all aspects of physical function. The status of medicine as a science is defended. Moreover, the subject is placed in the context of Aristotelian natural philosophy, through insistence on medicine's scientific character, the application to it of the concept of the four causes, and the assertion that the fundamental physical principles on which medicine rests are drawn from natural philosophy. The human body studied by the physician exists as part of the sublunary world of Aristotelian physics and is subject to its laws. At the same time the independence of medicine as a discipline is safeguarded by the warning that the *medicus* should not, *qua medicus,* investigate issues in natural philosophy. The significance of these assertions was not to escape Avicenna's Latin commentators.

In addition, the second of the two introductory sections, that on the elements, fulfills a transitional function. While it continues the Aristotelian and philosophical themes of *Doctrina* 1, it also leads directly into the mainly Galenic and physiological material of the rest of the treatise. The topics surveyed in the last four subdivisions of Fen 1 are *complexio* or temperament, the humors or bodily fluids, the parts of the body, and the virtues and operations, which include sensation, motion, pulsation, and so on. These categories, together with the elements and *spiritus* (discussed by Avicenna along with the virtues and operations), constitute the ancient scheme of the things natural. In composing Fen 1, Avicenna superimposed the Aristotelian scheme of the four causes upon the set of seven things natural, redefining the latter as a sequence that proceeded from the most remote to the most immediate material causes, and ended with the final causes of the human body. Thus *Doctrina* 1 informs the reader that the body's material causes are the elements (remote), the humors (somewhat remote), and the members and *spiritus* (immediate). The virtues and operations, which usually come last in the scheme of things natural, Avicenna regarded, appropriately enough, as the final or teleological causes of the human body. These definitions accounted for the things natural except *com-*

Iranian stamp honoring the millenary of Avicenna's birth and depicting his reconstructed mausoleum at Hamadhān.

plexio, which Avicenna proclaimed the body's formal cause. He discussed *complexio* in its accustomed place in the sequence of things natural between the elements and the humors. This position, somewhat awkward in terms of his arrangement according to the four causes, had perhaps to be retained because of the presence of another implied progression in the traditional order of the first four of the things natural (elements, *complexio,* humors, members), namely an ascending hierarchy of perceptibility to sense.

Within this whole scheme, each section leads logically to its successor, and all major bodily functions are neatly fitted into the system. Having learned that the human body, like all other sublunary bodies, is fundamentally composed of the four elements, each with its pair of qualities, the reader proceeds next to *Doctrina* 3 on *complexio.* The balance of the elementary qualities produces, in plant and animal species, in human individuals, in parts of the body, and in medicinal compounds, the *complexio,* which Avicenna, as transmitted by Gerard, defined as itself a quality. Complexion, used in this special sense, is either balanced or unbalanced, temperate or intemperate; in reality, however, complexion never achieves perfect balance, although in man it can come very close. A given complexion can only be identified by comparison with one of a series of norms (such as with the ideal for the species or the individual). According to Avicenna, eight varieties of temperate and eight varities of distemperate complexion can be identified in this way. Medicines, too, can only be described as, for example, temperate, hot, or cold, with regard to their effect on a particular body or kind of body. The same medicine may be hot in regard to a scorpion and cold in regard to a man, or hotter for Peter than it is for Paul. Whereas the elements in the human body were conceived of as not individually or directly perceptible to sense, complexion was supposedly to some extent detectable by physical means; in human beings, the skin of the palm of the hand is the most temperate organ and hence serves as the measure of the complexion of the other parts of the body and the manifestation of the complexion of the body as a whole. As is apparent from the foregoing, all the organs and humors of the body were thought of as individually complexionate. Avicenna accordingly provided his readers with four lists of bodily parts, each list being arranged in descending order from the extreme of hotness, coldness, wetness, or dryness to the palm of the hand.

Since complexion in human beings was considered both as a kind of individual constitution and as sex-linked and subject to change in scientifically predictable ways over time (as well as in response to climatic and other conditions), discussion of complexion necessarily involved consideration of growth and aging as well as sex differences. Avicenna devoted a chapter to these topics, in which he considered some of the implications of the doctrine that life involves a process of diminution of heat and moisture from infancy to old age and ultimately death. A long section of this chapter weighs the relative complexional heat of children and youths; the problem was of interest because the theory just mentioned implied that infants ought to be the hotter, but the vigor of youth seemed to suggest the contrary.

Doctrina 4 defines the humors as liquids into which nutriment is converted. In addition to the four primary humors (blood, phlegm, red bile, and black bile), four secondary humors are identified. All are said to be found in both good and bad varieties. The good varieties of the primary humors are absorbed into and nourish the substance of the body; the bad are "superfluities," which are either excreted or damaging to the body if retained. Thus, discussion of the humors and their role in the body's economy involves attention to digestion, nutrition, and excretion, processes treated in a chapter on the generation of the humors. Topics covered include the stages of digestion and functions of mastication, saliva, stomach, intestines, liver, kidneys, and bladder.

The topic of the humors is succeeded in *Doctrina* 5 by that of the *membra,* or parts of the body, which are here described as generated by the humors and sustained by their nutritive activity. The introductory chapter of this section contains generalizations about the members paralleling those about the humors and complexions in the two preceding parts of the work; it is, however, followed by five *summae* containing a total of seventy-six chapters on the anatomy of the bones, muscles, nerves, arteries, and veins. Well over half of Fen 1, in fact, consists of these chapters on anatomy. However, . . . the only part of *Doctrina* 5 normally taught in European universities was the introductory

chapter, and this is all that will be considered here. It is mainly concerned with various ways of classifying bodily parts. The first distinction made is between *membra similia* or *simplicia* (for example, bones, cartilage, nerves, ligaments, arteries, and veins) and composite or instrumental members (for example, the hands or the face); it will be observed that this distinction is not quite the same as that between tissues and organs, which it is sometimes said to resemble. Brief definitions of the nature and function of the more important *membra similia* follow. It is, of course, only such members that are treated in the subsequent anatomical chapters; for an account of the chief composite members as such the reader has to turn to the introductory chapters of each section of Book 3.

The next classification of members is according to whether they receive or emit virtue: examples of members that both receive and emit (*suscipiens et tribuens*) are the brain and the liver; a member that receives and does not emit is the flesh; one that emits and does not receive is, according to some, the heart, although others disagree. This allusion to the difference between the teaching of Aristotle and that of Galen on the role of the heart leads, appropriately enough, to consideration of the Galenic doctrine of the three, or four, primary or principal members. The discussion divides the parts into principal members and members that serve the principal members. The former are heart, brain, liver, and testicles; the subsidiary organs of the heart are the arteries and lungs, those of the liver the stomach and veins, and so on. Again, the members may be divided into those in whose generation the paternal sperm played a larger part (all *membra similia* other than flesh and blood) and those generated primarily from the retained menstrual blood of the mother (flesh and blood); discussion of this distinction leads into a brief excursus on embryology. Members may also be classified as fibrous (*villosa*) or nonfibrous in composition, the *membra villosa* being the stomach, intestines, urinary bladder, and gall bladder.

Discussion of the principal members leads naturally to consideration of the virtues, or powers, associated with each of them. These were divided into "natural," "vital" and "animal" virtues, a classification ultimately connected with the philosophical concept of the three-fold character of the soul. Hence, *Doctrina* 6, the concluding section of Fen 1, opens (after a brief introductory chapter) with an account of the natural virtues (or in other terminology, powers of the vegetative soul) associated with liver and testicles: growth, the ability to convert and assimilate nutriment, and reproduction. Avicenna then proceeded to a description of the role of *spiritus* in preparing the body for the reception of the animal virtues (that is, the powers associated with the sensitive soul possessed by all animals, including humankind) of motion and sensation. *Spiritus* in the Galenic tradition here followed by Avicenna was a highly refined bodily substance formed in part from inspired air; in Avicenna's version it was first generated in the liver from the vaporous part of the humors (to which, presumably, inspired air had contributed) and then received a second generation in the heart. Pervading the entire body, *spiritus,* which manifests itself in pulsation, serves as the vehicle of *virtus vitalis,* which keeps life itself in being. Specialized functions attributed to *spiritus*—the refinement of animal spirits in the brain and the role of visual spirits in seeing—were also briefly mentioned by Avicenna. The account of the animal virtues focuses mainly on the process whereby messages from the senses are received and interpreted in the brain. For the Latin Middle Ages and Renaissance, Avicenna was of course a leading authority on psychology, although his reputation in this field was chiefly based on his **De anima** rather than the **Canon**. Nonetheless, in the latter work, too, he weighed the validity of such classifications of brain function as *sensus communis, phantasia,* and imaginative, cogitative, estimative, and rational powers (the last of these being associated with the rational soul and reserved for humankind alone). Fen 1 finally concludes with a chapter in which it is pointed out that many of the body's actual operations require the cooperation of both natural and animal powers.

As will have become apparent from the foregoing summary, the first fen of Book 1 of the **Canon** is a compendium based almost entirely upon ancient Greek sources, chiefly Aristotle and Galen. Yet Avicenna's selection, organization, and interpretation of his material resulted in a work with a distinctive character of its own. Investigation of the relationship of Fen 1 to its sources is beyond the scope of the present work; however, consideration of the way in which a few somewhat arbitrarily chosen examples of Aristotelian and Galenic doctrines appear in Avicenna's treatise may serve to throw light upon the special characteristics and apparent goals of that work.

Avicenna was both physician and philosopher, although he distinguished quite sharply between the two roles. Repeatedly, he warned the readers of Fen 1 that the *medicus* should not himself investigate natural philosophy, but should rather accept the conclusions of experts in that field. However, information and ideas derived from philosophy in general and from Aristotle in particular in fact play quite a large part in Fen 1. The Aristotelian framework provided for the whole work in its opening sections has already been noted. In addition, Avicenna took every opportunity that offered itself to point out specific differences between the physiological and psychological views of Galen and his followers and those of Aristotle and his. The most important differences between Aristotle and Galen on the subject of physiology were those relating to the functions of heart and brain and to conception. Regarding heart and brain, Aristotle usually held the heart

to be the primary organ of the whole body, whereas the Galenists, as already noted, considered the heart only one of several primary organs (namely, heart, brain, and liver, a triad to which the testicles were often added as a fourth). The differing doctrines had extensive ramifications in that they also entailed differing views on sensation and motion, the blood vessels, and other topics. As regards conception, Aristotle held that the active or formative principle was contributed entirely by the male, whereas Galen maintained that both sexes contributed actively to the formation of the fetus and that females as well as males therefore emitted sperm.

Hence, in the first general chapter on the members, Avicenna informed his readers, according to the version attributed to Gerard, that the brain was held to be the *principium* of sense absolutely by some (the Galenists), but only intermediately by others (the Aristotelians). A little farther on, he remarked that

> . . . the *medici* differ from a great man among the philosophers. For this great man among the philosophers said that the heart is the member that gives out and does not receive. For it is the first root of all the virtues, and it gives to all the other members their virtues by which they are nourished and live and by which they know and move. But the *medici* and some of the first philosophers shared out these virtues among the members and they do not say that [the heart] gives out and does not take in. And the opinion of the philosopher is indeed more subtly proved and truer. But the opinion of the *medici* when it is attended to in the first place (*in primis*) is more obvious.

Later in the same chapter, referring to the simile used by "he who gave truth (*verificavit*) to the wise," likening the male contribution in conception to rennet and the female contribution to that of the milk passively acted upon by rennet, Avicenna observed:

> This word is to no small, nay, to a large extent, contrary to the words of Galen. For it seems to him that both the power of coagulating and the power of being coagulated is in each of the two [that is, male and female] sperms. . . .

In several passages of *Doctrina* 6, on the virtues, Avicenna returned at some length to the topic of the differences between the physiology of Aristotle and that of Galen, explaining that their differences over heart and brain were reflected in varying accounts of the vital, animal, and natural powers (associated with heart, brain, and liver, respectively). In one of these passages the *medicus* was instructed that though the Aristotelian view was correct, it was not his business in his capacity as *medicus* to investigate the issue, since whether or not a particular organ was or was not the *principium* of one of the powers made no difference from the standpoint of medical treatment.

Doctrina 6 also warns of differences between philosophical and medical terminology. Galenic medical writers normally described motion and sense as animal, and growth and reproduction as natural, powers. Avicenna, as Gerard represented him, pointed out that "the philosophers when they say *anima* mean *anima terrena,* the perfection of the natural instrumental body. And they mean the *principium* of every power, that principle indeed from which motion and diverse operations come." Hence, the powers of growth and reproduction termed natural by medical writers might be described as *animales* in philosophical texts, although on other occasions *animalis* might be used to refer to the power of comprehending and moving. Furthermore, the reader is also instructed that philosophers use the term natural for "every power (*virtus*) through which operation occurs in a body according to the diversity of its form," and this usage refers to a higher faculty than the powers of reproduction and growth designated by the medical term *virtus naturalis.* Finally, yet other passages in the same *doctrina* point out differences between philosophers and medical writers over the proper classification of the internal powers of the brain.

In Fen 1, the various discussions of the relationship of philosophical and medical teachings carry a double message. On the one hand, the *medicus* is repeatedly warned off philosophizing. He is, in effect, told on a number of occasions that although the Aristotelian teaching is true, he should for all practical purposes follow Galen and not worry about the discrepancy. On the other, the reader gets a good many tantalizing glimpses of philosophical views, and hints are not lacking that the dual roles of philosopher and physician may be combined in one person. That Avicenna himself had functioned in both capacities was, of course, well known to medieval and Renaissance readers of the *Canon* in Latin. Furthermore, in *Canon* 1.1 Avicenna referred readers of Fen 1 to his own philosophical writings; and he drew attention to Galen's philosophical interests with the remark that if Galen is to be attacked for his views on the division of medicine "he ought not to be attacked insofar as he is a *medicus* but insofar as he is a philosopher."

For the strictly physiological, as distinct from the natural philosophical, material in *Canon* 1.1, Galen is by far the most important source. Almost all the physiological concepts schematized and abbreviated in Avicenna's treatise can be found in Galen's works. Except for the instances noted above, in which Galen's views are weighted against those of Aristotle, to the ultimate advantage of the latter, the Latin text of *Canon* 1.1 contains few or no examples of clearly intentional divergence from Galen's teaching. Moreover, Galen is several times cited by name, and is always mentioned

with respect, even in instances when Aristotle's opinions are preferred from the standpoint of philosophy. Yet the spirit and approach of Avicenna in *Canon* 1.1 seems very different from that of Galen.

Avicenna's apparent goal in writing *Canon* 1.1 was to present a highly compressed yet comprehensive account of the whole of physiological theory; the work teaches a set of principles that have been, to a very large extent, effectively abstracted from any context of experience. Unified organization, clarity (usually), and brevity are achieved, but at a certain cost. Lacking, for the most part, are illustrative examples, admissions of uncertainty or limited knowledge, indications of divergence of views among ancient physicians, or acknowledgement of the presence of inconsistencies within the body of Galen's writings. By contrast, Galen's major treatises embody, as a rule, a leisurely and discursive investigation of a particular aspect of a unified science of medicine that is not sharply divided into theory and practice. Moreover, in Galen's writings physiological theory is generally interwoven into a context rich in detailed anatomical description, records of personal experience and observation, and, often, polemic against the holders of different scientific views. Without undertaking any detailed investigation of the way in which Avicenna used his Galenic sources (or the form in which these reached him), we may illustrate some of the ways in which the teaching of Galen is transformed by its presentation in the Latin text of *Canon* 1.1 by means of a comparison of a few passages therein with sections of three works of Galen that *Canon* 1.1 to some extent parallels in subject matter—namely, *De complexionibus (De temperamentis), De naturalibus facultatibus,* and *De usu partium.*

Let us take our first example from the treatment of the subject of *complexio.* Most of the main ideas expressed in *Doctrina* 3 of *Canon* 1.1 can also be found in Books 1 and 2 of Galen's *De complexionibus.* Among the themes present in Galen's work that are also treated in *Canon* 1.1 are the relation of complexion to the elementary qualities; the notion that the physician considers complexion not as a balance of weight (*ad pondus*) but *ad justitiam,* in terms of appropriateness for the species, individual, etc., under consideration; the idea that complexion can only be expressed in relative terms and that the point of reference must always be specified; the related idea that a given complexion may be cold in regard to one point of reference and hot in regard to another; the assertion that man is the most temperate of all complexionate beings and that the skin of the hand is the most temperate part of man; and discussions of the different complexions of various ages and sexes, of the inhabitants of different regions, and of the individual organs of the human body.

De complexionibus 1, however, also contains extensive passages of exposition of differing views and polemic against them that have no parallel in *Canon* 1.1.3; furthermore, Book 3 of *De complexionibus* is devoted to detailed exposition of the complexion of various medicinal substances and the therapeutic applications of complexion theory, topics excluded from *Canon* 1.1. But the characteristic that most significantly distinguishes Galen's treatment from Avicenna's handling of some of the same material is the inclusion throughout Book 2 of *De complexionibus* of lengthy descriptions of the physical manifestations of different kinds of complexion. In Galen's treatise, the whole subject is closely related to anatomical experience, to observation of the patient, and to medical care; in Avicenna's, summary of the topic is explained by means of clearly stated but abstract and apparently arbitrarily determined rules, and examples are deliberately deferred until later in the *Canon*. Thus, Galen's remarks on the complexion of the various organs relate the complexional characteristics of each part to its physical characteristics and especially to its consistency; the flesh of the heart is drier than that of the spleen, kidneys, and liver because it is harder. The reader is urged to find out for himself that the heat of the heart is greater than that of any other organ by thrusting his fingers into an incision in the chest of a living animal. By contrast, *Canon* 1.1's neatly schematized and readily memorable lists of organs in descending order of dryness and heat provide essentially the same information as that given by Galen—and a few gaps are filled in—but supporting references to physical experience are absent. In general, in Galen's much more than in Avicenna's account one is constantly reminded that complexion, and secondary characteristics dependent thereon, are to a significant extent accessible to sense.

Nowhere is this contrast more evident, perhaps, than in the treatment of the issue of whether the complexion of children or youths is hotter. In *Canon* 1.1, in one of the relatively few places in that treatise where a diversity of opinion among ancient physicians is acknowledged, otherwise unidentified *medici antiqui* are described as having been divided on the issue. Galen is said to have dissented from both views, and to have maintained that the heat of children and youths was *in radice* equal, but that the heat of children was greater in quantity and that of youths greater in quality. The rest of the passage is devoted to an explanation of Galen's supposed views, which turns on the two assertions: it is impossible to increase innate heat, and humidity declines throughout life. Thus, the heat of youths is conserved by less humidity than that of infants; they are at a stage of life in which the humidity is sufficient to preserve heat at a level that is qualitatively high, but not of such quantity as to permit further augmentation of the body in the form of growth.

Turning to the Galenic account as presented in *De complexionibus,* one is immediately struck by the much less abstract character of most of the discussion. Galen

pointed out that the physician's evaluation of actual (as distinct from potential) complexional heat depended on touch, which with the aid of memory was indeed a satisfactory way of detecting changes in the heat of a single individual. However, if different individuals or whole categories of individuals were to be compared, then it was essential to compare like with like in regard to as many characteristics and conditions as possible—body type, diet, environment, and so on. These remarks, interesting for the adumbration of the idea of controlled observation of numerous exemplars, find no echo in the Latin *Canon* 1.1.3. Moreover, Galen's conclusion in *De complexionibus* was firmly rooted in his clinical experience; he stated that having touched the bodies of numerous children and adolescents, he found it impossible to assert on the basis of the sense of touch that either group was simply and unequivocally hotter than the other. However, the perspiration (a manifestation of heat, evidently) of children, was, owing to their greater humidity, greater in quantity, and that of adolescents more acrid in quality. This difference is because children have more innate heat, but the heat of adolescents is drier. Comparing this chapter with the passage in the *Canon,* one notes that the latter, characteristically, elaborates on Galen's conclusion, but does not contain those of his supporting arguments that depend upon clinical experience and sense perception. (*Canon* 1.1.3.3 does, however, also explain a few perceptible characteristics of small children in complexional terms.)

One more illustration of the way in which Avicenna handled Galenic material may be drawn from his treatment of the topic of digestion and the digestive organs. We have seen that in *Canon* 1.1 there is a short narrative of the digestive process as a whole in the chapter on the generation of the humors (1.1.4.2); to this must be added the description of the coats of the stomach and intestines in the section on *membra villosa* in the general chapter on the members (1.1.5.1), and the account of the four nutritive powers (attractive, retentive, digestive, and expulsive) in the third chapter of *Doctrina* 6. Among the most important Galenic accounts of this part of physiology are Books 4 and 5 of *De usu partium* on the digestive organs and digestive process, and the lengthy discussion of nutritive power in *De naturalibus facultatibus.*

In its main outline, the brief summary of digestion in Avicenna's chapter on the generation of the humors is fairly similar to the much longer account presented by Galen in *De usu partium* and with parts of the account in *De naturalibus facultatibus.* Missing from Avicenna's highly compressed version are, however, both the emphasis on functional teleology and the richness of detail characteristic of *De usu partium* and the context of polemic against Erasistratus and his followers found in *De naturalibus facultatibus.* It is really only the opening generalities of *De usu partium* 4.1-4 that are paralleled in *Canon* 1.1.4.1. Any attempt at more detailed description of the individual digestive organs and their functions, similar to that occupying the remainder of Books 4 and 5 of Galen's work, is postponed in the *Canon* until scattered chapters of Book 3. Furthermore, even in passages that do closely parallel one another in Galen's account and in the *Canon,* Avicenna's version is greatly simplified. In some instances, the process of simplification, and the stripping away or deemphasis of the metaphors freely used by Galen to clarify his descriptions and render them more vivid, resulted in a presentation of Galenic ideas in the *Canon* in a form that was simultaneously both cryptic and perhaps more literal than Galen intended. One example will suffice. In both *De usu partium* and *De naturalibus facultatibus* Galen compared the concoction of the chyle in the liver to the fermentation of wine. In the former work, he said:

> Let us, then, compare the chyle to wine just pressed from the grapes and poured into casks, and still working, settling, fermenting, and bubbling with innate heat. The heavy, earthy part of its residues, which I think is called the dregs, is sinking to the bottom of the vessels and the other, light, airy part floats. This latter part is called the flower and forms on the top of light wines in particular, whereas the dregs are more abundant in heavy wines. In making this comparison, think of the chyle sent up from the stomach to the liver as bubbling and fermenting like new wine from the heat of the viscus and beginning to change into useful blood; consider too that in this effervescence the thick, muddy residue is being carried downward and the fine, thin residue is coming to the top and floating on the surface of the blood.

In *De naturalibus facultatibus* the same idea is presented as follows:

> What else, then, remains but to explain clearly what it is that happens in the generation of the humors, according to the belief and demonstration of the Ancients? This will be more clearly understood from a comparison. Imagine then some new wine which has been not long ago pressed from the grape, and which is fermenting and undergoing alteration through the agency of its continued heat. Imagine next two residual substances produced during this process of alteration, the one tending to be light and air-like and the other to be heavy and more of the nature of earth; of these the one, as I understand, they call the flower and the other the lees. Now you may correctly compare yellow bile to the first of these, and black bile to the latter. . . .

In the *Canon* the presentation of its idea runs as follows:

> In every concoction of this sort there is to be found foam and sediment. . . . The foam is red [yellow]

bile; and the sediment is melancholy [black bile].

Avicenna's drastic condensation of Galenic material is accompanied on occasion not only by oversimplification, as in the instance just noted, but also by inconsistency, the latter sometimes merely echoing Galen's own. Thus, in the account of the *membra villosa* in the Gerard version of *Canon* 1.1, the urinary bladder is said in passing to have a single tunic; but in the account of the bladder's anatomy in Book 3 it is described as having two tunics. This discrepancy presumably stems from the fact that Galen had assigned the bladder one tunic in *De usu partium* and in one passage of *De naturalibus facultatibus,* but in a second passage of the latter work had given it two. Moreover, while the details of Galen's—and Avicenna's own—experience were excised from *Canon* 1.1, certain concepts adumbrated in Galen's works in *Canon* 1.1 were elaborated to the point where they may be regarded as original contributions. A case of this kind that has been the subject of modern scholarly attention is Avicenna's development of the concept of so-called radical moisture as an explanation of the process of aging. It must be emphasized, however, that the focus in the physiological sections of *Canon* 1.1 upon the systematic presentation and explanation of principles, at the expense of detail and supporting evidence, is unquestionably part of the deliberate strategy of that treatise; other parts of the *Canon* are rich in material pertaining to the experience of the physician and the treatment of patients.

Avicenna was neither the first nor the earliest available in Latin among authors who had written in Arabic to produce a schematic general summary of Greco-Arabic medicine structured around a division into theory and practice. The collection of brief medical opinions attributed to Joannitius and known as the *Isagoge* begins with the assertion that medicine is divided into theoretical and practical branches and proceeds to a consideration of the naturals, the nonnaturals, and the things against nature (that is, diseases). Avicenna has been shown to have drawn some of his material from the medical encyclopedia of Rasis (d. 925); another predecessor and possible partial source of the *Canon* was the survey of medicine written by Haly Abbas (d. 994). As compared with these other works, the *Canon* offers a fuller and more intellectually demanding account of its subject matter than the highly abbreviated *Isagoge,* and its organization is somewhat easier to grasp than that of the work of Rasis. The work of Haly Abbas is fully comparable to the *Canon* in scope and sophistication as well as structure. It is divided into ten books on theory and ten books on practice, of which the first four books on theory roughly parallel *Canon* 1.1 in content. In organization, the *Liber totius medicinae* is in at least one respect superior to the *Canon*: Haly's entire account of physiology and anatomy is presented as a coherent unit in his opening books, whereas in the **Canon,** as we have seen, the treatment of internal organs is excluded from the physiological and anatomical material in Book 1, Fen 1. Like **Canon** 1.1, of which it may well have been one of the sources, the *Liber totius medicinae* contains lengthy passages summarizing Galenic concepts. But the Aristotelian element, which plays so marked a part in **Canon** 1.1 seems not to be found in the corresponding parts of the Latin version of Haly's work. It was precisely Avicenna's philosophical interests that gave **Canon** 1.1 its distinctive cast. In **Canon** 1.1, as in Avicenna's philosophical writings, elements of diverse origin were drawn together. It seems likely that, indeed, Avicenna's well-known readiness to incorporate both Aristotelian and Neoplatonic elements into his philosophical system stimulated his interest in considering the relationship between Aristotelian and Galenic thought, which also contained Platonic elements.

Such, in barest outline, was the **Canon** as translated by Gerard of Cremona or his associates. The scope and organization of the work, the mass of practical information it contained, the author's summaries of Galenic thought (inadequate though these might sometimes be in detail), and the philosophical context in which Avicenna succeeded in placing medicine while preserving its independence as a distinct science—all initially secured for the **Canon** a place of honor in medieval western European medicine. . . .

Levy on Avicenna's importance to the history of medicine:

What Avicenna's status is in the history of scientific progress is difficult to assess. Primarily he was a philosopher, and like others of his kind, took all learning for his province, with medicine as one of its parishes. He was reared under the shadow that Galen had thrown across the centuries and he relied in his practice upon ancient and long accepted dogma, namely the theories formulated in ages long past. Galen's shadow was not greatly lightened by Avicenna, but he appears to have made it easier for his colleagues to make their way about in the gloom. The **Canon** classified and systematized all the Greek medical knowledge that survived, so that part of it at any rate came to be required reading for every medical student in the Islamic world and, in a Latin translation, in Europe too. In its Latin garb, full of strange mutilations of the Arabic original, it was one of the earliest works produced once the European printers began to work.

Reuben Levy, "Avicenna—His Life and Times," in Medical History, *Vol. 1, July, 1957, pp. 249-61.*

FURTHER READING

Bibliography

Anawati, Georges C. *Mu'allafāt Ibn Sīnā.* Cairo, 1950, 435 p.

    Bibliography listing 276 titles attributed to Avicenna.

Biography

Avicenna. *The Life of Ibn Sina: A Critical Edition and Annotated Translation.* Trans. William E. Gohlman. Albany: State University of New York Press, 1974. 163 p.

    Contains the complete Arabic text and an English translation of *Sirat al-Shaykh al-Ra'īs,* Avicenna's autobiography, completed by his student Abū 'Ubayd al-Jūzjānī.

Criticism

Afnan, Soheil M. *Avicenna: His Life and Works.* London: George Allen & Unwin, 1958, 298 p.

    Examines Avicenna's life and social milieu, and his approaches to logic, metaphysics, psychology, religion, and science in historical context.

Courtois, V., ed. *Avicenna Commemoration Volume.* Calcutta: Iran Society, 1956, 324 p.

    Collection of essays on Avicenna's life and works, written in honor of the millenary of his birth. The book includes essays written in English, German, French, and Arabic.

Craig, William Lane. "Ibn Sīnā." In *The Cosmological Argument from Plato to Leibniz,* pp. 86-98. London: Macmillan, 1980.

    Outlines Avicenna's arguments for the existence of God.

Goodman, Lenn E. *Avicenna.* London: Routledge, 1992, 240 p.

    Discusses Avicenna's life in historical context; his metaphysics, especially his synthesis of necessity and contingency, and his distinction between essence and existence; his arguments for the immortality of the soul; and his views on logic, rhetoric, and poetics.

Heath, Peter. "Allegory and Philosophy." In *Allegory and Philosophy in Avicenna (Ibn Sînâ); with a Translation of the Book of the Prophet Muhammad's Ascent to Heaven,* pp. 33-106. Philadelphia: University of Pennsylvania Press, 1992.

    Examines "the degree to which Avicenna's cosmological, psychological, and epistemological theories find parallel, if diverse, expression in the different formats of philosophical exposition and allegorical narration."

Houben, J. "Avicenna and Mysticism." *Indo-Iranica* VI,

No. 3 (January 1953): 1-17.

> Explores Avicenna's ideas in relation to mid-Eastern mysticism and claims that Avicenna's philosophy is not mystical because of his monism and his (over)emphasis on reason.

Marmura, Michael. "Avicenna's Psychological Proof of Prophecy." *Journal of Near Eastern Studies* XXII, No. 1 (January 1963): 49-56.

> Elucidates Avicenna's argument for the existence of prophetic ability.

Morewedge, Parviz. "A Third Version of the Ontological Argument in the Ibn Sīnian Metaphysics." In *Islamic Philosophical Theology,* edited by Parviz Morewedge, pp. 188-222. Albany: State University of New York Press, 1979.

> Examines Avicenna's concept of the Necessary Existent in his argument for God's existence, with special focus on the argument's experiential, "mystical" approach.

Nasr, Seyyed Hossein. "Ibn Sīnā." In *An Introduction to Islamic Cosmological Doctrines: Conceptions of Nature and Methods Used for Its Study by the Ikhwān Al-Safā, Al-Bīrūnī, and Ibn Sīnā,* rev. ed., pp. 175-274. Albany: State University of New York Press, 1993.

> Explores Avicenna's metaphysics and natural philosophy, and in particular his views on the relation between man and the universe.

Nogales, Salvador Gómez. "Ibn Sina." In *Religion, Learning, and Science in the 'Abbasid Period,* edited by

M. J. L. Young, J. D. Latham, and R. B. Serjeant, pp. 389-404. Cambridge University Press, 1990.

> Claims that, rather than merely having transmitted Greek ideas, Avicenna uniquely fused Islamic religion and philosophy.

Riordan, Joseph D. "God, Intellect, and Avicenna." In *God Knowable and Unknowable,* edited by Robert J. Roth, pp. 23-41. New York: Fordham University Press, 1973.

> Contrasts European philosophy, as typified by Averroës and a neglect of a mystical relationship with God, with the philosophy of Islam, as represented by Avicenna and the preservation of "intellectual intuition."

Siraisi, Nancy G. *Avicenna in Renaissance Italy: The "Canon" and Medical Teaching in Italian Universities after 1500.* Princeton: Princeton University Press, 1987, 410 p.

> Explores the reception of Avicenna's *Canon on Medicine* in Italy and its use as a standard text on medical theory and physiology. Siraisi discusses the *Canon*'s Italian commentators and translators, and includes a bibliography of Latin editions of the *Canon* and commentary written after 1500.

Wickens, G. M., ed. *Avicenna: Scientist & Philosopher; a Millenary Symposium.* London: Luzac & Company, 1952, 128 p.

> A collection of six essays discussing Avicenna's life and his influence on the development of Arabic philosophy, on Jewish thought, on Medieval science, and on the thirteenth-century West.

Additional coverage of Avicenna's life and career is contained in the following source published by Gale Research: *Dictionary of Literary Biography,* Vol. 115.

Odyssey

c. Eighth Century B.C.

Greek poem.

INTRODUCTION

For information on the *Iliad,* see *CMLC,* Volume 1.

The *Odyssey* is considered one of the greatest literary achievements of Western civilization. Composed of twenty-four books totaling over 12,000 lines, it details the wanderings of Odysseus, King of Ithaca, and focuses on his honor, bravery, resourcefulness, and nobility. Although the *Odyssey* has been deemed inferior to Homer's other epic, the *Iliad,* by many critics, it has been praised for its structural sophistication, thematic consistency, and complex characterization.

Plot and Major Characters

The story of the *Odyssey* begins ten years after the fall of Troy, during which interval Odysseus has been trying to return to Ithaca, where his wife, Penelope, is faithfully waiting for his return. The reader is first introduced to the hero, Odysseus, in Book V, near the end of his seven-year captivity by the goddess Calypso. Under Zeus's orders, Calypso releases Odysseus, who, after building an improvised boat, resumes his journey home. Along the way Odysseus stops at the island of Phaeacia, where he meets the young princess Nausicaa and recounts to the Phaeacians his adventures during the first three years after the Trojan War—with the Lotus-Eaters, the Cyclops, Circe, Scylla and Charybdis, and the Sirens. Odysseus sets out to sea again and upon his arrival in his kingdom discovers that Penelope is being courted by suitors who are also plotting to kill his son, Telemachos. Disguised as a beggar, Odysseus mingles with the suitors in his palace, talks with Penelope, and is recognized by his old nurse, Eurycleia. He is also reunited with Telemachos, and together they plan their revenge against the suitors. Penelope, longing for Odysseus's return but realizing that she can no longer delay replying to the suitors' marriage requests, decides to hold a bow-and-arrow contest and offers herself as the prize. The suitors try in vain to string Odysseus's bow, and finally Odysseus (still dressed as a beggar) steps forward to try. He succeeds, revealing his identity, and together he and Telemachos kill the suitors; Odysseus then approaches Penelope, who is still not convinced that he is truly her husband. As a final test to determine if her husband has really returned home, Penelope asks Od-

ysseus a question about their marriage bed, and his correct answer proves his identity. They go to their bed, make love, and exchange stories of what has happened since they were last together. Odysseus then resumes his place as King of Ithaca and restores peace to his kingdom.

Major Themes

The central theme of the *Odyssey* is that of disguise and recognition. The clearest example of this is Odysseus's concealment of his identity from his friends and family in Ithaca and the subsequent private scenes of recognition that structure the second half of the poem. Odysseus reveals his identity to a number of characters in the poem: his son, Telemachos, who then makes plans to help him kill the suitors; his dog, Argus, who recognizes his scent and dies from the excitement of his master's return home; his nurse, who sees the scar on his thigh by which she recognizes Odysseus as she bathes him; his wife, Penelope, who is cautious to believe he has returned; his father, Laertes, who regains physical and emotional strength upon his son's return home; and the suitors, who are punished for their selfish and underhanded actions during Odysseus's absence. Sheila Murnaghan has noted that, furthermore, "the reunions of these characters with Odysseus involve these characters' own shedding of disguise and recognition as well as his." Laertes, for example, sheds his rags and the weakness of old age upon Odysseus's return, becoming the strong patriarch that Odysseus left behind twenty years earlier. Telemachos also undergoes a change, but, unlike that of Laertes, it is not a recovery of a previous state but growth into a new state of maturity. The complex nature of the two main characters, Odysseus and Penelope, also plays an important part in the *Odyssey*. W. B. Stanford has praised Odysseus as "one of the fullest and most versatile characters in literature: a symbol of the Ionic-Greek Everyman in his eloquence, cleverness, unscrupulousness, intellectual curiosity, courage, endurance, shrewdness," and Nancy Felson-Rubin has observed that, "the Penelope who emerges by the end of the poem is a forceful figure who operates imaginatively within the constraints of her situation and succeeds in keeping her options open until she reaches safety in her husband's embrace."

Textual History

Authorship of the *Odyssey* has traditionally been attributed to the blind Greek bard Homer, but his relation to the *Iliad* and the *Odyssey* has incited much scholarly inquiry and has brought together the efforts of experts in such fields as archeology, linguistics, art, and comparative literature. As a result of their research, three main theories regarding the composition of the poems have emerged: the analytic, the separatist, and the unitarian. Until the publication of Friedrich Adolph Wolf's *Prolegomena ad Homerum* in 1795, the notion that Homer was the author of the *Iliad* and the *Odyssey* was largely undisputed. However, citing certain inconsistencies and errors in the texts, Wolf asserted that the two works were not the compositions of one poet, but the products of many different authors at work on various traditional poems and stories over time. Wolf's argument convinced many critics—who were subsequently termed the analysts—but also inspired the notorious authorship controversy known as the "Homeric question." Another theory that escalated at this time was that of the separatists, who believed that the *Odyssey* and the *Iliad* were written by two different authors who may not have even known about each other's works. While these two views prevailed throughout the nineteenth and early twentieth centuries, they were ultimately challenged by an opposing group of critics, the unitarians, whose primary spokesman was Andrew Lang. The unitarians insisted that a single individual of genius composed the Homeric epics, supporting their claim by citing a unified sensibility, original style, and consistent use of themes and imag-

ery in the poems. Another theory, proposed by Samuel Butler in 1897, asserted that the *Odyssey* was written by Nausicaa, a young woman from Trapani and a member of King Alcinous's household, but this theory has been widely discredited among scholars.

The textual history of the *Odyssey* is assumed to have begun with an oral version of the poem which was transmitted by local bards and probably recorded on papyri shortly after Homer's death. Although Homeric Greece did not yet have a system of writing appropriate for literary texts, records indicate that a Phoenician alphabet may have been adapted and used for this purpose in the eighth century B.C. Once set down in writing, the poems most likely became the exclusive proprety of the *Homeridae*, or sons of Homer, a bardic guild whose members performed and preserved the poems. Scholars believe that in the second half of the sixth century B.C. the Athenian dictator Peisistratus, who ruled from 560-27 B.C., established a Commission of Editors of Homer to edit the text of the poems and remove any errors and interpolations that had accumulated in the process of transmission—thereby establishing a Canon of Homer. Fragments of papyrus have been found in Egypt, the earliest dating from the third century B.C., but the oldest complete manuscript is the Laurentianus of the tenth or eleventh century A.D. The first printed edition of Homer's poetry appeared in Europe in 1488 and remained in use until the seventeenth century. Many translations of the *Odyssey* have subsequently been published; critics agree that the most influential translations have been those by George Chapman, Alexander Pope, Samuel Butler, and Richmond Lattimore.

Critical Reception

The *Odyssey* has often been unfavorably compared to the *Iliad* by critics who have condemned it for its excessive repetitiveness, drawn-out narrative, and lack of unity. Yet in spite of its weaknesses, the *Odyssey* is still considered one of the greatest literary works of all time. G. S. Kirk has stated that, "no one in his senses can deny that the poem is a marvelous accomplishment," and Stephen V. Tracy has asserted that, "the *Odyssey* has something for everyone; it is a highly entertaining adventure story." One aspect of the poem on which scholars have focused is that of the origin and artistic merit of the first four books of the *Odyssey*, collectively known as the *Telemachia*. Cited by some critics as evidence in support of the analytic theory because of its distinctive treatment, the *Telemachia*, according to other critics, is indeed a part of the original story and figures prominently as a necessary link to establishing Odysseus's importance and stature within Ithaca. Pointing out the centrality of the *Telemachia* in the *Odyssey*, J. W. Mackail has commented that, "nothing in the *Iliad* is such a feat of design as the way in which the first four books of the *Odyssey* do not bring Odysseus onto the scene at all and yet imply him through every line as the central figure." Differences in style between the *Odyssey* and the *Iliad* have also prompted significant debate, particularly the *Odyssey*'s greater emphasis on myth, prominence of women in the poem, and downplaying the lore of warfare. Samuel Eliot Bassett has noted that, "the *Iliad* is a tale of war, unmarked by trickery: the *Odyssey* of domestic intrigue," and Andrew Lang has observed that, "the *Odyssey* is calmer, more reflective, more religious than the *Iliad*, being a poem of peace." Examining the role of the gods in the *Odyssey*, Samuel Butler has noted an evolution, contending that "in the *Odyssey* the gods no longer live in houses and sleep in four-post bedsteads, but the conception of their abode, like that of their existence altogether, is far more spiritual." As early as the eighteenth century, Alexander Pope cautioned, "whoever reads the *Odyssey* with an eye to the *Iliad*, expecting to find it of the same character, or of the same sort of spirit, will be grievously deceived." Although critics still debate the relative merits of the *Odyssey* compared to those of the *Iliad*, most agree with Stanford's assertion that "few long poems equal it in the variety and charm of its word-music, and few stories surpass it in sustained excitement and human interest."

PRINCIPAL ENGLISH TRANSLATIONS

The Odysseys of Homer (translated by George Chapman) 1614
The Odyssey of Homer (translated by Alexander Pope) 1725
Homer's Iliad and Odyssey (translated by William Cowper) 1791
The Odyssey of Homer (translated by Theodore Alois Buckley) 1855
The Odyssey of Homer (translated by William Cullen Bryant) 1871
The Odyssey of Homer (translated by S. H. Butcher and A. Lang) 1888
The Odyssey (translated by Samuel Butler) 1900
The Odyssey (translated by J. W. Mackail) 1903-10
The Odyssey (translated by A. T. Murray) 1919
The Odyssey of Homer (translated by T. E. Lawrence) 1932
The Odyssey (translated by E. V. Rieu) 1945
The Odyssey of Homer (translated by Ennis Rees) 1960
The Odyssey (translated by Robert Fitzgerald) 1961
The Odyssey of Homer (translated by Richmond Lattimore) 1967

CRITICISM

George Chapman (essay date 1614)

SOURCE: A dedication to the *Odyssey*, in *Chapman's*

Homer: The "Iliad," the "Odyssey," and the Lesser Homerica, Vol. 2, edited by Allardyce Nicoll, Pantheon Books, 1956, pp. 3-8.

[*A successful English dramatist and poet, Chapman is chiefly remembered as a scholar and translator of Homer's works. While his merits as a translator are often debated by scholars, his* Iliad *and* Odyssey *remain landmarks in Homer studies. In his 1614 dedication of the* Odyssey *to Robert Carr, Earl of Somerset, Chapman deems Homer "the most wise and most divine Poet."*]

TO THE
MOST WORTHILY HONORED,
MY SINGULAR GOOD LORD, ROBERT,
EARLE OF SOMERSET,
Lord Chamberlaine, & c

I have adventured, Right Noble Earle, out of my utmost and ever-vowed service to your Vertues, to entitle their Merits to the Patronage of Homer's English life—whose wisht naturall life the great Macedon would have protected as the spirit of his Empire—

That he to his unmeasur'd mightie Acts
Might adde a Fame as vast, and their extracts,
In fires as bright and endlesse as the starres,
His breast might breathe and thunder out his warres.
But that great Monark's love of fame and praise
Receives an envious Cloud in our foule daies—
For, since our Great ones ceasse themselves to do
Deeds worth their praise, they hold it folly too
To feed their praise in others. But what can
(Of all the gifts that are) be given to man
More precious than Eternitie and Glorie,
Singing their praises in unsilenc't storie
Which no blacke Day, no Nation, nor no Age,
No change of Time or Fortune, Force nor Rage,
Shall ever race? All which the Monarch knew
Where Homer liv'd entitl'd would ensew:
          —*Cuius de gurgite vivo*
*Combibit arcanos vatum omnis turba furores,
&c.—*
From whose deepe Fount of life the thirstie rout
Of Thespian Prophets have lien sucking out
Their sacred rages. And as th'influent stone
Of Father Jove's great and laborious Sonne
Lifts high the heavie Iron and farre implies
The wide Orbs that the Needle rectifies
In vertuous guide of every sea-driven course,
To all aspiring his one boundlesse force:

So from one Homer all the holy fire
That ever did the hidden heate inspire
In each true Muse came cleerly sparkling
    downe,
And must for him compose one flaming
    Crowne.
He, at Jove's Table set, fils out to us
Cups that repaire Age sad and ruinous,
And gives it Built of an eternall stand
With his all-sinewie Odyssean hand—
Shifts Time and Fate, puts Death in Life's
    free state
And Life doth into Ages propagate.
He doth in Men the Gods' affects inflame,
His fuell Vertue, blowne by Praise and Fame,
And, with the high soule's first impulsions
    driven,
Breakes through rude Chaos, Earth, the Seas
    and Heaven.
The Nerves of all things hid in Nature lie
Naked before him, all their Harmonie
Tun'd to his Accents, that in Beasts breathe
    Minds.
What Fowles, what Floods, what Earth, what
    Aire, what Winds,
What fires Æthereall, what the Gods conclude
In all their Counsels, his Muse makes indude
With varied voices, that even rockes have
    mov'd.
And yet for all this, naked Vertue lov'd,
Honors without her he as abject prises,
And foolish Fame deriv'd from thence
    despises—
When, from the vulgar taking glorious bound
Up to the Mountaine where the Muse is
    crownd,
He sits and laughs to see the jaded Rabble
Toile to his hard heights, t'all accesse unable,
    &c.

*And that your Lordship may in his Face take view
of his Mind, the first word of his **Iliads** is . . .
wrath; the first word of his **Odysses**, . . . Man—
contracting in either word his each worke's
Proposition. In one, Predominant Perturbation; in
the other, over-ruling Wisedome; in one, the Bodie's
fervour and fashion of outward Fortitude to all
possible height of Heroicall Action; in the other,
the Mind's inward, constant and unconquerd
Empire, unbroken, unalterd with any most insolent
and tyrannous infliction. To many most soveraigne
praises is this Poeme entitled, but to that Grace in
chiefe which sets on the Crowne both of Poets and
Orators, . . . Parva magnè dicere, pervulgata nove,
jejuna plenè: To speake things litle, greatly; things
commune, rarely; things barren and emptie,
fruitfully and fully. The returne of a man into his
Countrie is his whole scope and object, which in
itselfe, your Lordship may well say, is jejune and
fruitlesse enough, affoording nothing feastfull,
nothing magnificent. And yet even this doth the*
*divine inspiration render vast, illustrous and of
miraculous composure. And for this, my Lord, is
this Poeme preferred to his **Iliads**; for therein much
magnificence, both of person and action, gives great
aide to his industrie, but in this are these helpes
exceeding sparing or nothing; and yet is the
Structure so elaborate and pompous that the poore
plaine Groundworke (considered together) may
seeme the naturally rich wombe to it and produce
it needfully. Much wondered at, therefore, is the
Censure of Dionysius Longinus (a man otherwise
affirmed, grave and of elegant judgement),
comparing Homer in his **Iliads** to the Sunne rising,
in his **Odysses** to his descent or setting, or to the
Ocean robd of his aesture, many tributorie flouds
and rivers of excellent ornament withheld from their
observance—when this his worke so farre exceeds
the Ocean, with all his Court and concourse, that
all his Sea is onely a serviceable streame to it. Nor
can it be compared to any One power to be named
in nature, being an entirely wel-sorted and digested
Confluence of all—where the most solide and grave
is made as nimble and fluent as the most airie and
firie, the nimble and fluent as firme and well-
bounded as the most grave and solid. And (taking
all together) of so tender impression, and of such
Command to the voice of the Muse, that they knocke
heaven with her breath and discover their
foundations as low as hell. Nor is this all-comprising
Poesie phantastique, or meere fictive, but the most
material and doctrinall illations of Truth, both for
all manly information of Manners in the yong, all
prescription of Justice, and even Christian pietie,
in the most grave and high-governd. To illustrate
both which in both kinds, with all height of
expression, the Poet creates both a Bodie and a
Soule in them—wherein, if the Bodie (being the
letter, or historie) seemes fictive and beyond
Possibilitie to bring into Act, the sence then and
Allegorie (which is the Soule) is to be sought—
which intends a more eminent expressure of Vertue,
for her lovelinesse, and of Vice, for her uglinesse,
in their severall effects, going beyond the life than
any Art within life can possibly delineate. Why then
is Fiction to this end so hatefull to our true
Ignorants? Or why should a poore Chronicler of a
Lord Maior's naked Truth (that peradventure will
last his yeare) include more worth with our moderne
wizerds than Homer for his naked Ulysses, clad in
eternall Fiction? But this Prozer Dionysius and the
rest of these grave and reputatively learned (that
dare undertake for their gravities the headstrong
censure of all things, and challenge the
understanding of these Toyes in their childhoods,
when even these childish vanities retaine deepe and
most necessarie learning enough in them to make
them children in their ages and teach them while
they live) are not in these absolutely divine Infusions
allowed either voice or relish—for Qui Poeticas ad
fores accedit, &c., sayes the Divine Philosopher, he
that knocks at the Gates of the Muses, sine Musarum
furore, is neither to be admitted entrie nor a touch
at their Thresholds, his opinion of entrie ridiculous
and his presumption impious. Nor must Poets
themselves (might I a litle insist on these contempts,*

not tempting too farre your Lordship's Ulyssean patience) presume to these doores without the truly genuine and peculiar induction—there being in Poesie a twofold rapture (or alienation of soule, as the abovesaid Teacher termes it), one Insania, *a disease of the mind and a meere madnesse, by which the infected is thrust beneath all the degrees of humanitie,* et ex homine Brutum quodammodo redditur *(for which poore Poesie in this diseasd and impostorous age is so barbarously vilified); the other is* Divinus furor, *by which the sound and divinely healthfull* supra hominis naturam erigitur, et in Deum transit: *one a perfection directly infused from God, the other an infection obliquely and degenerately proceeding from man. Of the divine Furie, my Lord, your Homer hath ever bene both first and last Instance, being pronounced absolutely . . . the most wise and most divine Poet—against whom whosoever shall open his prophane mouth may worthily receive answer with this of his divine defender (Empedocles, Heraclitus, Protagoras, Epicharmus, &c. being of Homer's part) . . . &c., who against such an Armie and the Generall Homer dares attempt the assault but he must be reputed ridiculous? And yet against this hoast and this invincible Commander shall we have every Besogne and foole a Leader—the common herd (I assure myself) readie to receive it on their hornes, their infected Leaders*

Such men as sideling ride the ambling Muse,
Whose saddle is as frequent as the stuse,
Whose Raptures are in every Pageant seene,
In every Wassall rime and Dancing greene—
When he that writes by any beame of Truth
Must dive as deepe as he past shallow youth.
Truth dwels in Gulphs, whose Deepes hide shades so rich
That Night sits muffl'd there in clouds of pitch,
More Darke than Nature made her, and requires,
To cleare her tough mists, Heaven's great fire of fires,
To whom the Sunne it selfe is but a Beame.
For sicke soules then (but rapt in foolish Dreame)
To wrestle with these Heav'n-strong mysteries
What madnesse is it—when their light serves eies
That are not worldly in their least aspect
But truly pure and aime at Heaven direct.
Yet these none like but what the brazen head
Blatters abroad, no sooner borne but dead.

Holding then in eternal contempt, my Lord, those short-lived Bubbles, eternize your vertue and judgement with the Grecian Monark, esteeming not as the least of your New-yeare's Presents

Homer, three thousand yeares dead, now reviv'd

Even from that dull Death that in life he liv'd,
When none conceited him, none understood,
That so much life in so much death as blood
Conveys about it could mixe. But when Death
Drunke up the bloudie Mist that humane breath
Pour'd round about him (Povertie and Spight
Thickning the haplesse vapor), then Truth's light
Glimmerd about his Poeme; the pincht soule
(Amidst the Mysteries it did enroule)
Brake powrefully abroad. And as we see
The Sunne, all hid in clouds, at length got free,
Through some forc't covert, over all the wayes
Neare and beneath him, shootes his vented rayes
Farre off and stickes them in some litle Glade,
All woods, fields, rivers left besides in shade:
So your Apollo, from that world of light
Closde in his Poem's bodie, shot to sight
Some few forc't Beames, which neare him were not seene
(As in his life or countrie), Fate and Spleene
Clouding their radiance, which, when Death had clear'd,
To farre-off Regions his free beames appear'd—
In which all stood and wonderd, striving which
His Birth and Rapture should in right enrich.
Twelve Labours of your Thespian Hercules
I now present your Lorship. Do but please
To lend Life meanes till th' other Twelve receave
Equall atchievement—and let Death then reave
My life now lost in our Patrician Loves
That knocke heads with the herd, in whom there moves
One blood, one soule, both drownd in one set height
Of stupid Envie and meere popular Spight,
Whose loves with no good did my least veine fill,
And from their hates I feare as little ill.
Their Bounties nourish not when most they feed,
But where there is no Merit or no Need;
Raine into rivers still; and are such showres
As bubbles spring and overflow the flowres.
Their worse parts and worst men their Best subornes,
Like winter Cowes, whose milke runnes to their hornes.
And as litigious Clients' bookes of Law
Cost infinitely, taste of all the Awe
Bencht in our kingdome's Policie, Pietie, State,

Earne all their deepe explorings, satiate
All sorts there thrust together by the heart
With thirst of wisedome spent on either part,
Horrid examples made of Life and Death
From their fine stuffe woven—yet, when once
    the breath
Of sentence leaves them, all their worth is
    drawne
As drie as dust and weares like Cobweb
    Lawne:
So these men set a price upon their worth
That no man gives but those that trot it forth
Through Need's foule wayes, feed Humors
    with all cost
Though Judgement sterves in them, Rout
    State-engrost
(At all Tabacco benches, solemne Tables,
Where all that crosse their Envies are their
    fables)
In their ranke faction, Shame and Death
    approv'd
Fit Penance for their Opposites, none lov'd
But those that rub them, not a Reason heard
That doth not sooth and glorifie their preferd
Bitter Opinions—when, would Truth resume
The cause to his hands, all would flie in fume
Before his sentence, since the innocent mind
Just God makes good, to whom their worst is
    wind.
For that I freely all my Thoughts expresse
My Conscience is my Thousand witnesses,
And to this stay my constant Comforts vow:
You for the world I have, or God for you.

René Le Bossu (essay date 1675)

SOURCE: "Selections from *Treatise of the Epick Poem* (1675) translated by W. J.," in *The Continental Model: Selected French Critical Essays of the Seventeenth Century, in English Translation,* edited by Scott Elledge and Donald Schier; revised edition, Cornell, 1970, pp. 307-23.

[*Le Bossu was a French critic best known for his* Treatise on Epic Poetry, *written in 1675. Much discussed in England even before it was translated into English, the* Treatise *was severely criticized by Samuel Johnson and, in France, by Voltaire for its rigid rules concerning epic poetry. In the following excerpt from that work, Le Bossu analyzes Homer's crafting of the hero of the* Odyssey, *Ulysses.*]

The *Odyssey* was not designed, like the *Iliad,* for the instruction of all the states of Greece joined in one body, but for each state in particular. As a state is composed of two parts, the head which commands and the members which obey, there are instructions requisite for both, to teach the one to govern and the others to submit to government.

There are two virtues necessary to one in authority: prudence to order, and care to see his orders put in execution. The prudence of a politician is not acquired but by a long experience in all sorts of business, and by an acquaintance with all the different forms of governments and states. The care of the administration suffers not him that has the government to rely upon others, but requires his own presence, and kings who are absent from their states are in danger of losing them, and give occasion to great disorders and confusion.

These two points may be easily united in one and the same man. A king forsakes his kingdom to visit the courts of several princes, where he learns the manners and customs of different nations. From hence there naturally arises a vast number of incidents, of dangers, and of adventures, very useful for a political institution. On the other side, this absence gives way to the disorders which happen in his own kingdom, and which end not till his return, whose presence only can re-establish all things. Thus the absence of a king has the same effects in this fable as the division of the princes had in the former.

The subjects have scarce any need but of one general maxim, which is to suffer themselves to be governed and to obey faithfully, whatever reason they may imagine against the orders they receive. It is easy to join this instruction with the other by bestowing on this wise and industrious prince such subjects as in his absence would rather follow their own judgment than his commands, and by demonstrating the misfortunes which this disobedience draws upon them, the evil consequences which almost infallibly attend these particular notions, which are entirely different from the general idea of him who ought to govern.

But as it was necessary that the princes in the *Iliad* should be choleric and quarrelsome, so it is necessary in the fable of the *Odyssey* that the chief person should be sage and prudent. This raises a difficulty in the fiction, because this person ought to be absent for the two reasons aforementioned, which are essential to the fable and which constitute the principal aim of it; but he cannot absent himself without offending against another maxim of equal importance, viz., that a king should upon no account leave his country.

It is true there are sometimes such necessities as sufficiently excuse the prudence of a politician in this point. But such a necessity is a thing important enough of itself to supply matter for another poem, and this multiplication of the action would be vicious. To prevent which, in the first place, this necessity and the departure of the hero must be disjoined from the poem; and in the second place, the hero having been obliged to absent himself for a reason antecedent to the action and placed distinct from the fable, he ought not so far to embrace this opportunity of instructing himself as to absent himself voluntarily from his own government. For at this rate, his absence would be merely voluntary, and one might with reason lay to his charge all the disorders which might arise.

Thus in the constitution of the fable he ought not to take for his action and for the foundation of his poem the departure of a prince from his own country nor his voluntary stay in any other place, but his return, and this return retarded against his will. This is the first idea Homer gives us of it. His hero appears at first in a desolate island, sitting upon the side of the sea, which, with tears in his eyes, he looks upon as the obstacle which had so long opposed his return and detained him from revisiting his own dear country.

And lastly, since this forced delay might more naturally and usually happen to such as make voyages by sea, Homer has judiciously made choice of a prince whose kingdom was in an island.

Let us see then how he has feigned all this action, making his hero a person in years, because years are requisite to instruct a man in prudence and policy.

A prince had been obliged to forsake his native country and to head an army of his subjects in a foreign expedition. Having gloriously performed this enterprise, he was marching home again, and conducting his subjects to his own state. But spite of all the attempts with which his eagerness to return had inspired him, he was stopped by the way by tempests for several years, and cast upon several countries differing from each other in manners and government. In these dangers his companions, not always following his orders, perished through their own fault. The grandees of his country strangely abuse his absence, and raise no small disorders at home. They consume his estate, conspire to destroy his son, would constrain his queen to accept of one of them for her husband, and indulge themselves in all violence, so much the more because they were persuaded he would never return. But at last he returns, and discovering himself only to his son and some others who had continued firm to him, he is an eyewitness of the insolence of his enemies, punishes them according to their deserts, and restores to his island that tranquillity and repose to which they had been strangers during his absence.

As the truth which serves for foundation to this fiction is that the absence of a person from his own home or his neglect of his own affairs is the cause of great disorders, so the principal point of the action, and the most essential one, is the absence of the hero. This fills almost all the poem. For not only this real absence lasted several years, but even when the hero returned

A Greek vase decorated with a representation of Odysseus.

he does not discover himself; and this prudent disguise, from whence he reaped so much advantage, has the same effect upon the authors of the disorders, and all others who knew him not, as his real absence had before, so that he is absent as to them till the very moment of their punishment.

After the poet had thus composed his fable and joined the fiction to the truth, he then makes choice of Ulysses, the king of the isle of Ithaca, to maintain the character of his chief personage, and bestowed the rest upon Telemachus, Penelope, Antinous, and others, whom he calls by what names he pleases.

I shall not here insist upon the many excellent advices which are so many parts and natural consequences of the fundamental truth, and which the poet very dexterously lays down in those fictions which are the episodes and members of the entire action. Such for instance are these advices: not to intrude oneself into the mysteries of government which the prince keeps secret; (this is represented to us by the winds shut up in a bullhide, which the miserable companions of Ulysses would needs be so foolish as to pry into); not to suffer oneself to be led away by the seeming charms of an idle and inactive life, to which the Sirens' song invited; not to suffer oneself to be sensualized by pleasures, like those who were changed into brutes by Circe; and a great many other points of morality necessary for all sorts of people.

This poem is more useful to the people than the *Iliad,* where the subjects suffer rather by the ill conduct of their princes than through their own miscarriages. But in the *Odyssey* it is not the fault of Ulysses that is the ruin of his subjects. This wise prince leaves untried no method to make them partakers of the benefit of his return. Thus the poet in the *Iliad* says he sings the anger of Achilles, which had caused the death of so many Grecians, and, on the contrary, in the *Odyssey* he tells his readers that the subjects perished through their own fault.

Thomas Hobbes (essay date 1675)

SOURCE: "Preface to Homer (1675)," in *Critical Essays of the Seventeenth Century, Vol. II: 1650-1685,* edited by J.E. Spingarn, Oxford at the Clarendon Press, 1908, pp. 67-76.

[*Hobbes is best known for such philosophical writings as* Human Nature *(1650),* Elements of Law *(1650),* Leviathan; or, the Matter, Form, and Power of a Commonwealth, Ecclesiastical and Civil *(1651), and* Elements of Philosophy *(1655). As a young man he knew Francis Bacon and assisted the great Lord Chancellor in translating several of his essays into Latin. Hobbes was greatly influenced by the works of Galileo and his contemporary, Descartes. In his 1675 preface to the* Odyssey, *Hobbes examines the seven virtues of a heroic poem.*]

1675
To The
Reader,
concerning
The Vertues of an
Heroique Poem

The Vertues required in an Heroick Poem, and indeed in all Writings published, are comprehended all in this one word, *Discretion.*

And Discretion consisteth in this, That every part of the Poem be conducing, and in good order placed, to the End and Designe of the Poet. And the Designe is not only to profit, but also to delight the Reader.

By Profit, I intend not here any accession of Wealth, either to the Poet, or to the Reader; but accession of Prudence, Justice, Fortitude, by the example of such Great and Noble Persons as he introduceth speaking, or describeth acting. For all men love to behold, though

not to practise, Vertue. So that at last the work of an Heroique Poet is no more but to furnish an ingenuous Reader (when his leisure abounds) with the diversion of an honest and delightful Story, whether true or feigned.

But because there be many men called Critiques, and Wits, and Vertuosi, that are accustomed to censure the Poets, and most of them of divers Judgments: How is it possible (you'l say) to please them all? Yes, very well; if the Poem be as it should be. For men can judge what's good, that know not what is best. For he that can judge what is best, must have considered all those things (though they be almost innumerable) that concur to make the reading of an Heroique Poem pleasant. Whereof I'll name as many as shall come into my mind.

And they are contained, first, in the choice of words. Secondly, in the construction. Thirdly, in the contrivance of the Story or Fiction. Fourthly, in the Elevation of the Fancie. Fifthly, in the Justice and Impartiality of the Poet. Sixthly, in the clearness of Descriptions. Seventhly, in the Amplitude of the Subject.

And (to begin with words) the first Indiscretion is, The use of such words as to the Readers of Poesie (which are commonly Persons of the best Quality) are not sufficiently known. For the work of an Heroique Poem is to raise admiration, principally, for three Vertues, Valour, Beauty, and Love; to the reading whereof Women no less than Men have a just pretence, though their skill in Language be not so universal. And therefore forein words, till by long use they become vulgar, are unintelligible to them. Also the names of Instruments and Tools of Artificers, and words of Art, though of use in the Schools, are far from being fit to be spoken by a Heroe. He may delight in the Arts themselves, and have skill in some of them; but his Glory lies not in that, but in Courage, Nobility, and other Vertues of Nature, or in the Command he has over other men. Nor does *Homer* in any part of his Poem attribute any praise to *Achilles,* or any blame to *Alexander,* for that they had both learnt to play upon the Ghittarre. The character of words that become a Heroe are Property and Significancy, but without both the malice and lasciviousness of a Satyr.

Another Vertue of an Heroique Poem is the Perspicuity and the Facility of Construction, and consisteth in a natural contexture of the words, so as not to discover the labour but the natural ability of the Poet; and this is usually called a good Style. For the order of words, when placed as they ought to be, carries a light before it, whereby a man may foresee the length of his period, as a torch in the night shews a man the stops and unevenness in his way. But when plac'd unnaturally, the Reader will often find unexpected checks, and be forced to go back and hunt for the sense, and suffer such unease, as in a Coach a man unexpectedly finds in passing over a furrow. And though the Laws of Verse (which have bound the Greeks and Latines to number of Feet and quantity of Syllables, and the English and other Nations to number of Syllables and Rime) put great constraint upon the natural course of Language, yet the Poet, having the liberty to depart from what is obstinate, and to chuse somewhat else that is more obedient to such Laws, and no less fit for his purpose, shall not be, neither by the measure nor by the necessity of Rime, excused; though a Translation often may.

A third Vertue lies in the Contrivance. For there is difference between a Poem and a History in Prose. For a History is wholly related by the Writer; but in a Heroique Poem the Narration is, a great part of it, put upon some of the persons introduced by the Poet. So *Homer* begins not his **Iliad** with the injury done by *Paris,* but makes it related by *Menelaus,* and very briefly, as a thing notorious; nor begins he his **Odysses** with the departure of *Ulysses* from *Troy,* but makes *Ulysses* himself relate the same to *Alcinous,* in the midst of his Poem; which I think much more pleasant and ingenious than a too precise and close following of the time.

A fourth is in the Elevation of Fancie, which is generally taken for the greatest praise of Heroique Poetry; and is so, when governed by discretion. For men more generally affect and admire Fancie than they do either Judgment, or Reason, or Memory, or any other intellectual Vertue; and for the pleasantness of it, give to it alone the name of Wit, accounting Reason and Judgment but for a dull entertainment. For in Fancie consisteth the Sublimity of a Poet, which is that Poetical Fury which the Readers for the most part call for. It flies abroad swiftly to fetch in both Matter and Words; but if there be not Discretion at home to distinguish which are fit to be used and which not, which decent and which undecent for Persons, Times, and Places, their delight and grace is lost. But if they be discreetly used, they are greater ornaments of a Poem by much than any other. A Metaphor also (which is a Comparison contracted into a word) is not unpleasant; but when they are sharp and extraordinary, they are not fit for an Heroique Poet, nor for a publique consultation, but only for an Accusation or Defence at the Bar.

A fifth lies in the Justice and Impartiality of the Poet, and belongeth as well to History as to Poetry. For both the Poet and the Historian writeth only (or should do) matter of Fact. And as far as the truth of Fact can defame a man, so far they are allowed to blemish the reputation of Persons. But to do the same upon Report, or by inference, is below the dignity not only of a Heroe but of a Man. For neither a Poet nor an Historian ought to make himself an absolute Master of any

mans good name. None of the Emperors of *Rome* whom *Tacitus* or any other Writer hath condemned, was ever subject to the Judgment of any of them, nor were they ever heard to plead for themselves, which are things that ought to be antecedent to condemnation. Nor was, I think, *Epicurus* the Philosopher (who is transmitted to us by the Stoicks for a man of evil and voluptuous life) ever called, convented, and lawfully convicted, as all men ought to be before they be defamed. Therefore 'tis a very great fault in a Poet to speak evil of any man in their Writings Historical.

A sixth Vertue consists in the perfection and curiosity of Descriptions, which the ancient writers of Eloquence called *Icones,* that is, *Images.* And an Image is always a part, or rather the ground, of a Poetical comparison. As, for example, when *Virgil* would set before our eyes the fall of *Troy,* he describes perhaps the whole Labour of many men together in the felling of some great Tree, and with how much ado it fell. This is the Image. To which if you but add these words, So fell *Troy,* you have the Comparison entire; the grace whereof lieth in the lightsomness, and is but the description of all, even of the minutest, parts of the thing described; that not onely they that stand far off, but also they that stand near, and look upon it with the oldest spectacles of a Critique, may approve it. For a Poet is a Painter, and should paint Actions to the understanding with the most decent words, as Painters do Persons and Bodies with the choicest colours to the eye; which, if not done nicely, will not be worthy to be plac'd in a Cabinet.

The seventh Vertue which lying in the Amplitude of the Subject, is nothing but variety, and a thing without which a whole Poem would be no pleasanter than an Epigram, or one good Verse; nor a Picture of a hundred figures better than any one of them asunder, if drawn with equal art. And these are the Vertues which ought especially to be looked upon by the Critiques, in the comparing of the Poets, *Homer* with *Virgil,* or *Virgil* with *Lucan.* For these only, for their excellencie, I have read or heard compared.

If the comparison be grounded upon the first and second Vertues, which consist in known words and Style unforc'd, they are all excellent in their own Language, though perhaps the Latin than the Greek is apter to dispose it self into an Hexameter Verse, as having both fewer Monosyllables and fewer Polysyllables. And this may make the Latin Verse appear more grave and equal, which is taken for a kind of Majesty; though in truth there be no Majesty in words, but then when they seem to proceed from an high and weighty imployment of the minde. But neither *Homer,* nor *Virgil,* nor *Lucan,* nor any Poet writing commendably, though not excellently, was ever charged much with unknown words, or great constraint of Style, as being a fault proper to Translators, when they hold themselves too superstitiously to their Authors words.

In the third Vertue, which is Contrivance, there is no doubt but *Homer* excels them all. For their Poems, except the Introduction of their Gods, are but so many Histories in Verse; whereas *Homer* has woven so many Histories together as contain the whole Learning of his time (which the Greeks called *Cyclopædia*), and furnished both the Greek and Latin Stages with all the Plots and Arguments of their Tragedies.

The fourth Vertue, which is the height of Fancie, is almost proper to *Lucan,* and so admirable in him, that no Heroique Poem raises such admiration of the Poet as his hath done, though not so great admiration of the persons he introduceth. And though it be the mark of a great Wit, yet it is fitter for a Rhetorician than a Poet, and rebelleth often against Discretion, as when he says,

> *Victrix causa Diis placuit, sed victa Catoni;*

that is,

> *The Side that Won the Gods approved most,*
> *But* Cato *better lik'd the Side that lost.*

Than which nothing could be spoken more gloriously to the Exaltation of a man, nor more disgracefully to the Depression of the Gods. *Homer* indeed maketh some Gods for the *Greeks,* and some for the *Trojans,* but always makes *Jupiter* impartial: And never prefers the judgment of a man before that of *Jupiter,* much less before the judgment of all the Gods together.

The fifth Vertue, which is the Justice and Impartiality of a Poet, is very eminent in *Homer* and *Virgil,* but the contrary in *Lucan. Lucan* shews himself openly in the *Pompeyan* Faction, inveighing against *Cæsar* throughout his Poem, like *Cicero* against *Cataline* or *Marc Antony,* and is therefore justly reckon'd by *Quintilian* as a Rhetorician rather than a Poet. And a great part of the delight of his Readers proceedeth from the pleasure which too many men take to hear Great persons censured. But *Homer* and *Virgil* (especially *Homer*) do every where what they can to preserve the Reputation of their Heroes.

If we compare *Homer* and *Virgil* by the sixth Vertue, which is the clearness of Images, or Descriptions, it is manifest that *Homer* ought to be preferr'd, though *Virgil* himself were to be the Judge. For there are very few Images in *Virgil* besides those which he hath translated out of *Homer;* so that *Virgils* Images are *Homers* Praises. But what if he have added something to it of his own? Though he have, yet it is no addition of praise, because 'tis easie. But he hath some Images which are not in *Homer,* and better than his. It may be so; and so may other Poets have which never durst

compare themselves with *Homer.* Two or three fine sayings are not enough to make a Wit. But where is that Image of his better done by him than *Homer,* of those that have been done by them both? Yes, *Eustathius,* as Mr. *Ogilby* hath observ'd, where they both describe the falling of a Tree, prefers *Virgil's* description. But *Eustathius* is in that, I think, mistaken. The place of *Homer* is in the fourth of the **Iliads,** the sense whereof is this:

> *As when a man hath fell'd a Poplar Tree*
> *Tall, streight, and smooth, with all the fair*
>   *boughs on;*
> *Of which he means a Coach-wheel made shall*
>   *be,*
> *And leaves it on the Bank to dry i' th' Sun:*
> *So lay the comely* Simoisius,
> *Slain by great* Ajax, *Son of* Telamon.

It is manifest that in this place *Homer* intended no more than to shew how comely the body of *Simoisius* appeared as he lay dead upon the Bank of *Scamander,* streight and tall, with a fair head of hair, and like a streight and high Poplar with the boughs still on; and not at all to describe the manner of his falling, which, when a man is wounded through the breast, as he was with a Spear, is always sudden.

The description of how a great Tree falleth, when many men together hew it down, is in the second of *Virgil's Æneads.* The sense of it, with the comparison, is in English this;

> *And* Troy, *methought, then sunk in fire and*
>   *smoke,*
> *And overturned was in every part:*
> *As when upon the mountain an old Oak*
> *Is hewn about with keen steel to the heart,*
> *And pli'd by Swains with many heavy blows,*
> *It nods and every way it threatens round,*
> *Till overcome with many wounds, it bows,*
> *And leisurely at last comes to the ground.*

And here again it is evident that *Virgil* meant to compare the manner how *Troy* after many Battles, and after the losses of many Cities, conquer'd by the many nations under *Agamemnon* in a long War, and thereby weaken'd, and at last overthrown, with a great Tree hewn round about, and then falling by little and little leisurely.

So that neither these two Descriptions nor the two Comparisons can be compared together. The Image of a man lying on the ground is one thing; the Image of falling, especially of a Kingdom, is another. This therefore gives no advantage to *Virgil* over *Homer.* 'Tis true that this Description of the Felling and Falling of a Tree is exceeding graceful. But is it therefore more than *Homer* could have done if need had been? Or is

---

Longinus (c. 1-2 century) on the *Odyssey* as inferior to the *Iliad* :

The *Odyssey* . . . is an instance how natural it is to a great genius, when it begins to grow old and decline, to delight itself in *narrations* and *fables.* For that Homer composed the *Odyssey* after the *Iliad,* many proofs may be given . . . From hence, in my judgment, it proceeds, that as the *Iliad* was written while his *spirit* was in its greatest vigour, the whole structure of that work is dramatic, and full of action; whereas the greater part of the *Odyssey* is employed in narration, which is the taste of *old age:* so that in this latter piece we may compare him to the setting sun, which has still the same greatness, but not the same ardour or force. He speaks not in the same strain; we see no more that *sublime* of the *Iliad,* which marches on with a constant pace, without ever being stopped or retarded: there appears no more that hurry, and that strong tide of motions and passions, pouring one after another: there is no more the same fury, or the same volubility of diction, so suitable to action, and all along drawing in such innumerable images of nature. . . . But though all this be *age,* it is the age of Homer.—And it may be said, for the credit of these fictions, that they are *beautiful dreams,* or, if you will, the dreams of Jupiter himself. I spoke of the *Odyssey,* only to show that the greatest poets, when their genius wants strength and warmth for the *pathetic,* for the most part employ themselves in painting the *manners.* This Homer has done in characterizing the suitors, and describing their way of life; which is properly a branch of comedy, whose peculiar business it is to represent the manners of men.

Longinus, quoted in The "Iliad" and the "Odyssey" of Homer, *translated by Alexander Pope, Leavitt & Allen, 1848.*

---

there no Description in *Homer* of somewhat else as good as this? Yes, and in many of our English Poets now alive. If it then be lawful for *Julius Scaliger* to say, that if *Jupiter* would have described the fall of a Tree, he could not have mended this of *Virgil,* it will be lawful for me to repeat an old Epigram of *Antipater,* to the like purpose, in favour of *Homer:*

> The Writer of the famous Trojan *War,*
> And of Ulysses *Life, O* Jove, *make known,*
> Who, whence he was; for thine the Verses are,
> And he would have us think they are his own.

The seventh and last commendation of an Heroique Poem consisteth in Amplitude and Variety; and in this *Homer* exceedeth *Virgil* very much, and that not by superfluity of words, but by plenty of Heroique matter, and multitude of Descriptions and Comparisons (whereof *Virgil* hath translated but a small part into his

Æneads), such as are the Images of Shipwrecks, Battles, Single Combats, Beauty, Passions of the mind, Sacrifices, Entertainments, and other things, whereof *Virgil* (abating what he borrows of *Homer*) has scarce the twentieth part. It is no wonder therefore if all the ancient Learned men both of *Greece* and *Rome* have given the first place in Poetry to *Homer.* It is rather strange that two or three, and of late time and but Learners of the Greek tongue, should dare to contradict so many competent Judges both of Language and Discretion. But howsoever I defend *Homer,* I aim not thereby at any reflection upon the following Translation. Why then did I write it? Because I had nothing else to do. Why publish it? Because I thought it might take off my Adversaries from shewing their folly upon my more serious Writings, and set them upon my Verses to shew their wisdom. . . .

Alexander Pope (essay date 1725)

SOURCE: A postscript to The "Iliad" and the "Odyssey" of Homer, *edited by W. C. Armstrong, translated by Alexander Pope, Leavitt and Allen, 1848, pp. 401-19.*

[*Pope has been called the greatest English poet of his time and one of the most important in the history of world literature. As a critic and satirical commentator on eighteenth-century England, he was the author of work that represents the epitome of Neoclassicist thought. His greatness lies in his cultivation of style and wit, rather than sublimity and pathos, and this inclination shaped his criticism of other writers. In the following excerpt from the postscript to his 1725 translation of the* Odyssey, *Pope argues that the* Odyssey *should be analyzed separately from the* Iliad, *contending that "the* Odyssey *is the reverse of the* Iliad, *in moral, subject, manner and style."*]

I cannot dismiss [the *Odyssey*] without a few observations on the character and style of it. Whoever reads the *Odyssey* with an eye to the *Iliad,* expecting to find it of the same character or of the same sort of spirit, will be grievously deceived, and err against the first principle of criticism, which is, to consider the nature of the piece, and the intent of its author. The *Odyssey* is a moral and political work, instructive to all degrees of men, and filled with images, examples, and precepts of civil and domestic life. Homer is here a person,

> Qui didicit, *patriæ* quid debeat, et quid *amicis,*
> Quo sit amore *parens,* quo *frater* amandus, et *hospes:*
> Qui quid sit *pulcrum* quid *turpe,* quid *utile,* quid *non,*
> Plenius et melius Chrysippo et Crantore dicit.

The *Odyssey* is the reverse of the *Iliad,* in moral, subject, manner and style; to which it has no sort of relation, but as the story happens to follow in order of time, and as some of the same persons are actors in it. Yet from this incidental connection, many have been misled to regard it as a continuation or second part, and thence to expect a parity of character inconsistent with its nature.

It is no wonder that the common reader should fall into this mistake, when so great a critic as Longinus seems not wholly free from it; although what he has said, has been generally understood to import a severer censure of the *Odyssey* than it really does, if we consider the occasion on which it is introduced, and the circumstances to which it is confined.

> The *Odyssey* is an instance how natural it is to a great genius, when it begins to grow old and decline, to delight itself in *narrations* and *fables.* For that Homer composed the *Odyssey* after the *Iliad,* many proofs may be given. . . . From hence, in my judgment, it proceeds, that as the *Iliad* was written while his *spirit* was in its greatest vigour, the whole structure of that works is dramatic, and full of action; whereas the greater part of the *Odyssey* is employed in narration, which is the taste of *old age:* so that in this latter piece we may compare him to the setting sun, which has still the same greatness, but not the same ardour or force. He speaks not in the same strain; we see no more that *sublime* of the *Iliad,* which marches on with a constant pace, without ever being stopped or retarded: there appears no more that hurry, and that strong tide of motions and passions, pouring one after another: there is no more the same fury, or the same volubility of diction, so suitable to action, and all along drawing in such innumerable images of nature. But Homer, like the ocean, is always great, even when he ebbs and retires; even when he is lowest, and loses himself most in narrations and incredible fictions: as instances of this, we cannot forget the descriptions of tempests, the adventures of Ulysses with the Cyclops, and many others. But though all this be *age,* it is the age of Homer.—And it may be said, for the credit of these fictions, that they are *beautiful dreams,* or, if you will, the dreams of Jupiter himself. I spoke of the *Odyssey,* only to show that the greatest poets, when their genius wants strength and warmth for the *pathetic,* for the most part employ themselves in painting the *manners.* This Homer has done in characterizing the suitors, and describing their way of life; which is properly a branch of comedy, whose peculiar business it is to represent the manners of men.

We must first observe, it is the *sublime* of which Longinus is writing: that, and not the nature of Homer's poem, is his subject. After having highly extolled the sublimity and fire of the *Iliad,* he justly observes the *Odyssey* to have less of those qualities, and to turn more on the side of moral, and reflections on human life. Nor is it his business here to determine, whether the *elevated spirit* of the one, or the *just moral* of the other, be the greater excellence in itself.

Secondly, that fire and fury of which he is speaking, cannot well be meant of the general spirit and inspiration which is to run through a whole epic poem, but of that particular warmth and impetuosity necessary in some parts, to image or represent actions or passions, of haste, tumult, and violence. It is on occasions of citing some such particular passages in Homer, that Longinus breaks into this reflection; which seems to determine his meaning chiefly to that sense.

Upon the whole, he affirms the *Odyssey* to have less sublimity and fire that the *Iliad,* but he does not say it wants the sublime or wants fire. He affirms it to be narrative, but not that the narration is defective. He affirms it to abound in fictions, not that those fictions are ill invented or ill executed. He affirms it to be nice and particular in painting the manners, but not that those manners are ill painted. If Homer has fully in these points accomplished his own design, and done all that the nature of his poem demanded or allowed, it still remains perfect in its kind, and as much a master-piece as the *Iliad.*

The amount of the passage is this: that in his own particular taste, and with respect to the *sublime,* Longinus preferred the *Iliad:* and because the *Odyssey* was less active and lofty, he judged it the work of the old age of Homer.

If this opinion be true, it will only prove, that Homer's age might determine him in the choice of his subject, not that it affected him in the execution of it; and that which would be a very wrong instance to prove the decay of his imagination, is a very good one to evince the strength of his judgment. For had he (as Madame Dacier observed) composed the *Odyssey* in his youth, and the *Iliad* in his age, both must in reason have been exactly the same as they now stand. To blame Homer for his choice of such a subject, as did not admit the same incidents and the same pomp of style as his former, is to take offence at too much variety, and to imagine that when a man has written one good thing, he must ever after only copy himself.

The 'Battle of Constantine,' and the 'School of Athens,' are both pieces of Raphael: Shall we censure the 'School of Athens' as faulty, because it has not the fury and fire of the other? or shall we say that Raphael was grown grave and old, because he chose to represent the manners of old men and philosophers? There is all the silence, tranquillity, and composure in the one, and all the warmth hurry, and tumult in the other, which the subject of either required: both of them had been imperfect, if they had not been as they are. And let the poet or painter be young or old, who designs or performs in this manner, it proves him to have made the piece at a time of life when he was master not only of his art, but of his discretion.

Aristotle makes no such distinction between the two poems: he constantly cites them with equal praise, and draws the rules and examples of epic writing equally from both. But it is rather to the *Odyssey* that Horace gives the preference, in the Epistle to Lollius, and in the Art of Poetry. It is remarkable how opposite his opinion is to that of Longinus: and that the particulars he chooses to extol, are those very *fictions* and *pictures of the manners,* which the other seems least to approve. Those fables and manners are the very essence of the work: but even without that regard, the fables themselves have both more invention and more instruction, and the manners more moral and example, than those of the *Iliad.*

In some points (and those the most essential to the epic poem) the *Odyssey* is confessed to excel the *Iliad;* and principally in the great end of it, the *moral.* The conduct, turn, and disposition of the *fable* is also what the critics allow to be the better model for epic writers to follow; accordingly we find much more of the cast of this poem than of the other in the Æneid, and (what next to that is perhaps the greatest example) in the Telemachus. In the *manners,* it is no way inferior: Longinus is so far from finding any defect in these, that he rather taxes Homer with painting them too minutely. As to the *narrations,* although they are more numerous as the occasions are more frequent, yet they carry no more the marks of old age, and are neither more prolix, nor more circumstantial, than the conversations and dialogues of the *Iliad.* Not to mention the length of those of Phoenix in the ninth book, and of Nestor in the eleventh (which may be thought in compliance to their characters), those of Glaucus in the sixth, of Æneas in the twentieth, and some others, must be allowed to exceed any in the whole *Odyssey.* And that the propriety of style, and the numbers, in the narrations of each are equal, will appear to any who compare them.

To form a right judgment, whether the genius of Homer had suffered any decay; we must consider, in both his poems, such parts as are of a similar nature, and will bear comparison. And it is certain we shall find in each the same vivacity and fecundity of invention, the same life and strength of imagining and colouring, the particular descriptions as highly painted, the figures as bold, the metaphors as animated, and the numbers as harmonious and as various.

The *Odyssey* is a perpetual source of poetry: the stream is not the less full for being gentle; though it is true (when we speak only with regard to the *sublime*) that a river, foaming and thundering in cataracts from rocks and precipices, is what more strike amaze, and fills the mind, than the same body of water, flowing afterwards through peaceful vales and agreeable scenes of pasturage.

The *Odyssey,* as I have before said, ought to be considered according to its own nature and design, not with an eye to the *Iliad.* To censure Homer, because it is unlike what it was never meant to resemble, is as if a gardener, who had purposely cultivated two beautiful trees of contrary natures, as a specimen of his skill in the several kinds, should be blamed for not bringing them into *pairs;* when in root, stem, leaf, and flower, each was so entirely different, that one must have been spoiled, in the endeavour to match the other.

Longinus, who saw this poem was "partly of the nature of comedy," ought not, for that very reason, to have considered it with a view to the *Iliad.* How little any such resemblance was the intention of Homer, may appear from hence, that, although the character of Ulysses was there already drawn, yet here he purposely turns to another side of it, and shows him not in that full light of glory, but in the shade of common life, with a mixture of such qualities as are requisite to all the lowest accidents of it, struggling with misfortunes, and on a level with the meanest of mankind. As for the other persons, none of them are above what we call the higher comedy: Calypso, though a goddess, is a character of intrigue. The suitors yet more approaching to it; the Phæacians are of the same cast; the Cyclops, Melanthius, and Irus, descend even to droll characters; and the scenes that appear throughout are generally of the comic kind; banquets, revels, sports, loves, and the pursuit of a woman.

From the nature of the poem, we shall form an idea of the *style.* The diction is to follow the images, and to take its colour from the complexion of the thoughts. Accordingly the *Odyssey* is not always clothed in the majesty of verse proper to tragedy, but sometimes descends into the plainer narrative, and sometimes even to that familiar dialogue essential to comedy. However, where it cannot support a sublimity, it always preserves a dignity, or at least a propriety.

There is a real beauty in an easy, pure, perspicuous description, even of a *low action.* There are numerous instances of this both in Homer and Virgil: and perhaps those natural passages are not the least pleasing of their works. It is often the same in history, where the representations of common, or even domestic things, in clear, plain, and natural words, are frequently found to make the liveliest impression on the reader.

The question is, how far a poet, in pursuing the description or image of an action, can attach himself to *little circumstances,* without vulgarity or trifling? what particulars are proper, and enliven the image; or what are impertinent, and clog it? In this matter painting is to be consulted, and the whole regard had to those circumstances which contribute to form a full, and yet not a confused, idea of a thing.

Epithets are of vast service to this effect, and the right use of these is often the only expedient to render the narration poetical.

The great point of judgment is to distinguish when to speak simply, and when figuratively: but whenever the poet is obliged by the nature of his subject to descend to the lower manner of writing, an elevated style would be affected, and therefore ridiculous; and the more he was forced upon figures and metaphors to avoid that lowness, the more the image would be broken, and consequently obscure.

One may add, that the use of the grand style on little subjects, is not only ludicrous, but a sort of transgression against the rules of proportion and mechanics: it is using a vast force to lift a *feather*.

I believe, now I am upon this head, it will be found a just observation, that the *low actions of life* cannot be put into a figurative style, without being ridiculous; but *things natural can*. Metaphors raise the latter into dignity, as we see in the Georgics; but throw the former into ridicule as in the Lutrin. I think this may very well be accounted for: laughter implies censure; inanimate and irrational beings are not objects of censure, therefore they may be elevated as much as you please, and no ridicule follows: but when rational beings are represented above their real character, it becomes ridiculous in art, because it is vicious in morality. The bees in Virgil, were they rational beings, would be ridiculous by having their actions and manners represented on a level with creatures so superior as men; since it would imply folly or pride, which are the proper objects of ridicule.

The use of pompous expressions for low actions or thoughts, is the *true sublime* of Don Quixote. How far unfit it is for epic poetry, appears in its being the perfection of the mock epic. It is so far from being the sublime of *tragedy,* that it is the cause of all *bombast,* when poets, instead of being (as they imagine) constantly lofty, only preserve throughout a painful equality of fustian; that continued swell of language (which runs indiscriminately even through their lowest characters, and rattles like some mightiness of meaning in the most indifferent subjects) is of a piece with that perpetual elevation of tone which the players have learned from it; and which is not *speaking,* but *vociferating.*

There is still more reason for a variation of style in *epic* poetry than in *tragic,* to distinguish between that *language of the gods* proper to the *muse* who sings, and is inspired; and that of *men,* who are introduced speaking only according to nature. Farther, there ought to be a difference of style observed in the speeches of human persons, and those of deities; and again, in those which may be called set harangues or orations, and those which are only conversation and dialogue. Homer has more of the latter than any other poet; what Virgil does by two or three words of narration, Homer still performs by speeches: not only replies, but even rejoinders, are frequent in him, a practice almost unknown to Virgil. This renders his poems more animated, but less grave and majestic; and consequently necessitates the frequent use of a lower style. The writers of tragedy lie under the same necessity if they would copy nature; whereas that painted and poetical diction which they perpetually use, would be improper even in orations designed to move with all the arts of rhetoric: this is plain from the practice of Demosthenes and Cicero; and Virgil, in those of Drances and Turnus, gives an eminent example, how far removed the style of them ought to be from such an excess of figures and ornaments: which indeed fits only that *language of the gods* we have been speaking of, or that of a muse under inspiration.

To read through a whole work in this strain, is like travelling all along the ridge of a hill, which is not half so aggreable as sometimes gradually to rise, and sometimes gently to descend, as the way leads, and as the end of the journey directs.

Indeed, the true reason that so few poets have imitated Homer in these lower parts, has been the extreme difficulty of preserving that mixture of ease and dignity essential to them. For it is as hard for an epic poem to stoop to the narrative with success, as for a prince to descend to be familiar, without diminution to his greatness.

The *sublime* style is more easily counterfeited than the *natural:* something that passes for it, or sounds like it, is common in all false writers: but nature, purity, perspicuity, and simplicity, never walk in the clouds; they are obvious to all capacities, and where they are not evident, they do not exist.

The most plain narration not only admits of these, and of harmony (which are all the qualities of style), but it requires every one of them to render it pleasing. On the contrary, whatever pretends to a share of the sublime, may pass, notwithstanding any defects in the rest; nay, sometimes without any of them, and gain the admiration of all ordinary readers.

Homer, in his lowest narrations or speeches, is ever easy, flowing, copious, clear, and harmonious. He shows not less *invention,* in assembling the humbler, than the greater thoughts and images: nor less *judgment* in proportioning the style, and the versification to these, than to the other. Let it be remembered, that the same genius that soared the highest, and from whom the greatest models of the *sublime* are derived, was also he who stooped the lowest, and gave to the simple *narrative* its utmost perfection. Which of these was the harder task to Homer himself, I cannot pretend to determine; but to his translator I can affirm (however unequal all his imitations must be) that of the latter has been much the more difficult.

Whoever expects here the same pomp of verse, and the same ornaments of diction, as in the *Iliad,* he will, and he ought to be, disappointed. Were the original otherwise, it had been an offence against nature; and were the translation so, it were an offence against Homer, which is the same thing.

It must be allowed that there is a majesty and harmony in the Greek language, which greatly contribute to elevate and support the narration. But I must also observe, that this is an advantage grown upon the language since Homer's time: for things are removed from vulgarity by being out of use; and if the words we could find in any present language were equally sonorous or musical in themselves, they would still appear less poetical and uncommon than those of a dead one, from this only circumstances, of being in every man's mouth. I may add to this another disadvantage to a translator, from a different cause: Homer seems to have taken upon him the character of an historian, antiquary, divine, and professor of arts and sciences, as well as a poet. In one or other of these characters, he descends into many particularities which, as a poet only, perhaps he would have avoided. All these ought to be preserved by a faithful translator, who in some measure takes the place of Homer; and all that can be expected from him is to make them as poetical as the subject will bear. Many arts, therefore, are requisite to supply these disadvantages, in order to dignify and solemnize these plainer parts, which hardly admit of any poetical ornaments.

Some use has been made to this end of the style of Milton. A just and moderate mixture of old words may have an effect like the working of old abbey stones into a building, which I have sometimes seen to give a kind of venerable air, and yet not destroy the neatness, elegance, and equality, requisite to a new work; I mean, without rendering it too unfamiliar, or remote from the present purity of writing, or from that ease and smoothness which ought always to accompany narration or dialogue. In reading a style judiciously antiquated, one finds a pleasure not unlike that of travelling on an old Roman way: but then the road must be as *good* as the way is *ancient;* the style must be such in which we may evenly proceed, without being put to short stops by sudden abruptnesses, or puzzled by frequent turnings and transpositions. No man delights in furrows and stumbling-blocks: and let our love to antiquity be ever so great, a fine ruin is one thing, and

a heap of rubbish another. The imitators of Milton, like most other imitators, are not *copies,* but *caricatures* of their original; they are a hundred times more obsolete and cramp than he, and equally so in all places: whereas it should have been observed of Milton, that he is not lavish of his exotic words and phrases every where alike, but employs them much more where the subject is marvellous, vast, and strange, as in the scenes of heaven, hell, chaos, &c., than where it is turned to the natural and agreeable, as in the pictures of paradise, the loves of our first parents, entertainments of angels, and the like. In general, this unusual style better serves to awaken our ideas in the descriptions and in the imaging and picturesque parts, than it agrees with the lower sort of narrations, the character of which is simplicity and purity. Milton has several of the latter, where we find not an antiquated, affected, or uncouth word, for some hundred lines together; as in his fifth book, the latter part of the eighth, the former of the tenth and eleventh books, and in the narration of Michael in the twelfth. I wonder indeed that he, who ventured (contrary to the practice of all other epic poets) to imitate Homer's lownesses in the narrative, should not also have copied his plainness and perspicuity in the *dramatic* parts: since in his speeches (where clearness, above all, is necessary) there is frequently such transposition and forced construction, that the very sense is not to be discovered without a second or third reading, and in this certainly he ought to be no example.

To preserve the true character of Homer's style in the present translation, great pains have been taken to be easy and natural. The chief merit I can pretend to, is, not to have been carried into a more plausible and figurative manner of writing, which would better have pleased all readers, but the judicious ones. My errors had been fewer, had each of those gentlemen who joined with me shown as much of the severity of a friend to me, as I did to them, in a strict animadversion and correction. What assistance I received from them, was made known in general to the public, in the original proposals for this work, and the particulars are specified at the conclusion of it; to which I must add (to be punctually just) some part of the tenth and fifteenth books. The reader will now be too good a judge how much the greater part of it, and consequently of its faults, is chargeable upon me alone. But this I can with integrity affirm, that I have bestowed as much time and pains upon the whole, as were consistent with the indispensable duties and cares of life, and with that wretched state of health which God has been pleased to make my portion. At the least, it is a pleasure to me to reflect, that I have introduced into our language this other work of the greatest and the most ancient of poets, with some dignity; and I hope with as little disadvantage as the *Iliad.* And if, after the unmerited success of that translation, any one will wonder why I would enterprise the *Odyssey,* I think it sufficient to say, that Homer himself did the same, or the world would never have seen it. . . .

Thomas De Quincey (essay date 1841)

SOURCE: "Homer and the Homeridae," in *The Collected Writings of Thomas De Quincey,* edited by David Masson, A. & C. Black, 1897, pp. 7-95.

[*An English critic and essayist, De Quincey used his own life as the subject of his best-known work,* Confessions of an English Opium Eater *(1822), in which he chronicled his addiction to opium. He contributed reviews to a number of London journals and earned a reputation as an insightful if occasionally long-winded literary critic. At the time of his death, De Quincey's critical expertise was underestimated, though his talent as a prose writer had long been acknowledged. In the following excerpt from an article first published in* Blackwood's Magazine *in 1841, De Quincey studies the historical background of Homeric texts.*]

Up to . . . (the epoch of transplanting the ***Iliad*** from Greece insular and Greece colonial to Greece continental) the Homeric poems had been left to the custody of two schools or professional orders, interested in the text of these poems: *how* interested, or in what way their duties connected them with Homer, I will not at this point inquire. Suffice it, that these two separate orders of men *did* confessedly exist—one being elder, perhaps, than Homer himself, or even than Troy: viz. the *Aoidoi,* or Chanters, and *Citharœdi,* or Harpers. These, no doubt, had originally no more relation to Homer than to any other narrative poet; their duty of musical recitation had brought them connected with Homer, as it would have done with any other popular poet; and it was only the increasing current of Homer's predominance over all rival poets which gradually gave such a bias and inflection to these men's professional art as at length to suck them within the great Homeric tide. They became, but were not originally, a sort of Homeric choir and orchestra—a chapel of priests having a ministerial duty in the vast Homeric cathedral. Through them exclusively, or, if not, certainly through them chiefly, the two great objects were secured: first, that to each successive generation of men Homer was *published* with all the advantages of a musical accompaniment; secondly, that for distant generations Homer was *preserved.* I do not thus beg the question as to the existence of alphabetic writing in the days of Homer; on the contrary, I go along with Nitzsch and others in opposing Wolf upon that point. I believe that a laborious and painful art of writing *did* exist; but with such disadvantages as to writing materials that Homer (I am satisfied) would have fared ill as regarded his chance of reaching the polished age of Pericles had he relied on written memorials, or upon any mode of publication less impassioned than the orchestral chanting of the *Rhapsodoi.*

The other order of men dedicated to some Homeric interest, whatever that might be, were those technically known as the *Homeridœ.* The functions of these men have never been satisfactorily ascertained, or so as to discriminate them broadly and firmly from the *Citharœdi* and *Rhapsodoi.* But in two features it is evident that they differed essentially: first, that the *Homeridœ* constituted a more *local* and domestic college of Homeric ministers, confined originally to a single island, not diffused (as were the *Rhapsodoi*) over all Greece; secondly, that by their very name, which refers them back to Homer as a mere radiation from his life-breathing orb, this class of followers is barred from pretending in the Homeric equipage (like the *Citharœdi*) to any independent existence, still less to any anterior existence. The musical reciters had been originally a general and neutral class of public ministers, gradually sequestered into the particular service of Homer; but the *Homeridœ* were, in some way or other, possibly by blood, or by fiction of love and veneration, Homer's direct personal representatives,—like the green-turbaned Seyuds of Islamism, who claim a relation of consanguinity to the Prophet himself.

Thus far, however, though there is evidence of two separate colleges or incorporations who charged themselves with the general custody, transmission, and *publication* of the Homeric poems, we hear of no care applied to the periodical *review* of the Homeric text; we hear of no man taking pains to qualify himself for that office by collecting copies from all quarters, or by applying the supreme political authority of his own peculiar commonwealth to the conservation and the authentication of the Homeric poems. The text of no book can become an object of anxiety until by numerous corruptions it has become an object of doubt. Lycurgus, it is true, the Spartan lawgiver, *did* apply his own authority, in a very early age, to the general purpose of importing and naturalising the ***Iliad.*** But there his office terminated. Critical skill, applied to the investigation of an author's text, was a function of the human mind as much unknown in the Greece of Lycurgus as in the Germany of Tacitus, or in the Tonga-taboo of Captain Cook. And, of all places in Greece, such delicate reactions of the intellect upon its own creations were least likely to arise amongst the illiterate Dorian tribes of the Peloponnesus—wretches that hugged their own barbarising institutions as the very jewels of their birthright, and would most certainly have degenerated rapidly into African brutality had they not been held steady, hustled and forcibly shouldered into social progress, by the press of surrounding tribes, fortunately more intellectual than themselves.

Thus continued matters through about four centuries from Homer. And by that time we begin to feel anxious about the probable state of the Homeric text. Not that I suppose any *interregnum* in Homer's influence—not that I believe in any possible defect of links in that vast series of traditional transmitters; the integrity of that succession was guaranteed by its interwreathing itself with human pleasures, with religious ceremonies, with household and national festivals. It is not that Homer would have become apocryphal or obscure for *want* of public repetition; on the contrary, he would have suffered by too much repetition—too constant and too fervent a repetition would have been the main source of corruptions in the text. Sympathy in the audience must always have been a primary demand with the *Rhapsodoi;* and, to a perfect sympathy, it is one antecedent condition to be perfectly understood. Hence, when allusions were no longer intelligible or effectual, what result would be likely to follow? Too often it must happen that they would be dropped from the text; and, when any Homeric family or city had become extinct, the temptation would be powerful for substituting the names of others who could delight the chanter by fervid gratitude for such a vicarious distinction where it had been merited, or could reward him with gifts where it had not. But it is not necessary to go over the many causes in preparation, after a course of four centuries, for gradually sapping the integrity of Homer's text. Everybody will agree that it was at length high time to have some edition "by authority"; and that, had the *Iliad* and *Odyssey* received no freezing arrest in their licentious tendency towards a general interfusion of their substance, and an adulterating of their diction, with modern words and ideas, most certainly by the time of Alexander—*i.e.* about seven centuries from Homer—either poem would have existed only in fractions. The connecting parts between the several books would have dropped out; and all the . . . episodes dedicated to the honour of a particular hero, might, with regard to names less hallowed in the imagination of Greece, or where no representatives of the house remained, have perished utterly. Considering the great functions of the Greek language subsequently in propagating Christianity, it was a real providential provision which caused the era of state editions to supersede the *ad libitum* text of the careless or the interested, and just at that precise period when the rapidly rising tide of Athenian refinement would else soon have swept away all the landmarks of primitive Greece, and when the altered character of the public reciters would have co-operated with the other difficulties of the case to make a true Homeric text irrecoverable. For the *Rhapsodoi* were in a regular course of degradation to the rank of mere mercenary artists, from that of sacred minstrels who connected the past with the present, and who *sang*—precisely because their burden of truth was too solemn for unimpassioned speech. This was the station they *had* occupied; but it remains in evidence against them, that they were rapidly sinking under the changes of the times; were open to bribes; and, as one consequence (whilst partly it was one cause) of this degradation, that they had ceased to command the public respect. The very same changes, and through the very same steps, and under the very same agencies, have been since exhibited to Europe in the parallel history of our mediæval minstrels. The pig-headed [Joseph] Ritson, in mad pursuit of that single idea (no matter what) which might vex Bishop [Thomas] Percy, made it his business, in one essay, to prove, out of the statutes at large, and out of local court records, that the minstrel, so far from being that honoured guest in the courts of princes whom the bishop had described, was in fact, by Act of Parliament, a rogue and a vagabond, standing in awe of the parish beadle, and liable to be kicked out of any hundred or tithing where he should be found trespassing. But what nonsense! All that Ritson said was virtually false, though plausibly half-true. The minstrel was, and he was not, all that the bishop and others had affirmed. The contradiction lay in the *time:* Percy and Ritson were speaking of different periods; the bishop of the twelfth, thirteenth, and fourteenth centuries—the attorney of the sixteenth and seventeenth. Now, the Grecian *Rhapsodoi* passed through corresponding stages of declension. Having ministered through many centuries to advancing civilisation, finally they themselves fell before a higher civilisation; and the particular aspect of the new civilisation which proved fatal to *them* was the general diffusion of reading as an art of liberal education. In the age of Pericles every well-educated man could read; and one result from his skill, as no doubt it had also been one amongst its exciting causes, was that he had a fine copy at home, beautifully adorned, of the *Iliad* and *Odyssey*. Paper and vellum, for the last six centuries B.C. (that is, from the era of the Egyptian king Psammetichus), were much less scarce in Greece than during the ages immediately consecutive to Homer; and this scarcity it was that had retarded manuscript literature, as subsequently it retarded the art of printing.

How providential, therefore—and, with the recollection of that great part played by Greece in propagating Christianity through the previous propagation of her own literature and language, what is there in such an interference unworthy of Providence?—how providential, that precisely in that interval of one hundred and eleven years between the year 555 B.C., the *locus* of Pisistratus, and 444 B.C., the *locus* of Pericles, whilst as yet the traditional text of Homer was retrievable, though rapidly nearing to the time when it would be strangled with weeds, and whilst as yet the arts of reading and writing had not weakened the popular devotion to Homer by dividing it amongst multiplied books, just then, in that critical isthmus of transitional time, did two or three Athenians of rank—first Solon, next Pisistratus, and lastly (if Plato is right) Hipparchus—step forward to make a public, solemn, and *legally* operative review of the Homeric poems. They drew the old hulk into dock; laid bare its timbers; and stopped the further progress of decay. What more they did than this, and by what characteristic services each connected his name with a separate province in this memorable restoration of the *Iliad* and *Odyssey,* I shall inquire further on.

One century after Pisistratus we come to Pericles; or, counting from the *locus* of each (555 B.C., and 444 B.C.), exactly one hundred and eleven years divide them. One century after Pericles we come to Alexander the Great; or, counting from the *locus* of each (444 B.C., and 333 B.C., exactly one hundred and eleven years divide them. During this period of two hundred and twenty-two years Homer had rest. Nobody was tempted by any oblique interest to torment his text any more. And it is singular enough that this period of two hundred and twenty-two years, during which Homer reigned in the luxury of repose, having nothing to do but to let himself be read and admired, was precisely that ring-fence of years within which lies true Grecian history; for, if any man wishes to master the Grecian history, he needs not to ascend above Pisistratus, nor to come down below Alexander. Before Pisistratus all is mist and fable; after Alexander all is dependency and servitude. And remarkable it is that, soon after Alexander, and indirectly through changes caused by him, Homer was again drawn out for the pleasure of the tormentors. Among the dynasties founded by Alexander's lieutenants was one memorably devoted to literature. The Macedonian house of the Ptolemies, when seated on the throne of Egypt, had founded the very first public library and the first learned public. Alexander died in the year 320 B.C.; and already in the year 280 B.C., (that is, not more than forty years after) the learned Jews of Alexandria and Palestine had commenced, under the royal patronage, that translation of the Hebrew Scriptures into Greek which, from the supposed number of the translators—(viz. *septuaginta, seventy*)—has obtained the name of the "Septuagint." This was a service to posterity. But the earliest *Grecian* service to which this Alexandrian Library ministers was Homeric; and it strikes us as singular when we contrast it with the known idolatry towards Homer of that royal soldier from whom the city itself, with all its novelties, drew its name and foundation. Had Alexander survived forty years longer, as very easily he might if he had insisted upon leaving his heel-taps at Babylon, how angry it would have made him that the very first trial of this new and powerful galvanic battery, involved in the institution of a public library, should be upon the body of the *Iliad*!

From 280 B.C. to 160 B.C. there was a constant succession of Homeric critics. The immense material found in the public library towards a direct history of Homer and his fortunes would alone have sufficed to evoke a school of critics. But there was, besides, another invitation to Homeric criticism, more oblique, and eventually more effective. The Alexandrian Library contained vast collections towards the study of the Greek language through all its dialects, and through all its chronological stages. This study led back by many avenues to Homer. A verse or a passage which hitherto had passed for genuine, and which otherwise, perhaps, yielded no internal argument for suspicion, was now found to be veined by some phrase, dialect, terminal form, or mode of using words, that might be too modern for Homer's age, or too far removed in space from Homer's Ionian country. We moderns, from our vast superiority to the Greeks themselves in Greek metrical science, have in this science found an extra resource laid open to us for detecting the spurious in Greek poetry; and many are the condemned passages in our modern editions of Greek books against which no jealousy would ever have arisen amongst unmetrical scholars. Here, however, the Alexandrian critics, with all their slashing insolence, showed themselves sons of the feeble; they groped about in twilight. But, even without that resource, they contrived to riddle Homer through and through with desperate gashes. In fact, after being "treated" and "handled" by three generations of critics, Homer came forth (just as we may suppose one of Lucan's legionary soldiers from the rencounter with the amphisbæna, the dipsas, and the water-snake of the African wilderness) one vast wound, one huge system of confluent ulcers. Often, in reviewing the labours of three particularly amongst these Alexandrian scorpions, I think of the Æsopian fable, in which an old man with two wives, one aged as befitted him, and the other young, submits his head alternately to what may be called the Alexandrian revision of each. The old lady goes to work first; and upon "moral principle" she indignantly extirpates all the black hairs which could ever have inspired him with the absurd fancy of being young and making love to a girl. Next comes the young critic: she is disgusted with age; and upon system eliminates (or, to speak with Aristarchus, "obelises") all the grey hairs. And thus, between the two ladies and their separate editions of the old gentleman, he, poor Homeric creature, comes forth as bald as the back of one's hand. Aristarchus might well boast that he had cured Homer of the dry-rot! he *has,* and by leaving hardly one whole spar of his ancient framework. Nor can I, with my poor share of penetration, comprehend what sort of abortion it is which Aristarchus would have us to accept and entertain in the room of our old original *Iliad* and *Odyssey*. To cure a man radically of the toothache by knocking all his teeth down his throat seems a suspicious recommendation for "dental surgery." And, with respect to the Homer of Aristarchus, it is to be considered that, besides the lines, sentences, and long passages to which that Herod of critics affixed his *obelus* or stiletto, there were entire books which he found no use in obelising piecemeal; because it was not this line or that line into which he wished to thrust his dagger, but the whole rabble of lines—"tag, rag, and bobtail." Which reminds me of John Paul Richter, who suggests to some author anxiously revising the table of his own errata, that, perhaps, on reflection, he might see cause to put his whole book into the list of *errata,* requesting of the reader kindly to erase the total work as one entire oversight and continuous blunder, from page one down to the word *finis.* In such cases, as Martial observes, no plurality of cancellings or erasures will answer the critic's purpose: but "*una* litura potest." One mighty bucket of ink thrown over the whole will execute the critical sentence; but, as to obelising, *that* is no better than snapping pocket-pistols in a sea-fight.

With the Alexandrian tormentors we may say that Homer's pre-Christian martyrdom came to an end. His post-Christian sufferings have been due chiefly to the Germans, who have renewed the warfare not only of Alexandrian critics, but of the ancient *Chorizontes.* These people I have not mentioned separately, because, in fact, nothing remains of their labours, and the general spirit of their warfare may be best understood from that of modern Germany. They acquired their name of *Chorizontes* (or separators) from their principle of breaking up the *Iliad* into multiform groups of little tadpole *Iliads*; as also of splitting the one old hazy but golden Homer, that looms upon us so venerably through a mist of centuries, into a vast reverberation of little silver Homers, that twinkled up and down the world, and lived where they found it convenient.

Samuel Butler (essay date 1897)

SOURCE: "Who Was the Writer?", in *The Authoress of the Odyssey: Where and When She Wrote, Who She Was, the Use She Made of the "Iliad," and How the Poem Grew under Her Hands,* 1897. Reprint by University of Chicago Press, 1967, pp. 200-09.

[*An English novelist, satirist, essayist, and translator, Butler is best known for his* The Way of All Flesh (1903), *an autobiographical novel that satirizes Victorian church and family life. As a Homeric scholar, Butler achieved notoriety for his* The Authoress of the Odyssey, *in which he propounded the theory that the* Odyssey *was written by a woman. In the following excerpt from that work, he contends that the* Odyssey *was written by Nausicaa, a young woman from Trapani and a member of King Alcinous's household, rather than by Homer.*]

I Believe . . . that the *Odyssey* was written by one woman, and . . . that this woman knew no other neighbourhood than that of Trapani, and therefore must be held to have lived and written there.

Who, then, was she? . . .

We have to find a woman of Trapani, young, fearless, self-willed, and exceedingly jealous of the honour of her sex. She seems to have moved in the best society of her age and country, for we can imagine none more polished on the West coast of Sicily in Odyssean times than the one with which the writer shews herself familiar. She must have had leisure, or she could not have carried through so great a work. She puts up with men when they are necessary or illustrious, but she is never enthusiastic about them, and likes them best when she is laughing at them; but she is cordially interested in fair and famous women.

I think she should be looked for in the household of the person whom she is travestying under the name of King Alcinous. The care with which his pedigree and that of his wife Arēte is explained (vii. 54-77), and the warmth of affectionate admiration with which Arēte is always treated, have the same genuine flavour that has led scholars to see true history and personal interest in the pedigree of Æneas given in *Il.* xx. 200-241. Moreover, she must be a sufficiently intimate member of the household to be able to laugh at its head as much as she chose. No pedigree of any of the other of the *Odyssey* is given save that of Theoclymenus, whose presence in the poem at all requires more explanation than I can give. I can only note that he was of august descent, more than sub-clerical, and of a different stamp from any other character to whom we are introduced.

The fact that the writer should be looked for in a member of King Alcinous' household seems further supported by the zest with which this household and garden are described (vii. 81-132), despite the obviously subrisive exaggeration which pervades the telling. There is no such zest in the description of any other household, and the evident pleasure which the writer takes in it is more like that of a person drawing her own home, than either describing some one else's or creating an imaginary scene. See how having begun in the past tense she slides involuntarily into the present as soon as she comes to the women of the house and to the garden. She never does this in any other of her descriptions.

Lastly, she must be looked for in one to whom the girl described as Nausicaa was all in all. No one else is drawn with like livingness and enthusiasm, and no other episode is written with the same, or nearly the same, buoyancy of spirits and resiliency of pulse and movement, or brings the scene before us with anything approaching the same freshness, as that in which Nausicaa takes the family linen to the washing cisterns. The whole of Book vi. can only have been written by one who was throwing herself into it heart and soul.

All the three last paragraphs are based on the supposition that the writer was drawing real people. That she was drawing a real place, lived at that place, and knew no other, does not admit of further question; we can pin the writer down here by reason of the closeness with which she has kept to natural features that remain much as they were when she portrayed them; but no traces of Alcinous's house and garden, nor of the inmates of his household will be even looked for by any sane person; it is open, therefore, to an objector to contend that though the writer does indeed appear to have drawn permanent features from life, we have no evidence that she drew houses and gardens and men and women from anything but her own imagination.

Granted; but surely, in the first place, if we find her keeping to her own neighbourhood as closely as she can whenever the permanency of the feature described enables us to be certain of what she did, there is a presumption that she was doing the same thing in cases where the evidence has been too fleeting to allow of our bringing her to book. And secondly, we have abundant evidence that the writer did not like inventing.

Richly endowed with that highest kind of imagination which consists in wise selection and judicious application of materials derived from life, she fails, as she was sure to do, when cut off from a base of operation in her own surroundings. This appears most plainly in the three books which tell of the adventures of Ulysses after he has left Mt. Eryx and the Cyclopes. There is no local detail in the places described; nothing, in fact, but a general itinerary such as she could easily get from the mariners of her native town. With this she manages to rub along, helping herself out with fragments taken from nearer home, but there is no approach to such plausible invention as we find in *Gulliver's Travels, Robinson Crusoe,* or *Pilgrim's Progress;* and when she puts a description of the land of Hades into the mouth of Circe (x. 508-515)—which she is aware must be something unlike anything she had ever witnessed—she breaks down and gives as a scene which carries no conviction. Fortunately not much detail is necessary here; in Ithaca, however, a great deal is wanted, and feeling invention beyond her strength she does not even attempt it, but has recourse with the utmost frankness to places with which she is familiar.

Not only does she shirk invention as much as possible in respect of natural features, but she does so also as regards incident. She can vilipend her neighbours on Mt. Eryx as the people at Trapani continue doing to this day, for there is no love lost between the men of Trapani and those of Mte. S. Giuliano, as Eryx is now called. She knows Ustica: the wind comes thence, and she can make something out of that; then there is the other great Sican city of Cefalù—a point can be made here; but with the Lipari islands her material is running short. She has ten years to kill, for which, however, eight or eight-and-a-half may be made to pass. She cannot have killed more than three months before she lands her hero on Circe's island; here, then, in pity's name let him stay for at any rate twelve months—which he accordingly does.

She soon runs through her resources for the Sirens' island, and Scylla and Charybdis; she knows that there is nothing to interest her on the East coast of Sicily below Taormina—for Syracuse (to which I will return) was still a small pre-Corinthian settlement, while on the South coast we have no reason to believe that there was any pre-Hellenic city. What, she asked herself, could she do but shut Ulysses up in the most lonely island she could think of—the one from which he would have the least chance of escaping—for the remainder of his term? She chose, therefore, the island which the modern Italian Government has chosen, for exactly the same reasons, as the one in which to confine those who cannot be left at large—the island of Pantellaria; but she was not going to burden Calypso for seven long years with all Ulysses' men, so his ship had better be wrecked.

This way out of the difficulty does not indicate a writer of fecund or mature invention. She knew the existence of Sardinia, for Ulysses smiles a grim Sardinian smile (xx. 302). Why not send him there, and describe it with details taken not from the North side of Trapani but from the South? Or she need not have given details at all—she might have sent him very long journeys extending over ever so many years in half a page. If she had been of an inventive turn there were abundant means of keeping him occupied without having recourse to the cheap and undignified expedient of shutting him up first for a year in one island, and then for seven in another. Having made herself so noble a peg on which to hang more travel and adventure, she would have hung more upon it, had either strength or inclination pointed in that direction. It is one of the commonplaces of Homeric scholars to speak of the voyages of Ulysses as "a story of adventurous travel." So in a way they are, but one can see all through that the writer is trying to reduce the adventurous travel to a minimum.

See how hard put to it she is when she is away from her own actual surroundings. She does not repeat her incidents so long as she is at home, for she has plenty of material to draw from; when she is away from home, do what she may, she cannot realise things so easily, and has a tendency to fall back on something she has already done. Thus, at Pylos, she repeats the miraculous flight of Minerva (iii. 372) which she had used i. 320. On reaching the land of the Læstrygonians Ulysses climbs a high rock to reconnoitre, and sees no sign of inhabitants save only smoke rising from the ground—at the very next place he comes to he again climbs a high rock to reconnoitre, and apparently sees no sign of inhabitants but only the smoke of Circe's house rising from the middle of a wood. He is conducted to the house of Alcinous by a girl who had come out of the town to fetch a pitcher of water (vii. 20); this is repeated (x. 105) when Ulysses' men are conducted to the house of the Læstrygonian Antiphates, by a girl who had come out of the town to fetch a pitcher of water. The writer has invented a sleep to ruin Ulysses just as he was well in sight of Ithaca (x. 31, &c.). This is not good invention, for such a moment is the very last in which Ulysses would be likely to feel sleepy— but the effort of inventing something else to ruin him when his men are hankering after the cattle of the Sun is quite too much for her, and she repeats (xii. 338) the sleep which had proved so effectual already. So, as I have said above, she repeats the darkness on each occasion when Ulysses seems likely to stumble upon Trapani. Calypso, having been invented once, must do duty again as Circe—or *vice versâ,* for Book x. was probably written before Book v.

Such frequent examples of what I can only call consecutive octaves indicate a writer to whom invention does not come easily, and who is not likely to have recourse to it more than she can help. Having shown this as regards both places and incidents, it only remains to point out that the writer's dislike of invention extends to the invention of people as well as places. The principal characters in the *Odyssey* are all of them Scherian. Nestor, Ulysses, Menelaus and Alcinous are every one of them the same person playing other parts, and the greater zest with which Alcinous is drawn suggests . . . that the original from whom they are all taken was better known to the writer in the part of Alcinous than in that of any of the other three. Penelope, Helen, and Arēte are only one person, and I always suspect Penelope to be truer to the original than either of the other two. Idothea and Ino are both of them Nausicaa; so also are Circe and Calypso, only made up a little older, and doing as the writer thinks Nausicaa would do if she were a goddess and had an establishment of her own. I am more doubtful about these last two, for they both seem somewhat more free from that man-hatred which Nausicaa hardly attempts to conceal. Still, Nausicaa contemplates marrying as soon as she can find the right person, and, as we have seen, neither Circe nor Calypso had a single man-servant of their own, while Circe was in the habit of turning all men who came near her into pigs or wild beasts. Calypso, moreover, is only made a little angry by being compelled to send Ulysses away. She does not seem to have been broken-hearted about it. Neither of them, therefore, must be held to be more fond of men than the convenience of the poem dictated. Even the common people of Ithaca are Scherians, and make exactly the same fault-finding ill-natured remarks about Penelope (xxiii. 149-151) as the Phæacians did about Nausicaa in Book vi. 273-288.

If, then, we observe that where the writer's invention is more laboured she is describing places foreign to her own neighbourhood, while when she carries conviction she is at or near her own home, the presumption becomes very strong that the more spontaneous scenes are not so much invention as a rendering of the writer's environment, to which it is plain that she is

passionately attached, however much she may sometimes gird at it. I, therefore, dismiss the supposition of my supposed objector that the writer was not drawing Alcinous' household and garden from life, and am confirmed in this opinion by remembering that the house of Ulysses corresponds perfectly with that of Alcinous—even to the number of the women servants kept in each establishment.

Being limited to a young woman who was an intimate member of Alcinous' household, we have only to choose between some dependant who idolised Nausicaa and wished to celebrate her with all her surroundings, or Nausicaa (whatever her real name may have been) herself. Or again, it may be urged that the poem was written by some bosom friend of Nausicaa's who was very intimate with the family, as for example Captain Dymas's daughter.

The intimate friend theory may be dismissed at once. High spirited girls, brilliant enough to write the *Odyssey* are not so self effacing as to keep themselves entirely out of sight. If a friend had written the washing day episode, the friend would have come a washing too—especially after having said she would in Nausicaa's dream.

If, again, a dependent had written it, Nausicaa would neither have had the heart nor the power to suppress her altogether; for if she tried to do so the dependant— so daring and self-willed as the writer proves herself to be—would have been more than a match for her mistress. We may be sure that there were not two such spirits in Trapani, as we must suppose if we make Nausicaa able to bow the will of the authoress of the *Odyssey.* The fact that in the washing day episode, so far as possible, we find Nausicaa, all Nausicaa, and nothing but Nausicaa, among the female *dramatis personæ,* indicates that she was herself the young woman of Trapani, a member of the household of King Alcinous, whom we have got to find, and that she was giving herself the little niche in her work which a girl who was writing such a work was sure to give herself.

A dependant would not have dared to laugh at Alcinous with such playful malice as the writer has done. Again she would have made more of Nausicaa herself in the scenes that follow. At present she is left rather as a ragged edge, and says good bye to Ulysses in Book viii. 460, &c., with much less detail, both as regards her own speech and that of Ulysses in reply, than a courtier-like dependant would have permitted. She does not hear Ulysses' account of his adventures— which she might perfectly well have done under her mother's wing. She does not appear to take her meals with the rest of the family at all. When she returns from washing, Eurymedusa brings her supper into her own room. She is not present at any of Alcinous' banquets, nor yet at the games, and her absence from

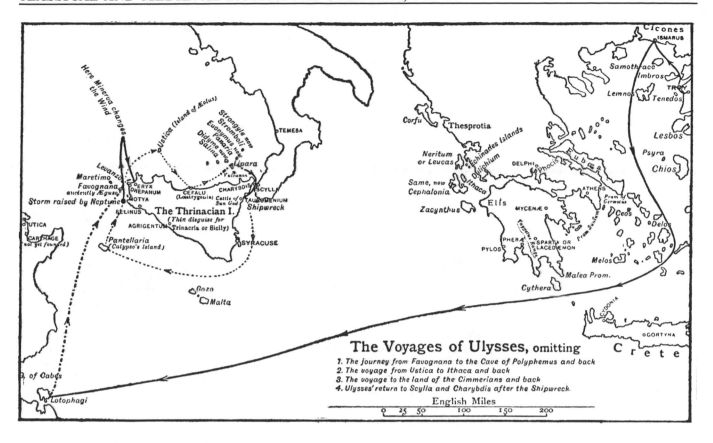

The voyages of Ulysses.

the farewell scene in Book xiii. is too marked to be anything but intentional. It seems as though she wished the reader to understand that she lived apart, and however much she might enjoy an outing with her maids, would have nothing to do with the men who came night after night drinking her father's best wine, and making havoc of his estate. She almost calls these people scoundrels to their faces by saying that they always made the final drink offering of the evening not to Jove but to Mercury, the god of thieves (vii. 137). In passing, I may say that the strangeness of the manner in which Nausicaa says good bye to Ulysses is one of the many things which convince me that the ***Odyssey*** has never been recast by a later hand. A person recasting the work would have been tolerably sure to have transferred the leave-taking to Book xiii.

Nausicaa, again, would have been more than human if she had permitted any one but herself to put into her mouth the ill-natured talk about her which she alleges to pass current among the Phæacians. She would not mind saying it herself when her audience, private or public, would know that she was doing so, but a dependant would have been requested to be less pungent.

I admit as I have already done that these arguments are

not absolutely demonstrative, but it being, I may say, demonstrated that we must choose between Nausicaa and some other young woman of Trapani who lived in, or was very closely intimate with, the household of King Alicnous, I have no hesitation in saying that I think Nausicaa herself more likely than this other unknown young woman to have been the writer we are seeking.

Let the reader look at [a portrait of Nausicaa] and say whether he would find the smallest difficulty in crediting the original of the portrait with being able to write the ***Odyssey***. Would he refuse so to credit her merely because all he happened to know about her for certain was that she once went out washing clothes with her attendants? Nausicaa enjoyed a jaunt on a fine spring morning and helped her maids at the washing cisterns; therefore it is absurd to suppose that she could have written the ***Odyssey***. I venture to think that this argument will carry little weight outside the rank and file of our Homerists—greatly as I dislike connecting this word however remotely with the ***Odyssey***.

No artist can reach an ideal higher than his own best actual environment. Trying to materially improve upon that with which he or she is fairly familiar invariably ends in failure. It is only adjuncts that may be arranged and varied—the essence may be taken or left, but it must not be bettered. The attempt to take nature and be content with her save in respect of details which after all are unimportant, leads to Donatello, Giovanni Bellini, Holbein, Rembrandt, and De Hooghe—the attempt to improve upon her leads straight to Michael Angelo and the *barocco,* to Turner and the modern drop scene. . . . [Women such as Nausicaa], though doubtless comparatively rare, yet existed, as they exist in Italy now, in considerable numbers. Is it a very great stretch of imagination to suppose that one among them may have shown to equal advantage whether as driver, washerwoman, or poetess? At the same time I think it highly probable that the writer of the **Odyssey** was both short and plain, and was laughing at herself, and intending to make her audience laugh also, by describing herself as tall and beautiful. She may have been either plain or beautiful without its affecting the argument.

I wish I could find some one who would give me any serious reason why Nausicaa should not have written the **Odyssey.** For the last five years I have pestered every scholar with whom I have been able to scrape acquaintance, by asking him to explain why the **Odyssey** should not have been written by a young woman. One or two have said that they could see none whatever, but should not like to commit themselves to a definite opinion without looking at the work again. One well-known and very able writer said that when he had first heard of the question as being mooted, he had supposed it to be some paradox of my own, but on taking up the **Odyssey** he had hardly read a hundred lines before he found himself saying "Why of course it is." The greater number, however, gave me to understand that they should not find it a difficult matter to expose the absurdity of my contention if they were not otherwise employed, but that for the present they must wish me a very good morning. They gave me nothing, but to do them justice before I had talked with them for five minutes I saw that they had nothing to give with which I was not already familiar. The **Odyssey** is far too easy, simple, and straightforward for the understanding of scholars—as I said in the *Life of Dr. Butler of Shrewsbury,* if it had been harder to understand, it would have been sooner understood—and yet I do not know; the **Iliad** is indeed much harder to understand, but scholars seem to have been very sufficiently able to misunderstand it.

Every scholar has read a Book or two of the **Odyssey** here and there; some have read the whole; a few have read it through more than once; but none that I have asked have so much as been able to tell me whether Ulysses had a sister or no—much less what her name was. Not one of those whom I have as yet had the good fortune to meet in England—for I have met with such in Sicily—have saturated themselves with the

poem, and that, too, unhampered by a single preconceived idea in connection with it. Nothing short of this is of the smallest use.

Andrew Lang (essay date 1906)

SOURCE: "Notes of Change in the *Odyssey,*" in *Homer and His Age,* 1906. Reprint by AMS Press, 1968, pp. 229-43.

[*Lang was one of England's most powerful men of letters during the closing decades of the nineteenth century. A romantic vision of the past imbued Lang's writings, coloring his work as a translator, poet, and revisionist historian. Among the chief proponents of Romanticism in a critical battle that pitted late-nineteenth-century revivalist Romanticists against the defenders of Naturalism and Realism, Lang espoused his strong preference for romantic adventure novels throughout his literary criticism. In this essay, Lang contends that there are few societal differences between the* Iliad *and the* Odyssey, *arguing that "all these so-called differences between* Iliad *and* Odyssey *do not point to the fact that the* Odyssey *belongs to a late and changed period of culture, of belief and customs."*]

If the Homeric descriptions of details of life contain anachronisms, points of detail inserted in later progressive ages, these must be peculiarly conspicuous in the **Odyssey**. Longinus regarded it as the work of Homer's advanced life, the sunset of his genius, and nobody denies that it assumes the existence of the **Iliad** and is posterior to that epic. In the **Odyssey,** then, we are to look, if anywhere, for indications of a changed society. That the language of the **Odyssey,** and of four Books of the **Iliad** (IX., X., XXIII., XXIV.), exhibits signs of change is a critical commonplace, but the language is matter for a separate discussion; we are here concerned with the ideas, manners, customary laws, weapons, implements, and so forth of the Epics.

Taking as a text Mr. Monro's essay, *The Relation of the Odyssey to the Iliad,* we examine the notes of difference which he finds between the twin Epics. As to the passages in which he discovers "borrowing or close imitation of passages" in the **Iliad** by the poet of the **Odyssey,** we shall not dwell on the matter, because we know so little about the laws regulating the repetition of epic formulæ. It is tempting, indeed, to criticise Mr. Monro's list of twenty-four Odyssean "borrowings," and we might arrive at some curious results. . . .

We might . . . urge that "to send a spear through the back of a stag" is not, as Mr. Monro thought, "an improbable feat," and that a man wounded to death as Leiocritus was wounded, would not, as Mr. Monro argued, fall backwards. He supposes that the poet of the *Odyssey* borrowed the forward fall from a passage in the *Iliad,* where the fall is in keeping. But, to make good our proof, it might be necessary to spear a human being in the same way as Leiocritus was speared.

The repetitions of the Epic, at all events, are not the result of the weakness of a poet who had to steal his expressions like a schoolboy. They have some other cause than the indolence or inefficiency of a *cento*-making undergraduate. Indeed, a poet who used the many terms in the *Odyssey* which do not occur in the *Iliad* was not constrained to borrow from any predecessor.

It is needless to dwell on the Odyssean novelties in vocabulary, which were naturally employed by a poet who had to sing of peace, not of war, and whose epic, as Aristotle says, is "ethical," not military. The poet's rich vocabulary is appropriate to his novel subject, that is all.

Coming to Religion (I) we find Mr. Leaf assigning to his original *Achilleis*—"the kernel"—the very same religious ideas as Mr. Monro takes to be marks of "lateness" and of advance when he finds them in the *Odyssey!*

In the original oldest part of the *Iliad,* says Mr. Leaf, "the gods show themselves just so much as to let us know what are the powers which control mankind from heaven. . . . Their interference is such as becomes the rulers of the world, not partisans in the battle." It is the later poets of the *Iliad,* in Mr. Leaf's view, who introduce the meddlesome, undignified, and extremely unsportsmanlike gods. The original early poet of the *Iliad* had the nobler religious conceptions.

In that case—the *Odyssey* being later than the original kernel of the *Iliad*—the *Odyssey* ought to give us gods as undignified and unworthy as those exhibited by the later continuators of the *Iliad.*

But the reverse is the case. The gods behave fairly well in Book XXIV. of the *Iliad,* which, we are to believe, is the latest, or nearly the latest, portion. They are all wroth with the abominable behaviour of Achilles to dead Hector (XXIV. 134). They console and protect Priam. As for the *Odyssey,* Mr. Monro finds that in this late Epic the gods are just what Mr. Leaf proclaims them to have been in his old original kernel. "There is now an Olympian concert that carries on something like a moral government of the world. It is very different in the *Iliad.* . . ."

But it was not very different; it was just the same, in Mr. Leaf's genuine old original germ of the *Iliad.* In fact, the gods are "very much like you and me." When their *ichor* is up, they misbehave as we do when our blood is up, during the fury of war. When Hector is

dead and when the war is over, the gods give play to their higher nature, as men do. There is no difference of religious conception to sever the *Odyssey* from the later but not from the original parts of the *Iliad.* It is all an affair of the circumstances in each case.

The *Odyssey* is calmer, more reflective, more *religious* than the *Iliad,* being a poem of peace. The *Iliad,* a poem of war, is more *mythological* than the *Odyssey;* the gods in the *Iliad* are excited, like the men, by the great war and behave accordingly. That neither gods nor men show any real sense of the moral weakness of Agamemnon or Achilles, or of the moral superiority of Hector, is an unacceptable statement. Even Achilles and Agamemnon are judged by men and by the poet according to their own standard of ethics and of customary law. There is really no doubt on this point. Too much (2) is made of the supposed different views of Olympus—a mountain in Thessaly in the *Iliad;* a snowless, windless, supra-mundane place in *Odyssey,* V. 41-47. Of the Odyssean passage Mr. Merry justly says, "the actual description is not irreconcilable with the general Homeric picture of Olympus." It is "an idealised mountain," and conceptions of it vary, with the variations which are essential to and inseparable from all mythological ideas. . . . In *Iliad,* V. 753, the poet "regarded the summit of Olympus as a half-way stage between heaven and earth," thus "departing from the oldest Homeric tradition, which made the earthly mountain Olympus, and not any aerial region, the dwelling of the gods." But precisely the same confusion of mythical ideas occurs among a people so backward as the Australian south-eastern tribes, whose All Father is now seated on a hill-top and now "above the sky." In *Iliad,* VIII. 25, 26, the poet is again said to have "entirely lost the real Epic conception of Olympus as a mountain in Thessaly," and to "follow the later conception, which removed it from earth to heaven." . . . The poet of *Iliad,* XI. 184, says plainly that Zeus descended *"from heaven"* to Mount Ida. In fact, all that is said of Olympus, of heaven, of the home of the gods, is poetical, is mythical, and so is necessarily subject to the variations of conception inseparable from mythology. This is certain if there be any certainty in mythological science, and here no hard and fast line can be drawn between *Odyssey* and *Iliad.*

(3) The next point of difference is that, "we hear no more of Iris as the messenger of Zeus;" in the *Odyssey,* "the agent of the will of Zeus is now Hermes, as in the Twenty-fourth Book of the *Iliad,*" a late "Odyssean" Book. But what does that matter, seeing that *Iliad,* Book VIII., is declared to be one of the latest additions; yet in Book VIII. Iris, not Hermes, is the messenger (VIII. 409-425). If in late times Hermes, not Iris, is the messenger, why, in a very "late" Book (VIII.) is Iris the messenger, not Hermes? *Iliad,* Book XXIII., is also a late "Odyssean" Book, but here Iris goes on her messages (XXIII. 199) moved merely by

the prayers of Achilles. In the late Odyssean Book (XXIV.) of the *Iliad,* Iris runs on messages from Zeus both to Priam and to Achilles. If Iris, in "Odyssean" times, had resigned office and been succeeded by Hermes, why did Achilles pray, not to Hermes, but to Iris? There is nothing in the argument about Hermes and Iris. There is nothing in the facts but the variability of mythical and poetical conceptions. Moreover, the conception of Iris as the messenger certainly existed through the age of the *Odyssey,* and later. In the *Odyssey* the beggar man is called "Irus," a male Iris, because he carries messages; and Iris does her usual duty as messenger in the Homeric Hymns, as well as in the so-called late Odyssean Books of the *Iliad*. The poet of the *Odyssey* knew all about Iris; there had arisen no change of belief; he merely employed Hermes as messenger, not of the one god, but of the divine Assembly.

(4) Another difference is that in the *Iliad* the wife of Hephæstus is one of the Graces; in the *Odyssey* she is Aphrodite. This is one of the inconsistencies which are the essence of mythology. Mr. Leaf points out that when Hephæstus is about exercising his craft, in making arms for Achilles, Charis "is made wife of Hephæstus by a more transparent allegory than we find elsewhere in Homer," whereas, when Aphrodite appears in a comic song by Demodocus (*Odyssey,* VIII. 266-366), "that passage is later and un-Homeric." Of this we do not accept the doctrine that the lay is un-Homeric. The difference comes to no more than *that;* the accustomed discrepancy of mythology, of story-telling about the gods. But as to the lay of Demodocus being un-Homeric and late, the poet at least knows the regular Homeric practice of the bride-price, and its return by the bride's father to the husband of an adulterous wife (*Odyssey,* VIII. 318, 319). The poet of this lay, which Mr. Merry defends as Homeric, was intimately familiar with Homeric customary law. Now, according to Paul Cauer, as we shall see, other "Odyssean" poets were living in an age of changed law, later than that of the author of the lay of Demodocus. All these so-called differences between *Iliad* and *Odyssey* do not point to the fact that the *Odyssey* belongs to a late and changed period of culture, of belief and customs. There is nothing in the evidence to prove that contention.

There (5) are two references to local oracles in the *Odyssey,* that of Dodona (XIV. 327; XIX. 296) and that of Pytho (VIII. 80). This is the old name of Delphi. Pytho occurs in *Iliad,* IX. 404, as a very rich temple of Apollo—the oracle is not named, but the oracle brought in the treasures. Achilles (XVI. 233) prays to Pelasgian Zeus of Dodona, whose priests were thickly tabued, but says nothing of the oracle of Dodona. Neither when in leaguer round Troy, nor when wandering in fairy lands forlorn, had the Achæans or Odysseus much to do with the local oracles of Greece;

perhaps not, in Homer's time, so important as they were later, and little indeed is said about them in either Epic.

(6) "The geographical knowledge shown in the *Odyssey* goes beyond that of the *Iliad* . . . especially in regard to Egypt and Sicily." But a poet of a widely wandering hero of Western Greece has naturally more occasion than the poet of a fixed army in Asia to show geographical knowledge. Egyptian Thebes is named, in *Iliad,* IX., as a city very rich, especially in chariots; while in the *Odyssey* the poet has occasion to show more knowledge of the way to Egypt and of Viking descents from Crete on the coast (*Odyssey,* III. 300; IV. 351; XIV. 257; XVII. 426). Archæology shows that the Mycenæan age was in close commercial relation with Egypt, and that the Mycenæan civilisation extended to most Mediterranean lands and islands, and to Italy and Sicily. There is nothing suspicious, as "late," in the mention of Sicily by Odysseus in Ithaca (*Odyssey,* XX. 383; XXIV. 307). In the same way, if the poet of a western poem does not dilate on the Troad and the people of Asia Minor as the poet of the *Iliad* does, that is simply because the scene of the *Iliad* is in Asia and the scene of the *Odyssey* is in the west, when it is not in No Man's land. From the same cause the poet of sea-faring has more occasion to speak of the Phænicians, great sea-farers, than the poet of the Trojan leaguer.

(7) We know so little about land tenure in Homeric times—and, indeed, early land tenure is a subject so complex and obscure that it is not easy to prove advance towards separate property in the *Odyssey*—beyond what was the rule in the time of the *Iliad.* In the Making of the Arms (XVIII. 541-549) we find many men ploughing a field, and this may have been a common field. But in what sense? Many ploughs were at work at once on a Scottish runrig field, and each farmer had his own strip on several common fields, but each farmer held by rent, or by rent and services, from the laird. These common fields were not common property. In XII. 422 we have "a common field," and men measuring a strip and quarrelling about the marking-stones, across the "baulk," but it does not follow that they are owners; they may be tenants. Such quarrels were common in Scotland when the runrig system of common fields, each man with his strip, prevailed.

A man had a . . . lot (*Iliad,* XV. 448), but what was a "lot"? At first, probably, a share in land periodically shifted—*le partage noir* of the Russian peasants. Kings and men who deserve public gratitude receive . . . a piece of public land, as Bellerophon did from the Lycians (VI. 194). In the case of Melager such an estate is offered to him, but by whom? Not by the people at large, but by the γέροντες (IX. 574).

Who are the γέροντες? They are not ordinary men

of the people; they are, in fact, the gentry. In an age so advanced from tribal conditions as is the Homeric time—far advanced beyond ancient tribal Scotland or Ireland—we conceive that, as in these countries during the tribal period, the γέροντες (in Celtic, the *Flaith*) held *in possession,* if not in accordance with the letter of the law, as *property,* much more land than a single "lot." The Irish tribal freeman had a right to a "lot," redistributed by rotation. Wealth consisted of cattle; and a *bogire,* a man of many kine, let *them* out to tenants. Such a rich man, a *flatha,* would, in accordance with human nature, use his influence with kineless dependents to acquire *in possession* several lots, avoid the partition, and keep the lots in possession though not legally in property. Such men were the Irish *flaith,* gentry under the *Ri,* or king, his γέροντες; each with his *ciniod,* or near kinsmen, to back his cause.

"*Flaith* seems clearly to mean land-owners," or squires, says Sir James Ramsay [in his *Foundations of England*]. If land, contrary to the tribal ideal, came into private hands in early Ireland, we can hardly suppose that, in the more advanced and settled Homeric society, no man but the king held land equivalent in extent to a number of "lots." The . . . gentry, the chariot-owning warriors, of whom there are hundreds not of kingly rank in Homer (as in Ireland there were many *flaith* to one *Ri*) probably, in an informal but tight grip, held considerable lands. When we note their position in the *Iliad,* high above the nameless host, can we imagine that they did not hold more land than the simple, perhaps periodically shifting, "lot"? There were "lotless" men (*Odyssey,* XI. 490), lotless *freemen,* and what had become of their lots? Had they not fallen into the hands of . . . the *flaith?*

Mr. Ridgeway in a very able essay [in *Journal of Hellenic Studies*, vi] holds different opinions. He points out that among a man's possessions, in the *Iliad,* we hear only of personal property and live stock. It is in one passage only in the *Odyssey* (XIV. 211) that we meet with men holding several lots of land; but *they,* we remark, occur in Crete—an isle, as we know, of very advanced civilisation from of old. Mr. Ridgeway also asks whether the lotless men may not be "outsiders," such as are attached to certain villages of Central and Southern India; or they may answer to the *Fuidhir,* or "broken men," of early Ireland, fugitives from one to another tribe. They would be "settled on the waste lands of a community." If so, they would not be lotless; they would have new lots.

Laertes, though a king, is supposed to have won his farm by his own labours from the waste (*Odyssey,* XXIV. 207). Mr. Monro says, "the land having thus been won from the wastes, . . . was a . . . separate possession of Laertes." The passage is in the rejected conclusion of the *Odyssey;* and if any man might go and squat in the waste, any man might have a lot, or better than one lot. In *Iliad,* XXIII. 832-835, Achilles says that his offered prize of iron will be useful to a man "whose rich fields are very remote from any town." Teucer and Meriones compete for the prize: probably they had such rich remote fields, not each a mere lot in a common field. These remote fields they are supposed to hold in perpetuity, apart from the τέμενος, which, in Mr. Ridgeway's opinion, reverted, on the death of each holder, to the community, save where kingship was hereditary. Now, if κλῆρος had come to mean "a lot of land," as we say "a building lot," obviously men like Teucer and Meriones had many lots, rich fields, which at death might sometimes pass to their heirs. Thus there was separate landed property in the *Iliad;* but the passage is denounced, though not by Mr. Ridgeway, as "late."

The absence of enclosures . . . proves nothing about absence of several property in land. In Scotland the laird's lands were unenclosed till deep in the eighteenth century.

My own case for land in private *possession,* in Homeric times, rests mainly on human nature in such an advanced society. Such *possession* as I plead for is in accordance with human nature, in a society so distinguished by degrees of wealth as is the Homeric.

Unless we are able to suppose that all the gentry of the *Iliad* held no "rich fields remote from towns," each having but one rotatory lot apiece, there is no difference in Iliadic and Odyssean land tenure, though we get clearer lights on it in the *Odyssey.*

The position of the man of several lots may have been indefensible, if the ideal of tribal law were ever made real, but wealth in growing societies universally tends to override such law. Mr. Keller justly warns us [in his *Homeric Society,* 1902] against the attempt "to apply universally certain fixed rules of property development. The passages in Homer upon which opinions diverge most are isolated ones, occurring in similes and fragmentary descriptions. Under such conditions the formulation of theories or the attempt rigorously to classify can be little more than an intellectual exercise."

We have not the materials for a scientific knowledge of Homeric real property; and, with all our materials in Irish law books, how hard it is for us to understand the early state of such affairs in Ireland! But does any one seriously suppose that the knightly class of the *Iliad,* the chariot-driving gentlemen, held no more land—legally or by permitted custom—than the two Homeric swains who vituperate each other across a baulk about the right to a few feet of a strip of a runrig field? Whosoever can believe *that* may also believe that the practice of adding "lot" to "lot" began in the period between the finished composition of the *Iliad* (or of the parts of it which allude to land tenure) and the beginning of the *Odyssey* (or of the parts of it which refer to land tenure). The inference is that, though the fact is not explicitly stated in the *Iliad,* there were men who held more "lots" than one in Iliadic times as well as in the Odyssean times, when, in a solitary passage of the *Odyssey,* we do hear of such men in Crete. But whosoever has pored over early European land tenures knows how dim our knowledge is, and will not rush to employ his lore in discriminating between the date of the *Iliad* and the date of the *Odyssey.*

Not much proof of change in institutions between Iliadic and Odyssean times can be extracted from two passages about the . . . bride-price of Penelope. The rule in both *Iliad* and *Odyssey* is that the wooer gives a bride-price to the father of the bride. . . . This was the rule known even to that painfully late and un-Homeric poet who made the Song of Demodocus about the loves of Ares and Aphrodite. In that song the injured husband, Hephæstus, claims back the bride-price which he had paid to the father of his wife, Zeus. This is the accepted custom throughout the *Odyssey* (VI. 159; XVI. 77; XX. 335; XXI. 162; XV. 17, &c.). So far there is no change of manners, no introduction of the later practice, a dowry given with the bride, in place of a bride-price given to the father by the bridegroom. But Penelope was neither maid, wife, nor widow; her husband's fate, alive or dead, was uncertain, and her son was so anxious to get her out of the house that he says he offered gifts *with* her (XX. 342). In the same way, to buy back the goodwill of Achilles, Agamemnon offers to give him his daughter without bride-price, and to add great gifts (*Iliad,* IX. 147). . . . People, of course, could make their own bargain; take as much for their daughter as they could get, or let the gifts go from husband to bride, and then return to the husband's home with her (as in Germany in the time of Tacitus, *Germania,* 18), or do that, and throw in more gifts. But in *Odyssey,* II. 53, Telemachus says that the Wooers shrink from going to the house of Penelope's father, Icarius, who would endow (?) his daughter. . . . And again (*Odyssey,* I. 277; II. 196), her father's folk will furnish a bridal feast. . . . Some critics think that the gifts here are *dowry,* a later institution than bride-price; others, that the father of the dear daughter merely chose to be generous, and returned the bride-price, or its equivalent, in whole or part. If the former view be correct, these passages in *Odyssey,* I., II. are later than the exceedingly "late" song of Demodocus. If the latter theory be correct the father is merely showing goodwill, and doing as the Germans did when they were in a stage of culture much earlier than the Homeric.

The position of Penelope is very unstable and legally perplexing. Has her father her marriage? has her son her marriage? is she not perhaps still a married woman with a living husband? Telemachus would give much to have her off his hands, but he refuses to send her to her father's house, where the old man might be ready enough to return the bride-price to her new husband, and get rid of her with honour. For if Telemachus sends his mother away against her will he will have to pay a heavy fine to her father, and to thole his mother's curse, and lose his character among men (*Odyssey,* II. 130-138). The Icelanders of the saga period gave dowries with their daughters. But when Njal [in *Story of Burnt Njal*] wanted Hildigunna for his foster-son, Hauskuld, he offered to give Ýáïï. "I will lay down as much money as will seem fitting to thy niece and thyself," he says to Flosi, "if thou wilt think of making this match."

Circumstances alter cases, and we must be hard pressed to discover signs of change of manners in the *Odyssey* as compared with the *Iliad* if we have to rely on a solitary mention of "men of many lots" in Crete, and on the perplexed proposals for the second marriage of Penelope. We must not be told that the many other supposed signs of change, Iris, Olympus, and the rest, have "cumulative weight." If we have disposed of each individual supposed note of change in beliefs and manners in its turn, then these proofs have, in each case, no individual weight and, cumulatively, are not more ponderous than a feather.

Arnold lauds Homer as the greatest Greek poet:

From Homer to Tryphiodorus and Quintus the line of [Greek poets], great and little, stretches down her history; but the first is greatest of all, and would be equally greatest had he written last. The verse of Homer is sufficient as the voices of nature are. It cannot be imagined as being better or completer, any more than the noise of the waving of the woods at dawn, or the rhythmical beating of the sea waves upon the shore. It appears as though his Achæan faith were true—as if the Goddess of Poesy, whom he invoked in his opening line, had indeed bowed her brows to him in visible favour; and given her own heaven-strung cithara into his hands, ready set and tuned.

Edwin Arnold, in The Poets of Greece, *Cassell, Petter, and Galpin, 1869.*

Franz Kafka (essay date 1924?)

SOURCE: "The Silence of the Sirens," translated by Willa and Edwin Muir, in *Parables in German and English,* Schocken Books, 1947, pp. 75-77.

[*Regarded as a major figure in twentieth-century literature, Kafka was an original, profoundly moral writer whose central concern was with the essential loneli-*

ness of modern man struggling to comprehend an in-comprehensible world. His literary reputation rests largely upon the posthumous publication of Der Prozess *(1925;* The Trial, *1935),* Das Schloss *(1926;* The Castle, *1930), and* Amerika *(1927;* America, *1938), which relate surreal, nightmarish stories of alienation. In the following essay, originally written in German and for which the exact date of composition is unknown, Kafka examines Ulysses's escape from the Sirens.]*

Proof that inadequate, even childish measures, may serve to rescue one from peril.

To protect himself from the Sirens Ulysses stopped his ears with wax and had himself bound to the mast of his ship. Naturally any and every traveller before him could have done the same, except those whom the Sirens allured even from a great distance; but it was known to all the world that such things were of no help whatever. The song of the Sirens could pierce through everything, and the longing of those they seduced would have broken far stronger bonds than chains and masts. But Ulysses did not think of that, although he had probably heard of it. He trusted absolutely to his handful of wax and his fathom of chain, and in innocent elation over his little stratagem sailed out to meet the Sirens.

Now the Sirens have a still more fatal weapon than their song, namely their silence. And though admittedly such a thing has never happened, still it is conceivable that someone might possibly have escaped from their singing; but from their silence certainly never. Against the feeling of having triumphed over them by one's own strength, and the consequent exaltation that bears down everything before it, no earthly powers could have remained intact.

And when Ulysses approached them the potent song-stresses actually did not sing, whether because they thought that this enemy could be vanquished only by their silence, or because the look of bliss on the face of Ulysses, who was thinking of nothing but his wax and his chains, made them forget their singing.

But Ulysses, if one may so express it, did not hear their silence; he thought they were singing and that he alone did not hear them. For a fleeting moment he saw their throats rising and falling, their breasts lifting, their eyes filled with tears, their lips half-parted, but believed that these were accompaniments to the airs which died unheard around him. Soon, however, all this faded from his sight as he fixed his gaze on the distance, the Sirens literally vanished before his resolution, and at the very moment when they were nearest to him he knew of them no longer.

But they—lovelier than ever—stretched their necks and

turned, let their cold hair flutter free in the wind, and forgetting everything clung with their claws to the rocks. They no longer had any desire to allure; all that they wanted was to hold as long as they could the radiance that fell from Ulysses' great eyes.

If the Sirens had possessed consciousness they would have been annihilated at that moment. But they remained as they had been; all that had happened was that Ulysses had escaped them.

A codicil to the foregoing has also been handed down. Ulysses, it is said, was so full of guile, was such a fox, that not even the goddess of fate could pierce his armor. Perhaps he had really noticed, although here the human understanding is beyond its depths, that the Sirens were silent, and opposed the afore-mentioned pretense to them and the gods merely as a sort of shield.

Werner Jaeger (essay date 1934)

SOURCE: "Nobility and Areté," in *Paideia: The Ideals of Greek Culture, Vol. I,* second edition, translated by Gilbert Highet, Oxford University Press, Inc., 1945, pp. 3-14.

[Jaeger was a German educator and classics scholar whose works include Aristotle: Fundamentals of the History of His Development *(1934) and* Paideia: The Ideals of Greek Culture *(1939-44). In the following excerpt from the latter work, originally published in German in 1934 under the title* Paideia: Die Formung des Griechischen Menschen, *Jaeger examines the* Iliad *and the* Odyssey *as examples of the early Greek aristocratic culture, noting the embodiment of those ideals in the poems' heroes.]*

Education is such a natural and universal function of society that many generations accept and transmit it without question or discussion: thus the first mention of it in literature is relatively late. Its content is roughly the same in every nation—it is both moral and practical. It consists partly of commandments like *Honour the gods, Honour thy father and thy mother, Respect the stranger;* partly of ancient rules of practical wisdom and prescriptions of external morality; and partly of those professional skills and traditions which (as far as they are communicable from one generation to another) the Greeks named *techné.* The several Greek states later embodied in their written laws the elementary rules of respect for gods, parents, and strangers: such legislation, of course, drew no fundamental distinction between law and morality. The rich stream of popular wisdom, on the other hand, carrying with it many ancient rules of conduct and many precepts sprung from old superstition, first flowed into daylight in the gnomic poetry of Hesiod. But the arts and handicrafts naturally resisted the exposure of their secrets in writing, as can be seen from the doctors' professional oath in the Hippocratic corpus.

The training of the young, in the above sense, must be distinguished from cultural education, which aims at fulfilling an ideal of man as he ought to be. In such an ideal pattern, utility is neglected, or at least relegated to the background. The vital factor is . . . the Beautiful as a determinant ideal. The contrast between these two views of education can be seen throughout history, for it is a fundamental part of human nature. It matters little in what words we choose to describe them, but we may, perhaps, use the word Education for the former, and Culture for the latter. It is obvious that culture and education have different origins. Culture is shown in the whole man—both in his external appearance and conduct, and in his inner nature. Both the outer and the inner man are deliberately produced, by a conscious process of selection and discipline which Plato compares to the breeding of good dogs. At first this process is confined to one small class within the state—the nobility. The aristocratic origin of the *kalos kagathos* in classical Greece is as clear as that of the gentleman of England. Both titles carry us back to the ideal of knightly aristocracy. But as the two types were taken over by the bourgeoisie in its rise to power, the ideals inspiring them became universal and at last affected the whole nation.

It is a fundamental fact in the history of culture that all higher civilisation springs from the differentiation of social classes—a differentiation which is created by natural variations in physical and mental capacity between man and man. Even when such social differentiations lead to the creation of a rigid and privileged class, the hereditary principle which rules it is counterbalanced by the new supplies of strength which pour in from the lower classes. And even if the ruling caste is deprived of all its rights, or destroyed, through some violent change, the new leaders rapidly and inevitably become an aristocracy in their turn. The nobility is the prime mover in forming a nation's culture. The history of Greek culture—that universally important aspect of the formation of the Greek national character—actually begins in the aristocratic world of early Greece, with the creation of a definite ideal of human perfection, an ideal towards which the élite of the race was constantly trained. Since our earliest literary evidence shows us an aristocratic civilization rising above the mass of the common people, we must start our historical survey with a sketch of that civilization. All later culture, however high an intellectual level it may reach, and however greatly its content may change, still bears the imprint of its aristocratic origin. Culture is simply the aristocratic ideal of a nation, increasingly intellectualized.

It would seem obvious for us to use the history of the word *paideia* as a clue to the origins of Greek culture.

But we cannot do so, since the word does not occur before the fifth century. That is of course merely an accident of transmission. If new sources were discovered, we might well find evidence of its occurrence at an earlier date. But even then we should be none the wiser; for the earliest examples of its use show that at the beginning of the fifth century it still had the narrow meaning of 'child-rearing' and practically nothing of its later, higher sense. We can find a more natural clue to the history of Greek culture in the history of the idea of *areté,* which goes back to the earliest times. There is no complete equivalent for the word areté in modern English: its oldest meaning is a combination of proud and courtly morality with warlike valour. But the idea of areté is the quintessence of early Greek aristocratic education.

The aristocracies of early Greece are first described by Homer—if we may use that name for the two great epics, the **Iliad** and the **Odyssey**. In Homer we find both the historical evidence for the life of that epoch and the permanent poetic expression of its ideals. We must study him from both points of view. We shall first use him to build up our picture of the aristocratic world, and then examine the ideals of that world as they are embodied in his heroes. For in the great figures of the epic the ideals of aristocracy attain a cultural significance which is far wider than their first narrow sphere of validity. We cannot, in fact, follow the history of culture unless we fix our attention on the ebb and flow of historical development, and at the same time on the artistic struggle to perpetuate the ideal which is the highest expression of every creative epoch.

In Homer, as elsewhere, the word areté is frequently used in a wide sense, to describe not only human merit but the excellence of non-human things—the power of the gods, the spirit and speed of noble horses. But ordinary men have no areté; and whenever slavery lays hold of the son of a noble race, Zeus takes away half of his areté—he is no longer the same man as he was. Areté is the real attribute of the nobleman. The Greeks always believed that surpassing strength and prowess were the natural basis of leadership; it was impossible to dissociate leadership and areté. The root of the word is the same as that of $\rho\iota\sigma\tau o s$ the word which shows superlative ability and superiority; and $\rho\iota\sigma\tau o s$ was constantly used in the plural to denote the nobility. It was natural for the Greeks, who ranked every man according to his ability, to use the same standard for the world in general. That is why they could apply the word areté to things and beings which were not human, and that is why the content of the word grew richer in later times. For a man's ability can be appraised by different standards, varying according to the duties he has to perform. Only now and then, in later books, does Homer use areté for moral or spiritual qualities. Everywhere else (in conformity with the ideas of primitive Greece) it denotes the strength and skill of a warrior or athlete, and above all his heroic valour. But such valour is not considered as a moral quality distinct from strength, in the modern sense; it is always closely bound up with physical power.

It is not probable that in living speech the word areté had only the narrow Homeric sense, at the time when the two poems came into being. The epics themselves recognise standards other than areté. The *Odyssey* constantly exalts intellectual ability—especially in its hero, whose courage is usually ranked lower than his cleverness and cunning. In Homer's time merits different from valour and strength may well have been contained in the notion of areté: apart from the above exceptions, we find such extensions elsewhere in early poetry. It is clear that the new meaning given to the word by everyday speech was then forcing its way into the language of poetry. But areté as a special description of heroic strength and courage was by then fast rooted in the traditional speech of heroic poetry, and was to remain as such for a long period. It was natural that, in the warlike age of the great migrations, men should be valued chiefly for their prowess in battle: there are analogies for this in other countries. Again, the adjective ἀγαϑός which corresponds to the noun areté though it derives from a different root, came to imply the combination of nobility and valour in war. It meant sometimes 'noble' and sometimes 'brave' or 'capable'; but it seldom meant 'good' in the later sense, any more than areté meant 'moral virtue'. This old meaning long survived, in such formalised expressions as 'he died like a brave hero'; and is often found in sepulchral inscriptions and accounts of battles.

Now, although the military connotation of these words predominates in Homer, they have also a more general ethical sense. Both meanings were derived from the same root: both denote the gentlemen who possess (both in war and in private life) standards which are not valid for the common people. Thus the code of the nobility had a twofold influence on Greek education. In the first place, the city-state inherited from it one of the finest elements in its ethical system—the obligation to be brave. (In the city-state courage was called manliness, a clear reminiscence of the Homeric identification of courage with manly areté.) And, secondly, the higher social standards of the polis were derived from aristocratic practice; as is shown not so much in any particular precepts of bourgeois morality as in the general ideals of liberality and a certain magnificence in the conduct of life.

In Homer, the real mark of the nobleman is his sense of duty. He is judged, and is proud to be judged, by a severe standard. And the nobleman educates others by presenting to them an eternal ideal, to which they have a duty to conform. His sense of duty is *aidos*. Anyone is free to appeal to aidos; and if it is slighted the slight

awakes in others the kindred emotion of *nemesis*. Both aidos and nemesis are essential parts of Homer's ideal of aristocracy. The nobleman's pride in high race and ancient achievement is partnered by his knowledge that his pre-eminence can be guaranteed only by the virtues which won it. The aristoi are distinguished by that name from the mass of the common people: and though there are many aristoi, they are always striving with one another for the prize of areté. The Greek nobles believed that the real test of manly virtue was victory in battle—a victory which was not merely the physical conquest of an enemy, but the proof of hard-won areté. This idea is exactly suited by the word *aristeia,* which was later used for the single-handed adventures of an epic hero. The hero's whole life and effort are a race for the first prize, an unceasing strife for supremacy over his peers. (Hence the eternal delight in poetic accounts of these aristeiai.) In peace-time too, the warriors match their aretai against one another in war-games: in the *Iliad* we see them in competition even in a brief pause in the war, at the funeral games of Patroclus. It was that chivalrous rivalry which struck out the motto of knighthood throughout the centuries. . . .

(This, motto, which teachers of all ages have quoted to their pupils, modern educational 'levellers' have now, for the first time, abandoned.) Into that one sentence the poet has condensed the whole educational outlook of the nobility. When Glaucus meets Diomede on the battlefield, and wishes to prove himself a worthy opponent, he first (in the Homeric manner) names his illustrious ancestors, and then continues: 'Hippolochus begat me, and I claim to be his son. He sent me to Troy, and often gave me this command, to strive always for the highest areté, and to excel all others.' It is the finest possible expression of the inspiration of heroic strife: and it was familiar to the author of the eleventh book of the *Iliad,* who makes Peleus give the same counsel to his son Achilles.

There is another way in which the *Iliad* bears witness to the high educational ideals of the early Greek aristocracy. It shows that the old conception of areté as warlike prowess could not satisfy the poets of a new age: their new ideal of human perfection was that character which united nobility of action with nobility of mind. And it is important to notice that the new concept is expressed by Phoenix, who is the old counsellor and teacher of Achilles, the pattern-hero of Greece. At a crisis in the action, he reminds his pupil of the ideal on which he has been moulded: 'to be both a speaker of words and a doer of deeds'. The later Greeks were right in believing this verse to be the earliest formulation of the Greek educational ideal, of its effort to express the whole of human potentialities. It was often quoted in the later ages of rhetoric and sophistication to set off the departed heroic world of action against the wordy and inactive present; but it can be interpreted in another way, for it shows the whole mental outlook of the aristocracy. They believed that mastery of words meant intellectual sovereignty. Phoenix speaks this line to Achilles when he has just received the envoys of the Greek chiefs with sullen anger. The poet presents the eloquent Odysseus and Ajax the laconic man of action as contrasts to Achilles himself. By this contrast he emphasises the highest ideal of developed humanity as personified in the greatest of the heroes—Achilles—who has been trained to it by the third envoy Phoenix. The word areté had originally meant warlike prowess; but it is clear from this passage that a later age found no difficulty in transforming the concept of nobility to suit its own higher ideals, and that the word itself was to acquire a broader meaning to suit this developing ideal.

An essential concomitant of areté is honour. In a primitive community it is inseparable from merit and ability. Aristotle has well described it as a natural standard for man's half-realised efforts to attain areté. 'Men,' he says, 'seem to pursue honour in order to assure themselves of their own worth—their areté. They strive to be honoured for it, by men who know them and who are judicious. It is therefore clear that they recognise areté as superior.' The philosophy of later times then bade man obey an inner standard: it taught him to regard honour as the external image of his inner value, reflected in the criticism of his fellows. But the Homeric man estimated his own worth exclusively by the standards of the society to which he belonged. He was a creature of his class: he measured his own areté by the opinion which others held of him. Yet the philosophic man of later times could dispense with such external recognition, although (as Aristotle says) he might not be entirely indifferent to it.

Homer and the aristocracy of his time believed that the denial of honour due was the greatest of human tragedies. The heroes treat one another with constant respect, since their whole social system depends on such respect. They have all an insatiable thirst for honour, a thirst which is itself a moral quality of individual heroes. It is natural for the great hero or the powerful prince to demand high and higher honour. When the Homeric man does a great deed, he never hesitates to claim the honour which is its fit reward. It is not chiefly the question of payment for services rendered which occupies him. The sources of honour and dishonour are praise and blame. . . . But praise and blame were considered by the philosophic morality of later times to be the foundations of social life, the expression of objective social standards. Nowadays we must find it difficult to imagine how entirely *public* was the conscience of a Greek. (In fact, the early Greeks never conceived anything like the personal conscience of modern times.) Yet we must strive to recognise that fact, before we can comprehend what they meant by honour. Christian sentiment will regard any claim to honour, any self-advancement, as an expression of sin-

ful vanity. The Greeks, however, believed such ambition to be the aspiration of the individual towards that ideal and supra-personal sphere in which alone he can have real value. Thus it is true in some sense to say that the areté of a hero is completed only in his death. Areté exists in mortal man. Areté *is* mortal man. But it survives the mortal, and lives on in his glory, in that very ideal of his areté which accompanied and directed him throughout his life. The gods themselves claim their due honour. They jealously avenge any infringement of it, and pride themselves on the praise which their worshippers give to their deeds. Homer's gods are an immortal aristocracy. And the essence of Greek worship and piety lay in giving honour to godhead: to be pious is 'to honour the divinity'. To honour both gods and men for their areté is a primitive instinct.

On this basis, we can comprehend the tragic conflict of Achilles in the *Iliad*. His indignation at his comrades and his refusal to help them do not spring from an exaggerated individual ambition. A great ambition is, for Greek sentiment, the quality of a great hero. When the hero's honour is offended, the very foundations of the alliance of the Achaean warriors against Troy are shaken. The man who infringes another's honour ends by losing sight of true areté itself. Such a difficulty would now be mitigated by feelings of patriotism; but patriotism is strange to the old aristocratic world. Agamemnon can only make a despotic appeal to his own sovereign power; and such an appeal is equally foreign to aristocratic sentiment, which recognises the leader only as *primus inter pares*. Achilles, when he is refused the honour which he has earned, feels that he is an aristocrat confronted by a despot. But that is not the chief issue. The head and front of the offence is that a pre-eminent areté has been denied its honour. The death of Ajax, the mightiest Greek hero after Achilles, is the second great tragedy of offended honour. The weapons of the dead Achilles are awarded to Odysseus, although Ajax has done more to earn them. The tragedy of Ajax ends in madness and death; the wrath of Achilles brings the Greek army to the edge of the abyss. Homer can scarcely say whether it is possible to repair honour once it has been injured. Phoenix advises Achilles not to bend the bow too far, and to accept Agamemnon's gift as an atonement—for the sake of his comrades in their affliction. But it is not only from obstinacy that Achilles in the original saga refuses the offers of atonement: as is shown once more by the parallel example of Ajax, who returns no answer to the sympathetic words of his former enemy Odysseus when they meet in the underworld, but silently turns away 'to the other souls, into the dark kingdom of the dead'. Thetis entreats Zeus thus: 'Honour my son, who must die sooner than all others. Agamemnon has robbed him of his honour; do you honour him, Olympian!' And the highest of the gods is gracious to Achilles, by allowing the Achaeans, deprived of his help, to be defeated; so that they see how unjustly they have acted in cheating their greatest hero of his honour.

In later ages, love of honour was not considered as a merit by the Greeks: it came to correspond to ambition as we know it. But even in the age of democracy we can see that love of honour was often held to be justifiable in the intercourse of both individuals and states. We can best understand the moral nobility of this idea by considering Aristotle's description of the *megalopsychos,* the proud or high-minded man. In many details, the ethical doctrines of Plato and Aristotle were founded on the aristocratic morality of early Greece: in fact, there is much need for a historical investigation (from that point of view) of the origin, development, and transmission of the ideas which we know as Platonic and Aristotelian. The class limitations of the old ideals were removed when they were sublimated and universalised by philosophy: while their permanent truth and their indestructible ideality were confirmed and strengthened by that process. Of course the thought of the fourth century is more highly detailed and elaborated than that of Homeric times. We cannot expect to find its ideas, or even their exact equivalents, in Homer. But in many respects Aristotle, like the Greeks of all ages, has his gaze fixed on Homer's characters, and he develops his ideals after the heroic patterns. That is enough to show that he was far better able to understand early Greek ideas than we are.

It is initially surprising for us to find that pride or high-mindedness is considered as a virtue. And it is also notable that Aristotle does not believe it to be an independent virtue like the others, but one which presupposes them and is 'in a way an ornament to them'. We cannot understand this unless we recognise that Aristotle is here trying to assign the correct place in his analysis of the moral consciousness to the high-minded areté of old aristocratic morality. In another connexion he says that he considers Achilles and Ajax to be the ideal patterns of this quality. High-mindedness is in itself morally worthless, and even ridiculous, unless it is backed by full areté, the highest unity of all excellences, which neither Aristotle nor Plato shrinks from describing as *kalokagathia*. The great Athenian thinkers bear witness to the aristocratic origin of their philosophy, by holding that areté cannot reach true perfection except in the high-minded man. Both Aristotle and Homer justify their belief that high-mindedness is the finest expression of spiritual and moral personality, by basing it on areté as worthy of honour. 'For honour is the prize of areté; it is the tribute paid to men of ability.' Hence pride is an enhancement of areté. But it is also laid down that to attain true pride, true magnanimity is the most difficult of all human tasks.

Here, then, we can grasp the vital significance of early aristocratic morality for the shaping of the Greek character. It is immediately clear that the Greek conception of man and his areté developed along an unbroken line throughout Greek history. Although it was transformed and enriched in succeeding centuries, it retained the shape which it had taken in the moral code of the nobility. The aristocratic character of the Greek ideal of culture was always based on this conception of areté.

Under the guidance of Aristotle, we may here investigate some of its further implications. He explains that human effort after complete areté is the product of an ennobled self-love. . . . This doctrine is not a mere caprice of abstract speculation—if it were, it would be misleading to compare it with early conceptions of areté. Aristotle is defending the ideal of fully justified self-love as against the current beliefs of his own enlightened and 'altruistic' age; and in doing so he has laid bare one of the foundations of Greek ethical thought. In fact, he admires self-love, just as he prizes high-mindedness and the desire for honour, because his philosophy is deeply rooted in the old aristocratic code of morality. We must understand that the Self is not the physical self, but the ideal which inspires us, the ideal which every nobleman strives to realise in his own life. If we grasp that, we shall see that it is the highest kind of self-love which makes man reach out towards the highest areté: through which he 'takes possession of the beautiful'. The last phrase is so entirely Greek that it is hard to translate. For the Greeks, beauty meant nobility also. To lay claim to the beautiful, to take possession of it, means to overlook no opportunity of winning the prize of the highest areté.

But what did Aristotle mean by the beautiful? Our thoughts turn at once to the sophisticated views of later ages—the cult of the individual, the humanism of the eighteenth century, with its aspirations towards aesthetic and spiritual self-development. But Aristotle's own words are quite clear. They show that he was thinking chiefly of acts of moral heroism. A man who loves himself will (he thought) always be ready to sacrifice himself for his friends or his country, to abandon possessions and honours in order to 'take possession of the beautiful'. The strange phrase is repeated: and we can now see why Aristotle should think that the utmost sacrifice to an ideal is a proof of a highly developed self-love. 'For,' he says, 'such a man would prefer short intense pleasures to long quiet ones; would choose to live nobly for a year rather than to pass many years of ordinary life; would rather do one great and noble deed than many small ones.'

These sentences reveal the very heart of the Greek view of life—the sense of heroism through which we feel them most closely akin to ourselves. By this clue we can understand the whole of Hellenic history—it is the psychological explanation of the short but glorious aristeia of the Greek spirit. The basic motive of Greek areté is contained in the words 'to take possession of

Odysseus beset by the sirens, a scene painted on a section of an ancient Greek vase.

the beautiful'. The courage of a Homeric nobleman is superior to a mad berserk contempt of death in this—that he subordinates his physical self to the demands of a higher aim, the beautiful. And so the man who gives up his life to win the beautiful, will find that his natural instinct for self-assertion finds its highest expression in self-sacrifice. The speech of Diotima in Plato's *Symposium* draws a parallel between the struggles of law-giver and poet to build their spiritual monuments, and the willingness of the great heroes of antiquity to sacrifice their all and to bear hardship, struggle, and death, in order to win the prize of imperishable fame. Both these efforts are explained in the speech as examples of the powerful instinct which drives mortal man to wish for self-perpetuation. That instinct is described as the metaphysical ground of the paradoxes of human ambition. Aristotle himself wrote a hymn to the immortal areté of his friend Hermias, the prince of Atarneus, who died to keep faith with his philosophical and moral ideals; and in that hymn he expressly connects his own philosophical conception of areté with that found in Homer, and with its Hom-

eric ideals Achilles and Ajax. And it is clear that many features in his description of self-love are drawn from the character of Achilles. The Homeric poems and the great Athenian philosophers are bound together by the continuing life of the old Hellenic ideal of areté.

Samuel Eliot Bassett (lecture date 1936?)

SOURCE: "The Epic Illusion (*Continued*)," in *The Poetry of Homer,* University of California Press, 1938, pp. 57-80.

[*Bassett was an influential Greek scholar and one of the foremost Homeric specialists of his time. In this excerpt from a posthumously published collection of lectures, he analyzes Homer's use of dialogue to create the "illusion of personality" in the characters of the* Odyssey *and the* Iliad.]

No poetic picture of past human life can produce the illusion of reality if it does no more than convince us with its general likeness to life. The real world that we know is peopled with other human beings no two of whom are identical. The more intimately we enter into the lives of others, the more we feel the uniqueness of their individualities. The universal human interest is never in typical "man"; it is in persons—because individuals, not types, belong to life. The most universally human presentation of life must therefore create above all the illusion of personality. This is the life principle of every great mythos. The biology of literature may abstract the elements of personality and describe them, but the secret of its synthesis has never been discovered. It differs from moral character as the story from its plot. It is not physical appearance or peculiarities of action. Shylock is a real personality, but who knows how he looked or moved? Much less is it revealed by an analysis of the contents of the mind. Personality is a complex intangible. It has been called a "fourth dimension," a term which in the theory of relativity describes ultimate physical reality. Literary art produces the illusion of the ultimate human reality chiefly by means of the form of self-expression which is most characteristic of our race. Man has been articulate ever since he became human. He makes known the uniqueness of his individuality best by his *ipsissima verba*.

The power of direct speech to create this illusion is seen in the Apologue, where the theme carries us far from reality. When Polyphemus says to Odysseus that he does not recognize the rights of suppliant and stranger, he tells us little more than we have learned from the poet's description of him: "Respect for the right had no place in his heart." But the Cyclops does not become to us a living personality until we not only see him, but also hear him speak. The speech both in Homer and in Attic drama is again and again used as the final and the supreme way of producing upon us the emotion caused by the illusion of personality. In the *Ajax* and in the *Oedipus Rex* of Sophocles the sufferings of the hero are first described, then we see him, and finally we hear from his lips the expression of his agony of mind. In the *Alcestis* of Euripides the handmaid describes the queen's farewell to her home and her failing strength; then we see her with her husband and children, taking her last look at the light of day, and, finally, she speaks, and becomes for the first time a real person. (The Attic drama uses the recital by the Messenger from within and from off-scene to prepare the minds of the audience and so to heighten the impressiveness of a scene of pathos.) Here, as often elsewhere, Homer showed tragedy the way. Homer first describes Cyclops; then after an interval we see him enter the cave and perform his evening tasks; and at last, when these are done and his fire is lighted, we hear his terrible voice and his brutal words. It is the words of Polyphemus to Odysseus, to the other Cyclopes, and to his pet ram, that made him a personality, destined to live throughout classical literature. The king of the Laestrygonians, on the contrary, and his wife

and daughter, all silent actors, lack this reality, and do not appear as characters in later literature. The hospitable Axylus and handsome Nireus are like interesting characters who are merely pointed out to us as they pass on the street. But Thersites and Phoenix are real persons, because we hear them speak. Out of the abundance of the heart the mouth speaketh; and the heart not only is the center of the physical life but also has become for us the center of personality.

The urge to create the illusion of personality through direct speech is primitive. It falls entirely within the sphere of the sensuous; it accords with the naïve personalization of the external world, and it results directly from the childlike tendency to imitate. Aesop's animals speak. The tales of the Old Testament abound in direct discourse. (In the Book of Ruth the story is told in seventy-five verses, I 6-IV 17; only fourteen verses contain no direct utterance, and of indirect discourse there is not a trace.) But the persistence of direct speech as the most universal characteristic of the imaginative picture of life expressed by means of words we cannot explain without recognizing in direct utterance the chief component in the illusion of personality. The term "dramatic illusion" disregards its origin and its debt to Homer. Plato identified Homer with drama in his use of the speeches. His discovery of this most potent ingredient in the "charm" of Homer—under which Plato himself fell—has been too much overlooked in recent years, especially by scholars in other fields than Greek. Both the *Aeneid* and the *Nibelungenlied* have been called more "dramatic" than the Homeric poems. It is true that the adjective is thus used in a derived sense. It describes the effect rather than the manner of drama. But its frequent and ambiguous use has obscured the significance of Aristotle's observation that in the use of the dramatic manner Homer was supreme among epic poets. For this reason, in examining the illusion of personality in Homer we shall discuss at some length the use of speeches, calling in the aid of statistics.

Homer employs direct speech more than any later Western epic poet. Of the three poetic manners in Homer, the objectively narrative, the subjectively explanatory, and the dramatically "imitative," the last is used more than the the first two taken together. If the verses which introduce the speeches and are little more than the stage direction "loquitur" of drama are included, three-fifths of Homer consists of speeches. This is almost exactly the same proportion as that of speech to choral lyrics in the *Suppliants* of Aeschylus.

Homer not only uses direct speech more than any other epic poet of Western literature; he uses it in a more dramatic way.

The characteristic feature of drama is the dialogue. This is literary mimesis in its truest sense, since conversation is the most common accompaniment of all human intercourse. Because Aeschylus added a second actor and thus made true dialogue possible, he was regarded as the father of tragedy. His debt to Homer has not been sufficiently recognized. His remark that his tragedies were "portions from Homer's great feasts," if taken at its face value, should mean that what he added to the embryonic drama of Thespis and his immediate successors was due to the inspiration and pattern of Homer. The evidence is worth considering here, since it also testifies to the dramatic character of Homer.

(1) The first great renascence of Homer fell during the formative years of Aeschylus. The recitation of the Homeric poems was made an important feature of the Panathenaic festival sometime in the sixth century, most probably by the Pisistratids, and was followed by a deep and widespread enthusiasm for Homer. During the fifth century the Homeric poems were familiar to every Athenian; they are likely to have been still more popular before they had to share with the drama the public interest. During the life of Socrates the rhapsode wore a festal costume and employed all the histrionic artifices: Plato makes no distinction between rhapsode and tragic actor. These features were most probably introduced in the sixth century. Homer was the only poet to whom Aeschylus in his early years could have turned for suggestions of the way to handle a tragic plot and present it dramatically. (2) Plato identifies Homer's epic with tragedy in its effect: " . . . the authors of tragic poetry in iambic and in heroic verse"; "When we listen to Homer or any other tragic poet"; "Next, consider tragedy, and its leader and guide, Homer"; "Homer, the first of the tragic poets." Plato, himself a poet, must have had good reason for this identification. (3) Aristotle says that tragedy "has all the elements of the epic." Chancellor [G. R.] Throop has shown [in "Epic and Dramatic, I, II," *Washington University Studies,* Vols. V, 1917, and XII, 1924] that most of the characteristic features of the tragic plot are found in Homer. Finally, Aristotle frequently illustrates from Homer a principle of the structure of a tragic plot. The recognized similarity between Homer and tragedy in plot, in mimesis, and in effect, the lack of other similar poetry (for the cyclic poems were rich in material, but poor in its use), and the great popularity of Homer at Athens just before Aeschylus began to write, seem sufficient to prove that his remark about the influence of Homer upon tragedy was literally true. We notice also that Athenaeus contrasts Aeschylus with a certain Ulpian: the latter took, not "slices" of meat, as Aeschylus did, but a bone or a thick piece of gristle. The *pièces de résistance* of Homer are the dialogues, which Aeschylus, by adding a second actor, introduced into the nascent tragedy.

In the use of the dialogue Homer is unequaled in Western epic. After Homer, Greek epic shows a steady decline in this respect, until in Nonnus there is an average of less than one dialogue to a book, and in the whole of the *Dionysiaca* only three which consist of as many as four speeches. The third book of the *Argonautica,* which is the most dramatic, falls far short of Homer. Vergil, too, restricts the dialogue within far narrower limits than Homer does.

A comparison of Homer's dialogues with those of Attic tragedy is illuminating. Of course, since stichomythy is barred from the epic, we cannot compare the number of speeches per dialogue. Yet Homer has one dialogue of 26 speeches, a greater number than is found in either of the first two epeisodia of the *Prometheus Bound.* We can, however, make the comparison with respect to length of dialogue. In the *Ajax* of Sophocles the six dialogues average about 185 verses each. Homer has seven dialogues, each of which is longer than this. In the *Medea* of Euripides there are eight dialogues containing from 79 to 196 verses each, averaging 131 verses. Homer has 30 dialogues of more than 79 verses each, and 15 of more than 131 verses. The dialogue which contains the Apologue contains 2298 verses, and is undoubtedly the longest dialogue in verse in Greek literature.

In the number of interlocutors Homer's dramatic manner is more free than that of either the primitive folk tale or Attic tragedy. The former limits the number to two, the latter practically to three—for where three actors participate, the words of the Coryphaeus are for the most part a pure formality. In Homer's dialogues three or four speakers often take part, and nine times there are from five to eight, most frequently without a single new entrance. It is noticeable, however, that where Homer is dramatic in effect as well as in manner, the number of speakers is limited to two or three or, at most, four. Plato observes the same freedom and the same limitations.

The *Odyssey* makes a more extensive use of the dialogue than does the *Iliad.* Hirzel [in *Der Dialog,* I, 1895] virtually denies this. He accepts the view of the Author On the Sublime, that the *Odyssey* was the work of the poet's old age: the *Iliad* is "full of action and conflict; the *Odyssey* is largely narrative"—which is characteristic of old age. Hirzel believes that dialogue belongs to youth, whether of the individual or of nations, because passionate youth delights in the external and make-up, while age withdraws within itself, and relates the external to its own ego. Aside from the preponderance of speaker's narratives in the *Odyssey*— . . . Hirzel's chief argument is that the *Odyssey* has no dialogues which compare in dramatic power with those between Hector and Andromache, between Achilles and the Envoys, and between Achilles and Priam. This view confuses theme and situation with the poet's manner of presenting them. The theme of the *Iliad* is more tragic. Hence the situations of the three dialogues just mentioned give rise to deeper emotions. In their effect some of the dialogues of the *Iliad* are more dramatic. But if "dramatic form" is proper to youth and not to old age, as Hirzel thinks, the inference that the *Odyssey* was composed in Homer's later years is not supported by the facts. . . .

The advance in the technique of the dramatic epic exhibited by the *Odyssey* is clear. That it is largely due to the theme and the resulting situations is almost equally so. . . . [Homer gives considerable] attention to rest, and it is here that the dialogue plays its part. On the battlefield combatants may speak as they approach, but if a dialogue ensues we must assume, and the poet often tells us, that they then stood still. On a journey or voyage there is rarely conversation in Homer, except when a halt is made. Priam and Idaeus pause at the river to let their steeds drink, and the long conversation with Hermes ensues. But as they drive on, no word is spoken until they reach the quarters of Achilles. The exchange of speeches at the assembly and the council, in the quarters of Agamemnon, Achilles, and Nestor, and in the palaces of Priam and Paris points to the conclusion that speech and action, the logos and the ergon, tend to exclude each other. Hence the *Odyssey* offers greater opportunity for the dialogue. The scenes at Ogygia, Ithaca, Pylus, Sparta, and Phaeacia are better adapted to the dialogue than is the battlefield at Troy.

The alternation between movement in the narrative and rest in the dialogue has its counterpart in the stasima and epeisodia of tragedy. The evolutions of the chorus offered a pleasing diversion after the comparative lack of action and movement of the actors, except in the entrances and exits. Homer, however, introduces action, even off-scene action, into many of his longer dialogues. The dialogue between Achilles and Priam is thrice interrupted thus: Achilles leaves the hall and prepares the body of Hector for its return; the meal is prepared and eaten; and a couch is prepared for Priam. Attic tragedy had no place for eating and sleeping: the *Alcestis* is "rather like comedy."

This blending of action with dialogue is particularly noticeable in the *Odyssey*. It is less appropriate in the *Iliad* because the violent action of the battlefield demands for the listener's relaxation more completely motionless scenes between the accounts of fighting. Yet the manner is the same in both. In Book XV, in Hera's return from Mount Ida, her chief errand is postponed by the angry exit of Ares to avenge the death of his son Ascalaphus, and his recall to his senses by Athena. This adds much to the picture of the unhappy Olympian family, but has nothing to do with the chief purpose of the episode. It would be impossible in Attic tragedy. Nor could Hera give her message to Iris and Apollo off-scene. Yet these off-scene words, and Athena's "big sister" interference with the plan of

Ares, undoubtedly deepen the perspective in which we view the Olympians, and also contribute to the realism of the story.

Let us test the closeness with which Homer in his long dialogues approaches drama in both manner and effect. At the same time let us try to see how nearly alike the two poems are in both these respects by taking an episode from each, the Presbeia and the Niptra.

In the Presbeia (186-668), the scene is laid in the quarters of Achilles. Achilles, seated, is singing of exploits of heroes, accompanying himself on the lyre. Opposite to him sits Patroclus, listening to his song. Automedon and perhaps other squires are clearing away the dinner. A knock is heard, one of the squires opens the door, and Odysseus and Ajax enter, followed by Phoenix and the two heralds. Achilles and his friend spring to their feet and warmly greet the two envoys. The latter sit while food is prepared and eaten. Then there is an awkward pause—Odysseus, as always, is "the deliberate." Ajax nods to Phoenix to speak, but Odyseus is now ready and begins. The dialogue continues for more than four hundred verses, with six long speeches, a speech by Odysseus, by Phoenix, and by Ajax, and the reply of Achilles to each. This long dialogue is interrupted only by the "loquiturs" and by six verses of stage directions, describing the silence that followed Achilles' rejection of the plea of Odysseus, the emotion of Phoenix (430 f., 433), and the gesture of Achilles to Patroclus to prepare a bed for Phoenix, thus telling the envoys that the interview is over. With the usual libations the envoys and heralds exeunt.

This episode contains nothing that makes it unsuitable for presentation on the stage. It shows not only Homer's ability to dramatize action, but still more his manner of selecting the essential details of setting, of action, and of speeches. If the effect of a narrative is to be deep it must be distinct. Therefore the attention of the hearer must not be diverted by unessential details nor overburdened by too many. We know that Phoenix and the heralds accompanied the envoys; hence no mention is made of their entrance, just as Automedon's presence is not indicated until he is brought into the action (vs. 209). The exchange of greetings and the conversation during the preparation of the food are reduced to a minimum. As listeners we can follow at one time only the action of a single person, or of a small group acting together. Hence our attention is focused on Achilles. His two short speeches—one expressing his glad surprise and his joy at the coming of his friends, the other bidding Patroclus assist in giving them a hearty welcome—are sufficient to create the emotional atmosphere of the action which follows, and to impart to it reality. Of course, we are not to suppose that the envoys maintained an absolute silence until Odysseus spoke, or that there was no conversation while the meal was being prepared and eaten. But realism here would defeat the poet's aim. His interest, and ours, is in the play of spirit on spirit in the debate.

This episode could be presented in a Greek theater by laying the scene before Achilles' door. The envoys would enter and summon him forth from within—at least, this would be the simplest arrangement. Instead of the meal, there must be a brief dialogue to introduce the Debate. It seems unlikely that even Sophocles could have created a greater emotional tension by this dialogue than Homer does by the meal and the two short speeches which precede it.

In the Niptra (51-601), Odysseus, a ragged beggar, is for the first time in twenty years alone in his own hall (51 f.). He is standing at one side, at some distance from the fire. Penelope enters (from the other side) with her attendants, who place for her, near the fire, a chair with a fleece for a cushion. She sits (53-59). The house servants (including Eurycleia) enter, remove the food, the goblets and the tables, and replenish the braziers. Melantho taunts Odysseus because he lingers. He chides her for failing to remember that ill fortune may come to any mortal, and warns her of her own fate if she persists in her disloyal conduct. Penelope overhears the conversation and sternly rebukes Melantho for her unnecessary insolence to the Beggar. He remains, she says, by her own command. She bids Eurynome bring a cushioned stool for the stranger. The stewardess does so. Odysseus takes his seat by the fire, and the conversation with Penelope begins, and continues through eleven speeches, ending with the Queen's command to the old nurse to bathe the Beggar's feet. Aside from the "loquiturs," the poet interrupts only three times to indicate the emotions of the three chief characters. He describes (I) Penelope's burst of tears, called forth by the fictitious account of Odysseus' visit to the Beggar twenty years before, and the pity of Odysseus for his wife—which he stoutly conceals (203-213), (2) her second burst of tears when the Beggar describes the garment and brooch which she herself had given Odysseus at his departure (249-251), and (3) the gesture and tears of Eurycleia when told by Penelope to wash the feet of the Beggar (361 f.). At verse 385, after a speech by Eurycleia, the poet narrates: "The old slave woman took a shining basin and poured in cold water, then hot, until it was the right temperature. Odysseus, sitting at the hearth, quickly turned away from the bright fire, for suddenly the thought came to him that when she took his foot in her hands she would know him by the scar. She came near her master, and began to bathe his feet, and quickly recognized him by the scar, which—" The narrative pauses at this tense moment while the poet tells how Odysseus came by the scar (393-466). The listener is tense with interest, not so much in the outcome, for he knows this will be "happy," as in how the critical situation will be treated. The poet postpones the solution

for seventy-four verses, while he narrates this incident of the past, deliberately, with details, and even with direct speech (404-412). Yet even this part of the Niptra, like all the rest, could be produced on the stage. The water for bathing the feet, we know from verse 503, must be brought in from without. For the stage version, when Penelope bids Eurycleia bathe the stranger's feet, the nurse must leave the hall to get the basin and water (the poet omitted this action as unessential). Odysseus suddenly moves away from the hearth and turns toward the darkened part of the hall, expressing his fears about the scar in a long soliloquy in which he tells the story of the Boar Hunt. Penelope has no interest whatsoever in the act of hospitality to a stranger, and therefore falls into a deep revery—possibly she even nods. Hence she would not hear the soliloquy of Odysseus, nor would she notice the agitation of the old slave when she recognizes her master, nor the look with which Eurycleia tries to draw her attention to her discovery (vss. 476 f.). The poet has a briefer, and altogether sufficient way of indicating the inattention of the Queen: Athena turned her thoughts elsewhere (vss. 478 f.). When Eurycleia has brought fresh water and has bathed and dried the feet of her master, the latter resumes his position by the fire, and the conversation with Penelope is taken up once more and continues until the exeunt of Penelope, the women servants, and, finally, Odysseus (vss. 600 f.).

In external form the two episodes are remarkably alike. They are of the same length. Time (evening) and place (a hall) are the same. There are four speaking actors and mutes or supernumeraries in both. In both the Crowd (the army and the Suitors) are absent. Both begin with the entrance of chief characters and end with "Exeunt omnes." Both lack off-stage action. On the scene the chief movements are due to the proximity of a meal, and minor actions by the chief characters—the lyre song . . . and the spinning of Penelope—contribute to ethos.

But the themes are contrastingly different, and this difference is sufficient to account for many of the dissimilarities. The *Iliad* is a tale of war, unmarked by trickery: the *Odyssey,* of domestic intrigue. Odysseus is the only man in the Niptra, and Eurycleia's rôle is in many ways like that of Phoenix. Achilles is the straightforward, peerless champion. Odysseus excels in $\delta \alpha \lambda o s$. This complicates the situation. The path of the lie is always devious. The Debate in the Presbeia takes the straight course of truth. Its theme is single: Shall Achilles return to the fighting? Hence the speeches of the episode can be limited to seven, and the Debate is not interrupted by action. The Niptra contains twenty-six speeches, all concerned with the intrigue which arises from the return of Odysseus. The main dialogue falls into three parts. Two questions are to be answered: Is it likely that Odysseus will return? and Shall Penelope select a new husband by the ordeal of the Bow?

Between these two "debates" both action and dialogue are inserted which deepen the impression that Penelope's first question has already been answered happily, and that the ordeal will not result as she forebodes.

The themes determine the kind and the degree of emotion aroused by the two episodes. The Presbeia consolidates its effect because the emotion which it arouses is strictly tragic. But the tragedy with a happy ending may also be highly dramatic in its effect. The Niptra does not suffer by comparison with the famous recognition scene in the *Iphigenia in Tauris*. In both, the situation permits two recognitions. Euripides presents them both, because both situation and plot demand the second, inferior though it is. The Niptra, like the *Oedipus Rex,* successfully postpones the second and major recognition, and the resulting suspense enhances the effect. Now, as the recognition in the *Iphigenia* is as "dramatic" but not as "tragic" as that of the *Oedipus,* so the Niptra is quite as "dramatic" as the Presbeia though not equally "tragic." In the same way the parting between Hector and Andromache, and the scene between Achilles and Prima, are no more "dramatic" than the Argus episode and the recognitions of Odysseus by Penelope and Laertes. The theme of the *Iliad* is the greater one: the dramatic art of the poet is essentially the same in both *Iliad* and *Odyssey*.

The theme of the *Odyssey* also explains sufficiently its greater use of the narratives contained in the dialogues. We need not resort to the explanation offered by the Author On the Sublime, that the love of tales is a token of the old age of genius. These tales, with very rare exceptions, are told only in the dialogue. Like the dialogue itself, they bulk larger in the *Odyssey,* but the technique of their use is found in the *Iliad*.

Corinna's advice to the youthful Pindar to use more myth in his odes contains a universal truth. Poetry, prose, and every speaker, use the tale because it illustrates one's thoughts, from experience real or imagined. Thus Agamemnon tells the tale of the birth of Heracles as an instance of the infatuation to which great kings, whether of Olympus or of Argos, are liable. The modern public speaker's tale or anecdote has a similar use, and often the story is remembered long after its moral has been forgotten. Hephaestus told the story of his fall from Heaven to illustrate the danger of crossing the purpose of Zeus. The tale is firmly embedded in literature; its moral is usually forgotten.

Men must converse about something, and small talk is not "memorable speech." The tale gives body to many of the longer dialogues of Homer. Remove from the only speech that Phoenix makes, the allegory, the story of his own youth, and the tale of Meleager, and the residue is too meager to justify the speech. What else could the Swineherd and the Beggar do during a long day and a long night, except to tell of their own past

lives? Without these long conversations the two episodes would lack both extent and content.

In addition to the three uses just described—to give body to the dialogue, to enrich it with matters in themselves interesting, and to illustrate an argument or strengthen a plea—the tale within the tale is employed to give the needful exposition of the past. It is this function which explains its more extensive use in the *Odyssey*.

The *Iliad* and the *Odyssey* contain each about a score of these narratives, but in the *Odyssey* their average length is much greater (including the Apologue, about six times as great; without the Apologue, at least twice). In the *Iliad* the account of the past is of comparatively little importance. With a few exceptions, the previous years of the war are for the most part ignored. We are told of incidents in the previous fighting of Achilles, and of the negotiations for the return of Helen. Aulis is mentioned in one episode. But for the reconstruction of a history of the earlier years of the war we must rely on casual references. It is the same with the past lives of the major heroes, except Achilles, Diomede, and a few others. Hence (in the *Iliad*) the tales which enrich the dialogues are largely taken from, or include, well-known myths and legends, like those of the Centaurs and Amazons, Heracles, and the Seven Against Thebes.

The *Iliad* tells of a tragic incident near the close of the war. The *Odyssey* includes the events of the next ten years. It is a Nostoi as well as a Nostos, for it tells of the death or the safe homecoming of every major Greek hero of the *Iliad*. Of this part of the theme we are given a hint at the beginning of the poem. Now it is significant that of about twenty tales within a dialogue in the *Odyssey* fourteen are of events, real or fictitious, in the lives of Odysseus or of some major hero of the *Iliad* between the end of the *Iliad* and the beginning of the *Odyssey,* and five more concern Odysseus or some member of his family. Only the tale of Eumaeus is of matters outside the theme.

The richness of the dialogue . . . is undoubtedly due to the Ionian *Lust zur Fabulierung,* but the art with which the tales are inserted is one of the many indications that with Homer the intuitive power to impart to a narrative the reality of life reached an all-time peak. The German term *Rahmenerzählung* fails to do full justice to this innate power. In Homer the frame and the tale blend into one, so that the tale becomes an organic element in the conversation of living persons. . . .

In Homer the Apologue grows out of the previous action and blends imperceptibly with what follows. Its setting and its beginning and end are truer to life. Odysseus, always "the deliberate," has avoided telling his name. But he knows he must do so, as Alcinous says, if the

Phaeacian ship is to carry him home. The time for this has come. So he asks Demodocus to sing of . . . the Wooden Horse. This is, as it were, the overture to the recognition. The questions of Alcinous spring naturally from the situation: "Who are you? Where is your home? Where have you wandered? [He knew from the conversation of the previous evening that his guest had suffered much.] Why do you weep when the bard sings of the Trojan War?" The reply of Odysseus contains more than the tale of his wanderings. It is treated as an after-dinner speech. There is first the delicate compliment to host and bard; then the modest hint that the speaker can add nothing to the enjoyment of the feast, and the equally modest and tactful remark that one's own simple home is far dearer than luxury in a foreign land. At the middle of the speech—also at the one point where the narrative threatens to become wearisome—the speaker suggests that he has spoken long enough, and is complimented and urged to go on. At the end the dialogue is continued, with the appreciation of the speech, and the life which the poet is presenting goes on without a break. Homer's *Rahmenerzählung* is not an artifice; it is the unconscious result of the consummate art of the master of oral narrative, which relies for the illusion of reality chiefly on the *ipsissima verba* of individuals.

The oral narrative uses the direct utterance of its characters also for other subordinate purposes. A reader with print before his eyes can reread the words if their full import is not clear at first, or if he wishes to enjoy again the emotion which they arouse. But the "winged word" cannot be thus recalled. This is perhaps one reason why Homer uses the single speech, either in or outside of the dialogue, which might easily be omitted in written narrative. Sometimes the single speech does little more than "hold the picture" and give the listener time to enter it emotionally. The speeches of Odysseus to the leaders and the common soldiers in the Diapeira are quite unnecessary for the printed narrative: "Whenever he met a prince or a man of prominence, he would stop and with gentle and courteous words check his flight to the ships [the words of the speech follow]. But if he saw a common soldier and found him joining in the cry [to launch the ships], he would smite him with his scepter and with harsh words rebuke him [the harsh words follow]. Thus with authority he went through the camp, and the army rushed back to the assembly." The *ipsissima verba* of Odysseus (vss. 190-197, 200-206) bring him more closely before our attention, and present him less as a fact than as a personal character in the story. But they also give us time to picture the turning back of the army from its purpose to sail home.

The words of exultation over a fallen enemy often serve the same purpose. When Othryoneus, suitor for Cassandra's hand, is slain by Idomeneus, or Cebriones by Patroclus, or Iphition by Achilles, the victor's boast tells us almost exactly what we have learned just before from the poet about the importance of the slain warrior or the manner of his fall. But the repetition of the same idea helps the listener to grasp them better. Similes are used for a similar purpose. But rarely do we find both the victor's boast and the simile used together. The fall of Asius, slain by Idomeneus just after Othryoneus, is pictured with the aid of a simile; that of Alcathous, which follows soon after, not by a simile, but by a speech of exultation. The fall of Sarpedon is described by a simile, and Patroclus does not exult over his body; but no simile is used when Hector falls; instead, Achilles exults over him. Both simile and speech of exultation "hold the picture" and, in different ways, present the death of a warrior as the carrier of some emotion, and not merely as a historical fact.

Perhaps the commonest secondary use of single speech is to make clearer the action which is to follow. On these single speeches the poet, or the bards who preceded him, seem to have bestowed special attention. With all their variety they show a far greater tendency to be typical than do the dialogues, especially the longer ones. It is the same technique of specialization which Euripides shows in his speeches of prologist and messenger. . . . Fully 90 per cent of the 350-odd single speeches of the *Iliad,* and 80 per cent of the 70-odd in the *Odyssey,* fall into one or other of the following categories: (1) the prayer; (2) the soliloquy; (3) the "Voice from the crowd"; (4) the Messenger's repetition of a command; (5) the exhortation of a general to his army, or of a warrior to his comrade; (6) the flyting of a foe, or the exultation over his fall; (7) the dirge; (8) the command.

Of the more than 400 single speeches in the two poems, about 40 per cent are commands. Furthermore, the last speech of a dialogue often expresses a command or a purpose. By this means the listener is informed of the action which is to be described. The speeches of Zeus in the *Iliad* and of Athena in the *Odyssey* serve this purpose. Helenus thus twice announces the program of the following episode. Nestor often plays the rôle of announcer. In the *Odyssey,* Nestor's command to his sons is carried out almost to the letter in the account of the sacrifice to Athena.

The repetition of the same command by other single speeches often helps to emphasize action which is of unusual importance in the plot. The thrice repeated description of the proposed journey of Telemachus gives the listener fair warning that this episode is to bulk large in the sequel. We, who find in a novel a table of contents and often chapter headings, are apt to forget that to the simple and unsophisticated listener this kind of information must have been very welcome. The tendency of some readers to turn to the last pages of a novel to see how it ends, shows how this kind of curiosity may interfere with the enjoyment of the immediate action. The latter is always Homer's chief concern. If the narrator had given the information *in propria persona* and at length, he would have diverted the attention of his hearer to the fact that he was listening to a story. The illusion would have been partly effaced.

Speeches which forecast the action of an episode often add its ethos, which likewise gains by repetition. The "baneful Dream" repeats to Agamemnon, and Agamemnon to the council, the command of Zeus to arm the long-haired Achaeans with all speed, for now Hera has prevailed over the Olympians, and Troy may be captured. Homer has prepared for the "baneful Dream" by the ironical words of Achilles to Agamemnon: "[Consult some seer or priest,] aye, or a reader of dreams, *for the dream comes from Zeus.*" The first Olympian episode has made it clear that Zeus is deceiving Agamemnon when he says that Hera's entreaties have won over all the Olympians to the side of the Greeks. The first speech in Book II therefore not only gives the program of the marshaling of the troops, but also helps to create the atmosphere with which the poet surrounds Agamemnon throughout the poem.

The terms of the truce are recited four times: by Hector, by Iris, by the Trojan herald, and by Agamemnon. They are of extreme importance, because after the Trojans have broken the truce—and not till then,—Greeks, Trojans, and the listeners are sure that Troy is doomed. The truce and its violation add an undertone to the rest of the story.

Whatever their secondary functions may be, the speeches have as their major purpose the presentation of the characters as living personalities. The reality of the characters is shown by the way they live today. Homer gave them, indeed, a kind of immortality. In this respect his only rival in Greek literature is Plato. The Platonic Socrates and his friends and acquaintances still live for us, because we hear them converse as men of that day must have spoken. The illusion of personality is not created best by the analysis of a few characters, possibly because one's nature is best revealed by the varied contact with many other individuals. Dickens, with fifty or more characters in some of his novels, portrays personality quite as well as Thackeray with far fewer. The half-dozen characters of an Attic tragedy cannot compare in this respect with Shakespeare's far more numerous *dramatis personae*. There are about seventy-five speaking characters in the *Iliad,* and nearly as many in the *Odyssey,* if we include the Apologue and the tale of Proteus. No two of these are alike. As Aristotle says, by their words they all reveal different individual traits. We should not mistake Eidothea for Leucothea if we could talk with these two sea nymphs. The more we hear the characters speak, the better we know their personal peculiarities. . . .

The primitive man personalizes his thoughts of the world. The oral narrative must present a tale dramatically both because it is primitive and because its method of presentation lends itself to pure mimesis. Long generations during which the attention of bards was concentrated on this one genre would, with fortune, produce ever greater attention to the persons of the tale. It is not surprising that in Homer there are more numerous, more varied, and perhaps more living characters than we find in the work of any other poet before Shakespeare.

Butler on humor in the *Odyssey* (c. 1902):

[Let] me point out the irony of literature in connection with this astonishing work. Here is a poem in which the hero and heroine have already been married many years before it begins: it is marked by a total absence of love-business in such sense as we understand it: its interest centres mainly in the fact of a bald elderly gentleman, whose little remaining hair is red, being eaten out of house and home during his absence by a number of young men who are courting the supposed widow—a widow who, if she be fair and fat, can hardly also be less than forty. Can any subject seem more hopeless? Moreover, this subject so initially faulty is treated with a carelessness in respect of consistency, ignorance of commonly known details, and disregard of ordinary canons, that can hardly be surpassed, and yet I cannot think that in the whole range of literature there is a work which can be decisively placed above it. I am afraid you will hardly accept this; I do not see how you can be expected to do so, for in the first place there is no even tolerable prose translation, and in the second, the *Odyssey,* like the *Iliad,* has been a school book for over two thousand five hundred years, and what more cruel revenge than this can dullness take on genius?

Samuel Butler, in The Humour of Homer and Other Essays, *Mitchell Kennerley, 1914.*

Erich Auerbach (essay date 1946)

SOURCE: "Odysseus' Scar," in *Mimesis: The Representation of Reality in Western Literature,* translated by Willard R. Trask, Princeton University Press, 1953, pp. 3-23.

[Auerbach was a German-born American philologist and critic. He is best known for his Mimesis: Dargestellte Wirklichkeit in der Abendländischen Literatur *(1946;* Mimesis, The Representation of Reality in Western Literature, *1953), a landmark study in which the critic explores the interpretation of reality through literary representation. In the following excerpt from that work, Auerbach compares the discourse, perspec-*

tive, detail, and historical development of the Odyssey *with that of several Old Testament stories.*]

Readers of the **Odyssey** will remember the well-prepared and touching scene in book 19, when Odysseus has at last come home, the scene in which the old housekeeper Euryclea, who had been his nurse, recognizes him by a scar on his thigh. The stranger has won Penelope's good will; at his request she tells the housekeeper to wash his feet, which, in all old stories, is the first duty of hospitality toward a tired traveler. Euryclea busies herself fetching water and mixing cold with hot, meanwhile speaking sadly of her absent master, who is probably of the same age as the guest, and who perhaps, like the guest, is even now wandering somewhere, a stranger; and she remarks how astonishingly like him the guest looks. Meanwhile Odysseus, remembering his scar, moves back out of the light; he knows that, despite his efforts to hide his identity, Euryclea will now recognize him, but he wants at least to keep Penelope in ignorance. No sooner has the old woman touched the scar than, in her joyous surprise, she lets Odysseus' foot drop into the basin; the water spills over, she is about to cry out her joy; Odysseus restrains her with whispered threats and endearments; she recovers herself and conceals her emotion. Penelope, whose attention Athena's foresight had diverted from the incident, has observed nothing.

All this is scrupulously externalized and narrated in leisurely fashion. The two women express their feelings in copious direct discourse. Feelings though they are, with only a slight admixture of the most general considerations upon human destiny, the syntactical connection between part and part is perfectly clear, no contour is blurred. There is also room and time for orderly, perfectly well-articulated, uniformly illuminated descriptions of implements, ministrations, and gestures; even in the dramatic moment of recognition, Homer does not omit to tell the reader that it is with his right hand that Odysseus takes the old woman by the throat to keep her from speaking, at the same time that he draws her closer to him with his left. Clearly outlined, brightly and uniformly illuminated, men and things stand out in a realm where everything is visible; and not less clear—wholly expressed, orderly even in their ardor—are the feelings and thoughts of the persons involved.

In my account of the incident I have so far passed over a whole series of verses which interrupt it in the middle. There are more than seventy of these verses—while to the incident itself some forty are devoted before the interruption and some forty after it. The interruption, which comes just at the point when the housekeeper recognizes the scar—that is, at the moment of crisis—describes the origin of the scar, a hunting accident which occurred in Odysseus' boyhood, at a boar hunt, during the time of his visit to his grandfather Autolycus. This first affords an opportunity to inform the reader about Autolycus, his house, the precise degree of the kinship, his character, and, no less exhaustively than touchingly, his behavior after the birth of his grandson; then follows the visit of Odysseus, now grown to be a youth; the exchange of greetings, the banquet with which he is welcomed, sleep and waking, the early start for the hunt, the tracking of the beast, the struggle, Odysseus' being wounded by the boar's tusk, his recovery, his return to Ithaca, his parents' anxious questions—all is narrated, again with such a complete externalization of all the elements of the story and of their interconnections as to leave nothing in obscurity. Not until then does the narrator return to Penelope's chamber, not until then, the digression having run its course, does Euryclea, who had recognized the scar before the digression began, let Odysseus' foot fall back into the basin.

The first thought of a modern reader—that this is a device to increase suspense—is, if not wholly wrong, at least not the essential explanation of this Homeric procedure. For the element of suspense is very slight in the Homeric poems; nothing in their entire style is calculated to keep the reader or hearer breathless. The digressions are not meant to keep the reader in suspense, but rather to relax the tension. And this frequently occurs, as in the passage before us. The broadly narrated, charming, and subtly fashioned story of the hunt, with all its elegance and self-sufficiency, its wealth of idyllic pictures, seeks to win the reader over wholly to itself as long as he is hearing it, to make him forget what had just taken place during the foot-washing. But an episode that will increase suspense by retarding the action must be so constructed that it will not fill the present entirely, will not put the crisis, whose resolution is being awaited, entirely out of the reader's mind, and thereby destroy the mood of suspense; the crisis and the suspense must continue, must remain vibrant in the background. But Homer—and to this we shall have to return later—knows no background. What he narrates is for the time being the only present, and fills both the stage and the reader's mind completely. So it is with the passage before us. When the young Euryclea (vv. 401ff.) sets the infant Odysseus on his grandfather Autolycus' lap after the banquet, the aged Euryclea, who a few lines earlier had touched the wanderer's foot, has entirely vanished from the stage and from the reader's mind.

Goethe and Schiller, who, though not referring to this particular episode, exchanged letters in April 1797 on the subject of "the retarding element" in the Homeric poems in general, put it in direct opposition to the element of suspense—the latter word is not used, but is clearly implied when the "retarding" procedure is opposed, as something proper to epic, to tragic procedure (letters of April 19, 21, and 22). The "retarding element," the "going back and forth" by means of episodes, seems to me, too, in the Homeric poems, to be opposed to any tensional and suspensive striving toward a goal, and doubtless Schiller is right in regard to Homer when he says that what he gives us is "simply the quiet existence and operation of things in accordance with their natures"; Homer's goal is "already present in every point of his progress." But both Schiller and Goethe raise Homer's procedure to the level of a law for epic poetry in general, and Schiller's words quoted above are meant to be universally binding upon the epic poet, in contradistinction from the tragic. Yet in both modern and ancient times, there are important epic works which are composed throughout with no "retarding element" in this sense but, on the contrary, with suspense throughout, and which perpetually "rob us of our emotional freedom"—which power Schiller will grant only to the tragic poet. And besides it seems to me undemonstrable and improbable that this procedure of Homeric poetry was directed by aesthetic considerations or even by an aesthetic feeling of the sort postulated by Goethe and Schiller. The effect, to be sure, is precisely that which they describe, and is, furthermore, the actual source of the conception of epic which they themselves hold, and with them all writers decisively influenced by classical antiquity. But the true cause of the impression of "retardation" appears to me to lie elsewhere—namely, in the need of the Homeric style to leave nothing which it mentions half in darkness and unexternalized.

The excursus upon the origin of Odysseus' scar is not basically different from the many passages in which a newly introduced character, or even a newly appearing object or implement, though it be in the thick of a battle, is described as to its nature and origin; or in which, upon the appearance of a god, we are told where he last was, what he was doing there, and by what road he reached the scene; indeed, even the Homeric epithets seem to me in the final analysis to be traceable to the same need for an externalization of phenomena in terms perceptible to the senses. Here is the scar, which comes up in the course of the narrative; and Homer's feeling simply will not permit him to see it appear out of the darkness of an unilluminated past; it must be set in full light, and with it a portion of the hero's boyhood—just as, in the *Iliad*, when the first ship is already burning and the Myrmidons finally arm that they may hasten to help, there is still time not only for the wonderful simile of the wolf, not only for the order of the Myrmidon host, but also for a detailed account of the ancestry of several subordinate leaders (vv. 155ff.). To be sure, the aesthetic effect thus produced was soon noticed and thereafter consciously sought; but the more original cause must have lain in the basic impulse of the Homeric style: to represent phenomena in a fully externalized form, visible and palpable in all their parts, and completely fixed in their spatial and temporal relations. Nor do psychological processes receive any other treatment: here too nothing must remain hidden and unexpressed. With the utmost fullness, with an orderliness which even passion does not disturb, Homer's personages vent their inmost hearts in speech; what they do not say to others, they speak in their own minds, so that the reader is informed of it. Much that is terrible takes place in the Homeric poems, but it seldom takes place wordlessly: Polyphemus talks to Odysseus; Odysseus talks to the suitors when he begins to kill them; Hector and Achilles talk at length, before battle and after; and no speech is so filled with anger or scorn that the particles which express logical and grammatical connections are lacking or out of place. This last observation is true, of course, not only of speeches but of the presentation in general. The separate elements of a phenomenon are most clearly placed in relation to one another; a large number of conjunctions, adverbs, particles, and other syntactical tools, all clearly circumscribed and delicately differentiated in meaning, delimit persons, things, and portions of incidents in respect to one another, and at the same time bring them together in a continuous and ever flexible connection; like the separate phenomena themselves, their relationships—their temporal, local, causal, final, consecutive, comparative, concessive, antithetical, and conditional limitations—are brought to light in perfect fullness; so that a continuous rhythmic procession of phenomena passes by, and never is there a form left fragmentary or half-illuminated, never a lacuna, never a gap, never a glimpse of unplumbed depths.

And this procession of phenomena takes place in the foreground—that is, in a local and temporal present which is absolute. One might think that the many interpolations, the frequent moving back and forth, would create a sort of perspective in time and place; but the Homeric style never gives any such impression. The way in which any impression of perspective is avoided can be clearly observed in the procedure for introducing episodes, a syntactical construction with which every reader of Homer is familiar; it is used in the passage we are considering, but can also be found in cases when the episodes are much shorter. To the word scar (v. 393) there is first attached a relative clause ("which once long ago a boar . . ."), which enlarges into a voluminous syntactical parenthesis; into this an independent sentence unexpectedly intrudes (v. 396: "A god himself gave him . . ."), which quietly disentangles itself from syntactical subordination, until, with verse 399, an equally free syntactical treatment of the new content begins a new present which continues unchallenged until, with verse 467 ("The old woman now touched it . . ."), the scene which had been broken off is resumed. To be sure, in the case of such long episodes as the one we are considering, a purely syntactical connection with the principal theme would hardly have been possible; but a connection with it through perspective would have been all the easier had the content been arranged with that end in view; if, that is, the entire story of the scar had been presented as a recollection which awakens in Odysseus' mind at this particular moment. It would have been perfectly easy to do; the story of the scar had only to be inserted two verses earlier, at the first mention of the word scar, where the motifs "Odysseus" and "recollection" were already at hand. But any such subjectivistic-perspectivistic procedure, creating a foreground and background, resulting in the present lying open to the depths of the past, is entirely foreign to the Homeric style; the Homeric style knows only a foreground, only a uniformly illuminated, uniformly objective present. And so the excursus does not begin until two lines later, when Euryclea has discovered the scar—the possibility for a perspectivistic connection no longer exists, and the story of the wound becomes an independent and exclusive present.

The genius of the Homeric style becomes even more apparent when it is compared with an equally ancient and equally epic style from a different world of forms. I shall attempt this comparison with the account of the sacrifice of Isaac, a homogeneous narrative produced by the so-called Elohist. The King James version translates the opening as follows (Genesis 22:1): "And it came to pass after these things, that God did tempt Abraham, and said to him, Abraham! and he said, Behold, here I am." Even this opening startles us when we come to it from Homer. Where are the two speakers? We are not told. The reader, however, knows that they are not normally to be found together in one place on earth, that one of them, God, in order to speak to Abraham, must come from somewhere, must enter the earthly realm from some unknown heights or depths. Whence does he come, whence does he call to Abraham? We are not told. He does not come, like Zeus or Poseidon, from the Aethiopians, where he has been enjoying a sacrificial feast. Nor are we told anything of his reasons for tempting Abraham so terribly. He has not, like Zeus, discussed them in set speeches with other gods gathered in council; nor have the deliberations in his own heart been presented to us; unexpected and mysterious, he enters the scene from some unknown height or depth and calls: Abraham! It will at once be said that this is to be explained by the particular concept of God which the Jews held and which was wholly different from that of the Greeks. True enough—but this constitutes no objection. For how is the Jewish concept of God to be explained? Even their earlier God of the desert was not fixed in form and content, and was alone; his lack of form, his lack of local habitation, his singleness, was in the end not only maintained but developed even further in competition with the comparatively far more manifest gods of the surrounding Near Eastern world. The concept of God held by the Jews is less a cause than a symptom of their manner of comprehending and representing things.

This becomes still clearer if we now turn to the other

person in the dialogue, to Abraham. Where is he? We do not know. He says, indeed: Here I am—but the Hebrew word means only something like "behold me," and in any case is not meant to indicate the actual place where Abraham is, but a moral position in respect to God, who has called to him—Here am I awaiting thy command. Where he is actually, whether in Beersheba or elsewhere, whether indoors or in the open air, is not stated; it does not interest the narrator, the reader is not informed; and what Abraham was doing when God called to him is left in the same obscurity. To realize the difference, consider Hermes' visit to Calypso, for example, where command, journey, arrival and reception of the visitor, situation and occupation of the person visited, are set forth in many verses; and even on occasions when gods appear suddenly and briefly, whether to help one of their favorites or to deceive or destroy some mortal whom they hate, their bodily forms, and usually the manner of their coming and going, are given in detail. Here, however, God appears without bodily form (yet he "appears"), coming from some unspecified place—we only hear his voice, and that utters nothing but a name, a name without an adjective, without a descriptive epithet for the person spoken to, such as is the rule in every Homeric address; and of Abraham too nothing is made perceptible except the words in which he answers God: *Hinne-ni,* Behold me here—with which, to be sure, a most touching gesture expressive of obedience and readiness is suggested, but it is left to the reader to visualize it. Moreover the two speakers are not on the same level: if we conceive of Abraham in the foreground, where it might be possible to picture him as prostrate or kneeling or bowing with outspread arms or gazing upward, God is not there too: Abraham's words and gestures are directed toward the depths of the picture or upward, but in any case the undetermined, dark place from which the voice comes to him is not in the foreground.

After this opening, God gives his command, and the story itself begins: everyone knows it; it unrolls with no episodes in a few independent sentences whose syntactical connection is of the most rudimentary sort. In this atmosphere it is unthinkable that an implement, a landscape through which the travelers passed, the serving-men, or the ass, should be described, that their origin or descent or material or appearance or usefulness should be set forth in terms of praise; they do not even admit an adjective: they are serving-men, ass, wood, and knife, and nothing else, without an epithet; they are there to serve the end which God has commanded; what in other respects they were, are, or will be, remains in darkness. A journey is made, because God has designated the place where the sacrifice is to be performed; but we are told nothing about the journey except that it took three days, and even that we are told in a mysterious way: Abraham and his followers rose "early in the morning" and "went unto" the place of which God had told him; on the third day he lifted up his eyes and saw the place from afar. That gesture is the only gesture, is indeed the only occurrence during the whole journey, of which we are told; and though its motivation lies in the fact that the place is elevated, its uniqueness still heightens the impression that the journey took place through a vacuum; it is as if, while he traveled on, Abraham had looked neither to the right nor to the left, had suppressed any sign of life in his followers and himself save only their footfalls.

Thus the journey is like a silent progress through the indeterminate and the contingent, a holding of the breath, a process which has no present, which is inserted, like a blank duration, between what has passed and what lies ahead, and which yet is measured: three days! Three such days positively demand the symbolic interpretation which they later received. They began "early in the morning." But at what time on the third day did Abraham lift up his eyes and see his goal? The text says nothing on the subject. Obviously not "late in the evening," for it seems that there was still time enough to climb the mountain and make the sacrifice. So "early in the morning" is given, not as an indication of time, but for the sake of its ethical significance; it is intended to express the resolution, the promptness, the punctual obedience of the sorely tried Abraham. Bitter to him is the early morning in which he saddles his ass, calls his serving-men and his son Isaac, and sets out; but he obeys, he walks on until the third day, then lifts up his eyes and sees the place. Whence he comes, we do not know, but the goal is clearly stated: Jeruel in the land of Moriah. What place this is meant to indicate is not clear—"Moriah" especially may be a later correction of some other word. But in any case the goal was given, and in any case it is a matter of some sacred spot which was to receive a particular consecration by being connected with Abraham's sacrifice. Just as little as "early in the morning" serves as a temporal indication does "Jeruel in the land of Moriah" serve as a geographical indication; and in both cases alike, the complementary indication is not given, for we know as little of the hour at which Abraham lifted up his eyes as we do of the place from which he set forth—Jeruel is significant not so much as the goal of an earthly journey, in its geographical relation to other places, as through its special election, through its relation to God, who designated it as the scene of the act, and therefore it must be named.

In the narrative itself, a third chief character appears: Isaac. While God and Abraham, the serving-men, the ass, and the implements are simply named, without mention of any qualities or any other sort of definition, Isaac once receives an appositive; God says, "Take Isaac, thine only son, whom thou lovest." But this is not a characterization of Isaac as a person, apart from his relation to his father and apart from the story; he may be handsome or ugly, intelligent or stupid, tall or short, pleasant or unpleasant—we are not told. Only what we need to know about him as a personage in the action, here and now, is illuminated, so that it may become apparent how terrible Abraham's temptation is, and that God is fully aware of it. By this example of the contrary, we see the significance of the descriptive adjectives and digressions of the Homeric poems; with their indications of the earlier and as it were absolute existence of the persons described, they prevent the reader from concentrating exclusively on a present crisis; even when the most terrible things are occurring, they prevent the establishment of an overwhelming suspense. But here, in the story of Abraham's sacrifice, the overwhelming suspense is present; what Schiller makes the goal of the tragic poet—to rob us of our emotional freedom, to turn our intellectual and spiritual powers (Schiller says "our activity") in one direction, to concentrate them there—is effected in this Biblical narrative, which certainly deserves the epithet epic.

We find the same contrast if we compare the two uses of direct discourse. The personages speak in the Bible story too; but their speech does not serve, as does speech in Homer, to manifest, to externalize thoughts—on the contrary, it serves to indicate thoughts which remain unexpressed. God gives his command in direct discourse, but he leaves his motives and his purpose unexpressed; Abraham, receiving the command, says nothing and does what he has been told to do. The conversation between Abraham and Isaac on the way to the place of sacrifice is only an interruption of the heavy silence and makes it all the more burdensome. The two of them, Isaac carrying the wood and Abraham with fire and a knife, "went together." Hesitantly, Isaac ventures to ask about the ram, and Abraham gives the well-known answer. Then the text repeats: "So they went both of them together." Everything remains unexpressed.

It would be difficult, then, to imagine styles more contrasted than those of these two equally ancient and equally epic texts. On the one hand, externalized, uniformly illuminated phenomena, at a definite time and in a definite place, connected together without lacunae in a perpetual foreground; thoughts and feeling completely expressed; events taking place in leisurely fashion and with very little of suspense. On the other hand, the externalization of only so much of the phenomena as is necessary for the purpose of the narrative, all else left in obscurity; the decisive points of the narrative alone are emphasized, what lies between is nonexistent; time and place are undefined and call for interpretation; thoughts and feeling remain unexpressed, are only suggested by the silence and the fragmentary speeches; the whole, permeated with the most unrelieved suspense and directed toward a single goal (and to that extent far more of a unity), remains mysterious and "fraught with background."

I will discuss this term in some detail, lest it be mis-understood. I said above that the Homeric style was "of the foreground" because, despite much going back and forth, it yet causes what is momentarily being narrated to give the impression that it is the only present, pure and without perspective. A consideration of the Elohistic text teaches us that our term is capable of a broader and deeper application. It shows that even the separate personages can be represented as possess-ing "background"; God is always so represented in the Bible, for he is not comprehensible in his presence, as is Zeus; it is always only "something" of him that appears, he always extends into depths. But even the human beings in the Biblical stories have greater depths of time, fate, and consciousness than do the human beings in Homer; although they are nearly always caught up in an event engaging all their faculties, they are not so entirely immersed in its present that they do not remain continually conscious of what has happened to them earlier and elsewhere; their thoughts and feel-ings have more layers, are more entangled. Abraham's actions are explained not only by what is happening to him at the moment, nor yet only by his character (as Achilles' actions by his courage and his pride, and Odysseus' by his versatility and foresightedness), but by his previous history; he remembers, he is constantly conscious of, what God has promised him and what God has already accomplished for him—his soul is torn between desperate rebellion and hopeful expecta-tion; his silent obedience is multilayered, has back-ground. Such a problematic psychological situation as this is impossible for any of the Homeric heroes, whose destiny is clearly defined and who wake every morn-ing as if it were the first day of their lives: their emo-tions, though strong, are simple and find expression instantly.

How fraught with background, in comparison, are characters like Saul and David! How entangled and stratified are such human relations as those between David and Absalom, between David and Joab! Any such "background" quality of the psychological situa-tion as that which the story of Absalom's death and its sequel (II Samuel 18 and 19, by the so-called Jahvist) rather suggests than expresses, is unthinkable in Hom-er. Here we are confronted not merely with the psy-chological processes of characters whose depth of background is veritably abysmal, but with a purely geographical background too. For David is absent from the battlefield; but the influence of his will and his feelings continues to operate, they affect even Joab in his rebellion and disregard for the consequences of his actions; in the magnificent scene with the two messen-gers, both the physical and psychological background is fully manifest, though the latter is never expressed. With this, compare, for example, how Achilles, who sends Patroclus first to scout and then into battle, loses almost all "presentness" so long as he is not physically present. But the most important thing is the "multilay-eredness" of the individual character; this is hardly to be met with in Homer, or at most in the form of a conscious hesitation between two possible courses of action; otherwise, in Homer, the complexity of the psychological life is shown only in the succession and alternation of emotions; whereas the Jewish writers are able to express the simultaneous existence of various layers of consciousness and the conflict between them.

The Homeric poems, then, though their intellectual, linguistic, and above all syntactical culture appears to be so much more highly developed, are yet compara-tively simple in their picture of human beings; and no less so in their relation to the real life which they describe in general. Delight in physical existence is everything to them, and their highest aim is to make that delight perceptible to us. Between battles and passions, adventures and perils, they show us hunts, banquets, palaces and shepherds' cots, athletic con-tests and washing days—in order that we may see the heroes in their ordinary life, and seeing them so, may take pleasure in their manner of enjoying their savory present, a present which sends strong roots down into social usages, landscape, and daily life. And thus they bewitch us and ingratiate themselves to us until we live with them in the reality of their lives; so long as we are reading or hearing the poems, it does not matter whether we know that all this is only legend, "make-believe." The oft-repeated reproach that Homer is a liar takes nothing from his effectiveness, he does not need to base his story on historical reality, his reality is powerful enough in itself; it ensnares us, weaving its web around us, and that suffices him. And this "real" world into which we are lured, exists for itself, con-tains nothing but itself; the Homeric poems conceal nothing, they contain no teaching and no secret second meaning. Homer can be analyzed, as we have essayed to do here, but he cannot be interpreted. Later allego-rizing trends have tried their arts of interpretation upon him, but to no avail. He resists any such treatment; the interpretations are forced and foreign, they do not crys-tallize into a unified doctrine. The general consider-ations which occasionally occur (in our episode, for example, v. 360: that in misfortune men age quickly) reveal a calm acceptance of the basic facts of human existence, but with no compulsion to brood over them, still less any passionate impulse either to rebel against them or to embrace them in an ecstasy of submission.

It is all very different in the Biblical stories. Their aim is not to bewitch the senses, and if nevertheless they produce lively sensory effects, it is only because the moral, religious, and psychological phenomena which are their sole concern are made concrete in the sensi-ble matter of life. But their religious intent involves an absolute claim to historical truth. The story of Abra-ham and Isaac is not better established than the story of Odysseus, Penelope, and Euryclea; both are legend-ary. But the Biblical narrator, the Elohist, had to believe in the objective truth of the story of Abraham's sacrifice—the existence of the sacred ordinances of life rested upon the truth of this and similar stories. He had to believe in it passionately; or else (as many rationalistic interpreters believed and perhaps still believe) he had to be a conscious liar—no harmless liar like Homer, who lied to give pleasure, but a political liar with a definite end in view, lying in the interest of a claim to absolute authority.

To me, the rationalistic interpretation seems psychologically absurd; but even if we take it into consideration, the relation of the Elohist to the truth of his story still remains a far more passionate and definite one than is Homer's relation. The Biblical narrator was obliged to write exactly what his belief in the truth of the tradition (or, from the rationalistic standpoint, his interest in the truth of it) demanded of him—in either case, his freedom in creative or representative imagination was severely limited; his activity was perforce reduced to composing an effective version of the pious tradition. What he produced, then, was not primarily oriented toward "realism" (if he succeeded in being realistic, it was merely a means, not an end); it was oriented toward truth. Woe to the man who did not believe it! One can perfectly well entertain historical doubts on the subject of the Trojan War or of Odysseus' wanderings, and still, when reading Homer, feel precisely the effects he sought to produce; but without believing in Abraham's sacrifice, it is impossible to put the narrative of it to the use for which it was written. Indeed, we must go even further. The Bible's claim to truth is not only far more urgent than Homer's, it is tyrannical—it excludes all other claims. The world of the Scripture stories is not satisfied with claiming to be a historically true reality—it insists that it is the only real world, is destined for autocracy. All other scenes, issues, and ordinances have no right to appear independently of it, and it is promised that all of them, the history of all mankind, will be given their due place within its frame, will be subordinated to it. The Scripture stories do not, like Homer's, court our favor, they do not flatter us that they may please us and enchant us—they seek to subject us, and if we refuse to be subjected we are rebels.

Let no one object that this goes too far, that not the stories, but the religious doctrine, raises the claim to absolute authority; because the stories are not, like Homer's, simply narrated "reality." Doctrine and promise are incarnate in them and inseparable from them; for that very reason they are fraught with "background" and mysterious, containing a second, concealed meaning. In the story of Isaac, it is not only God's intervention at the beginning and the end, but even the factual and psychological elements which come between, that are mysterious, merely touched upon, fraught with background; and therefore they require subtle investigation and interpretation, they demand them. Since so much in the story is dark and incomplete, and since the reader knows that God is a hidden God, his effort to interpret it constantly finds something new to feed upon. Doctrine and the search for enlightenment are inextricably connected with the physical side of the narrative—the latter being more than simple "reality"; indeed they are in constant danger of losing their own reality, as very soon happened when interpretation reached such proportions that the real vanished.

If the text of the Biblical narrative, then, is so greatly in need of interpretation on the basis of its own content, its claim to absolute authority forces it still further in the same direction. Far from seeking, like Homer, merely to make us forget our own reality for a few hours, it seeks to overcome our reality: we are to fit our own life into its world, feel ourselves to be elements in its structure of universal history. This becomes increasingly difficult the further our historical environment is removed from that of the Biblical books; and if these nevertheless maintain their claim to absolute authority, it is inevitable that they themselves be adapted through interpretative transformation. This was for a long time comparatively easy; as late as the European Middle Ages it was possible to represent Biblical events as ordinary phenomena of contemporary life, the methods of interpretation themselves forming the basis for such a treatment. But when, through too great a change in environment and through the awakening of a critical consciousness, this becomes impossible, the Biblical claim to absolute authority is jeopardized; the method of interpretation is scorned and rejected, the Biblical stories become ancient legends, and the doctrine they had contained, now dissevered from them, becomes a disembodied image.

As a result of this claim to absolute authority, the method of interpretation spread to traditions other than the Jewish. The Homeric poems present a definite complex of events whose boundaries in space and time are clearly delimited; before it, beside it, and after it, other complexes of events, which do not depend upon it, can be conceived without conflict and without difficulty. The Old Testament, on the other hand, presents universal history: it begins with the beginning of time, with the creation of the world, and will end with the Last Days, the fulfilling of the Covenant, with which the world will come to an end. Everything else that happens in the world can only be conceived as an element in this sequence; into it everything that is known about the world, or at least everything that touches upon the history of the Jews, must be fitted as an ingredient of the divine plan; and as this too became possible only by interpreting the new material as it poured in, the need for interpretation reaches out beyond the original Jewish-Israelitish realm of reality—for example to Assyrian, Babylonian, Persian, and Roman history; interpretation in a determined direction becomes a general method of comprehending reality; the new and strange world which now comes into view and which, in the form in which it presents itself, proves to be wholly unutilizable within the Jewish religious frame, must be so interpreted that it can find a place there. But this process nearly always also reacts upon the frame, which requires enlarging and modifying. The most striking piece of interpretation of this sort occurred in the first century of the Christian era, in consequence of Paul's mission to the Gentiles: Paul and the Church Fathers reinterpreted the entire Jewish tradition as a succession of figures prognosticating the appearance of Christ, and assigned the Roman Empire its proper place in the divine plan of salvation. Thus while, on the one hand, the reality of the Old Testament presents itself as complete truth with a claim to sole authority, on the other hand that very claim forces it to a constant interpretative change in its own content; for millennia it undergoes an incessant and active development with the life of man in Europe.

The claim of the Old Testament stories to represent universal history, their insistent relation—a relation constantly redefined by conflicts—to a single and hidden God, who yet shows himself and who guides universal history by promise and exaction, gives these stories an entirely different perspective from any the Homeric poems can possess. As a composition, the Old Testament is incomparably less unified than the Homeric poems, it is more obviously pieced together—but the various components all belong to one concept of universal history and its interpretation. If certain elements survived which did not immediately fit in, interpretation took care of them; and so the reader is at every moment aware of the universal religio-historical perspective which gives the individual stories their general meaning and purpose. The greater the separateness and horizontal disconnection of the stories and groups of stories in relation to one another, compared with the *Iliad* and the *Odyssey,* the stronger is their general vertical connection, which holds them all together and which is entirely lacking in Homer. Each of the great figures of the Old Testament, from Adam to the prophets, embodies a moment of this vertical connection. God chose and formed these men to the end of embodying his essence and will—yet choice and formation do not coincide, for the latter proceeds gradually, historically, during the earthly life of him upon whom the choice has fallen. How the process is accomplished, what terrible trials such a formation inflicts, can be seen from our story of Abraham's sacrifice. Herein lies the reason why the great figures of the Old Testament are so much more fully developed, so much more fraught with their own biographical past, so much more distinct as individuals, than are the Homeric heroes. Achilles and Odysseus are splendidly described in many well-ordered words, epithets cling to them, their emotions are constantly displayed in their words and deeds—but they have no development, and their life-histories are clearly set forth

once and for all. So little are the Homeric heroes presented as developing or having developed, that most of them—Nestor, Agamemnon, Achilles—appear to be of an age fixed from the very first. Even Odysseus, in whose case the long lapse of time and the many events which occurred offer so much opportunity for biographical development, shows almost nothing of it. Odysseus on his return is exactly the same as he was when he left Ithaca two decades earlier. But what a road, what a fate, lie between the Jacob who cheated his father out of his blessing and the old man whose favorite son has been torn to pieces by a wild beast!— between David the harp player, persecuted by his lord's jealousy, and the old king, surrounded by violent intrigues, whom Abishag the Shunnamite warmed in his bed, and he knew her not! The old man, of whom we know how he has become what he is, is more of an individual than the young man; for it is only during the course of an eventful life that men are differentiated into full individuality; and it is this history of a personality which the Old Testament presents to us as the formation undergone by those whom God has chosen to be examples. Fraught with their development, sometimes even aged to the verge of dissolution, they show a distinct stamp of individuality entirely foreign to the Homeric heroes. Time can touch the latter only outwardly, and even that change is brought to our observation as little as possible; whereas the stern hand of God is ever upon the Old Testament figures; he has not only made them once and for all and chosen them, but he continues to work upon them, bends them and kneads them, and, without destroying them in essence, produces from them forms which their youth gave no grounds for anticipating. The objection that the biographical element of the Old Testament often springs from the combination of several legendary personages does not apply; for this combination is a part of the development of the text. And how much wider is the pendulum swing of their lives than that of the Homeric heroes! For they are bearers of the divine will, and yet they are fallible, subject to misfortune and humiliation—and in the midst of misfortune and in their humiliation their acts and words reveal the transcendent majesty of God. There is hardly one of them who does not, like Adam, undergo the deepest humiliation—and hardly one who is not deemed worthy of God's personal intervention and personal inspiration. Humiliation and elevation go far deeper and far higher than in Homer, and they belong basically together. The poor beggar Odysseus is only masquerading, but Adam is really cast down, Jacob really a refugee, Joseph really in the pit and then a slave to be bought and sold. But their greatness, rising out of humiliation, is almost superhuman and an image of God's greatness. The reader clearly feels how the extent of the pendulum's swing is connected with the intensity of the personal history—precisely the most extreme circumstances, in which we are immeasurably forsaken and in despair, or immeasurably joyous and exalted, give us, if we survive them, a personal stamp which is recognized as the product of a rich existence, a rich development. And very often, indeed generally, this element of development gives the Old Testament stories a historical character, even when the subject is purely legendary and traditional.

Homer remains within the legendary with all his material, whereas the material of the Old Testament comes closer and closer to history as the narrative proceeds; in the stories of David the historical report predominates. Here too, much that is legendary still remains, as for example the story of David and Goliath; but much—and the most essential—consists in things which the narrators knew from their own experience or from firsthand testimony. Now the difference between legend and history is in most cases easily perceived by a reasonably experienced reader. It is a difficult matter, requiring careful historical and philological training, to distinguish the true from the synthetic or the biased in a historical presentation; but it is easy to separate the historical from the legendary in general. Their structure is different. Even where the legendary does not immediately betray itself by elements of the miraculous, by the repetition of well-known standard motives, typical patterns and themes, through neglect of

clear details of time and place, and the like, it is generally quickly recognizable by its composition. It runs far too smoothly. All cross-currents, all friction, all that is casual, secondary to the main events and themes, everything unresolved, truncated, and uncertain, which confuses the clear progress of the action and the simple orientation of the actors, has disappeared. The historical event which we witness, or learn from the testimony of those who witnessed it, runs much more variously, contradictorily, and confusedly; not until it has produced results in a definite domain are we able, with their help, to classify it to a certain extent; and how often the order to which we think we have attained becomes doubtful again, how often we ask ourselves if the data before us have not led us to a far too simple classification of the original events! Legend arranges its material in a simple and straightforward way; it detaches it from its contemporary historical context, so that the latter will not confuse it; it knows only clearly outlined men who act from few and simple motives and the continuity of whose feelings and actions remains uninterrupted. In the legends of martyrs, for example, a stiff-necked and fanatical persecutor stands over against an equally stiff-necked and fanatical victim; and a situation so complicated—that is to say, so real and historical—as that in which the

An archaic bronze of one of Odysseus's companions escaping from the cave of Polyphemus under a ram.

"persecutor" Pliny finds himself in his celebrated letter to Trajan on the subject of the Christians, is unfit for legend. And that is still a comparatively simple case. Let the reader think of the history which we are ourselves witnessing; anyone who, for example, evaluates the behavior of individual men and groups of men at the time of the rise of National Socialism in Germany, or the behavior of individual peoples and states before and during the last war, will feel how difficult it is to represent historical themes in general, and how unfit they are for legend; the historical comprises a great number of contradictory motives in each individual, a hesitation and ambiguous groping on the part of groups; only seldom (as in the last war) does a more or less plain situation, comparatively simple to describe, arise, and even such a situation is subject to division below the surface, is indeed almost constantly in danger of losing its simplicity; and the motives of all the interested parties are so complex that the slogans of propaganda can be composed only through the crudest simplification—with the result that friend and foe alike can often employ the same ones. To write history is so difficult that most historians are forced to make concessions to the technique of legend.

It is clear that a large part of the life of David as given in the Bible contains history and not legend. In Absalom's rebellion, for example, or in the scenes from David's last days, the contradictions and crossing of motives both in individuals and in the general action have become so concrete that it is impossible to doubt the historicity of the information conveyed. Now the men who composed the historical parts are often the same who edited the older legends too; their peculiar religious concept of man in history, which we have attempted to describe above, in no way led them to a legendary simplification of events; and so it is only natural that, in the legendary passages of the Old Testament, historical structure is frequently discernible—of course, not in the sense that the traditions are examined as to their credibility according to the methods of scientific criticism; but simply to the extent that the tendency to a smoothing down and harmonizing of events, to a simplification of motives, to a static definition of characters which avoids conflict, vacillation, and development, such as are natural to legendary structure, does not predominate in the Old Testament world of legend. Abraham, Jacob, or even Moses produces a more concrete, direct, and historical impression than the figures of the Homeric world—not because they are better described in terms of sense (the contrary is the case) but because the confused, contradictory multiplicity of events, the psychological and factual cross-purposes, which true history reveals, have not disappeared in the representation but still remain clearly perceptible. In the stories of David, the legendary, which only later scientific criticism makes recognizable as such, imperceptibly passes into the historical; and even in the legendary, the problem of the classi-

fication and interpretation of human history is already passionately apprehended—a problem which later shatters the framework of historical composition and completely overruns it with prophecy; thus the Old Testament, in so far as it is concerned with human events, ranges through all three domains: legend, historical reporting, and interpretative historical theology.

Connected with the matters just discussed is the fact that the Greek text seems more limited and more static in respect to the circle of personages involved in the action and to their political activity. In the recognition scene with which we began, there appears, aside from Odysseus and Penelope, the housekeeper Euryclea, a slave whom Odysseus' father Laertes had bought long before. She, like the swineherd Eumaeus, has spent her life in the service of Laertes' family; like Eumaeus, she is closely connected with their fate, she loves them and shares their interests and feelings. But she has no life of her own, no feelings of her own; she has only the life and feelings of her master. Eumaeus too, though he still remembers that he was born a freeman and indeed of a noble house (he was stolen as a boy), has, not only in fact but also in his own feeling, no longer a life of his own, he is entirely involved in the life of his masters. Yet these two characters are the only ones whom Homer brings to life who do not belong to the ruling class. Thus we become conscious of the fact that in the Homeric poems life is enacted only among the ruling class—others appear only in the role of servants to that class. The ruling class is still so strongly patriarchal, and still itself so involved in the daily activities of domestic life, that one is sometimes likely to forget their rank. But they are unmistakably a sort of feudal aristocracy, whose men divide their lives between war, hunting, marketplace councils, and feasting, while the women supervise the maids in the house. As a social picture, this world is completely stable; wars take place only between different groups of the ruling class; nothing ever pushes up from below. In the early stories of the Old Testament the patriarchal condition is dominant too, but since the people involved are individual nomadic or half-nomadic tribal leaders, the social picture gives a much less stable impression; class distinctions are not felt. As soon as the people completely emerges—that is, after the exodus from Egypt—its activity is always discernible, it is often in ferment, it frequently intervenes in events not only as a whole but also in separate groups and through the medium of separate individuals who come forward; the origins of prophecy seem to lie in the irrepressible politico-religious spontaneity of the people. We receive the impression that the movements emerging from the depths of the people of Israel-Judah must have been of a wholly different nature from those even of the later ancient democracies—of a different nature and far more elemental.

With the more profound historicity and the more profound social activity of the Old Testament text, there is connected yet another important distinction from Homer: namely, that a different conception of the elevated style and of the sublime is to be found here. Homer, of course, is not afraid to let the realism of daily life enter into the sublime and tragic; our episode of the scar is an example, we see how the quietly depicted, domestic scene of the foot-washing is incorporated into the pathetic and sublime action of Odysseus' homecoming. From the rule of the separation of styles which was later almost universally accepted and which specified that the realistic depiction of daily life was incompatible with the sublime and had a place only in comedy or, carefully stylized, in idyl—from any such rule Homer is still far removed. And yet he is closer to it than is the Old Testament. For the great and sublime events in the Homeric poems take place far more exclusively and unmistakably among the members of a ruling class; and these are far more untouched in their heroic elevation than are the Old Testament figures, who can fall much lower in dignity (consider, for example, Adam, Noah, David, Job); and finally, domestic realism, the representation of daily life, remains in Homer in the peaceful relam of the idyllic, whereas, from the very first, in the Old Testament stories, the sublime, tragic, and problematic take shape precisely in the domestic and commonplace: scenes such as those between Cain and Abel, between Noah and his sons, between Abraham, Sarah, and Hagar, between Rebekah, Jacob, and Esau, and so on, are inconceivable in the Homeric style. The entirely different ways of developing conflicts are enough to account for this. In the Old Testament stories the peace of daily life in the house, in the fields, and among the flocks, is undermined by jealousy over election and the promise of a blessing, and complications arise which would be utterly incomprehensible to the Homeric heroes. The latter must have palpable and clearly expressible reasons for their conflicts and enmities, and these work themselves out in free battles; whereas, with the former, the perpetually smouldering jealousy and the connection between the domestic and the spiritual, between the paternal blessing and the divine blessing, lead to daily life being permeated with the stuff of conflict, often with poison. The sublime influence of God here reaches so deeply into the everyday that the two realms of the sublime and the everyday are not only actually unseparated but basically inseparable.

We have compared these two texts, and, with them, the two kinds of style they embody, in order to reach a starting point for an investigation into the literary representation of reality in European culture. The two styles, in their opposition, represent basic types: on the one hand fully externalized description, uniform illumination, uninterrupted connection, free expression, all events in the foreground, displaying unmistakable meanings, few elements of historical development and

of psychological perspective; on the other hand, certain parts brought into high relief, others left obscure, abruptness, suggestive influence of the unexpressed, "background" quality, multiplicity of meanings and the need for interpretation, universal-historical claims, development of the concept of the historically becoming, and preoccupation with the problematic.

Homer's realism is, of course, not to be equated with classical-antique realism in general; for the separation of styles, which did not develop until later, permitted no such leisurely and externalized description of everyday happenings; in tragedy especially there was no room for it; furthermore, Greek culture very soon encountered the phenomena of historical becoming and of the "multilayeredness" of the human problem, and dealt with them in its fashion; in Roman realism, finally, new and native concepts are added. We shall go into these later changes in the antique representation of reality when the occasion arises; on the whole, despite them, the basic tendencies of the Homeric style, which we have attempted to work out, remained effective and determinant down into late antiquity.

Since we are using the two styles, the Homeric and the Old Testament, as starting points, we have taken them as finished products, as they appear in the texts; we have disregarded everything that pertains to their origins, and thus have left untouched the question whether their peculiarities were theirs from the beginning or are to be referred wholly or in part to foreign influences. Within the limits of our purpose, a consideration of this question is not necessary; for it is in their full development, which they reached in early times, that the two styles exercised their determining influence upon the representation of reality in European literature.

Mark Van Doren (essay date 1946)

SOURCE: "The *Odyssey*," in *The Noble Voice: A Study of Ten Great Poems,* Henry Holt and Company, 1946, pp. 45-85.

[*Van Doren was one of the most prolific men of letters in twentieth-century American writing. He wrote accomplished studies of Shakespeare, John Dryden, Nathaniel Hawthorne, and Henry David Thoreau, and served as the literary editor and film critic for the* Nation *during the 1920s and 1930s. Van Doren's criticism is aimed at the general reader, rather than the scholar or specialist, and is noted for its lively perception and wide interest. Like his fiction and poetry (for which he won the Pulitzer Prize in 1939), his criticism consistently examines the inner life of the individual. In this essay, Van Doren praises the* Odyssey's *"relaxed and spacious" spirit, deeming it "still the finest tale in print."*]

The first two sentences of the *Odyssey* are enough to inform us that now we are in another world of poetry. "Tell me, O Muse, of the man of many devices, who wandered full many ways after he had sacked the sacred citadel of Troy. Many were the men whose cities he saw and whose mind he learned, aye, and many the woes he suffered in his heart upon the sea, seeking to win his own life and the return of his comrades." Many devices, many ways, many men, many cities, many minds, many woes, and upon the sea to boot—the view opens and becomes multiple. This world is wide, and there is so much to report about it that Homer cannot decide where to begin. "Of these things, goddess, daughter of Zeus, beginning where thou wilt—at some place or other—tell thou even to us."

Homer does know, of course, where such a tale should start. It is still the finest tale in print, and its author was no fumbler. It concerns itself with the final stage of Odysseus' journey home from Troy, and with his return to Ithaca in a disguise which lasts until all the necessary recognitions are accomplished, including that by the suitors who have infested his house, after which they are promptly dispatched. The beginning is in this very house, where Telemachus, the young son whom Odysseus had left there twenty years before as an infant in arms, is stung by his mother Penelope's position—and furthermore is inspired by a visit from Pallas Athene, his father's intimate deity—to set forth in his chariot so that he may find out what he can about the missing wanderer from old Nestor in Pylos and from Menelaus in the hollow land of Lacedaemon with its many ravines. Even while he is absent, learning little, Odysseus is enduring the last of his adventures on an island where he is the comfortable prisoner of the nymph Calypso; whom he leaves, only to be wrecked on the shores of Phaeacia, where he remains until for our benefit he has told the king of all his adventures to date. He gets home in advance of his son, midway through the poem; and then romance contracts into drama.

No art is lacking in Homer which is needed to tell this tale and tell it perfectly. But neither is there lacking in him a sense of the difference we must feel, now that we are free in a universe as loose as that of the *Iliad* was tight. Aristotle put the difference when he said the *Iliad* was simple and disastrous, the *Odyssey* complicated and moral. Lawrence of Arabia said the *Iliad* was huge and terrible, the *Odyssey* gay, fine, and vivid. If further epithets are in order, the following might do. The *Iliad* is tense, of great density, with no neutral territory to travel in, no free air to breathe; the *Odyssey* is relaxed and spacious, occupying as it does a porous world in which the prevailing sanity and serenity will not be disturbed or clogged by any human event.

The spirit of the *Odyssey* is something like that which

breathes in the *History* of Herodotus. What the subject of Herodotus is can be debated. Is it the big story of Greece and Persia, or is it the little stories—of Gyges and Candaules' queen, of Adrastus, of Croesus and Solon, of Cyrus' youth, of Rhampsinitus, of Sataspes, of Xerxes and the five sons of Pythius, of the Spartans at Thermopylae, combing their long hair—of which the big one is stuck full, interrupting it as cloves do a ham? Or is it a third thing: the customs of distant peoples, Scythian, Ethiopian, which Herodotus pauses so frequently to describe? It is perhaps more, much more, than all that. It is perhaps the whole world as Herodotus in his curiosity now knows it, and as he certainly loves it. This world is more stationary than moving, no matter how many figures dot its foreground. It is a timeless world that keeps its own equilibrium, shining brightly clear out to its extremities; it has a vast life which is more important than the life of any one man or people, it has a fixed truth which even wars between continents may not alter. It is a universe of strangers, an immense field of leisure where time seeks its level and space its calm. It is a universe in which no conceivable thing is missing, just as it is a place where, given enough time, anything can happen. But you will not know its wonders unless you travel. If you do travel, the farther you go the more you will find—"the extreme regions of the earth are blessed" with the most gold and the greatest marvels: races of utterly bald men, people in mountains with feet like goats, countries where a half of every year is spent in sleep and the oxen walk backwards, troglodytes who feed on serpents and lizards and whose language is like the screeching of bats, or the natives of Atlas who eat no living thing and never dream. Not that the extremities are all, or marvels everything. The whole includes home, of which Herodotus is proud. But it is an immense whole, which the historian's constant effort is to keep in focus.

The world of the *Odyssey* is something like that. It is so immense and free that the reminders we are sometimes given of Agamemnon and Achilles fall strangely on our ears; those were tragic figures, and this is not a tragedy. The parallel of Agamemnon's disastrous return is maintained indeed throughout the poem. Telemachus is told by Athene, by Nestor, and by Menelaus that he may have to avenge his father as Orestes did his; and the two episodes in Hades, in the eleventh and the twenty-fourth books, are eloquent of Agamemnon's murder by his queen. But Agamemnon, for all his shade believes that "no longer is there faith in women," admits in the gloom of the underworld that Penelope is no Clytemnestra; she is the faithful wife in a story that turns out happily. So Helen, as Telemachus beholds her in Lacedaemon, is restored to her former role as the good wife of Menelaus. Eumaeus, the old swineherd of Odysseus back in Ithaca, echoes the *Iliad* when he wishes she had perished with all her kindred; but the old man of the sea who tells Menelaus that he will spend eternity in the Elysian plain because "thou hast Helen to wife and art the husband of the daughter of Zeus" is talking with surer accent the language of the *Odyssey*. As for Achilles, we hear him wondering in Hades whether his father ever suffered dishonor as Agamemnon did, or even as Odysseus still does from the absurd suitors; and the rage he feels when he realizes his incapacity in such a case to be Orestes, or even to be Telemachus, only reminds us of furies we shall never feel here. Achilles, true to the character he had at Troy, is the unhappiest man in Hades. Odysseus hails him as the mighty ruler of the dead, but the son of Thetis answers: "Nay, seek not to speak soothingly to me of death, glorious Odysseus. I should choose, so I might live on earth, to serve as the hireling of another, of some portionless man whose livelihood was but small, rather than to be lord over all the dead."

The *Odyssey* is anything but tragedy. "I am a man of many sorrows," says Odysseus more than once; and at least once, as the raft bearing him away from Calypso is about to break up, he wishes he had died at Troy. He is moved on another occasion to deliver himself as Zeus had to the horses of Achilles: "Nothing feebler does earth nurture than man, of all things that on earth are breathing and moving," he says to Amphinomus the suitor, lifting a cup of honey-sweet wine when he has finished. But we do not forget his many devices, and we do not believe he will be put down, as indeed he never is. Even if we doubted him there is always Athene to foretell the successful outcome of his career. Penelope, praying once to Artemis, speaks of Zeus who "knows all things, both the happiness and the haplessness of mortal men." But there it is—the happiness along with the unhappiness. The two alternate in the *Odyssey,* and in the right order for our pleasure. The miseries of its people are many, but they have not the dimension of terror.

If the gods write tragedy in this world they write it as men write songs, to soothe the mind with remembered woe, and to make still further poetry possible. "There is time for sleep," says Eumaeus to the old man he does not yet know to be Odysseus, "and there is time to take joy in hearing tales. . . . We two will drink and feast in the hut, and will take delight each in the other's grievous woes, as we recall them to mind. For in after time a man finds joy even in woes, whosoever has suffered much, and wandered much." King Alcinous of Phaeacia supposes that the gods wrought so much havoc at Troy, and spun such a skein of ruin, "that there might be a song for those yet to be born." He could sit up all night, he insists, listening to the woes of Odysseus, they are so sweet to hear.

The tears of the *Odyssey* are copious beyond record, but they do not scald like the fewer and fiercer ones of the *Iliad*. Everybody weeps, and often, but it seems easy to do so; easy, and even sweet, for these are free dispositions, and tears are their native tongue, in which the truth is spoken. Nobody, least of all Odysseus, can resist a minstrel; Telemachus cannot, nor Penelope either; tears flow like rain, wetting the beautiful sad words which accompany the lyre. At the house of Menelaus, when the master has ended his recital of the uncertainties in which Odysseus must be enmeshed, all of the company are seized with a desire to have a good cry. "Argive Helen wept, the daughter of Zeus, Telemachus wept, and Menelaus, son of Atreus, nor could the son of Nestor keep his eyes tearless." In Ithaca Telemachus weeps for his father, Penelope for both her husband and her son, as well as for herself. Our first sight of the hero is of a strong man weeping on Calypso's shore: "and his eyes were never dry of tears, and his sweet life was ebbing away, as he longed mournfully for his return." Twice in the hall of Alcinous, listening with the others to the bard Demodocus as he sings the sufferings of Troy, Odysseus is overcome at the mention of his own name, so that he must grasp his great purple cloak in his stout hands and draw it down over his head to keep secret the tears he cannot prevent. Home in Ithaca, watching the efforts of his old hound Argos to get up and come to him, he must turn his head and wipe his eyes. Near the end, as Eurycleia brings the women of the household in to greet him, a sweet longing seizes him to weep and wail, "for in his heart he knew them all." In the arms of Penelope at last he weeps without restraint, as later in the orchard with his father. Once, when it was still necessary to keep his disguise with Penelope, he had with the most painful difficulty held back the tears which would have blended with hers: "his eyes stood fixed between his lids as though they were horn or iron." But such difficulty is rare in the poem. The most natural thing is what happens to Penelope on the same occasion:

> He spoke, and made the many falsehoods of his tale seem like the truth, and as she listened her tears flowed and her face melted as the snow melts on the lofty mountains, the snow which the East Wind thaws when the West Wind has strewn it, and as it melts the streams of the rivers flow full: so her fair cheeks melted as she wept and mourned for her husband, who even then was sitting by her side.

Relief is regularly available to the good people of the *Odyssey,* as dew comes daily to ferns and grass.

The relief of sleep is likewise constant, bestowing upon the poem a soft atmosphere in which it easily keeps its health. This atmosphere has fairy quality, reminding us of many an ancient tale wherein a princess or an old man, a Beauty or a Rip Van Winkle, slept years away. The promise of Alcinous which Odysseus likes best is that on the morrow the Phaeacians will take him home in one of their magic ships:

Then shalt thou lie down, overcome by sleep, and they shall row thee over the calm sea until thou comest to thy country and thy house, or to whatsoever place thou wilt, aye though it be even far beyond Euboea, which those of our people who saw it, when they carried fair-haired Rhadamanthus to visit Tityus, the son of Gaea, say is the furthest of lands. Thither they went, and without toil accomplished their journey, and on the selfsame day came back home.

And the promise is true.

Then for Odysseus they spread a rug and a linen sheet on the deck of the hollow ship at the stern, that he might sleep soundly; and he too went aboard, and laid him down in silence. . . . And as soon as they leaned back, and tossed the brine with their oar-blades, sweet sleep fell upon his eyelids, an unawakening sleep, most sweet, and most like to death. . . . Now he slept in peace, forgetful of all he had suffered. . . . Then they stepped forth from the benched ship upon the land, and first they lifted Odysseus out of the hollow ship, with the linen sheet and bright rug as they were, and laid him down on the sand, still overpowered by sleep. . . . But Odysseus awoke out of his sleep in his native land.

Meanwhile Penelope's life is passed in alternate weeping and sleeping. "And she sank back and slept, and all her joints relaxed." She too finds sleep a little death. "Ah," she cries when she awakens from one long nap which Athene has blessed her with as an escape from misery, "in my utter wretchedness soft slumber enfolded me. Would that pure Artemis would even now give me so soft a death, that I might no more waste my life away with sorrow at heart, longing for the manifold excellence of my dear husband." Death in the *Odyssey* is no more stern than that. It is an enveloping cloud, beneficent, without edges.

Penelope, to be sure, has her difficulties with sleep. Sometimes it does not come, and she tosses in her chamber. And sometimes this excellent thing which "makes one forget all things, the good and the evil, when once it envelops the eyelids," does come but brings bad dreams. Increasingly as it comes, however, she loves it, so that it grows to be almost a disease with her, a drug to which she is addicted. Even when Eurycleia runs upstairs to her, laughing and stumbling and saying "Odysseus is here," Penelope tells her to go away. "Why dost thou mock me, who have a heart full of sorrow, to tell me this wild tale, and dost rouse me out of slumber, the sweet slumber that bound me and enfolded my eyelids?" Only at the end, when she knows her husband and lies by his side while he goes over his adventures since he left her twenty years ago, is she cured of her desire to absent herself from life. She listens to the last chapter of his tale.

The hardness of heart which various persons find in one another is not the caked hardness, the bitter bafflement, of Hecuba or Achilles. It is at the worst an excess of caution or suspicion, pardonable in these Ithacans who have been fooled so many times by false rumors of their lord's return, or by pretenders who have come and been exposed. "Verily," says Odysseus to Eumaeus, "thou hast in thy bosom a heart that is slow to believe." But on the whole Odysseus is pleased that this is so, because it argues fidelity in those to whom he is returning. Penelope's hopelessness is his best hope; though to Eurycleia and Telemachus it can be enraging, as when the young man, desperate because she will not believe that this is Odysseus, denounces her thus:

My mother, cruel mother, that hast an unyielding heart, why dost thou thus hold aloof from my father, and dost not sit by his side and ask and question him? No other woman would harden her heart as thou dost, and stand aloof from her husband, who after many grievous toils had come back to her in the twentieth year to his native land; but thy heart is ever harder than stone.

Even Odysseus makes use of the same terms a little later. But that is after Athene has restored his good looks, the good looks which have been Penelope's image of him all the while, and he is sure she knows him. "Be not vexed with me, Odysseus," she says. It is unnecessary, for it has suited him well that she should be so slow to believe a stranger. She has in fact been faithful to the image now restored, the image of the husband she remembers. The old beggar he had seemed to be was of course not her Odysseus. It is touching that her son and nurse have misunderstood her on this score, but it is not tragic.

Eumaeus once regrets that Odysseus had not died at Troy and thus achieved a hero's end instead of the ragged, anonymous state of one who wanders unknown in the world. But the author of the *Odyssey* prefers now to be occupied with the raveled extremity of a legend, with the tale of a return, and of a recognition. Such savagery as is here—the torture of Melanthius, the hanging of the maids, the madness of the suitors just before they die—is soon over, and it is simple as poetic justice is simple. A number of persons in the *Odyssey* lay up grief for themselves, and the grief comes; but it comes with an almost amusing promptness, a clean completeness suitable to romance which will forget that evil ever was. When at the Phaeacian games Euryalus sizes Odysseus up and says: "Thou dost not look like an athlete," he is only preparing himself for what we know must happen, namely that Odysseus will throw the discus farther than anybody.

The woes of Odysseus are numerous but serial; they are not interlocked and towered like those of Hector or Achilles. His mind is often divided in counsel, so that he must stand a while and ponder what he should do next. It is never difficult, however, to do so; the decisions of Odysseus are so brisk as almost to be instantaneous. It is as if they were forced by the certainty that the story must go the way of its foretelling. We are regularly informed that Odysseus will return, and once returned that he will execute the suitors; and if in passing we are worried about the ambush that has been prepared for Telemachus upon his arrival from Pylos and Lacedaemon, Athene takes the trouble to assure us that we need not be. A strong tide of success runs in the poem. The main direction is clear, and the decisions of Odysseus therefore cannot be hesitant or wrong. Foretelling here is not foreshortening, as it was in the fatal atmosphere of the *Iliad*. If anything, it is the opposite—the tendency of the tale is to string itself out, multiplying artificial uncertainties as it goes. Suspense is linear, it takes the form of mere delay. We are teased rather than tormented; told, simply, that we must wait a little longer. Such a function is served by Penelope's reluctance to believe; by the interpolation, just as we stop breathing to watch the recognition by Eurycleia, of the long tale of the boar hunt years ago when Autolycus was host to young Odysseus; by many hitches before the bow is tried. So irony in this narrative is of the elementary sort. It consists at the most in someone's not knowing who Odysseus is, and saying or doing things at which we shall shiver or smile. The identity of Odysseus is everything; we know it from the start, but nobody else does. Hence the complications, the discoveries, which according to Aristotle were the essence of the *Odyssey*. They are the most primitive complications possible to story.

Hence, nevertheless, their power. The irony latent in Penelope's direction to the swineherd: "Go, goodly Eumaeus, and bid the stranger come hither, that I may give him greeting, and ask him if haply he has heard of Odysseus, or has seen him with his eyes," or in her sitting then and talking with this stranger, and mourning for her husband "who even then was sitting by her side," is as sure as it is unsubtle. And the recognitions of the poem have no rival in their kind.

The *Odyssey* is a riot of recognition, and not of its hero alone. The poet makes excellent game of the discovery, first by Nestor and then by Menelaus and Helen, that the young man sitting before them with so many questions about Odysseus on his lips is none other than Telemachus, son of that same Odysseus. It is exciting to see Nestor in the amazement that falls on him when Mentor, the friend of Telemachus who has been talking at Pylos, suddenly departs in the likeness of a sea-eagle and so reveals that the boy is distinguished by the guardianship of Athene, "maid most glorious." Athene has a fine time appearing to Odysseus in new forms he must puzzle out. It is not always the hero who shines in the scenes of discovery. But his share of them is the lion's share, even to the point of

his having twice the privilege of recognizing his own name and deeds in the songs Demodocus sings.

His first recognition by others occurs at the court of Alcinous, when the simple sentence, "I am Odysseus," perhaps does not surprise Alcinous himself, who has been watching the business of the singing and the purple robe, but certainly floods with light the minds of those in the court who have underestimated their stranger. So the Cyclops groans when he hears the name of the man who has blinded him. "Lo now, verily a prophecy uttered long ago is come upon me. There lived here a soothsayer, and he told me that all these things should be brought to pass in days to come, that by the hands of Odysseus I should lose my sight." Circe also has been waiting for her day in this immortal tale. "Surely thou art Odysseus, the man of ready device, who Argeïphontes of the golden wand ever said to me would come hither on his way home from Troy with his swift, black ship."

The major recognition scenes are saved, however, for the second half, at the beginning of which Odysseus comes home to Ithaca. Then, curiously enough, it is Ithaca that must be identified to him, not he to Ithaca. For when he awakes from his deep Phaeacian sleep he does not know where he is. "The goddess had shed a mist . . . that she might render him unknown, and tell him all things, so that his wife might not know him, nor his townfolk, nor his friends, until the wooers had paid the full price of all their transgressions. Therefore all things seemed strange to their lord, the long paths, the bays offering safe anchorage, the sheer cliffs, and the luxuriant trees." The arrival of Athene to tell him that this is Ithaca, his pretense that he never heard of such a country, and her smiling delight in his effort to deceive her, make up a charming moment. But before long the serious business of getting himself known to the right persons in the right order is under way.

The first such person is Telemachus, who when his doubts are overcome flings his arms about his father and sheds tears; which start Odysseus weeping too, so that "they wailed aloud more vehemently than birds, sea-eagles, or vultures with crooked talons"; and the sun would have set on their weeping if Telemachus had not suddenly thought of a question to ask. In what manner of ship had his father come to Ithaca?

The next person—if the hound Argos may be passed over as he wags his tail and drops his ears, knowing it is Odysseus who stands there—is one whom the time has not yet come to tell, but who learns anyway. This is Eurycleia, whom in a careless moment Odysseus chooses to wash his feet. Penelope has asked the stranger if he wishes that attention, and he has said that no serving-woman of hers shall touch him "unless there is some old, true-hearted dame who has suffered in her heart as many woes as I." "I have an old dame," answers Penelope, "with a heart of understanding in her breast, who lovingly nursed and cherished my hapless husband, and took him in her arms on the day when his mother bore him. She shall wash thy feet, weak with age though she be. Come now, wise Eurycleia, arise and wash the feet of one of like age with thy master." And Eurycleia proceeds to do so, letting fall hot tears because this stranger is most like Odysseus of all men who have come to Ithaca since its master left. "So say all men," remarks Odysseus, still thinking himself safe; for although there is one sign by which she may know him, he believes he can conceal it.

> So he spoke, and the old dame took the shining cauldron with water wherefrom she was about to wash his feet, and poured in cold water in plenty, and then added thereto the warm. But Odysseus sat him down away from the hearth and straightway turned himself toward the darkness, for he at once had a foreboding at heart that, as she touched him, she might note a scar, and the truth be made manifest. So she drew near and began to wash her lord, and straightway knew the scar of the wound which long ago a boar had dealt him with his white tusk, when Odysseus had gone to Parnassus to visit Autolycus and the sons of Autolycus, his mother's noble father, who excelled all men in thievery and in oaths.

Then Homer, as if he knew that one of the high moments in his poem was preparing, as indeed it is, and as of course he knows, tantalizes us with seventy lines of history about the scar, resuming only when every detail of that old day with Autolycus has been exhausted:

> This scar the old dame, when she had taken the limb in the flat of her hands, knew by the touch, and she let fall the foot. Into the basin the leg fell, and the brazen vessel rang. Over it tilted, and the water was spilled upon the ground. Then upon her soul came joy and grief in one moment, and both her eyes were filled with tears and the flow of her voice was checked. But she touched the chin of Odysseus, and said:

> "Verily thou art Odysseus, dear child, and I knew thee not, till I had handled all the body of my lord."

One sentence, beginning with "dear child" and ending with "my lord," is all she speaks before she turns toward Penelope, hoping she too will see. But Penelope, must not see; so Odysseus has to seize Eurycleia by the throat and draw her to him, whispering: "Mother, why wilt thou destroy me? Since thou hast found me out, and a god has put this in thy heart, be silent lest any other in the halls learn hereof."

No other scene of the series will be more exciting than this, though each one to come will have a beauty proper to its nature. The revelation to Eumaeus and Philo-

etius is rapid, as the situation requires. The stringing of the bow is long delayed, for we know that it is the sign by which the suitors will know Odysseus. When it does come—

> And he held it in his right hand, and tried the string, which sang sweetly beneath his touch, like to a swallow in tone—

it is swift and tremendous. The excitement of that moment in the hall, if in truth it surpasses the excitement of Eurycleia's discovery, does so with the aid of the fact that the scene is central to the poem; this moment is the one toward which time has been hastening since Telemachus first felt shame because his father's honor was abused; and the moment is soon over. The persuasion of Penelope takes longer because the poem can now afford to luxuriate in the spectacle of the long-suffering wife's perplexity, and in the grave comedy of joy postponed. Even after the right appearance of Odysseus has been restored, Penelope must subject him to one more test: she orders Eurycleia to make his bed outside the bridal chamber he once had built with his own hands. His anger at this—for one post of the bed had been a rooted olive tree, and it was therefore immovable—is what she wishes to see. Only then, with a burst of entirely natural tears, does she run straight at him and fling her arms about his neck, kissing his head; and he weeps, "and from his neck she could in no wise let her white arms go." It is the gods, she cries, who have "begrudged that we two should remain with each other and enjoy our youth." But it is a goddess, the bright-eyed Athene, who prolongs the night for them so that they may first have their fill of love and then take delight in the mutual chronicle of twenty years. Hereafter there is but one more necessary scene in the list. Odysseus, finding his father in the vineyard, "digging about a plant," with a patched, foul tunic on his body and greaves of oxhide on his shins to guard against scratches, thinks to begin with playful words, mocking the old man; but the outcome is that Laertes groans and strews dust over his head, whereupon Odysseus, his heart stirred and his nostrils shot through with pain, announces abruptly who he is. It is not enough. Laertes must have a sign. So Odysseus shows his scar; but better yet, he says to his father:

> Come, I will tell thee also the trees in the well-ordered garden which once thou gavest me, and I, who was but a child, was following thee through the garden, and asking thee for this and that. It was through these very trees that we passed, and thou didst name them, and tell me each one. Pear-trees thirteen thou gavest me, and ten apple-trees, and forty fig-trees. And rows of vines too didst thou promise to give me, even as I say, fifty of them, which ripened severally at different times—and upon them are clusters of all sorts—whensoever the seasons of Zeus weighed them down from above.

After which no major recognition remains to be strung on Homer's well-woven string.

It is a string and not a structure, for the organization of the *Odyssey* is loose and free, like its refrains: "Now the sun set and all the ways grew dark"; "So the wind filled the body of the sail, and the dark wave sang loudly about the stem of the ship as she went." Its similes are fewer than those of the *Iliad,* and less powerful, because less required; though the bow that sings like a swallow could not be surpassed for its purpose. But the similes of the *Iliad* were needed to pack the tight world Homer had decided to confine us in; or else they were breathing spaces in that world, reminding us of the greater one without. Whereas the world of the *Odyssey* is nothing but the one without. It is among other things a world of old men—Nestor, Eumaeus, Laertes, and the Old Man of the Sea—who have far memories because they have traveled much.

It is above all a bright world, open under space; and itself is full of space. Reality shines in it like mica; objects strike us because they have first been struck by the sun, as the white stones are upon which Nestor likes to go forth and sit in the early morning. The heaven of Olympus, whence Athene speeds with her flashing eyes, is a place without wind or rain, "but the air is outspread clear and cloudless, and over it hovers a radiant whiteness." The house of Menelaus, like the palace of Alcinous, has a gleam over its high roof "as of sun or moon." The epithet for Ithaca is "clear-seen." The epithet for night is "baneful," and the place where Homer's imagination least likes to dwell is the land and city of the Cimmerians, "wrapped in mist and cloud; never does the bright sun look down on them." The most grievous sin of the hero's comrades is the one they commit against Helios. And the most brilliant picture in a poem hung everywhere with pictures—for the *Odyssey* illustrates itself—is that which shows Pallas Athene preceding Odysseus and Telemachus into the hall where the weapons are, "bearing a golden lamp."

> Then Telemachus suddenly spoke to his father, and said: "Father, verily this is a great marvel that my eyes behold; certainly the walls of the house and the fair beams and crossbeams of fir and the pillars that reach on high, glow in my eyes as with the light of blazing fire. Surely some god is within."
>
> Then Odysseus of many wiles answered him, and said: "Hush, check thy thought, and ask no question; this, I tell thee, is the way of the gods that hold Olympus."

Distance and strangeness are the stuff of which narrative in the *Odyssey* is made. The poem lies under a sun that shines impartially on far and near. Nestor tells Telemachus that Menelaus may know something about his father because he has "but lately come from a strange land, from a folk whence no one would hope in his heart to return, whom the storms had once driven astray into a sea so great, whence the very birds do not fare in the space of a year." Strangers are the population of this world; they come and go, taking with them tales of where they have been. "There is a land called Crete," Odysseus tells Penelope, "in the midst of the wine-dark sea, a fair, rich land, begirt with water, and therein are many men, past counting, and ninety cities." It is a broad world, full of folk and fate, and the strangers who walk it are privileged persons whom it is the morality of the poem to receive with dignity in the halls they enter; though it is also the custom to shower them with questions—"Who art thou among men, and from whence? Where is thy city, and where thy parents? On what manner of ship didst thou come?" In such a world a man may move in anonymity if he pleases, but the custom is for him to reply; if his host has a good heart he loves strangers even as he fears the gods, and he will listen well. Frequently the wanderer spins yarns until he is sure of his host's heart—for safety, and perhaps for the mere fun of it. Nestor had the reputation of being so masterful and insistent a host that many a visitor to Pylos must have done as Telemachus did on his return from Lacedaemon—avoided the old man altogether, in his haste to get elsewhere. Yet certain citizens of the poem would have gone there with relish and regaled the horseman of Gerenia with mythical biographies. The poem is populated with excellent liars, of whom Athene is one, but of whom, naturally, Odysseus is king. Odysseus at a moment's notice can tell whoppers so circumstantial, so thicket-rich with detail, that only a cynic could disbelieve him. He invents families for himself, and remembers lands where he has never been unless he has been everywhere. He has the imagination of a minstrel—the person whom this society honors even more than it honors strangers. "For among all men that are upon the earth," Odysseus remarks at the court of Alcinous, "minstrels win honor and reverence, for that the Muse has taught them the paths of song." It is bad luck to kill a minstrel. Odysseus saves the one he had left at home.

It is a world on which the stars shine: "the Pleiads, and late-setting Boötes, and the Bear, which men also call the Wain, which ever circles where it is and watches Orion, and alone has no part in the baths of Ocean." But the sea which the Bear watches and never enters—that is the element in which the poem chiefly lives, showing its back among tempestuous waves. The sea of the *Odyssey* is real to its bottom. "When the sun hath reached mid heaven," says Menelaus, "the unerring old man of the sea is wont to come forth from the brine at the breath of the West Wind, hidden by the dark ripple. And when he is come forth, he lies down to sleep in the hollow caves; and around him the seals, the brood of the fair daughter of the sea, sleep in a herd, coming forth from the grey water, and bitter is the smell they breathe of the depths of the sea." No lines could bring more water with them than these do, or more of its smell when it is old and wild.

Over such water Odysseus had come to Phaeacia from faraway Troy, through the many adventures of which he told Alcinous: those of the Cicones, the Lotus-eaters, the Cyclops, Aeolus, the Laestrygonians, Circe, Hades, the Sirens, Scylla and Charybdis, the island of Helios Hyperion, and at last Calypso's isle. Through such water Odysseus swims, wades, sails, and drifts on a raft of his own making. With it under and around him he obeys that curiosity—his ruling passion—which causes as many deaths as were ever caused by the wrath of Achilles, for it pushes him to go where his comrades cannot survive. The sea is both his savior and his foe; and it is something from which the end of the poem releases him, dedicating him henceforth to life on the land he kisses in joy at being safe.

The prophet Teiresias instructed him thus in Hades:

> When thou hast slain the wooers in thy halls, then do thou go forth, taking a shapely oar, until thou comest to men that know naught of the sea and eat not of food mingled with salt, aye, and they know naught of ships with purple sails, or of shapely oars that are as wings unto ships. And I will tell thee of a sign right manifest, which will not escape thee. When another wayfarer, on meeting thee, shall say that thou hast a winnowing-fan on thy stout shoulder, then do thou fix in the earth thy shapely oar and make goodly offerings to lord Poseidon—a ram, and a bull, and a boar that mates with sows—and depart for thy home and offer sacred hecatombs to the immortal gods who hold broad heaven, to each one in due order. And death shall come to thee thyself far from the sea, a death so gentle, that shall lay thee low when thou art overcome with sleek old age, and thy people shall dwell in prosperity around thee. In this have I told thee sooth.

And Odysseus does not forget the prophecy. He repeats it to Penelope while their night is prolonged, to let her know that they will not be together always even now. But she is content if it means that his old age will be happy, an escape at last from evil. He will die so far from the sea that nobody whom he meets there will know an oar from a winnowing-fan. So be it, yet then there will be an end to evil.

The sea was foe to Odysseus in the person of Poseidon, its god, because Odysseus in blinding Polyphemus the Cyclops had blinded Poseidon's own son. The sea-god's punishment of the Phaeacians for their hospitality to the hero, and for their help to him in reaching home, springs from the same root: a friend of Odysseus must be an enemy of Polyphemus, and therefore of Poseidon. But more than that lurks in the mysterious Phaeacian background. These fairy people had once been neighbors of the Cyclops, and like

them are still in some measure children of the gods. They are a misty folk, living in a land of incredible beauty which is the last item needed to make the landscape of the *Odyssey* altogether wonderful.

As Odysseus approached this land of shadowy mountains "it shewed like unto a shield in the misty deep." Its folk were fostered of Zeus, who left them in peace "far off in the surging sea, the furthermost of men, and no other mortals have dealings with us." The Phaeacians are the ultimate strangers; they extend the beautiful world of the *Odyssey* to its limit. They care for nothing but ships, which for them are magic ships, "swift as a bird on the wing or as a thought." Their harbor is crowned with palisades; the palace of Alcinous has doors of silver and gold, and they are guarded by immortal dogs. The inhabitants of this land are favored by visits from the gods in manifest form. At sacrifices gods sit among them, feasting as they do. "Aye," says Alcinous, "and if one of us a lone wayfarer meets them, they use no concealment, for we are of near kin to them, as are the Cyclopes and the wild tribes of the Giants." The Phaeacians are Cronos-folk, of an earlier generation than mankind. No wonder they are wonderful to behold. And no wonder Poseidon punishes them for dishonoring their divine origin by the assistance they give Odysseus, who is a rank mortal if any man ever was. They are, however, the final stroke of light, and the fairest hue of distance, with which the universe of our hero paints itself.

But houses nearer home have almost an equal splendor. For the author of the *Odyssey* there is something important about any house, particularly if it is ruled by a member of that superior race, that breed of natural kings, to which Menelaus admits Telemachus and Peisistratus because they are the sons, respectively, of Odysseus and Nestor. The houses of such men, and indeed of any men that fear the gods and love strangers, are entered by the poet with awe and described with a ceremony befitting the rituals which go on there. The forms of courtesy, even the daily forms, are given full attention; there seems to be plenty of time for them in a work devoted as this one is to the task of revealing the charms of human life when it is gloriously provisioned. Such is the case not only at Phaeacia, where the reception of Odysseus is royal in its generosity—golden youths standing on pedestals in the hall, holding torches aloft to light the banqueters by night; a fair handmaiden bringing water in a gold pitcher so that the stranger may wash in a silver basin; delectable fruits brought always to his side from an orchard which never stops bearing "pear upon pear, apple upon apple, cluster upon cluster, and fig upon fig," and where the farewells as he leaves would be grateful to the most exacting god. It is the case as well in any household we are privileged to see, and certainly in that one which Penelope is keeping for Odysseus to see again. Telemachus and Peisistratus depart from the palace of Menelaus with their chariots full of shining gifts which match the exalted compliments ringing in their ears. As they speed homeward over the sand—for houses in the *Odyssey* are far apart, and the hooves of horses have much flying to do—they have leisure to reflect upon the splendid, spacious world they live in.

Even Calypso in her cave, though doubtless in her divinity she could have lived without effort, keeps excellent house. When Hermes arrived there with the message that she must release Odysseus he found that "a great fire was burning on the hearth, and from afar over the isle there was a fragrance of cleft cedar and juniper, as they burned; but she within was singing with a sweet voice as she went to and fro before the loom, weaving with a golden shuttle." And outside the cave she tends a Homeric garden—rich vines fed by four fountains, and beyond them soft meadows of violet and parsley.

We are so long in Penelope's house, once we arrive, that we grow accustomed to its beauty and begin to take it for granted. But it is the most interesting of all the establishments, as of course it should be. The hall of weapons, the mistress's high chamber, the great hall where the suitors revel, the corridors where mendicants can sit and gnaw the bones thrown at them, the cups, the plates, the tables, the tended fires, and the soft fleeces that line chairs—the poem lives here, as well as in the outlying premises of the swineherd and among the rows of trees Laertes once planted, during eleven of its books, and makes itself at home. When the suitors are killed there is much blood to be cleaned up, and we are told how this is done. "First they bore forth the bodies of the slain and set them down beneath the portico of the well-fenced court, propping them one against the other; and Odysseus himself gave them orders and hastened on the work. Then they cleansed the beautiful high seats and the tables with water and porous sponges. But Telemachus and the neatherd and the swineherd scraped with hoes the floor of the well-built house, and the women bore the scrapings forth and threw them out of doors." No domestic detail is ignored.

The human body in this world is assumed to have great grace, and is treated with utmost affection. It is kissed all over—on the head, the shoulders, the hands, and finally where it is brightest, on "both beautiful eyes." The person of Odysseus must be beautified on numerous occasions, for his rough adventures make him a sorry sight, and as such he is not fit to be seen by the fine folk of the tale. Nausicaa of the white arms, the child princess of Phaeacia who is washing garments at the shore when Odysseus is cast up there, is given 'courage by Athene to look at the strange man, befouled with brine, who stares at her like a rain-beaten lion. But his attendant goddess soon makes him more presentable:

> With water from the river goodly Odysseus washed from his skin the brine which clothed his back and broad shoulders, and from his head he wiped the scurf of the unresting sea. But when he had washed his whole body and anointed himse!f with oil, and had put on him the raiment which the unwedded maid had given him, then Athene, the daughter of Zeus, made him taller to look upon and mightier, and from his head she made the locks to flow in curls like unto the hyacinth flower. And as when a man overlays silver with gold, a cunning workman whom Hephaestus and Pallas Athene have taught all manner of craft, and full of grace is the work he produces, even so the goddess shed grace upon his head and shoulders.

A similar transformation is worked before he offers himself to the sight of Alcinous and his court; and exactly the same words are used to describe his being made ready for Penelope. In the case of Laertes, however, beautification comes after he has been made happy by the sight of Odysseus, not before. For the old man too receives the attention of Athene, growing in stature and might, so that his son, seeing him come forth from the bath, marvels at him and is glad.

The deities of the poem are seldom formidable like those of the *Iliad*. Even Poseidon, who causes Odysseus endless trouble, is not the terrible force that waited to level the wall before Troy. He is rather the god of shipwreck, presiding over accidents and preparing further toils. The Cyclopes over whom he watches wish only to be left alone, and indeed Odysseus is not attractive when he disturbs the solitude of Polyphemus, however exciting the hazards of the game played in a smoky cave where sheep and men are eaten with identical relish. Odysseus, describing the adventure to Alcinous, speaks with the condescension of a civilized man concerning this "overweening and lawless folk"

> who, trusting in the immortal gods, plant nothing with their hands nor plough; but all these things spring up for them without sowing or ploughing, wheat, and barley, and vines, which bear the rich clusters of wine, and the rain of Zeus gives them increase. Neither assemblies for council have they, nor appointed laws, but they dwell on the peaks of lofty mountains in hollow caves, and each one is lawgiver to his children and his wives, and they reck nothing one of another.

The Cyclopes, that is to say, dwell in primitive peace, innocent of law and war. They are earth-born, and live in simplicity.

The immortals most native to the *Odyssey* are Hermes and Athene, because they are the most beautiful. The divine messenger whom Zeus sends to Calypso goes as the poem likes all things to go, speedily, with strength and grace.

> Straightway he bound beneath his feet his beautiful sandals, immortal, golden, which were wont to bear him over the waters of the sea and over the boundless land swift as the blasts of the wind. And he took the wand wherewith he lulls to sleep the eyes of whom he will, while others again he awakens even out of slumber. With this in his hand the strong Argeïphontes flew. On to Pieria he stepped from the upper air, and swooped down upon the sea, and then sped over the wave like a bird, the cormorant, which in quest of fish over the dread gulfs of the unresting sea wets its thick plumage in the brine. In such wise did Hermes ride upon the multitudinous waves.

But Athene is the divine heroine of the tale. She is its presiding genius, memorable forever.

Athene is never long absent from Odysseus' life, and consequently from our sight. As a young maiden carrying a pitcher, as a young herdsman of sheep, as a woman "comely and tall, and skilled in glorious handiwork," and finally as the swallow that flies up to the roof-beam of the smoky hall in Ithaca where Odysseus is warring with the suitors—as anything that takes her charming fancy she comes when Odysseus needs her; or when, as sometimes it is possible to imagine, she desires to see this mortal for whom she has such deathless affection. "Hard is it, goddess," he tells her once, "for a mortal man to know thee when he meets thee, how wise soever he be, for thou takest what shape thou wilt." But he is only complaining of his supreme good fortune, for she is such a companion as any man might desire. The two of them are almost lovers. "I cannot leave thee in thy sorrow," she says, "for thou art soft of speech, keen of wit, and prudent." These are the reasons she chooses to give for the delight she takes in him—and takes particularly in his lies. When he has told her one of them she smiles and strokes his hand, changing herself to the form of a woman as she says:

> Cunning must he be and knavish, who would go beyond thee in all manner of guile, aye, though it were a god that met thee. Bold man, crafty in counsel, insatiate in deceit, not even in thine own land, it seems, wast thou to cease from guile and deceitful tales, which thou lovest to the bottom of thine heart. But come, let us no longer talk of this, being both well versed in craft. . . . Now am I come hither to weave a plan for thee.

She has loved his pretense that he is a stranger to the Ithaca whither she brought him. There was no good reason for his lie. It was merely his talent at work, and she adores his talent, as he on every occasion adores her. In the likeness of Mentes, and later on of Mentor, she has been of assistance to his son; and once she sent a phantom to his wife, so that Penelope might cease her weeping and recover the warm comfort of sleep. Now that Odysseus is home she is constantly at his side, taking clever care of him as he proceeds with his revenge. The goddess who had guided him to Phaeacia and exposed him to Nausicaa attends to each necessary detail. She assures him of success; she bears a golden lamp before him when he and Telemachus need light; she maddens the wooers and makes them miss their aim; she delays the dawn. And once she appears to him in manifest presence. Telemachus, who is with him in the swineherd's hut, does not notice her there. "But Odysseus saw her, and the hounds, and they barked not, but with whining slunk in fear to the further side of the farmstead."

The mortal she never deserts is due the preëminence his poem gives him. Odysseus is built into the **Odyssey** as the olive tree was built into his bed. Many another person is of the clearest interest. Eurycleia, the truehearted dame who guards the treasure room and tries to keep the young master from going on his journey to Pylos, but who when he has gone is strict with Penelope lest she grieve foolishly and disturb Laertes with the news; who rejoices over the death of the suitors a little too soon to suit Odysseus, though he is more than ready to let her give him the list of the maids who must be hanged; who hovers always in the house, a servant and yet the mistress of her ancient self—Eurycleia is one of Rembrandt's women, so carved and so lighted. Nausicaa at the other extreme of life, wondering whether such a man as Odysseus—of all men—might be her husband, and when he sets sail reminding him of what he owes her, is a maiden with white arms who flashes at the center of the poem, an image never to be lost from that essential place. Telemachus, who wants so badly to be older and wiser than he is, remains boyish to the end, when he commits the error of leaving the door of the storeroom open, and apologizes for it. Odysseus magnanimously discusses things with him as man to man, but his life is yet to be. The nicest stroke lavished upon his character is that in which Homer has him refuse the gift of horses from Menelaus because there is no room for horses on rocky Ithaca. But he speaks up for his little country, saying it is "pleasanter than one that pastures horses." And Menelaus smiles, stroking the boy's hand.

Penelope is not privileged to be a heroine of tragedy; the hard heart that Telemachus laments in her is something he only thinks is there. What actually is there we discover almost as soon as the poem begins. It is a pure capacity for feeling, and for saying, or singing, what is felt. That she is wrong about the facts— Odysseus *is* coming, and Telemachus *will* return from Lacedaemon—does not qualify the force of her grief when she fears that both may be lost; it merely makes her a lyric heroine.

> And on her fell a cloud of soul-consuming grief, and she had no more the heart to sit upon one of the many seats that were in the room, but down upon the threshold of her fair-wrought chamber she sank, moaning piteously, and round about her wailed her handmaids.

> "Hear me, my friends, for to me the Olympian has given sorrow above all the women who were bred and born with me. For long since I lost my noble husband of the lion heart. . . . And now again my well-loved son have the storm-winds swept away from our halls without tidings, nor did I hear of his setting forth."

It is madness in the suitors to desire a woman who will never be out of love with Odysseus, or, as she says to them when she proposes the trial of the bow, with this fair house "which methinks I shall ever remember even in my dreams." She may be chargeable with lyric exaggeration when she insists: "All excellence of mine, both of beauty and of form, the immortals destroyed on the day when the Argives embarked for Ilios, and with them went my husband." Yet Athene is sufficiently aware of what twenty years can do in such a case to see that she must make Penelope's face fair with the ambrosial balm of no less a beauty than Cytherea's herself, that she must increase her stature and stateliness, and leave her whiter than new-sawn ivory. The function of Penelope is to intensify our excitement as we see Odysseus approach the climax of his homecoming, and she performs it by providing a series of scenes in which he is so near to her, and yet so unknown, that suspense can scarcely go further. Not the least rich of these is concerned with the dreams they have of each other during the last night before the suitors are slain.

No reader of the *Iliad* forgets Priam's description of Odysseus when in the third book he discusses with Helen the Greek warriors they can see from the walls:

> Come now, tell me also of yonder man, dear child, who he is. Shorter is he by a head than Agamemnon, son of Atreus, but broader of shoulder and of chest to look upon. His battlegear lieth upon the bounteous earth, but himself he rangeth like the bell-wether of a herd through the ranks of warriors. Like a ram he seemeth to me, a ram of thick fleece, that paceth through a great flock of white ewes.

Or the answer which Antenor adds to Helen's; for Antenor had once entertained both Menelaus and Odysseus when they came to Troy on an embassage concerning Helen:

> Now when they mingled with the Trojans, as they were

gathered together, while men stood up Menelaus overtopped all with his broad shoulders; howbeit when the twain were seated Odysseus was the more royal. When they began to weave the web of speech, Menelaus in truth spake fluently, with few words, but very clearly. But whenever Odysseus of many wiles arose, he would stand and look down with eyes fixed upon the ground, and his staff he would move neither backwards nor forwards, but would hold it stiff, like a man of no understanding; thou wouldst have deemed him a churlish man and a fool. But when he uttered his great voice from his chest, and words like snowflakes on a winter's day, then could no mortal man beside vie with Odysseus.

And in the funeral games for Patroclus this burly fellow, with a torso longer than his legs, had taken many prizes—sometimes trickily, sometimes with Athene's aid. Even then he had not been young. Antilochus had marveled at his swiftness of foot in a race run with men perhaps no more than half his age. "Odysseus is of an earlier generation and of earlier men—a green old age is his, men say." That was how Antilochus explained the success of Odysseus. The immortals show special honor to older men.

But the favors of Athene are bestowed here upon a man who is neither young nor old. A son of Alcinous observes at Phaeacia: "In build, surely, he is no mean man, in thighs and calves, and in his two arms above, his stout neck, and his great might. In no wise does he lack aught of the strength of youth, but he has been broken by many troubles." And Odysseus, replying to the taunts of Euryalus, admits that he may have lost something in his passage through wars of men and the grievous waves. It is hard to see, however, what he has lost. The mortal to whom Athene is so faithful seems to have everything still, and timelessly. It is only to those at Ithaca who cannot see through the disguise she has given him that he manifests the feebleness of age. To be sure, the disguise is good. Athene shrivels his skin, she makes him bald, she clothes him in tatters, she sticks a staff in his hand, and she slings over his back a miserable wallet full of holes. And above all she makes good her final promise: "I will dim thy two eyes that were so beautiful." The brine-crusted, sea-beaten stranger washed naked on the shore of Phaeacia was less transformed than this; he still looked like a lion to the startled Nausicaa, and in her childish fancy he might some day be her husband.

The entrance of Odysseus is not until the fifth book; not, that is to say, until it has been prepared with all the skill available to Homer, which means all the skill there is. We have seen him awaited by everyone at Ithaca; we have heard him praised by Nestor and Menelaus; we have learned that he is "great-hearted," and that as a father—three persons say this, including Athene—he is "gentle." Now on Ogygia, the island of Calypso, we find him longing for home. He admits to the immortal nymph that Penelope is less beautiful than she. "But even so I wish and long day by day to reach my home. And if again some god shall smite me on the wine-dark sea, I will endure it, having in my breast a heart that endures affliction."

The stout heart he has is altogether his, and human, just as his tongue is what a good mind makes it. For the mortal nature of which he boasts at Phaeacia shows itself in both body and mind. He is not Samson. He is spirit, too, and art personified. He is good at anything; "no man can vie with me," he tells Eumaeus, "in piling well a fire, in splitting dry faggots, in carving and roasting meat, and in pouring wine." This is when he is applying to the swineherd for a position as servant to the suitors, but we do not doubt that the real Odysseus has watched every human action and can imitate it. He makes convincing gestures among the wooers in the hall, "beginning on the right, stretching out his hand on every side, as if he had been long a beggar."

To say that he is mind as well as body is not to say that he forgets his body. The man who had urged Achilles to eat before he mourned Patroclus still has an appetite. He curses this "ravening belly" which demands so much attention, but he seems not to be sorry that he is alive there also. Neither is it to say that he denies himself the pleasures of possession. In one of his lying tales about himself he says it is greed that so long delays his return from Troy. "Yea, and Odysseus would long since have been here," he tells Penelope, "only it seemed to his mind more profitable to gather wealth by roaming over the wide earth." Greed is not the word, but it is true that when he awakes at Ithaca he counts the presents Alcinous has given him, thinking the sailors may have slipped something out and gone away with it. Nothing has disappeared, and he is pleased. He is the sort of man who expresses himself in his possessions. He must have everything right—his bed was so and so, and it should still be that way. His bow with its long pedigree, once he has it in his hands, is fingered carefully: turned round and round, and tried this way and that, "lest worms might have eaten the horns." Penelope, taking it from its peg in the storeroom, had suddenly sat down with it on her knees, and wept. A thing that Odysseus owns is Odysseus.

His suspicion of the Phaeacian sailors is in character. He suspects everybody, including the gods. He is slow to believe either that his own luck is turning or that other people mean the good things they say. He has seen too many chances unwisely taken, and been too many times deceived. He moves through the final stages of recognition and revenge with a professional caution. He is no amateur in adventure, even though he is blessed with its essential spirit, the spirit of curiosity. His curiosity is always at war with his caution. There is no need for him to see what the Cyclopes are like,

and his men tell him so, protesting. But there across the water, as darkness comes down, he notices smoke and hears the voices of men, sheep, and goats, and the first thing he must do next morning is to set off in that direction, though it will mean the loss of comrades who go with him. The Sirens recognize in Odysseus a victim made to order: a man not only curious, but certain to take delight in songs concerning himself. For that is what they will sing, they say, if he comes close enough to hear. It takes the strongest ropes to keep him bound upright by his mast, safe from the seduction.

Suspicion and curiosity in Odysseus are the signs of a nimble wit that explores the ground before him. A still more famous one is his guile; he is ever ready with devices which his imagination, measuring persons and predicaments, is quick and accurate to supply him with. He is at home in the entire world, for he is never lost from himself. "Thou art a knave," Calypso exclaims to him in admiration when he demands that she swear an oath not to deal doubly with him; for that is what she might indeed have done. As he sees his strategy working against the Cyclops his heart laughs within him, proud of its cunning. Polyphemus had supposed that the Odysseus destined to come and blind him would be a giant like himself, not this puny weakling who first overpowered him with wine. The greatness of Odysseus is where the Cyclops cannot see it, in his wit. It is what makes him so successful in flattery, as when he calls Nausicaa a queen. It is the chief thing that guarantees Athene's continuing love.

The song of the Sirens would have seduced his vanity, if vanity is the name for the delight he takes in himself. "My fame reaches unto heaven," he tells Alcinous; and the old beggar of Ithaca tells Penelope that her husband is "like unto the gods." The mountain-top which Polyphemus hurls after his retreating ship does not discourage him from shouting back: "Cyclops, if any one of mortal men shall ask thee about the shameful blinding of thine eye, say that Odysseus, the sacker of cities, blinded it, even the son of Laertes, whose home is in Ithaca." He cannot hear too much from Eumaeus about the Odysseus who is gone; and his challenge to Eurymachus the suitor, when Eurymachus has insulted his character and strength, loses no glory by being for the moment hypothetical:

> Eurymachus, I would that we two might have a match in working, in the season of spring, when the long days come, at mowing the grass, I with a curved scythe in my hands and thou with another like it, and that the grass might be in plenty that so we might test our work, fasting till late evening. Or I would again that there were oxen to drive best there are, tawny and large, both well fed with grass, of like age and like power to bear the yoke, tireless in strength—and that there were a field of four acres, and the soil should yield before the plough: then

shouldest thou see me, whether or no I could cut a straight furrow to the end.

If these are boasts, they are the boasts of one who is praising life. If Odysseus loves himself, he loves the moving world still more. That world, concentrated in him, is what he loves and praises.

Peisistratus touching his horses with the whip so that they speed onward, nothing loath; Demodocus sitting and singing with a cup of wine which he has been shown how to reach with his hand, for he is blind; Telemachus standing by his father's side with sword and spear, armed with gleaming bronze; Achilles in the underworld, departing with long strides over the field of asphodel, joyful because he has been told that his son is preëminent—these, with Nestor on his white stones, Nausicaa with her white arms, Menelaus under his golden roof, Eurycleia with her torches and linen, Penelope in her grave chamber, are precious persons who adorn the tale created to contain them. But Odysseus is priceless, and he is not contained. The tale is of a dark storm that gathered over Ithaca, growing in secret mass until the land could be wholly cleansed by the lightning of its lord. This lord, still free, walks in the world. There has never been another poem to match either his or that of his young comrade-in-arms Achilles.

Mackail on the imperfect genius of the *Odyssey*:

The *Odyssey* is planned more ambitiously, more dexterously [than the *Iliad*]; construction is passing from an art into a science, architecture into engineering. Nothing in the *Iliad* is such a feat of design as the way in which the first four books of the *Odyssey* do not bring Odysseus on to the scene at all and yet imply him through every line as the central figure. A faultless sense of proportion keeps the poem wholly clear of divided interest. But, from whatever reasons, the genius flagged later. The *Odyssey* reminds one of a church begun when architecture had reached its perfection, on which the age lavished all its skill and riches, but where the imaginative impulse gave out before it was completed, or where part of the structure, built hastily or recklessly, collapsed and was rebuilt poorly by feebler hands.

J. W. Mackail, in Lectures on Greek Poetry, *Longmans, Green and Co., 1911.*

E. M. W. Tillyard (essay date 1954)

SOURCE: "Homer: The *Odyssey*," in *The English Epic and Its Background*, Oxford University Press, 1954, pp. 21-39.

[*Tillyard was an English scholar of Renaissance liter-* ature *who remains highly reputed for his studies of John Milton, William Shakespeare, and the epic form. In the essay below, Tillyard details similarities between the* Iliad *and the* Odyssey, *maintaining that they are different but equally brilliant poems*.]

Some readers think the *Odyssey* greatly inferior to the *Iliad*. T. E. Lawrence's chilly preface to his translation is a modern example of such an opinion, and Longinus's remark on the *Odyssey,* with its fabulous element, being the work of an old man is an ancient one. To both Pope gives the best answer in his postscript to his translation:

Whoever reads the *Odyssey* with an eye to the *Iliad,* expecting to find it of the same character, or of the same sort of spirit, will be grievously deceived, and err against the first principle of Criticism, which is to consider the nature of the piece, and the intent of its author. . . . The *Odyssey* is the reverse of the *Iliad,* in *Moral, Subject, Manner* and *Style;* to which it has no sort of relation, but as the story happens to follow in order of time, and as some of the same persons are actors in it. Yet from this incidental connection many have been misled to regard it as a continuation or second part, and thence to expect a parity of character inconsistent with its nature.

But Pope recognises common qualities too, and thinks that by comparing these you can judge whether Homer's powers have declined in the *Odyssey*. Comparing the common parts, he says we shall find in each the same vivacity and fecundity of invention, the same life and strength of imaging and colouring, the particular descriptions as highly painted, the figures as bold, the metaphors as animated, and the numbers as harmonious and various. And he thinks that in its way the simple narrative perfection of the *Odyssey* cost Homer as much to achieve as the sublime of the *Iliad*. Here I need do no more than use Pope's authority for asserting that the parts of the *Odyssey* are of high quality and that there is no initial bar to its epic character.

The *Odyssey* embraces the same area of life as the *Iliad,* but it sets out from a different point of the compass and chooses different portions for prolonged occupation. The Greek political unit of Homer's day was the city-state with its not too autocratic king; and however many towns were sacked, the norm was peaceful life in such a city. Whereas the *Iliad* dealt with exceptional happenings and their results, though constantly reminding us of the norm, the *Odyssey* was centred in it. This is clear from the outset. After the opening scene among the gods we are shown Ithaca and how the lawless suitors defy decency and threaten the domestic order. But that order, though threatened, still persists, and it is the moral centre of the poem. Telemachus, Odysseus's heir, is still in occupation of his own house and feels himself responsible for his mother, even if the suitors consume his father's goods. He succeeds in calling a general assembly at Ithaca and in appealing to the people at large against the suitors. And we gather that the people are on the side of order, though the suitors terrorise them. Anyhow Mentor still has the freedom of speech to blame the people for their lethargy.

There is another touch at the beginning which both confirms the domestic theme and links the *Odyssey* with the *Iliad*. It occurs in the first book during the conversation between Telemachus and Athena in the guise of Mentes. Athena has complimented Telemachus on his bearing and says he indeed resembles his father. To which Telemachus replies. . . .

> My mother indeed says I am his son. But for myself
> I am ignorant, for no one ever knew his own father.
> If only I had been the son of a fortunate man
> enjoying his possessions when death overtook him!
> But as it is, he is the most miserable of mortal men,
> the man, I mean, who they say is my father, now
> you ask me the question.

Telemachus yearns for the well-ordered state, with the old, legitimate king, dying among his possessions. But he also recalls by contrast Achilles and his problems as set forth in the ninth book of the *Iliad*. Whereas Peleus had grown old among his possessions and his son had chosen to seek honour in Troy rather than to repeat the pattern set by his father, Odysseus was growing into middle age through all kinds of foreign adventure while his goods were being dissipated and his son, unlike Achilles, was trying to regain the ordered social life. In both poems these elements are the same; they are contrasted not in themselves but in the way they are blended.

When the scene shifts from Ithaca, we witness the quiet routine and the ordered transaction of civilised life in Pylos and Sparta. Even in Phaeacia, where the inhabitants belong to an antique world nearer the gods and where supernatural events are habitual, the prevailing temper is one of domestic order. And the main action consists not only, indeed not principally, in the return of the wandering hero but in re-establishing the domestic and political norm in Ithaca, which though terribly threatened has not quite given way. This great action is completed only in the last book. There we are shown Laertes, now recovered and rejuvenated, joining son and grandson to repel the dead suitors' kinfolk. The proper hereditary norm has been re-established. And in the final heavenly conversation, between Zeus and Athena, it is decreed that Odysseus and the suitors' kin shall be reconciled and he reign in perpetuity. The old mutual goodwill shall be restored.

If the centre of the *Odyssey* is different from the *Iliad*'s, so too is the style. I noted how in the first book of the *Iliad* the principal episode, the quarrel between Agamemnon and Achilles, was followed by the subsidiary episode, much quieter but equally intense, of the two heralds fetching away Briseis from Achilles's tent; and I mentioned a slight suggestion of comedy. In the *Odyssey* this vein of quiet, intense description predominates and it answers the mainly social theme. This uncommon clarity of description, where the details are few but necessary and telling to the utmost, is what constitutes the *Odyssey*'s basic charm. It depends on powers of observation and enjoyment primitively fresh but wielded by a highly sophisticated art. Here are two samples of Homer's economical clarity in the *Odyssey*. In the last book Odysseus and Telemachus, fearing revenge for having killed the suitors, withdraw from the town and seek out Laertes, now retired from his rule and living a farmer's life in an up-country farm. The context is important: Laertes does not know of his son's return and victory and that there is now no reason for his living in this rough squalor. To Odysseus, now triumphant, the squalor must have appeared doubly pathetic. These things we must bear in mind as we read Homer's description of Laertes on his farm . . . :

> And he found his father alone, in the neat vineyard,
> breaking up the soil round a vine-stock. He was
> wearing a dirty tunic, disgracefully patched, his shins
> bound round with stitched leather gaiters to prevent
> scratches, with gloves on his hands against the
> brambles, while on his head, to make matters worse,
> he had a cap of goatskin.

There is much of the *Odyssey* here in little: the typically human, pathetic situation; the details clear and separate and not too many; the slight comedy of the old man's very forgivable masochism in dressing just a little more miserably than he need, the goatskin hat being (unlike Robinson Crusoe's) more Spartan than the case required. The other passage describes Odysseus, waiting for sleep in beggar's disguise in his own house, hearing the girls of his household who were the suitors' mistresses stealing away to join their lovers. Again, the context is essential, Odysseus has had a terrible day, suffering insults in his own home from the suitors, on whom he is thinking out revenge. The girls' laughter breaks in on an overwrought man. . . .

> So Odysseus lay there unable to sleep, thinking out
> mischief for the suitors; when out of the women's
> quarters came the girls whom the suitors had for
> mistresses, laughing and chaffing among themselves.
> And his heart was stirred up within him.

As the final touch to an exhausting day's experience, could anything be more apt?

Of English authors Chaucer comes nearest Homer in this convincing power of description, the power which is so certain of itself that the reader's suspension of disbelief is not merely willing but as instantaneous as the working of the new anaesthetics. This is Canacee retiring from the feast early so as not to spoil her complexion:

> She was ful mesurable, as wommen be;
> For of hir fader hadde she take leve
> To goon to reste soone after it was eve.
> Hir liste nat appalled for to be
> Ne on the morwe unfeestlich for to se,
> And slepte hire firste sleep and thanne awook.

And this is the gigantic stadium Theseus put up for the tournament between Palamon and Arcite:

> The circuit a myle was aboute,
> Walled of stoon and dyched al withoute.
> Round was the shap in manere of compas,
> Ful of degrees, the heighte of sixty pas,
> That whan a man was set on o degree
> He letted not his felowe for to see.

It might be the first grandstand ever to be constructed and Chaucer the first man to see it, but the art has the smoothness of a finished diplomat.

Set against the realism of the domestic norm is the element of the fabulous. And here one must guard against the error of Longinus and of many (if not most) recent readers: that of giving this element a dominant place. Through the way Homer ordered his plot it is obvious that he meant the fabulous element not to dominate but to set off the domestic. The domestic theme is firmly established in the first four books with the troubles of Penelope and Telemachus in Ithaca and Telemachus's journey to the Peloponnese; it remains strong in the scenes on Calypso's island and in Phaeacia, that is for four more books; and the fabulous element dominates only in Books Nine to Twelve, making indeed a wonderful diversity and variety, but remaining strictly subordinate. A section of antiquity was wiser than Longinus in this matter, for the papyrus finds point to the last four books having been the most popular in Egypt between the third century before and the third after Christ. Of course, there is no denying the enchantment of the wanderings of Odysseus. The point is that it is more than self-valuable. The love of home can never be truly perceived in separation from the other love of freedom to wander and from the desire for change; it can never be truly prized in separation from the chaos and barbarism out of which the domestic pieties were painfully won. Homer gives us the whole picture.

There is another contrast: important both in itself and in the connections it makes with the *Iliad*. Right through the poem the misfortune of Agamemnon and the guilt of Clytaemnestra are compared with the better domestic fortune of Odysseus and with Penelope's virtue; and the action is not complete till Agamemnon in Hades

hears from the suitors' ghosts of domestic reunion in Ithaca. That comparison Homer plainly meant to be as important as it is close. We hear of it at the very beginning in the council in heaven, where Aegisthus, Agamemnon, Clytaemnestra, and Orestes all are mentioned. Homer wished us to think of a whole pattern of correspondences: Agamemnon-Odysseus, Clytaemnestra-Penelope, Aegisthus-the suitors, Orestes-Telemachus. Only, in one story the issue is unhappy, the wife is false, and the son has to do an unnatural deed; while in the other the issue is happy, the wife faithful, and the son's deed of violence legitimate. But the two stories are not only parallel, they typify the stories of all the Achaean chiefs who had survived the Trojan War. In fact, the story of Odysseus's return corresponds to the wrath of Achilles in implying a wider context or theme: the combined home-comings of the Homeric heroes.

The **Odyssey** usually passes for a comedy, and rightly. But tragedy is never far off, and we are constantly reassured that the author had it at his call. Telemachus's helpless plight among the suitors is almost intolerable. His growing manhood was constantly being insulted. Penelope's grief for Odysseus is great and prolonged. It culminates in her refusal to acknowledge him when he declares himself; and the lovely passage when her reluctant self-defence breaks barely escapes from tragedy to pathos, like the recognition scenes in *Pericles* and the *Winter's Tale*. Odysseus's longing for home is intense and almost tragic when thwarted for so long. But though intense it is steady and untempestuous: unlike the emotion that corresponds to it in the **Iliad** the anger of Achilles. Nevertheless, Homer at least twice reassures us that Odysseus too can feel violently as well as obstinately. The first time is when, having bent his bow, he leaps from his rags, pours out his arrows at his feet, tells the suitors that he will now strike a target which no man yet has struck, and shoots the chief of the suitors, Antinous. The rest, though thinking the blow accidental, are about to set upon him and kill him, when he throws at them his tremendous indictment. . . . :

> You dogs, you never thought I should come back from the people of Troy; and so you wasted my household goods, you forced the maid-servants to sleep with you. You wooed my wife behind my back though I was still alive, fearing neither the gods in high heaven nor any retribution that might fall on you from men. And now, for all of you, your fate is sealed.

And terror seized them all. And right at the end of the poem, when the suitors' friends and relatives seek revenge, Odysseus becomes a terrific figure, giving a great shout, swooping on them like an eagle, until restrained by a thunderbolt from Zeus. It is almost as if Homer, having rounded off the domestic theme with

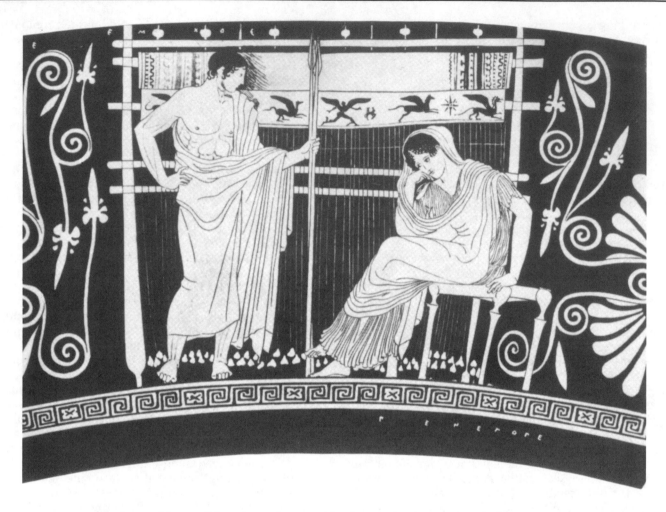

Penelope and her son Telemachos gather around her loom in this drawing on a skyphos c. 450 B.C.

the union of the three generations in the resistance to the suitors' avengers, wished as a last touch to establish a momentary union with his other great poem.

The *Iliad* is not worse plotted than the *Odyssey,* but the lines of the *Odyssey* are more immediately clear: with the result that the *Odyssey* has supplied the classic shape for the formal epic. Both poems begin at a late stage of the total action, but in the *Iliad* past events are recalled by the unemphatic method of scattered hints. The *Odyssey* by making one of the characters narrate past history established a great precedent. The *Aeneid,* the *Lusiad, Paradise Lost* all follow it. The precedent also of making a journey (or journeys) lead to a narrower stage of action was also set by the *Odyssey*. Here the resemblance with *Paradise Lost* is particularly close. In the *Odyssey* the various travels converge in the narrow stage of the palace hall in Ithaca, after which the scene expands somewhat to include the island. In *Paradise Lost* the various travels from Hell and Heaven converge in Adam's garden, after which the scene, though never expanding to its

old dimensions, includes the earth. But the Odyssean analogy is not confined to the formal epic. The journey is a simple and universal symbol of human life; and the voyager, of man living his normal span. The stock phrase 'soul-Odyssey' unconsciously testifies to the fact of this symbol and to the instinct to see it in Homer. Man's pilgrimage was a great medieval theme: so it is the *Odyssey* above all epics that stands, by reason of its plot, at the head of a great succession.

As in the *Iliad,* there is abundant evidence that Homer held the whole content of the *Odyssey* in his mind during composition. One piece of evidence has been mentioned already in another context: Homer's unrelaxed attention to the parallel theme of Agamemnon and his household and his care to complete the theme by causing the suitors' ghosts to bear to Agamemnon in Hades the news of Odysseus's return and of Penelope's successful resistance and fidelity. Another piece is the careful mention in the first book (189-90) of Laertes living aloof on his farm with an old attendant, nursing his grief; a mention to be taken up in the last book by the wonderful description of Laertes in his orchard, quoted earlier. Again, just as Thetis is introduced in the first and last books of the *Iliad,* so an assembly is summoned in the first and last books of the *Odyssey*. The people do the wrong thing in both, but in different ways. In the first, they fail to speak up in support of Telemachus through fear of the suitors; in the second they are frivolously weak in supporting Eupeithes, the father of Antinous, in his demand for vengeance, and, far from remaining silent, they burst into an uproar. Homer had the assembly in the first book in his mind till he was near the end of his poem.

In this matter of will-power and the predetermined plan as revealed in the composition of the *Odyssey* it is more apt to express astonished admiration than to present more evidence for the obvious.

W. B. Stanford (essay date 1954)

SOURCE: "The Untypical Hero," in *The Ulysses Theme: A Study in the Adaptability of a Traditional Hero,* second edition, Basil Blackwell, 1963, pp. 66-80.

[*Stanford was a writer on Greek literature, politics, and ecclesiastical affairs. In this essay, first published in 1954, he explores Odysseus's unconventionality as a hero, noting that Homer "skilfully succeeded in distinguishing Odysseus by slight deviations from the norm in almost every heroic feature."*]

There is nothing freakish about Odysseus's personality in the Homeric poems. In the *Iliad* Homer endows him with the normal qualities of an Achaean hero—princely birth, good physique, strength, skill in athletics and battle, courage, energy, and eloquence. But in most of these Odysseus is surpassed or equalled by some of his colleagues at Troy. The Atreidae and Aeacids are of more illustrious lineage. Agamemnon and Menelaus are of more impressive stature. Achilles and Ajax surpass him in strength and force of arms. Diomedes is more gallant and dashing in battle. Even in oratory he is not unrivalled.

The fact is, of course, that Odysseus is not the chief hero of the *Iliad*. Achilles, and after him Ajax, Hector, Diomedes, and the Atreidae, are more prominent. Not that the *Iliad* presents Odysseus as a minor hero: he has his triumphs in the council and in the assembly, on the field of battle and in the athletic contests. But his unique personality is not allowed to divert attention from the *Iliad's* main themes, the wrath of Achilles and the death of Hector. On the other hand, in the *Odyssey* he, 'the man of many turns', is the main theme, and his personal qualities become specially luminous against the sordidness of his environment, as he makes his way among foolish shipmates, ruthless monsters,

and greedy usurpers. Yet here, too, Odysseus meets his equals at times. Eumaeus the swineherd shows a loyalty and gentle courtesy quite as fine as his, and Penelope is wily enough to outwit him in their final recognition scene.

By endowing Odysseus with a share of the normal heroic qualities Homer avoided any suggestion that he was an eccentric figure or a narrowly limited type. But at the same time Homer, especially in the *Iliad,* skilfully succeeded in distinguishing Odysseus by slight deviations from the norm in almost every heroic feature. In his ancestry there was the unique Autolycan element. In physique he had the unusually short legs and long torso described by Antenor and Helen in *Il.* 3, 190 ff. He reminded Helen of a sturdy ram, she said, as he marshalled the Achaean ranks. Any hint of the ludicrous in this comparison is removed by Antenor's subsequent description of Odysseus's imposing presence. But there is something a little unaristocratic, or at least non-Achaean, in this portrait, contrasting with the tall, long-limbed stature of the other heroes. Napoleon would have looked like that beside Wellington; or Cuchulain, that 'short, dark man', among the taller champions of the Red Branch Knights. Possibly Homer meant to imply something more than a personal peculiarity here. It may be intended as an indication of some racial difference between Odysseus and the other Achaeans. Perhaps—but it is a pure guess—Homer regarded Odysseus as being partly a survival of the pre-Greek stock in Greece, an 'Aegean' or 'Mediterranean' type. At any rate, the physical difference serves to mark Odysseus out as exceptional, without giving an impression of ugliness, oddity, or deformity.

One finds the same distinction in a quite different kind of trait—in Odysseus's unusually frank and realistic remarks on the importance of food in human life. All the Homeric heroes were hearty eaters and drinkers. But, whether by accident or convention, none of them except Odysseus had anything notable to say about eating. Perhaps it was regarded as a plebeian subject, unfit for high-born Achaeans; or perhaps they simply were not interested in it as a subject for conversation. It was typical of the average Homeric hero that he was prepared on occasion to ignore the need for food, both for himself and for others. The contrast with Odysseus's attitude is well illustrated in a scene between him and Achilles in *Iliad* Nineteen. Achilles, now equipped with new armour and ready for battle, is impatient to launch a general attack against the Trojans to take vengeance for Patroclus's death. Odysseus objects. The Greek soldiers have been kept awake all night in lamenting Patroclus and in preparing his body for burial. The Trojans, on the contrary, have been able to enjoy a quiet supper and a night's rest. Odysseus, not being blinded by personal feeling like Achilles, knows that unless soldiers get a good meal first they will not be able to fight all day: even if they are eager to continue the battle, 'yet their limbs are treacherously weighed down as hunger and thirst overtake them, and their knees fail them as they go'. There is both compassionate understanding and Napoleonic common sense here: the spirit may be willing, but the flesh is weak; an army marches on its stomach. Odysseus adds some further remarks on the strengthening and cheering effect of food and wine, and ends by demanding that the army should have a full meal before being ordered to attack.

Achilles's reply to Odysseus's reasonable objection is characteristic: '*You* go and busy yourselves with food: *I* shall not touch a morsel until Patroclus is avenged. And, let me tell you, if I were in supreme command, the whole army would have to fight fasting, too, till sunset. Then, with vengeance achieved, we should have a great supper.' What is one to call such arrogant confidence as this—with no thought of fatigue or death, no consideration for himself or for others? Is it heroic, or is it schoolboyish? Is it superb singleness of purpose or callow rashness? Odysseus in his reply deftly and gently suggests that youthful heedlessness is partly, at least, to blame. Addressing Achilles with great deference as 'Much the mightiest of the Achaeans' he admits his own inferiority to him in martial valour. But he claims definite superiority in thinking things out. Then after an appeal to Achilles to listen patiently for a moment (Odysseus clearly wants to avoid provoking Achilles's wrath again in any way: but he insists on making his point about the need for food), he emphasizes the danger of fatigue in war, and mildly ridicules Achilles's notion that fasting is a good way for warriors to mourn those slain in battle. Bury the dead with pitiless heart, bewail them for a day, yes—but those who survive must eat to get energy for punishing the enemy. Odysseus is trying to persuade Achilles to eat with the others. If Achilles fights fasting against a well-fed Hector, even Achilles may be conquered. Odysseus's arguments fail, as in the Embassy scene, to overcome Achilles's passionate resolve. But, significantly, Athene intervenes later, at Zeus's request, and feeds Achilles with nectar and ambrosia 'so that', the poet remarks, 'joyless hunger should not reach his knees'. Thus obliquely Homer, Athene, and Zeus agree with Odysseus's advice.

But the typical Homeric hero would probably have admired Achilles's intransigence more than Odysseus's more practical policy. One does in fact find an indication elsewhere in the *Iliad* that Odysseus had already got a reputation for being too much interested in the pleasures of eating. In *Iliad* 4, 343-6, Agamemnon accuses Odysseus and the Athenian Menestheus of being quick to hear invitations to a feast, but slow to answer the call to arms. Odysseus emphatically denies any reluctance to join the fight, but he passes over the accusation of unusual alacrity in coming to feasts. Probably he thought it beneath contempt. Yet, as in

Agamemnon's accompanying accusation of evil deceitfulness, it may well be that Homer intends us to catch a glimpse here of a general tendency to regard Odysseus as rather more partial to good fare than a hero should have been.

This is uncertain. But there is no uncertainty about the attitude of post-Homeric writers. Attic comedians, fourth-century philosophers, Alexandrian critics, late classical chroniclers, agree in accusing Odysseus of greed and gluttony. They based their slanders chiefly on some of his actions and remarks in the *Odyssey* which, considered out of their contexts, certainly do give a bad impression. Thus in *Od.* 6, 250, Odysseus eats 'greedily'. In *Od.* 7, 215-18 he asks Alcinous to let him go on with his supper without interruption, remarking that there is no more shameful compulsion than that of 'the abominable belly' which compels even a mourner to eat and forget his grief for a while. In *Od.* 9, 1 ff., after the Phaeacians have given him a splendid banquet, Odysseus pronounces that he knows of no more beautiful consummation in life than a feast with good food, good wine, good song, and general good cheer. Later, after his arrival in Ithaca, when still in his beggar's disguise, Odysseus returns to the theme of hunger and appetite. He tells Eumaeus that it is for the sake of 'the accursed belly' that vagabonds are compelled to suffer all the hardships of wandering from place to place (*Od.* 15, 344-5). Later he tells Eumaeus again (*Od.* 17, 286-9) that in his opinion it is impossible to conceal the 'accursed belly' when it is in its full fury: it brings many evils to men, and for its sake men sail the barren seas to attack their enemies. Soon afterwards (vv. 473-4) he attributes a violent assault by Antinous to the promptings of his 'baneful accursed belly'. In the following book he pretends that he wants to attack the rival beggar, Irus, at the behest of 'the evil-working belly' (18, 53-4), but repudiates a suggestion by a Suitor (18, 362-4) that he was good for nothing but gross eating (18, 376-81).

If one remembers that no other hero in the *Iliad,* nor any Homeric heroine in either poem, even uses the word for 'belly' and still less discusses its effects, it is clear that Odysseus is an untypical hero in this respect. And it is obvious how easy it was for comic writers to portray him as a glutton, courtly critics as a crudely indelicate eater, and philosophers as confirmed voluptuary, by concentrating on a few passages out of their contexts. Thus Plato was shocked at Odysseus's praise of banquets, as being one of the finest 'consummations' in life. But surely the effusive remarks of an after-dinner speaker at a royal banquet are not to be judged as a solemn philosophical pronouncement. Besides, should not Odysseus's more sober aphorisms on the harmful effects of appetite in human life be weighed against this? And should it not have been remembered to Odysseus's credit how he had rejected the temptation of the Lotus-fruit and had resolutely held out against eating the Cattle of the Sun? When he eats 'greedily' after his reception in Alcinous's palace, should we not bear in mind that (apart from a snack from the remains of Nausicaa's picnic in Book Six) he had not eaten for three days and had suffered terrible physical and mental agonies in Poseidon's long storm? Indeed, he had shown supreme self-control during his first supplication to Nausicaa: he had never mentioned food, but modestly asked only for a scrap of clothing and for information about the city. One almost loses patience with armchair critics who censure the conduct of a ravenous shipwrecked mariner for not conforming with the court etiquette of Alexandria or Versailles, and with moralists who demand the scruples of the confessional in the speeches of the banqueting-hall.

Odysseus's remarks on food in the second half of the *Odyssey* were less criticized, because he was obviously playing up to his rôle as a beggar in all of them. Further, as the Cynics noticed, he was a philosophical beggar. He showed that he understood the effects of appetite on men in general: how it drives men to war as well as to trade; how it moves the languid fingers of the courtier as well as the clutching fists of the starveling outcast. Yet he never suggested, as the more cynical Cynics did, that the belly was lord of all, and that he and his dog Argos were equally its slaves. He simply accepted it as one of the inescapable elemental forces in human life. Heroes like Agamemnon, Ajax, and Achilles, who had, as far as we know, never been compulsorily deprived of food in their lives, could nonchalantly disregard its demands. But Odysseus, by the time of his return to Ithaca, had become painfully familiar with the effects of involuntary hunger. Homer himself, if he was a bard wandering from audience to audience 'for the sake of accursed belly', may well have made Odysseus his own spokesman here. He, too, if we can deduce his personal feelings from the vivid description of the blind bard Demodocus in *Od.* 8, 62 ff., appreciated the comfort of having a basket of food and a cup of wine within reach to take 'whenever his spirit prompted him'.

The contrast here between the conventional hero's insouciance, or reticence, on the subject of food and Odysseus's frequent attention to it is one of the best illustrations of Odysseus's unconventionality as a hero. But Homer, perhaps for fear that his less philosophical hearers might fail to appreciate this kind of example, also exemplified Odysseus's uniqueness in a small matter that all warriors would notice. It is frequently emphasized in the *Odyssey* (and also mentioned in *Iliad* Ten) that Odysseus had unusual skill as an archer. His triumph over the Suitors at the end of the *Odyssey* depended on this. But only a few, and those not the most illustrious, of the other heroes at Troy show any interest in the use of the bow. Indeed, there are some indications that archery was despised as plebeian or unmanly, much as a medieval knight of the sword and

lance scorned to assail another knight with arrows. Perhaps Odysseus was merely old fashioned in his military technique. Or perhaps it was because the plot of the *Odyssey* demanded a triumph by means of the bow. But the trait does also serve to distinguish him from the other chief heroes. Another feature is far more peculiar. It is once mentioned in the *Odyssey* that Odysseus possessed, and so he presumably used, poisoned arrows. This, however, like his Autolycan ancestry, is never referred to in the *Iliad*.

Though Odysseus's Homeric speeches were the admiration of every age of classical rhetoric, their excellence is not that of an orator among tongue-tied men. Oratory was a recognized part of heroic training. Thus in the Embassy scene Achilles's reply is fully as powerful and eloquent as Odysseus's pleadings. At times, too, Nestor's speeches in council are as wise and as cogent as Odysseus's. The difference is not one of skill. It lies more in the fact that, when the other heroes speak, their minds are obsessed with conventions and prerogatives or weakened by passion and self-concern. Achilles's wrath and Nestor's tendency to garrulous reminiscences tend to make their orations more effective as expressions of prejudices and personal feelings than as instruments of policy. In contrast, Odysseus's speeches are strictly functional, as a rule. When he shows passion or introduces a personal touch it is almost always because it will help to achieve his aim—to quell Thersites and to rebuke the wavering Agamemnon or an insolent prince of Phaeacia. Those who consider passionate self-esteem an essential quality of the genuine heroic type may find this kind of self-possession mean or machiavellian. But, as Sophocles indicates in his *Ajax,* it is the faculty that maintains justice and humanity among passionate men.

Besides this functional difference between Odysseus's speeches and those of other heroes, Homer signalizes his oratory by a peculiar personal trait. In Antenor's speech, as already mentioned, there is a description of Odysseus's curious habitual pose before beginning an important speech. He would stand with his eyes fixed on the ground, his body and gestures stiff 'like an ignorant fellow's'. His voice, Antenor adds, was of great power. But he seems to have controlled this Gladstonian organ with the deftness of a Disraeli: his words came smoothly, lightly, continuously, flake after flake like falling snow—perhaps in the quiet, level tone characteristic of adepts in the art of plausibility. The general effect, we are told, was overwhelming. Homer corroborates this impression in several scenes in the *Odyssey,* where he describes how Odysseus could hold an audience spellbound 'like a skilled bard'. Homer could hardly have paid a higher tribute to his oratory. Once again he identifies Odysseus's powers with his own.

In the later tradition Odysseus was often accused of

cowardice. The charge was based less on incidents mentioned by Homer than on others first recorded in the post-Homeric tradition, Odysseus's attempt to evade conscription, for example, and in later versions of his conduct with Palamedes and Philoctetes. There is nothing of that kind in the Homeric poems. But one ambiguous incident in *Iliad* Eight left a shadow on his reputation for courage. The circumstances are these. A general rout of the Achaeans has begun. Agamemnon, the two Ajaxes, and Idomeneus retreat rapidly. Nestor is left behind in grave danger. Hector rushes forward to cut him down. Diomedes sees the danger and calls to Odysseus for help in rescuing the old king. 'But', Homer records, 'Odysseus did not hear (or listen to) his call, and sped on to the Achaean ships'. The crucial verb is capable of two interpretations. It was left open to Odysseus's defenders in post-Homeric controversies to argue that Odysseus had simply not heard Diomedes's cry in the confusion of the general retreat. But his detractors could take it as a deliberate ignoring of a comrade's cry for help. Homer's own intention is hidden in the ambiguity. However, no matter what he meant here, he soon makes it clear that none of his heroes attached any blame to Odysseus for his conduct. On the contrary, Odysseus's prestige is at its highest in the next three books.

If one considers the whole of Odysseus's career, a general accusation of cowardice is plainly absurd. In *Iliad* 11, 395 ff., he stands valorously alone against the whole Trojan host. His bravery in the Doloneia is incontestable. Similarly it took the highest courage to vanquish the Cyclops, to resist Scylla, to overthrow the horde of Suitors. Yet Homer does seem to hint occasionally, not at cowardice, but at a kind of tension between prudence and boldness. Thus in Odysseus's brief spell as supreme champion of the Greeks in *Iliad* Eleven, he pauses for a moment to wonder whether it would not be wiser to retreat with the rest. He immediately reminds himself of his heroic duty, and, with a touch of fatalism, unusual in him, fights on. There is obviously no cowardice in this. On the contrary, the man who fully foresees danger and then goes on to meet it is more truly courageous than a stubborn Ajax or a furious Achilles. The best illustration of this tension between prudence and heroic valour is found in Odysseus's attempt to avoid conscription by feigning madness. . . . Unfortunately it is not certain that Homer knew the legend.

A commentator on Euripides's version of the Cyclops incident has seen something of a Hamletesque figure in Odysseus as portrayed there. This was possible in the atmosphere of the late fifth century. But Homer's Odysseus is obviously no indecisive princeling sicklied o'er with the pale cast of thought. His decisive boldness is made clear both at the beginning of the *Iliad* in his handling of the Thersites affair, and at the outset of his Odyssean adventures when he sacks Is-

marus like any Elizabethan buccaneer or Spanish conquistador. He is 'the great-hearted', 'the sacker of cities', as well as the prudent and resourceful Odysseus. Yet in both these bold deeds his prudence is not entirely in abeyance. While he faces Thersites uncompromisingly, he coaxes, amuses, and flatters the other Greeks. Again in the sack of Ismarus he orders a withdrawal as soon as a counter-attack seems likely. His comrades refuse, with disastrous results. Odysseus calls them 'great fools' for not obeying his prudent command. But when he first gave it, they, for their part, may well have thought his prudence was mere timidity.

The fact is that, even though no real cowardice was involved, Odysseus's gift for anticipating dangers and his readiness to avoid them when it best served his purpose, did separate him from the normal hero of his time. Whether one admires it or not, a certain mulish stubbornness in the manner of Ajax, a reckless *élan* like that of Diomedes, a readiness to let everything be turned upside down for the sake of some point of honour in the manner of Achilles, was more characteristic of the early heroic temperament than a prudent resourcefulness. When the typical hero found his path to fame and glory blocked, his instinct was to batter his own or someone else's head against the obstacle until something broke. The gentle Hector and the tough Ajax were alike in this intransigence. Odysseus was no less determined to gain his purpose; but he was far less intransigent. He was prepared to undermine an obstacle or to look for another path, to imitate the mole or the fox rather than the rhinoceros.

In the later tradition, admirers of the simpler, prouder kind of hero will despise this quality, calling it cowardly or opportunistic. Homer suggests no such disapproval. On the contrary the *Odyssey* implies that some such resourcefulness is necessary to overcome the trials of human life in general. Almost all Homer's more intransigent heroes die unhappily, Agamemnon murdered by his wife, Ajax killed by his own hand, Achilles slain by a cowardly arrow. Odysseus, like Nestor and Menelaus, returns home at last to live in peace and prosperity.

Odysseus was also the 'much-enduring' man. Among the other Homeric heroes only Nestor, whose life had extended over three normal generations, shared this epithet with him. Why? After all, many of the rest showed great endurance in battle. The answer seems to lie in a special implication in Homer's use of epithets in *poly-* meaning 'much'. . . . [It] seems to imply variety rather than degree, especially in its active compounds. The other heroes were 'much-enduring' in their own special forte, namely, fighting. But Odysseus and Nestor were men who had shown their endurance in an unusual variety of circumstances: Nestor because of his abnormally long life, Odysseus because of his enterprising nature. Here once again a clash between Odysseus's qualities and the typical heroic temperament emerges. Ajax or Achilles would never have been willing to undergo some of Odysseus's experiences— his three adventures in beggar's disguise, for instance, and his ignominious escape from the Cyclops's cave by hanging under a ram's belly (which was a kind of Trojan Horse stratagem in reverse). In the later tradition Odysseus is accused of ignobleness, even cowardice, for his readiness to employ disguise or stealth when necessary to achieve his purpose. Undoubtedly one can detect an element of Autolycanism here. But what was often forgotten was that these various examples of combined resourcefulness and endurance were generally used *pro bono publico*.

We shall see all this argued out in the later tradition. Here it need only be emphasized that without this quality Odysseus could never have been so serviceable to the Greek cause. This serviceability varied from such an ordinary task as that of pacifying the indignant Chryses in *Iliad* One to the final triumph of Ulyssean cleverness in the ruse of the Wooden Horse. But it is the common fate of serviceable men to be despised by their more self-centred associates.

All these deviations from the heroic norm are exemplified in the *Iliad* as well as in the *Odyssey*. The next quality to be considered has little or no scope in the restricted Iliadic *milieu*. It needs the more expansive background of the *Odyssey*. It is a quality that points away from the older Heroic Age with its code of static conventions and prerogatives, and on to a coming era, the era of Ionian exploration and speculation. This is Odysseus's desire for fresh knowledge. Homer does not emphasize it. But it can be seen plainly at work in two of the most famous of Odysseus's Odyssean exploits. It becomes the master passion of his whole personality in the post-classical tradition, notably in Dante, Tennyson, Arturo Graf, and Kazantzakis.

This eagerness to learn more about God, man, and nature is the most characteristic feature of the whole Greek tradition. To quote a recent commentator on Dante's conception of Ulysses:

> To be a Greek was to seek to know; to know the primordial substance of matter, to know the meaning of number, to know the world as a rational whole. In no spirit of paradox one may say that Euclid is the most typical Greek: he would fain know to the bottom, and know as a rational system, the laws of the measurement of the earth. . . . No doubt the Greek genius means many things. To one school . . . it means an aesthetic ideal. . . . To others, however, it means an austere thing, which delights in logic and mathematics; which continually wondering and always inquisitive, is driven by its wonder into philosophy, and into inquiry about the why and wherefore, the whence

and whither, of tragedy, of the State, indeed, of all things.

This eagerness to learn is not, of course, entirely a Greek quality. Every child, scholar, and scientist, shares it. But it can hardly be denied that the Greeks were endowed more richly with intellectual curiosity than any other ancient people. More conservative cultures like the Egyptian and the Roman judged the Greek spirit of experiment and inquiry either childlike or dangerous. But, for good and ill, it has been the strongest force in the development of modern European civilization and science.

Odysseus is alone among Homer's heroes in displaying this intellectual curiosity strongly. There is an obvious reason for this. A spirit of inquiry would naturally get more stimulus from the unexplored territories of Odysseus's fabulous wanderings than from the conventional environment of the *Iliad*. But it was hardly accidental that Odysseus should have had these special opportunities for acquiring fresh knowledge. To him that hath shall be given: adventures are to the adventurous. One may well doubt whether an Ajax or a Nestor would have shown as much alert curiosity even in the cave of the Cyclops or near the island of the Sirens if they had been there instead of Odysseus. Odysseus's personality and exploits are indivisible: he has curious adventures because he is Odysseus, and he is Odysseus because he has curious adventures. Set another hero in Circe's palace or in Phaeacia and you may have some story like *Innocents Abroad*, or a *Childe Harold's Pilgrimage*, or an *Aeneid*, but not an *Odyssey*.

Odysseus's desire to know is most clearly illustrated in the episodes with the Cyclops and the Sirens. He himself asserts that his original motive for landing on the Cyclops's island was to see whether its unknown inhabitants were 'violent, savage and lawless, or else hospitable men with god-fearing mind'—almost as if, in modern terms, he wanted to do some anthropological research. It is more the motive of a Malinowski approaching the Trobriand Islands, than of a pirate or a conquistador. But his crew did not share this zeal for knowledge. When they entered the Cyclops's cave, the Companions felt a presentiment of danger and begged him to withdraw. Odysseus refused, still eager to see what the giant was like. In describing the consequences Odysseus admits his folly here in the strongest words of self-denunciation that he ever uses (*Od.* 9, 228-30). As a result of his imprudence six of his companions were devoured. It becomes clear later, in the Sirens incident, when Odysseus meets a similar temptation to dangerous knowledge, that he had learned a lesson from his rash curiosity, for he takes great care to prevent any danger to his companions from hearing their deadly song.

But Odysseus's motives in the Cyclops episode were

not unmixed. He admits that his second reason for wanting to meet the ogre was a hope of extracting some guest-gifts from him—acquisitiveness as well as inquisitiveness. The post-Homeric tradition was inclined to censure Odysseus for unheroic cupidity here and elsewhere. But other Homeric heroes were quite as eager to receive gifts as he. It was a normal part of heroic etiquette; and in general the Greeks always had a flair for trade as well as for science. Odysseus's fault lay not in his hope of getting gifts but in his allowing that hope (combined with curiosity) to endanger the lives of his companions. Homer left it to others to draw a moral.

But there is a deeper difficulty in this incident. To anyone who has followed Odysseus's career from the beginning of the *Iliad* up to his encounter with the Cyclops, Odysseus's general lack of prudence and self-control in it must seem quite uncharacteristic of his usual conduct, especially his foolhardy boastfulness after his escape from the Cyclops's clutches (*Od.* 9, 490 ff.). By this last imprudence, despite his companions' entreaties, he nearly brought disaster on them all from the Monster's missiles. Perhaps the explanation is that this particular episode retains much of its pre-Homeric shape and ethos. It may have been fairly fully worked out before Homer incorporated it into his poem. Its outline is almost pure folklore. Homer's additions seem to consist mainly of vivid descriptions of scenery and the motivation of Odysseus's conduct. In order to fit Odysseus into the traditional plot, and also in order to make him incur the wrath of Poseidon, Homer may have had to strain his own conception of Odysseus's character more than elsewhere. So while in one way the victory over the Cyclops was Odysseus's greatest Autolycan triumph—especially in the typically Autolycan equivocation of his No-man formula—it was also his greatest failure as the favourite of Athene. And, significantly, by provoking Poseidon's enmity it was the main cause of his losing Athene's personal protection for nine years. In other words, in this episode Odysseus relapses for a while nearer to his original character as the Wily Lad than anywhere else in the Homeric poems.

To return to Odysseus's intellectual curiosity: it is presented in a much purer light in his encounter with the Sirens. Here no greed for gain, or indifference to his companions' safety, intrudes. Circe (who in Athene's absence takes her place for a while in advising Odysseus) has warned Odysseus of the Sirens' fatal attractions, telling him of 'the great heap of men rotting on their bones' which lies in the flowery meadow beside them. Better not to hear their seductive song at all; but if he, Odysseus cannot resist a desire to hear it—and Circe knows Odysseus well enough to expect that he cannot resist it—he must fill his comrades' ears with wax and have himself bound tightly to the mast.

What happens in the actual encounter became one of the most famous stories in European literature and a rich source of allegorical and symbolical interpretations. Its significance for the present study lies in the nature of the Sirens' temptation. This was not based on any amorous enticements. Instead the Sirens offered information about the Trojan war and knowledge of 'whatever has happened on the wide, fertile earth'. To put it in modern jargon, the Sirens guaranteed to supply a global news-service to their clients, an almost irresistible attraction to the typical Greek whose chief delight, as observed in the Acts of the Apostles (xvii. 21) was 'to tell or to hear some new thing'.

As Homer describes the incident, the attractions of the Sirens were primarily intellectual. Merely sensual pleasures would not, Homer implies (and Cicero [in De finibus] later insists), have allured him so strongly. He had resisted the temptation to taste of the fruit of the Lotus. But one must not overlook, with Cicero, the effect of their melodious song and their unrivalled voices. Music for the Greeks was the most moving of the arts. Besides, as Montaigne observes in his essay on *Glory,* there was a subtle touch of flattery in their first words:

> Deca vers nous, deca, O treslouable Ulysse,
> Et le plus grand honneur dont la Grece
>   fleurisse.

And perhaps their subtlest flattery was in recognizing Odysseus's calibre at once and in appealing only to his intellect. If an Agamemnon or a Menelaus had been in his place, they might have changed their tune.

For some reason Odysseus's intellectual curiosity, as displayed in his encounter with the Sirens, was not much emphasized in the earlier classical tradition. Presumably so typical a quality of the early Greeks (as distinct from the Achaean heroes) was taken for granted. But the later allegorists, both pagan and Christian, made it a favourite theme for imaginative moralization. . . .

It might rashly be concluded from the preceding analysis that Homer's Odysseus was a man distracted by psychological conflicts and distressed by social tensions. The general impression derived from the Homeric poems suggests nothing of the kind. The inner and outer tensions are skilfully implied, but the total portrait is that of a man well integrated both in his own temperament and with his environment. As Athene emphasized, he was essentially 'self-possessed', fully able to control conflicting passions and motives. His psychological tensions never reach a breaking-point. They serve rather to give him his dynamic force. As a result his purposefulness is like an arrow shot from a well-strung bow, and his energy has the tirelessness of coiled springs. Resilience, elasticity, concentration, these are the qualities that maintain his temperamental balance. In contrast the Ajax-like hero was superficially firm and strong. His code of conduct and his heroic pride encased his heart like archaic armour. Once this psychological carapace was pierced by some violent shock the inner parts were as soft as any crustacean's. Odysseus's strength and self-possession did not depend on any outer armour. He could be as firm and enduring in the role of a beggar or in the cave of a Cyclops as in full battle-dress at Troy. This was the quality that the Cynic and Stoic philosophers were most to admire later.

Such was his inner harmony and strength. His conduct in matters of major importance shows a similar purposeful integrity. He had a remarkable power of taking the long view, of seeing actions in their widest context, of disciplining himself to the main purpose in hand. Thus while other heroes at Troy are squabbling like children over questions of honour and precedence, Odysseus presses on steadily towards victory. And why? Not, Homer implies, for the sake of triumph and plunder, but in order to return to his beloved Ithaca as soon as possible. Here Odysseus's efforts for the Greek cause are integrated with his fundamental love of home; *pro bono publico* is ultimately *pro domo sua.* Similarly his loyalty to the Companions during the fabulous voyages, and his patience with their infuriating alternations of rashness and timidity, were part of the same enlightened egotism: he needed a crew to sail his ship home. His love for Penelope, too, was, as has been suggested already, not based entirely on *eros* or *agape,* but also contained that *philia,* that attachment to one's normal and natural social environment which underlies so much of Greek happiness. And his piety is the piety of one who wishes to keep on good terms with the gods.

Such mixed motives may seem impure or ignoble to those who take their ideals from self-sacrificing patriotism, or from self-effacing saintliness, or from self-forgetting romanticism. But these are post-Homeric concepts. Within the context of the Heroic Age and perhaps of the Homeric Age, too, this identification of one's own best interests with the general welfare of one's kith, kin, and comrades, with one's *philoi* in fact, was a saving grace for both the individual and society. All the Homeric heroes are egotists; but Odysseus's egotism has sent its roots out more widely into his personal environment than that of Agamemnon, Achilles, or Ajax.

One other aspect of Odysseus's Homeric character needs to be kept in mind at the last. In a way it is the most important of all for the development of the tradition. This is the fundamental ambiguity of his essential qualities. We have seen how prudence may decline towards timidity, tactfulness towards a blame-

worthy *suppressio veri,* serviceability towards servility, and so on. The ambiguity lies both in the qualities themselves and in the attitudes of others towards them. Throughout the later tradition this ambiguity in Odysseus's nature and in his reputation will vacillate between good and bad, between credit and infamy. Odysseus's personality and reputation at best are poised, as it were, on a narrow edge between Aristotelian faults of excess and deficiency. Poised between rashness and timorousness, he is prudently brave; poised between rudeness and obsequiousness he is 'civilized'; poised between stupidity and overcleverness he, at his best, is wise.

Homer was large-minded enough to comprehend a unity in apparent diversity, a structural consistency within an external changefulness, in the character of Ulysses. But few later authors were as comprehending. Instead, in the post-Homeric tradition Odysseus's complex personality becomes broken up into various simple types—the *politique,* the romantic amorist, the sophisticated villain, the sensualist, the philosophic traveller, and others. Not till James Joyce wrote his *Ulysses* was a successful effort made to recreate Homer's polytropic hero in full. Similarly after Homer judgments on Odysseus's ethical status became narrower and sharper. Moralists grew angry in disputing whether he was a 'good' man or not—good, that is to say, according to the varying principles of Athens, or Alexandria, or Rome, or Florence, or Versailles, or Madrid, or Weimar. Here is another long Odyssey for Odysseus to endure. But Homer, the unmoved mover in this chaotic cosmos of tradition, does not vex his own or his hero's mind with any such problems in split personality or ambivalent ethics. He is content to portray a man of many turns.

Tolstoy praises the universality of Homer's writings:

However distant Homer is from us we can without the slightest effort transport ourselves into the life he describes. And we are thus transported chiefly because, however alien to us may be the events Homer describes, he believes in what he says and speaks seriously of what he is describing, and therefore he never exaggerates and the sense of measure never deserts him. And therefore it happens that, not to speak of the wonderfully distinct, lifelike, and excellent characters of Achilles, Hector, Priam, Odysseus, and the eternally touching scenes of Hector's farewell, of Priam's embassy, of the return of Odysseus, and so forth, the whole of the *Iliad* and still more the *Odyssey,* is as naturally close to us all as if we had lived and were now living among the gods and heroes.

Leo Tolstoy, in Recollections and Essays, *translated by Aylmer Maude, Oxford University Press, 1937.*

Cedric H. Whitman (essay date 1958)

SOURCE: "The *Odyssey* and Change," in *Homer and the Heroic Tradition,* Cambridge, Mass.: Harvard University Press, 1958, pp. 285-309.

[*An American classics scholar specializing in Greek literature, Whitman is highly esteemed as a Homer critic. In the following essay, he explores some societal and artistic changes that took place between the time of the* Iliad *and that of the* Odyssey, *and notes how these changes are reflected in the latter work.*]

A study of Homer oriented . . . through the *Iliad* is bound to differ widely from one whose focus is primarily the *Odyssey.* For all their identity of style, the contrast between the two poems is vast and obvious, and it is unnecessary to recall the numerous statements of their difference, from Aristotle's "passionate" versus "ethical," to more recent formulations such as "tragic" versus "comic," or "Aeolic" versus "Ionic." As to the last, there is certainly nothing Aeolic about the *Iliad* except perhaps, in origin, Achilles himself, and the numerous Aeolic dialectal forms, which occur equally in the *Odyssey.* In a more real sense the latter may be Ionic, in that the spirit of sea adventuring may have been stimulated anew as an epic subject by the colonization of Ionia. On the other hand, the character of Odysseus cannot in any sense be connected with the intellectualism and versatility which characterized the rise of Ionia later. In the time when the *Odyssey* must have been composed, the Ionians could have created as yet little of the civilization which is so admired in the sixth century. The character of Odysseus, as Homer received it, must have been of complex origin, a conflation of quasi-historical saga elements with the familiar folk-tale figure of the picaresque wanderer. What Homer made of it is again something else, for the *Odyssey* is no mere retelling of a traditional story. It is, like the *Iliad,* a profoundly original creation, a vast expansion of a controlling poetic idea. It is the work of a master, though perhaps of a master whose zenith, as Longinus suggests, has gone by.

Whether or not it was the same master who wrote the *Iliad* is a question which must probably remain unanswered, except in the personal convictions of individuals. Suffice it to say here that, for all the real and even extreme contrast between the two poems, there has yet to be produced a single cogent argument to the effect that they must belong to different hands, or different eras. Arguments drawn from minor points of subject matter, such as Phoenicians, the knowledge of riding astride of horses, familiarity with Egypt, and all such, provide intolerable examples of argument from silence, at best, and at worst betray convictions about Homer more positivistic than well-informed. Attempts on linguistic grounds to prove the *Odyssey* later fail utterly; the epic language, save for what differences must exist because of the differences in the setting and the story, is the same for both poems, and in the *Odyssey* no neologisms exist of such a convincing sort that we must put the poem very much later than the *Iliad.* Also, on the grounds of oral theory, the *Odyssey* cannot be pushed very far into the period when literacy and a changing society were popularizing the various forms of lyric poetry, and relegating oral composition to the obscure corners of the Greek world. If the *Odyssey* belonged in any real sense to the seventh century, it must have been composed in some such obscure corner by a poet with old-fashioned tastes, bent on following in the wake of the *Iliad,* and essentially unmoved by the world around him. If such a poet existed—and many may have—it is hard to see how his work ever became known as Homer's. In the seventh century, the least of poets signed his work, and even the poems of the *Cycle* have names other than Homer's (and sometimes several) attached to them. To say the least, it is an uneconomical hypothesis to put the *Odyssey* so late. Both great epics belong to the most mature period of oral composition; both reflect the synthetic and formalized vision of the heroic Bronze Age in essentially the same way; both have ecumenical breadth, and tend to draw into their schemes large sections of the myth of Troy not immediately involved in the plot; both are complex, monumental, and retrospective; and both show much in common with the Athenian artistic approach, at once vivid, lucid, and subtle.

Such basic similarities point to similar poetic concerns and a similar period of composition. But if one looks at certain differences of compositional approach, one may be able to guess the relation between the two poems a little more accurately. That the *Odyssey* is later than the *Iliad* most will agree, albeit the agreement is often based on the groundless assumption that the *Odyssey* is more "civilized," because more concerned with civilization as such, and the *Iliad* more primitive. The reverse could be asserted with equal truth, and, in any event, the *Iliad* penetrates further into the frontier mysteries of human psychology. But the relative outlooks upon character and experience cannot be decisive in such a matter. More significant is the relative structure of the two poems. The *Iliad,* as already shown, follows a strict Geometric design comparable to nothing except the sepulchral vases of the Dipylon. Very little of the sort occurs in the *Odyssey,* and where it does occur, asymmetrical elements are more frequent, the responsions less careful and less significant. The antithetical polarities of the hysteron-proteron technique enhance meaning in the *Iliad*; insofar as they exist in the *Odyssey,* they are somewhat perfunctory, and the sense of form which one derives from the poem comes far less from repeated or inverted themes and episodes than from the substance of the narrative itself, its progress through time, and its achievement of a long-awaited end. The *Iliad* is tightly designed in every instant; the *Odyssey* sings itself, proceeding with a natural, leisurely pace, entirely suited to the prevailing mood of a large landscape with figures. For this reason, perhaps, the *Odyssey* has far fewer similes than the *Iliad*: the latter concentrates on one *mise en scène,* one major action, one monolithic idea of the heroic; visions of the rest of the world therefore knot themselves into hard images which cluster luminously around the rush of action. The *Odyssey* has a wider lens; it peers less deeply, but takes time to describe. Its object, like that of its hero, is often simply to see:

> Standing there, divine long-suffering Odysseus
>   gazed.

And there is very little which Odysseus will not take time to look at. The same objective scrutiny falls on Cyclops, Circe, the suitors, Eumaeus' steading, the gardens of Alcinous, the faithless maidservants, and weeping Penelope—"eyes like horn or iron." The *Odyssey* keeps building scenic episodes, typical and often static, and in these lie its chief symbols, not, as in the *Iliad,* in continuous and ever-shifting motifs.

This is not to say, however, that no evidences of Geometric design are to be found in the *Odyssey*. Certain parts, especially the *Adventures* and the Phaeacian episode, show conscious scenic antithesis and framing patterns. The *Adventures* are particularly elegant, grouped as they are around the supreme adventure, the Journey to the Dead. This central episode, with its retrospect upon the whole heroic tradition in the ghosts of Ajax, Achilles, Agamemnon, and Heracles, and its mysterious prospect of peace at last and "death from the sea" in the prophecy of Teiresias, is carefully framed, first by the two Elpenor episodes, and then by the two scenes with Circe. For the rest, the poet summarizes two out of every three adventures rather briefly, and dramatizes one at greater length. . . . Calypso, of course, is dramatized in her own right in Book 5, but not in the narrative of the hero. Book 8 offers, perhaps, a more interesting Geometric structure. Here Odysseus is deliberately contrasted with his Phaeacian hosts, who grow more and more impressed and mystified by him until finally nothing will satisfy save the full narrative of his adventures. The whole book turns on the two principles of music and gymnastic, keynotes of civilization to the Greek mind, and both highly developed by the peace-loving and somewhat soft Phaeacians. Odysseus proves the supremacy in bodily arts of the lonely and experienced hero over those who dwell in the ivory tower on the edge of the world. As for music, he is not a singer, but he emerges as the living substance of the heroic lays of Demodocus, which are mere amusement to the Phaeacians. Of Demodocus' three songs, the middle one of Ares and Aphrodite, with its ring of Olympian laughter, is a lighthearted romance appropriate to the people who love warm baths

and bed; the first and the last are Trojan songs appropriate to Odysseus, deeply involved with his identity, and prompting those tears which in turn lead to the full revelation of his experience. Few episodes in Homer are more skillfully handled than the Eighth *Odyssey*; form and purpose are truly one. . . .

Other parts of the *Odyssey* might be shown to have comparable, though less perfect, symmetry of design, but wherever such is to be found, it is confined to sections and does not spread over the whole. Total design is no longer a matter of inner strains and balances; instead, it is achieved through scenes marking stages of the advancement of the story, and the effect is not annular, but linear. Antithesis is certainly omnipresent, but it centers around the primary moral concern of the poem, the goodness and evil of men, especially in the category of hospitality and in images of righteous and unrighteous feasting. Antithesis is, therefore, more concerned with explicit meaning in the *Odyssey* than with total external form, and hence the poem does not lead back into itself to enclose a single experience with finality, but proceeds to the point at which it wishes to stop. And even as the circular pattern was appropriate to the *Iliad,* as a poem of heroic being, the linear movement of the *Odyssey* is wholly inevitable for a poem of becoming. The line may be produced to infinity, and in some sense, the *Odyssey,* overshadowed by the prophecy of Tiresias, never really ends. The *Iliad* ends with a funeral, the symbol of utter finality, and the image of Niobe in stone, weeping forever. The *Odyssey* closes with Odysseus at home, but fated to wander still and at last to meet death from the sea, that shifting and chaotic substratum of boundless possibility which gives the whole poem its atmosphere of haunting and unfathomable romance.

The breakdown of pure geometricity as a formal principle in favor of scene for its own sake, immediacy and even homeliness of description, and in general a wider horizon of possibility, if these traits are in fact characteristic of the *Odyssey,* imply some comparable change in the poet's audience and his world in general. About the turn of the century, and even somewhat before, such a change is indeed visible in the work of the Attic vase-painters. By rapid degrees the controlled, contained manner of the Dipylon gives way to a freer and more experimental style, the so-called proto-Attic, in which the governing concern is pictorial, while the close rhythms and muted formalism of the Geometric dwindle and eventually disappear. The vases of this period are less admired than most Attic ware, partly because they are eclipsed by the fine proto-Corinthian development, and partly because proto-Attic is essentially transitional, and leads to the triumphant Black Figure style. But the proto-Attic is not without its accomplishments. The manner is breezy, open, and slightly orientalizing. A new awareness of life in its immediacy, and not without humor appears in contrast to the somber reserve of Geometric painting. Human and animal figures appear with new and sometimes realistic details; outline drawing is born, incision begins, and monochrome yields to the use of various new colors. It is clearly a somewhat undisciplined phase, where careless workmanship, especially in the traditional motifs maintained from the Geometric, often goes hand in hand with bold naturalism and realistic representation in the principal picture. The new techniques with color and incision are by no means mastered, and the glaze is far below the quality of proto-Corinthian or the better Geometric ware. Each pot seems a little more like a sketch than a finished painting. There is something also distinctly romantic about it, in contrast to the heroic austerity of the former period. There is no longer much concern, at least in most vases, to adjust the decoration to the shape of the vase. Subject matter wins the day more and more decisively, as the style progresses, until it is all refined into the new formalism of Black Figure. But in the earlier stages of proto-Attic, one feels the strong sudden impact of nature disintegrating the rigid rationale of the Geometric method, and especially in the human figure, which is no longer an anonymous bundle of sticks and triangles, but begins to swell with a kind of personality. The scene itself is all-engrossing; total design retreats. The old, sure-handed sophistication is gone, and if the new product is often naive, there is nevertheless tremendous spirit in it. The horizon is suddenly vast; almost anything can appear on a proto-Attic pot, and the subjects vary all the way from scenes of myth to the prosaic details of everyday life.

It can hardly be entirely fanciful to see in the change from the Geometric to the proto-Attic approach an analogy to the shift of outlook from the *Iliad* to the *Odyssey*. This is no mere matter of subject. It involves the whole instinct about the inner relationship of part to whole, of decoration to structure, as well as the basic conception of humanity and its context. The triumph of scenic episode over totality of design is perhaps the most striking parallel between the *Odyssey* and proto-Attic art. Yet the parallel extends also to many details of the creative approach. In the *Iliad,* battle scenes contain many summaries of unknown men slain by unknown men, *androktasiae*; these anonymities are, however, always named, and their little entries, as in the *Catalogue,* pass by with formulaic rigidity, like the rows of identical warriors on Geometric ware. Individuals become visible only through the shape of a norm. But in the *Odyssey,* the companions of Odysseus are treated differently. They fall into no formalized pattern of the whole, and only one or two are named at all. For the most part, they disappear until they have to do something, and are treated, in contrast to the brief tragic histories of the *Iliad,* as simple expendabilities. Proto-Attic art is not concerned to represent generalities of men, but particularities of event; and hence, instead of the typical scene, formu-

laic yet possibly individualized to a faint degree, there is either full individualization or nothing. Two of the companions emerge as people, the young, heedless and ill-fated Elpenor, and the presumptuous, sane, and slightly insubordinate Eurylochus. The rest are vapor. It is often said that the characters in the *Odyssey* are types, and some are. But they are regularly types of something in human experience, and never, with the exception of Odysseus himself, typical simply of humanity, as are the rows of names in the *Iliad*. No such generality runs through the *Odyssey*: its pictures seize the foreground and thrust out the binding continuous friezes.

Moreover, in the matter of characterization the methods of the *Iliad* and *Odyssey* differ. As described elsewhere, the secondary characters of the *Iliad* find their individuality through a series of subtle contrasts, either with the heroic norm, or with another character, usually Achilles. Personal details, especially of a trivial sort, play little or no part. But the *Odyssey* is directly descriptive, as a rule through illustrative action, sometimes even in minor detail. We learn the character of Eumaeus from his defense of the stranger from the dogs, from his manner of putting food before a guest, from his tears at the sight of Telemachus, from his strict obedience to orders, from his sedulous care of the swine, and a hundred other touches. Here is no characterization by reference to a single formulaic social norm. The poet is interested both in Eumaeus and in his total context; he wants to fill him out. He is interested in the behavior of dogs, too. In the *Iliad* they only tear dead bodies, a purely formulaic function. In *Odyssey* 16 they keep interrupting the progress of the plot with actions which the poet includes, presumably, out of a concern with naturalistic representation: they assail Odysseus, fawn on Telemachus, and whimper with fear at the apparition of Athena. These are real dogs, not symbols of death with disgrace, and they resemble in their vividness a fine proto-Attic sherd in the Agora Museum at Athens, showing a donkey's head, painted and incised, with mouth open in a most convincing and hilarious asinine grin. So too of the details of personal appearance, one hears little or nothing in the *Iliad,* but in the *Odyssey* the hero's dark hair and stout limbs are often mentioned, especially in connection with his transformation by Athena. In particular, skin quality has newly impressed itself on the poet's imagination: Odysseus is darkly tanned, Penelope's skin is like cut ivory. Such minutiae are unknown to the Geometric *Iliad,* though women in general are "white-armed"; but in the proto-Attic period, the vase-painters were beginning to represent flesh tones with different colors, white as a rule, but sometimes black for men, and it is perhaps no wonder that this new pictorial element has crept into the epic consciousness. Finally, in the matter of landscape and milieu, it is hard to find any descriptive passages in the *Iliad* comparable to that of the island of Calypso or the gardens of Alcinous. Here simple delight in the setting has tempted the poet to sing on and on, regardless of symmetry or waiting issues. New fields of content have revealed themselves, and the older concept of form has become attenuated amid the new preoccupation with the immediacy of life.

The change in epic, however, must not be looked upon as either sudden or radical. The traditional nature of oral verse precludes radical changes. It must be assumed that the bardic repertoire comprised in advance the formulae and other typological materials necessary to produce the *Odyssey* as well as the *Iliad*. The language of the *Odyssey* offers no foothold to the assertion that it is younger. But its motivating artistic concern is younger, and so is its idea of form. Hence it arises, once more, that the creativity of the poet in such a traditional medium consists in the deployment of his given material, which includes not only plot, but also the whole gamut of visionary, formalized detail which was the singers' thesaurus. It is a matter of selectivity and degree, operating in the service of a sharply focused artistic purpose. In the broadest sense, the *Iliad* draws upon the formulae of heroic warfare, the *Odyssey* upon those of peace, the norms of social existence, and of the adventures of long-existent popular folk tales. It is truistic to point out that the polarities involved exist side by side in the *Shield* of Achilles. The tradition embraced it all, and the poet needed to invent little or nothing in order to create either poem. But the principle governing his selection and emphasis must in some sense follow the artistic spirit of the age, and in the *Odyssey* one may observe the new suppleness, the naturalism, and even occasionally the carefree blunders of the proto-Attic times.

If one attempts to fix the date of the poem more accurately, there is evident risk of pressing the argument too far. Yet there is some reason to feel that the *Odyssey* corresponds to the early stages of the proto-Attic period, and not to that phase, well on in the seventh century, when the style was already approaching Black Figure. Startling as some proto-Attic painting may be, it does not represent an instantaneous revolution. Some later Geometric vases show far less rigidity than the earlier ones; lines become sketchy, poses more supple, knees bend a little, the figures gain a little flesh on their bones; the contiguous warriors in a row may not be all in the same position. [In his *Greek Sculpture and Painting*, 1932, J. D. Beazley] says eloquently: ". . . a strong wind seems to be blowing against the neat fabric and making it bend, totter and reel." The change is rapid but the steps are observable. Moreover, the new animal motifs seem to be only partly the product of Oriental influence; partly they recall Mycenaean tradition. Later, Orientalism triumphed, breeding sphinxes, griffins, and gorgons everywhere, and thrusting out the last traces of Geometric order. But at the end of the eighth century and beginning of the

seventh century, the proto-Attic style clearly had its roots in tradition, and had by no means freed itself utterly from the Geometric. The *Odyssey* seems equally transitional. Geometric design, as seen above, has not totally vanished, but it does "totter and reel." The wind is blowing vigorously, but it has not yet blown away the epic form. If one were to choose a single vase as an illustration of the creative temper underlying the *Odyssey* the best choice might be the famous Attic Analatos vase, dated about 700. Geometric motifs are still present, notably the frieze of traditional waterfowl. But on the neck, the dance of long-haired girls and men, one with a lyre, responds with pristine freshness to the pictorial urge, the pressure of a new awareness in visual experience. It is descriptive, not symbolic. Reserved space allows the picture to breathe, as in the *Odyssey* Homer gives his descriptions as much time as they want. The atmosphere is spring-like and unprejudiced by previous conceptions, and suggests a feeling of direct delight in life which is essentially foreign to Geometric painting. One cannot yet quite see, but one can foresee, the lyricism of the seventh century, the choirs of Alcman and Stesichorus, or the bright vignettes of Archilochus. The *Odyssey* and the Analatos vase both seem to stand exquisitely poised between two ages, not quite belonging to either, but drawing breath from both.

To arrive by such means at a date of about 700 B.C. for the *Odyssey* may seem both rash and impressionistic. Yet the phenomena involved are specific enough: the decay of Geometric design, the arrival at self-existent pictures for their own sake, greater variety and suppleness of individuation, a freer naturalism, and what might be called the opening of surfaces, whether by space in painting or by a more luxuriant expenditure of time in verse—all these are traceable facts and tendencies. What is more, they are tokens of attitude and motivation, the semiconscious theorizing of the artist as he sets to work, and as such they are hallmarks of a time, never quite to be imitated at any other time. When all the necessary allowances therefore have been made for the difficulty both of dating exactly the early pottery of Greece, and of comparing poetry and painting, the period around the turn of the eighth century still seems more reasonable for the *Odyssey* than any date which, by reason of tenuous and superficially more factual-seeming points of subject matter, would push the poem down to a time when it could only have been archaistic. The inner side of artistic creation is what must be decisive, for it alone is characteristic of its time.

One final comparison with the situation in vase-painting leads to broader considerations. The masterpieces of the Geometric Age were funerary, and their memorial purpose is revealed in the death-like quietude of their formality. They have the heroic death-consciousness which pervades the *Iliad*. The focus of the *Odyssey*, on the other hand, is life in all its variety and directness, and again recalls the more lyrical responses of proto-Attic art, where life as daily lived and observed, unmediated by anything but the senses, finds its first expression since the fall of the Bronze Age, and thereby lays the foundation of the so-called "Greek renaissance." Such a shift reflects a shift in the psychology of a people. Ordinarily it is said that the Greek renaissance was a period of rising individualism and the discovery of the self as such. Yet the *Iliad* is a poem of self-knowledge in every sense as much as the *Odyssey,* but whereas the latter exhibits a hero whose will is proverbial for its unity and tenacity, the *Iliad*'s hero is the first in our history to be divided by the metaphysical paradox of human nature. Achilles allies himself with equal intensity, both to his own human nature, with all its concern and commitments, and to that intuition of the absolute in being and value which is the besetting demon of the spiritual hero. These opposites can be joined only in the mysterious flame of a love at once detached and entire, self-discovery in self-destruction. Achilles stands representative in and of an architectonic world in which everything is known and in its place, except himself; his learning of himself is a creating of himself. Death is always imminently upon him, a formative limitation which reveals itself at last as the inevitable framework of his tragic being. By contrast, the life-consciousness of the *Odyssey* involves a vastly different view of the individual soul. In and of himself, the hero is a fixed personality, confronted by no hopeless division in himself; he is equipped, as if by magic, with every skill which any situation might require, so that he needs only to deliberate ways and means; in the whole course of the poem, his celebrated intellect deals with no problem which can even remotely be called intellectual, and least of all does he deal with that deepest of all intellectual problems, the self. He is himself—at least if viewed from one point of view. Yet from another point of view, the matter is more mysterious. Life's paradox now appears not in the man but in his external experience, and the adventures of Odysseus, both on the sea and in Ithaca, cast upon him a constantly shifting cloud of disguise, from which he never fully emerges until he has revealed himself to the last person to whom he must—Laertes. And it is by no means tactless of the poet to have saved Laertes till last, incidentally, for recognition by one's father is, in a way, the final legitimation which establishes a man in his world. And it is the world which is the overt concern of Odysseus. Achilles created himself; Odysseus creates his world, by risk, choice, tenacity, and action, and the world thus created reveals the selfhood of its creator. By contact with the "limits of the earth," Odysseus defines, rather than discovers, himself, each experience involving, and at last dissipating, a particular shade of that anonymity which overhangs a man until his context is complete. Hence in the first part of the poem Odysseus is regularly an unknown man to those who receive him, until by some word or action he makes his identity known.

In the second part, his disguise conceals him, except at such times when the truth peeps out a little, for the astute to read. Mephistopheles promised to show Faust "first the small world, then the great," and through such experience Faust expands beyond the limits of his earlier self to a transcendent knowledge. The *Odyssey* exactly reverses this process. Odysseus begins, equipped with knowledge so various as to be in a sense transcendental, in the great world of magic and mysterious, absolute existences, and slowly by determination narrows it all down to the small circle of his own family household. And by contrast with the *Iliad,* where the world was architectonic and the hero the measure of the infinite, the *Odyssey* presents an infinite and rather amorphous world, under the image of the sea, out of whose mists any monstrosity or beguiling vision may arise, while the hero is the measure of fixity and definition. Perhaps for this reason the *Odyssey* has always seemed the more closely allied, of the two epics, to the classical period, for then too the prevailing outlook centered the legislating mind of the individual as the measure amid unpredictable experience, and infinite possibility. Indeed, it was precisely this view of the individual self, not the *Iliad*'s view, which began to take conscious shape in the seventh century, and to create the new lyrical forms. The *Iliad*'s view returns only in Sophoclean tragedy.

It is an unanswerable question how much of this view existed already in the tale which Homer found, and how much is his own emphasis. The nature of myth, or folk tale, is to reflect in external form the psyche's subconscious exploration of itself and its experience. Myths contain from the moment of their inception all the meanings which can be extracted from them. If Homer therefore created a poem in which the hero reveals himself, not so much directly as through the steady battery of experiences which rub against him, the reasons perhaps are, first that the tale he chose included the possibility of such, and second that such an approach would be welcomed and understood by his audience. The oral poet did not compose in solitude and publish at his own expense; he sang for gatherings of friends and strangers. And if one looks for the time when the stream of direct experience becomes of primary concern to the Greek artistic spirit and fills the foreground with the ideated shapes which to the archaic mind are knowledge, it is to be found precisely in this early proto-Attic period, when fragments of Geometric form, a few Orientalized motifs, and above all direct observations of life itself, merged, sometimes chaotically, sometimes into tapestries of vigor and finesse. All these elements merge also in the *Odyssey*. . . .

[If] the *Odyssey* marks the end of the great oral period of Greek literature, it is an end implied by the material, and a few symptoms of slackened technique do not prevent the poem from presenting a final apotheosis of the whole tradition. It is less intense than the *Iliad* and more external in its view of everything, not from disinterest in the profound, but from the distancing and detachment which comes of retrospect from new vantage points. Already by 700, the Greek world was showing a new face, and quicker changes were in progress than any which had taken place for centuries. Colonization, expansion of trade, contact with foreign parts, and hence wider geographical cognizance, the strong growth of oligarchy, a rising ethnic consciousness, and experimentation in all the arts—all these were forces energetically at work from the beginning of the seventh century, and all are, in one way or another, reflected in the *Odyssey*. The subject of epic was the past, but the approach, insofar as the traditional medium allowed, took on colors from the present. Some of these have been described, but the perspective which they create upon the heroic past, the real matter of the poem, is in itself one of the chief notes of difference between this poem and the *Iliad*. Here one is no longer in the midst of the heroic Achaean world; one follows instead a wanderer from that world, a wanderer who becomes more and more generalized through the first books into an image of Everyman in his experience, and in the last books, reparticularized into a commanding but somewhat altered personality in a world which is also changed. The old Achaean world reappears in Pylos and Sparta, in order to acquaint Telemachus with his heritage. One hears high tales of it from Demodocus, but the people to whom he sings are not of it, except for Odysseus himself. We see its representative string the great bow where the new men fail. But it is a thing of the past. Menelaus, Helen, and Nestor, active once, are now only receptacles of memory, glorious or sorrowful, of the deeds at Troy:

> There lies Ajax, scion of Ares, there lies
>   Achilles,
> There also Patroclus, a councillor like the
>   gods,
> There too my own dear son, both mighty and
>   stainless,
> Antilochus, exceeding in swiftness of foot,
>   and a spearman.

If one seeks the Achaean world in the *Odyssey,* it is to be found far in the west, in the Islands of the Dead. The men of bronze slew each other, as Hesiod says, and Odysseus, nearly the last of them, is undergoing changes. The superb and panoramic dream of the *Nekyia* revisits and summarizes it all for the last time, fixing once more in deathly eternity the great persons of the tradition. Sad, but detached, it is an elegy for heroes who had lived in songs for future men; and now, the songs are changing. In the new world of Hellas, one sees them differently; they are still the verities of the culture, but the immediacy of life itself is already setting them further apart, while a new kind of man, and a new sense of artistic and intellectual form takes the foreground. The fierce purity of Achilles' spirit, disdainful of phenomena, yields place to a heroic conception more available to a time of widening horizons, the man who wades eagerly through the phenomena of experience, to define himself by the limits of action, perception and understanding. The tale of Menelaus and Proteus in Book 4 presents the paradigm: hold fast to the changing, chaotic shapes, and the truth will come in the end.

In the long run, both *Iliad* and *Odyssey* contributed their share to the perfecting of what we call the classical spirit. Embodying as they do the polarities of that spirit, they remain for us the archetypes of the Classical, the Hellenic, and like all Hellenic things, they stand by a structural tension of passion and form, at once mysterious and profoundly clear.

Albert B. Lord (essay date 1960)

SOURCE: "The *Odyssey,*" in *The Singer of Tales,* Cambridge, Mass.: Harvard University Press, 1960, pp. 158-85.

[*A specialist in Slavic studies and contemporary literature, Lord has written extensively on folklore and folk epics. In this essay, he analyzes the structure of the* Odyssey *as oral epic, emphasizing its place within the context of other narrative oral poetry.*]

In reading the *Odyssey* or the *Iliad* we are at a distinct disadvantage because we are reading isolated texts in a tradition. The comparison with other traditions shows us very clearly that songs are not isolated entities, but that they must be understood in terms of other songs that are current. Had we an adequate collection of ancient Greek epic songs, we could view the Homeric poems from a truer perspective. Much of the difficulty in interpretation in the past has arisen from this lack. Yet the situation would be even worse had only one song survived, and that a short one; at least there are two poems adding up to some 27,000 lines, and the two poems are on different subjects. Hesiod and especially the Cyclic fragments may be of some help in supplying a hint of other thematic material current in Homer's day. And the poems themselves may point to still more such themes. We can even, with some caution, appeal to the Greek dramatists for versions of epic stories. . . . Our task is not then entirely hopeless. Other traditions can assist us particularly in indicating what we should look for.

Of great interest and value for Homeric study are the texts on clay tablets that have been unearthed in Mesopotamia and the nearer Near East. Their deciphering and interpretation are marvels of scholarship, imaginative scholarship at its best. Homer is no longer the earliest epic singer whose songs we know. Rather he stands perhaps a little before the midpoint, chronologically, of our knowledge. For we now have epic tales going back to the third millennium B.C. from peoples and cultures contiguous to Greek and with which the Greeks had contact. In other words, we have access to thematic material of Homer's neighbors before his day; we know the story climate of the Near East which taught Greece so much. If we find parallel tales and themes among these peoples they may be of service in interpreting Homer; they may verify or even help us to discover story patterns in the Homeric songs.

We should be daring enough, as well, to make use of later epic stories which follow the same or similar patterns, provided that they are traditional and oral. Medieval and modern songs, if our theory of composition and transmission is correct, are extremely conservative in regard to essential story pattern. . . . Our best material will be in the Homeric songs themselves and in what we know of Greek Cyclic poets and Greek drama. Next in importance is the Near Eastern corpus. And last, but by no means least, the medieval and modern parallels can be useful. For it is the essential pattern and the significant detail that concern us, not the accidental and incidental.

The *Odyssey* was one of many return songs told in the time of Homer. Some of them were surely in Homer's own repertory. It is clear that he had the tale of the return of Agamemnon in his mind while composing the *Odyssey,* and also the return of Menelaus. A son played no vital role in this story, but it contained wanderings and strange adventures, shipwreck and storm, and a visit to the "other" world in the many shapes of Proteus. The romance of the journey of the Argonauts was known to Homer. These songs were all, and many more, in the repertory of epic singers in his day. They surround the *Odyssey.* Together with it they make up a body of related thematic material.

Yet the *Odyssey* does not draw from the tradition; it is a part of it. I do not wish to imply that Homer used these other songs as sources, borrowing here and there, modeling this or that incident on one in another song. We should not forget . . . that songs are fluid in content. The question as to whether an incident "belongs" in a song, the question of proprietary rights, as it were, is relative in oral tradition. It is vastly important for us to understand the place of the *Odyssey* in the repertory of Homer and in the repertory of other singers. It is the place of one song among many others with related themes in an oral epic tradition.

. . . . .

After an invocation which stresses the wanderings of Odysseus and the loss of his men (but has no mention of Telemachus), the *Odyssey* opens with a council of the gods in which we find Zeus meditating on the sto-

ry of the return of Agamemnon. Such a reference to another tale is highly sophisticated and unusual for oral epic. . . .

Such a device of reference is, of course, far from inconsistent with the analogical thinking or associative thinking of oral poets everywhere. But I do not believe that this explains the presence of these references in the *Odyssey.* They make sense, however, if they are taken as part of a song telling the story of the return of the heroes of Troy, a song, in other words, that would include both the events of the Cyclic epic, the *Nostoi,* and the *Odyssey,* and possibly also the *Telegony.* They are not an anomaly in such a setting. Indeed, they presuppose it. This larger song with which we are dealing is the song of the returns of the Greek heroes from the Trojan War, including Agamemnon, Menelaus, Nestor, Odysseus, and, to a lesser extent, others. Perhaps the returns of the Atridae and the return of Odysseus were sometimes sung as a single song, and without the extensive ornamentation of Homer this would not have to be an inordinately long song. We know that Odysseus, Telemachus, and Telegonus all appeared in the Greek return stories in some way. We can therefore postulate that we could have (a) a song including all the heroes, not emphasizing one above another, (b) a song including all, but emphasizing the return of the Atridae, and (c) a song including all, but emphasizing Odysseus. This is thoroughly consistent with oral technique. Homer probably sang the return of the Atridae as a separate song as well as the *Odyssey,* and it is very likely that he may sometimes have sung them together. The opening of the *Odyssey,* I believe, indicates just that.

The allusion to the return of Agamemnon points, then, to the scope of tales in the tradition of ancient Greece. It also provides later generations of readers, who are no longer listeners to the old songs, with an indication of another pattern of return story from that of the tale of Odysseus. Moreover, we know not only of the existence of this different pattern, but also that Homer started his *Odyssey* with an awareness of that pattern. The divergences in the two stories are clear: Agamemnon returns home openly and is murdered by his wife's lover, whereas Odysseus returns in disguise and murders his wife's suitors; Clytemnestra is unfaithful to her husband, but Penelope is a model of fidelity. Later in the *Odyssey* Homer emphasizes these *differences* between the two stories. But in the opening of the song Homer is thinking of the parallels, of Aegisthus and Orestes, of the violator and the avenger, of suitor and son. And as soon as the plan is laid for the release of Odysseus from Ogygia, the singer turns to the suitors of Odysseus' wife and to the actions of Odysseus' son. The pattern of release and return is scarcely begun before Homer has shifted emphasis to enclose within that pattern a multiform of the related suitor and son them. . . .

It may be that Telemachus enters the *Odyssey* because of the parallel between the story of Agamemnon and the story of Odysseus, the two return stories par excellence involving return to wife and family. The plan of Athena to send Telemachus away from Ithaca so that he will not be present when Odysseus lands on the island has a certain parallel in the exiling of Orestes, which results in his absence at the time of Agamemnon's return and murder. It is noteworthy too that when Telemachus returns, like Orestes, he brings a friend. Theoclymenus has been thought of as being a vestige of many people, but I am not sure that anyone has suggested him as a Pylades. Theoclymenus thus considered is an extension of Peisistratus, son of Nestor, who makes a better Pylades to Telemachus' Orestes. Moreover, the attitude of the suitors to Telemachus as they plot to kill him is like that of Aegisthus. Since Homer opens his song with reference of the Agamemnon pattern we may not be far wrong in suggesting that this pattern was at some time influential in introducing Telemachus as the son plotted against and absented first by the suitors and then, in a later interpretation, sent by Athena to seek news of his father.

Yet as soon as Telemachus becomes an "exile," he also falls into the pattern of the young hero who sets forth to win his own spurs in the world with borrowed equipment. Like Beowulf, Telemachus is thought a weakling, and like the Sirotan Alija of Yugoslav Moslem tradition he must borrow the means of his transportation. . . . Invariably the young man who sets out on adventures is fatherless and aided by mother, uncle, or friend. The usual pattern is that the equipment and the assistance are denied by one group and granted, often through intervention, by another group. . . .

Athena has said that she will go to Ithaca in order to arouse Telemachus to more vigorous action and that she will send him on his journey "to win a good report among mankind." She has thus emphasized the journey as a maturing—should we say initiatory—adventure for the young man. The pattern of the tale of the youthful hero setting out on his first adventure sometimes contains the rescue of someone from the hands of an enemy, often by killing the enemy, who is possibly a supernatural monster. Sometimes the journey takes the hero into the other world, and as such entails experience with the guardians, entrances, and exits of that world. Sometimes, too, the purpose of the journey is to obtain power-bestowing knowledge or information, to be used on the return by the hero, or perhaps, if not used in a specific situation, to make a powerful magician or simply "a man" of the hero. This last is actually Athena's avowed purpose in sending Telemachus to the mainland:

> Near him came Athene, likened to Mentor in her form and voice, and speaking in winged words she said:

> "Telemachus, henceforth you shall not be a base man nor a foolish, if in you stirs the brave soul of your father, and you like him can give effect to deed and word. Then shall this voyage not be vain and ineffective. But if you are no son of him and of Penelope, then am I hopeless of your gaining what you seek. Few sons are like their fathers; most are worse, few better than the father. Yet because you henceforth will not be base nor foolish, nor has the wisdom of Odysseus wholly failed you, therefore there is a hope you will one day accomplish all. . . ." (2.267-280)

It makes extraordinarily good sense that the son of Odysseus of many wiles should seek knowledge in his first journey from home. His visit to Nestor and to Menelaus is, therefore, not a vain one in the deeper meanings of such journeys.

On the most obvious level Telemachus discovers from Menelaus where his father is, namely, on an island with Calypso. This was the information he was seeking; he knows now that his father is not dead. From Nestor and Menelaus Telemachus has also heard the full story of the return of the other Greeks and especially of Agamemnon. The parallel between Telemachus and Orestes has been almost painfully pointed out to Telemachus; likewise emphasized is the correspondence between affairs in Ithaca and affairs in Argos before Agamemnon's return. Orestes has proved his worth, and Homer's audience can be optimistic about Telemachus' future once Nestor's doubts of Telemachus' promise are cleared away with the knowledge that Athena is at the boy's side.

It is at Book 4, line 624, in the *Odyssey* that we are faced, I believe, for the first time, with a really serious problem. As long as we were following the Telemachus portion of Athena's plan, we were forgetful not of Odysseus, who is actually always in our minds, but of Athena's intention of releasing him from Calypso's island and of bringing him home. Even though it was never promised that Telemachus would find Odysseus and return with him—in fact we knew very well that this would not be so and we had been told that Telemachus' journey even overtly was merely for news—the realization that we were in a tale of the young man's first adventure, the exploit that would make a man of him, led us subconsciously to expect a rescue. There were, it would seem, versions in which Telemachus did meet his father and return to Ithaca with him. In the tale of Dictys the Cretan [*Ephemeris de Historia Belli Trojani,* edited by F. Meister, 1872], Telemachus hears of his father's presence as a guest of Antenor and goes to meet Odysseus there. In this tale Telemachus is married to Nausicaa, daughter of Antenor, after he and Odysseus have slain the suitors. With Telemachus feasting in Sparta and ready to return home we are now prepared for the release of Odysseus, which might well be followed eventually by the meeting of father and son. In reality this is what happens, but so much intervenes that we tend to lose sight of the fact that Telemachus' meeting with Odysseus at Eumaeus' hut (Book 16) is in essence a meeting of the two before either of them returns to the palace of Odysseus in Ithaca. Meeting there is, but postponed almost to the last moment. Yet the traditional bard has too deep a feeling for the meanings and forces in the story patterns to allow himself to violate them altogether.

When we analyze the recognitions . . . we shall note Homer postponing actions because other material, chiefly that related to Telemachus, interrupts. In the second half of Book 4 there is such an interruption, which postpones briefly the expected release of Odysseus from Ogygia. The scene shifts from Sparta back to Ithaca and to the discovery by the suitors and by Penelope of Telemachus' absence. Antinous now lays the plot to ambush Telemachus on his return voyage from Pylos, and Penelope's fears are allayed by a dream in which her sister assures her that the gods will protect her son. The plot against Telemachus comes, I believe, from the Agamemnon-Orestes story pattern, which is ever on Homer's mind in these early books, and it is that pattern which interrupts the action at this point.

And here a question comes to mind, consideration of which may add further depth to our understanding of the first four books of the *Odyssey*. Telemachus is a parallel to Orestes, but he is also in part a parallel to his own father Odysseus, especially insofar as the Odysseus pattern coincides with the Agamemnon pattern. It is not mere chance that in Greek tragedy Orestes returns to Argos in disguise and tells a deceptive tale about his identity. Here Orestes and Odysseus both share the same thematic complex, that is, that of return of the hero in disguise. It is a thematic complex fraught with latent mythic meanings, the disguise being the weeds of the other world which still cling to the hero; this complex is not merely narrative framework. Orestes' return is like Odysseus' return. There is trouble awaiting both. Telemachus as he returns circumspectly to Ithaca shares with Orestes and his father Odysseus the dangers of encounter with the forces of evil at home. At the other end of Telemachus' journey he has been given instructions in regard to Penelope, and he himself repeats them, instructions that mimic the counsel given by a departing husband on his way to war. "If I do not return, then go back to your father or marry again." On the journey Telemachus is honored as his father, and first Nestor, then Helen, and then Menelaus point out how strikingly like his father he is. The patterns of Odysseus, Telemachus, Agamemnon, and Orestes merge and separate and then merge again.

Homer begins the *Odyssey* again in Book 5. He has let Telemachus and Orestes get a little out of hand; he has enjoyed the story and the weaving of its telling. But he is aware that it has gone a little far. Facetiously we might say that he tricked himself by that initial speech of Zeus with its introduction of the Agamemnon parallel. So Homer takes up the story of the release of Odysseus by a return to the gods in council with Athena starting off as if she had never mentioned Odysseus to Zeus before. Zeus' reply is Homer chiding Homer:

> "My child," replied the Gatherer of the Clouds, "I never thought to hear such words from you. Did you not plan the whole affair yourself? Was it not your idea that Odysseus should return and settle accounts with these men? As for Telemachus, you are well able to look after him: use your own skill to bring him back to Ithaca safe and sound, and let the Suitors sail home again in their ship with nothing accomplished."

> (5.21-27)

At any rate we leave Agamemnon, Orestes, and Telemachus until Book 11, where Odysseus meets Agamemnon in the lower world, and inquires from his mother Anticlea about his son.

If the return of Agamemnon has been a potent influence in shaping the part of the *Odyssey* that concerns Telemachus, the return of Menelaus, narrated in *Nostoi* and also in Book 4 of the *Odyssey,* has been effective in fashioning the Circe and Underworld episodes. Menelaus, it will be recalled, was detained on an island off the coast of Egypt waiting for favorable winds. He meets the daughter of Proteus, Eidothea, who advises him to question her father as to why he is kept from proceeding further with his ships. She tells him how to capture the old man of the sea. Proteus, when finally subdued, first answers Menelaus' questions as to who of the gods is keeping him in Egypt and what his homeward way is. After this Menelaus asks Proteus about the returns of the other heroes from Troy, and Proteus prophesies Menelaus' own future.

The points of coincidence of pattern with the story of Odysseus are clear: (1) Menelaus and Odysseus are both being detained on an island; (2) they are both advised by a supernatural female to seek information from an aged second-sighter; (3) there is a certain ritual to be gone through in order to get the seer to talk; (4) the seer tells them both why they are having difficulty with the immortals, how they can overcome these difficulties, and he prophesies the nature of the death of each.

Menelaus first asks Eidothea: "Rather tell me—for gods know all—which of the immortals chains me here and bars my progress; and tell me of my homeward way, how I may pass along the swarming sea" (4.379-381). In her advice about her father she says: "He would tell you of your course, the stages of your journey, and of your homeward way, how you may pass along the swarming sea. And he would tell you, heaven-descended man, if you desire, all that has happened at your home, of good or ill, while you have wandered on your long and toilsome way" (4.389-393). This last has more relevance to Odysseus, it will be noted, than it does to Menelaus. At the close of her instructions to Menelaus as to how to capture Proteus, Eidothea tells him: "Then, hero, cease from violence and set the old man free, but ask what god afflicts you, and ask about your homeward way, how you may pass along the swarming sea" (4.422-424). Menelaus' actual question to the captive Proteus is word-for-word the same as his original question to Eidothea, given above.

Odysseus on his part in Book 10 is told by Circe, when he asks her permission to return home, that he "must first perform a different journey, and go to the halls of Hades and of dread Persephone, there to consult the spirit of Teiresias of Thebes, the prophet blind, whose mind is steadfast still" (10.490-493). Odysseus objects and asks who will pilot them, and Circe gives full instructions which end: "Thither the seer will quickly come, O chief of men, and he will tell your course, the stages of your journey, and of your homeward way, how you may pass along the swarming sea" (10.538-540). Odysseus then tells his men that they are to leave, saying: "For potent Circe has at last made known to me the way" (10.549)—and later when they were mustered: "But Circe has marked out for us a different journey, even to the halls of Hades and of dread Persephone, there to consult the spirit of Teiresias of Thebes" (10.563-565). In the land of the dead, after the ritual, after talking with Elpenor, Teiresias comes up and speaks to Odysseus, without the latter asking him any questions (11.99).

It will be noted that the reason for the journey to the lower world to consult Teiresias is given only once, at the end of Circe's instructions about the ritual to be performed. Odysseus himself, incidentally, does not ask why he must go. The journey is imposed by Circe, not suggested as the consultation with Proteus is suggested by Eidothea. Hence one has the impression of a labor, like that of Heracles. In the case of Menelaus there is a plethora of questions and reasons for the journey. The closest version in the Menelaus passage (Book 4) to the words of Circe in Book 10 about inquiring concerning the journey home occurs at the close of Eidothea's first advice (not the ritual instructions) to Menelaus, in which she uses exactly the same words: "He would tell you of your course, the stages of your journey, and of your homeward way, how you may pass along the swarming sea" (4.389-390). And it is here that she adds . . . "and he would tell you, heaven-descended man, if you desire, all that has happened at your home, of good or ill, while you have wandered on your long and toilsome way" (4.391-393). This would have made sense in reference to Odysseus. Of the three questions which Odysseus might have been

sent to ask, the three, indeed, that the seer answers without being asked, namely, (1) who of the gods is angry, (2) how can I get home, and (3) what is going on at home, only one is made explicit in the instructions. We know the others partly from the answers given by Teiresias and partly from the parallel with another multiform of the theme, the questioning of Proteus by Menelaus. Actually it would have been better on the part of the bard to let us infer from the answers what the questions to be asked were. The first question would not make much sense under the circumstances, because the only immortal holding Odysseus and his men back at this point seems to be Circe herself, and she will release them (if they go to Hades?). The second question would make sense if Teiresias really answered it, but he doesn't, and Odysseus gets the answer when he returns from Circe herself. In other words, the question which is really listed is not answered. And even if the third question had been asked, no one could have been less interested than Odysseus in the answer, to judge from his reaction to what Teiresias tells him of affairs at home. Odysseus says: "Teiresias, these are the threads of destiny the gods themselves have spun (referring to the prophecy of his own death). Nevertheless, declare me this, and plainly tell: I see the spirit of my dead mother here . . ." (11.139-141). He completely ignores the information given him. This is in contrast to the weeping of Menelaus in the earlier passage.

From the parallel of the Menelaus-Proteus passage we understand why Teiresias gives the "replies" he does—to questions that are not asked. But we are still left with several difficult questions ourselves: (1) Why did Circe send him to consult Teiresias, if not to find out how to get home? (2) What is the role of Elpenor? (3) Why does Odysseus ignore the information about affairs at home? and (4) Why does his mother's account of things at home differ from that of Teiresias?

The parallel with Menelaus-Proteus may suggest an answer to the question of why Odysseus ignores Teiresias' information about things at home. The earlier passage has influenced the inclusion of this account in the speech of the seer, but it does not belong as things stand because it duplicates the questions and answers of Odysseus and his mother. (It contradicts them, too, of course.) In regard to this question and answer, in other words, Teiresias is a duplication of Odysseus' mother (or *vice versa?*). And note, please, that the account of affairs at Ithaca in that it describes an evil situation at home parallels the Agamemnon tale. Once again the Agamemnon pattern, with its Telemachus-Orestes correspondence, interrupts the story of Odysseus. Now, from the account of Ithacan affairs given by Anticleia, one would judge that Odysseus was not supposed to learn about the suitors from anyone in Hades. This part of the scene indicates either that there was no trouble at home, or else that Odysseus was to find out about it elsewhere. In the Dictys version, it is worth mentioning, he finds out about it from Telemachus, who meets him at Antenor's home! We have several patterns conflicting at this point, each one contributing something to the story. Just as there were forms of the story in which Odysseus did not find out about the suitors from anyone in Hades, so there may well have been versions of the Return in which all was well at home and the wife was not besieged by suitors, as Anticleia's tale would seem to indicate. . . .

The story of Menelaus may help us in other parts of our puzzle also. Elpenor has at least a partial counterpart in Nestor's tale of Menelaus' journey as related to Telemachus in Book 3. Thus: "Now as we came from Troy, the son of Atreus and myself set sail together full of loving thoughts; but when we were approaching sacred Sunion, a cape of Athens, Phoebus Apollo smote the helmsman of Menelaus and slew him with his gentle arrows while he held the rudder of the running ship within his hands. Phrontis it was, Onetor's son, one who surpassed all humankind in piloting a ship when winds were wild. So Menelaus tarried, though eager for his journey, to bury his companion and to pay the funeral rites" (3.276-285). This incident is like the death of another helmsman, even Tiphys in the Argonauts; and all together are the ancestors of Palinurus in the *Aeneid* and a host of others. True, Elpenor is not a helmsman, and he is not buried until later. But the loss of a man who must be given burial rites, occurring in a story in which there are other more striking parallels, tends to confirm what we have said about the force of thematic correspondences.

Corroborative also is another detail from Menelaus' journeyings, this time as told by the hero himself in Book 4. After the prophecy of Proteus: "So back again to Egypt's waters, to its heaven-descended stream, I brought my ships and made the offerings due. And after appeasing the anger of the gods that live forever, I raised a mound to Agamemnon, that his fame might never die" (4.581-584). Thus also Odysseus and his men returned to Circe's island and there buried Elpenor with due ceremony and piled a mound for him, topped by the oar he pulled when alive.

Professor [Cedric H.] Whitman's analysis [*Homer and the Heroic Tradition;* 1958] of Odysseus' *Adventures* exhibits the kind of geometric scheme that he has found elsewhere in Homer, particularly in the **Iliad**. In it Elpenor frames the all-important central episode of the Journey to the Dead. The picture that emerges is neat, but a question arises when we consider the *connections* between the several parts. The implication of Whitman's scheme is that Homer had the pattern, CIRCE, Elpenor, NEKYIA, Elpenor, CIRCE in his mind and was fitting the events to this configuration. Are we to infer that Elpenor remains unburied so that Homer can fulfill his program of returning to Aeaea, to the Elpe-

nor theme, and hence to Circe, purely for the aesthetic effect of geometric regularity? It does not seem likely that the force of the artistic pattern, *qua* artistic pattern, in a traditional oral song would be great enough in itself to cause either the placing or displacing of incidents. I doubt if the artistic pattern is dynamic to this degree and in this way. This is not to deny that such balances of pattern are felt by the singers—we have seen them operative on the level of interlinear connections, where they play a part in determining the position of words in a line and perhaps even thereby the choice of words. But to suppose that such patterns would be the cause of changes of essential idea and meaning may be carrying their influence too far.

There is real difficulty, I think, with understanding the role of Elpenor, unless we try to analyze his part in the story on the basis of the dynamic mythic patterns involved. Only these have the power needed. The difficulty begins when Elpenor is left unburied. The Menelaus pattern to which we referred above supplies room for the loss of a companion, but time is taken for burial. It may well be that the death of a companion in this configuration is sacrificial and a necessary element for the successful journey to the land of the dead. I think that in a sacrificial death, due burial would be expected, and thus it happens in the Menelaus pattern.

The Menelaus pattern, however, does not provide for the return of the hero to the woman who sends him into the other world to consult with a seer. We are left with one question for which no answer has been suggested: why did Circe send Odysseus to the Underworld? There are two parts to that question: why Circe? and why the Underworld?

The parallel with the Menelaus episode suggests that the excursion to the world of mystery belongs to the story pattern wherein the journey is planned or ordered by the daughter of a sage or sorcerer, herself a sorceress. Any hero who has been away a long period from home and returns is fit subject for the lower world journey, because he has already followed the pattern of the myth by reason of a long absence in the other world and a return to this. The journey to the Underworld is but a microcosm of the macrocosm. *Nostoi,* we are told, also contained a visit to Hades—we do not know just where in *Nostoi*—a Hades that probably included Tantalus, hence of the old-fashioned kind similar to the end of the Underworld narrative in the **Odyssey**. Odysseus visited there a seer, one, indeed, whose death and burial are narrated in *Nostoi*. There is no journey to the Underworld in Dictys, but it is related that Odysseus went to an island on which was a certain oracle and that the oracle answered his questions about everything except what happens to the souls of men in the hereafter. It is not recorded what the questions and answers were, nor where the oracle was. But the event occurred after his visit to Circe and

In a drawing on a pot c. 450 B.C., Odysseus dismays the suitors before slaying them with his bow.

Calypso, sisters who lived in Aulis, whose realms he visited in the order given, Circe's and then Calypso's. It is not said that Calypso sent him to the oracle; it is said rather "and then I came to an island. . . ."

In these two sections we have seen how a knowledge of other traditional multiforms in the charged atmosphere of oral literature helps to explain the structure and even the "inconsistencies" of any given multiform. Just as any single return tale . . . must be understood in terms of the others which surround it, and, in a real sense, are contained in it themselves, so the *Odyssey* must be read with an awareness of the multiforms operative in its own structure.

. . . . .

From the time that Odysseus leaves the farm with Eumaeus for his own house until the recognition of the wanderer by his wife, the singer of the *Odyssey* is elaborating the central and most vital portion of the return story. We shall shortly be concerned with the recognitions before the hero enters the town of Ithaca and after he has left it for his father's farm. Now let us examine the central core, which is to say, the recognition of Odysseus by his wife. At his home Odysseus is recognized by or revealed to a dog, a nurse, two farm hands, and his wife, in addition, of course, to the suitors. The dog recognizes him instinctively; the nurse knows him by the scar; the suitors find out about

his identity by the trial of the bow; he tells the farm hands who he is. His wife recognizes him by three different methods: (a) by the trial of the bow, (b) by the bath, and (c) by the token of the bed. Any one of these means would have been sufficient, but Homer, or the tradition before him, has woven them all together, making only the last final. The singer renders many lines of story before he finally reaches this recognition. Odysseus departs from the swineherd's hut and arrives at his own palace in the middle of Book 17, but recognition is consummated near the close of Book 23. It is, I believe, legitimate to ask why the narration takes so long, why the recognition is postponed several times, including a last minute delay while Odysseus bathes and his wife waits.

It should first be noted that there are two returns to the palace recorded here: that of Telemachus and that of Odysseus. The two returns are kept separate. That of Telemachus deserves special scrutiny. The opening scene of Book 17 (Telemachus asks Eumaeus to take the stranger, Odysseus, to the city to beg his living, while he, Telemachus goes ahead to tell his mother of his return) parallels in part the scene in Book 15 when Telemachus arrives on the shores of Ithaca and sends Peiraeus with Theoclymenus on to the city while he goes to Eumaeus' hut. In both passages Telemachus is sending to the city someone whom he has met before his own return to Ithaca, and this stranger is accompanied by a friend. These two scenes look like multiforms of the same theme, and it is not surprising that scholars have sometimes thought that Theoclymenus is a duplication of Odysseus. The impression that this is so is strengthened when we see that Telemachus goes home and awaits the coming first of Theoclymenus and then of Odysseus. In fact, Book 17 begins with a twofold plan, the first part of which is concerned with Telemachus and the second with Odysseus. As at the beginning of the *Odyssey,* the first plan is followed, Telemachus goes home and the narrative continues with his return with Theoclymenus, and then the second plan, the return from the farm of Odysseus and Eumaeus, is fulfilled.

The parallel between these two plans in Book 17 and those set forth in Book 1 is made even more compelling by the similarity in the technique of moving from plan one to plan two in both parts of the song. In Book 4 Menelaus has concluded his account of his meeting with Proteus and has invited Telemachus to stay for a while with him, then he will send him forth with goodly gifts. Telemachus has requested him to let him go, and asks for some small gift rather than horses and chariot, and Menelaus has said he will give him a bowl of silver with a rim of gold. At this moment the singer says: "So they conversed together. But banqueters were coming to the palace of the noble king. Men drove up sheep, and brought the cheering wine, and their veiled wives sent bread. Thus they were busied with their dinner in the hall. Meanwhile before the palace of Odysseus the suitors were making merry, throwing the discus and the hunting spear upon the level pavement, holding riot as of old" (4.620-627).

Compare with this passage that in Book 17 which is the transition from Telemachus at home with Penelope and Theoclymenus to the suitors. Telemachus has reported to Penelope (and Theoclymenus) his conversation with Menelaus in Sparta; Theoclymenus has prophesied that Odysseus is already in Ithaca, when Penelope says with a sigh that she wishes this were so; if it were she would give him, Theoclymenus, many a gift. "So they conversed together. Meanwhile before the palace of Odysseus the suitors were making merry, throwing the discus and the hunting spear upon the level pavement, holding riot as of old" (17.166-169).

The two passages given above are like watersheds between the plot of Telemachus' journey to the mainland and the suitors at home. On the other hand the subsequent passages about the suitors lead to, or are at the least themselves followed by, the narrative which directly concerns Odysseus. It is true that there is great difference in length between the passage about the suitors in Book 4 and that in Book 17; the former is over two hundred lines long and the latter less than twenty. Nevertheless, they have the same plot material before them, and the same after them.

The scene in Book 17 ending with the passage given above begins with the arrival of Telemachus at the palace of his father. Because this entire theme has affinities with the final recognition theme between Odysseus and Penelope in Book 23, we may learn something of importance by analyzing the theme in Book 17 and its earlier relatives. Let us first, however, note the points of similarity between the scene in Book 17 and that in Book 23, the goal of our present investigation. Telemachus returns to the palace and is greeted first by Eurycleia, then by the other maids, and after this his mother enters, greets him, and asks what he saw on his journey. At the end of Book 22, after the slaughter of the suitors, Odysseus talks with Eurycleia, has a fire lighted and the house fumigated, and next is greeted by the faithful maids; then Eurycleia, at the beginning of Book 23, goes and finally brings Penelope to meet Odysseus. Although the conversation between Eurycleia and Penelope is of some length and, therefore, has no parallel itself in the earlier passage, nevertheless, there is a similarity of pattern in the order of persons greeted. Father and son follow the same pattern, in the beginning of the two scenes.

In both these passages something strange happens after the entrance of Penelope. In Book 17 she asks, as we have seen, for a report from Telemachus. Instead of giving her a report, he tells her to take a bath, change, and pray to Zeus while her son goes to the market place to pick up a stranger to bring home for supper! Penelope does as he orders, he fetches Theoclymenus, they bathe and eat with Penelope nearby spinning. Finally she says that she is going to bed and she asks him for the report, stating that he had not dared to give it before because of the suitors—yet the suitors were not present at the time of his return. At any rate, now at last Telemachus tells his mother what he learned from Nestor and Menelaus. So much at the moment for Book 17. In Book 23 at this point Penelope and Odysseus sit staring at one another until Telemachus upbraids his mother for not speaking to his father after so many years. Penelope says that she and Odysseus have ways of knowing one another; then he suggests that he and Telemachus carry out a ruse to protect them against the suitors' relatives. He takes a bath and then comes back to where Penelope is sitting patiently. There is clearly hugger-mugger of some sort at both these points! Penelope is kept waiting first for the report of her husband from her son and then for a report from her husband. In both passages the report is delayed by one or more baths, by the departure and return of the person who is to give the report.

Conversations between Telemachus and his mother (and it is a conversation of mother and son that is the focal point of the difficulty in both these passages) have had special significance since the very beginning of the song. It could also be said that the arrival of a stranger at the palace of Odysseus, or elsewhere, for that matter, has also been of significance from the opening of the *Odyssey*. Moreover, both a conversation between Telemachus and Penelope and the arrival of a stranger are frequently combined in the same scene. We are concerned with two of these scenes. Can other similar combinations give us any clues to the strange puzzles of this pair? What can other multiforms show us about the two in question?

Once again in connection with the beginning of Book 17 are we referred back to Book 1. In the first scene in Ithaca, the arrival of a stranger precedes rather than follows the conversation between Telemachus and Penelope, but both these elements are present. We are reminded by Telemachus' words to his mother when she complains about the bard's song that the son's role now is to give orders to his mother; for Athena has visited him, and the days of his maturity are at hand. In Book 1 as in Book 17 he orders Penelope to go upstairs; in both cases she obeys without a word. There is no meeting of mother and son between that in Book 1 and that in Book 17, but in Book 4 we note that when the news of Telemachus' absence is reported to Penelope, she is comforted by Eurycleia and then bathes, changes, goes to her upper chamber, and prays, this time to Athena. Although she does not talk with Telemachus between Book 1 and Book 17, she does enter the great hall once in Book 16 to rebuke Antinous for the plot to kill her son. Eurymachus swears falsely that no harm will come to Telemachus from the suitors; thereupon Penelope, without further word, returns to her chamber to weep for Odysseus—the same words being used here as in the passage in Book 1.

A pattern emerges, then, in which we see Penelope enter the scene to rebuke someone and to be herself in turn rebuked or ignored and, especially by her son, sent back to her room. For this reason we do not question Telemachus' sending her back to bathe and pray in Book 17; the sense of Penelope's theme is thus being carried out. This is what happened to her both times when she has appeared before. And it is in part what happens when we see her again in Book 18 after the match between Irus and Odysseus, when she comes into the hall and rebukes Telemachus for allowing a stranger to be badly treated. Telemachus corrects her; matters have turned out well for the stranger in this match. When Penelope enters again in Book 19, Telemachus has gone to bed, but by a sort of attraction there is rebuking in the scene that follows; the maid Melantho rebukes Odysseus and is rebuked in her turn by both Odysseus and Penelope. The pattern is kept with different actors. Whatever the logic of the situation, the sense of the patterns prepares us to accept Telemachus' rebuke of his mother's silence in Book 23. This has ever been the general tenor of their exchanges of words and, indeed, of most of the entrances of Penelope.

Such comparison with other appearances of a theme may show us in this case why we accept without much question the postponing of Telemachus' report to Penelope, and it is possible that the habit of a pattern may have caused such an illogical situation in the narrative. But it is not enough here, because Homer has himself given a reason, although late, for the postponement, namely that the suitors were present and their presence deterred Telemachus. Perhaps Homer thought that it was clear that hostile people were on the scene when Telemachus was greeted by Penelope. It is more likely that Telemachus' story had to be saved until Theoclymenus was present. The preserving of smaller habitual patterns has helped to gloss over or to make palatable to the hearer a breaking, or at least mingling of larger patterns. Theoclymenus is a nuisance, a disturbing influence, yet Homer insists on him.

When Athena at the beginning of Book 15 appears to Telemachus in Sparta, urging him to return home, she makes no mention of this hitchhiker, but she advises Telemachus to leave his ship before it reaches the city and to spend a night at Eumaeus' hut, sending the swineherd ahead to tell Penelope that he has returned safe and sound. This is not what happens. It is clear by now, I believe, that we are dealing with a song that is a conflation, an oral conflation, I maintain, of a number of versions of the return song. Formula analysis of a passage is useful in establishing the orality of a text, in textual criticism, and in poetic evaluation. The study of thematic repetitions, as we have just seen, also helps to establish orality; to confirm textual readings; in limited ways to explain structural patterns; to provide the aura around the theme which corresponds to that around a formula. As units of composition, formula and theme are as indispensable to the scholar as they are to the singer. Yet we have, I think, demonstrated that there is a class of problems that can be answered only by reference to a multiple-text study like that in the appendix—in other words, by awareness of the multiplicity of versions in and around songs belonging to an oral tradition.

The singer begins in Book 17 to follow a pattern of the return of Telemachus that is correct for a Telemachus (or anyone else) returning home with a report, provided there is no Theoclymenus who should be either with him or at someone else's house. Similarly, in Book 23 the singer is following a pattern that is perfectly all right if there were no Telemachus in the hall with Odysseus when Penelope entered. Other factors are involved in both these cases, but part of the difficulty is that the patterns are suitable for simple not for complex situations; for straight-line versions rather than for mixed versions.

But, if I am not mistaken, it is not merely that two themes have been juxtaposed, or that one was started and then interrupted by another. It seems that themes have been telescoped together in a distinctive way. Telemachus' report is postponed; what takes its place is a different thematic complex beginning with the arrival of the stranger and his entertainment. The stranger has news of Odysseus also, and this fact links the two themes, the theme of Telemachus' report and that of Theoclymenus. The two reports are juxtaposed, that of Telemachus which is the tale of Menelaus; that of Theoclymenus, which is the prophecy of a seer. This is one way of looking at the telescoping, but it does not provide a motive strong enough for such radical countering of logic as Telemachus' lack of response to his mother's first question. Suppose, however, that the Theoclymenus episode were really the arrival of Odysseus disguised as Theoclymenus, with Penelope wishing to ask him about Odysseus. We have a hint of something of this sort with Mentes in Book 1, when it is suggested that if he had only stayed he might have given information about Odysseus. . . . But this version simply cannot stand with one in which an Odysseus is already on his way to town or about to leave for town with Eumaeus. What are telescoped together, then, are not a report of Telemachus and a prophecy, but a report of Telemachus and a deceptive story by Odysseus. There seems to be evidence, in other words, of a version in which Telemachus met his father at Pylos and returned with him, and another version in which he met Odysseus at Eumaeus' hut. They have been put together in oral tradition as we have it in this song of Homer's. The result is duplication often with one element in the duplication being vestigial or partial, and hence an apparent postponement and suspense, or an inconsistency.

Duplication or repetition is a characteristic of the portion of the song we are now analyzing. For example, there are repeated buffetings and insulting of Odysseus. Blows begin when he is on the road to the palace with Eumaeus and they are joined by the goatherd Melanthius, who abuses Odysseus with words and then kicks him on the hip, after he has prophesied that "many a footstool from men's hands flying around his head his ribs shall rub, as he is knocked about the house" (17.231-232). This pattern is indeed found again in Book 17 when Antinous insults Odysseus as he begs food from him and the suitor hurls a footstool at him. Near the close of Book 18 the same theme occurs again. Eurymachus abuses Odysseus and hurls a footstool at him, missing him, but striking the right hand of the winepourer. And at line 284 of Book 20 the theme is introduced with the same words as the quarrel with Eurymachus: "Yet Athena allowed the haughty suitors not altogether yet to cease from biting scorn. She wished more pain to pierce the heart of Laertes' son, Odysseus." Ctesippus now taunts the hero and throws an ox-hoof at him. It misses him and strikes the wall. These actions all incur rebuke: Melanthius is rebuked by the swineherd, Antinous by the suitors, Eurymachus by Telemachus, and Ctesippus also by Telema-

chus. These incidents are multiforms of a single theme four times repeated, whose meaning, deeply bedded in the myth underlying the story, is that the resurrected god in disguise is rejected by the unworthy, who cannot recognize him. These episodes are actually testings.

The boxing match with Irus in Book 18 is a different kind of incident. It is a set contest between the representative or champion of the suitors and Odysseus, and its parallel is to be found in the trial of the bow! Odysseus in reality abandons his disguise in both scenes. For the boxing match Athena fills out his limbs and men wonder; Irus quakes and wants to run away. Here is a frustrated, a vestigial recognition scene brought about by accomplishing a feat of strength possible only to the returned hero. The match follows after the scene in which Penelope summons Eumaeus, asking him to bring the beggar to her so that she may question him about Odysseus; she has heard of his being struck by Antinous. Proceeding in the reverse order, we begin with (a) the abuse of Odysseus by Antinous, (b) rebuke by the suitors, (c) Penelope tries to meet Odysseus but is put off, and (d) vestigial recognition scene in the match with Irus. We can begin the pattern again with (a) the abuse by Eurymachus, (b) the rebuke by Telemachus, (c) Odysseus and Telemachus remove the armor from the hall, and (d) the recognition scene with Eurycleia. If we begin a third time, we have (a) the abuse by Ctesippus, (b) the rebuke by Telemachus, (c) Theoclymenus' prophecy of doom, the abuse of him, and his departure, and (d) the trial of the bow and recognition. This thrice-repeated general pattern is strengthened even more by the realization that in Book 17 (a) the abuse of Odysseus by Melanthius is followed by (b) the rebuke by Eumaeus, and (d) the recognition by the dog Argus! The third element in this pattern is variable but the other three elements are clear: abuse, rebuke, "x," recognition.

Now the trial of the bow brings about the revelation of Odysseus to the farm hands and then to all else. The tale proceeds untroubled until line 58 of Book 23, when to our amazement (and that of Eurycleia as well) Penelope still has doubts. Thus what might have been the first recognition by Penelope, that of the trial of the bow, ceases to be a recognition and becomes only one link in a chain of evidence. When she descends to see her son, the suitors who are dead, and him who slew them—as she herself says—it is her first appearance since the setting of the trial by the bow. As she descends she even debates within her heart whether she should question Odysseus apart or whether she should rush to him as to her husband. We may wonder whether Homer is himself debating this question. At any rate, we find that a scene that begins to lead toward recognition is side-tracked into plans for safety following the slaying of the suitors, plans concocted by

Odysseus and Telemachus while Penelope, as it were, "stands by."

Loosely associated with these plans is a bath taken by Odysseus. This bath has caused Homerists much trouble; for Penelope simply, it seems, waits for Odysseus' return, their recognition scene being suddenly postponed again in a most brutal way. It is the second time at least (the first being the refusal of Odysseus to go to Penelope's chamber) that poorly motivated postponement has occurred. The bath belongs in the tale of the return—it surely has ritual significance. Even on the most realistic grounds it should be required after the grime and blood of the slaughter. Eurycleia urged a change of clothes on Odysseus earlier, right after the slaughter, at the end of Book 22, which Odysseus refused, thus putting off the doffing of his disguise until the scene with Penelope. This earlier reference makes one suspect that the placing here by Homer may be deliberate. He indicated that he had a choice—as he does fairly frequently. The bath cannot be delayed any longer; it must come before Odysseus and Penelope begin to speak in earnest about the signs which they alone understand.

It seems to me that the singer was about to embark on the final recognition scene between husband and wife— Penelope will know him when he emerges from the bath without disguise, whether the bath was taken before she came on the stage or while she waited— when he was once again turned from it by Telemachus material. Yet the ingredients of the "second" recognition by Penelope (the trial by the bow being the first) stay in place, namely, there is conversation about the state of his clothes, he bathes, he emerges in bright glory. This recognition also then has become another link in the chain of evidence, and the final recognition now follows immediately. Although it would seem that Penelope has not moved from her chair in the hall, one might argue that she now "appears" again on the stage of the singer's and hearer's attention. And this will be her final appearance in the song.

Just as the accumulating of disguises emphasizes by duplication the force of the testing of recognition, so the threefold recognition by Penelope, the last following the ritual cleansing and loss of the traces of death, leaves no doubt of the importance of this element in the story. Logical inconsistency there may be, but there is no mythic ambiguity. The conflation in oral tradition has resulted in increased power of the myth.

In terms of mythic meanings the coming of age of Telemachus is emphasized by his journey and its success, by the presence of a god on his side, ultimately by his ability to draw the bow of Odysseus, if it were not that he was restrained by his father. We tend to forget that Penelope tells us that Odysseus had instructed her to wait until Telemachus' beard grew before

she remarried. The dramatic piling up of evidence of Telemachus' change to manhood stresses the fact that the time for remarriage has come. It is the last moment for Odysseus' return. In the myth of death and resurrection the darkest hour of devastation is at hand, and the return of the dying god, still in the weeds of the other world of deformity but potent with new life, is imminent.

. . . . .

The inner logic of the tale of Odysseus makes it impossible that the story could be stopped at line 296 of Book 23. I do not believe in interpolators any more than I believe in ghosts, even less, but had Homer not continued beyond that point, someone would have had to or the narrative would have remained unfinished.

The first section of this "continuation" really contains no difficulty, and [in his *The Homeric Odyssey*, 1955, Denys] Page seems to me to be entirely correct when he says that were it not for the Alexandrains this passage would not have come under question. Such résumés are perfectly normal in oral poetry, and numerous examples can be found.

The second scene of the continuation (23.344-the end; 24.205-411), the recognition of the returned hero by his parent, in the case of the *Odyssey,* his father, is a well-established element in the general story of return. . . . For some reason the return of the hero is associated with the death of one of the characters in his immediate circle upon recognition. (In the case of the *Odyssey* it is the dog Argus who dies when he recognizes his master. . . .) Recognition by a parent is a necessary element in the story and a regularly recurring part of the theme of recognitions.

It is not the recognition itself, then, which causes trouble in the *Odyssey,* but its *position* in the poem. That its place after the recognition by Penelope is not governed by rational or sentimental reasons is clear. Eumaeus told Odysseus straightway about his father's situation. They are already outside of town, and nothing would seem easier than for Odysseus to relieve his father's distress by going at once to him. This might have involved an earlier recognition by Eumaeus, but there seems to be no earthly reason why this would have done any harm, since Eumaeus has been proved loyal. Obviously the oral poet is not motivated by such considerations of reasoning. This approach is clearly not productive. . . .

There seems then to be reason to believe that the singer of the *Odyssey* was following a common practice in the order of recognitions in respect to that of wife, parent. . . . In the *Odyssey,* once Odysseus has gone to town, the recognition with Laertes can take place only after affairs have been settled in the city.

The objection that the structure of the scene of recognition itself is faulty because it is so long drawn out has no basis in the logic of oral epic. The lengthy deceptive story may seem merciless to us, but it is so integral a part of the recognition scene, particularly of one so elaborately told as this, that it would have been illogical to omit it. Anyone versed in recognition scenes would scarcely think to question it. . . . Whatever the reason may be for the deceptive story in return songs, it is so much part of the thematic complex, that we should not label as faulty any recognition scene in which it occurs. It is natural and right in that context.

In spite of all this, there is something wrong with this scene from the point of view of oral epic. Equally as important as the deceptive story is the element of disguise. Indeed the deceptive story makes no sense without the disguise. . . . When Odysseus left his palace he put on his own splendid armor! The only kind of recognition scene which could have been used after this (unless Laertes was blind, which he was not) was the variety in which the hero comes up and says, "Here I am, your son is back." But the elaborate recognition by scar and trees depends on disguise and is associated with deceptive story.

That the recognition by Laertes belongs earlier, before Odysseus has changed his disguise, even before he went into town, is indicated in the beginning of the scene. When he accosts his father, Odysseus pretends that he has just arrived in the island and inquires if he is really in Ithaca and if the old man knows anything about a friend of his named Odysseus. Although there is logically no objection to these questions as they are and where they stand, they would certainly be as well situated earlier in the song, soon after Odysseus' arrival in Ithaca, even better placed indeed. It seems most likely, therefore, that a multiform of the recognition theme designed for one place has been transferred to a position normally taken by another multiform of the theme. Thus an inconsistency has arisen. . . .

Homer does his best as always to gloss this over. Odysseus tells Telemachus, "But I will put my father to the proof, and try if he will recognize and know me by the sight, or if he will fail to know me who have been absent long" (24.216-218). He also disposes of his weapons (but not his armor) before he goes to meet his father. He is hesitant whether to go straight to his father and tell him directly of his return to Ithaca. These bits make me strongly suspect that Homer was aware of the difficulty, but that the traditional recognition scene with Laertes could not be eschewed.

We have seen that Homer probably had authority for the position of the recognition by the parent following that of recognition by the wife. This undoubtedly facilitated the shift. But there was also authority for meeting and even recognition by parent and son earlier

in the song. . . . Recognition comes only after an interval. There is, then, good authority for the earlier position of this theme, at least for the encounter and the deceptive story; but also for the recognition itself.

If we have information to show us that the scene is really out of place (provided one can use this term in discussing oral epic), we ought to have some basis also for hazarding an opinion as to where the scene would have been "in place." There are, I think, three points at which it might well have occurred, in two of which at least Homer himself indicates that he was about to embark upon a scene with Laertes but gave it up. We can learn much about the structure of the *Odyssey* as oral epic by examining these three passages.

The first is toward the end of Book 15, after line 389. In Book 14 Odysseus was received by Eumaeus; he told his deceptive tale, tested Eumaeus, and found him both good and loyal. As Book 14 closes, we could expect either a recognition of Odysseus by Eumaeus or the meeting of Odysseus with another person whom he tests with the deceptive story. . . . Instead of either of these, however, we are directed to Sparta with Athena and Telemachus. The pattern is interrupted by the return to the Telemachus thread in the poem. The return to this thread here may have been made easier by the fact that one of our expectations is of another meeting and deceptive story. In Book 15, line 301, while Telemachus is on his voyage home, we are back with Odysseus in Eumaeus' hut. Odysseus turns the conversation to affairs in the palace in town and asks about his father and mother. Eumaeus tells him about them. Here, at line 389, I think, we are ready for the expedition with Eumaeus to Laertes' farm for the recognition with the father. But the flow is interrupted again by Eumaeus' tale of his own life, which lasts late into the night. This tale, if I read the signs correctly, should be part of a recognition scene between Eumaeus and Odysseus. We saw that the stage had already been set for this recognition before the interlude with Telemachus in Sparta. . . . Eumaeus' tale, then, may be a fragment of a recognition scene that is never completed, but is attracted to this position because such a scene is expected here. Moreover, it is also the kind of tale that Odysseus might tell as a deceptive story, another part, as we know, of the recognition complex. From this point of view it might be said to take the place of the deceptive story to Laertes, which could have come at this point. Surely at the end of Eumaeus' story (line 495) we might have gone on to the Laertes recognition scene on the following day.

But once again the Telemachus thread interrupts, and instead of the recognition scene with Laertes we have one with Telemachus. The pattern is kept, but Telemachus has taken Laertes' place and the singer has again postponed the recognition with the parent! In other words, by this point, Eumaeus' recognition has been twice postponed and so has the recognition with Laertes. In each case the interruption has been caused by the Telemachus part of the story: at the end of Book 14 and at 15.495 for Eumaeus; at 15.389 and 495 for Laertes. The first interruption may contain a vestigial recognition scene (or at least the deceptive story part of it, including disguise) between Telemachus and Theoclymenus-Odysseus; the second interruption is a full-fledged recognition. By these maneuvers the first recognition remains that between Odysseus and his son.

What an amazing feat of construction. How cleverly indeed have the two threads been woven together! Telemachus and Odysseus have met and recognition has taken place. Homer and the singers of ancient Greece (for we have no proof that Homer did this himself, but must realize the probability that this was the way he heard the story) have accomplished the masterly interweaving of plots by following the lead of the elementary forces in the story itself!

The last opportunity for the recognition by Eumaeus and by Laertes before the whole party goes to town comes in Book 16 at line 298, after the recognition by Telemachus. At this point the singer shows his awareness of the possibility and excludes it once and for all. Odysseus instructs Telemachus not to tell Laertes, nor the swineherd, nor anyone else until they have sounded them out, although he suggests that they might make trial of some of the men. Telemachus objects even to this. At line 456, just before Eumaeus' return from town, Athena transforms Odysseus into a beggar again, and the singer comments: "for fear the swineherd looking in his face might know, and go and tell the tale to steadfast Penelope, not holding fast the secret in his heart" (16.457-459). At this point Homer is clearly and consciously following a pattern that will have the recognitions by the swineherd and the father later in the song.

There are two matters worthy of notice in connection with this final opportunity for Laertes' recognition of his son. At the time when Telemachus arrives and sends Eumaeus to town to tell his mother that he is safely back (thus, incidentally, duplicating the messenger sent from the ship to tell Penelope the news), Eumaeus suggests that he stop by the farm on his way and inform Laertes of his grandson's safety. Telemachus hinders him from this and states that the best news to tell the old man and anyone else would be that his father has returned. Laertes is certainly on the singer's mind.

The second valuable clue is in Odysseus' suggestion that they sound out some of the men, the suggestion voted down by Telemachus. By rejecting the recognition of Laertes the singer has also rejected the possible assistance of certain minor characters scarcely noticed

in reading the poem, namely the old man Dolius and his sons, who are actually the last people to recognize Odysseus. It may be pure speculation, but it is possible that Eumaeus is a duplication of the group of Laertes, Dolius, et al., or that in some songs of the tradition we would find him either completely absent or a member of that group. By having him as a separate figure, the singer is forced later to associate the neatherd with him. There are real signs of the traditional, oral combining and recombining of configurations in this part of the *Odyssey* as elsewhere. Certainly if any scene in the poem is a part of it, that scene is the recognition of Laertes. We have no less an authority than Homer himself, as well as Greek tradition, and the whole tradition of the Return since Homer's day.

Having investigated the question of where the scene might have been, there being doubt that as constituted it is in its "proper" place, we must now consider why it is where it is. Actually, it has been put at one of the most significant places in the story. After the recognition by the wife and the essential remarriage and the settlement of affairs with the suitors, as represented at least by their slaying, Odysseus, or the returned hero, must depart from home. Teiresias has told Odysseus this in the Underworld, and Odysseus has just told Penelope that this is his fate. The *Telegony* takes Odysseus, after the burial of the suitors by their kinsmen, first to inspect his herds in Elis, then to Thesprotis, and after each of these journeys back again to Ithaca, where he is finally killed by Telegonus. We are told that when Odysseus returned from Elis he performed the "sacrifices ordered by Teiresias," action which does not gibe very well with what we know of Teiresias' instructions from the *Odyssey* (although all we learn about what happened in Elis is that he was entertained by Polyxenus and received a mixing bowl as a gift, and that the story of Trophonius and Agamedes and Augeas followed). But that is in the *Telegony*. It helps to show that Greek epic tradition relates that Odysseus did continue his travels. . . .

In the *Telegony* the journey to Thesprotis, at least, seems . . . to be a return. The deceptive story told to Eumaeus (Book 14) and to Penelope (Book 19) tells of Odysseus in that land. Visiting the herds in Elis may be parallel to the visit to Laertes' farm.

But the references to herds in Elis, to Proxenus, and to the story of Trophonius seem to be of special interest. . . . [All] these elements are in some way connected with the lower world and with chthonic cult. Thesprotis too in Epirus is distinguished by the river Acheron, a well-known entrance to the Underworld, and the gateway to Dodona. The *Telegony* provides evidence, therefore, that Odysseus not only went on further travels but that those further travels were somehow connected with the other world from which he had just come. Everything in oral tradition points to the conclusion that at this moment in the story of Odysseus' return there should be departure from Penelope and another visit to that strange world from which the hero had been rescued or released. The journey out to the country to Laertes' farm for the recognition with the hero's parent suits the requirement of departure from Penelope and, perhaps, a mild idea of return in the fact that he had come into town from the country.

The singer is, to be sure, not satisfied with this substitute. As soon as Odysseus and Telemachus have set out from town, the singer lets them go their way, and the story continues without them in that strange puzzle that is the Second Nekyia (Book 24.1-204). In some form or other a journey to the other world belongs, and is in fact required, here, as we have seen above. The pull of the significant pattern is strong. Whatever problems the present form of the Underworld journey in the last book of the *Odyssey* poses for us (and they are many and not to be ignored), however abrupt its introduction here, and the return to the Laertes scene when this passage is completed, the forces that hold together a song in oral tradition demand that some such journey occur at this moment in the tale. If there is any passage that could be termed "out of place" in the ending of the *Odyssey* it is not the Second Nekyia.

The first difficulty brought forth in the passage itself is that Hermes Psychopompos is not found elsewhere in Homer and is hence unhomeric, in fact not at home in Greek epic. We cannot take this too seriously, I think. Actually we have two songs. Anyone acquainted with traditional material can realize how infinitesimal a part of any tradition are two texts, no matter how long and how rich. True, souls go to the Underworld fairly frequently in the Homeric poems and Hermes might have been introduced to conduct them, but he is not. It seems to me that there is something special about this particular departure of souls on their journey to Hades that requires someone as companion if not guide for them, something special that does not occur elsewhere in Homeric song.

The journeyer in this case should have been Odysseus; for there is some reason to think that he was supposed to bring these suitors back as ransom or sacrifice or for purification. . . . Yet Odysseus. . . . cannot make this journey. For one thing, he is busy elsewhere. But the feeling is strong that there must be someone at their head, and Hermes is a good choice. Was it not he who brought the message from Zeus to Calypso releasing him from the other world? Was not Hermes involved in some way with his coming back into the world of reality?

It is also objected that the geography of the journey is peculiar and unlike that of other Homeric journeys, or references to such, to the lower world, with the exception, at least, of Ocean Stream. I submit that the geog-

raphy here is especially fitting for Odysseus. At least it takes the suitors off in the direction of Thesprotis, whence Odysseus pretended he had come and whither the *Telegony* says he later went. For Hermes guides the suitors from Ithaca across the Ocean, past Leucas to the Gates of the Sun, which is to say to the entrance to the lower world. With all that has been written about Leucas, I cannot understand Page's rhetorical question: "Who ever heard, before or since, of a Rock Leucas, or White Rock, near the entrance of Hades across the river Oceanus?" The river Oceanus is where you want it to be, it seems to me, and if you are in Ithaca, or anywhere else in Greece, it is not far away, unless you want it to be, of course. The Island or promontory of Leucas, noted for its white rock from which human sacrifice was made for purification or to appease Apollo, as any traveler knows, is across a narrow strait from Corcyra, not far north of Ithaca. The White Rock is a clue not merely geographically but also ideologically to this journey; it indicates, I believe, the nature of the slaughter of the suitors, as sacrifice or purification for Odysseus. As for its being near the entrance to Hades, one needs only to look again at the map to see that it is not far south of Thesprotis and the river Acheron; indeed, for anyone going there from Ithaca, it is right on the road. This is, in short, another version of the journey of Odysseus to Thesprotis, exactly what one might expect to find just at this point.

It would be wrong to leave any discussion of the Second Nekyia without referring to the likelihood that both its position and its content—and perhaps its very existence—are due to the parallel with the Agamemnon type of return story, which we have noted as being often on Homer's mind in the dictating of the *Odyssey*. We know from the *Nostoi* that there was a descent to the land of Hades and we have assumed that it was made by one of the heroes in his wanderings before returning home. Is it possible that the journey to the Underworld in the *Nostoi* occurred at the end and that the traveler was Agamemnon after his murder, or since we do not know whether Orestes' vengeance was included in the *Nostoi,* might the traveler have been Aegisthus himself? If the parallel is still operating here, then not only the Second Nekyia but also the final reconciliation at the close of the *Odyssey* is not merely the tying together of loose threads but as necessary a conclusion of the feud as either the murder of Aegisthus by Orestes or the final placating of the Furies. Viewed from this light these final sections of the *Odyssey* are inevitable because of the influence of the related pattern of the Orestes story.

On the level of myth the existence of these two parallel Returns, both in the same song, but also in the same tradition, must give us pause. They are contradictory. One of them would seem to be the return from the other world to set aright devastation at home, to bring new life, to be ever repeated, the myth of death and resurrection, the other a myth of return to death, of tragedy and annihilation, demanding righteous vengeance, the inexorability of original sin, as exemplified in the curse on the House of Atreus. Yet the coupling of two such contradictory patterns, the one concerned with life and the other with death, should not amaze us. They are complementary, not contradictory.

G. S. Kirk (essay date 1962)

SOURCE: "The *Odyssey*," in *The Songs of Homer,* Cambridge University Press, 1962, pp. 355-71.

[*An English professor of Greek, Kirk is the author of numerous critical works on classical authors, including several books on Homer. In this essay, Kirk assesses the flaws of the* Odyssey, *contending that while "the poem is a marvellous accomplishment" it "fails to achieve the profound monumental effect of the* Iliad*."*]

The *Odyssey* is a poem of greater structural sophistication than the *Iliad*. This is seen particularly in the division of the action between Ithaca, the Peloponnese, Calypso's island, Scherie and, by reminiscence, the scenes of Odysseus's preceding adventures. The coalescence of these parts was in no way beyond the powers of a great oral poet working with the example of the *Iliad* in his mind and with the help of a highly developed system of formulas and minor themes. Moreover the composer of the monumental *Odyssey* seems to have had the advantage of using certain quite extensive poems on important elements of his subject-matter: certainly on the courting of Penelope and her treatment of the suitors, on the recognition of Odysseus and the concerting of a plan for killing the intruders. It may be that some of this material had been worked up previously by the monumental singer himself, into a song of say four or five thousand lines; we cannot tell. Yet there were also other pre-existing versions, as can be seen from signs of inconsistency and conflation in the matter of when and how Odysseus made himself known to his wife. The adventures of Odysseus, too, were certainly founded on earlier poems of wanderings in far-off lands; and the journey of Telemachus to the Peloponnese, though it bears every sign of having been put together by the main composer, probably makes use of much existing material on the . . . Returns of the Achaean heroes from Troy, and perhaps on life in the great Mycenaean palaces. It seems probable, then, that the poet of the *Odyssey* worked with larger prepared units than the poet of the *Iliad,* and that made the interweaving of major themes correspondingly easier.

The main plan of the poem is not difficult: the decision of the gods to release Odysseus, the crisis in Ith-

aca between Telemachus and the suitors, Telemachus's journey, Odysseus's stay among the Phaeacians and the retrospective recital of his adventures, his arrival in Ithaca and at Eumaeus's hut, Telemachus's return and meeting with his father, Odysseus in disguise at the palace, the plan for vengeance and its successful accomplishment, his recognition by Penelope. This narrative falls into well-defined and substantial episodes: for example the journey of Telemachus (first Pylos, then Sparta, with reminiscences of Achaean fortunes), the adventures of Odysseus, the scenes with Eumaeus, Odysseus in disguise among the suitors. The main difficulty lay in passing from one field of action to another and in adjusting and relating the temporal sequence. Here the *Iliad,* which is much more strictly annalistic, provided little help. In fact the solution of these problems was often made very simple: . . .

> Thus they [*sc.* Odysseus and Eumaeus in Eumaeus's hut] spoke such words to each other; and they slept for no long time, but a little while, for fair-throned Dawn quickly came. But they, by the shore, Telemachus's companions, loosed the sails . . . (15. 493-6)

Sometimes there is a slight chronological deception, but nothing that is detectable in recitation or indeed in ordinary reading; the regular epic convention is observed that events, wherever they take place, follow each other successively and leave no gaps. The inconsistencies and harsh transitions in the *Odyssey* do not in general arise out of this complex structure, but rather from the conflation of variant accounts on the one hand and from rhapsodic expansions on the other— whether by the later insertion of summaries designed to introduce an episode chosen for special recitation, or by the expansion of the main underworld scene and the supplementation of the ending.

The narrative of the *Odyssey* stands out in retrospect as tense, varied and compelling. Taken as a whole this story of return and vengeance is satisfying and successful: no one in his senses can deny that the poem is a marvellous accomplishment. Nevertheless it contains weaknesses, especially when judged by some of the standards that we apply to the *Iliad;* and it is essential to recognize and understand those weaknesses, even at the risk—which anyone runs who treats either poem with less than open-mouthed and uncritical adulation— of being accused of boorish impercipience. I shall consider these first and at much greater length than the positive qualities of felicity and genius, which in this poem are unusually self-evident where they exist and which tend to wilt under the blast of exposition.

The main fault of the *Odyssey* is that at many points the narrative content is drawn out to excessive length. At these points one feels that the monumental singer is consciously and almost painfully elaborating his material so as to make a great poem which will match the scale of the *Iliad*. He is doing the kind of thing that Avdo Mededovi did when encouraged by Parry to expand a theme to monumental length; though with the difference that the singer of the *Odyssey* did not simply drag in every kind of thematic accretion and accessory of detail from the oral singer's repertoire, but rather expanded his scenes either by free composition of an excessively leisurely kind or by sheer repetition. This does not happen, or rather it does not become noticeable as a fault, in scenes where the action is rapid and enthralling and the plot-content relatively high. On the contrary there are many points, for example in some of the adventures (like the Lotus-eaters, the Laestrygonians, the Sirens) or in Telemachus's evading of the ambush set by the suitors, at which the narrative is all too brief and elliptical. At these points expansion and elaboration would have been well justified; though admittedly the main singer was right not to make the recital of Odysseus's adventures too long in total. There it might have been better to omit one or two of the lesser episodes and to have expanded certain of the others; though it seems profane to suggest a course by which the world might never have known of the Lotus-Eaters, and one cannot wish it on absolute grounds. It is not at points like these, then, that expansion becomes vicious: rather it is in conversations between some of the main characters—between the suitors and Telemachus, or the disguised Odysseus and Eumaeus or later Penelope herself—that a certain lack of tension, an excessive leisureliness, becomes obtrusive. These conversations are perhaps largely the work of the main composer himself; he sought to gain length not so much in the expansion of pre-existing narrative elements as by an increase in scale in the preparatory and transitional passages that he had to supply in order to make a unified poem. Some reservation is necessary, since the same excessive leisureliness shows itself in books 3 and 4—in Telemachus's visit to the palaces of Nestor and Menelaus and in the long conversations and reminiscences that take place there. Here the poet was probably expanding well-known epic themes of the Returns of the heroes from Troy and the fate which met them at home. His method and technique differ, then, from those of book 14 or 19. Yet the effect of slowness and monotony and the excessive use of repetition remain the same. It is no use arguing that a deliberate slowing of the pace was necessary at these points. I doubt whether such compositional subtleties occurred to the oral poet, even to the monumental poets themselves; and though their experience and good taste might instinctively achieve variations of tempo where necessary, it is doubtful if extreme leisureliness *was* necessary either so early in the poem as 3 and 4 or between 13 and 19, in which there is comparatively little action anyway and many plans and minor movements have to be described. In short, then, if such long-drawn-out sections of the poem exist, they exist

because of a fault of method on the part of the main composer; or perhaps a fault of intention, to produce a poem to match the *Iliad* in length and scale.

That *longueurs* do exist can be confirmed, though admittedly with some risk of error, by reading the poem through, fairly rapidly and preferably in Greek, and at least with an open mind. It will be observed that in 3 and 4 genre passages of the preparation of food, sacrifices, and arrival and departure are very frequent, as is perhaps inevitable, and that such repeated passages are commoner throughout the *Odyssey* as a whole than in the *Iliad*. Similes are almost wholly absent from these books, partly because much digressionary material was being offered in the form of reminiscences by Nestor, Menelaus and Helen, and partly because similes are almost entirely restricted to narrative and do not come easily in speeches. Indeed one might almost say that these reminiscences, and the information they supply about what happened between the end of the *Iliad* and the beginning of the *Odyssey* over ten years later, are the main point of the third and fourth book. Certainly Telemachus discovers little about his father, and apart from the subsidiary theme of his education and development the so-called Telemachy contributes little to the main plot of the poem. This is no reason for suspecting its authenticity or supposing that it must have existed as an independent poem before the formation of the *Odyssey*. It seems to me to be a potentially entertaining episode which has the advantage of giving a certain interest to the character of the boy Telemachus, and showing how up to this moment he has been too young and too weak to prevent the suitors from establishing themselves in his mother's house. It also summarizes events from the end of the Trojan war, which had to be referred to somehow—even though the audience of the *Odyssey* may be presumed to have known many of them from short poems like those that seem to have been used as source by the monumental composer; and it gives them additional point by the contrast between Agamemnon's wife and Odysseus's and by the exemplar of the heroic son Orestes which is constantly stressed by Athene-Mentes and others. The leisureliness of narrative in these books, the rambling and repetitious reminiscences and the wordy conversations, the emphasis on food and drink, sunrise and sunset, going to bed and getting up, and on the small details of life in a peacetime palace, the flatness of the particular formular style and the absence of similes (to all of which Menelaus's story of his encounter with Proteus, 4. 351ff., is an exception)—all this reminds one strongly of the methods of books 14 to 19, the preparations for action in Ithaca, and persuades one that the Telemachy, though it uses earlier material, is essentially the work of the main composer of the *Odyssey*.

It is tenable that this main composer elaborated the conversations between Odysseus and Eumaeus, or

Odysseus and Penelope, in order to deepen the characterization and explain the motives of the main figures of the poem. If so he was not particularly successful. One cannot feel that Odysseus's false tales, or his claim to have seen the real Odysseus in Thesprotia and his assertions that this Odysseus is or soon will be in Ithaca, met as they are by obstinate and despondent disbelief on the part of the swineherd or Penelope, really do much to illustrate character in depth; nor indeed is this a common epic intention. They substantiate Odysseus's craftiness, but that is already well-established—his false tale to the disguised Athene in 13, at which she is so delighted that she smiles and fondles and praises him, has already made this point in the same kind of way but infinitely better. They also substantiate Penelope's habit of despair, her repeated disappointment caused by visitors who tried to please her by claiming to have news of her husband—but in fact this theme is over-emphasized, and eventually leads to the highly improbable picture of Penelope maintaining complete disbelief even in the face of a perspicuous dream plainly interpreted and other information that clearly portends her husband's return. The flagging tempo after Odysseus has reached Eumaeus's hut is emphasized by one of the poorest digressions in the whole poem (14. 457ff.), the story which the hero tells Eumaeus in order to secure the loan of a cloak or other warm clothes for the night. No such elaborate trick was necessary, since Eumaeus had already shown himself the soul of hospitality; and the story that Odysseus concocts, of how he had once won the use of a cloak in an ambush on a cold night, is weak and rather pointless. This complicated wrangle about cloaks is unfortunately a not completely inappropriate conclusion to the fourteenth book, which is surely the least satisfactory, poetically and dramatically, of any in either poem. The preoccupation with trivialities reminds one of the tiresome arguments about whether Achilles will or will not take any food in book XIX of the *Iliad*—a theme repeated, with little more success but at least more briefly, at 7. 215ff.

This occasional weakness in the narrative is sometimes aggravated by the language. In general it is true that the language of the *Odyssey* is smoother and flatter than that of the earlier poem. It is more polished, less stark and angular, yet more diffuse and much less lively. It is not particularly that its formular vocabulary is slightly different from that of the *Iliad,* for though there are significant differences there are far more similarities; and the harshness of some of its untraditional neologisms is balanced by the occasional linguistic crudity of the Iliad. Nor is a tired or second-hand formular style . . . , in which in certain passages the high proportion of repeated lines and half-lines and the overworking of certain common formulas begin to obtrude themselves, particularly to blame. Indeed the formular phrases of the *Odyssey* give the impression of being less mechanically used, more variegated by mi-

nor adjustments and alterations, than those of the *Iliad*. The language is in a way less stereotyped, and I conjecture that the proportion of more or less free composition to strictly formular composition is higher in the *Odyssey* than in the *Iliad;* in certain respects the main poet of the later poem is technically superior to the singer of the monumental *Iliad*. The main trouble with this smoother and less angular language is precisely parallel to that of the narrative structure, that it is plethoric, redundant and over-digested. It is typical that the formular stock of the *Odyssey* contains far more tautologous phrases than the *Iliad,* phrases like . . . 'have accomplished and done', . . . 'knows and has learned', . . . 'word and tale', . . . 'utters and declares', . . . Admittedly the repeated use of functional half-lines tends to encourage the unnecessary expansion of an idea to fill the other half of the verse, and the language of Homer in general is often rather full and imprecise—so that one finds sentences like . . . 'and he perceiving it with his mind marvelled in his spirit', 1. 322-3. Yet the *Odyssey* goes further in this way than the *Iliad*—taken as a whole, that is; obviously there are parts of the earlier poem that are 'Odyssean' in style and vocabulary, like much of XXIV, and parts of the *Odyssey,* like book 22, which possess the greater sharpness and force of most of the Iliad.

The impression of redundancy in language is heightened not only by the *Odyssey*'s greater use of repeated genre passages, of food and sacrifice and ships, but also by its tendency to reuse a preceding passage in a shortened form—so that one has an impression not of archaic simplicity, directness and economy but of anticlimax and repletion. The repetition of the prophecy of Odysseus's last journey at different points throughout the poem is dramatically effective, and the repetition of Penelope's ruse with the web is acceptable for the same reason; but Odysseus's false tales are too similar to each other, and the recital to Antinous at 17. 427-41 of part of a longer story told to Eumaeus in 14 makes a frigid effect. One has no right to complain of the magnificent scenes of shipwreck in the *Odyssey,* but the brilliant description of the destruction of Odysseus's ship at 12. 403-25 is sadly and unnecessarily attenuated by being dragged into one of the false tales at 14. 301 ff. A large part of the nineteenth book consists of repetitions. Finally the epic convention by which a messenger's speech is repeated more or less verbatim, when the messenger receives it and when he delivers it, is seriously overworked at certain points in the *Odyssey,* where it is applied to prophecies, instructions, and the actual performance of those instructions: thus Circe tells Odysseus how to pass the Sirens, then Odysseus tells his crew, and finally the actual journey is narrated in much the same language, by now all too familiar. The same feeling of extensive repetition is produced by Circe's instructions to Odysseus at the end of 10 about his visit to Hades, and the description of the actual visit that follows early in 11; though it is possible that constructional difficulties played some part in this instance.

The main events of the *Odyssey* are more varied in themselves and allow a more varied and therefore potentially more lively treatment than those of the *Iliad,* which is so heavily concerned with the progress of battle and the martial reactions of its chief participants. In fact, however, the vitality and tension that fill even some of the slightest episodes of the *Iliad* are often absent from the *Odyssey*. And yet, of course, the later poem still contains many brilliant evocations and descriptive *tours de force:* the landing in Scherie and the encounter with Nausicaa in 6, the semi-lyrical picture of the islet facing the island of the Cyclopes at 9. 116ff., Polyphemus's tender speech to his ram and his furious prayer against Odysseus later in the same book, the famous episode of the dog Argos in 17, the description of the early morning bustle of the palace servants at 20. 147-65, the strange but powerful episode of the suitors' mad laughter and Theoclymenus's vision and departure—the one and only time when his appearance has any dramatic force—at the end of that book, the rout of the suitors and the blood-thirsty vengeance on the treacherous servants in 22—these and more reach the heights of inspiration and virtuosity. Apart from such set-pieces the singer of this poem, and presumably some of his immediate predecessors, were capable of extraordinary touches of irony, subtlety, tenderness and fantasy—indeed in these gentler qualities they exceeded the normal range of heroic poetry and at least equalled the powers of the singer of the *Iliad*. The description of the Phaeacians, though it contains some odd anomalies, shows all these qualities, and particularly the gift for fantasy and lyrical other-worldliness which is one of the special splendours of the main composer of this poem. This is seen as the Phaeacian ship carries Odysseus homeward:

> Then they leaned back and threw up the salt sea with the oar, and for Odysseus delightful sleep fell upon his eyelids, unbroken and very sweet, most like to death. And the ship—as in a plain stallions four-yoked all leap forward together at the lashes of the whip, and rising high swiftly achieve their course, so did the ship's stern rise, and behind, dark and huge, the wave of the boisterous sea rushed along. Safely the ship ran all the time, nor would a falcon have kept pace with it, the fastest of birds: so swiftly running along did it cut the waves of the sea, bearing a man who possessed counsel like the gods, who before did suffer very many griefs in his heart, wars of men and cleaving the grievous waves, yet then slept motionless, in forgetfulness of all that he had undergone. When the star rose that is brightest, which most of all comes announcing the light of early-born Dawn, then it was that to the island approached the sea-travelling ship. There is a certain harbour of Phorkys, the old man of the sea, in the community of Ithaca . . . (13. 78-97)

To the shore of this harbour Odysseus is carried, still sleeping, by his magical escorts, who are destined to be turned to stone by Poseidon on their return to Scherie: Athene disguises the landscape by shrouding everything in mist, and when Odysseus wakes he does not recognize it but everything remains fantastic, menacing and strange.

Despite such marvellous scenes the *Odyssey* as a whole fails to achieve the profound monumental effect of the *Iliad*. This is partly because the main theme is less universal and less tragic; but to a large extent it is caused by the actual character of Odysseus. The man of many trials and many devices, the canny, suspicious, boastful and ruseful victim of fortune and his own qualities, is obviously less magnificent than the god-like Achilles, the swift and insanely proud warrior; he is also less real, strangely enough, and less credible. Achilles is often petty and unimaginative, in many ways like a destructive and acquisitive child, but there is something sympathetic in him: he represents some of the commonest aspirations and failings of human nature, though on a superhuman scale. Odysseus is a more specialized being, a curious mixture of heroic and intellectual qualities that can never have been frequent in any society. Moreover he is not drawn in much depth: partly the difficulty lies in reconciling the Iliadic Odysseus, who is clever and persuasive but still a great warrior in the classic mould, with the ingenious braggart, poisoned arrows and all, that he has become in some parts of the *Odyssey*. For even within the *Odyssey* itself his character is inconsistent in—for the unitarian audience—a rather unfathomable way. The faithful husband who rejects a life of divinity with Circe and Calypso is estimable enough; he makes a nice symbol of the conservative and social demands of man and the power of his affections, even at the cost of survival; yet he does not accord with the dangerously conceived victor over the Cyclops. In fact this Odysseus of the sea-adventures makes too strong an impression for the good of the whole poem, in the rest of which the hero's character is more consistently sound and gentle—though always suspicious. Admittedly the hero of the false tales is not usually an appealing figure, and one suspects that the real Odysseus quite admired his creations; but otherwise the generous master of servants, the patient victim of insults, the determined and ultimately affectionate husband, is admirable enough. The trouble is that he does not turn out to be very interesting. Largely this is because of the role the main poet has seen fit to assign to Athene, and to the altered conception, different from that of the *Iliad,* of the way in which the gods rule the life of mortals. During the sea-adventures, at least, Athene is absent from Odysseus's side—because she could not risk offending Poseidon, as she explains later, but also perhaps because some of the earlier sea-tales did not have this kind of divine participant; and, though the audience still knows that the hero will survive, his ordeals seem more terrifying as a consequence. Once he is accompanied at almost every step by the goddess, either heavily disguised or in her plainest anthropomorphic form of a tall, beautiful and accomplished woman, the tension of Odysseus's actions and dangers is surely reduced. This may not seriously affect his moral stature, but it diminishes his interest as a hero developing with his circumstances. The growth of Telemachus's character under the goddess's guidance is heavily emphasized; but his father is too mature and too cunning for this kind of unfolding, and the only quirks and anomalies of his character, as we have seen, are probably the rather worrying product of the conflation of different themes and different kinds of epic material. The Achilles of the *Iliad* stands in contrast: he is fascinating because he occasionally rebels against the traditions of the hero. In IX he sublimates his personal affront into a temporary inquietude with the whole concept of heroic warfare and heroic guest-friend obligations, and shows a touch of schizophrenia (or at least hysteria) in the process; while at the poem's end his frenetic mutilation of Hector is followed by a mercurial and heroic acceptance of Zeus's rebuke, and his treatment of Priam reveals a touchy and evanescent humanity that was neither impossible nor entirely expected of him.

A similar difference affects the drawing of other figures in the two poems. Although they are placed in fewer situations that might be expected to reveal the finer points of character, Agamemnon, Nestor, Hector and Paris stand out more solidly from the *Iliad* than do Eumaeus, Telemachus of Antinous from the *Odyssey*. Even Ajax, whose main role is martial, is better defined than most of the second-rank personalities of the later poem, of which there are many. Helen in the *Iliad* enters the action at only a few points, yet she still seems more a creature of flesh and blood than Penelope, who is described and talked about throughout the *Odyssey*. Perhaps it is partly because flesh and blood are Helen's speciality, and there is little moral complexity about her; while there is all too much complexity in Penelope, in fact a great deal of doubt about what precisely she is up to—some of which doubt, it is fair to say, probably arises from structural anomalies and the conflation of two variant accounts. Nevertheless Penelope never becomes much more than a paradigm of wifely constancy or of feminine illogicality, uncertainty and despair: an adult figure, but lacking the spark of life that touches the lesser female characters, Nausicaa and Circe and Calypso. It is a commonplace that Homer's most felicitous descriptions are often brief, allusive, and almost accidental: 'No cause for reproach that Trojans and well-greaved Achaeans for such a woman so long a time should suffer griefs; marvellously like the immortal goddesses is she to look upon' (III. 156-8)—that is how Helen's signal beauty was described in the *Iliad*. The same unemphatic allusiveness distinguishes Nausicaa, and even more the

two demi-goddesses, and makes them more remarkable in retrospect than Penelope herself. It is admittedly harder for the poet to vivify a middle-aged wife than a divine mistress; but one senses the same flatness in many of the lesser characters of the *Odyssey*, too, in comparison with their counterparts in the *Iliad*. Admittedly the martial poem almost completely neglects the humble people below heroic rank; steersmen, stewards and the common ruck of soldiers are occasionally referred to in the mass, and so are a favourite captive-woman or two; the upstart Thersites is beaten up by Odysseus; but the *Odyssey* has the advantage in social universality, and in places—as in the description of the anonymous corn-grinding woman who, weaker than the others, was kept working even at dawn and prayed aloud for the destruction of the suitors (20. 105ff.)—it achieves great pathos. Yet scores of Iliadic fighters both on the Achaean and on the Trojan side come alive, if only for a line or two; the poet imagines them as people, with a home and a living background, and this turns their death or their moment of triumph into something more than a mere statistic of warfare. This simply does not happen in the *Odyssey:* Odysseus's crew in the adventures, even the demoralized Eurylochus, hardly exist except as a necessary group, labouring or complaining, weeping or expiring as events demand.

The same reproach can be made to a lesser degree about the suitors. In terms of sheer bulk of description they play a large part in the poem. Yet my own feeling is that most of them are uninteresting—Antinous and Eurymachus mere bully-boys and cheats, Amphinomus a bit better because unusual, with signs of decency, Ctesippus a mere replica of Antinous, and most of the rest anonymous until the moment when, as the victims of Odysseus, they gain a name and a patronymic and a brief semblance of actual existence. None of these men makes a dangerous suitor for Penelope, someone really likely to turn her head. In a way the treatment of the suitors as an indistinct, sinister and almost anonymous *bloc* might be dramatic; but this effect is spoiled by the poet's plain efforts to give individuality to some of them. An even more serious criticism concerns Eumaeus. The story in 15 of his kidnapping as a child is a brilliant digression, but otherwise comparatively little about him is subtle, memorable or deeply interesting: he is shown at length as the faithful swineherd, conscientiously guarding his master's property, wishing for his return, cursing the suitors, and acting as a loyal friend and retainer of Telemachus and (in spite of her neglect) of Penelope. Country life and servitude have sapped the heroic qualities that his noble birth promised; Odysseus does not take him into his confidence before he has to, and then his role in the plan against the suitors is relatively minor. Eurycleia, the faithful elderly nurse, again has an important part in the narrative, especially in her recognition of Odysseus by his scar, but only comes powerfully alive in her rather gruesome approval of the horrors perpetrated later.

The *Odyssey* shares with the *Iliad* the great virtue of a well-defined central theme which is worked out at length but inexorably. By its nature, though, the Odyssean theme is less profound and less pathetic. The restoration of Odysseus to his home and fortune and family, the reward of Penelope's constancy and the removal of the manifold dangers to Telemachus, are not rendered trivial simply because they are not tragic, but nevertheless these things lack the depth and severity of the wrath of Achilles and its dire consequences. At times the complicated narrative of Odysseus's return, his intricate plan, his disguise, his methodical and cool-headed progress to the goal that Athene has guaranteed him, entail stretches of narration in which major events are lacking. That is particularly so of books 13 to 19 or 20; and the same leisureliness of action is apparent in many parts of the journey of Telemachus. In these places the possibility of tedium, a slight wilting of attention in the audience, might be excluded by spirited composition and by flashes of digression. A similar danger existed with much of the battle-poetry in the *Iliad*, but the earlier poet was more successful in meeting it. One of his devices for doing so is the extended simile. Now while it is true that an image can be used almost anywhere for its own sake, it is rightly accepted that frequent similes are more necessary in the battle-poetry of the *Iliad* than in much of the *Odyssey;* yet there are many places in the latter poem where the greater use of imagery would have been a welcome improvement. The *Odyssey* contains far fewer similes than the *Iliad*, and they are not a very conspicuous element in the Odyssean style. They are almost entirely absent from the Telemachy and the preparatory period in Ithaca; they become more frequent, indeed, in places where the action itself quickens up and where they are consequently less necessary. One disadvantage, already remarked, was that convention evidently excluded their use in speeches. Book 22, which describes the slaughter of the suitors, has many good similes to add to the Iliadic effect of the poetry of battle. Doubtless this is intentional: the model of the *Iliad* showed that similes were commonest in poetry of action and warfare. Yet there they were commonest in such contexts because the contexts themselves were so numerous that there was danger of monotony. In the *Odyssey,* though, martial contexts are rare and the danger of monotony exists elsewhere; could the main composer with advantage have used more similes in the quieter passages and fewer in the violent ones? Some of those he does use, at least, are fresh and lively and come up to the highest standard of the *Iliad*.

In other digressionary devices, too, the *Odyssey* lags behind the *Iliad*. The abolition of scenes among the gods, once the poem is under way, removes one glorious and effective kind of diversion. The singer may have felt that to introduce a fourth major scene of action into an already complicated plot would be too much, but the chief reason for the change is the new and less dramatic conception of a daimon-like personal protector. The lack of life and detail in the minor characters, in comparison with the *Iliad,* has already been noticed; Nestor's reminiscences have no real parallel in the *Odyssey,* and Theoclymenus is a less successful diversionary figure; portents come thick and fast in the second part of the poem, but many of them are obscure in significance and casual in description. One new device, which belongs to a poem about noble courts and not to one about expeditionary war, is the description of singers in action and the report at less or greater length of some of their songs: the illicit love of Ares and Aphrodite, sung by Demodocus for a Phaeacian dance and lasting a hundred lines, is a brilliant and unusual episode. Most of the Odyssean references to happenings outside the action of the poem are to the Trojan war and the returns of the heroes; the first four books are full of these—for example Helen's tale of Odysseus's entry into Troy in disguise, at 4. 240ff., in which the emphasis on his disguise may be a deliberate echo of what is to happen later in the action; and Menelaus's subsequent account of the Trojan Horse. There is less relief and less contrast in these references to recent events, though no less intrinsic interest, than in the Iliadic type of historical digression on the vanished world of earlier generations. The boar-hunt on Parnassus is one example of an Odyssean digression which succeeds in evoking a fresh atmosphere, and so do certain parts of Odysseus's fabrications. The exchange of gifts and the description of rich and unusual objects, as at 15. 99ff., excited the Homeric audience more than a modern reader, and had something of the effect of an extended simile. One common Iliadic diversion arose from a request to be told a hero's parentage—such a request stimulated, for example, the whole Bellerophon story in VI. This device is used only rarely in the *Odyssey,* though Theoclymenus's genealogy is given at length, and in a confused and abbreviated style, at 15. 225-56; a more successful example, again in a convoluted style suggesting a more extensive poetical model, is seen in the description of Iphitus, the previous owner of Odysseus's great bow, who was treacherously murdered by Heracles (21. 13-41).

Sometimes a lack of realism, permissible in the more impressionistic narrative of the *Iliad,* damages the tension of the *Odyssey,* which relies more heavily on the careful, logical and progressive narration of events. Occasionally this is due to the difficulties of binding together the complex elements of the poem and is a hardly avoidable consequence of large-scale oral poetry. Often this reason does not apply, as when Odysseus's manifest distress at hearing songs about the return from Troy is only very belatedly and hesitantly recognized by Alcinous (who is, however, a bit of a fool);

or in the failure of either Telemachus or Leodes to demand another attempt at stringing the bow once Antinous had had the new idea of softening it with grease. Yet this is a small complaint, less important than those that preceded it. They, I believe, have real substance. Different people will have different opinions here, but I think the conclusion will stand that the *Odyssey* is stylistically flatter and less continuously moving than the *Iliad;* also that there are long sections where the interest is allowed to flag, partly because of an abandonment of some of the technical resources of the earlier poem but also because the main composer was trying to draw out the pure narrative thread to an excessive length, with little more than brute magnitude in view. The plain fact is, though, that if there had been no *Iliad* many of these criticisms would not, and perhaps could not, have been made. By any but quite exceptional standards the *Odyssey* is a superb narrative epic. The technical analysis of its relative strengths and weaknesses neither disguises this truth nor rivals it in importance.

Pound notes the accuracy of the *Odyssey*

I have never read half a page of *Homer* without finding melodic invention, I mean melodic invention that I didn't already know. I have, on the other hand, found also in Homer the imaginary spectator, which in 1918 I still thought was Henry James's particular property.

Homer says, "an experienced soldier would have noticed." The sheer literary qualities in Homer are such that a physician has written a book to prove that Homer must have been an army doctor. (When he describes certain blows and their effect, the wounds are said to be accurate, and the description fit for coroner's inquest.)

Another French scholar has more or less shown that the geography of the *Odyssey* is correct geography; not as you would find it if you had a geography book and a map, but as it would be in a "periplum," that is, as a coasting sailor would find it.

The news in the *Odyssey* is still news. Odysseus is still "very human," by no means a stuffed shirt, or a pretty figure taken down from a tapestry. . . .

You can't tuck Odysseus away with Virgil's Aeneas. Odysseus is emphatically "the wise guy," the downy, the hard-boiled Odysseus.

Ezra Pound, in ABC of Reading, *New Directions, 1951 (?).*

Howard W. Clarke (essay date 1963)

SOURCE: "Telemachus and the *Telemacheia,*" in *The Art of the Odyssey,* Prentice-Hall, Inc., 1967, pp. 30-44.

[*In the following essay, first published in the* American Journal of Philology *in 1963, Clarke discusses the first four books of the* Odyssey, *known collectively as the* Telemacheia, *which deal with Telemachus' journey and his gradual coming of age.*]

The criticism of Homeric epic has become so formalized over the centuries that it has developed denominations to accommodate scholars of various persuasions. There are, first, the "Separatists," who believe that the *Iliad* and the *Odyssey* are by two different poets, who may not have even known of each other's work. Then there are the "Analysts," who believe that different poets worked on different parts of the two poems at different stages in their evolution, with "Homer" being credited with whatever was most meritorious in this process. Opposed to the analytical critics are the "Unitarians," who maintain, with varying degrees of persistence, that one poet—whom they agree on calling Homer—composed both poems. Complicating this division is the fact that few of the adherents to any of these sects have ever held the faith pure, and the quarrels within and between them have long provided the scholarly world with controversies that were sometimes diverting but more often dispiriting. Recent research into the ways of composing oral poetry has weakened the meaningfulness of these labels, and the angry and abusive essays once written in defense of one or another of these views have now acquired a quaintness never intended by their authors.

When the Analysts dealt with the *Odyssey* (and they always dealt very harshly with the *Odyssey*), it was one of their standard truths that if Books I-IV of the poem were not by another hand, then they were certainly distinct enough in treatment and integration to deserve a special name—the *Telemacheia*. The books of the *Telemacheia*—along with Book XV, which tells of Telemachus' return—are separate from the poem in that they are generally concerned with Telemachus, Odysseus' son. Telemachus is an important character in the *Odyssey* [as noted by S. Bassett, "The Proems of the *Iliad* and the *Odyssey,*" *American Journal of Philology,* XLIV, 1923].

Telemachus appears in sixteen books of the *Odyssey* in all except V-XIII . . . and he speaks more often than any other of the characters in either poem, except their respective heroes . . . Telemachus also furnishes the incentive for the plot of the Suitors, which both emphasizes their *hybris* and increases the interest as we approach the climax of the story. In fact, the Suitors, without Telemachus, lose half of their importance, just as there would be no tragic outcome of the Wrath if there were no Hector. And, finally, a lonely, tearful, vacillating, and altogether human Penelope would be impossible if there were no Telemachus or his equivalent; she would have to be more decisive and energetic—more the queen, and less the woman.

Certainly the Telemachus we meet in Book I has his problems in Ithaca, but his position in the *Odyssey* raises problems for the poem too. Either the political structure of Ithaca is highly irregular or else Homer has left much unsaid about the conditions of kingship there. First of all, why is not Odysseus' father Laertes king of Ithaca? He is still alive, and we meet him in the last books of the poem out in the country where he has withdrawn in sorrow over the loss of his son, but even before his retirement he does not seem to have ruled as king.

The dilemma in which this situation involves the Ithacans is obvious. On the one hand, old Laertes has been made unfit for kingship, presumably through infirmity; on the other hand, Telemachus is unqualified because of youth and inexperience. Since strength and vigor seem the qualifications for rule in Ithaca, the people are victimized by the weakness of their leaders—the weakness of old age and of youth, the senility of Laertes and the adolescence of Telemachus. Odysseus alone combines exuberance and experience, and he is desperately needed. It is noteworthy, too, that when he returns not only does he save his family and his land, but the vitality of his presence extends to his father and his son. For Laertes there is a sudden and miraculous transformation. "Athena herself intervened to increase his royal stature. As he stepped out of the bath she made him seem taller and sturdier than before, so that his own son was amazed when he saw him looking like an immortal god" (XXIV, 368-71). Athena's powers here show symbolically how the presence of his beloved son has revitalized the aged Laertes. In the same way, the Telemachus whom Odysseus meets in Book XVI and fights beside in XXII is not the young man whom Athena found in Book I; but if his transformation is gradual, it is because not even a goddess can immediately infuse into a young man the wisdom accumulated in a lifetime's experience as hero and king. Where Laertes had, like Odysseus, already known the meaning of the heroic life and needed only to be rejuvenated, Telemachus must be introduced, or initiated, into it. The process of this introduction, this initiation, is one of the purposes of the four books (and part of Book XV) commonly referred to as the *Telemacheia*. In a society, like Ithaca, where kingship depends not so much on inheritance as on merit, it is not enough for Telemachus to have the title of prince; he must be prepared to prove his worth, as he will in Book XXII, but before the crucial test comes he must know what it is he is fighting for. Pylos and Sparta, the two cities he visits in Books III and IV, can offer him the examples he will need of heroic civilization. Hence we should understand these opening four books of the poem as educative—as Telemachus' preparation for heroism.

The *Telemacheia* properly begins after the Council of the Gods when Athena visits Ithaca to hearten Odysseus' son and urge him to call an assembly of Ithacans and then set off to Sparta and Pylos in search of news about his father. Here she finds a despairing Telemachus lost in the dreamworld that has become his since the Suitors made the real world intolerable. He is hoping that somehow Odysseus will appear "from somewhere" (115). It will be Athena's purpose in the next few books to rid Telemachus of his melancholy, to show him how in the heroic world dreams can be translated into realities. Although the goddess is at once impressed by Telemachus' physical resemblance to his famous father, his insecurity is such that he is even unsure of his own identity and never refers to his father by name. "My mother certainly says I am his son; but for myself I cannot tell" (I, 215-16). It will be the burden of the next few books to harmonize Telemachus' inner and outer selves, to make him be his father's son not merely in name but in deed. The example Athena offers him is of another famous son, from the Agamemnon myth. "You are no longer a child: you must put childish thoughts away. Have you not heard what a name Prince Orestes made for himself in the world when he killed the traitor Aegisthus for murdering his noble father? You, my friend—and what a tall and splendid fellow you have grown!—must be as brave as Orestes. Then future generations will sing your praises" (I, 297-302). This encouragement by Athena—to be repeated by Nestor in Book III—is not without its effect, but Telemachus' adolescent attempts to take charge are a fiasco. He shocks Penelope quite unnecessarily, even cruelly, and then turns on the Suitors in a tone of voice that must have been totally unexpected by them, for at first they are taken aback. "This is sheer insolence" (368), he says, using the Greek word *hybris,* and they bite their lips in astonishment at his boldness. But the new Telemachus lapses back into the old Telemachus as soon as Antinous, one of the Suitors' ringleaders, has a chance to distract him. Poor Telemachus discourses vaguely on the nature of kingship, then is so uncertain of his own position (if, indeed, he is to succeed Odysseus) that he concedes the claims of the other princes. He then concludes lamely that he intends at least to control his own house. This has not been a very convincing display of newly found authority or spirit, but in his confusion Telemachus has at least raised the great question which Odysseus will answer: Who is to be king of Ithaca? He has also asked what kingship means; and his tentative answer—an enrichment of one's house and an increase of honor (392-93)—will soon be confirmed in the glory and wealth of the courts of Nestor and Menelaus. Thus, in this book, Telemachus has been awakened by Athena to an awareness of royalty and its prerogatives. This is important, for it is his initial preparation for the coming struggle to preserve the same prerogatives of rightful kingship in Ithaca. When the first book ends with the quiet and touching scene of Eurycleia tending Telemachus as he prepares for bed, Homer has completed the picture of Telemachus' surroundings. He is in some way subject to Penelope, although he has now dared to bridle at her authority; he is attended by an aged nursemaid; and he is bedeviled and oppressed by insolent Suitors. Father Odysseus is away, grandfather Laertes is off on his farm, and Telemachus has only two women to support him against the menace of a hundred and eight young men determined to marry his mother and take over his father's throne.

In Book II we read little that particularly convinces us that Telemachus has profited by Athena's encouragement. He denounces the Suitors at a public assembly and appeals, without much hope, to their nonexistent sense of justice. When he then goes on to invoke Zeus and Themis, we feel that this is clearly not the kind of speech his father would deliver, and whatever faint effect it might have had on the hard hearts of the Suitors is dissipated when he concludes his words with a sudden burst of tears. The crowd pities Telemachus, but the Suitors do not, particularly the cynical Antinous, who goes on to shift the blame to Penelope for her funeral-shroud ruse. Once again Telemachus' attempt at oratory has been abortive and ineffective, but once again he has raised a central theme of the ***Odyssey***: the justice of Odysseus, the injustice of the Suitors. As spokesman for his family, and speaking in an assembly of the citizens of Ithaca, Telemachus has publicly arraigned the Suitors for their crimes against his father's household, an indictment that will still obtain when Odysseus seeks a terrible swift vengeance in Book XXII. Furthermore, the terms of his speech, just as in Book I, foreshadow elements of experience in Books III and IV. He describes Odysseus' kingship as fatherly in its gentleness (47), and he will see gentle and exemplary fathers in Nestor and Menelaus; the food squandered by the Suitors in their incessant parties in Ithaca (55-56) will be consumed in order and harmony at the feasts in Pylos and Sparta; the wine that intoxicates the Suitors in Ithaca (57) will become a tranquilizer in Sparta; and the weakness Telemachus protests here (60-61) will be overcome by confidence and resolve before he sees Ithaca again.

After his speech Telemachus commences his preparations for his journey, but runs into the astonished protests of his nurse Eurycleia: "But there's no need at all for you to endure the hardships of wandering over the barren sea" (369-70). This feminine attraction to place is partly what Telemachus must overcome by becoming acquainted with the ways of the heroes who did suffer hardships at Troy and then had to return over the seas to the great centers of the Mycenaean Age. But for all Telemachus' determination, Eurycleia's objection still stands, and to assert that Telemachus must rid himself of inhibitions induced by the women who have brought him up is not a very convincing justification for his trip. Indeed, the fact that Telemachus intends to go off on a junket at this crucial time, with the Suitors growing impatient and poor Penelope

at her wit's end, was duly noted by Analyst critics and made one of their reasons for believing in the original separateness of the *Telemacheia*. In this objection they were anticipated here by Homer himself, by Odysseus at XIII, 417 ("Do you want him too to scour the barren seas in misery while strangers eat him out of house and home?"), and by Eumaeus in XIV, 178 ("Suddenly some god deprived him of his wits—or perhaps it was a man who fooled him—and off he went to holy Pylos on his father's trail").

They are right—this does seem like the worst conceivable time to leave Ithaca. To them the answer is provided by Athena in XIII, 422. Yes, she could have told Telemachus the truth about his father, but she sent him off to win what the Greeks called *kleos,* reputation, a hero's highest reward: "I myself arranged the journey for him, in order that he might win a noble *kleos*." The fact is that nothing Athena *told* Telemachus would have had any lasting cffcct; what he needed before meeting his father was experience in heroic society, the kind of experience he had never known in Ithaca, and this journey to two of the great centers of heroic civilization, Pylos and Sparta, was the only way he could gain it. To put it in religious terms, Telemachus had to be baptized into the heroic life, to commune with its leaders, and to be confirmed in its values, or he would never be a trusted ally to his father or a fit successor to the kingship. *Kleos* ranks with *aretê,* excellence, as an honorific word in the heroic vocabulary, and it is only in places like Pylos and Sparta that Telemachus can absorb their meanings and prepare himself to merit them. It is true that this is a critical juncture in the affairs of Ithaca, but far from impeding Telemachus, it makes his journey all the more necessary. For it is at the truly critical periods of man's life—when he is most exposed—that he must appeal to an extra source of strength, an access of grace. Hence Telemachus' journey is neither unnecessary nor unmotivated, for the necessity is Telemachus himself—his youthfulness, his inexperience—and the motive transcends the averred search for information.

The beginning of Telemachus' journey is particularly significant. It is traditional in primitive societies for the young candidate to be taken at night from the care of the women, either forcibly or without their knowledge, and given over to the elders of the tribe who will conduct the tests and trials by which the novice must prove his worth and fitness as a member of his tribe. In the same way, Telemachus leaves in the dark of night, his mother Penelope unaware of his departure and his nurse Eurycleia bound by an oath not to reveal the reason for his absence. He is accompanied by Athena who is disguised as Mentor—a name that has come into English as the word for teacher or coach. The first stage of their journey is Nestor's citadel at Pylos. Here we are in the heroic world and we notice that Telemachus does not know how to act, what to do, how to approach the great man. "Remember that I have had no practice in making speeches; and a young man may well hesitate to cross-examine one so much his senior" (III, 23-24). Athena encourages him, tells him not to be so shy, to rely on his native wit, and to have faith in the assistance of the gods. It is she who passes the cup to Telemachus as the libation is being offered and it is she who offers a prayer that Telemachus can repeat after her. Telemachus manages nicely in his first bout with the social forms of a kingly court, though not as deftly as Nestor's son Peisistratus, who had, after all, the benefit of growing up within this mannered society. (And how polite they are, as Homer here as elsewhere emphasizes manners and ceremony.) Nestor then delivers a long speech—he rarely delivered a short one—luxuriating in the recollected sorrows of the Trojan War and remarking Telemachus' resemblance to his famous father. (We notice here the continuing reference to faithful sons—Antilochus, Peisistratus, Orestes.) In reminiscing about Troy, Nestor passes from Achilles to Ajax to Patroclus and finally to his own son Antilochus. He praises Odysseus for his good sense, tells how, out of allegiance and piety, Odysseus stayed behind at Troy with Agamemnon, and does not forget to remind Telemachus approvingly of the sterling example of Agamemnon's son Orestes. Telemachus picks up the hint, but then awkwardly blurts out his despair of ever seeing his father again "even if it proves to be god's will" (228), for which he is promptly chided by Athena, who gives him a one-sentence lesson in the power of the gods. In the fully integrated society piety and manners are identical and Telemachus must learn to trim his private doubts accordingly. That evening Athena leaves and Telemachus is received into Nestor's palace where he sleeps beside Nestor's son Peisistratus. The next day Nestor arranges an elaborate banquet for Telemachus' crew and even has his youngest daughter, Polycaste, give Telemachus a bath. This might seem an odd way to honor a guest, but in the intimate and domestic setting of this book it is both appropriate and charming. At any rate, to continue with religious terminology, it acts almost as a kind of baptism, for out of it Telemachus emerges, "looking like a god" (468). Nestor then gives him horses and a chariot and sends Peisistratus to accompany him on his way to Sparta. Athena is no longer with Telemachus, but he has been accepted into Nestor's household, bathed by his daughter, and is now being escorted by his son. For Telemachus this breif visit to Pylos has been a tonic experience after the noisy desperation of his life at Ithaca, and at last he is ready to break out of the shell of his depression and uncertainty and to make his way in broad heroic society.

Book IV opens with a scene of feasting and family cheer in the splendid palace of Menelaus, where King Menelaus is celebrating the marriages of his son and daughter. Here in Sparta there is a prosperity, a security, and a family intimacy that Telemachus had never known in Ithaca and had only lately met in Pylos. Again we are aware how subtly and exactly Homer chooses details to contrast Menelaus and Sparta with Odysseus and Ithaca. The primary complication of the *Odyssey* is the disunion of a family, whereas here we have an immediate awareness of union (the double marriage) and reunion (Helen). And compare the joy and harmony of Menelaus' banquet with the pointless carousing of the Suitors. Nor has anything in Telemachus' limited experience prepared him for the magnificance of Menelaus' palace, before which even Peisistratus is impressed. Nevertheless, Telemachus is making progress; at the beginning of Book III the mere sight of a hero panicked him; here he seems quite sure of himself before Menelaus, and he can be forgiven his awe before the royal palace—after all his father, who has seen everything, is no less impressed by Alcinous' palace in Book VII. Manners are once again stressed: Menelaus' anger when a servant suggests the possibility of sending Telemachus and Peisistratus "on for someone else to entertain" (29), and his embarrassment when Telemachus weeps as he reminisces of Odysseus. And in the stories Menelaus tells there are little morals which can also be of use to Telemachus. Proteus, for example, tells Menelaus that he should have sacrificed to Zeus before embarking; Ajax's fate is an example to those who would blaspheme; and when Proteus tells Menelaus of what happened to Agamemnon and then urges him to hurry back to his land as quickly as he can, Homer shows us that the point is not lost on Telemachus. He refuses to protract his stay in Sparta, and when Menelaus offers him three horses he has the wit and the temerity to ask for a gift he can carry, not horses which are so impractical on Ithaca. Menelaus is impressed.

Book IV (along with Book XIV) has generally found little favor with critics of the *Odyssey*. Admittedly, Menelaus, the cuckolded warrior of the *Iliad,* is not much more interesting in the *Odyssey* as a slightly blowsy rich man, and some of Helen's radiance has diminished in her translation from the walls of Troy. But the Homer of the *Odyssey* rarely likes to compete with the Homer of the *Iliad,* a fact which has led some Separatist critics to posit two Homers. The Nestor of Book III does not quite sound like the Nestor of the *Iliad,* who so often compared the debased present with the glorious past of his own young manhood, and the domestic calm of Menelaus' menage in Book IV should not be troubled by memories of old loves and old hates. Only Helen still feels the rankling memory of that old infatuation, "shameless creature that I was" (145), but she shows a proper remorse and has equipped herself with a drug that has "the power of robbing grief and anger of their sting and banishing all painful memories" (220). But it is all to Homer's purpose to deflect the attention from these commanding figures of the

Iliad, because the center of these books is Telemachus. For him and for the whole poem Book IV is effective and meaningful; it not only extends the *Telemacheia,* but it also prepares the reader for Book V, easing him, as it were, into the *Odyssey* proper. For Menelaus' fate closely approaches Odysseus', since his return was recently as uncertain as is Odysseus' now. Menelaus is also proof to Telemachus and to us that even after the weariest of journeys one can return home safely and enjoy a happy and prosperous future. Further, Menelaus' range of experience is considerably broader than Nestor's, extending beyond the known Greek sea routes into the areas of the fabulous where creatures like Proteus live. It is only from this strange Old Man of the Sea that fairly specific information about Odysseus is available, and this information is, after all, the purpose of Telemachus' trip. Also, the Proteus episode is just the sort of adventure Odysseus might have had, and thus the Nestor-Menelaus-Proteus progression prepares us for the fantastic adventures of Books V to XII and gives us a richer view of Odysseus than if we had first seen him when Hermes was sent to Calypso. Proteus' advice to Menelaus to return home as quickly as possible is also a warning that Odysseus and Telemachus have no time to lose either. The accounts given in Books III and IV of the returns of the various heroes are also deftly arranged by Homer to isolate Odysseus' situation. Nestor was one of the first to return, Menelaus one of the last; Ajax, son of Oileus, was killed off the coast of Asia Minor, Agamemnon after his return home. In this milieu of rescue and death, all possibilities are exhausted except one, which transcends them all—Odysseus' fate—of travels compared with which Menelaus' were child's play, of the multiple threats of death in the distance still to be covered, of a home and family near ruin, as was Agamemnon's, and of the loss of ship and company. Odysseus still belongs neither to the saved nor to the lost, and he can perish like Agamemnon or he can come safely home to peace and quiet like Menelaus and Nestor. With the latter he is connected by his wisdom, with the former by his wanderings, with both by the divine favor he enjoys. But yet Odysseus surpasses them all in ways that the *Odyssey* will describe and for which the *Telemacheia,* and particularly Book IV, has prepared us.

Before the *Odyssey* proper begins with Odysseus on Calypso's island in Book V, the scene changes to Ithaca where the Suitors hatch their plot to ambush and slay Telemachus and where Penelope hears from the herald Medon about Telemachus' trip and also about the Suitors' designs on her son. The transition from Sparta is abrupt, but again we notice how everything in the poem returns to Ithaca—Odysseus from his wanderings, Telemachus from his trip; and now, just before Odysseus appears, Homer returns us to Ithaca for a final glimpse of what Odysseus is returning to—homicidal Suitors and a suffering Penelope. It is this impression of home and wife—and not of Helen and Menelaus—that we have when we first see Odysseus in the next book.

The last scene of what we can still call the *Telemacheia*—that is, before Telemachus meets his father and they both challenge the Suitors—takes place in Book XV, when Athena again visits Telemachus, this time in Sparta, and urges him to hasten back to Ithaca. His reaction is almost as precipitate as it was in Book I, but Peisistratus checks him; after all, there are proper ways to do these things, and "a guest never forgets a host who has shown him kindness' (54-55). Telemachus is impatient, and he frets through Menelaus' moralizing and the rituals of gift-giving, but by now he is aware of his responsibilities and feels himself a man of action; now it is more than he can stand to have to return to Pylos to brave Nestor's oppressive hospitality. Telemachus has been schooled in the forms of the heroic life in Books III and IV; in XV he has earned the right to transcend them. He can now dispense with social obligations, for his own obligations are infinitely more demanding. He must be about his father's business.

The last scene of the *Telemacheia,* the Theoclymenus episode, is puzzling. Why is Theoclymenus brought in? Perhaps to palliate murder in the face of Odysseus' subsequent treatment of the Suitors? Certainly Theoclymenus, like Odysseus, can say, "It is my fate to wander about the world" (XV, 276), for he is being pursued by the kinsmen of the man he has slain. And for the rest of the poem this relic of the feuds of the heroic world will hover uneasily in the background like Conrad's Leggat, the secret sharer in Odysseus' revenge and a disturbing reminder of the random violence and blood guilt of the heroic age. But for Telemachus the decision to accept Theoclymenus demonstrates his newly won authority: he has the right to give asylum, even hospitality, if he wants, to a murderer. Through Theoclymenus Homer can underscore the identity of Telemachus, show that he is now coming into his own and can afford his father the assistance Odysseus might have received from another Achaean hero on the fields before Troy. In this sense it is appropriate that the *Telemacheia* end with Theoclymenus interpreting an omen, a hawk appearing on the right with a dove in its talons, which he sees as signifying that, "No family in Ithaca is kinglier than yours; you will have power forever" (533-34). As a professional performance this is indeed shabby, and as a prophecy it is so vague as to be meaningless. But it is not a prophecy; it is an accolade, a ceremony to complete the *Telemacheia* by marking Telemachus' attainment to true manhood. His doubts about his right to his royal patrimony are allayed, and he is rewarded with an assurance of future success. Theoclymenus' words signal an access of power that Telemachus will need in the days ahead.

*Odysseus and Circe, caricatured by the Boetians about 400 B.C. when Odysseus's adventures
in the Septentrionales had become a subject for satire.*

Telemachus now returns to Ithaca.

> On the voyage from Ithaca to Pylos, Telemachus was as he himself said only a passenger. . . . He had little to do either with the preparation of the cargo or the sailing of the ship; everything was under the immediate control of Athena; but on the return trip he was the sole commander and cared for all matters which concerned both ship and crew with the assurance of a veteran seaman. [J.A. Scott, in "The Journey Made by Telemachus and Its Influence on the Action of the *Odyssey*," *The Classical Journal*, XIII, 1918]

After Telemachus is back in Ithaca his fortunes merge with those of his father and his role is clearly subordinated to Odysseus'. This somewhat diminishes the impact of Telemachus' personality, and Homer is not always successful in giving him something to do. Although he is potentially his father's most powerful ally against the Suitors, even Odysseus seems to ignore him when he tells Athena, "I am alone" (XX, 40). Of course, Telemachus shows his mettle: only a nod from Odysseus in Book XXI keeps him from stringing the bow, and he seems to do his share in the fight with the Suitors. He is exceptional in his mercy, checking Odysseus from slaying Phemius the minstrel and Medon the herald, and relentless in his revenge, personally stringing up the unfaithful serving women. (Perhaps his savagery toward the servant girls, like his occasional harshness with his mother, is part of a deep-seated reaction against an adolescence spent among women.) But if Telemachus does acquire some of his father's heroism, it is at the price of his own individuality. Homer seems conscious of this and goes to great lengths to let us know that Telemachus is still around. But the glimpses he gives us are often of the "old" Telemachus, laughing (XXI, 105), sneezing (XVII, 541), and absentmindedly botching his father's plans (XXII, 154); Telemachus speaks out of turn (XXIII, 97-103), parades in borrowed feathers.

One answer to the problem presented by Telemachus' role seems to be that the second half of the *Odyssey* belongs to its hero alone. . . . Odysseus, so long absent and so often disguised, must dominate the action of the final books, both by the vitality of his own presence and by the revivifying effect he has on his family. Penelope subjects Odysseus to one more trial, devising a test—the bedpost ploy—her husband could be proud of. Later on, this transformation also affects Laertes, who, as we have noted, is rejuvenated by Athena. Telemachus, for his part, becomes so like Odysseus that he is indistinguishable from him, being so much a replica of his father as his own name (Far-fighter?) is—or sounds like—a title for Odysseus. The problem Homer faced was technical: how to show the maturity, individuality, and heroism of Telemachus without detracting from the dominance of Odysseus. If his compromises were not always successful, it is large-ly because the pre-logical situations of myth will not readily conform to the logic of literature.

Yet even though Telemachus yields place to Odysseus in the final books of the poem, in his own "epic" he can stand a thorough comparison with his more famous father; and at the same time we can see how skillfully Homer uses the *Telemacheia* as a kind of "little epic" to balance and contrast with the rest of the *Odyssey*. First, both Telemachus and his father make journeys, from which both must return home indirectly and in constant danger. Odysseus has to survive the world's perils and disorders while preserving his identity and his purpose. For Telemachus the world is precisely the opposite, centering in the well-ordered kingdoms of Nestor and Menelaus. Telemachus' progress is from the chaos of Ithaca to the cosmos of Pylos and Sparta; Odysseus seeks the stability of his home across the ragged edges of the world—he must go, literally, through hell and back. Furthermore, in their separate worlds there is an important difference between the two: Odysseus acts, Telemachus reacts. Although Odysseus, in his struggles with giants and monsters and witches, more than once comes within an inch of his life, Telemachus' experiences, apart from the social, are vicarious—he listens, observes, absorbs. He learns about his father—not his whereabouts, but rather the full story of the Odyssean exploits at Troy. He can now better appreciate his father (particularly when it comes to infiltrating a hostile city), because he has learned of his derring-do from the greatest living authorities on heroic *aretê*.

It is important, therefore, that in this atmosphere of wartime heroism recollected in the tranquility of peace Telemachus do nothing, just as it is for Odysseus in the Underworld of Book XI. And yet, through his own faltering efforts to make this trip and share the memories of Nestor and Menelaus, Telemachus is able to rehearse privately many of the great crises of the *Odyssey*. The stories of the heroes fighting at Troy and returning to Greece prepare him for the coming struggle by expanding his knowledge, if not his experience, of the world. He sees two families, those of Nestor and Menelaus, that are as happy as his own is unhappy; and when he visits with Helen he sees a woman who suffered for love as bitterly as his own mother Penelope is suffering. He hears of a prophet Proteus who is much like the prophet Tiresias whom Odysseus meets in the Underworld (Book XI), and yet this Proteus is at the same time a sea monster like those who threaten his father; and, finally, he too must hurry home at the warning of Athena to save Penelope from the Suitors. Homer has succeeded in packing a version of the *Odyssey* into a little more than two books, all in the passive voice.

In the *Telemacheia* Telemachus frees himself from the women who have reared him, the Suitors who harass him, and the island that inhibits him, and visits a world that is rich and new. Within the scope of the whole poem the adventure of Odysseus that most nearly corresponds to his son's journey is in Book XI, where Odysseus visits the Underworld. This adventure, called the *Nekyia* in Greek, may not be one of Homer's best efforts, but it does define the special quality of the *Telemacheia* and it is interesting to compare them. Both of these episodes, for example, presume to show us the hero learning something vital to his future welfare, yet in each the information is either not forthcoming as supposed or else could have been acquired elsewhere. Further, it is only in the *Nekyia* that Odysseus assumes the stance of Telemachus in Books III and IV—that of the passive observer of an unfamiliar ceremony. However, there are significant differences. Whereas Telemachus is introduced to the heroic tradition in the front parlors of the returned chieftains where manners saturate conduct, where worldly prudence and social maturity have a climactic importance, and where the storms and struggles of life seem comfortably remote, Odysseus on the other hand has to break through the world's surfaces, has to pass, indeed, from life to death. Telemachus hears about Agamemnon and Achilles; Odysseus goes to see them. Odysseus' fate is cosmic; hence he must penetrate to the mist-bound areas beyond this life. His living presence in Hades prefigures the life that he will restore to the stricken land of Ithaca. Odysseus must go beneath the levels of the world, the very levels which Telemachus must come to know with tact and nicety. Ordinarily Odysseus is satisfied with his knack for survival in a hostile and perplexing world, but in the *Nekyia* he is in touch with powers beyond his techniques and he is immobilized by them. He comes for specific information from Tiresias, but he stays to meet the ghostly representatives of the heroic Establishment. Odysseus needs no education in the ways of this world; now his experience has been deepened by exposure to the ways of the next world. But if the **Odyssey** in Book XI breaks through the forms of life, the *Telemacheia* is content to slide along their surface, initiating its young hero into the rites of a faith in which he was born but never reared. Its high priest is Nestor, its catechism the legends of Troy.

The escorts of the two heroes are another point of contrast. For much of his return Odysseus is saddled with the burden of his company, the responsibility for their safety and the accountability for their lesser talents. Within his larger fate are subsumed the fates of his companions. With Telemachus, however, the situation is reversed—Odysseus has men under him; Telemachus has men over him, for he is under the divine protection of Athena and the fraternal guidance of Peisistratus. Since Odysseus either overshadows the men who accompany him or else travels alone, his personality everywhere dominates the action even when

the forces opposing him are most critical or catastrophic. Telemachus does not dominate the action; instead he is usually at its mercy. He finds himself in social impasses, situations where he fears that his training and experience are not adequate. He is never alone; Athena and Peisistratus are ever with him, and his final character is shaped by their initial tutoring and example. Their salutary presence, their promptings, assurances, and commendations are the background of his development.

From the time of Porphyrio, who called it a *paideusis,* or "education," the *Telemacheia* has sometimes been taken as a kind of *Bildungsroman,* or "novel of education"; and it is true that all the elements are there. Telemachus at the beginning is the callow youth; Pylos and Sparta are the open world; Athena is the guide, the mentor. And the result is Telemachus beside his father fighting with skill and courage against the Suitors. It is not simply an education, though. What Telemachus experiences is not something taught, but something imparted—one young man's initiation into a world he has inherited and whose values he will soon have to defend by force. (One notices that what one would most expect to happen fails to materialize—namely, that either Nestor or Menelaus would volunteer to send off a detachment of their palace guard to Ithaca to restrain the Suitors, protect Penelope, and confirm Telemachus in his patrimony. Instead they seem to assume that this is exclusively the problem of Telemachus and Odysseus.) And yet it is not a rite of initiation in the anthropological sense of a set of artificial dangers contrived to test a candidate's reactions. Growing up fatherless in a house recently occupied by scheming Suitors has given Telemachus a taste of danger; now, in the *Telemacheia,* Pylos and Sparta demonstrate to him the possibilities of peace, and the examples of Nestor and Menelaus expose him to the precedents of heroism. In a sense, then, the *Telemacheia* is a kind of reverse *Bildungsroman,* because it exposes the young hero not so much to danger as to safety. Telemachus' life was already perilous enough back in Ithaca; now in Pylos and Sparta he has a vision of peace, security, happiness, and family reunion, all the values he has never known but will soon have to win back in a bloody and desperate battle. Goethe named the hero of his *Bildungsroman* Wilhelm Meister to foreshadow the master he would become; likewise there is something appropriate in the sound of Telemachus' name, "Far-fighter," so apt for this young Ithacan who in the not so far future will be the kind of fighter his father can trust and admire. For in the final books of the **Odyssey** Telemachus will meet his greatest trial, the challenge to prove his worth by successful deeds, to demonstrate before his elders and his peers that he is truly the son of his father. For Telemachus the meetings with Nestor and Menelaus are sacraments, the visible means to the graces of heroism. Hence the search he makes is for more than news of his father:

"Telemachos Remembers":

Twenty years, every day,

The figures in the web she wove
Came and stood and went away.
Her fingers in their pitiless play
Beat downward as the shuttle drove.

Slowly, slowly did they come,
With horse and chariot, spear and bow,
Half-finished heroes sad and mum,
Came slowly to the shuttle's hum.
Time itself was not so slow.

And what at last was there to see?
A horse's head, a trunkless man,
Mere odds and ends about to be,
And the thin line of augury
Where through the web the shuttle ran.

How could she bear the mounting load,
Dare once again her ghosts to rouse?
Far away Odysseus trod
The treadmill of the turning road
That did not bring him to his house.

The weary loom, the weary loom,
The task grown sick from morn to night,
From year to year. The treadle's boom
Made a low thunder in the room.
The woven phantoms mazed her sight.

If she had pushed it to the end,
Followed the shuttle's cunning song
So far she had no thought to rend
In time the web from end to end,
She would have worked a matchless wrong.

Instead, that jumble of heads and spears,
Forlorn scraps of her treasure trove.
I wet them with my childish tears
Not knowing she wove into her fears
Pride and fidelity and love.

Edwin Muir, in One Foot in Eden, *Faber and
Faber, 1956.*

he seeks the social and family assurance of the heroic age, where sons are like their fathers because they have grown up in their shadows, as Antilochus was like Nestor, or where sons inherit their father's bravery and defend their memories, as Orestes avenged the death of Agamemnon. Telemachus has never had a father to provide the scenes and cues for his glory, and so this journey is not only for information but, as Athena admits (XIII, 422), to win him his first *kleos*. Since Homer's time the fatherless child has been a major figure in Western literature—Oedipus, Hamlet, Stephen Dedalus, Dickens' waifs—because the quest for the father reflects the profounder theme of the spiritual condition of children deprived of faith and security. Telemachus leaves the menace of the Suitors behind in Ithaca, experiences the harmony and stability of Pylos and Sparta, and then returns to help his father purge the contaminated land and restore justice and the social conventions. The heroic society Telemachus traverses is an enclosed world with its own laws and conventions and ceremonies, its own mystique of wisdom and virtue, its own concept of honor. Out of it emerges a new Telemachus. For the meaning of these five books, the final purpose of the *Telemacheia* is to delineate the birth of a hero. As such it parallels in its way the **Odyssey** proper—which presents the return of the hero and, with Laertes, the rebirth of a hero—and thereby completes the picture of heroic life which the **Odyssey** celebrates.

H. D. F. Kitto (essay date 1966)

SOURCE: "The *Odyssey*," in *Poiesis: Structure and Thought,* University of California Press, 1966, pp. 116-52.

[*A British critic, translator, and specialist on Hellenic drama, Kitto has written extensively on ancient Greek literature, theater, and history. In this excerpt, he defends the structure and theme of the* Odyssey.]

There are two Homeric questions. There is the one first asked by Lachmann and eagerly debated ever since: one Homer, or two, or a multitude? The other is: What are the poems about? How did Homer think? We can consider the poems either as historic monuments (which they are), or as poems (which they are). I admit that the two questions are not entirely separable. It is indeed possible to examine some purely archaeological, philological, or historical aspects of the poems without considering their poetic qualities at all, but, ideally, one cannot do the converse. If this [study] takes very little notice of the more famous Homeric Question, the reason is that it is concerned with the **Odyssey,** as a poem, from a particular point of view: we shall be using it as a means of testing Aristotle's assertion that structure, "the disposition of the material", is all-important. . . . I choose the **Odyssey** rather than the **Iliad** because its structure is more taut, and it is more taut because the **Iliad**—notably in the Catalogue of the Ships—incorporates much more quasi-historical material. If the same poet wrote both poems, on which question I need express no opinion here, he was much more conscious in the **Iliad** of having a function additional to that of being a profoundly tragic epic poet. . . .

I shall assume what is in any case obvious, that some major poet gave to the *Odyssey* what is substantially its present shape. Book XI may be a later addition; I can afford to express no opinion, because the present argument would not be affected; still less would minor interpolations affect it. Other suspected passages will be considered as they turn up.

It is traditional to say that the structure of the poem is one of the surest signs of the poet's genius. The raw material of which it is composed is abundant and diverse, far flung both in time and space, yet it is organised by Homer into a plot of the utmost clarity and simplicity, so that the action occupies only thirty-seven days. Is this not a masterstroke? Certainly—but let us not suppose that when we say this we are saying anything of great importance. The plot is an example of poiesis on the grand scale, and poiesis has to do with more than literary skill: it has something to do with mind and thought. . . .

Let us first review some . . . criticisms, beginning, as is right and proper, with that excellent early-modern critic Longinus—for Longinus, after all, was separated from Homer by about a thousand years, and in social structure and habits of thought the Roman Empire was as alien from the Homeric age as our own is. In his impressive comparison of the *Odyssey* with the *Iliad* Longinus writes like this:

> The *Odyssey* shows that when a great genius is in decline, a special mark of old age is the love of telling stories. The *Odyssey* is Homer's later poem, an epilogue to the *Iliad*. The *Iliad,* written when Homer's inspiration was at its height, is full of action and conflict; the *Odyssey* for the most part consists of narrative, the characteristic of old age. It is the sunset of Homer: the grandeur remains, but not the intensity. You seem to see the ebb and flow of greatness, a fancy that roams through the fabulous and the incredible; it is as if the Ocean were withdrawing into itself, leaving its bed here and there high and dry. I have not forgotten the tempests of the *Odyssey,* the story of the Cyclops, and the like; if I speak of old age, it is nevertheless the old age of Homer. Yet throughout the poem as a whole, the fabulous prevails over the real. Genius, when it has passed its prime, can sink into absurdity—for example, the incident of the wine-skin, of a hero on a wreck for ten days without food, of the incredible slaying of the Suitors. Another sign of old age is fondness for the delineation of manners; for such are the details that Homer gives, with an eye for description, of life in the house of Odysseus; they form, as it were, a Comedy of Manners. . . .

Longinus, then, found that the *Odyssey* lacks the grandeur and intensity of the *Iliad*—and few will quarrel with him for that—but his criticism fails; it illuminates Longinus, but not Homer. It fails because he comes to the poem with a specific demand, namely that it should display epic sublimity, and when he finds that it does not do this, instead of asking whether it meets different demands he finds a less laborious explanation: Homer, when he came to write the *Odyssey,* was quite an old gentleman, past his best, a bit garrulous, . . . interested now in quiet things like the delineation of character and manners. It is of course an impressive passage, but the criticism is of that unconstructive kind that is content with negatives: "Aeschylus was not so clever as Sophocles in constructing plots"; "Thucydides had no idea of the importance of economic affairs"; "the slaying of the Suitors is incredible".

From this springboard I jump to a modern critic of the poem—a scientist, once a colleague of my own, therefore an intelligent and civilised man. He read the *Odyssey,* in E. V. Rieu's translation, and told me how much he had enjoyed it: so vivid and entrancing a story. But he, like Longinus, boggled at the slaying of the Suitors, though not for the same reason. What was merely incredible—the wine-skin and suchlike, he, being a scientist, could take in his stride; what worried him was the gods, especially Athena, popping up from time to time to make things easier for Odysseus, particularly in the fight with the Suitors, stealing the hero's thunder, "making him look half a fool".

This critic, like Longinus, was looking at the poem, naturally, from his own point of view, and that was something like this: "In the poem I find things familiar to me. There is a hero in distress. He has one ambition, to get home. He meets difficulties of all kinds, but being bold, resourceful, and courageous he surmounts them. Some of the incidents are marvellous, but *that* does not upset me. He does get back home, is confronted with a final test, passes it triumphantly, and all is well. It is that familiar thing, an adventure story, and it is supremely well told. Incidents like those of Circe or the Cyclops confirm my diagnosis. But in a tale of this kind, gods are a nuisance—at least, gods who pull the strings for the hero at a crisis."

And what do we say in reply? Useless to talk to a scientist about "the epic tradition of divine machinery". He would be quick to point out that this only says again, in different words, that Homer used gods even when they are a nuisance to his story; and he might well ask if the Greeks were such that the greatest of their poets lacked the courage or the originality to throw overboard a tradition when it was cramping and cumbrous.

Then there is Telemachus' journey to Sparta. It is an attractive episode, and, as Aristotle wisely said, the epic form is hospitable to such—but does it *do* anything for us, and for the poem, other than decorate it, at rather undue length? Because when at last Telemachus does return, the little news that he has been able to pick up is already out of date, since Homer contrives that Odysseus should get home first. Naturally, it has been suggested that this part of the *Odyssey* was originally a separate lay, having Telemachus for its hero. Very well; but whose idea was it to bring it into the *Odyssey?* It may indeed be a law of nature that an interpolator is a fool as well as a nuisance, but if the interpolation is so obviously useless, why ever did it remain in the poem? In fact, as Delabecque has shown, in his *Télémaque et la structure de l'Odyssée,* the episode is so carefully worked into the main fabric, with so many deft links, that if Homer did not himself compose it (which he may well have done), he at least adopted it, quite deliberately, and therefore with some idea in mind. What was it?

One part of the episode is even more challenging, namely the long description in Book II of the Assembly held in Ithaca, for it accomplishes practically nothing. Telemachus calls the meeting, makes a protest against the Suitors, and receives very little support; then he demands a ship, gets consent of a kind—and immediately acquires a ship by other means: through the agency of Athena. What is the point of it all? It is easy to make it sound inept; what is not so easy is to make such a degree of ineptitude sound plausible, even by invoking an interpolator.

One might also ask, about the whole theme of the Suitors, if it is not a little bourgeois. That young gallants should riot in the house of an absent man, waste his substance and persecute his wife (or widow), is deplorable conduct indeed, but is it of epic dignity, worthy of being set alongside the tragic theme of Achilles' wrath? Longinus evidently thought not; to him it was only Comedy of Manners.

Then, naturally, there is the ending of the poem. (I say "naturally" because the Greeks were notoriously bad at endings: the *Iliad, Odyssey,* Antigone, Ajax, Trachiniae, Medea: an impressive list.) There is some consensus of opinion that Homer ended his poem at XXIII 296, where Odysseus and Penelope are reunited and Athena prolongs the night for their comfort and joy. The poem we have goes past this point to what Myres called "a poor, drivelling, misbegotten end": the friends of the slain Suitors (as Myres put it) prepare to take vengeance on Odysseus and his party; these in turn arm themselves with zest, so that old Laertes cries out in delight: "Dear gods! What a day is this to warm my heart! My son and grandson are competing in valour". But Athena intervenes with a great cry to make them all drop their weapons and conclude a peace—and Myres, himself the gallant commander of a gunboat in the First World War, is bitterly disappointed, and refuses to debit an ending like this to Homer. . . .

To my scientific friend, as to many others, including

perhaps Longinus, the help given by Athena to Odysseus and Telemachus in the fight was matter for regret: Odysseus is the hero, and he would have been more of a hero without the divine aid that caused the Suitors' weapons to fly askew. From an unhellenic point of view, yes; from Homer's, no. From his, an Odysseus who should conquer without divine aid would be nearly meaningless; he would lack a certain seriousness, a certain public stature. What is at stake, for Homer, is rather more than the heroic triumph of his Odysseus; behind this, or rather *in* this, there is the triumph of Order over Disorder. That is something to which the gods are not indifferent; something that concerns any member of human society—which is the reason why I have just spoken of the "public" stature of the hero. Athena's help is essential to the poem. But if so, why is the heroism of Odysseus necessary? Why *both?* Briefly, because the maxim *Do it yourself* never commended itself to Olympus. "The god" did not stop Xerxes with a thunderbolt; in Aeschylus' recreation of the war, the Persians are already ruined by the courage and intelligence of the Greeks, and by certain natural causes before the god openly declares his interest by freezing the Strymon. Orestes, in the *Choephori,* is not only directly commanded by Apollo; he also has his own commanding private reasons. It is the standard conception. We should not fail to notice that at XIII 375 f., although Athena promises her help to Odysseus, she leaves it to him to devise the means. The world of these poets is not really a world of magic, even though Athena can become a bird, or appear to Telemachus as Mentes or Mentor: indeed, when she does choose to appear as one of these wise and intelligent men, it is noticeable that oftener than not what she says is no more than what he might have said; but the fact that it is Athena, not Mentes or Mentor, who says it gives to the advice a certain resonance: it matters nothing to the mechanics of the plot, but it does make the incident somewhat more than a detail in a purely personal story. Athena may have her "special means of transport", namely golden and imperishable sandals, and a "special weapon", accurately described: a great, heavy spear with a blade of sharp bronze, but not on this account does she cease to embody a perfectly clear moral idea. In the *Iliad* a god will show his, or her, power through a Diomedes or Hector—but these had power to start with; a god never magically transforms and uses a nonentity. A god could "help" such a man as Thersites only by making him, as we too might say, supernaturally ugly and vulgar. It is a poetic and vividly imagined world, but not an irrational one. The really irrational world, in which men cowered in bewilderment before discordant demons, did not arrive (as we have seen) until the fifth century—and in Athens. In Homer, men and gods are in a real sense partners, . . . as Aeschylus remarked, in a forgetful moment. Odysseus' victory without Athena would have been romantic and unhellenic because not significant of anything in particular, but no more unhellenic than would be Athena's without Odysseus.

We will move on to Longinus' Comedy of Manners, and to the idea that the whole theme of the Suitors falls below epic standards of dignity.

To be fair to Homer, we might first remind ourselves of a subsidiary point. In a rich country, the United States for instance, food and drink do not have the same status as in a poor country like Greece, where the gods are more grudging. Wastefulness was moral obliquity, not an economic virtue. But apart from this, in his handling of the Suitors Homer works two ideas for all he is worth, and Longinus appears to have taken neither into account. One is their moral violence, on which Homer insists more and more as the poem goes on: they are ill-mannered, wasteful, plunderers of another man's wealth, loose-living, and finally plotters of murder, and, in the case of Antinous, of usurpation. All this is brought to a climax that is by no means undramatic when Athena, taking the form of Mentor, comes to Odysseus' help in the fight. Agelaus threatens him (her): "Mentor, keep out of the way. We are going to kill these two men, the father and the son. Then we shall kill you as well; we shall confiscate your estate too, and reduce your family to beggary and shame". The fool does not know, of course, that he is talking to a goddess; even so, it is hardly Comedy of Manners.

The second idea is one that would not perhaps naturally impose itself on a critic living under the Roman Empire. As we have seen, Homer's plot, unlike mine, has a political reference, provided that we use the word "political" in its wide Greek sense. Homer of course does not make much fuss about this; as he was a Greek, composing for Greeks, there was no reason why he should; but there are several passages that do not make the degree of sense that we expect of a great poet until we realise that the political framework is present to Homer's mind, whether consciously or quite unconsciously. It does something, perhaps quite a lot, to explain his structure.

First of all, it goes without saying that Odysseus is always the good, wise, and just king, and this is more than a simple characterising of the hero. A picture of such a king is given (as it happens) by Odysseus himself, in a speech that he makes to Penelope (XIX 106 ff.), in which he represents her as the queenly counterpart. He says, in E. V. Rieu's translation:

> Your fame has reached to Heaven itself, like that of some perfect king, who rules over a populous and mighty state with the fear of the gods in his heart, and he upholds the right. Therefore the dark soil yields its wheat and barley, and the trees are laden

with ripe fruit, the sheep never fail to bring forth their lambs nor the sea to provide its fish, all because of his wise government; and his people prosper under him.

We notice the same assumption—unless indeed we should say, the same imagery—as in Aeschylus: Dike, Order, is indivisible; the moral, physical and (here) economic worlds are one. So in the *Eumenides* (930 f.) Athena says of the Erinyes, as the ministers of Dike, that it is their function to order everything for mortals. . . . Accordingly they invoke upon Attica fruitfulness and wealth, the implied condition being (vv. 1018 ff.) that the Athenians revere the Erinyes, the defenders of Dike. The same feeling underlies the long prayer in the *Supplices* (625 ff.): because Argos has chosen to reverence Zeus Hikesios the chorus prays that the city may be free of war and pestilence, that its crops may be abundant and its cattle fertile. It pervades too Homer's description of Scheria: the people are just, generous, and god-fearing, and (or therefore?) everything is orderly and beautiful; the fruit trees bear at every time of the year. Under the government of a just king "the sheep never fail to bring forth their lambs nor the sea to provide its fish"; and such a king was Odysseus. . . . [Lawlessness] is not a moral phenomenon only.

But in Ithaca, order and government are in abeyance: this is implied throughout. For nineteen years the king has been absent; his son, at the beginning of the poem, is a mere lad, quite helpless; Laertes has given up and gone to his vineyard on the hillside (I 188 ff.); even Penelope laments that her troubles have caused her to neglect her duties toward guests, beggars, and messengers who have come on public business (XIX 133 ff.). The royal line is in danger of extinction. Antinous admits (I 386 f.) that Telemachus is the natural successor, though Eurymachus at once hints that another might be chosen; but in any case the Suitors are planning to murder him. In the end, when Eurymachus turns king's evidence, hoping to save his own life, he asserts what we can well believe, that Antinous was the ringleader, anxious not so much to marry Penelope as to make himself king (XXII 48 ff.). All this intelligibly connects itself with several notable features of the poem, and they in turn with each other.

We saw that much of the first four books can be accused of having little organic connexion with the rest of the poem, however delightful it may be in itself. But, as many have pointed out, the episode of Telemachus' journey, instigated by Athena, had an ulterior purpose, and one that Athena declares more than once, namely that Telemachus should win renown. It is the poet's way of making the helpless lad grow up; so that at the end of the poem, although it is only thirty-seven days distant counting by the calendar, he is a mere lad no longer, but a young hero, one who can stand valiantly by his father's side, his destined and worthy successor. The real point, of course, is not what happens to Telemachus as if he were a real person, but what happens to our conception of Telemachus as the poem goes on. At his first meeting with Athena, when she is Mentes, he is simply a charming, well-mannered boy. Mentes-Athena tells him that his own qualities and parentage are such that surely his house will continue to be glorious; he can say in answer only that his father is dead, his property being wasted, and he himself likely to be killed. It is Athena-Mentes who urges him to *do* something: to call an Assembly, and to undertake the journey.

During the journey, two things happen to Telemachus—that is, to our conception of Telemachus: he gains in poise, and he gains in stature. At III 21 ff., he contemplates with alarm the prospect of accosting the great Nestor, but Athena, who is now Mentor, reassures him: he has his native wit, and if that fails, the gods will inspire him. From that moment he speaks to the great with confidence and dignity. Equally important is that the great accept him instantly, both as the son of the renowned Odysseus, and on his own obvious merits. Even before the journey, but after his talk with Athena-Mentes, he spoke to Penelope with a new authority that took her aback (I 356 ff.); then he firmly told the Suitors, to their surprise, that he intended to be master in his own house, and would be willing to succeed Odysseus as king. Towards the end of IV, Penelope laments that he, a mere boy, should have gone into such danger; when we see him home again, he is much more than a boy: at XX 266 ff. and 304 ff. he speaks with great authority to the Suitors, and at XVII 45 very firmly to his mother. On each occasion, Homer tells us, his behaviour caused astonishment. We moderns know that a young gentleman should not speak like this to his mother, but how did Homer's audiences respond? With the reflection, I suspect, that under Athena's guidance Telemachus is becoming quite kingly. It is perhaps no accident that in this part of the poem Homer twice makes him improve on a course of action proposed, the one by Eumaeus and the other by Odysseus himself (XVI 146 ff. and 308 ff.).

The whole episode then, leisurely and delightful though it is, has its close relationship with the rest of the poem; but what about the abortive meeting of the Assembly? It is easy to say that it does nothing to advance the action; one can say the same of the Herald scene in the *Agamemnon,* if one has not understood the play; but in each case the episode does a great deal for the composition and the idea that is shaping it.

Anyone who is disposed to regard this part of II as an interpolation should consider two facts. It is already foreshadowed by Athena at I 272 ff., so that the two passages stand or fall together; and there is a signifi-

cant repetition of the same theme at XVI 376 ff., when Antinous has just returned from his unsuccessful ambush. He is now taking Telemachus very seriously indeed, and openly warns the others that the time has come to dispose of him. He is dangerous, says Antinous; he may summon an Assembly and denounce us; we may find ourselves banished, for the people now are regarding us with disfavour—a fact for which we must, and easily can, take the speaker's own word. Here, the point is clear enough: what happens to the Suitors is so much more decisive than what Antinous feared: they are not banished, but put to death; and not by order of any Assembly, but by Odysseus himself. If Homer found some use in one passage for the idea of an Assembly, he may have found it in two. Perhaps the first is worth looking at in detail.

It is on Athena's prompting that Telemachus summons the meeting. Old Aegyptius opens the discussion: "This is the first time that we have been called together since Odysseus left for Troy. What is the reason? Is the army returning? Is an enemy approaching? Is it something that concerns the public welfare?" Such indeed it is, as we soon learn, even though at first it may seem to be only a private matter.

In response to Aegyptius Telemachus comes forward: in the names of Zeus and Themis (Right) he challenges Ithaca to protect his house from unlawful spoliation. Antinous, in answer, makes an impossible demand. Again Telemachus invokes Zeus—and at once two eagles appear in the sky and hover above the meeting. Haliserthes can read the omen: unless the Suitors give way at once, vengeance will come upon them. The next speaker, contemptuous and defiant, is Eurymachus. He does not believe in birds, nor in justice or moderation either. Finally, Telemachus demands that a ship be given him at least, in order that he may find out, if he can, whether his father is alive or dead; if dead, he will give his mother to a new husband.

Then Mentor rises; he makes a speech that may explain to us why it was his form that Athena chose to assume. He denounces, not so much the Suitors, who are indulging their wickedness (he says) at the risk of their own lives, as the rest of Ithaca, which is doing nothing to stop them. The last speaker, Leiocritus, is another of the Suitors. He defies Mentor, the rest of Ithaca, and Odysseus himself, should he return. He does however suggest that Telemachus should have a ship, though with the sneer that it will be a long time before he sails from Ithaca.

So the Assembly breaks up; and since in the event it is Athena who provides the ship, despite the Suitors, it is understandable if one or two literally-minded critics have found the whole episode a waste of their time. But we should remember that all this was written in

Greek, for Greeks. There was a period in English literature too when the connexion between religion, morality, and politics was both close and obvious; it did not long survive Shakespeare, and when we today meet it in Shakespeare, as often as not we fail to see it. The fact that this Assembly accomplishes nothing is the whole point. In the first book we saw the lawless behaviour of the Suitors within the palace, with Telemachus unable to check it. What Book II does for the poem is to bring the lawlessness out of the seclusion of the palace and put it upon the public stage: it is not a Greek idea that . . . lawlessness is a matter only of private conduct and consequence. Telemachus challenges the *polis* to deal with it, and the *polis* either cannot or will not. Aegyptius asked: "Or is it something that concerns the public welfare?" But of course it is: what was the *polis* for, if not to see justice done between man and man? But in the absence of Odysseus the King, public order has broken down; the Assembly has not even met. Zeus sends two warning eagles to signify his displeasure.

It all coheres intelligibly. In Homer's *Odyssey,* . . . more is at stake than the return and triumph of the hero. There is the question, expressly raised by Athena, if the gods are content that disorder should prevail unchecked; there is the constant picture of Odysseus as the good king, and for that matter of Penelope as the virtuous queen, contrasted so often with Clytemnestra; there is the moral disorder in the palace; there is its counterpart, the breakdown of public justice in Ithaca, both crying out for the return of the King and the reassertion of authority. It was this wide frame of reference that made the ternary form inevitable: at the outset Homer needed to show us what is at stake.

All this, as it seems to me, makes quite impossible the idea, accepted by several scholars, that Homer's poem ended at XXIII 296, with the reunion of Odysseus and Penelope. . . . Certainly, before we can feel sure that the whole of Book XXIV is Homer's work there is much philological and other evidence to consider, but if Homer did not compose it as it stands, the composer was surely working on Homer's own foundations. It is not merely that the idea of counter-vengeance has been raised twice already, once by Odysseus to Athena (XX 36 f.) and once by Odysseus to Telemachus (XXIII 117 ff.): obviously, an interpolator of XXIV could be clever enough to interpolate these passages too, by way of preparation. One could indeed maintain, rightly, that a counter-vengeance, or something like it, is implied in what Antinous said in his remark . . . about a possible meeting of the Assembly; but the major point is that the existence and the well-being of the body politic is implied throughout the poem—implied rather than insisted on, for why should Homer insist upon something that any Greek audience would take for granted? As Telemachus brought his private wrongs upon

the public stage, to be recognised by Mentor, not to mention Zeus, as a grave public matter, so it is natural, even inevitable, that Odysseus' personal reassertion of justice, within his own house, should have its public counterpart. The palace may have been purified by sulphur, but Ithaca too needs something of a purification—at least, a reassertion of authority and order. In any case, no Greek audience could think that the tale had reached its conclusion in a bedroom, when over a hundred young men of Ithaca were lying dead just outside the house. The old Laertes is, surely, using words that Homer wrote for him, when he cries: "Dear gods! What a day to warm my heart! My son and grandson are competing in valour." The King, so long absent, has had his just vengeance, and is ready, with his son, to quell counter-vengeance. But the end is to be conciliation and peace, and it will be strange if Athena is not there to bring it about. . . .

C. M. Bowra (essay date 1971?)

SOURCE: "The *Odyssey:* Its Shape and Character," in *Homer,* Gerald Duckworth & Company Limited, 1972, pp. 117-40.

[*Bowra, an English critic and literary historian, was considered among the foremost classical scholars of the first half of the twentieth century. He also wrote extensively on modern literature, particularly modern European poetry, in studies noted for their erudition, lucidity, and straightforward style. In this posthumously published essay, Bowra examines the characters, structure, and sources of the* Odyssey. *Textual references to the* Iliad *have been rendered in roman numerals, while references to the* Odyssey *are in arabic numerals.*]

The *Odyssey,* like the *Iliad,* begins with an invocation to the Muse:

> Tell, Muse, of the man of many devices, who wandered far indeed, when he had sacked the holy citadel of Troy. He saw the cities of many men and knew their minds, and many were the sorrows which he suffered in his spirit on the sea, when he tried to win his own life and the return of his companions. But not even so, for all his desire, did he save his companions; for they were destroyed by their own insolence, when they ate the cattle of the Sun Hyperion; and he robbed them of the day of their return. From what point you will, goddess, daughter of Zeus, speak to us also. (1.1-10)

This presents several surprises. Unlike Achilles at the start of the *Iliad,* the hero of the *Odyssey* is not named but called 'the man of many devices', which indicates that his story is familiar, and this is confirmed by the last words when the muse is asked to 'speak to us also'. But the familiar story is outlined in a peculiar way. The fantastic adventures of Odysseus are inadequately, almost deceptively, suggested in the reference to cities and minds; almost the only city seen by him is the capital of Phaeacia, and minds are not what he marks in the Cyclops and other monsters. Next, the emphasis on his struggle to save his own life is fair enough and anticipates some of his bravest efforts, but he hardly does so much to secure the return of his comrades. He looks after them, but he takes risks with their lives, and more than once he is the cause of their loss. Finally, not a word is said about the Suitors and the vengeance on them. They occupy more than half the poem and provide its central theme. The opening lines of the *Odyssey* are much less apt and less relevant than those of *Iliad*.

Odysseus must have been the subject of many different stories, some of which survive outside the *Odyssey,* and even of the more constant stories there were variations, as we can see from the Homeric text. When Homer announces his theme at the start, he assumes that much will be known about Odysseus, and the special surprises which he has in store are not of the kind to be publicised now. It is enough that he should refer vaguely to the wanderings and the sufferings of Odysseus and that he should hint at his ultimate return home. It is more striking that he makes such a point of the comrades and their untoward doom, and this is more than a passing whim. One of the chief features of the *Odyssey* is that at the crisis of his fortunes Odysseus has to act alone. Calypso can do little to help him, and on Ithaca he has to find what support he can, first from Eumaeus and then from Telemachus. Therefore his comrades must be disposed of, and their eating of the cattle of the sun meets a real need in the story. Because of this Odysseus' last ship is wrecked, and he himself is cast up on Calypso's island. Homer does not actually give false clues, but his clues are a little delusive. His aim is to keep his audience guessing about how he will treat a familiar mass of stories, which none the less have to be selected and remodelled to suit his own taste.

The material of the *Odyssey* differs greatly from that of the *Iliad* and gives it a different character. While the *Iliad* tells of the 'glorious doings of men' and is heroic in the sense that heroes struggle against other heroes, the *Odyssey* uses a less specific and less exalted material. Its stories are ultimately fairy-tales or folk-tales, and are unheroic in the sense that the unquestionable hero Odysseus is faced not by his equals but by his inferiors or by monsters. In its own compass it displays two kinds of narrative. Books 1-4 and 13-24 tell the age-old tale of the Wanderer's Return and his vengeance on the Suitors who devour his substance and try to marry his wife. In this there is not much fantasy or marvel. Instead we find what 'Longinus' calls 'a comedy of manners' (*On the Sublime*). By this he means that it is concerned with the behaviour of

human beings at a familiar and not very exalted level, as he himself knew it in the comedies of Menander. So far as it goes, this is fair enough, as is also his judgment on Books v-xii, in which he speaks of 'a fancy roving in the fabulous and incredible'. The two parts differ greatly in matter, scale, temper and outlook. The second consists of stories so ancient that they seem to have been polished and perfected by constant telling, while the first class, which deals with stories hardly less ancient but of a different kind, has a less confident and less accomplished, even more experimental and more tentative, air.

The *Odyssey* serves in some sense as a sequel to the *Iliad*. No doubt there were many such sequels, especially in the creative heyday of oral song. The tale of Troy had many consequences, and among these were the adventures of Odysseus. In time he became the chief of the surviving heroes, and his return the most famous of many. Once a figure becomes known for certain qualities, appropriate adventures, with which he may originally have had no connexion, are attached to him and marked with his personal imprint. Odysseus seems from the start to have been 'wily' and 'much-enduring', and stories which turned on wiliness or endurance were annexed to him. The relation of the *Odyssey* to the *Iliad* is obvious throughout. The past in retrospect is seen to have been disastrous, the story of 'evil Ilium not to be named' (19.260,597; 23.19), words which do not occur in the *Iliad* and suggest a shift of attitude towards the Trojan War. At the start of the *Odyssey,* when the gods discuss the fate of Odysseus as he languishes on Calypso's island, they turn at once to the fate of his old comrade, Agamemnon, who has been murdered by his wife and her lover (1.35 ff.), and this broaches the topic of what happens to the heroes of Troy. The audience knows all about the Trojan War and can take any reference to it. So now it lies in the background as they hear about Odysseus and Ithaca.

In the *Odyssey* certain characters appear who have played a substantial part in the *Iliad* but need not necessarily play any part in the return of Odysseus. When Telemachus sails off to find news of his father, he visits first Nestor at Pylos and then Menelaus and Helen at Sparta. Nestor is just the same as in the *Iliad,* garrulous, generous, helpful, even wise. Actually he contributes very little to Telemachus' knowledge of his father, and Homer shows a flicker of playful malice when Telemachus, eager to embark on his ship at Pylos and get home, decides to do so without seeing Nestor, since this would waste a lot of time (15.199-201), and sends the young Peisistratus to fix things with him. Menelaus is a less marked personality than Nestor, but he shows the kingly qualities which we expect from him, and especially loyalty to the son of his old friend Odysseus. More striking is Helen, who makes only a few appearances in the *Iliad* but in all of them reveals the pathos of her doom and her desire to escape from it. Her capacity for affection is clear from what she says to Priam (iii 172), to Hector in his lifetime (vi 344 ff.) and about him after his death (xxiv 762 ff.). The whole adventure with Paris has been a sorrow and a disaster for her, but she has not been able to avoid it (iii 399 ff.). Now she is back with Menelaus at Sparta, happy and at peace. She recalls without distress episodes from the war, but the scope of her character is revealed when she sees that Menelaus and his guests are distressing themselves with reminiscences, and mixes a drug which she has brought from Egypt and which deadens pain and sorrow (4.219 ff.). She has learned from her sufferings, and the tenderness which is already hers in the *Iliad* is turned to new purposes.

Odysseus himself in the *Odyssey* is an enlarged and elaborated version of what he is in the *Iliad*. His main qualities there are cunning and endurance. He keeps his head when others lose theirs, notably after Agamemnon's ill-judged test of the army's morale (ii 166 ff.). He is throughout a notable leader, resourceful and brave. In the *Odyssey*, where he is far longer on the stage, some of his qualities are turned in new directions. First, his cunning is tested in unfamiliar conditions, as in the cave of the Cyclops, where he takes on some qualities of a folk-hero and sustains them quite convincingly. Secondly, his need for cunning is enforced by his own recklessness. It is his fault that he is trapped in the cave of the Cyclops, since he has insisted on entering it, and equally it is his fault that he seeks out Circe's dwelling by himself. Thirdly, his abundant appetites, known from his taste for food and drink in the *Iliad*, are extended in the *Odyssey* to living with Circe and with Calypso, not perhaps in entire satisfaction but still competently. Lastly, the warrior of the *Iliad* becomes the returned wanderer of the *Odyssey* and needs all his powers of decision, command and improvisation. These he amply displays. The man who strikes Thersites and kills Dolon is not likely to spare the Suitors or the servants, male and female, who have worked for them. Odysseus in the *Odyssey* is a magnified version of Odysseus in the *Iliad*, but he remains substantially the same man and recognizable in his main being.

Finally, there are in the *Odyssey* two passages where Homer presents ghosts of the dead, and each includes some chief figures of the *Iliad*. At 11.385-567 Odysseus, at the end of the world, summons ghosts with an offering of blood, and among those who appear are Agamemnon, Achilles and Aias. All three have died since the end of the *Iliad*. Agamemnon has been murdered by his wife, in marked contrast with Odysseus, whose faithful Penelope holds out bravely against the Suitors. His story emphasizes the dangers that await those who return from Troy, but sheds no new light on his personality. Aias, in a brief appearance,

adds a new dimension to his simple character in the *Iliad*, for in the interval he has killed himself because his honour has been wounded by Odysseus. Odysseus does his best to appease him, but Aias takes no notice and makes no answer. The most striking figure is Achilles, for his words complement by contrast what he says in Book ix when momentarily he rejects the heroic life. Now he knows what he has lost, for he would rather 'work on the land as the serf of a man with no property, with no great means of life, than reign over all the perished dead' (11.489-91). His only consolation is to know that his son Neoptolemus is already a stout warrior (11.540). These three ghosts form a link with the *Iliad*, and when Odysseus speaks to them he speaks to his peers, as he does nowhere else in the *Odyssey*.

More mysterious is 24.1-204, where the ghosts of the Suitors are escorted by Hermes to the land of the dead and met by some heroes of the *Iliad*, notably Achilles and Agamemnon. Though the passage is thought to be a later addition, at least it has a part in the whole plan of the *Odyssey*. Achilles hears of his own death and funeral from Agamemnon (24.36 ff.); at it the Muses sang and the ceremony is a fitting climax to a heroic life. To this the Suitors present a complete antithesis. Their ignominious deaths are the proper end to their squalid careers. In this passage the poet seems to have aimed at more than one effect. First, when he makes Agamemnon say that Odysseus is indeed fortunate to have a wife like Penelope (24.192 ff.) and very unlike Clytaemnestra, he emphasizes a subsidiary theme of the *Odyssey*, but does not gain much by it. Secondly, the parade of the ghosts of Troy, in which Patroclus, Aias and Antilochus are named as well as Achilles and Agamemnon (24.16-17), provides a final curtain for great figures of the *Iliad* and of the heroic age. Their place here recalls them at the end of a long story, and the renewed attention paid to them brings various themes together in a last bow. Thirdly, there is a real contrast between the death and glory of Achilles, immortalized in song, and the miserable careers of the Suitors, who are at the other extreme from the true nobility of the heroic ideal. Whoever composed this passage, must have felt that the *Odyssey* must be brought into contact with the *Iliad*, and this he did by stressing what real heroes are.

When we look at the structure of the *Odyssey*, Books 1-4 look as if they could be omitted by bards who were pressed for time and wished to plunge *in medias res* with the more thrilling adventures of Odysseus, but this does not mean that these books do not serve a dramatic purpose. In fact they serve more than one. First, they show the general plight of Ithaca and the particular plight of Penelope in the absence of Odysseus. This is indispensable to any understanding of his difficulties on his return and of the character of the Suitors, from whom he is to exact vengeance. It is bad enough that they should harry his wife and devour his substance and corrupt his servants, but they soon put themselves brutally in the wrong by plotting the death of Telemachus. In this situation everything turns on the possible return of Odysseus. The poet shows how little is known of him, how anticipations of his return vary between irrational hope and not impossible despair. This creates the suspense at which the poet excels. It is to some extent lessened when Telemachus gets news of Odysseus from Menelaus, but it remains vague and unsubstantiated, though omens and portents suggest that something is going to happen. These books build up a growing assurance in the return of Odysseus, and incidentally introduce the other characters with whom he will be associated. The *Odyssey* can be imagined without them, but they add to its range and richness and do much to set its plot to work.

Books 1-4 do more than this. They prepare the way for much that comes later. For instance, Telemachus is cast for a large part, and is not yet ready for it. But he begins to face his responsibilities and to test his powers. His access of courage takes the Suitors by surprise (1.381-2; 2.85-6), and before long they are sufficiently afraid of him to plot his death. By this means he becomes an important participant in the action, and he gives sturdy help in the vengeance. Again, these books anticipate in their manner the dual nature of the *Odyssey,* its element of domestic comedy and its element of fable and fancy. The first is to the fore here, and has a special charm. This manner is unadventurous and unexciting, but its human normality presents a fine contrast with the gluttonous revels and gross manners of the Suitors. Against this are set the stories told by Telemachus' hosts at Sparta, which take us either back to the heroic world of Troy, as when Helen tells how she recognized Odysseus when he came disguised as a beggar to spy in Troy (4.240-64), or forward to the world of marvels, as when Menelaus tells how he tricked Proteus, the old man of the sea, into revealing the fate of Odysseus (4.351 ff.). The main notes of the *Odyssey* are struck at the start, and in due course each is taken up to make its contribution to the whole design.

The middle section of the *Odyssey,* Books 5-12, has a notably distinctive character. Though its more extravagant actions are told by Odysseus himself, the first part, his departure from Calypso and his arrival and welcome in Phaeacia, are told in the third person with an outstanding objectivity, in which Odysseus emerges in all his gifts and dominates the scene. These books provide a skilful transition to the wonders that follow. The events are not yet marvellous, nor are there any monsters. Odysseus shows his physical powers by swimming in a rough sea for two days and two nights, and his resourcefulness by winning the help of the Phaecian royal family. Yet Phaeacia is not real in the same sense as Ithaca. The seasons allow crops all the year round; the servants in the palace are made of metal by Hephaestus; the Phaeacians hardly mingle with other peoples and are consciously proud of their singularity; unlike authentic heroes they live not for war but for dance and song. Once Odysseus has arrived and been handsomely welcomed, we are ready to hear of the wilder wonders which he is about to tell. In Phaeacia these seem less improbable than in Ithaca, and the lively entertainment in Phaeacia prepares us for what lies outside the known world. At the start we have even left the sea, but it is soon present again when Odysseus tells his tale.

Even at this stage, and still more in the narrative of Odysseus, it is clear that the poet is familiar with different versions of a tale and has to make his choice between them. This is easy enough when Odysseus meets Nausicaa. The theme of Wanderer meeting the king's daughter is old and widely spread. A less human version is known from Egypt. A man is shipwrecked on an island. He finds it rich in fruit and trees, and is royally entertained, loaded with gifts and given a safe passage home to Egypt. But his hostess is a snake, thirty ells long, and her family is like her. She treats the castaway with much kindness and courtesy; this is a primitive version of the Nausicaa story, which has not yet assumed its fully human character. The episode in the *Odyssey* shows no misfits or oddities, and looks like a complete tale, but it may well have grown from humble origins. What is remarkable is that while Homer hints at a story in which the Wanderer marries the Princess, the Egyptian tale suggests nothing of the kind. So the treatment of Nausicaa by Odysseus has an ancient precedent. In this case variants have been absorbed into a final version, and Homer's choice was forced upon him by Odysseus' destiny to be joined again to Penelope.

In their long and widely scattered careers such tales develop variations, and the poet has to choose between alternatives. This is very much the case with the Cyclops. As the *Odyssey* tells it, the substantial, unchanged element is that the hero and his companion are caught in the cave of a one-eyed cannibal giant, and after suffering losses in their own number blind him and escape. This story occurs in many countries and is clearly primordial. Homer knew more than one version and made his own choice. First, there is the trick by which Odysseus says that his name is 'No-man', and so when the Cyclops calls for help and says 'No-man is hurting me' (9.408), his friends go away. The trick throve happily in other contexts, but is well in place here. To set the Cyclops among other monsters of his kind makes him more formidable and increases the danger to Odysseus; the trick saves him at a critical point. Second, the Cyclops is blinded with a stake lying in the cave which is not yet ready for use. That is why the Cyclops will not take it with him when he goes out, and Odysseus can use it to blind him. The Cyclops eats his visitors raw after breaking their heads on the floor like puppies (9.289-90). This is perhaps more bestial than to cook them first, and since there is no need for a spit, the stake takes its place. Thirdly, in the escape from the cave there is one version in which Odysseus and his companions kill the ram and the sheep, clothe themselves in their skins, and behave like them as they walk out on all fours. But the Homeric version brings advantages, notably when the ram goes out, with Odysseus under its belly, and we are simultaneously afraid that the Cyclops will catch the escapers and touched by his affectionate words to the ram. Choices between competing versions had to be made, and were, usually with good results.

The episode of Circe, which reads very easily, contains traces of competing versions. She is a witch, daughter of the sun, who lives in a stone palace among woods on an otherwise uninhabited island. This is common form, and suggests her dangerous character. In such stories the adventurer is guided to her by some chance, and behind the story in the *Odyssey* we may discern a stag who did the guiding. Odysseus meets such a stag but kills it and with some effort carries it to his companions for their supper (10.156 ff.). Then having seen the palace, he decides to send a party to investigate. He does not go himself or take the lead, but divides his crew into two companies, one of which is chosen by lot to go. This procedure creates suspense and leaves Odysseus free to take action later and remedy the evils that have befallen the first party. This party finds wolves and lions which greet it in a friendly way, and are in fact men transformed by Circe. But this is their only appearance. When the companions are turned back into men from swine, nothing is said about these earlier victims. Their function is to reveal something sinister in Circe's dwelling, and when they have done that, they are forgotten. When Odysseus' companions are turned into swine, we are expressly told that they keep their wits as before (10.240), and this is not usual in this kind of theme, where the witch tends to instil forgetfulness of former lives. We may guess why Homer does what he does. He has already dealt with the theme of forgetfulness in telling of the Lotus-eaters, who forget all about their return home (9.94-7), and the theme is not suitable for repetition. Finally, on his way to Circe Odysseus meets Hermes, who tells him of the danger ahead and gives him a plant, *moly,* to protect him from Circe's spells. The plant is carefully described, and then we hear no more. We do not know how Odysseus uses it, or how it works; what we do know is that Circe's spells have no effect on him. In these ways Homer keeps the episode of Circe simple and circumvents obstacles in the tradition.

In the passage of years a traditional theme may assume new shapes, which are so different that they are really new tales. The *Odyssey* deals twice with the ancient theme of the witch who detains the hero on his return by making him live with her. She need not be malevolent but she hinders his desire to go home. In the *Odyssey* she appears in two quite different forms, as Circe and Calypso. If Circe, who has a ruthless, cruel side, is the Hawk, Calypso is the Concealer, who keeps Odysseus hidden on Ogygia for eight years. Both live alone on remote islands, in circumstances of some beauty. Yet, allowing for this degree of likeness, the differences are great. Circe is subdued by the superior cunning and courage of Odysseus, and after admitting her defeat, welcomes him as her lover; Calypso saves him from the sea after shipwreck and her devotion to him is complete. Circe keeps Odysseus for a year and then releases him without complaint; Calypso keeps him for eight years, hoping to make him immortal but is told by the gods to give him up, which she does unhappily but graciously. Circe at the start has a sinister glamour; there is nothing sinister in Calypso. The two are distinct and distinguishable, but we can see why both are needed. The adventure with Circe is exciting for its own sake and entirely appropriate to the hero on his wanderings; the sojourn with Calypso has much charm and beauty but lacks dramatic variety. It is needed to fill a gap in the story. After his ten years of war at Troy Odysseus is away from home for another ten years before he returns to Ithaca. By the time of his shipwreck and the loss of all his companions only ten years have passed, and the remaining eight have to be accounted for. Homer does this by confining him to Calypso's island, where nothing can be heard of him and his fate remains a mystery to his family and his friends, and is almost forgotten by the gods.

Circe begins as a malevolent witch, but once Odysseus has subdued her, she becomes his helper and shows no signs of her sinister past. She then takes up another part which may belong to her original character—she foretells the future and gives advice about it. That heroes should have this happen is common enough, but Homer seems to have been faced by two traditional characters who prophesy. Circe is one, but she insists that Odysseus should consult the other—the ghost of the seer Tiresias. This is a very ancient theme and bears some resemblance to *Gilgamesh,* where the hero crosses the waters of death to consult Uta-Napishtim. Odysseus sails to the edge of the world and calls up the ghost of Tiresias, who says very little about the immediate future, except in warning him not to eat the cattle of the Sun in Thrinacia (11.104 ff.), but gives him a precise forecast of his last days and quiet ending (11.121 ff.), with advice on the ritual that will appease Poseidon. We may perhaps assume that in earlier versions Tiresias said more than this, and that his warning about the cattle is only part of a set of warnings and forecasts. But Homer transfers these to Circe. When

Odysseus comes back to her, she gives him a careful forecast of the dangers that lie before him (12.37-141). This device keeps Circe still powerful, even if she has reformed her habits, but at the cost of a lengthy prevision of what will come soon afterwards. It all happens according to plan, but lacks the element of surprise.

In Books 13-24 we are back in Ithaca and a familiar world. Yet here too the main actions are derived largely from folk-tale, and old themes exploited with novelty. At some point the Wanderer must be recognized. No doubt there were many versions of this, and the recognition need not all come at once. Homer moves through a series of recognitions, each separate and distinct, and each marking a step forward. The first is when Odysseus, transformed into a shrunken old beggar is for a short time given back his old shape and reveals himself to Telemachus (16.166 ff.). Athene makes it possible, and to that degree it is supernatural. What matters is that Odysseus must not start on his vengeance entirely alone, and his obvious companion is his son, who stays with him for the rest of the poem. The second recognition is a stroke of genius. When Odysseus arrives at his palace, he sees lying in his midden outside the gates his dog Argos, whom he trained twenty years before. The dog is neglected and full of ticks, but he wags his tail and drops his ears and struggles towards his old master (17.291-304). Odysseus knows him at once and says a few words about him, and then the dog dies 'having seen Odysseus again in the twentieth year' (17.327). This recognition is based on affection and loyalty and conveys swiftly and surely how Odysseus belongs to Ithaca and how deep his roots there are. The third comes when Odysseus has his feet washed by his old nurse, Euryclea. It is dark, and Penelope is sitting in the shadow not far away. The nurse recognizes a scar which Odysseus got long ago on a boar-hunt, and is on the point of crying out, when the basin of water is upset and Odysseus puts his hand on her throat and enjoins her silence (19.386 ff.). This is the most dramatic of the recognitions, and the one in which the scar, used twice elsewhere, really creates a situation. Through it the recognition by Penelope is postponed until it can be most effective. In the fourth recognition, during the fight in the hall, Odysseus reveals himself to Eumaeus, who accepts his word and, like the nurse, recognizes the scar, but without any exciting reaction (21.207 ff.). Fifth is the recognition by Penelope, and this is the most unexpected. The signs that have satisfied others do not satisfy her, and she tries to test the stranger by telling Euryclea to make a bed, but the stranger knows that Penelope and he have their own special, secret bed made out of an olive-trunk in the heart of the palace. This is highly appropriate, as Odysseus and Penelope are man and wife and the bed is an intimate sign of it. Finally, Odysseus goes off to see his old father Laertes in the country and identifies himself first by the scar (24.331 ff.) and then by knowing the details of Laertes' orchard which he helped to plant. All these recognitions have a certain simplicity. If the scar does the most work, that is perhaps because it comes from the oldest tradition, while the dog Argos, who needs no sign, looks as if he were Homer's own invention. The accumulation of six recognitions suggests that there were many variants in the tradition, and that Homer gave a subordinate purpose to some which might have been of primary importance in earlier versions.

Somewhat different from the recognitions are two events which do not reveal the identity of the Wanderer but show that he is someone remarkable. These are the stringing of the great bow which Odysseus left behind when he went to Troy (21.39), and the exhibition-shot with it through a line of axes planted in the ground. It is conceivable that in earlier versions the two events were alternative and that either of them would suffice to prove who Odysseus is. Nor must we assume that, once the bow had been strung, the slaughter of the Suitors followed immediately. The *Odyssey* finds its climax in the combination of these events, but it is possible that originally neither event served just this purpose. The stringing of the bow may have been no more than a test of the Wanderer's identity, proposed by his wife, who is still not sure of him. So the exhibition-shot may have come from some other context, as when the Suitors compete for marriage with Penelope, and even then Odysseus need not take a part. In its present place it establishes his preeminence, and leaves him with the bow in his hands as an instrument for vengeance.

When a story belongs to a cycle centred on some main point, it may not fit in easily with others in a like position. Tradition is aware of its place, and the poet may feel that he owes it some attention, but it may lead to difficulties and to some awkwardness in his main scheme. This is the case, in the *Odyssey,* with the shroud which Penelope claims to be weaving for Laertes when he dies. She tells the Suitors that when it is finished, she will make her choice among them, but every night she undoes the work of the day, until a point comes when the Suitors catch her at it and know that she is deceiving them (2.85-110). We can see the story behind this. The shroud is a device to put off a decision as long as possible, and as such Penelope reports it to the unrecognized Odysseus (19.136 ff.). The theme is not in itself very conclusive, and the discovery of Penelope's trickery by the Suitors does not force the issue of her marriage as we might expect. There was moreover a different version, which appears when the ghost of Amphimedon says that when Penelope finished the shroud, 'in that hour an evil spirit brought Odysseus from somewhere to the border of the land' (24.146-50). This comes from the suspicious conclusion of the *Odyssey,* but its author uses good and independent material; for this is just what the trick of the shroud should have done. Homer must have known it and rejected it for his own less emphatic version because he did not wish Penelope's marriage to be confused with the return of Odysseus, and because he wished this return to be both prolonged and secret.

Another slightly inconclusive theme is that of the seer Theoclymenus. When Telemachus is about to sail from Pylos, Theoclymenus suddenly appears and asks for protection, since he is guilty of murder. Telemachus takes him on board (15.256-81). On arriving in Ithaca Theoclymenus asks where he is to stay, and Telemachus, rather strangely, says with Eurymachus, who is one of the Suitors and a prominent enemy. This conveys the depressed and defeated mood of Telemachus. At this point a hawk flies overhead carrying a dove, and Theoclymenus interprets this as an omen of success, with the result that Telemachus changes his mind and gives other orders for the reception of Theoclymenus (15.525 ff.). Later, at the palace, Theoclymenus meets Penelope and tells her with full assurance that Odysseus is already in his own country and plotting evil for the Suitors (17.152-61). As a seer he knows this from the omen of the hawk and the dove. Finally, when the doom of the Suitors is near and one of them has just thrown an ox's foot at Odysseus, they are seized with a frenzy of madness, and Theoclymenus in ringing tones foresees their doom (20.345-57). It is an apocalyptic moment, but it is the last for Theoclymenus. He has done his task, which is to forecast events by augury and vision, but we suspect that in some other version he must have done more, that he may have played a more prominent part in letting Penelope know of her husband's presence or in driving the Suitors to their destruction. The element of the supernatural which he represents adds something to the story but is not fully exploited.

In these loose ends and imperfectly exploited themes we can see traces of the different variants which Homer must have known and from which he had to make his selection. But this is not the problem with the end of the *Odyssey* from 23.297 to 24.548. Here there are indeed unexpected contradictions, and there is perhaps an explanation of them. The two great Alexandrian scholars, Aristarchus and Aristophanes, regarded 23.296, 'Then they came gladly to the place of their old bed', as the 'end' or the 'limit' of the *Odyssey*. We do not know why they thought this. They may conceivably have had external evidence that some good manuscripts ended at this point, or they may have made their decision on the strength of anomalies of language and narrative after this point. We cannot dismiss their view, nor can we deny that in some ways the 'continuation' differs in some ways from the rest of the poem, not merely in linguistic solecisms but in actual episodes, like Penelope's web. It is unlikely that the main

poet of the *Odyssey* composed this part, but that does not deprive it of all significance. At least it shows how the Homeric manner persisted with adaptations, and how someone felt that the end of the *Odyssey* called for some sort of epilogue.

The *Odyssey* might, in our view, have had a perfectly satisfactory end when Odysseus and Penelope go to bed at 23.296. But someone must have felt that more should be said, and we may ask what advantages, if any, were gained by adding the last passages. Odysseus gives Penelope an account of his adventures, tactfully omitting his infidelities. The audience hardly needs this, and we could assume that Penelope will get the story sooner or later. The appearance of the Suitors in Hades indicates their inferiority to the men of Troy, but not much is made of this, and what is stressed is the comparison between Clytaemnestra and Penelope, which the audience might make for itself. On the other hand the recognition of Odysseus by Laertes has a quiet charm and shows Odysseus in a playful, teasing mood. It is family poetry, and there is something to be said for making Odysseus meet his father after he has met his son and his wife. Moreover the fight between the supporters of Odysseus and the kinsmen of the Suitors indicates that the slaying was not as final as it seemed, and it may have provided a start for new adventures in which Odysseus leaves Ithaca, as he seems to have done in the *Telegony*. The continuation serves no clear single purpose, but suggests a poet who would like to prolong the story in various ways for different reasons. He may have used old material, at least in Penelope's web, and he has a gift for quiet narrative in the scene with Laertes. Otherwise we miss the swing and the strength of the main poem.

The sources of the *Odyssey* are different from those of the *Iliad* and the difference explains some of its character. If it deals with marvels and monsters, so to a smaller extent does the *Iliad*. In both poems gods interfere with the course of nature. When Aphrodite spirits Paris away from the battlefield (iii 380) or protects Aeneas (v. 315-17), it is not very different from when Athene covers Odysseus with a mist in Phaeacia (7.15) or changes his appearance to prevent him being recognized (13.430-3). Though the *Iliad* contains the remarkable scene when the horse of Achilles speaks to him, it is because Hera has for this one occasion given it a human voice (xix 407 ff.), and this is well within the power of the gods. The *Odyssey* differs when its marvels are not caused by the gods but belong to the world of legend. The wind-bag of Aeolus, the transformations of Circe, the summoning of ghosts at the end of the world, the monstrosity of Scylla, are outside human experience and do not belong to the strictly heroic world of the *Iliad*. In face of them Odysseus conducts himself heroically, as when he insists on hearing the Sirens' song but forestalls disaster by getting himself lashed to the mast (12.178-9). But the monsters which he has to face are outside both human and heroic experience.

Homer evidently saw this and tried to bring his monsters as near as possible to humanity, to relate them to it, and even in some degree to humanize them. This is certainly the case with the Cyclops, who despite his single eye, his bulk 'like a wooded peak of tall mountains' (9.190-2), and his cannibalistic gluttony, is made real by his pastoral life, by his care for his flocks, by his affection for his ram. He is hideous and horrible, but not outside comprehension. Comparable in some respects to him is the queen of the Laestrygonians. She lives in a rocky fjord, and all looks easy until the scouts of Odysseus entering her palace, 'saw a woman as big as a mountain-peak, and they hated her' (10.113). She grabs one of them and plans to make her supper of him. She is of the same loathsome breed as the Cyclops, but since he has recently received full treatment, she is deftly conveyed in a short sketch. The Sirens, despite their gift of song which lures men to death and the bones of decaying bodies round them (12.45-6), are careful to do no more than invite Odysseus to listen to them on the latest subjects of song (12.184-92). The exception to this realism is Scylla, who is a monster among monsters, aptly and fully described, with her twelve feet, her six necks, each with a head and three rows of teeth (12.89-91); she seizes six men from the ship of Odysseus and eats them while they are still crying for help and stretching out their hands, so that Odysseus comments:

> That was the most piteous thing that I saw with my eyes of all that I suffered searching out the ways of the sea. (12.258-9)

Scylla must be descended from tales of sea-monsters, of giant krakens and man-slaying cuttle-fish, and perhaps because she has some basis in fact Homer feels that he must describe her exactly. She is far from ordinary, and yet one small touch brings her into the compass of living things—her voice is like that of a puppy (12.86). It is quite unexpected and almost absurd, and it is just this that brings it home. The monsters of the *Odyssey* are clearly visualized. Their horror comes not from vagueness but from clearly imagined actions and the menace of a horrible death which they offer. The only approximation to them in the *Iliad* is the Chimaera:

> It was a divine creature, not of human race, in front a lion, in the rear a snake, and in the middle a goat, and it breathed the terrible strength of flaming fire. (vi 180-2)

Description is reduced to the barest essentials, but the Chimaera emerges clearly. This is the Homeric way of looking at monsters, and it is fully developed in the *Odyssey*. It is quite different from the shapeless horrors which the long northern night gives to its dragons.

This controlling realism informs most parts of the *Odyssey* and gives much of its special flavour. It accounts for a certain quiet poetry which is not very noticeable in the *Iliad,* but makes the *Odyssey* friendly and familiar. It finds poetry in quite unassuming and humble subjects, as when Telemachus goes to bed and Euryclea folds his clothes and hangs them on a peg (1.439-40), or his ship sets out in the evening and the wind fills the sail and the dark waves resound about the stern (2.427-9). Life in the palace, despite the disruption caused by the Suitors, follows a routine, and there is a quiet dignity in the reception of guests, the laying out of tables, the scrubbing of them with sponges. In making his raft Odysseus shows a high technical accomplishment, and the mere making has its own interest. It was this that Racine admired so greatly [in *Oeuvres complètes,* ed. pléiade, II], when he compared its language with Latin:

> Calypso lui donne encore un vilebrequin et des clous, tant Homère est exact à décrire les moindres particularités, ce qui a bonne grace dans le grec, au lieu que le latin est beaucoup plus réservé, et ne s'amuse pas à de si petites choses.

Yet, though the Homeric language can say anything that it likes and not lose its force, that is because the poetical vision for which it works is so direct and straightforward. It finds interest and charm everywhere, and is happy to say so.

The same kind of realism can be seen in the characters. We have marked how Odysseus is developed from his old self in the *Iliad,* but he is the only character of any complexity, and that is because legend insisted upon a more than common personality. The others go their own way, and make their individual mark. At the start Telemachus is only a boy, and conscious of it. But he wishes to assert himself, even though he lacks the authority and the experience to do so. His voyage to Pylos makes a man of him. On it he settles his own decisions, and, when he comes back to Ithaca, he is ready for action, and follows and helps his father. Penelope presents rather a special problem. Legend marked her as prudent, and she has kept the Suitors off for ten years, not merely by the stratagem of the web but by other postponements and evasions. Despite long hours of tearful lamentation for her lost husband she keeps her courage, and her sudden appearances among the Suitors reduce them to momentary acquiescence, which cannot all be ascribed to good manners. Her prudence makes her suspicious, and that is why she is so slow to recognize Odysseus as her husband. She and Telemachus are supported by the swineherd Eumaeus and the old nurse Euryclea, and though the first claim of these is their unswerving loyalty to their master, they display an innate nobility in their response to the demands made of them. The party of Odysseus on Ithaca is homogeneous in that it is held together by loyalty to him and hatred of the Suitors. It contains no very powerful personality except the great man himself, but its members are sufficiently distinctive to set him in a full perspective.

The Suitors are beyond dispute deplorable, not in the plebeian way of Thersites but as a degenerate corruption of heroes. They have a high opinion of themselves and no scruples about getting what they want. Antinous differs from Eurymachus only in being more outspokenly brutal. The others conform to type, except perhaps Amphinomus, who has some relics of decency but does not escape death because of them (22.89-94). Their deaths are deserved, as are those of the household of Odysseus who follow them. The beggar Irus, the goatherd Melanthius, the serving-woman Melantho, begin by insulting the unrecognized Odysseus and come to suitable ends. In the Suitors it is hard not to see an embodiment of a heroic society in decay. This is the generation that did not fight at Troy, and their lack of heroic qualities fits the relatively unheroic temper of the *Odyssey*. It makes little attempt to maintain the lofty level of the *Iliad,* and the hero who holds it together is never matched by anyone of his own calibre. Even Alcinous, despite his wealth and kingly condescension, is not heroic, and some of his court, notably Laodamas and Euryalus, lack proper courtesy (8.132 ff.). This lower tone comes partly from the material of the *Odyssey,* which is concerned not with heroic prowess in war but with wild adventures and a cunning vengeance. It is significant that, when Odysseus kills the Suitors, he has every advantage over them, and though this is due to his foresight, it is not the way in which Achilles would take on an enemy.

In the *Iliad* the intermittent interventions of the gods and the frivolity of some of their actions provide a contrast to the dangers and destructiveness of heroic life; in the *Odyssey* such a contrast is not needed, and the gods are treated with a different intention. The nearest approximation to the spirit of the Deception of Zeus is the song of Demodocus about Ares and Aphrodite (8.266-366), but its purpose is to provide relief before Odysseus starts on the tale of his adventures, and incidentally to throw light on the Phaeacians, who, having no heroic obligations or challenges, are well served by this kind of song. Otherwise the *Odyssey* treats the gods less freely than the *Iliad* and in a more calculated way. They are concerned with human actions, and the council on Olympus, which decides to do something about Odysseus, keeps an eye on such wrongdoing as the behaviour of Aegisthus (1.32-41). Poseidon is entirely justified in

maintaining his wrath against Odysseus for blinding Polyphemus (1.20-1), which leads to his being wrecked on his raft, and incidentally to the ship of the Phaeacians, which takes him to Ithaca, being turned to stone (13.163-4). But apart from these special cases, the dominating part played by the gods in the *Odyssey* is the friendship between Athene and Odysseus. This recalls such occasions in the *Iliad* as when, in the panic after Agamemnon's false proposal to withdraw from Troy, Athene sets Odysseus to restore order (ii 173-82) or on night-operations keeps an eye on him (x 245, 277, 482, 497). In the *Odyssey* she is seldom far away. Both on Phaeacia and in Ithaca she is a constant helper and gives Odysseus advice and practical assistance, while in the intervals she instils confidence into his son. She even takes part in the slaughter of the Suitors by deflecting weapons aimed at Odysseus (22.256, 273) and frightening the Suitors by flashing her aegis from the roof (22.297-8). Her character as a virgin-goddess makes it impossible for her to be in love with Odysseus but she holds him in great affection and admiration. They treat each other on equal terms, as when she praises him for his cunning (13.291 ff.), or he recalls her kindness to him at Troy (13.314). The Homeric poems have no parallel to so close a companionship between a goddess and a mortal, and though later Greek literature occasionally allows such friendships, it makes much less of them than Homer does of this. It enhances the position of Odysseus as a heroic survivor in an unheroic world. A man of this quality deserves the affection and the support of the gods. . . .

Denys Page (lecture date 1972)

SOURCE: "The Lotus-Eaters," in *Folktales in Homer's "Odyssey,"* Cambridge, Mass.: Harvard University Press, 1973, pp. 3-21.

[*Page is a classics scholar and the author of the highly regarded* Sappho and Alcaeus *(1955). In the following excerpt from a lecture delivered in 1972, he speculates on the historical basis of the tale of the Lotus-Eaters.*]

Odyssey 9.80-104: Odysseus and his companions set sail from the coast of Thrace. Their course lay down the east coast of the Peloponnese, round its southern promontories, and up the west coast to Ithaca:

> But as I was doubling Cape Malea, the waves and current and northwind drove me off course and drifted me away from Cythera. From there, for nine days I was swept over the fishy sea by ruinous winds; and on the tenth we landed in the country of the Lotus-Eaters, who live on a food of flowers. There we set foot on the mainland and drew water, and my companions quickly took their dinner beside the swift ships. When we had tasted of food

and drink, I sent some of my company to inquire what sort of men ate their bread in the country. I chose two men, and gave them a third for company as spokesman. So they went and very soon were in the midst of men who were Lotus-Eaters. Now the Lotus-Eaters did not plan to kill my companions, but gave them lotus to taste. And when anyone of them ate the honeysweet fruit of the lotus, he no longer wished to bring a message back, or to return, but wanted to stay there and feed on lotus among the Lotus-Eaters, and to forget about going home. I myself brought them weeping to the ships by force, and dragged them under the rowing-benches and tied them up in the hollow ships. And I commanded my other trusty companions to make haste and embark in the swift ships, fearing that someone else might eat of the lotus and forget about going home. They quickly embarked and sat on the benches, and sitting in order smote the gray water with their oars.

Here is very little said about the Lotus-Eaters. They ate lotus; they meant you no harm; they gave you lotus to eat, and you wanted to stay with them for ever. That is all: and for the rest of time nobody has ever known anything more about the Lotus-Eaters. For hundreds of years geographers argued about their location, botanists debated what sort of lotus they ate. But if we look for other facts about them, we must wait almost a thousand years from the time of Herodotus, when Stephanus of Byzantium will publish his great geographical dictionary. There . . . we read a cryptic notice: the Germara are 'a Celtic people, who do not see the sunlight; as Aristotle says in his book *On Wonderful Things,* "the Lotus-Eaters sleep for six months"'. This is the only new thing ever said about the Lotus-Eaters; it is plainly fiction, and the alleged authority is bogus. Aristotle was not the author of the book *On Wonderful Things to Hear* . . . , nor in fact does that collection of improbabilities say anything about Lotus-Eaters, asleep or waking.

There is nothing particularly surprising in the fact that the *Odyssey* contains the only information about the Lotus-Eaters that was ever known to any post-Homeric Greek. What I find surprising is the fact that this episode, which has a certain charm, made no impact on the imagination of the poetical and romantic writers of Greece and Rome. Nor is it represented in Greek or Roman art. There is nothing but brief allusion, and even that is rare. Not counting geographers and botanists, I reckon about a dozen brief allusions in Greek from Xenophon to Palladas, not so many in Latin from Cicero to Ammianus. Only from the dismal soul of the mythographer Hyginus, in the second century A.D., was wrung a rare cry. Dullest of mortals, he has the unique distinction, among the ancients, of being emotionally aroused when he contemplates the Lotus-Eaters: *Lotophagos,* he cries, *homines minime malos*; 'they were really very good

people'. This is not much, but it is something; it is an ember aglow in the ash-heap. Warm your hands while you may, for it will be long enough before you find another.

From the eighth century B.C. up to the year A.D. 1832 the Lotus-Eaters lived only in the *Odyssey*. Then the heart of Lord Tennyson was moved by these lines of Homer, and he published *The Lotos-Eaters,* a poem which has the atmosphere of a steamy hot-house over-filled with exotic odorous blooms; some very beautiful, some drooping and faded, but altogether heavy-scented and enervating.

Odysseus and his companions reach the land of the Lotus-Eaters:

> In the afternoon they came unto a land
> In which it seemed always afternoon. . . .
> A land where all things always seemed the same;
> And round about the keel with faces pale,
> Dark faces pale against that rosy flame,
> The mild-eyed melancholy Lotos-Eaters came.
> Branches they bore of that enchanted stem,
> Laden with flower and fruit, whereof they gave
> To each, but those who did receive of them,
> And taste, to him the gushing of the wave
> Far, far away did seem to mourn and rave
> On alien shores; and if his fellow spake,
> His voice was thin, as voices from the grave;
> And deep-asleep he seemed, yet all awake,
> And music in his ears his beating heart did make.
> They sat them down upon the yellow sand
> Between the sun and moon upon the shore;
> And sweet it was to dream of Fatherland,
> Of child, and wife, and slave; but evermore
> Most weary seem'd the sea, weary the oar,
> Weary the wandering fields of barren foam.
> Then some one said, 'We will return no more';
> And all at once they sang, 'Our island home
> Is far beyond the wave; we will no longer roam'.

No such romantic note is struck by the ancients. They have no interest in the Lotus-Eaters, except to inquire just where they lived and what they ate.

Locating the Lotus-Eaters has been for many the pastime of idle hours, from Herodotus to the present day. Herodotus placed them in Tripolitania, as western neighbours of the Gindánes, whose women (he says) wear many ankle-bracelets of leather, one for each lover; and the woman with the greatest number of anklets is thought to be the best woman, as being the most loved. Now (he continues) 'there is a headland jutting out to sea from the land of these Gindánes. It is inhabited by Lotus-Eaters, who live by eating nothing but the fruit of the lotus. The fruit of the lotus is the size of the mastichberry, similar in sweetness to the fruit of the date-palm. The Lotus-Eaters make wine of it too'.

The geographical position is clear enough, because the eastern neighbours of the Lotus-Eaters, the Machlyes, are bounded on the west by an identifiable feature, Lake Tritonis. So the Lotus-Eaters lived (roughly speaking) on the North African coast facing *Syrtis Minor*.

I shall not repeat the variations on this theme composed by later geographers. There is a choice between various points on, and islands off, the coast of North Africa from Morocco to Cyrene. Or you might find Lotus-Eaters in Sicily, at Acragas or Camarina. Nor were they wanting in Illyria or Scythia or somewhere beyond the Straits of Gibraltar. Nothing in all this has anything to do with the Homeric Lotus-Eaters. Nobody ever knew anything about them not already known to Herodotus; and he knew nothing.

His process of thought is transparent: the Lotus-Eaters of Homer are assumed to be a living nation; Homer says that Odysseus could not weather the southeastern cape of the Peloponnese and was driven by storm-winds for nine days over the sea; where will he land, if not in North Africa? Now by happy chance we have a tale about a tribe on the coast of Tripolitania living on the fruit of a shrub or tree; let us call the shrub 'lotus', and our work is done. True, a wind which prevents you from rounding Cape Malea is not the one to carry you west of Tripoli; true also that the shrub or tree—*Jujúba, Zizyphus*—of which the tribe eats the fruit has nothing whatsoever to do with any of the plants called lotus; true, finally, that the result of our researches is disenchanting, for it is not more remarkable that an African tribe should eat these berries than that Greeks should eat olives. There is not, however, time to raise objections. We are quickly diverted to new and much greater marvels—the tale of the Atlantes, who have no dreams; of the land where donkeys never drink; of men whose eyes are in their chests, for they have no heads.

Herodotus is not always to be believed, but he is enchanting; wearisome are most of his followers. Nor are modern speculations more rewarding, though occasionally more risible: have not the Lotus-Eaters lately been made real and relevant, a colony of drop-outs living on drugs, *bhang* possibly, or *hashish*?

Enough of all this pseudo-geography. The Lotus-Eaters of Homer have no home in the real world. They are as fanciful as the Cyclops or Circe. We might say simply, they are figures of folktale; but it is not quite

so easy. We have first to ask a question or two.

From Homer's brief story we learnt very little, and were left wondering. What sort of creatures were the Lotus-Eaters? Why did they eat lotus, of all flowers? Did they know what effect their diet would have upon the stranger? Were they perhaps waiting for a victim? They had not in mind (says Odysseus) the killing of his companions; what then did they have in mind? In a folktale, it is very unlikely that the hosts will allow their guests to be taken away, as Odysseus takes them, after they have eaten the magical food. We suspect that these Lotus-Eaters are not ordinary men: creatures of fairyland, perhaps; but whether kindly or malignant? Surely they have a story of their own.

We shall have to look in universal folklore to see if we can identify the tale which Homer has in mind. But, first, there is a curious matter to be perpended. *Lotophagos* means 'eater of lotus'; and it is a fair question to ask, why *lotus*? Of all plants in the world, why has the Homeric story chosen the lotus for the diet of our mild-eyed melancholy friends? Now it happens that there were regions of the world where a flower called 'lotus' was in fact the common food of people; and it is worthwhile to consider what those regions were, and what is meant by 'lotus' in this context.

The name 'lotus' was applied by the ancients indifferently to a number of quite different families of plants, notably (1) the true lotus, of which more in a moment; (2) the shrub or tree *Zizyphus, Jujúba*, whose berries were eaten by tribes in North Africa; (3) trefoils, clovers, and melilots. Of these, I leave *Jujúba* and the clovers out of account. The *Jujúba*, which belongs to the family *Rhamnaceae*, owes its inclusion in the list of lotuses solely to the determination of ancient geographers and botanists to find a living tribe which they might identify with the Homeric Lotus-Eaters. The trefoils, clovers, and melilots, which belong to the family *Leguminosae*, have always and rightly been regarded as irrelevant: the spellbinding delicacy of the Lotus-Eaters was certainly not to be identified with this common cattle-fodder.

The lotus which men really ate was what I have called the true lotus, of which there are two varieties to be considered: (1) *Nelumbo*, the Indian lotus, and (2) *Nymphaea*, the Egyptian lotus, both of the family *Nymphaeaceae*.

Begin, O Muse, the tale of *Nelumbo* and *Nymphaea*, from the point where the Sanskrit poems of ancient India leave off. It is necessary to say enough to establish two facts: First, that there were (and are) two kinds of edible lotus, one Indian and one Egyptian; for India and Egypt are places from which the knowledge of the edible lotus could have been transmitted to Homer through poetry or folklore. Secondly, that the Indian lotus could not have been known to Homer except through continuous tradition from the remote period when the Indo-European peoples had not yet divided into Indians and Europeans.

So first, *Nelumbo*. This is the Indian lotus, a beautiful flower, both holy and useful. [W. H. Goodyear, in *The Grammar of the Lotus,* says,] 'When Buddha was born, a lotus bloomed where he first touched the ground; he stepped seven steps northward, and a lotus marked each footfall'. Its seeds, which are 'the size of filberts', were, as they still are, a common food. *Nymphaea* is the Egyptian lotus, associated in cult with Isis, Osiris, and Horus. Its seeds are edible; they are small grains, like poppy-seeds. The two plants are alike in being aquatic, with edible seeds; in other respects there is very little resemblance between them. *Nelumbo* is rosy; its leaves are raised high above the water by cylindrical petioles. *Nymphaea* is white or blue; its leaves lie more or less flat on the water. There are differences in the number, shape, and arrangement of the sepals, in the shape and appearance of the petals, in the shape of the leaves, and in the size and structure of the seedpods and their fruits.

Herodotus describes both flowers quite accurately, first *Nymphaea* as follows: 'When the river is full and inundates the plains, many lilies, which the Egyptians call "lotus", grow in the water. They pluck these and dry them in the sun, then they crush the poppy-like centre of the lotus and make loaves of it baked over the fire. The root of this lotus is edible too, and fairly sweet; it is round, about the size of an apple'. So much for *Nymphaea*; now he describes *Nelumbo*: 'There are other lilies, which look like roses, growing in the river too. The fruit of these grows in a separate calyx growing at the side from the root, shaped very like a wasp's nest. Within this are numerous edible seeds, as big as olivestones. They are eaten both soft and dried'. The account in Theophrastus is similar, but with much additional detail, keenly observed and accurately described. Modern descriptions of *Nelumbo* and *Nymphaea* correct the ancient in a few details only; they add that *Nelumbo* has been a common food in our own times.

Now it is as certain as such things can be that the Indian lotus, *Nelumbo,* well-known to Herodotus, was in his day a recent immigrant from the East. It was not familiar to the Egyptians till the later years of the sixth century B.C. The eating of *Nelumbo* could not have been known to Homer, unless the knowledge had been transmitted through saga or folklore from the remote 'Indo-European' period, a couple of thousand years before the **Odyssey**.

There is much more that might be said about *Nelumbo* and *Nymphaea*; but we already have what we need. We asked, why eaters of lotus, of all flowers in the world? And we have found that the lotus is a flower of which the seeds were in fact a common food, in India and in Egypt. Homer's tale is plainly fiction; but it is fiction blended with dimly remembered fact.

I call it dimly remembered, because the lotus would not have been chosen by Homer if its true nature had not been forgotten. What Homer needed was a mysterious flower with fruits of magical quality; but the flower of which he tells was one of the commonest, in India and in Egypt, and its fruits were the normal food of the masses. This truth must have been long forgotten by Homer's time. In the Dark Age of Greece, from the fall of the Mycenaean kings down to the eighth century B.C., nothing whatsoever was known about India except the little that had survived in saga and folklore from the very remote past. Nor was anything known about Egypt, except scraps of information (and not many of them) preserved from the Mycenaean period mainly in the tradition of epic verse. But there will have been, at some early period, a traveller's tale of remote regions of the world full of great wonders, such as a tribe of men who lived on flowers which they called 'lotus'. After the lapse of hundreds of years, all contact with reality is lost. Nothing is remembered except that there was an old story about people called 'lotus-eaters'. They were once a traveller's tale, and a true one. Now they no longer have a home in the real world; and we no longer know (or care) what sort of flower this 'lotus' is. If it be asked whether India or Egypt is likelier to be the source of the tale about eaters of lotus, the best evidence may be the fact (if it is one) that 'lotus' is a word of Semitic origin. If the Homeric lotus reflects the Indian *Nelumbo*—a plant unknown to the Western world until long after Homer's time—I do not understand how the flower could be known to Homer by a Semitic name. So I suppose that Egyptian *Nymphaea* was the diet of the real and remote ancestors of the fictitious Lotus-Eaters of the **Odyssey**. The Mycenaeans traded with Egypt for two or three hundred years; their products are found as far up the Nile as Assouan. Traders returned home with much to tell; and among their tales was this, that people in Egypt lived on a flower which they called 'lotus'.

By Homer's time the Lotus-Eaters have degenerated into figures of folktale. At least that is what they seem to be, in the **Odyssey**. But have they any history as such? The essence of the episode is this: that creatures, whether human or not, living in a remote place, offer food to the traveller; who, if he eats it, loses the desire or the power to return home, and will stay with his hosts forever. Is this a common folktale, like the stories of the Cyclops and Circe?

The answer is that, in one special connexion, it is as common a story as you may find. The special connexion is with the underworld, the abode of the dead. The traveller who visits the underworld may be sure of his return, provided that he refuses food or drink offered by his ghostly entertainers; if he partakes, he must stay there forever.

Thus in the Homeric *Hymn to Demeter,* Persephone has good hope of returning from the underworld to the earth above; but Hades, with a sinister smile and furtive glances round, gave her honeysweet seeds of pomegranate to eat before she left him. She ate them; and not even Zeus could then do more than compromise, granting her eight months of the year on earth and four in the underworld. . . .

The essence of this very widespread story is that a person, whether living or dead, cannot enter the world of the dead unless he first eats their food, and cannot return from that world if he does eat it. Now there is not the faintest indication in the *Odyssey* that Odysseus has arrived at the threshold of the underworld, or that the Lotus-Eaters are ghosts or demons beyond the grave. Let us therefore briefly consider something else which they might be; for this motif, though specially common in connexion with visits to the world of the dead, is not wholly restricted to that connexion. It is applied (in various forms) also to the world of fairies, goblins, gnomes, giants, and other such daydream and nightmare figures of folklore. . . .

So the Lotus-Eaters might be either ghosts in the underworld or goblins in fairyland; and it is characteristic of our poet that he should portray them as neither the one thing nor the other. Homer takes the motif from folktale and transplants it into a quite different soil. He is, as usual, at pains to suppress, or at least to minimize, the unreal elements in the folktales from which he freely borrows. He makes the scene lifelike and credible. His travellers are ordinary persons on their way home, driven by storm-winds to a distant but not supernatural place; they are not visitors to the underworld or adventurers on the border of fairyland. And the Lotus-Eaters seem quite normal people, except for their peculiar diet. They seem unaware of the effect which their food will have on the strangers. They mean no great harm (we are told); and certainly no great harm is done. Odysseus can take his companions away, none the worse; and the Lotus-Eaters offer no resistance. This characteristic of Homeric art, the adaptation of common folktale motifs to realistic settings, is to be observed throughout the *Odyssey*; especially in the story of the return from Troy to Ithaca, but also elsewhere.

So much for this episode. We have lived an hour with the Lotus-Eaters and learnt a little of their history. They have their origin in a true but dimly remembered tale about men in Egypt who lived on lotus. Now to their lotus the poet ascribes a certain magical effect which

he takes from common folklore. But the magic is hardly done before it is undone. We—the audience of Homer—are in a real world, and we believe every word we are told. . . .

Lesky compares the structure of the *Odyssey* to that of the *Iliad* (1957-58):

The *Odyssey,* like the *Iliad,* has a very compressed time-scale: all the events occur within forty days. But this concentration is effected by very different means. In the *Iliad* the wrath theme forms a solid core round which all the other elements are ultimately wrapped. This is concentration in the truest sense: the way in which the fates of Achilles, Patroclus and Hector are bound up one with another and with the central wrath motif allows us to speak of a weaving together of several thematic strands in a manner that is not parallelled in the *Odyssey*. There the devices of composition are basically simpler, easier to grasp, and consequently more effective. A continuous narrative of events is broken up into sections and put together anew, without losing the continuity. Odysseus relates to the Phaeacians his adventures from the beginning until his landing on the island of Calypso. The poet is thus enabled to put much of the narrative into the first person. The first four books—the so-called *Telemachia*—can also be said to serve a useful end in the structure as a whole. Apart from the picture they give of the suitors and of Odysseus' character, the events in Ithaca make a kind of picture-frame around the wanderings related in the middle books.

Albin Lesky, in A History of Greek Literature, *translated by James Willis and Cornelius de Heer, Thomas Y. Crowell Company, 1966.*

Jasper Griffin (essay date 1980)

SOURCE: "Characterization," in *Homer on Life and Death,* Oxford at the Clarendon Press, 1980, pp. 50-80.

[*In the following essay, Griffin addresses the issue of inconsistent characterization in the* Odyssey, *contending that the complexity of the characters gives them "depth and significance."*]

Some people have inclined to deny the possibility of there being in the Homeric poems any consistent characterization at all. Old-fashioned analysts and modern oralists agree on this point. For the former, separate authorship of the different parts into which they resolved the poems made it hopeless to look for psychological consistency; for the latter, the rigorous constraints of the formulaic system must, it seems, prevent the singer from allowing his characters to speak or think differently from each other. Another question of principle arises: How far is it legitimate to read psychology into what happens in the poems, when this is not made explicit by the poet? The analyst Von der Mühll states [in *Kritisches Hypomnema Zur Ilias*] as an axiom that 'to depict characters, beyond the objective wording of the text, did not lie within the intentions or the powers of Homer', while the neo-analyst Kakridis insists [in *Festschrift W. Schadewaldt,* 1970], against those who supply psychological motivations for the actions of the poet's characters, that 'in poetry only what is recorded exists: nothing else.' From the point of view of oral composition, [G. S.] Kirk warns [*The Songs of Homer*] that 'the depiction of the heroic character is limited both by the technique and aims of oral poetry and by the simplicity of heroic virtues and vices', and when, despite these limitations, genuine characterization is still found, he thinks it right to express this in an extraordinarily guarded fashion: 'These characters achieve a complexity which has the appearance [*sic*] of being consistently developed as each poem progresses. Even so we must take care not to deduce too much about the methods and the scope of operation of the main poets . . .' It almost seems as though we become so scrupulous that in the end it seems fair to question not only what is not on the surface of the poems, but even what is.

. . . I hope to make three points, of a fairly general character, which together will prove helpful in considering this tangled question, and which also will show the poet at work conferring depth and significance upon his creation. First, characters in the poems can be different from each other; second, they can be seen to intend things which they do not explicitly reveal as their intention; third, they can be complex, in ways which are rather different in the two poems. . . .

[In the **Odyssey**,] Odysseus is entertained and loved by two goddesses, Calypso and Circe, and he has to detach himself from each of them and also to say farewell to Nausicaa. With the glamorous Circe Odysseus happily spends a year in pleasure, 'feasting on meat inexhaustible and sweet wine'. Eventually his crew urge on him that it is time to go, and he embraces her knees in supplication, begging her to let him depart: his men are melting his heart with their lamentations, when she is not there to see. At once she answers: 'Son of Laertes, sprung from Zeus, Odysseus of the many wiles, do not remain longer in my house against your will . . .' Forthwith she plans their departure.

Very different is the loving Calypso. For seven years Odysseus has been kept prisoner on her island, without means of escape; she wishes to marry him and make him immortal, but he will have none of it. Day after day he sits gazing out to sea and weeping. At last the

gods intervene and send Hermes to tell Calypso that she must let him go home. She pours out her feelings to Hermes in bitterness against the gods; then she finds Odysseus and tells him that he can go, if he will, 'for I shall send you off with all my heart.' The hero is naturally astonished, and she reassures him with a smile, saying 'My mind is righteous and my heart within me is not of iron; no, it is kindly.' The pair have a last interview, recorded with great delicacy and charm. She asks if he is really so anxious to see his wife, 'for whom you yearn every day', and suggests that she, as a goddess, must be far better-looking. The tactful Odysseus at once admits that Penelope is inferior in beauty but says, 'Yet even so I wish and long every day to come home . . .' Calypso never tells him why she lets him go, and Odysseus never knows; she claims the credit for her own soft heart, and in his presence only hints at her bitterness and the real reason when she says 'I shall send a favourable wind for you, so that you may reach your homeland in safety—if that is the will of the gods in heaven, who are stronger than I to devise and to carry out.' We see through these words her expression of the fact that, were it not for the gods, she would not be letting him go; but for Odysseus that meaning is lost.

Lastly, there is Nausicaa. The night before she meets Odysseus, she dreamt of getting married. When he appears, at first she does not find him impressive; but when he is bathed and glorified by Athena, she says to her maids, 'I wish that such a man might be called my husband, living here, and that he might be pleased to stay here!' She goes on to give a broad hint to Odysseus: 'If you come into town with me, malicious people will talk, saying "Who is this tall and handsome stranger with Nausicaa? Where did she find him? He will be her husband next."' And even her father seems to think the match an attractive one. But of course Odysseus is off home to his wife, and there is no place for Nausicaa. She does, however, manage to be in his way as he goes in to dinner and to have a last word with him. 'Farewell, stranger, and when you are in your homeland think sometimes of me and remember that to me first you owe the saving of your life.' Odysseus replies that if he returns home safely, 'There I shall honour you like a god all my days, for your rescued me, princess.' Three scenes of parting, each of them coloured by love, and all very different.

The situation of parting with a woman in love is an emotional and difficult one, which is calculated to bring out the real nature of both parties. It was to have a great future in literature. Virgil's Dido and the *Heroides* of Ovid are among its forms. The variants on the theme in the **Odyssey** show us three very different women: the hard-boiled Circe, to whom the affair has been one of pleasure which there is no point in trying to prolong; the young Nausicaa, with whom nothing is put into words and yet everything is there, in essence rather than in actuality; and the suffering Calypso, retaining her dignity as she loses her love. Each represents a type and offers a different relationship, to which the wandering hero might have abandoned himself, forgetting his wife and home. That he resists them all brings out his unconquerable resolution, the central fact of the *Odyssey*. But we observe also two other things: these women are inscrutable, and they are complex.

Before Odysseus met Circe, Hermes gave him a marvellous herb which would defend him against her magic. When her spell failed to work, Odysseus should attack her with drawn sword, as if intending to kill her; 'and she in fear will bid you come to her bed.' This duly happens. Circe tries and fails to turn the hero into a pig, recognizes him as Odysseus, whose coming had been often foretold, and says, 'Come now, sheathe your sword, and then let us go to our bed, so that we may have union in love and sleep together, and trust each other.' This is not the behaviour of a fully human person. The immediate transition from hostile magic to the act of love—and after it Circe really is trustworthy—is dreamlike, recalling the transitions in fairy stories. The transformation of a frankly magical tale into one of complex and real humanity is clear when Circe says to the hero, not that the magic herb has protected him, but 'your mind is proof against enchantment.' Odysseus and his men never understand the formidable Circe. 'Now my heart longs to be gone, and that of my comrades, who melt my heart as they wail around me, when you are not present', he says to her, when he begs her to allow him to depart; but she has not the least reluctance in the world. She tells them that they must go to the land of the dead, and the news breaks their hearts. As they make their way to the ship, she 'passes them by easily', taking the animals they need to sacrifice to the dead. They do not see her go; as Odysseus puts it, 'who could see a god against his will, passing hither or thither?' From first to last she is mysterious, and they are all aware of it.

When we turn to Calypso, we find that she is inscrutable in a very different way. There is not, as there was with Circe, any doubt or mystery about her basic motive: she regards Odysseus as belonging to her, she saved him from the sea, and she intends to keep him for ever and make him immortal. She conceals her motive for letting him go . . . —a neat contrast with the behaviour of Achilles in the last book of the *Iliad*. Achilles, who told Odysseus that he hated like the gates of Hell the man who thought one thing in his heart and said another, does not try to claim the credit for releasing Hector's body to Priam, saying, 'I am minded to give you Hector, and a messenger has come to me from Zeus, my own mother . . .' She conceals her motive; and Hermes avoids directly threatening her, in case she is minded to disobey the order of Zeus. When she asks, 'Why have you come?' he replies, 'Zeus sent me here, much against my will. Who would choose to cross so vast an expanse of salt water, without a single city where men offer sacrifices and hecatombs to the gods? But it is impossible for another god to cross or frustrate the will of aegis-bearing Zeus. They say there is a man with you . . .' On this passage the scholiast comments: 'While seeming to defend himself on the ground that it was unavoidable that he obey Zeus, he is really preparing her, too, to accept the facts. For disobedience to Zeus is impossible.' He also is too gallant to make any allusion to Calypso's love for Odysseus, saying only that 'The wind and wave brought him here, and now Zeus orders you to send him away.' It is only the unhappy goddess who talks of her love and her hopes—to Hermes, but not to the hero himself.

Their last conversation is distinguished for what is not said but hinted at.

> Are you so very anxious to sail for home at once? Then farewell; but if you only knew what sufferings are in store for you before you reach your home, you would stay here, and live with me, and be immortal—however you long to see your wife, for whom you yearn every day.—But in truth I think I am not inferior to her in beauty or stature, since it is not right that mortal women should rival immortals in form and beauty.

Such a speech invites and rewards treatment as being psychologically sophisticated. The goddess is saying: 'You can go if you want to, but you would do better to stay with me; I can do so much for you! I suspect you only want to go because of that wife of yours, whom you refuse to forget: but I don't see why you prefer her to me, when I am so much better looking.' Such a speech is not easy to answer. Odysseus' reply could serve as a model for embarrassed males. He begins by granting and underlining her final point. 'Mighty goddess, be not angry with me; I know full well that prudent Penelope is inferior to you in beauty and in stature, for she is mortal, while you are immortal and for ever young.' She is a mighty goddess, he insists, separated by a great gulf from a mere mortal man; and as for his wife, of course she is far less attractive than Calypso. 'Yet still I wish and long every day to go home and see the day of my return . . .' The ancients read psychology into this speech, pointing out that Odysseus cleverly began by clearing himself on the charge of love for his wife, 'since nothing wounded Calypso as much as being slighted in comparison with her', and that he was careful to reassure Calypso that it was not for his wife's sake that he was so anxious to leave, but simply to 'go home'. Avoiding any question of invidious comparison between the two ladies, making no explicit refusal of the appeal she makes to him in such delicately indirect form, he allows her to keep her dignity, as Hermes tried to do. The question of principle, whether such psychological refinements, not explicitly underlined by the poet, are really to be read into the poem, will be considered after we have glanced at the scene of parting from Nausicaa.

We have seen that Nausicaa had marriage in her mind the day she met Odysseus, that her father was also thinking about it, and that both of them had thoughts of Odysseus in the role of her husband. When events take their different course, and he is about to leave, she contrives to be where he passes and to have a last exchange with him. 'Remember me when you are far away'—'I will remember you and feel grateful to you for saving my life.' The exchange is inconclusive, on the surface, and yet the audience feels it to be satisfying and perfect. This is so because we naturally supply what is not said, what might have been; Nausicaa was ready to fall in love with Odysseus, and hopes at least to live in his memory. She has secured a last word from the glamorous stranger, and she can be confident that it will be something sweet to hear. We have in fact the equivalent, in terms of the softer ethos of the *Odyssey,* of the tragic wish of Andromache after Hector's death, that he had at least 'in dying stretched out his arms to me and spoken some memorable word, which I might remember ever after as I weep night and day' (24.743). In the *Iliad,* tragedy; in the *Odyssey,* a touching but gentle pathos.

It is time to confront the question of principle. As we have seen, some people deny that any psychology is to be read into or behind the bare words of the text. This view was heroically supported by Adolf Kirchhoff, at a passage which can serve as a test case. In the sixth book of the *Odyssey,* Nausicaa told Odysseus not to accompany her into town, as their appearance together would cause talk, and even rumours of marriage. Odysseus complies with these instructions and makes his own way to her father's palace. But when her father says to him, 'I find fault with my daughter for one thing, that she did not bring you to our house with her maidservants', he replies 'Do not blame your innocent daughter. She did tell me to follow with her servants, but I refused, from fear and respect, lest your heart be angered by the sight; we men on earth are prompt to resentment.' What are we to make of this? Most scholars, from antiquity onwards, have seen in the passage a white lie to protect Nausicaa from her father's displeasure. Even Kakridis, in the same article in which he asserts the axiom that 'in poetry only what is recorded exists', says of this passage, 'The epic poet trusts his audience to detect the intention of the lie: the girl was to be protected from her father's anger', and only Kirchhoff insisted [in *Die homerische Odyssee*] that 'If Homer meant to make Odysseus act chivalrously, he should have said so; this is not psychologically subtle, it is merely slapdash.'

Now, there are passages in the *Odyssey* in which the poet does explicitly tell us of a character's hidden motive. At the simplest level there is the hypocrisy of a character like Eurymachus, who swears to Penelope that no man will lay hands on Telemachus while he is alive, or his blood will spurt round Eurymachus' spear; he has not forgotten the kindness of Odysseus towards him when he was a child. 'So he spoke to cheer her, but he himself was planning Telemachus' destruction.' Odysseus is famous for his power to conceal his feelings, and one of the constant pleasures of the poem is observing him as he does things which have a secret meaning for him, unknown to the other characters; from asking, when incognito, for the song of the Wooden Horse, 'which Odysseus brought into Troy', to serving as a beggarly hanger-on in his own home and saying, 'I too once was wealthy and had a fine house.' Achilles, who himself always speaks from the heart, is aware that others do not.

More specifically, the poems contain examples of tact and delicacy, marked as such. Athena comes to Nausicaa in a dream and tells her that she should take a party of maids and friends on a day's laundry by the river: 'Your wedding day is near at hand, when you must have clean clothes to wear . . . the cream of the young men of Phaeacia are seeking your hand . . .' The real motive of the goddess is of course to get Nausicaa and her company to the isolated spot where Odysseus is in urgent need of her help, but she prefers to go about it indirectly. Nausicaa is delighted with the idea of the excursion, and asks her father for a waggon for the day. She does not mention her own marriage, but instead says that her brothers are constantly going to dances, her father needs to be well dressed, and she herself has many dirty things. 'So she spoke, for she felt shame about mentioning lusty marriage to her father; but he understood it all . . .' Here we have a whole net of unspoken feelings and reticences. Athena acts indirectly, Nausicaa says something other than what she means, her father sees through the screen but makes no comment upon it.

Slightly less explicit is the following passage: the first song which the Muse inspires Demodocus to sing among the Phaeacians is the story of a great quarrel at Troy between Odysseus and Achilles. The rest of the audience is delighted with the song, but Odysseus himself, for whom it has an unsuspected and personal meaning, hides his face in his garment and weeps. 'Then the other Phaeacians did not observe that he was shedding tears, but Alcinous alone observed it, sitting beside him, and heard his deep sighs. At once he spoke out among the Phaeacian oarsmen, "Listen, leaders and counsellors of Phaeacia: we have had our fill now of the feast and the music which goes with it. Now let us go out and turn to sport" . . .' If we press here the principle that only what is made explicit is to be accepted as present, then the poet has not told us that

Alcinous acts as he does because he wishes to spare Odysseus, and to do it tactfully. He has not given us, expressly, any motive at all for Alcinous' action. But it is perfectly clear what is meant, and the reader who insisted on more would try our patience. The 'white lie' of Odysseus about Nausicaa belongs in the same box, and so does, for instance, a delicate touch in the first book.

Athena has come to Ithaca to rouse Telemachus into action. Odysseus is still alive, she says, on an island in the sea, 'and fierce men have him, cruel men who hold him there against his will.' Now in fact Odysseus is of course on the island of Calypso, detained by a loving nymph who wants to make him immortal. Who are these 'fierce men'? Even in the palmy days of analytic scholarship this contradiction was not seized on as evidence for a separate origin and a different version of the story, because it is so obvious that the goddess is avoiding a truth which, if revealed, would reduce poor Telemachus to despair. These passages help us to understand a more vexed one in the nineteenth book. Disguised as a beggar, the hero has a confidential conversation with Penelope, and tells her that her husband will very soon be home. He gives her a summary account of his adventures, which he claims to have heard from the king of Thesprotia; and this account entirely omits Calypso, taking Odysseus straight from the shipwreck to the land of the Phaeacians. Analysts failed to resist the temptation here, and 'earlier versions' and the like were freely invented. In the light of our discussion we see that the hero spares Penelope's feelings. She would not like to hear from an anonymous beggar that the talk of Thesprotia was her husband's intrigue with a goddess.

This brief survey has shown that the *Odyssey* contains passages in which the poet explicitly tells us of the psychology which we are to see underlying the words and acts of characters, and also that other passages, where this is not made explicit, come so close to them in nature that we can have no reasonable doubt that there, too, the instinctive response of the audience, to interpret the passages in the light of the psychology of human beings, is sound. We need not fear that there is an objection in principle to doing this in the Homeric poems. This does not of course mean that every possible nuance which can be read into the text by perverse ingenuity is really there, nor that we are helpless to choose between plausible and implausible interpretations. The standard must continue to be that of taste and sense, here as elsewhere in the study of literature; we cannot banish them and replace them with a rule, which will give us with objective certainty the answers to aesthetic questions. . . .

The idea that Homeric men are simple, without depths, and with everything on the surface, has often led scholars to find contradictory features in the charac-

ters depicted in the poems. For J. A. Scott [*The Unity of Homer*], 'the character of Paris in the *Iliad* involves constant contradictions.' In Achilles, [E.] Bethe found [in *Homer*] 'two fundamentally different creations by two great but fundamentally different poets', which it is 'an absolute psychological impossibility' that one poet can have entertained, while Wilamowitz argued [in *Die Ilias and Homer*] that in Book 9 he is 'altogether a quite different character' from what he is in Book 1. Of Agamemnon, [Karl] Reinhardt thought [in *Der Dichter der Ilias*] that 'The anxious brother of Menelaus, the admirer of the wise Nestor, is a different man from the excitable and overbearing one who wrongs Achilles', the two sides being irreconcilable and deriving from separate stories. When Diomede, after fighting and wounding two gods in the fifth book, says at the beginning of the sixth that 'If you are a god, I will not fight with heavenly gods', Von der Mühll finds it 'undeniably unsatisfactory and unworthy'. [In his "Die Schreckliche Calypso," *Festschrift R. Sühnel*, F.] Dirlmeier finds two separate conceptions in the figure of Calypso, which he refuses to try to reconcile, on the ground that we do not know that the poet wanted to create consistent characters. . . .

We have seen that in the *Odyssey* characters are remarkable for their opaqueness. The greater prominence in the poem of women, who even in the *Iliad* are more inscrutable and evasive than the male, goes with this. But so do other considerations. For instance, the inhuman and superhuman figures whom Odys-

Part woman, part hound, part serpent, the monster Scylla is shown below a crab on a silver coin of the fifth century.

seus meets on his wanderings behave in an utterly unpredictable way, not only Circe but also the queen of the Laestrygons. Odysseus' scouts met her daughter, apparently an ordinary girl drawing water at a well; they asked her the name of the king of the country, and she directed them to her father's palace. There they found the queen 'as huge as a mountain peak, and they loathed her at sight. She called her husband . . . and at once he seized one of my men and made ready his meal . . .' The appalling suddenness and unexpectedness of this event and its aftermath, the destruction of all but one of Odysseus' ships by creatures 'not like men but like giants', is fresh in the memory of the survivors when they come to the deceitful hospitality of Circe. Again we see the dreamlike and inexplicable logic of the events of a fairy story, all the more striking when it is juxtaposed with a more fully realized and human character like Odysseus. The psychology of Aeolus, on his floating island with his six sons married to his six daughters, who gives Odysseus the winds in a leather bag but, when he returns despairing, drives him away with insults, is also clearly not to be analysed like that of a human person. And this sort of inscrutability goes deeper and is more puzzling than mere deception, which also abounds in the adventures; even the Sirens know how to sound friendly and benevolent.

Such persons shade off into the more fully human people of the poem. Over dinner in Sparta, Menelaus, reconciled with Helen and an affectionate husband, listens with apparent complacency to her story of the time when she alone, in Troy, recognized Odysseus, who had entered the city in disguise; he slew many men, 'and the other women of Troy wept aloud, but my soul rejoiced, for my heart was turned and I longed to go back home, and I lamented the madness which Aphrodite gave me, when she took me away from my own country, forsaking my marriage bed and my husband, who lacked nothing, either in mind or in beauty.' To this edifying recital by a contrite wife Menelaus replies by saying that indeed Odysseus was remarkable for intelligence and strength of will. For instance, when we were all hidden in the Trojan Horse, 'you came to the spot; doubtless a god who planned victory for the Trojans must have brought you. Deiphobus, handsome as a god, followed you. Three times you went round the horse, touching it, and calling to us each by his name, imitating the voice of the wife of each man.' Odysseus prevented any of us from replying, and put his hand forcibly over the mouth of Anticlus to keep him silent. 'So Odysseus saved all the Argives; and he held Anticlus until Pallas Athena led you away.' From antiquity onwards readers have been preplexed to know what to make of this. Did Helen try to betray her husband and the other Achaeans to death? With what purpose and to what effect does Menelaus now tell this story? The characters make no comment upon it, and sixteen lines later Menelaus is in bed,

'and beside him lay Helen of the long robe, that divine lady.' Helen, in fact, is inscrutable. We cannot reconcile her story and that of her husband, and we have no way of analysing the situation in terms of their particular characters. Helen has a glamorous if shady past; she is quicker than her husband, whether to recognize a guest, or to interpret an omen; he gives Telemachus a foolish present which has to be changed, she gives him a suggestive one, a wedding-dress for his bride, 'a keepsake of the hands of Helen'. She has acquired in Egypt drugs to cheer people up. The archetype of deceitful wives, she is also the daughter of Zeus. We cannot read her mind.

That is less surprising when we reflect that Queen Arete of the Phaeacians also remains enigmatic. Odysseus is told by Nausicaa and also by Athena to make his supplication to her; she is honoured by her husband as no other mortal woman is honoured, and her favour will mean success. Yet when he does this the result is an embarrassed silence, broken at last by an aged counsellor. Queen Arete does not speak at all for eighty lines, and when she does it is to say something quite unexpected. The temptation to add to the number of psychological explanations of her behaviour will be resisted. The point, for us, is that we find another character, and another woman, who is inscrutable, and whose character is not elucidated by the poet. Odysseus finds the goddess Athena no less opaque, as he complains bitterly to her when she has appeared to him in disguise on his first return to Ithaca. Penelope herself is not less mysterious. Her behaviour towards the disguised Odysseus is so ambiguous that some have been led to suppose that really she recognized him all the time; and the scene in which she appears before the Suitors in all her beauty and induces them to give her gifts, while Odysseus is delighted with her conduct, has also perplexed many readers. And she gives us a last surprise by not recognizing the victorious Odysseus, after his triumph, as her husband.

Deception is one of the poem's great subjects. Odysseus is famous for his tricks and guile; Penelope has more tricks than any heroine known to mythology, as the frustrated Suitors complain; Telemachus learns how to conceal his feelings and fool his enemies. Odysseus tells mighty lies in Ithaca and evidently delights in them. But not all deception is of this ultimately cheery and successful sort. Every vagrant who appeared in Ithaca while Odysseus was away told lies about him and his imminent return, breaking the heart of Penelope and Eumaeus, so that now the lonely wife cannot believe in his return even when he has come home and slain his enemies. Eumaeus' own life was blighted when cheating Phoenicians seduced his nurse and carried him away as a little child, selling him into slavery. The Suitors lie to Penelope and plan the murder of Telemachus. Agamemnon's ghost tells Odysseus how he was tricked and murdered by his wife and her lover: 'Indeed I thought I should come home most welcome to my children and my household', he says bitterly, and he urges the hero to keep his return a secret, 'for there is no more trusting in women'. Trust is the hardest thing in such a world. Athena tells Telemachus, when he lingers in Sparta, to hurry home, or his mother will marry again and carry off some of his goods for her new husband: 'You know what the heart of woman is like; she wants to increase the household of the man who marries her, and she forgets her former children and her husband once he is dead; she asks no more about him . . .' And Telemachus himself, in his lethargy of despair in the first book, answers Athena's question whether he is Odysseus' son with the cynical reply that 'My mother says I am his son, but I do not know; no man ever knew his own parentage . . .' From the Suitors' point of view, their destruction too, was a treacherous trick.

For the *Iliad* the world, though terrible, remains a place in which heroism is possible. The situations round which the poem is built are scenes which embody attitudes to the fundamental questions of acceptance of death, patriotism, heroic anger, heroic shame. The characters, too, are defined by their relation to these questions. Agamemnon mistakes his position with Zeus, thinking that he is the man whom the god delights to honour; he loses his contest with Achilles for supremacy and as a hero is not of the highest quality. Hector, brave and loyal, is deceived by the temporary help of Zeus and his own short-sightedness; he too mistakes the intentions of the god for him, and he discovers, when he cannot face Achilles and turns to run from his onset, that he had also mistaken his own prowess as a hero. Paris and Helen are characterized by their attitudes to fate and duty, he as frivolous, she as more deeply tragic. In the *Odyssey* the world is menacing, not with the sharp clarity of heroic death, but with the mysteriousness of undeclared motives, inscrutable people, liars and cheats. Disloyalty and deception, not heroic rage and strife for honour, are the causes of disaster, and Odysseus must struggle not against the clear and passionate will of Achilles, as he does in the ninth and the nineteenth books of the *Iliad,* nor with the heroes of Troy in battle, but with mutinous sailors, offensive servants, disloyal subjects, and with monsters and goddesses against whom heroic prowess is useless. The *Odyssey* is intensely interested in individuals, and it is not an accident that the people whom the hero meets, even his patron goddess and his wife, are represented almost without exception as mysterious; while Odysseus himself moves unrecognized and enigmatic among the Phaeacians, as he moves disguised about his own house. That was what interested the poet about his characters. That was what made them fit into his world.

Sheila Murnaghan (essay date 1987)

SOURCE: "Recognition and the Return of Odysseus," in *Disguise and Recognition in the "Odyssey,"* Princeton University Press, 1987, pp. 20-55.

[*Here, Murnaghan explores the theme of disclosure and recognition as it relates to Odysseus and Laertes, Telemachos, Eumaeus, and Penelope, as well as discussing Odysseus's need to re-establish his past relationships with these characters.*]

During their meeting in Book 13, Athena and Odysseus sit down together at the base of an olive tree and concoct the plot through which, imitating the story of a disguised god, he will defeat his enemies. This then becomes the plot, in a literary sense, of the second half of the poem, a plot shaped by the deployment of a divine strategy to make possible a story of mortal revenge. Its climactic moment is Odysseus' imitation of a divine epiphany when, having strung the bow, he reveals himself to the suitors with bewildering suddenness and proceeds to punish them for their transgressions against him.

But while Odysseus' moment of triumph over the suitors resembles a divine epiphany, it also differs from one in that it is only possible with the aid of certain human accomplices, whose help is secured in a series of private scenes of recognition that structure the second half of the poem. As he advances geographically towards the center of his house, where he will confront and defeat the suitors, Odysseus also advances strategically. He accumulates a group of supporters who will make his success possible in a series of reunions that take the form of recognition scenes: with Athena when he arrives on the shore of Ithaca; with Telemachus when he has arrived at the hut of the swineherd Eumaeus at the edge of his own holdings; with the dog Argus when he arrives at the threshold of his house; with his nurse Eurycleia at the hearth; with Eumaeus and Philoetius in the courtyard outside the megaron as he embarks on his action against the suitors.

When the decisive moment of the contest of the bow is at hand, Odysseus is able to rely on the aid of all those to whom his true identity is known, and they act as a kind of team to bring about his success. Penelope—who, uniquely, acts as his accomplice without knowing who he is—proposes the contest and insists that Odysseus be allowed to take part. Telemachus orders that the bow be placed in Odysseus' hands and urges Eumaeus on when he falters. Eumaeus hands Odysseus the bow and tells Eurycleia, in Telemachus' name, to close the doors. Similarly, when Odysseus has moved from his recovery of the house to his recovery of the estate as a whole and has been recognized by Laertes and by Dolius and his sons, he forms from them, and Telemachus, a band of followers with whom to face the attack of the suitors' relatives. These encounters diminish the success of the suitors' challenge, both in the sense that they reduce the number of people from whom Odysseus' return is concealed, of whose recognition he is deprived as a result of the suitors' presence, and in the sense that they give him the allies he will need to remove the suitors from his house.

Odysseus' time-defying defeat of the suitors requires this acquisition of accomplices and thus depends on the conquest of time in another, more ordinary way as well: it depends on the reanimation of past relationships. The permanence of Odyseus' claim to his position may mimic the timeless power of the gods, but it actually rests on the durability of his domestic relationships, his capacity to recover a series of roles defined by his relations with others: father, son, husband, and master. The success of his return is dependent on the qualities that make such relationships last, the close identification of interests that makes the association beneficial to both participants. The successive scenes of recognition in which Odysseus' base of support in Ithaca is reconstructed articulate the *Odyssey's* account of his return in two senses: through their sequence, these scenes provide the structure of the plot; and through their internal form, they express the interdependence of the relationships that make it possible for Odysseus to come back.

In their typical form, the *Odyssey's* recognition scenes act out the essential mutuality of the relationships that are being revived. They involve a process of identification and testing leading to emotionally-charged reunions, which are experienced in gestures of physical union such as embracing, kissing, or in the case of Odysseus and Penelope, making love. Within these episodes there is often a progression from expressions of solitary, one-sided emotion, which often evoke the pain of the separation that is now to be cured, to the shared emotion of reunion. These reunions are achieved through a two-sided process consisting of disclosure of identity on one side and recognition of identity on the other, gestures which are not neutral but have the broader connotations of mutual acknowledgment or praise, implying a willing concession of honor or service on both sides.

When, under the dangerous, necessarily clandestine conditions of Odysseus' return, he identifies himself to one of his loyal supporters, that gesture of self-disclosure is also a gesture of acknowledgment; it acknowledges, sometimes after a considerable period of testing, the demonstrated reliability and loyalty that make him willing to risk disclosing himself. At the same time, when Odysseus identifies himself, he stakes a claim to a certain status, and those who recognize him acquiesce in that claim. Their recognition of his iden-

tity is not unlike the modern idea of political recognition, acknowledgment of legitimacy in a position of power. Penelope's suitors, who withhold this acknowledgment from Odysseus, prove to be incapable of recognizing his identity, while each of his loyal supporters acts out his acquiescence to Odysseus' claims by recognizing him. The importance of mutual loyalty to the meaning of recognition scenes is underscored by the way these scenes regularly end with the two figures who have been reunited plotting together against their shared enemies.

The account of Odysseus' self-disclosure to Eumaeus and Philoetius illustrates well how these episodes of recognition of identity also act out an identification of interests that is based on mutual recognition in a broader sense and outweighs in importance the immediate occasion of the removal of one figure's disguise. First, Odysseus asks for a hypothetical show of loyalty by asking what Eumaeus and Philoetius would do if Odysseus were to return. When Eumaeus responds by praying to all the gods for Odysseus' return, then Odysseus discloses himself. . . .

> But, when he had recognized their unswerving mind,
> he spoke to them again, answering them with words,
> "Here I am, myself, within the house, having struggled much;
> I have returned in the twentieth year to the land of my fathers.
> I recognize that I come wished for by you alone of my servants . . ."
>   (*Od.* 21.205-210)

Here the language of recognition . . . is applied to Odysseus' apprehension of Eumaeus and Philoetius' loyalty, their willingness to recognize him, which he acknowledges through his self-disclosure. The words with which Odysseus discloses himself are at once the announcement of a prayed-for benefit and a boast containing a bid for acknowledgment of his achievement in returning home and for aid in his further struggle. An action consisting of the revelation and recognition of identity becomes the occasion for a dialogue articulating a series of mutual claims and obligations, a dialogue involving expressions of praise that are verbal tokens of a mutual commitment to material aid.

The mutuality and interdependence of Odysseus' relationships with members of his household is, then, represented formally in the structure of the scenes of recognition in which, as his identity becomes more and more widely known, his disguise is gradually dispelled. But the mutuality of experience between Odysseus and the loyal members of his household is more complex and pervasive. As his dependents, these characters derive their identities and capacities from their place in the *oikos,* "household," of which he is the head. In his absence, Laertes, Telemachus, Eumaeus, and Penelope cling to their literal identities as father, son, loyal servant, and wife of Odysseus. But Odysseus' absence and the presence of the suitors make it difficult for them to enjoy the status, to exercise the power, that ought to be inextricable from those roles. Like Odysseus when he lands on the shore of Ithaca, they experience a disjunction between their nominal identities and the places they ought to occupy in the social world. And that disjunction is similarly represented in their cases as a kind of disguise. Theirs is not the deliberately contrived and willfully assumed disguise that Odysseus takes on, but rather genuine experience of the unimpressive appearance, powerlessness, subjugation to time, foreignness to the house of Odysseus, and lowered social status that are elements in his disguise. But these experiences nonetheless take on the character of disguises because they prove reversible, and like Odysseus' more literal disguise, are removed with the revelation of his return.

Thus the reunions of these characters with Odysseus involve these characters' own shedding of disguise and recognition as well as his. And Odysseus, in the course of repossessing his house, imitates Athena not only by revealing himself but also by bringing out of disguise those on whom his recovery of Ithaca depends, much as she uncovers Ithaca from its obscuring mist. In different ways, depending on the nature of their relationships to Odysseus, the members of Odysseus' household rehearse their own versions of return and recognition. The way in which each recognition scene functions as a climactic moment in both of two intersecting stories of recovery and recognition conditions, in each case, its particular timing and construction; in responding to these factors, these episodes become precise depictions of how the distinct but interdependent characters involved are related to one another.

That the effects of Odysseus' absence create a kind of disguise is most apparent in the case of the last of the figures by whom Odysseus is recognized, his father Laertes. The condition into which Laertes has fallen is described to Odysseus by his mother Anticleia when he meets her in the underworld. . . .

> Your father stays there
> on the farm, and does not go to town. He has
>   no bed
> or bed clothes or blankets or shining
>   coverings,
> but in the winter he sleeps in the house where
>   the servants do
> in the dust near the fire, and wears vile
>   clothing;
> but when summer comes and the fruitful

> harvest-time,
> everywhere along the slope of his vineyard,
> he throws together his bed of fallen leaves.
> And there he lies grieving, and a great sorrow
>   grows in his mind
> as he longs for your homecoming. And harsh
>   old age comes over him.
>
>   (*Od.* 11.187-196)

In response to Odysseus' absence, Laertes himself has withdrawn from both home and society. He has fallen into a state of grief that combines elements of Odysseus' anonymous persona on Phaeacia and his deliberate disguise on Ithaca. Like Odysseus when he arrives on the Phaeacian shore, Laertes is barely alive and barely participating in civilized life. In both cases this virtually uncivilized state is represented through sleeping, not indoors in a bed or at least in a fixed place, but outdoors on the ground in a random pile of leaves. In fact, Laertes is dressed in an anomalous costume that seems to suggest a kind of animal suit, as if he were no longer fully human (*Od.* 24.229-231). Like Odysseus when he disguises himself both on his return to Ithaca and during the spying mission to Troy (as is recounted to Telemachus by Helen in *Odyssey* 4), Laertes has taken on the rags and activities of a poor servant and the outward signs of old age.

When Odysseus meets Laertes in *Odyssey* 24, Laertes is much more conspicuously disguised than Odysseus is. When Odysseus first addresses his father, he comments on his appearance, saying to him, in essence, "You seem to be in disguise." . . .

> Old man, you show no lack of skill in tending
> the orchard. It is well cared for, and there is
>   no
> tree, no fig, no vine, nor any olive,
> no pear, and no bed of greens uncared for in
>   your garden.
> But I will tell you something else, and you
>   must not be angry:
> you yourself are not well cared for. For you
>   are wretchedly old
> and miserably dirty and you wear shabby
>   clothes.
> It is not on account of laziness that your lord
>   neglects you,
> and nothing about you suggests a slave,
> neither your form nor your size, for you seem
>   like a king.
> You seem like the kind who, when he has
>   bathed and eaten,
> sleeps comfortably. That is the way of the
>   elders.
>
>   (*Od.* 24.244-255)

In this speech Odysseus contrasts Laertes' current

appearance with what appears to be his proper role, and he does so in a way that associates Laertes' proper role with qualities and gestures that are, in the *Odyssey,* specifically associated with the removal of disguise or the establishment of identity. He contrasts Laertes' shabby appearance to his careful tending of the orchard; when he proves his own identity to Laertes, it is by recalling how he learned to tend that very orchard. Then he goes on to say that Laertes looks as if he could be altered by a bath and that he might end up by sleeping more comfortably, presumably in a bed. In the *Odyssey* a bath is often the occasion of the removal of disguise, and sleeping in a bed is often its result—most notably, of course, in the recognition scene between Odysseus and Penelope in which Odysseus proves his identity and regains his marriage bed all at once.

Odysseus counters this disguise by bringing himself to his father's attention; first he evokes an absent, fictitious version of himself in the false tale that he tells, and then he identifies himself openly and announces that he has defeated the suitors. The sequel to this revelation is the removal of Laertes' disguise. When Laertes returns to his house, he has a bath, through which both his rags and his old age are cast aside, and he emerges looking like the gods (*Od.* 24.365-370). When Odysseus comments on this change, he is, in a sense, recognizing his father. Laertes answers with a wish: that he could have been as he was during one of the great victories of his youth and could have joined in the previous day's battle against the suitors (*Od.* 24.376-382). This wish is reminiscent of the wishes of Odysseus' friends that Odysseus would return as he was on some past occasion. Odysseus' success in fulfilling those wishes is here transferred to Laertes, who, by recognizing Odysseus, also puts aside the effects of time and then goes on to play a leading role in the battle with the suitors' relatives, which reenacts the battle with the suitors themselves.

The reunion of Odysseus and Laertes, then, combines a graphic reversal of the effects of time with a demonstration of reciprocity: Odysseus brings Laertes out of the state of weakness and grief that oppresses him and obscures his identity, and Laertes helps Odysseus ward off the final threat to his own recovery of his proper position and identity. This reciprocity is reinforced by the effective leveling of their ages that occurs as Laertes is restored to his prime. The reversal of the effects of time involved in Laertes' reanimation not only signals the return of the past but also removes the imbalance inherent in the chronologically unequal relationship of father and son, an imbalance which, at this time in their lives, makes the son more powerful than his aged father. This imbalance is also countered by the proof that Odyssecus is obliged to offer his father. Odysseus may be a more

powerful figure in this encounter, confronting a father who is his dependent and controlling his own self-disclosure, but he cannot win Laertes' recognition without satisfying his demand for proof. In meeting this demand he recalls times in their lives when the balance of their relationship was different. He shows him the scar, which evokes the time when he was only just entering manhood and underwent a kind of initiation; and he recalls an even earlier time when Laertes showed him the orchard, taught him the names of the trees, and gave him some of them—a time when he was Laertes' dependent and received only a token portion of his inheritance (*Od.* 24.330-344).

But at the same time that this episode, in one way, plays down the imbalance in their relationship (by making it clear that the imbalance stems only from this particular point in their history), it also, in other ways, draws attention to that imbalance. It does so especially through two related features: the extremity of Laertes' destitution, which is expressed in the transfer of the motifs of disguise to him, and the placement of the episode late in the narrative, which gives it a belated or tacked-on quality. Laertes' condition of extreme dependency means that Odysseus can only appear to him late in the story when his return is virtually complete. Only then is Odysseus' presence sufficiently powerful to bring Laertes out of the decline that has been his response to the suitors' presence. Simply the prospect or likelihood of Odysseus' return is insufficient to revive Laertes, as is clear when he responds to Odysseus' false tale by nearly dying. Thus Odysseus appears to Laertes virtually undisguised himself and couples the revelation of his identity with the announcement that he has destroyed the suitors. The confrontation with the suitors' relatives, which still remains and with which Laertes does help, is not as essential to Odysseus' recovery as the defeat of the suitors themselves. That this confrontation lies before him is not as great a challenge to his identity as the presence of the suitors has been, and the help that Laertes gives him is not as decisive as the help he has received from other supporters within the house.

This depiction of the imbalance between father and son, even in an encounter which also does away with it, is partly a reflection of the *Odyssey*'s partiality for its hero, which causes him to be portrayed to best advantage, and thus at that time in his life when his glory cannot be rightly challenged, even by his own father. It also expresses a constant feature of the relationships between fathers and sons as they are affected by the passage of time. It is always the case that, while the father is the chief source of the son's identity, his continued presence is not necessary for the continuation of that identity. The father is likely to die while the son is still alive, but the son must be able to continue on without him and thus must not depend on him to retain the position he inherits. Odysseus can, and must, remain the son of Laertes with all that that means, even after Laertes is no longer alive. On the other hand, it is only through his son's possession of this heritage that the father's identity can, in any sense, continue after his death, as the loss of selfhood with which Laertes responds to Odysseus' absence attests. The sense of many readers from antiquity on that the recognition between Odysseus and Laertes is an inessential appendage is appropriate, but that does not mean that our *Odyssey* has been added to; rather it gives in this way an accurate account of the relationship of father and son. The *Odyssey* would be presenting a less true picture if it made it seem indispensable that Odysseus be reunited with his father in order to resume his place in his home. At the same time, the poem recognizes that Odysseus' place derives above all from his relationship to his father and acknowledges this in its final episode.

The same features of the relationship of father and son that cause Odysseus' reunion with his father to be the last in the series that makes up the account of his return cause his reunion with his son Telemachus to be the first (or first with an actual member of his household). Odysseus encounters Laertes only after his victory over the suitors is complete because Laertes' recovery is so thoroughly dependent on his return and because he does not need Laertes' help very much. He encounters Telemachus when he has still made very little progress towards the achievement of his return and because Telemachus needs the assurance of his presence relatively little and is more in a position to help his father than to be helped by him.

Like Laertes, Telemachus is not fully himself when the story opens but becomes so by the end; the way in which, by the poem's conclusion, events have brought both of them into a similar state of paramount vigor is expressed in the final tableau in which they both fight at Odysseus' side in his battle against the suitors' relatives. But while Telemachus' distance from his proper state also manifests itself in powerlessness in the face of the suitors' presence and mournful longing for Odysseus' return, what keeps him from asserting himself is not his father's absence but his own immaturity. The change in him that comes to be recognized in his encounter with his father is not the recovery of a previous state but growth into a new state of maturity, and the role played in this change by Odysseus is consequently different.

Laertes has become Odysseus' permanent dependent whose survival depends absolutely on his return. But it is Telemachus' role to stop being Odysseus' dependent eventually and to become his successor. When that happens, Telemachus must be able to survive even if Odysseus is not present, even if, as will sooner or later be the case, Odysseus is dead. Furthermore, he must be capable of succeeding his father on the basis of his own comparable merits. It is essential to the poem's celebration of inherited excellence that Telemachus be able to take his father's place even if his father does not return to hand it to him personally. Therefore Telemachus must be seen not to need his father's direct influence in order to attain to a state in which he can take hold of what is rightfully his.

When the poem opens, Telemachus is in a state of unreadiness to assert himself that is reminiscent of Odysseus' reticence on Phaeacia. This is a less extreme version of disguise than that displayed by Laertes, which depends on Odysseus' miraculous presence for its reversal; Telemachus' state is not a debilitating decline but an indication of still-unfulfilled potential. Much as Odysseus holds back his identity unnecessarily on Phaeacia, Telemachus refuses the recognition spontaneously offered him by "Mentes." When "Mentes" suggests to Telemachus that he must be the son of Odysseus, Telemachus gives a noncommittal answer: his mother says that he is, but he is not sure; no one knows for sure who his father is, and he would rather have been the son of someone more fortunate, someone who died at home among his possessions (*Od.* 1.214-220).

While Telemachus believes that his father's absence is his problem and dreams of his father's return as the solution (*Od.* 1.113-117), his discernable resemblance to Odysseus suggests that the capacity to heal the Ithacan situation is also present in him. As it turns out, he does not overcome this uncertainty about himself by being exposed to Odysseus and recognizing him. At the prompting of Athena, he adopts another, more satisfactory and realistic solution: rather than simply waiting for his father to return, he grows up independently. He asserts himself against the suitors and takes a voyage to Pylos and Sparta, where he comes to know his father from others' memories of him. He undertakes an independent voyage that is in its structure and import parallel to the return of Odysseus. Like Laertes, he responds to Odysseus' absence with an absence of his own, but his absence takes the form of an autonomous voyage from which he can make a more forceful return.

Telemachus' voyage, like Odysseus' return, takes the form of a series of encounters; in each of these encounters Telemachus is recognized as his father's son and heir: by "Mentes," by Nestor, by Helen and Menelaus—an episode in which the discovery of his identity is a central element—by Theoclymenus, and finally by Odysseus himself in a reunion that marks simultaneously the return of Odysseus and the return of Telemachus. In these encounters Telemachus meets people who both recognize him as Odysseus' son and tell him stories that reveal Odysseus' greatness. As a result, he learns both that he actually resembles Odysseus—that his connection to Odysseus is inherent and apparent and not simply something his mother asserts—and that Odysseus is someone whose son he would want to be, a great hero whether he succeeds in returning to Ithaca or not. By the last of these encounters, the meeting with the stranger in Eumaeus' hut, Telemachus identifies himself unhesitatingly not only as the son of Odysseus but also as part of a line that includes Arcesius and Laertes (*Od.* 16.117-120).

The story of Telemachus' journey is an adaptation of the disguise-and-recognition plot structure that shapes the story of Odysseus' return to the particular dimensions of Telemachus' situation. Although elements in Telemachus' story—most notably his recognition by Menelaus and Helen because of his secret weeping at the mention of Odysseus—are reminiscent of Odysseus' visit to Phaeacia, Telemachus has a much easier time establishing his identity than Odysseus does in that episode. Telemachus is able to benefit from some of the privileges of his position as Odysseus' son; his discovery of his identity is paralleled by his learning to take advantage of that legacy. While he arrives at Pylos and Sparta in the anonymous condition of all strangers, Telemachus is also traveling with the proper trappings of his station, especially a ship full of companions. He goes among people who have a connection to his father, and who are prepared to recognize him and welcome him because of that connection. Telemachus also inherits the help of his father's supporters, in particular his father's divine patron Athena, who helps him in the guise of old friends of his father. Because of his father's connection with Nestor, Telemachus gains his own companion, Peisistratus, whose capacity to help him be recognized is seen when he speaks up to confirm Menelaus' and Helen's spontaneous identification (*Od.* 4.155-167).

The way Telemachus discovers his identity reflects the degree of dependence that a son has on his father at Telemachus' stage of life. His father must be in his background—the son must inherit some advantages from him and must have access to memories of him—but he no longer needs to be an actual presence in his life. Telemachus' journey is not at all an attempt to bring Odysseus back: it is an attempt to bring about his own emergence as the son of Odysseus so that he can take control of his household in his father's absence. When "Mentes" tells Telemachus to go on the journey, he does not tell him to look for Odysseus but to look for information about him (*Od.* 1.279-283).

Telemachus' reunion with Odysseus is the culminating moment of Telemachus' growth to a point where he no

longer needs Odysseus' return. Thus, the scene is placed at the beginning of Odysseus' homecoming, when Odysseus can offer little support and needs a good deal of help. At the same time, Telemachus' attainment of this condition is made premature by Odysseus' return, and his new prominence must be suspended as long as Odysseus is still alive. This suspension is dramatized during the contest of the bow, when Telemachus nearly succeeds in stringing the bow himself but steps aside at a signal from Odysseus (*Od.* 21.101-135). Thus, although the placement of their recognition acknowledges Telemachus' newfound maturity, other aspects of the subsequent scene are designed to play down this maturity or to counter it in the light of Odysseus' return.

While still disguised, Odysseus as the stranger suggests that the situation on Ithaca could be remedied either by a son of Odysseus or by Odysseus himself (*Od.* 16.100-101). But he does not recognize at first that Telemachus is ready for recognition; he has to be told by Athena not to wait any longer before disclosing himself to him. The words Odysseus uses to impress his identity on Telemachus also emphasize Telemachus' dependence on him. . . .

> I am no god. Why do you compare me to the immortals?
> But I am your father, the one for whom you have been grieving
> as you suffer many hardships, receiving the insults of men.
>
> (*Od.* 16.187-189)

As they make his own presence known, Odysseus' words return Telemachus to the helpless condition he was in when the poem opened, when Athena came upon him, grieving and dreaming of his father's return (*Od.* 1.113-117). They serve to deny the effects of his intervening voyage on Telemachus, effects that must, for the time being, be suspended.

These two recognition scenes, the one between Odysseus and Telemachus and the one between Odysseus and Laertes, frame the story of Odysseus' return, but are segregated from the central action and central arena of the narrative, Odysseus' defeat of the suitors in his own house. The recognition scenes that cluster around the defeat of the suitors involve the recreation of more difficult relationships with people to whom Odysseus is not related by blood: his loyal servants, Eurycleia, Eumaeus, and Philoetius, and his wife Penelope. Because these relationships are not based on any natural tie but are artificial social constructs, their continuity over time is genuinely subject to question as the continuity of the indissoluble kinship of father and son is not. Thus the aspects of Odysseus' identity affirmed by his relations with these figures are more seriously threatened by his absence than is his identity as son of Laertes or father of Telemachus. This great threat is registered in the narrative by the way in which reunions with those figures take place close to the center of his home and of the story of his recovery and, especially in the cases of Eumaeus and Penelope, only after a long period of testing and re-negotiation.

Odysseus' ties to his servants are even more vulner-able to the effects of his absence than is his tie to his wife. While a marriage begins without any kinship between husband and wife, it creates kinship between them through their children. But the relationship of master and servant is permanently unequal in status and, on the part of the servants, or more properly slaves, originally involuntary. Although the poem refers to the acts of generosity with which masters win the loyalty of their servants, it also acknowledg-es that slaves are won by force (for example, *Od.* 1.398). And it shows, especially in its portrayal of the majority of Odysseus' servants who have not re-mained loyal to him, that such gracious acts are not sufficient to create ties that automatically endure when the master is not present.

The *Odyssey* registers the inherent difficulty of such relationships by making their revival important and far from routine prerequisites to the hero's triumphant self-revelation. It has often seemed to interpreters of the poem that the placement of the recognitions involving Eumaeus and Eurycleia is determined by considerations having to do with the treatment of other, more impor-tant characters. A recognition with Eumaeus in his hut seems to have been postponed to make way for the reunion with Telemachus; the recognition by Eurycleia seems to have been inserted to avert a premature rec-ognition with Penelope. In other words, these charac-ters' subordinate, servile status has seemed to be reca-pitulated in the way in which their allotment of narra-tive attention is designed to serve the presentation of other, more socially elevated characters. But it is pos-sible to read the distribution of Odysseus' recognitions in another way, to see it as a means of highlighting his dependence on the loyalty of his social subordinates, a loyalty that is far from automatic. The tense moment of real danger to Odysseus' whole project created by Eurycleia's recognition of him dramatizes how much he needs to be able to rely on her and on others like her. The recognition by Eumaeus comes as a crucial prelude to Odysseus' participation in the contest of the bow and is given weight both by the long account of Odysseus' preceding encounter with Eumaeus and by the way Eumaeus' role is duplicated in the figure of Philoetius.

In addition, the *Odyssey* makes sense of the contin-ued voluntary submission of unrelated subordinates by assimilating these relationships to the socially equal and involuntary relationships of kinship. As they rec-ognize Odysseus and are recognized by him, the poem suggests that Eurycleia and Eumaeus are more like relatives than like servants. The capacity of mutual recognition to bring to light kinship where none has been apparent is here used to imply a metaphorical kinship where none actually exists. Odysseus' retain-ers lose their social inferiority as if it were, like his, a disguise.

As their similar names suggest, Eurycleia is, in many ways, a doublet for Odysseus' mother, Anticleia. Her role of nurse is naturally very close to that of mother. The account of her history given at *Odyssey* 1.429-433 makes it clear that she is Anticleia's equal in social status and nearly her equal in position in the house-hold of Laertes. Although she is now a slave, she was originally an aristocrat, as the provision of her father's and grandfather's names at 1.429 attests, and has re-ceived as much honor as his wife from Laertes, who has only refrained from sharing his bed with her out of fear of his wife's anger (*Od.* 1.432-433). In the ac-count of how Odysseus got his scar that evokes their past relationship, Eurycleia is virtually identified with Odysseus' mother. . . .

> Autolycus came to the rich land of Ithaca
> and there found a child newly born to his
>   daughter;
> this child Eurycleia laid on his knees
> as he finished his dinner, and called him by
>   name and said to
>   him,
> "Autolycus, you yourself find a name to be
>   given
> to this child of your child. You have prayed
>   much for him."
> Then Autolycus spoke and gave her an
>   answer,
> "My son-in-law and daughter, give him the
>   name I tell you . . ."
>
>   (*Od.* 19.399-406)

The child of his daughter whom Autolycus has come to see is presented to him by Eurycleia, and she poses a question to which the answer is addressed to Odys-seus' father and mother. Any reader of these lines who did not know otherwise would assume that Eurycleia was Odysseus' mother.

Eumaeus has a history similar both to the history that goes with Odysseus' disguise and to Eurycleia's histo-ry. He, too, is originally of noble birth and has occu-pied a place in the house of Laertes comparable to that of a member of the family. He has been raised almost as if he were Odysseus' brother, only a little less hon-ored than Odysseus' sister Ctimene (*Od.* 15.363-365). Only on reaching adulthood has he been relegated to a farm on the periphery of the estate and to the status of a servant (*Od.* 15.370). And only with the advent of the suitors has he been truly confined to that place and role.

Odysseus' recognition of Eumaeus repairs Eumaeus' social subordination. As they are recognized by Odysseus, Eumaeus and Philoetius are absorbed into Odysseus' family as brothers to Telemachus. Between his declaration and his show of proof, Odysseus promises, . . .

> If by my hand a god destroys the arrogant
> suitors,
> then I will get you both wives, and allot you
> possessions
> and houses built next to mine. And then
> you both will be companions and brothers of
> Telemachus.
>
> *(Od.* 21.213-216)

The assimilation that is implicit in the recognition scene with Eurycleia is here made explicit.

Eumaeus' recognition comes not at a hut at the edge of the estate but in the courtyard of the house, only a small distance from the center of Odysseus' power. Similarly, Eumaeus' relationship to Odysseus is revealed to be not that of a distant inferior but one that involves only a relatively minor degree of subordination. Eumaeus' subordination is that of a son to his father (which is, after all, only temporary) or that of a great hero's companion, neither of which involves social inferiority. Eumaeus' servile status, like Laertes' old age and peasant's rags, is not an inescapable condition but a form of disguise that Odysseus' return, rather than reaffirming their unequal relationship, removes.

Like his reunion with Eumaeus, Odysseus' reunion with Penelope comes only after a long period of testing and negotiation and involves a more complex interrelation of two separate stories of recovery and recognition than do his reunions with Laertes and Telemachus. The recognition of Penelope and Odysseus occurs only after a series of meetings that are difficult to interpret and that are interwined with Odysseus' other interactions with his household. This greater complexity is a reflection of the nature of Odysseus and Penelope's relationship, which is more definitive, more nearly balanced, and less intrinsically secure than Odysseus' relationships with his father and with his son. As husband and wife Odysseus and Penelope are closer in age and are involved in a more nearly equal relationship than fathers and sons usually are. While Laertes may have been the source of Odysseus' identity in the past, and Telemachus may represent the greatest prospect of its continuation into the future, Penelope is the figure on whom the recovery of his power to assert it in the present most depends. In the middle of his life, Odysseus is most

decisively defined by his role as her husband. At the same time, that role, because it is created through an artificial and reversible social tie rather than through an unalterable bond of blood kinship, is vulnerable in a way that his identity as Laertes' son and Telemachus' father is not. Odysseus is not naturally Penelope's husband, as he is naturally Laertes' son; that role could have been played by any of a number of men and now that he is absent could be taken over by someone else. Consequently, the most serious challenge to Odysseus' identity comes from Penelope's suitors, rivals who would like to replace him in that role.

The inherent instability of the roles of husband and wife as expressions of identity can only be countered by the willingness of the partners to see it as inviolable, as having the irreversible quality of a tie of blood. A successful marriage comes to resemble kinship both because husband and wife come to be related through their children and because they invest their relationship with the particularity and permanence of kinship. But this kinship always remains metaphorical, the product not of biology but of an attitude of mind. This notion of mental kinship is expressed in the idea of *homophrosyn* , "likeness of mind," which is identified by Odysseus in his speech to Nausicaa as the central quality of a successful marriage *(Od.* 6.180-185). Because the form of kinship represented by marriage is in this way entirely voluntary, its recognition—expressed in this poem by Penelope's recognition of Odysseus as her husband and by Odysseus' recognition of Penelope as his wife—signals not the effects of heredity but the virtue of marital fidelity.

Odysseus' definitive yet inherently difficult relationship to Penelope is expressed in the plot of the *Odyssey* in Penelope's decisive role in the suitor's defeat through her setting of the contest of the bow, and in the placement of their recognition scene. Because the status of this relationship is so profoundly affected by the suitors' presence, the relationship is reinstated immediately after, but only after, the suitors have been eliminated. Thus, Odysseus can neither wait to be reunited with Penelope, as he can with Laertes, nor reveal himself at once and plot openly with her, as he does with Telemachus. And because Penelope's continued identity as Odysseus' wife is dependent on his actual return in a way that Telemachus' identity as his son is not, that identity can appropriately be resumed only when Odysseus' homecoming is truly secure.

Penelope's dependence on Odysseus' presence for her identity is reflected in her response to his absence, which, like Laertes', combines elements of mourning and disguise. It involves partly physical withdrawal to the inner portion of the house, from which she emerges only rarely, but primarily emotional withdrawal into grief, despair, and inactivity. Furthermore, she is in a state of physical decline that resembles a disguise. She describes this condition to the stranger during their meeting in Book 19. When he compliments her by saying that she has been able to take Odysseus' place in his absence, she quite correctly denies it. . . .

> Stranger, all my excellence, my form and
>   appearance,
> were destroyed by the immortals, when the
>   Argives
> embarked for Ilium and my husband Odysseus
>   went with them.
> If he were to come back and take care of my
>   life,
> my glory would be greater and so more
>   beautiful.
>
> (*Od.* 19.124-128)

As in the case of Laertes, the outward effects of time and unhappy experience are here given the obscuring and reversible qualities of a disguise, but a disguise that can only be lifted with Odysseus' return.

Penelope's recognition of Odysseus, then, represents for her, as it does for him, emergence from a debilitating state of eclipse. Like the reunion of Odysseus and Telemachus, the reunion of Odysseus and Penelope marks a double return. But Penelope's return is emotional rather than physical, and so resembles Odysseus' only metaphorically. This metaphorical resemblance is delineated in the simile describing the embrace which marks their reunion. . . .

> He wept holding his beloved wife, whose
>   thoughts were sound.
> And as the land appears welcome to men who
>   are swimming,
> whose well-built ship Poseidon has smashed
> on the sea, driven on with winds and big
>   swells.
> A few escape from the gray sea to dry land
> swimming, with sea-salt coating their skin,
> and rejoicing they step on shore, escaping
>   evil,
> so welcome was her husband to her as she
>   saw him before her,
> and she clung to his neck with her white
>   arms.
>
> (*Od.* 23.232-240)

The way this simile identifies Odysseus and Penelope's experiences is enhanced by its construction: a reader or listener first assumes that the simile applies to Odysseus and realizes only at line 239 that it applies to Penelope. This poetic relocation of experiences like Odysseus' in Penelope's emotional life not only suggests an internalized version of the withdrawal

and return plot that is basic to heroic narrative but also evokes the necessarily imaginary or notional kinship on which their marriage is based: Penelope's ability to experience Odysseus' trials in her imagination is a sign of their *homophrosynē*, their "likeness of mind."

Not only does the recognition scene of Odysseus and Penelope mark Penelope's return as well as Odysseus', but there is also a notable similarity between her experiences in the second half of the poem and his. Just as Odysseus undergoes a series of preliminary, clandestine recognitions that lead up to his open self-disclosure and general acknowledgment, so Penelope undergoes a series of experiences that in important ways resemble recognition scenes, in which she somehow acknowledges Odysseus' presence and is recognized by him and through which important steps are taken towards securing Odysseus' reinstatement: her appearance in the hall in Book 18, her meeting with the stranger in Book 19, and her institution of the contest of the bow in Book 21. But while Odysseus' recognitions remain generally unacknowledged, in the sense that they are kept secret by the participants, Penelope's recognitions remain unacknowledged in a further sense. They are not perceived as recognition scenes by the characters involved; they are recognition scenes only at the level of their thematic and structural affinities.

The ambiguous status of these episodes as both recognition scenes and not recognition scenes can be understood as the narrative accommodation of a certain necessary paradox. On the one hand, Penelope must not know that Odysseus is back until the end of her gradual recovery because her recognition of him actually signals its completion; on the other hand, she must know that Odysseus is back from the beginning because she cannot begin to recover until she does know. Only as she recovers does she become capable of helping Odysseus in his operations against the suitors, and thereby of bringing about the circumstances under which her actual recognition of Odysseus can take place. This means that, for most of the narrative, she must somehow know and acknowledge that Odysseus is back but still not recognize him.

These paradoxical conditions are met through a narrative characterized by ambiguity and indirection. Odysseus remains disguised from Penelope but makes his presence known to her in indirect ways. He impresses himself upon her in two distinct forms—as her absent, remembered husband and as the present stranger—while refraining from the crucial revelation that would collapse these two figures into one. He evokes his absent self by making predictions of his own return, by introducing himself as a character into his own false tales, and by encouraging the hopes that still linger in Penelope's dreams and private thoughts. As the stranger, he stirs up the household, reenacts their courtship, and . . . reawakens her interest in performing the duties of a host. In response to these gestures, Penelope acts out a kind of recognition of Odysseus but does not actually recognize him. Thus, like Odysseus after each episode of recognition, she, after each of these encounters, firmly disavows what has just occurred. But while Odysseus denies his own return by reassuming his beggar's disguise, she denies it by asserting her certainty that Odysseus will never return (for example, *Od.* 19.568-569).

Perhaps the best illustration of the kind of scene of self-revelation that Odysseus' presence causes Penelope to stage is her appearance before the suitors in Book 18. While this scene does not involve actual revelation of identity, it is very much an episode of recognition in the broader sense. Athena implants in Penelope a desire to appear before the suitors, . . .

> . . . so that she might open as much as
>   possible
> the hearts of the suitors and become even
>   more honored
> in the eyes of her husband and son than she
>   was before.
>
> > (*Od.* 18.160-162)

Penelope's appearance is an opportunity for her to display before a gathering of those best suited to acknowledge them her most glorious attributes, the combination of sexual attractiveness and chastity that makes her at once desired by the suitors and valued by her husband and son. In the course of her appearance, she wins praise from the suitors (*Od.* 18.244-249) and then insists that that be followed with material recognition in the form of gifts. In addition, she earns Odysseus' admiration for the way she uses trickery to elicit the suitors' gifts (*Od.* 18.281-283).

The timing of this episode is like that of Odysseus' self-disclosures, for it marks a significant moment in Penelope's psychological return. It is her first response to a cluster of events that have brought Odysseus to her notice: Telemachus' report of what he has learned on his journey, Theoclymenus' "prophecy" that Odysseus has already returned, Odysseus' actual entrance into the house in disguise, and Eumaeus' praise of his guest of the night before.

While Penelope's behavior in this episode is inspired by Odysseus' presence, the workings of this inspiration are obscured in the narrative both by what she doesn't know and by what she won't admit. No indication is given of precisely how the impulse to descend to the hall, which Athena sends her, presents itself to Penelope's mind. As she expresses it to her nurse, she seems to be openly puzzled by her wish to

show herself to the suitors, but to have already formulated a justification for acting on it based on her maternal duty to Telemachus. . . .

> She laughed in an idle way and called her by
>   name and addressed her.
> "Eurynome, my heart desires, although before
>   it did not,
> to appear to the suitors, although they are still
>   hateful to me.
> I would speak a word to my son, for it would
>   be more to his advantage
> not always to go among the arrogant suitors,
> who speak nicely, but have evil intentions."
>
> > (*Od.* 18.164-168)

Penelope's own words point to the way in which this desire represents a change in her and thus reveal that, however unaware of it she may be, her action is a response to the changes that have occured in the household, of which the most important is Odysseus' entrance into it as the stranger.

During her appearance, Penelope effectively acknowledges that Odysseus is somehow behind her actions, although she does not know that that is literally the case and she does so in statements whose sincerity is impossible to assess. When she confronts Telemachus, she does not warn him against the suitors as she has suggested she would; rather, she scolds him for the mistreatment that the disguised Odysseus has suffered (*Od.* 18.215-225). When she turns to her other purpose of extracting gifts from the suitors, she says she has finally reached the point when she must marry again and claims that this decision is in accord with instructions given her by Odysseus when he left for the Trojan War (*Od.* 18.251-280). Her gesture of acting more like a potential bride so that the suitors will act more like proper suitors is, in this way, tied to an evocation of Odysseus as he was when she last saw him, the point at which his image was left in her memory and from which she herself dates her decline. Odysseus' role in motivating Penelope's behavior is thus expressed, but indirectly and in a sense inaccurately in speeches that are far from straightforward. She alludes to him as he presents himself, in disguised or distanced forms, as either the present beggar or the long-absent Odysseus of the past.

Penelope's self-revelation in this scene is further allied to more narrowly defined scenes of recognition by the element of physical transformation. As Odysseus' disguise often is, Penelope's careworn appearance is suspended temporarily for a preliminary scene of recognition. With Athena's aid, she is suddenly transformed so that she looks more beautiful and resembles the gods (*Od.* 18.190-196). In this case, though, she is herself unaware of her transformation and denies that it has taken place, responding to

Eurymachus' praise in the same words with which she denies the stranger's praise in the passage quoted above (*Od.* 18.251-255). In fact, when this transformation occurs, she actively resists it. When she tells Eurynome that she would like to show herself to the suitors, Eurynome suggests that she should wash and anoint herself, that is, that she should willfully change her appearance, and links the cessation of mourning that this would signal to Telemachus' maturity (*Od.* 18.171-176). Penelope responds by saying, in effect, that Telemachus' maturity is not sufficient to rouse her from her present condition; she must remain disguised as long as Odysseus is absent. . . .

> Eurynome, don't suggest such things, much as you care for me,
> as washing my body and anointing myself with oil.
> For the gods who live on Olympus destroyed my beauty
> since the day when that man embarked in the hollow ships.
>
>   (*Od.* 18.178-181)

From her perspective, the event that is necessary for her deliverance has not occurred. Not knowing that Odysseus has returned (however much she may be acknowledging Odysseus' return in her behavior) Penelope cannot cooperate with Athena in bringing about the transformation that precedes her descent into the hall. Instead, Athena must first make her unconscious by putting her to sleep in order to accomplish it.

The way in which, throughout this episode, Penelope persistently denies and resists those aspects of her own behavior that make it most like the combination of revelation of oneself and recognition of another of which episodes of recognition consist, highlights the paradoxical or ambiguous character of her preliminary encounters with Odysseus. In many of their formal characteristics, these encounters are episodes of recognition, but they are not acknowledged as such by any of the participants. This is particularly apparent during their meeting in Book 19 where the growing psychological sympathy that precedes recognition is achieved through a series of displaced gestures of recognition. In the early part of the episode Penelope recognizes, not the stranger, but the absent figure of Odysseus whom the stranger claims to have met, in a process that shares the formal features of actual recognition scenes: the expression of solitary emotion (*Od.* 19.209-212); a demand for proof (*Od.* 19.215-219); the presentation of tokens (*Od.* 19.220-248); even the formula describing recognition, . . . "as she recognized the sure signs that Odysseus had pointed out" (*Od.* 19.250, cf. *Od.* 23.206, *Od.* 24.346). Later, Odysseus' recognition is evoked obliquely through Penelope's account of her dream and the stranger's response to it. But

again the recognition does not actually occur. Yet, this interchange leads directly to the typical conclusion of a recognition scene, the construction of a plot (*Od.* 19.570-587), a plot that so strongly suggests the sequel to recognition that it is interpreted as a sure sign that a recognition has taken place by at least one of the suitors (*Od.* 24.167-169) and by many readers of the poem.

At the surface level of the plot, Odysseus does not reveal himself to Penelope and she does not recognize him until after the suitors have been dealt with. But in terms of the patterns their actions fulfill, Odysseus and Penelope participate in a series of encounters in which they go through the motions of recognition, each acknowledging the other, which anticipate and lead up to their openly-avowed reunion in Book 23. These encounters are, in a sense, recognition scenes that have gone underground: they resemble the moment of open recognition that they anticipate, but do not share its openness; they are recognitions on the level of the underlying import of the actions that make them up but not in the consciousness of the characters. In the case of Penelope, the meaning that her actions derive from their formal and thematic associations assumes special importance as a guide for interpreting them, because the poem is silent about her thoughts and feelings at crucial junctures in the narrative. . . .

The plot of Odysseus' return to Ithaca is thus complicated by the interwined stories of the loyal supporters who recognize him, stories that, in various ways, resemble his own. The differences between these stories and the ways in which they intersect delineate the important distinction that always remains between Odysseus, as the dominant heroic figure on whom the poem centers, and his followers. Just as Odysseus' extraordinary voyage remains different from Telemachus' tame trip to the mainland and from Penelope's difficulties at home, so there is finally a significant difference between the literal disguises that Odysseus assumes and discards at will and the metaphorical disguises of Laertes, Telemachus, Penelope, and Eumaeus. These characters' oppressive conditions take on the reversible quality of disguise only because of Odysseus' return against all odds and against all expectations. In various ways, the encounters discussed above all delineate relationships that, while reciprocal, also involve dependence on Odysseus. Odysseus' single-handed self-restoration in Phaeacia and his resort to literal disguise on Ithaca set him apart as a hero who is not subject to these limitations, a hero who is so thoroughly in control of his situation that he can adopt and abandon these limitations at will, and who can serve as the agent of their transcendence by others. With these characters Odysseus is able to play the role of a god, to act towards them as Athena acts towards him.

Odysseus' disguise is an artificial device that allows

him to structure the plot of his return by controlling the timing of his self-revelations so that he can, at the proper moment, disclose himself like a disguised god instead of running headlong into destruction like that ordinary mortal Agamemnon. Similarly, the ***Odyssey's*** plot of the hero's return in disguise and recognition is an artificial device through which the poem organizes and controls the celebration of its hero Odysseus. And just as the success of Odysseus' strategies and of the divine scheme into which they are subsumed depends on proper timing, so the poem's success in presenting Odysseus playing this godlike role with the various dependent members of his household also depends on timing, on the story being set at a particular point in Odysseus' life.

The importance of the story's timing is suggested most urgently by the mounting pressures on Penelope to marry again, to cast someone else in the role of her husband. It is also seen in relation to the two members of Odysseus' own family who recognize him: his father, who was once a more powerful figure than he, and his son, who someday will be. The challenge to Odysseus' preeminence that these figures represent is implicit in the poem's nearly final image of Odysseus fighting the suitors' relatives with Laertes and Telemachus, both in a state of paramount vigor, at his side. Only because the poem is set at the time when Telemachus is still too young and Laertes is already too old to assert himself effectively can Odysseus remain the dominant figure in this tableau.

The significance of timing is further reflected in the way Odysseus times the self-revelations that animate the heroism of his father and son. Telemachus is encountered soon after Odysseus' arrival and is consigned to the role of his father's lieutenant. Laertes does not realize his wish of recovering his youth in time to fight against the suitors. Odysseus' delay in revealing himself to Laertes assures that his father is not able to share the limelight when Odysseus performs his most glorious feat. Only in the context of what is represented as a secondary challenge, the battle with the suitors' relatives, does the poem directly represent the competition between the generations. And then this generational competition is depicted as a welcome rivalry: Odysseus reminds Telemachus of the tradition of heroism he must live up to (*Od.* 24.506-509); Telemachus responds that he will do his best (*Od.* 24.511-512); and Laertes rejoices that his son and his grandson are vying in *aret,* "excellence" (*Od.* 24.514-515). This final vision, which stresses the family's figurative conquest of time through the continuity of the line, cannot outweigh the singularity of Odysseus' achievements as revealed in the actions that lead up to it.

Finally, the poem's success in depicting Odysseus as extraordinary is aided by its geographical as well as its temporal setting. For it is only at home in Ithaca that Odysseus can find people with whom he has relations of mutual support capable of being revived after many years in which he plays this dominant role. Only there can he defeat his enemies by putting together a band of followers consisting solely of family members and personal retainers. Outside his own home he must cooperate with others who are not naturally subordinated to him by virtue of their age, gender, or social status. Only at home can he count on being able to play the central part in a godlike scenario. The setting and the action that occurs in it are entirely interdependent, and what is in one sense the goal of the story is in another its precondition. The apparent conquest of limitation implied in the hero's achievements is inextricable from an acceptance of limitation, the limitation of his sphere of action to his own home. What appears to be a story of godlike transcendence is in fact bounded by the restricted conditions of ordinary human life.

Lloyd-Jones on the morality of the *Odyssey*:

In the *Odyssey,* moral issues are infinitely simpler [than in the *Iliad*], not only during the adventures narrated by Odysseus, with their marked element of folktale, but even in Ithaca, where daily life is depicted with such great naturalism, good and bad and right and wrong are separated almost as clearly as in a Western film. True, one or two characters have an intermediate status; . . . but these exceptions hardly do more than heighten the contrast between black and white. It seems most unsafe to conclude that the comparative moral simplicity of the *Odyssey* is due simply to ethical progress made by the Greek world in the interval between the composition of the two poems. The truth is that the *Odyssey* is not an epic poem of the same kind as the *Iliad*. It is a poem linked with the true heroic epic through the person of its hero and other characters, yet containing a strong element of folklore and distinguished by a marked moralising strain, conductive to the triumph of the hero, and a happy ending, from the tragic character of the other epic. The difference in theology and morality between the two poems reflects a difference in style and purpose, and is of no value in fixing their temporal relation to each other.

Hugh Lloyd-Jones, in The Justice of Zeus, *University of California Press, 1971.*

Nancy Felson-Rubin (essay date 1994)

SOURCE: "Wife," in *Regarding Penelope: From Character to Poetics,* Princeton University Press, 1994, pp. 43-65.

[In the essay below, Felson-Rubin examines the husband-wife relationship of Odysseus and Penelope and

details "the formal pattern of their second courtship."]

Odysseus's image of Penelope once he is home differs radically from the image that drew him there. While he journeyed, he envisioned Penelope as a fixed point, a stable goal, a *telos* or "fulfillment." So long as he remembered her and Ithaka, he never strayed too far nor roamed too recklessly. Once he is on Ithaka, however, Penelope becomes an enigma for him (as she is for other characters). In a sense, she *is* his human condition. Face-to-face, the two engage in a courtship dance in which now one, now the other takes the lead. They reverse roles, take risks, dominate, and outwit each other, until finally they reunite on their implanted marriage-bed. There they mingle in lovemaking and exchange stories of their adventures.

Evident in the dance Homer choreographs for Odysseus and Penelope on Ithaka is the *homophrosunê* or "like-mindedness" that Odysseus wishes for Nausikäa as the foundation of a good marriage (6.181-85). This principle, as we shall see, describes both the marriage reenacted between Odysseus and Penelope and the architecture of the ***Odyssey***.

To probe Odysseus's understanding of Penelope requires that we concoct Odysseus's character (as we did Penelope's), to see whether elements dispersed in the text allow us to capture him as he gazes upon her. Does he understand the complex, intricate, polytropic, "periphronic" Penelope? Or does Homer weave gaps in Odysseus's vision which create [as stated by Teresa de Lauretis in *Alice Doesn't. Feminism Semiotics Cinema,* 1984] "an effect of distance, like a discordant echo, which ruptures the coherence of address and dislocates meaning"?

According to the descriptions other characters give of Odysseus before and during the Trojan War, he was a generous, gentle, and pious king. He ruled like a gentle father (*êpios patêr*), even seating upon his knees and feeding the young Eurymakhos (16.442-44). He accepted refugees, such as the father of Antinoös (16.424-30), and regularly transported strangers, exchanged hospitality, and sacrificed to the gods (cf. 1.66-67). He was master of an orderly and prosperous household, in which servants and livestock and even Argos the hunting dog flourished. The loyal swineherd ruefully reminisces to the beggar about the relaxed and prosperous days of old, when Odysseus was in the palace and the help were treated well. Under Odysseus, the Ithakans prospered like the subjects of the ideal king to whom the stranger compares Penelope at 19.109-14.

Odysseus and Penelope once shared responsibilities, such as the care of his parents, as Odysseus's departing words reveal. These are the words that Penelope repeats to Antinoös in the presence of the disguised Odysseus, when she tells how her husband took her by the wrist and said:

> here let everything be in your charge.
> You must take thought for my father and
>   mother here in our palace,
> as you do now, or even more, since I shall be
>   absent.
> But when you see our son grown up and
>   bearded, then you may
> marry whatever man you might please,
>   forsaking your household.
>
>   18.266-70

Whereas Agamemnon enjoined a bard to watch over Klytaimestra, and thus virtually to command his kingdom, Odysseus left everything in Penelope's care, a sign in itself of his confidence in their like-mindedness.

Some of Odysseus's traits as a warrior would also grace an egalitarian husband. When Telemakhos, yearning for news of his father, hears Nestor, Menelaos, and Helen recount exploits of the heroic Odysseus in Troy, he learns of his father's cunning (*mêtis*), daring, and capacity to endure. Nestor tells of Odysseus's stratagem of the Trojan Horse, which ended the War (3.118-22), but also of his thoughtfulness as a leader and of their accord (3.127-29), in contrast to the discord between Menelaos and Agamemnon (3.141-50). Helen's tale of Odysseus the beggar reconnoitering in Troy reveals, again, his cunning and daring. Menelaos depicts Odysseus inside the Trojan horse, hearing Helen impersonate each Akhaian's wife (4.271-89), restraining his comrades, and holding himself back. Though he does not use epithets, these actions correspond to what is meant by *ekhephrôn* ("temperate; prudent; discreet") and *polutlas* ("much-enduring"). Such traits, as we shall see, also distinguish Odysseus as he courts Penelope anew.

Several critical choices toward the end of his journey empower Odysseus to engage in a courtship dance with Penelope. On Ogygia, the penultimate stop before Ithaka, he picks a life of endurance with Penelope over an unchanging and inglorious life with Kalypso the Concealer. Kalypso tries her best to undermine his decision to return to the land of his fathers and to Penelope:

> but if you only knew . . .
> you would stay here with me and be the lord
>   of this household
> and be an immortal, for all your longing once
>   more to look on
> that wife for whom you are pining all your
>   days here. And yet
> I think that I can claim that I am not her
>   inferior

A coin bearing on the obverse the legend Iakin, and on the reverse a representation of the brooch described by Odysseus.

either in build or stature, since it is not likely
    that mortal
women can challenge the goddesses for build
    and beauty.

                    5.206-13

The goddess derides Penelope as a mere mortal woman, calling her *keinês,* "that one." Odysseus concedes Kalypso's superiority, as one who is immortal and ageless (218), but refuses her attractive offer, tactfully shifting the terms of the comparison by substituting "house" and "homecoming" for "wife." Accepting his own mortality, with a mortal partner, Odysseus declines to stay: "I will endure (*tlêsomai*)," he tells Kalypso, "keeping a stubborn spirit (*talapenthea thumon*) inside me" (5.222). To endure means, in the context of the **Odyssey,** to embrace human contingency and uncertainty; this involves accepting a Penelope who is neither static nor predictable but who requires of her partner a willingness to take risks. Seen thus, marriage with Penelope epitomizes the human condition.

Odysseus's yearning for Penelope and for Ithaka is graphically portrayed in the here-and-now, whereas his relationship (*philotês*) with Kalypso is told only in retrospect. What we experience directly is the captive lover, whose eyes are "never / wiped dry of tears, and the sweet lifetime was draining out of him / as he wept for a way home, since the nymph was no longer pleasing / to him" (5.151-53). Despite a surrounding so lush and idyllic that Hermes marvels seeing it (5.59-75),

Odysseus yearns to rejoin Penelope at home. Homer adds (perhaps playing to male auditors) that once Odysseus obtains a promise of release, he and Kalypso "enjoyed themselves in love and stayed all night by each other." (5.227)

As he tells his Kalypso adventure to the Phaiakians, in order to dramatize their ongoing battle of wills Odysseus counterbalances one iterative against another. That is, he matches his own *dueskon* (7.259-60: "I . . . forever was drenching with tears / that clothing, immortal stuff, Kalypso had given") against Kalypso's *ephaske* (7.256-57: "she promised [lit., "kept saying"] / to make me an immortal and all my days to be ageless").

On Skheria Odysseus resists the enticement of princess Nausikäa. From the start he understands the implications of their differences in age and experience. Their first meeting at the shore opens with a simile that underscores his self-restraint. The naked hero, awakened by Nausikäa and her age-mates, strides confidently, "trusting in his might" (*alki pepoithôs*),

            like some hill-kept lion,
  who advances, though he is rained on and
    blown by the wind, and both eyes
  kindle; he goes out after cattle or sheep, or it
    may be
  deer in the wilderness, and his belly is urgent
    upon him
  to get inside of a close steading and go for

the sheepflocks.
So Odysseus was ready to face (lit., "mingle
    with") young girls with well-ordered
hair, naked though he was, for the need
    (*khreiô*) was on him; and yet
he appeared terrifying to them, all crusted
    with dry spray,
and they scattered one way and another down
    the jutting beaches.

6.130-38

The simile casts an immediate shadow on the encounter to follow. The hungry lion clearly intends to devour his prey once he goes after them; likewise, Odysseus could victimize the young maidens by "mingling" in their midst. [In *Similes in the Homeric Poems, Hypomnemata,* Vol. 49, 1977, Carroll] Moulton rightly interprets the violence as seen from the maidens' perspective; i.e., it is their focalization that Homer captures in the simile. This does not in itself eliminate violence as a possibility; i.e., for Homer's audience, the maidens' fear of a ravenous, overconfident lion *raises* the possibility that Odysseus will behave that way in the present circumstances.

On the violence inherent in the simile, [William T.] Magrath comments [in "Progression of the Lion Similes in the *Odyssey,*" *Classical Journal,* Vol. 77, 1982], "This lion is obviously prone to violence, driven by maddening hunger, desperately in search of flesh-meat." But after what does the leonine Odysseus hunger? Clearly he has a need (*khreiô*) for food and hospitality; perhaps he "needs" to conquer innocent maidens as well.

The verb *miksesthai,* "to mingle," commonly used in Homer for "have sexual intercourse with," suggests that this is a scene of potential rape. Nausikää soon uses this verb to express her disapproval of a girl who would "mingle with men" (6.288: *andrasi misgêtai*) before she comes openly to marriage. Two explicitly sexual uses of the verb occur. First, at 1.73, Thoösa, daughter of Phorkys, bore Polyphemos after mingling (*migeisa*) with Poseidon. Then, at 23.219, Penelope explains that, if Helen had known she would be brought back home again, she would not "have lain in love (*emigê philotêti kai eunêi,* lit., "have mingled in lovemaking and the bed") with an outlander from another country."

The lion simile bolsters this interpretation. Its inclusion of deer (133, *elaphous*) as the lion's potential victims recalls the Artemis simile, some lines earlier (102-4): Nausikää leads in the dancing like Artemis "delighting in boars and deer [*elaphoisi*] in their running." Homer's comparison of Nausikää, the "virgin unwedded" (109: *admês,* lit., "untamed"), to Artemis underscores the maiden's simultaneous vulnerability and inviolability, because Artemis and her attendants are frequent victims of sexual assault, but at a high risk to the attacker.

Thus the lion simile evokes Odysseus's latent power to victimize Nausikää and her maidens as a predator his prey; yet no victimization, no rape takes place. Instead, Odysseus supplicates Nausikää as if she were a goddess, anticipating the suppliant role he will assume in Ithaka. Comparing Nausikää to Artemis, he begs for her protection and prays that the gods grant what her heart desires, "a husband and a house and sweet agreement / in all things (*homophrosunên esthlên,* lit., "noble like-mindedness"), for nothing is better than this, more steadfast, / than when two people, a man and his wife, keep a harmonious / household (*homophroneonte noêmasin,* lit., "being like-minded in their thoughts")." (6.181-84) By wishing Nausikää a like-minded marriage, Odysseus gently communicates to her, early on, that he is not her match.

Nausikää's role as savior restores the balance between them and permits a measure of reciprocity. This is heightened, for the audience (and presumably for Nausikää), when Odysseus names the very thing her heart desires. Later, their parting also attests to a reciprocity between them (8.457-68).

Odysseus's speech to Nausikää, designed to win her over by verbal seduction, is labeled "soothing" (*meilikhion*) and "profit-turning" (*kerdaleon*) (6.148). This suggests that Odysseus might take advantage of her youth and innocence, yet compared to what the lion simile suggests *could* have happened, his motives are benign. He merely charms Nausikää into granting his request for refuge. This combination of expediency and restraint prefigures Odysseus's manner during his prolonged second courtship of Penelope.

When Odysseus meets Alkinoös and Arete, his first task is to deflect any Skherian notion that he might wed Nausikää. What he most wants is safe transport home and gifts, *not* pressure to stay and marry. He tells his Adventures for these purposes, and we are asked to consider their content in light of his intent. Odysseus uses his legendary status to influence the royal couple, cleverly enhancing his self-image as he enchants them individually with his tales. Even his fib to deflect blame from Nausikää for her apparent inhospitality is self-enhancing. He deliberately and cunningly weaves an image of himself as an adventurer who erred at times but paid dearly and now knows better. His ultimate enticement is a place for the Phaiakians, as rescuers, in his song: the better he sings, the more likely they are to help him.

Odysseus narrates his encounters in the Underworld so as to characterize himself sympathetically for his Phaiakian audience and to catalyze them to act on his behalf. First, he describes with feeling his meeting with his mother and then catalogues the heroines of old in detail—tales that would enchant the queen. He has the murdered king Agamemnon raise the spectre of a Klytaimestran Penelope to prod the Phaiakians to convey him to Ithaka with caution, just in case. By manipulating the stories about heroines and treacherous wives, Odysseus subtly and tactfully builds up to his climactic point, voicing (as he leaves Skheria) the hope that he will find a blameless wife (*amumona akoitin*) in *his* halls (13.42-43).

In his Adventures Odysseus exercises power through kindliness and example, as in his kingly role in Ithaka in the recollections of his people. He depicts himself, to the Phaiakians, as leading his men not so much by intimidation as by eliciting unanimity and consensus. The function of debate in their deliberations foreshadows Periclean Athens, as does the fact that no one, not even Odysseus, has a monopoly on right thinking. Hence, when the outcome is calamitous, blame falls on everyone, not just on a misguided leader. That Odysseus uses persuasion, not force, is evident from incidents where someone challenges his leadership, usually Eurylokhos. On Kirke's island, instead of eliminating his challenger or struggling with him for power, Odysseus restrains his rage (e.g., at 10.438-41), goes along with his men, and leaves Eurylokhos behind. He and his men eventually triumph over the situation, though they need to remind him not to dally. That is, they take the leadership role, and he follows along. In a second example, on the island of Helios, the crew is misled by Eurylokhos to consume the sun god's cattle, breaking their oath to Odysseus. All perish through their own recklessness (cf. 1.7-9 and 12.415-19); that is, they are to blame along with Eurylokhos, who led them astray. Odysseus, however, as a leader who fell asleep, cannot entirely be absolved.

Because, of all the Adventures, Homer authenticates only the episodes with Kalypso, the Kyklops, and Helios, listeners are entitled to be skeptical about the rest. Indeed the ironic wording of Alkinoös's compliment to Odysseus, when he likens him to a bard (11.367-69), invites us to question the latter's veracity (and, incidentally and by extension, that of Homer himself); some episodes may be fabricated, others exaggerated, to help the singer-narrator Odysseus achieve his ends.

Odysseus's varied relations to Kalypso, Kirke, the Sirens, and Arete and Nausikää, in his Adventures and in Homer's narrations, all foreshadow his eventual courtship of Penelope. Each female offers him something, and at little cost. Willing to embrace the first three, he gains what he needs without irrevocably endangering himself by becoming stuck, trapped, eclipsed, or frozen. Something in Penelope's relationship to him offers him the freedom to explore this female world

without jeopardizing their ultimate reunion. Odysseus's adventures with Kalypso, Kirke, and the Sirens seem to satisfy his desire and need to rove. By the time he meets Arete and Nausikää, he has exhausted his need for exotic adventures and an exotic lover or spouse.

His choice to leave Ogygia and to reject Kalypso's offer enables Odysseus to coalesce as a self. It is this self that Athena recognizes and affirms at their reunion in Book 13. Indeed, Athena's acknowledgement of his "polytropy" as a distinctive feature of his personality facilitates our task of "making sense" of *Odusseus polutropos* "Odysseus of the many turns."

Other characters have already contributed to our growing impression of Odysseus's coherence. For example, Nestor described him as *poikilomêtis* ("full of various wiles") at 3.163, Helen as possessing *kerdosunê* ("cunning; craft; an eye to profit") at 4.251, and Helen and Menelaos as *talasiphrôn* ("patient of mind; stout-hearted; of enduring spirit") at 4.241 and 4.270, respectively. In addition, Kirke repeatedly recognized him as *polumêkhanos* ("resourceful; inventive; of many devices") at 10.456, 488, and 504. Odysseus himself expands our growing image of him by the way he portrays himself in the Adventures that he narrates in Skheria.

The reunion of Odysseus and Athena on Ithaka rehearses the reunion between husband and wife. With Athena, Odysseus is alternately dominant and submissive, active and passive; and this flexibility prepares him to court Penelope. To the goddess disguised first as a shepherd, then as a stately girl, he fibs, "forever using to advantage the mind that is within him" (13.255), delighting his "partner." His ingenuity at lying leads her to portray him as *polukerdeos, poikilomêtis, polutlas, epetês, angkhinoos, ekhephrôn, polumêkhanos*—epithets that epitomize his distinctive heroic qualities.

Odysseus's continued skepticism about whether he is really on Ithaka elicits not only more delight from Athena but more precise characterization:

> Always you are the same, and such is the
> mind within you,
> and so I cannot abandon you when you are
> unhappy,
> because you are fluent, and reason closely,
> and keep your head always.
>
>   13.330-32

Emphasizing his paternal line just as he is returning to his *oikos,* the goddess addresses him as "son of Laertes and seed of Zeus, resourceful Odysseus" (13.375). Together, they plan the slaughter of the suitors. Athena neither affirms Odysseus's marital bond with Penelope nor challenges it. On the one hand, she applies a common epithet, *ekhephrôn,* to Penelope (at 13.406) and Odysseus (at 13.332) and emphasizes that both are temperate and discreet. On the other, she focuses more on survival traits in Odysseus than on those traits that enable him to reunite with Penelope.

The traits Athena assigns Odysseus confirm those already manifest in his first boar hunt and in the Odysseus of legend: he is much-enduring, of much cunning, of dappled cunning, of many strategies, with a mind to much profit, restrained in his mind, close-thinking. These traits overlap and are mutually compatible. Missing from Athena's characterization and epithetization of Odysseus are certain domestic traits evident in his roles as father-husband-king-friend and manifest in reminiscences of characters from before and during the Trojan War. Two refrains describe Odysseus of old: "he ruled gently like a father" and "if he were to come back and take care of my life (*emon bion amphipoleuoi*), then / my reputation (*kleos*) would be great and splendid" (18.254-55 = 19.127-28). Except for *polutlas* and *ekhephrôn,* the traits enumerated by Athena would not especially enhance Odysseus's capacity for a relationship with Penelope based on *homophrosunê,* except insofar as the "polytropy" of each partner contributes to like-mindedness and mutual admiration.

While Odysseus's affinity with Athena is based on a common ability to maneuver words and thoughts, his affinity with Penelope seems to exceed this. Versatility, or "polytropy," indeed contributes to the quality of their second courtship as a combat, a hunt, a pursuit and chase by predator of prey, even as a playful dance; but "polytropy" could just as easily undermine the stability of their marriage.

Odysseus focuses on the issue of Penelope's fidelity. "Is Penelope still waiting for me, after twenty years?" is his recurrent question. Each piece of news of Penelope, from his mother Antikleia, from the seer Teiresias, and from Athena, adds nuances to his understanding. Odysseus bids the shade of Antikleia to tell him about the wife he married, "what she wants (her *boulê*), what she is thinking (her *noos*), / and whether she stays fast by my son, and guards everything, / or if she has married the best man among the Akhaians" (11.177-79). Antikleia responds:

> All too much with enduring heart she does
>   wait for you
> there in your own palace, and always with her
>   the wretched
> nights and the days also waste her away with
>   weeping.
>
>   11.181-83

With this empathic portrait of Penelope, Antikleia reassures Odysseus.

The prophet Teiresias describes Odysseus's domestic situation with more reserve and in greater detail:

> but if you yourself get clear,
> you will come home in bad case, with the loss
>   of all your companions,
> in someone else's ship, and find troubles in
>   your household,
> insolent men, who are eating away your
>   livelihood,
> and courting your godlike wife and offering
>   gifts to win her.
> You may punish the violences of these men,
>   when you come home.
> But after you have killed these suitors in your
>   own palace,
> either by treachery, or openly with the sharp
>   bronze,
> then you must . . .
>
>   11.113-21

Teiresias does not mention Penelope's reaction to the suitors but his statement, "offering gifts to win her," does leave the possibility open that one of them will indeed persuade her.

Both Antikleia's depiction of Penelope weeping and Teiresias's of her being courted lead into Odysseus's encounter with the shade of Agamemnon, whose tale of his own slaughter by a treacherous wife and her lover raises questions implicitly and explicitly about the future action of Penelope.

Once in Ithaka, Odysseus again hears of the courtship of Penelope, this time from Athena:

> Son of Laertes and seed of Zeus, resourceful
>   Odysseus,
> consider how you can lay your hands on these
>   shameless suitors,
> who for three years now have been as lords in
>   your palace,
> and courting your godlike wife, and offering
>   gifts to win her.
> And she, though her heart forever grieves over
>   your homecoming,
> holds out some hope for all, and makes
>   promises to each man,
> sending them messages, but her mind has
>   other intentions.
>
>   13.375-81

He exclaims in response:

> Surely I was on the point of perishing by an
>   evil
> fate in my palace, like Atreus's son
>   Agamemnon, unless
> you had told me, goddess, the very truth of

all that has happened.
Come then, weave the design . . .

13.383-86

O pôpoi . . . indicates Odysseus's surprise at Penelope's extension of hope to her suitors. This exclamation, which some take as sheer flattery of Athena, reveals his awareness of the deep ambiguity in Penelope's outward gestures of encouragement to the suitors. He understands that she is living dangerously; the question is, How will he respond?

Odysseus's disguise gives him an immediate edge on Penelope. It affords him an opportunity, as with Nausikäa, to exploit, dominate, and overpower her. Always lurking as a possible plot is brutality toward a wayward wife, brutality that in our text is played out against the twelve wayward maidservants (metonyms of Penelope).

When the swineherd Eumaios speaks of Penelope, he never mentions her words of encouragement to the suitors. To Telemakhos he says only:

> All too much with enduring heart she does
>   wait for him
> there in your own palace, and always with her
>   the wretched
> nights and the days also waste her away with
>   weeping.

16.37-39

These are almost the exact words of Antikleia in the Underworld quoted earlier, with appropriate changes in the formula for person (from "for you" to "for him").

Upon returning from his journey Telemakhos underscores Penelope's ambivalence when he tells Eumaios, in Odysseus's presence:

>   it was for your sake I came here,
> to look upon you with my eyes, and to hear a
>   word from you,
> whether my mother endures still in the halls,
>   or whether
> some other man has married her, and the bed
>   of Odysseus
> lies forlorn of sleepers with spider webs
>   grown upon it.

16.31-35

A bit later, he reminds Eumaios of the problem of entertaining a guest in the palace and complains about his mother:

> I myself am young and have no faith in my
>   hand's strength
> to defend a man, if anyone else picks a quarrel
>   with him;

and my mother's heart is divided in her, and
    ponders two ways,
whether to remain here with me, and look
    after the household,
keep faith with her husband's bed, and regard
    the voice of the people,
or go away at last with the best man of the
    Akhaians
who pays her court in her palace, and brings
    her the most presents.

16.71-77

Telemakhos's concerns reinforce what Odysseus already knows from Athena of the courtship of Penelope.

Reports of Penelope's activities have a cumulative effect on Odysseus, causing sometimes faint concern, sometimes sharp anxiety about whether she will wait or act precipitously. Odysseus takes control of the time and place of their interview. He achieves this indirectly, through an intermediary, Eumaios the swineherd. The swineherd himself does not know the role he is playing as he transmits messages back and forth. In this way, Odysseus and Penelope "converse" via Eumaios.

First, on his own, Eumaios tells Penelope that the stranger "would charm out (*thelgoito*) the dear heart within you . . . so he enchanted me" (17.514 and 521). This verb "enchant, or charm" appears elsewhere in erotic contexts, as when Penelope charms the suitors' hearts with *erôs* (18.212) and with soft words (18.283). So here *thelgoito* has meaning beyond Eumaios's intention, which listeners pick up but which may also stimulate Penelope. In her energetic reply, she emphatically summons Odysseus (via the intermediary) to her side: the swineherd should "tell the stranger to come" (17.508-9), "call him here, so he can tell me directly" (529), and "go, please, and summon the stranger into my presence" (544). Eumaios carries the message, translating the three requests: "Penelope . . . / summons you, for her heart is urgent to find out / from you about her husband, though she is suffering troubles" (553-55). In response, and on the grounds of avoiding rough treatment from the suitors, Odysseus asks the swineherd:

> Tell Penelope, therefore for all her eagerness
>   (*epeigomenên per*), to wait
> for me in the palace until the sun has set. Let
>   her
> then question me about her husband's day of
>   homecoming,
> giving me a seat close to the fire.

17.569-72

Trimming the beggar's message, the swineherd omits *epeigomenên per* (582, "for all her eagerness," lit. "although being eager" or "howevermuch eager"). This participle appears in Penelope's pronouncement to the suitors in her ruse of the shroud, recounted first by Antinoös to Telemakhos, next by Penelope to the stranger, and finally by Amphimedon in the Underworld:

> Young men, my suitors now that the great Odysseus has perished,
> Wait, though you are eager (*epeigomenoi*) to marry me until I finish
> this web, so that my weaving will not be useless and wasted.
> 2.96-98 = 19.141-43 = 24.131-33

The participial phrase formulaically describes the impatience of a lover. Thus Odysseus's inclusion of it in his message to Penelope and Eumaios's deletion of it when he delivers the message suggest that Odysseus alone recognizes Penelope's state of mind.

In their interchange, Eumaios refers to Penelope as "mother of Telemakhos" (17.554). Odysseus substitutes "daughter of Ikarios," which may suggest that, as he requests his first rendezvous through an unwitting intermediary, he thinks of Penelope as her father's daughter, as if he were once again asking her father for her hand in marriage.

Before they meet for their private interview at the hearth, Penelope appears before her suitors, motivated by Athena and by her own unexamined intentions. Athena adorns her, decking her out like a maiden to be married. She charms and arouses the suitors (18.212-13), and she stirs Odysseus (and Telemakhos) besides.

Penelope's display before the suitors might have offended Odysseus and incurred his blame. Indeed, later, after the recognition, Penelope exonerates herself from blame (23.209-30). But here, as she wheedles gifts out of her suitors, Odysseus is happy "because she beguiled gifts out of them and enchanted their spirits / with blandishing words, though her own mind had other intentions" (18.282-83). He values the economic gains that will replenish the household, and he recognizes both their like-mindedness in esteeming household wealth and her wiliness, which matches his. Her act, as he interprets it, reveals a wife still taking thought for their common possessions and a wife still shrewd in promoting their common goals.

Most importantly, Odysseus is now among Penelope's many suitors. She is "much wooed," like Pero in Odysseus's Catalogue of Heroines (11.287-90), Nausikäa on Skheria, and Helen. Because Odysseus hopes to win Penelope, competition for her hand, far from intimidating or discouraging him, enhances her value and stimulates his desire. He is now confident of Penelope's intentions. In fact, Homer's formulaic "though her mind had other intentions" may represent Odysseus's focalization, as a character who intuits his wife's attitudes from within. Compare, however, the impact of Athena's "reassurance" to Odysseus about Penelope's steadfastness at 13.381, where, after informing him that Penelope sends secret promises to each suitor, she employs the same formula: "but her mind has other intentions." Odysseus responds by emphasizing his narrow escape from an evil death. To the external audience the reassuring words on both occasions may even raise suspicions about Penelope's intentions; in neither case is the evaluation of her intentions authoritative.

Because he expects to survive even if Penelope betrays him, he watches, with equanimity, as she charms the suitors. His confident reaction would baffle an audience still skeptical about Penelope's motives. Moreover, by inviting the live audience to watch Odysseus watch Penelope flirt, Homer heightens suspense.

Several parallels between Penelope and Odysseus become clear. As she enjoys enchanting her suitors, so he once took pleasure with Kalypso and presumably with Kirke. As her behavior toward the suitors is incautious, in that it overlooks the possible costs of pleasure, especially the endangerment of her son, so Odysseus was incautious with Polyphemos and only retrospectively acknowledged his own poor judgment.

During Penelope's "flirtation" Odysseus overhears her tell Eurymakhos what Odysseus said to her when he left for Troy:

> Dear wife, since I do not think the strong-greaved Akhaians
> will all come safely home from Troy without hurt . . . ,
> here let everything be in your charge. . . .
> But when you see our son grown up and bearded, then you may
> marry whatever man you might please, forsaking your household.
> 18.259-70

Penelope's reminiscence should remind Odysseus that his wife deserves no blame for doing precisely what he had long ago prescribed.

The appointed interview is preceded by an exchange between Odysseus and Melantho. Odysseus warns her:

> Beware of your mistress, who may grow angry with you and hate you.
> Or Odysseus may come back. There is still time for hope there.
> And even if he has perished and will no longer come back,
> here is Telemakhos, his son, by grace of Apollo

grown such a man, and in his palace none of
the women
will be sinful and escape, since he is a child
no longer.

19.83-88

In these lines Odysseus shows how harshly he can
react to an affront, for the maid has rebuked him
twice (18.321ff and 19.65-69). Earlier, however, we
learned that she regularly sleeps with Eurymakhos
(18.325). Though the scolding ostensibly answers her
harsh words to the beggar, it also obliquely refers to
her reckless dalliance with a suitor—a form of infi-
delity and betrayal of the household and its master
and mistress.

Melantho is both a metonym for Penelope and her
mistress's foil. As her servant, linked to Penelope by
contiguity, she actualizes what in her mistress remains
potential. Thus we can see, via this vignette, how
Odysseus would react were Penelope to betray his bed:
if she acted recklessly and treacherously, she would
not escape his notice. Penelope calls Melantho a bold
and shameless bitch (19.92), dissociating herself from
the maidservant's wanton behavior. Penelope's remark
suggests that she sees through Melantho—recognizing
(as [John J.] Winkler suggests [in *The Constraints of
Desire. The Anthropology of Sex and Gender in Ancient Greece,* 1990]) her betrayal of Penelope's ruse of
the loom and perhaps even her affair with Eurymakhos. The pair, husband and wife, react toward Melantho with like minds.

To Penelope's uncustomarily direct query as to his
identity, "What man are you and whence? Where is
your city? Your parents?" (19.105) Odysseus responds
with an ornate compliment to her that recalls his earlier compliment to Nausikäa as he sought her protection. Once again, he is a suppliant and a wayfarer.
This time his advantage is his disguise and superior
knowledge; then it was Nausikäa's age and innocence.
His compliment, as a ploy, deflects the focus onto
Penelope, to whom, in a "reverse-gender simile," he
attributes the qualities of a good king:

> Lady, no mortal man on the endless earth
>   could have cause
> to find fault with you; your fame goes up into
>   the wide heaven,
> as of some king who, as a blameless man and
>   god-fearing,
> and ruling as lord over many powerful people,
> upholds the way of good government, and the
>   black earth yields him
> barley and wheat, his trees are heavy with
>   fruit, his sheepflocks
> continue to bear young, the sea gives him
>   fish, because of
> his good leadership, and his people prosper

(*aretôsi*) under him.

19.108-14

Penelope reclaims authority when she herself deflects
the compliment by claiming that Odysseus's departure
brought the ruin of her excellence and that, if he were
to return and tend to (*amphipoleuei*) her, then her glory (*kleos*) would be greater and more splendid (19.124-
63). As it is, she grieves and her suitors wear out her
house.

Penelope does not mention to the stranger the messages and words of encouragement of which others (Telemakhos and Athena) have informed Odysseus. Instead
she says:

> I waste away at the inward heart, longing for
>   Odysseus.
> These men try to hasten the marriage. I weave
>   my own wiles (*dolous tolupeuô*).

19.136-37

A *daimôn,* she says, put the idea of the web in her
mind, and she announced the plan to the suitors. (Penelope quotes her words, as Amphimedon's shade does
later to Agamemnon's shade). Her maidservants betrayed her, and the suitors compelled her, against her
will, to complete the shroud. She ends by confessing
aporia:

> Now I cannot escape from this marriage; I can
>   no longer
> think of another plan; my parents are urgent
>   with me
> to marry; my son is vexed as they eat away
>   our livelihood.

19.157-59

After revealing her dilemma, Penelope insists that the
stranger tell her who he is: "You were not born from
any fabulous oak or a boulder" (163). Odysseus tells a
lie, that he knew and entertained Odysseus on his way
to Troy and for twelve days gave him proper hospitality. This lie immediately affects Penelope, and her body
is melted,

> as the snow melts . . .
> so that her beautiful cheeks were streaming
>   tears, as Penelope
> wept for her man, who was sitting there by
>   her side.

19.204-9

But Odysseus himself, instead of enjoying inflicting
trouble and pain on his wife, "in his heart had pity for
his wife as she mourned him." (210) Still, he hides his
tears and continues to deceive her.

As Odysseus hears Penelope describe her wiliness in

her ruse of the loom, he edges toward reunion with her. Her admission of helplessness (155-56: "I cannot escape from this marriage; I can no longer / think of another plan" [*mêtis*]), both recalls Odysseus's helplessness (*amêkhania*) in the cave of the Kyklops and anticipates his quandry at 20.18-21 when he witnesses his maidservants mingling with the suitors. Those in the audience, making this connection, sense the couple's *homophrosunê* as each moves from powerlessness to triumph.

To prove that he indeed entertained Odysseus, the beggar describes the mantle his guest was wearing, with a pin double-sheathed and intricately carved, made of gold:

> the front part of it was artfully
> done: a hound held in his forepaws a dappled
> fawn, preying on it as it struggled; and all
>   admired it,
> how, though they were golden, it preyed on
>   the fawn and strangled it
> and the fawn struggled with his feet as he
>   tried to escape him.

> 19.227-31

Knowing that this very clasp was his wife's own gift to him, Odysseus teases Penelope by alluding to it and using it as a recognition sign or *sêma*. The description itself causes not only acceptance of his lie as truth (he did entertain her husband) but a weakening of her defenses. Odysseus manipulates Penelope's emotions and awakens *erôs* by evoking in her a memory of a gift that, in multiple semiosis, conveys the *erôs* in their relationship. His casual allusion to the clasp-gift, when he is pretending to have trouble remembering what Odysseus wore, heightens the erotic tension of the interview.

The clasp is a complicated symbol, signifying both as an object and through its decorations. As a departure gift from wife to husband, it binds Odysseus, reminding him of Penelope's claims. The scene depicted on it suggests an erotic conquest: the capture of a fawn by a hound who "preyed on the fawn and strangled it and the fawn struggled with his feet as it tried to escape him." In archaic and later Greek poetry, fawn imagery occurs in erotic contexts, as in Arkhilokhos's erotic fragment and the *Homeric Hymn to Demeter*. The scene on the clasp suggests an erotic chase, perhaps even the first capture of Penelope by Odysseus. Odysseus is the hound pursuing Penelope, and her flirtations with others (a resistance of sorts) intensify his pursuit. The chase itself is not unambiguously "male captures female." Rather, it playfully suggests capture and entrapment, but because the gender of both animals is masculine, and because of Homer's propensity for reverse-gender similes, Penelope could as well be the hound catching with her clasp an escaping Odysseus

as he departs from home. Thus the reciprocity that is key to the *homophroneonte noêmasin* of Odysseus and Penelope is a feature as well of Penelope's gift, long ago, to Odysseus.

Odysseus continues his half-truth with a story that Odysseus will return soon, within the year, "either at the waning of the moon or at its onset" (306), and that he is now accumulating wealth. This detail suggests to Penelope that her husband will return with an ample bridal gift, in no way inferior to the gifts she had to elicit from her suitors. With the detail that Odysseus will stop at Dodona, to find out whether to arrive openly or in secret, the beggar gives Penelope reason for hope but also accents the theme of secrecy and disclosure so prominent in their interview.

Lest his audience relax too much in anticipation of mutual recognition, Homer offers them a close call. The recognition by Eurykleia as she bathes the stranger's feet and the diverting of Penelope's attention tease the audience. So too does Homer's long digression, perhaps representing Eurykleia's remembrances, about Odysseus's coming of age at the boar hunt.

Odysseus's sudden threat to Eurykleia, when she is about to divulge his identity, that he will not spare her life if she does so, shows how intent he is to hide his identity from Penelope. Those who argue for a communication in code between husband and wife need to explain this urgent desire for secrecy. What appears as covert or subtle communication occurs on the global, not local level, between text and listeners, not among characters. We see their compatibility and like-mindedness; Penelope feels only erotic vibrations between them and her own attraction to this stranger, who may even supplant Odysseus in her affections. Athena, as the guiding hand of the poet, turns aside Penelope's perception, so that the stranger and Odysseus will not collapse, too soon, into a single identity.

As Penelope's attention returns, she resumes her conversation. It is time to close the interview, because she has the information she set out to acquire; yet, convinced that the stranger once hosted Odysseus and inexplicably drawn to him, she stays and talks with her new guest-friend "just for a little" (19.509). In their new intimacy, she divulges her sharpest anxieties to him. Like Pandareos's daughter (518-24), the greenwood nightingale, who once killed her child with the bronze when the madness was on her, she is anxious, especially over the recent abortive ambush of Telemakhos, for which she feels responsible.

Penelope explains her dilemma, whether or not to remarry, and then tells the guest-stranger her dream (535-53), which is fraught with ambiguities about her feelings toward the suitors. To the generous-spirited Odysseus, a complex Penelope lamenting over her geese

/ suitors is a challenge, not a candidate for blame. Odysseus ignores (or doesn't "hear") her triple mention of lamenting over the death of her geese and focuses instead on the opportunity that her narration affords him to encourage her with a strong prophecy:

> Lady, it is impossible to read this dream and
>   avoid it
> by turning another way, since Odysseus
>   himself has told you
> its meaning, how it will end. The suitors'
>   doom is evident
> for one and all. Not one will avoid his death
>   and destruction.
>
>   19.555-58

Odysseus-in-the-dream consoled Penelope (she reports) and interpreted the dream symbols to her:

> The geese are the suitors and I, the eagle,
>   have been
> a bird of portent, but now I am your own
>   husband, come home,
> and shall inflict shameless destruction on all
>   the suitors.
>
>   19.548-50

Odysseus-at-the-hearth, hearing the dream, validates the clear interpretation in the dream by dream-Odysseus, who has affirmed his own polymorphism and polytropy. But Odysseus-at-the-hearth still insists on remaining the stranger. Not yet ready to reveal himself, he offers Penelope only limited consolation. Though he sympathizes with the sorrowing and perplexed Penelope, he holds onto his disguise.

Professing skepticism, and denying that the dream can be taken as prophetic, Penelope proposes to set a bow-contest for her hand. Odysseus, in response, while endorsing this move and thus in a sense co-sponsoring it, maintains the secrecy of his disguise:

> O respected wife of Odysseus, son of Laertes,
> do not put off this contest in your house any
>   longer.
> Before these people can handle the well-
>   wrought bow, and manage
> to hook the string and bend it, and send a
>   shaft through the iron,
> Odysseus of the many designs will be back
>   here with you.
>
>   19.583-87

At this juncture, the husband who had enjoyed watching his wife charm the suitors and wrest gifts from them welcomes the bride-contest. It both helps shape his master plan for revenge and enables him to compete for Penelope's hand. Having to reclaim Penelope enhances her value for him; he is confident of victory yet uncertain what that victory will mean to her. (For the audience, witnessing all this, the bow-contest becomes a bride-contest, wherein the husband is the leading suitor and the wife the bride-prize.)

Penelope's behavior shortly after the interview, in the privacy of her chambers, underscores the difference in their situations. She weeps profusely as she gathers Odysseus's weapons for the contest (19.603) and prays fervently to Artemis for sudden death, begging to be snatched away like the daughters of Pandareos rather than to have to remarry (20.61-83). Odysseus neither witnesses her weeping nor hears her prayer for death. Despite the dissonance in their lives at this point, global *homophrosunê* is established to an extent: just as Penelope dreamt that "there was one who lay by me, like him / as he was when he went with the army, so that my own heart / was happy" (20.88-90), so too, when Odysseus awoke from a deep sleep induced by Athena, "it seemed to him in his mind that now / she was standing by his head, and had recognized him already" (20.93-94). In both cases, the "as if" quality of the recognition assures us that neither has yet firmly recognized the other and so neither one is secure. Odysseus, as he gazes on Penelope, struggles to fathom what she knows.

During the actual contest Penelope insists on handing her husband's bow to her guest, despite vociferous objections by the suitors (21.285-310). To one protester, Antinoös, she replies:

> Do you imagine that if this stranger, in the
>   confidence
> of hands and strength, should string the great
>   bow of Odysseus,
> that he would take me home with him and
>   make me his wife? No,
> he himself has no such thought in the heart
>   within him.
> Let none of you be sorrowful at heart in his
>   feasting
> here, for such a reason. There is no likelihood
>   of it.
>
>   21.314-19

Penelope professes that the beggar is no match for a queen, yet she insists he be given a try at the bow. Why? Is this a gesture of politeness, or does the stranger intrigue her, or does she suspect he is Odysseus come home? Does she know it is Odysseus yet pretend before the suitors? We cannot be sure. Her reply, with its denial, introduces a hypothetical plot-type, MARRIAGE TO A STRANGER, which was latent in the intimate conversation before the hearth.

Odysseus's recognition by Penelope is near at hand. During the slaughter, Penelope remains in her chamber, sent there by Telemakhos. Afterward, Odysseus's emissary, Eurykleia, summons her and tells her of the SLAUGHTER OF THE SUITORS. Claiming to remain skeptical (not about the slaughter but about her husband's return), Penelope descends "to see my son, so that I can look on / these men who courted me lying dead, and the man who killed them" (23.83-84). She sits opposite her husband at the hearth, in silence.

In this reunion scene, as Odysseus finally reassumes his identity and desires to embrace his wife, his control of the courtship dance begins to falter. He encounters a Penelope who cannot look at him directly, a Penelope midway between Artemis and Aphrodite. Now he faces the challenge of any suitor: how to respect the maiden's sense of shame and chastity yet press his claim and move things along.

Odysseus dissuades Telemakhos from interfering, with remarkable and characteristic sensitivity. He understands that Penelope, like a *parthenos* on the verge of marriage, is at a critical, liminal moment of her life cycle, as if she were on the verge of marriage. Odysseus, who earlier asked Antikleia of his wife's plans and intentions, now dismisses their impatient son in order to allow Penelope to question him in her own way, at her own pace. He understands that the secrets they alone share need reaffirmation if their marriage is to resume. In his patience, Odysseus respects Penelope's subjectivity (her qualms, her hesitations). He acknowledges her possible reluctance to embrace a husband twenty years older than when they parted and still defiled and dirty (23.115); it is as if he had overheard her earlier fantasy, when she dreamed he lay beside her "as he was when he went with the army" (20.89-90).

Penelope makes a key move at this juncture: she orders Eurykleia to make up the marriage-bed outside the bridal chamber. She tells her:

> Come then, Eurykleia, and make up a firm
>   bed for him
> outside the well-fashioned chamber: that very
>   bed that he himself
> built. Put the firm bed here outside for him,
>   and cover it
> over with fleeces and blankets, and with
>   shining coverlets.
>
>   23.177-80

With this move, Penelope takes charge of their reunion and assumes the initiative. Reciprocity results, as in the hunting scene on the clasp and in the maturation-boar-hunt of Odysseus. The "hunter" (Odysseus), who had the advantage until now (owing to disguise, which resembles ambush), is suddenly turned upon, as the cornered boar once turned on youthful Odysseus (19.449-51). Penelope wounds Odysseus with her fib, which counterbalances his previous lies and disguises.

His angry response and loss of control are short-lived. He recounts in detail how he constructed the bed from a live tree. His "story," which reveals his knowledge of the secret of the bed's construction, is the *sêma* that enables him to reclaim his bride and culminate (or complete) his second wooing of Penelope.

Penelope recognizes the *sêma,* especially the description of the construction of the bed, a sign they alone share. After he spoke, "her knees and the heart within her went slack (*luto*) / as she recognized the clear proofs (*sêmat'*) that Odysseus had given" (23.205-6). The phrase *luto gounata* echoes the description of the loosening of the knees of each suitor when Penelope appeared before them and enchanted their hearts with *erôs* (18.212-13: *erôi d'ara thumon ethelkhthen, / pantes d'êrêsanto parai lekheessi klithênai*). Cf. *lusimelês,* an epithet of Eros, the loosener of limbs (Hesiod, *Theogony*). Similar language describes one defeated in battle, as in Telemakhos's prayer to Zeus, Athena, and Apollo at 18.235-42: "if only . . . the limbs [would] be unstrung (*leluto de guia*) in each of them; / as now for Iros . . . / lolling his head like a drunken man, and unable / to stand upright on his feet again and make his way homeward / . . . since there is no strength in his body." The moment of Penelope's recognition of Odysseus is a moment of mutual surrender, of release for them and for the audience.

Two scenes round out their reunion. First, by her "Helen apology," Penelope placates Odysseus for her "stubborn spirit" and at the same time precludes future recriminations from him for encouraging the suitors. Second, Penelope trims her adventure story so as to leave out any incriminating details. Through their exchange of stories, Homer matches the two tales, reinforcing the audience's sense of their *homophrosunê.* Odysseus too equates their sufferings. The partners, in their marriage-bed, through lovemaking and exchange of stories, express and enact *homophrosunê.*

Two intersubjective symbols, the marriage-bed and the engraved clasp, illuminate the courtship dance of Penelope and Odysseus. Both are objects the couple share: Odysseus built the bed for his wife; she gave him the pin. This makes them ideal signs (*sêmata*) for mutual recognition. Each appears twice in a crucial interchange: the engraved pin in Odysseus's lie to Penelope at the hearth and in her response (19.225-35 and 255-57) and the bed in Penelope's trick lie to Odysseus and in his elaborate and angry response (23.177-80 and 182-204).

At the core of the fictional marriage of Penelope and Odysseus lies an oxymoron that is perhaps at the core of all enduring marriages: two quintessentially fluid characters form a lasting bond. They reunite on a marriage-bed, hewn long before by the bridegroom Odysseus, a bed whose roots go deep into the earth. On that rooted bed they exchanges stories of the adventures each underwent in the other's absence. They put their stories next to one another.

The interactions of Odysseus and Penelope constitute, in effect, a second wooing of a wife by her husband and of a husband by his wife. Some elements of plot fit under other plot-types as well, notably RETURN, CRIME AND PUNISHMENT, and MARRIAGE TO A STRANGER. Their second wooing enables each to evaluate the possibility of renewed like-mindedness between them. At the same time, Homer asks his audience to be persuaded and join in the merriment.

In the early stages of her courtship, Penelope gives promises to each suitor; with Odysseus already in the palace, she appears alluringly before them and beguiles gifts from them through enchantment. Through an intermediary, the couple arrange an interview, their first rendezvous. Penelope responds to the stranger's suggestion for the time and place.

During the first private encounter of the couple since Odysseus's departure, the dialogue between them and the playful ritual of their courtship begin. At first Odysseus takes the lead, owing to his disguise. He watches Penelope from a distance, tests her, and manipulates her emotions, holding back his own.

In a sense, Penelope enjoys three separate courtships: by the suitors, by the stranger, and by the returned Odysseus. In each, she plays with her expected role as an object of desire. For the suitors, she manipulates the time frame through her ruse of the loom, confronting them with obstacles that only entice them further, as if she is playing "hard-to-get." Then, as a second possible ruse, she determines the time, place, and nature of the final contest for her hand in marriage. The event tests all "three" of her possible partners in marriage. Once the stranger / Odysseus triumphs and thereby proves his claims, the still unsatisfied Penelope tests him further with her ruse of the marriage-bed, giving him a further obstacle to surmount. Essential to her success is his capacity to reverse roles in their courtship. Because her lie entraps him, he becomes her prey.

This reversibility of their roles annuls the gender hierarchy so prevalent in other couples' relations in the text, with Alkinoös and Arete as an interesting exception. The *homophroneonte noêmasin* that Odysseus posits as the foundation of a good marriage and the marriage-bed rooted in the earth, constructed from an olive tree, and made with his own hands, eliminate gender hierarchy and reverse domination and subordination. The love-hunt in Greek poetry usually presupposes an aggressor and a victim. By introducing a reversibility for the two participants, Homer interjects cooperation into the pursuit and chase.

The marriage of Penelope and Odysseus exhibits *erôs*

and *philotês*. The *philotês* is based in part on Odysseus's ideology about marriage (because in Homeric society, Penelope could not exercise power if he denied it to her); it is also based, in part, on their mutual recognition of traits in each other that reflect their similarity. Finally, it is based on Odysseus's capacity to survive the wound of Penelope's lie, a capacity foreshadowed by his survival of the boar's preemptive strike at 19.449-51.

Homer sets forth the reunion as the climax of the *Odyssey* plot. He affirms this clumination in the face of a propensity of each figure toward *dis*traction and *de*viation (in other words, separation as opposed to reunion). To each "polytrope" he assigns an overriding desire to return to home, hearth, and marriage-bed. Despite the intrinsic implausibility, despite the oxymoron, their final reunion feels natural and inevitable—the way things are. Homer makes the implausible plausible, charming us into acquiescence and unanimity through machinations of plot, character, theme, and diction. His epic produces not only "delight" (*terpsis*) but also "enchantment" or "beguilement" (*thelksis*).

FURTHER READING

Austin, Norman. *Archery at the Dark of the Moon: Poetic Problems in Homer's "Odyssey."* Berkeley: University of California Press, 1975, 297 p.

Detailed analysis of poetics, structure, and unity in the *Odyssey*.

Beye, Charles Rowan. *"The Odyssey,"* in his "The Odyssey" and the Epic Tradition., pp. 158-205. Anchor Books, 1966.

Focuses on the *Odyssey's* recurring themes of wandering, recognition, temptation, and hjomecoming.

Bremer, J. M., De Jong, I. J. F., and Kalff, J., eds. *Homer Beyond Oral Poetry*. Amsterdam: B. R. Grtner Publishing Co., 1987, 212 p.

A collection of essays that attempts to address the full range of Homer's artistry, covering such topics as myth, language, and characterization.

Butler, Samuel. "The Humour of Homer." In *The Humour of Homer and Other Essays,* edited by R. A. Streatfeild, pp. 59-98. New York: Mitchell Kennerley, 1914.

Compares authorial tone and treatment of humor in the *Iliad* and the *Odyssey*.

Clarke, Howard. *Homer's Readers: A Historical Introduction to the "Iliad" and the "Odyssey."* Newark: University of Delaware Press, 1981, 327 p.

Examines the various ways in which readers and

critics have perceived Homer and his works.

————, ed. *Twentieth Century Interpretations of the "Odyssey": A Collection of Critical Essays*. Englewood Cliffs, N. J.: Prentice-Hall, Inc., 1983, 131 p.

Essays on various aspects of the *Odyssey* by such critics as Richmond Lattimore, Cedric H. Whitman, and Dorothea Wender.

Clay, Jenny Strauss. *The Wrath of Athena: Gods and Men in the "Odyssey."* Princeton: Princeton University Press, 1983, 268 p.

Deals with the relationship between the divine and the human in the *Odyssey* from various perspectives.

Crane, Gregory. *Calypso: Backgrounds and Conventions of the "Odyssey."* Frankfurt: Athenaum, 1988, 190 p.

Explores, "to the extent that this is now possible, traditions and conventions that lie behind the *Odyssey,*" with emphasis on "Odysseus's wanderings and upon some of the figures whom he encounters on his way."

Dimock, George E. *The Unity of the "Odyssey."* Amherst: The University of Massachusetts Press, 1989, 343 p.

Detailed, episode-by-episode exploration of thematic consistency within the *Odyssey*.

Fenik, Bernard. *Studies in the "Odyssey."* Wiesbaden: Franz Steiner Verlag GMBH, 1974, 248 p.

Aims "to isolate and identify certain dominant stylistic characteristics of the *Odyssey,* and to interpret on the basis of both individual incidents and longer stretches of the narrative, and also to explain the origin and genesis of these techniques as a factor influencing the way they are used."

Finley, John H. *Homer's "Odyssey."* Cambridge: Harvard University Press, 1978, 245 p.

Examines the unity of the *Odyssey* through a study of "the chief characters' ultimate self-recognition" and "their simultaneous understanding of their moral stance toward the world-revealing gods."

Finley, M. I. "Bards and Heroes." In *The World of Odysseus*. New York: Viking Press, 1954, pp. 17-45.

Emphasizes the role of the bard in ancient Greece while analyzing the *Iliad* and *Odyssey* as heroic poems.

Friedrich, Rainer. "The Hybris of Odysseus." *The Journal of Hellenic Studies,* CXI (1991): 16-28.

Portrays Odysseus's pride as an important part of the poem's central theme.

Gray, Wallace. "Homer: *Odyssey*." In his *Homer to Joyce,* pp. 17-33. New York: Macmillan Publishing Co., 1985.

Focuses on Odysseus's physical and spiritual journeys, contending that "the hero's fate is largely determined

by the choices he makes rather than by fate or accident."

Griffin, Jasper. *Homer: The "Odyssey."* Cambridge: Cambridge University Press, 1987, 107 p.

Concise overview of the poem that includes discussion of its historical setting as well as of its individual style.

Huxley, Aldous. "Tragedy and the Whole Truth." In his *Music at Night and Other Essays,"* pp. 3-16. New York: Doubleday Doran & Co., 1930.

Praises Homer's accurate rendering of events in his writings, stating that "the experiences he records correspond fairly closely with our own actual or potential experiences."

Lattimore, Richmond. "Introduction." In his *The "Odyssey" of Homer,* translated by Richmond Lattimore, pp. 1-24. New York: Harper & Row, 1967.

Basic outline of the stucture of the *Odyssey* and its relationship to the *Iliad* from one of the foremost translators of Homer.

Lawrence, T. E. "Translator's Note." In *The Odyssey of Homer*, translated by T. E. Lawrence, pp. v-vii. 1932. Reprint. Oxford University Press, 1991.

In a note (signed "T. E. Shaw") to his translation, Lawrence speculates on Homer's attitudes and occupation.

Murray, Gilbert. *The Rise of the Greek Epic*. New York: Oxford University Press, A Galaxy Book, 1960. 356 p.

Respected study that presents background material for reading Homeric works. This work was first published in 1907.

Murray, Oswyn. *Early Greece*. Second edition. Cambridge: Harvard University Press, 1993, 353p.

Comprehensive survey of the history, archaeology, and myths of early Greece.

Pocock, L. G. *Odyssean Essays*. Oxford: Basil Blackwell, 1965, 132 p.

Collection of critical essays stemming from Pocock's premises that the *Odyssey* originated in Sicily and regarding its treatment of reality and allegory.

Rexroth, Kenneth. "Homer: *The Odyssey,*" in his *Classics Revisited,* pp. 12-16. Quadrangle Books, 1968.

Examines the *Odyssey*'s unique dream-like quality. This essay was first published in 1965.

Rieu, E. V. "Introduction." In *Homer: The "Odyssey,"* translated by E. V. Rieu, pp. 9-21. Baltimore: Penguin Books, 1946.

Brief overview for the first-time reader of the poem.

Scott, John A. "The *Odyssey*." In his *Homer and His Influence,* pp. 54-67, Boston: Marshall Jones Co., 1925.

Discusses similarites and differences between the *Odyssey* and the *Iliad,* supporting the thesis that the *Odyssey* is the work of an older poet. Scott asserts that, "it is doubtful if the skill with which the poet of the *Odyssey* weaves the individual strands of poetry into a great epic plot has ever been equalled."

————. *The Unity of Homer.* New York: Biblo and Tannen, 1965, 275 p.

Detailed examination of the question of unity in Homer, with a chapter partially devoted to the *Odyssey.*

Standford, W. B. "Introduction." In his *The "Odyssey" of Homer,* edited by W. B. Stanford, pp. ix-xlviii. London: Macmillan & Co. Ltd., 1958.

Comprehensive introduction to the characters, style, text, geography, and historical context of the *Odyssey.*

Taylor, Charles H., Jr., ed. *Essays on the "Odyssey": Selected Modern Criticism.* Bloomington: Indiana University Press, 1963, 136 p.

Includes essays by W. K. C. Guthrie, W. B. Stanford, George deF. Lord, George E. Dimock, Jr., William S. Anderson, Charles H. Taylor, Jr., and Anne Amory.

Tracy, Stephen V. *The Story of the "Odyssey."* Princeton: Princeton University Press, 1990, 160 p.

Details the adventures in Books 9-12 of the *Odyssey,* in which Odysseus gives a first-person account of his wanderings.

Vivante, Paolo. *Homer.* New Haven: Yale University Press, 1985, 218 p.

Studies the narrative, characters, and rendering of nature in the *Iliad* and the *Odyssey.*

Wender, Dorothea. *The Last Scenes of the "Odyssey."* Leiden: E. J. Brill, 1978, 83 p.

Defends the theory that the ending is indeed of a piece with the rest of the *Odyssey.*

Woodhouse, W. J. *The Composition of Homer's "Odyssey."* Oxford: Oxford at the Clarendon Press, 1930, 251 p.

Detailed study of the narrative of the *Odyssey,* including its methodology and sources.

Razón de amor

c. Thirteenth Century

Spanish poem.

INTRODUCTION

A medieval poem composed in two parts and written in Castilian Spanish, *Razón de amor* is valued both for its artistic merit and because it is the oldest extant lyrical poem in Castilian literature. Although scholars believe that it dates to the early thirteenth century, *Razón* was accidentally rediscovered in 1887 when A. Morel-Fatio, a French Hispanist, was researching some medieval sermon literature in the south of France. Bundled with texts of the sermons was a copy of the *Razón,* along with some prose pieces about the Ten Commandments. The poem is signed "Lupus de Moros," but scholars are in agreement that Lupus was most likely only the scribe who transcribed the text, not its author; nothing is known about the original writer except that, as he claims within the poem, he seems to have been educated in France and Germany, and to have lived in Lombardy. Today, the Morel-Fatio, located at the *Bibliothèque nationale* in Paris, remains the only known manuscript of the *Razón.* Scholarly editions, besides that of Morel-Fatio, include those of R. Menéndez Pidal (1905), Alfred Jacob (1956), and Mario DiPinto (1959); only a partial translation, by Charles C. Stebbins, is available in English.

Style and Themes

Razón de amor is comprised of two poems written in polymetric couplets—"Razón de amor," a love poem in the Provençal style, and "Denuestos del agua y del vino," which follows in the manuscript and is a burlesque dispute between water and wine. In the first part, two lovers are to meet in an orchard in the month of April. The lover, by his own description a young, educated cleric, waits lying on the grass near a cool fountain. He overhears a maiden nearby who is lamenting the fact that her beloved has fallen in love with another lady. The narrator then tells us that he and the lady with whom he has arranged an assignation have never actually seen each other before, although they have kept in touch by exchanging certain love tokens. After he and the lady in the orchard recognize each other, they engage in a love idyll under the trees. Many scholars have pointed out that the "Razón" exhibits several stylistic aspects typical of Provençal poetry of that period—for example, the use of a springtime, pastoral setting, the idea of the lover admiring his beloved from

afar, and the lover's use of the masculine term *senor* to refer to his lady. The second part of the *Razón,* the "Denuestos," is thematically and stylistically very different from the "Razón": it is a poetic debate between water and wine, written in a colloquial, brisk manner, in which the two substances each extol their own virtues and criticize the faults or inadequacies of the other. Critics have pointed out that the "Denuestos" clearly demonstrates its connection to the poetic tradition of the *conflictus,* popular in Medieval romance literature in Europe, where a debate is carried on between two types or personifications.

Critical Reception

One of the most vexing problems confronting critics who have written about the *Razón de amor* is the question of its thematic and structural unity. Some have argued that the two parts of the poem, so different in nature, were never meant to be viewed as an artistic whole, but were probably randomly joined together by the scribe who copied the manuscript. Others, however, have suggested that the "Razón" and the "Denuestos" were definitely planned as a single entity. As evidence, they have cited images that carry over from one part to the other (for example, that of water and wine) and have presented a case for considering the "Razón" an introduction to the "Denuestos." Still other critics have debated whether the *Razón de amor* is the work of one or more poets. Most recently, Harriet Goldberg has asserted that the two halves of the poem are indeed unified if they are viewed as parts of a dream-poem. Other approaches to the *Razón* have included exploring its relationship to the Medieval debate tradition and to the Provençal biographical genres of the *vida* and the *razo*; examining its allegorical aspects, use of Christian symbolism, and echoes of the biblical "Song of Songs"; and probing the ways in which the work blends popular Spanish folk elements with those of the European courtly tradition. While the *Razón*'s historical and linguistic importance has always been acknowledged by scholars, modern critical studies have increasingly focused on its characteristics as a work of art, thereby giving it an even more prominent place in Spanish and world literature.

PRINCIPAL ENGLISH TRANSLATION

"The *Razón de amor*: An Old Spanish Lyrical Poem of the 13th Century" (partial translation by Charles

C. Stebbins in *Allegorica,* Vol. 2, No.1) 1977

CRITICISM

James Holly Hanford (essay date 1913)

SOURCE: "The Medieval Debate between Wine and Water," in *PMLA,* Vol. XXVIII, No. 3, 1913, pp. 315-67.

[*In the following excerpt, Hanford discusses the* Razón de amor *in the context of the Medieval European tradition of the* conflictus, *or debate poetry, noting the origins and main characteristics of the genre.*]

Among the mediæval debates which have enjoyed the widest currency and have retained their hold on popular interest for the longest time is the contention between Wine and Water. Poems on this subject are extant in most of the languages of mediæval Europe; and the tradition has persisted with surprising vitality through more than seven centuries down to the present day. The bickerings of these two ancient foes may still be heard on the lips of the peasantry of Germany, France, and Spain, and a fragment of the same dispute was sung not long since as a nursery rhyme in Devon.

The history of this typical example of the *conflictus,* that species of disputation in which the contestants are not individuals but personifications or types, possesses considerable interest, first as a record of popular taste, secondly because of its bearing on the distribution of such material in the middle ages and on the relation between the literary and popular treatments of the same theme.

The literary debate of Wine and Water found its way early into Spanish literature. It appears in a thirteenth-century Castilian poem, probably of Provençal origin, in which the debate proper is curiously combined with an amatory dialogue in the style of the *pastourelle.* Originally the two parts of the "romance" must have existed as separate poems. In combining them the copyist or translator appears to have telescoped the two similar introductions. As it stands the narrative runs as follows: The poet, taking an April walk in an olive orchard, sees in the branches of one of the trees a vase full of clear cool wine. It was placed there, we are told, by the lady of the garden for her lover, and whoever drinks of it shall never fall sick. Coming nearer, the poet discovers another vase, full of cold water. He is about to drink, but desists for fear of enchantment. So much apparently constituted the opening of the original debate. It is sufficiently characteristic. At this point the poet lies down by a lovely fountain not previously mentioned, sees a beautiful woman, his own beloved, coming through the orchard, and holds conversation with her. We hear no more of the vases until the close of the love poem, when the author reverts to them. As he is about to sleep, a white dove flies toward the fountain, but, seeing him there, turns and enters the vase of water instead. As the bird flies out again in fright, the water is upset into the wine. In this astonishing manner the author makes his transition to the dispute between the two drinks.

There is little to distinguish the course of the argument which follows, from that of the debates which we have been considering. The tone of the dispute is colloquial; the contestants indulge in personalities and epithets much in the manner of the "flyting." The precious pair are visualized with a good deal of humor. The following passage may be quoted:

> Ell agua iaze muerta rridiendo
> De lo qu'el vino esta diziendo.
> Don vino, si vos de Dios salut,
> Que vos me fagades agora una vertud:
> Fartad bien un villano,
> No lo prenda ninguno de la mano,
> Et si, antes d'una passada, no cayere en el
>   lodo,
> Dios sodes de tod en todo;
> E si esto fazedes,
> Otorgo que vençuda m'avedes.
> En una blanca paret
> .V. kandelas ponet,
> E si el beudo non dixiere que son .c.,
> De quanto digo de todo miento.

The suggestion of a judicial test in these lines is a very early instance of the adoption of legal language in the vernacular debate.

In substance the poem is most nearly parallel to the *Denudata Veritate,* some passages being practically paraphrases of the Latin. Specific resemblances between the Spanish and the other Latin and French versions of the dispute are in comparison trifling. Yet they are sufficiently numerous to make it seem unlikely that the author of this poem or its original was influenced by the *Denudata* alone. The widely known *Dialogus* may have furnished a few hints in this case as it appears to have done in others where the *Denudata* tradition is in the main adhered to. The problem of relations becomes increasingly complicated and baffling as we examine more versions of the debate.

Without belonging in the first instance to popular tradition, this material circulated throughout Europe as freely and in as many forms as the great romantic stories, the beast epic, or the fabliaux. Each succeeding writer [on the wine-water theme] might draw upon his recollection of more than one predecessor, following no one of them as a model, but elaborating the theme in his own way. Hence the bewildering confusion of similarities and differences in the extant poems. Without, however, attempting to relate the different versions too exactly, we may draw some fairly certain conclusions regarding the general history of the dispute. The main features of this history may now be summarized.

The debate originated with the Latin rhythmic poets, the *Goliardi,* in the twelfth century, having been developed under the influence of the debate type in general out of motives familiar to the potatory literature of the time. It appears first in two forms, one more popular in character and apparently designed for recitation or singing, the other pedantic and smacking of religious parody. The two are probably related, but neither can be called a version of the other. The more popular is probably the earlier. In what country either of them was written cannot be determined, though one is inclined to look toward Germany; nor is it a matter of much importance, since they belong to a class of literature which is essentially non-national. From this very characteristic, such literature circulates freely through all nations and is easily taken over into the vernacular. The two Latin debates, we know, from the evidence of the manuscripts, to have been read and copied throughout Europe at least as late as the fifteenth century. Meanwhile the dispute had been adapted in French and Spanish, where it appears as early as the thirteenth century, probably through intermediaries now lost. The type of these as of practically all other vernacular versions of the debate is that of the more popular *Denudata* rather than of the biblical *Dialogus,* but the latter certainly contributed some of the material which was incorporated in the later tradition.

Going back directly to the *Denudata* or to some form of the dispute much like it is a second French poem, belonging to the fourteenth or fifteenth century, which appears to have been an important influence in the later history of the dispute. Like the earlier French and Spanish pieces it is characterized by a tendency to romanticize the debate and to elaborate the narrative element.

The early sixteenth century saw the beginning of a wide distribution of the debate in France, Spain, Italy, and Germany, in the form of *fliegende Blätter,* and similar prints are said to have been circulated by *colporteurs* in very recent times. Of these printed debates some few are of the elaborate type set by the French *Débat;* others, while belonging in a general way to the same tradition, show signs of having been adapted to the uses of popular entertainers. They are comparatively brief and simple; the narrative setting is generally absent; and the argument proceeds in alternate stanzas. Such adaptations may have been made independently by the street singers of different countries; or the material may have been passed from one group of minstrels to another.

Through these channels the dispute became familiar throughout Europe, finding its way even into such out of the way dialects as Rhæto-Romanic and Basque, and becoming very popular with the modern Hebrew and Yiddish writers. It is not surprising, therefore, that it should have been taken up into oral tradition. Pop-

ular versions have been recorded in modern times from France, Spain, England, and Germany. In the last named country, at least, the debate received a very general currency. The oral versions there evidently go back to the form of the dispute represented in the sixteenth-century German prints.

With respect to the breadth of its distribution, the variety of its forms, and the tenacity of its hold on popular interest, this debate is surpassed by only two dialogues of its class, the debate between the Body and the Soul, and the debate between Winter and Summer.

They, like it, are the common property of Europe, and they, too, appear in both literary and popular form. In comparison with these themes the debate of Wine and Water seems barren and circumscribed. It has little more than mother wit, a touch of the ridiculous, and a certain homeliness, as concerning the things of every day, to oppose to the imaginative appeal of the great drama of the seasons, or the eternal human interest of the conflict between flesh and spirit. Yet these slighter qualities are even dearer to the popular heart, and if other subjects aroused deeper emotions, none, apparently, afforded more delight. The mere fact that this theme should have lived for centuries in many tongues is full of interest for the student of literary history.

Chandler Rathfon Post (essay date 1915)

SOURCE: "The Thirteenth Century," in *Medieval Spanish Allegory,* Cambridge, Mass.: Harvard University Press, 1915, pp. 118-37.

[*In the excerpt below, Post explores the allegorical aspects of the* Razón de amor, *comparing it with other conventional allegories of the period.*]

The "Poème d'Amour," usually called now from the opening lines the **Razón de Amor,** is an idyll describing a scholar's more or less imaginary encounter with his lady, and thus belongs to a class which . . . may be regarded as allegorical; the "Debate of Water and Wine" is seen by its name to be a member of a large and well known category of mediaeval verse. It is a question whether they are to be considered as separate poems or parts of the same poem. The protagonists of disunion are Petraglione and Carolina Michaëlis de Vasconcellos, who ascribe the awkward juncture to some lumbering copyist; the latter differs from the former only in suppressing certain lines that she regards as added to the original compositions for a makeshift at a transition. Monaci, Gorra, Baist, and lastly Menéndez Pidal maintain that the two fragments were meant by the author to constitute a single poem. Gorra surmises that he has translated and united two foreign pieces without heed to the artistic discord. Baist, on what ground I do not know, would trace the juncture to the French original. Monaci and Menéndez Pidal suggest that the author had the specific intent of exhibiting the dexterity of his trade by joining two incongruous scenes. Though the links between the love poem and the debate, adduced by Menéndez Pidal as impossible for a mere copyist, are by no means conclusive evidence, they tend to inspire a belief in the unity of the whole composition. The difficulties, however, are of little importance to us: whether the two parts are to be conceived as originally distinct, or one as a digression within the other, for our present purpose we need only note the two diverse themes. It is, in any case, an error, as Petraglione was the first to point out, to print the whole first part separately and to call it with Morel-Fatio *Poème d'Amour* or with Menéndez y Pelayo *Aventura Amorosa;* for this also is subdivided into two separate parts, the one forming an introduction and setting to the Debate, the other consisting of the detached amorous episode and having no apparent logical connection with the theme of the Debate.

After a preface in which he discusses the excellence of his poem and his own cosmopolitan education in courtliness, the writer imagines himself, in the month of April, a popular time for such experiences, as lying down after his meal under an olive tree and as seeing in the branches of an apple orchard a silver vessel full of red wine, placed there by the mistress of the garden and possessing the magical property of curing whosoever drinks of it daily. He discerns also, in some vague spot above the wine, a vessel of cold water, which rises from the apple orchard and which he hesitates to drink for fear of enchantment. Here commences the long digression of the meeting with his mistress, which for the moment I pass over. When she has departed, he continues without transition the allegorical setting to the Debate by describing the appearance of a dove, which, frightened from bathing in the spring of the olive orchard by the sight of the author, seeks the vessel of water in the apple orchard. Having refreshed itself, the bird in its rapid flight overturns the water into the wine below, thus precipitating the encounter and consequent quarrel of the two liquids. The introduction and the Debate itself are further riveted together by a double reference in the latter to the commixture as the motive for the argument.

The mingling of the two liquids is a common setting for the mediaeval subject of a debate between Wine and Water. Thus in the French *Débat du Vin et de l'Eaue,* Pierre Jamec, also after a meal, provokes the dispute by mixing the two in his glass. In our anonymous composition the device of the dove and the basins of wine and water hidden away amidst the foliage of an orchard is more ingenious and poetical, and possesses a certain charm of mystery. Although, strictly, Wine and Water are personifications rather than allegorical figures, the treatment does not differ from that of the ordinary allegorical debate. The introductory fiction, though somewhat more extended, serves the purpose, as in the debates of Ruy Páez de Ribera, of a framework for a

didactic argument. It is an instructive comment on the attempt of those who would trace Ribera's inclination for allegory to Dantesque influence that there exists in Spain two centuries before his day, not a general, but an exact prototype to his poems, and that the imaginative setting in the identical sort of composition plays a more important rôle prior to the entrance of Dante into Spain.

The erotic episode itself is more or less on the plane of allegory. Lying in a meadow bedight with varied flowers, and watered by a spring the coolness of which spreads a hundred feet around, the writer, as he is about to sing of *fin amor,* beholds a fair lady approaching and likewise singing of love. After the mediaeval fashion, he describes her loveliness in most scrupulous detail. Her song is of the scholar who is unfaithful to her. She does not perceive the writer until, grasping her by the hand, he draws her to his side beneath the olive tree and questions her of her lover. Learning that she does not know him except by reputation, and by the gloves, hat, coral, and ring that he has sent her, he recognizes her forthwith by his own gifts, and she him by the belt that she has embroidered with her own hands. Like Basiliola in D'Annunzio's *La Nave,* she slips the mantle from her shoulders, they have their pleasure, and she leaves him.

The background of the episode is one of the conventional gardens that are to form so frequent a feature of literary landscape in the fifteenth century. The first lines, assigning the events to the springtime and laying the scene in an orchard, belong both to the erotic episode and to the Debate, but in the former they are later much augmented by a lengthy description of the fountain and a detailed list of the flowers. The whole passage is closely parallel to the beginning of the *Decir de las Siete Virtudes.* Just as the earlier poet is surprised by the lady of his heart, so, in the midst of a garden surrounded by a sweetly murmuring stream, carpeted by flowers, and redolent with soft odours, Imperial perceives Leah singing and gathering blossoms. The similarity to the dream of the twenty-seventh canto of the *Purgatorio* and to the fulfilment of the dream in the twenty-eighth might seem exact enough to suggest a relationship, were that possible, and once more proves how hazardous it is to dogmatize about specific imitations, unless they be extended or verbal.

The lapse of two centuries brings with it no appreciable difference in the verses that tell of Imperial's amorous wound and captivity. The same emphasis is given to the flowers and their perfume, and the many and varied constituents of the lady's beauty are enumerated with the same meticulous care. The surprisingly unmasculine familiarity with feminine costume finds an analogue in the description of the French lady whom Imperial in another poem discovers hunting along the bank of the Guadalquivir.

The presence of all this material in the thirteenth century renders it absurd to speak in very decided terms about any new allegorical school at the beginning of the fifteenth century. Since the Marquis of Santillana, the chief exponent of allegory during the later period, does not employ this form in at least half of his productions, if we are to speak at all of a Spanish allegorical school, Berceo should not improperly have a place in it. If he is responsible for the *Alexandre,* his title is all the stronger; if not, allegory of these early days occupies a still broader field, for another poet not only imports allegorical elements from his sources but adds touches of his own.

Alfred Jacob (essay date 1952)

SOURCE: "The *Razon de amor* as Christian Symbolism," *Hispanic Review* Vol. XX, No. 4, October, 1952, pp. 282-301.

[*In the following essay, Jacob presents a detailed account of the Christian symbolism in the* Razón de amor, *formulating a new interpretation of the poem based on his findings.*]

> Qui triste tiene su coraçon
> benga oyr esta razon.

So begins a poem of the early thirteenth century which, like the *Libro de buen amor,* is a composite of familiar themes ranging from *idealidad cortesana* in that part of it which sometimes separately bears the title **Razon de amor,** to *bufonerìa callejera* in the remainder, which comprises the "Denuestos del agua y el vino." Within the popular *juglaresco* framework of the day a *locus amoenus,* a damsel, and a gentleman are described; a *cantiga de amigo* is sung, and a recognition, a separation, a vision, and a dispute are presented, with original connecting narrative. There are in addition some unusual particulars: two vessels in an apple tree, one with wine and the other with water; a bird with a little bell attached, which upsets one vessel into the other; and a curious exchange of gifts between genteel lovers who never before have seen each other.

Little has been written on this poem since R. Menéndez Pidal published the definitive version in the *Revue Hispanique,* XIII (1905), as a single, unified piece. José Filguera Valverde in his article on the "Lìrica medieval gallega" in the first volume of *Historia general de las literaturas hispánicas* (1949), . . . is the first to suggest its possible "alegorismo" in common with the Introduction to Berceo's *Milagros;* and Leo Spitzer, in *Romania,* LXXI (1950), has offered a valuable overall reinterpretation stressing the human side. There still remains, however, the possibility of a definite didactic purpose couched in the Christian symbolism familiar to the Middle Ages.

The symbolist, according to C. S. Lewis (*The Allegory of Love,* 1936), leaves the given to find that which is more real. To the mediaeval mind, a tree standing in a garden and bearing a vessel of red wine would almost certainly suggest the "tree" of the Crucifixion and the blood of Jesus. Modern readers shy from tropology, preferring to see in a tree its simple beauty as a tree, and declaring that the further meaning it is said to conceal exists only in the oversubtle mind of the inquirer. But it is hardly fair to the artists of the Middle Ages to take beauty of form and color as the stimulus and justification of their enterprise. The value of nature, art, and antiquity lay in their didactic theological potential; the facts were nothing until they became symbols, and the most highly trained minds found no created thing too commonplace to illustrate spiritual verity. This way of thinking and writing was carried so far that its intricate results seem to us little more than masterpieces of eager ingenuity. We must however project ourselves back to the earlier age. "Nous sommes donc ici," writes Professor Spitzer of the **Razon,** "comme dans tant d'œuvres médiévales, en présence d'un plan surnaturel, érigé audessus d'une scène terrestre." Of this much we may be confident; beyond this, the uncertainties of any interpretation of one age by another permit only a range of plausibility. The following is therefore offered as possible, not as conclusive.

The initial clue to the appropriateness of the proposed interpretation is given by Gonzalo de Berceo, whose Introduction to the *Milagros de Nuestra Seõra* begins in a similar way: "Yo maestro Gonçalvo de Verçeo nomnado / Iendo en romeria caeçi en un prado / Verde e bien sençido, de flores bien poblado,/ Logar cobdiçiadero pora omne cansado." After describing the luxuriance of the flowers, trees and fruits, he removes his cloak, lies down in the cool shade, and listens to the birds. Seeing the fruits, he is reminded of Adam, and proceeds to a tropological interpretation of all other details: "Prendamos lo de dentro, lo de fuera dessemos./Todos quantos vevimos que en piedes andamos,/ . . . Todos somos romeos que camino andamos / . . . La nuestra romeria estonz la acabamos/ Quando a paraiso las almas enviamos."

From this point forward, Berceo converts the whole scene into a set of symbols and emblems. The meadow is the Blessed Virgin. Its green color is her decorum; its four fountains the Gospels, inspired by her; the shadows of trees, her prayers for sinners, whether kings or commoners; the trees, her miracles; the birds, the church fathers, prophets, apostles and priests who sing of her; the flowers, her many revealing names.

The poet of La Rioja was using an established didactic technique. Hugh of St. Victor had earlier stated: "Omnis natura Deum loquitur, omnis natura hominem docet, omnis natura rationem parit, et nihil in universitate infecundum est" (*Didascalicon de studio legendi,* VI, 5), and Vedel and Huizinga confirm that "Toda la

Naturaleza no era . . . sino otro tratado mellizo . . . de la Sagrada Escritura," and "There is not an object nor an action, however trivial, that is not constantly correlated with Christ or salvation. All thinking tends to religious interpretation of individual things." It remains to apply this method, which is also Berceo's, to the contemporaneous *Razon de amor*.

The poet's self-introduction, a *juglaresco* convention of doubtful autobiographical veridity, but part of a convenient framework for the piece, continues:

> odra razon acabada,
> feyta d'amor e bien rymada.
> Un escolar la rrimo
> que siempre duenas amo;
> mas siempre ouo cryança
> en Alemania y en Françia;
> moro mucho en Lombardia
> pora aprender cortesia.

He takes pride in his poetic accomplishment, the result of having been raised in the several domains of Frederick the Second and in polite society (*siempre duenas amo*), followed by prolonged residence in Northern Italy for study of *cortesia*, where he may have caught some of the beginnings of religious and moral poetry which later developed there. Having given the mood of his recitation and his self-introduction, he states the time and place of the first scene:

> En el mes d'abril, depues yantar,
> estaua so un oliuar.

In a country with a folk tradition of May songs, according to Menéndez Pidal (*Estudios literarios,* 1946), the month is given as April. May is the full release of Spring, the month of floral festivals; but April is the last month of Lent, when the attitude of the Christian world is one resembling *tristeza:* penitence. It was to these *tristes* that the *juglar* addressed his recital, offering them not gaiety but artistic skill. In its theme, which is now to be developed (Berceo's *meollo,* not the visible *corteza*), it belongs, like Dante's Divine Comedy, to the pre-Easter season.

The poet has already given his only description of the area he now occupies: "estaba so un oliuar." The later fragrant garden does not appear until after he has fallen asleep. The olive tree grows best on sparse rocky ground, and its lanceolate leaves do not offer dense shade. He is still outside the formal garden, in a position where

> Entre çimas d'un mançanar
> un uaso de plata ui estar;
> pleno era d'un claro uino
> que era uermeio e fino;
> cubierto era de tal mesura

no lo tocas la calentura.

In the whole range of symbolism no emblem is more widespread or has exerted greater influence upon the institutions of mankind than the branch or tree. Its meaning in mediaeval literary gardens is made clear by D. W. Robertson. ["The Doctrine of Charity in Mediaeval Gardens: a Topical Approach through Symbolism and Allegory," *Speculum,* XXVI (1951)]. Many gardens are little more than groves of trees and still others have a tree as a central feature. To the mediaeval mind, the very important position of the tree of life and the tree of knowledge of good and evil in the Biblical narrative, and the symmetry between the tree of the temptation in Eden and the tree of the redemption on Calvary, meant that any literary tree could be considered as an aspect of one of the Biblical trees, or as a transitional growth between the two extremes. The apple tree in particular figures frequently as the tree of life.

The tree under observation, then, may be no other than the symbol of the cross of Christ; and if it is, then the silver vessel on it (silver being the second in the sequence of metals), and its content of fine red wine, are readily identified as the body and blood of Jesus. If this is the end of the Lenten season, the traveller may well elevate his eyes to the symbol of the Crucifixion, and feel within himself that *tristeza* which the opening line attributes to the listeners. If, in common with Dante's great work, this is intended to be an Easter poem of the redemption of Man, it may be no accident that the traveller has reached this place at this time. It may figure the Jerusalem of the courtier who has changed his ways and makes the typically mediaeval expiatory pilgrimage. This is the more plausible since Grace Frank, in "The Distant Love of Jaufré Rudel," *MLN,* LVII (1942), and LXIX (1944), showed that a troubadour could sing of the Holy City in the figure of a damsel. Man, for Berceo as for St. Augustine, St. Bernard and Dante, was a stranger and a pilgrim in the world; and so the poetic subject of the *Razon de amor*, who not inaptly emblematizes Man seeking the New Jerusalem, may tentatively be called the penitent or the pilgrim.

> Una duena lo y eua puesto
> que era senora del uerto,
> que quan su amigo uiniese,
> d'a quel uino a beuer le disse.

Mary had given her Son to be crucified for the sins of mankind, and is often referred to under the symbolism of a garden—stemming from the "garden inclosed" of Song of Solomon, iv, 12. When the garden stands for the Church, she is its mistress. But do we dare to attribute an *amigo* to Mary? The wise Alfonso X, in the sixteenth *Cantiga,* has Mary say: "—Se me por amiga queres auer, máis rafez,/ tanto que est' ano rezes por mì outra uez / quanto pola outra antano fuste rezar." Mary was the friend of everyone who turned to her with utter devotion; and though the fact is here expressed in terms of love imagery, it is none the less a fact. St. Thomas Aquinas clarifies this sort of difficulty in the *Summa Theologica* (Pt. I, Q. 1, Art. 10) by saying: "When Scripture speaks of God's arm, the literal sense is not that God has such a member but only what is signified by this member, namely, operative power." That the word *dueã* is used here and *doncela* a little later, leads Professor Spitzer to infer two ladies; but at this date the words were still synonyms. Berceo in *Santa Oria* refers to the same four girls in stanza 41 as *virgenes,* in 45 as *donçellas,* and in 46 as *duenas,* and line 1764 of the *Cantar de Mio Cid* reveals the same: "Estas duenas que aduxiestes, que vos sirven tanto,/ Quierolas casar con de aquestos mios vassallos."

> Qui de tal uino ouiesse
> en la mana quan comiesse:
> e dello ouiesse cada dia,
> nuncas mas enfermarya.

The only wine which traditionally has this healing quality is the wine of communion or the eucharist, which is the blood of Jesus. Whoever communicates each morning, having of necessity been previously absolved, will never, according to the poem, fall back into the *tristeza* or *enfermedad* of mortal existence.

> Arriba del mançanar
> otro uaso ui estar;
> pleno era d'un agua fryda
> que en el mançanar se naçia.
> Beuiera d'ela de grado,
> mas oui miedo que era encantado.

There is an upper vessel, of a material not named, filled with cool water from the garden spring. The pilgrim fears to drink it. He senses something supernatural about it; and this clue, together with the statement that the water it contains is the same as that of the spring, identifies it clearly as the water of life, which is always described as flowing from the roots of the tree of life in the garden of Paradise, whether in Revelation (xxii.2), in the Vision of Saint Paul (Howard R. Patch, *The Other World,* 1950), or in the Muslim tradition (*La Escala de Mahoma,* ed. Muõz Sendino, 1949). Its position in the high spot of the garden; the fact that it is water or perfect purity relative to wine of more material reference; and that this vessel is unnamed, while the lower one is of silver, the second metal; and that it was not placed there by anyone and does not invite direct approach, all point to the symbolic divine Substance, near all but superior to all. This possibility is strengthened by the *Vision of St. Paul:* "And I entered in further, and saw a tree planted, out of whose roots flowed waters . . . and the spirit of God rested upon that tree."

The traveller twice again mentioning the discomfort of extreme heat, which may symbolically be a reminder

of the burden of mortal existence, or may connote the justice of God which envelops and consumes him inexorably, loosens or lays aside his outer clothing and lies down, bringing the first scene to a close. There has been no other action and no amenity. It is as if the pilgrim had approached, but yet remained outside the garden of his desire, thirsting for that water of life which he perceived above. Dante, too, emerged from the sinister woods and raised his eyes to another symbol of divine source high beyond the shoulder of the mountain and inaccessible to him: "Guardai in alto, e vidi le sue spalle/ vestite già de' raggi del pianeta,/ che mena dritto altrui per ogni calle."

Before examining the second scene, let us look again at the objects just appraised. Symbols, like words, have fluid and multiple meanings, and recognition of them is not an equivocation; rather, all meanings are necessary if mediaeval thinking is not to remain an enigma. . . . The scene observed from the olive grove, without in any way losing its paschal significance, can in addition give another perspective, back to the book of Genesis, and show the primitive cause of the Passion. The apple tree with its wine-fruit is now the tree of the temptation, and the fruit is offered by the mistress of the garden of Eden, Eve, to her lover Adam ('Adam' is Hebrew for Man, as a race) in the conviction that he "nuncas mas enfermarya." "In the day ye eat thereof . . . ye shall be as gods." ". . . a tree to be desired to make one wise" (Genesis iii.5-6). In early paintings it was often recognizably an apple tree; but any fruit tree in a garden recalled Eden, as we have already observed in the case of Berceo. "Da das Paradies ein Garten ist, kann umgekehrt ein Garten Paradies heissen" (E. R. Curtius, *Europäische Literatur . . .*).

The second of the four scenes into which the poem conveniently divides begins

> Pleguem a una fuente perenal,
> nunca fue omne que vies tall

and it represents the dream-vision of the thirsty penitent; thirsty for water, for reassurance that his quest will be successful, and for salvation, if the pilgrimage is that of this world's mortal journey. He envisions himself in a wonderfully cool, shady, aromatic garden close to an ever-flowing spring irrigating veriagated flowers and refreshing the atmosphere for a hundred paces around. This is like the second of the three paradises described by Hugh of St. Victor in his *De Arca Noe Morali.* . . . The first is that of man's innocence, and in it was the material tree of life; the second is the Church, and of it the tree of life is Christ who gave his life on the cross and gives it daily in the Eucharist. It is here that preparation is made for the paradise of God, whereof the tree is the divine wisdom, fountain of life, and origin of all good. We must not expect, however, since this is symbolical, and is moreover a vision with the consequent blurring of borders, that the dreamer's impressions will be sharply differentiated. It is a dream-fulfilment in terms of his own sense of need.

The *locus amoenus,* then, is the Christian Church. The water of the spring is baptism. Its purifying, regenerative quality circulates through the Church and makes fruition possible. The thirsty traveller marvels for fourteen verses at the sights and aromas, before taking a sip of the water of life. A single sip is sufficient because the sacrament of baptism is administered only once, and because "Whosoever drinketh of the water that I shall give him shall never thirst; but the water that I shall give him shall be in him a well of water springing up into everlasting life" (St. John iv.14). Instantly there is a total transformation in the penitent's attitude. His outreaching to nature and his joyful song

> en mi mano prys una flor,
> sabet non toda la peyor,
> e quis cantar de fin amor

betoken the loss of the separateness and fearfulness which had possessed him when he first saw the vessels, and his present restoration to inner security. It is at this moment that

> mas ui uenir una doncela,
> pues naçi non ui tan bella:
> blanca era e bermeia,
> cabelos cortos sobr' ell oreia,

followed by sixteen verses of description not materially distinguishable from that of any mediaeval lady of quality. Like Matelda of the *Purgatorio* xxviii she sings and gathers flowers as she goes. Her song is a sort of *cantiga de amigo* based on absence and jealousy, and is not intended to portray her own situation. If it were, the traveller's question "Dezit, la mia senor, si supiestes nunca d'amor?" would already have been answered. Rather, it is an interpolated lyric, bringing the damozel to the forefront of attention while the stranger observes her. Her physical description differs little from the established pattern of real and allegorical women as found in *Santa Marìa Egipcìaca, Libro de buen amor, Roman de la rose,* and *L'Intelligenza.* The poet's effort is to present the lady as attractive, according to the norms of the day.

The garden, too, should be viewed as a whole. True, the four flowers near the spring—sage, rose, lily and violet—may all share a flower symbolism, or individually may represent mercy, purity, humility and other virtues, or, as Berceo suggests (*Introducción*), they may be names of the Virgin. It is not necessary to establish a factual correspondence, because the mediaeval mind built more on suggestiveness. The same is true of the four gifts mentioned later: gloves, coif, *coral,* and ring; and the one gift from the damozel, the handmade belt. Symbolic

value may more probably attach to the numbers four and one than to the specific gifts. The four, on the side of man is a double dichotomy, hence complexity, hence experience or manifestation, while the one, on the side of the representative of Divinity is simplicity, purity, source. The world is in a sense fourfold with its four elements, four seasons, four directions, four qualities, and the four humours of man; while the world beyond is the realm of the One Supreme. The importance of number to the Middle Ages is made clear by Vincent Foster Hopper in *Mediaeval Number Symbolism* (1938). Symbolic numbers were a part of the Eternal Pattern, and numerical significance was found everywhere.

The presumed penitent approaches the damozel with perfect courtesy ("Yo non fiz aqui como uilano"), invites her to sit down under the tree of peace, beauty, and reconciliation, the olive, and not under the tree of the temptation or of the Passion (the apple tree with its two vessels is not a part of this scene), and without any courtly expressions at all, asks her two simple questions: "Si supiestes nunca d'amor?", which is an echo from the pastorelles, and "Que donas tenedes de la su amor?" With notable caution he is seeking to ascertain whether she is in fact the object of his *amor lonh,* and whether his gifts have found favor in her sight. She answers the first query with a description by hearsay of her unknown lover: a scholar rather than a knight, accomplished in poetry, well read, musical, of good family, young and rough-bearded (*barva punniente*); that is, between the full beard of an older man and the mere *bozo* of a youth. Her answer to the second question has already been touched upon. Most simply, the gifts are worthy of a lady of quality. They, together with the fact that his reserve permits no declaration or advances, help to reveal her as the lady of his highest aspiration, the Queen of Heaven. If he is a pilgrim, his vision will encompass no lesser fulfilment of the devout purpose which has brought him to this place. Since he has made offerings to her in absentia and she has received them, she has thereby accepted as it were the expression of his devotion, and his pilgrimage and penance are favored. Her effusive welcome is typical of that of the shepherd for one sheep recovered and of the Church for one sinner redeemed. Any human being who turns to her in full devotion is in truth "meu amado" and "meo amigo," and with utmost sincerity she may praise God because "agora e tod bien comigo, quant conozco meo amigo."

The modern reader must not for a moment overlook that this interpretation assumes a theological truth to be given in a poetic idiom. It is therefore not unseemly that the expression of Mary's welcoming love for the penitent at the end of his pilgrimage, as he dreams it, should be such a *galardón:* the kiss and the speechless raptured gazing on the traveller returned, the sinner delivered. The precarious dream world of mediaeval love poetry does not sharply distinguish between lady-worship and Mary-worship; terms suited to the Virgin are applied to ladies, and expressions apt for ladies are sung to the Queen of Heaven. What to us in our day would be a term of insufficient reverence was not held to be so in the day of Berceo and Alfonso.

Further confirmation that the kiss, the greeting, and the ensuing scene are not of necessity erotic (though in the confused borderland of the pilgrim's dream they may be) is found in the fact that in Italy, where the poet had studied *cortesìa,* Guinicelli was shortly to develop the courtly theme of praise, to the hyperbole that the lady is a creature sent from heaven to reveal here some of the splendor of God's kingdom; and Dante was to transform this *donna angelicata,* an angel or messenger from heaven, into a guide to heaven. Love of her is love directed to heaven. The poet of the ***Razon*** could already have had this imagery in mind; could, indeed, have communicated it to Brunetto Latini during the latter's reported embassy in Spain around 1260. In Brunetto's *Tesoretto* the poet, alone in a natural setting, meets a noble damsel. She is Nature, second only to God. She gives the poet instruction and reveals to him the wonders of the world. Dante looked upon Brunetto with filial affection, and part of *Purgatorio* xxviii is reminiscent of the *Tesoretto.* In it Matelda, already mentioned, a lady of great beauty and grace, singing and gathering flowers in a cool grove, greets the poet (not however with effusive affection), awakens his love, counsels him about his future course, and assists him, preliminary to the vision of Beatrice.

Thus the meeting beneath the olive tree may mark the completion of one stage of the pilgrim's quest, with the acceptance of his gifts and of his devotion, and the launching of another stage under the guidance of the *donna angelicata.* During the "grant pieça ali estando, / De nuestro amor ementando" the pair may be described by words of St. John of the Cross, commenting his "Allì me enseñó ciencia muy sabrosa" in *Cántico espiritual,* xxvii: "La ciencia sabrosa que dize aquì que la enseñó es la Teologìa mìstica, que es ciencia secreta de Dios, que llaman los espirituales contemplación; la cual es muy sabrosa, porque es ciencia por amor." This is no earthly love nor earthly garden. The enveloping and elevating atmosphere is rather that described by Hugh of St. Victor: "Amoris plena sunt omnia, et omnia amorem resonant: flores, odor, canticum. Nihil hic est quod animum non subeat, quod cor non penetret, et quod affectum non transigat" (*Sermo de assumption Beatae Virginis*). The possibility of mystical instruction must be considered here because of partial similarities with subsequent poems: Brunetto's *Tesoretto, L'Intelligenza* attributed to Dino Compagni, in which the damsel of the early stanzas is revealed to be Intelligence in the 299th; the *Documenti d'Amore* of Francesco da Barberino, in which Love teaches allegorically without any trace of erotic tendency, and the final cantos of the *Purgatorio.*

At the conclusion of their meeting (which, it must be remembered, takes place within the pilgrim's dream, and so is cast in the mold of his desire), the damozel begs leave to depart. Her final words, "Bien seguro seyt de mi amor" are not so much a statement as a reassurance, invited by his urgent "Mas de mi amor pensat," which, in view of her answer, is clearest if read as an objective genitive: "mi amor" here means "your love of me," just as in the *Poema del Cid,* 1206, "Sonando van sus nuevas" means "reports of him are spreading," and in the *Caballero Zifar,* ed. Wagner (1929), "De cuyo amor?" "Del vuestro," mean "Love of whom?" "Love of you." The penitent's parting request, then, to which she so graciously responds, is "Continue me in your love." In the poem he has made no affectionate advance whatever, but rather by his two careful (if conventional) queries has invited this reassurance of her acceptance of his devotion. If, as this interpretation posits, he is a pilgrim to some shrine of Mary, he wants above all things to know that his penance has earned her approbation, and that she will continue to favor him.

The vision is ended and the penitent is alone. Even in his dream (for he is probably still in fact asleep under the olive tree), he finds, with Ibn Hazm, that separation is the brother of death, a concept which Garcilaso expressed for all time in his first *Egloga,* 318-323:

> Tal es la tenebrosa
> noche de tu partir, en que he quedado
> de sombra y de temor atormentado,
> hasta que muerte el tiempo determine
> que a ver el deseado
> sol de tu clara vista me encamine,

and which in Herrera's commentary is traced back to Homer.

He seeks refuge, as before, in sleep, and in this dream-within-a-dream constituting the third scene he sees a dove, white as snow on the heights, fly toward the fountain where he lies, then to the tree, then quickly away. The dove is of rich Christian symbolism, and may here be seen, like the damozel, as a messenger and guide. It served this function for Noah preliminary to his release from the ark, and for Berceo's Santa Oria as described in stanzas 26, 30, 37, and 40, to aid in her ascent. The relevant verses are as follows:

> 37 Guarda esta palonba, todo lo al oluyda;
>   Tu ue do ella fuere, non seas deçebida,
>   Guiate por nos, fija, ca Christus te conbida.
> 40 Moujosse la palonba, començo de uolar,
>   Suso contra los çielos començo de pujar.
> 47 Catando la palonba como bien acordada,
>   Subio en pos las otras en essa grant posada.

The poet, who prided himself on his learning, could have seen two earlier Spanish poems in which this theme was used or implied; one in Hebrew by Zerahya ben Ishaq Ha-levi (No. 115 in Millás y Vallicrosa's *Poesìa sagrada hebraicoespaõla,* 2nd edition [1948]): "Vuelve como paloma y al palomar vuela, hasta que logres subir al trono de realeza. Aguas de salud saca para ti de la Fuente de vida, y con tus pies no enturbies sus claras linfas."

The other is in Arabic by Abu-l-Hasan Ali ben Hisn (the first poem in Garcìa Gomez's, *Poemas arabigo-andaluces,* 3rd edition [1946]), and includes the lines: "Nada me turbó más que un pichón que zureaba sobre una rama, entre la isla y el río. . . . Se recostaba en el ramo del <u>arak</u> como en un trono, escondiendo la garganta en el repliegue del ala. Mas al ver correr mis lágrimas, le asustó mi llanto, e irguiéndose sobre la verde rama, desplegó sus alas y las batïó en su vuelo, llevándose mi corazón. ¿Adónde? No lo sé."

Both Millás, following Peres cited by him, and Lawrence Ecker, in *Arabischer, Provenzalischer und Deutscher Minnesang* (1934), have shown the considerable interrelation between Northern and Andalusian poetry, little impeded by difference of language. But even within purely Christian antecedents, the dove was an early symbol of soul, and is used as such by Berceo in his "El naufrago salvado," stanza 600:

> Vidieron palonbiellas essir de so la mar,
> Más blancas que las nieves contral cielo volar:
> Credien que eran almas que querie Dios levar
> Al sancto paraiso, un glorioso logar.

The dove's entry immediately after the damozel's departure, its flight toward the pilgrim as if in recognition, its avoidance of the fountain of baptism or the water of life as made available to the Christian within the Church, and its immersion in the upper vessel or higher form of the same water, can now be seen as a figure of the soul or angelic essence of the damozel ascending to the Divine Nature, which, as seen by men, is Grace. The effect of this ascent is that the upper vessel overflows into the lower: Divine Grace is poured into the Eucharist. Now, while Grace is self-existent and not accessible to man through his own outreaching, Eucharist is a sacrament established for man—the vessel of wine was placed on the tree for him—and he may grasp it through his own will. Mary, who placed it there (gave her Son to be crucified), has now by her intervention (as the dove) endowed it with mystical efficacy, by commingling with it the divine ("encantado" or mysterious) fluid. The pilgrim, having known "baptism" in the second scene, followed by an intimate "confession," may now approach "communion," the symbol of union which he aspires ultimately to know as immortality, in the unknown region to which the dove has flown.

There remains the fourth and final scene, that of the "Denuestos". In a poem of pure entertainment it would serve to provide contrast, comic relief, and a spirited

ending, and the same pattern is followed here by the *ajuglarado* author. The Archpriest of Hita did the same at a later date, and similar variety was also practiced earlier by the Spanish Muslim poets of the South. According to Schack, "a menudo se advierte esta diversidad en una misma composición, la cual está formada de muchas partes, conteniendo cada una distinto asunto, como si fuesen varias composiciones" (*Poesìa y arte de los árabe,* 1945). In view of the interrelation between the Arabic and Romance branches of Spanish poetry, mentioned also by Schack, the essential unity of the poem as confirmed by Pidal and Spitzer need not be questioned. But what has a dispute in common with an idyllic or a mystical piece?

As in the earlier cases of the conventional descriptions of damsel and gallant, of a garden, the use of a conventional love song, and the *topoi* of recognition and separation, the poet employs familiar means to achieve a more exalted end. The details matter less than the impact of the whole. The argument between wine and water is an inverted echo of the colloquy between the pilgrim and the damozel. They, speaking in human terms, symbolize a sacred meaning. Wine and water, sacred symbols in the earlier part, are here humanized. The man and woman, having enjoyed spiritual harmony, are afterwards physically separated; the wine and water having experienced physical commixture, are morally separated. The dramatic technique involved is simply that of Gil and Menga who ludicrously imitate their master and mistress, but get everything topsy turvey.

From the point of view of the dreaming penitent, who has just had a vision of hope and the assurance of Grace, and now overhears, or further dreams, this dispute, it is the caricature or degradation of the most exalted symbols. The damozel has disappeared; the eucharistic wine has become the contrary of the Prince of humility: an arrogant braggart; while the water of Grace and Baptism has become the companion of dirty linen and constituent of mud.

A similar literary technique was to be employed by later authors, notably by Rodrigo Cota in his *Diálogo entre el amor y un viejo,* and by Torres Naharro in his *Addición del diálogo,* where in each case the tenor of the work alters and ends on a note more likely to delight the masses than the learned. Torres concludes his skit with a sacrilegious farced version of the *Ave maris stella* which must have appealed to the devotees of the Boy Bishop revels. It is not unexpected, then, to find a serious piece terminated by some form of jocularity.

The wine-water nightmare occupies the same place in the spiritual history of the penitent at this moment as the ordeal in Grail symbolism and in the society romances. The possibility of parallelism is suggested by two important coincidences between the **Razon de amor,** the Quest of the Grail, and the quest of Dante in the *Divine*

Comedy. They depend on the aid and inspiration of a woman; and the complete outward vision of the sacred symbol is followed by expulsion from its effective presence. There is a preliminary vision; then the vision is lost and there are trials of endurance: Gawain is pelted out of town, Perceval is expelled from the castle, Dante's way is blocked by wild beasts. And in Canto xxx of the *Purgatorio,* no sooner has Dante achieved the vision of Beatrice than she offers sharp rebuke, driving him to tears of penance and ultimately to a swoon. In each case there is some sort of trial or testing of the aspirant before he can achieve the final goal. Within this pattern, if, as seems to be the case, it may be applied to our poem, the ordeal of the pilgrim is purely psychological. With the departure of the damozel the luxuriant garden too has seemed to disappear, and the traveller is again in the relative bareness of the first scene, witnessing again the tree of the Passion on Calvary where blood and water issued together from the wound, and the earth did quake and the rocks rent (St. John xix.34; St. Matthew xxvii.51). This is the dramatic picture of the dreamer's state of soul within his dream, brought on by his new loneliness. Or, for the moment he may have slipped into another symbolic realm where water represents the things of God and wine the things of earth, and he envisions the conflict yet to come before his eventual release. There is of course nothing godly about the attitudes taken up by Water in this *disputa,* but that fact does not upset the water symbolism.

We cannot know how far the poet wished to carry the possible analogies. He has painted a very positive scene, then a messenger to the skies, then a very negative scene, and the reader is left to make what he can of it. In symbolic interpretation there is no fixed factual truth. It is clear, however, to the modern mind, and may have been so to the medieval, that the pilgrim must learn to see in all wine the potential presence of the Lord's body sacrificed for him, and in all water the power and grace of God inherent. "We cannot be enlightened by the Divine rays," wrote Dionysius, as quoted by St. Thomas, "except they be hidden within the covering of many sacred veils." And St. Thomas Aquinas in his comment adds: "What He is not is clearer to us than what He is. Therefore similitudes drawn from things farthest away from God form within us a truer estimate that God is above whatsoever we may say or think of Him" (*Summa Theologica,* I, Q. i, Art. 9). For Hugh of St. Victor there is also no incompatibility in spiritual things: "Spiritualis autem intelligentia nullam admittit repugnantiam, in qua diversa multa, adversa nulla esse possunt" (*Eruditionis didascalicae,* VI, iv).

The poet, having given his audience the refreshment of the earlier part of the argument, having carefully avoided the heavy theological humour of the *Goliae Dialogus inter Aquam et Vinum* (No. 22 in Wright's *Latin Poems commonly attributed to Walter Mapes,* 1841), returns to a final summary of his teaching, i.e. "Que entre reir y

reir / Bueno es la verdad decir. / Y por esto soy venido" (Diego Sánchez de Badajoz, *Farsa Teologal, Introito*). As in the beginning the vessel of wine was first mentioned, and Vino was the first to argue in the *disputa,* so it is Wine who now announces his true nature and power. "Yo fago al çiego ueyer / y al coxo correr / y al mudo faublar y al enfermo organar," though said as a joke, is nothing other than a repetition of the earlier "Qui de tal uino ouiesse . . . nuncas mas enfermarya." In stating plainly now that Wine is "el cuerpo de Iesu Cristo," the author confirms our initial symbolism of the tree as Cross and its strange fruit as the crucified body of Jesus. Water, which was superior in the tree, now closes the poem by ascribing to itself the power of baptism, thus confirming the symbolism of the fountain, and indeed the arbitrament of the Day of Judgment:

> e dize Dios que los que de agua fueren
>   bautizados
> fillos de Dios seran clamados,
> e llos que de agua non fueren bautizados
> fillos de Dios non seran clamados.

The author apparently is thinking of St. Matthew xxv.31: "When the Son of Man shall come in his glory, and all the holy angels with him, then shall he sit upon the throne of his glory: 32 And before him shall be gathered all nations; and he shall separate them one from another, as a shepherd divideth his sheep from the goats." Heaven or Hell, the ultimates in mediaeval experience, depended entirely on Water; that is, on Baptism and Grace, the lower fountain and the upper vessel.

Much more might be said of this little poem and its possible relation to the Platonic, Troubadour, Arabic, Hebrew, and Latin traditions; but the immediate purpose is to present the possibility of a symbolic interpretation embodying those transcendent correspondences of which, for the mediaeval mind, the earth and its beauties were shadows.

Roger M. Walker (essay date 1973)

SOURCE: "Two Notes on Spanish Debate Poems," in *Medieval Studies in Honor of Robert White Linker,* Brian Dutton, J. Woodrow Hassell, Jr., John E. Keller, eds., Editorial Castalia, 1973, pp. 177-84.

[*Here, Walker theorizes that the* Razón de amor *may have been parodied by Alfonso X in his poem about the famous courtesan Maria Peres.*]

The ***Razón de amor,*** dating from the early thirteenth century, is the earliest surviving Castilian poem to show considerable influence of the poetry of the Provençal troubadours. The *locus amoenus* setting, the beautiful girl and her cultured *amigo,* the exchange of elegant gifts, the courtly behaviour of the lovers, their long-standing *amor de lonh,* and many other features all suggest a solid familiarity with the ideals and conventions of the poets of Southern France as well as with those of the derivative Galician-Portuguese school. The poet introduces his work by telling his audience that he has studied *cortesìa* over a long period in a number of countries where courtliness flourished:

> 5 Un escolar la rrimó
>   que siempre dueñas amó;
>   mas siempre ovo cryança
>   en Alemania y en Francia,
>   moró mucho en Lombardìa
> 10 pora aprender cortesìa.

It is well known that the Provençal poets and their minstrels travelled widely outside Southern France during the hey-day of their civilization; and after the Albigensian Crusade had brutally shattered this civilization in the early years of the thirteenth century, many of them were forced to take permanent refuge in foreign courts. Both in travel, and in exile they took with them into Northern France, Italy, Germany, Spain, and places even farther afield, their concept of love and their poetic ideals. One of the courts which extended a warm welcome to the refuge poets was that of Alfonso X, el Sabio, king of Castile and León, himself an accomplished poet and the author of the poem I wish to consider in relation to the *Razón de amor*.

The poem in question is one of Alfonso's *cantigas de maldizer,* which concerns Maria Peres, known as *a Balteyra,* the most notorious *soldadera* of the royal court. This woman's scandalous behaviour is the subject of a considerable number of ribald verses in Galician-Portuguese. In the king's poem the joke centres on Joham Rodriguiz's *madeyra,* the yard-stick of which Maria is told she will have to take full measure. The last stanza reads:

> 16 E [J. R.] disse: esta he a midida d'Espanha,
>   ca nom de Lombardia, nem d'Alamanha,
>   e porque he grossa non vos seja mal,
>   ca delgada, pera gata, rren non val,
> 20 e d'esto muy mais sey eu c'abondanha.

How significant is it that the poet, in extolling Rodriguiz's *madeyra,* should contrast its size with that of the apparently less well-endowed inhabitants of Lombardy and Germany, two of the three centres of courtliness specifically singled out by the poet of the *Razón de amor? Alamanha,* of course, provides an easy rhyme with *Espanha;* but this does not explain either why Rodriguiz should wish to make his sexual organ a matter of national pride, or why the masculinity of the Italians should also be gratuitously impugned. If, however, we interpret these final lines as a satirical attack on the conventions of courtly love as exemplified by the *Razón de amor,* this scurrilous poem takes on a further humorous dimension. Alfonso would then seem to be implying, through Joham Rodriguiz, that the famous service of love, with its concomitant pleading, moaning and extravagant fidelity, is not the Spanish way of wooing; he might well be saying that the men of the peninsula prefer *coito* to *coita.* At the same time he appears to be suggesting that the elaborate ritual of courtly love is merely a cover for timidity and lack of sexual potency.

Unfortunately we have no knowledge of the popularity and diffusion of the *Razón de amor* during the later thirteenth century. We do know, however, that Alfonso was passionately interested in the development of Castilian as a literary instrument, that he was very well-versed in its heroic poetry, drawing extensively on epics for his *Estoria de España,* and that he himself composed one of the tiny number of lyric poems in Castilian that exist from before the fourteenth century. In view of this, it is reasonably probable that Alfonso knew the *Razón de amor.* Moreover, we have enough evidence concerning the high cultural level of the learned king's court to justify the assumption that if the king knew the **Razón** at least some of his courtiers would too, and so would be able to appreciate the satirical implications of his references to Germany and Lombardy in this *cantiga de maldizer.*

For all his breadth of learning and his international contacts, Alfonso remained a fervent nationalist and advocate of Castilian supremacy. Is it not possible that in this poem he is not only making an obscene joke at the expense of the luckless Maria Peres, but also indirectly extolling the notorious Spanish *hombría* at the expense of the dubious masculinity of the trans-Pyrenean *fin amors?*

Margo De Ley (essay date 1976)

SOURCE: "Provençal Biographical Tradition and the *Razón de amor,*" in *Journal of Hispanic Philology,* Vol. I, No. 1, Autumn, 1976, pp. 1-17.

[*In the essay below, De Ley probes the many connections between the* Razón de amor *and Provençal writings known as* vidas *and* razos, *suggesting that the author of the poem consciously chose to work within that biographical tradition.*]

Since its discovery in 1887 by Alfred Morel-Fatio, the *Razón de amor* has inspired studies by a number of scholars, but the problems it presents are far from a definite solution. These problems arise, in part, from the poet's statements about his work and from its apparently heterogeneous nature. Believed to have been written in the first half of the thirteenth century, the poem begins with an apparently biographical introduction. It then presents a sometimes-lyrical love-narrative which has a number of aspects in common with the Portuguese *can-*

tiga de amigo and *pastorela* as well as with Provençal courtly poetry. A debate follows between wine and water, drawn for the most part from a slightly earlier Latin poem, *Denudata veritate*. The **Razón** ends abruptly with a brief juglaresque request for wine, in Spanish, and the scribe's *explicit* in Latin. The introduction and a number of other lines in the poem resemble, as we shall see, the Provençal *vidas* and *razos* which were composed by minstrels to introduce the works of the troubadours and later included with them in the troubadour songbooks. By examining the **Razón de amor** and its relationship to these contemporary genres, I hope to shed new light on the problems of unity, authorship, and inspiration in the poem.

Previous studies . . . have discussed such aspects of the **Razón de amor** as the poet's origin, the interpretation of individual words and of the work as a whole, the rhythm, and the possible sources of the poem. While approaching the **Razón** from rather different points of view, almost all of these studies have touched on the problem of unity, and the majority have concluded that it was intended to be a single poem. Scholars generally agree on the influence of the Provençal courtly lyric on the love-narrative, but none mentions the biographies as a possible source of inspiration for that part of the poem. While some critics have pointed out that the word *razón* is used in the Spanish poem with the same meaning as the Provençal *razo,* in that they both refer to a literary composition, they have not discussed the influence of the Provençal genre on the poem itself.

In his study of the origins of the Romance literatures, Ramón Menéndez Pidal [in *Poesìa juglaresca y juglares,* 1957] draws heavily on the *razos* and *vidas,* while at times indicating their historical inaccuracies. The biographies, he points out, "nos han dado a conocer la condición y costumbres del juglar, sus viajes, su influencia y otros datos importantes para la historia de la cultura; con razón se ha observado que la vida de los trovadores y juglares es a menudo más interesante y más poética que sus canciones; al menos suele ser inseparable de las mismas." It is thanks to these brief documents that he is able to paint a portrait of the *clérigo ajuglarado,* and give evidence of the travels of poets and minstrels between Spanish courts and France and Italy.

It is generally believed that the biographies were composed no earlier than the beginning of the thirteenth and no later than the beginning of the fourteenth century by minstrels who were trying to maintain or revive interest in poems which had already been part of their repertory for a number of years. Guido Favati, in his thorough study of the biographies, comes to the more precise conclusions that the *razos* were written before the *vidas,* and that the *vidas* were composed at the earliest in the 1230's or 1240's, for the most part by Uc de Saint Circ while he was in Lombardy. The troubadour songbooks, which included the biographies, were complied later—

beginning around the middle of the thirteenth century—, apparently, by someone other than Uc de Saint Circ.

Nearly all of the *vidas* begin with the birthplace of the poet and about a quarter of them include his father's profession and the feudal domain of his home town. Most of the *vidas* mention as well the troubadour's profession, usually that of knight. In a dozen or so *vidas,* however, out of a total of just under a hundred, the poet is a monk, clerk, student, or man of letters. The fact that a courtly poet or minstrel was at first, or continued to be, connected in some way with the Church did not seem surprising or unnatural to the biographers. While religious decrees throughout the thirteenth century attempted to forbid the clergy to perform in public, the biographers continued to describe clerks who became minstrels. In the *vidas* over a third of the poets were minstrels or travelled "per lo mon," presumably performing their works in public. The fact that a poet earned his living as a minstrel or was of humble origin did not necessarily mean that his poetry was reputed to be lower in quality. There were of course troubadours who tended to disdain the role of public performer, and who, in some cases, employed minstrels to perform their works. The overlapping of roles, while not found in the majority of the biographies, was nevertheless not unusual, and in fact, some poets managed to pursue, either successively or concurrently, the varied careers of clerk, wandering minstrel, and courtly troubadour.

A large number of *vidas* are rather brief and contain little information beyond the poet's origins and profession. The longer ones go on to discuss the travels and loves of the poet. Travel was essential to the poets, for it added to their experience and prestige and permitted them to meet generous patrons and courtly ladies. About a third of the *vidas* mention the poet's travels, and within this group the most frequently mentioned court outside Southern France is that of Aragon. The courts of Catalonia and Castile were visited as well, and in all, over a dozen of the Provençal poets visited the Peninsula between the mid-twelfth and mid-thirteenth centuries. The courts of Lombardy were visited by more than half a dozen poets, almost all during the first half of the thirteenth century: Aimeric de Peguillan (c. 1208-30); Elias Cairel (c. 1215-25); Guillem Augier Novella (c. 1212-25); Raimbaut de Vaqueiras (end of twelfth century); Guillem de la Tor (c. 1215-25); Guillem Figueira (c. 1231-40); Uc de Saint Circ (1220-53). It was in Lombardy, as we saw earlier, that the courtly biographies were composed and recited, and the first songbooks were complied.

Nearly a quarter of thc *vidas* discuss the poet's relationship with women, and with only a few exceptions, the poet is depicted as a handsome and refined pursuer of ladies who often return his love and admiration. The *vidas* end, in nearly all cases, with the biographer's comment on the type and quality of the poet's work. This latter information seems to have been considered, along with the poet's origin, the most important information contained in them.

In the majority of *razos* the "reason" or motive for the composition of the poem is a particular incident in a poet's relationship with a lady; in a smaller number it is related to a political conflict. In any case the "reason" is presented in the form of a narrative, usually longer and more elaborate than the *vidas*.

In those *razos* which deal with love relationships the people involved are beautiful, intelligent, and courtly. The poet or his lady may have a rival, they may love or be loved by hearsay. The characters seek to acquire gifts, honor, and courtly reputations; they send messengers in the hope of inspiring or maintaining the affection of their would-be or actual lovers. They may express openly the desire for a physical relationship. In some cases they are fulfilled and in others they suffer deceit and disillusionment. The terms and the themes in the *razos* thus fall clearly within the Provençal courtly tradition. The use of prose and of a narrative form, the attempt at realism, the juglaresque framework, however, make of the *razos* a separate and unique genre. The extent to which the author of the **Razón de amor** found inspiration in the *vidas* and *razos* will become apparent in the comparison which follows.

The ten-line introduction of the **Razón de amor** serves essentially the same purpose as a Provençal *vida,* for it provides biographical information concerning the author of the piece to follow. In lines 1-4, "Qui triste tiene su coraçon / benga oyr esta razon / Odra razon acabada, / feyta d'amor e bien rymada," the poet presents his text as a "razon," a term which has reminded scholars of the Provençal *razo.* As Mario di Pinto points out, the reference to a literary work as a *razón,* and in fact one which deals with love, recalls the *razos.* The Spanish word *razón* had basically the same uses as the Provençal *razo,* and those uses were numerous: reason, a reason or explanation for something; a story (an unwritten one), the subject of a poem or story; a topic under discussion, a point of view, the verbal material which one uses to put across that point of view. Being so rich in meanings, the term appears frequently in Spanish and Provençal medieval literatures, including the biographies and the **Razón de amor,** but it occurs only very rarely as a literary label. In the biographies the term initially signifies a reason for, a commentary, or an explanation; it secondarily comes to refer to a particular literary form. In the Spanish poem it may possibly refer to a story or tale or to the expression of the poet's point of view on love, but even more likely it was chosen to refer to a narrative which, like the *razos,* recounts a poet's amorous adventure. Such an explanation makes more meaningful lines 3-5, in which the author emphasizes that the *razón* in question is in verse and that it has been worked on, polished by its author; he would thus hope to distin-

guish it from the prose *razos,* which often seemed rudimentary and less refined.

With line 5, "Vn-escolar la Rimo," begins the biographical description of the author of the love-narrative. While the Provençal equivalent of the word *escolar* does not appear in the biographies, the words *escola* and *scola* each appear once. Uc de Saint Circ was, according to his *vida,* sent to "la scola a Monpeslier." The famous but infortunate Guiraut de Borneil, who visited the court of Castile and perhaps other peninsular courts as well, was both a student and a troubadour: "la soa vida si era aitals que tot l'invern estava en escola et aprendia letras, e tota la estat anava per cortz e menava ab se dos cantadors que cantavon las soas chansos." The Provençal texts contain other words which refer to learning and letters: Peire Cardenal's *vida* states that "sos paires lo mes per quanorque . . . et apres letras"; Uc Brunet "fo clerges et enparet ben letras"; and Arnaut Daniel "amaret ben letras." In addition, six biographies, without discussing the poet's studies, emphasize his knowledge of letters.

Line 6 of the **Razón de amor,** "que sie[m]pre duenas amo," also presents, in a modified form, a biographical motif which appears in a variety of ways in the Provençal texts: Gui de Cavaillo was "mout amatz de dompnas"; Savaric de Malleo "Plus fo fins amics de dompnas e d'amadors que nuillz autres cavalliers"; and Raimbaut d'Aurenga "mout se deleitet en domnas onradas et en donnei onrat." Some troubadours were apparently exceptions to the typical courtly lover stereotype. Sordel, for example, according to his *vida,* "mout fo truans e fals vas dompnas."

Lines 7-10, "mas sie[m]pre ouo tryança / en-Alemania y-en-Fra[n]çia, / moro mucho en-Lombardia / pora [a]prender cortesia," discuss the poet's wide travels, and last, his courtliness. Judging from the *vidas* and *razos* travel between French courts was common (we can assume that in the Spanish poem "Fra[n]çia" was intended to include Provence), and, as we saw earlier, a handful of troubadours spent time in Lombardy. Aimeric de Peguillan, writing during the first quarter of the thirteenth century, "si fo de Tolosa. . . . Et anet s'en en Cataloingna. E'N Guillems de Berguedan . . . presentet lo al rei Anfos de Castella. . . . Puois s'en venc en Lombardia." Uc Brunet visited several courts within France and that of Aragon as well: "si fo de la ciutat de Rodes. . . . E briget ab lo rei d'Arragon et ab lo comte de Tolosa et ab lo comte de Rodes, lo sieu seingnor, et ab Bernart d'Andusa et ab lo Dalfin d'Alverne." The word *cortesia* is used in a number of *vidas* and *razos:* Savaric de Malleo, "era, razitz de tota la cortezia dal mon," Gaucelm Faidit was "paire e maistre de valor e de cortezia" and Guillem de Cabestaing "Molt of avinenz e prezatz d'armas e de servir e de cortesia."

Looking at the introduction as a whole, it seems that

its author was certainly aware of the language and motifs used in the Provençal *vidas,* but being Spanish and not Provençal he did not feel the same need to keep to the rules of the genre. He felt free to adapt it— most obviously from prose to verse—, to make it more concise, to blend its qualities with those of the Spanish verse tradition, and thus provide a more entertaining and inviting address to his audience.

In the narrative section of the **Razón de amor** the young lovers love each other by hearsay. This situation, found in courtly poetry as well as in the biographies, is first implied in lines 84-85, "Nunqua odi de homne deçir / que-tanta bona manera ouo en-si," where the young lady mentions her absent lover's excellent reputation. It is expressed later more directly by the *doncella* in her conversation with the narrator-poet in lines 108-09: "Diz ella 'a-plan, con grant amor ando, / mas non connozco mi amado.'" Such love or admiration by reputation (and similar use of the words *hear* and *say* in lines 84-85) can be seen in five biographies, one of which is the *vida* of the well-known Jaufre Rudel, who "enamoret se de la comtessa de Tripol, ses vezer, per lo ben qu'el n'auzi dire als pelerins que venguen d'Antiocha." A *razo* of Savaric de Malleo states that the countess of Manchac was "diziroza de pretz e de vezer En Savaric, per lo be qu'en auzia dire." Bertran de Born also fell in love with lady Guiscart by hearsay: "si la lauzava fort en comtan et en chantan. Bertrans, enans qu'el la vis, era sos amics per lo ben qu'el auzi[a] d'ella." Don Bernartz N'Arnautz, who eventually became the lover of lady Lombarda, "ausi contar de le bontaz e del valor de le; e venc s'en a Tolosa per le veser" (Na Lombarda). And Raimbaut d'Aurenga, according to one of his *razos,* loved the countess of Urgel by hearsay as well: "Rambauz, senes veser leis, per lo gran ben que n'ausia dire, si s'enamoret d'ella et ella de lui."

In line 110, "pero dizem un-su mesaiero," the young lady in the Spanish poem says that it is her lover's messenger who has brought her information about him. Messengers appear in a handful of biographies and in one, that of Raimbaut d'Aurenga, the messenger plays an important role in a love by hearsay, for he carries the troubadour's songs to his unseen beloved: "E si fez puois sas chansos d'ella; e si.l manda sas chansos per un joglar que avia nom Rasignol." Other troubadours and ladies used messengers to overcome the misunderstandings between themselves and their beloveds. Pons de Capdoill, hoping to win back the love of lady N'Alazais sent songs to her via a messenger: "manda sos mesatges e sas letras az ela; mas ella no volc escoutar ni auzir. Et el comensa esser tritz e dolens; e mandet letras e cotblas humils ab gran precs az ela" and lady Guillelma, in love with the noncommittal troubadour Guillem de Balaun, "li mandet un son mesatge cun soas letras fort amorosas, meraveillan se qe era so q'el tan estes de leis veser, o qe sos mesatges no l'ages mandat. Et el, com fols amans, no volc ausir ni entendre lo mesatge ni las letras,

e fetz li dar comjat del castel vilanamen." The biographer Uc de Saint Circ says in one of the *razos* attached to the poems of Savaric de Malleo that he wrote the *razo* and also that he served as messenger for his aristocratic patron. According to the *razo,* the lady Guillelma, in love with Savaric de Malleo, was eager to win back his affection: "fes far sas letras e sos mans e sas salutz. . . . E sapias per ver que ieu, Uc de San Sirc, que ay escrichas estas razos, fuy lo mesatje que lay aniey e.l portey totz los mans e.ls escrisz." It seems possible that the messenger mentioned in the Spanish poem is a minstrel employed by the poet-protagonist to sing his love songs to the young lady whom he loves from afar. The messenger is also, apparently, a composer of a brief introductory biography concerning his employer, for it is biographical information like that found in the *vidas* which he transmits to the lady, as we shall see in the following discussion.

The young lady's description of her lover's courtly talents and qualities in lines 111-13, "que-es clerygo e non caualero, / sabe muio de trobar / de leyer e de cantar," is strongly reminiscent of the courtly qualities of the troubadours in the biographies. Uc Brunet, according to his *vida,* "fo clerges et enparet ben letras, e de trobar of fort suptils, et de sen natural; e fez se joglars e trobet cansos bonas," and Aimeric de Belenoi "Clercs fo, e fez se joglars, et trobet bonas cansos e bellas e avinenz." The following examples from the biographies are briefer and even closer to the **Razón de amor:** Cadenet "saup ben cantar e parlar, et apres a trobar coblas"; Guillem Figueira "saup ben trobar e cantar"; Peire Cardenal "saup ben lezer e chantar"; and the knight Pons de Capdoill "sabia ben trobar e violar e cantar."

The last two lines in the *doncella's* description, lines 114-15, "dizem que es de buenas yentes, / mencebo barua punnientes," depart from the biographies. Line 115 has no connection with the *vidas* and the *razos,* and in line 114 the author of the **Razón de amor** seems to be using the term "buenas yentes" in a manner which is rare in the Provençal texts. The only occurrence in the latter which is suggestive of the **Razón** is in the *vida* of Peire Cardenal: "fo d'onradas gens de paratge." A more common usage in the Provençal pieces is: "cortes hom e ben avinenz d'estar entre las bonas genz" (Peire Guillem de Toloza).

In the **Razón de amor** lines 90-94, "que dizen que otra duena / cortesa e bela e bona, / te-quiere tan gran ben, / por-ti pie[r]de su sen," the girl discusses specific information which she has learned by hearsay about her lover in terms which were very common in the biographies. Rivals of the lady, while not as common as a male lover's rivals, appear nevertheless in a handful of *vidas* and *razos.* Two poets, Savaric de Malleo and Uc de Saint Circ, already in love with courtly ladies, were sought after by others. Savaric is unsuccessful in his attempt to seduce lady Guillerma de Benauzatz, and his friends tell him of another lady equally beautiful, and more willing, they believe, to share his bed. She is "joves e bela e avinens, e diziroza de pretz e de vezer En Savaric." And Uc de Saint Circ, in love with lady Clara, was temporarily lured away from her by her neighbor, "una vizina mout bella, qe avia nom ma dompna Ponsa. Mout era cortesa et ensegnada; et ac gran enveja a ma dompna Clara del pretz et de l'henor qe N'Uc li avia facha gasagnar; si se penset et penet con pogues faire q'ella tolgues N'Uc de la soa amistat et traes lo a si."

The young lady in the *Razón* describes her rival as "cortesa e bela e bona." Pairs of these three words appear in several biographies: The countess of Dia was "bela domna e bona"; the lady Eleina was "Bella dompna . . . e molt cortesa e enseingnada" (Bertrand de Born); a lady in Peirol's *vida* was "bella e bona e molt presada"; and Jordana d'Ebreu, beloved of the troubadour Gaucelm Faidit, "era bella dompna et gentilz ct avinen[s] et ensengnada e cortesa."

As in the introduction to the *Razón de amor,* the author of the love-narrative part of the poem presents a sort of composite portrait of his courtly personages, bringing together in a concise form elements which appear more diffusely in the biographies, and adding other material. And again as in the first ten lines, the author here modifies the Provençal material to fit into a poetic framework.

In lines 96-97, "Mas s'io-te uies una uegada, / a-plananc querves por amada!," the *doncella* expresses the belief that if she and her absent lover were to meet, he would certainly prefer her over her rival. While such sentiments are not expressed directly by any lady in the biographies, they are implied in the two passages quoted above in which one lady is hoping to replace another as the beloved of a troubadour. Such a wish is also implied—and comes true—in a *razo* of Savaric de Malleo, quoted above. The *razo* continues: "En Savaric, can vi la dona, azautet li mot a meravihas e preget la d'amor. E la dona, per la gran valor que vi en el, retenc lo per son cavayer."

The last two lines in the Spanish poem, 260-61, "Mi Razon aqui la fino, / e mandat nos dar uino," like the first four lines, have no counterpart in the biographies, since the latter were meant to precede, not to conclude, a poetic work. Here the poet who is finishing the piece adopts it as his own (*Mi*) or perhaps reveals himself to be the author—it does not seem possible to say which. In any case, this brief ending gives the poem a juglaresque rather than troubadouresque flavor and framework. As we saw earlier, however, the two professions were not necessarily mutually exclusive and there were poets who spent time in refined as well as popular milieux. Thus a minstrel such as Marcabru was capable of composing a courtly *pastorela* and the aristocratic troubadours were ridiculed by two of their contemporaries for

trying to sound simple-minded and unrefined. Meanwhile, drinking—mentioned in line 261—and courtly poetry were inseparable, according to Jeanroy, in certain parts of Italy, so much so that courts both rich and renowned and small and remote were beseiged by would-be troubadours seeking free drink. Two poets are said in the biographies to have a weakness for taverns. One was Uc de Pena, of bourgeois origin, a good singer, knowledgeable on the lives and works of the great men of his region: "fez se joglars; e cantet ben, e saup gran ren de las autrui cansos; e sabia molt las generasios dels grans homes d'aquellas encontradas, e fetz cansos. Grans baratiers fo de jogar e d'estar en taverna; per que ades fo paubres e ses arnes." Another example was Guillem Magret, who "si fo uns joglars de Vianes, jogaire e taverniers. E fez bonas cansos e bons sirventes e bonas coblas. E fo ben volgutz et onratz; mas anc mais non anet en arnes, que tot qant gazaingnava el jogava e despendia malamen en taverna."

While the lines from the *Razón de amor* which have been discussed here are reminiscent of courtly literature in general, most have no close verbal resemblance to the courtly lyric. The poetry of the troubadours, written in an entirely different framework, the great majority from a subjective point of view, contains few third-person descriptions such as we see in the *Razón de amor*. When such descriptions do appear, the social prestige and courtly qualities of a lover may be mentioned, but not troubadouresque talents such as writing or singing, or such experiences as travels. A *pastorela* written towards the middle of the twelfth century by the usually satirical and juglaresque Marcabru, shows the closest resemblance. It begins with the narrator-poet overhearing a courtly young lady who is wandering through a *locus amoenus* lamenting the absence of her *amics*. The narrator presents himself and engages her in conversation in the hope of seducing her, but the girl steadfastly refuses to be untrue to her absent lover. Despite certain similarities, however, the Provençal poem could not have inspired the lines quoted above from the *Razón de amor*. The sources of those sections of the Spanish poem are to be found elsewhere.

It seems evident after a comparison of the *Razón de amor* with the *vidas* and *razos* that these Provençal genres are sources of inspiration for the introduction and for a number of lines in the love-narrative. Since the poem's introduction states that the poet-protagonist of the love-narrative went to Lombardy, and since the poem is believed to have been written around the same time that the courtly biography was being cultivated there, it seems highly possible that the author of the *Razón de amor* was directly acquainted with the Provençal pieces. Such a knowledge of the *vidas* would point to the conclusion that the *Razón* was composed at the earliest in the 1230's, and possibly even after 1240, if we accept Favati's dating of the *vidas*.

In both the introduction and the love-narrative the author alters the Provençal tradition according to his own tastes and needs. In both parts of the poem he depersonalizes the poet-narrator-protagonist by omitting his name and origin and thus uses the biographical material to portray a universal type, a more purely literary personage, rather than to exalt the reputation of an individual. He gives a poetic rhythm and concision to material which appears in a rambling and occasionally picturesque prose form in the *vidas* and *razos*.

Borrowing from and modifying the Provençal texts in similar ways, the introduction and the love-narrative seem most likely to be the work of one author, but this conclusion is not the only possibility. The poet-minstrel who presents the biographical introduction and then speaks, in the final lines of the poem, of "Mi Razón," could well be adopting as his own material originally composed by others, but which he feels he has the right to use for his own purpose.

Such a conception of authorship in the Middle Ages makes it difficult solve the problem of unity in the *Razón de amor*. The juglaresque author of the first ten lines of the poem seems to be playing with the idea of double authorship and then, in the final two lines, denies it. The difference in style and tone between the love-narrative and the debate adds to the thorniness of the problem. For these reasons, it has seemed to some critics that there were two or more authors involved. Without agreeing with such a theory, I should like nevertheless to present some other possible conjectures, in addition to the one which I have offered above, concerning the poem's unity, in the light of the Provençal texts.

One possibility is that the author of the introduction had no knowledge of the author of the *Razón* other than what he could learn from the poem itself. This shortcut was used by the Provençal biographers also. There is no mention in the Spanish text of a specific person or of his origin, and the *Razón* contains all of the information necessary for the composition of the introduction: the *escolar* of line 5 comes from line 82; the courtliness mentioned in line 6 can be inferred from lines 55, 84-85, 112-13, and from the love-narrative in general; Germany and France may have been included to impress the audience with the poet's wide travels and Lombardy may have come to mind because it was, in the first half of the thirteenth century, the center of courtly literary activity and perhaps also because the minstrel-biographer was aware that certain lines seemed to be inspired by the biographical genres which were being cultivated there at that time.

One weakness of this view lies in the fact that the biographical introduction of the *Razón de amor* could not have been written very long after the love-narrative, since the *vidas* were probably composed closer to the middle than to the beginning of the thirteenth cen-

tury, and the Spanish poem was completed, it is generally believed, before 1250. The author of the introduction would then be commenting on the work of a contemporary and thus should have had more specific information about him. The authors of both parts seem equally acquainted with the Provençal biographies and equally interested in using material from them. The inclusion in the love-narrative of material which is taken from a purely biographical genre, makes of that part of the poem a sort of biography of the author as well, and the theme of love by reputation makes of it, at the same time, a poem about a biography. It therefore seems reasonable to assume that the authors of those two parts are one. If we consider the possibility that the author of the introduction was a separate person who was indeed acquainted with the author of the rest of the poem we still must contend with the similar use of biographical material in both parts.

The comparison of the Spanish text with passages from the Provençal biographies leads by a new route to the conclusion that a single poet was probably responsible for the whole work. The author of the *Razón de amor* incorporated both courtly and popular tastes in his repertory, and his poem is the expression of a variety of talents and experiences. There is ample evidence in the biographies of a tradition of such multi-talented poets. Uc de Saint Circ, Marcabru, Uc Brunet, and Aimeric de Belenoi can be included in this group, and the latter two are good examples of the clerk-troubadour-minstrel. . .

I hope that the above discussion of these poets has enabled the reader to better understand the type of author who, it seems, composed the entire *Razón*.

Such an entertainer-poet would thus have resembled another thirteenth-century cleric, Gonzalo de Berceo, whose *Milagros de Nuestra Señora* have their humorous moments, such as the "Milagro del clérigo embriagado," and others in which he expresses with refined lyricism his adoration for the Virgin Mary. He was, at the same time, a *trovador* (he refers to himself as such in *Loores de Nuestra Señora,* stanza 232) and a *joglar* (*Vida de Santo Domingo,* 289, 759, and 755-76), the latter because he wrote in the vernacular and addressed himself to a popular audience. In *Santo Domingo,* 2, in the manner of a minstrel he offers his listeners a brief description of the work he is about to present, and requests a glass of wine as reward:

> Quiero fer una prosa en roman paladino,
> en cual suele el pueblo fablar a su vecino,
> ca non soy tan letrado por fer otro latino;
> vien valdra, como creo, un vaso de bon vino.

As does the author of the *Razón de amor,* Berceo incorporates into his literary creation elements which in other more rudimentary compositions are simply the task of minstrels. The author of the *Razón* differs from him, however, in that his work serves to exalt no individual, either courtly or Christian. He differs also in choosing to remain completely removed from his text, using the third person in his description of himself, rather than the first—creating a sort of third-person autobiography.

The author of the **Razón de amor** is both a raconteur who tells of someone else's experiences, and a man writing about his own experiences. This dual position of the poet vis-à-vis his work recalls yet another "clérigo-juglar," the Archpriest of Hita, whose *Libro de buen amor* similarly shows shifts in the relationship of the author to his work. At times Juan Ruiz appears in the foreground, as when he introduces himself as author, yet at times he fades out of the limelight to allow other personages to speak, and even to offer a description of him—a description whose terms and tone are purely Spanish, but which is nevertheless reminiscent of the Provençal biographies:

> Es ligero, valiente, byen mançebo de dias,
> sabe los instrumentos e todas juglerias,
> doñeador alegre ¡para las çapatas mias!
> tal omne como este, non es en todas erias.

Critics have been able to conclude that the Archpriest's choice of an autobiographical framework was based on purely literary considerations and that he adopted such a stance to serve his artistic aims rather than because the experiences which he recounted were really his own. Similarly, it seems possible to conclude that the author of the **Razón de amor** chose a biographical framework less out of a desire for any kind of rudimentary realism than out of his fascination with the literary possibilities of such a technique.

Margaret Van Antwerp (essay date 1978)

SOURCE: "*Razón de amor* and the Popular Tradition," in *Romance Philology,* Vol. XXXII, No. 1, August, 1978, pp. 1-17.

[*Here, Van Antwerp sketches a detailed overview of the mingling of popular folk elements with the courtly tradition as evidenced in the style of the* Razón de amor.]

Few works of the Spanish Middle Ages have attracted more critical attention than the problematic **Razón de amor con los denuestos del agua y el vino**. The poem begins with the presentation of a courtly *amor de lonh*. Resting from the midday heat in a pleasant orchard, an *escolar* encounters a lovely maiden singing of a distant lover whom she has never met. He recognizes her as his own theretofore unseen beloved and presents himself to her. They make love in the shade of an olive tree growing near a miraculously cold "fuente perenal", and their long-awaited first meeting comes abruptly to an end. As the maiden departs from the orchard, a small white dove

appears, seeking a place to cool itself. The dove bathes in a vessel of water suspended throughout the poem from one of the highest limbs of an apple tree. This action of the dove overturns the vessel, causing it to spill into another, of wine, carefully hung in a lower branch of the same tree. Here the lyrical **Razón de amor** concludes, and the "Denuestos del agua y el vino" begin in which water and wine, now personified, comically debate their own strengths and weaknesses.

Aptly summarized by the daulity of its title, this complex text has been studied from various perspectives, including the scrutiny of linguistic peculiarities, the discussion of generic classification, and the investigation of poetic sources. The critics remain, however, in wide disagreement. Alicia C. de Ferraresi [in "Sentido y unidad de *Razón de amor,*" F, XIV (1970), and "*Locus amoenus* y vergel visionario en *Razón de amor,*" H R, XLII (1974),] views the poem as an embryonic "*enseignement* de amor", designed to illustrate the doctrines of courtly love, while Arsenio Pacheco argues, unconvincingly, that the lyrical **Razón de amor** is essentially a poetic prelude to the common medieval debate between wine and water [in "*¿Razón de amor o Denuestos del agua y el vino?*" BHS, LI (1974)]. Enrique de Rivas believes that the poem's "razón secreta" lies in the teachings of the Cathar heresy [in "La razón secreta de la *Razón de amor,*" Anuario de Filologia, VI-VII (1967-68)]; Alfred Jacob considers the piece conventional Christian allegory [in "The *Razón de amor* as Christian Symbolism," H R, XX (1952),]; and Leo Spitzer identifies the unified **Razón** and "Denuestos" as the product of the medieval conception of profane, human love [in "*Razón de amor,*" R, LXXI (1950)].

The diverse efforts of these critics are, in essence, quite similar: each accepts the poem as a work belonging to the tradition of courtly love into which some delightful although "alien" snatches of traditional-type song (the maiden's *cantigas de amigo* addressed to her lover from afar) have been introduced. All attempt to explain the apparent lack of thematic unity which characterizes the work, thus prolonging the debate initiated in 1887 by A. Morel-Fatio over whether the **Razón** and the "Denuestos" constitute a single poem or a fusion of two. Although the debate has produced many valuable insights, it has had at least one unfortunate result: The importance of the **Razón de amor** as the first manifestation of the cultured Castilian lyric has been largely overlooked.

This continuing academic clamor to ascertain the autonomy of the lyrical **Razón** or to establish its relationship to the "Denuestos" ignores one important lesson taught all Hispanists by S. M. Stern's publication of the *kharjas* in 1948: Convenient generalizations which label one poem "popular" and another "learned", although often necessary, are no longer absolutely valid, since the sophisticated love lyric (in the Peninsula as elsewhere) most certainly arose from a popular basis, of which much has been lost. As Alan D. Deyermond points out, this folk tradition is very much alive in the first written examples of the lyric that we possess. The clearly present influence of medieval Latin or Arabic verse in the writings of the first poets using the vernacular is of distinctly less consequence than it was once thought to be; "Latin and Arabic influences are in points of detail, whereas the popular tradition is not an influence but a fundamental cause" [*The Middle Ages,* 1971].

As the first cultured lyric written down and preserved in the Castilian language, the ***Razón de amor*** attests to the validity of Deyermond's statement. Despite the undeniable courtliness and artistic sophistication of this poem in which rapidly changing scenes are tied together by a complex set of structural parallels, the ***Razón de amor*** is intimately and inextricably bound to the popular tradition. Convincing linguistic evidence of this confluence of two traditions has recently been set forth by Daniel M. Cárdenas, who identifies the ***Razón***'s "lyrical nucleus" as vv. 78 to 146, containing little more than the maiden's traditional-type *cantigas de amigo* to her lover ["Nueva luz sobre *Razón de amor y denuestos del agua y del vino,*" RHM, XXXIV (1968)]. For Cárdenas, these nuclear verses, around which both the preceding *amorosa visione* and the subsequent debate were composed, represent "una poesá ya aprendida o escrita que alcanzó un estado estático" whose form and language the anonymous "juglar-refundidor" wished to respect. They are "un vestigio de una lìrica castellana más antigua"; more than mere "incrustaciones de villancicos", they constitute an integral part of the poem which "ensalza el valor del conjunto y la destreza del poeta".

Cárdenas' analysis is based upon a study of the phonological, morphological, and syntactic features of the poem. A literary analysis complements and reinforces him findings. Thematic and symbolic commonplaces reminiscent of the *cancionero de tipo tradicional* abound in the ***Razón***. Indeed, these recognizable vestiges of what Cárdenas terms "una lìrica castellana más antigua" lie at the center of each of the various scenes carefully woven together in the medieval masterpiece, as the early sophisticated poet draws inevitably upon the tradition which he begins to move away from but, of course, can never leave behind. One particularly striking example of the kinship between the ***Razón de amor*** and the lyrical folk tradition merits attention before we begin to scrutinize the text. It is found in a perplexing, decidedly popular song recorded in the fifteenth-century *Cancionero musical de Palacio:*

> No pueden dormir mis ojos,
> no pueden dormir.
>
> Y soñaba yo, mi madre,
> dos horas antes del día
> que me florecía la rosa:
> ell vino so ell agua frida.

No pueden dormir.

Despite its brevity, this folk song is strangely similar to the cultured ***Razón***. Like the sophisticated medieval lyric, it possesses a mysterious, somnolent air; it draws its force from the counterposition of water and wine, symbolic images reflected in the opening verses of the text under scrutiny. As in the cultured lyric, the water and wine of the folk song are matter-of-factly set forth; as symbols, they are expected to stand by themselves. To be appreciated most fully, this symbolic pair must be reintegrated into the folk tradition from which it ultimately sprang and evolved. That is to say, if we are to understand the symbolic implications of the wine and water, and, more important, the learned recollection of this pair by the anonymous poet of the ***Razón,*** we must return to Deyermond's "fundamental cause", to the vast corpus of traditional-type verse in which themes, images, and symbols define themselves—their limitations and nuances—through constant repetition and interaction with one another.

This process sheds light upon the problematic vessels of wine and water which appear in our text, as well as upon several other enigmatic yet decidedly symbolic elements of the medieval masterpiece. It fosters, in turn, an entirely new reading of this poem "feyta d'amor". With its complex architecture and subtle echoes of popular verse, the ***Razón*** confirms the inseparability of the *popular* and the *culto* traditions in poetry and points significantly to the popular origins of all cultured verse.

The confluence of the erudite and the popular is evident from the first moments. After a brief courtly introduction to the work, we are confronted by a scene displaying vestiges of folk tradition. Like so many lovers in traditional song, the poet rests from the heat beneath an olive tree growing in an orchard which does not belong to him. Folk lyric poeticizes this situation in a series of interrelated songs which warn of the consequences awaiting one who dares trespass upon a "huerto ajeno". In one of the simplest of these songs, the consequences are drastically understated; a gentle scolding seems sufficient punishment for the offense:

> No entréis en huerto ajeno,
> que os dirá mal su dueño;
> no entréis en huerto vcdado,
> que [os] dirá mal su amo.

More elaborate poems treating this same theme disclose, however, that the trespasser is pledged in love, both spiritually and physically, to the owner of the orchard. Accordingly, the lonely prioress in one well-known traditional song exacts a physical "prenda" from a bold *caballero,* caught stealing lemons from the convent orchard:

> —Gentil caballero,

dedesme hora un beso,
siquiera por el daño
que me habéis hecho.

Venía el caballero,
venía de Sevilla,
en huerto de monjas
limones cogía,
y la prioresa
prendas le pedía:
—Siquiera por el daño
que me habéis hecho.

The prioress' request is, in a sense, symbolically restated in a third folk song embroidering on the "huerto ajeno" theme. Here the physical nature of the trespasser's obligatory love pledge is succinctly set forth, for the *prenda* demanded is a "camisa", the most intimate article of apparel worn "a rayz de las carnes". If the thieving lady of the following folk song surrenders the *camisa,* as the proprietor of the orchard insists, she surrenders herself, since in the logic of folk magic the gift of a *camisa* (or of any similarly personal garment) represents simultaneously the promise and fulfillment of sexual love:

—Que no me desnudéis,
amores de mi vida,
que no me desnudéis,
que yo me iré en camisa.
—Entrastes, mi señora.
en el huerto ajeno,
cogiste tres pericas
del peral en medio:
dejáredes la prenda
de un amor verdadero.
—Que no me desnudéis,
que yo me iré en camisa.

In the *Razón de amor,* the poet-protagonist's entrance into the orchard of another retains several elements essential in the folkloric treatment of the theme. Spiritual commitment to the beloved is emphasized by the poet's careful enumeration of love tokens which, exchanged by the lovers from afar, help them to recognize each other when at last they meet in the orchard:

Yo connoçi luego las alfayas,
que yo ie las auia enbiadas;
ela connoçio una mi ci[n]ta man a mano
qu'ela la fiziera con la su mano.

The simultaneous pledging of love, implicit in the lemon- or pear-picking of folk song, is echoed in the *Razón* by the trespassing *escolar*'s sampling of the flowers which adorn the verdant orchard in which he rests:

En mi mano prys una flor,
sabet non toda la peyor;

e quis cantar de fin amor.
Mas ui uenir una doncela;
pues naçi, non ui tan bella.

Significantly, the arrival of the poet's beloved in the *Razón de amor* coincides with this "theft". It is as if she appears to exact payment for the "crime"; the pledge formalized by the exchange of love tokens has finally come due.

The poet's worldless pledge of love, suggested by the foray into the orchard, is matched by the symbolic offering of wine also introduced in the opening verses. Having entered the orchard to rest, the poet notes the presence of a silver vessel in the treetops. As he knowingly describes its contents and its purpose, it seems from the first to be destined for him:

Entre çimas d'un mançanar
un uaso de plata ui estar;
pleno era d'un claro uino
que era uermeio e fino;
cubierto era de tal mesura
no lo tocas la calentura.
Vna duena lo y eua puesto,
que era senora del uerto,
que quan su amigo uiniese,
d'a quel uino a beuer le disse.

A subtle parallelism establishes the single identity of the "dueña", proprietress of the orchard and donor of the wine, and the "doncella", beloved of the poet. Both *dueña* and *doncella* await the advent of a distant lover; both, more importantly, demonstrate a cautious awareness of the potentially harmful midday heat. The *dueña* carefully covers her gift of wine so that "no lo tocas la calentura", while the *doncella,* we later learn, avails herself of a hat "que nol fiziese mal la siesta". With the detail of the hat—unique in an otherwise stereotyped medieval description of feminine beauty—the poet turns the reader back to his earlier, similarly unusual presentation of the vessel of wine. The two ladies are fused into one. The poet emerges unquestionably as the "amigo" (as he is later addressed by his lover) for whom the wine has been set out, and the *dueña-doncella,* through her gift of wine, pledges herself to the poet, as he had promised himself to her upon entering the ochard.

Like the intrusion into a "huerto ajeno" and the commitment of love which it demands, the choice of wine as a "prenda de amor verdadero" is best explained by verses from the folkloric tradition. A universal referent for passion, wine appears in the emotion-charged verses of more than one *kharja* to represent love's comforts, both spiritual and physical. In one of these brief Mozarabic lyrics, a frantic young woman cries out for the tonic of an absent *amigo*'s love:

Y MAMMÀ, ŠI NO LĒŠA L-ẎINNA

> ALTESA, MORRÉY.
> TRAÝDE JAMRI MIN AL-HĀYIB:
> ASÀ SANARÉY.

The maiden's offer of wine in the **Razón** is poetically quite similar to the desperate plea expressed in the *kharja*. Both poems associate a gift of wine with the arrival of a distant lover and with the satisfying effects of his love. Both emphasize, moreover, the marvellous healing power of the wine. To the young woman of the *kharja*, it represents not only relief but also salvation from the madness to which unfulfilled passion drives her. To our poet it offers a foolproof safeguard against the emotional suffering involved in loving from afar. The wine, like the end of absence, promises health and contentment:

> Qui de tal uino ouiesse
> en la mana quan comiesse:
> e dello ouiesse cada dia,
> nu[n]cas mas enfermarya.

The sensuous nature of this soothing wine of love, expressed implicitly in the concise *kharja,* is emphatically suggested in the **Razón** by the strange, lofty position of the silver goblet in the treetop. Like the unique detail of the *doncella*'s hat, the high perch designated for the love offering is unprecedented in sophisticated medieval lyric. Folk song, however, commonly associates love and lovemaking with treetops or other high places and with the act of climbing up to them. Often these songs are exceedingly brief; as in the **Razón de amor** the association is matter-of-factly set forth, but never explained:

> Por encima de la oliva
> Mírame el Amor, mira.

At times, however, the identification of treetops and sexual activity is euphemistically betrayed, as in the following song's use of the verb *luchar:*

> Arribica, arribica
> de un verde sauze,
> luchaba la niña
> con su adorante.

Closely related traditional-type songs hesitatingly spell out the euphemism, linking the elevated meeting place to the sexual act itself, and enhancing, by extension, the erotic connotations of the vessel of wine in the **Razón**. In the following verses the rather graphic symbolism of "los caños [que] corren agua", flooding the fragrant "toronjil", combines with the calculated ambiguity of certain key phrases to produce a highly imaginative and suggestive song:

> La sierra es alta
> y áspera de sobir;
> los caños corren agua

> y dan en el toronjil.

> Madre, la mi madre,
> de cuerpo atán garrido,
> por aquella sierra,
> de aquel lomo erguido,
> iba una mañana
> el mi lindo amigo;
> llaméle con mi toca
> y con mis dedos cinco.
> Los caños corren agua
> y dan en el toronjil.

The success of this poem depends upon the reader's (or listener's) familiarity with poetic tradition, which clarifies the song's grammatically unclear antecedents: "el mi lindo amigo", more than the rightfully suspicious "madre", is the one praised for his "cuerpo atán garrido". The reference to "aquel lomo erguido" is similarly ambiguous; it is topographical and sexual as well. The entire poem is simultaneously a description of the lovers' elevated trysting place and of the lovemaking carried out there.

In light of popular tradition, the lofty perch chosen by the **Razón**'s damsel for her passionate offering of wine accentuates her desire not only to meet her lover from afar but also to know him in the carnal sense. As the **Razón de amor** begins, symbolic gestures of yearning, commitment, and love have been made by both the damsel and the trespassing poet. The satisfying realization of desire is, however, postponed until the two lovers actually meet. A mood of anxious anticipation, of rapidly growing desire and its attendant frustration, is established and maintained by the poet's constant references to the all-pervasive, metaphorical heat of "la siesta", which threatens to spoil the gift of fine wine, prompts the damsel to don a hat, and forces the *escolar* to recline on the grass and peel off some clothing:

> Sobre un prado pusmi tiesta,
> que nom fizies mal la siesta;
> parti de mi las uistiduras,
> que nom fizies mal la calentura.

Relief, however, is at hand. To the heat-ravaged vessel of wine suspended from the branches, the poet counterposes another goblet, filled with cooling water:

> Ariba del mançanar
> otro uaso ui estar;
> pleno era d'un agua fryda
>
> que en el mançanar se naçia.

After the rather elaborate description of the vessel of wine, this introduction of the second vessel seems disturbingly concise: The poet neither discloses the material of which the goblet is made nor comments upon the purpose of the vessel and its contents. The deliberate construction of parallels pervading the poem is lacking here, and this apparent poetic imbalance focuses attention on the mysterious container of water.

The water occupies a higher position in the tree—"Ariba del mançanar"—than the vessel of wine, indicating its participation, to perhaps an even greater degree, in the erotic connotations traditionally associated with a lofty trysting place. The fact that the poet neglects both to mention the purpose of this second vessel and to name the person responsible for its suspension in the tree suggests that the goblet of water, although essentially similar to that of wine, is somehow symbolically different. The omission of significant details in the presentation of the water and the poetic tension maintained between the two precariously-balanced goblets imply that the container of water represents some sort of constant vis-à-vis that of wine, placed in the tree by the proprietress of the orchard for a specific purpose. It is the goal to which the lovers aspire, a physical embodiment of the satisfaction and fulfillment sought by both the *escolar* and his beloved, eager to meet one another after a lengthy love from afar.

The tense relationship between desire and fulfillment, introduced by the two vessels, is emphasized by the poet's insistent counterposition of heat and cold. The passionate, almost painful yearning suggested by the all-consuming noonday heat and by the symbolic offering of wine is balanced by the promise of coolness proffered by the water in the second vessel, drawn from an uncannily cold spring "que en el mançanar se naçia". The poet's description of the spring is elaborate. As he approaches the "fuente perenal" he is at once impressed by its seductive, nearly magical qualities, by its triple promise of relief from the heat, of sensual pleasure, and of a new kind of life:

> Plegem a una fuente p(er)erenal,
> nu[n]ca fue omne que uies tall;
> tan grant uirtud en si auia,
> que de la frydor que d'i yxia,
> cient pasadas adeRedor
> non sintryades la calor.
>
> Todas yeruas que bien olien
> la fuent çerca si las tenie:
> y es la saluia, y sson as Rosas
> y el liryo e las uiolas;
> otras tantas yeruas y auia
> que sol no[m]bra no las sabria;
> mas ell olor que d'i yxia
> a omne muerto Ressuçitarya.

Appearing in a verdant setting, the "fuente perenal" vividly recalls the folkloric *fuente* or *baños de amor,* the lovers' favorite trysting place in traditional lyric of the Middle Ages. As it appears in the sophisticated *Razón*

de amor, the spring is a magical reservoir of "renovación" and "fecundidad", the two most salient characteristics of the folkloric *fuente de amor*. From the fertile ground nourished by its waters sprout countless lovely flowers, whose miraculous powers are worthy of note. Their fragrance alone, the poet points out, is apt to raise the dead, to renew life or re-create it, much as the spring or *baño* of folk song is able to convert empty existences into amorous adventures marked, as in the following song, by love's sweet suffering:

> Enviárame mi madre
> por agua a la fonte fría:
> vengo del amor ferida.

or, more often, by the physical pleasures of love, represented by the common bathing in the following song. Here lovemaking is as simple and elemental as the straightforward poetic style used to described the mutual face-washing of "la niña y el doncel":

> En la fuente del rosel,
> lavan la niña y el doncel.
>
> En la fuente de agua clara.
> con sus manos lavan la cara.
> Él a ella y ella a él
> lavan la niña y el doncel.

When protestations are heard, they concern the *qué dirán* of the spectators (chanting the choral *glosa,* as in the following song), without ever questioning the widely and tacitly accepted symbolism of the erotic *fuente* or *baños:*

> Caballero, queráisme dejar,
>   que me dirán mal.
> ¡Oh, qué mañanica, mañana,
> la mañana de San Juan,
> cuando la niña y el caballero
> ambos se iban a bañar!
>   Que me dirán mal.
> Caballero, queráisme dejar,
>   que me dirán mal.

It is as Gonzalo de Correas notes in a discussion of traditional merrymaking on the feast of Saint John. These Christianized rites of spring, he remarks, are characterized by three symbolic customs: "Bañar-se, coger hierbas y enramar las puertas", and the symbolic connotations of the *baños* are especially well-known: "La que del baño viene, bien sabe lo que quiere. Juntarse con el varón".

Like the spring in folk song, the "fuente perenal" of the *Razón* unifies: Its waters mysteriously join the *escolar* and the *doncella* together, nurturing their love and forming unbreakable bonds between them. The poet's discovery of the *fuente* is, in fact, a significant turning-point in the action of the **Razón de amor**. He takes a sip of cooling water from the spring, plucks a nearby flower, and prepares to sing of love. These sequential, almost ritualistic actions seem to have a magical effect. It is as if the poet's draught of spring water were a kind of love potion. As he sips the cooling liquid, he is temporarily released from the torturous effects of the heat ("Prys del agua un bocado / e fuy todo esfryado"). The drink of water (like the flower-picking) serves as a symbolic prelude to the fulfillment of desire, for just as he finishes drinking and prepares to sing of love, the lady he has worshipped from afar appears. The erotic promise of the *fuente* of the love tokens earlier exchanged, and of the lofty vessels of wine and water can now be realized in the long-awaited consummation of their love.

As in popular bathing songs, in the **Razón** the consummation is not forthrightly described. The details of the amorous encounter are merely suggested and the reader (or listener), with his knowledge of poetic tradition, is called upon to participate in the creative process by making good their absence. In the **Razón de amor** the poet and his beloved first "come together" beneath an olive tree ("junniemos amos en par / e posamos so ell oliuar"). They speak of love. Their physical activity is tastefully presented as the poet proudly describes his lady's caresses:

> Tolios el manto de los o[n]bros,
> besome la boca e por los oios;
> tan gran sabor de mi auia,
> sol fablar non me podia.

It is the lady who summarizes the joyous encounter in a traditional-type *cantiga de amigo* giving thanks for the pleasure of at last knowing her love:

> "Dios senor, a ti loa[do]
> quant conozco meu amado!
> agora e tod bien [comigo]
> quant conozco meo amigo!"

The sensuous tone of this understated love scene stems, in part, from the poet's learned recollection of several erotic commonplaces of traditional song, brought together in anticipation of the lovers' meeting. Their physical encounter is foreshadowed by the constellation of symbolic settings, objects, and gestures with which the poem begins, and is carefully rounded out by the concluding episode of the work—again reminiscent of folk tradition—involving the white dove.

After making love, the poet's beloved departs abruptly from the orchard. Her presence is, however, immediately replaced by that of a white dove, poetically associated with the lovers in several ways. The torments of the heat endured by the poet and his friend are similarly suffered by the dove, which seems to enter the orchard seeking a cooling place to bathe. When the bird finally finds relief, splashing clumsily in the vessel of water, it is described in terms nearly identical to those previously applied to the poet, soothed by his draught of water from the spring. The dove, "quando en el uaso fue entrada / . . . fue toda bien esfryada". Like the poet, the dove tests all possible sources of relief from the heat before partaking of one: It goes first to bathe in the "fuente perenal" but settles finally in the goblet, as the poet earlier considers a drink from the vessel ("Beuiera d'ela de grado, / mas oui miedo que era encantado"), but sips instead from the spring. Parallelism suggests an intimate relationship between poet and bird.

More significant, however, is the parallelistic association of the dove and the paramour which establishes a symbolic identification between the two and sheds light upon the concluding scene of the **Razón**. This identification is evoked through the remarkably similar poetic circumstances and events which accompany the sojourns in the orchard of both the maiden and the dove. Both the maiden's approach and the dove's advent are immediately preceded in the text by the poet's two curious references to an "omne muerto", soon to be restored to life. The poet's initial mention of the fragrance of the orchard flowers, which "a omne muerto Ressuçitarya", anticipates his first, vital experience with his beloved. His second apparently casual allusion to death occurs immediately prior to the arrival of the dove as the poet refers specifically to himself, disconsolate, emotionally deceased after the departure of his beloved:

> La mia senor se ua priuado,
> dexa a mi desconortado.
> Q[ue]que la ui fuera del uerto,
> por (por) poco non fuy muerto.

This second, well-placed reference to death is designed to turn the reader carefully back to the verses leading up to the arrival of the maiden, since the sequence of events involving the introduction, description, and actions of the dove nearly duplicates that presented with regard to the maiden.

Both the damsel and the bird intrude suddenly upon the poet's solitude, and each causes an abrupt change in his announced plans. The maiden's presence thwarts the lovesick poet's desire to sing (" . . . quis cantar de fin amor. / Mas ui uenir una doncela"), while the entrance of the dove disrupts his preparations to sleep ("Por uerdat quisieram adormir, / mas una palomela ui"). The poet reacts in like manner to these pleasant intrusions upon his aloneness: Seeing the *doncella,* he pours forth a detailed praise of her beauty; observing the dove, he comments upon the extraordinary whiteness of the bird, upon whose foot a small golden bell emerges. The poet then interacts with both the maiden and the dove. From a nearby hiding place he overhears the maiden's song of love and absence, and decides to surprise her as she sings:

Quant la mia senor esto dizia,
sabet, a mi non uidia;
pero se que no me conoçia,
que de mi non foyrya.
Yo non fiz aqui como uilano,
leuem e pris la por la mano;
junniemos amos en par
e posamos so el oliuar.

His action leads to the scene beneath the olive tree in which their love is consummated and their formal recognition of one another takes place.

The poet's interaction with the dove follows a similar pattern. He spots the bird, then startles it with his unexpected presence. The enigmatic scene above the apple (pomegranate) tree ensues:

[La paloma] uolando uiene por medio del uerto,
(en la funte quiso entra
mas quando a mi uido estar
e[n]tros en la del malgranar). . . .
ela que quiso ex[ir] festino,
uertios al agua sobr 'l uino!

The dove's spilling of the water into the wine above the apple tree is the high point of the episode involving the poet and the bird, as the earlier interlude beneath the olive tree is the culmination of events involving the poet and his beloved *doncella*. In each case it is the poet who makes the first move; it is his unexpected visitor whose actions round out the scene. The dove upsets the goblet of water; the maiden makes joyful love to the poet. Through another parallelistic configuration (similar to that revealing the single identity of *dueña* and *doncella*), the poet's beloved assumes the symbolic identity of the dove.

This careful and deliberate association of the maiden and the dove recalls the common thematic tradition of the folk known as *la caza de amor* in which the beloved most often takes the form of a bird. The learned poet's reminiscence of this thematic tradition in the *Razón de amor* is an effective complement to his earlier sophisticated variations on other well-known, essentially folkloric themes, since in poems dealing with *la caza de amor* the lover assumes the role of a predator or hunter whose pursuit of his prey promises not only spiritual but also physical rewards. The *garza* stalked in a familiar *estribillo* glossed by Gil Vicente clearly and succinctly emblematizes the woman in love. She is characterized in human terms, an "enamorada", wounded "en el alma" by what might anachronistically (and euphemistically) be described as a "Freudian" arrow of love:

Mal ferida va la garza
enamorada;

A las orillas de un río

la garza tenía el nido,
ballestero la ha herido
en el alma.
Sola va y gritos daba.

In the epico-lyrical works of the *Romancero viejo,* the sexual dynamism of the hunt, poeticized in Gil Vicente's song and alluded to in the *Razón,* is often forthrightly expressed. In the ballad of Conde Claros, for example, the rôle of the predator is assigned to the Count, whose aggressiveness makes him resemble "un gavilán". He is in love with Claraniña, and asks, as the ballad begins, her sexual favors if only for a night. When Claraniña demurs, the Count attempts to strengthen his demand with a threatening appeal to the terminology of the hunt:

"Bien sabedes vos, señora,
que soy cazador real;
caza que tengo en la mano
nunca la puedo dejar".

He is the hunter. She is his prey. The success of the chase depends upon her physical surrender. In the ballad, hunting imagery prefigures the graphic presentation of lovemaking which takes place between the two:

Tomárala por la mano,
para un vergel se van; . . .
de la cintura arriba
tan dulces besos se dan,
de la cintura abajo
como hombre y mujer se han.

Like Claraniña and other symbolic prey of the traditional *caza de amor,* the damsel of the *Razón de amor* has long eluded the poet; she has constantly motivated his hunt for both spiritual and physical fulfillment, a hunt which has led him at last to the luxuriant orchard of the *Razón*. This poetic kinship of the damsel-turned-dove and the many victims of the folkloric hunt, at first parallelistically suggested, is fully developed in the final verses of the poem under study. Here the poet discloses the success of his love-hunt through his significant description of the dove which bears "un cascauielo dorado / . . . al pie atado". Commonly employed to protect a bird from hunters or predators, the bell attests to the dove's domesticity. She has been hunted, ensnared, tamed; she belongs to someone. It is with good reason that the poet only alludes to the hunt and capture of the symbolic dove in the episode involving the bird: The *caza de amor* has ended triumphantly earlier in the poem as the poet wins the heart of his beloved maiden, not yet transformed into her symbolic counterpart, the dove.

When the dove enters the orchard, immediately after the damsel's departure, it is as if the recent love scene begins anew in the mind of the drowsing poet. Weary from emotion, the poet envisions his lady as a tame white dove, reënacting their joyful moments together with the symbolic spilling of the water into the wine. The dove's rearrangement, high in the tree, of the erotically-charged vessels of water and wine corresponds to the consummation of love which took place under the tree; the previously unattainable water of satisfaction is mixed with the wine of desire. The constant poetic tension between wine and water, heat and cold is at last relaxed, as the dove's action brings together the numerous recollections of folk song evident in the *Razón de amor* to conclude this poem "made of love" with a brilliant summary of all that has gone before.

Besides providing a fitting resolution to the quest for and discovery of love central to the *Razón,* the dove's spilling of the water into the wine brings to mind once more the popular verses of "No pueden dormir mis ojos", with dreamlike atmosphere and enigmatic symbols strangely like those of the *Razón de amor*. Presenting the restless, image-ridden sleep of a young girl, the folk poem sets forth in the *glosa* the dreamer's vision of a fresh, new rose, following it at once with a second, inseparable vision of the mysteriously placed wine and water:

> Y soñaba yo, mi madre,
> dos horas antes del día
> que me florecía la rosa:
> ell vino so ell agua frida.

With her description of the rose (a common folk symbol associated with all aspects of lovemaking) as bursting into bloom, the girl seemingly alludes to herself, to her blossoming womanhood, and to the first awakening to the pleasure of love which such an experience brings.

Inextricably bound to her representation of awakening womanhood as a flowering rose is her hazy vision of "ell vino so ell agua frida". Well-known folk symbols whose persistence is essential to the sophisticated development of the *Razón,* the counterposed wine and water are central to the wholly popular "No pueden dormir mis ojos", tensely placed one above the other to constitute yet another dreamlike representation of love's first stirrings within the young woman. Like the damsel of the *Razón de amor* who reveals her unsatisfied longing by placing a silver goblet of wine in the treetops, the restless peasant girl of the folk song is haunted by love's nascent desires, which have taken the form of wine in her semi-conscious mind. This wine is somehow separated from the higher-placed water, emblematic of the satisfaction sought by the young dreamer as she longs to make a first encounter with love. Although the tension which exists between the wine and the water of "No pueden dormir mis ojos" is never relaxed, the adolescent girl's dream vision, her unspoken, subconscious desire for love, is identical to the passionate and hopeful yearning of both the poet and his beloved in the *Razón de amor*.

With its symbolic expression of a passionate longing similar to that presented in the *Razón,* the folk poem, "No pueden dormir mis ojos", emerges as a vital link in the chain connecting the sophisticated medieval lyric to the spontaneity and charm of the popular tradition. Joined also to the folk tradition by its popular lyrical nucleus, as identified by Cárdenas, and by its insistent recollection of traditional folk song, the *Razón* is of special importance as the first known cultured lyric of the Castilian language. Marking the very beginnings of a genre which did not come into its own until well on into the fifteenth century, the poem demonstrates its early cultured author's inescapable dependence upon the popular tradition, the first cause of all Peninsular verse. More, then, than a curious work mingling traditional-type *cantigas de amigo* with the tenets of courtly love, the *Razón de amor* is a complex and sophisticated piece whose verses point to the popular origins of all lyric. Its many erudite reminiscences of both themes and images well-known to the folk not only clarify and enhance the learned contexts in which they appear but also bear witness to the virtual inseparability of the *popular* and *culto* traditions in the early days when artistic lyric was born.

Harriet Goldberg (essay date 1984)

SOURCE: "The *Razón de amor* and *Los denuestos del agua y el vino* as a Unified Dream Report," in *Kentucky Romance Quarterly,* Vol. 31, No. 1, 1984, pp. 4-49.

[*In the following essay, Goldberg argues that the* Razón de amor *is indeed a unified work, basing her assertions on her interpretation of the piece as a dream-poem.*]

The *Razón de amor,* an erudite lyric poem of the thirteenth century has been approached critically from various points of view. Alfred Jacob performed a feat of twentieth-century exegesis to show that the poet made use of amorous imagery to write a mystical Christian allegory. Alicia C. de Ferraresi identified it as an amorous vision in conformity with the courtly love tradition. She writes: "La amada nunca vista cobra en esta dimensión visionaria la realidad humana, corporal y psícica que corresponde al ideal del 'fin amor'." She too sees Christian symbolism in the poem—the kiss of the lovers is the kiss of peace; the baptismal water and the eucharistic wine serve jointly to make possible the communion of the soul with the "Amor Supremo"; the intrusive dove is both earthly *cupiditas* and divine *caritas*. Margot de Ley finds interesting new correspondences between the autobiographical passages in the *Razón* and the biographical tradition in Provencal poetry. She notes in particular the incidence of the topic of the travel account during which the poet has an amorous encounter. More recently Margaret Antwerp called attention to the mixture of the popular lyric in the poem which she identifies as the consciously literary production of a sophisticated poet. Perhaps the most vexing problem in connection with the poem is the question of its unity with the "Denuestos del agua y el vino", a traditional debate with which it was copied with some transitional lines. Leo Spitzer, seeing a thematic unity, complained that the poem suffered when it was considered to be the fusion of two different poems by a poet-scribe, a solution proposed earlier by Carolina Michaëlis.

Accepting Margaret Antwerp's image of a sophisticated poet who made use of traditional lyrics in the composition of the amorous nucleus of the poem, we can use her own argument to take exception to her stand on the unity of the poem. She writes: "The anthologists' separation of the courtly poem from the "Denuestos" is certainly justifiable. Comical in tone and traceable to medieval sources, the debate between the wine and the water cannot be properly said to belong to the same genre or tradition as the lyrical love poem, the *Razón de amor*." However, is it not possible that a poet who was imaginative enough to rely on popular lyrics, even reproducing a *cantiga de amigo* in his courtly poem, might have also considered the use of a traditional debate as a part of his total composition? Is it not also possible to imagine Michaëlis' poet-scribe, who, at the moment of transcribing two poems, saw in a creative flash a relationship between them? After all, creativity has been defined as the perception of relationships between seemingly unrelated ideas. The creative link in this case might have been a familiarity with contemporary dream lore, and, of course, an insight into human dream patterns stemming from personal experience.

This is not to suggest that the new element is the connection between dreams and amorous visions. Alicia C. de Ferraresi called attention to the use of a dream as the beginning of an amorous vision in the *Cancionero de Ripoll*. We find a striking parallel in the *Rota Veneris* of Boncompagno da Signa (b. 1170). In this guide to the composition of love letters the Bolognese scholar wrote: "Lovers have . . . been wont to say that they have witnessed in a dream what they have done." In a sample letter the lover writes of a time when he entered a garden where there were two rivulets. Tired after the hunt, he lies down under a pine tree and listens to the song of the birds. It is spring. A lovely virgin appears to him after he has fallen asleep sweetly: "She took me by the hand and began to tarry beside me for a while. First she made use of the most refined eloquence, introducing herself in colorful words; then after much had been spoken, she twined her arms around me, embraced me sweetly and, pressing her ruby lips upon mine, she gave me ineffable kisses." What is new in the unified *Razón* is the creative combination of a lyrical dream with an abrasively didactic debate as a subsequent scene in the same dream.

Having agreed that the amorous nucleus, the *Razón,* is a dream vision, then we can consider the possibility

that the arrival of the dove whose actions provoke the debate is a transitional dream scene which leads the reader to the final episode of the dream, the noisy doctrinaire debate. We can then propose that we are confronted with a new poem in whose unity rings the authorial voice of a particular poet-scribe who made the creative connection between the dream in which wine and water figured prominently and the traditional debate. In a sense, the new work, a re-formation of two previous poems, is a translation in the most basic meaning of the word. An artistic creation has been transferred in a new version in which the meaning has been altered instead of the language.

Before going about the task of examining the entire poem as a dream narrative, it is appropriate to present a brief summary of the presentation of dream material in medieval texts. First, we can acknowledge that the medieval author and his audience shared a common fund of dream lore—classical, Scriptural and folkloric. Since dreaming is a normal part of the human experience, we can also conjecture a shared familiarity with the phenomenon of dreaming. Medieval authors presented dream accounts in realistic circumstances, frequently giving the date, the time of day, the physical condition of the dreamer, the preparations for sleep, his location, the rapidity with which the dream began, the quality of the sleep, the duration of the dream, the part of the sleep period in which the dream occurred, the awakening, the recounting of the dream to another and a reaction to the content. It was not at all uncommon, however, to find one or more of these realistic details omitted from what was nevertheless clearly a dream. In fact, Ruy Paez denied that he was sleeping but reported that he had awakened in fear. Modern psychologists make use of waking dreams as therapeutic tools recognizing their kinship with those that take place during a sleep period. For our purpose, the consideration of the *Razón* as a dream vision need not depend on our recognition of its having been either a sleeping or a waking dream, since in both cases most of the circumstances are similar.

We are now ready to examine the *Razón de amor con los denuestos del agua e el vino* as a unified poem transcribed by an imaginative poet-scribe whose intention it was to accommodate the material to the structure of a dream report.

After introducing himself and giving his credentials, poetic and courtly, the poet begins his narrative with the information that he has just eaten his midday meal. One of the six generators of dreams according to St. Gregory was a full stomach. It should be noted that dreams resulting from this kind of stimulus (*ex parte corporibus* in Macrobius' scheme) were prophetically unreliable because the body's digestive activities impeded the soul's capacity to receive spiritual or divine messages. Having posited a shared familiarity with scientific dream lore between author and reader, we must begin to doubt the view that the poem is a Christian allegory since it occurs specifically "despues yantar" (v. 11). In the *Gran conquista de ultramar,* Corvalan has a singularly unreliable dream after an evening of eating and drinking. In fact, when the author of *Amadís de Gaula* wanted to convey the idea that his hero was going to dream prophetically, he writes that he had eaten very little before going to sleep.

In the manner of traditional dream reports, the poet tells us that he was in an olive grove after his meal giving his location and his condition (vv. 11-12). He gives us the time mentioning the *siesta,* and the date saying that it is April. In the last few moments of waking reality he sees two glasses placed up high in a tree—we know what his thoughts were upon falling asleep. Although Spitzer, following Michaëlis' line of thought considered this to be a supernatural touch, and Antwerp regarded the arrangement as the symbolic expression of the *dueña/ doncella's* carnal desire for her lover, anyone who has spent time living out of doors can testify to the practical logic of placing containers of liquid (susceptible to spillage, theft or sun spoilage) high up in the crook of a tree for safety and for shade. As part of his waking thoughts, he speculates about the contents of the glasses. The first one, a silver goblet is filled with fine red wine and is covered to keep out the heat. Idly he thinks that it must have been placed there by the woman who owns the orchard in preparation for the visit of her lover. Perhaps the wine has magical properties—perpetual immunity from illness, activated if it is taken daily with the morning meal (presumably after a night spent with the *dueña*): "Qui de tal uino ouiesse / en-la-mana quan comiesse: / e dello ouiesse cada-dia, / nu[n] cas mas enfermarya" (vv. 23-26). His thoughts are erotic as he imagines the relationship between the *dueña* of the orchard and her lover. His eye moves upward in the tree and he sees another glass full of water from the spring in the grove: "que en-el mançanar se nacia" (v. 30). This water frightens him. Although he is thirsty he is afraid that it might be enchanted (vv. 27-32).

The poet has noted the beginnings of the subsequent debate giving the water a sinister connotation and the wine a salutary one. Quite possibly he is in that interim pre-dream state called *phantasma, visum* by Macrobius during which the dreamer is sometimes a victim of succubi. In this state the dreamer frequently denies that he has been dreaming or even that he was asleep. Thus his recall of having disrobed and having put his head down in the meadow is a part of his memory of that period in which the boundary between the waking state and the sleeping state is uncertain. Spitzer, noting that the poet had not mentioned falling asleep, commented nevertheless on the dream-like quality of the scene. As we have noted above, the omission of one or another of the circumstantial details of a dream account did not preclude the possibility that the author was describing a dream experience. Two other dream accounts

which began in a *locus amoenus* are also sketchy in their details—Paris' dream in the *Corónica troyana* and the vision of Berceo, the pilgrim, in the *Milagros.*

Rather than seizing upon the omission of any mention of falling asleep as a sign of a scribal lapse, I suggest an alternate explanation. The so-called lapse might be one more realistic circumstantial detail—dreamers often were unsure if they were awake or asleep. Often dreamers in medieval dream reports, upon awakening tell of having been asked by their angelic visitors if they were asleep or awake. Sometimes an author used this uncertainty to mask an apparent falsehood as in the case of Queen Brisena who tried to explain the loss of property entrusted to her under lock and key by saying that she remembered having given the key to someone: "Digovos que no puedo entender si esto me auino en sueños o en realidad" (*Amadís de Gaula,* I, 255).

Ready for his rest, the poet of the *Razón* says abruptly that he arrived at a spring: "Pleguem a una fuente perenal" (v. 37). This is a crucial point in the poem. Spitzer interprets the verb as "yo aproximé" 'I came close to' assuming that the spring in question is still the spring in the orchard. However, if we take the verb literally as an arrival, then he has suddenly found himself in a new setting, in a change of scene typical of the brusque transitions common to dreams which are in a sense interior voyages. The very suddenness of the arrival conforms to the rapid, unexplained changes common to dreams.

Preoccupied by the events of the day (dreams that resulted from recent experience or thoughts were *ex parte anime*), the poet's dream revolves around his erotic thoughts upon sinking into the dream which had centered on the two glasses, the woman who had put them there, her lover and the heat of the day. He names the flowers that surround the spring, instead of just saying that they were lovely and profuse (salvia, lilies, roses and violas) and then translates them dream fashion into the medieval commonplace that in Paradise there are flowers whose fragrance will magically revive the dead. This resuscitative property is reminiscent of his waking thoughts about the curative powers of the wine in the silver goblet in the tree. The refrigerative property of the spring (vv. 39-42) is an echo of his thoughts about the enchanted water in the other glass.

We have been following the poet's dream adaptation of his waking thoughts about love, about the dangers of enchantments and about the heat in his dream report. Modern psychologists (post-Freudians) emphasize the usefulness of dream imagery in our learning to deal with waking reality: "In the Jungian scheme things appear differently because dreams are viewed not as symptoms of a sickness but as visions or images of meaning." In this dream, the poet makes the connection between the wine glass and the owner of the orchard who had put it there, and the woman who is the object of his love. This is the blurring of identity to which Antwerp refers. Viewed thus this dream is a fantasy in the Augustinian sense—a dream of images conserved in the dreamer's memory, as opposed to a phantasm which is a dream of an image without correspondence to reality, and *ostensio* which is a dream in which the images stem from divine intervention.

In the first part of the dream, the lover drank the water of the spring, an action of which he had been afraid when he was awake (vv. 51-4). Bolder in his dream, he picks one of the magical flowers, although he never even considered trying any of the curative wine when awake. He is inspired to sing of "fin amor" but the impulse is arrested by the sudden arrival of a lovely young woman, the most beautiful he has ever seen (a typically non-visual superlative allusion). Because this is a dream, the poet is free to depart from the usual standard rhetorical portrait of the beautiful woman. C. B. Hieatt explains this descriptive freedom speaking about dream poetry (the *Roman de la rose* in particular): "The imagery and description of the poem are richly visual, and the poem is to a very large extent an account of what the poet *sees* [her italics] rather than what he hears or thinks." In the *Razón* the poet actually describes the young woman's hair style instead of referring to her remarkably lovely hair ("cabelos cortos sobr'ell oreia" [v. 59]). She wears a hat to protect her from the noon-day sun: "Un sombrero tien en la tiesta / que nol fiziese mal la siesta" (vv. 73-4). Here the poet repeats his waking thoughts about the sun using parallel language: "que nom fiziese mal la siesta; / parti me mi las uistaduras" (vv. 34-5). Another pictorial detail is the mention of the gloves she carries in her hand. Often the subject of a drawing in a medieval miniature was made identifiable by an object he held in his hand. In the *Razón* the poet uses this visual device to prefigure the information that the poet has some previous connection with the young woman (v. 75 and 122-23). Professor de Ferraresi sees this line as evidence that the dream vision is a courtly one: "Como ya hemos dicho, ella es la dama lejana, el amor de *lonh* (vv. 96, 108), la amada nunca vista, real e irreal como un sueño." She relates the dream device to the courtly poetic need to possess and yet not to possess the object of the poet's love.

In contrast to this position Margaret Antwerp establishes most clearly the blend of the popular lyric (a most uncourtly genre) in the *Razón*. However she does not mention the frankly aggressive and sexual tone of the young woman's song. It appears that the "dama lejana" is more akin to the women who sang the *jarchas* than she is to the *belle dame sans merci* (who may even have been a nineteenth century invention). In a sequence of events beginning with the taking of the young woman's hand, the lovers engage in a teasing little interplay while sitting under a tree, until they embrace and consummate their love. Whether the poet intended to suggest actual sexual union or as de Fer-

raresi proposes the tantalizing contemplation of the woman's unclothed figure he ends the scene abruptly. The lovers don't exchange pledges of devotion; rather she begs his pardon for having to leave so soon and he begs her to think of him (vv. 136-39).

No sooner has she left than a white dove interrupts the dreaming poet's post-coital languors. For Antwerp this is the beginning of the dream as the drowsy poet re-enacts symbolically his recent sexual encounter. If, as I maintain, the entire poem is a unified dream report, then the episode of the dove's arrival is a brusque transition which links the two principal parts of the poem. It is not at all uncommon in dream lore to find a dreamer who has a dream within a dream. Here the dreamer distressed by her abrupt departure says that he wanted to fall asleep: "que que la-ui fuera del uerto, / por (por) poco non fuy muerto. Por uerdat quisiera adormir, / mas una palomela ui;" (vv. 144-46), and then dreams another repetition of his erotic thoughts upon falling asleep in the orchard. Recalling dream-fashion his fear of the water and the magical qualities of the wine, the debate which follows is a logical, censorious episode with which to end an erotic dream. Its shrill angry tone is consistent with the idea of dreams as censors of our waking thoughts. I find intriguing the connection made by Antwerp between the contents of the *Razón* and the popular lyric: "No pueden dormir mis ojos, / no pueden dormir. / Y soñaba yo, mi madre / dos horas antes del dìa / que me florecìa la rosa: / ell vino so ell agua frida. / No pueden dormir." This little song is a complete dream report since it includes the restlessness of the sleeper, the hour of the dream, and even a dream account made to the mother of the dreamer. According to Antwerp, the wine represents the longings of the young girl who sings the song and the water stands for the satisfaction she seeks. If our hypothetical poet-scribe made a similar connection, then the spilling of the water into the wine is a dream reaction of conscience to the satisfaction derived from having bathed in the water: "Quando en-el-uaso fue entrada / e fue toda bien esfryada, / ela que quiso ex[ir] festino, / uertios al-agua sobre 'l uino" (vv. 158-61).

In this little scene we find some of the characteristic techniques of dream accounts. The dove is described comparatively at first: "tan blanca era como la nieu del puerto" (v. 148), and then more specifically: "un-cas-cauielo dorado / tray al pie atado" (vv. 153-54). Merely symbolic doves characteristically do not wear the bell of a domestic pet, nor are they usually clumsy enough to spill their bath water. The bird's caution about the spring leads it to the glass, an echo of the poet's fear of the water before he fell asleep. As we have noted, it is the satisfaction of a bodily need that leads to the noisy moralizing of the debate, further reinforcing the logical nature of the sequence of events in the new poem. A drastically sudden change of mood is entirely consistent with human dream experiences, a fact which the Marqués de Santillana recognized when he made dramatic use of the transformation of a *locus amoenus* into a dreadful place where even the tree trunks became "fieros, ñudosos" and the song birds turned into poisonous snakes. Although the water has the last word in the debate, we can wonder if the poet-scribe did not intend to convey extra meaning when he asks for the traditional reward of wine, making a final vinous allusion.

Patricia E. Grieve (essay date 1986)

SOURCE: "Through the Silver Goblet: A Note on the 'vaso de plata' in *Razón de amor*," in *Revista de Estudios Hispánicos,* Vol. XX, No. 2, May, 1986, pp. 15-20.

[*Below, Grieve embellishes on Harriet Goldberg's interpretation of the* Razón de amor *(see above), attempting to define the exact point in the poem where the dream state begins.*]

Although critics continue to debate the structure, meaning and unity of the thirteenth-century poem *Razón de amor,* there seems to be little disagreement that the anonymous poet's composition is complex enough to keep critics busy ever since Morel-Fatio first published it in 1887. Investigations designed to support or dispute the unity of the poem through the elaboration of the generic elements which inform the work have produced theories of the poem's relationship to Christian allegory, the courtly love tradition, its incorporation of popular lyric, and its correspondences to the biographical tradition in Provençal poetry. Ramón Menéndez Pidal and Leo Spitzer, while differing in their supporting arguments, agree that *Razón de amor,* an *amorosa visione,* and the debate, "Denuestos del agua y el vino," are two parts which form a single composition.

Continuing in the line of those who favor the view of a unified work, Harriet Goldberg proposes that the entire poem, that is to say, *Razón de amor y Denuestos del agua y el vino,* be considered in the context of "human dream patterns stemming from personal experience." She says:

> This is not to suggest that the new element is the connection between dreams and amorous visions. . . . What is new in the unified *Razón* is the creative combination of a lyrical dream with an abrasively didactic debate as a subsequent scene in the same dream. [*Kentucky Romance Quarterly* 31 (1984)]

Goldberg provides convincing evidence of the poet-scribe's knowledge of dream lore, and she examines the poem in light of scientific discoveries on the states of dreaming and pre-dreaming. She discusses the difficulty in determining precisely where in the poem the dream-state begins, for in the recounting of the amorous adventure, which is the subject of *Razón de amor,* it appears that the author does not linguistically distin-guish between a waking and a dreaming state. In this short study, I propose to show that the poet indeed offers indirect evidence of his moment of falling asleep, that it occurs near the beginning of the poem, and that this evidence strengthens the unity of the poem.

After the opening stanza in which it is stated that the poem was composed by "un-escolar . . . que sie[m]pre duens amo" (5-6), the poet begins his tale of what happened after his midday meal:

> En-el-mes d'abril, depues yantar,
> estaua so un-oliuar.
> Entre-çimas d'un mançanar
> un-uaso de plata ui-estar;
> pleno era d'un claro uino
> que era uermeio e fino;
> cubierto era de-tal mesura
> no-lo tocas la calentura.
> Vna-duena lo-y-eua-puesto,
> que era senora del uerto,
> que quan su amigo uiniese,
> d'a quel uino a-beuer-le-disse.
> Qui de tal uino ouisse
> en-la-mana quan comiesse:
> e dello ouisse cada-dia,
> nu[n]cas mas enfermarya.
> Ariba del mançanar
> otro uaso ui estar;
> pleno era d'un agua fryda
> que en-el mançanar se-naçia.
> Beuiera d'ela de grado,
> mas oui-miedo que era encantado.
> Sobre un-prado pusmi tiesta,
> que nom fiziese mal la siesta;
> parti de mi-las uistiduras,
> que nom fizies mal la calentura. (11-36)

Spitzer regarded the inclusion of the mysterious vessels in the tree as a supernatural touch and commented on the dream-like quality of this part of the poem. Goldberg, however, is the first to examine the poem as a dream with a dream: the "Denuestos del agua y el vino" contained within the frame of the amorous dream of the poet. She seems unworried by the lack of a concrete reference to the moment of falling asleep, relying instead on scientific data for the possible cause: "Rather than seizing upon the omission of any mention of falling asleep as a sign of a scribal lapse, I suggest an alternate explanation. The so-called lapse might be one more realistic circumstantial detail—dreamers often were unsure if they were awake or asleep." Goldberg goes on to describe why the poet might be unsure of his own state of mind:

> The poet has noted the beginnings of the subsequent debate giving the water a sinister connotation and the wine a salutary one. Quite possibly he is in that interim pre-dream state called *phantasma visum* by Macrobius during which the dreamer is sometimes

a victim of succubi. In this state the dreamer frequently denies that he has been dreaming or even that he was asleep. Thus his recall of having disrobed and having put is head down in the meadow is a part of that period in which the boundary between the waking state and sleeping state is uncertain.

Interestingly enough, Goldberg considers the description of the vessels to be part of the waking state:

> In the last few moments of waking reality he sees two glasses placed up high in a tree—we know what his thoughts were upon falling asleep. . . . Anyone who has spent time living out of doors can testify to the practical logic of placing containers of liquid (susceptible to spillage, theft or sun spoilage) high up in the crook of a tree for safety and for shade. As part of his waking thoughts, he speculates about the contents of the glasses. The first one, a silver goblet, is filled with fine red wine and is covered to keep out the heat.

This is possible, but I submit that the line of demarcation between waking and sleeping occurs both abruptly and near the beginning of the poem with a physical impossibility: the description of the silver goblet, the "vaso de plata."

In Lewis Carroll's *Through the Looking Glass,* a masterpiece of the illogical logic of dreams, the King asks Alice who she sees coming down the road:

> "I see nobody on the road," said Alice.

> "I only wish *I* had such eyes," the King remarked in a fretful tone. "To be able to see Nobody! And at that distance too! Why, it's as much as *I* can do to see real people, by this light!"

If we are to believe what the poet says in *Razón de amor,* he, too, was able to "see Nobody." The poet describes from his position *below* the branches of the tree that contents of an opaque object, a silver goblet. Not only is the goblet metal, but it is covered. If we see this section as a dream report, and here I agree with Goldberg's proposal, what better place to start than with the recounting of the "seeing" of something that, logically, could not be seen? It is not infrequent in dreams to stand apart from oneself and see and do things wh ich humanly could not be achieved. To regard this description as an oversight on the part of the author is one answer, but it fails to ring true in a poem which reflects, in many ways, an admirable level of poetic sophistication.

The description of the contents of an opaque object is not the only example of an unusual phenomenon in the poem. Near the end of the first part of the work, the poet describes how the contents of the second vessel managed to get into the first:

En-la fuent [the dove] quiso entra,
[mas] quando a-mi uido estar,
[entros] en-el [uaso del] malgranar.
Quando en-el-uaso fue entrada
e fue toda bien effryada,
ela que quiso ex[ir] festino,
uertios al-agua sobre 'l-uino! (155-61)

As far as can be determined, Arsenio Pacheco is the only critic to comment that the wine vessel has somehow become uncovered so that the dove could tip the water into the wine: "Debe notarse que, en algún momento que no se precisa, el vaso de vino ha sido destapado, pues en otro caso no se explicarìa que pudiera verterse en él el agua derramada por la paloma" [in *Bulletin of Hispanic Studies* 51 (1974)].

One or two errors, or minor slips, on the part of the poet are possible, certainly, but it should strike us as unusual that in this case both items in question deal with the silver goblet. Is it not more likely, then, that there exists a reasonable, calculated link between the "slips" which might explain the so-called errors? The first example, the description of the vessel's contents, could well occur in the context of a dream. In the second case, this kind of jump from covered to uncovered, again, quite simply poses no problem to the logic of a dream. The net result of this link is that the amorous adventure, *Razón de amor,* becomes circular in its reference to the two vessels and in its presentation, or lack of presentation of detail, of two unexplained phenomena.

What this reveals about the poem, therefore, is that *Razón de amor* is perhaps even more cleverly unified than had been thought previously. The vessels mentioned at the beginning of the poem appear not to be important to the development of the poem until the end of the amorous adventure and have been criticized for being placed there only to enable the poet to continue with the debate later. If, in fact, both references to the vessels, at the onset of the amorous adventure as well as at the beginning of the debate, serve to signal the start of dream sequences, then the question of gratuitous references, unexplained phenomena, and structural unity are happily resolved in favor of the view of a poet's highly developed awareness of sophisticated poetic composition.

Colbert I. Nepaulsingh (essay date 1986)

SOURCE: "The Song of Songs and the Unity of the *Razón de amor,*" in *Towards a History of Literary Composition in Medieval Spain,* University of Toronto Press, 1986, pp. 41-62.

[*In the following essay, Nepaulsingh presents a detailed exploration of the biblical Song of Songs as a source for the* Razón de amor.]

[The] garden in the Song of Songs was by no means the only one that impressed its symbolism upon the minds of medieval writers. The garden of Ave in the Song was frequently compared with the garden of Eva in Genesis, or, as Alfonso el Sabio of Spain put it in his 'cantiga de loor': 'Ca Eva nos tolleu / o Parays' e Deus / Ave nos y meteu.' In Spain there also existed knowledge of the luscious gardens described in the Koran, a veritable paradise through which flowed magic rivers of water and of wine. And there were other literary gardens, gardens of song, like the one described by Todros Abulafia as a preface to his book of poems, and the one described by Moses ben Jacob Ibn Ezra: . . .

> All who are sick at heart and cry in bitterness
> Let not your soul complain in grief.
> Enter the garden of my songs, and find balm
> for your sorrow, and sing there with open
>   mouth.
>
> Honey compared with them is bitter to the
>   taste,
> And before their scent, flowing myrrh is rank.
> Through them the deaf hear, the stutterers
>   speak,
> The blind see, and the halting run.
> The troubled and grief-stricken rejoice in them,
> All who are sick at heart, and cry in bitterness.

The countless earthly gardens where ordinary mortal lovers held their trysts and ordinary workers sought, from the heat of the noon-day sun, the shade of a brook-watered tree were, of course, commonplace in Spain as anywhere else in the world. Toss these elements into the air a thirteenth-century Spanish poet breathed and, with the help of twentieth-century hindsight, it should be not unexpected that out of Ave, Eva, magic wine and magic water, lustful song and ordinary debate, should arise a poem of consummate medieval artistry—the *Razón de amor*. All the details of *Razón de amor* cannot be made to coincide with those of the Song of Songs or with the garden of Eva in Genesis, or with any other garden of either courtly literature or folklore where 'boy meets girl'; but the Song of Songs is such an important *locus classicus* for all such details, including ideas about courtly literature (King Solomon's court), that it would be worthwhile to examine how works far removed from it vary its contents.

The composition of the *Razón de amor* has been a subject of much debate ever since A. Morel-Fatio published the work as two separate poems in 1887. In 1905 Ramón Menéndez Pidal argued convincingly, in the introduction to his edition and facsimile reproduction of the manuscript, that the two parts of the poem constitute a unit. In 1950 Leo Spitzer declared that Menéndez Pidal's arguments for unity were definitive, and he added to those arguments his own aesthetic reasons for believing that the work was one single,

complete poem composed on the medieval principle of the harmony of contraries, *sic et non*. Nevertheless, as recently as 1974, it has been correctly pointed out that literary historians and anthologists remain divided in their opinions about the unity of the work, a fact that is reflected in the failure to drop the second part, 'Denuestos del agua y el vino,' from the bipartite title normally used for the work.

The search for the unity of the *Razón de amor* has led many able critics into several interrelated sources of information. Spitzer argued for Roman mythology, and other critics have tried to show how Christian symbolism, cathar heresy, grail legends, troubador poetry, linguistics, folk lyrics, and structural analysis can be used to prove or disprove the unity of the poem. All of this critical material includes many convincing insights about the lyrical tradition to which the *Razón de amor* belongs, and yet no single source that has been cited, nor any eclectic combination of those sources, can claim to have satisfied the critical queries that have arisen out of the search for the unity of the poem. There are missing links.

I should like to suggest that one of these missing links is the Song of Songs, which is mentioned only in passing in the critical material on the *Razón de amor,* except by Alicia de Colombì-Monguió [*De Amor y Poesìa*], who states explicitly that 'ningún clérigo-escolar pudo ignorar nunca el *Cantar de los Cantares.* Cierto es que, de darse algún eco suyo en el *Razón de amor,* se da tan quedo que debe llegar de muy lejos. Pero la posibilidad de su presencia ayudarìa a explicarnos ese manzanar-malgranar, árbol de la fecundidad, de la unión amorosa, del paraìso terrenal y de la salvación.' I shall not claim that the Song of Songs is a direct source for the composition of the *Razón*. Rather, I hope to illustrate that many of the problems left unanswered by searches elsewhere, including the problem of unity, can be resolved by a careful reading of the Song of Songs and its commentaries.

I shall attempt to justify my reference to the Song of Songs by listing some of the main motifs that it has in common with the *Razón de amor*. On the basis of this justification I shall then discuss the question of unity. By listing common motifs I do not mean to suggest exact relationships between the Song of Songs and the *Razón*. My point is that from the widespread tradition of the Song, the poet had available to him many motifs that could be repeated exactly, or altered, to suit artistic purposes. In other words, my emphasis is on identifying the tradition itself correctly, not on finding exact parallels. I am convinced that mutations take place constantly within the same tradition, and I do not believe that medieval artists were capable of only imitating a source exactly.

I should also make clear from the outset that if it can

be established satisfactorily that the **Razón** was composed in the tradition of the Song of Songs, the ambiguities in the **Razón,** to which critics like Colombì-Monguió have correctly referred would be adequately explained. Scholars of the Song have always omnilaterally conceded its inherent ambiguity, and there has never been universal agreement among biblical scholars that the Song should be included among the canon of holy books. Advocates of its holiness, like Rabbi Akiva and St Bernard, were keenly aware of the erotic qualities of the work, but considered it holy in spite of, even because of, its erotic content. Other scholars, of course, have refused to concede any divine content to the Song, choosing to consider it simply as a collection of erotic wedding songs. So a similar debate about the content of the **Razón** helps to confirm its composition within the tradition of the Song.

It has been noted that the invocation to the poem ('Sancti spiritus adsid nobis gratia amen') is different from the invocations in the works of other medieval Spanish authors. But its appropriateness becomes clear if this invocation is interpreted within the context of medieval attempts to understand the Song of Songs. The invocation to the **Razón de amor** is most probably a direct reference to the Book of Wisdom: 'Spiritus enim sanctus disciplinae effugiet fictum.' Because Solomon was believed to be the author of both the Book of Wisdom and the Song of Songs, this verse was used by commentators to explain how Solomon was divinely inspired to write the Song of Songs. St Bernard cites the verse from the Book of Wisdom in his sermon on the title 'Song of Songs,' and Abraham Ibn Ezra makes oblique reference to it in his interpretation of the title: 'Quoniam autem testificatur contextus scripturae Dominum Salomoni bis apparuisse, quid eum mirum est vaticinatum de re futura, cum praesertim afflatu Spiritussancti hunc librum fuderit." I shall have reason to return to the invocation when I discuss the unity of the **Razón**. At that time I will also explain how the second line of the poem ('qui triste tiene su coraçón benga oir esta razón') is related to the Song, and how that relationship helps to clarify the problem of unity.

In line 3 the motif of a perfect composition ('razón acabada') is clearly linked to interpretations of the title of the Song of Songs. Abraham Ibn Ezra, for example, in his commentary on the title refers to the excellence of the Song of Songs above all other songs of Solomon, and to its perfection ('Hoc enim sive carmen sive canticum dignius excellentiusque est caeteris . . . Itaque cum sit suis numeris perfectum, illud exposui tribus modis.' St Bernard also refers to its excellence in his sermon on the title. The idea that this perfect composition was 'feyta d'amor' (1. 3) is one that medieval poets associated with the Song of Songs seem to have known; a twelfth-century French version of the Song of Songs explains in its introductory lines 'Quar d'amor est li livres faiz.'

In line 4 the author of the **Razón** is described in terms that apply as well to the author of the Song of Songs: Solomon was well known as one who 'siepre dueñas amó.' In the context of 'loving women,' if the word *tyrança* in line 5 has a negative connotation (meaning trials, tribulations, or bad dealings), the author of the **Razón** shares this motif with that of King Solomon: 'Rex autem Solomon adamavit mulieres alienigenas multas, filiam quoque Pharaonis, et Moabitidas, et Ammonitidas, Idumaeas, et Sidonias, et Hethaeas: de gentibus, super quibus dixit Dominus filiis Israel: Non ingrediemini ad eas . . .' (1 Kings 11:1-2). In spite of differences in geographical locations (Lombardy, Moab), the tradition is discernible in the **Razón:** Solomon's court was considered to be a court of love and wisdom, and it must have been, ultimately, one of the models for other students of courtly love, like Andreas Capellanus.

The spring motif in line 7 ('en el mes d'abril') echoes one of the most famous passages of the Song of Songs: 'Iam enim hiems transiit; imber abiit et recessit. Flores apparuerunt in terra nostra' (2:11-12). In the same line of the **Razón** the motif of the noonday meal ('depués yantar') is reminiscent of 'Indica mihi, quem diligit anima mea, ubi pascas, ubi cubes in meridie' in the Song of Songs (1:6).

The olive tree, named in lines 7 and 54 of the **Razón,** is not found in the Song of Songs, but the apple tree and its shade are mentioned twice in a manner that reminds one of lines in the **Razón;** ('Sicut malus inter ligna silvarum, sic dilectus meus inter filios. Sub umbra illius quem desideraveram sedi . . . Sub arbore malo suscitavi te' 2:3, 8:5). By referring to the olive tree the poet probably seeks comparison with the great songwriter David, who described himself as an olive tree growing in the house of God: 'Ego autem sicut oliva virens in domo Dei' (Psalms 51:10). The likelihood of this comparison increases if it is noted that St Bernard refers to this verse of the Psalms in his sermon on Song of Songs 1:3. In addition, the olive was probably more common in Spain at the time of the poem's composition than were the palms and pomegranates and other exotic trees mentioned in the Song of Songs. Impey suggests that the olive is the tree of wisdom, as in the *Siervo libre de amor.*

The motifs of the wine, water, 'dueña,' and their special qualities appearing in lines 9 to 17 of the **Razón** are central to, and will be treated in, the discussion of unity. The siesta mentioned in line 18 is echoed in Song of Songs 1:7, a verse one modern commentator explains in this way: 'The violent heat of noonday compels people in the East to desist from labour, and recline in some cool part of the house. Shepherds especially, being more exposed to the burning rays of the sun, lead their flocks under some shady tree near wells and streams. We have beautiful descriptions of the same custom by Greeks and Romans.' The motif of disrobing is common to both works, but in the **Razón** both lovers disrobe—the man in the heat of the siesta (1. 19), and the woman in heat of passion at the sight of her lover (1. 66); in the Song, only the woman disrobes, not in a siesta but after she has gone to sleep ('Ego dormio, et cor meum vigilate . . . Exploliavime tunica mea, quomodo induar illa' 5:2-3).

The *locus amoenus* of the **Razón** (11. 20-8) with its fountain, flowers, and aromatic herbs, belongs clearly to the tradition of the *hortus conclusus* described in the Song (4:12-16). The description of a beautiful woman, from the top down, in this *locus amoenus* is also common to both works (11. 29-39; 4:1-5), although the descriptions differ in detail. It has been noted that the 'doncela' of the **Razón** is like most other medieval women except that she wears a hat to shield her from the sun (1. 38). There is a curiously close relationship between this descriptive detail of the beautiful white doncela of the **Razón** and the fact that the famous woman of the Song of Songs is beautiful but black because she had been scorched by the sun in the vineyards she had tended ('Nigra sum, sed formosa . . . Nolite me considerare quod fusca sim, quia decoloravit me sol. Filii matris meae pugnaverunt contra me; posuerunt me custodem in vineis,' 1:4-5).

Several motifs in the song sung by the doncela in the **Razón** (11. 41-50) are found also in the Song of Songs. The doncela's song expresses the desire of a woman to be with a lover about whom she has heard much but whom she does not know (11. 41-4); similarly, the ancient commentators described the entire Song of Songs as the desire of a wife (Israel) to be united with her husband (God) whom she has long forsaken and now knows only through the sayings of her forefathers. In line 45 the doncela sings that she would rather be with her lover than be queen of Spain; she repeats a similar choice in line 75 ('no vos camiar por un emperad—'). With regard to the doncela's preference, at least one medieval Spanish commentator of the Song of Songs noted that the story concerned a love triangle in which the woman chose her shepherd lover instead of King Solomon.

The doncela of the **Razón** has one fear resulting from her jealousy of another woman who is said to be deeply in love with the same lover (11. 46-9); but in spite of her jealousy she is confident that the lover will choose her (1. 50). This combination of jealousy and self-confidence is found also in the Song of Songs where the woman first acknowledges that other women love her lover; but towards the end of the book she is described as a confident winner by her lover ('Oleum effusum nomen tuum; ideo adolescentulae dilexerunt te . . . Sexaginta sunt reginae, et octoginta concubinae, et adolescentularum non est numerus. Una est columba mea, perfecta mea . . . Viderunt eam filiae, et beatissimam praedicaverunt; reginae et concubinae, et

laudaverunt eam' 1:2; 6:7-8).

The motif in line 51 of the **Razón**—of the woman who goes into a garden to work and is surprised there by a man—is found also in the Song of Songs ('Descendi in hortum nucum, ut viderem poma convallium, et inspicerem si floruisset vinea, et germinassent mala punica. Nescivi: anima mea conturbavit me, propter quadrigas Aminadab,' 6:11-12). Because the woman in the **Razón** has never seen her lover she cannot describe him precisely. Nevertheless, her description of him as intelligent and circumspect (11. 56-9) fits the more detailed description of the lover in the Song of Songs: 'Dilectus meus candidus et rubicundus; electus ex millibus . . . Guttur illius suavissimum, et totus desiderabilis' (5:10-16). The fact that the lover has made expensive gifts to the woman (11. 60-9) is yet another motif found in the Song of Songs ('Murenulas aureas faciemus tibi, vermiculatas argento, 1:10). Finally, the kiss in line 66 of the **Razón** and the long time the lovers spend savouring their love reflect motifs in the Song. 'Osculetur me osculo oris sui . . . Ut inveniam te foris, et deosculer te . . . Adiuro vos, filiae Jerusalem . . . ne suscitetis, neque evigilare faciatis dilectam, quoadusque ipsa velit' (1:1; 8:1; 2:7; 3:5).

Thus far I have commented on the **Razón de amor** line by line, and in the first seventy lines of the poem I have found very few sections that are not echoes of the Song of Songs. These echoes do not necessarily mean that the poet was working with a version of the Song of Songs in front of him; many of the motifs I have mentioned are ordinary themes that the author could have culled from numerous sources. Yet, by going directly to a mother lode of sources for medieval love lyrics, I believe I have been able to demonstrate that half of the **Razón de amor** belongs to the tradition of the Song of Songs. If it can be demonstrated that the second part of the poem, which has come to be known as the 'Duenestos del agua y el vino,' is also related to the Song of Songs, another reason will have been added to those arguments already made for the poem's unity. It does not much matter now when such a unity may have been conceived and executed, and by whom, whether by one poet before the composition of the entire poem or by another poet who attached a second part and reworked an earlier poem. The question is whether or not the poem in its present state is an artistic unit, and more specifically, whether or not the Song of Songs can help to clarify such thematic unity.

The second part of the **Razón** consists of three main elements, all of which can be related to the Song of Songs: the actions of a dove, a debate between wine and water, and the superiority of wine over water mainly because of wine's relationship to Christ. The dove is mentioned in several passages in the Song of Songs, and its behaviour in **Razón,** as represented by the spirit of wisdom, is clearly connected with the tradition of the

Song of Songs. The idea that wine and water are adversaries and should be made to debate with each other can be derived from the Song of Songs. Wine is repeatedly compared with love in the Song ('Quia meliora sunt ubera tua vino . . . Memores uberum tuorum super vinum . . . Pulchriora sunt ubera tua vino . . . Guttur tuum sicut vinum optimum,' 1:1,3; 4:10; 7:9). In the Song of Songs wine is the favoured drink of lovers ('Bibi vinum meum cum lacte meo. Comedite, amici, et bibite; et inebriamini, carissimi,' 5:1), and water is placed in an adversary position to love ('Aquae multae non potuerunt extinguere charitatem,' 8:7). The narrative unity of the *Razón* seems to be based on a question implied by the poet: Which substance leads to true love ('fin amor'), water or wine? The protagonist drinks water and immediately experiences an amorous encounter which, though pleasant enough while it lasts, leaves him sad and almost kills him (11. 76-7). A dove then appears to the poet and in a debate teaches him the wisdom of choosing wine over water.

The wise choice of wine over water is based on both wine's relationship to Christ and the equation found in commentaries on the Song of Songs that love is equal to wine because Christ is the true vine. We can be certain that medieval readers associated love with a special kind of wine because St Bernard, in his sermon on the Song of Songs verse beginning 'Introduxit me in cellam vinariam' (2:4), says explicitly that love is wine: 'Respondit mirum minime esse, si vino aestuaret, quae in cellam vinariam introisset. Et secundum litteram ita. Secundum spiritum quoque non negat ebriam, sed amore, non vino, nisi quod amor vinum est.' St Bernard's interpretation cannot be surprising since it is common in Christian commentaries that Christ is the bridegroom in the Song of Songs. If, therefore, in the *Razón* there are indications that love is equivalent to wine, the equation that love is wine (because of Christ) and water is the enemy will be seen as common to the Song of Songs and the *Razón*.

The language of both halves of the *Razón de amor* indicates that, in the mind of the poet, love is equivalent to wine. Wine is described in the first half of the poem as 'fino' (1. 9), and this is the same adjective used to describe love ('fin amor,' 1. 29). Moreover, it is evident that the courtly-love concept of *amor purus* and *amor mixtus* is based on an analogy to pure and mixed wine. This and many other courtly-love concepts are rooted ultimately in the Song of Songs. It is even easier in the second half of the *Razón de amor* to demonstrate that love is wine, because here everything that is said about wine applies equally to love. It can reasonably be said that love dislikes to be weakened by bad companions (11. 88-90); love does strange things to people's heads, making good people sceptical and wise ones mad (11. 95-8); love has no hands or feet and yet it has the power to conquer valiant men even as it conquered Sampson (11. 113-18); a table set

without love is worthless (1. 117); any rustic Romeo, giddy with love, will, if unassisted, stumble and fall (11. 120-2); love alters perception (11. 123-5); love is always stored as an honourable possession (1. 132); and that love works miracles, making the blind man see, the lame man walk, the dumb man speak, the sick man well, just as it says in the Bible that Jesus Christ, the source of love, worked miracles (11. 133-7). There can be no doubt that in the second half of the *Razón de amor* love is wine. Since, in the same section of the poem, water is engaged in verbal combat with wine, it follows logically that water is enemy to love.

Once it has been demonstrated that the equations that love is wine (because of Christ) and water is the enemy are common to both the tradition of the Song of Songs and the *Razón*, the thematic unity of the *Razón* can be considered established. The entire poem, not just the first half, is a 'razón acabada feyta de amor'— a title that reflects the title Canticum Canticorum Salomonis, The Song of Songs, which is Solomon's. The poet captures the full meaning of the biblical superlative with his 'acabada,' and uses the same enigmatic genitive that kept medieval commentators wondering whether the Song was written by Solomon, about him, or both. The title 'Denuestos' could be dropped, and the poem could be called *Razón* (compare Song), *Razón acabada* (compare Song of Songs), or *Razón de amor* (compare Song of Solomon).

With the wine-love-Christ equation in mind, a number of difficulties that have plagued previous interpretations of the poem can be clarified. Again I comment line by line, highlighting those lines that have not been sufficiently explained in the first part of this [essay]. I do not intend interpretations that precede or follow as definitive readings of *Razón;* nor do I mean to suggest that *Razón* must henceforth be understood always in the tradition of the Song of Songs. As Alicia de Colombí-Monguió has correctly pointed out, ambiguity in *Razón* is a necessary poetic device without which much of the work's artistry would be lost. I use the tradition of the Song of Songs throughout this chapter only as an heuristic tool to help explain the poem's unity, but other meanings and interpretations are surely elicited by this polysemous text. What follows, therefore, is a test to see if a reading of *Razón* in the tradition of the Song of Songs can be sustained justifiably throughout the poem.

Some editors follow Morel-Fatio and omit the invocation in line 1 entirely ('Sancti spiritus adsid nobis gratia amen'); others, after Menéndez Pidal, include it, but apart from the rest of the poem. But there seems sufficient reason to follow London's edition and count the invocation as the first line of the poem. The poet writing in the tradition of the Song of Songs chooses an appropriate invocation closely related to King Solomon. King Solomon asked God for wisdom (1 Kings 3:6-9), and in return he received divine inspiration to compose his works, including, according to the medieval commentators, the Song of Songs (1 Kings 4:29-32). Likewise, the poet of the *Razón* invokes the presence of the Holy Spirit and by implication, like Solomon, appeals for wisdom. Since both wisdom and the Holy Spirit are represented in the poem, this invocation, in so far as it foreshadows the appearance of wisdom and the Holy Spirit, ought to be considered an integral part of the whole work.

A careful analysis of the invocation alerts the reader to the fact that what seems commonplace in the poem might be of greater aesthetic significance. This is certainly true of line 2 of the poem, which on the surface seems to be a minstrel's stereotyped invitation to listeners. In fact, this line is a direct reference to the text in the Psalms beginning 'Et vinum laetificet cor hominis' (103:15), and is appropriate in the *Razón* for two reasons. First, the text was quoted by commentators on the passages about wine in the Song of Songs; St Bernard, for example, quotes it in his sermon on the third verse of the first chapter of the Song. Second, the same text forms a part of the literary tradition of the debate between wine and water; it is found, for example, in one of the Hebrew wine-and-water debates. The poet has therefore told careful readers in the second line of the poem exactly what the outcome of the *razón* will be: they should drink wine if they are sad at heart because 'wine makes the heart glad.' There is, in the second half of the poem, a similarly subtle use of cliché when the poet makes wine say 'placem de coraçó' (l. 112); it is fitting, according to Psalm 103:15, that wine should say that it is pleased at heart.

The poet promises in lines 3-6 to tell from experience why those who are lovesick should drink wine; not any kind of wine (note 'qui de *tal* vino,' l. 13), but a special kind of clear, red, fine wine that he once saw in a silver vessel, covered from the heat, in the bough of an apple tree; it had been placed there by the lady who owned the garden. Now these details do not make complete sense if they are to be taken only literally. How could the poet see what was inside a vessel in the bough of a tree if he was under another tree ('so un olivar,' l. 7)? Either he had prior knowledge of the contents of the vessel and of how it got on the bough, or his words are not to be taken only literally. If the poem was composed in the tradition of the Song of Songs, and it is accepted that this tradition is at the very core of allegory in Western literature, it can be safely assumed that the poet means these words to be taken figuratively as well as literally, as appropriate. What then do the apple tree, the covered silver vessel of wine, and the lady of the garden represent on the figurative level?

The apple tree is like the tree of knowledge of good and evil mentioned in Genesis 2:9-17. By choosing the tree from the book of Genesis the poet has not left the tradi-

tion of the Song of Songs. It was accepted medieval practice to compare the gardens of the Song of Songs with the gardens described in Genesis; and more importantly, when Solomon asked for wisdom he asked to be able to choose between good and evil ('Dabis ergo servo tuo . . . discernere inter bonum et malum,' 1 Kings 3:9).

The 'señora del huerto,' like the bride in the Song of Songs, is, in a Christian context, like the Church. In the Song of Songs she prepares a special wine for her lover ('Et dabo tibi poculum ex vino condito,' 8:2), and therefore was identified, by commentators on the Song, with wisdom who, in Proverbs 9:1-5, invites all to partake of her specially mixed wine: 'Sapientia aedificavit sibi domum . . . miscuit vinum, et proposuit mensam suam. Misit ancillas suas ut vocarent . . . "Venite . . . . . . et bibite vinum quod miscui vobis."' The wine in the silver vessel therefore is the good fruit placed on the apple tree of knowledge of good and evil; it is the wine of wisdom, the wine prepared by the Church. Note that the vessel of wine does not grow naturally on this tree but has been placed there (l. 11). The poet affirms that whoever drinks of this communion chalice every day while taking the host ('quan comiesse,' l. 13) shall never again fall ill. The poet probably knows this at first hand as a result of the experience about to be narrated; the words in lines 11-14, like those in the opening and closing lines (ll. 1-6, 145-6), refer to the moment of narration and must be distinguished from words referring to the events that occurred before the moment of narration (for example, ll. 7-10, 15-144).

The passage about the cup of water (ll. 15-29), like the one about wine, must be interpreted figuratively as well as literally because it is not explained how the poet could literally see the contents of the cup; it is not important to decide whether or not the poet fell asleep after line 19 and experienced in a dream what is related after that line. The entire passage is figurative as well as literal. So is the rest of the poem, for that matter, since wine and water cannot be understood, literally, to have debated with each other.

The cup of water represents the evil fruit on the tree of knowledge of good and evil. But water is not always evil. Since it is born of the tree of good as well as of evil water sometimes serves good purposes. For example, water nurtures the very tree on which it was born; it feeds the miracle-working aromatic herbs and flowers around the fountain (ll. 20-23); it makes the long-dried-up mother vine pregnant again (ll. 105-10); it cleans up dirty places (ll. 127-31); and it is used in the sacrament of baptism to give new life to Christians (ll. 139-44). But in spite of its good life-giving qualities, this water represents evil and is associated with death (note 'encantado,' l. 17, 'omme muerto,' l. 26, and 'muerta,' l. 118) because in Genesis 2:17 God promised man that if he ate of the evil fruit, he would surely die. Water is also associated with nakedness and with sex or carnal knowledge, because Adam realized his nakedness after he ate the fruit and 'knew' his wife, Eve. In this carnal sense, this water gives new life, in the form of sexual potency, to 'dead' lovers, a potency that, in terms of some common interpretations of Genesis, is the ultimate cause of death among mankind. Note that, unlike the vessel of wine, this evil fruit grows naturally on the tree ('en el mançanar s-nacía,' l. 16).

The water cup itself is not described as being of a precious metal, as is the silver vessel of wine, and wine later reminds water of this: 'C'a mi siepre me tiennen ornado de entro en buenna cubas condesado' (1. 132). The cup of water, unlike the vessel of wine, is uncovered, naked like Adam after he had eaten the fruit. So when the man (1. 19) and the woman (1. 66) disrobe, they align themselves symbolically with the cup of nakedness and carnal knowledge. For all these potentially evil reasons, the cup of water is described as being farther away from man's reach than the wine ('arriba del mançanar, 1. 15), not simply, as some have supposed, to facilitate the spilling of the water into the wine; if the water were below the wine, the dove—if it flew upwards out of the water—would still have been able to spill water into the wine.

There are, it seems, two fountains: one that rises out of the apple tree of knowledge of good and evil (1. 16), and another that feeds the herbs and flowers (11. 20-8). This interpretation of two fountains is later supported by lines 81-2 in which the dove avoids one fountain and flies to another, but the meaning of the text here is not as clear as it might be. These fountains, if there are two, are alike, since both contain a special kind of cold water (11. 16 and 21-2) which is to be compared with the two kinds of fountain waters described in the Song of Songs: the well of living waters (4:15), and the waters associated with death that cannot quench love (8:6-7). As with the tree of good and evil in Genesis and the waters of life and death in the Song, the waters of the fountains in the *Razón* can serve a double purpose. When the fountain is a baptismal font the purpose is good and the water gives new spiritual life to a spiritually dead person. But when the fountain is used for ordinary purposes, the water acts as an aphrodisiac which, through the smell of the flowers it feeds, arouses a sexually inactive man ('a omne muerto Ressucytarya,' 1. 26) without being able to quench his thirst for love.

It is crucial to the understanding of the *Razón de amor* to note that the man, an 'escolar,' does not use the water of the fountain for good, baptismal, purposes. Clearly, since he is a 'clergyo' (1. 57), he is already baptized. When he drinks of the water, ignoring the special wine of the church, he uses the fountain for ordinary purposes and the consequences of this use are immediately predictable. First of all he suffers a thorough chill (1. 27). (This is what biblical scholars and clerics described as the 'chill of Satan.') Then he takes

a flower in his hand. The smell of this flower, under good, baptismal circumstances, would have given him a spiritual resurrection and he would have then been able to sing of 'fin amor.' Instead, he is unable to sing of 'fin amor' (1. 29) because the sight of the 'doncela,' the most beautiful woman he has ever seen, sets his carnal waters flowing; the 'fin amor' this woman represents is unable to quench the escolar's thirst for love.

This beautiful 'doncela' is, like her surroundings, not evil; some of her qualities are like those of the wine: her complexion is clear and ruddy (11. 31-2, 35), and she is clothed. But she also possesses some qualities of the evil fruit: her face is as fresh as an apple (1. 32), reminiscent of the apple with which Eve tempted Adam, and her eyes are black and smiling (1. 34), not unlike the water described later in the poem as 'muerta Ridiendo' (1. 118). It becomes clear from the woman's song, and especially from her repeated use of the verb *conocer,* that the love she represents is not a spiritual 'fin amor,' but the carnal, perhaps illicit, love for a cleric. She is, in fact, Scientia, and she must be distinguished from Sapientia, the 'señora del huerto.' Scientia is not wisdom, which is probably represented by her rival, the 'dueña cortesa e bela e bona' (1. 47); she is worldly, carnal knowledge that comes but does not linger (compare 1 Corinthians 13:8), the noonday devil to whom St Bernard dedicates an entire sermon on verse 6 of the first chapter of the Song of Songs. Scientia, like the waters of the Song, cannot quench love's thirst, and, as a consequence, leaves the love-sick cleric as sad ('desconortado,' 1. 76) as the listeners to whom he appeals in line 2, and almost dead (1. 77).

It is a well-worn theme in medieval literature that someone who has come very close to death experiences a visionary insight into truth. Such an experience is often described as taking place in the twilight world between sleep and wakefulness, which is why the cleric explains that he really wanted to sleep ('por verdat quisieram adormir,' 1. 78). Because of the visionary nature of this experience, the dove and its actions should be interpreted both literally and figuratively.

The dove is mentioned several times in the Song of Songs (1:15, 2:14; 4:1; 5:2, 12; 6:9), but the verse that fits most closely the scene in the *Razón* is the one in which the lover's eyes are described as doves, bathed in milk, beside streams of water ('Oculi eius sicut columbae super rivulos aquarum, quae lacte sunt lotae, et resident iuxta fluenta plenissima,' 5:12). The motifs of whiteness (1. 79) and bathing (1. 82) are present also in the *Razón*. In order to understand what the dove represents on a figurative level, one must note that, on the literal level, the dove's behaviour is exactly the opposite of that of the doncela. The cleric is certain that the doncela, although she does not know him, will not flee when she sees him (1. 52); but this is exactly what the dove does ('en la funte quiso entra mas quando a mi vido estar / etros' en la del malgranar,' 11. 81-2). The fact that the dove flees from the cleric makes it easy to identify the bird on the figurative level. In Solomon's Book of Wisdom, in the sentence before the one to which the invocation of the **Razón** refers, the wisdom of the Holy Spirit is described as refusing to enter a sinful body or soul and fleeing from deceit ('Quoniam in malevolam animam non introibit sapientia, nec habitabit in corpore subdito peccatis. Spiritus enim sanctus disciplinae effugiet fictum').

The dove, therefore, is the wisdom of the Holy Spirit, which rejected the sinful cleric when he was a disciple of water and taught him to be a disciple of the right wine. The dove does not attempt to *drink* the water of evil. It enters the fountain/cup and, like the poet, feels or pretends to feel the chill of cupidity (1. 85), but it flies out immediately ('festino,') 1. 86), shaking the water from its body on to the wine of wisdom. The dove thus gives a graphic lesson to the cleric about how he should behave, and the lesson is further impressed upon the cleric's mind by wine's victory in the debate with water.

Before some points in the debate are clarified, it would be well to examine closely two 'mistakes' attributed to the poet or to the scribe. It has been noted that the vessel of wine is never uncovered; at least one critic believes that this detail is an error because, if the vessel remained covered, the water could not have been spilled into it. But we have already shown that the vessel of wine remains covered for very sound aesthetic and symbolic reasons related to the nakedness of Adam and Eve. Clearly the wine must have been covered with a fine porous cloth (like a ritual corporal) through which water would pass as easily as through a sieve. The poet is also supposed to have erred in lines 82-3 in which 'malgranar' should have been 'mançanar.' Since this passage is not only repeated but also garbled, there is good reason to suppose the cause was either scribal error or the poet's bad memory. However, the poet might have deliberately used 'malgranar' for at least two valid reasons: first, pomegranates are mentioned three times in the Song (4:12, 7:12; 8:2), twice juxtaposed with reference to wine; second, the Latin name for pomegranate (*malum granatum*) describes a kind of apple that, because of its first by syllable in Spanish (mal-), connotes evil.

We have seen how the subtlety of the debate between wine and water lies mainly in the facts that everything said about wine applies equally well to love, and everything said about water belies its dual function as a fruit on the tree of knowledge of good and evil. As early as the poem's second line, we have seen a subtle anticipation of the outcome of the debate, namely, that those who are sad at heart should drink wine, not water. Not everyone will agree that this is the outcome of the debate. Some will want to agree with Spitzer that the

outcome of the debate is a reconciliation between two warring elements, a *concordia discors:* 'C'est comme si l'auteur, fine mouche, nous disait, "L'eau est aussi nécessaire que le vin—donnez-moi *donc* du vin!"' Others may want to claim that water has won the debate because it seems to have the last word. This claim rests on the assumption that the extant version is complete, which is not necessarily true. It remains to be demonstrated, therefore, even in spite of all that has been said about the wine of wisdom and the water of evil, precisely how water has been made to concede defeat.

Water's final claim (11. 139-44) is characteristic of its duplicitous nature throughout the poem: what seems like a solid defence and victory is, in fact, a self-defeating argument. It seems conclusive for water to imply that since baptism is essential in Christianity, wine must be baptized (hence watered down) in order to be called a child of God—a very clever argument on the surface. But wine does not need to reply to this argument because water has already conceded, in line 106, that everybody knows that wine is the child of God ('que no a homne que no lo sepa que fillo *sodes* de la çepa'); everybody knows that Christ is reported to have said, 'I am the true vine' (John 15:1); so everybody also knows, as water admits, that wine, the fruit of the vine, is the child of God.

Wine does not need to repeat itself because it has already said precisely that it is the child of God in its much misunderstood climactic argument in line 137 ('asi co dize en el scripto de fazem' el cuerpo de iesu Xo'). This line is normally assumed to refer directly to the sacrament of Communion, but this cannot be, because in this sacrament wine becomes the *blood* of Jesus, not the 'cuerpo de iesu Xo' (Matthew 26:26-8). The subject of 'fazem' is 'el cuerpo de iesu Xo,' not 'el scripto.' So the meaning of the line is, 'just as it tells in the Scripture about the body of Christ making me,' not 'where it [the Scripture] makes me the body of Christ.'

It is clear that the poet intends to refer vaguely to Communion with the well-known phrase 'cuerpo de iesu Xo,' but he means to refer specifically to instances where the body of Christ associates itself with wine. The most memorable of such instances is at the wedding at Cana where Jesus worked the miracle of changing water into wine (John 2:1-11). We can be certain that line 137 refers to this miracle because it comes at the end of references to other miracles Christ performed—making the blind see, the lame walk, the dumb speak, and the sick well (11. 135-6). Another memorable instance where Christ associates himself with wine is when he says, in John 15:1, 'I am the true vine.' So line 137 must be interpreted to mean 'just as it tells in the Scripture about the body of Christ, the true vine, making me, wine.' In other words, since the body of Christ, the true vine, made wine, everybody knows that wine is the child of God, which is exactly what water concedes in line 106 ('que fillo sodes de la çepa').

The poet's ending of the debate after water's self-defeating argument is, therefore, by no means abrupt. What water says in lines 138-44 not only has no effect on wine's argument but also proves wine correct, *quod erat demonstrandum*. Similarly, what water says in lines 138-44 not only has no effect on the narrator's experience, but also proves the decision artistically correct to end the debate and call for wine in line 145 ('Mi razón aqui la fino e mandat nos dar vino'). What water says about baptism convinces the narrator that he should end the debate and call for wine because he knows that when he drank the water he could not possibly have been thinking about baptism. Baptism is a sacrament usually performed only once, and not only was he, a cleric, already baptized, but (if Jacob is right about a Lenten setting) baptism was forbidden during Lent. The narrator is forced to concede that water and baptism, though essential, are not sufficient to cure his lovesickness, because even though baptized, he drank water and ended up sick again ('desconortado,' 1.76). This is theologically sound in a Christian context: baptism is essential for salvation, but is not sufficient to guarantee it. Spitzer is therefore not correct in asserting that the poet orders wine because, since both water and wine are essential, either will suffice. The poet orders wine because he has learned that water will make him sick again, and that only wine can cure his illness, as claimed in lines 14 and 136 of the poem.

Line 146 offers further proof of why the narrator orders wine. In the light of how subtly the poet has used stereotyped expressions throughout the poem, it would be unwise to treat this line as a mere cliché typical of an explicit. Like the invocation, which also reads like a cliché, the explicit is an integral part of the poem. When the text says, 'Seper cum Domino bibat,' the poet is not just punning ('bibat' for 'vivat'), nor does the text mean, 'May he drink [either water or wine] forever with the Lord.' Instead he is referring specifically to the promise Christ made to his disciples that they would drink wine with him in the Kingdom of Heaven: 'Dico autem vobis: non bibam amodo de hoc genimine vitis usque in diem illum, cum illud bibam vobiscum novum in regno Patris mei' (Matthew 26:29). The key word in this text, 'vobiscum,' is what causes the poet to write 'cum Domino.'

It would be equally unwise to dismiss the signature of the poem ('Lupus me fecit de moros') as simply the name of a poet from a town, in Saragossa, north of Ateca. There is ample reason to suppose that even if Lupus de Moros were a real person, the name also alludes to the fact that the poem thus signed is an attack on Moorish customs, written by a wolf among the Moors. It is well known that Muslims are prohibited from drinking wine on earth, and a poem that

urges the drinking of wine on earth obviously flies in the face of a Muslim religious precept. It is also well known that although Muslims are prohibited from wine on earth, they are repeatedly promised wine in Paradise. (Indeed, numerous passages of the Koran sound much like the scene in the *locus amoenus* of the **Razón de amor**.) Here are three typical examples:

> The righteous shall surely dwell in bliss . . . They shall drink of a pure wine, securely sealed . . . a wine tempered with the waters of Tasnim, a spring at which the favoured will refresh themselves. (83:22-8)

> Allah . . . will reward them for their steadfastness with robes of silk and the delights of Paradise. Reclining there upon soft couches, they shall feel neither the scorching heat nor the biting cold. Trees will spread their shade around them, and fruits will hang in clusters over them. They shall be served with silver dishes, and beakers large as goblets; silver goblets which they themselves shall measure: and cups brim-full with ginger flavoured water from the Fount of Selsabil. (76:12-17)

> They shall recline on jewelled couches face to face, and there shall wait on them immortal youths with bowls and ewers and a cup of wine (that will neither pain their heads nor take away their reason); with fruits of their own choice and flesh of fowls that they relish. And theirs shall be the dark-eyed houris, chaste as hidden pearls: a guerdon for their deeds. (56:15-23)

The pure wine securely covered, the springs, the special water, the silver vessels, the heat and cold, the shady trees, the dark-eyed houri, all are reminiscent of the *Razón de amor*. As well, the Koran has a passage about disrobing at noon: 'Believers, let your slaves and children ask your leave when they come in to see you before the morning prayer, when you have put off your garments in the heat of noon, and after the evening prayer' (24:57).

The Koran alludes to the twofold function of water—as the original good substance from which all life was created, and as the dirty substance in carnal love: 'Are the disbelievers unaware that the heavens and the earth were one solid mass which We tore asunder, and that We made every living thing of water? (21:31) . . . 'Let man reflect from what he is created. He is created from an ejected fluid, that issues from between the loin and the ribs' (86:57). The descriptions of Paradise in the Koran are filled with streams of pure water. Since water is such an important substance in the Muslim pre-prayer ritual (wudu), one wonders whether the references in the *Razón* to water and baptism are not also attacks on Muslim ablutions, which have been compared to Christian baptism. It is important to note that these quotations from the Koran are by no means a departure from the tradition of the Song of Songs. The descriptions of Paradise in the Koran are either directly dependent upon the Song of Songs and its parallel in Genesis or, if not directly dependent, at the very least were written in the same Semitic tradition. The *Razón de amor* could hardly have been written other than in Spain where Jews, Christians, and Muslims scrutinized each other's religious practices for centuries.

To sum up: the *Razón de amor* is a Judaeo-Christian poem written (perhaps in an environment in which there were many Moors) to warn clerics against the sin of *luxuria*. Additional circumstantial support for this claim exists in the document attached to the poem and written in the same hand. This document on the Ten Commandments was attached to the *Razón de amor* probably because both works are aimed at the instruction of priests and both sets of instructions deal mainly with luxuria. The *Razón de amor* tells priests how to avoid luxuria themselves, while the attached document tells priests how to deal with luxuria when they hear the confessions of their parishioners. Consequently, although the general tendency in *Razón de amor* criticism has been to ignore the attached addendum, this document merits a more careful examination to see if it reveals how a priest who read it might have interpreted the *Razón*.

The document can be divided into two parts. The first part lists the Commandments one by one and explains how sins are committed against each one, in order that the priest will know how to question the confessant concerning each commandment. The second part instructs the priest how to probe the confessant about sins committed through the five senses, on the job, with the body, mind, and soul, through omission, and with one's wife. This second part also reminds the priest that sins are of three kinds (against God, against one's neighbour, and against oneself), and explains how to exact proper penance for sins, to process serious sins, to dismiss the confessant, and lastly, how to pray for the scribe who wrote the work.

It is not surprising to read in this document that the priest is instructed to probe for luxuria in the commandments against fornication and coveting a neighbour's wife. But it is revealing to observe that luxuria is discussed even under a commandment like 'keeping the Sabbath holy,' where the priest is told to ask if the confessant 'canto cantares luxoriosos en vigilias.' Luxuria is also implied in the commandment against murder: 'E quinto es: *Non mataras*. En este peca qui mata de feito o de voluntat o por mal exemplo, o, si, pudo, que no liuro de muerte a so cristiano, o si mato nino chiquielo [en] el vientre de so madre, o ensenno erbas con que lo matasen o dieu erbas a alguno con que mories.'

It is well to remember that instructions like these were written partly because they were ignored. Nevertheless, since the medieval Christian world was made up of confessors and confessants in constant contact with each other, it is easy to imagine an ordinary priest who took his job seriously wondering, as he read the *Razón de amor,* if the doncela ever sang lustful songs on the Sabbath, or if she had anything to do with the special water her lover drank that almost killed him, or if she collected special flowers and herbs for purposes of abortion. If he were a more learned priest, he would, of course, understand the tradition of allegorized lust in which the poem was written.

In the second part of the document an entire paragraph is devoted to lust, even lust between husband and wife. Here the priest is instructed that the third category of sin (against oneself) is committed 'por comer e por beber e por luxuria,' that the penance for this category is fasting, flagellation, and pilgrimage, and that the sin of lying with a virgin is serious enough to be referred to the bishop. But the most revealing passage of this part is the one about the five senses:

> E deve demandar el preste al pecador si va veder fornicaciones o las mulleres, como non deviese bolver sos ollos a la vanidat, e demandel si vaveder lo[s] juegos los dias domingos o de las fiestas; el del odor: si porta con si musco [o] otras odores; del odir: si ode buenaminetre cantares o otros omnes que dicen paraulas feas, que los pecadores enujan se de odir la misa e las paraulas de Dios, e de los cantares de la[s] caçurias non se enuyan e beven el vino puro e las carnes calentes e muytas por raçon de luxuria e beven huevos por exa raçon, ed es mayor pecado que si quebrantas la quaresma: del taner: si toco muller en las tetas o en otro lugar de vergonça.

Again it is easy to imagine a literal-minded priest wondering, as he read the *Razón,* if the *locus amoenus* where the lovers disrobed was a favourite spot for voyeurs, if anything in the garden smelled of lustful musk oil, if the cleric enjoyed listening to the doncela's song as much as he enjoyed listening to mass. He might also wonder where the cleric touched the doncela, and, especially, if the cleric drank pure wine for lustful aphrodisiac purposes.

The priest would probably classify the cleric's offence in the category of sins against oneself (since it involved eating, drinking, and luxuria), and would have either ordered the confessant to fast and flagellate (but not go on pilgrimage since that is where he seemed to have met a lot of dueñas). For lying with a virgin, the priest would have referred the poet to the bishop. The bishop, a more learned reader, would probably have been pleased that the poet had either confessed his sin or invented a cleric who could narrate a subtle and learned autobiographical testimony for the benefit of other clerics; he would have probably reminded the poet of how God punished King Solomon for his lustfulness, and urged him to continue taking Holy Communion daily to either avoid recidivism or prevent his autobiographical fiction from ever becoming fact.

As far as the Moorish environment is concerned, the evidence in the document on confession is as slight as it is in the *Razón de amor*. This evidence is implied in the translation of the biblical *neighbour* in the first part of the document on confession. The Vulgate uses 'proximus' for 'neighbour,' and the author of the document was aware of this because he used 'próximo' twice in the second part, in the paragraph about the three kinds of sins. But in the first part of the document 'neighbour' is translated as 'cristiano' (for example, 'que no livro de muerte a so cristiano,' 'Non cobdiciaras ren de to cristiano,' and 'Non cobdiciaras de to cristiano la muller'). The implication is that the author was probably writing in a context in which one's neighbour was not necessarily Christian.

In the history of literary composition in medieval Spain, the document on confession is, of course, more important to the study of works that are arranged around the Ten Commandments and the five senses (like Talavera's *Corbacho*) than to the study of the *Razón de amor*. Nevertheless, the document does demonstrate that luxuria was a subject important enough to cause a prosaic tract on confession to be copied in the same manuscript in the same hand as a subtle allegorical poem written in the tradition of the Song of Songs. This juxtaposition adds support for the working hypothesis that questions posed from a European perspective about Christian symbolism, Cathar heresies, grail legends, troubadours, classical traditions, and goliards, though often essential, are not always sufficient without questions about luxuria and the biblical tradition in the composition of certain medieval Spanish works. This is not to say that in the rest of Europe confession is incompatible with lust, but simply to suggest that in medieval Spain the universal debate about wine, women, and song (common to both the document on confession and the *Razón de amor*) sometimes has a special biblical and Semitic flavour.

The pagan paradise described in the *Razón de amor,* although resembling the *locus amoenus* of world literature, has a greater affinity with the Koran than with European literature; this is the negative paradise that later evolved in Spain into the 'infierno de los enamorados' so popular with Santillana and his fifteenth-century contemporaries. After the *Razón de amor,* medieval Spanish writers did not forget the exegetical tradition of the Song of Songs. Santillana, for example, refers to the Church, in one of his sonnets, as 'la sancta esposa'; he quotes the Song directly in his 'Goços de nuestra Señora'; in his 'Canonización de los bienaventurados sanctos' he dresses the Virgin Mary

in the words of Solomon; and he begins his 'Triunfete de amor' with a noonday vision. In fact it can be said with fairness of Santillana and his contemporaries that their constant reference to classical literature is in large measure a superficial varnish, a thick 'fermosa cobertura,' for their fundamental commitment to biblical themes, and especially to the Song of Songs, which the Spanish love lyric imitates. Even in *Celestina,* in which there is so much Petrarch, the prime mover of the story is that Calisto has dared to transform the *hortus conclusus* and the Virgin Mary of the Song of Songs into his own church/garden and god ('Melibeo so e a Melibea adoro e en Melibea creo e a Melibea amo . . . Por Dios la creo'). But although the Song and its motifs remain present in medieval Spanish literature, they do not predominate aesthetically and artistically after the *Razón de amor* until, of course, the work of the mystics in the sixteenth century, beyond the medieval period.

In the light of this strong reliance in Spain on the Bible, it is not surprising that the references in the *Razón de amor* are, in its first part, to the Old Testament, and in its second part to the New Testament, and that events in the first part prefigure those in the second part. The bipartite composition, which has caused critics to consider it two poems, is therefore precisely what lends it unity, a unity reflected in the composition of the Christian Bible and its exegesis. This method of composition remains faithful to the tradition of the Song of Songs because Christian exegetes have interpreted Christ, the true vine in the New Testament, to be prefigured as the bridegroom in the Song.

FURTHER READING

Deyermond, A. D. "The Literature of the Thirteenth-Century Expansion." In his *A Literary History of Spain: The Middle Ages*, 55-81. London: Ernest Benn, 1971.
> Discusses *Razón de amor* in the context of other Medieval Spanish debate-poems, referring to it as "puzzling."

Goldberg, Harriet. "The Dream Report as a Literary Device in Medieval Hispanic Literature." *Hispania* 66, No. 1 (March, 1983): 21-31.
> Survey of Medieval Spanish dream literature that briefly refers to the *Razón de amor.*

London, G. H. "The *Razón de amor* and the 'Denuestos del agua y el vino': New Readings and Interpretations." *Romance Philology* XIX, No. 1, (August, 1965): 28-47.
> A translation along with technical notes on the manuscript, language, and transcription.

Spitzer, Leo. *"Razón de amor."* *Romania* 71 (1950): 145-65.

> Seminal critical article on the *Razón de amor,* available only in French.

CLASSICAL
AND MEDIEVAL
LITERATURE
CRITICISM

INDEXES

Literary Criticism Series
Cumulative Author Index

Literary Criticism Series
Cumulative Topic Index

CMLC Cumulative Nationality Index

CMLC Cumulative Title Index

CMLC Cumulative Critic Index

How to Use This Index

The main references

Calvino, Italo
1923-1985.....CLC 5, 8, 11, 22, 33, 39,
73; SSC 3

list all author entries in the following Gale Literary Criticism series:

BLC = *Black Literature Criticism*
CLC = *Contemporary Literary Criticism*
CLR = *Children's Literature Review*
CMLC = *Classical and Medieval Literature Criticism*
DA = *DISCovering Authors*
DC = *Drama Criticism*
HLC = *Hispanic Literature Criticism*
LC = *Literature Criticism from 1400 to 1800*
NCLC = *Nineteenth-Century Literature Criticism*
PC = *Poetry Criticism*
SSC = *Short Story Criticism*
TCLC = *Twentieth-Century Literary Criticism*
WLC = *World Literature Criticism, 1500 to the Present*

The cross-references

See also CANR 23; CA 85-88;
obituary CA 116

list all author entries in the following Gale biographical and literary sources:

AAYA = *Authors & Artists for Young Adults*
AITN = *Authors in the News*
BEST = *Bestsellers*
BW = *Black Writers*
CA = *Contemporary Authors*
CAAS = *Contemporary Authors Autobiography Series*
CABS = *Contemporary Authors Bibliographical Series*
CANR = *Contemporary Authors New Revision Series*
CAP = *Contemporary Authors Permanent Series*
CDALB = *Concise Dictionary of American Literary Biography*
CDBLB = *Concise Dictionary of British Literary Biography*
DLB = *Dictionary of Literary Biography*
DLBD = *Dictionary of Literary Biography Documentary Series*
DLBY = *Dictionary of Literary Biography Yearbook*
HW = *Hispanic Writers*
JRDA = *Junior DISCovering Authors*
MAICYA = *Major Authors and Illustrators for Children and Young Adults*
MTCW = *Major 20th-Century Writers*
NNAL = *Native North American Literature*
SAAS = *Something about the Author Autobiography Series*
SATA = *Something about the Author*
YABC = *Yesterday's Authors of Books for Children*

Literary Criticism Series
Cumulative Author Index

A. E.........................TCLC 3, 10
See also Russell, George William

Abasiyanik, Sait Faik 1906-1954
See Sait Faik
See also CA 123

Abbey, Edward 1927-1989......CLC 36, 59
See also CA 45-48; 128; CANR 2, 41

Abbott, Lee K(ittredge) 1947-......CLC 48
See also CA 124; DLB 130

Abe, Kobo 1924-1993.....CLC 8, 22, 53, 81
See also CA 65-68; 140; CANR 24; MTCW

Abelard, Peter c. 1079-c. 1142 ... CMLC 11
See also DLB 115

Abell, Kjeld 1901-1961............CLC 15
See also CA 111

Abish, Walter 1931-..............CLC 22
See also CA 101; CANR 37; DLB 130

Abrahams, Peter (Henry) 1919- .....CLC 4
See also BW 1; CA 57-60; CANR 26;
DLB 117; MTCW

Abrams, M(eyer) H(oward) 1912-... CLC 24
See also CA 57-60; CANR 13, 33; DLB 67

Abse, Dannie 1923-.............CLC 7, 29
See also CA 53-56; CAAS 1; CANR 4, 46;
DLB 27

Achebe, (Albert) Chinua(lumogu)
1930- .....CLC 1, 3, 5, 7, 11, 26, 51, 75;
BLC; DA; WLC
See also BW 2; CA 1-4R; CANR 6, 26, 47;
CLR 20; DLB 117; MAICYA; MTCW;
SATA 40; SATA-Brief 38

Acker, Kathy 1948- ....CLC 45
See also CA 117; 122

Ackroyd, Peter 1949-..........CLC 34, 52
See also CA 123; 127

Acorn, Milton 1923-..............CLC 15
See also CA 103; DLB 53

Adamov, Arthur 1908-1970 ......CLC 4, 25
See also CA 17-18; 25-28R; CAP 2; MTCW

Adams, Alice (Boyd) 1926- ... CLC 6, 13, 46
See also CA 81-84; CANR 26; DLBY 86;
MTCW

Adams, Andy 1859-1935..........TCLC 56
See also YABC 1

Adams, Douglas (Noel) 1952- ... CLC 27, 60
See also AAYA 4; BEST 89:3; CA 106;
CANR 34; DLBY 83; JRDA

Adams, Francis 1862-1893...... NCLC 33

Adams, Henry (Brooks)
1838-1918 .... TCLC 4, 52; DA
See also CA 104; 133; DLB 12, 47

Adams, Richard (George)
1920- ....CLC 4, 5, 18
See also AITN 1, 2; CA 49-52; CANR 3,
35; CLR 20; JRDA; MAICYA; MTCW;
SATA 7, 69

Adamson, Joy(-Friederike Victoria)
1910-1980 ....CLC 17
See also CA 69-72; 93-96; CANR 22;
MTCW; SATA 11; SATA-Obit 22

Adcock, Fleur 1934-..............CLC 41
See also CA 25-28R; CANR 11, 34;
DLB 40

Addams, Charles (Samuel)
1912-1988 ....CLC 30
See also CA 61-64; 126; CANR 12

Addison, Joseph 1672-1719.........LC 18
See also CDBLB 1660-1789; DLB 101

Adler, C(arole) S(chwerdtfeger)
1932-........................CLC 35
See also AAYA 4; CA 89-92; CANR 19,
40; JRDA; MAICYA; SAAS 15;
SATA 26, 63

Adler, Renata 1938-............CLC 8, 31
See also CA 49-52; CANR 5, 22; MTCW

Ady, Endre 1877-1919...........TCLC 11
See also CA 107

Aeschylus
525B.C.-456B.C......... CMLC 11; DA

Afton, Effie
See Harper, Frances Ellen Watkins

Agapida, Fray Antonio
See Irving, Washington

Agee, James (Rufus)
1909-1955...............TCLC 1, 19
See also AITN 1; CA 108;
CDALB 1941-1968; DLB 2, 26, 152

Aghill, Gordon
See Silverberg, Robert

Agnon, S(hmuel) Y(osef Halevi)
1888-1970 ....CLC 4, 8, 14
See also CA 17-18; 25-28R; CAP 2; MTCW

Agrippa von Nettesheim, Henry Cornelius
1486-1535 ....LC 27

Aherne, Owen
See Cassill, R(onald) V(erlin)

Ai 1947-....................CLC 4, 14, 69
See also CA 85-88; CAAS 13; DLB 120

Aickman, Robert (Fordyce)
1914-1981 ....CLC 57
See also CA 5-8R; CANR 3

Aiken, Conrad (Potter)
1889-1973 ... CLC 1, 3, 5, 10, 52; SSC 9
See also CA 5-8R; 45-48; CANR 4;
CDALB 1929-1941; DLB 9, 45, 102;
MTCW; SATA 3, 30

Aiken, Joan (Delano) 1924-........CLC 35
See also AAYA 1; CA 9-12R; CANR 4, 23,
34; CLR 1, 19; JRDA; MAICYA;
MTCW; SAAS 1; SATA 2, 30, 73

Ainsworth, William Harrison
1805-1882 ....NCLC 13
See also DLB 21; SATA 24

Aitmatov, Chingiz (Torekulovich)
1928-......................CLC 71
See also CA 103; CANR 38; MTCW;
SATA 56

Akers, Floyd
See Baum, L(yman) Frank

Akhmadulina, Bella Akhatovna
1937-........................CLC 53
See also CA 65-68

Akhmatova, Anna
1888-1966 ....CLC 11, 25, 64; PC 2
See also CA 19-20; 25-28R; CANR 35;
CAP 1; MTCW

Aksakov, Sergei Timofeyvich
1791-1859 ....NCLC 2

Aksenov, Vassily
See Aksyonov, Vassily (Pavlovich)

Aksyonov, Vassily (Pavlovich)
1932-....................CLC 22, 37
See also CA 53-56; CANR 12, 48

Akutagawa Ryunosuke
1892-1927 ....TCLC 16
See also CA 117

Alain 1868-1951 ....TCLC 41

Alain-Fournier....................TCLC 6
See also Fournier, Henri Alban
See also DLB 65

Alarcon, Pedro Antonio de
1833-1891 ....NCLC 1

Alas (y Urena), Leopoldo (Enrique Garcia)
1852-1901 ....TCLC 29
See also CA 113; 131; HW

Albee, Edward (Franklin III)
1928-......CLC 1, 2, 3, 5, 9, 11, 13, 25,
53, 86; DA; WLC
See also AITN 1; CA 5-8R; CABS 3;
CANR 8; CDALB 1941-1968; DLB 7;
MTCW

Alberti, Rafael 1902- ....CLC 7
See also CA 85-88; DLB 108

Albert the Great 1200(?)-1280.... CMLC 16
See also DLB 115

Alcala-Galiano, Juan Valera y
See Valera y Alcala-Galiano, Juan

Alcott, Amos Bronson 1799-1888 .. NCLC 1
See also DLB 1

Alcott, Louisa May
1832-1888 ....NCLC 6; DA; WLC
See also CDALB 1865-1917; CLR 1, 38;
DLB 1, 42, 79; JRDA; MAICYA;
YABC 1

Aldanov, M. A.
See Aldanov, Mark (Alexandrovich)

Aldanov, Mark (Alexandrovich)
1886(?)-1957 ....TCLC 23
See also CA 118

Aldington, Richard 1892-1962...... **CLC 49**
See also CA 85-88; CANR 45; DLB 20, 36, 100, 149

Aldiss, Brian W(ilson)
1925- .... **CLC 5, 14, 40**
See also CA 5-8R; CAAS 2; CANR 5, 28; DLB 14; MTCW; SATA 34

Alegria, Claribel 1924-........... **CLC 75**
See also CA 131; CAAS 15; DLB 145; HW

Alegria, Fernando 1918-.......... **CLC 57**
See also CA 9-12R; CANR 5, 32; HW

Aleichem, Sholom .... **TCLC 1, 35**
See also Rabinovitch, Sholem

Aleixandre, Vicente 1898-1984 ... **CLC 9, 36**
See also CA 85-88; 114; CANR 26; DLB 108; HW; MTCW

Alepoudelis, Odysseus
See Elytis, Odysseus

Aleshkovsky, Joseph 1929-
See Aleshkovsky, Yuz
See also CA 121; 128

Aleshkovsky, Yuz .... **CLC 44**
See also Aleshkovsky, Joseph

Alexander, Lloyd (Chudley) 1924- .. **CLC 35**
See also AAYA 1; CA 1-4R; CANR 1, 24, 38; CLR 1, 5; DLB 52; JRDA; MAICYA; MTCW; SAAS 19; SATA 3, 49, 81

Alfau, Felipe 1902-............... **CLC 66**
See also CA 137

Alger, Horatio, Jr. 1832-1899..... **NCLC 8**
See also DLB 42; SATA 16

Algren, Nelson 1909-1981 .... **CLC 4, 10, 33**
See also CA 13-16R; 103; CANR 20; CDALB 1941-1968; DLB 9; DLBY 81, 82; MTCW

Ali, Ahmed 1910- .... **CLC 69**
See also CA 25-28R; CANR 15, 34

Alighieri, Dante 1265-1321 .... **CMLC 3**

Allan, John B.
See Westlake, Donald E(dwin)

Allen, Edward 1948-.............. **CLC 59**

Allen, Paula Gunn 1939-.......... **CLC 84**
See also CA 112; 143; NNAL

Allen, Roland
See Ayckbourn, Alan

Allen, Sarah A.
See Hopkins, Pauline Elizabeth

Allen, Woody 1935-............ **CLC 16, 52**
See also AAYA 10; CA 33-36R; CANR 27, 38; DLB 44; MTCW

Allende, Isabel 1942- .... **CLC 39, 57; HLC**
See also CA 125; 130; DLB 145; HW; MTCW

Alleyn, Ellen
See Rossetti, Christina (Georgina)

Allingham, Margery (Louise)
1904-1966 .... **CLC 19**
See also CA 5-8R; 25-28R; CANR 4; DLB 77; MTCW

Allingham, William 1824-1889 ... **NCLC 25**
See also DLB 35

Allison, Dorothy E. 1949-......... **CLC 78**
See also CA 140

Allston, Washington 1779-1843.... **NCLC 2**
See also DLB 1

Almedingen, E. M. .... **CLC 12**
See also Almedingen, Martha Edith von
See also SATA 3

Almedingen, Martha Edith von 1898-1971
See Almedingen, E. M.
See also CA 1-4R; CANR 1

Almqvist, Carl Jonas Love
1793-1866 .... **NCLC 42**

Alonso, Damaso 1898-1990 .... **CLC 14**
See also CA 110; 131; 130; DLB 108; HW

Alov
See Gogol, Nikolai (Vasilyevich)

Alta 1942-....................... **CLC 19**
See also CA 57-60

Alter, Robert B(ernard) 1935-...... **CLC 34**
See also CA 49-52; CANR 1, 47

Alther, Lisa 1944-.............. **CLC 7, 41**
See also CA 65-68; CANR 12, 30; MTCW

Altman, Robert 1925-............. **CLC 16**
See also CA 73-76; CANR 43

Alvarez, A(lfred) 1929-.......... **CLC 5, 13**
See also CA 1-4R; CANR 3, 33; DLB 14, 40

Alvarez, Alejandro Rodriguez 1903-1965
See Casona, Alejandro
See also CA 131; 93-96; HW

Alvaro, Corrado 1896-1956 .... **TCLC 60**

Amado, Jorge 1912-..... **CLC 13, 40; HLC**
See also CA 77-80; CANR 35; DLB 113; MTCW

Ambler, Eric 1909-............ **CLC 4, 6, 9**
See also CA 9-12R; CANR 7, 38; DLB 77; MTCW

Amichai, Yehuda 1924- ...... **CLC 9, 22, 57**
See also CA 85-88; CANR 46; MTCW

Amiel, Henri Frederic 1821-1881 .. **NCLC 4**

Amis, Kingsley (William)
1922- .. **CLC 1, 2, 3, 5, 8, 13, 40, 44; DA**
See also AITN 2; CA 9-12R; CANR 8, 28; CDBLB 1945-1960; DLB 15, 27, 100, 139; MTCW

Amis, Martin (Louis)
1949- .... **CLC 4, 9, 38, 62**
See also BEST 90:3; CA 65-68; CANR 8, 27; DLB 14

Ammons, A(rchie) R(andolph)
1926- .... **CLC 2, 3, 5, 8, 9, 25, 57**
See also AITN 1; CA 9-12R; CANR 6, 36; DLB 5; MTCW

Amo, Tauraatua i
See Adams, Henry (Brooks)

Anand, Mulk Raj 1905-........... **CLC 23**
See also CA 65-68; CANR 32; MTCW

Anatol
See Schnitzler, Arthur

Anaya, Rudolfo A(lfonso)
1937- .... **CLC 23; HLC**
See also CA 45-48; CAAS 4; CANR 1, 32; DLB 82; HW 1; MTCW

Andersen, Hans Christian
1805-1875 .. **NCLC 7; DA; SSC 6; WLC**
See also CLR 6; MAICYA; YABC 1

Anderson, C. Farley
See Mencken, H(enry) L(ouis); Nathan, George Jean

Anderson, Jessica (Margaret) Queale
.... **CLC 37**
See also CA 9-12R; CANR 4

Anderson, Jon (Victor) 1940- .... **CLC 9**
See also CA 25-28R; CANR 20

Anderson, Lindsay (Gordon)
1923-1994 .... **CLC 20**
See also CA 125; 128; 146

Anderson, Maxwell 1888-1959 ..... **TCLC 2**
See also CA 105; DLB 7

Anderson, Poul (William) 1926- .... **CLC 15**
See also AAYA 5; CA 1-4R; CAAS 2; CANR 2, 15, 34; DLB 8; MTCW; SATA-Brief 39

Anderson, Robert (Woodruff)
1917- .... **CLC 23**
See also AITN 1; CA 21-24R; CANR 32; DLB 7

Anderson, Sherwood
1876-1941 .... **TCLC 1, 10, 24; DA; SSC 1; WLC**
See also CA 104; 121; CDALB 1917-1929; DLB 4, 9, 86; DLBD 1; MTCW

Andouard
See Giraudoux, (Hippolyte) Jean

Andrade, Carlos Drummond de ...... **CLC 18**
See also Drummond de Andrade, Carlos

Andrade, Mario de 1893-1945..... **TCLC 43**

Andreas-Salome, Lou 1861-1937... **TCLC 56**
See also DLB 66

Andrewes, Lancelot 1555-1626 .... **LC 5**
See also DLB 151

Andrews, Cicily Fairfield
See West, Rebecca

Andrews, Elton V.
See Pohl, Frederik

Andreyev, Leonid (Nikolaevich)
1871-1919 .... **TCLC 3**
See also CA 104

Andric, Ivo 1892-1975 .... **CLC 8**
See also CA 81-84; 57-60; CANR 43; DLB 147; MTCW

Angelique, Pierre
See Bataille, Georges

Angell, Roger 1920-.............. **CLC 26**
See also CA 57-60; CANR 13, 44

Angelou, Maya
1928- .... **CLC 12, 35, 64, 77; BLC; DA**
See also AAYA 7; BW 2; CA 65-68; CANR 19, 42; DLB 38; MTCW; SATA 49

Annensky, Innokenty Fyodorovich
1856-1909 .... **TCLC 14**
See also CA 110

Anon, Charles Robert
See Pessoa, Fernando (Antonio Nogueira)

Anouilh, Jean (Marie Lucien Pierre)
1910-1987 ...... **CLC 1, 3, 8, 13, 40, 50**
See also CA 17-20R; 123; CANR 32; MTCW

Anthony, Florence
See Ai

Anthony, John
See Ciardi, John (Anthony)

Anthony, Peter
See Shaffer, Anthony (Joshua); Shaffer, Peter (Levin)

Anthony, Piers 1934- .... **CLC 35**
See also AAYA 11; CA 21-24R; CANR 28; DLB 8; MTCW

Antoine, Marc
See Proust, (Valentin-Louis-George-Eugene-) Marcel

Antoninus, Brother
See Everson, William (Oliver)

Antonioni, Michelangelo 1912- ..... **CLC 20**
See also CA 73-76; CANR 45

Antschel, Paul 1920-1970
See Celan, Paul
See also CA 85-88; CANR 33; MTCW

Anwar, Chairil 1922-1949 .... **TCLC 22**
See also CA 121

Apollinaire, Guillaume .. **TCLC 3, 8, 51; PC 7**
See also Kostrowitzki, Wilhelm Apollinaris de

Appelfeld, Aharon 1932- .... **CLC 23, 47**
See also CA 112; 133

Apple, Max (Isaac) 1941-........ **CLC 9, 33**
See also CA 81-84; CANR 19; DLB 130

Appleman, Philip (Dean) 1926- ..... **CLC 51**
See also CA 13-16R; CAAS 18; CANR 6, 29

Appleton, Lawrence
See Lovecraft, H(oward) P(hillips)

Apteryx
See Eliot, T(homas) S(tearns)

Apuleius, (Lucius Madaurensis)
125(?)-175(?) .... **CMLC 1**

Aquin, Hubert 1929-1977.......... **CLC 15**
See also CA 105; DLB 53

Aragon, Louis 1897-1982........ **CLC 3, 22**
See also CA 69-72; 108; CANR 28; DLB 72; MTCW

Arany, Janos 1817-1882......... **NCLC 34**

Arbuthnot, John 1667-1735.......... **LC 1**
See also DLB 101

Archer, Herbert Winslow
See Mencken, H(enry) L(ouis)

Archer, Jeffrey (Howard) 1940- .... **CLC 28**
See also BEST 89:3; CA 77-80; CANR 22

Archer, Jules 1915- .... **CLC 12**
See also CA 9-12R; CANR 6; SAAS 5; SATA 4

Archer, Lee
See Ellison, Harlan (Jay)

Arden, John 1930- .... **CLC 6, 13, 15**
See also CA 13-16R; CAAS 4; CANR 31; DLB 13; MTCW

Arenas, Reinaldo
1943-1990 .... **CLC 41; HLC**
See also CA 124; 128; 133; DLB 145; HW

Arendt, Hannah 1906-1975 .... **CLC 66**
See also CA 17-20R; 61-64; CANR 26; MTCW

Aretino, Pietro 1492-1556 .... **LC 12**

Arghezi, Tudor................... **CLC 80**
See also Theodorescu, Ion N.

Arguedas, Jose Maria
1911-1969 .... **CLC 10, 18**
See also CA 89-92; DLB 113; HW

Argueta, Manlio 1936-............ **CLC 31**
See also CA 131; DLB 145; HW

Ariosto, Ludovico 1474-1533........ **LC 6**

Aristides
See Epstein, Joseph

Aristophanes
450B.C.-385B.C.... **CMLC 4; DA; DC 2**

Arlt, Roberto (Godofredo Christophersen)
1900-1942 .... **TCLC 29; HLC**
See also CA 123; 131; HW

Armah, Ayi Kwei 1939-.... **CLC 5, 33; BLC**
See also BW 1; CA 61-64; CANR 21; DLB 117; MTCW

Armatrading, Joan 1950-.......... **CLC 17**
See also CA 114

Arnette, Robert
See Silverberg, Robert

Arnim, Achim von (Ludwig Joachim von Arnim) 1781-1831 .... **NCLC 5**
See also DLB 90

Arnim, Bettina von 1785-1859.... **NCLC 38**
See also DLB 90

Arnold, Matthew
1822-1888 ..... **NCLC 6, 29; DA; PC 5; WLC**
See also A. E.
See also CDBLB 1832-1890; DLB 32, 57

Arnold, Thomas 1795-1842 ...... **NCLC 18**
See also DLB 55

Arnow, Harriette (Louisa) Simpson
1908-1986 .... **CLC 2, 7, 18**
See also CA 9-12R; 118; CANR 14; DLB 6; MTCW; SATA 42; SATA-Obit 47

Arp, Hans
See Arp, Jean

Arp, Jean 1887-1966............... **CLC 5**
See also CA 81-84; 25-28R; CANR 42

Arrabal
See Arrabal, Fernando

Arrabal, Fernando 1932- ... **CLC 2, 9, 18, 58**
See also CA 9-12R; CANR 15

Arrick, Fran..................... **CLC 30**
See also Gaberman, Judie Angell

Artaud, Antonin 1896-1948 ..... **TCLC 3, 36**
See also CA 104

Arthur, Ruth M(abel) 1905-1979.... **CLC 12**
See also CA 9-12R; 85-88; CANR 4; SATA 7, 26

Artsybashev, Mikhail (Petrovich)
1878-1927 .... **TCLC 31**

Arundel, Honor (Morfydd)
1919-1973 .... **CLC 17**
See also CA 21-22; 41-44R; CAP 2; CLR 35; SATA 4; SATA-Obit 24

Asch, Sholem 1880-1957 .... **TCLC 3**
See also CA 105

Ash, Shalom
See Asch, Sholem

Ashbery, John (Lawrence)
1927- ...... **CLC 2, 3, 4, 6, 9, 13, 15, 25, 41, 77**
See also CA 5-8R; CANR 9, 37; DLB 5; DLBY 81; MTCW

Ashdown, Clifford
See Freeman, R(ichard) Austin

Ashe, Gordon
See Creasey, John

Ashton-Warner, Sylvia (Constance)
1908-1984 .... **CLC 19**
See also CA 69-72; 112; CANR 29; MTCW

Asimov, Isaac
1920-1992 ...... **CLC 1, 3, 9, 19, 26, 76**
See also AAYA 13; BEST 90:2; CA 1-4R; 137; CANR 2, 19, 36; CLR 12; DLB 8; DLBY 92; JRDA; MAICYA; MTCW; SATA 1, 26, 74

Astley, Thea (Beatrice May)
1925- .... **CLC 41**
See also CA 65-68; CANR 11, 43

Aston, James
See White, T(erence) H(anbury)

Asturias, Miguel Angel
1899-1974 .... **CLC 3, 8, 13; HLC**
See also CA 25-28; 49-52; CANR 32; CAP 2; DLB 113; HW; MTCW

Atares, Carlos Saura
See Saura (Atares), Carlos

Atheling, William
See Pound, Ezra (Weston Loomis)

Atheling, William, Jr.
See Blish, James (Benjamin)

Atherton, Gertrude (Franklin Horn)
1857-1948 .... **TCLC 2**
See also CA 104; DLB 9, 78

Atherton, Lucius
See Masters, Edgar Lee

Atkins, Jack
See Harris, Mark

Atticus
See Fleming, Ian (Lancaster)

Atwood, Margaret (Eleanor)
1939- ..... **CLC 2, 3, 4, 8, 13, 15, 25, 44, 84; DA; PC 8; SSC 2; WLC**
See also AAYA 12; BEST 89:2; CA 49-52; CANR 3, 24, 33; DLB 53; MTCW; SATA 50

Aubigny, Pierre d'
See Mencken, H(enry) L(ouis)

Aubin, Penelope 1685-1731(?)........ **LC 9**
See also DLB 39

Auchincloss, Louis (Stanton)
1917- .... **CLC 4, 6, 9, 18, 45**
See also CA 1-4R; CANR 6, 29; DLB 2; DLBY 80; MTCW

Auden, W(ystan) H(ugh)
1907-1973 ...... **CLC 1, 2, 3, 4, 6, 9, 11, 14, 43; DA; PC 1; WLC**
See also CA 9-12R; 45-48; CANR 5; CDBLB 1914-1945; DLB 10, 20; MTCW

Audiberti, Jacques 1900-1965 ...... **CLC 38**
See also CA 25-28R

Audubon, John James
1785-1851 .... **NCLC 47**

Auel, Jean M(arie) 1936- . . . . CLC 31
  See also AAYA 7; BEST 90:4; CA 103;
  CANR 21

Auerbach, Erich 1892-1957 . . . . TCLC 43
  See also CA 118

Augier, Emile 1820-1889 . . . . NCLC 31

August, John
  See De Voto, Bernard (Augustine)

Augustine, St. 354-430 . . . . CMLC 6

Aurelius
  See Bourne, Randolph S(illiman)

Austen, Jane
  1775-1817 . . . . . NCLC 1, 13, 19, 33, 51;
                                        DA; WLC
  See also CDBLB 1789-1832; DLB 116

Auster, Paul 1947- . . . . CLC 47
  See also CA 69-72; CANR 23

Austin, Frank
  See Faust, Frederick (Schiller)

Austin, Mary (Hunter)
  1868-1934 . . . . TCLC 25
  See also CA 109; DLB 9, 78

Autran Dourado, Waldomiro
  See Dourado, (Waldomiro Freitas) Autran

Averroes 1126-1198 . . . . CMLC 7
  See also DLB 115

Avicenna 980-1037 . . . . CMLC 16
  See also DLB 115

Avison, Margaret 1918- . . . . CLC 2, 4
  See also CA 17-20R; DLB 53; MTCW

Axton, David
  See Koontz, Dean R(ay)

Ayckbourn, Alan
  1939- . . . . CLC 5, 8, 18, 33, 74
  See also CA 21-24R; CANR 31; DLB 13;
  MTCW

Aydy, Catherine
  See Tennant, Emma (Christina)

Ayme, Marcel (Andre) 1902-1967 . . . CLC 11
  See also CA 89-92; CLR 25; DLB 72

Ayrton, Michael 1921-1975 . . . . CLC 7
  See also CA 5-8R; 61-64; CANR 9, 21

Azorin . . . . CLC 11
  See also Martinez Ruiz, Jose

Azuela, Mariano
  1873-1952 . . . . TCLC 3; HLC
  See also CA 104; 131; HW; MTCW

Baastad, Babbis Friis
  See Friis-Baastad, Babbis Ellinor

Bab
  See Gilbert, W(illiam) S(chwenck)

Babbis, Eleanor
  See Friis-Baastad, Babbis Ellinor

Babel, Isaak (Emmanuilovich)
  1894-1941(?) . . . . . . TCLC 2, 13; SSC 16
  See also CA 104

Babits, Mihaly 1883-1941 . . . . TCLC 14
  See also CA 114

Babur 1483-1530 . . . . LC 18

Bacchelli, Riccardo 1891-1985 . . . . . CLC 19
  See also CA 29-32R; 117

Bach, Richard (David) 1936- . . . . CLC 14
  See also AITN 1; BEST 89:2; CA 9-12R;
  CANR 18; MTCW; SATA 13

Bachman, Richard
  See King, Stephen (Edwin)

Bachmann, Ingeborg 1926-1973 . . . . . CLC 69
  See also CA 93-96; 45-48; DLB 85

Bacon, Francis 1561-1626 . . . . LC 18
  See also CDBLB Before 1660; DLB 151

Bacon, Roger 1214(?)-1292 . . . . . . CMLC 14
  See also DLB 115

Bacovia, George. . . . . TCLC 24
  See also Vasiliu, Gheorghe

Badanes, Jerome 1937- . . . . CLC 59

Bagehot, Walter 1826-1877 . . . . . . NCLC 10
  See also DLB 55

Bagnold, Enid 1889-1981 . . . . CLC 25
  See also CA 5-8R; 103; CANR 5, 40;
  DLB 13; MAICYA; SATA 1, 25

Bagritsky, Eduard 1895-1934 . . . . . TCLC 60

Bagrjana, Elisaveta
  See Belcheva, Elisaveta

Bagryana, Elisaveta. . . . . CLC 10
  See also Belcheva, Elisaveta
  See also DLB 147

Bailey, Paul 1937- . . . . CLC 45
  See also CA 21-24R; CANR 16; DLB 14

Baillie, Joanna 1762-1851 . . . . NCLC 2
  See also DLB 93

Bainbridge, Beryl (Margaret)
  1933- . . . . CLC 4, 5, 8, 10, 14, 18, 22, 62
  See also CA 21-24R; CANR 24; DLB 14;
  MTCW

Baker, Elliott 1922- . . . . CLC 8
  See also CA 45-48; CANR 2

Baker, Nicholson 1957- . . . . CLC 61
  See also CA 135

Baker, Ray Stannard 1870-1946 . . . TCLC 47
  See also CA 118

Baker, Russell (Wayne) 1925- . . . . . . CLC 31
  See also BEST 89:4; CA 57-60; CANR 11,
  41; MTCW

Bakhtin, M.
  See Bakhtin, Mikhail Mikhailovich

Bakhtin, M. M.
  See Bakhtin, Mikhail Mikhailovich

Bakhtin, Mikhail
  See Bakhtin, Mikhail Mikhailovich

Bakhtin, Mikhail Mikhailovich
  1895-1975 . . . . CLC 83
  See also CA 128; 113

Bakshi, Ralph 1938(?)- . . . . CLC 26
  See also CA 112; 138

Bakunin, Mikhail (Alexandrovich)
  1814-1876 . . . . NCLC 25

Baldwin, James (Arthur)
  1924-1987 . . . . . CLC 1, 2, 3, 4, 5, 8, 13,
             15, 17, 42, 50, 67; BLC; DA; DC 1;
                                        SSC 10; WLC
  See also AAYA 4; BW 1; CA 1-4R; 124;
  CABS 1; CANR 3, 24;
  CDALB 1941-1968; DLB 2, 7, 33;
  DLBY 87; MTCW; SATA 9;
  SATA-Obit 54

Ballard, J(ames) G(raham)
  1930- . . . . CLC 3, 6, 14, 36; SSC 1
  See also AAYA 3; CA 5-8R; CANR 15, 39;
  DLB 14; MTCW

Balmont, Konstantin (Dmitriyevich)
  1867-1943 . . . . TCLC 11
  See also CA 109

Balzac, Honore de
  1799-1850 . . . . NCLC 5, 35; DA; SSC 5;
                                        WLC
  See also DLB 119

Bambara, Toni Cade
  1939- . . . . CLC 19, 88; BLC; DA
  See also AAYA 5; BW 2; CA 29-32R;
  CANR 24, 49; DLB 38; MTCW

Bamdad, A.
  See Shamlu, Ahmad

Banat, D. R.
  See Bradbury, Ray (Douglas)

Bancroft, Laura
  See Baum, L(yman) Frank

Banim, John 1798-1842 . . . . NCLC 13
  See also DLB 116

Banim, Michael 1796-1874 . . . . . . NCLC 13

Banks, Iain
  See Banks, Iain M(enzies)

Banks, Iain M(enzies) 1954- . . . . CLC 34
  See also CA 123; 128

Banks, Lynne Reid . . . . CLC 23
  See also Reid Banks, Lynne
  See also AAYA 6

Banks, Russell 1940- . . . . CLC 37, 72
  See also CA 65-68; CAAS 15; CANR 19;
  DLB 130

Banville, John 1945- . . . . CLC 46
  See also CA 117; 128; DLB 14

Banville, Theodore (Faullain) de
  1832-1891 . . . . NCLC 9

Baraka, Amiri
  1934- . . . . CLC 1, 2, 3, 5, 10, 14, 33;
                                        BLC; DA; PC 4
  See also Jones, LeRoi
  See also BW 2; CA 21-24R; CABS 3;
  CANR 27, 38; CDALB 1941-1968;
  DLB 5, 7, 16, 38; DLBD 8; MTCW

Barbauld, Anna Laetitia
  1743-1825 . . . . NCLC 50
  See also DLB 107, 109, 142

Barbellion, W. N. P. . . . . TCLC 24
  See also Cummings, Bruce F(rederick)

Barbera, Jack (Vincent) 1945- . . . . . . CLC 44
  See also CA 110; CANR 45

Barbey d'Aurevilly, Jules Amedee
  1808-1889 . . . . NCLC 1; SSC 17
  See also DLB 119

Barbusse, Henri 1873-1935 . . . . TCLC 5
  See also CA 105; DLB 65

Barclay, Bill
  See Moorcock, Michael (John)

Barclay, William Ewert
  See Moorcock, Michael (John)

Barea, Arturo 1897-1957 . . . . TCLC 14
  See also CA 111

Barfoot, Joan 1946- .... **CLC 18**
See also CA 105

Baring, Maurice 1874-1945 .... **TCLC 8**
See also CA 105; DLB 34

Barker, Clive 1952- .... **CLC 52**
See also AAYA 10; BEST 90:3; CA 121;
129; MTCW

Barker, George Granville
1913-1991 .... **CLC 8, 48**
See also CA 9-12R; 135; CANR 7, 38;
DLB 20; MTCW

Barker, Harley Granville
See Granville-Barker, Harley
See also DLB 10

Barker, Howard 1946- .... **CLC 37**
See also CA 102; DLB 13

Barker, Pat 1943- .... **CLC 32**
See also CA 117; 122

Barlow, Joel 1754-1812 .... **NCLC 23**
See also DLB 37

Barnard, Mary (Ethel) 1909- ...... **CLC 48**
See also CA 21-22; CAP 2

Barnes, Djuna
1892-1982 ... **CLC 3, 4, 8, 11, 29; SSC 3**
See also CA 9-12R; 107; CANR 16; DLB 4,
9, 45; MTCW

Barnes, Julian 1946- .... **CLC 42**
See also CA 102; CANR 19; DLBY 93

Barnes, Peter 1931- .... **CLC 5, 56**
See also CA 65-68; CAAS 12; CANR 33,
34; DLB 13; MTCW

Baroja (y Nessi), Pio
1872-1956 .... **TCLC 8; HLC**
See also CA 104

Baron, David
See Pinter, Harold

Baron Corvo
See Rolfe, Frederick (William Serafino
Austin Lewis Mary)

Barondess, Sue K(aufman)
1926-1977 .... **CLC 8**
See Kaufman, Sue
See also CA 1-4R; 69-72; CANR 1

Baron de Teive
See Pessoa, Fernando (Antonio Nogueira)

Barres, Maurice 1862-1923 .... **TCLC 47**
See also DLB 123

Barreto, Afonso Henrique de Lima
See Lima Barreto, Afonso Henrique de

Barrett, (Roger) Syd 1946- .... **CLC 35**

Barrett, William (Christopher)
1913-1992 .... **CLC 27**
See also CA 13-16R; 139; CANR 11

Barrie, J(ames) M(atthew)
1860-1937 .... **TCLC 2**
See also CA 104; 136; CDBLB 1890-1914;
CLR 16; DLB 10, 141; MAICYA;
YABC 1

Barrington, Michael
See Moorcock, Michael (John)

Barrol, Grady
See Bograd, Larry

Barry, Mike
See Malzberg, Barry N(athaniel)

Barry, Philip 1896-1949 .... **TCLC 11**
See also CA 109; DLB 7

Bart, Andre Schwarz
See Schwarz-Bart, Andre

Barth, John (Simmons)
1930- ...... **CLC 1, 2, 3, 5, 7, 9, 10, 14,
27, 51, 89; SSC 10**
See also AITN 1, 2; CA 1-4R; CABS 1;
CANR 5, 23, 49; DLB 2; MTCW

Barthelme, Donald
1931-1989 ...... **CLC 1, 2, 3, 5, 6, 8, 13,
23, 46, 59; SSC 2**
See also CA 21-24R; 129; CANR 20;
DLB 2; DLBY 80, 89; MTCW; SATA 7;
SATA-Obit 62

Barthelme, Frederick 1943- .... **CLC 36**
See also CA 114; 122; DLBY 85

Barthes, Roland (Gerard)
1915-1980 .... **CLC 24, 83**
See also CA 130; 97-100; MTCW

Barzun, Jacques (Martin) 1907- .... **CLC 51**
See also CA 61-64; CANR 22

Bashevis, Isaac
See Singer, Isaac Bashevis

Bashkirtseff, Marie 1859-1884 ... **NCLC 27**

Basho
See Matsuo Basho

Bass, Kingsley B., Jr.
See Bullins, Ed

Bass, Rick 1958- .... **CLC 79**
See also CA 126

Bassani, Giorgio 1916- .... **CLC 9**
See also CA 65-68; CANR 33; DLB 128;
MTCW

Bastos, Augusto (Antonio) Roa
See Roa Bastos, Augusto (Antonio)

Bataille, Georges 1897-1962 .... **CLC 29**
See also CA 101; 89-92

Bates, H(erbert) E(rnest)
1905-1974 .... **CLC 46; SSC 10**
See also CA 93-96; 45-48; CANR 34;
MTCW

Bauchart
See Camus, Albert

Baudelaire, Charles
1821-1867 ..... **NCLC 6, 29; DA; PC 1;
SSC 18; WLC**

Baudrillard, Jean 1929- .... **CLC 60**

Baum, L(yman) Frank 1856-1919 ... **TCLC 7**
See also CA 108; 133; CLR 15; DLB 22;
JRDA; MAICYA; MTCW; SATA 18

Baum, Louis F.
See Baum, L(yman) Frank

Baumbach, Jonathan 1933- ...... **CLC 6, 23**
See also CA 13-16R; CAAS 5; CANR 12;
DLBY 80; MTCW

Bausch, Richard (Carl) 1945- ...... **CLC 51**
See also CA 101; CAAS 14; CANR 43;
DLB 130

Baxter, Charles 1947- .... **CLC 45, 78**
See also CA 57-60; CANR 40; DLB 130

Baxter, George Owen
See Faust, Frederick (Schiller)

Baxter, James K(eir) 1926-1972 .... **CLC 14**
See also CA 77-80

Baxter, John
See Hunt, E(verette) Howard, (Jr.)

Bayer, Sylvia
See Glassco, John

Baynton, Barbara 1857-1929 ..... **TCLC 57**

Beagle, Peter S(oyer) 1939- .... **CLC 7**
See also CA 9-12R; CANR 4; DLBY 80;
SATA 60

Bean, Normal
See Burroughs, Edgar Rice

Beard, Charles A(ustin)
1874-1948 .... **TCLC 15**
See also CA 115; DLB 17; SATA 18

Beardsley, Aubrey 1872-1898 ..... **NCLC 6**

Beattie, Ann
1947- .... **CLC 8, 13, 18, 40, 63; SSC 11**
See also BEST 90:2; CA 81-84; DLBY 82;
MTCW

Beattie, James 1735-1803 .... **NCLC 25**
See also DLB 109

Beauchamp, Kathleen Mansfield 1888-1923
See Mansfield, Katherine
See also CA 104; 134; DA

Beaumarchais, Pierre-Augustin Caron de
1732-1799 .... **DC 4**

**Beauvoir, Simone (Lucie Ernestine Marie
Bertrand) de**
1908-1986 .... **CLC 1, 2, 4, 8, 14, 31, 44,
50, 71; DA; WLC**
See also CA 9-12R; 118; CANR 28;
DLB 72; DLBY 86; MTCW

Becker, Jurek 1937- .... **CLC 7, 19**
See also CA 85-88; DLB 75

Becker, Walter 1950- .... **CLC 26**

Beckett, Samuel (Barclay)
1906-1989 ...... **CLC 1, 2, 3, 4, 6, 9, 10,
11, 14, 18, 29, 57, 59, 83; DA; SSC 16;
WLC**
See also CA 5-8R; 130; CANR 33;
CDBLB 1945-1960; DLB 13, 15;
DLBY 90; MTCW

Beckford, William 1760-1844 .... **NCLC 16**
See also DLB 39

Beckman, Gunnel 1910- .... **CLC 26**
See also CA 33-36R; CANR 15; CLR 25;
MAICYA; SAAS 9; SATA 6

Becque, Henri 1837-1899 .... **NCLC 3**

Beddoes, Thomas Lovell
1803-1849 .... **NCLC 3**
See also DLB 96

Bedford, Donald F.
See Fearing, Kenneth (Flexner)

Beecher, Catharine Esther
1800-1878 .... **NCLC 30**
See also DLB 1

Beecher, John 1904-1980 .... **CLC 6**
See also AITN 1; CA 5-8R; 105; CANR 8

Beer, Johann 1655-1700 .... **LC 5**

Beer, Patricia 1924- .... **CLC 58**
See also CA 61-64; CANR 13, 46; DLB 40

Beerbohm, Henry Maximilian
1872-1956 .... TCLC 1, 24
See also CA 104; DLB 34, 100

Beerbohm, Max
See Beerbohm, Henry Maximilian

Beer-Hofmann, Richard
1866-1945 .... TCLC 60
See also DLB 81

Begiebing, Robert J(ohn) 1946-..... CLC 70
See also CA 122; CANR 40

Behan, Brendan
1923-1964 .... CLC 1, 8, 11, 15, 79
See also CA 73-76; CANR 33;
CDBLB 1945-1960; DLB 13; MTCW

Behn, Aphra
1640(?)-1689 ...... LC 1, 30; DA; DC 4;
PC 12; WLC
See also DLB 39, 80, 131

Behrman, S(amuel) N(athaniel)
1893-1973 .... CLC 40
See also CA 13-16; 45-48; CAP 1; DLB 7,
44

Belasco, David 1853-1931 .... TCLC 3
See also CA 104; DLB 7

Belcheva, Elisaveta 1893- .... CLC 10
See also Bagryana, Elisaveta

Beldone, Phil "Cheech"
See Ellison, Harlan (Jay)

Beleno
See Azuela, Mariano

Belinski, Vissarion Grigoryevich
1811-1848 .... NCLC 5

Belitt, Ben 1911-................. CLC 22
See also CA 13-16R; CAAS 4; CANR 7;
DLB 5

Bell, James Madison
1826-1902 .... TCLC 43; BLC
See also BW 1; CA 122; 124; DLB 50

Bell, Madison (Smartt) 1957- ...... CLC 41
See also CA 111; CANR 28

Bell, Marvin (Hartley) 1937-..... CLC 8, 31
See also CA 21-24R; CAAS 14; DLB 5;
MTCW

Bell, W. L. D.
See Mencken, H(enry) L(ouis)

Bellamy, Atwood C.
See Mencken, H(enry) L(ouis)

Bellamy, Edward 1850-1898 ...... NCLC 4
See also DLB 12

Bellin, Edward J.
See Kuttner, Henry

Belloc, (Joseph) Hilaire (Pierre)
1870-1953 .... TCLC 7, 18
See also CA 106; DLB 19, 100, 141;
YABC 1

Belloc, Joseph Peter Rene Hilaire
See Belloc, (Joseph) Hilaire (Pierre)

Belloc, Joseph Pierre Hilaire
See Belloc, (Joseph) Hilaire (Pierre)

Belloc, M. A.
See Lowndes, Marie Adelaide (Belloc)

Bellow, Saul
1915- ...... CLC 1, 2, 3, 6, 8, 10, 13, 15,
25, 33, 34, 63, 79; DA; SSC 14; WLC
See also AITN 2; BEST 89:3; CA 5-8R;
CABS 1; CANR 29; CDALB 1941-1968;
DLB 2, 28; DLBD 3; DLBY 82; MTCW

Belser, Reimond Karel Maria de
See Ruyslinck, Ward

Bely, Andrey .... TCLC 7; PC 11
See also Bugayev, Boris Nikolayevich

Benary, Margot
See Benary-Isbert, Margot

Benary-Isbert, Margot 1889-1979... CLC 12
See also CA 5-8R; 89-92; CANR 4;
CLR 12; MAICYA; SATA 2;
SATA-Obit 21

Benavente (y Martinez), Jacinto
1866-1954 .... TCLC 3
See also CA 106; 131; HW; MTCW

Benchley, Peter (Bradford)
1940- .... CLC 4, 8
See also AAYA 14; AITN 2; CA 17-20R;
CANR 12, 35; MTCW; SATA 3

Benchley, Robert (Charles)
1889-1945 .... TCLC 1, 55
See also CA 105; DLB 11

Benda, Julien 1867-1956 .... TCLC 60
See also CA 120

Benedict, Ruth 1887-1948 .... TCLC 60

Benedikt, Michael 1935- .... CLC 4, 14
See also CA 13-16R; CANR 7; DLB 5

Benet, Juan 1927-................. CLC 28
See also CA 143

Benet, Stephen Vincent
1898-1943 .... TCLC 7; SSC 10
See also CA 104; DLB 4, 48, 102; YABC 1

Benet, William Rose 1886-1950 ... TCLC 28
See also CA 118; DLB 45

Benford, Gregory (Albert) 1941-.... CLC 52
See also CA 69-72; CANR 12, 24, 49;
DLBY 82

Bengtsson, Frans (Gunnar)
1894-1954 .... TCLC 48

Benjamin, David
See Slavitt, David R(ytman)

Benjamin, Lois
See Gould, Lois

Benjamin, Walter 1892-1940 ...... TCLC 39

Benn, Gottfried 1886-1956........ TCLC 3
See also CA 106; DLB 56

Bennett, Alan 1934-........... CLC 45, 77
See also CA 103; CANR 35; MTCW

Bennett, (Enoch) Arnold
1867-1931 .... TCLC 5, 20
See also CA 106; CDBLB 1890-1914;
DLB 10, 34, 98, 135

Bennett, Elizabeth
See Mitchell, Margaret (Munnerlyn)

Bennett, George Harold 1930-
See Bennett, Hal
See also BW 1; CA 97-100

Bennett, Hal .... CLC 5
See also Bennett, George Harold
See also DLB 33

Bennett, Jay 1912-................. CLC 35
See also AAYA 10; CA 69-72; CANR 11,
42; JRDA; SAAS 4; SATA 41;
SATA-Brief 27

Bennett, Louise (Simone)
1919-.................. CLC 28; BLC
See also BW 2; DLB 117

Benson, E(dward) F(rederic)
1867-1940 .... TCLC 27
See also CA 114; DLB 135, 153

Benson, Jackson J. 1930-......... CLC 34
See also CA 25-28R; DLB 111

Benson, Sally 1900-1972 .... CLC 17
See also CA 19-20; 37-40R; CAP 1;
SATA 1, 35; SATA-Obit 27

Benson, Stella 1892-1933........ TCLC 17
See also CA 117; DLB 36

Bentham, Jeremy 1748-1832 ..... NCLC 38
See also DLB 107

Bentley, E(dmund) C(lerihew)
1875-1956 .... TCLC 12
See also CA 108; DLB 70

Bentley, Eric (Russell) 1916-....... CLC 24
See also CA 5-8R; CANR 6

Beranger, Pierre Jean de
1780-1857 .... NCLC 34

Berendt, John (Lawrence) 1939-.... CLC 86
See also CA 146

Berger, Colonel
See Malraux, (Georges-)Andre

Berger, John (Peter) 1926- ...... CLC 2, 19
See also CA 81-84; DLB 14

Berger, Melvin H. 1927-.......... CLC 12
See also CA 5-8R; CANR 4; CLR 32;
SAAS 2; SATA 5

Berger, Thomas (Louis)
1924-......... CLC 3, 5, 8, 11, 18, 38
See also CA 1-4R; CANR 5, 28; DLB 2;
DLBY 80; MTCW

Bergman, (Ernst) Ingmar
1918-.................... CLC 16, 72
See also CA 81-84; CANR 33

Bergson, Henri 1859-1941........ TCLC 32

Bergstein, Eleanor 1938-.......... CLC 4
See also CA 53-56; CANR 5

Berkoff, Steven 1937-............. CLC 56
See also CA 104

Bermant, Chaim (Icyk) 1929- ...... CLC 40
See also CA 57-60; CANR 6, 31

Bern, Victoria
See Fisher, M(ary) F(rances) K(ennedy)

Bernanos, (Paul Louis) Georges
1888-1948 .... TCLC 3
See also CA 104; 130; DLB 72

Bernard, April 1956- .... CLC 59
See also CA 131

Berne, Victoria
See Fisher, M(ary) F(rances) K(ennedy)

Bernhard, Thomas
1931-1989 .... CLC 3, 32, 61
See also CA 85-88; 127; CANR 32;
DLB 85, 124; MTCW

Berriault, Gina 1926-............. CLC 54
See also CA 116; 129; DLB 130

Berrigan, Daniel 1921-............ **CLC 4**
See also CA 33-36R; CAAS 1; CANR 11,
43; DLB 5

Berrigan, Edmund Joseph Michael, Jr.
1934-1983
See Berrigan, Ted
See also CA 61-64; 110; CANR 14

Berrigan, Ted.................... **CLC 37**
See also Berrigan, Edmund Joseph Michael,
Jr.
See also DLB 5

Berry, Charles Edward Anderson 1931-
See Berry, Chuck
See also CA 115

Berry, Chuck.................... **CLC 17**
See also Berry, Charles Edward Anderson

Berry, Jonas
See Ashbery, John (Lawrence)

Berry, Wendell (Erdman)
1934-............. **CLC 4, 6, 8, 27, 46**
See also AITN 1; CA 73-76; DLB 5, 6

Berryman, John
1914-1972 ...... **CLC 1, 2, 3, 4, 6, 8, 10,
13, 25, 62**
See also CA 13-16; 33-36R; CABS 2;
CANR 35; CAP 1; CDALB 1941-1968;
DLB 48; MTCW

Bertolucci, Bernardo 1940- .... **CLC 16**
See also CA 106

Bertrand, Aloysius 1807-1841 .... **NCLC 31**

Bertran de Born c. 1140-1215 ..... **CMLC 5**

Besant, Annie (Wood) 1847-1933 ... **TCLC 9**
See also CA 105

Bessie, Alvah 1904-1985.......... **CLC 23**
See also CA 5-8R; 116; CANR 2; DLB 26

Bethlen, T. D.
See Silverberg, Robert

Beti, Mongo................ **CLC 27; BLC**
See also Biyidi, Alexandre

Betjeman, John
1906-1984 .... **CLC 2, 6, 10, 34, 43**
See also CA 9-12R; 112; CANR 33;
CDBLB 1945-1960; DLB 20; DLBY 84;
MTCW

Bettelheim, Bruno 1903-1990 ...... **CLC 79**
See also CA 81-84; 131; CANR 23; MTCW

Betti, Ugo 1892-1953 .... **TCLC 5**
See also CA 104

Betts, Doris (Waugh) 1932-.... **CLC 3, 6, 28**
See also CA 13-16R; CANR 9; DLBY 82

Bevan, Alistair
See Roberts, Keith (John Kingston)

Bialik, Chaim Nachman
1873-1934 .... **TCLC 25**

Bickerstaff, Isaac
See Swift, Jonathan

Bidart, Frank 1939-.............. **CLC 33**
See also CA 140

Bienek, Horst 1930-........... **CLC 7, 11**
See also CA 73-76; DLB 75

Bierce, Ambrose (Gwinett)
1842-1914(?) .... **TCLC 1, 7, 44; DA;
SSC 9; WLC**
See also CA 104; 139; CDALB 1865-1917;
DLB 11, 12, 23, 71, 74

Billings, Josh
See Shaw, Henry Wheeler

Billington, (Lady) Rachel (Mary)
1942-....................... **CLC 43**
See also AITN 2; CA 33-36R; CANR 44

Binyon, T(imothy) J(ohn) 1936- .... **CLC 34**
See also CA 111; CANR 28

Bioy Casares, Adolfo
1914-... **CLC 4, 8, 13, 88; HLC; SSC 17**
See also CA 29-32R; CANR 19, 43;
DLB 113; HW; MTCW

Bird, Cordwainer
See Ellison, Harlan (Jay)

Bird, Robert Montgomery
1806-1854 .... **NCLC 1**

Birney, (Alfred) Earle
1904-................**CLC 1, 4, 6, 11**
See also CA 1-4R; CANR 5, 20; DLB 88;
MTCW

Bishop, Elizabeth
1911-1979 ...... **CLC 1, 4, 9, 13, 15, 32;
DA; PC 3**
See also CA 5-8R; 89-92; CABS 2;
CANR 26; CDALB 1968-1988; DLB 5;
MTCW; SATA-Obit 24

Bishop, John 1935-............... **CLC 10**
See also CA 105

Bissett, Bill 1939-................ **CLC 18**
See also CA 69-72; CAAS 19; CANR 15;
DLB 53; MTCW

Bitov, Andrei (Georgievich) 1937-... **CLC 57**
See also CA 142

Biyidi, Alexandre 1932-
See Beti, Mongo
See also BW 1; CA 114; 124; MTCW

Bjarme, Brynjolf
See Ibsen, Henrik (Johan)

Bjornson, Bjornstjerne (Martinius)
1832-1910 .... **TCLC 7, 37**
See also CA 104

Black, Robert
See Holdstock, Robert P.

Blackburn, Paul 1926-1971 ...... **CLC 9, 43**
See also CA 81-84; 33-36R; CANR 34;
DLB 16; DLBY 81

Black Elk 1863-1950 .... **TCLC 33**
See also CA 144; NNAL

Black Hobart
See Sanders, (James) Ed(ward)

Blacklin, Malcolm
See Chambers, Aidan

Blackmore, R(ichard) D(oddridge)
1825-1900 .... **TCLC 27**
See also CA 120; DLB 18

Blackmur, R(ichard) P(almer)
1904-1965 .... **CLC 2, 24**
See also CA 11-12; 25-28R; CAP 1; DLB 63

Black Tarantula, The
See Acker, Kathy

Blackwood, Algernon (Henry)
1869-1951 .... **TCLC 5**
See also CA 105; DLB 153

Blackwood, Caroline 1931- .... **CLC 6, 9**
See also CA 85-88; CANR 32; DLB 14;
MTCW

Blade, Alexander
See Hamilton, Edmond; Silverberg, Robert

Blaga, Lucian 1895-1961 .... **CLC 75**

Blair, Eric (Arthur) 1903-1950
See Orwell, George
See also CA 104; 132; DA; MTCW;
SATA 29

Blais, Marie-Claire
1939-............ **CLC 2, 4, 6, 13, 22**
See also CA 21-24R; CAAS 4; CANR 38;
DLB 53; MTCW

Blaise, Clark 1940-............... **CLC 29**
See also AITN 2; CA 53-56; CAAS 3;
CANR 5; DLB 53

Blake, Nicholas
See Day Lewis, C(ecil)
See also DLB 77

Blake, William
1757-1827 .... **NCLC 13, 37; DA;
PC 12; WLC**
See also CDBLB 1789-1832; DLB 93;
MAICYA; SATA 30

Blasco Ibanez, Vicente
1867-1928 .... **TCLC 12**
See also CA 110; 131; HW; MTCW

Blatty, William Peter 1928-......... **CLC 2**
See also CA 5-8R; CANR 9

Bleeck, Oliver
See Thomas, Ross (Elmore)

Blessing, Lee 1949-.............. **CLC 54**

Blish, James (Benjamin)
1921-1975 .... **CLC 14**
See also CA 1-4R; 57-60; CANR 3; DLB 8;
MTCW; SATA 66

Bliss, Reginald
See Wells, H(erbert) G(eorge)

Blixen, Karen (Christentze Dinesen)
1885-1962
See Dinesen, Isak
See also CA 25-28; CANR 22; CAP 2;
MTCW; SATA 44

Bloch, Robert (Albert) 1917-1994... **CLC 33**
See also CA 5-8R; 146; CAAS 20; CANR 5;
DLB 44; SATA 12

Blok, Alexander (Alexandrovich)
1880-1921 .... **TCLC 5**
See also CA 104

Blom, Jan
See Breytenbach, Breyten

Bloom, Harold 1930- .... **CLC 24**
See also CA 13-16R; CANR 39; DLB 67

Bloomfield, Aurelius
See Bourne, Randolph S(illiman)

Blount, Roy (Alton), Jr. 1941- ..... **CLC 38**
See also CA 53-56; CANR 10, 28; MTCW

Bloy, Leon 1846-1917............ **TCLC 22**
See also CA 121; DLB 123

Blume, Judy (Sussman) 1938-... **CLC 12, 30**
See also AAYA 3; CA 29-32R; CANR 13,
37; CLR 2, 15; DLB 52; JRDA;
MAICYA; MTCW; SATA 2, 31, 79

Blunden, Edmund (Charles)
1896-1974 .... **CLC 2, 56**
See also CA 17-18; 45-48; CAP 2; DLB 20,
100; MTCW

Bly, Robert (Elwood)
1926- .... **CLC 1, 2, 5, 10, 15, 38**
See also CA 5-8R; CANR 41; DLB 5;
MTCW

Boas, Franz 1858-1942.......... **TCLC 56**
See also CA 115

Bobette
See Simenon, Georges (Jacques Christian)

Boccaccio, Giovanni
1313-1375 .... **CMLC 13; SSC 10**

Bochco, Steven 1943-............. **CLC 35**
See also AAYA 11; CA 124; 138

Bodenheim, Maxwell 1892-1954 ... **TCLC 44**
See also CA 110; DLB 9, 45

Bodker, Cecil 1927- .... **CLC 21**
See also CA 73-76; CANR 13, 44; CLR 23;
MAICYA; SATA 14

Boell, Heinrich (Theodor)
1917-1985 .... **CLC 2, 3, 6, 9, 11, 15, 27,
32, 72; DA; WLC**
See also CA 21-24R; 116; CANR 24;
DLB 69; DLBY 85; MTCW

Boerne, Alfred
See Doeblin, Alfred

Boethius 480(?)-524(?) .... **CMLC 15**
See also DLB 115

Bogan, Louise
1897-1970 ...... **CLC 4, 39, 46; PC 12**
See also CA 73-76; 25-28R; CANR 33;
DLB 45; MTCW

Bogarde, Dirk .... **CLC 19**
See also Van Den Bogarde, Derek Jules
Gaspard Ulric Niven
See also DLB 14

Bogosian, Eric 1953- .... **CLC 45**
See also CA 138

Bograd, Larry 1953-.............. **CLC 35**
See also CA 93-96; SATA 33

Boiardo, Matteo Maria 1441-1494 .... **LC 6**

Boileau-Despreaux, Nicolas
1636-1711 .... **LC 3**

Boland, Eavan (Aisling) 1944-... **CLC 40, 67**
See also CA 143; DLB 40

Bolt, Lee
See Faust, Frederick (Schiller)

Bolt, Robert (Oxton) 1924-1995 .... **CLC 14**
See also CA 17-20R; 147; CANR 35;
DLB 13; MTCW

Bombet, Louis-Alexandre-Cesar
See Stendhal

Bomkauf
See Kaufman, Bob (Garnell)

Bonaventura................... **NCLC 35**
See also DLB 90

Bond, Edward 1934-....... **CLC 4, 6, 13, 23**
See also CA 25-28R; CANR 38; DLB 13;
MTCW

Bonham, Frank 1914-1989........ **CLC 12**
See also AAYA 1; CA 9-12R; CANR 4, 36;
JRDA; MAICYA; SAAS 3; SATA 1, 49;
SATA-Obit 62

Bonnefoy, Yves 1923-........ **CLC 9, 15, 58**
See also CA 85-88; CANR 33; MTCW

Bontemps, Arna(ud Wendell)
1902-1973 .... **CLC 1, 18; BLC**
See also BW 1; CA 1-4R; 41-44R; CANR 4,
35; CLR 6; DLB 48, 51; JRDA;
MAICYA; MTCW; SATA 2, 44;
SATA-Obit 24

Booth, Martin 1944-.............. **CLC 13**
See also CA 93-96; CAAS 2

Booth, Philip 1925-............... **CLC 23**
See also CA 5-8R; CANR 5; DLBY 82

Booth, Wayne C(layson) 1921- ..... **CLC 24**
See also CA 1-4R; CAAS 5; CANR 3, 43;
DLB 67

Borchert, Wolfgang 1921-1947 ..... **TCLC 5**
See also CA 104; DLB 69, 124

Borel, Petrus 1809-1859........ **NCLC 41**

Borges, Jorge Luis
1899-1986 ... **CLC 1, 2, 3, 4, 6, 8, 9, 10,
13, 19, 44, 48, 83; DA; HLC; SSC 4;
WLC**
See also CA 21-24R; CANR 19, 33;
DLB 113; DLBY 86; HW; MTCW

Borowski, Tadeusz 1922-1951...... **TCLC 9**
See also CA 106

Borrow, George (Henry)
1803-1881 .... **NCLC 9**
See also DLB 21, 55

Bosman, Herman Charles
1905-1951 .... **TCLC 49**

Bosschere, Jean de 1878(?)-1953... **TCLC 19**
See also CA 115

Boswell, James
1740-1795 .... **LC 4; DA; WLC**
See also CDBLB 1660-1789; DLB 104, 142

Bottoms, David 1949-............. **CLC 53**
See also CA 105; CANR 22; DLB 120;
DLBY 83

Boucicault, Dion 1820-1890...... **NCLC 41**

Boucolon, Maryse 1937-
See Conde, Maryse
See also CA 110; CANR 30

Bourget, Paul (Charles Joseph)
1852-1935 .... **TCLC 12**
See also CA 107; DLB 123

Bourjaily, Vance (Nye) 1922- .... **CLC 8, 62**
See also CA 1-4R; CAAS 1; CANR 2;
DLB 2, 143

Bourne, Randolph S(illiman)
1886-1918 .... **TCLC 16**
See also CA 117; DLB 63

Bova, Ben(jamin William) 1932-.... **CLC 45**
See also CA 5-8R; CAAS 18; CANR 11;
CLR 3; DLBY 81; MAICYA; MTCW;
SATA 6, 68

Bowen, Elizabeth (Dorothea Cole)
1899-1973 ..... **CLC 1, 3, 6, 11, 15, 22;
SSC 3**
See also CA 17-18; 41-44R; CANR 35;
CAP 2; CDBLB 1945-1960; DLB 15;
MTCW

Bowering, George 1935-........ **CLC 15, 47**
See also CA 21-24R; CAAS 16; CANR 10;
DLB 53

Bowering, Marilyn R(uthe) 1949-... **CLC 32**
See also CA 101; CANR 49

Bowers, Edgar 1924- .... **CLC 9**
See also CA 5-8R; CANR 24; DLB 5

Bowie, David .... **CLC 17**
See also Jones, David Robert

Bowles, Jane (Sydney)
1917-1973 .... **CLC 3, 68**
See also CA 19-20; 41-44R; CAP 2

Bowles, Paul (Frederick)
1910- .... **CLC 1, 2, 19, 53; SSC 3**
See also CA 1-4R; CAAS 1; CANR 1, 19;
DLB 5, 6; MTCW

Box, Edgar
See Vidal, Gore

Boyd, Nancy
See Millay, Edna St. Vincent

Boyd, William 1952-........ **CLC 28, 53, 70**
See also CA 114; 120

Boyle, Kay
1902-1992 ..... **CLC 1, 5, 19, 58; SSC 5**
See also CA 13-16R; 140; CAAS 1;
CANR 29; DLB 4, 9, 48, 86; DLBY 93;
MTCW

Boyle, Mark
See Kienzle, William X(avier)

Boyle, Patrick 1905-1982.......... **CLC 19**
See also CA 127

Boyle, T. C.
See Boyle, T(homas) Coraghessan

Boyle, T(homas) Coraghessan
1948- .... **CLC 36, 55; SSC 16**
See also BEST 90:4; CA 120; CANR 44;
DLBY 86

Boz
See Dickens, Charles (John Huffam)

Brackenridge, Hugh Henry
1748-1816 .... **NCLC 7**
See also DLB 11, 37

Bradbury, Edward P.
See Moorcock, Michael (John)

Bradbury, Malcolm (Stanley)
1932- .... **CLC 32, 61**
See also CA 1-4R; CANR 1, 33; DLB 14;
MTCW

Bradbury, Ray (Douglas)
1920- ... **CLC 1, 3, 10, 15, 42; DA; WLC**
See also AITN 1, 2; CA 1-4R; CANR 2, 30;
CDALB 1968-1988; DLB 2, 8; MTCW;
SATA 11, 64

Bradford, Gamaliel 1863-1932..... **TCLC 36**
See also DLB 17

Bradley, David (Henry, Jr.)
1950- .... **CLC 23; BLC**
See also BW 1; CA 104; CANR 26; DLB 33

Bradley, John Ed(mund, Jr.)
1958- .... CLC 55
See also CA 139

Bradley, Marion Zimmer   1930- ..... CLC 30
See also AAYA 9; CA 57-60; CAAS 10;
CANR 7, 31; DLB 8; MTCW

Bradstreet, Anne
1612(?)-1672 ...... LC 4, 30; DA; PC 10
See also CDALB 1640-1865; DLB 24

Brady, Joan   1939- .... CLC 86
See also CA 141

Bragg, Melvyn   1939- .... CLC 10
See also BEST 89:3; CA 57-60; CANR 10,
48; DLB 14

Braine, John (Gerard)
1922-1986 .... CLC 1, 3, 41
See also CA 1-4R; 120; CANR 1, 33;
CDBLB 1945-1960; DLB 15; DLBY 86;
MTCW

Brammer, William   1930(?)-1978 .... CLC 31
See also CA 77-80

Brancati, Vitaliano   1907-1954 ..... TCLC 12
See also CA 109

Brancato, Robin F(idler)   1936- ..... CLC 35
See also AAYA 9; CA 69-72; CANR 11,
45; CLR 32; JRDA; SAAS 9; SATA 23

Brand, Max
See Faust, Frederick (Schiller)

Brand, Millen   1906-1980 .... CLC 7
See also CA 21-24R; 97-100

Branden, Barbara .... CLC 44

Brandes, Georg (Morris Cohen)
1842-1927 .... TCLC 10
See also CA 105

Brandys, Kazimierz   1916- .... CLC 62

Branley, Franklyn M(ansfield)
1915- .... CLC 21
See also CA 33-36R; CANR 14, 39;
CLR 13; MAICYA; SAAS 16; SATA 4,
68

Brathwaite, Edward Kamau   1930- ... CLC 11
See also BW 2; CA 25-28R; CANR 11, 26,
47; DLB 125

Brautigan, Richard (Gary)
1935-1984 .... CLC 1, 3, 5, 9, 12, 34, 42
See also CA 53-56; 113; CANR 34; DLB 2,
5; DLBY 80, 84; MTCW; SATA 56

Braverman, Kate   1950- .... CLC 67
See also CA 89-92

Brecht, Bertolt
1898-1956 ...... TCLC 1, 6, 13, 35; DA;
DC 3; WLC
See also CA 104; 133; DLB 56, 124; MTCW

Brecht, Eugen Berthold Friedrich
See Brecht, Bertolt

Bremer, Fredrika   1801-1865 ..... NCLC 11

Brennan, Christopher John
1870-1932 .... TCLC 17
See also CA 117

Brennan, Maeve   1917- .... CLC 5
See also CA 81-84

Brentano, Clemens (Maria)
1778-1842 .... NCLC 1
See also DLB 90

Brent of Bin Bin
See Franklin, (Stella Maraia Sarah) Miles

Brenton, Howard   1942- .... CLC 31
See also CA 69-72; CANR 33; DLB 13;
MTCW

Breslin, James   1930-
See Breslin, Jimmy
See also CA 73-76; CANR 31; MTCW

Breslin, Jimmy .... CLC 4, 43
See also Breslin, James
See also AITN 1

Bresson, Robert   1901- .... CLC 16
See also CA 110; CANR 49

Breton, Andre   1896-1966... CLC 2, 9, 15, 54
See also CA 19-20; 25-28R; CANR 40;
CAP 2; DLB 65; MTCW

Breytenbach, Breyten   1939(?)- .. CLC 23, 37
See also CA 113; 129

Bridgers, Sue Ellen   1942- .... CLC 26
See also AAYA 8; CA 65-68; CANR 11,
36; CLR 18; DLB 52; JRDA; MAICYA;
SAAS 1; SATA 22

Bridges, Robert (Seymour)
1844-1930 .... TCLC 1
See also CA 104; CDBLB 1890-1914;
DLB 19, 98

Bridie, James..................... TCLC 3
See also Mavor, Osborne Henry
See also DLB 10

Brin, David   1950- .... CLC 34
See also CA 102; CANR 24; SATA 65

Brink, Andre (Philippus)
1935- .... CLC 18, 36
See also CA 104; CANR 39; MTCW

Brinsmead, H(esba) F(ay)   1922- .... CLC 21
See also CA 21-24R; CANR 10; MAICYA;
SAAS 5; SATA 18, 78

Brittain, Vera (Mary)
1893(?)-1970 .... CLC 23
See also CA 13-16; 25-28R; CAP 1; MTCW

Broch, Hermann   1886-1951....... TCLC 20
See also CA 117; DLB 85, 124

Brock, Rose
See Hansen, Joseph

Brodkey, Harold   1930- .... CLC 56
See also CA 111; DLB 130

Brodsky, Iosif Alexandrovich   1940-
See Brodsky, Joseph
See also AITN 1; CA 41-44R; CANR 37;
MTCW

Brodsky, Joseph .. CLC 4, 6, 13, 36, 50; PC 9
See also Brodsky, Iosif Alexandrovich

Brodsky, Michael Mark   1948- ..... CLC 19
See also CA 102; CANR 18, 41

Bromell, Henry   1947- .... CLC 5
See also CA 53-56; CANR 9

Bromfield, Louis (Brucker)
1896-1956 .... TCLC 11
See also CA 107; DLB 4, 9, 86

Broner, E(sther) M(asserman)
1930- .... CLC 19
See also CA 17-20R; CANR 8, 25; DLB 28

Bronk, William   1918- .... CLC 10
See also CA 89-92; CANR 23

Bronstein, Lev Davidovich
See Trotsky, Leon

Bronte, Anne   1820-1849 .... NCLC 4
See also DLB 21

Bronte, Charlotte
1816-1855 ... NCLC 3, 8, 33; DA; WLC
See also CDBLB 1832-1890; DLB 21

Bronte, (Jane) Emily
1818-1848 .... NCLC 16, 35; DA; PC 8;
WLC
See also CDBLB 1832-1890; DLB 21, 32

Brooke, Frances   1724-1789 .... LC 6
See also DLB 39, 99

Brooke, Henry   1703(?)-1783 .... LC 1
See also DLB 39

Brooke, Rupert (Chawner)
1887-1915 .... TCLC 2, 7; DA; WLC
See also CA 104; 132; CDBLB 1914-1945;
DLB 19; MTCW

Brooke-Haven, P.
See Wodehouse, P(elham) G(renville)

Brooke-Rose, Christine   1926- ...... CLC 40
See also CA 13-16R; DLB 14

Brookner, Anita   1928- ...... CLC 32, 34, 51
See also CA 114; 120; CANR 37; DLBY 87;
MTCW

Brooks, Cleanth   1906-1994 ..... CLC 24, 86
See also CA 17-20R; 145; CANR 33, 35;
DLB 63; DLBY 94; MTCW

Brooks, George
See Baum, L(yman) Frank

Brooks, Gwendolyn
1917- ...... CLC 1, 2, 4, 5, 15, 49; BLC;
DA; PC 7; WLC
See also AITN 1; BW 2; CA 1-4R;
CANR 1, 27; CDALB 1941-1968;
CLR 27; DLB 5, 76; MTCW; SATA 6

Brooks, Mel...................... CLC 12
See also Kaminsky, Melvin
See also AAYA 13; DLB 26

Brooks, Peter   1938- .... CLC 34
See also CA 45-48; CANR 1

Brooks, Van Wyck   1886-1963...... CLC 29
See also CA 1-4R; CANR 6; DLB 45, 63,
103

Brophy, Brigid (Antonia)
1929- .... CLC 6, 11, 29
See also CA 5-8R; CAAS 4; CANR 25;
DLB 14; MTCW

Brosman, Catharine Savage   1934-.... CLC 9
See also CA 61-64; CANR 21, 46

Brother Antoninus
See Everson, William (Oliver)

Broughton, T(homas) Alan   1936- ... CLC 19
See also CA 45-48; CANR 2, 23, 48

Broumas, Olga   1949- .... CLC 10, 73
See also CA 85-88; CANR 20

Brown, Charles Brockden
1771-1810 .... NCLC 22
See also CDALB 1640-1865; DLB 37, 59,
73

Brown, Christy   1932-1981 .... CLC 63
See also CA 105; 104; DLB 14

Brown, Claude   1937- .... CLC 30; BLC
See also AAYA 7; BW 1; CA 73-76

Brown, Dee (Alexander) 1908- .. CLC 18, 47
See also CA 13-16R; CAAS 6; CANR 11, 45; DLBY 80; MTCW; SATA 5

Brown, George
See Wertmueller, Lina

Brown, George Douglas
1869-1902 . . . . TCLC 28

Brown, George Mackay 1921-.... CLC 5, 48
See also CA 21-24R; CAAS 6; CANR 12, 37; DLB 14, 27, 139; MTCW; SATA 35

Brown, (William) Larry 1951-...... CLC 73
See also CA 130; 134

Brown, Moses
See Barrett, William (Christopher)

Brown, Rita Mae 1944-..... CLC 18, 43, 79
See also CA 45-48; CANR 2, 11, 35; MTCW

Brown, Roderick (Langmere) Haig-
See Haig-Brown, Roderick (Langmere)

Brown, Rosellen 1939-............ CLC 32
See also CA 77-80; CAAS 10; CANR 14, 44

Brown, Sterling Allen
1901-1989 .... CLC 1, 23, 59; BLC
See also BW 1; CA 85-88; 127; CANR 26; DLB 48, 51, 63; MTCW

Brown, Will
See Ainsworth, William Harrison

Brown, William Wells
1813-1884 . . . . NCLC 2; BLC; DC 1
See also DLB 3, 50

Browne, (Clyde) Jackson 1948(?)-... CLC 21
See also CA 120

Browning, Elizabeth Barrett
1806-1861 . . . . . NCLC 1, 16; DA; PC 6; WLC
See also CDBLB 1832-1890; DLB 32

Browning, Robert
1812-1889 . . . . NCLC 19; DA; PC 2
See also CDBLB 1832-1890; DLB 32; YABC 1

Browning, Tod 1882-1962 . . . . CLC 16
See also CA 141; 117

Brownson, Orestes (Augustus)
1803-1876 . . . . NCLC 50

Bruccoli, Matthew J(oseph) 1931- .. CLC 34
See also CA 9-12R; CANR 7; DLB 103

Bruce, Lenny . . . . CLC 21
See also Schneider, Leonard Alfred

Bruin, John
See Brutus, Dennis

Brulard, Henri
See Stendhal

Brulls, Christian
See Simenon, Georges (Jacques Christian)

Brunner, John (Kilian Houston)
1934- . . . . CLC 8, 10
See also CA 1-4R; CAAS 8; CANR 2, 37; MTCW

Bruno, Giordano 1548-1600 . . . . LC 27

Brutus, Dennis 1924- . . . . CLC 43; BLC
See also BW 2; CA 49-52; CAAS 14; CANR 2, 27, 42; DLB 117

Bryan, C(ourtlandt) D(ixon) B(arnes)
1936- . . . . CLC 29
See also CA 73-76; CANR 13

Bryan, Michael
See Moore, Brian

Bryant, William Cullen
1794-1878 . . . . NCLC 6, 46; DA
See also CDALB 1640-1865; DLB 3, 43, 59

Bryusov, Valery Yakovlevich
1873-1924 . . . . TCLC 10
See also CA 107

Buchan, John 1875-1940 . . . . TCLC 41
See also CA 108; 145; DLB 34, 70; YABC 2

Buchanan, George 1506-1582 . . . . LC 4

Buchheim, Lothar-Guenther 1918- ... CLC 6
See also CA 85-88

Buchner, (Karl) Georg
1813-1837 . . . . NCLC 26

Buchwald, Art(hur) 1925-.......... CLC 33
See also AITN 1; CA 5-8R; CANR 21; MTCW; SATA 10

Buck, Pearl S(ydenstricker)
1892-1973 . . . . CLC 7, 11, 18; DA
See also AITN 1; CA 1-4R; 41-44R; CANR 1, 34; DLB 9, 102; MTCW; SATA 1, 25

Buckler, Ernest 1908-1984........ CLC 13
See also CA 11-12; 114; CAP 1; DLB 68; SATA 47

Buckley, Vincent (Thomas)
1925-1988 . . . . CLC 57
See also CA 101

Buckley, William F(rank), Jr.
1925- . . . . CLC 7, 18, 37
See also AITN 1; CA 1-4R; CANR 1, 24; DLB 137; DLBY 80; MTCW

Buechner, (Carl) Frederick
1926- . . . . CLC 2, 4, 6, 9
See also CA 13-16R; CANR 11, 39; DLBY 80; MTCW

Buell, John (Edward) 1927-........ CLC 10
See also CA 1-4R; DLB 53

Buero Vallejo, Antonio 1916- ... CLC 15, 46
See also CA 106; CANR 24, 49; HW; MTCW

Bufalino, Gesualdo 1920(?)-........ CLC 74

Bugayev, Boris Nikolayevich 1880-1934
See Bely, Andrey
See also CA 104

Bukowski, Charles
1920-1994 . . . . CLC 2, 5, 9, 41, 82
See also CA 17-20R; 144; CANR 40; DLB 5, 130; MTCW

Bulgakov, Mikhail (Afanas'evich)
1891-1940 . . . . TCLC 2, 16; SSC 18
See also CA 105

Bulgya, Alexander Alexandrovich
1901-1956 . . . . TCLC 53
See also Fadeyev, Alexander
See also CA 117

Bullins, Ed 1935- . . . . CLC 1, 5, 7; BLC
See also BW 2; CA 49-52; CAAS 16; CANR 24, 46; DLB 7, 38; MTCW

Bulwer-Lytton, Edward (George Earle Lytton)
1803-1873 . . . . NCLC 1, 45
See also DLB 21

Bunin, Ivan Alexeyevich
1870-1953 . . . . TCLC 6; SSC 5
See also CA 104

Bunting, Basil 1900-1985.... CLC 10, 39, 47
See also CA 53-56; 115; CANR 7; DLB 20

Bunuel, Luis 1900-1983 .. CLC 16, 80; HLC
See also CA 101; 110; CANR 32; HW

Bunyan, John 1628-1688 .. LC 4; DA; WLC
See also CDBLB 1660-1789; DLB 39

Burckhardt, Jacob (Christoph)
1818-1897 . . . . NCLC 49

Burford, Eleanor
See Hibbert, Eleanor Alice Burford

Burgess, Anthony
CLC 1, 2, 4, 5, 8, 10, 13, 15, 22, 40, 62, 81
See also Wilson, John (Anthony) Burgess
See also AITN 1; CDBLB 1960 to Present; DLB 14

Burke, Edmund
1729(?)-1797 . . . . LC 7; DA; WLC
See also DLB 104

Burke, Kenneth (Duva)
1897-1993 . . . . CLC 2, 24
See also CA 5-8R; 143; CANR 39; DLB 45, 63; MTCW

Burke, Leda
See Garnett, David

Burke, Ralph
See Silverberg, Robert

Burney, Fanny 1752-1840 . . . . NCLC 12
See also DLB 39

Burns, Robert 1759-1796............ PC 6
See also CDBLB 1789-1832; DA; DLB 109; WLC

Burns, Tex
See L'Amour, Louis (Dearborn)

Burnshaw, Stanley 1906-..... CLC 3, 13, 44
See also CA 9-12R; DLB 48

Burr, Anne 1937- . . . . CLC 6
See also CA 25-28R

Burroughs, Edgar Rice
1875-1950 . . . . TCLC 2, 32
See also AAYA 11; CA 104; 132; DLB 8; MTCW; SATA 41

Burroughs, William S(eward)
1914- . . . . CLC 1, 2, 5, 15, 22, 42, 75; DA; WLC
See also AITN 2; CA 9-12R; CANR 20; DLB 2, 8, 16, 152; DLBY 81; MTCW

Burton, Richard F. 1821-1890.... NCLC 42
See also DLB 55

Busch, Frederick 1941- ... CLC 7, 10, 18, 47
See also CA 33-36R; CAAS 1; CANR 45; DLB 6

Bush, Ronald 1946- . . . . CLC 34
See also CA 136

Bustos, F(rancisco)
See Borges, Jorge Luis

Bustos Domecq, H(onorio)
See Bioy Casares, Adolfo; Borges, Jorge Luis

Butler, Octavia E(stelle) 1947- ..... CLC 38
See also BW 2; CA 73-76; CANR 12, 24,
38; DLB 33; MTCW

Butler, Robert Olen (Jr.) 1945-..... CLC 81
See also CA 112

Butler, Samuel 1612-1680 .... LC 16
See also DLB 101, 126

Butler, Samuel
1835-1902 ...... TCLC 1, 33; DA; WLC
See also CA 143; CDBLB 1890-1914;
DLB 18, 57

Butler, Walter C.
See Faust, Frederick (Schiller)

Butor, Michel (Marie Francois)
1926- .... CLC 1, 3, 8, 11, 15
See also CA 9-12R; CANR 33; DLB 83;
MTCW

Buzo, Alexander (John) 1944-...... CLC 61
See also CA 97-100; CANR 17, 39

Buzzati, Dino 1906-1972 .... CLC 36
See also CA 33-36R

Byars, Betsy (Cromer) 1928-....... CLC 35
See also CA 33-36R; CANR 18, 36; CLR 1,
16; DLB 52; JRDA; MAICYA; MTCW;
SAAS 1; SATA 4, 46, 80

Byatt, A(ntonia) S(usan Drabble)
1936- .... CLC 19, 65
See also CA 13-16R; CANR 13, 33;
DLB 14; MTCW

Byrne, David 1952-............... CLC 26
See also CA 127

Byrne, John Keyes 1926-
See Leonard, Hugh
See also CA 102

Byron, George Gordon (Noel)
1788-1824 ...... NCLC 2, 12; DA; WLC
See also CDBLB 1789-1832; DLB 96, 110

C. 3. 3.
See Wilde, Oscar (Fingal O'Flahertie Wills)

Caballero, Fernan 1796-1877..... NCLC 10

Cabell, James Branch 1879-1958 ... TCLC 6
See also CA 105; DLB 9, 78

Cable, George Washington
1844-1925 .... TCLC 4; SSC 4
See also CA 104; DLB 12, 74

Cabral de Melo Neto, Joao 1920-... CLC 76

Cabrera Infante, G(uillermo)
1929- .... CLC 5, 25, 45; HLC
See also CA 85-88; CANR 29; DLB 113;
HW; MTCW

Cade, Toni
See Bambara, Toni Cade

Cadmus and Harmonia
See Buchan, John

Caedmon fl. 658-680............. CMLC 7
See also DLB 146

Caeiro, Alberto
See Pessoa, Fernando (Antonio Nogueira)

Cage, John (Milton, Jr.) 1912-..... CLC 41
See also CA 13-16R; CANR 9

Cain, G.
See Cabrera Infante, G(uillermo)

Cain, Guillermo
See Cabrera Infante, G(uillermo)

Cain, James M(allahan)
1892-1977 .... CLC 3, 11, 28
See also AITN 1; CA 17-20R; 73-76;
CANR 8, 34; MTCW

Caine, Mark
See Raphael, Frederic (Michael)

Calasso, Roberto 1941- .... CLC 81
See also CA 143

Calderon de la Barca, Pedro
1600-1681 .... LC 23; DC 3

Caldwell, Erskine (Preston)
1903-1987 .... CLC 1, 8, 14, 50, 60;
SSC 19
See also AITN 1; CA 1-4R; 121; CAAS 1;
CANR 2, 33; DLB 9, 86; MTCW

Caldwell, (Janet Miriam) Taylor (Holland)
1900-1985 .... CLC 2, 28, 39
See also CA 5-8R; 116; CANR 5

Calhoun, John Caldwell
1782-1850 .... NCLC 15
See also DLB 3

Calisher, Hortense
1911- .... CLC 2, 4, 8, 38; SSC 15
See also CA 1-4R; CANR 1, 22; DLB 2;
MTCW

Callaghan, Morley Edward
1903-1990 .... CLC 3, 14, 41, 65
See also CA 9-12R; 132; CANR 33;
DLB 68; MTCW

Calvino, Italo
1923-1985 ..... CLC 5, 8, 11, 22, 33, 39,
73; SSC 3
See also CA 85-88; 116; CANR 23; MTCW

Cameron, Carey 1952-............ CLC 59
See also CA 135

Cameron, Peter 1959-............. CLC 44
See also CA 125

Campana, Dino 1885-1932........ TCLC 20
See also CA 117; DLB 114

Campbell, John W(ood, Jr.)
1910-1971 .... CLC 32
See also CA 21-22; 29-32R; CANR 34;
CAP 2; DLB 8; MTCW

Campbell, Joseph 1904-1987 .... CLC 69
See also AAYA 3; BEST 89:2; CA 1-4R;
124; CANR 3, 28; MTCW

Campbell, Maria 1940-............ CLC 85
See also CA 102; NNAL

Campbell, (John) Ramsey
1946- .... CLC 42; SSC 19
See also CA 57-60; CANR 7

Campbell, (Ignatius) Roy (Dunnachie)
1901-1957 .... TCLC 5
See also CA 104; DLB 20

Campbell, Thomas 1777-1844 .... NCLC 19
See also DLB 93; 144

Campbell, Wilfred................. TCLC 9
See also Campbell, William

Campbell, William 1858(?)-1918
See Campbell, Wilfred
See also CA 106; DLB 92

Campos, Alvaro de
See Pessoa, Fernando (Antonio Nogueira)

Camus, Albert
1913-1960 .... CLC 1, 2, 4, 9, 11, 14, 32,
63, 69; DA; DC 2; SSC 9; WLC
See also CA 89-92; DLB 72; MTCW

Canby, Vincent 1924-............. CLC 13
See also CA 81-84

Cancale
See Desnos, Robert

Canetti, Elias
1905-1994 ...... CLC 3, 14, 25, 75, 86
See also CA 21-24R; 146; CANR 23;
DLB 85, 124; MTCW

Canin, Ethan 1960-............... CLC 55
See also CA 131; 135

Cannon, Curt
See Hunter, Evan

Cape, Judith
See Page, P(atricia) K(athleen)

Capek, Karel
1890-1938 ..... TCLC 6, 37; DA; DC 1;
WLC
See also CA 104; 140

Capote, Truman
1924-1984 ...... CLC 1, 3, 8, 13, 19, 34,
38, 58; DA; SSC 2; WLC
See also CA 5-8R; 113; CANR 18;
CDALB 1941-1968; DLB 2; DLBY 80,
84; MTCW

Capra, Frank 1897-1991.......... CLC 16
See also CA 61-64; 135

Caputo, Philip 1941-............. CLC 32
See also CA 73-76; CANR 40

Card, Orson Scott 1951- .... CLC 44, 47, 50
See also AAYA 11; CA 102; CANR 27, 47;
MTCW

Cardenal (Martinez), Ernesto
1925- .... CLC 31; HLC
See also CA 49-52; CANR 2, 32; HW;
MTCW

Carducci, Giosue 1835-1907....... TCLC 32

Carew, Thomas 1595(?)-1640........ LC 13
See also DLB 126

Carey, Ernestine Gilbreth 1908-.... CLC 17
See also CA 5-8R; SATA 2

Carey, Peter 1943-............. CLC 40, 55
See also CA 123; 127; MTCW

Carleton, William 1794-1869...... NCLC 3

Carlisle, Henry (Coffin) 1926-...... CLC 33
See also CA 13-16R; CANR 15

Carlsen, Chris
See Holdstock, Robert P.

Carlson, Ron(ald F.) 1947-......... CLC 54
See also CA 105; CANR 27

Carlyle, Thomas 1795-1881 .. NCLC 22; DA
See also CDBLB 1789-1832; DLB 55; 144

Carman, (William) Bliss
1861-1929 .... TCLC 7
See also CA 104; DLB 92

Carnegie, Dale 1888-1955 .... TCLC 53

Carossa, Hans 1878-1956........ TCLC 48
See also DLB 66

Carpenter, Don(ald Richard)
1931- .... CLC 41
See also CA 45-48; CANR 1

Carpentier (y Valmont), Alejo
    1904-1980 . . . . **CLC 8, 11, 38; HLC**
    See also CA 65-68; 97-100; CANR 11;
    DLB 113; HW

Carr, Caleb 1955(?)- . . . . **CLC 86**
    See also CA 147

Carr, Emily 1871-1945 . . . . **TCLC 32**
    See also DLB 68

Carr, John Dickson 1906-1977 . . . . . . **CLC 3**
    See also CA 49-52; 69-72; CANR 3, 33;
    MTCW

Carr, Philippa
    See Hibbert, Eleanor Alice Burford

Carr, Virginia Spencer 1929- . . . . **CLC 34**
    See also CA 61-64; DLB 111

Carrere, Emmanuel 1957- . . . . **CLC 89**

Carrier, Roch 1937- . . . . **CLC 13, 78**
    See also CA 130; DLB 53

Carroll, James P. 1943(?)- . . . . **CLC 38**
    See also CA 81-84

Carroll, Jim 1951- . . . . **CLC 35**
    See also CA 45-48; CANR 42

Carroll, Lewis . . . . **NCLC 2; WLC**
    See also Dodgson, Charles Lutwidge
    See also CDBLB 1832-1890; CLR 2, 18;
    DLB 18; JRDA

Carroll, Paul Vincent 1900-1968 . . . . **CLC 10**
    See also CA 9-12R; 25-28R; DLB 10

Carruth, Hayden
    1921- . . . . . . **CLC 4, 7, 10, 18, 84; PC 10**
    See also CA 9-12R; CANR 4, 38; DLB 5;
    MTCW; SATA 47

Carson, Rachel Louise 1907-1964 . . . **CLC 71**
    See also CA 77-80; CANR 35; MTCW;
    SATA 23

Carter, Angela (Olive)
    1940-1992 . . . . . . **CLC 5, 41, 76; SSC 13**
    See also CA 53-56; 136; CANR 12, 36;
    DLB 14; MTCW; SATA 66;
    SATA-Obit 70

Carter, Nick
    See Smith, Martin Cruz

Carver, Raymond
    1938-1988 . . . **CLC 22, 36, 53, 55; SSC 8**
    See also CA 33-36R; 126; CANR 17, 34;
    DLB 130; DLBY 84, 88; MTCW

Cary, Elizabeth 1585-1639 . . . . **LC 30**

Cary, (Arthur) Joyce (Lunel)
    1888-1957 . . . . **TCLC 1, 29**
    See also CA 104; CDBLB 1914-1945;
    DLB 15, 100

Casanova de Seingalt, Giovanni Jacopo
    1725-1798 . . . . **LC 13**

Casares, Adolfo Bioy
    See Bioy Casares, Adolfo

Casely-Hayford, J(oseph) E(phraim)
    1866-1930 . . . . **TCLC 24; BLC**
    See also BW 2; CA 123

Casey, John (Dudley) 1939- . . . . **CLC 59**
    See also BEST 90:2; CA 69-72; CANR 23

Casey, Michael 1947- . . . . **CLC 2**
    See also CA 65-68; DLB 5

Casey, Patrick
    See Thurman, Wallace (Henry)

Casey, Warren (Peter) 1935-1988 . . . **CLC 12**
    See also CA 101; 127

Casona, Alejandro . . . . **CLC 49**
    See also Alvarez, Alejandro Rodriguez

Cassavetes, John 1929-1989 . . . . **CLC 20**
    See also CA 85-88; 127

Cassill, R(onald) V(erlin) 1919- . . . **CLC 4, 23**
    See also CA 9-12R; CAAS 1; CANR 7, 45;
    DLB 6

Cassity, (Allen) Turner 1929- . . . . **CLC 6, 42**
    See also CA 17-20R; CAAS 8; CANR 11;
    DLB 105

Castaneda, Carlos 1931(?)- . . . . **CLC 12**
    See also CA 25-28R; CANR 32; HW;
    MTCW

Castedo, Elena 1937- . . . . **CLC 65**
    See also CA 132

Castedo-Ellerman, Elena
    See Castedo, Elena

Castellanos, Rosario
    1925-1974 . . . . **CLC 66; HLC**
    See also CA 131; 53-56; DLB 113; HW

Castelvetro, Lodovico 1505-1571 . . . . . **LC 12**

Castiglione, Baldassare 1478-1529 . . . **LC 12**

Castle, Robert
    See Hamilton, Edmond

Castro, Guillen de 1569-1631 . . . . **LC 19**

Castro, Rosalia de 1837-1885 . . . . . **NCLC 3**

Cather, Willa
    See Cather, Willa Sibert

Cather, Willa Sibert
    1873-1947 . . . . **TCLC 1, 11, 31; DA;**
                                                SSC 2; WLC
    See also CA 104; 128; CDALB 1865-1917;
    DLB 9, 54, 78; DLBD 1; MTCW;
    SATA 30

Catton, (Charles) Bruce
    1899-1978 . . . . **CLC 35**
    See also AITN 1; CA 5-8R; 81-84;
    CANR 7; DLB 17; SATA 2;
    SATA-Obit 24

Cauldwell, Frank
    See King, Francis (Henry)

Caunitz, William J. 1933- . . . . **CLC 34**
    See also BEST 89:3; CA 125; 130

Causley, Charles (Stanley) 1917- . . . . . **CLC 7**
    See also CA 9-12R; CANR 5, 35; CLR 30;
    DLB 27; MTCW; SATA 3, 66

Caute, David 1936- . . . . **CLC 29**
    See also CA 1-4R; CAAS 4; CANR 1, 33;
    DLB 14

Cavafy, C(onstantine) P(eter) . . . . . . **TCLC 2, 7**
    See also Kavafis, Konstantinos Petrou

Cavallo, Evelyn
    See Spark, Muriel (Sarah)

Cavanna, Betty . . . . **CLC 12**
    See also Harrison, Elizabeth Cavanna
    See also JRDA; MAICYA; SAAS 4;
    SATA 1, 30

Cavendish, Margaret Lucas
    1623-1673 . . . . **LC 30**
    See also DLB 131

Caxton, William 1421(?)-1491(?) . . . . . **LC 17**

Cayrol, Jean 1911- . . . . **CLC 11**
    See also CA 89-92; DLB 83

Cela, Camilo Jose
    1916- . . . . **CLC 4, 13, 59; HLC**
    See also BEST 90:2; CA 21-24R; CAAS 10;
    CANR 21, 32; DLBY 89; HW; MTCW

Celan, Paul . . . . . . **CLC 10, 19, 53, 82; PC 10**
    See also Antschel, Paul
    See also DLB 69

Celine, Louis-Ferdinand
    . . . . **CLC 1, 3, 4, 7, 9, 15, 47**
    See also Destouches, Louis-Ferdinand
    See also DLB 72

Cellini, Benvenuto 1500-1571 . . . . **LC 7**

Cendrars, Blaise . . . . **CLC 18**
    See also Sauser-Hall, Frederic

Cernuda (y Bidon), Luis
    1902-1963 . . . . **CLC 54**
    See also CA 131; 89-92; DLB 134; HW

Cervantes (Saavedra), Miguel de
    1547-1616 . . . . . . **LC 6, 23; DA; SSC 12;**
                                                WLC

Cesaire, Aime (Fernand)
    1913- . . . . **CLC 19, 32; BLC**
    See also BW 2; CA 65-68; CANR 24, 43;
    MTCW

Chabon, Michael 1965(?)- . . . . **CLC 55**
    See also CA 139

Chabrol, Claude 1930- . . . . **CLC 16**
    See also CA 110

Challans, Mary 1905-1983
    See Renault, Mary
    See also CA 81-84; 111; SATA 23;
    SATA-Obit 36

Challis, George
    See Faust, Frederick (Schiller)

Chambers, Aidan 1934- . . . . **CLC 35**
    See also CA 25-28R; CANR 12, 31; JRDA;
    MAICYA; SAAS 12; SATA 1, 69

Chambers, James 1948-
    See Cliff, Jimmy
    See also CA 124

Chambers, Jessie
    See Lawrence, D(avid) H(erbert Richards)

Chambers, Robert W. 1865-1933 . . . **TCLC 41**

Chandler, Raymond (Thornton)
    1888-1959 . . . . **TCLC 1, 7**
    See also CA 104; 129; CDALB 1929-1941;
    DLBD 6; MTCW

Chang, Jung 1952- . . . . **CLC 71**
    See also CA 142

Channing, William Ellery
    1780-1842 . . . . **NCLC 17**
    See also DLB 1, 59

Chaplin, Charles Spencer
    1889-1977 . . . . **CLC 16**
    See also Chaplin, Charlie
    See also CA 81-84; 73-76

Chaplin, Charlie
    See Chaplin, Charles Spencer
    See also DLB 44

Chapman, George 1559(?)-1634 . . . . . . **LC 22**
    See also DLB 62, 121

Chapman, Graham 1941-1989 . . . . . . **CLC 21**
See also Monty Python
See also CA 116; 129; CANR 35

Chapman, John Jay 1862-1933 . . . . . **TCLC 7**
See also CA 104

Chapman, Walker
See Silverberg, Robert

Chappell, Fred (Davis) 1936- . . . . **CLC 40, 78**
See also CA 5-8R; CAAS 4; CANR 8, 33;
DLB 6, 105

Char, Rene(-Emile)
1907-1988 . . . . **CLC 9, 11, 14, 55**
See also CA 13-16R; 124; CANR 32;
MTCW

Charby, Jay
See Ellison, Harlan (Jay)

Chardin, Pierre Teilhard de
See Teilhard de Chardin, (Marie Joseph)
Pierre

Charles I 1600-1649 . . . . **LC 13**

Charyn, Jerome 1937- . . . . **CLC 5, 8, 18**
See also CA 5-8R; CAAS 1; CANR 7;
DLBY 83; MTCW

Chase, Mary (Coyle) 1907-1981 . . . . . . **DC 1**
See also CA 77-80; 105; SATA 17;
SATA-Obit 29

Chase, Mary Ellen 1887-1973 . . . . **CLC 2**
See also CA 13-16; 41-44R; CAP 1;
SATA 10

Chase, Nicholas
See Hyde, Anthony

Chateaubriand, Francois Rene de
1768-1848 . . . . **NCLC 3**
See also DLB 119

Chatterje, Sarat Chandra 1876-1936(?)
See Chatterji, Saratchandra
See also CA 109

Chatterji, Bankim Chandra
1838-1894 . . . . **NCLC 19**

Chatterji, Saratchandra . . . . **TCLC 13**
See also Chatterje, Sarat Chandra

Chatterton, Thomas 1752-1770 . . . . **LC 3**
See also DLB 109

Chatwin, (Charles) Bruce
1940-1989 . . . . **CLC 28, 57, 59**
See also AAYA 4; BEST 90:1; CA 85-88;
127

Chaucer, Daniel
See Ford, Ford Madox

Chaucer, Geoffrey
1340(?)-1400 . . . . **LC 17; DA**
See also CDBLB Before 1660; DLB 146

Chaviaras, Strates 1935-
See Haviaras, Stratis
See also CA 105

Chayefsky, Paddy . . . . **CLC 23**
See also Chayefsky, Sidney
See also DLB 7, 44; DLBY 81

Chayefsky, Sidney 1923-1981
See Chayefsky, Paddy
See also CA 9-12R; 104; CANR 18

Chedid, Andree 1920- . . . . **CLC 47**
See also CA 145

Cheever, John
1912-1982 . . . . . . **CLC 3, 7, 8, 11, 15, 25,
64; DA; SSC 1; WLC**
See also CA 5-8R; 106; CABS 1; CANR 5,
27; CDALB 1941-1968; DLB 2, 102;
DLBY 80, 82; MTCW

Cheever, Susan 1943- . . . . **CLC 18, 48**
See also CA 103; CANR 27; DLBY 82

Chekhonte, Antosha
See Chekhov, Anton (Pavlovich)

Chekhov, Anton (Pavlovich)
1860-1904 . . . . . **TCLC 3, 10, 31, 55; DA;
SSC 2; WLC**
See also CA 104; 124

Chernyshevsky, Nikolay Gavrilovich
1828-1889 . . . . **NCLC 1**

Cherry, Carolyn Janice 1942-
See Cherryh, C. J.
See also CA 65-68; CANR 10

Cherryh, C. J. . . . . **CLC 35**
See also Cherry, Carolyn Janice
See also DLBY 80

Chesnutt, Charles W(addell)
1858-1932 . . . . **TCLC 5, 39; BLC; SSC 7**
See also BW 1; CA 106; 125; DLB 12, 50,
78; MTCW

Chester, Alfred 1929(?)-1971 . . . . **CLC 49**
See also CA 33-36R; DLB 130

Chesterton, G(ilbert) K(eith)
1874-1936 . . . . **TCLC 1, 6; SSC 1**
See also CA 104; 132; CDBLB 1914-1945;
DLB 10, 19, 34, 70, 98, 149; MTCW;
SATA 27

Chiang Pin-chin 1904-1986
See Ding Ling
See also CA 118

Ch'ien Chung-shu 1910- . . . . **CLC 22**
See also CA 130; MTCW

Child, L. Maria
See Child, Lydia Maria

Child, Lydia Maria 1802-1880 . . . . **NCLC 6**
See also DLB 1, 74; SATA 67

Child, Mrs.
See Child, Lydia Maria

Child, Philip 1898-1978 . . . . **CLC 19, 68**
See also CA 13-14; CAP 1; SATA 47

Childress, Alice
1920-1994 . . **CLC 12, 15, 86; BLC; DC 4**
See also AAYA 8; BW 2; CA 45-48; 146;
CANR 3, 27; CLR 14; DLB 7, 38; JRDA;
MAICYA; MTCW; SATA 7, 48, 81

Chislett, (Margaret) Anne 1943- . . . . **CLC 34**

Chitty, Thomas Willes 1926- . . . . **CLC 11**
See also Hinde, Thomas
See also CA 5-8R

Chivers, Thomas Holley
1809-1858 . . . . **NCLC 49**
See also DLB 3

Chomette, Rene Lucien 1898-1981
See Clair, Rene
See also CA 103

Chopin, Kate . . . . . . **TCLC 5, 14; DA; SSC 8**
See also Chopin, Katherine
See also CDALB 1865-1917; DLB 12, 78

Chopin, Katherine 1851-1904
See Chopin, Kate
See also CA 104; 122

Chretien de Troyes
c. 12th cent. - . . . . **CMLC 10**

Christie
See Ichikawa, Kon

Christie, Agatha (Mary Clarissa)
1890-1976 . . . . . . **CLC 1, 6, 8, 12, 39, 48**
See also AAYA 9; AITN 1, 2; CA 17-20R;
61-64; CANR 10, 37; CDBLB 1914-1945;
DLB 13, 77; MTCW; SATA 36

Christie, (Ann) Philippa
See Pearce, Philippa
See also CA 5-8R; CANR 4

Christine de Pizan 1365(?)-1431(?) . . . . **LC 9**

Chubb, Elmer
See Masters, Edgar Lee

Chulkov, Mikhail Dmitrievich
1743-1792 . . . . **LC 2**
See also DLB 150

Churchill, Caryl 1938- . . . **CLC 31, 55; DC 5**
See also CA 102; CANR 22, 46; DLB 13;
MTCW

Churchill, Charles 1731-1764 . . . . **LC 3**
See also DLB 109

Chute, Carolyn 1947- . . . . **CLC 39**
See also CA 123

Ciardi, John (Anthony)
1916-1986 . . . . **CLC 10, 40, 44**
See also CA 5-8R; 118; CAAS 2; CANR 5,
33; CLR 19; DLB 5; DLBY 86;
MAICYA; MTCW; SATA 1, 65;
SATA-Obit 46

Cicero, Marcus Tullius
106B.C.-43B.C. . . . . **CMLC 3**

Cimino, Michael 1943- . . . . **CLC 16**
See also CA 105

Cioran, E(mil) M. 1911- . . . . **CLC 64**
See also CA 25-28R

Cisneros, Sandra 1954- . . . . . . **CLC 69; HLC**
See also AAYA 9; CA 131; DLB 122, 152;
HW

Clair, Rene . . . . **CLC 20**
See also Chomette, Rene Lucien

Clampitt, Amy 1920-1994 . . . . **CLC 32**
See also CA 110; 146; CANR 29; DLB 105

Clancy, Thomas L., Jr. 1947-
See Clancy, Tom
See also CA 125; 131; MTCW

Clancy, Tom . . . . **CLC 45**
See also Clancy, Thomas L., Jr.
See also AAYA 9; BEST 89:1, 90:1

Clare, John 1793-1864 . . . . **NCLC 9**
See also DLB 55, 96

Clarin
See Alas (y Urena), Leopoldo (Enrique
Garcia)

Clark, Al C.
See Goines, Donald

Clark, (Robert) Brian 1932- . . . . **CLC 29**
See also CA 41-44R

Clark, Curt
See Westlake, Donald E(dwin)

Clark, Eleanor 1913- .... CLC 5, 19
See also CA 9-12R; CANR 41; DLB 6

Clark, J. P.
See Clark, John Pepper
See also DLB 117

Clark, John Pepper
1935- .... CLC 38; BLC; DC 5
See also Clark, J. P.
See also BW 1; CA 65-68; CANR 16

Clark, M. R.
See Clark, Mavis Thorpe

Clark, Mavis Thorpe 1909- .... CLC 12
See also CA 57-60; CANR 8, 37; CLR 30;
MAICYA; SAAS 5; SATA 8, 74

Clark, Walter Van Tilburg
1909-1971 .... CLC 28
See also CA 9-12R; 33-36R; DLB 9;
SATA 8

Clarke, Arthur C(harles)
1917- ...... CLC 1, 4, 13, 18, 35; SSC 3
See also AAYA 4; CA 1-4R; CANR 2, 28;
JRDA; MAICYA; MTCW; SATA 13, 70

Clarke, Austin 1896-1974........ CLC 6, 9
See also CA 29-32; 49-52; CAP 2; DLB 10,
20

Clarke, Austin C(hesterfield)
1934- .... CLC 8, 53; BLC
See also BW 1; CA 25-28R; CAAS 16;
CANR 14, 32; DLB 53, 125

Clarke, Gillian 1937- .... CLC 61
See also CA 106; DLB 40

Clarke, Marcus (Andrew Hislop)
1846-1881 .... NCLC 19

Clarke, Shirley 1925-............. CLC 16

Clash, The
See Headon, (Nicky) Topper; Jones, Mick;
Simonon, Paul; Strummer, Joe

Claudel, Paul (Louis Charles Marie)
1868-1955 .... TCLC 2, 10
See also CA 104

Clavell, James (duMaresq)
1925-1994.........CLC 6, 25, 87
See also CA 25-28R; 146; CANR 26, 48;
MTCW

Cleaver, (Leroy) Eldridge
1935- .... CLC 30; BLC
See also BW 1; CA 21-24R; CANR 16

Cleese, John (Marwood) 1939- ..... CLC 21
See also Monty Python
See also CA 112; 116; CANR 35; MTCW

Cleishbotham, Jebediah
See Scott, Walter

Cleland, John 1710-1789 .... LC 2
See also DLB 39

Clemens, Samuel Langhorne 1835-1910
See Twain, Mark
See also CA 104; 135; CDALB 1865-1917;
DA; DLB 11, 12, 23, 64, 74; JRDA;
MAICYA; YABC 2

Cleophil
See Congreve, William

Clerihew, E.
See Bentley, E(dmund) C(lerihew)

Clerk, N. W.
See Lewis, C(live) S(taples)

Cliff, Jimmy..................... CLC 21
See also Chambers, James

Clifton, (Thelma) Lucille
1936- .... CLC 19, 66; BLC
See also BW 2; CA 49-52; CANR 2, 24, 42;
CLR 5; DLB 5, 41; MAICYA; MTCW;
SATA 20, 69

Clinton, Dirk
See Silverberg, Robert

Clough, Arthur Hugh 1819-1861.. NCLC 27
See also DLB 32

Clutha, Janet Paterson Frame 1924-
See Frame, Janet
See also CA 1-4R; CANR 2, 36; MTCW

Clyne, Terence
See Blatty, William Peter

Cobalt, Martin
See Mayne, William (James Carter)

Cobbett, William 1763-1835 ..... NCLC 49
See also DLB 43, 107

Coburn, D(onald) L(ee) 1938- ...... CLC 10
See also CA 89-92

Cocteau, Jean (Maurice Eugene Clement)
1889-1963 .... CLC 1, 8, 15, 16, 43; DA;
WLC
See also CA 25-28; CANR 40; CAP 2;
DLB 65; MTCW

Codrescu, Andrei 1946- .... CLC 46
See also CA 33-36R; CAAS 19; CANR 13,
34

Coe, Max
See Bourne, Randolph S(illiman)

Coe, Tucker
See Westlake, Donald E(dwin)

Coetzee, J(ohn) M(ichael)
1940- .... CLC 23, 33, 66
See also CA 77-80; CANR 41; MTCW

Coffey, Brian
See Koontz, Dean R(ay)

Cohan, George M. 1878-1942 ..... TCLC 60

Cohen, Arthur A(llen)
1928-1986 .... CLC 7, 31
See also CA 1-4R; 120; CANR 1, 17, 42;
DLB 28

Cohen, Leonard (Norman)
1934- .... CLC 3, 38
See also CA 21-24R; CANR 14; DLB 53;
MTCW

Cohen, Matt 1942-................ CLC 19
See also CA 61-64; CAAS 18; CANR 40;
DLB 53

Cohen-Solal, Annie 19(?)- .... CLC 50

Colegate, Isabel 1931- .... CLC 36
See also CA 17-20R; CANR 8, 22; DLB 14;
MTCW

Coleman, Emmett
See Reed, Ishmael

Coleridge, Samuel Taylor
1772-1834 .. NCLC 9; DA; PC 11; WLC
See also CDBLB 1789-1832; DLB 93, 107

Coleridge, Sara 1802-1852...... NCLC 31

Coles, Don 1928- .... CLC 46
See also CA 115; CANR 38

Colette, (Sidonie-Gabrielle)
1873-1954 ...... TCLC 1, 5, 16; SSC 10
See also CA 104; 131; DLB 65; MTCW

Collett, (Jacobine) Camilla (Wergeland)
1813-1895 .... NCLC 22

Collier, Christopher 1930-......... CLC 30
See also AAYA 13; CA 33-36R; CANR 13,
33; JRDA; MAICYA; SATA 16, 70

Collier, James L(incoln) 1928- ..... CLC 30
See also AAYA 13; CA 9-12R; CANR 4,
33; CLR 3; JRDA; MAICYA; SATA 8,
70

Collier, Jeremy 1650-1726.......... LC 6

Collier, John 1901-1980
See also CA 65-68; 97-100; CANR 10;
DLB 77; SSC 19

Collins, Hunt
See Hunter, Evan

Collins, Linda 1931-.............. CLC 44
See also CA 125

Collins, (William) Wilkie
1824-1889 .... NCLC 1, 18
See also CDBLB 1832-1890; DLB 18, 70

Collins, William 1721-1759 .... LC 4
See also DLB 109

Colman, George
See Glassco, John

Colt, Winchester Remington
See Hubbard, L(afayette) Ron(ald)

Colter, Cyrus 1910- .... CLC 58
See also BW 1; CA 65-68; CANR 10;
DLB 33

Colton, James
See Hansen, Joseph

Colum, Padraic 1881-1972......... CLC 28
See also CA 73-76; 33-36R; CANR 35;
CLR 36; MAICYA; MTCW; SATA 15

Colvin, James
See Moorcock, Michael (John)

Colwin, Laurie (E.)
1944-1992 ....CLC 5, 13, 23, 84
See also CA 89-92; 139; CANR 20, 46;
DLBY 80; MTCW

Comfort, Alex(ander) 1920-........ CLC 7
See also CA 1-4R; CANR 1, 45

Comfort, Montgomery
See Campbell, (John) Ramsey

Compton-Burnett, I(vy)
1884(?)-1969 ... CLC 1, 3, 10, 15, 34
See also CA 1-4R; 25-28R; CANR 4;
DLB 36; MTCW

Comstock, Anthony 1844-1915 .... TCLC 13
See also CA 110

Conan Doyle, Arthur
See Doyle, Arthur Conan

Conde, Maryse 1937-............. CLC 52
See also Boucolon, Maryse
See also BW 2

Condillac, Etienne Bonnot de
1714-1780 .... LC 26

Condon, Richard (Thomas)
1915- .... CLC 4, 6, 8, 10, 45
See also BEST 90:3; CA 1-4R; CAAS 1;
CANR 2, 23; MTCW

Congreve, William
1670-1729 ... **LC 5, 21; DA; DC 2; WLC**
See also CDBLB 1660-1789; DLB 39, 84

Connell, Evan S(helby), Jr.
1924- .... **CLC 4, 6, 45**
See also AAYA 7; CA 1-4R; CAAS 2;
CANR 2, 39; DLB 2; DLBY 81; MTCW

Connelly, Marc(us Cook)
1890-1980 .... **CLC 7**
See also CA 85-88; 102; CANR 30; DLB 7;
DLBY 80; SATA-Obit 25

Connor, Ralph .... **TCLC 31**
See also Gordon, Charles William
See also DLB 92

Conrad, Joseph
1857-1924 .... **TCLC 1, 6, 13, 25, 43, 57;**
DA; SSC 9; WLC
See also CA 104; 131; CDBLB 1890-1914;
DLB 10, 34, 98; MTCW; SATA 27

Conrad, Robert Arnold
See Hart, Moss

Conroy, Pat 1945- .... **CLC 30, 74**
See also AAYA 8; AITN 1; CA 85-88;
CANR 24; DLB 6; MTCW

Constant (de Rebecque), (Henri) Benjamin
1767-1830 .... **NCLC 6**
See also DLB 119

Conybeare, Charles Augustus
See Eliot, T(homas) S(tearns)

Cook, Michael 1933- .... **CLC 58**
See also CA 93-96; DLB 53

Cook, Robin 1940- .... **CLC 14**
See also BEST 90:2; CA 108; 111;
CANR 41

Cook, Roy
See Silverberg, Robert

Cooke, Elizabeth 1948- .... **CLC 55**
See also CA 129

Cooke, John Esten 1830-1886 ..... **NCLC 5**
See also DLB 3

Cooke, John Estes
See Baum, L(yman) Frank

Cooke, M. E.
See Creasey, John

Cooke, Margaret
See Creasey, John

Cooney, Ray .... **CLC 62**

Cooper, Douglas 1960- .... **CLC 86**

Cooper, Henry St. John
See Creasey, John

Cooper, J. California .... **CLC 56**
See also AAYA 12; BW 1; CA 125

Cooper, James Fenimore
1789-1851 .... **NCLC 1, 27**
See also CDALB 1640-1865; DLB 3;
SATA 19

Coover, Robert (Lowell)
1932- .. **CLC 3, 7, 15, 32, 46, 87; SSC 15**
See also CA 45-48; CANR 3, 37; DLB 2;
DLBY 81; MTCW

Copeland, Stewart (Armstrong)
1952- .... **CLC 26**

Coppard, A(lfred) E(dgar)
1878-1957 .... **TCLC 5**
See also CA 114; YABC 1

Coppee, Francois 1842-1908 ...... **TCLC 25**

Coppola, Francis Ford 1939- .... **CLC 16**
See also CA 77-80; CANR 40; DLB 44

Corbiere, Tristan 1845-1875 ..... **NCLC 43**

Corcoran, Barbara 1911- .... **CLC 17**
See also AAYA 14; CA 21-24R; CAAS 2;
CANR 11, 28, 48; DLB 52; JRDA;
SAAS 20; SATA 3, 77

Cordelier, Maurice
See Giraudoux, (Hippolyte) Jean

Corelli, Marie 1855-1924 .... **TCLC 51**
See also Mackay, Mary
See also DLB 34

Corman, Cid .... **CLC 9**
See also Corman, Sidney
See also CAAS 2; DLB 5

Corman, Sidney 1924-
See Corman, Cid
See also CA 85-88; CANR 44

Cormier, Robert (Edmund)
1925- .... **CLC 12, 30; DA**
See also AAYA 3; CA 1-4R; CANR 5, 23;
CDALB 1968-1988; CLR 12; DLB 52;
JRDA; MAICYA; MTCW; SATA 10, 45

Corn, Alfred (DeWitt III) 1943- .... **CLC 33**
See also CA 104; CANR 44; DLB 120;
DLBY 80

Corneille, Pierre 1606-1684 .... **LC 28**

Cornwell, David (John Moore)
1931- .... **CLC 9, 15**
See also le Carre, John
See also CA 5-8R; CANR 13, 33; MTCW

Corso, (Nunzio) Gregory 1930- ... **CLC 1, 11**
See also CA 5-8R; CANR 41; DLB 5, 16;
MTCW

Cortazar, Julio
1914-1984 ...... **CLC 2, 3, 5, 10, 13, 15,**
33, 34; HLC; SSC 7
See also CA 21-24R; CANR 12, 32;
DLB 113; HW; MTCW

Corwin, Cecil
See Kornbluth, C(yril) M.

Cosic, Dobrica 1921- .... **CLC 14**
See also CA 122; 138

Costain, Thomas B(ertram)
1885-1965 .... **CLC 30**
See also CA 5-8R; 25-28R; DLB 9

Costantini, Humberto
1924(?)-1987 .... **CLC 49**
See also CA 131; 122; HW

Costello, Elvis 1955- .... **CLC 21**

Cotter, Joseph Seamon Sr.
1861-1949 .... **TCLC 28; BLC**
See also BW 1; CA 124; DLB 50

Couch, Arthur Thomas Quiller
See Quiller-Couch, Arthur Thomas

Coulton, James
See Hansen, Joseph

Couperus, Louis (Marie Anne)
1863-1923 .... **TCLC 15**
See also CA 115

Coupland, Douglas 1961- .... **CLC 85**
See also CA 142

Court, Wesli
See Turco, Lewis (Putnam)

Courtenay, Bryce 1933- .... **CLC 59**
See also CA 138

Courtney, Robert
See Ellison, Harlan (Jay)

Cousteau, Jacques-Yves 1910- ...... **CLC 30**
See also CA 65-68; CANR 15; MTCW;
SATA 38

Coward, Noel (Peirce)
1899-1973 .... **CLC 1, 9, 29, 51**
See also AITN 1; CA 17-18; 41-44R;
CANR 35; CAP 2; CDBLB 1914-1945;
DLB 10; MTCW

Cowley, Malcolm 1898-1989 .... **CLC 39**
See also CA 5-8R; 128; CANR 3; DLB 4,
48; DLBY 81, 89; MTCW

Cowper, William 1731-1800 ...... **NCLC 8**
See also DLB 104, 109

Cox, William Trevor 1928- ... **CLC 9, 14, 71**
See also Trevor, William
See also CA 9-12R; CANR 4, 37; DLB 14;
MTCW

Coyne, P. J.
See Masters, Hilary

Cozzens, James Gould
1903-1978 .... **CLC 1, 4, 11**
See also CA 9-12R; 81-84; CANR 19;
CDALB 1941-1968; DLB 9; DLBD 2;
DLBY 84; MTCW

Crabbe, George 1754-1832 .... **NCLC 26**
See also DLB 93

Craig, A. A.
See Anderson, Poul (William)

Craik, Dinah Maria (Mulock)
1826-1887 .... **NCLC 38**
See also DLB 35; MAICYA; SATA 34

Cram, Ralph Adams 1863-1942 .... **TCLC 45**

Crane, (Harold) Hart
1899-1932 .... **TCLC 2, 5; DA; PC 3;**
WLC
See also CA 104; 127; CDALB 1917-1929;
DLB 4, 48; MTCW

Crane, R(onald) S(almon)
1886-1967 .... **CLC 27**
See also CA 85-88; DLB 63

Crane, Stephen (Townley)
1871-1900 .... **TCLC 11, 17, 32; DA;**
SSC 7; WLC
See also CA 109; 140; CDALB 1865-1917;
DLB 12, 54, 78; YABC 2

Crase, Douglas 1944- .... **CLC 58**
See also CA 106

Crashaw, Richard 1612(?)-1649 ...... **LC 24**
See also DLB 126

Craven, Margaret 1901-1980 .... **CLC 17**
See also CA 103

Crawford, F(rancis) Marion
1854-1909 .... **TCLC 10**
See also CA 107; DLB 71

Crawford, Isabella Valancy
1850-1887 .... **NCLC 12**
See also DLB 92

Crayon, Geoffrey
See Irving, Washington

Creasey, John 1908-1973 . . . . CLC 11
See also CA 5-8R; 41-44R; CANR 8;
DLB 77; MTCW

Crebillon, Claude Prosper Jolyot de (fils)
1707-1777 . . . . LC 28

Credo
See Creasey, John

Creeley, Robert (White)
1926- . . . . . CLC 1, 2, 4, 8, 11, 15, 36, 78
See also CA 1-4R; CAAS 10; CANR 23, 43;
DLB 5, 16; MTCW

Crews, Harry (Eugene)
1935- . . . . CLC 6, 23, 49
See also AITN 1; CA 25-28R; CANR 20;
DLB 6, 143; MTCW

Crichton, (John) Michael
1942- . . . . CLC 2, 6, 54
See also AAYA 10; AITN 2; CA 25-28R;
CANR 13, 40; DLBY 81; JRDA;
MTCW; SATA 9

Crispin, Edmund . . . . CLC 22
See also Montgomery, (Robert) Bruce
See also DLB 87

Cristofer, Michael 1945(?)- . . . . CLC 28
See also CA 110; DLB 7

Croce, Benedetto 1866-1952 . . . . . . TCLC 37
See also CA 120

Crockett, David 1786-1836 . . . . NCLC 8
See also DLB 3, 11

Crockett, Davy
See Crockett, David

Crofts, Freeman Wills
1879-1957 . . . . TCLC 55
See also CA 115; DLB 77

Croker, John Wilson 1780-1857 . . NCLC 10
See also DLB 110

Crommelynck, Fernand 1885-1970 . . CLC 75
See also CA 89-92

Cronin, A(rchibald) J(oseph)
1896-1981 . . . . CLC 32
See also CA 1-4R; 102; CANR 5; SATA 47;
SATA-Obit 25

Cross, Amanda
See Heilbrun, Carolyn G(old)

Crothers, Rachel 1878(?)-1958 . . . . . TCLC 19
See also CA 113; DLB 7

Croves, Hal
See Traven, B.

Crowfield, Christopher
See Stowe, Harriet (Elizabeth) Beecher

Crowley, Aleister . . . . TCLC 7
See also Crowley, Edward Alexander

Crowley, Edward Alexander 1875-1947
See Crowley, Aleister
See also CA 104

Crowley, John 1942- . . . . CLC 57
See also CA 61-64; CANR 43; DLBY 82;
SATA 65

Crud
See Crumb, R(obert)

Crumarums
See Crumb, R(obert)

Crumb, R(obert) 1943- . . . . CLC 17
See also CA 106

Crumbum
See Crumb, R(obert)

Crumski
See Crumb, R(obert)

Crum the Bum
See Crumb, R(obert)

Crunk
See Crumb, R(obert)

Crustt
See Crumb, R(obert)

Cryer, Gretchen (Kiger) 1935- . . . . . . CLC 21
See also CA 114; 123

Csath, Geza 1887-1919 . . . . TCLC 13
See also CA 111

Cudlip, David 1933- . . . . CLC 34

Cullen, Countee
1903-1946 . . . . . . TCLC 4, 37; BLC; DA
See also BW 1; CA 108; 124;
CDALB 1917-1929; DLB 4, 48, 51;
MTCW; SATA 18

Cum, R.
See Crumb, R(obert)

Cummings, Bruce F(rederick) 1889-1919
See Barbellion, W. N. P.
See also CA 123

Cummings, E(dward) E(stlin)
1894-1962 . . . . . . CLC 1, 3, 8, 12, 15, 68;
DA; PC 5; WLC 2
See also CA 73-76; CANR 31;
CDALB 1929-1941; DLB 4, 48; MTCW

Cunha, Euclides (Rodrigues Pimenta) da
1866-1909 . . . . TCLC 24
See also CA 123

Cunningham, E. V.
See Fast, Howard (Melvin)

Cunningham, J(ames) V(incent)
1911-1985 . . . . CLC 3, 31
See also CA 1-4R; 115; CANR 1; DLB 5

Cunningham, Julia (Woolfolk)
1916- . . . . CLC 12
See also CA 9-12R; CANR 4, 19, 36;
JRDA; MAICYA; SAAS 2; SATA 1, 26

Cunningham, Michael 1952- . . . . CLC 34
See also CA 136

Cunninghame Graham, R(obert) B(ontine)
1852-1936 . . . . TCLC 19
See also Graham, R(obert) B(ontine)
Cunninghame
See also CA 119; DLB 98

Currie, Ellen 19(?)- . . . . CLC 44

Curtin, Philip
See Lowndes, Marie Adelaide (Belloc)

Curtis, Price
See Ellison, Harlan (Jay)

Cutrate, Joe
See Spiegelman, Art

Czaczkes, Shmuel Yosef
See Agnon, S(hmuel) Y(osef Halevi)

Dabrowska, Maria (Szumska)
1889-1965 . . . . CLC 15
See also CA 106

Dabydeen, David 1955- . . . . CLC 34
See also BW 1; CA 125

Dacey, Philip 1939- . . . . CLC 51
See also CA 37-40R; CAAS 17; CANR 14,
32; DLB 105

Dagerman, Stig (Halvard)
1923-1954 . . . . TCLC 17
See also CA 117

Dahl, Roald 1916-1990 . . . . . CLC 1, 6, 18, 79
See also CA 1-4R; 133; CANR 6, 32, 37;
CLR 1, 7; DLB 139; JRDA; MAICYA;
MTCW; SATA 1, 26, 73; SATA-Obit 65

Dahlberg, Edward 1900-1977 . . . CLC 1, 7, 14
See also CA 9-12R; 69-72; CANR 31;
DLB 48; MTCW

Dale, Colin . . . . TCLC 18
See also Lawrence, T(homas) E(dward)

Dale, George E.
See Asimov, Isaac

Daly, Elizabeth 1878-1967 . . . . CLC 52
See also CA 23-24; 25-28R; CAP 2

Daly, Maureen 1921- . . . . CLC 17
See also AAYA 5; CANR 37; JRDA;
MAICYA; SAAS 1; SATA 2

Damas, Leon-Gontran 1912-1978 . . . CLC 84
See also BW 1; CA 125; 73-76

Daniel, Samuel 1562(?)-1619 . . . . LC 24
See also DLB 62

Daniels, Brett
See Adler, Renata

Dannay, Frederic 1905-1982 . . . . CLC 11
See also Queen, Ellery
See also CA 1-4R; 107; CANR 1, 39;
DLB 137; MTCW

D'Annunzio, Gabriele
1863-1938 . . . . TCLC 6, 40
See also CA 104

d'Antibes, Germain
See Simenon, Georges (Jacques Christian)

Danvers, Dennis 1947- . . . . CLC 70

Danziger, Paula 1944- . . . . CLC 21
See also AAYA 4; CA 112; 115; CANR 37;
CLR 20; JRDA; MAICYA; SATA 36,
63; SATA-Brief 30

Da Ponte, Lorenzo 1749-1838 . . . . NCLC 50

Dario, Ruben 1867-1916 . . . . TCLC 4; HLC
See also CA 131; HW; MTCW

Darley, George 1795-1846 . . . . NCLC 2
See also DLB 96

Daryush, Elizabeth 1887-1977 . . . . CLC 6, 19
See also CA 49-52; CANR 3; DLB 20

Daudet, (Louis Marie) Alphonse
1840-1897 . . . . NCLC 1
See also DLB 123

Daumal, Rene 1908-1944 . . . . TCLC 14
See also CA 114

Davenport, Guy (Mattison, Jr.)
1927- . . . . CLC 6, 14, 38; SSC 16
See also CA 33-36R; CANR 23; DLB 130

Davidson, Avram 1923-
See Queen, Ellery
See also CA 101; CANR 26; DLB 8

Davidson, Donald (Grady)
1893-1968 . . . . CLC 2, 13, 19
See also CA 5-8R; 25-28R; CANR 4;
DLB 45

Davidson, Hugh
See Hamilton, Edmond

Davidson, John 1857-1909 . . . . TCLC 24
See also CA 118; DLB 19

Davidson, Sara 1943- . . . . CLC 9
See also CA 81-84; CANR 44

Davie, Donald (Alfred)
1922- . . . . CLC 5, 8, 10, 31
See also CA 1-4R; CAAS 3; CANR 1, 44;
DLB 27; MTCW

Davies, Ray(mond Douglas) 1944- . . CLC 21
See also CA 116; 146

Davies, Rhys 1903-1978 . . . . CLC 23
See also CA 9-12R; 81-84; CANR 4;
DLB 139

Davies, (William) Robertson
1913- . . . . . CLC 2, 7, 13, 25, 42, 75; DA;
WLC
See also BEST 89:2; CA 33-36R; CANR 17,
42; DLB 68; MTCW

Davies, W(illiam) H(enry)
1871-1940 . . . . TCLC 5
See also CA 104; DLB 19

Davies, Walter C.
See Kornbluth, C(yril) M.

Davis, Angela (Yvonne) 1944- . . . . . . CLC 77
See also BW 2; CA 57-60; CANR 10

Davis, B. Lynch
See Bioy Casares, Adolfo; Borges, Jorge
Luis

Davis, Gordon
See Hunt, E(verette) Howard, (Jr.)

Davis, Harold Lenoir 1896-1960 . . . . CLC 49
See also CA 89-92; DLB 9

Davis, Rebecca (Blaine) Harding
1831-1910 . . . . TCLC 6
See also CA 104; DLB 74

Davis, Richard Harding
1864-1916 . . . . TCLC 24
See also CA 114; DLB 12, 23, 78, 79

Davison, Frank Dalby 1893-1970 . . . CLC 15
See also CA 116

Davison, Lawrence H.
See Lawrence, D(avid) H(erbert Richards)

Davison, Peter (Hubert) 1928- . . . . . CLC 28
See also CA 9-12R; CAAS 4; CANR 3, 43;
DLB 5

Davys, Mary 1674-1732 . . . . LC 1
See also DLB 39

Dawson, Fielding 1930- . . . . CLC 6
See also CA 85-88; DLB 130

Dawson, Peter
See Faust, Frederick (Schiller)

Day, Clarence (Shepard, Jr.)
1874-1935 . . . . TCLC 25
See also CA 108; DLB 11

Day, Thomas 1748-1789 . . . . LC 1
See also DLB 39; YABC 1

Day Lewis, C(ecil)
1904-1972 . . . . CLC 1, 6, 10; PC 11
See also Blake, Nicholas
See also CA 13-16; 33-36R; CANR 34;
CAP 1; DLB 15, 20; MTCW

Dazai, Osamu . . . . TCLC 11
See also Tsushima, Shuji

de Andrade, Carlos Drummond
See Drummond de Andrade, Carlos

Deane, Norman
See Creasey, John

**de Beauvoir, Simone (Lucie Ernestine Marie
Bertrand)**
See Beauvoir, Simone (Lucie Ernestine
Marie Bertrand) de

de Brissac, Malcolm
See Dickinson, Peter (Malcolm)

de Chardin, Pierre Teilhard
See Teilhard de Chardin, (Marie Joseph)
Pierre

Dee, John 1527-1608 . . . . LC 20

Deer, Sandra 1940- . . . . CLC 45

De Ferrari, Gabriella 1941- . . . . CLC 65
See also CA 146

Defoe, Daniel
1660(?)-1731 . . . . LC 1; DA; WLC
See also CDBLB 1660-1789; DLB 39, 95,
101; JRDA; MAICYA; SATA 22

de Gourmont, Remy
See Gourmont, Remy de

de Hartog, Jan 1914- . . . . CLC 19
See also CA 1-4R; CANR 1

de Hostos, E. M.
See Hostos (y Bonilla), Eugenio Maria de

de Hostos, Eugenio M.
See Hostos (y Bonilla), Eugenio Maria de

Deighton, Len . . . . CLC 4, 7, 22, 46
See also Deighton, Leonard Cyril
See also AAYA 6; BEST 89:2;
CDBLB 1960 to Present; DLB 87

Deighton, Leonard Cyril 1929-
See Deighton, Len
See also CA 9-12R; CANR 19, 33; MTCW

Dekker, Thomas 1572(?)-1632 . . . . LC 22
See also CDBLB Before 1660; DLB 62

de la Mare, Walter (John)
1873-1956 . . TCLC 4, 53; SSC 14; WLC
See also CDBLB 1914-1945; CLR 23;
DLB 19, 153; SATA 16

Delaney, Franey
See O'Hara, John (Henry)

Delaney, Shelagh 1939- . . . . CLC 29
See also CA 17-20R; CANR 30;
CDBLB 1960 to Present; DLB 13;
MTCW

Delany, Mary (Granville Pendarves)
1700-1788 . . . . LC 12

Delany, Samuel R(ay, Jr.)
1942- . . . . CLC 8, 14, 38; BLC
See also BW 2; CA 81-84; CANR 27, 43;
DLB 8, 33; MTCW

De La Ramee, (Marie) Louise 1839-1908
See Ouida
See also SATA 20

de la Roche, Mazo 1879-1961 . . . . . . CLC 14
See also CA 85-88; CANR 30; DLB 68;
SATA 64

Delbanco, Nicholas (Franklin)
1942- . . . . CLC 6, 13
See also CA 17-20R; CAAS 2; CANR 29;
DLB 6

del Castillo, Michel 1933- . . . . CLC 38
See also CA 109

Deledda, Grazia (Cosima)
1875(?)-1936 . . . . TCLC 23
See also CA 123

Delibes, Miguel . . . . CLC 8, 18
See also Delibes Setien, Miguel

Delibes Setien, Miguel 1920-
See Delibes, Miguel
See also CA 45-48; CANR 1, 32; HW;
MTCW

DeLillo, Don
1936- . . . . . CLC 8, 10, 13, 27, 39, 54, 76
See also BEST 89:1; CA 81-84; CANR 21;
DLB 6; MTCW

de Lisser, H. G.
See De Lisser, Herbert George
See also DLB 117

De Lisser, Herbert George
1878-1944 . . . . TCLC 12
See also de Lisser, H. G.
See also BW 2; CA 109

Deloria, Vine (Victor), Jr. 1933- . . . . CLC 21
See also CA 53-56; CANR 5, 20, 48;
MTCW; NNAL; SATA 21

Del Vecchio, John M(ichael)
1947- . . . . CLC 29
See also CA 110; DLBD 9

de Man, Paul (Adolph Michel)
1919-1983 . . . . CLC 55
See also CA 128; 111; DLB 67; MTCW

De Marinis, Rick 1934- . . . . CLC 54
See also CA 57-60; CANR 9, 25

Demby, William 1922- . . . . CLC 53; BLC
See also BW 1; CA 81-84; DLB 33

Demijohn, Thom
See Disch, Thomas M(ichael)

de Montherlant, Henry (Milon)
See Montherlant, Henry (Milon) de

Demosthenes 384B.C.-322B.C. . . . . CMLC 13

de Natale, Francine
See Malzberg, Barry N(athaniel)

Denby, Edwin (Orr) 1903-1983 . . . . . CLC 48
See also CA 138; 110

Denis, Julio
See Cortazar, Julio

Denmark, Harrison
See Zelazny, Roger (Joseph)

Dennis, John 1658-1734 . . . . LC 11
See also DLB 101

Dennis, Nigel (Forbes) 1912-1989 . . . . CLC 8
See also CA 25-28R; 129; DLB 13, 15;
MTCW

De Palma, Brian (Russell) 1940- . . . . CLC 20
See also CA 109

De Quincey, Thomas 1785-1859 . . . NCLC 4
See also CDBLB 1789-1832; DLB 110; 144

Deren, Eleanora   1908(?)-1961
See Deren, Maya
See also CA 111

Deren, Maya . . . . CLC 16
See also Deren, Eleanora

Derleth, August (William)
1909-1971 . . . . CLC 31
See also CA 1-4R; 29-32R; CANR 4;
DLB 9; SATA 5

Der Nister   1884-1950 . . . . TCLC 56

de Routisie, Albert
See Aragon, Louis

Derrida, Jacques   1930- . . . . CLC 24, 87
See also CA 124; 127

Derry Down Derry
See Lear, Edward

Dersonnes, Jacques
See Simenon, Georges (Jacques Christian)

Desai, Anita   1937- . . . . CLC 19, 37
See also CA 81-84; CANR 33; MTCW;
SATA 63

de Saint-Luc, Jean
See Glassco, John

de Saint Roman, Arnaud
See Aragon, Louis

Descartes, Rene   1596-1650 . . . . LC 20

De Sica, Vittorio   1901(?)-1974 . . . . . CLC 20
See also CA 117

Desnos, Robert   1900-1945 . . . . TCLC 22
See also CA 121

Destouches, Louis-Ferdinand
1894-1961 . . . . CLC 9, 15
See also Celine, Louis-Ferdinand
See also CA 85-88; CANR 28; MTCW

Deutsch, Babette   1895-1982 . . . . CLC 18
See also CA 1-4R; 108; CANR 4; DLB 45;
SATA 1; SATA-Obit 33

Devenant, William   1606-1649 . . . . LC 13

Devkota, Laxmiprasad
1909-1959 . . . . TCLC 23
See also CA 123

De Voto, Bernard (Augustine)
1897-1955 . . . . TCLC 29
See also CA 113; DLB 9

De Vries, Peter
1910-1993 . . . . CLC 1, 2, 3, 7, 10, 28, 46
See also CA 17-20R; 142; CANR 41;
DLB 6; DLBY 82; MTCW

Dexter, Martin
See Faust, Frederick (Schiller)

Dexter, Pete   1943- . . . . CLC 34, 55
See also BEST 89:2; CA 127; 131; MTCW

Diamano, Silmang
See Senghor, Leopold Sedar

Diamond, Neil   1941- . . . . CLC 30
See also CA 108

di Bassetto, Corno
See Shaw, George Bernard

Dick, Philip K(indred)
1928-1982 . . . . CLC 10, 30, 72
See also CA 49-52; 106; CANR 2, 16;
DLB 8; MTCW

Dickens, Charles (John Huffam)
1812-1870 . . . . . . NCLC 3, 8, 18, 26, 37,
50; DA; SSC 17; WLC
See also CDBLB 1832-1890; DLB 21, 55,
70; JRDA; MAICYA; SATA 15

Dickey, James (Lafayette)
1923- . . . . CLC 1, 2, 4, 7, 10, 15, 47
See also AITN 1, 2; CA 9-12R; CABS 2;
CANR 10, 48; CDALB 1968-1988;
DLB 5; DLBD 7; DLBY 82, 93; MTCW

Dickey, William   1928-1994 . . . . . CLC 3, 28
See also CA 9-12R; 145; CANR 24; DLB 5

Dickinson, Charles   1951- . . . . CLC 49
See also CA 128

Dickinson, Emily (Elizabeth)
1830-1886 . . NCLC 21; DA; PC 1; WLC
See also CDALB 1865-1917; DLB 1;
SATA 29

Dickinson, Peter (Malcolm)
1927- . . . . CLC 12, 35
See also AAYA 9; CA 41-44R; CANR 31;
CLR 29; DLB 87; JRDA; MAICYA;
SATA 5, 62

Dickson, Carr
See Carr, John Dickson

Dickson, Carter
See Carr, John Dickson

Diderot, Denis   1713-1784 . . . . LC 26

Didion, Joan   1934- . . . . . CLC 1, 3, 8, 14, 32
See also AITN 1; CA 5-8R; CANR 14;
CDALB 1968-1988; DLB 2; DLBY 81,
86; MTCW

Dietrich, Robert
See Hunt, E(verette) Howard, (Jr.)

Dillard, Annie   1945- . . . . CLC 9, 60
See also AAYA 6; CA 49-52; CANR 3, 43;
DLBY 80; MTCW; SATA 10

Dillard, R(ichard) H(enry) W(ilde)
1937- . . . . CLC 5
See also CA 21-24R; CAAS 7; CANR 10;
DLB 5

Dillon, Eilis   1920-1994 . . . . CLC 17
See also CA 9-12R; 147; CAAS 3; CANR 4,
38; CLR 26; MAICYA; SATA 2, 74

Dimont, Penelope
See Mortimer, Penelope (Ruth)

Dinesen, Isak . . . . CLC 10, 29; SSC 7
See also Blixen, Karen (Christentze
Dinesen)

Ding Ling . . . . CLC 68
See also Chiang Pin-chin

Disch, Thomas M(ichael)   1940- . . . CLC 7, 36
See also CA 21-24R; CAAS 4; CANR 17,
36; CLR 18; DLB 8; MAICYA; MTCW;
SAAS 15; SATA 54

Disch, Tom
See Disch, Thomas M(ichael)

d'Isly, Georges
See Simenon, Georges (Jacques Christian)

Disraeli, Benjamin   1804-1881 . . NCLC 2, 39
See also DLB 21, 55

Ditcum, Steve
See Crumb, R(obert)

Dixon, Paige
See Corcoran, Barbara

Dixon, Stephen   1936- . . . . . CLC 52; SSC 16
See also CA 89-92; CANR 17, 40; DLB 130

Dobell, Sydney Thompson
1824-1874 . . . . NCLC 43
See also DLB 32

Doblin, Alfred . . . . TCLC 13
See also Doeblin, Alfred

Dobrolyubov, Nikolai Alexandrovich
1836-1861 . . . . NCLC 5

Dobyns, Stephen   1941- . . . . CLC 37
See also CA 45-48; CANR 2, 18

Doctorow, E(dgar) L(aurence)
1931- . . . . . CLC 6, 11, 15, 18, 37, 44, 65
See also AITN 2; BEST 89:3; CA 45-48;
CANR 2, 33; CDALB 1968-1988; DLB 2,
28; DLBY 80; MTCW

Dodgson, Charles Lutwidge   1832-1898
See Carroll, Lewis
See also CLR 2; DA; MAICYA; YABC 2

Dodson, Owen (Vincent)
1914-1983 . . . . CLC 79; BLC
See also BW 1; CA 65-68; 110; CANR 24;
DLB 76

Doeblin, Alfred   1878-1957 . . . . TCLC 13
See also Doblin, Alfred
See also CA 110; 141; DLB 66

Doerr, Harriet   1910- . . . . CLC 34
See also CA 117; 122; CANR 47

Domecq, H(onorio) Bustos
See Bioy Casares, Adolfo; Borges, Jorge
Luis

Domini, Rey
See Lorde, Audre (Geraldine)

Dominique
See Proust, (Valentin-Louis-George-Eugene-)
Marcel

Don, A
See Stephen, Leslie

Donaldson, Stephen R.   1947- . . . . CLC 46
See also CA 89-92; CANR 13

Donleavy, J(ames) P(atrick)
1926- . . . . CLC 1, 4, 6, 10, 45
See also AITN 2; CA 9-12R; CANR 24, 49;
DLB 6; MTCW

Donne, John
1572-1631 . . . . LC 10, 24; DA; PC 1
See also CDBLB Before 1660; DLB 121,
151

Donnell, David   1939(?)- . . . . CLC 34

Donoghue, P. S.
See Hunt, E(verette) Howard, (Jr.)

Donoso (Yanez), Jose
1924- . . . . CLC 4, 8, 11, 32; HLC
See also CA 81-84; CANR 32; DLB 113;
HW; MTCW

Donovan, John   1928-1992 . . . . CLC 35
See also CA 97-100; 137; CLR 3;
MAICYA; SATA 72; SATA-Brief 29

Don Roberto
See Cunninghame Graham, R(obert)
B(ontine)

Doolittle, Hilda
  1886-1961 ..... **CLC 3, 8, 14, 31, 34, 73;**
                   DA; PC 5; WLC
  See also H. D.
  See also CA 97-100; CANR 35; DLB 4, 45;
  MTCW

Dorfman, Ariel 1942-.... **CLC 48, 77; HLC**
  See also CA 124; 130; HW

Dorn, Edward (Merton) 1929-... **CLC 10, 18**
  See also CA 93-96; CANR 42; DLB 5

Dorsan, Luc
  See Simenon, Georges (Jacques Christian)

Dorsange, Jean
  See Simenon, Georges (Jacques Christian)

Dos Passos, John (Roderigo)
  1896-1970 ..... **CLC 1, 4, 8, 11, 15, 25,**
                  34, 82; DA; WLC
  See also CA 1-4R; 29-32R; CANR 3;
  CDALB 1929-1941; DLB 4, 9; DLBD 1;
  MTCW

Dossage, Jean
  See Simenon, Georges (Jacques Christian)

Dostoevsky, Fedor Mikhailovich
  1821-1881 ...... **NCLC 2, 7, 21, 33, 43;**
                   DA; SSC 2; WLC

Doughty, Charles M(ontagu)
  1843-1926 .... **TCLC 27**
  See also CA 115; DLB 19, 57

Douglas, Ellen .... **CLC 73**
  See also Haxton, Josephine Ayres;
  Williamson, Ellen Douglas

Douglas, Gavin 1475(?)-1522........ **LC 20**

Douglas, Keith 1920-1944 .... **TCLC 40**
  See also DLB 27

Douglas, Leonard
  See Bradbury, Ray (Douglas)

Douglas, Michael
  See Crichton, (John) Michael

Douglass, Frederick
  1817(?)-1895 .... **NCLC 7; BLC; DA;**
                      WLC
  See also CDALB 1640-1865; DLB 1, 43, 50,
  79; SATA 29

Dourado, (Waldomiro Freitas) Autran
  1926- .... **CLC 23, 60**
  See also CA 25-28R; CANR 34

Dourado, Waldomiro Autran
  See Dourado, (Waldomiro Freitas) Autran

Dove, Rita (Frances)
  1952- .... **CLC 50, 81; PC 6**
  See also BW 2; CA 109; CAAS 19;
  CANR 27, 42; DLB 120

Dowell, Coleman 1925-1985....... **CLC 60**
  See also CA 25-28R; 117; CANR 10;
  DLB 130

Dowson, Ernest Christopher
  1867-1900 .... **TCLC 4**
  See also CA 105; DLB 19, 135

Doyle, A. Conan
  See Doyle, Arthur Conan

Doyle, Arthur Conan
  1859-1930 .... **TCLC 7; DA; SSC 12;**
                   WLC
  See also AAYA 14; CA 104; 122;
  CDBLB 1890-1914; DLB 18, 70; MTCW;
  SATA 24

Doyle, Conan
  See Doyle, Arthur Conan

Doyle, John
  See Graves, Robert (von Ranke)

Doyle, Roddy 1958(?)-............ **CLC 81**
  See also AAYA 14; CA 143

Doyle, Sir A. Conan
  See Doyle, Arthur Conan

Doyle, Sir Arthur Conan
  See Doyle, Arthur Conan

Dr. A
  See Asimov, Isaac; Silverstein, Alvin

Drabble, Margaret
  1939- .... **CLC 2, 3, 5, 8, 10, 22, 53**
  See also CA 13-16R; CANR 18, 35;
  CDBLB 1960 to Present; DLB 14;
  MTCW; SATA 48

Drapier, M. B.
  See Swift, Jonathan

Drayham, James
  See Mencken, H(enry) L(ouis)

Drayton, Michael 1563-1631........ **LC 8**

Dreadstone, Carl
  See Campbell, (John) Ramsey

Dreiser, Theodore (Herman Albert)
  1871-1945 .... **TCLC 10, 18, 35; DA;**
                   WLC
  See also CA 106; 132; CDALB 1865-1917;
  DLB 9, 12, 102, 137; DLBD 1; MTCW

Drexler, Rosalyn 1926- .... **CLC 2, 6**
  See also CA 81-84

Dreyer, Carl Theodor 1889-1968.... **CLC 16**
  See also CA 116

Drieu la Rochelle, Pierre(-Eugene)
  1893-1945 .... **TCLC 21**
  See also CA 117; DLB 72

Drinkwater, John 1882-1937..... **TCLC 57**
  See also CA 109; DLB 10, 19, 149

Drop Shot
  See Cable, George Washington

Droste-Hulshoff, Annette Freiin von
  1797-1848 .... **NCLC 3**
  See also DLB 133

Drummond, Walter
  See Silverberg, Robert

Drummond, William Henry
  1854-1907 .... **TCLC 25**
  See also DLB 92

Drummond de Andrade, Carlos
  1902-1987 .... **CLC 18**
  See also Andrade, Carlos Drummond de
  See also CA 132; 123

Drury, Allen (Stuart) 1918-....... **CLC 37**
  See also CA 57-60; CANR 18

Dryden, John
  1631-1700 ... **LC 3, 21; DA; DC 3; WLC**
  See also CDBLB 1660-1789; DLB 80, 101,
  131

Duberman, Martin 1930-.......... **CLC 8**
  See also CA 1-4R; CANR 2

Dubie, Norman (Evans) 1945-...... **CLC 36**
  See also CA 69-72; CANR 12; DLB 120

Du Bois, W(illiam) E(dward) B(urghardt)
  1868-1963 ...... **CLC 1, 2, 13, 64; BLC;**
                  DA; WLC
  See also BW 1; CA 85-88; CANR 34;
  CDALB 1865-1917; DLB 47, 50, 91;
  MTCW; SATA 42

Dubus, Andre 1936-... **CLC 13, 36; SSC 15**
  See also CA 21-24R; CANR 17; DLB 130

Duca Minimo
  See D'Annunzio, Gabriele

Ducharme, Rejean 1941-.......... **CLC 74**
  See also DLB 60

Duclos, Charles Pinot 1704-1772 ..... **LC 1**

Dudek, Louis 1918- .... **CLC 11, 19**
  See also CA 45-48; CAAS 14; CANR 1;
  DLB 88

Duerrenmatt, Friedrich
  1921-1990 ...... **CLC 1, 4, 8, 11, 15, 43**
  See also CA 17-20R; CANR 33; DLB 69,
  124; MTCW

Duffy, Bruce (?)-................ **CLC 50**

Duffy, Maureen 1933- .... **CLC 37**
  See also CA 25-28R; CANR 33; DLB 14;
  MTCW

Dugan, Alan 1923-.............. **CLC 2, 6**
  See also CA 81-84; DLB 5

du Gard, Roger Martin
  See Martin du Gard, Roger

Duhamel, Georges 1884-1966 .... **CLC 8**
  See also CA 81-84; 25-28R; CANR 35;
  DLB 65; MTCW

Dujardin, Edouard (Emile Louis)
  1861-1949 .... **TCLC 13**
  See also CA 109; DLB 123

Dumas, Alexandre (Davy de la Pailleterie)
  1802-1870 ...... **NCLC 11; DA; WLC**
  See also DLB 119; SATA 18

Dumas, Alexandre
  1824-1895 .... **NCLC 9; DC 1**

Dumas, Claudine
  See Malzberg, Barry N(athaniel)

Dumas, Henry L. 1934-1968 ..... **CLC 6, 62**
  See also BW 1; CA 85-88; DLB 41

du Maurier, Daphne
  1907-1989 ...... **CLC 6, 11, 59; SSC 18**
  See also CA 5-8R; 128; CANR 6; MTCW;
  SATA 27; SATA-Obit 60

Dunbar, Paul Laurence
  1872-1906 ...... **TCLC 2, 12; BLC; DA;**
                  PC 5; SSC 8; WLC
  See also BW 1; CA 104; 124;
  CDALB 1865-1917; DLB 50, 54, 78;
  SATA 34

Dunbar, William 1460(?)-1530(?) .... **LC 20**
  See also DLB 132, 146

Duncan, Lois 1934-.............. **CLC 26**
  See also AAYA 4; CA 1-4R; CANR 2, 23,
  36; CLR 29; JRDA; MAICYA; SAAS 2;
  SATA 1, 36, 75**

Duncan, Robert (Edward)
1919-1988 .... **CLC 1, 2, 4, 7, 15, 41, 55;**
PC 2
See also CA 9-12R; 124; CANR 28; DLB 5,
16; MTCW

Duncan, Sara Jeannette
1861-1922 .... **TCLC 60**
See also DLB 92

Dunlap, William 1766-1839 .... **NCLC 2**
See also DLB 30, 37, 59

Dunn, Douglas (Eaglesham)
1942- .... **CLC 6, 40**
See also CA 45-48; CANR 2, 33; DLB 40;
MTCW

Dunn, Katherine (Karen) 1945- ..... **CLC 71**
See also CA 33-36R

Dunn, Stephen 1939- .... **CLC 36**
See also CA 33-36R; CANR 12, 48;
DLB 105

Dunne, Finley Peter 1867-1936 .... **TCLC 28**
See also CA 108; DLB 11, 23

Dunne, John Gregory 1932- .... **CLC 28**
See also CA 25-28R; CANR 14; DLBY 80

Dunsany, Edward John Moreton Drax
Plunkett 1878-1957
See Dunsany, Lord
See also CA 104; DLB 10

Dunsany, Lord................. **TCLC 2, 59**
See also Dunsany, Edward John Moreton
Drax Plunkett
See also DLB 77, 153

du Perry, Jean
See Simenon, Georges (Jacques Christian)

Durang, Christopher (Ferdinand)
1949- .... **CLC 27, 38**
See also CA 105

Duras, Marguerite
1914- ...... **CLC 3, 6, 11, 20, 34, 40, 68**
See also CA 25-28R; DLB 83; MTCW

Durban, (Rosa) Pam 1947- .... **CLC 39**
See also CA 123

Durcan, Paul 1944- .... **CLC 43, 70**
See also CA 134

Durkheim, Emile 1858-1917 ...... **TCLC 55**

Durrell, Lawrence (George)
1912-1990 .... **CLC 1, 4, 6, 8, 13, 27, 41**
See also CA 9-12R; 132; CANR 40;
CDBLB 1945-1960; DLB 15, 27;
DLBY 90; MTCW

Durrenmatt, Friedrich
See Duerrenmatt, Friedrich

Dutt, Toru 1856-1877 .... **NCLC 29**

Dwight, Timothy 1752-1817 ...... **NCLC 13**
See also DLB 37

Dworkin, Andrea 1946- .... **CLC 43**
See also CA 77-80; CAAS 21; CANR 16,
39; MTCW

Dwyer, Deanna
See Koontz, Dean R(ay)

Dwyer, K. R.
See Koontz, Dean R(ay)

Dylan, Bob 1941- ...... **CLC 3, 4, 6, 12, 77**
See also CA 41-44R; DLB 16

Eagleton, Terence (Francis) 1943-
See Eagleton, Terry
See also CA 57-60; CANR 7, 23; MTCW

Eagleton, Terry .... **CLC 63**
See also Eagleton, Terence (Francis)

Early, Jack
See Scoppettone, Sandra

East, Michael
See West, Morris L(anglo)

Eastaway, Edward
See Thomas, (Philip) Edward

Eastlake, William (Derry) 1917- ..... **CLC 8**
See also CA 5-8R; CAAS 1; CANR 5;
DLB 6

Eastman, Charles A(lexander)
1858-1939 .... **TCLC 55**
See also NNAL; YABC 1

Eberhart, Richard (Ghormley)
1904- .... **CLC 3, 11, 19, 56**
See also CA 1-4R; CANR 2;
CDALB 1941-1968; DLB 48; MTCW

Eberstadt, Fernanda 1960- .... **CLC 39**
See also CA 136

Echegaray (y Eizaguirre), Jose (Maria Waldo)
1832-1916 .... **TCLC 4**
See also CA 104; CANR 32; HW; MTCW

Echeverria, (Jose) Esteban (Antonino)
1805-1851 .... **NCLC 18**

Echo
See Proust, (Valentin-Louis-George-Eugene-)
Marcel

Eckert, Allan W. 1931- .... **CLC 17**
See also CA 13-16R; CANR 14, 45;
SATA 29; SATA-Brief 27

Eckhart, Meister 1260(?)-1328(?) .. **CMLC 9**
See also DLB 115

Eckmar, F. R.
See de Hartog, Jan

Eco, Umberto 1932- .... **CLC 28, 60**
See also BEST 90:1; CA 77-80; CANR 12,
33; MTCW

Eddison, E(ric) R(ucker)
1882-1945 .... **TCLC 15**
See also CA 109

Edel, (Joseph) Leon 1907- ...... **CLC 29, 34**
See also CA 1-4R; CANR 1, 22; DLB 103

Eden, Emily 1797-1869 .... **NCLC 10**

Edgar, David 1948- .... **CLC 42**
See also CA 57-60; CANR 12; DLB 13;
MTCW

Edgerton, Clyde (Carlyle) 1944- .... **CLC 39**
See also CA 118; 134

Edgeworth, Maria 1767-1849 ... **NCLC 1, 51**
See also DLB 116; SATA 21

Edmonds, Paul
See Kuttner, Henry

Edmonds, Walter D(umaux) 1903- .. **CLC 35**
See also CA 5-8R; CANR 2; DLB 9;
MAICYA; SAAS 4; SATA 1, 27

Edmondson, Wallace
See Ellison, Harlan (Jay)

Edson, Russell................... **CLC 13**
See also CA 33-36R

Edwards, Bronwen Elizabeth
See Rose, Wendy

Edwards, G(erald) B(asil)
1899-1976 .... **CLC 25**
See also CA 110

Edwards, Gus 1939- .... **CLC 43**
See also CA 108

Edwards, Jonathan 1703-1758 .... **LC 7; DA**
See also DLB 24

Efron, Marina Ivanovna Tsvetaeva
See Tsvetaeva (Efron), Marina (Ivanovna)

Ehle, John (Marsden, Jr.) 1925- .... **CLC 27**
See also CA 9-12R

Ehrenbourg, Ilya (Grigoryevich)
See Ehrenburg, Ilya (Grigoryevich)

Ehrenburg, Ilya (Grigoryevich)
1891-1967 .... **CLC 18, 34, 62**
See also CA 102; 25-28R

Ehrenburg, Ilyo (Grigoryevich)
See Ehrenburg, Ilya (Grigoryevich)

Eich, Guenter 1907-1972 .... **CLC 15**
See also CA 111; 93-96; DLB 69, 124

Eichendorff, Joseph Freiherr von
1788-1857 .... **NCLC 8**
See also DLB 90

Eigner, Larry...................... **CLC 9**
See also Eigner, Laurence (Joel)
See also DLB 5

Eigner, Laurence (Joel) 1927-
See Eigner, Larry
See also CA 9-12R; CANR 6

Eiseley, Loren Corey 1907-1977 ..... **CLC 7**
See also AAYA 5; CA 1-4R; 73-76;
CANR 6

Eisenstadt, Jill 1963- .... **CLC 50**
See also CA 140

Eisenstein, Sergei (Mikhailovich)
1898-1948 .... **TCLC 57**
See also CA 114

Eisner, Simon
See Kornbluth, C(yril) M.

Ekeloef, (Bengt) Gunnar
1907-1968 .... **CLC 27**
See also CA 123; 25-28R

Ekelof, (Bengt) Gunnar
See Ekeloef, (Bengt) Gunnar

Ekwensi, C. O. D.
See Ekwensi, Cyprian (Odiatu Duaka)

Ekwensi, Cyprian (Odiatu Duaka)
1921- .... **CLC 4; BLC**
See also BW 2; CA 29-32R; CANR 18, 42;
DLB 117; MTCW; SATA 66

Elaine......................... **TCLC 18**
See also Leverson, Ada

El Crummo
See Crumb, R(obert)

Elia
See Lamb, Charles

Eliade, Mircea 1907-1986 .... **CLC 19**
See also CA 65-68; 119; CANR 30; MTCW

Eliot, A. D.
See Jewett, (Theodora) Sarah Orne

Eliot, Alice
See Jewett, (Theodora) Sarah Orne

Eliot, Dan
See Silverberg, Robert

Eliot, George
1819-1880 ..... **NCLC 4, 13, 23, 41, 49;
DA; WLC**
See also CDBLB 1832-1890; DLB 21, 35, 55

Eliot, John 1604-1690 .... **LC 5**
See also DLB 24

Eliot, T(homas) S(tearns)
1888-1965 ..... **CLC 1, 2, 3, 6, 9, 10, 13,
15, 24, 34, 41, 55, 57; DA; PC 5; WLC 2**
See also CA 5-8R; 25-28R; CANR 41;
CDALB 1929-1941; DLB 7, 10, 45, 63;
DLBY 88; MTCW

Elizabeth 1866-1941 .... **TCLC 41**

Elkin, Stanley L(awrence)
1930-1995 ...... **CLC 4, 6, 9, 14, 27, 51;
SSC 12**
See also CA 9-12R; 148; CANR 8, 46;
DLB 2, 28; DLBY 80; MTCW

Elledge, Scott .... **CLC 34**

Elliott, Don
See Silverberg, Robert

Elliott, George P(aul) 1918-1980 ..... **CLC 2**
See also CA 1-4R; 97-100; CANR 2

Elliott, Janice 1931- .... **CLC 47**
See also CA 13-16R; CANR 8, 29; DLB 14

Elliott, Sumner Locke 1917-1991 ... **CLC 38**
See also CA 5-8R; 134; CANR 2, 21

Elliott, William
See Bradbury, Ray (Douglas)

Ellis, A. E. .... **CLC 7**

Ellis, Alice Thomas .... **CLC 40**
See also Haycraft, Anna

Ellis, Bret Easton 1964- .... **CLC 39, 71**
See also AAYA 2; CA 118; 123

Ellis, (Henry) Havelock
1859-1939 .... **TCLC 14**
See also CA 109

Ellis, Landon
See Ellison, Harlan (Jay)

Ellis, Trey 1962- .... **CLC 55**
See also CA 146

Ellison, Harlan (Jay)
1934- .... **CLC 1, 13, 42; SSC 14**
See also CA 5-8R; CANR 5, 46; DLB 8;
MTCW

Ellison, Ralph (Waldo)
1914-1994 .... **CLC 1, 3, 11, 54, 86;
BLC; DA; WLC**
See also BW 1; CA 9-12R; 145; CANR 24;
CDALB 1941-1968; DLB 2, 76;
DLBY 94; MTCW

Ellmann, Lucy (Elizabeth) 1956- .... **CLC 61**
See also CA 128

Ellmann, Richard (David)
1918-1987 .... **CLC 50**
See also BEST 89:2; CA 1-4R; 122;
CANR 2, 28; DLB 103; DLBY 87;
MTCW

Elman, Richard 1934- .... **CLC 19**
See also CA 17-20R; CAAS 3; CANR 47

Elron
See Hubbard, L(afayette) Ron(ald)

Eluard, Paul .... **TCLC 7, 41**
See also Grindel, Eugene

Elyot, Sir Thomas 1490(?)-1546 ..... **LC 11**

Elytis, Odysseus 1911- .... **CLC 15, 49**
See also CA 102; MTCW

Emecheta, (Florence Onye) Buchi
1944- .... **CLC 14, 48; BLC**
See also BW 2; CA 81-84; CANR 27;
DLB 117; MTCW; SATA 66

Emerson, Ralph Waldo
1803-1882 ...... **NCLC 1, 38; DA; WLC**
See also CDALB 1640-1865; DLB 1, 59, 73

Eminescu, Mihail 1850-1889 ..... **NCLC 33**

Empson, William
1906-1984 .... **CLC 3, 8, 19, 33, 34**
See also CA 17-20R; 112; CANR 31;
DLB 20; MTCW

Enchi Fumiko (Ueda) 1905-1986.... **CLC 31**
See also CA 129; 121

Ende, Michael (Andreas Helmuth)
1929- .... **CLC 31**
See also CA 118; 124; CANR 36; CLR 14;
DLB 75; MAICYA; SATA 61;
SATA-Brief 42

Endo, Shusaku 1923- ..... **CLC 7, 14, 19, 54**
See also CA 29-32R; CANR 21; MTCW

Engel, Marian 1933-1985.......... **CLC 36**
See also CA 25-28R; CANR 12; DLB 53

Engelhardt, Frederick
See Hubbard, L(afayette) Ron(ald)

Enright, D(ennis) J(oseph)
1920- .... **CLC 4, 8, 31**
See also CA 1-4R; CANR 1, 42; DLB 27;
SATA 25

Enzensberger, Hans Magnus
1929- .... **CLC 43**
See also CA 116; 119

Ephron, Nora 1941- .... **CLC 17, 31**
See also AITN 2; CA 65-68; CANR 12, 39

Epsilon
See Betjeman, John

Epstein, Daniel Mark 1948- .... **CLC 7**
See also CA 49-52; CANR 2

Epstein, Jacob 1956- .... **CLC 19**
See also CA 114

Epstein, Joseph 1937- .... **CLC 39**
See also CA 112; 119

Epstein, Leslie 1938- .... **CLC 27**
See also CA 73-76; CAAS 12; CANR 23

Equiano, Olaudah
1745(?)-1797 .... **LC 16; BLC**
See also DLB 37, 50

Erasmus, Desiderius 1469(?)-1536.... **LC 16**

Erdman, Paul E(mil) 1932- .... **CLC 25**
See also AITN 1; CA 61-64; CANR 13, 43

Erdrich, Louise 1954-.......... **CLC 39, 54**
See also AAYA 10; BEST 89:1; CA 114;
CANR 41; DLB 152; MTCW; NNAL

Erenburg, Ilya (Grigoryevich)
See Ehrenburg, Ilya (Grigoryevich)

Erickson, Stephen Michael 1950-
See Erickson, Steve
See also CA 129

Erickson, Steve .... **CLC 64**
See also Erickson, Stephen Michael

Ericson, Walter
See Fast, Howard (Melvin)

Eriksson, Buntel
See Bergman, (Ernst) Ingmar

Ernaux, Annie 1940- .... **CLC 88**
See also CA 147

Eschenbach, Wolfram von
See Wolfram von Eschenbach

Eseki, Bruno
See Mphahlele, Ezekiel

Esenin, Sergei (Alexandrovich)
1895-1925 .... **TCLC 4**
See also CA 104

Eshleman, Clayton 1935-........... **CLC 7**
See also CA 33-36R; CAAS 6; DLB 5

Espriella, Don Manuel Alvarez
See Southey, Robert

Espriu, Salvador 1913-1985........ **CLC 9**
See also CA 115; DLB 134

Espronceda, Jose de 1808-1842... **NCLC 39**

Esse, James
See Stephens, James

Esterbrook, Tom
See Hubbard, L(afayette) Ron(ald)

Estleman, Loren D. 1952- .... **CLC 48**
See also CA 85-88; CANR 27; MTCW

Eugenides, Jeffrey 1960(?)- .... **CLC 81**
See also CA 144

Euripides c. 485B.C.-406B.C. .... **DC 4**
See also DA

Evan, Evin
See Faust, Frederick (Schiller)

Evans, Evan
See Faust, Frederick (Schiller)

Evans, Marian
See Eliot, George

Evans, Mary Ann
See Eliot, George

Evarts, Esther
See Benson, Sally

Everett, Percival L. 1956- .... **CLC 57**
See also BW 2; CA 129

Everson, R(onald) G(ilmour)
1903- .... **CLC 27**
See also CA 17-20R; DLB 88

Everson, William (Oliver)
1912-1994 .... **CLC 1, 5, 14**
See also CA 9-12R; 145; CANR 20; DLB 5,
16; MTCW

Evtushenko, Evgenii Aleksandrovich
See Yevtushenko, Yevgeny (Alexandrovich)

Ewart, Gavin (Buchanan)
1916- .... **CLC 13, 46**
See also CA 89-92; CANR 17, 46; DLB 40;
MTCW

Ewers, Hanns Heinz 1871-1943 ... **TCLC 12**
See also CA 109

Ewing, Frederick R.
See Sturgeon, Theodore (Hamilton)

Exley, Frederick (Earl)
   1929-1992 .... CLC 6, 11
   See also AITN 2; CA 81-84; 138; DLB 143;
   DLBY 81

Eynhardt, Guillermo
   See Quiroga, Horacio (Sylvestre)

Ezekiel, Nissim   1924- .... CLC 61
   See also CA 61-64

Ezekiel, Tish O'Dowd   1943- .... CLC 34
   See also CA 129

Fadeyev, A.
   See Bulgya, Alexander Alexandrovich

Fadeyev, Alexander .... TCLC 53
   See also Bulgya, Alexander Alexandrovich

Fagen, Donald   1948- .... CLC 26

Fainzilberg, Ilya Arnoldovich   1897-1937
   See Ilf, Ilya
   See also CA 120

Fair, Ronald L.   1932- .... CLC 18
   See also BW 1; CA 69-72; CANR 25;
   DLB 33

Fairbairns, Zoe (Ann)   1948- .... CLC 32
   See also CA 103; CANR 21

Falco, Gian
   See Papini, Giovanni

Falconer, James
   See Kirkup, James

Falconer, Kenneth
   See Kornbluth, C(yril) M.

Falkland, Samuel
   See Heijermans, Herman

Fallaci, Oriana   1930- .... CLC 11
   See also CA 77-80; CANR 15; MTCW

Faludy, George   1913- .... CLC 42
   See also CA 21-24R

Faludy, Gyoergy
   See Faludy, George

Fanon, Frantz   1925-1961 ..... CLC 74; BLC
   See also BW 1; CA 116; 89-92

Fanshawe, Ann   1625-1680 .... LC 11

Fante, John (Thomas)   1911-1983 ... CLC 60
   See also CA 69-72; 109; CANR 23;
   DLB 130; DLBY 83

Farah, Nuruddin   1945- .... CLC 53; BLC
   See also BW 2; CA 106; DLB 125

Fargue, Leon-Paul   1876(?)-1947 ... TCLC 11
   See also CA 109

Farigoule, Louis
   See Romains, Jules

Farina, Richard   1936(?)-1966 .... CLC 9
   See also CA 81-84; 25-28R

Farley, Walter (Lorimer)
   1915-1989 .... CLC 17
   See also CA 17-20R; CANR 8, 29; DLB 22;
   JRDA; MAICYA; SATA 2, 43

Farmer, Philip Jose   1918- .... CLC 1, 19
   See also CA 1-4R; CANR 4, 35; DLB 8;
   MTCW

Farquhar, George   1677-1707 .... LC 21
   See also DLB 84

Farrell, J(ames) G(ordon)
   1935-1979 .... CLC 6
   See also CA 73-76; 89-92; CANR 36;
   DLB 14; MTCW

Farrell, James T(homas)
   1904-1979 .... CLC 1, 4, 8, 11, 66
   See also CA 5-8R; 89-92; CANR 9; DLB 4,
   9, 86; DLBD 2; MTCW

Farren, Richard J.
   See Betjeman, John

Farren, Richard M.
   See Betjeman, John

Fassbinder, Rainer Werner
   1946-1982 .... CLC 20
   See also CA 93-96; 106; CANR 31

Fast, Howard (Melvin)   1914- ...... CLC 23
   See also CA 1-4R; CAAS 18; CANR 1, 33;
   DLB 9; SATA 7

Faulcon, Robert
   See Holdstock, Robert P.

Faulkner, William (Cuthbert)
   1897-1962 ..... CLC 1, 3, 6, 8, 9, 11, 14,
            18, 28, 52, 68; DA; SSC 1; WLC
   See also AAYA 7; CA 81-84; CANR 33;
   CDALB 1929-1941; DLB 9, 11, 44, 102;
   DLBD 2; DLBY 86; MTCW

Fauset, Jessie Redmon
   1884(?)-1961 .... CLC 19, 54; BLC
   See also BW 1; CA 109; DLB 51

Faust, Frederick (Schiller)
   1892-1944(?) .... TCLC 49
   See also CA 108

Faust, Irvin   1924- .... CLC 8
   See also CA 33-36R; CANR 28; DLB 2, 28;
   DLBY 80

Fawkes, Guy
   See Benchley, Robert (Charles)

Fearing, Kenneth (Flexner)
   1902-1961 .... CLC 51
   See also CA 93-96; DLB 9

Fecamps, Elise
   See Creasey, John

Federman, Raymond   1928- ...... CLC 6, 47
   See also CA 17-20R; CAAS 8; CANR 10,
   43; DLBY 80

Federspiel, J(uerg) F.   1931- .... CLC 42
   See also CA 146

Feiffer, Jules (Ralph)   1929- .... CLC 2, 8, 64
   See also AAYA 3; CA 17-20R; CANR 30;
   DLB 7, 44; MTCW; SATA 8, 61

Feige, Hermann Albert Otto Maximilian
   See Traven, B.

Feinberg, David B.   1956-1994 ...... CLC 59
   See also CA 135; 147

Feinstein, Elaine   1930- .... CLC 36
   See also CA 69-72; CAAS 1; CANR 31;
   DLB 14, 40; MTCW

Feldman, Irving (Mordecai)   1928- .... CLC 7
   See also CA 1-4R; CANR 1

Fellini, Federico   1920-1993 ..... CLC 16, 85
   See also CA 65-68; 143; CANR 33

Felsen, Henry Gregor   1916- .... CLC 17
   See also CA 1-4R; CANR 1; SAAS 2;
   SATA 1

Fenton, James Martin   1949- .... CLC 32
   See also CA 102; DLB 40

Ferber, Edna   1887-1968 .... CLC 18
   See also AITN 1; CA 5-8R; 25-28R; DLB 9,
   28, 86; MTCW; SATA 7

Ferguson, Helen
   See Kavan, Anna

Ferguson, Samuel   1810-1886 ..... NCLC 33
   See also DLB 32

Fergusson, Robert   1750-1774 ...... LC 29
   See also DLB 109

Ferling, Lawrence
   See Ferlinghetti, Lawrence (Monsanto)

Ferlinghetti, Lawrence (Monsanto)
   1919(?)- .... CLC 2, 6, 10, 27; PC 1
   See also CA 5-8R; CANR 3, 41;
   CDALB 1941-1968; DLB 5, 16; MTCW

Fernandez, Vicente Garcia Huidobro
   See Huidobro Fernandez, Vicente Garcia

Ferrer, Gabriel (Francisco Victor) Miro
   See Miro (Ferrer), Gabriel (Francisco
   Victor)

Ferrier, Susan (Edmonstone)
   1782-1854 .... NCLC 8
   See also DLB 116

Ferrigno, Robert   1948(?)- .... CLC 65
   See also CA 140

Feuchtwanger, Lion   1884-1958 ..... TCLC 3
   See also CA 104; DLB 66

Feuillet, Octave   1821-1890 ...... NCLC 45

Feydeau, Georges (Leon Jules Marie)
   1862-1921 .... TCLC 22
   See also CA 113

Ficino, Marsilio   1433-1499 .... LC 12

Fiedeler, Hans
   See Doeblin, Alfred

Fiedler, Leslie A(aron)
   1917- .... CLC 4, 13, 24
   See also CA 9-12R; CANR 7; DLB 28, 67;
   MTCW

Field, Andrew   1938- .... CLC 44
   See also CA 97-100; CANR 25

Field, Eugene   1850-1895 .... NCLC 3
   See also DLB 23, 42, 140; MAICYA;
   SATA 16

Field, Gans T.
   See Wellman, Manly Wade

Field, Michael .... TCLC 43

Field, Peter
   See Hobson, Laura Z(ametkin)

Fielding, Henry
   1707-1754 .... LC 1; DA; WLC
   See also CDBLB 1660-1789; DLB 39, 84,
   101

Fielding, Sarah   1710-1768 .... LC 1
   See also DLB 39

Fierstein, Harvey (Forbes)   1954- ... CLC 33
   See also CA 123; 129

Figes, Eva   1932- .... CLC 31
   See also CA 53-56; CANR 4, 44; DLB 14

Finch, Robert (Duer Claydon)
   1900- .... CLC 18
   See also CA 57-60; CANR 9, 24, 49;
   DLB 88

Findley, Timothy 1930- . . . . CLC 27
See also CA 25-28R; CANR 12, 42;
DLB 53

Fink, William
See Mencken, H(enry) L(ouis)

Firbank, Louis 1942-
See Reed, Lou
See also CA 117

Firbank, (Arthur Annesley) Ronald
1886-1926 . . . . TCLC 1
See also CA 104; DLB 36

Fisher, M(ary) F(rances) K(ennedy)
1908-1992 . . . . CLC 76, 87
See also CA 77-80; 138; CANR 44

Fisher, Roy 1930- . . . . CLC 25
See also CA 81-84; CAAS 10; CANR 16;
DLB 40

Fisher, Rudolph
1897-1934 . . . . TCLC 11; BLC
See also BW 1; CA 107; 124; DLB 51, 102

Fisher, Vardis (Alvero) 1895-1968 . . . . CLC 7
See also CA 5-8R; 25-28R; DLB 9

Fiske, Tarleton
See Bloch, Robert (Albert)

Fitch, Clarke
See Sinclair, Upton (Beall)

Fitch, John IV
See Cormier, Robert (Edmund)

Fitzgerald, Captain Hugh
See Baum, L(yman) Frank

FitzGerald, Edward 1809-1883 . . . . NCLC 9
See also DLB 32

Fitzgerald, F(rancis) Scott (Key)
1896-1940 . . . . TCLC 1, 6, 14, 28, 55;
DA; SSC 6; WLC
See also AITN 1; CA 110; 123;
CDALB 1917-1929; DLB 4, 9, 86;
DLBD 1; DLBY 81; MTCW

Fitzgerald, Penelope 1916- . . . CLC 19, 51, 61
See also CA 85-88; CAAS 10; DLB 14

Fitzgerald, Robert (Stuart)
1910-1985 . . . . CLC 39
See also CA 1-4R; 114; CANR 1; DLBY 80

FitzGerald, Robert D(avid)
1902-1987 . . . . CLC 19
See also CA 17-20R

Fitzgerald, Zelda (Sayre)
1900-1948 . . . . TCLC 52
See also CA 117; 126; DLBY 84

Flanagan, Thomas (James Bonner)
1923- . . . . CLC 25, 52
See also CA 108; DLBY 80; MTCW

Flaubert, Gustave
1821-1880 . . . . NCLC 2, 10, 19; DA;
SSC 11; WLC
See also DLB 119

Flecker, (Herman) James Elroy
1884-1915 . . . . TCLC 43
See also CA 109; DLB 10, 19

Fleming, Ian (Lancaster)
1908-1964 . . . . CLC 3, 30
See also CA 5-8R; CDBLB 1945-1960;
DLB 87; MTCW; SATA 9

Fleming, Thomas (James) 1927- . . . . CLC 37
See also CA 5-8R; CANR 10; SATA 8

Fletcher, John Gould 1886-1950 . . . TCLC 35
See also CA 107; DLB 4, 45

Fleur, Paul
See Pohl, Frederik

Flooglebuckle, Al
See Spiegelman, Art

Flying Officer X
See Bates, H(erbert) E(rnest)

Fo, Dario 1926- . . . . CLC 32
See also CA 116; 128; MTCW

Fogarty, Jonathan Titulescu Esq.
See Farrell, James T(homas)

Folke, Will
See Bloch, Robert (Albert)

Follett, Ken(neth Martin) 1949- . . . . CLC 18
See also AAYA 6; BEST 89:4; CA 81-84;
CANR 13, 33; DLB 87; DLBY 81;
MTCW

Fontane, Theodor 1819-1898 . . . . . NCLC 26
See also DLB 129

Foote, Horton 1916- . . . . CLC 51
See also CA 73-76; CANR 34; DLB 26

Foote, Shelby 1916- . . . . CLC 75
See also CA 5-8R; CANR 3, 45; DLB 2, 17

Forbes, Esther 1891-1967 . . . . CLC 12
See also CA 13-14; 25-28R; CAP 1;
CLR 27; DLB 22; JRDA; MAICYA;
SATA 2

Forche, Carolyn (Louise)
1950- . . . . CLC 25, 83, 86; PC 10
See also CA 109; 117; DLB 5

Ford, Elbur
See Hibbert, Eleanor Alice Burford

Ford, Ford Madox
1873-1939 . . . . TCLC 1, 15, 39, 57
See also CA 104; 132; CDBLB 1914-1945;
DLB 34, 98; MTCW

Ford, John 1895-1973 . . . . CLC 16
See also CA 45-48

Ford, Richard 1944- . . . . CLC 46
See also CA 69-72; CANR 11, 47

Ford, Webster
See Masters, Edgar Lee

Foreman, Richard 1937- . . . . CLC 50
See also CA 65-68; CANR 32

Forester, C(ecil) S(cott)
1899-1966 . . . . CLC 35
See also CA 73-76; 25-28R; SATA 13

Forez
See Mauriac, Francois (Charles)

Forman, James Douglas 1932- . . . . . . CLC 21
See also CA 9-12R; CANR 4, 19, 42;
JRDA; MAICYA; SATA 8, 70

Fornes, Maria Irene 1930- . . . . . . CLC 39, 61
See also CA 25-28R; CANR 28; DLB 7;
HW; MTCW

Forrest, Leon 1937- . . . . CLC 4
See also BW 2; CA 89-92; CAAS 7;
CANR 25; DLB 33

Forster, E(dward) M(organ)
1879-1970 . . . . . CLC 1, 2, 3, 4, 9, 10, 13,
15, 22, 45, 77; DA; WLC
See also AAYA 2; CA 13-14; 25-28R;
CANR 45; CAP 1; CDBLB 1914-1945;
DLB 34, 98; DLBD 10; MTCW;
SATA 57

Forster, John 1812-1876 . . . . NCLC 11
See also DLB 144

Forsyth, Frederick 1938- . . . . . . CLC 2, 5, 36
See also BEST 89:4; CA 85-88; CANR 38;
DLB 87; MTCW

Forten, Charlotte L. . . . . TCLC 16; BLC
See also Grimke, Charlotte L(ottie) Forten
See also DLB 50

Foscolo, Ugo 1778-1827 . . . . NCLC 8

Fosse, Bob . . . . CLC 20
See also Fosse, Robert Louis

Fosse, Robert Louis 1927-1987
See Fosse, Bob
See also CA 110; 123

Foster, Stephen Collins
1826-1864 . . . . NCLC 26

Foucault, Michel
1926-1984 . . . . CLC 31, 34, 69
See also CA 105; 113; CANR 34; MTCW

Fouque, Friedrich (Heinrich Karl) de la Motte
1777-1843 . . . . NCLC 2
See also DLB 90

Fourier, Charles 1772-1837 . . . . . . NCLC 51

Fournier, Henri Alban 1886-1914
See Alain-Fournier
See also CA 104

Fournier, Pierre 1916- . . . . CLC 11
See also Gascar, Pierre
See also CA 89-92; CANR 16, 40

Fowles, John
1926- . . . . . . CLC 1, 2, 3, 4, 6, 9, 10, 15,
33, 87
See also CA 5-8R; CANR 25; CDBLB 1960
to Present; DLB 14, 139; MTCW;
SATA 22

Fox, Paula 1923- . . . . CLC 2, 8
See also AAYA 3; CA 73-76; CANR 20,
36; CLR 1; DLB 52; JRDA; MAICYA;
MTCW; SATA 17, 60

Fox, William Price (Jr.) 1926- . . . . . CLC 22
See also CA 17-20R; CAAS 19; CANR 11;
DLB 2; DLBY 81

Foxe, John 1516(?)-1587 . . . . LC 14

Frame, Janet . . . . CLC 2, 3, 6, 22, 66
See also Clutha, Janet Paterson Frame

France, Anatole . . . . TCLC 9
See also Thibault, Jacques Anatole Francois
See also DLB 123

Francis, Claude 19(?)- . . . . CLC 50

Francis, Dick 1920- . . . . CLC 2, 22, 42
See also AAYA 5; BEST 89:3; CA 5-8R;
CANR 9, 42; CDBLB 1960 to Present;
DLB 87; MTCW

Francis, Robert (Churchill)
1901-1987 . . . . CLC 15
See also CA 1-4R; 123; CANR 1

Frank, Anne(lies Marie)
1929-1945 . . . . TCLC 17; DA; WLC
See also AAYA 12; CA 113; 133; MTCW;
SATA-Brief 42

Frank, Elizabeth 1945- . . . . CLC 39
See also CA 121; 126

Franklin, Benjamin
See Hasek, Jaroslav (Matej Frantisek)

Franklin, Benjamin 1706-1790. . . LC 25; DA
See also CDALB 1640-1865; DLB 24, 43,
73

Franklin, (Stella Maraia Sarah) Miles
1879-1954 . . . . TCLC 7
See also CA 104

Fraser, (Lady) Antonia (Pakenham)
1932- . . . . CLC 32
See also CA 85-88; CANR 44; MTCW;
SATA-Brief 32

Fraser, George MacDonald 1925- . . . . CLC 7
See also CA 45-48; CANR 2, 48

Fraser, Sylvia 1935- . . . . CLC 64
See also CA 45-48; CANR 1, 16

Frayn, Michael 1933- . . . . . . CLC 3, 7, 31, 47
See also CA 5-8R; CANR 30; DLB 13, 14;
MTCW

Fraze, Candida (Merrill) 1945- . . . . . CLC 50
See also CA 126

Frazer, J(ames) G(eorge)
1854-1941 . . . . TCLC 32
See also CA 118

Frazer, Robert Caine
See Creasey, John

Frazer, Sir James George
See Frazer, J(ames) G(eorge)

Frazier, Ian 1951- . . . . CLC 46
See also CA 130

Frederic, Harold 1856-1898 . . . . . . NCLC 10
See also DLB 12, 23

Frederick, John
See Faust, Frederick (Schiller)

Frederick the Great 1712-1786 . . . . . . LC 14

Fredro, Aleksander 1793-1876 . . . . . NCLC 8

Freeling, Nicolas 1927- . . . . CLC 38
See also CA 49-52; CAAS 12; CANR 1, 17;
DLB 87

Freeman, Douglas Southall
1886-1953 . . . . TCLC 11
See also CA 109; DLB 17

Freeman, Judith 1946- . . . . CLC 55

Freeman, Mary Eleanor Wilkins
1852-1930 . . . . TCLC 9; SSC 1
See also CA 106; DLB 12, 78

Freeman, R(ichard) Austin
1862-1943 . . . . TCLC 21
See also CA 113; DLB 70

French, Albert 1943- . . . . CLC 86

French, Marilyn 1929- . . . . . . CLC 10, 18, 60
See also CA 69-72; CANR 3, 31; MTCW

French, Paul
See Asimov, Isaac

Freneau, Philip Morin 1752-1832 . . NCLC 1
See also DLB 37, 43

Freud, Sigmund 1856-1939 . . . . TCLC 52
See also CA 115; 133; MTCW

Friedan, Betty (Naomi) 1921- . . . . . . CLC 74
See also CA 65-68; CANR 18, 45; MTCW

Friedman, B(ernard) H(arper)
1926- . . . . CLC 7
See also CA 1-4R; CANR 3, 48

Friedman, Bruce Jay 1930- . . . . CLC 3, 5, 56
See also CA 9-12R; CANR 25; DLB 2, 28

Friel, Brian 1929- . . . . CLC 5, 42, 59
See also CA 21-24R; CANR 33; DLB 13;
MTCW

Friis-Baastad, Babbis Ellinor
1921-1970 . . . . CLC 12
See also CA 17-20R; 134; SATA 7

Frisch, Max (Rudolf)
1911-1991 . . . . CLC 3, 9, 14, 18, 32, 44
See also CA 85-88; 134; CANR 32;
DLB 69, 124; MTCW

Fromentin, Eugene (Samuel Auguste)
1820-1876 . . . . NCLC 10
See also DLB 123

Frost, Frederick
See Faust, Frederick (Schiller)

Frost, Robert (Lee)
1874-1963 . . . . CLC 1, 3, 4, 9, 10, 13, 15,
26, 34, 44; DA; PC 1; WLC
See also CA 89-92; CANR 33;
CDALB 1917-1929; DLB 54; DLBD 7;
MTCW; SATA 14

Froude, James Anthony
1818-1894 . . . . NCLC 43
See also DLB 18, 57, 144

Froy, Herald
See Waterhouse, Keith (Spencer)

Fry, Christopher 1907- . . . . CLC 2, 10, 14
See also CA 17-20R; CANR 9, 30; DLB 13;
MTCW; SATA 66

Frye, (Herman) Northrop
1912-1991 . . . . CLC 24, 70
See also CA 5-8R; 133; CANR 8, 37;
DLB 67, 68; MTCW

Fuchs, Daniel 1909-1993 . . . . CLC 8, 22
See also CA 81-84; 142; CAAS 5;
CANR 40; DLB 9, 26, 28; DLBY 93

Fuchs, Daniel 1934- . . . . CLC 34
See also CA 37-40R; CANR 14, 48

Fuentes, Carlos
1928- . . . . . . CLC 3, 8, 10, 13, 22, 41, 60;
DA; HLC; WLC
See also AAYA 4; AITN 2; CA 69-72;
CANR 10, 32; DLB 113; HW; MTCW

Fuentes, Gregorio Lopez y
See Lopez y Fuentes, Gregorio

Fugard, (Harold) Athol
1932- . . . . CLC 5, 9, 14, 25, 40, 80; DC 3
See also CA 85-88; CANR 32; MTCW

Fugard, Sheila 1932- . . . . CLC 48
See also CA 125

Fuller, Charles (H., Jr.)
1939- . . . . CLC 25; BLC; DC 1
See also BW 2; CA 108; 112; DLB 38;
MTCW

Fuller, John (Leopold) 1937- . . . . CLC 62
See also CA 21-24R; CANR 9, 44; DLB 40

Fuller, Margaret . . . . NCLC 5, 50
See also Ossoli, Sarah Margaret (Fuller
marchesa d')

Fuller, Roy (Broadbent)
1912-1991 . . . . CLC 4, 28
See also CA 5-8R; 135; CAAS 10; DLB 15,
20

Fulton, Alice 1952- . . . . CLC 52
See also CA 116

Furphy, Joseph 1843-1912 . . . . TCLC 25

Fussell, Paul 1924- . . . . CLC 74
See also BEST 90:1; CA 17-20R; CANR 8,
21, 35; MTCW

Futabatei, Shimei 1864-1909 . . . . . . TCLC 44

Futrelle, Jacques 1875-1912 . . . . . . TCLC 19
See also CA 113

Gaboriau, Emile 1835-1873 . . . . . . NCLC 14

Gadda, Carlo Emilio 1893-1973 . . . . CLC 11
See also CA 89-92

Gaddis, William
1922- . . . . . CLC 1, 3, 6, 8, 10, 19, 43, 86
See also CA 17-20R; CANR 21, 48; DLB 2;
MTCW

Gaines, Ernest J(ames)
1933- . . . . CLC 3, 11, 18, 86; BLC
See also AITN 1; BW 2; CA 9-12R;
CANR 6, 24, 42; CDALB 1968-1988;
DLB 2, 33, 152; DLBY 80; MTCW

Gaitskill, Mary 1954- . . . . CLC 69
See also CA 128

Galdos, Benito Perez
See Perez Galdos, Benito

Gale, Zona 1874-1938 . . . . TCLC 7
See also CA 105; DLB 9, 78

Galeano, Eduardo (Hughes) 1940- . . . CLC 72
See also CA 29-32R; CANR 13, 32; HW

Galiano, Juan Valera y Alcala
See Valera y Alcala-Galiano, Juan

Gallagher, Tess 1943- . . . . CLC 18, 63; PC 9
See also CA 106; DLB 120

Gallant, Mavis
1922- . . . . CLC 7, 18, 38; SSC 5
See also CA 69-72; CANR 29; DLB 53;
MTCW

Gallant, Roy A(rthur) 1924- . . . . CLC 17
See also CA 5-8R; CANR 4, 29; CLR 30;
MAICYA; SATA 4, 68

Gallico, Paul (William) 1897-1976 . . . CLC 2
See also AITN 1; CA 5-8R; 69-72;
CANR 23; DLB 9; MAICYA; SATA 13

Gallup, Ralph
See Whitemore, Hugh (John)

Galsworthy, John
1867-1933 . . . . TCLC 1, 45; DA; WLC 2
See also CA 104; 141; CDBLB 1890-1914;
DLB 10, 34, 98

Galt, John 1779-1839 . . . . NCLC 1
See also DLB 99, 116

Galvin, James 1951- . . . . CLC 38
See also CA 108; CANR 26

Gamboa, Federico 1864-1939 . . . . . . TCLC 36

Gandhi, M. K.
See Gandhi, Mohandas Karamchand

Gandhi, Mahatma
See Gandhi, Mohandas Karamchand

Gandhi, Mohandas Karamchand
1869-1948 . . . . **TCLC 59**
See also CA 121; 132; MTCW

Gann, Ernest Kellogg 1910-1991 . . . . **CLC 23**
See also AITN 1; CA 1-4R; 136; CANR 1

Garcia, Cristina 1958- . . . . **CLC 76**
See also CA 141

Garcia Lorca, Federico
1898-1936 . . . . **TCLC 1, 7, 49; DA;**
DC 2; HLC; PC 3; WLC
See also CA 104; 131; DLB 108; HW;
MTCW

Garcia Marquez, Gabriel (Jose)
1928- . . . . **CLC 2, 3, 8, 10, 15, 27, 47, 55,**
68; DA; HLC; SSC 8; WLC
See also AAYA 3; BEST 89:1, 90:4;
CA 33-36R; CANR 10, 28; DLB 113;
HW; MTCW

Gard, Janice
See Latham, Jean Lee

Gard, Roger Martin du
See Martin du Gard, Roger

Gardam, Jane 1928- . . . . **CLC 43**
See also CA 49-52; CANR 2, 18, 33;
CLR 12; DLB 14; MAICYA; MTCW;
SAAS 9; SATA 39, 76; SATA-Brief 28

Gardner, Herb . . . . **CLC 44**

Gardner, John (Champlin), Jr.
1933-1982 . . . . . **CLC 2, 3, 5, 7, 8, 10, 18,**
28, 34; SSC 7
See also AITN 1; CA 65-68; 107;
CANR 33; DLB 2; DLBY 82; MTCW;
SATA 40; SATA-Obit 31

Gardner, John (Edmund) 1926- . . . . . **CLC 30**
See also CA 103; CANR 15; MTCW

Gardner, Noel
See Kuttner, Henry

Gardons, S. S.
See Snodgrass, W(illiam) D(e Witt)

Garfield, Leon 1921- . . . . **CLC 12**
See also AAYA 8; CA 17-20R; CANR 38,
41; CLR 21; JRDA; MAICYA; SATA 1,
32, 76

Garland, (Hannibal) Hamlin
1860-1940 . . . . **TCLC 3; SSC 18**
See also CA 104; DLB 12, 71, 78

Garneau, (Hector de) Saint-Denys
1912-1943 . . . . **TCLC 13**
See also CA 111; DLB 88

Garner, Alan 1934- . . . . **CLC 17**
See also CA 73-76; CANR 15; CLR 20;
MAICYA; MTCW; SATA 18, 69

Garner, Hugh 1913-1979 . . . . **CLC 13**
See also CA 69-72; CANR 31; DLB 68

Garnett, David 1892-1981 . . . . **CLC 3**
See also CA 5-8R; 103; CANR 17; DLB 34

Garos, Stephanie
See Katz, Steve

Garrett, George (Palmer)
1929- . . . . **CLC 3, 11, 51**
See also CA 1-4R; CAAS 5; CANR 1, 42;
DLB 2, 5, 130, 152; DLBY 83

Garrick, David 1717-1779 . . . . **LC 15**
See also DLB 84

Garrigue, Jean 1914-1972 . . . . **CLC 2, 8**
See also CA 5-8R; 37-40R; CANR 20

Garrison, Frederick
See Sinclair, Upton (Beall)

Garth, Will
See Hamilton, Edmond; Kuttner, Henry

Garvey, Marcus (Moziah, Jr.)
1887-1940 . . . . **TCLC 41; BLC**
See also BW 1; CA 120; 124

Gary, Romain . . . . **CLC 25**
See also Kacew, Romain
See also DLB 83

Gascar, Pierre . . . . **CLC 11**
See also Fournier, Pierre

Gascoyne, David (Emery) 1916- . . . . **CLC 45**
See also CA 65-68; CANR 10, 28; DLB 20;
MTCW

Gaskell, Elizabeth Cleghorn
1810-1865 . . . . **NCLC 5**
See also CDBLB 1832-1890; DLB 21, 144

Gass, William H(oward)
1924- . . . **CLC 1, 2, 8, 11, 15, 39; SSC 12**
See also CA 17-20R; CANR 30; DLB 2;
MTCW

Gasset, Jose Ortega y
See Ortega y Gasset, Jose

Gates, Henry Louis, Jr. 1950- . . . . . . **CLC 65**
See also BW 2; CA 109; CANR 25; DLB 67

Gautier, Theophile
1811-1872 . . . . **NCLC 1; SSC 20**
See also DLB 119

Gawsworth, John
See Bates, H(erbert) E(rnest)

Gaye, Marvin (Penze) 1939-1984 . . . **CLC 26**
See also CA 112

Gebler, Carlo (Ernest) 1954- . . . . **CLC 39**
See also CA 119; 133

Gee, Maggie (Mary) 1948- . . . . **CLC 57**
See also CA 130

Gee, Maurice (Gough) 1931- . . . . **CLC 29**
See also CA 97-100; SATA 46

Gelbart, Larry (Simon) 1923- . . . **CLC 21, 61**
See also CA 73-76; CANR 45

Gelber, Jack 1932- . . . . **CLC 1, 6, 14, 79**
See also CA 1-4R; CANR 2; DLB 7

Gellhorn, Martha (Ellis) 1908- . . **CLC 14, 60**
See also CA 77-80; CANR 44; DLBY 82

Genet, Jean
1910-1986 . . . **CLC 1, 2, 5, 10, 14, 44, 46**
See also CA 13-16R; CANR 18; DLB 72;
DLBY 86; MTCW

Gent, Peter 1942- . . . . **CLC 29**
See also AITN 1; CA 89-92; DLBY 82

Gentlewoman in New England, A
See Bradstreet, Anne

Gentlewoman in Those Parts, A
See Bradstreet, Anne

George, Jean Craighead 1919- . . . . . . **CLC 35**
See also AAYA 8; CA 5-8R; CANR 25;
CLR 1; DLB 52; JRDA; MAICYA;
SATA 2, 68

George, Stefan (Anton)
1868-1933 . . . . **TCLC 2, 14**
See also CA 104

Georges, Georges Martin
See Simenon, Georges (Jacques Christian)

Gerhardi, William Alexander
See Gerhardie, William Alexander

Gerhardie, William Alexander
1895-1977 . . . . **CLC 5**
See also CA 25-28R; 73-76; CANR 18;
DLB 36

Gerstler, Amy 1956- . . . . **CLC 70**
See also CA 146

Gertler, T. . . . . **CLC 34**
See also CA 116; 121

Ghalib 1797-1869 . . . . **NCLC 39**

Ghelderode, Michel de
1898-1962 . . . . **CLC 6, 11**
See also CA 85-88; CANR 40

Ghiselin, Brewster 1903- . . . . **CLC 23**
See also CA 13-16R; CAAS 10; CANR 13

Ghose, Zulfikar 1935- . . . . **CLC 42**
See also CA 65-68

Ghosh, Amitav 1956- . . . . **CLC 44**
See also CA 147

Giacosa, Giuseppe 1847-1906 . . . . . . **TCLC 7**
See also CA 104

Gibb, Lee
See Waterhouse, Keith (Spencer)

Gibbon, Lewis Grassic . . . . **TCLC 4**
See also Mitchell, James Leslie

Gibbons, Kaye 1960- . . . . **CLC 50, 88**

Gibran, Kahlil
1883-1931 . . . . **TCLC 1, 9; PC 9**
See also CA 104

Gibson, William 1914- . . . . **CLC 23; DA**
See also CA 9-12R; CANR 9, 42; DLB 7;
SATA 66

Gibson, William (Ford) 1948- . . . **CLC 39, 63**
See also AAYA 12; CA 126; 133

Gide, Andre (Paul Guillaume)
1869-1951 . . . . **TCLC 5, 12, 36; DA;**
SSC 13; WLC
See also CA 104; 124; DLB 65; MTCW

Gifford, Barry (Colby) 1946- . . . . **CLC 34**
See also CA 65-68; CANR 9, 30, 40

Gilbert, W(illiam) S(chwenck)
1836-1911 . . . . **TCLC 3**
See also CA 104; SATA 36

Gilbreth, Frank B., Jr. 1911- . . . . **CLC 17**
See also CA 9-12R; SATA 2

Gilchrist, Ellen 1935- . . **CLC 34, 48; SSC 14**
See also CA 113; 116; CANR 41; DLB 130;
MTCW

Giles, Molly 1942- . . . . **CLC 39**
See also CA 126

Gill, Patrick
See Creasey, John

Gilliam, Terry (Vance) 1940- . . . . **CLC 21**
See also Monty Python
See also CA 108; 113; CANR 35

Gillian, Jerry
See Gilliam, Terry (Vance)

Gilliatt, Penelope (Ann Douglass)
1932-1993 . . . . CLC **2, 10, 13, 53**
See also AITN 2; CA 13-16R; 141;
CANR 49; DLB 14

Gilman, Charlotte (Anna) Perkins (Stetson)
1860-1935 . . . . TCLC **9, 37; SSC 13**
See also CA 106

Gilmour, David 1949- . . . . CLC **35**
See also CA 138, 147

Gilpin, William 1724-1804 . . . . . . NCLC **30**

Gilray, J. D.
See Mencken, H(enry) L(ouis)

Gilroy, Frank D(aniel) 1925- . . . . CLC **2**
See also CA 81-84; CANR 32; DLB 7

Ginsberg, Allen
1926- . . . . . . CLC **1, 2, 3, 4, 6, 13, 36, 69;**
DA; PC **4**; WLC **3**
See also AITN 1; CA 1-4R; CANR 2, 41;
CDALB 1941-1968; DLB 5, 16; MTCW

Ginzburg, Natalia
1916-1991 . . . . CLC **5, 11, 54, 70**
See also CA 85-88; 135; CANR 33; MTCW

Giono, Jean 1895-1970 . . . . CLC **4, 11**
See also CA 45-48; 29-32R; CANR 2, 35;
DLB 72; MTCW

Giovanni, Nikki
1943- . . . . . . CLC **2, 4, 19, 64; BLC; DA**
See also AITN 1; BW 2; CA 29-32R;
CAAS 6; CANR 18, 41; CLR 6; DLB 5,
41; MAICYA; MTCW; SATA 24

Giovene, Andrea 1904- . . . . CLC **7**
See also CA 85-88

Gippius, Zinaida (Nikolayevna) 1869-1945
See Hippius, Zinaida
See also CA 106

Giraudoux, (Hippolyte) Jean
1882-1944 . . . . TCLC **2, 7**
See also CA 104; DLB 65

Gironella, Jose Maria 1917- . . . . CLC **11**
See also CA 101

Gissing, George (Robert)
1857-1903 . . . . TCLC **3, 24, 47**
See also CA 105; DLB 18, 135

Giurlani, Aldo
See Palazzeschi, Aldo

Gladkov, Fyodor (Vasilyevich)
1883-1958 . . . . TCLC **27**

Glanville, Brian (Lester) 1931- . . . . . . CLC **6**
See also CA 5-8R; CAAS 9; CANR 3;
DLB 15, 139; SATA 42

Glasgow, Ellen (Anderson Gholson)
1873(?)-1945 . . . . TCLC **2, 7**
See also CA 104; DLB 9, 12

Glaspell, Susan (Keating)
1882(?)-1948 . . . . TCLC **55**
See also CA 110; DLB 7, 9, 78; YABC 2

Glassco, John 1909-1981 . . . . CLC **9**
See also CA 13-16R; 102; CANR 15;
DLB 68

Glasscock, Amnesia
See Steinbeck, John (Ernst)

Glasser, Ronald J. 1940(?)- . . . . CLC **37**

Glassman, Joyce
See Johnson, Joyce

Glendinning, Victoria 1937- . . . . CLC **50**
See also CA 120; 127

Glissant, Edouard 1928- . . . . CLC **10, 68**

Gloag, Julian 1930- . . . . CLC **40**
See also AITN 1; CA 65-68; CANR 10

Glowacki, Aleksander
See Prus, Boleslaw

Glueck, Louise (Elisabeth)
1943- . . . . CLC **7, 22, 44, 81**
See also CA 33-36R; CANR 40; DLB 5

Gobineau, Joseph Arthur (Comte) de
1816-1882 . . . . NCLC **17**
See also DLB 123

Godard, Jean-Luc 1930- . . . . CLC **20**
See also CA 93-96

Godden, (Margaret) Rumer 1907- . . . CLC **53**
See also AAYA 6; CA 5-8R; CANR 4, 27,
36; CLR 20; MAICYA; SAAS 12;
SATA 3, 36

Godoy Alcayaga, Lucila 1889-1957
See Mistral, Gabriela
See also BW 2; CA 104; 131; HW; MTCW

Godwin, Gail (Kathleen)
1937- . . . . CLC **5, 8, 22, 31, 69**
See also CA 29-32R; CANR 15, 43; DLB 6;
MTCW

Godwin, William 1756-1836 . . . . . . NCLC **14**
See also CDBLB 1789-1832; DLB 39, 104,
142

Goethe, Johann Wolfgang von
1749-1832 . . . . NCLC **4, 22, 34; DA;**
PC **5**; WLC **3**
See also DLB 94

Gogarty, Oliver St. John
1878-1957 . . . . TCLC **15**
See also CA 109; DLB 15, 19

Gogol, Nikolai (Vasilyevich)
1809-1852 . . . . NCLC **5, 15, 31; DA;**
DC **1**; SSC **4**; WLC
See also DLB 198

Goines, Donald
1937(?)-1974 . . . . CLC **80; BLC**
See also AITN 1; BW 1; CA 124; 114;
DLB 33

Gold, Herbert 1924- . . . . CLC **4, 7, 14, 42**
See also CA 9-12R; CANR 17, 45; DLB 2;
DLBY 81

Goldbarth, Albert 1948- . . . . CLC **5, 38**
See also CA 53-56; CANR 6, 40; DLB 120

Goldberg, Anatol 1910-1982 . . . . CLC **34**
See also CA 131; 117

Goldemberg, Isaac 1945- . . . . CLC **52**
See also CA 69-72; CAAS 12; CANR 11,
32; HW

Golding, William (Gerald)
1911-1993 . . . . CLC **1, 2, 3, 8, 10, 17, 27,**
58, 81; DA; WLC
See also AAYA 5; CA 5-8R; 141;
CANR 13, 33; CDBLB 1945-1960;
DLB 15, 100; MTCW

Goldman, Emma 1869-1940 . . . . . . TCLC **13**
See also CA 110

Goldman, Francisco 1955- . . . . CLC **76**

Goldman, William (W.) 1931- . . . . CLC **1, 48**
See also CA 9-12R; CANR 29; DLB 44

Goldmann, Lucien 1913-1970 . . . . . . CLC **24**
See also CA 25-28; CAP 2

Goldoni, Carlo 1707-1793 . . . . LC **4**

Goldsberry, Steven 1949- . . . . CLC **34**
See also CA 131

Goldsmith, Oliver
1728-1774 . . . . LC **2; DA; WLC**
See also CDBLB 1660-1789; DLB 39, 89,
104, 109, 142; SATA 26

Goldsmith, Peter
See Priestley, J(ohn) B(oynton)

Gombrowicz, Witold
1904-1969 . . . . CLC **4, 7, 11, 49**
See also CA 19-20; 25-28R; CAP 2

Gomez de la Serna, Ramon
1888-1963 . . . . CLC **9**
See also CA 116; HW

Goncharov, Ivan Alexandrovich
1812-1891 . . . . NCLC **1**

Goncourt, Edmond (Louis Antoine Huot) de
1822-1896 . . . . NCLC **7**
See also DLB 123

Goncourt, Jules (Alfred Huot) de
1830-1870 . . . . NCLC **7**
See also DLB 123

Gontier, Fernande 19(?)- . . . . CLC **50**

Goodman, Paul 1911-1972 . . . . CLC **1, 2, 4, 7**
See also CA 19-20; 37-40R; CANR 34;
CAP 2; DLB 130; MTCW

Gordimer, Nadine
1923- . . . . CLC **3, 5, 7, 10, 18, 33, 51, 70;**
DA; SSC **17**
See also CA 5-8R; CANR 3, 28; MTCW

Gordon, Adam Lindsay
1833-1870 . . . . NCLC **21**

Gordon, Caroline
1895-1981 . . . CLC **6, 13, 29, 83; SSC 15**
See also CA 11-12; 103; CANR 36; CAP 1;
DLB 4, 9, 102; DLBY 81; MTCW

Gordon, Charles William 1860-1937
See Connor, Ralph
See also CA 109

Gordon, Mary (Catherine)
1949- . . . . CLC **13, 22**
See also CA 102; CANR 44; DLB 6;
DLBY 81; MTCW

Gordon, Sol 1923- . . . . CLC **26**
See also CA 53-56; CANR 4; SATA 11

Gordone, Charles 1925- . . . . CLC **1, 4**
See also BW 1; CA 93-96; DLB 7; MTCW

Gorenko, Anna Andreevna
See Akhmatova, Anna

Gorky, Maxim . . . . TCLC **8; WLC**
See also Peshkov, Alexei Maximovich

Goryan, Sirak
See Saroyan, William

Gosse, Edmund (William)
1849-1928 . . . . TCLC **28**
See also CA 117; DLB 57, 144

Gotlieb, Phyllis Fay (Bloom)
1926- . . . . CLC **18**
See also CA 13-16R; CANR 7; DLB 88

Gottesman, S. D.
See Kornbluth, C(yril) M.; Pohl, Frederik

Gottfried von Strassburg
　　fl. c. 1210-.................. **CMLC 10**
　See also DLB 138

Gould, Lois .... **CLC 4, 10**
　See also CA 77-80; CANR 29; MTCW

Gourmont, Remy de 1858-1915.... **TCLC 17**
　See also CA 109

Govier, Katherine 1948-........... **CLC 51**
　See also CA 101; CANR 18, 40

Goyen, (Charles) William
　　1915-1983 .... **CLC 5, 8, 14, 40**
　See also AITN 2; CA 5-8R; 110; CANR 6;
　　DLB 2; DLBY 83

Goytisolo, Juan
　　1931- .... **CLC 5, 10, 23; HLC**
　See also CA 85-88; CANR 32; HW; MTCW

Gozzano, Guido 1883-1916 .... **PC 10**
　See also DLB 114

Gozzi, (Conte) Carlo 1720-1806 .. **NCLC 23**

Grabbe, Christian Dietrich
　　1801-1836 .... **NCLC 2**
　See also DLB 133

Grace, Patricia 1937-............. **CLC 56**

Gracian y Morales, Baltasar
　　1601-1658 .... **LC 15**

Gracq, Julien................. **CLC 11, 48**
　See also Poirier, Louis
　See also DLB 83

Grade, Chaim 1910-1982 .... **CLC 10**
　See also CA 93-96; 107

Graduate of Oxford, A
　See Ruskin, John

Graham, John
　See Phillips, David Graham

Graham, Jorie 1951-............. **CLC 48**
　See also CA 111; DLB 120

Graham, R(obert) B(ontine) Cunninghame
　See Cunninghame Graham, R(obert)
　　B(ontine)
　See also DLB 98, 135

Graham, Robert
　See Haldeman, Joe (William)

Graham, Tom
　See Lewis, (Harry) Sinclair

Graham, W(illiam) S(ydney)
　　1918-1986 .... **CLC 29**
　See also CA 73-76; 118; DLB 20

Graham, Winston (Mawdsley)
　　1910- .... **CLC 23**
　See also CA 49-52; CANR 2, 22, 45;
　　DLB 77

Grant, Skeeter
　See Spiegelman, Art

Granville-Barker, Harley
　　1877-1946 .... **TCLC 2**
　See also Barker, Harley Granville
　See also CA 104

Grass, Guenter (Wilhelm)
　　1927- ..... **CLC 1, 2, 4, 6, 11, 15, 22, 32,
　　　　　　　　　　　　　49, 88; DA; WLC**
　See also CA 13-16R; CANR 20; DLB 75,
　　124; MTCW

Gratton, Thomas
　See Hulme, T(homas) E(rnest)

Grau, Shirley Ann
　　1929- .... **CLC 4, 9; SSC 15**
　See also CA 89-92; CANR 22; DLB 2;
　　MTCW

Gravel, Fern
　See Hall, James Norman

Graver, Elizabeth 1964-.......... **CLC 70**
　See also CA 135

Graves, Richard Perceval 1945- .... **CLC 44**
　See also CA 65-68; CANR 9, 26

Graves, Robert (von Ranke)
　　1895-1985 ...... **CLC 1, 2, 6, 11, 39, 44,
　　　　　　　　　　　　　　　45; PC 6**
　See also CA 5-8R; 117; CANR 5, 36;
　　CDBLB 1914-1945; DLB 20, 100;
　　DLBY 85; MTCW; SATA 45

Gray, Alasdair (James) 1934-...... **CLC 41**
　See also CA 126; CANR 47; MTCW

Gray, Amlin 1946- .... **CLC 29**
　See also CA 138

Gray, Francine du Plessix 1930-.... **CLC 22**
　See also BEST 90:3; CA 61-64; CAAS 2;
　　CANR 11, 33; MTCW

Gray, John (Henry) 1866-1934 .... **TCLC 19**
　See also CA 119

Gray, Simon (James Holliday)
　　1936- .... **CLC 9, 14, 36**
　See also AITN 1; CA 21-24R; CAAS 3;
　　CANR 32; DLB 13; MTCW

Gray, Spalding 1941-............. **CLC 49**
　See also CA 128

Gray, Thomas
　　1716-1771 ...... **LC 4; DA; PC 2; WLC**
　See also CDBLB 1660-1789; DLB 109

Grayson, David
　See Baker, Ray Stannard

Grayson, Richard (A.) 1951- .... **CLC 38**
　See also CA 85-88; CANR 14, 31

Greeley, Andrew M(oran) 1928- .... **CLC 28**
　See also CA 5-8R; CAAS 7; CANR 7, 43;
　　MTCW

Green, Brian
　See Card, Orson Scott

Green, Hannah
　See Greenberg, Joanne (Goldenberg)

Green, Hannah .... **CLC 3**
　See also CA 73-76

Green, Henry................... **CLC 2, 13**
　See also Yorke, Henry Vincent
　See also DLB 15

Green, Julian (Hartridge) 1900-
　See Green, Julien
　See also CA 21-24R; CANR 33; DLB 4, 72;
　　MTCW

Green, Julien................ **CLC 3, 11, 77**
　See also Green, Julian (Hartridge)

Green, Paul (Eliot) 1894-1981...... **CLC 25**
　See also AITN 1; CA 5-8R; 103; CANR 3;
　　DLB 7, 9; DLBY 81

Greenberg, Ivan 1908-1973
　See Rahv, Philip
　See also CA 85-88

Greenberg, Joanne (Goldenberg)
　　1932-...................... **CLC 7, 30**
　See also AAYA 12; CA 5-8R; CANR 14,
　　32; SATA 25

Greenberg, Richard 1959(?)-....... **CLC 57**
　See also CA 138

Greene, Bette 1934-.............. **CLC 30**
　See also AAYA 7; CA 53-56; CANR 4;
　　CLR 2; JRDA; MAICYA; SAAS 16;
　　SATA 8

Greene, Gael .... **CLC 8**
　See also CA 13-16R; CANR 10

Greene, Graham
　　1904-1991 .... **CLC 1, 3, 6, 9, 14, 18, 27,
　　　　　　　　　　　37, 70, 72; DA; WLC**
　See also AITN 2; CA 13-16R; 133;
　　CANR 35; CDBLB 1945-1960; DLB 13,
　　15, 77, 100; DLBY 91; MTCW; SATA 20

Greer, Richard
　See Silverberg, Robert

Gregor, Arthur 1923-.............. **CLC 9**
　See also CA 25-28R; CAAS 10; CANR 11;
　　SATA 36

Gregor, Lee
　See Pohl, Frederik

Gregory, Isabella Augusta (Persse)
　　1852-1932 .... **TCLC 1**
　See also CA 104; DLB 10

Gregory, J. Dennis
　See Williams, John A(lfred)

Grendon, Stephen
　See Derleth, August (William)

Grenville, Kate 1950-............. **CLC 61**
　See also CA 118

Grenville, Pelham
　See Wodehouse, P(elham) G(renville)

Greve, Felix Paul (Berthold Friedrich)
　　1879-1948
　See Grove, Frederick Philip
　See also CA 104; 141

Grey, Zane 1872-1939 .... **TCLC 6**
　See also CA 104; 132; DLB 9; MTCW

Grieg, (Johan) Nordahl (Brun)
　　1902-1943 .... **TCLC 10**
　See also CA 107

Grieve, C(hristopher) M(urray)
　　1892-1978 .... **CLC 11, 19**
　See also MacDiarmid, Hugh
　See also CA 5-8R; 85-88; CANR 33;
　　MTCW

Griffin, Gerald 1803-1840 .... **NCLC 7**

Griffin, John Howard 1920-1980.... **CLC 68**
　See also AITN 1; CA 1-4R; 101; CANR 2

Griffin, Peter 1942- .... **CLC 39**
　See also CA 136

Griffiths, Trevor 1935-......... **CLC 13, 52**
　See also CA 97-100; CANR 45; DLB 13

Grigson, Geoffrey (Edward Harvey)
　　1905-1985 .... **CLC 7, 39**
　See also CA 25-28R; 118; CANR 20, 33;
　　DLB 27; MTCW

Grillparzer, Franz 1791-1872...... **NCLC 1**
　See also DLB 133

Grimble, Reverend Charles James
　See Eliot, T(homas) S(tearns)

Grimke, Charlotte L(ottie) Forten
1837(?)-1914
See Forten, Charlotte L.
See also BW 1; CA 117; 124

Grimm, Jacob Ludwig Karl
1785-1863 .... NCLC 3
See also DLB 90; MAICYA; SATA 22

Grimm, Wilhelm Karl 1786-1859 .. NCLC 3
See also DLB 90; MAICYA; SATA 22

Grimmelshausen, Johann Jakob Christoffel
von 1621-1676 .... LC 6

Grindel, Eugene 1895-1952
See Eluard, Paul
See also CA 104

Grisham, John 1955- .... CLC 84
See also AAYA 14; CA 138; CANR 47

Grossman, David 1954- .... CLC 67
See also CA 138

Grossman, Vasily (Semenovich)
1905-1964 .... CLC 41
See also CA 124; 130; MTCW

Grove, Frederick Philip .... TCLC 4
See also Greve, Felix Paul (Berthold
Friedrich)
See also DLB 92

Grubb
See Crumb, R(obert)

Grumbach, Doris (Isaac)
1918- .... CLC 13, 22, 64
See also CA 5-8R; CAAS 2; CANR 9, 42

Grundtvig, Nicolai Frederik Severin
1783-1872 .... NCLC 1

Grunge
See Crumb, R(obert)

Grunwald, Lisa 1959- .... CLC 44
See also CA 120

Guare, John 1938- .... CLC 8, 14, 29, 67
See also CA 73-76; CANR 21; DLB 7;
MTCW

Gudjonsson, Halldor Kiljan 1902-
See Laxness, Halldor
See also CA 103

Guenter, Erich
See Eich, Guenter

Guest, Barbara 1920- .... CLC 34
See also CA 25-28R; CANR 11, 44; DLB 5

Guest, Judith (Ann) 1936- .... CLC 8, 30
See also AAYA 7; CA 77-80; CANR 15;
MTCW

Guevara, Che .... CLC 87; HLC
See also Guevara (Serna), Ernesto

Guevara (Serna), Ernesto 1928-1967
See Guevara, Che
See also CA 127; 111; HW

Guild, Nicholas M. 1944- .... CLC 33
See also CA 93-96

Guillemin, Jacques
See Sartre, Jean-Paul

Guillen, Jorge 1893-1984 .... CLC 11
See also CA 89-92; 112; DLB 108; HW

Guillen (y Batista), Nicolas (Cristobal)
1902-1989 ..... CLC 48, 79; BLC; HLC
See also BW 2; CA 116; 125; 129; HW

Guillevic, (Eugene) 1907- .... CLC 33
See also CA 93-96

Guillois
See Desnos, Robert

Guiney, Louise Imogen
1861-1920 .... TCLC 41
See also DLB 54

Guiraldes, Ricardo (Guillermo)
1886-1927 .... TCLC 39
See also CA 131; HW; MTCW

Gumilev, Nikolai Stephanovich
1886-1921 .... TCLC 60

Gunn, Bill .... CLC 5
See also Gunn, William Harrison
See also DLB 38

Gunn, Thom(son William)
1929- .... CLC 3, 6, 18, 32, 81
See also CA 17-20R; CANR 9, 33;
CDBLB 1960 to Present; DLB 27;
MTCW

Gunn, William Harrison 1934(?)-1989
See Gunn, Bill
See also AITN 1; BW 1; CA 13-16R; 128;
CANR 12, 25

Gunnars, Kristjana 1948- .... CLC 69
See also CA 113; DLB 60

Gurganus, Allan 1947- .... CLC 70
See also BEST 90:1; CA 135

Gurney, A(lbert) R(amsdell), Jr.
1930- .... CLC 32, 50, 54
See also CA 77-80; CANR 32

Gurney, Ivor (Bertie) 1890-1937 ... TCLC 33

Gurney, Peter
See Gurney, A(lbert) R(amsdell), Jr.

Guro, Elena 1877-1913 .... TCLC 56

Gustafson, Ralph (Barker) 1909- .... CLC 36
See also CA 21-24R; CANR 8, 45; DLB 88

Gut, Gom
See Simenon, Georges (Jacques Christian)

Guthrie, A(lfred) B(ertram), Jr.
1901-1991 .... CLC 23
See also CA 57-60; 134; CANR 24; DLB 6;
SATA 62; SATA-Obit 67

Guthrie, Isobel
See Grieve, C(hristopher) M(urray)

Guthrie, Woodrow Wilson 1912-1967
See Guthrie, Woody
See also CA 113; 93-96

Guthrie, Woody .... CLC 35
See also Guthrie, Woodrow Wilson

Guy, Rosa (Cuthbert) 1928- .... CLC 26
See also AAYA 4; BW 2; CA 17-20R;
CANR 14, 34; CLR 13; DLB 33; JRDA;
MAICYA; SATA 14, 62

Gwendolyn
See Bennett, (Enoch) Arnold

H. D. .... CLC 3, 8, 14, 31, 34, 73; PC 5
See also Doolittle, Hilda

H. de V.
See Buchan, John

Haavikko, Paavo Juhani
1931- .... CLC 18, 34
See also CA 106

Habbema, Koos
See Heijermans, Herman

Hacker, Marilyn 1942- .... CLC 5, 9, 23, 72
See also CA 77-80; DLB 120

Haggard, H(enry) Rider
1856-1925 .... TCLC 11
See also CA 108; DLB 70; SATA 16

Hagiwara Sakutaro 1886-1942 .... TCLC 60

Haig, Fenil
See Ford, Ford Madox

Haig-Brown, Roderick (Langmere)
1908-1976 .... CLC 21
See also CA 5-8R; 69-72; CANR 4, 38;
CLR 31; DLB 88; MAICYA; SATA 12

Hailey, Arthur 1920- .... CLC 5
See also AITN 2; BEST 90:3; CA 1-4R;
CANR 2, 36; DLB 88; DLBY 82; MTCW

Hailey, Elizabeth Forsythe 1938-... CLC 40
See also CA 93-96; CAAS 1; CANR 15, 48

Haines, John (Meade) 1924- .... CLC 58
See also CA 17-20R; CANR 13, 34; DLB 5

Haldeman, Joe (William) 1943-..... CLC 61
See also CA 53-56; CANR 6; DLB 8

Haley, Alex(ander Murray Palmer)
1921-1992 .... CLC 8, 12, 76; BLC; DA
See also BW 2; CA 77-80; 136; DLB 38;
MTCW

Haliburton, Thomas Chandler
1796-1865 .... NCLC 15
See also DLB 11, 99

Hall, Donald (Andrew, Jr.)
1928- .... CLC 1, 13, 37, 59
See also CA 5-8R; CAAS 7; CANR 2, 44;
DLB 5; SATA 23

Hall, Frederic Sauser
See Sauser-Hall, Frederic

Hall, James
See Kuttner, Henry

Hall, James Norman 1887-1951 ... TCLC 23
See also CA 123; SATA 21

Hall, (Marguerite) Radclyffe
1886(?)-1943 .... TCLC 12
See also CA 110

Hall, Rodney 1935- .... CLC 51
See also CA 109

Halleck, Fitz-Greene 1790-1867 .. NCLC 47
See also DLB 3

Halliday, Michael
See Creasey, John

Halpern, Daniel 1945- .... CLC 14
See also CA 33-36R

Hamburger, Michael (Peter Leopold)
1924- .... CLC 5, 14
See also CA 5-8R; CAAS 4; CANR 2, 47;
DLB 27

Hamill, Pete 1935- .... CLC 10
See also CA 25-28R; CANR 18

Hamilton, Alexander
1755(?)-1804 .... NCLC 49
See also DLB 37

Hamilton, Clive
See Lewis, C(live) S(taples)

Hamilton, Edmond 1904-1977 .... CLC 1
See also CA 1-4R; CANR 3; DLB 8

Hamilton, Eugene (Jacob) Lee
See Lee-Hamilton, Eugene (Jacob)

Hamilton, Franklin
See Silverberg, Robert

Hamilton, Gail
See Corcoran, Barbara

Hamilton, Mollie
See Kaye, M(ary) M(argaret)

Hamilton, (Anthony Walter) Patrick
1904-1962 . . . . **CLC 51**
See also CA 113; DLB 10

Hamilton, Virginia 1936- . . . . **CLC 26**
See also AAYA 2; BW 2; CA 25-28R;
CANR 20, 37; CLR 1, 11; DLB 33, 52;
JRDA; MAICYA; MTCW; SATA 4, 56,
79

Hammett, (Samuel) Dashiell
1894-1961 . . . . **CLC 3, 5, 10, 19, 47;**
SSC 17
See also AITN 1; CA 81-84; CANR 42;
CDALB 1929-1941; DLBD 6; MTCW

Hammon, Jupiter
1711(?)-1800(?) . . . . **NCLC 5; BLC**
See also DLB 31, 50

Hammond, Keith
See Kuttner, Henry

Hamner, Earl (Henry), Jr. 1923- . . . **CLC 12**
See also AITN 2; CA 73-76; DLB 6

Hampton, Christopher (James)
1946- . . . . **CLC 4**
See also CA 25-28R; DLB 13; MTCW

Hamsun, Knut . . . . **TCLC 2, 14, 49**
See also Pedersen, Knut

Handke, Peter 1942- . . **CLC 5, 8, 10, 15, 38**
See also CA 77-80; CANR 33; DLB 85,
124; MTCW

Hanley, James 1901-1985 . . . **CLC 3, 5, 8, 13**
See also CA 73-76; 117; CANR 36; MTCW

Hannah, Barry 1942- . . . . **CLC 23, 38**
See also CA 108; 110; CANR 43; DLB 6;
MTCW

Hannon, Ezra
See Hunter, Evan

Hansberry, Lorraine (Vivian)
1930-1965 . . . . . . **CLC 17, 62; BLC; DA;**
DC 2
See also BW 1; CA 109; 25-28R; CABS 3;
CDALB 1941-1968; DLB 7, 38; MTCW

Hansen, Joseph 1923- . . . . **CLC 38**
See also CA 29-32R; CAAS 17; CANR 16,
44

Hansen, Martin A. 1909-1955 . . . . . **TCLC 32**

Hanson, Kenneth O(stlin) 1922- . . . . **CLC 13**
See also CA 53-56; CANR 7

Hardwick, Elizabeth 1916- . . . . **CLC 13**
See also CA 5-8R; CANR 3, 32; DLB 6;
MTCW

Hardy, Thomas
1840-1928 . . . . . **TCLC 4, 10, 18, 32, 48,**
53; DA; PC 8; SSC 2; WLC
See also CA 104; 123; CDBLB 1890-1914;
DLB 18, 19, 135; MTCW

Hare, David 1947- . . . . **CLC 29, 58**
See also CA 97-100; CANR 39; DLB 13;
MTCW

Harford, Henry
See Hudson, W(illiam) H(enry)

Hargrave, Leonie
See Disch, Thomas M(ichael)

Harjo, Joy 1951- . . . . **CLC 83**
See also CA 114; CANR 35; DLB 120;
NNAL

Harlan, Louis R(udolph) 1922- . . . . . **CLC 34**
See also CA 21-24R; CANR 25

Harling, Robert 1951(?)- . . . . **CLC 53**
See also CA 147

Harmon, William (Ruth) 1938- . . . . . **CLC 38**
See also CA 33-36R; CANR 14, 32, 35;
SATA 65

Harper, F. E. W.
See Harper, Frances Ellen Watkins

Harper, Frances E. W.
See Harper, Frances Ellen Watkins

Harper, Frances E. Watkins
See Harper, Frances Ellen Watkins

Harper, Frances Ellen
See Harper, Frances Ellen Watkins

Harper, Frances Ellen Watkins
1825-1911 . . . . **TCLC 14; BLC**
See also BW 1; CA 111; 125; DLB 50

Harper, Michael S(teven) 1938- . . **CLC 7, 22**
See also BW 1; CA 33-36R; CANR 24;
DLB 41

Harper, Mrs. F. E. W.
See Harper, Frances Ellen Watkins

Harris, Christie (Lucy) Irwin
1907- . . . . **CLC 12**
See also CA 5-8R; CANR 6; DLB 88;
JRDA; MAICYA; SAAS 10; SATA 6, 74

Harris, Frank 1856(?)-1931 . . . . . . **TCLC 24**
See also CA 109

Harris, George Washington
1814-1869 . . . . **NCLC 23**
See also DLB 3, 11

Harris, Joel Chandler
1848-1908 . . . . **TCLC 2; SSC 19**
See also CA 104; 137; DLB 11, 23, 42, 78,
91; MAICYA; YABC 1

Harris, John (Wyndham Parkes Lucas)
Beynon 1903-1969
See Wyndham, John
See also CA 102; 89-92

Harris, MacDonald . . . . **CLC 9**
See also Heiney, Donald (William)

Harris, Mark 1922- . . . . **CLC 19**
See also CA 5-8R; CAAS 3; CANR 2;
DLB 2; DLBY 80

Harris, (Theodore) Wilson 1921- . . . . **CLC 25**
See also BW 2; CA 65-68; CAAS 16;
CANR 11, 27; DLB 117; MTCW

Harrison, Elizabeth Cavanna 1909-
See Cavanna, Betty
See also CA 9-12R; CANR 6, 27

Harrison, Harry (Max) 1925- . . . . . . **CLC 42**
See also CA 1-4R; CANR 5, 21; DLB 8;
SATA 4

Harrison, James (Thomas)
1937- . . . . **CLC 6, 14, 33, 66; SSC 19**
See also CA 13-16R; CANR 8; DLBY 82

Harrison, Jim
See Harrison, James (Thomas)

Harrison, Kathryn 1961- . . . . **CLC 70**
See also CA 144

Harrison, Tony 1937- . . . . **CLC 43**
See also CA 65-68; CANR 44; DLB 40;
MTCW

Harriss, Will(ard Irvin) 1922- . . . . . . **CLC 34**
See also CA 111

Harson, Sley
See Ellison, Harlan (Jay)

Hart, Ellis
See Ellison, Harlan (Jay)

Hart, Josephine 1942(?)- . . . . **CLC 70**
See also CA 138

Hart, Moss 1904-1961 . . . . **CLC 66**
See also CA 109; 89-92; DLB 7

Harte, (Francis) Bret(t)
1836(?)-1902 . . . . **TCLC 1, 25; DA;**
SSC 8; WLC
See also CA 104; 140; CDALB 1865-1917;
DLB 12, 64, 74, 79; SATA 26

Hartley, L(eslie) P(oles)
1895-1972 . . . . **CLC 2, 22**
See also CA 45-48; 37-40R; CANR 33;
DLB 15, 139; MTCW

Hartman, Geoffrey H. 1929- . . . . **CLC 27**
See also CA 117; 125; DLB 67

Hartmann von Aue
c. 1160-c. 1205 . . . . **CMLC 15**
See also DLB 138

Haruf, Kent 19(?)- . . . . **CLC 34**

Harwood, Ronald 1934- . . . . **CLC 32**
See also CA 1-4R; CANR 4; DLB 13

Hasek, Jaroslav (Matej Frantisek)
1883-1923 . . . . **TCLC 4**
See also CA 104; 129; MTCW

Hass, Robert 1941- . . . . **CLC 18, 39**
See also CA 111; CANR 30; DLB 105

Hastings, Hudson
See Kuttner, Henry

Hastings, Selina . . . . **CLC 44**

Hatteras, Amelia
See Mencken, H(enry) L(ouis)

Hatteras, Owen . . . . **TCLC 18**
See also Mencken, H(enry) L(ouis); Nathan,
George Jean

Hauptmann, Gerhart (Johann Robert)
1862-1946 . . . . **TCLC 4**
See also CA 104; DLB 66, 118

Havel, Vaclav 1936- . . . . **CLC 25, 58, 65**
See also CA 104; CANR 36; MTCW

Haviaras, Stratis . . . . **CLC 33**
See also Chaviaras, Strates

Hawes, Stephen 1475(?)-1523(?) . . . . . **LC 17**

Hawkes, John (Clendennin Burne, Jr.)
1925- . . . . . . **CLC 1, 2, 3, 4, 7, 9, 14, 15,**
27, 49
See also CA 1-4R; CANR 2, 47; DLB 2, 7;
DLBY 80; MTCW

Hawking, S. W.
See Hawking, Stephen W(illiam)

Hawking, Stephen W(illiam)
1942- . . . . CLC 63
See also AAYA 13; BEST 89:1; CA 126;
129; CANR 48

Hawthorne, Julian 1846-1934 . . . . . TCLC 25

Hawthorne, Nathaniel
1804-1864 . . . . . . NCLC 39; DA; SSC 3;
WLC
See also CDALB 1640-1865; DLB 1, 74;
YABC 2

Haxton, Josephine Ayres 1921-
See Douglas, Ellen
See also CA 115; CANR 41

Hayaseca y Eizaguirre, Jorge
See Echegaray (y Eizaguirre), Jose (Maria
Waldo)

Hayashi Fumiko 1904-1951 . . . . TCLC 27

Haycraft, Anna
See Ellis, Alice Thomas
See also CA 122

Hayden, Robert E(arl)
1913-1980 . . . . . . CLC 5, 9, 14, 37; BLC;
DA; PC 6
See also BW 1; CA 69-72; 97-100; CABS 2;
CANR 24; CDALB 1941-1968; DLB 5,
76; MTCW; SATA 19; SATA-Obit 26

Hayford, J(oseph) E(phraim) Casely
See Casely-Hayford, J(oseph) E(phraim)

Hayman, Ronald 1932- . . . . CLC 44
See also CA 25-28R; CANR 18

Haywood, Eliza (Fowler)
1693(?)-1756 . . . . LC 1

Hazlitt, William 1778-1830 . . . . . . NCLC 29
See also DLB 110

Hazzard, Shirley 1931- . . . . CLC 18
See also CA 9-12R; CANR 4; DLBY 82;
MTCW

Head, Bessie 1937-1986 . . . CLC 25, 67; BLC
See also BW 2; CA 29-32R; 119; CANR 25;
DLB 117; MTCW

Headon, (Nicky) Topper 1956(?)- . . . CLC 30

Heaney, Seamus (Justin)
1939- . . . . CLC 5, 7, 14, 25, 37, 74
See also CA 85-88; CANR 25, 48;
CDBLB 1960 to Present; DLB 40;
MTCW

Hearn, (Patricio) Lafcadio (Tessima Carlos)
1850-1904 . . . . TCLC 9
See also CA 105; DLB 12, 78

Hearne, Vicki 1946- . . . . CLC 56
See also CA 139

Hearon, Shelby 1931- . . . . CLC 63
See also AITN 2; CA 25-28R; CANR 18,
48

Heat-Moon, William Least . . . . CLC 29
See also Trogdon, William (Lewis)
See also AAYA 9

Hebbel, Friedrich 1813-1863 . . . . . NCLC 43
See also DLB 129

Hebert, Anne 1916- . . . . CLC 4, 13, 29
See also CA 85-88; DLB 68; MTCW

Hecht, Anthony (Evan)
1923- . . . . CLC 8, 13, 19
See also CA 9-12R; CANR 6; DLB 5

Hecht, Ben 1894-1964 . . . . CLC 8
See also CA 85-88; DLB 7, 9, 25, 26, 28, 86

Hedayat, Sadeq 1903-1951 . . . . TCLC 21
See also CA 120

Hegel, Georg Wilhelm Friedrich
1770-1831 . . . . NCLC 46
See also DLB 90

Heidegger, Martin 1889-1976 . . . . . . CLC 24
See also CA 81-84; 65-68; CANR 34;
MTCW

Heidenstam, (Carl Gustaf) Verner von
1859-1940 . . . . TCLC 5
See also CA 104

Heifner, Jack 1946- . . . . CLC 11
See also CA 105; CANR 47

Heijermans, Herman 1864-1924 . . . TCLC 24
See also CA 123

Heilbrun, Carolyn G(old) 1926- . . . . . CLC 25
See also CA 45-48; CANR 1, 28

Heine, Heinrich 1797-1856 . . . . NCLC 4
See also DLB 90

Heinemann, Larry (Curtiss) 1944- . . CLC 50
See also CA 110; CAAS 21; CANR 31;
DLBD 9

Heiney, Donald (William) 1921-1993
See Harris, MacDonald
See also CA 1-4R; 142; CANR 3

Heinlein, Robert A(nson)
1907-1988 . . . . . . CLC 1, 3, 8, 14, 26, 55
See also CA 1-4R; 125; CANR 1, 20;
DLB 8; JRDA; MAICYA; MTCW;
SATA 9, 69; SATA-Obit 56

Helforth, John
See Doolittle, Hilda

Hellenhofferu, Vojtech Kapristian z
See Hasek, Jaroslav (Matej Frantisek)

Heller, Joseph
1923- . . . . CLC 1, 3, 5, 8, 11, 36, 63; DA;
WLC
See also AITN 1; CA 5-8R; CABS 1;
CANR 8, 42; DLB 2, 28; DLBY 80;
MTCW

Hellman, Lillian (Florence)
1906-1984 . . . . . . CLC 2, 4, 8, 14, 18, 34,
44, 52; DC 1
See also AITN 1, 2; CA 13-16R; 112;
CANR 33; DLB 7; DLBY 84; MTCW

Helprin, Mark 1947- . . . . . CLC 7, 10, 22, 32
See also CA 81-84; CANR 47; DLBY 85;
MTCW

Helvetius, Claude-Adrien
1715-1771 . . . . LC 26

Helyar, Jane Penelope Josephine 1933-
See Poole, Josephine
See also CA 21-24R; CANR 10, 26

Hemans, Felicia 1793-1835 . . . . . . NCLC 29
See also DLB 96

Hemingway, Ernest (Miller)
1899-1961 . . . . CLC 1, 3, 6, 8, 10, 13, 19,
30, 34, 39, 41, 44, 50, 61, 80; DA; SSC 1;
WLC
See also CA 77-80; CANR 34;
CDALB 1917-1929; DLB 4, 9, 102;
DLBD 1; DLBY 81, 87; MTCW

Hempel, Amy 1951- . . . . CLC 39
See also CA 118; 137

Henderson, F. C.
See Mencken, H(enry) L(ouis)

Henderson, Sylvia
See Ashton-Warner, Sylvia (Constance)

Henley, Beth . . . . CLC 23
See also Henley, Elizabeth Becker
See also CABS 3; DLBY 86

Henley, Elizabeth Becker 1952-
See Henley, Beth
See also CA 107; CANR 32; MTCW

Henley, William Ernest
1849-1903 . . . . TCLC 8
See also CA 105; DLB 19

Hennissart, Martha
See Lathen, Emma
See also CA 85-88

Henry, O. . . . . TCLC 1, 19; SSC 5; WLC
See also Porter, William Sydney

Henry, Patrick 1736-1799 . . . . LC 25

Henryson, Robert 1430(?)-1506(?). . . . LC 20
See also DLB 146

Henry VIII 1491-1547 . . . . LC 10

Henschke, Alfred
See Klabund

Hentoff, Nat(han Irving) 1925- . . . . . CLC 26
See also AAYA 4; CA 1-4R; CAAS 6;
CANR 5, 25; CLR 1; JRDA; MAICYA;
SATA 42, 69; SATA-Brief 27

Heppenstall, (John) Rayner
1911-1981 . . . . CLC 10
See also CA 1-4R; 103; CANR 29

Herbert, Frank (Patrick)
1920-1986 . . . . . . CLC 12, 23, 35, 44, 85
See also CA 53-56; 118; CANR 5, 43;
DLB 8; MTCW; SATA 9, 37;
SATA-Obit 47

Herbert, George 1593-1633 . . . . LC 24; PC 4
See also CDBLB Before 1660; DLB 126

Herbert, Zbigniew 1924- . . . . CLC 9, 43
See also CA 89-92; CANR 36; MTCW

Herbst, Josephine (Frey)
1897-1969 . . . . CLC 34
See also CA 5-8R; 25-28R; DLB 9

Hergesheimer, Joseph
1880-1954 . . . . TCLC 11
See also CA 109; DLB 102, 9

Herlihy, James Leo 1927-1993 . . . . . . CLC 6
See also CA 1-4R; 143; CANR 2

Hermogenes fl. c. 175- . . . . CMLC 6

Hernandez, Jose 1834-1886 . . . . . . NCLC 17

Herrick, Robert
1591-1674 . . . . LC 13; DA; PC 9
See also DLB 126

Herring, Guilles
See Somerville, Edith

Herriot, James 1916-1995 . . . . CLC 12
See also Wight, James Alfred
See also AAYA 1; CA 148; CANR 40

Herrmann, Dorothy 1941- . . . . CLC 44
See also CA 107

Herrmann, Taffy
See Herrmann, Dorothy

Hersey, John (Richard)
1914-1993 .... **CLC 1, 2, 7, 9, 40, 81**
See also CA 17-20R; 140; CANR 33;
DLB 6; MTCW; SATA 25;
SATA-Obit 76

Herzen, Aleksandr Ivanovich
1812-1870 .... **NCLC 10**

Herzl, Theodor 1860-1904 .... **TCLC 36**

Herzog, Werner 1942- .... **CLC 16**
See also CA 89-92

Hesiod c. 8th cent. B.C.- .... **CMLC 5**

Hesse, Hermann
1877-1962 .... **CLC 1, 2, 3, 6, 11, 17, 25,**
69; DA; SSC 9; WLC
See also CA 17-18; CAP 2; DLB 66;
MTCW; SATA 50

Hewes, Cady
See De Voto, Bernard (Augustine)

Heyen, William 1940- .... **CLC 13, 18**
See also CA 33-36R; CAAS 9; DLB 5

Heyerdahl, Thor 1914- .... **CLC 26**
See also CA 5-8R; CANR 5, 22; MTCW;
SATA 2, 52

Heym, Georg (Theodor Franz Arthur)
1887-1912 .... **TCLC 9**
See also CA 106

Heym, Stefan 1913- .... **CLC 41**
See also CA 9-12R; CANR 4; DLB 69

Heyse, Paul (Johann Ludwig von)
1830-1914 .... **TCLC 8**
See also CA 104; DLB 129

Heyward, (Edwin) DuBose
1885-1940 .... **TCLC 59**
See also CA 108; DLB 7, 9, 45; SATA 21

Hibbert, Eleanor Alice Burford
1906-1993 .... **CLC 7**
See also BEST 90:4; CA 17-20R; 140;
CANR 9, 28; SATA 2; SATA-Obit 74

Higgins, George V(incent)
1939- .... **CLC 4, 7, 10, 18**
See also CA 77-80; CAAS 5; CANR 17;
DLB 2; DLBY 81; MTCW

Higginson, Thomas Wentworth
1823-1911 .... **TCLC 36**
See also DLB 1, 64

Highet, Helen
See MacInnes, Helen (Clark)

Highsmith, (Mary) Patricia
1921-1995 .... **CLC 2, 4, 14, 42**
See also CA 1-4R; 147; CANR 1, 20, 48;
MTCW

Highwater, Jamake (Mamake)
1942(?)- .... **CLC 12**
See also AAYA 7; CA 65-68; CAAS 7;
CANR 10, 34; CLR 17; DLB 52;
DLBY 85; JRDA; MAICYA; SATA 32,
69; SATA-Brief 30

Higuchi, Ichiyo 1872-1896 ...... **NCLC 49**

Hijuelos, Oscar 1951- ...... **CLC 65; HLC**
See also BEST 90:1; CA 123; DLB 145; HW

Hikmet, Nazim 1902(?)-1963 ...... **CLC 40**
See also CA 141; 93-96

Hildesheimer, Wolfgang
1916-1991 .... **CLC 49**
See also CA 101; 135; DLB 69, 124

Hill, Geoffrey (William)
1932- .... **CLC 5, 8, 18, 45**
See also CA 81-84; CANR 21;
CDBLB 1960 to Present; DLB 40;
MTCW

Hill, George Roy 1921- .... **CLC 26**
See also CA 110; 122

Hill, John
See Koontz, Dean R(ay)

Hill, Susan (Elizabeth) 1942- .... **CLC 4**
See also CA 33-36R; CANR 29; DLB 14,
139; MTCW

Hillerman, Tony 1925- .... **CLC 62**
See also AAYA 6; BEST 89:1; CA 29-32R;
CANR 21, 42; SATA 6

Hillesum, Etty 1914-1943 .... **TCLC 49**
See also CA 137

Hilliard, Noel (Harvey) 1929- ...... **CLC 15**
See also CA 9-12R; CANR 7

Hillis, Rick 1956- .... **CLC 66**
See also CA 134

Hilton, James 1900-1954 .... **TCLC 21**
See also CA 108; DLB 34, 77; SATA 34

Himes, Chester (Bomar)
1909-1984 .... **CLC 2, 4, 7, 18, 58; BLC**
See also BW 2; CA 25-28R; 114; CANR 22;
DLB 2, 76, 143; MTCW

Hinde, Thomas .... **CLC 6, 11**
See also Chitty, Thomas Willes

Hindin, Nathan
See Bloch, Robert (Albert)

Hine, (William) Daryl 1936- .... **CLC 15**
See also CA 1-4R; CAAS 15; CANR 1, 20;
DLB 60

Hinkson, Katharine Tynan
See Tynan, Katharine

Hinton, S(usan) E(loise)
1950- .... **CLC 30; DA**
See also AAYA 2; CA 81-84; CANR 32;
CLR 3, 23; JRDA; MAICYA; MTCW;
SATA 19, 58

Hippius, Zinaida .... **TCLC 9**
See also Gippius, Zinaida (Nikolayevna)

Hiraoka, Kimitake 1925-1970
See Mishima, Yukio
See also CA 97-100; 29-32R; MTCW

Hirsch, E(ric) D(onald), Jr. 1928- ... **CLC 79**
See also CA 25-28R; CANR 27; DLB 67;
MTCW

Hirsch, Edward 1950- .... **CLC 31, 50**
See also CA 104; CANR 20, 42; DLB 120

Hitchcock, Alfred (Joseph)
1899-1980 .... **CLC 16**
See also CA 97-100; SATA 27;
SATA-Obit 24

Hitler, Adolf 1889-1945 .... **TCLC 53**
See also CA 117; 147

Hoagland, Edward 1932- .... **CLC 28**
See also CA 1-4R; CANR 2, 31; DLB 6;
SATA 51

Hoban, Russell (Conwell) 1925- .. **CLC 7, 25**
See also CA 5-8R; CANR 23, 37; CLR 3;
DLB 52; MAICYA; MTCW; SATA 1,
40, 78

Hobbs, Perry
See Blackmur, R(ichard) P(almer)

Hobson, Laura Z(ametkin)
1900-1986 .... **CLC 7, 25**
See also CA 17-20R; 118; DLB 28;
SATA 52

Hochhuth, Rolf 1931- .... **CLC 4, 11, 18**
See also CA 5-8R; CANR 33; DLB 124;
MTCW

Hochman, Sandra 1936- .... **CLC 3, 8**
See also CA 5-8R; DLB 5

Hochwaelder, Fritz 1911-1986 ...... **CLC 36**
See also CA 29-32R; 120; CANR 42;
MTCW

Hochwalder, Fritz
See Hochwaelder, Fritz

Hocking, Mary (Eunice) 1921- ..... **CLC 13**
See also CA 101; CANR 18, 40

Hodgins, Jack 1938- .... **CLC 23**
See also CA 93-96; DLB 60

Hodgson, William Hope
1877(?)-1918 .... **TCLC 13**
See also CA 111; DLB 70, 153

Hoffman, Alice 1952- .... **CLC 51**
See also CA 77-80; CANR 34; MTCW

Hoffman, Daniel (Gerard)
1923- .... **CLC 6, 13, 23**
See also CA 1-4R; CANR 4; DLB 5

Hoffman, Stanley 1944- .... **CLC 5**
See also CA 77-80

Hoffman, William M(oses) 1939- ... **CLC 40**
See also CA 57-60; CANR 11

Hoffmann, E(rnst) T(heodor) A(madeus)
1776-1822 .... **NCLC 2; SSC 13**
See also DLB 90; SATA 27

Hofmann, Gert 1931- .... **CLC 54**
See also CA 128

Hofmannsthal, Hugo von
1874-1929 .... **TCLC 11; DC 4**
See also CA 106; DLB 81, 118

Hogan, Linda 1947- .... **CLC 73**
See also CA 120; CANR 45; NNAL

Hogarth, Charles
See Creasey, John

Hogg, James 1770-1835 .... **NCLC 4**
See also DLB 93, 116

Holbach, Paul Henri Thiry Baron
1723-1789 .... **LC 14**

Holberg, Ludvig 1684-1754 .... **LC 6**

Holden, Ursula 1921- .... **CLC 18**
See also CA 101; CAAS 8; CANR 22

Holderlin, (Johann Christian) Friedrich
1770-1843 .... **NCLC 16; PC 4**

Holdstock, Robert
See Holdstock, Robert P.

Holdstock, Robert P. 1948- .... **CLC 39**
See also CA 131

Holland, Isabelle 1920- .... **CLC 21**
See also AAYA 11; CA 21-24R; CANR 10,
25, 47; JRDA; MAICYA; SATA 8, 70

Holland, Marcus
See Caldwell, (Janet Miriam) Taylor
(Holland)

Hollander, John 1929- ...... CLC **2, 5, 8, 14**
See also CA 1-4R; CANR 1; DLB 5;
SATA 13

Hollander, Paul
See Silverberg, Robert

Holleran, Andrew 1943(?)- .... CLC **38**
See also CA 144

Hollinghurst, Alan 1954- .... CLC **55**
See also CA 114

Hollis, Jim
See Summers, Hollis (Spurgeon, Jr.)

Holmes, John
See Souster, (Holmes) Raymond

Holmes, John Clellon 1926-1988.... CLC **56**
See also CA 9-12R; 125; CANR 4; DLB 16

Holmes, Oliver Wendell
1809-1894 .... NCLC **14**
See also CDALB 1640-1865; DLB 1;
SATA 34

Holmes, Raymond
See Souster, (Holmes) Raymond

Holt, Victoria
See Hibbert, Eleanor Alice Burford

Holub, Miroslav 1923- .... CLC **4**
See also CA 21-24R; CANR 10

Homer
c. 8th cent. B.C.- ...... CMLC **1, 16; DA**

Honig, Edwin 1919- .... CLC **33**
See also CA 5-8R; CAAS 8; CANR 4, 45;
DLB 5

Hood, Hugh (John Blagdon)
1928- .... CLC **15, 28**
See also CA 49-52; CAAS 17; CANR 1, 33;
DLB 53

Hood, Thomas 1799-1845........ NCLC **16**
See also DLB 96

Hooker, (Peter) Jeremy 1941-...... CLC **43**
See also CA 77-80; CANR 22; DLB 40

Hope, A(lec) D(erwent) 1907- .... CLC **3, 51**
See also CA 21-24R; CANR 33; MTCW

Hope, Brian
See Creasey, John

Hope, Christopher (David Tully)
1944- .... CLC **52**
See also CA 106; CANR 47; SATA 62

Hopkins, Gerard Manley
1844-1889 .... NCLC **17; DA; WLC**
See also CDBLB 1890-1914; DLB 35, 57

Hopkins, John (Richard) 1931-...... CLC **4**
See also CA 85-88

Hopkins, Pauline Elizabeth
1859-1930 .... TCLC **28; BLC**
See also BW 2; CA 141; DLB 50

Hopkinson, Francis 1737-1791 ...... LC **25**
See also DLB 31

Hopley-Woolrich, Cornell George 1903-1968
See Woolrich, Cornell
See also CA 13-14; CAP 1

Horatio
See Proust, (Valentin-Louis-George-Eugene-)
Marcel

Horgan, Paul (George Vincent O'Shaughnessy)
1903-1995 .... CLC **9, 53**
See also CA 13-16R; 147; CANR 9, 35;
DLB 102; DLBY 85; MTCW; SATA 13

Horn, Peter
See Kuttner, Henry

Hornem, Horace Esq.
See Byron, George Gordon (Noel)

Hornung, E(rnest) W(illiam)
1866-1921 .... TCLC **59**
See also CA 108; DLB 70

Horovitz, Israel (Arthur) 1939-..... CLC **56**
See also CA 33-36R; CANR 46; DLB 7

Horvath, Odon von
See Horvath, Oedoen von
See also DLB 85, 124

Horvath, Oedoen von 1901-1938... TCLC **45**
See also Horvath, Odon von
See also CA 118

Horwitz, Julius 1920-1986......... CLC **14**
See also CA 9-12R; 119; CANR 12

Hospital, Janette Turner 1942-..... CLC **42**
See also CA 108; CANR 48

Hostos, E. M. de
See Hostos (y Bonilla), Eugenio Maria de

Hostos, Eugenio M. de
See Hostos (y Bonilla), Eugenio Maria de

Hostos, Eugenio Maria
See Hostos (y Bonilla), Eugenio Maria de

Hostos (y Bonilla), Eugenio Maria de
1839-1903 .... TCLC **24**
See also CA 123; 131; HW

Houdini
See Lovecraft, H(oward) P(hillips)

Hougan, Carolyn 1943- .... CLC **34**
See also CA 139

Household, Geoffrey (Edward West)
1900-1988 .... CLC **11**
See also CA 77-80; 126; DLB 87; SATA 14;
SATA-Obit 59

Housman, A(lfred) E(dward)
1859-1936 ...... TCLC **1, 10; DA; PC 2**
See also CA 104; 125; DLB 19; MTCW

Housman, Laurence 1865-1959..... TCLC **7**
See also CA 106; DLB 10; SATA 25

Howard, Elizabeth Jane 1923- ... CLC **7, 29**
See also CA 5-8R; CANR 8

Howard, Maureen 1930- ..... CLC **5, 14, 46**
See also CA 53-56; CANR 31; DLBY 83;
MTCW

Howard, Richard 1929- ...... CLC **7, 10, 47**
See also AITN 1; CA 85-88; CANR 25;
DLB 5

Howard, Robert Ervin 1906-1936... TCLC **8**
See also CA 105

Howard, Warren F.
See Pohl, Frederik

Howe, Fanny 1940- .... CLC **47**
See also CA 117; SATA-Brief 52

Howe, Irving 1920-1993.......... CLC **85**
See also CA 9-12R; 141; CANR 21;
DLB 67; MTCW

Howe, Julia Ward 1819-1910 ..... TCLC **21**
See also CA 117; DLB 1

Howe, Susan 1937-............... CLC **72**
See also DLB 120

Howe, Tina 1937-................ CLC **48**
See also CA 109

Howell, James 1594(?)-1666 .... LC **13**
See also DLB 151

Howells, W. D.
See Howells, William Dean

Howells, William D.
See Howells, William Dean

Howells, William Dean
1837-1920 .... TCLC **7, 17, 41**
See also CA 104; 134; CDALB 1865-1917;
DLB 12, 64, 74, 79

Howes, Barbara 1914- .... CLC **15**
See also CA 9-12R; CAAS 3; SATA 5

Hrabal, Bohumil 1914-......... CLC **13, 67**
See also CA 106; CAAS 12

Hsun, Lu
See Lu Hsun

Hubbard, L(afayette) Ron(ald)
1911-1986 .... CLC **43**
See also CA 77-80; 118; CANR 22

Huch, Ricarda (Octavia)
1864-1947 .... TCLC **13**
See also CA 111; DLB 66

Huddle, David 1942- .... CLC **49**
See also CA 57-60; CAAS 20; DLB 130

Hudson, Jeffrey
See Crichton, (John) Michael

Hudson, W(illiam) H(enry)
1841-1922 .... TCLC **29**
See also CA 115; DLB 98, 153; SATA 35

Hueffer, Ford Madox
See Ford, Ford Madox

Hughart, Barry 1934-.............. CLC **39**
See also CA 137

Hughes, Colin
See Creasey, John

Hughes, David (John) 1930- .... CLC **48**
See also CA 116; 129; DLB 14

Hughes, (James) Langston
1902-1967 ..... CLC **1, 5, 10, 15, 35, 44;**
BLC; DA; DC 3; PC 1; SSC 6; WLC
See also AAYA 12; BW 1; CA 1-4R;
25-28R; CANR 1, 34; CDALB 1929-1941;
CLR 17; DLB 4, 7, 48, 51, 86; JRDA;
MAICYA; MTCW; SATA 4, 33

Hughes, Richard (Arthur Warren)
1900-1976 .... CLC **1, 11**
See also CA 5-8R; 65-68; CANR 4;
DLB 15; MTCW; SATA 8;
SATA-Obit 25

Hughes, Ted
1930- .... CLC **2, 4, 9, 14, 37; PC 7**
See also CA 1-4R; CANR 1, 33; CLR 3;
DLB 40; MAICYA; MTCW; SATA 49;
SATA-Brief 27

Hugo, Richard F(ranklin)
1923-1982 .... CLC **6, 18, 32**
See also CA 49-52; 108; CANR 3; DLB 5

Hugo, Victor (Marie)
1802-1885 .. NCLC **3, 10, 21; DA; WLC**
See also DLB 119; SATA 47

Huidobro, Vicente
See Huidobro Fernandez, Vicente Garcia

Huidobro Fernandez, Vicente Garcia
1893-1948 . . . . **TCLC 31**
See also CA 131; HW

Hulme, Keri 1947- . . . . **CLC 39**
See also CA 125

Hulme, T(homas) E(rnest)
1883-1917 . . . . **TCLC 21**
See also CA 117; DLB 19

Hume, David 1711-1776 . . . . **LC 7**
See also DLB 104

Humphrey, William 1924- . . . . **CLC 45**
See also CA 77-80; DLB 6

Humphreys, Emyr Owen 1919- . . . . . **CLC 47**
See also CA 5-8R; CANR 3, 24; DLB 15

Humphreys, Josephine 1945- . . . . **CLC 34, 57**
See also CA 121; 127

Hungerford, Pixie
See Brinsmead, H(esba) F(ay)

Hunt, E(verette) Howard, (Jr.)
1918- . . . . **CLC 3**
See also AITN 1; CA 45-48; CANR 2, 47

Hunt, Kyle
See Creasey, John

Hunt, (James Henry) Leigh
1784-1859 . . . . **NCLC 1**

Hunt, Marsha 1946- . . . . **CLC 70**
See also BW 2; CA 143

Hunt, Violet 1866-1942 . . . . **TCLC 53**

Hunter, E. Waldo
See Sturgeon, Theodore (Hamilton)

Hunter, Evan 1926- . . . . **CLC 11, 31**
See also CA 5-8R; CANR 5, 38; DLBY 82;
MTCW; SATA 25

Hunter, Kristin (Eggleston) 1931- . . . **CLC 35**
See also AITN 1; BW 1; CA 13-16R;
CANR 13; CLR 3; DLB 33; MAICYA;
SAAS 10; SATA 12

Hunter, Mollie 1922- . . . . **CLC 21**
See also McIlwraith, Maureen Mollie
Hunter
See also AAYA 13; CANR 37; CLR 25;
JRDA; MAICYA; SAAS 7; SATA 54

Hunter, Robert (?)-1734 . . . . **LC 7**

Hurston, Zora Neale
1903-1960 . . . . **CLC 7, 30, 61; BLC; DA;
SSC 4**
See also BW 1; CA 85-88; DLB 51, 86;
MTCW

Huston, John (Marcellus)
1906-1987 . . . . **CLC 20**
See also CA 73-76; 123; CANR 34; DLB 26

Hustvedt, Siri 1955- . . . . **CLC 76**
See also CA 137

Hutten, Ulrich von 1488-1523 . . . . . . **LC 16**

Huxley, Aldous (Leonard)
1894-1963 . . . . . **CLC 1, 3, 4, 5, 8, 11, 18,
35, 79; DA; WLC**
See also AAYA 11; CA 85-88; CANR 44;
CDBLB 1914-1945; DLB 36, 100;
MTCW; SATA 63

Huysmans, Charles Marie Georges
1848-1907
See Huysmans, Joris-Karl
See also CA 104

Huysmans, Joris-Karl . . . . **TCLC 7**
See also Huysmans, Charles Marie Georges
See also DLB 123

Hwang, David Henry
1957- . . . . **CLC 55; DC 4**
See also CA 127; 132

Hyde, Anthony 1946- . . . . **CLC 42**
See also CA 136

Hyde, Margaret O(ldroyd) 1917- . . . **CLC 21**
See also CA 1-4R; CANR 1, 36; CLR 23;
JRDA; MAICYA; SAAS 8; SATA 1, 42,
76

Hynes, James 1956(?)- . . . . **CLC 65**

Ian, Janis 1951- . . . . **CLC 21**
See also CA 105

Ibanez, Vicente Blasco
See Blasco Ibanez, Vicente

Ibarguengoitia, Jorge 1928-1983 . . . . **CLC 37**
See also CA 124; 113; HW

Ibsen, Henrik (Johan)
1828-1906 . . . . **TCLC 2, 8, 16, 37, 52;
DA; DC 2; WLC**
See also CA 104; 141

Ibuse Masuji 1898-1993 . . . . **CLC 22**
See also CA 127; 141

Ichikawa, Kon 1915- . . . . **CLC 20**
See also CA 121

Idle, Eric 1943- . . . . **CLC 21**
See also Monty Python
See also CA 116; CANR 35

Ignatow, David 1914- . . . . . . **CLC 4, 7, 14, 40**
See also CA 9-12R; CAAS 3; CANR 31;
DLB 5

Ihimaera, Witi 1944- . . . . **CLC 46**
See also CA 77-80

Ilf, Ilya . . . . **TCLC 21**
See also Fainzilberg, Ilya Arnoldovich

Immermann, Karl (Lebrecht)
1796-1840 . . . . **NCLC 4, 49**
See also DLB 133

Inclan, Ramon (Maria) del Valle
See Valle-Inclan, Ramon (Maria) del

Infante, G(uillermo) Cabrera
See Cabrera Infante, G(uillermo)

Ingalls, Rachel (Holmes) 1940- . . . . . **CLC 42**
See also CA 123; 127

Ingamells, Rex 1913-1955 . . . . **TCLC 35**

Inge, William Motter
1913-1973 . . . . **CLC 1, 8, 19**
See also CA 9-12R; CDALB 1941-1968;
DLB 7; MTCW

Ingelow, Jean 1820-1897 . . . . **NCLC 39**
See also DLB 35; SATA 33

Ingram, Willis J.
See Harris, Mark

Innaurato, Albert (F.) 1948(?)- . . **CLC 21, 60**
See also CA 115; 122

Innes, Michael
See Stewart, J(ohn) I(nnes) M(ackintosh)

Ionesco, Eugene
1909-1994 . . . . **CLC 1, 4, 6, 9, 11, 15, 41,
86; DA; WLC**
See also CA 9-12R; 144; MTCW; SATA 7;
SATA-Obit 79

Iqbal, Muhammad 1873-1938 . . . . . **TCLC 28**

Ireland, Patrick
See O'Doherty, Brian

Iron, Ralph
See Schreiner, Olive (Emilie Albertina)

Irving, John (Winslow)
1942- . . . . **CLC 13, 23, 38**
See also AAYA 8; BEST 89:3; CA 25-28R;
CANR 28; DLB 6; DLBY 82; MTCW

Irving, Washington
1783-1859 . . . . **NCLC 2, 19; DA; SSC 2;
WLC**
See also CDALB 1640-1865; DLB 3, 11, 30,
59, 73, 74; YABC 2

Irwin, P. K.
See Page, P(atricia) K(athleen)

Isaacs, Susan 1943- . . . . **CLC 32**
See also BEST 89:1; CA 89-92; CANR 20,
41; MTCW

Isherwood, Christopher (William Bradshaw)
1904-1986 . . . . **CLC 1, 9, 11, 14, 44**
See also CA 13-16R; 117; CANR 35;
DLB 15; DLBY 86; MTCW

Ishiguro, Kazuo 1954- . . . . . . **CLC 27, 56, 59**
See also BEST 90:2; CA 120; CANR 49;
MTCW

Ishikawa Takuboku
1886(?)-1912 . . . . **TCLC 15; PC 10**
See also CA 113

Iskander, Fazil 1929- . . . . **CLC 47**
See also CA 102

Ivan IV 1530-1584 . . . . **LC 17**

Ivanov, Vyacheslav Ivanovich
1866-1949 . . . . **TCLC 33**
See also CA 122

Ivask, Ivar Vidrik 1927-1992 . . . . **CLC 14**
See also CA 37-40R; 139; CANR 24

Jackson, Daniel
See Wingrove, David (John)

Jackson, Jesse 1908-1983 . . . . **CLC 12**
See also BW 1; CA 25-28R; 109; CANR 27;
CLR 28; MAICYA; SATA 2, 29;
SATA-Obit 48

Jackson, Laura (Riding) 1901-1991
See Riding, Laura
See also CA 65-68; 135; CANR 28; DLB 48

Jackson, Sam
See Trumbo, Dalton

Jackson, Sara
See Wingrove, David (John)

Jackson, Shirley
1919-1965 . . . . **CLC 11, 60, 87; DA;
SSC 9; WLC**
See also AAYA 9; CA 1-4R; 25-28R;
CANR 4; CDALB 1941-1968; DLB 6;
SATA 2

Jacob, (Cyprien-)Max 1876-1944 . . . **TCLC 6**
See also CA 104

Jacobs, Jim 1942- . . . . **CLC 12**
See also CA 97-100

Jacobs, W(illiam) W(ymark)
1863-1943 .... **TCLC 22**
See also CA 121; DLB 135

Jacobsen, Jens Peter 1847-1885 .. **NCLC 34**

Jacobsen, Josephine 1908-......... **CLC 48**
See also CA 33-36R; CAAS 18; CANR 23, 48

Jacobson, Dan 1929- .... **CLC 4, 14**
See also CA 1-4R; CANR 2, 25; DLB 14; MTCW

Jacqueline
See Carpentier (y Valmont), Alejo

Jagger, Mick 1944-............... **CLC 17**

Jakes, John (William) 1932-....... **CLC 29**
See also BEST 89:4; CA 57-60; CANR 10, 43; DLBY 83; MTCW; SATA 62

James, Andrew
See Kirkup, James

James, C(yril) L(ionel) R(obert)
1901-1989 .... **CLC 33**
See also BW 2; CA 117; 125; 128; DLB 125; MTCW

James, Daniel (Lewis) 1911-1988
See Santiago, Danny
See also CA 125

James, Dynely
See Mayne, William (James Carter)

James, Henry
1843-1916 ...... **TCLC 2, 11, 24, 40, 47; DA; SSC 8; WLC**
See also CA 104; 132; CDALB 1865-1917; DLB 12, 71, 74; MTCW

James, M. R.
See James, Montague (Rhodes)

James, Montague (Rhodes)
1862-1936 .... **TCLC 6; SSC 16**
See also CA 104

James, P. D. .... **CLC 18, 46**
See also White, Phyllis Dorothy James
See also BEST 90:2; CDBLB 1960 to Present; DLB 87

James, Philip
See Moorcock, Michael (John)

James, William 1842-1910..... **TCLC 15, 32**
See also CA 109

James I 1394-1437 .... **LC 20**

Jameson, Anna 1794-1860 .... **NCLC 43**
See also DLB 99

Jami, Nur al-Din 'Abd al-Rahman
1414-1492 .... **LC 9**

Jandl, Ernst 1925- .... **CLC 34**

Janowitz, Tama 1957- .... **CLC 43**
See also CA 106

Jarrell, Randall
1914-1965 .... **CLC 1, 2, 6, 9, 13, 49**
See also CA 5-8R; 25-28R; CABS 2; CANR 6, 34; CDALB 1941-1968; CLR 6; DLB 48, 52; MAICYA; MTCW; SATA 7

Jarry, Alfred
1873-1907 .... **TCLC 2, 14; SSC 20**
See also CA 104

Jarvis, E. K.
See Bloch, Robert (Albert); Ellison, Harlan (Jay); Silverberg, Robert

Jeake, Samuel, Jr.
See Aiken, Conrad (Potter)

Jean Paul 1763-1825 .... **NCLC 7**

Jefferies, (John) Richard
1848-1887 .... **NCLC 47**
See also DLB 98, 141; SATA 16

Jeffers, (John) Robinson
1887-1962 .... **CLC 2, 3, 11, 15, 54; DA; WLC**
See also CA 85-88; CANR 35; CDALB 1917-1929; DLB 45; MTCW

Jefferson, Janet
See Mencken, H(enry) L(ouis)

Jefferson, Thomas 1743-1826 .... **NCLC 11**
See also CDALB 1640-1865; DLB 31

Jeffrey, Francis 1773-1850....... **NCLC 33**
See also DLB 107

Jelakowitch, Ivan
See Heijermans, Herman

Jellicoe, (Patricia) Ann 1927-...... **CLC 27**
See also CA 85-88; DLB 13

Jen, Gish .... **CLC 70**
See also Jen, Lillian

Jen, Lillian 1956(?)-
See Jen, Gish
See also CA 135

Jenkins, (John) Robin 1912-....... **CLC 52**
See also CA 1-4R; CANR 1; DLB 14

Jennings, Elizabeth (Joan)
1926- .... **CLC 5, 14**
See also CA 61-64; CAAS 5; CANR 8, 39; DLB 27; MTCW; SATA 66

Jennings, Waylon 1937-........... **CLC 21**

Jensen, Johannes V. 1873-1950.... **TCLC 41**

Jensen, Laura (Linnea) 1948- ...... **CLC 37**
See also CA 103

Jerome, Jerome K(lapka)
1859-1927 .... **TCLC 23**
See also CA 119; DLB 10, 34, 135

Jerrold, Douglas William
1803-1857 .... **NCLC 2**

Jewett, (Theodora) Sarah Orne
1849-1909 .... **TCLC 1, 22; SSC 6**
See also CA 108; 127; DLB 12, 74; SATA 15

Jewsbury, Geraldine (Endsor)
1812-1880 .... **NCLC 22**
See also DLB 21

Jhabvala, Ruth Prawer
1927- .... **CLC 4, 8, 29**
See also CA 1-4R; CANR 2, 29; DLB 139; MTCW

Jiles, Paulette 1943-........... **CLC 13, 58**
See also CA 101

Jimenez (Mantecon), Juan Ramon
1881-1958 .... **TCLC 4; HLC; PC 7**
See also CA 104; 131; DLB 134; HW; MTCW

Jimenez, Ramon
See Jimenez (Mantecon), Juan Ramon

Jimenez Mantecon, Juan
See Jimenez (Mantecon), Juan Ramon

Joel, Billy .... **CLC 26**
See also Joel, William Martin

Joel, William Martin 1949-
See Joel, Billy
See also CA 108

John of the Cross, St. 1542-1591 .... **LC 18**

Johnson, B(ryan) S(tanley William)
1933-1973 .... **CLC 6, 9**
See also CA 9-12R; 53-56; CANR 9; DLB 14, 40

Johnson, Benj. F. of Boo
See Riley, James Whitcomb

Johnson, Benjamin F. of Boo
See Riley, James Whitcomb

Johnson, Charles (Richard)
1948- .... **CLC 7, 51, 65; BLC**
See also BW 2; CA 116; CAAS 18; CANR 42; DLB 33

Johnson, Denis 1949-............. **CLC 52**
See also CA 117; 121; DLB 120

Johnson, Diane 1934-........ **CLC 5, 13, 48**
See also CA 41-44R; CANR 17, 40; DLBY 80; MTCW

Johnson, Eyvind (Olof Verner)
1900-1976 .... **CLC 14**
See also CA 73-76; 69-72; CANR 34

Johnson, J. R.
See James, C(yril) L(ionel) R(obert)

Johnson, James Weldon
1871-1938 .... **TCLC 3, 19; BLC**
See also BW 1; CA 104; 125; CDALB 1917-1929; CLR 32; DLB 51; MTCW; SATA 31

Johnson, Joyce 1935-............. **CLC 58**
See also CA 125; 129

Johnson, Lionel (Pigot)
1867-1902 .... **TCLC 19**
See also CA 117; DLB 19

Johnson, Mel
See Malzberg, Barry N(athaniel)

Johnson, Pamela Hansford
1912-1981 .... **CLC 1, 7, 27**
See also CA 1-4R; 104; CANR 2, 28; DLB 15; MTCW

Johnson, Samuel
1709-1784 .... **LC 15; DA; WLC**
See also CDBLB 1660-1789; DLB 39, 95, 104, 142

Johnson, Uwe
1934-1984 .... **CLC 5, 10, 15, 40**
See also CA 1-4R; 112; CANR 1, 39; DLB 75; MTCW

Johnston, George (Benson) 1913- ... **CLC 51**
See also CA 1-4R; CANR 5, 20; DLB 88

Johnston, Jennifer 1930-........... **CLC 7**
See also CA 85-88; DLB 14

Jolley, (Monica) Elizabeth
1923- .... **CLC 46; SSC 19**
See also CA 127; CAAS 13

Jones, Arthur Llewellyn 1863-1947
See Machen, Arthur
See also CA 104

Jones, D(ouglas) G(ordon) 1929-.... **CLC 10**
See also CA 29-32R; CANR 13; DLB 53

Jones, David (Michael)
1895-1974 . . . . **CLC 2, 4, 7, 13, 42**
See also CA 9-12R; 53-56; CANR 28;
CDBLB 1945-1960; DLB 20, 100; MTCW

Jones, David Robert   1947-
See Bowie, David
See also CA 103

Jones, Diana Wynne   1934- . . . . **CLC 26**
See also AAYA 12; CA 49-52; CANR 4,
26; CLR 23; JRDA; MAICYA; SAAS 7;
SATA 9, 70

Jones, Edward P.   1950- . . . . **CLC 76**
See also BW 2; CA 142

Jones, Gayl   1949- . . . . **CLC 6, 9; BLC**
See also BW 2; CA 77-80; CANR 27;
DLB 33; MTCW

Jones, James   1921-1977 . . . . **CLC 1, 3, 10, 39**
See also AITN 1, 2; CA 1-4R; 69-72;
CANR 6; DLB 2, 143; MTCW

Jones, John J.
See Lovecraft, H(oward) P(hillips)

Jones, LeRoi . . . . **CLC 1, 2, 3, 5, 10, 14**
See also Baraka, Amiri

Jones, Louis B. . . . . **CLC 65**
See also CA 141

Jones, Madison (Percy, Jr.)   1925- . . . **CLC 4**
See also CA 13-16R; CAAS 11; CANR 7;
DLB 152

Jones, Mervyn   1922- . . . . **CLC 10, 52**
See also CA 45-48; CAAS 5; CANR 1;
MTCW

Jones, Mick   1956(?)- . . . . **CLC 30**

Jones, Nettie (Pearl)   1941- . . . . **CLC 34**
See also BW 2; CA 137; CAAS 20

Jones, Preston   1936-1979 . . . . **CLC 10**
See also CA 73-76; 89-92; DLB 7

Jones, Robert F(rancis)   1934- . . . . **CLC 7**
See also CA 49-52; CANR 2

Jones, Rod   1953- . . . . **CLC 50**
See also CA 128

Jones, Terence Graham Parry
1942- . . . . **CLC 21**
See also Jones, Terry; Monty Python
See also CA 112; 116; CANR 35

Jones, Terry
See Jones, Terence Graham Parry
See also SATA 67; SATA-Brief 51

Jones, Thom   1945(?)- . . . . **CLC 81**

Jong, Erica   1942- . . . . . . **CLC 4, 6, 8, 18, 83**
See also AITN 1; BEST 90:2; CA 73-76;
CANR 26; DLB 2, 5, 28, 152; MTCW

Jonson, Ben(jamin)
1572(?)-1637 . . . . **LC 6; DA; DC 4; WLC**
See also CDBLB Before 1660; DLB 62, 121

Jordan, June   1936- . . . . **CLC 5, 11, 23**
See also AAYA 2; BW 2; CA 33-36R;
CANR 25; CLR 10; DLB 38; MAICYA;
MTCW; SATA 4

Jordan, Pat(rick M.)   1941- . . . . **CLC 37**
See also CA 33-36R

Jorgensen, Ivar
See Ellison, Harlan (Jay)

Jorgenson, Ivar
See Silverberg, Robert

Josephus, Flavius   c. 37-100 . . . . . **CMLC 13**

Josipovici, Gabriel   1940- . . . . **CLC 6, 43**
See also CA 37-40R; CAAS 8; CANR 47;
DLB 14

Joubert, Joseph   1754-1824 . . . . **NCLC 9**

Jouve, Pierre Jean   1887-1976 . . . . . . **CLC 47**
See also CA 65-68

Joyce, James (Augustine Aloysius)
1882-1941 . . . . **TCLC 3, 8, 16, 35, 52;**
DA; SSC 3; WLC
See also CA 104; 126; CDBLB 1914-1945;
DLB 10, 19, 36; MTCW

Jozsef, Attila   1905-1937 . . . . **TCLC 22**
See also CA 116

Juana Ines de la Cruz   1651(?)-1695 . . . **LC 5**

Judd, Cyril
See Kornbluth, C(yril) M.; Pohl, Frederik

Julian of Norwich   1342(?)-1416(?) . . . . **LC 6**
See also DLB 146

Juniper, Alex
See Hospital, Janette Turner

Just, Ward (Swift)   1935- . . . . **CLC 4, 27**
See also CA 25-28R; CANR 32

Justice, Donald (Rodney)   1925- . . **CLC 6, 19**
See also CA 5-8R; CANR 26; DLBY 83

Juvenal   c. 55-c. 127 . . . . **CMLC 8**

Juvenis
See Bourne, Randolph S(illiman)

Kacew, Romain   1914-1980
See Gary, Romain
See also CA 108; 102

Kadare, Ismail   1936- . . . . **CLC 52**

Kadohata, Cynthia . . . . **CLC 59**
See also CA 140

Kafka, Franz
1883-1924 . . . . **TCLC 2, 6, 13, 29, 47, 53;**
DA; SSC 5; WLC
See also CA 105; 126; DLB 81; MTCW

Kahanovitsch, Pinkhes
See Der Nister

Kahn, Roger   1927- . . . . **CLC 30**
See also CA 25-28R; CANR 44; SATA 37

Kain, Saul
See Sassoon, Siegfried (Lorraine)

Kaiser, Georg   1878-1945 . . . . **TCLC 9**
See also CA 106; DLB 124

Kaletski, Alexander   1946- . . . . **CLC 39**
See also CA 118; 143

Kalidasa   fl. c. 400- . . . . **CMLC 9**

Kallman, Chester (Simon)
1921-1975 . . . . **CLC 2**
See also CA 45-48; 53-56; CANR 3

Kaminsky, Melvin   1926-
See Brooks, Mel
See also CA 65-68; CANR 16

Kaminsky, Stuart M(elvin)   1934- . . . **CLC 59**
See also CA 73-76; CANR 29

Kane, Paul
See Simon, Paul

Kane, Wilson
See Bloch, Robert (Albert)

Kanin, Garson   1912- . . . . **CLC 22**
See also AITN 1; CA 5-8R; CANR 7;
DLB 7

Kaniuk, Yoram   1930- . . . . **CLC 19**
See also CA 134

Kant, Immanuel   1724-1804 . . . . . . **NCLC 27**
See also DLB 94

Kantor, MacKinlay   1904-1977 . . . . . . **CLC 7**
See also CA 61-64; 73-76; DLB 9, 102

Kaplan, David Michael   1946- . . . . . . **CLC 50**

Kaplan, James   1951- . . . . **CLC 59**
See also CA 135

Karageorge, Michael
See Anderson, Poul (William)

Karamzin, Nikolai Mikhailovich
1766-1826 . . . . **NCLC 3**
See also DLB 150

Karapanou, Margarita   1946- . . . . **CLC 13**
See also CA 101

Karinthy, Frigyes   1887-1938 . . . . . . **TCLC 47**

Karl, Frederick R(obert)   1927- . . . . . **CLC 34**
See also CA 5-8R; CANR 3, 44

Kastel, Warren
See Silverberg, Robert

Kataev, Evgeny Petrovich   1903-1942
See Petrov, Evgeny
See also CA 120

Kataphusin
See Ruskin, John

Katz, Steve   1935- . . . . **CLC 47**
See also CA 25-28R; CAAS 14; CANR 12;
DLBY 83

Kauffman, Janet   1945- . . . . **CLC 42**
See also CA 117; CANR 43; DLBY 86

Kaufman, Bob (Garnell)
1925-1986 . . . . **CLC 49**
See also BW 1; CA 41-44R; 118; CANR 22;
DLB 16, 41

Kaufman, George S.   1889-1961 . . . . . **CLC 38**
See also CA 108; 93-96; DLB 7

Kaufman, Sue . . . . **CLC 3, 8**
See also Barondess, Sue K(aufman)

Kavafis, Konstantinos Petrou   1863-1933
See Cavafy, C(onstantine) P(eter)
See also CA 104

Kavan, Anna   1901-1968 . . . . . . **CLC 5, 13, 82**
See also CA 5-8R; CANR 6; MTCW

Kavanagh, Dan
See Barnes, Julian

Kavanagh, Patrick (Joseph)
1904-1967 . . . . **CLC 22**
See also CA 123; 25-28R; DLB 15, 20;
MTCW

Kawabata, Yasunari
1899-1972 . . . . . **CLC 2, 5, 9, 18; SSC 17**
See also CA 93-96; 33-36R

Kaye, M(ary) M(argaret)   1909- . . . . . **CLC 28**
See also CA 89-92; CANR 24; MTCW;
SATA 62

Kaye, Mollie
See Kaye, M(ary) M(argaret)

Kaye-Smith, Sheila   1887-1956 . . . . . **TCLC 20**
See also CA 118; DLB 36

Kaymor, Patrice Maguilene
See Senghor, Leopold Sedar

Kazan, Elia 1909-. . . . . **CLC 6, 16, 63**
See also CA 21-24R; CANR 32

Kazantzakis, Nikos
1883(?)-1957 . . . . **TCLC 2, 5, 33**
See also CA 105; 132; MTCW

Kazin, Alfred 1915- . . . . **CLC 34, 38**
See also CA 1-4R; CAAS 7; CANR 1, 45;
DLB 67

Keane, Mary Nesta (Skrine) 1904-
See Keane, Molly
See also CA 108; 114

Keane, Molly. . . . . **CLC 31**
See also Keane, Mary Nesta (Skrine)

Keates, Jonathan 19(?)-. . . . . **CLC 34**

Keaton, Buster 1895-1966 . . . . **CLC 20**

Keats, John
1795-1821 . . . **NCLC 8; DA; PC 1; WLC**
See also CDBLB 1789-1832; DLB 96, 110

Keene, Donald 1922- . . . . **CLC 34**
See also CA 1-4R; CANR 5

Keillor, Garrison. . . . . **CLC 40**
See also Keillor, Gary (Edward)
See also AAYA 2; BEST 89:3; DLBY 87;
SATA 58

Keillor, Gary (Edward) 1942-
See Keillor, Garrison
See also CA 111; 117; CANR 36; MTCW

Keith, Michael
See Hubbard, L(afayette) Ron(ald)

Keller, Gottfried 1819-1890 . . . . **NCLC 2**
See also DLB 129

Kellerman, Jonathan 1949- . . . . **CLC 44**
See also BEST 90:1; CA 106; CANR 29

Kelley, William Melvin 1937-. . . . . . **CLC 22**
See also BW 1; CA 77-80; CANR 27;
DLB 33

Kellogg, Marjorie 1922-. . . . . **CLC 2**
See also CA 81-84

Kellow, Kathleen
See Hibbert, Eleanor Alice Burford

Kelly, M(ilton) T(erry) 1947-. . . . . . . **CLC 55**
See also CA 97-100; CANR 19, 43

Kelman, James 1946-. . . . . **CLC 58, 86**

Kemal, Yashar 1923- . . . . **CLC 14, 29**
See also CA 89-92; CANR 44

Kemble, Fanny 1809-1893 . . . . **NCLC 18**
See also DLB 32

Kemelman, Harry 1908-. . . . . **CLC 2**
See also AITN 1; CA 9-12R; CANR 6;
DLB 28

Kempe, Margery 1373(?)-1440(?) . . . . . **LC 6**
See also DLB 146

Kempis, Thomas a 1380-1471 . . . . **LC 11**

Kendall, Henry 1839-1882. . . . . . . **NCLC 12**

Keneally, Thomas (Michael)
1935- . . . . . . **CLC 5, 8, 10, 14, 19, 27, 43**
See also CA 85-88; CANR 10; MTCW

Kennedy, Adrienne (Lita)
1931-. . . . . **CLC 66; BLC; DC 5**
See also BW 2; CA 103; CAAS 20; CABS 3;
CANR 26; DLB 38

Kennedy, John Pendleton
1795-1870 . . . . **NCLC 2**
See also DLB 3

Kennedy, Joseph Charles 1929-
See Kennedy, X. J.
See also CA 1-4R; CANR 4, 30, 40;
SATA 14

Kennedy, William 1928-. . . **CLC 6, 28, 34, 53**
See also AAYA 1; CA 85-88; CANR 14,
31; DLB 143; DLBY 85; MTCW;
SATA 57

Kennedy, X. J.. . . . . **CLC 8, 42**
See also Kennedy, Joseph Charles
See also CAAS 9; CLR 27; DLB 5

Kenny, Maurice (Francis) 1929-. . . . **CLC 87**
See also CA 144; NNAL

Kent, Kelvin
See Kuttner, Henry

Kenton, Maxwell
See Southern, Terry

Kenyon, Robert O.
See Kuttner, Henry

Kerouac, Jack . . . . . **CLC 1, 2, 3, 5, 14, 29, 61**
See also Kerouac, Jean-Louis Lebris de
See also CDALB 1941-1968; DLB 2, 16;
DLBD 3

Kerouac, Jean-Louis Lebris de 1922-1969
See Kerouac, Jack
See also AITN 1; CA 5-8R; 25-28R;
CANR 26; DA; MTCW; WLC

Kerr, Jean 1923-. . . . . **CLC 22**
See also CA 5-8R; CANR 7

Kerr, M. E. . . . . **CLC 12, 35**
See also Meaker, Marijane (Agnes)
See also AAYA 2; CLR 29; SAAS 1

Kerr, Robert . . . . **CLC 55**

Kerrigan, (Thomas) Anthony
1918-. . . . . **CLC 4, 6**
See also CA 49-52; CAAS 11; CANR 4

Kerry, Lois
See Duncan, Lois

Kesey, Ken (Elton)
1935- . . . . . . **CLC 1, 3, 6, 11, 46, 64; DA;**
WLC
See also CA 1-4R; CANR 22, 38;
CDALB 1968-1988; DLB 2, 16; MTCW;
SATA 66

Kesselring, Joseph (Otto)
1902-1967 . . . . **CLC 45**

Kessler, Jascha (Frederick) 1929-. . . . **CLC 4**
See also CA 17-20R; CANR 8, 48

Kettelkamp, Larry (Dale) 1933- . . . . **CLC 12**
See also CA 29-32R; CANR 16; SAAS 3;
SATA 2

Keyber, Conny
See Fielding, Henry

Keyes, Daniel 1927-. . . . . **CLC 80; DA**
See also CA 17-20R; CANR 10, 26;
SATA 37

Khanshendel, Chiron
See Rose, Wendy

Khayyam, Omar
1048-1131 . . . . **CMLC 11; PC 8**

Kherdian, David 1931-. . . . . **CLC 6, 9**
See also CA 21-24R; CAAS 2; CANR 39;
CLR 24; JRDA; MAICYA; SATA 16, 74

Khlebnikov, Velimir . . . . **TCLC 20**
See also Khlebnikov, Viktor Vladimirovich

Khlebnikov, Viktor Vladimirovich 1885-1922
See Khlebnikov, Velimir
See also CA 117

Khodasevich, Vladislav (Felitsianovich)
1886-1939 . . . . **TCLC 15**
See also CA 115

Kielland, Alexander Lange
1849-1906 . . . . **TCLC 5**
See also CA 104

Kiely, Benedict 1919-. . . . . **CLC 23, 43**
See also CA 1-4R; CANR 2; DLB 15

Kienzle, William X(avier) 1928- . . . . **CLC 25**
See also CA 93-96; CAAS 1; CANR 9, 31;
MTCW

Kierkegaard, Soren 1813-1855. . . . **NCLC 34**

Killens, John Oliver 1916-1987. . . . . **CLC 10**
See also BW 2; CA 77-80; 123; CAAS 2;
CANR 26; DLB 33

Killigrew, Anne 1660-1685. . . . . **LC 4**
See also DLB 131

Kim
See Simenon, Georges (Jacques Christian)

Kincaid, Jamaica 1949- . . . **CLC 43, 68; BLC**
See also AAYA 13; BW 2; CA 125;
CANR 47

King, Francis (Henry) 1923- . . . . . **CLC 8, 53**
See also CA 1-4R; CANR 1, 33; DLB 15,
139; MTCW

King, Martin Luther, Jr.
1929-1968 . . . . **CLC 83; BLC; DA**
See also BW 2; CA 25-28; CANR 27, 44;
CAP 2; MTCW; SATA 14

King, Stephen (Edwin)
1947-. . . . . . **CLC 12, 26, 37, 61; SSC 17**
See also AAYA 1; BEST 90:1; CA 61-64;
CANR 1, 30; DLB 143; DLBY 80;
JRDA; MTCW; SATA 9, 55

King, Steve
See King, Stephen (Edwin)

King, Thomas 1943-. . . . . **CLC 89**
See also CA 144; NNAL

Kingman, Lee. **CLC 17**
See also Natti, (Mary) Lee
See also SAAS 3; SATA 1, 67

Kingsley, Charles 1819-1875 . . . . . **NCLC 35**
See also DLB 21, 32; YABC 2

Kingsley, Sidney 1906-1995. . . . . . . **CLC 44**
See also CA 85-88; 147; DLB 7

Kingsolver, Barbara 1955-. . . . . . **CLC 55, 81**
See also CA 129; 134

Kingston, Maxine (Ting Ting) Hong
1940-. . . . . **CLC 12, 19, 58**
See also AAYA 8; CA 69-72; CANR 13,
38; DLBY 80; MTCW; SATA 53

Kinnell, Galway
1927-. . . . . **CLC 1, 2, 3, 5, 13, 29**
See also CA 9-12R; CANR 10, 34; DLB 5;
DLBY 87; MTCW

Kinsella, Thomas 1928- . . . . **CLC 4, 19**
See also CA 17-20R; CANR 15; DLB 27;
MTCW

Kinsella, W(illiam) P(atrick)
1935- . . . . **CLC 27, 43**
See also AAYA 7; CA 97-100; CAAS 7;
CANR 21, 35; MTCW

Kipling, (Joseph) Rudyard
1865-1936 . . . . . . **TCLC 8, 17; DA; PC 3;**
SSC 5; WLC
See also CA 105; 120; CANR 33;
CDBLB 1890-1914; DLB 19, 34, 141;
MAICYA; MTCW; YABC 2

Kirkup, James 1918- . . . . **CLC 1**
See also CA 1-4R; CAAS 4; CANR 2;
DLB 27; SATA 12

Kirkwood, James 1930(?)-1989 . . . . . . **CLC 9**
See also AITN 2; CA 1-4R; 128; CANR 6,
40

Kis, Danilo 1935-1989 . . . . **CLC 57**
See also CA 109; 118; 129; MTCW

Kivi, Aleksis 1834-1872 . . . . **NCLC 30**

Kizer, Carolyn (Ashley)
1925- . . . . **CLC 15, 39, 80**
See also CA 65-68; CAAS 5; CANR 24;
DLB 5

Klabund 1890-1928 . . . . **TCLC 44**
See also DLB 66

Klappert, Peter 1942- . . . . **CLC 57**
See also CA 33-36R; DLB 5

Klein, A(braham) M(oses)
1909-1972 . . . . **CLC 19**
See also CA 101; 37-40R; DLB 68

Klein, Norma 1938-1989 . . . . **CLC 30**
See also AAYA 2; CA 41-44R; 128;
CANR 15, 37; CLR 2, 19; JRDA;
MAICYA; SAAS 1; SATA 7, 57

Klein, T(heodore) E(ibon) D(onald)
1947- . . . . **CLC 34**
See also CA 119; CANR 44

Kleist, Heinrich von
1777-1811 . . . . **NCLC 2, 37**
See also DLB 90

Klima, Ivan 1931- . . . . **CLC 56**
See also CA 25-28R; CANR 17

Klimentov, Andrei Platonovich 1899-1951
See Platonov, Andrei
See also CA 108

Klinger, Friedrich Maximilian von
1752-1831 . . . . **NCLC 1**
See also DLB 94

Klopstock, Friedrich Gottlieb
1724-1803 . . . . **NCLC 11**
See also DLB 97

Knebel, Fletcher 1911-1993 . . . . **CLC 14**
See also AITN 1; CA 1-4R; 140; CAAS 3;
CANR 1, 36; SATA 36; SATA-Obit 75

Knickerbocker, Diedrich
See Irving, Washington

Knight, Etheridge
1931-1991 . . . . **CLC 40; BLC**
See also BW 1; CA 21-24R; 133; CANR 23;
DLB 41

Knight, Sarah Kemble 1666-1727 . . . . . **LC 7**
See also DLB 24

Knister, Raymond 1899-1932 . . . . . . **TCLC 56**
See also DLB 68

Knowles, John
1926- . . . . **CLC 1, 4, 10, 26; DA**
See also AAYA 10; CA 17-20R; CANR 40;
CDALB 1968-1988; DLB 6; MTCW;
SATA 8

Knox, Calvin M.
See Silverberg, Robert

Knye, Cassandra
See Disch, Thomas M(ichael)

Koch, C(hristopher) J(ohn) 1932- . . . **CLC 42**
See also CA 127

Koch, Christopher
See Koch, C(hristopher) J(ohn)

Koch, Kenneth 1925- . . . . **CLC 5, 8, 44**
See also CA 1-4R; CANR 6, 36; DLB 5;
SATA 65

Kochanowski, Jan 1530-1584 . . . . **LC 10**

Kock, Charles Paul de
1794-1871 . . . . **NCLC 16**

Koda Shigeyuki 1867-1947
See Rohan, Koda
See also CA 121

Koestler, Arthur
1905-1983 . . . . **CLC 1, 3, 6, 8, 15, 33**
See also CA 1-4R; 109; CANR 1, 33;
CDBLB 1945-1960; DLBY 83; MTCW

Kogawa, Joy Nozomi 1935- . . . . **CLC 78**
See also CA 101; CANR 19

Kohout, Pavel 1928- . . . . **CLC 13**
See also CA 45-48; CANR 3

Koizumi, Yakumo
See Hearn, (Patricio) Lafcadio (Tessima
Carlos)

Kolmar, Gertrud 1894-1943 . . . . . . **TCLC 40**

Komunyakaa, Yusef 1947- . . . . **CLC 86**
See also CA 147; DLB 120

Konrad, George
See Konrad, Gyoergy

Konrad, Gyoergy 1933- . . . . . . **CLC 4, 10, 73**
See also CA 85-88

Konwicki, Tadeusz 1926- . . . . . **CLC 8, 28, 54**
See also CA 101; CAAS 9; CANR 39;
MTCW

Koontz, Dean R(ay) 1945- . . . . **CLC 78**
See also AAYA 9; BEST 89:3, 90:2;
CA 108; CANR 19, 36; MTCW

Kopit, Arthur (Lee) 1937- . . . . **CLC 1, 18, 33**
See also AITN 1; CA 81-84; CABS 3;
DLB 7; MTCW

Kops, Bernard 1926- . . . . **CLC 4**
See also CA 5-8R; DLB 13

Kornbluth, C(yril) M. 1923-1958 . . . . **TCLC 8**
See also CA 105; DLB 8

Korolenko, V. G.
See Korolenko, Vladimir Galaktionovich

Korolenko, Vladimir
See Korolenko, Vladimir Galaktionovich

Korolenko, Vladimir G.
See Korolenko, Vladimir Galaktionovich

Korolenko, Vladimir Galaktionovich
1853-1921 . . . . **TCLC 22**
See also CA 121

Kosinski, Jerzy (Nikodem)
1933-1991 . . . . **CLC 1, 2, 3, 6, 10, 15, 53,**
70
See also CA 17-20R; 134; CANR 9, 46;
DLB 2; DLBY 82; MTCW

Kostelanetz, Richard (Cory) 1940- . . **CLC 28**
See also CA 13-16R; CAAS 8; CANR 38

Kostrowitzki, Wilhelm Apollinaris de
1880-1918
See Apollinaire, Guillaume
See also CA 104

Kotlowitz, Robert 1924- . . . . **CLC 4**
See also CA 33-36R; CANR 36

Kotzebue, August (Friedrich Ferdinand) von
1761-1819 . . . . **NCLC 25**
See also DLB 94

Kotzwinkle, William 1938- . . . **CLC 5, 14, 35**
See also CA 45-48; CANR 3, 44; CLR 6;
MAICYA; SATA 24, 70

Kozol, Jonathan 1936- . . . . **CLC 17**
See also CA 61-64; CANR 16, 45

Kozoll, Michael 1940(?)- . . . . **CLC 35**

Kramer, Kathryn 19(?)- . . . . **CLC 34**

Kramer, Larry 1935- . . . . **CLC 42**
See also CA 124; 126

Krasicki, Ignacy 1735-1801 . . . . **NCLC 8**

Krasinski, Zygmunt 1812-1859 . . . . **NCLC 4**

Kraus, Karl 1874-1936 . . . . **TCLC 5**
See also CA 104; DLB 118

Kreve (Mickevicius), Vincas
1882-1954 . . . . **TCLC 27**

Kristeva, Julia 1941- . . . . **CLC 77**

Kristofferson, Kris 1936- . . . . **CLC 26**
See also CA 104

Krizanc, John 1956- . . . . **CLC 57**

Krleza, Miroslav 1893-1981 . . . . **CLC 8**
See also CA 97-100; 105; DLB 147

Kroetsch, Robert 1927- . . . . . . **CLC 5, 23, 57**
See also CA 17-20R; CANR 8, 38; DLB 53;
MTCW

Kroetz, Franz
See Kroetz, Franz Xaver

Kroetz, Franz Xaver 1946- . . . . **CLC 41**
See also CA 130

Kroker, Arthur 1945- . . . . **CLC 77**

Kropotkin, Peter (Aleksieevich)
1842-1921 . . . . **TCLC 36**
See also CA 119

Krotkov, Yuri 1917- . . . . **CLC 19**
See also CA 102

Krumb
See Crumb, R(obert)

Krumgold, Joseph (Quincy)
1908-1980 . . . . **CLC 12**
See also CA 9-12R; 101; CANR 7;
MAICYA; SATA 1, 48; SATA-Obit 23

Krumwitz
See Crumb, R(obert)

Krutch, Joseph Wood 1893-1970 . . . . **CLC 24**
See also CA 1-4R; 25-28R; CANR 4;
DLB 63

Krutzch, Gus
See Eliot, T(homas) S(tearns)

Krylov, Ivan Andreevich
1768(?)-1844 . . . . NCLC 1
See also DLB 150

Kubin, Alfred 1877-1959 . . . . TCLC 23
See also CA 112; DLB 81

Kubrick, Stanley 1928- . . . . CLC 16
See also CA 81-84; CANR 33; DLB 26

Kumin, Maxine (Winokur)
1925- . . . . CLC 5, 13, 28
See also AITN 2; CA 1-4R; CAAS 8;
CANR 1, 21; DLB 5; MTCW; SATA 12

Kundera, Milan
1929- . . . . CLC 4, 9, 19, 32, 68
See also AAYA 2; CA 85-88; CANR 19;
MTCW

Kunene, Mazisi (Raymond) 1930-. . . CLC 85
See also BW 1; CA 125; DLB 117

Kunitz, Stanley (Jasspon)
1905- . . . . CLC 6, 11, 14
See also CA 41-44R; CANR 26; DLB 48;
MTCW

Kunze, Reiner 1933- . . . . CLC 10
See also CA 93-96; DLB 75

Kuprin, Aleksandr Ivanovich
1870-1938 . . . . TCLC 5
See also CA 104

Kureishi, Hanif 1954(?)- . . . . CLC 64
See also CA 139

Kurosawa, Akira 1910- . . . . CLC 16
See also AAYA 11; CA 101; CANR 46

Kushner, Tony 1957(?)- . . . . CLC 81
See also CA 144

Kuttner, Henry 1915-1958 . . . . TCLC 10
See also CA 107; DLB 8

Kuzma, Greg 1944- . . . . CLC 7
See also CA 33-36R

Kuzmin, Mikhail 1872(?)-1936 . . . . TCLC 40

Kyd, Thomas 1558-1594 . . . . . . LC 22; DC 3
See also DLB 62

Kyprianos, Iossif
See Samarakis, Antonis

La Bruyere, Jean de 1645-1696 . . . . . . LC 17

Lacan, Jacques (Marie Emile)
1901-1981 . . . . CLC 75
See also CA 121; 104

Laclos, Pierre Ambroise Francois Choderlos
de 1741-1803 . . . . NCLC 4

Lacolere, Francois
See Aragon, Louis

La Colere, Francois
See Aragon, Louis

La Deshabilleuse
See Simenon, Georges (Jacques Christian)

Lady Gregory
See Gregory, Isabella Augusta (Persse)

Lady of Quality, A
See Bagnold, Enid

La Fayette, Marie (Madelaine Ploche de la
Vergne Comtes 1634-1693 . . . . . . LC 2

Lafayette, Rene
See Hubbard, L(afayette) Ron(ald)

Laforgue, Jules
1860-1887 . . . . NCLC 5; SSC 20

Lagerkvist, Paer (Fabian)
1891-1974 . . . . CLC 7, 10, 13, 54
See also Lagerkvist, Par
See also CA 85-88; 49-52; MTCW

Lagerkvist, Par
See Lagerkvist, Paer (Fabian)
See also SSC 12

Lagerloef, Selma (Ottiliana Lovisa)
1858-1940 . . . . TCLC 4, 36
See also Lagerlof, Selma (Ottiliana Lovisa)
See also CA 108; SATA 15

Lagerlof, Selma (Ottiliana Lovisa)
See Lagerloef, Selma (Ottiliana Lovisa)
See also CLR 7; SATA 15

La Guma, (Justin) Alex(ander)
1925-1985 . . . . CLC 19
See also BW 1; CA 49-52; 118; CANR 25;
DLB 117; MTCW

Laidlaw, A. K.
See Grieve, C(hristopher) M(urray)

Lainez, Manuel Mujica
See Mujica Lainez, Manuel
See also HW

Lamartine, Alphonse (Marie Louis Prat) de
1790-1869 . . . . NCLC 11

Lamb, Charles
1775-1834 . . . . NCLC 10; DA; WLC
See also CDBLB 1789-1832; DLB 93, 107;
SATA 17

Lamb, Lady Caroline 1785-1828 . . NCLC 38
See also DLB 116

Lamming, George (William)
1927- . . . . CLC 2, 4, 66; BLC
See also BW 2; CA 85-88; CANR 26;
DLB 125; MTCW

L'Amour, Louis (Dearborn)
1908-1988 . . . . CLC 25, 55
See also AITN 2; BEST 89:2; CA 1-4R;
125; CANR 3, 25, 40; DLBY 80; MTCW

Lampedusa, Giuseppe (Tomasi) di . . . TCLC 13
See also Tomasi di Lampedusa, Giuseppe

Lampman, Archibald 1861-1899 . . NCLC 25
See also DLB 92

Lancaster, Bruce 1896-1963 . . . . CLC 36
See also CA 9-10; CAP 1; SATA 9

Landau, Mark Alexandrovich
See Aldanov, Mark (Alexandrovich)

Landau-Aldanov, Mark Alexandrovich
See Aldanov, Mark (Alexandrovich)

Landis, John 1950- . . . . CLC 26
See also CA 112; 122

Landolfi, Tommaso 1908-1979 . . . CLC 11, 49
See also CA 127; 117

Landon, Letitia Elizabeth
1802-1838 . . . . NCLC 15
See also DLB 96

Landor, Walter Savage
1775-1864 . . . . NCLC 14
See also DLB 93, 107

Landwirth, Heinz 1927-
See Lind, Jakov
See also CA 9-12R; CANR 7

Lane, Patrick 1939- . . . . CLC 25
See also CA 97-100; DLB 53

Lang, Andrew 1844-1912 . . . . TCLC 16
See also CA 114; 137; DLB 98, 141;
MAICYA; SATA 16

Lang, Fritz 1890-1976 . . . . CLC 20
See also CA 77-80; 69-72; CANR 30

Lange, John
See Crichton, (John) Michael

Langer, Elinor 1939- . . . . CLC 34
See also CA 121

Langland, William
1330(?)-1400(?) . . . . LC 19; DA
See also DLB 146

Langstaff, Launcelot
See Irving, Washington

Lanier, Sidney 1842-1881 . . . . NCLC 6
See also DLB 64; MAICYA; SATA 18

Lanyer, Aemilia 1569-1645 . . . . . . LC 10, 30
See also DLB 121

Lao Tzu . . . . CMLC 7

Lapine, James (Elliot) 1949- . . . . CLC 39
See also CA 123; 130

Larbaud, Valery (Nicolas)
1881-1957 . . . . TCLC 9
See also CA 106

Lardner, Ring
See Lardner, Ring(gold) W(ilmer)

Lardner, Ring W., Jr.
See Lardner, Ring(gold) W(ilmer)

Lardner, Ring(gold) W(ilmer)
1885-1933 . . . . TCLC 2, 14
See also CA 104; 131; CDALB 1917-1929;
DLB 11, 25, 86; MTCW

Laredo, Betty
See Codrescu, Andrei

Larkin, Maia
See Wojciechowska, Maia (Teresa)

Larkin, Philip (Arthur)
1922-1985 . . . . CLC 3, 5, 8, 9, 13, 18, 33,
39, 64
See also CA 5-8R; 117; CANR 24;
CDBLB 1960 to Present; DLB 27;
MTCW

Larra (y Sanchez de Castro), Mariano Jose de
1809-1837 . . . . NCLC 17

Larsen, Eric 1941- . . . . CLC 55
See also CA 132

Larsen, Nella 1891-1964 . . . . . CLC 37; BLC
See also BW 1; CA 125; DLB 51

Larson, Charles R(aymond) 1938- . . . CLC 31
See also CA 53-56; CANR 4

Lasker-Schueler, Else 1869-1945 . . TCLC 57
See also DLB 66, 124

Latham, Jean Lee 1902- . . . . CLC 12
See also AITN 1; CA 5-8R; CANR 7;
MAICYA; SATA 2, 68

Latham, Mavis
See Clark, Mavis Thorpe

Lathen, Emma . . . . CLC 2
See also Hennissart, Martha; Latsis, Mary
J(ane)

Lathrop, Francis
See Leiber, Fritz (Reuter, Jr.)

Latsis, Mary J(ane)
See Lathen, Emma
See also CA 85-88

Lattimore, Richmond (Alexander)
1906-1984 .... **CLC 3**
See also CA 1-4R; 112; CANR 1

Laughlin, James 1914-........... **CLC 49**
See also CA 21-24R; CANR 9, 47; DLB 48

Laurence, (Jean) Margaret (Wemyss)
1926-1987 .. **CLC 3, 6, 13, 50, 62; SSC 7**
See also CA 5-8R; 121; CANR 33; DLB 53;
MTCW; SATA-Obit 50

Laurent, Antoine 1952- .... **CLC 50**

Lauscher, Hermann
See Hesse, Hermann

Lautreamont, Comte de
1846-1870 .... **NCLC 12; SSC 14**

Laverty, Donald
See Blish, James (Benjamin)

Lavin, Mary 1912-...... **CLC 4, 18; SSC 4**
See also CA 9-12R; CANR 33; DLB 15;
MTCW

Lavond, Paul Dennis
See Kornbluth, C(yril) M.; Pohl, Frederik

Lawler, Raymond Evenor 1922- .... **CLC 58**
See also CA 103

Lawrence, D(avid) H(erbert Richards)
1885-1930 ...... **TCLC 2, 9, 16, 33, 48;**
DA; SSC 4, 19; WLC
See also CA 104; 121; CDBLB 1914-1945;
DLB 10, 19, 36, 98; MTCW

Lawrence, T(homas) E(dward)
1888-1935 .... **TCLC 18**
See also Dale, Colin
See also CA 115

Lawrence of Arabia
See Lawrence, T(homas) E(dward)

Lawson, Henry (Archibald Hertzberg)
1867-1922 .... **TCLC 27; SSC 18**
See also CA 120

Lawton, Dennis
See Faust, Frederick (Schiller)

Laxness, Halldor .... **CLC 25**
See also Gudjonsson, Halldor Kiljan

Layamon fl. c. 1200-............. **CMLC 10**
See also DLB 146

Laye, Camara 1928-1980 ... **CLC 4, 38; BLC**
See also BW 1; CA 85-88; 97-100;
CANR 25; MTCW

Layton, Irving (Peter) 1912-..... **CLC 2, 15**
See also CA 1-4R; CANR 2, 33, 43;
DLB 88; MTCW

Lazarus, Emma 1849-1887........ **NCLC 8**

Lazarus, Felix
See Cable, George Washington

Lazarus, Henry
See Slavitt, David R(ytman)

Lea, Joan
See Neufeld, John (Arthur)

Leacock, Stephen (Butler)
1869-1944 .... **TCLC 2**
See also CA 104; 141; DLB 92

Lear, Edward 1812-1888 .... **NCLC 3**
See also CLR 1; DLB 32; MAICYA;
SATA 18

Lear, Norman (Milton) 1922- ...... **CLC 12**
See also CA 73-76

Leavis, F(rank) R(aymond)
1895-1978 .... **CLC 24**
See also CA 21-24R; 77-80; CANR 44;
MTCW

Leavitt, David 1961-.............. **CLC 34**
See also CA 116; 122; DLB 130

Leblanc, Maurice (Marie Emile)
1864-1941 .... **TCLC 49**
See also CA 110

Lebowitz, Fran(ces Ann)
1951(?)-.................. **CLC 11, 36**
See also CA 81-84; CANR 14; MTCW

Lebrecht, Peter
See Tieck, (Johann) Ludwig

le Carre, John .... **CLC 3, 5, 9, 15, 28**
See also Cornwell, David (John Moore)
See also BEST 89:4; CDBLB 1960 to
Present; DLB 87

Le Clezio, J(ean) M(arie) G(ustave)
1940- .... **CLC 31**
See also CA 116; 128; DLB 83

Leconte de Lisle, Charles-Marie-Rene
1818-1894 .... **NCLC 29**

Le Coq, Monsieur
See Simenon, Georges (Jacques Christian)

Leduc, Violette 1907-1972........ **CLC 22**
See also CA 13-14; 33-36R; CAP 1

Ledwidge, Francis 1887(?)-1917 ... **TCLC 23**
See also CA 123; DLB 20

Lee, Andrea 1953- .... **CLC 36; BLC**
See also BW 1; CA 125

Lee, Andrew
See Auchincloss, Louis (Stanton)

Lee, Don L. .... **CLC 2**
See also Madhubuti, Haki R.

Lee, George W(ashington)
1894-1976 .... **CLC 52; BLC**
See also BW 1; CA 125; DLB 51

Lee, (Nelle) Harper
1926-............ **CLC 12, 60; DA; WLC**
See also AAYA 13; CA 13-16R;
CDALB 1941-1968; DLB 6; MTCW;
SATA 11

Lee, Helen Elaine 1959(?)- .... **CLC 86**

Lee, Julian
See Latham, Jean Lee

Lee, Larry
See Lee, Lawrence

Lee, Lawrence 1941-1990......... **CLC 34**
See also CA 131; CANR 43

Lee, Manfred B(ennington)
1905-1971 .... **CLC 11**
See also Queen, Ellery
See also CA 1-4R; 29-32R; CANR 2;
DLB 137

Lee, Stan 1922-.................. **CLC 17**
See also AAYA 5; CA 108; 111

Lee, Tanith 1947-................ **CLC 46**
See also CA 37-40R; SATA 8

Lee, Vernon .... **TCLC 5**
See also Paget, Violet
See also DLB 57, 153

Lee, William
See Burroughs, William S(eward)

Lee, Willy
See Burroughs, William S(eward)

Lee-Hamilton, Eugene (Jacob)
1845-1907 .... **TCLC 22**
See also CA 117

Leet, Judith 1935- .... **CLC 11**

Le Fanu, Joseph Sheridan
1814-1873 .... **NCLC 9; SSC 14**
See also DLB 21, 70

Leffland, Ella 1931- .... **CLC 19**
See also CA 29-32R; CANR 35; DLBY 84;
SATA 65

Leger, Alexis
See Leger, (Marie-Rene Auguste) Alexis
Saint-Leger

Leger, (Marie-Rene Auguste) Alexis
Saint-Leger 1887-1975........ **CLC 11**
See also Perse, St.-John
See also CA 13-16R; 61-64; CANR 43;
MTCW

Leger, Saintleger
See Leger, (Marie-Rene Auguste) Alexis
Saint-Leger

Le Guin, Ursula K(roeber)
1929- .... **CLC 8, 13, 22, 45, 71; SSC 12**
See also AAYA 9; AITN 1; CA 21-24R;
CANR 9, 32; CDALB 1968-1988; CLR 3,
28; DLB 8, 52; JRDA; MAICYA;
MTCW; SATA 4, 52

Lehmann, Rosamond (Nina)
1901-1990 .... **CLC 5**
See also CA 77-80; 131; CANR 8; DLB 15

Leiber, Fritz (Reuter, Jr.)
1910-1992 .... **CLC 25**
See also CA 45-48; 139; CANR 2, 40;
DLB 8; MTCW; SATA 45;
SATA-Obit 73

Leimbach, Martha 1963-
See Leimbach, Marti
See also CA 130

Leimbach, Marti .... **CLC 65**
See also Leimbach, Martha

Leino, Eino .... **TCLC 24**
See also Loennbohm, Armas Eino Leopold

Leiris, Michel (Julien) 1901-1990... **CLC 61**
See also CA 119; 128; 132

Leithauser, Brad 1953-............ **CLC 27**
See also CA 107; CANR 27; DLB 120

Lelchuk, Alan 1938-................ **CLC 5**
See also CA 45-48; CAAS 20; CANR 1

Lem, Stanislaw 1921-........ **CLC 8, 15, 40**
See also CA 105; CAAS 1; CANR 32;
MTCW

Lemann, Nancy 1956-............. **CLC 39**
See also CA 118; 136

Lemonnier, (Antoine Louis) Camille
1844-1913 .... **TCLC 22**
See also CA 121

Lenau, Nikolaus 1802-1850 ...... **NCLC 16**

L'Engle, Madeleine (Camp Franklin)
1918- .... CLC 12
See also AAYA 1; AITN 2; CA 1-4R;
CANR 3, 21, 39; CLR 1, 14; DLB 52;
JRDA; MAICYA; MTCW; SAAS 15;
SATA 1, 27, 75

Lengyel, Jozsef 1896-1975.......... CLC 7
See also CA 85-88; 57-60

Lennon, John (Ono)
1940-1980 .... CLC 12, 35
See also CA 102

Lennox, Charlotte Ramsay
1729(?)-1804 .... NCLC 23
See also DLB 39

Lentricchia, Frank (Jr.) 1940-...... CLC 34
See also CA 25-28R; CANR 19

Lenz, Siegfried 1926-............. CLC 27
See also CA 89-92; DLB 75

Leonard, Elmore (John, Jr.)
1925- .... CLC 28, 34, 71
See also AITN 1; BEST 89:1, 90:4;
CA 81-84; CANR 12, 28; MTCW

Leonard, Hugh.................... CLC 19
See also Byrne, John Keyes
See also DLB 13

Leopardi, (Conte) Giacomo
1798-1837 .... NCLC 22

Le Reveler
See Artaud, Antonin

Lerman, Eleanor 1952-............. CLC 9
See also CA 85-88

Lerman, Rhoda 1936-............. CLC 56
See also CA 49-52

Lermontov, Mikhail Yuryevich
1814-1841 .... NCLC 47

Leroux, Gaston 1868-1927........ TCLC 25
See also CA 108; 136; SATA 65

Lesage, Alain-Rene 1668-1747....... LC 28

Leskov, Nikolai (Semyonovich)
1831-1895 .... NCLC 25

Lessing, Doris (May)
1919- ..... CLC 1, 2, 3, 6, 10, 15, 22, 40;
DA; SSC 6
See also CA 9-12R; CAAS 14; CANR 33;
CDBLB 1960 to Present; DLB 15, 139;
DLBY 85; MTCW

Lessing, Gotthold Ephraim
1729-1781 .... LC 8
See also DLB 97

Lester, Richard 1932-............. CLC 20

Lever, Charles (James)
1806-1872 .... NCLC 23
See also DLB 21

Leverson, Ada 1865(?)-1936(?) .... TCLC 18
See also Elaine
See also CA 117; DLB 153

Levertov, Denise
1923- ...... CLC 1, 2, 3, 5, 8, 15, 28, 66;
PC 11
See also CA 1-4R; CAAS 19; CANR 3, 29;
DLB 5; MTCW

Levi, Jonathan.................... CLC 76

Levi, Peter (Chad Tigar) 1931-..... CLC 41
See also CA 5-8R; CANR 34; DLB 40

Levi, Primo
1919-1987 .... CLC 37, 50; SSC 12
See also CA 13-16R; 122; CANR 12, 33;
MTCW

Levin, Ira 1929- .... CLC 3, 6
See also CA 21-24R; CANR 17, 44;
MTCW; SATA 66

Levin, Meyer 1905-1981 .... CLC 7
See also AITN 1; CA 9-12R; 104;
CANR 15; DLB 9, 28; DLBY 81;
SATA 21; SATA-Obit 27

Levine, Norman 1924- .... CLC 54
See also CA 73-76; CANR 14; DLB 88

Levine, Philip 1928-.. CLC 2, 4, 5, 9, 14, 33
See also CA 9-12R; CANR 9, 37; DLB 5

Levinson, Deirdre 1931-.......... CLC 49
See also CA 73-76

Levi-Strauss, Claude 1908- .... CLC 38
See also CA 1-4R; CANR 6, 32; MTCW

Levitin, Sonia (Wolff) 1934- ...... CLC 17
See also AAYA 13; CA 29-32R; CANR 14,
32; JRDA; MAICYA; SAAS 2; SATA 4,
68

Levon, O. U.
See Kesey, Ken (Elton)

Lewes, George Henry
1817-1878 .... NCLC 25
See also DLB 55, 144

Lewis, Alun 1915-1944........... TCLC 3
See also CA 104; DLB 20

Lewis, C. Day
See Day Lewis, C(ecil)

Lewis, C(live) S(taples)
1898-1963 ..... CLC 1, 3, 6, 14, 27; DA;
WLC
See also AAYA 3; CA 81-84; CANR 33;
CDBLB 1945-1960; CLR 3, 27; DLB 15,
100; JRDA; MAICYA; MTCW;
SATA 13

Lewis, Janet 1899-............... CLC 41
See also Winters, Janet Lewis
See also CA 9-12R; CANR 29; CAP 1;
DLBY 87

Lewis, Matthew Gregory
1775-1818 .... NCLC 11
See also DLB 39

Lewis, (Harry) Sinclair
1885-1951 ..... TCLC 4, 13, 23, 39; DA;
WLC
See also CA 104; 133; CDALB 1917-1929;
DLB 9, 102; DLBD 1; MTCW

Lewis, (Percy) Wyndham
1884(?)-1957 .... TCLC 2, 9
See also CA 104; DLB 15

Lewisohn, Ludwig 1883-1955...... TCLC 19
See also CA 107; DLB 4, 9, 28, 102

Lezama Lima, Jose 1910-1976 ... CLC 4, 10
See also CA 77-80; DLB 113; HW

L'Heureux, John (Clarke) 1934-.... CLC 52
See also CA 13-16R; CANR 23, 45

Liddell, C. H.
See Kuttner, Henry

Lie, Jonas (Lauritz Idemil)
1833-1908(?) .... TCLC 5
See also CA 115

Lieber, Joel 1937-1971............. CLC 6
See also CA 73-76; 29-32R

Lieber, Stanley Martin
See Lee, Stan

Lieberman, Laurence (James)
1935- .... CLC 4, 36
See also CA 17-20R; CANR 8, 36

Lieksman, Anders
See Haavikko, Paavo Juhani

Li Fei-kan 1904-
See Pa Chin
See also CA 105

Lifton, Robert Jay 1926-.......... CLC 67
See also CA 17-20R; CANR 27; SATA 66

Lightfoot, Gordon 1938-.......... CLC 26
See also CA 109

Lightman, Alan P. 1948- .... CLC 81
See also CA 141

Ligotti, Thomas (Robert)
1953- .... CLC 44; SSC 16
See also CA 123; CANR 49

Li Ho 791-817.................... PC 12

Liliencron, (Friedrich Adolf Axel) Detlev von
1844-1909 .... TCLC 18
See also CA 117

Lilly, William 1602-1681............ LC 27

Lima, Jose Lezama
See Lezama Lima, Jose

Lima Barreto, Afonso Henrique de
1881-1922 .... TCLC 23
See also CA 117

Limonov, Edward 1944-.......... CLC 67
See also CA 137

Lin, Frank
See Atherton, Gertrude (Franklin Horn)

Lincoln, Abraham 1809-1865..... NCLC 18

Lind, Jakov .... CLC 1, 2, 4, 27, 82
See also Landwirth, Heinz
See also CAAS 4

Lindbergh, Anne (Spencer) Morrow
1906- .... CLC 82
See also CA 17-20R; CANR 16; MTCW;
SATA 33

Lindsay, David 1878-1945 .... TCLC 15
See also CA 113

Lindsay, (Nicholas) Vachel
1879-1931 .... TCLC 17; DA; WLC
See also CA 114; 135; CDALB 1865-1917;
DLB 54; SATA 40

Linke-Poot
See Doeblin, Alfred

Linney, Romulus 1930- .... CLC 51
See also CA 1-4R; CANR 40, 44

Linton, Eliza Lynn 1822-1898.... NCLC 41
See also DLB 18

Li Po 701-763.................... CMLC 2

Lipsius, Justus 1547-1606 .... LC 16

Lipsyte, Robert (Michael)
1938-.................... CLC 21; DA
See also AAYA 7; CA 17-20R; CANR 8;
CLR 23; JRDA; MAICYA; SATA 5, 68

Lish, Gordon (Jay) 1934-.. CLC 45; SSC 18
See also CA 113; 117; DLB 130

Lispector, Clarice 1925-1977....... CLC 43
  See also CA 139; 116; DLB 113

Littell, Robert 1935(?)- .... CLC 42
  See also CA 109; 112

Little, Malcolm 1925-1965
  See Malcolm X
  See also BW 1; CA 125; 111; DA; MTCW

Littlewit, Humphrey Gent.
  See Lovecraft, H(oward) P(hillips)

Litwos
  See Sienkiewicz, Henryk (Adam Alexander
    Pius)

Liu E 1857-1909............... TCLC 15
  See also CA 115

Lively, Penelope (Margaret)
  1933-.................... CLC 32, 50
  See also CA 41-44R; CANR 29; CLR 7;
    DLB 14; JRDA; MAICYA; MTCW;
    SATA 7, 60

Livesay, Dorothy (Kathleen)
  1909-.................. CLC 4, 15, 79
  See also AITN 2; CA 25-28R; CAAS 8;
    CANR 36; DLB 68; MTCW

Livy c. 59B.C.-c. 17 .... CMLC 11

Lizardi, Jose Joaquin Fernandez de
  1776-1827 .... NCLC 30

Llewellyn, Richard
  See Llewellyn Lloyd, Richard Dafydd
    Vivian
  See also DLB 15

Llewellyn Lloyd, Richard Dafydd Vivian
  1906-1983 .... CLC 7, 80
  See also Llewellyn, Richard
  See also CA 53-56; 111; CANR 7;
    SATA 11; SATA-Obit 37

Llosa, (Jorge) Mario (Pedro) Vargas
  See Vargas Llosa, (Jorge) Mario (Pedro)

Lloyd Webber, Andrew 1948-
  See Webber, Andrew Lloyd
  See also AAYA 1; CA 116; SATA 56

Llull, Ramon c. 1235-c. 1316..... CMLC 12

Locke, Alain (Le Roy)
  1886-1954 .... TCLC 43
  See also BW 1; CA 106; 124; DLB 51

Locke, John 1632-1704 .... LC 7
  See also DLB 101

Locke-Elliott, Sumner
  See Elliott, Sumner Locke

Lockhart, John Gibson
  1794-1854 .... NCLC 6
  See also DLB 110, 116, 144

Lodge, David (John) 1935-......... CLC 36
  See also BEST 90:1; CA 17-20R; CANR 19;
    DLB 14; MTCW

Loennbohm, Armas Eino Leopold 1878-1926
  See Leino, Eino
  See also CA 123

Loewinsohn, Ron(ald William)
  1937-..................... CLC 52
  See also CA 25-28R

Logan, Jake
  See Smith, Martin Cruz

Logan, John (Burton) 1923-1987..... CLC 5
  See also CA 77-80; 124; CANR 45; DLB 5

Lo Kuan-chung 1330(?)-1400(?)...... LC 12

Lombard, Nap
  See Johnson, Pamela Hansford

London, Jack.. TCLC 9, 15, 39; SSC 4; WLC
  See also London, John Griffith
  See also AAYA 13; AITN 2;
    CDALB 1865-1917; DLB 8, 12, 78;
    SATA 18

London, John Griffith 1876-1916
  See London, Jack
  See also CA 110; 119; DA; JRDA;
    MAICYA; MTCW

Long, Emmett
  See Leonard, Elmore (John, Jr.)

Longbaugh, Harry
  See Goldman, William (W.)

Longfellow, Henry Wadsworth
  1807-1882 .... NCLC 2, 45; DA
  See also CDALB 1640-1865; DLB 1, 59;
    SATA 19

Longley, Michael 1939-........... CLC 29
  See also CA 102; DLB 40

Longus fl. c. 2nd cent. -.......... CMLC 7

Longway, A. Hugh
  See Lang, Andrew

Lopate, Phillip 1943-............ CLC 29
  See also CA 97-100; DLBY 80

Lopez Portillo (y Pacheco), Jose
  1920-.................... CLC 46
  See also CA 129; HW

Lopez y Fuentes, Gregorio
  1897(?)-1966 .... CLC 32
  See also CA 131; HW

Lorca, Federico Garcia
  See Garcia Lorca, Federico

Lord, Bette Bao 1938-............ CLC 23
  See also BEST 90:3; CA 107; CANR 41;
    SATA 58

Lord Auch
  See Bataille, Georges

Lord Byron
  See Byron, George Gordon (Noel)

Lorde, Audre (Geraldine)
  1934-1992 .... CLC 18, 71; BLC; PC 12
  See also BW 1; CA 25-28R; 142; CANR 16,
    26, 46; DLB 41; MTCW

Lord Jeffrey
  See Jeffrey, Francis

Lorenzo, Heberto Padilla
  See Padilla (Lorenzo), Heberto

Loris
  See Hofmannsthal, Hugo von

Loti, Pierre .... TCLC 11
  See also Viaud, (Louis Marie) Julien
  See also DLB 123

Louie, David Wong 1954- .... CLC 70
  See also CA 139

Louis, Father M.
  See Merton, Thomas

Lovecraft, H(oward) P(hillips)
  1890-1937 .... TCLC 4, 22; SSC 3
  See also AAYA 14; CA 104; 133; MTCW

Lovelace, Earl 1935-.............. CLC 51
  See also BW 2; CA 77-80; CANR 41;
    DLB 125; MTCW

Lovelace, Richard 1618-1657....... LC 24
  See also DLB 131

Lowell, Amy 1874-1925.. TCLC 1, 8; PC 12
  See also CA 104; DLB 54, 140

Lowell, James Russell 1819-1891 .. NCLC 2
  See also CDALB 1640-1865; DLB 1, 11, 64,
    79

Lowell, Robert (Traill Spence, Jr.)
  1917-1977 ... CLC 1, 2, 3, 4, 5, 8, 9, 11,
    15, 37; DA; PC 3; WLC
  See also CA 9-12R; 73-76; CABS 2;
    CANR 26; DLB 5; MTCW

Lowndes, Marie Adelaide (Belloc)
  1868-1947 .... TCLC 12
  See also CA 107; DLB 70

Lowry, (Clarence) Malcolm
  1909-1957 .... TCLC 6, 40
  See also CA 105; 131; CDBLB 1945-1960;
    DLB 15; MTCW

Lowry, Mina Gertrude 1882-1966
  See Loy, Mina
  See also CA 113

Loxsmith, John
  See Brunner, John (Kilian Houston)

Loy, Mina .... CLC 28
  See also Lowry, Mina Gertrude
  See also DLB 4, 54

Loyson-Bridet
  See Schwob, (Mayer Andre) Marcel

Lucas, Craig 1951-............... CLC 64
  See also CA 137

Lucas, George 1944-............. CLC 16
  See also AAYA 1; CA 77-80; CANR 30;
    SATA 56

Lucas, Hans
  See Godard, Jean-Luc

Lucas, Victoria
  See Plath, Sylvia

Ludlam, Charles 1943-1987..... CLC 46, 50
  See also CA 85-88; 122

Ludlum, Robert 1927- .... CLC 22, 43
  See also AAYA 10; BEST 89:1, 90:3;
    CA 33-36R; CANR 25, 41; DLBY 82;
    MTCW

Ludwig, Ken...................... CLC 60

Ludwig, Otto 1813-1865.......... NCLC 4
  See also DLB 129

Lugones, Leopoldo 1874-1938 ..... TCLC 15
  See also CA 116; 131; HW

Lu Hsun 1881-1936 ...... TCLC 3; SSC 20
  See also Shu-Jen, Chou

Lukacs, George .... CLC 24
  See also Lukacs, Gyorgy (Szegeny von)

Lukacs, Gyorgy (Szegeny von) 1885-1971
  See Lukacs, George
  See also CA 101; 29-32R

Luke, Peter (Ambrose Cyprian)
  1919-1995 .... CLC 38
  See also CA 81-84; 147; DLB 13

Lunar, Dennis
  See Mungo, Raymond

Lurie, Alison 1926-........CLC 4, 5, 18, 39
See also CA 1-4R; CANR 2, 17; DLB 2;
MTCW; SATA 46

Lustig, Arnost 1926-.............CLC 56
See also AAYA 3; CA 69-72; CANR 47;
SATA 56

Luther, Martin 1483-1546...........LC 9

Luzi, Mario 1914-...............CLC 13
See also CA 61-64; CANR 9; DLB 128

Lynch, B. Suarez
See Bioy Casares, Adolfo; Borges, Jorge
Luis

Lynch, David (K.) 1946-...........CLC 66
See also CA 124; 129

Lynch, James
See Andreyev, Leonid (Nikolaevich)

Lynch Davis, B.
See Bioy Casares, Adolfo; Borges, Jorge
Luis

Lyndsay, Sir David 1490-1555 ......LC 20

Lynn, Kenneth S(chuyler) 1923-....CLC 50
See also CA 1-4R; CANR 3, 27

Lynx
See West, Rebecca

Lyons, Marcus
See Blish, James (Benjamin)

Lyre, Pinchbeck
See Sassoon, Siegfried (Lorraine)

Lytle, Andrew (Nelson) 1902-......CLC 22
See also CA 9-12R; DLB 6

Lyttelton, George 1709-1773........LC 10

Maas, Peter 1929-..............CLC 29
See also CA 93-96

Macaulay, Rose 1881-1958 .....TCLC 7, 44
See also CA 104; DLB 36

Macaulay, Thomas Babington
1800-1859 ....NCLC 42
See also CDBLB 1832-1890; DLB 32, 55

MacBeth, George (Mann)
1932-1992 ....CLC 2, 5, 9
See also CA 25-28R; 136; DLB 40; MTCW;
SATA 4; SATA-Obit 70

MacCaig, Norman (Alexander)
1910- ....CLC 36
See also CA 9-12R; CANR 3, 34; DLB 27

MacCarthy, (Sir Charles Otto) Desmond
1877-1952 ....TCLC 36

MacDiarmid, Hugh
............CLC 2, 4, 11, 19, 63; PC 9
See also Grieve, C(hristopher) M(urray)
See also CDBLB 1945-1960; DLB 20

MacDonald, Anson
See Heinlein, Robert A(nson)

Macdonald, Cynthia 1928-......CLC 13, 19
See also CA 49-52; CANR 4, 44; DLB 105

MacDonald, George 1824-1905.....TCLC 9
See also CA 106; 137; DLB 18; MAICYA;
SATA 33

Macdonald, John
See Millar, Kenneth

MacDonald, John D(ann)
1916-1986 ....CLC 3, 27, 44
See also CA 1-4R; 121; CANR 1, 19;
DLB 8; DLBY 86; MTCW

Macdonald, John Ross
See Millar, Kenneth

Macdonald, Ross..... CLC 1, 2, 3, 14, 34, 41
See also Millar, Kenneth
See also DLBD 6

MacDougal, John
See Blish, James (Benjamin)

MacEwen, Gwendolyn (Margaret)
1941-1987 ....CLC 13, 55
See also CA 9-12R; 124; CANR 7, 22;
DLB 53; SATA 50; SATA-Obit 55

Macha, Karel Hynek 1810-1846.. NCLC 46

Machado (y Ruiz), Antonio
1875-1939 ....TCLC 3
See also CA 104; DLB 108

Machado de Assis, Joaquim Maria
1839-1908 ....TCLC 10; BLC
See also CA 107

Machen, Arthur.......... TCLC 4; SSC 20
See also Jones, Arthur Llewellyn
See also DLB 36

Machiavelli, Niccolo 1469-1527 .. LC 8; DA

MacInnes, Colin 1914-1976......CLC 4, 23
See also CA 69-72; 65-68; CANR 21;
DLB 14; MTCW

MacInnes, Helen (Clark)
1907-1985 ....CLC 27, 39
See also CA 1-4R; 117; CANR 1, 28;
DLB 87; MTCW; SATA 22;
SATA-Obit 44

Mackay, Mary 1855-1924
See Corelli, Marie
See also CA 118

Mackenzie, Compton (Edward Montague)
1883-1972 ....CLC 18
See also CA 21-22; 37-40R; CAP 2;
DLB 34, 100

Mackenzie, Henry 1745-1831 .... NCLC 41
See also DLB 39

Mackintosh, Elizabeth 1896(?)-1952
See Tey, Josephine
See also CA 110

MacLaren, James
See Grieve, C(hristopher) M(urray)

Mac Laverty, Bernard 1942-.......CLC 31
See also CA 116; 118; CANR 43

MacLean, Alistair (Stuart)
1922-1987 ....CLC 3, 13, 50, 63
See also CA 57-60; 121; CANR 28; MTCW;
SATA 23; SATA-Obit 50

Maclean, Norman (Fitzroy)
1902-1990 ....CLC 78; SSC 13
See also CA 102; 132; CANR 49

MacLeish, Archibald
1892-1982 ....CLC 3, 8, 14, 68
See also CA 9-12R; 106; CANR 33; DLB 4,
7, 45; DLBY 82; MTCW

MacLennan, (John) Hugh
1907-1990 ....CLC 2, 14
See also CA 5-8R; 142; CANR 33; DLB 68;
MTCW

MacLeod, Alistair 1936- ....CLC 56
See also CA 123; DLB 60

MacNeice, (Frederick) Louis
1907-1963 ....CLC 1, 4, 10, 53
See also CA 85-88; DLB 10, 20; MTCW

MacNeill, Dand
See Fraser, George MacDonald

Macpherson, James 1736-1796 .....LC 29
See also DLB 109

Macpherson, (Jean) Jay 1931-......CLC 14
See also CA 5-8R; DLB 53

MacShane, Frank 1927-...........CLC 39
See also CA 9-12R; CANR 3, 33; DLB 111

Macumber, Mari
See Sandoz, Mari(e Susette)

Madach, Imre 1823-1864........ NCLC 19

Madden, (Jerry) David 1933- .... CLC 5, 15
See also CA 1-4R; CAAS 3; CANR 4, 45;
DLB 6; MTCW

Maddern, Al(an)
See Ellison, Harlan (Jay)

Madhubuti, Haki R.
1942-.......... CLC 6, 73; BLC; PC 5
See also Lee, Don L.
See also BW 2; CA 73-76; CANR 24;
DLB 5, 41; DLBD 8

Maepenn, Hugh
See Kuttner, Henry

Maepenn, K. H.
See Kuttner, Henry

Maeterlinck, Maurice 1862-1949 ... TCLC 3
See also CA 104; 136; SATA 66

Maginn, William 1794-1842...... NCLC 8
See also DLB 110

Mahapatra, Jayanta 1928-......... CLC 33
See also CA 73-76; CAAS 9; CANR 15, 33

Mahfouz, Naguib (Abdel Aziz Al-Sabilgi)
1911(?)-
See Mahfuz, Najib
See also BEST 89:2; CA 128; MTCW

Mahfuz, Najib................. CLC 52, 55
See also Mahfouz, Naguib (Abdel Aziz
Al-Sabilgi)
See also DLBY 88

Mahon, Derek 1941-.............. CLC 27
See also CA 113; 128; DLB 40

Mailer, Norman
1923-...... CLC 1, 2, 3, 4, 5, 8, 11, 14,
28, 39, 74; DA
See also AITN 2; CA 9-12R; CABS 1;
CANR 28; CDALB 1968-1988; DLB 2,
16, 28; DLBD 3; DLBY 80, 83; MTCW

Maillet, Antonine 1929-.......... CLC 54
See also CA 115; 120; CANR 46; DLB 60

Mais, Roger 1905-1955 .... TCLC 8
See also BW 1; CA 105; 124; DLB 125;
MTCW

Maistre, Joseph de 1753-1821 .... NCLC 37

Maitland, Sara (Louise) 1950-...... CLC 49
See also CA 69-72; CANR 13

Major, Clarence
1936-............. CLC 3, 19, 48; BLC
See also BW 2; CA 21-24R; CAAS 6;
CANR 13, 25; DLB 33

Major, Kevin (Gerald) 1949- . . . . . . **CLC 26**
See also CA 97-100; CANR 21, 38;
CLR 11; DLB 60; JRDA; MAICYA;
SATA 32

Maki, James
See Ozu, Yasujiro

Malabaila, Damiano
See Levi, Primo

Malamud, Bernard
1914-1986 . . . . . . **CLC 1, 2, 3, 5, 8, 9, 11,**
18, 27, 44, 78, 85; DA; SSC 15; WLC
See also CA 5-8R; 118; CABS 1; CANR 28;
CDALB 1941-1968; DLB 2, 28, 152;
DLBY 80, 86; MTCW

Malaparte, Curzio 1898-1957 . . . . . **TCLC 52**

Malcolm, Dan
See Silverberg, Robert

Malcolm X . . . . **CLC 82; BLC**
See also Little, Malcolm

Malherbe, Francois de 1555-1628 . . . . . **LC 5**

Mallarme, Stephane
1842-1898 . . . . **NCLC 4, 41; PC 4**

Mallet-Joris, Francoise 1930- . . . . . . **CLC 11**
See also CA 65-68; CANR 17; DLB 83

Malley, Ern
See McAuley, James Phillip

Mallowan, Agatha Christie
See Christie, Agatha (Mary Clarissa)

Maloff, Saul 1922- . . . . **CLC 5**
See also CA 33-36R

Malone, Louis
See MacNeice, (Frederick) Louis

Malone, Michael (Christopher)
1942- . . . . **CLC 43**
See also CA 77-80; CANR 14, 32

Malory, (Sir) Thomas
1410(?)-1471(?) . . . . **LC 11; DA**
See also CDBLB Before 1660; DLB 146;
SATA 59; SATA-Brief 33

Malouf, (George Joseph) David
1934- . . . . **CLC 28, 86**
See also CA 124

Malraux, (Georges-)Andre
1901-1976 . . . . . **CLC 1, 4, 9, 13, 15, 57**
See also CA 21-22; 69-72; CANR 34;
CAP 2; DLB 72; MTCW

Malzberg, Barry N(athaniel) 1939- . . . **CLC 7**
See also CA 61-64; CAAS 4; CANR 16;
DLB 8

Mamet, David (Alan)
1947- . . . . **CLC 9, 15, 34, 46; DC 4**
See also AAYA 3; CA 81-84; CABS 3;
CANR 15, 41; DLB 7; MTCW

Mamoulian, Rouben (Zachary)
1897-1987 . . . . **CLC 16**
See also CA 25-28R; 124

Mandelstam, Osip (Emilievich)
1891(?)-1938(?) . . . . **TCLC 2, 6**
See also CA 104

Mander, (Mary) Jane 1877-1949 . . . **TCLC 31**

Mandiargues, Andre Pieyre de . . . . . . **CLC 41**
See also Pieyre de Mandiargues, Andre
See also DLB 83

Mandrake, Ethel Belle
See Thurman, Wallace (Henry)

Mangan, James Clarence
1803-1849 . . . . **NCLC 27**

Maniere, J.-E.
See Giraudoux, (Hippolyte) Jean

Manley, (Mary) Delariviere
1672(?)-1724 . . . . **LC 1**
See also DLB 39, 80

Mann, Abel
See Creasey, John

Mann, (Luiz) Heinrich 1871-1950 . . . **TCLC 9**
See also CA 106; DLB 66

Mann, (Paul) Thomas
1875-1955 . . . . **TCLC 2, 8, 14, 21, 35, 44,**
60; DA; SSC 5; WLC
See also CA 104; 128; DLB 66; MTCW

Manning, David
See Faust, Frederick (Schiller)

Manning, Frederic 1887(?)-1935 . . . **TCLC 25**
See also CA 124

Manning, Olivia 1915-1980 . . . . . . **CLC 5, 19**
See also CA 5-8R; 101; CANR 29; MTCW

Mano, D. Keith 1942- . . . . **CLC 2, 10**
See also CA 25-28R; CAAS 6; CANR 26;
DLB 6

Mansfield, Katherine
. . . . **TCLC 2, 8, 39; SSC 9; WLC**
See also Beauchamp, Kathleen Mansfield

Manso, Peter 1940- . . . . **CLC 39**
See also CA 29-32R; CANR 44

Mantecon, Juan Jimenez
See Jimenez (Mantecon), Juan Ramon

Manton, Peter
See Creasey, John

Man Without a Spleen, A
See Chekhov, Anton (Pavlovich)

Manzoni, Alessandro 1785-1873 . . **NCLC 29**

Mapu, Abraham (ben Jekutiel)
1808-1867 . . . . **NCLC 18**

Mara, Sally
See Queneau, Raymond

Marat, Jean Paul 1743-1793 . . . . **LC 10**

Marcel, Gabriel Honore
1889-1973 . . . . **CLC 15**
See also CA 102; 45-48; MTCW

Marchbanks, Samuel
See Davies, (William) Robertson

Marchi, Giacomo
See Bassani, Giorgio

Margulies, Donald . . . . **CLC 76**

Marie de France c. 12th cent. - . . . . **CMLC 8**

Marie de l'Incarnation 1599-1672 . . . **LC 10**

Mariner, Scott
See Pohl, Frederik

Marinetti, Filippo Tommaso
1876-1944 . . . . **TCLC 10**
See also CA 107; DLB 114

Marivaux, Pierre Carlet de Chamblain de
1688-1763 . . . . **LC 4**

Markandaya, Kamala . . . . **CLC 8, 38**
See also Taylor, Kamala (Purnaiya)

Markfield, Wallace 1926- . . . . **CLC 8**
See also CA 69-72; CAAS 3; DLB 2, 28

Markham, Edwin 1852-1940 . . . . . **TCLC 47**
See also DLB 54

Markham, Robert
See Amis, Kingsley (William)

Marks, J
See Highwater, Jamake (Mamake)

Marks-Highwater, J
See Highwater, Jamake (Mamake)

Markson, David M(errill) 1927- . . . . **CLC 67**
See also CA 49-52; CANR 1

Marley, Bob . . . . **CLC 17**
See also Marley, Robert Nesta

Marley, Robert Nesta 1945-1981
See Marley, Bob
See also CA 107; 103

Marlowe, Christopher
1564-1593 . . . . . **LC 22; DA; DC 1; WLC**
See also CDBLB Before 1660; DLB 62

Marmontel, Jean-Francois
1723-1799 . . . . **LC 2**

Marquand, John P(hillips)
1893-1960 . . . . **CLC 2, 10**
See also CA 85-88; DLB 9, 102

Marquez, Gabriel (Jose) Garcia
See Garcia Marquez, Gabriel (Jose)

Marquis, Don(ald Robert Perry)
1878-1937 . . . . **TCLC 7**
See also CA 104; DLB 11, 25

Marric, J. J.
See Creasey, John

Marrow, Bernard
See Moore, Brian

Marryat, Frederick 1792-1848 . . . . **NCLC 3**
See also DLB 21

Marsden, James
See Creasey, John

Marsh, (Edith) Ngaio
1899-1982 . . . . **CLC 7, 53**
See also CA 9-12R; CANR 6; DLB 77;
MTCW

Marshall, Garry 1934- . . . . **CLC 17**
See also AAYA 3; CA 111; SATA 60

Marshall, Paule
1929- . . . . **CLC 27, 72; BLC; SSC 3**
See also BW 2; CA 77-80; CANR 25;
DLB 33; MTCW

Marsten, Richard
See Hunter, Evan

Martha, Henry
See Harris, Mark

Martial c. 40-c. 104 . . . . **PC 10**

Martin, Ken
See Hubbard, L(afayette) Ron(ald)

Martin, Richard
See Creasey, John

Martin, Steve 1945- . . . . **CLC 30**
See also CA 97-100; CANR 30; MTCW

Martin, Valerie 1948- . . . . **CLC 89**
See also BEST 90:2; CA 85-88; CANR 49

Martin, Violet Florence
1862-1915 . . . . **TCLC 51**

Martin, Webber
See Silverberg, Robert

Martindale, Patrick Victor
See White, Patrick (Victor Martindale)

Martin du Gard, Roger
1881-1958 .... TCLC 24
See also CA 118; DLB 65

Martineau, Harriet 1802-1876.... NCLC 26
See also DLB 21, 55; YABC 2

Martines, Julia
See O'Faolain, Julia

Martinez, Jacinto Benavente y
See Benavente (y Martinez), Jacinto

Martinez Ruiz, Jose 1873-1967
See Azorin; Ruiz, Jose Martinez
See also CA 93-96; HW

Martinez Sierra, Gregorio
1881-1947 .... TCLC 6
See also CA 115

Martinez Sierra, Maria (de la O'LeJarraga)
1874-1974 .... TCLC 6
See also CA 115

Martinsen, Martin
See Follett, Ken(neth Martin)

Martinson, Harry (Edmund)
1904-1978 .... CLC 14
See also CA 77-80; CANR 34

Marut, Ret
See Traven, B.

Marut, Robert
See Traven, B.

Marvell, Andrew
1621-1678 ..... LC 4; DA; PC 10; WLC
See also CDBLB 1660-1789; DLB 131

Marx, Karl (Heinrich)
1818-1883 .... NCLC 17
See also DLB 129

Masaoka Shiki .... TCLC 18
See also Masaoka Tsunenori

Masaoka Tsunenori 1867-1902
See Masaoka Shiki
See also CA 117

Masefield, John (Edward)
1878-1967 .... CLC 11, 47
See also CA 19-20; 25-28R; CANR 33;
CAP 2; CDBLB 1890-1914; DLB 10, 19,
153; MTCW; SATA 19

Maso, Carole 19(?)- .... CLC 44

Mason, Bobbie Ann
1940- .... CLC 28, 43, 82; SSC 4
See also AAYA 5; CA 53-56; CANR 11,
31; DLBY 87; MTCW

Mason, Ernst
See Pohl, Frederik

Mason, Lee W.
See Malzberg, Barry N(athaniel)

Mason, Nick 1945- .... CLC 35

Mason, Tally
See Derleth, August (William)

Mass, William
See Gibson, William

Masters, Edgar Lee
1868-1950 ...... TCLC 2, 25; DA; PC 1
See also CA 104; 133; CDALB 1865-1917;
DLB 54; MTCW

Masters, Hilary 1928- .... CLC 48
See also CA 25-28R; CANR 13, 47

Mastrosimone, William 19(?)- ...... CLC 36

Mathe, Albert
See Camus, Albert

Matheson, Richard Burton 1926- ... CLC 37
See also CA 97-100; DLB 8, 44

Mathews, Harry 1930- .... CLC 6, 52
See also CA 21-24R; CAAS 6; CANR 18,
40

Mathews, John Joseph 1894-1979... CLC 84
See also CA 19-20; 142; CANR 45; CAP 2;
NNAL

Mathias, Roland (Glyn) 1915- ...... CLC 45
See also CA 97-100; CANR 19, 41; DLB 27

Matsuo Basho 1644-1694........... PC 3

Mattheson, Rodney
See Creasey, John

Matthews, Greg 1949- .... CLC 45
See also CA 135

Matthews, William 1942-......... CLC 40
See also CA 29-32R; CAAS 18; CANR 12;
DLB 5

Matthias, John (Edward) 1941-...... CLC 9
See also CA 33-36R

Matthiessen, Peter
1927- .... CLC 5, 7, 11, 32, 64
See also AAYA 6; BEST 90:4; CA 9-12R;
CANR 21; DLB 6; MTCW; SATA 27

Maturin, Charles Robert
1780(?)-1824 .... NCLC 6

Matute (Ausejo), Ana Maria
1925- .... CLC 11
See also CA 89-92; MTCW

Maugham, W. S.
See Maugham, W(illiam) Somerset

Maugham, W(illiam) Somerset
1874-1965 ...... CLC 1, 11, 15, 67; DA;
SSC 8; WLC
See also CA 5-8R; 25-28R; CANR 40;
CDBLB 1914-1945; DLB 10, 36, 77, 100;
MTCW; SATA 54

Maugham, William Somerset
See Maugham, W(illiam) Somerset

Maupassant, (Henri Rene Albert) Guy de
1850-1893 .... NCLC 1, 42; DA; SSC 1;
WLC
See also DLB 123

Maurhut, Richard
See Traven, B.

Mauriac, Claude 1914-............ CLC 9
See also CA 89-92; DLB 83

Mauriac, Francois (Charles)
1885-1970 .... CLC 4, 9, 56
See also CA 25-28; CAP 2; DLB 65;
MTCW

Mavor, Osborne Henry 1888-1951
See Bridie, James
See also CA 104

Maxwell, William (Keepers, Jr.)
1908- .... CLC 19
See also CA 93-96; DLBY 80

May, Elaine 1932- .... CLC 16
See also CA 124; 142; DLB 44

Mayakovski, Vladimir (Vladimirovich)
1893-1930 .... TCLC 4, 18
See also CA 104

Mayhew, Henry 1812-1887 ...... NCLC 31
See also DLB 18, 55

Mayle, Peter 1939(?)-............ CLC 89
See also CA 139

Maynard, Joyce 1953- .... CLC 23
See also CA 111; 129

Mayne, William (James Carter)
1928- .... CLC 12
See also CA 9-12R; CANR 37; CLR 25;
JRDA; MAICYA; SAAS 11; SATA 6, 68

Mayo, Jim
See L'Amour, Louis (Dearborn)

Maysles, Albert 1926- .... CLC 16
See also CA 29-32R

Maysles, David 1932-............ CLC 16

Mazer, Norma Fox 1931- .... CLC 26
See also AAYA 5; CA 69-72; CANR 12,
32; CLR 23; JRDA; MAICYA; SAAS 1;
SATA 24, 67

Mazzini, Guiseppe 1805-1872 .... NCLC 34

McAuley, James Phillip
1917-1976 .... CLC 45
See also CA 97-100

McBain, Ed
See Hunter, Evan

McBrien, William Augustine
1930- .... CLC 44
See also CA 107

McCaffrey, Anne (Inez) 1926-...... CLC 17
See also AAYA 6; AITN 2; BEST 89:2;
CA 25-28R; CANR 15, 35; DLB 8;
JRDA; MAICYA; MTCW; SAAS 11;
SATA 8, 70

McCall, Nathan 1955(?)- .... CLC 86
See also CA 146

McCann, Arthur
See Campbell, John W(ood, Jr.)

McCann, Edson
See Pohl, Frederik

McCarthy, Charles, Jr. 1933-
See McCarthy, Cormac
See also CANR 42

McCarthy, Cormac 1933-..... CLC 4, 57, 59
See also McCarthy, Charles, Jr.
See also DLB 6, 143

McCarthy, Mary (Therese)
1912-1989 ... CLC 1, 3, 5, 14, 24, 39, 59
See also CA 5-8R; 129; CANR 16; DLB 2;
DLBY 81; MTCW

McCartney, (James) Paul
1942- .... CLC 12, 35
See also CA 146

McCauley, Stephen (D.) 1955- ..... CLC 50
See also CA 141

McClure, Michael (Thomas)
1932- . . . . **CLC 6, 10**
See also CA 21-24R; CANR 17, 46;
DLB 16

McCorkle, Jill (Collins) 1958- . . . . . . **CLC 51**
See also CA 121; DLBY 87

McCourt, James 1941- . . . . **CLC 5**
See also CA 57-60

McCoy, Horace (Stanley)
1897-1955 . . . . **TCLC 28**
See also CA 108; DLB 9

McCrae, John 1872-1918 . . . . **TCLC 12**
See also CA 109; DLB 92

McCreigh, James
See Pohl, Frederik

McCullers, (Lula) Carson (Smith)
1917-1967 . . . . **CLC 1, 4, 10, 12, 48; DA;**
SSC 9; WLC
See also CA 5-8R; 25-28R; CABS 1, 3;
CANR 18; CDALB 1941-1968; DLB 2, 7;
MTCW; SATA 27

McCulloch, John Tyler
See Burroughs, Edgar Rice

McCullough, Colleen 1938(?)- . . . . . . **CLC 27**
See also CA 81-84; CANR 17, 46; MTCW

McElroy, Joseph 1930- . . . . **CLC 5, 47**
See also CA 17-20R

McEwan, Ian (Russell) 1948- . . . **CLC 13, 66**
See also BEST 90:4; CA 61-64; CANR 14,
41; DLB 14; MTCW

McFadden, David 1940- . . . . **CLC 48**
See also CA 104; DLB 60

McFarland, Dennis 1950- . . . . **CLC 65**

McGahern, John
1934- . . . . **CLC 5, 9, 48; SSC 17**
See also CA 17-20R; CANR 29; DLB 14;
MTCW

McGinley, Patrick (Anthony)
1937- . . . . **CLC 41**
See also CA 120; 127

McGinley, Phyllis 1905-1978 . . . . . . **CLC 14**
See also CA 9-12R; 77-80; CANR 19;
DLB 11, 48; SATA 2, 44; SATA-Obit 24

McGinniss, Joe 1942- . . . . **CLC 32**
See also AITN 2; BEST 89:2; CA 25-28R;
CANR 26

McGivern, Maureen Daly
See Daly, Maureen

McGrath, Patrick 1950- . . . . **CLC 55**
See also CA 136

McGrath, Thomas (Matthew)
1916-1990 . . . . **CLC 28, 59**
See also CA 9-12R; 132; CANR 6, 33;
MTCW; SATA 41; SATA-Obit 66

McGuane, Thomas (Francis III)
1939- . . . . **CLC 3, 7, 18, 45**
See also AITN 2; CA 49-52; CANR 5, 24,
49; DLB 2; DLBY 80; MTCW

McGuckian, Medbh 1950- . . . . **CLC 48**
See also CA 143; DLB 40

McHale, Tom 1942(?)-1982 . . . . . . **CLC 3, 5**
See also AITN 1; CA 77-80; 106

McIlvanney, William 1936- . . . . **CLC 42**
See also CA 25-28R; DLB 14

McIlwraith, Maureen Mollie Hunter
See Hunter, Mollie
See also SATA 2

McInerney, Jay 1955- . . . . **CLC 34**
See also CA 116; 123; CANR 45

McIntyre, Vonda N(eel) 1948- . . . . . **CLC 18**
See also CA 81-84; CANR 17, 34; MTCW

McKay, Claude . . . . . **TCLC 7, 41; BLC; PC 2**
See also McKay, Festus Claudius
See also DLB 4, 45, 51, 117

McKay, Festus Claudius 1889-1948
See McKay, Claude
See also BW 1; CA 104; 124; DA; MTCW;
WLC

McKuen, Rod 1933- . . . . **CLC 1, 3**
See also AITN 1; CA 41-44R; CANR 40

McLoughlin, R. B.
See Mencken, H(enry) L(ouis)

McLuhan, (Herbert) Marshall
1911-1980 . . . . **CLC 37, 83**
See also CA 9-12R; 102; CANR 12, 34;
DLB 88; MTCW

McMillan, Terry (L.) 1951- . . . . . **CLC 50, 61**
See also BW 2; CA 140

McMurtry, Larry (Jeff)
1936- . . . . **CLC 2, 3, 7, 11, 27, 44**
See also AITN 2; BEST 89:2; CA 5-8R;
CANR 19, 43; CDALB 1968-1988;
DLB 2, 143; DLBY 80, 87; MTCW

McNally, T. M. 1961- . . . . **CLC 82**

McNally, Terrence 1939- . . . . . . **CLC 4, 7, 41**
See also CA 45-48; CANR 2; DLB 7

McNamer, Deirdre 1950- . . . . **CLC 70**

McNeile, Herman Cyril 1888-1937
See Sapper
See also DLB 77

McNickle, (William) D'Arcy
1904-1977 . . . . **CLC 89**
See also CA 9-12R; 85-88; CANR 5, 45;
NNAL; SATA-Obit 22

McPhee, John (Angus) 1931- . . . . . . **CLC 36**
See also BEST 90:1; CA 65-68; CANR 20,
46; MTCW

McPherson, James Alan
1943- . . . . **CLC 19, 77**
See also BW 1; CA 25-28R; CAAS 17;
CANR 24; DLB 38; MTCW

McPherson, William (Alexander)
1933- . . . . **CLC 34**
See also CA 69-72; CANR 28

Mead, Margaret 1901-1978 . . . . **CLC 37**
See also AITN 1; CA 1-4R; 81-84;
CANR 4; MTCW; SATA-Obit 20

Meaker, Marijane (Agnes) 1927-
See Kerr, M. E.
See also CA 107; CANR 37; JRDA;
MAICYA; MTCW; SATA 20, 61

Medoff, Mark (Howard) 1940- . . . **CLC 6, 23**
See also AITN 1; CA 53-56; CANR 5;
DLB 7

Medvedev, P. N.
See Bakhtin, Mikhail Mikhailovich

Meged, Aharon
See Megged, Aharon

Meged, Aron
See Megged, Aharon

Megged, Aharon 1920- . . . . **CLC 9**
See also CA 49-52; CAAS 13; CANR 1

Mehta, Ved (Parkash) 1934- . . . . **CLC 37**
See also CA 1-4R; CANR 2, 23; MTCW

Melanter
See Blackmore, R(ichard) D(oddridge)

Melikow, Loris
See Hofmannsthal, Hugo von

Melmoth, Sebastian
See Wilde, Oscar (Fingal O'Flahertie Wills)

Meltzer, Milton 1915- . . . . **CLC 26**
See also AAYA 8; CA 13-16R; CANR 38;
CLR 13; DLB 61; JRDA; MAICYA;
SAAS 1; SATA 1, 50, 80

Melville, Herman
1819-1891 . . . . . **NCLC 3, 12, 29, 45, 49;**
DA; SSC 1, 17; WLC
See also CDALB 1640-1865; DLB 3, 74;
SATA 59

Menander
c. 342B.C.-c. 292B.C. . . . . **CMLC 9; DC 3**

Mencken, H(enry) L(ouis)
1880-1956 . . . . **TCLC 13**
See also CA 105; 125; CDALB 1917-1929;
DLB 11, 29, 63, 137; MTCW

Mercer, David 1928-1980 . . . . **CLC 5**
See also CA 9-12R; 102; CANR 23;
DLB 13; MTCW

Merchant, Paul
See Ellison, Harlan (Jay)

Meredith, George 1828-1909 . . . **TCLC 17, 43**
See also CA 117; CDBLB 1832-1890;
DLB 18, 35, 57

Meredith, William (Morris)
1919- . . . . **CLC 4, 13, 22, 55**
See also CA 9-12R; CAAS 14; CANR 6, 40;
DLB 5

Merezhkovsky, Dmitry Sergeyevich
1865-1941 . . . . **TCLC 29**

Merimee, Prosper
1803-1870 . . . . **NCLC 6; SSC 7**
See also DLB 119

Merkin, Daphne 1954- . . . . **CLC 44**
See also CA 123

Merlin, Arthur
See Blish, James (Benjamin)

Merrill, James (Ingram)
1926-1995 . . . . **CLC 2, 3, 6, 8, 13, 18, 34**
See also CA 13-16R; 147; CANR 10, 49;
DLB 5; DLBY 85; MTCW

Merriman, Alex
See Silverberg, Robert

Merritt, E. B.
See Waddington, Miriam

Merton, Thomas
1915-1968 . . **CLC 1, 3, 11, 34, 83; PC 10**
See also CA 5-8R; 25-28R; CANR 22;
DLB 48; DLBY 81; MTCW

Merwin, W(illiam) S(tanley)
1927- . . . **CLC 1, 2, 3, 5, 8, 13, 18, 45, 88**
See also CA 13-16R; CANR 15; DLB 5;
MTCW

Metcalf, John 1938- . . . . CLC 37
See also CA 113; DLB 60

Metcalf, Suzanne
See Baum, L(yman) Frank

Mew, Charlotte (Mary)
1870-1928 . . . . TCLC 8
See also CA 105; DLB 19, 135

Mewshaw, Michael 1943- . . . . CLC 9
See also CA 53-56; CANR 7, 47; DLBY 80

Meyer, June
See Jordan, June

Meyer, Lynn
See Slavitt, David R(ytman)

Meyer-Meyrink, Gustav 1868-1932
See Meyrink, Gustav
See also CA 117

Meyers, Jeffrey 1939- . . . . CLC 39
See also CA 73-76; DLB 111

Meynell, Alice (Christina Gertrude Thompson)
1847-1922 . . . . TCLC 6
See also CA 104; DLB 19, 98

Meyrink, Gustav . . . . TCLC 21
See also Meyer-Meyrink, Gustav
See also DLB 81

Michaels, Leonard
1933- . . . . CLC 6, 25; SSC 16
See also CA 61-64; CANR 21; DLB 130;
MTCW

Michaux, Henri 1899-1984 . . . . . . CLC 8, 19
See also CA 85-88; 114

Michelangelo 1475-1564 . . . . LC 12

Michelet, Jules 1798-1874 . . . . NCLC 31

Michener, James A(lbert)
1907(?)- . . . . CLC 1, 5, 11, 29, 60
See also AITN 1; BEST 90:1; CA 5-8R;
CANR 21, 45; DLB 6; MTCW

Mickiewicz, Adam 1798-1855 . . . . . NCLC 3

Middleton, Christopher 1926- . . . . . . CLC 13
See also CA 13-16R; CANR 29; DLB 40

Middleton, Richard (Barham)
1882-1911 . . . . TCLC 56

Middleton, Stanley 1919- . . . . CLC 7, 38
See also CA 25-28R; CANR 21, 46;
DLB 14

Middleton, Thomas 1580-1627 . . . . DC 5
See also DLB 58

Migueis, Jose Rodrigues 1901- . . . . . CLC 10

Mikszath, Kalman 1847-1910 . . . . . TCLC 31

Miles, Josephine
1911-1985 . . . . CLC 1, 2, 14, 34, 39
See also CA 1-4R; 116; CANR 2; DLB 48

Militant
See Sandburg, Carl (August)

Mill, John Stuart 1806-1873 . . . . . NCLC 11
See also CDBLB 1832-1890; DLB 55

Millar, Kenneth 1915-1983 . . . . CLC 14
See also Macdonald, Ross
See also CA 9-12R; 110; CANR 16; DLB 2;
DLBD 6; DLBY 83; MTCW

Millay, E. Vincent
See Millay, Edna St. Vincent

Millay, Edna St. Vincent
1892-1950 . . . . . TCLC 4, 49; DA; PC 6
See also CA 104; 130; CDALB 1917-1929;
DLB 45; MTCW

Miller, Arthur
1915- . . . . CLC 1, 2, 6, 10, 15, 26, 47, 78;
DA; DC 1; WLC
See also AITN 1; CA 1-4R; CABS 3;
CANR 2, 30; CDALB 1941-1968; DLB 7;
MTCW

Miller, Henry (Valentine)
1891-1980 . . . . CLC 1, 2, 4, 9, 14, 43, 84;
DA; WLC
See also CA 9-12R; 97-100; CANR 33;
CDALB 1929-1941; DLB 4, 9; DLBY 80;
MTCW

Miller, Jason 1939(?)- . . . . CLC 2
See also AITN 1; CA 73-76; DLB 7

Miller, Sue 1943- . . . . CLC 44
See also BEST 90:3; CA 139; DLB 143

Miller, Walter M(ichael, Jr.)
1923- . . . . CLC 4, 30
See also CA 85-88; DLB 8

Millett, Kate 1934- . . . . CLC 67
See also AITN 1; CA 73-76; CANR 32;
MTCW

Millhauser, Steven 1943- . . . . . . CLC 21, 54
See also CA 110; 111; DLB 2

Millin, Sarah Gertrude 1889-1968 . . CLC 49
See also CA 102; 93-96

Milne, A(lan) A(lexander)
1882-1956 . . . . TCLC 6
See also CA 104; 133; CLR 1, 26; DLB 10,
77, 100; MAICYA; MTCW; YABC 1

Milner, Ron(ald) 1938- . . . . CLC 56; BLC
See also AITN 1; BW 1; CA 73-76;
CANR 24; DLB 38; MTCW

Milosz, Czeslaw
1911- . . . CLC 5, 11, 22, 31, 56, 82; PC 8
See also CA 81-84; CANR 23; MTCW

Milton, John 1608-1674 . . . LC 9; DA; WLC
See also CDBLB 1660-1789; DLB 131, 151

Min, Anchee 1957- . . . . CLC 86
See also CA 146

Minehaha, Cornelius
See Wedekind, (Benjamin) Frank(lin)

Miner, Valerie 1947- . . . . CLC 40
See also CA 97-100

Minimo, Duca
See D'Annunzio, Gabriele

Minot, Susan 1956- . . . . CLC 44
See also CA 134

Minus, Ed 1938- . . . . CLC 39

Miranda, Javier
See Bioy Casares, Adolfo

Mirbeau, Octave 1848-1917 . . . . TCLC 55
See also DLB 123

Miro (Ferrer), Gabriel (Francisco Victor)
1879-1930 . . . . TCLC 5
See also CA 104

Mishima, Yukio
. . . . . . CLC 2, 4, 6, 9, 27; DC 1; SSC 4
See also Hiraoka, Kimitake

Mistral, Frederic 1830-1914 . . . . . . TCLC 51
See also CA 122

Mistral, Gabriela . . . . TCLC 2; HLC
See also Godoy Alcayaga, Lucila

Mistry, Rohinton 1952- . . . . CLC 71
See also CA 141

Mitchell, Clyde
See Ellison, Harlan (Jay); Silverberg, Robert

Mitchell, James Leslie 1901-1935
See Gibbon, Lewis Grassic
See also CA 104; DLB 15

Mitchell, Joni 1943- . . . . CLC 12
See also CA 112

Mitchell, Margaret (Munnerlyn)
1900-1949 . . . . TCLC 11
See also CA 109; 125; DLB 9; MTCW

Mitchell, Peggy
See Mitchell, Margaret (Munnerlyn)

Mitchell, S(ilas) Weir 1829-1914 . . TCLC 36

Mitchell, W(illiam) O(rmond)
1914- . . . . CLC 25
See also CA 77-80; CANR 15, 43; DLB 88

Mitford, Mary Russell 1787-1855 . . NCLC 4
See also DLB 110, 116

Mitford, Nancy 1904-1973 . . . . CLC 44
See also CA 9-12R

Miyamoto, Yuriko 1899-1951 . . . . . TCLC 37

Mo, Timothy (Peter) 1950(?)- . . . . . . CLC 46
See also CA 117; MTCW

Modarressi, Taghi (M.) 1931- . . . . . . CLC 44
See also CA 121; 134

Modiano, Patrick (Jean) 1945- . . . . . CLC 18
See also CA 85-88; CANR 17, 40; DLB 83

Moerck, Paal
See Roelvaag, O(le) E(dvart)

Mofolo, Thomas (Mokopu)
1875(?)-1948 . . . . TCLC 22; BLC
See also CA 121

Mohr, Nicholasa 1935- . . . . . . CLC 12; HLC
See also AAYA 8; CA 49-52; CANR 1, 32;
CLR 22; DLB 145; HW; JRDA; SAAS 8;
SATA 8

Mojtabai, A(nn) G(race)
1938- . . . . CLC 5, 9, 15, 29
See also CA 85-88

Moliere 1622-1673 . . . . LC 28; DA; WLC

Molin, Charles
See Mayne, William (James Carter)

Molnar, Ferenc 1878-1952 . . . . TCLC 20
See also CA 109

Momaday, N(avarre) Scott
1934- . . . . CLC 2, 19, 85; DA
See also AAYA 11; CA 25-28R; CANR 14,
34; DLB 143; MTCW; NNAL; SATA 48;
SATA-Brief 30

Monette, Paul 1945-1995 . . . . CLC 82
See also CA 139; 147

Monroe, Harriet 1860-1936 . . . . TCLC 12
See also CA 109; DLB 54, 91

Monroe, Lyle
See Heinlein, Robert A(nson)

Montagu, Elizabeth 1917- . . . . NCLC 7
See also CA 9-12R

Montagu, Mary (Pierrepont) Wortley
1689-1762 . . . . **LC 9**
See also DLB 95, 101

Montagu, W. H.
See Coleridge, Samuel Taylor

Montague, John (Patrick)
1929- . . . . **CLC 13, 46**
See also CA 9-12R; CANR 9; DLB 40;
MTCW

Montaigne, Michel (Eyquem) de
1533-1592 . . . . **LC 8; DA; WLC**

Montale, Eugenio
1896-1981 . . . . **CLC 7, 9, 18; PC 12**
See also CA 17-20R; 104; CANR 30;
DLB 114; MTCW

Montesquieu, Charles-Louis de Secondat
1689-1755 . . . . **LC 7**

Montgomery, (Robert) Bruce 1921-1978
See Crispin, Edmund
See also CA 104

Montgomery, L(ucy) M(aud)
1874-1942 . . . . **TCLC 51**
See also AAYA 12; CA 108; 137; CLR 8;
DLB 92; JRDA; MAICYA; YABC 1

Montgomery, Marion H., Jr. 1925- . . **CLC 7**
See also AITN 1; CA 1-4R; CANR 3, 48;
DLB 6

Montgomery, Max
See Davenport, Guy (Mattison, Jr.)

Montherlant, Henry (Milon) de
1896-1972 . . . . **CLC 8, 19**
See also CA 85-88; 37-40R; DLB 72;
MTCW

Monty Python
See Chapman, Graham; Cleese, John
(Marwood); Gilliam, Terry (Vance); Idle,
Eric; Jones, Terence Graham Parry; Palin,
Michael (Edward)
See also AAYA 7

Moodie, Susanna (Strickland)
1803-1885 . . . . **NCLC 14**
See also DLB 99

Mooney, Edward 1951-
See Mooney, Ted
See also CA 130

Mooney, Ted . . . . **CLC 25**
See also Mooney, Edward

Moorcock, Michael (John)
1939- . . . . **CLC 5, 27, 58**
See also CA 45-48; CAAS 5; CANR 2, 17,
38; DLB 14; MTCW

Moore, Brian
1921- . . . . **CLC 1, 3, 5, 7, 8, 19, 32**
See also CA 1-4R; CANR 1, 25, 42; MTCW

Moore, Edward
See Muir, Edwin

Moore, George Augustus
1852-1933 . . . . **TCLC 7; SSC 19**
See also CA 104; DLB 10, 18, 57, 135

Moore, Lorrie . . . . **CLC 39, 45, 68**
See also Moore, Marie Lorena

Moore, Marianne (Craig)
1887-1972 . . . . **CLC 1, 2, 4, 8, 10, 13, 19,
47; DA; PC 4**
See also CA 1-4R; 33-36R; CANR 3;
CDALB 1929-1941; DLB 45; DLBD 7;
MTCW; SATA 20

Moore, Marie Lorena 1957-
See Moore, Lorrie
See also CA 116; CANR 39

Moore, Thomas 1779-1852 . . . . **NCLC 6**
See also DLB 96, 144

Morand, Paul 1888-1976 . . . . **CLC 41**
See also CA 69-72; DLB 65

Morante, Elsa 1918-1985 . . . . **CLC 8, 47**
See also CA 85-88; 117; CANR 35; MTCW

Moravia, Alberto . . . . . . **CLC 2, 7, 11, 27, 46**
See also Pincherle, Alberto

More, Hannah 1745-1833 . . . . **NCLC 27**
See also DLB 107, 109, 116

More, Henry 1614-1687 . . . . **LC 9**
See also DLB 126

More, Sir Thomas 1478-1535 . . . . **LC 10**

Moreas, Jean . . . . **TCLC 18**
See also Papadiamantopoulos, Johannes

Morgan, Berry 1919- . . . . **CLC 6**
See also CA 49-52; DLB 6

Morgan, Claire
See Highsmith, (Mary) Patricia

Morgan, Edwin (George) 1920- . . . . . **CLC 31**
See also CA 5-8R; CANR 3, 43; DLB 27

Morgan, (George) Frederick
1922- . . . . **CLC 23**
See also CA 17-20R; CANR 21

Morgan, Harriet
See Mencken, H(enry) L(ouis)

Morgan, Jane
See Cooper, James Fenimore

Morgan, Janet 1945- . . . . **CLC 39**
See also CA 65-68

Morgan, Lady 1776(?)-1859 . . . . . . **NCLC 29**
See also DLB 116

Morgan, Robin 1941- . . . . **CLC 2**
See also CA 69-72; CANR 29; MTCW;
SATA 80

Morgan, Scott
See Kuttner, Henry

Morgan, Seth 1949(?)-1990 . . . . **CLC 65**
See also CA 132

Morgenstern, Christian
1871-1914 . . . . **TCLC 8**
See also CA 105

Morgenstern, S.
See Goldman, William (W.)

Moricz, Zsigmond 1879-1942 . . . . . **TCLC 33**

Morike, Eduard (Friedrich)
1804-1875 . . . . **NCLC 10**
See also DLB 133

Mori Ogai . . . . **TCLC 14**
See also Mori Rintaro

Mori Rintaro 1862-1922
See Mori Ogai
See also CA 110

Moritz, Karl Philipp 1756-1793 . . . . . . **LC 2**
See also DLB 94

Morland, Peter Henry
See Faust, Frederick (Schiller)

Morren, Theophil
See Hofmannsthal, Hugo von

Morris, Bill 1952- . . . . **CLC 76**

Morris, Julian
See West, Morris L(anglo)

Morris, Steveland Judkins 1950(?)-
See Wonder, Stevie
See also CA 111

Morris, William 1834-1896 . . . . **NCLC 4**
See also CDBLB 1832-1890; DLB 18, 35, 57

Morris, Wright 1910- . . . **CLC 1, 3, 7, 18, 37**
See also CA 9-12R; CANR 21; DLB 2;
DLBY 81; MTCW

Morrison, Chloe Anthony Wofford
See Morrison, Toni

Morrison, James Douglas 1943-1971
See Morrison, Jim
See also CA 73-76; CANR 40

Morrison, Jim . . . . **CLC 17**
See also Morrison, James Douglas

Morrison, Toni
1931- . . . . **CLC 4, 10, 22, 55, 81, 87;
BLC; DA**
See also AAYA 1; BW 2; CA 29-32R;
CANR 27, 42; CDALB 1968-1988;
DLB 6, 33, 143; DLBY 81; MTCW;
SATA 57

Morrison, Van 1945- . . . . **CLC 21**
See also CA 116

Mortimer, John (Clifford)
1923- . . . . **CLC 28, 43**
See also CA 13-16R; CANR 21;
CDBLB 1960 to Present; DLB 13;
MTCW

Mortimer, Penelope (Ruth) 1918- . . . . **CLC 5**
See also CA 57-60; CANR 45

Morton, Anthony
See Creasey, John

Mosher, Howard Frank 1943- . . . . . . **CLC 62**
See also CA 139

Mosley, Nicholas 1923- . . . . **CLC 43, 70**
See also CA 69-72; CANR 41; DLB 14

Moss, Howard
1922-1987 . . . . **CLC 7, 14, 45, 50**
See also CA 1-4R; 123; CANR 1, 44;
DLB 5

Mossgiel, Rab
See Burns, Robert

Motion, Andrew (Peter) 1952- . . . . . . **CLC 47**
See also CA 146; DLB 40

Motley, Willard (Francis)
1909-1965 . . . . **CLC 18**
See also BW 1; CA 117; 106; DLB 76, 143

Motoori, Norinaga 1730-1801 . . . . **NCLC 45**

Mott, Michael (Charles Alston)
1930- . . . . **CLC 15, 34**
See also CA 5-8R; CAAS 7; CANR 7, 29

Moure, Erin 1955- . . . . **CLC 88**
See also CA 113; DLB 60

Mowat, Farley (McGill) 1921- ..... **CLC 26**
See also AAYA 1; CA 1-4R; CANR 4, 24,
42; CLR 20; DLB 68; JRDA; MAICYA;
MTCW; SATA 3, 55

Moyers, Bill 1934- .... **CLC 74**
See also AITN 2; CA 61-64; CANR 31

Mphahlele, Es'kia
See Mphahlele, Ezekiel
See also DLB 125

Mphahlele, Ezekiel 1919- ..... **CLC 25; BLC**
See also Mphahlele, Es'kia
See also BW 2; CA 81-84; CANR 26

Mqhayi, S(amuel) E(dward) K(rune Loliwe)
1875-1945 .... **TCLC 25; BLC**

Mr. Martin
See Burroughs, William S(eward)

Mrozek, Slawomir 1930- .... **CLC 3, 13**
See also CA 13-16R; CAAS 10; CANR 29;
MTCW

Mrs. Belloc-Lowndes
See Lowndes, Marie Adelaide (Belloc)

Mtwa, Percy (?)- .... **CLC 47**

Mueller, Lisel 1924- .... **CLC 13, 51**
See also CA 93-96; DLB 105

Muir, Edwin 1887-1959 .... **TCLC 2**
See also CA 104; DLB 20, 100

Muir, John 1838-1914 .... **TCLC 28**

Mujica Lainez, Manuel
1910-1984 .... **CLC 31**
See also Lainez, Manuel Mujica
See also CA 81-84; 112; CANR 32; HW

Mukherjee, Bharati 1940- .... **CLC 53**
See also BEST 89:2; CA 107; CANR 45;
DLB 60; MTCW

Muldoon, Paul 1951- .... **CLC 32, 72**
See also CA 113; 129; DLB 40

Mulisch, Harry 1927- .... **CLC 42**
See also CA 9-12R; CANR 6, 26

Mull, Martin 1943- .... **CLC 17**
See also CA 105

Mulock, Dinah Maria
See Craik, Dinah Maria (Mulock)

Munford, Robert 1737(?)-1783 .... **LC 5**
See also DLB 31

Mungo, Raymond 1946- .... **CLC 72**
See also CA 49-52; CANR 2

Munro, Alice
1931- .... **CLC 6, 10, 19, 50; SSC 3**
See also AITN 2; CA 33-36R; CANR 33;
DLB 53; MTCW; SATA 29

Munro, H(ector) H(ugh) 1870-1916
See Saki
See also CA 104; 130; CDBLB 1890-1914;
DA; DLB 34; MTCW; WLC

Murasaki, Lady .... **CMLC 1**

Murdoch, (Jean) Iris
1919- ...... **CLC 1, 2, 3, 4, 6, 8, 11, 15,
22, 31, 51**
See also CA 13-16R; CANR 8, 43;
CDBLB 1960 to Present; DLB 14;
MTCW

Murnau, Friedrich Wilhelm
See Plumpe, Friedrich Wilhelm

Murphy, Richard 1927- .... **CLC 41**
See also CA 29-32R; DLB 40

Murphy, Sylvia 1937- .... **CLC 34**
See also CA 121

Murphy, Thomas (Bernard) 1935-... **CLC 51**
See also CA 101

Murray, Albert L. 1916- .... **CLC 73**
See also BW 2; CA 49-52; CANR 26;
DLB 38

Murray, Les(lie) A(llan) 1938- ..... **CLC 40**
See also CA 21-24R; CANR 11, 27

Murry, J. Middleton
See Murry, John Middleton

Murry, John Middleton
1889-1957 .... **TCLC 16**
See also CA 118; DLB 149

Musgrave, Susan 1951- .... **CLC 13, 54**
See also CA 69-72; CANR 45

Musil, Robert (Edler von)
1880-1942 .... **TCLC 12; SSC 18**
See also CA 109; DLB 81, 124

Musset, (Louis Charles) Alfred de
1810-1857 .... **NCLC 7**

My Brother's Brother
See Chekhov, Anton (Pavlovich)

Myers, L. H. 1881-1944 .... **TCLC 59**
See also DLB 15

Myers, Walter Dean 1937- ... **CLC 35; BLC**
See also AAYA 4; BW 2; CA 33-36R;
CANR 20, 42; CLR 4, 16, 35; DLB 33;
JRDA; MAICYA; SAAS 2; SATA 41, 71;
SATA-Brief 27

Myers, Walter M.
See Myers, Walter Dean

Myles, Symon
See Follett, Ken(neth Martin)

Nabokov, Vladimir (Vladimirovich)
1899-1977 ..... **CLC 1, 2, 3, 6, 8, 11, 15,
23, 44, 46, 64; DA; SSC 11; WLC**
See also CA 5-8R; 69-72; CANR 20;
CDALB 1941-1968; DLB 2; DLBD 3;
DLBY 80, 91; MTCW

Nagai Kafu .... **TCLC 51**
See also Nagai Sokichi

Nagai Sokichi 1879-1959
See Nagai Kafu
See also CA 117

Nagy, Laszlo 1925-1978 .... **CLC 7**
See also CA 129; 112

Naipaul, Shiva(dhar Srinivasa)
1945-1985 .... **CLC 32, 39**
See also CA 110; 112; 116; CANR 33;
DLBY 85; MTCW

Naipaul, V(idiadhar) S(urajprasad)
1932- .... **CLC 4, 7, 9, 13, 18, 37**
See also CA 1-4R; CANR 1, 33;
CDBLB 1960 to Present; DLB 125;
DLBY 85; MTCW

Nakos, Lilika 1899(?)- .... **CLC 29**

Narayan, R(asipuram) K(rishnaswami)
1906- .... **CLC 7, 28, 47**
See also CA 81-84; CANR 33; MTCW;
SATA 62

Nash, (Frediric) Ogden 1902-1971 .. **CLC 23**
See also CA 13-14; 29-32R; CANR 34;
CAP 1; DLB 11; MAICYA; MTCW;
SATA 2, 46

Nathan, Daniel
See Dannay, Frederic

Nathan, George Jean 1882-1958 ... **TCLC 18**
See also Hatteras, Owen
See also CA 114; DLB 137

Natsume, Kinnosuke 1867-1916
See Natsume, Soseki
See also CA 104

Natsume, Soseki .... **TCLC 2, 10**
See also Natsume, Kinnosuke

Natti, (Mary) Lee 1919-
See Kingman, Lee
See also CA 5-8R; CANR 2

Naylor, Gloria
1950- .... **CLC 28, 52; BLC; DA**
See also AAYA 6; BW 2; CA 107;
CANR 27; MTCW

Neihardt, John Gneisenau
1881-1973 .... **CLC 32**
See also CA 13-14; CAP 1; DLB 9, 54

Nekrasov, Nikolai Alekseevich
1821-1878 .... **NCLC 11**

Nelligan, Emile 1879-1941 .... **TCLC 14**
See also CA 114; DLB 92

Nelson, Willie 1933- .... **CLC 17**
See also CA 107

Nemerov, Howard (Stanley)
1920-1991 .... **CLC 2, 6, 9, 36**
See also CA 1-4R; 134; CABS 2; CANR 1,
27; DLB 6; DLBY 83; MTCW

Neruda, Pablo
1904-1973 ..... **CLC 1, 2, 5, 7, 9, 28, 62;
DA; HLC; PC 4; WLC**
See also CA 19-20; 45-48; CAP 2; HW;
MTCW

Nerval, Gerard de
1808-1855 ..... **NCLC 1; PC 12; SSC 18**

Nervo, (Jose) Amado (Ruiz de)
1870-1919 .... **TCLC 11**
See also CA 109; 131; HW

Nessi, Pio Baroja y
See Baroja (y Nessi), Pio

Nestroy, Johann 1801-1862 ...... **NCLC 42**
See also DLB 133

Neufeld, John (Arthur) 1938- ...... **CLC 17**
See also AAYA 11; CA 25-28R; CANR 11,
37; MAICYA; SAAS 3; SATA 6, 81

Neville, Emily Cheney 1919- ...... **CLC 12**
See also CA 5-8R; CANR 3, 37; JRDA;
MAICYA; SAAS 2; SATA 1

Newbound, Bernard Slade 1930-
See Slade, Bernard
See also CA 81-84; CANR 49

Newby, P(ercy) H(oward)
1918- .... **CLC 2, 13**
See also CA 5-8R; CANR 32; DLB 15;
MTCW

Newlove, Donald 1928- .... **CLC 6**
See also CA 29-32R; CANR 25

Newlove, John (Herbert) 1938- ..... **CLC 14**
See also CA 21-24R; CANR 9, 25

Newman, Charles 1938- .... **CLC 2, 8**
See also CA 21-24R

Newman, Edwin (Harold) 1919- .... **CLC 14**
See also AITN 1; CA 69-72; CANR 5

Newman, John Henry
1801-1890 .... **NCLC 38**
See also DLB 18, 32, 55

Newton, Suzanne 1936- .... **CLC 35**
See also CA 41-44R; CANR 14; JRDA;
SATA 5, 77

Nexo, Martin Andersen
1869-1954 .... **TCLC 43**

Nezval, Vitezslav 1900-1958 ...... **TCLC 44**
See also CA 123

Ng, Fae Myenne 1957(?)- .... **CLC 81**
See also CA 146

Ngema, Mbongeni 1955- .... **CLC 57**
See also BW 2; CA 143

Ngugi, James T(hiong'o) .... **CLC 3, 7, 13**
See also Ngugi wa Thiong'o

Ngugi wa Thiong'o 1938- ..... **CLC 36; BLC**
See also Ngugi, James T(hiong'o)
See also BW 2; CA 81-84; CANR 27;
DLB 125; MTCW

Nichol, B(arrie) P(hillip)
1944-1988 .... **CLC 18**
See also CA 53-56; DLB 53; SATA 66

Nichols, John (Treadwell) 1940- .... **CLC 38**
See also CA 9-12R; CAAS 2; CANR 6;
DLBY 82

Nichols, Leigh
See Koontz, Dean R(ay)

Nichols, Peter (Richard)
1927- .... **CLC 5, 36, 65**
See also CA 104; CANR 33; DLB 13;
MTCW

Nicolas, F. R. E.
See Freeling, Nicolas

Niedecker, Lorine 1903-1970.... **CLC 10, 42**
See also CA 25-28; CAP 2; DLB 48

Nietzsche, Friedrich (Wilhelm)
1844-1900 .... **TCLC 10, 18, 55**
See also CA 107; 121; DLB 129

Nievo, Ippolito 1831-1861 .... **NCLC 22**

Nightingale, Anne Redmon 1943-
See Redmon, Anne
See also CA 103

Nik. T. O.
See Annensky, Innokenty Fyodorovich

Nin, Anais
1903-1977 ...... **CLC 1, 4, 8, 11, 14, 60;
SSC 10**
See also AITN 2; CA 13-16R; 69-72;
CANR 22; DLB 2, 4, 152; MTCW

Nissenson, Hugh 1933- .... **CLC 4, 9**
See also CA 17-20R; CANR 27; DLB 28

Niven, Larry .... **CLC 8**
See also Niven, Laurence Van Cott
See also DLB 8

Niven, Laurence Van Cott 1938-
See Niven, Larry
See also CA 21-24R; CAAS 12; CANR 14,
44; MTCW

Nixon, Agnes Eckhardt 1927- ...... **CLC 21**
See also CA 110

Nizan, Paul 1905-1940 .... **TCLC 40**
See also DLB 72

Nkosi, Lewis 1936- .... **CLC 45; BLC**
See also BW 1; CA 65-68; CANR 27

Nodier, (Jean) Charles (Emmanuel)
1780-1844 .... **NCLC 19**
See also DLB 119

Nolan, Christopher 1965- .... **CLC 58**
See also CA 111

Norden, Charles
See Durrell, Lawrence (George)

Nordhoff, Charles (Bernard)
1887-1947 .... **TCLC 23**
See also CA 108; DLB 9; SATA 23

Norfolk, Lawrence 1963- .... **CLC 76**
See also CA 144

Norman, Marsha 1947- .... **CLC 28**
See also CA 105; CABS 3; CANR 41;
DLBY 84

Norris, Benjamin Franklin, Jr.
1870-1902 .... **TCLC 24**
See also Norris, Frank
See also CA 110

Norris, Frank
See Norris, Benjamin Franklin, Jr.
See also CDALB 1865-1917; DLB 12, 71

Norris, Leslie 1921- .... **CLC 14**
See also CA 11-12; CANR 14; CAP 1;
DLB 27

North, Andrew
See Norton, Andre

North, Anthony
See Koontz, Dean R(ay)

North, Captain George
See Stevenson, Robert Louis (Balfour)

North, Milou
See Erdrich, Louise

Northrup, B. A.
See Hubbard, L(afayette) Ron(ald)

North Staffs
See Hulme, T(homas) E(rnest)

Norton, Alice Mary
See Norton, Andre
See also MAICYA; SATA 1, 43

Norton, Andre 1912- .... **CLC 12**
See also Norton, Alice Mary
See also AAYA 14; CA 1-4R; CANR 2, 31;
DLB 8, 52; JRDA; MTCW

Norton, Caroline 1808-1877 ...... **NCLC 47**
See also DLB 21

Norway, Nevil Shute 1899-1960
See Shute, Nevil
See also CA 102; 93-96

Norwid, Cyprian Kamil
1821-1883 .... **NCLC 17**

Nosille, Nabrah
See Ellison, Harlan (Jay)

Nossack, Hans Erich 1901-1978 ..... **CLC 6**
See also CA 93-96; 85-88; DLB 69

Nostradamus 1503-1566 .... **LC 27**

Nosu, Chuji
See Ozu, Yasujiro

Notenburg, Eleanora (Genrikhovna) von
See Guro, Elena

Nova, Craig 1945- .... **CLC 7, 31**
See also CA 45-48; CANR 2

Novak, Joseph
See Kosinski, Jerzy (Nikodem)

Novalis 1772-1801 .... **NCLC 13**
See also DLB 90

Nowlan, Alden (Albert) 1933-1983 .. **CLC 15**
See also CA 9-12R; CANR 5; DLB 53

Noyes, Alfred 1880-1958 .... **TCLC 7**
See also CA 104; DLB 20

Nunn, Kem 19(?)- .... **CLC 34**

Nye, Robert 1939- .... **CLC 13, 42**
See also CA 33-36R; CANR 29; DLB 14;
MTCW; SATA 6

Nyro, Laura 1947- .... **CLC 17**

Oates, Joyce Carol
1938- ...... **CLC 1, 2, 3, 6, 9, 11, 15, 19,
33, 52; DA; SSC 6; WLC**
See also AITN 1; BEST 89:2; CA 5-8R;
CANR 25, 45; CDALB 1968-1988;
DLB 2, 5, 130; DLBY 81; MTCW

O'Brien, Darcy 1939- .... **CLC 11**
See also CA 21-24R; CANR 8

O'Brien, E. G.
See Clarke, Arthur C(harles)

O'Brien, Edna
1936- ... **CLC 3, 5, 8, 13, 36, 65; SSC 10**
See also CA 1-4R; CANR 6, 41;
CDBLB 1960 to Present; DLB 14;
MTCW

O'Brien, Fitz-James 1828-1862... **NCLC 21**
See also DLB 74

O'Brien, Flann .... **CLC 1, 4, 5, 7, 10, 47**
See also O Nuallain, Brian

O'Brien, Richard 1942- .... **CLC 17**
See also CA 124

O'Brien, Tim 1946- .... **CLC 7, 19, 40**
See also CA 85-88; CANR 40; DLB 152;
DLBD 9; DLBY 80

Obstfelder, Sigbjoern 1866-1900 ... **TCLC 23**
See also CA 123

O'Casey, Sean
1880-1964 ...... **CLC 1, 5, 9, 11, 15, 88**
See also CA 89-92; CDBLB 1914-1945;
DLB 10; MTCW

O'Cathasaigh, Sean
See O'Casey, Sean

Ochs, Phil 1940-1976 .... **CLC 17**
See also CA 65-68

O'Connor, Edwin (Greene)
1918-1968 .... **CLC 14**
See also CA 93-96; 25-28R

O'Connor, (Mary) Flannery
1925-1964 .... **CLC 1, 2, 3, 6, 10, 13, 15,
21, 66; DA; SSC 1; WLC**
See also AAYA 7; CA 1-4R; CANR 3, 41;
CDALB 1941-1968; DLB 2, 152;
DLBD 12; DLBY 80; MTCW

O'Connor, Frank .... **CLC 23; SSC 5**
See also O'Donovan, Michael John

O'Dell, Scott   1898-1989. . . . .   **CLC 30**
    See also AAYA 3; CA 61-64; 129;
    CANR 12, 30; CLR 1, 16; DLB 52;
    JRDA; MAICYA; SATA 12, 60

Odets, Clifford   1906-1963 . . . . . .   **CLC 2, 28**
    See also CA 85-88; DLB 7, 26; MTCW

O'Doherty, Brian   1934-. . . . .   **CLC 76**
    See also CA 105

O'Donnell, K. M.
    See Malzberg, Barry N(athaniel)

O'Donnell, Lawrence
    See Kuttner, Henry

O'Donovan, Michael John
    1903-1966 . . . .   **CLC 14**
    See also O'Connor, Frank
    See also CA 93-96

Oe, Kenzaburo
    1935- . . . .   **CLC 10, 36, 86; SSC 20**
    See also CA 97-100; CANR 36; MTCW

O'Faolain, Julia   1932-. . . . . . .   **CLC 6, 19, 47**
    See also CA 81-84; CAAS 2; CANR 12;
    DLB 14; MTCW

O'Faolain, Sean
    1900-1991 . . . .   **CLC 1, 7, 14, 32, 70;**
                                                    SSC 13
    See also CA 61-64; 134; CANR 12;
    DLB 15; MTCW

O'Flaherty, Liam
    1896-1984 . . . .   **CLC 5, 34; SSC 6**
    See also CA 101; 113; CANR 35; DLB 36;
    DLBY 84; MTCW

Ogilvy, Gavin
    See Barrie, J(ames) M(atthew)

O'Grady, Standish James
    1846-1928 . . . .   **TCLC 5**
    See also CA 104

O'Grady, Timothy   1951- . . . .   **CLC 59**
    See also CA 138

O'Hara, Frank
    1926-1966 . . . .   **CLC 2, 5, 13, 78**
    See also CA 9-12R; 25-28R; CANR 33;
    DLB 5, 16; MTCW

O'Hara, John (Henry)
    1905-1970 . . . .   **CLC 1, 2, 3, 6, 11, 42;**
                                                    SSC 15
    See also CA 5-8R; 25-28R; CANR 31;
    CDALB 1929-1941; DLB 9, 86; DLBD 2;
    MTCW

O Hehir, Diana   1922- . . . .   **CLC 41**
    See also CA 93-96

Okigbo, Christopher (Ifeanyichukwu)
    1932-1967 . . . . .   **CLC 25, 84; BLC; PC 7**
    See also BW 1; CA 77-80; DLB 125;
    MTCW

Okri, Ben   1959- . . . .   **CLC 87**
    See also BW 2; CA 130; 138

Olds, Sharon   1942-. . . . .   **CLC 32, 39, 85**
    See also CA 101; CANR 18, 41; DLB 120

Oldstyle, Jonathan
    See Irving, Washington

Olesha, Yuri (Karlovich)
    1899-1960 . . . .   **CLC 8**
    See also CA 85-88

Oliphant, Laurence
    1829(?)-1888 . . . .   **NCLC 47**
    See also DLB 18

Oliphant, Margaret (Oliphant Wilson)
    1828-1897 . . . .   **NCLC 11**
    See also DLB 18

Oliver, Mary   1935-. . . . .   **CLC 19, 34**
    See also CA 21-24R; CANR 9, 43; DLB 5

Olivier, Laurence (Kerr)
    1907-1989 . . . .   **CLC 20**
    See also CA 111; 129

Olsen, Tillie
    1913- . . . .   **CLC 4, 13; DA; SSC 11**
    See also CA 1-4R; CANR 1, 43; DLB 28;
    DLBY 80; MTCW

Olson, Charles (John)
    1910-1970 . . . . .   **CLC 1, 2, 5, 6, 9, 11, 29**
    See also CA 13-16; 25-28R; CABS 2;
    CANR 35; CAP 1; DLB 5, 16; MTCW

Olson, Toby   1937- . . . .   **CLC 28**
    See also CA 65-68; CANR 9, 31

Olyesha, Yuri
    See Olesha, Yuri (Karlovich)

Ondaatje, (Philip) Michael
    1943- . . . .   **CLC 14, 29, 51, 76**
    See also CA 77-80; CANR 42; DLB 60

Oneal, Elizabeth   1934-
    See Oneal, Zibby
    See also CA 106; CANR 28; MAICYA;
    SATA 30

Oneal, Zibby . . . .   **CLC 30**
    See also Oneal, Elizabeth
    See also AAYA 5; CLR 13; JRDA

O'Neill, Eugene (Gladstone)
    1888-1953 . . . . . .   **TCLC 1, 6, 27, 49; DA;**
                                                    WLC
    See also AITN 1; CA 110; 132;
    CDALB 1929-1941; DLB 7; MTCW

Onetti, Juan Carlos   1909-1994 . . .   **CLC 7, 10**
    See also CA 85-88; 145; CANR 32;
    DLB 113; HW; MTCW

O Nuallain, Brian   1911-1966
    See O'Brien, Flann
    See also CA 21-22; 25-28R; CAP 2

Oppen, George   1908-1984 . . . .   **CLC 7, 13, 34**
    See also CA 13-16R; 113; CANR 8; DLB 5

Oppenheim, E(dward) Phillips
    1866-1946 . . . .   **TCLC 45**
    See also CA 111; DLB 70

Orlovitz, Gil   1918-1973 . . . .   **CLC 22**
    See also CA 77-80; 45-48; DLB 2, 5

Orris
    See Ingelow, Jean

Ortega y Gasset, Jose
    1883-1955 . . . .   **TCLC 9; HLC**
    See also CA 106; 130; HW; MTCW

Ortese, Anna Maria   1914-. . . . .   **CLC 89**

Ortiz, Simon J(oseph)   1941- . . . .   **CLC 45**
    See also CA 134; DLB 120; NNAL

Orton, Joe . . . .   **CLC 4, 13, 43; DC 3**
    See also Orton, John Kingsley
    See also CDBLB 1960 to Present; DLB 13

Orton, John Kingsley   1933-1967
    See Orton, Joe
    See also CA 85-88; CANR 35; MTCW

Orwell, George
    . . . .   **TCLC 2, 6, 15, 31, 51; WLC**
    See also Blair, Eric (Arthur)
    See also CDBLB 1945-1960; DLB 15, 98

Osborne, David
    See Silverberg, Robert

Osborne, George
    See Silverberg, Robert

Osborne, John (James)
    1929-1994 . . . . .   **CLC 1, 2, 5, 11, 45; DA;**
                                                    WLC
    See also CA 13-16R; 147; CANR 21;
    CDBLB 1945-1960; DLB 13; MTCW

Osborne, Lawrence   1958- . . . .   **CLC 50**

Oshima, Nagisa   1932- . . . .   **CLC 20**
    See also CA 116; 121

Oskison, John Milton
    1874-1947 . . . .   **TCLC 35**
    See also CA 144; NNAL

Ossoli, Sarah Margaret (Fuller marchesa d')
    1810-1850
    See Fuller, Margaret
    See also SATA 25

Ostrovsky, Alexander
    1823-1886 . . . .   **NCLC 30**

Otero, Blas de   1916-1979. . . . .   **CLC 11**
    See also CA 89-92; DLB 134

Otto, Whitney   1955-. . . . .   **CLC 70**
    See also CA 140

Ouida . . . .   **TCLC 43**
    See also De La Ramee, (Marie) Louise
    See also DLB 18

Ousmane, Sembene   1923- . . . .   **CLC 66; BLC**
    See also BW 1; CA 117; 125; MTCW

Ovid   43B.C.-18(?). . . . .   **CMLC 7; PC 2**

Owen, Hugh
    See Faust, Frederick (Schiller)

Owen, Wilfred (Edward Salter)
    1893-1918 . . . . . .   **TCLC 5, 27; DA; WLC**
    See also CA 104; 141; CDBLB 1914-1945;
    DLB 20

Owens, Rochelle   1936-. . . . .   **CLC 8**
    See also CA 17-20R; CAAS 2; CANR 39

Oz, Amos   1939- . . .   **CLC 5, 8, 11, 27, 33, 54**
    See also CA 53-56; CANR 27, 47; MTCW

Ozick, Cynthia
    1928- . . . .   **CLC 3, 7, 28, 62; SSC 15**
    See also BEST 90:1; CA 17-20R; CANR 23;
    DLB 28, 152; DLBY 82; MTCW

Ozu, Yasujiro   1903-1963 . . . .   **CLC 16**
    See also CA 112

Pacheco, C.
    See Pessoa, Fernando (Antonio Nogueira)

Pa Chin . . . .   **CLC 18**
    See also Li Fei-kan

Pack, Robert   1929-. . . . .   **CLC 13**
    See also CA 1-4R; CANR 3, 44; DLB 5

Padgett, Lewis
    See Kuttner, Henry

Padilla (Lorenzo), Heberto   1932-. . .   **CLC 38**
    See also AITN 1; CA 123; 131; HW

Page, Jimmy   1944-. . . . .   **CLC 12**

Page, Louise   1955-. . . . .   **CLC 40**
    See also CA 140

Page, P(atricia) K(athleen)
  1916- . . . . **CLC 7, 18; PC 12**
  See also CA 53-56; CANR 4, 22; DLB 68;
  MTCW

Paget, Violet 1856-1935
  See Lee, Vernon
  See also CA 104

Paget-Lowe, Henry
  See Lovecraft, H(oward) P(hillips)

Paglia, Camille (Anna) 1947- . . . . . . **CLC 68**
  See also CA 140

Paige, Richard
  See Koontz, Dean R(ay)

Pakenham, Antonia
  See Fraser, (Lady) Antonia (Pakenham)

Palamas, Kostes 1859-1943 . . . . **TCLC 5**
  See also CA 105

Palazzeschi, Aldo 1885-1974 . . . . . . **CLC 11**
  See also CA 89-92; 53-56; DLB 114

Paley, Grace 1922- . . . . **CLC 4, 6, 37; SSC 8**
  See also CA 25-28R; CANR 13, 46;
  DLB 28; MTCW

Palin, Michael (Edward) 1943- . . . . . **CLC 21**
  See also Monty Python
  See also CA 107; CANR 35; SATA 67

Palliser, Charles 1947- . . . . **CLC 65**
  See also CA 136

Palma, Ricardo 1833-1919 . . . . **TCLC 29**

Pancake, Breece Dexter 1952-1979
  See Pancake, Breece D'J
  See also CA 123; 109

Pancake, Breece D'J . . . . **CLC 29**
  See also Pancake, Breece Dexter
  See also DLB 130

Panko, Rudy
  See Gogol, Nikolai (Vasilyevich)

Papadiamantis, Alexandros
  1851-1911 . . . . **TCLC 29**

Papadiamantopoulos, Johannes 1856-1910
  See Moreas, Jean
  See also CA 117

Papini, Giovanni 1881-1956 . . . . **TCLC 22**
  See also CA 121

Paracelsus 1493-1541 . . . . **LC 14**

Parasol, Peter
  See Stevens, Wallace

Parfenie, Maria
  See Codrescu, Andrei

Parini, Jay (Lee) 1948- . . . . **CLC 54**
  See also CA 97-100; CAAS 16; CANR 32

Park, Jordan
  See Kornbluth, C(yril) M.; Pohl, Frederik

Parker, Bert
  See Ellison, Harlan (Jay)

Parker, Dorothy (Rothschild)
  1893-1967 . . . . **CLC 15, 68; SSC 2**
  See also CA 19-20; 25-28R; CAP 2;
  DLB 11, 45, 86; MTCW

Parker, Robert B(rown) 1932- . . . . . . **CLC 27**
  See also BEST 89:4; CA 49-52; CANR 1,
  26; MTCW

Parkin, Frank 1940- . . . . **CLC 43**
  See also CA 147

Parkman, Francis, Jr.
  1823-1893 . . . . **NCLC 12**
  See also DLB 1, 30

Parks, Gordon (Alexander Buchanan)
  1912- . . . . **CLC 1, 16; BLC**
  See also AITN 2; BW 2; CA 41-44R;
  CANR 26; DLB 33; SATA 8

Parnell, Thomas 1679-1718 . . . . **LC 3**
  See also DLB 94

Parra, Nicanor 1914- . . . . **CLC 2; HLC**
  See also CA 85-88; CANR 32; HW; MTCW

Parrish, Mary Frances
  See Fisher, M(ary) F(rances) K(ennedy)

Parson
  See Coleridge, Samuel Taylor

Parson Lot
  See Kingsley, Charles

Partridge, Anthony
  See Oppenheim, E(dward) Phillips

Pascoli, Giovanni 1855-1912 . . . . . **TCLC 45**

Pasolini, Pier Paolo
  1922-1975 . . . . **CLC 20, 37**
  See also CA 93-96; 61-64; DLB 128;
  MTCW

Pasquini
  See Silone, Ignazio

Pastan, Linda (Olenik) 1932- . . . . . . **CLC 27**
  See also CA 61-64; CANR 18, 40; DLB 5

Pasternak, Boris (Leonidovich)
  1890-1960 . . . . . . **CLC 7, 10, 18, 63; DA;
  PC 6; WLC**
  See also CA 127; 116; MTCW

Patchen, Kenneth 1911-1972 . . . **CLC 1, 2, 18**
  See also CA 1-4R; 33-36R; CANR 3, 35;
  DLB 16, 48; MTCW

Pater, Walter (Horatio)
  1839-1894 . . . . **NCLC 7**
  See also CDBLB 1832-1890; DLB 57

Paterson, A(ndrew) B(arton)
  1864-1941 . . . . **TCLC 32**

Paterson, Katherine (Womeldorf)
  1932- . . . . **CLC 12, 30**
  See also AAYA 1; CA 21-24R; CANR 28;
  CLR 7; DLB 52; JRDA; MAICYA;
  MTCW; SATA 13, 53

Patmore, Coventry Kersey Dighton
  1823-1896 . . . . **NCLC 9**
  See also DLB 35, 98

Paton, Alan (Stewart)
  1903-1988 . . . . . . **CLC 4, 10, 25, 55; DA;
  WLC**
  See also CA 13-16; 125; CANR 22; CAP 1;
  MTCW; SATA 11; SATA-Obit 56

Paton Walsh, Gillian 1937-
  See Walsh, Jill Paton
  See also CANR 38; JRDA; MAICYA;
  SAAS 3; SATA 4, 72

Paulding, James Kirke 1778-1860 . . **NCLC 2**
  See also DLB 3, 59, 74

Paulin, Thomas Neilson 1949-
  See Paulin, Tom
  See also CA 123; 128

Paulin, Tom . . . . **CLC 37**
  See also Paulin, Thomas Neilson
  See also DLB 40

Paustovsky, Konstantin (Georgievich)
  1892-1968 . . . . **CLC 40**
  See also CA 93-96; 25-28R

Pavese, Cesare
  1908-1950 . . . . . **TCLC 3; PC 12; SSC 19**
  See also CA 104; DLB 128

Pavic, Milorad 1929- . . . . **CLC 60**
  See also CA 136

Payne, Alan
  See Jakes, John (William)

Paz, Gil
  See Lugones, Leopoldo

Paz, Octavio
  1914- . . . . **CLC 3, 4, 6, 10, 19, 51, 65;
  DA; HLC; PC 1; WLC**
  See also CA 73-76; CANR 32; DLBY 90;
  HW; MTCW

Peacock, Molly 1947- . . . . **CLC 60**
  See also CA 103; CAAS 21; DLB 120

Peacock, Thomas Love
  1785-1866 . . . . **NCLC 22**
  See also DLB 96, 116

Peake, Mervyn 1911-1968 . . . . . . **CLC 7, 54**
  See also CA 5-8R; 25-28R; CANR 3;
  DLB 15; MTCW; SATA 23

Pearce, Philippa . . . . **CLC 21**
  See also Christie, (Ann) Philippa
  See also CLR 9; MAICYA; SATA 1, 67

Pearl, Eric
  See Elman, Richard

Pearson, T(homas) R(eid) 1956- . . . . **CLC 39**
  See also CA 120; 130

Peck, Dale 1968(?)- . . . . **CLC 81**

Peck, John 1941- . . . . **CLC 3**
  See also CA 49-52; CANR 3

Peck, Richard (Wayne) 1934- . . . . . . **CLC 21**
  See also AAYA 1; CA 85-88; CANR 19,
  38; CLR 15; JRDA; MAICYA; SAAS 2;
  SATA 18, 55

Peck, Robert Newton 1928- . . . . **CLC 17; DA**
  See also AAYA 3; CA 81-84; CANR 31;
  JRDA; MAICYA; SAAS 1; SATA 21, 62

Peckinpah, (David) Sam(uel)
  1925-1984 . . . . **CLC 20**
  See also CA 109; 114

Pedersen, Knut 1859-1952
  See Hamsun, Knut
  See also CA 104; 119; MTCW

Peeslake, Gaffer
  See Durrell, Lawrence (George)

Peguy, Charles Pierre
  1873-1914 . . . . **TCLC 10**
  See also CA 107

Pena, Ramon del Valle y
  See Valle-Inclan, Ramon (Maria) del

Pendennis, Arthur Esquir
  See Thackeray, William Makepeace

Penn, William 1644-1718 . . . . **LC 25**
  See also DLB 24

Pepys, Samuel
  1633-1703 . . . . **LC 11; DA; WLC**
  See also CDBLB 1660-1789; DLB 101

Percy, Walker
   1916-1990 .... **CLC 2, 3, 6, 8, 14, 18, 47,**
                                              65
   See also CA 1-4R; 131; CANR 1, 23;
   DLB 2; DLBY 80, 90; MTCW

Perec, Georges 1936-1982 .... **CLC 56**
   See also CA 141; DLB 83

Pereda (y Sanchez de Porrua), Jose Maria de
   1833-1906 .... **TCLC 16**
   See also CA 117

Pereda y Porrua, Jose Maria de
   See Pereda (y Sanchez de Porrua), Jose
   Maria de

Peregoy, George Weems
   See Mencken, H(enry) L(ouis)

Perelman, S(idney) J(oseph)
   1904-1979 ... **CLC 3, 5, 9, 15, 23, 44, 49**
   See also AITN 1, 2; CA 73-76; 89-92;
   CANR 18; DLB 11, 44; MTCW

Peret, Benjamin 1899-1959 .... **TCLC 20**
   See also CA 117

Peretz, Isaac Loeb 1851(?)-1915... **TCLC 16**
   See also CA 109

Peretz, Yitzkhok Leibush
   See Peretz, Isaac Loeb

Perez Galdos, Benito 1843-1920 ... **TCLC 27**
   See also CA 125; HW

Perrault, Charles 1628-1703 .... **LC 2**
   See also MAICYA; SATA 25

Perry, Brighton
   See Sherwood, Robert E(mmet)

Perse, St.-John .... **CLC 4, 11, 46**
   See also Leger, (Marie-Rene Auguste) Alexis
   Saint-Leger

Perutz, Leo 1882-1957 .... **TCLC 60**
   See also DLB 81

Peseenz, Tulio F.
   See Lopez y Fuentes, Gregorio

Pesetsky, Bette 1932- .... **CLC 28**
   See also CA 133; DLB 130

Peshkov, Alexei Maximovich 1868-1936
   See Gorky, Maxim
   See also CA 105; 141; DA

Pessoa, Fernando (Antonio Nogueira)
   1888-1935 .... **TCLC 27; HLC**
   See also CA 125

Peterkin, Julia Mood 1880-1961.... **CLC 31**
   See also CA 102; DLB 9

Peters, Joan K. 1945-............. **CLC 39**

Peters, Robert L(ouis) 1924- .... **CLC 7**
   See also CA 13-16R; CAAS 8; DLB 105

Petofi, Sandor 1823-1849 .... **NCLC 21**

Petrakis, Harry Mark 1923- .... **CLC 3**
   See also CA 9-12R; CANR 4, 30

Petrarch 1304-1374................. **PC 8**

Petrov, Evgeny .... **TCLC 21**
   See also Kataev, Evgeny Petrovich

Petry, Ann (Lane) 1908- ...... **CLC 1, 7, 18**
   See also BW 1; CA 5-8R; CAAS 6;
   CANR 4, 46; CLR 12; DLB 76; JRDA;
   MAICYA; MTCW; SATA 5

Petursson, Halligrimur 1614-1674 .... **LC 8**

Philips, Katherine 1632-1664....... **LC 30**
   See also DLB 131

Philipson, Morris H. 1926- .... **CLC 53**
   See also CA 1-4R; CANR 4

Phillips, David Graham
   1867-1911 .... **TCLC 44**
   See also CA 108; DLB 9, 12

Phillips, Jack
   See Sandburg, Carl (August)

Phillips, Jayne Anne
   1952- .... **CLC 15, 33; SSC 16**
   See also CA 101; CANR 24; DLBY 80;
   MTCW

Phillips, Richard
   See Dick, Philip K(indred)

Phillips, Robert (Schaeffer) 1938-... **CLC 28**
   See also CA 17-20R; CAAS 13; CANR 8;
   DLB 105

Phillips, Ward
   See Lovecraft, H(oward) P(hillips)

Piccolo, Lucio 1901-1969.......... **CLC 13**
   See also CA 97-100; DLB 114

Pickthall, Marjorie L(owry) C(hristie)
   1883-1922 .... **TCLC 21**
   See also CA 107; DLB 92

Pico della Mirandola, Giovanni
   1463-1494 .... **LC 15**

Piercy, Marge
   1936- .... **CLC 3, 6, 14, 18, 27, 62**
   See also CA 21-24R; CAAS 1; CANR 13,
   43; DLB 120; MTCW

Piers, Robert
   See Anthony, Piers

Pieyre de Mandiargues, Andre 1909-1991
   See Mandiargues, Andre Pieyre de
   See also CA 103; 136; CANR 22

Pilnyak, Boris .... **TCLC 23**
   See also Vogau, Boris Andreyevich

Pincherle, Alberto 1907-1990 ... **CLC 11, 18**
   See also Moravia, Alberto
   See also CA 25-28R; 132; CANR 33;
   MTCW

Pinckney, Darryl 1953- .... **CLC 76**
   See also BW 2; CA 143

Pindar 518B.C.-446B.C.......... **CMLC 12**

Pineda, Cecile 1942-............. **CLC 39**
   See also CA 118

Pinero, Arthur Wing 1855-1934 ... **TCLC 32**
   See also CA 110; DLB 10

Pinero, Miguel (Antonio Gomez)
   1946-1988 .... **CLC 4, 55**
   See also CA 61-64; 125; CANR 29; HW

Pinget, Robert 1919- .... **CLC 7, 13, 37**
   See also CA 85-88; DLB 83

Pink Floyd
   See Barrett, (Roger) Syd; Gilmour, David;
   Mason, Nick; Waters, Roger; Wright,
   Rick

Pinkney, Edward 1802-1828 ..... **NCLC 31**

Pinkwater, Daniel Manus 1941-.... **CLC 35**
   See also Pinkwater, Manus
   See also AAYA 1; CA 29-32R; CANR 12,
   38; CLR 4; JRDA; MAICYA; SAAS 3;
   SATA 46, 76

Pinkwater, Manus
   See Pinkwater, Daniel Manus
   See also SATA 8

Pinsky, Robert 1940- .... **CLC 9, 19, 38**
   See also CA 29-32R; CAAS 4; DLBY 82

Pinta, Harold
   See Pinter, Harold

Pinter, Harold
   1930- ..... **CLC 1, 3, 6, 9, 11, 15, 27, 58,**
                                         73; DA; WLC
   See also CA 5-8R; CANR 33; CDBLB 1960
   to Present; DLB 13; MTCW

Pirandello, Luigi
   1867-1936 ..... **TCLC 4, 29; DA; DC 5;**
                                              WLC
   See also CA 104

Pirsig, Robert M(aynard)
   1928-....................**CLC 4, 6, 73**
   See also CA 53-56; CANR 42; MTCW;
   SATA 39

Pisarev, Dmitry Ivanovich
   1840-1868 .... **NCLC 25**

Pix, Mary (Griffith) 1666-1709....... **LC 8**
   See also DLB 80

Pixerecourt, Guilbert de
   1773-1844 .... **NCLC 39**

Plaidy, Jean
   See Hibbert, Eleanor Alice Burford

Planche, James Robinson
   1796-1880 .... **NCLC 42**

Plant, Robert 1948- .... **CLC 12**

Plante, David (Robert)
   1940- .... **CLC 7, 23, 38**
   See also CA 37-40R; CANR 12, 36;
   DLBY 83; MTCW

Plath, Sylvia
   1932-1963 ..... **CLC 1, 2, 3, 5, 9, 11, 14,**
                        17, 50, 51, 62; DA; PC 1; WLC
   See also AAYA 13; CA 19-20; CANR 34;
   CAP 2; CDALB 1941-1968; DLB 5, 6,
   152; MTCW

Plato 428(?)B.C.-348(?)B.C.... **CMLC 8; DA**

Platonov, Andrei .... **TCLC 14**
   See also Klimentov, Andrei Platonovich

Platt, Kin 1911- .... **CLC 26**
   See also AAYA 11; CA 17-20R; CANR 11;
   JRDA; SAAS 17; SATA 21

Plick et Plock
   See Simenon, Georges (Jacques Christian)

Plimpton, George (Ames) 1927-..... **CLC 36**
   See also AITN 1; CA 21-24R; CANR 32;
   MTCW; SATA 10

Plomer, William Charles Franklin
   1903-1973 .... **CLC 4, 8**
   See also CA 21-22; CANR 34; CAP 2;
   DLB 20; MTCW; SATA 24

Plowman, Piers
   See Kavanagh, Patrick (Joseph)

Plum, J.
   See Wodehouse, P(elham) G(renville)

Plumly, Stanley (Ross) 1939- ...... **CLC 33**
   See also CA 108; 110; DLB 5

Plumpe, Friedrich Wilhelm
   1888-1931 .... **TCLC 53**
   See also CA 112**

Poe, Edgar Allan
    1809-1849 ..... **NCLC 1, 16; DA; PC 1;**
                              SSC 1; WLC
    See also AAYA 14; CDALB 1640-1865;
    DLB 3, 59, 73, 74; SATA 23

Poet of Titchfield Street, The
    See Pound, Ezra (Weston Loomis)

Pohl, Frederik 1919- .... **CLC 18**
    See also CA 61-64; CAAS 1; CANR 11, 37;
    DLB 8; MTCW; SATA 24

Poirier, Louis 1910-
    See Gracq, Julien
    See also CA 122; 126

Poitier, Sidney 1927- .... **CLC 26**
    See also BW 1; CA 117

Polanski, Roman 1933- .... **CLC 16**
    See also CA 77-80

Poliakoff, Stephen 1952- .... **CLC 38**
    See also CA 106; DLB 13

Police, The
    See Copeland, Stewart (Armstrong);
    Summers, Andrew James; Sumner,
    Gordon Matthew

Polidori, John William
    1795-1821 .... **NCLC 51**
    See also DLB 116

Pollitt, Katha 1949- .... **CLC 28**
    See also CA 120; 122; MTCW

Pollock, (Mary) Sharon 1936-...... **CLC 50**
    See also CA 141; DLB 60

Polo, Marco 1254-1324 .... **CMLC 15**

Pomerance, Bernard 1940-......... **CLC 13**
    See also CA 101; CANR 49

Ponge, Francis (Jean Gaston Alfred)
    1899-1988 .... **CLC 6, 18**
    See also CA 85-88; 126; CANR 40

Pontoppidan, Henrik 1857-1943 ... **TCLC 29**

Poole, Josephine .... **CLC 17**
    See also Helyar, Jane Penelope Josephine
    See also SAAS 2; SATA 5

Popa, Vasko 1922- .... **CLC 19**
    See also CA 112

Pope, Alexander
    1688-1744 .... **LC 3; DA; WLC**
    See also CDBLB 1660-1789; DLB 95, 101

Porter, Connie (Rose) 1959(?)- ..... **CLC 70**
    See also BW 2; CA 142; SATA 81

Porter, Gene(va Grace) Stratton
    1863(?)-1924 .... **TCLC 21**
    See also CA 112

Porter, Katherine Anne
    1890-1980 ...... **CLC 1, 3, 7, 10, 13, 15,**
                              27; DA; SSC 4
    See also AITN 2; CA 1-4R; 101; CANR 1;
    DLB 4, 9, 102; DLBD 12; DLBY 80;
    MTCW; SATA 39; SATA-Obit 23

Porter, Peter (Neville Frederick)
    1929- .... **CLC 5, 13, 33**
    See also CA 85-88; DLB 40

Porter, William Sydney 1862-1910
    See Henry, O.
    See also CA 104; 131; CDALB 1865-1917;
    DA; DLB 12, 78, 79; MTCW; YABC 2

Portillo (y Pacheco), Jose Lopez
    See Lopez Portillo (y Pacheco), Jose

Post, Melville Davisson
    1869-1930 .... **TCLC 39**
    See also CA 110

Potok, Chaim 1929-....... **CLC 2, 7, 14, 26**
    See also AITN 1, 2; CA 17-20R; CANR 19,
    35; DLB 28, 152; MTCW; SATA 33

Potter, Beatrice
    See Webb, (Martha) Beatrice (Potter)
    See also MAICYA

Potter, Dennis (Christopher George)
    1935-1994 .... **CLC 58, 86**
    See also CA 107; 145; CANR 33; MTCW

Pound, Ezra (Weston Loomis)
    1885-1972 ...... **CLC 1, 2, 3, 4, 5, 7, 10,**
        13, 18, 34, 48, 50; DA; PC 4; WLC
    See also CA 5-8R; 37-40R; CANR 40;
    CDALB 1917-1929; DLB 4, 45, 63;
    MTCW

Povod, Reinaldo 1959-1994 .... **CLC 44**
    See also CA 136; 146

Powell, Adam Clayton, Jr.
    1908-1972 .... **CLC 89; BLC**
    See also BW 1; CA 102; 33-36R

Powell, Anthony (Dymoke)
    1905- .... **CLC 1, 3, 7, 9, 10, 31**
    See also CA 1-4R; CANR 1, 32;
    CDBLB 1945-1960; DLB 15; MTCW

Powell, Dawn 1897-1965 .... **CLC 66**
    See also CA 5-8R

Powell, Padgett 1952-............. **CLC 34**
    See also CA 126

Powers, J(ames) F(arl)
    1917- .... **CLC 1, 4, 8, 57; SSC 4**
    See also CA 1-4R; CANR 2; DLB 130;
    MTCW

Powers, John J(ames) 1945-
    See Powers, John R.
    See also CA 69-72

Powers, John R. .... **CLC 66**
    See also Powers, John J(ames)

Pownall, David 1938-............. **CLC 10**
    See also CA 89-92; CAAS 18; CANR 49;
    DLB 14

Powys, John Cowper
    1872-1963 .... **CLC 7, 9, 15, 46**
    See also CA 85-88; DLB 15; MTCW

Powys, T(heodore) F(rancis)
    1875-1953 .... **TCLC 9**
    See also CA 106; DLB 36

Prager, Emily 1952-.............. **CLC 56**

Pratt, E(dwin) J(ohn)
    1883(?)-1964 .... **CLC 19**
    See also CA 141; 93-96; DLB 92

Premchand...................... **TCLC 21**
    See also Srivastava, Dhanpat Rai

Preussler, Otfried 1923-.......... **CLC 17**
    See also CA 77-80; SATA 24

Prevert, Jacques (Henri Marie)
    1900-1977 .... **CLC 15**
    See also CA 77-80; 69-72; CANR 29;
    MTCW; SATA-Obit 30

Prevost, Abbe (Antoine Francois)
    1697-1763 .... **LC 1**

Price, (Edward) Reynolds
    1933- .... **CLC 3, 6, 13, 43, 50, 63**
    See also CA 1-4R; CANR 1, 37; DLB 2

Price, Richard 1949- .... **CLC 6, 12**
    See also CA 49-52; CANR 3; DLBY 81

Prichard, Katharine Susannah
    1883-1969 .... **CLC 46**
    See also CA 11-12; CANR 33; CAP 1;
    MTCW; SATA 66

Priestley, J(ohn) B(oynton)
    1894-1984 .... **CLC 2, 5, 9, 34**
    See also CA 9-12R; 113; CANR 33;
    CDBLB 1914-1945; DLB 10, 34, 77, 100,
    139; DLBY 84; MTCW

Prince 1958(?)-.................. **CLC 35**

Prince, F(rank) T(empleton) 1912-... **CLC 22**
    See also CA 101; CANR 43; DLB 20

Prince Kropotkin
    See Kropotkin, Peter (Aleksieevich)

Prior, Matthew 1664-1721.......... **LC 4**
    See also DLB 95

Pritchard, William H(arrison)
    1932-........................ **CLC 34**
    See also CA 65-68; CANR 23; DLB 111

Pritchett, V(ictor) S(awdon)
    1900- .... **CLC 5, 13, 15, 41; SSC 14**
    See also CA 61-64; CANR 31; DLB 15,
    139; MTCW

Private 19022
    See Manning, Frederic

Probst, Mark 1925- .... **CLC 59**
    See also CA 130

Prokosch, Frederic 1908-1989.... **CLC 4, 48**
    See also CA 73-76; 128; DLB 48

Prophet, The
    See Dreiser, Theodore (Herman Albert)

Prose, Francine 1947-............. **CLC 45**
    See also CA 109; 112; CANR 46

Proudhon
    See Cunha, Euclides (Rodrigues Pimenta) da

Proulx, E. Annie 1935- .... **CLC 81**

Proust, (Valentin-Louis-George-Eugene-)
Marcel
    1871-1922 ... **TCLC 7, 13, 33; DA; WLC**
    See also CA 104; 120; DLB 65; MTCW

Prowler, Harley
    See Masters, Edgar Lee

Prus, Boleslaw 1845-1912 .... **TCLC 48**

Pryor, Richard (Franklin Lenox Thomas)
    1940-........................ **CLC 26**
    See also CA 122

Przybyszewski, Stanislaw
    1868-1927 .... **TCLC 36**
    See also DLB 66

Pteleon
    See Grieve, C(hristopher) M(urray)

Puckett, Lute
    See Masters, Edgar Lee

Puig, Manuel
    1932-1990 ... **CLC 3, 5, 10, 28, 65; HLC**
    See also CA 45-48; CANR 2, 32; DLB 113;
    HW; MTCW

Purdy, Al(fred Wellington)
1918- . . . . CLC 3, 6, 14, 50
See also CA 81-84; CAAS 17; CANR 42;
DLB 88

Purdy, James (Amos)
1923- . . . . CLC 2, 4, 10, 28, 52
See also CA 33-36R; CAAS 1; CANR 19;
DLB 2; MTCW

Pure, Simon
See Swinnerton, Frank Arthur

Pushkin, Alexander (Sergeyevich)
1799-1837 . . . . NCLC 3, 27; DA; PC 10;
WLC
See also SATA 61

P'u Sung-ling 1640-1715 . . . . LC 3

Putnam, Arthur Lee
See Alger, Horatio, Jr.

Puzo, Mario 1920- . . . . CLC 1, 2, 6, 36
See also CA 65-68; CANR 4, 42; DLB 6;
MTCW

Pym, Barbara (Mary Crampton)
1913-1980 . . . . CLC 13, 19, 37
See also CA 13-14; 97-100; CANR 13, 34;
CAP 1; DLB 14; DLBY 87; MTCW

Pynchon, Thomas (Ruggles, Jr.)
1937- . . . . . CLC 2, 3, 6, 9, 11, 18, 33, 62,
72; DA; SSC 14; WLC
See also BEST 90:2; CA 17-20R; CANR 22,
46; DLB 2; MTCW

Qian Zhongshu
See Ch'ien Chung-shu

Qroll
See Dagerman, Stig (Halvard)

Quarrington, Paul (Lewis) 1953- . . . . CLC 65
See also CA 129

Quasimodo, Salvatore 1901-1968 . . . CLC 10
See also CA 13-16; 25-28R; CAP 1;
DLB 114; MTCW

Queen, Ellery . . . . CLC 3, 11
See also Dannay, Frederic; Davidson,
Avram; Lee, Manfred B(ennington);
Sturgeon, Theodore (Hamilton); Vance,
John Holbrook

Queen, Ellery, Jr.
See Dannay, Frederic; Lee, Manfred
B(ennington)

Queneau, Raymond
1903-1976 . . . . CLC 2, 5, 10, 42
See also CA 77-80; 69-72; CANR 32;
DLB 72; MTCW

Quevedo, Francisco de 1580-1645 . . . . LC 23

Quiller-Couch, Arthur Thomas
1863-1944 . . . . TCLC 53
See also CA 118; DLB 135, 153

Quin, Ann (Marie) 1936-1973 . . . . CLC 6
See also CA 9-12R; 45-48; DLB 14

Quinn, Martin
See Smith, Martin Cruz

Quinn, Simon
See Smith, Martin Cruz

Quiroga, Horacio (Sylvestre)
1878-1937 . . . . TCLC 20; HLC
See also CA 117; 131; HW; MTCW

Quoirez, Francoise 1935- . . . . CLC 9
See also Sagan, Francoise
See also CA 49-52; CANR 6, 39; MTCW

Raabe, Wilhelm 1831-1910 . . . . TCLC 45
See also DLB 129

Rabe, David (William) 1940- . . . CLC 4, 8, 33
See also CA 85-88; CABS 3; DLB 7

Rabelais, Francois
1483-1553 . . . . LC 5; DA; WLC

Rabinovitch, Sholem 1859-1916
See Aleichem, Sholom
See also CA 104

Racine, Jean 1639-1699 . . . . LC 28

Radcliffe, Ann (Ward) 1764-1823 . . NCLC 6
See also DLB 39

Radiguet, Raymond 1903-1923 . . . . TCLC 29
See also DLB 65

Radnoti, Miklos 1909-1944 . . . . TCLC 16
See also CA 118

Rado, James 1939- . . . . CLC 17
See also CA 105

Radvanyi, Netty 1900-1983
See Seghers, Anna
See also CA 85-88; 110

Rae, Ben
See Griffiths, Trevor

Raeburn, John (Hay) 1941- . . . . CLC 34
See also CA 57-60

Ragni, Gerome 1942-1991 . . . . CLC 17
See also CA 105; 134

Rahv, Philip 1908-1973 . . . . CLC 24
See also Greenberg, Ivan
See also DLB 137

Raine, Craig 1944- . . . . CLC 32
See also CA 108; CANR 29; DLB 40

Raine, Kathleen (Jessie) 1908- . . . CLC 7, 45
See also CA 85-88; CANR 46; DLB 20;
MTCW

Rainis, Janis 1865-1929 . . . . TCLC 29

Rakosi, Carl . . . . CLC 47
See also Rawley, Callman
See also CAAS 5

Raleigh, Richard
See Lovecraft, H(oward) P(hillips)

Rallentando, H. P.
See Sayers, Dorothy L(eigh)

Ramal, Walter
See de la Mare, Walter (John)

Ramon, Juan
See Jimenez (Mantecon), Juan Ramon

Ramos, Graciliano 1892-1953 . . . . . TCLC 32

Rampersad, Arnold 1941- . . . . CLC 44
See also BW 2; CA 127; 133; DLB 111

Rampling, Anne
See Rice, Anne

Ramsay, Allan 1684(?)-1758 . . . . LC 29
See also DLB 95

Ramuz, Charles-Ferdinand
1878-1947 . . . . TCLC 33

Rand, Ayn
1905-1982 . . . . . . CLC 3, 30, 44, 79; DA;
WLC
See also AAYA 10; CA 13-16R; 105;
CANR 27; MTCW

Randall, Dudley (Felker)
1914- . . . . CLC 1; BLC
See also BW 1; CA 25-28R; CANR 23;
DLB 41

Randall, Robert
See Silverberg, Robert

Ranger, Ken
See Creasey, John

Ransom, John Crowe
1888-1974 . . . . CLC 2, 4, 5, 11, 24
See also CA 5-8R; 49-52; CANR 6, 34;
DLB 45, 63; MTCW

Rao, Raja 1909- . . . . CLC 25, 56
See also CA 73-76; MTCW

Raphael, Frederic (Michael)
1931- . . . . CLC 2, 14
See also CA 1-4R; CANR 1; DLB 14

Ratcliffe, James P.
See Mencken, H(enry) L(ouis)

Rathbone, Julian 1935- . . . . CLC 41
See also CA 101; CANR 34

Rattigan, Terence (Mervyn)
1911-1977 . . . . CLC 7
See also CA 85-88; 73-76;
CDBLB 1945-1960; DLB 13; MTCW

Ratushinskaya, Irina 1954- . . . . CLC 54
See also CA 129

Raven, Simon (Arthur Noel)
1927- . . . . CLC 14
See also CA 81-84

Rawley, Callman 1903-
See Rakosi, Carl
See also CA 21-24R; CANR 12, 32

Rawlings, Marjorie Kinnan
1896-1953 . . . . TCLC 4
See also CA 104; 137; DLB 9, 22, 102;
JRDA; MAICYA; YABC 1

Ray, Satyajit 1921-1992 . . . . CLC 16, 76
See also CA 114; 137

Read, Herbert Edward 1893-1968 . . . . CLC 4
See also CA 85-88; 25-28R; DLB 20, 149

Read, Piers Paul 1941- . . . . . . CLC 4, 10, 25
See also CA 21-24R; CANR 38; DLB 14;
SATA 21

Reade, Charles 1814-1884 . . . . NCLC 2
See also DLB 21

Reade, Hamish
See Gray, Simon (James Holliday)

Reading, Peter 1946- . . . . CLC 47
See also CA 103; CANR 46; DLB 40

Reaney, James 1926- . . . . CLC 13
See also CA 41-44R; CAAS 15; CANR 42;
DLB 68; SATA 43

Rebreanu, Liviu 1885-1944 . . . . TCLC 28

Rechy, John (Francisco)
1934- . . . . CLC 1, 7, 14, 18; HLC
See also CA 5-8R; CAAS 4; CANR 6, 32;
DLB 122; DLBY 82; HW

Redcam, Tom 1870-1933 . . . . TCLC 25

Reddin, Keith..................... CLC 67

Redgrove, Peter (William)
    1932-...................... CLC 6, 41
    See also CA 1-4R; CANR 3, 39; DLB 40

Redmon, Anne .... CLC 22
    See also Nightingale, Anne Redmon
    See also DLBY 86

Reed, Eliot
    See Ambler, Eric

Reed, Ishmael
    1938-... CLC 2, 3, 5, 6, 13, 32, 60; BLC
    See also BW 2; CA 21-24R; CANR 25, 48;
    DLB 2, 5, 33; DLBD 8; MTCW

Reed, John (Silas) 1887-1920 ...... TCLC 9
    See also CA 106

Reed, Lou....................... CLC 21
    See also Firbank, Louis

Reeve, Clara 1729-1807 .... NCLC 19
    See also DLB 39

Reich, Wilhelm 1897-1957....... TCLC 57

Reid, Christopher (John) 1949-..... CLC 33
    See also CA 140; DLB 40

Reid, Desmond
    See Moorcock, Michael (John)

Reid Banks, Lynne 1929-
    See Banks, Lynne Reid
    See also CA 1-4R; CANR 6, 22, 38;
    CLR 24; JRDA; MAICYA; SATA 22, 75

Reilly, William K.
    See Creasey, John

Reiner, Max
    See Caldwell, (Janet Miriam) Taylor
    (Holland)

Reis, Ricardo
    See Pessoa, Fernando (Antonio Nogueira)

Remarque, Erich Maria
    1898-1970 .... CLC 21; DA
    See also CA 77-80; 29-32R; DLB 56;
    MTCW

Remizov, A.
    See Remizov, Aleksei (Mikhailovich)

Remizov, A. M.
    See Remizov, Aleksei (Mikhailovich)

Remizov, Aleksei (Mikhailovich)
    1877-1957 .... TCLC 27
    See also CA 125; 133

Renan, Joseph Ernest
    1823-1892 .... NCLC 26

Renard, Jules 1864-1910 .... TCLC 17
    See also CA 117

Renault, Mary .... CLC 3, 11, 17
    See also Challans, Mary
    See also DLBY 83

Rendell, Ruth (Barbara) 1930-.. CLC 28, 48
    See also Vine, Barbara
    See also CA 109; CANR 32; DLB 87;
    MTCW

Renoir, Jean 1894-1979 .... CLC 20
    See also CA 129; 85-88

Resnais, Alain 1922-.............. CLC 16

Reverdy, Pierre 1889-1960 .... CLC 53
    See also CA 97-100; 89-92

Rexroth, Kenneth
    1905-1982 ...... CLC 1, 2, 6, 11, 22, 49
    See also CA 5-8R; 107; CANR 14, 34;
    CDALB 1941-1968; DLB 16, 48;
    DLBY 82; MTCW

Reyes, Alfonso 1889-1959 .... TCLC 33
    See also CA 131; HW

Reyes y Basoalto, Ricardo Eliecer Neftali
    See Neruda, Pablo

Reymont, Wladyslaw (Stanislaw)
    1868(?)-1925 .... TCLC 5
    See also CA 104

Reynolds, Jonathan 1942-....... CLC 6, 38
    See also CA 65-68; CANR 28

Reynolds, Joshua 1723-1792 .... LC 15
    See also DLB 104

Reynolds, Michael Shane 1937-.... CLC 44
    See also CA 65-68; CANR 9

Reznikoff, Charles 1894-1976 .... CLC 9
    See also CA 33-36; 61-64; CAP 2; DLB 28,
    45

Rezzori (d'Arezzo), Gregor von
    1914-...................... CLC 25
    See also CA 122; 136

Rhine, Richard
    See Silverstein, Alvin

Rhodes, Eugene Manlove
    1869-1934 .... TCLC 53

R'hoone
    See Balzac, Honore de

Rhys, Jean
    1890(?)-1979 .... CLC 2, 4, 6, 14, 19, 51
    See also CA 25-28R; 85-88; CANR 35;
    CDBLB 1945-1960; DLB 36, 117; MTCW

Ribeiro, Darcy 1922-............. CLC 34
    See also CA 33-36R

Ribeiro, Joao Ubaldo (Osorio Pimentel)
    1941-................... CLC 10, 67
    See also CA 81-84

Ribman, Ronald (Burt) 1932- .... CLC 7
    See also CA 21-24R; CANR 46

Ricci, Nino 1959-................. CLC 70
    See also CA 137

Rice, Anne 1941- .... CLC 41
    See also AAYA 9; BEST 89:2; CA 65-68;
    CANR 12, 36

Rice, Elmer (Leopold)
    1892-1967 .... CLC 7, 49
    See also CA 21-22; 25-28R; CAP 2; DLB 4,
    7; MTCW

Rice, Tim(othy Miles Bindon)
    1944-...................... CLC 21
    See also CA 103; CANR 46

Rich, Adrienne (Cecile)
    1929- .... CLC 3, 6, 7, 11, 18, 36, 73, 76;
                                        PC 5
    See also CA 9-12R; CANR 20; DLB 5, 67;
    MTCW

Rich, Barbara
    See Graves, Robert (von Ranke)

Rich, Robert
    See Trumbo, Dalton

Richard, Keith..................... CLC 17
    See also Richards, Keith

Richards, David Adams 1950-...... CLC 59
    See also CA 93-96; DLB 53

Richards, I(vor) A(rmstrong)
    1893-1979................ CLC 14, 24
    See also CA 41-44R; 89-92; CANR 34;
    DLB 27

Richards, Keith 1943-
    See Richard, Keith
    See also CA 107

Richardson, Anne
    See Roiphe, Anne (Richardson)

Richardson, Dorothy Miller
    1873-1957 .... TCLC 3
    See also CA 104; DLB 36

Richardson, Ethel Florence (Lindesay)
    1870-1946
    See Richardson, Henry Handel
    See also CA 105

Richardson, Henry Handel......... TCLC 4
    See also Richardson, Ethel Florence
    (Lindesay)

Richardson, Samuel
    1689-1761 .... LC 1; DA; WLC
    See also CDBLB 1660-1789; DLB 39

Richler, Mordecai
    1931-....... CLC 3, 5, 9, 13, 18, 46, 70
    See also AITN 1; CA 65-68; CANR 31;
    CLR 17; DLB 53; MAICYA; MTCW;
    SATA 44; SATA-Brief 27

Richter, Conrad (Michael)
    1890-1968 .... CLC 30
    See also CA 5-8R; 25-28R; CANR 23;
    DLB 9; MTCW; SATA 3

Ricostranza, Tom
    See Ellis, Trey

Riddell, J. H. 1832-1906 .... TCLC 40

Riding, Laura..................... CLC 3, 7
    See also Jackson, Laura (Riding)

Riefenstahl, Berta Helene Amalia 1902-
    See Riefenstahl, Leni
    See also CA 108

Riefenstahl, Leni.................. CLC 16
    See also Riefenstahl, Berta Helene Amalia

Riffe, Ernest
    See Bergman, (Ernst) Ingmar

Riggs, (Rolla) Lynn 1899-1954 .... TCLC 56
    See also CA 144; NNAL

Riley, James Whitcomb
    1849-1916 .... TCLC 51
    See also CA 118; 137; MAICYA; SATA 17

Riley, Tex
    See Creasey, John

Rilke, Rainer Maria
    1875-1926 .... TCLC 1, 6, 19; PC 2
    See also CA 104; 132; DLB 81; MTCW

Rimbaud, (Jean Nicolas) Arthur
    1854-1891 ..... NCLC 4, 35; DA; PC 3;
                                        WLC

Rinehart, Mary Roberts
    1876-1958 .... TCLC 52
    See also CA 108

Ringmaster, The
    See Mencken, H(enry) L(ouis)

Author Index

Ringwood, Gwen(dolyn Margaret) Pharis
  1910-1984 . . . . CLC 48
  See also CA 112; DLB 88

Rio, Michel 19(?)- . . . . CLC 43

Ritsos, Giannes
  See Ritsos, Yannis

Ritsos, Yannis 1909-1990 . . . . . CLC 6, 13, 31
  See also CA 77-80; 133; CANR 39; MTCW

Ritter, Erika 1948(?)- . . . . CLC 52

Rivera, Jose Eustasio 1889-1928 . . . TCLC 35
  See also HW

Rivers, Conrad Kent 1933-1968 . . . . . . CLC 1
  See also BW 1; CA 85-88; DLB 41

Rivers, Elfrida
  See Bradley, Marion Zimmer

Riverside, John
  See Heinlein, Robert A(nson)

Rizal, Jose 1861-1896 . . . . NCLC 27

Roa Bastos, Augusto (Antonio)
  1917- . . . . CLC 45; HLC
  See also CA 131; DLB 113; HW

Robbe-Grillet, Alain
  1922- . . . . . . CLC 1, 2, 4, 6, 8, 10, 14, 43
  See also CA 9-12R; CANR 33; DLB 83;
  MTCW

Robbins, Harold 1916- . . . . CLC 5
  See also CA 73-76; CANR 26; MTCW

Robbins, Thomas Eugene 1936-
  See Robbins, Tom
  See also CA 81-84; CANR 29; MTCW

Robbins, Tom . . . . CLC 9, 32, 64
  See also Robbins, Thomas Eugene
  See also BEST 90:3; DLBY 80

Robbins, Trina 1938- . . . . CLC 21
  See also CA 128

Roberts, Charles G(eorge) D(ouglas)
  1860-1943 . . . . TCLC 8
  See also CA 105; CLR 33; DLB 92;
  SATA-Brief 29

Roberts, Kate 1891-1985 . . . . CLC 15
  See also CA 107; 116

Roberts, Keith (John Kingston)
  1935- . . . . CLC 14
  See also CA 25-28R; CANR 46

Roberts, Kenneth (Lewis)
  1885-1957 . . . . TCLC 23
  See also CA 109; DLB 9

Roberts, Michele (B.) 1949- . . . . CLC 48
  See also CA 115

Robertson, Ellis
  See Ellison, Harlan (Jay); Silverberg, Robert

Robertson, Thomas William
  1829-1871 . . . . NCLC 35

Robinson, Edwin Arlington
  1869-1935 . . . . TCLC 5; DA; PC 1
  See also CA 104; 133; CDALB 1865-1917;
  DLB 54; MTCW

Robinson, Henry Crabb
  1775-1867 . . . . NCLC 15
  See also DLB 107

Robinson, Jill 1936- . . . . CLC 10
  See also CA 102

Robinson, Kim Stanley 1952- . . . . . . CLC 34
  See also CA 126

Robinson, Lloyd
  See Silverberg, Robert

Robinson, Marilynne 1944- . . . . CLC 25
  See also CA 116

Robinson, Smokey . . . . CLC 21
  See also Robinson, William, Jr.

Robinson, William, Jr. 1940-
  See Robinson, Smokey
  See also CA 116

Robison, Mary 1949- . . . . CLC 42
  See also CA 113; 116; DLB 130

Rod, Edouard 1857-1910 . . . . TCLC 52

Roddenberry, Eugene Wesley 1921-1991
  See Roddenberry, Gene
  See also CA 110; 135; CANR 37; SATA 45;
  SATA-Obit 69

Roddenberry, Gene . . . . CLC 17
  See also Roddenberry, Eugene Wesley
  See also AAYA 5; SATA-Obit 69

Rodgers, Mary 1931- . . . . CLC 12
  See also CA 49-52; CANR 8; CLR 20;
  JRDA; MAICYA; SATA 8

Rodgers, W(illiam) R(obert)
  1909-1969 . . . . CLC 7
  See also CA 85-88; DLB 20

Rodman, Eric
  See Silverberg, Robert

Rodman, Howard 1920(?)-1985 . . . . . CLC 65
  See also CA 118

Rodman, Maia
  See Wojciechowska, Maia (Teresa)

Rodriguez, Claudio 1934- . . . . CLC 10
  See also DLB 134

Roelvaag, O(le) E(dvart)
  1876-1931 . . . . TCLC 17
  See also CA 117; DLB 9

Roethke, Theodore (Huebner)
  1908-1963 . . . . . . CLC 1, 3, 8, 11, 19, 46
  See also CA 81-84; CABS 2;
  CDALB 1941-1968; DLB 5; MTCW

Rogers, Thomas Hunton 1927- . . . . . CLC 57
  See also CA 89-92

Rogers, Will(iam Penn Adair)
  1879-1935 . . . . TCLC 8
  See also CA 105; 144; DLB 11; NNAL

Rogin, Gilbert 1929- . . . . CLC 18
  See also CA 65-68; CANR 15

Rohan, Koda . . . . TCLC 22
  See also Koda Shigeyuki

Rohmer, Eric . . . . CLC 16
  See also Scherer, Jean-Marie Maurice

Rohmer, Sax . . . . TCLC 28
  See also Ward, Arthur Henry Sarsfield
  See also DLB 70

Roiphe, Anne (Richardson)
  1935- . . . . CLC 3, 9
  See also CA 89-92; CANR 45; DLBY 80

Rojas, Fernando de 1465-1541 . . . . . . LC 23

Rolfe, Frederick (William Serafino Austin
  Lewis Mary) 1860-1913 . . . . . . TCLC 12
  See also CA 107; DLB 34

Rolland, Romain 1866-1944 . . . . TCLC 23
  See also CA 118; DLB 65

Rolvaag, O(le) E(dvart)
  See Roelvaag, O(le) E(dvart)

Romain Arnaud, Saint
  See Aragon, Louis

Romains, Jules 1885-1972 . . . . CLC 7
  See also CA 85-88; CANR 34; DLB 65;
  MTCW

Romero, Jose Ruben 1890-1952 . . . TCLC 14
  See also CA 114; 131; HW

Ronsard, Pierre de
  1524-1585 . . . . LC 6; PC 11

Rooke, Leon 1934- . . . . CLC 25, 34
  See also CA 25-28R; CANR 23

Roper, William 1498-1578 . . . . LC 10

Roquelaure, A. N.
  See Rice, Anne

Rosa, Joao Guimaraes 1908-1967 . . . CLC 23
  See also CA 89-92; DLB 113

Rose, Wendy 1948- . . . . CLC 85; PC 12
  See also CA 53-56; CANR 5; NNAL;
  SATA 12

Rosen, Richard (Dean) 1949- . . . . . . CLC 39
  See also CA 77-80

Rosenberg, Isaac 1890-1918 . . . . . . TCLC 12
  See also CA 107; DLB 20

Rosenblatt, Joe . . . . CLC 15
  See also Rosenblatt, Joseph

Rosenblatt, Joseph 1933-
  See Rosenblatt, Joe
  See also CA 89-92

Rosenfeld, Samuel 1896-1963
  See Tzara, Tristan
  See also CA 89-92

Rosenthal, M(acha) L(ouis) 1917- . . . CLC 28
  See also CA 1-4R; CAAS 6; CANR 4;
  DLB 5; SATA 59

Ross, Barnaby
  See Dannay, Frederic

Ross, Bernard L.
  See Follett, Ken(neth Martin)

Ross, J. H.
  See Lawrence, T(homas) E(dward)

Ross, Martin
  See Martin, Violet Florence
  See also DLB 135

Ross, (James) Sinclair 1908- . . . . CLC 13
  See also CA 73-76; DLB 88

Rossetti, Christina (Georgina)
  1830-1894 . . . . . NCLC 2, 50; DA; PC 7;
                                      WLC
  See also DLB 35; MAICYA; SATA 20

Rossetti, Dante Gabriel
  1828-1882 . . . . NCLC 4; DA; WLC
  See also CDBLB 1832-1890; DLB 35

Rossner, Judith (Perelman)
  1935- . . . . CLC 6, 9, 29
  See also AITN 2; BEST 90:3; CA 17-20R;
  CANR 18; DLB 6; MTCW

Rostand, Edmond (Eugene Alexis)
  1868-1918 . . . . TCLC 6, 37; DA
  See also CA 104; 126; MTCW

Roth, Henry 1906- . . . . CLC 2, 6, 11
  See also CA 11-12; CANR 38; CAP 1;
  DLB 28; MTCW

Roth, Joseph 1894-1939......... **TCLC 33**
See also DLB 85

Roth, Philip (Milton)
1933-...... **CLC 1, 2, 3, 4, 6, 9, 15, 22,**
31, 47, 66, 86; DA; WLC
See also BEST 90:3; CA 1-4R; CANR 1, 22,
36; CDALB 1968-1988; DLB 2, 28;
DLBY 82; MTCW

Rothenberg, Jerome 1931-....... **CLC 6, 57**
See also CA 45-48; CANR 1; DLB 5

Roumain, Jacques (Jean Baptiste)
1907-1944............. **TCLC 19; BLC**
See also BW 1; CA 117; 125

Rourke, Constance (Mayfield)
1885-1941.................. **TCLC 12**
See also CA 107; YABC 1

Rousseau, Jean-Baptiste 1671-1741 ... **LC 9**

Rousseau, Jean-Jacques
1712-1778........... **LC 14; DA; WLC**

Roussel, Raymond 1877-1933..... **TCLC 20**
See also CA 117

Rovit, Earl (Herbert) 1927-......... **CLC 7**
See also CA 5-8R; CANR 12

Rowe, Nicholas 1674-1718.......... **LC 8**
See also DLB 84

Rowley, Ames Dorrance
See Lovecraft, H(oward) P(hillips)

Rowson, Susanna Haswell
1762(?)-1824............... **NCLC 5**
See also DLB 37

Roy, Gabrielle 1909-1983....... **CLC 10, 14**
See also CA 53-56; 110; CANR 5; DLB 68;
MTCW

Rozewicz, Tadeusz 1921-........ **CLC 9, 23**
See also CA 108; CANR 36; MTCW

Ruark, Gibbons 1941-............. **CLC 3**
See also CA 33-36R; CANR 14, 31;
DLB 120

Rubens, Bernice (Ruth) 1923-... **CLC 19, 31**
See also CA 25-28R; CANR 33; DLB 14;
MTCW

Rudkin, (James) David 1936-...... **CLC 14**
See also CA 89-92; DLB 13

Rudnik, Raphael 1933-............. **CLC 7**
See also CA 29-32R

Ruffian, M.
See Hasek, Jaroslav (Matej Frantisek)

Ruiz, Jose Martinez.............. **CLC 11**
See also Martinez Ruiz, Jose

Rukeyser, Muriel
1913-1980.... **CLC 6, 10, 15, 27; PC 12**
See also CA 5-8R; 93-96; CANR 26;
DLB 48; MTCW; SATA-Obit 22

Rule, Jane (Vance) 1931-.......... **CLC 27**
See also CA 25-28R; CAAS 18; CANR 12;
DLB 60

Rulfo, Juan 1918-1986.... **CLC 8, 80; HLC**
See also CA 85-88; 118; CANR 26;
DLB 113; HW; MTCW

Runeberg, Johan 1804-1877...... **NCLC 41**

Runyon, (Alfred) Damon
1884(?)-1946................ **TCLC 10**
See also CA 107; DLB 11, 86

Rush, Norman 1933-.............. **CLC 44**
See also CA 121; 126

Rushdie, (Ahmed) Salman
1947-................. **CLC 23, 31, 55**
See also BEST 89:3; CA 108; 111;
CANR 33; MTCW

Rushforth, Peter (Scott) 1945- ..... **CLC 19**
See also CA 101

Ruskin, John 1819-1900.......... **TCLC 20**
See also CA 114; 129; CDBLB 1832-1890;
DLB 55; SATA 24

Russ, Joanna 1937-.............. **CLC 15**
See also CA 25-28R; CANR 11, 31; DLB 8;
MTCW

Russell, George William 1867-1935
See A. E.
See also CA 104; CDBLB 1890-1914

Russell, (Henry) Ken(neth Alfred)
1927-....................... **CLC 16**
See also CA 105

Russell, Willy 1947-.............. **CLC 60**

Rutherford, Mark............... **TCLC 25**
See also White, William Hale
See also DLB 18

Ruyslinck, Ward 1929-............ **CLC 14**
See also Belser, Reimond Karel Maria de

Ryan, Cornelius (John) 1920-1974 ... **CLC 7**
See also CA 69-72; 53-56; CANR 38

Ryan, Michael 1946-............. **CLC 65**
See also CA 49-52; DLBY 82

Rybakov, Anatoli (Naumovich)
1911-.................... **CLC 23, 53**
See also CA 126; 135; SATA 79

Ryder, Jonathan
See Ludlum, Robert

Ryga, George 1932-1987.......... **CLC 14**
See also CA 101; 124; CANR 43; DLB 60

S. S.
See Sassoon, Siegfried (Lorraine)

Saba, Umberto 1883-1957........ **TCLC 33**
See also CA 144; DLB 114

Sabatini, Rafael 1875-1950....... **TCLC 47**

Sabato, Ernesto (R.)
1911-.............. **CLC 10, 23; HLC**
See also CA 97-100; CANR 32; DLB 145;
HW; MTCW

Sacastru, Martin
See Bioy Casares, Adolfo

Sacher-Masoch, Leopold von
1836(?)-1895.............. **NCLC 31**

Sachs, Marilyn (Stickle) 1927-..... **CLC 35**
See also AAYA 2; CA 17-20R; CANR 13,
47; CLR 2; JRDA; MAICYA; SAAS 2;
SATA 3, 68

Sachs, Nelly 1891-1970........... **CLC 14**
See also CA 17-18; 25-28R; CAP 2

Sackler, Howard (Oliver)
1929-1982.................. **CLC 14**
See also CA 61-64; 108; CANR 30; DLB 7

Sacks, Oliver (Wolf) 1933- .... **CLC 67**
See also CA 53-56; CANR 28; MTCW

Sade, Donatien Alphonse Francois Comte
1740-1814................ **NCLC 47**

Sadoff, Ira 1945-.................. **CLC 9**
See also CA 53-56; CANR 5, 21; DLB 120

Saetone
See Camus, Albert

Safire, William 1929-............. **CLC 10**
See also CA 17-20R; CANR 31

Sagan, Carl (Edward) 1934-........ **CLC 30**
See also AAYA 2; CA 25-28R; CANR 11,
36; MTCW; SATA 58

Sagan, Francoise........ **CLC 3, 6, 9, 17, 36**
See also Quoirez, Francoise
See also DLB 83

Sahgal, Nayantara (Pandit) 1927-... **CLC 41**
See also CA 9-12R; CANR 11

Saint, H(arry) F. 1941-........... **CLC 50**
See also CA 127

St. Aubin de Teran, Lisa 1953-
See Teran, Lisa St. Aubin de
See also CA 118; 126

Sainte-Beuve, Charles Augustin
1804-1869.................. **NCLC 5**

Saint-Exupery, Antoine (Jean Baptiste Marie
Roger) de
1900-1944......... **TCLC 2, 56; WLC**
See also CA 108; 132; CLR 10; DLB 72;
MAICYA; MTCW; SATA 20

St. John, David
See Hunt, E(verette) Howard, (Jr.)

Saint-John Perse
See Leger, (Marie-Rene Auguste) Alexis
Saint-Leger

Saintsbury, George (Edward Bateman)
1845-1933.................. **TCLC 31**
See also DLB 57, 149

Sait Faik....................... **TCLC 23**
See also Abasiyanik, Sait Faik

Saki.................... **TCLC 3; SSC 12**
See also Munro, H(ector) H(ugh)

Sala, George Augustus........... **NCLC 46**

Salama, Hannu 1936-............. **CLC 18**

Salamanca, J(ack) R(ichard)
1922-..................... **CLC 4, 15**
See also CA 25-28R

Sale, J. Kirkpatrick
See Sale, Kirkpatrick

Sale, Kirkpatrick 1937-........... **CLC 68**
See also CA 13-16R; CANR 10

Salinas (y Serrano), Pedro
1891(?)-1951................ **TCLC 17**
See also CA 117; DLB 134

Salinger, J(erome) D(avid)
1919-...... **CLC 1, 3, 8, 12, 55, 56; DA;**
SSC 2; WLC
See also AAYA 2; CA 5-8R; CANR 39;
CDALB 1941-1968; CLR 18; DLB 2, 102;
MAICYA; MTCW; SATA 67

Salisbury, John
See Caute, David

Salter, James 1925- .... **CLC 7, 52, 59**
See also CA 73-76; DLB 130

Saltus, Edgar (Everton)
1855-1921.................. **TCLC 8**
See also CA 105

Saltykov, Mikhail Evgrafovich
1826-1889 .... **NCLC 16**

Samarakis, Antonis 1919- .... **CLC 5**
See also CA 25-28R; CAAS 16; CANR 36

Sanchez, Florencio 1875-1910 ..... **TCLC 37**
See also HW

Sanchez, Luis Rafael 1936-........ **CLC 23**
See also CA 128; DLB 145; HW

Sanchez, Sonia 1934-... **CLC 5; BLC; PC 9**
See also BW 2; CA 33-36R; CANR 24, 49;
CLR 18; DLB 41; DLBD 8; MAICYA;
MTCW; SATA 22

Sand, George
1804-1876 ...... **NCLC 2, 42; DA; WLC**
See also DLB 119

Sandburg, Carl (August)
1878-1967 .... **CLC 1, 4, 10, 15, 35; DA;**
                            PC 2; WLC
See also CA 5-8R; 25-28R; CANR 35;
CDALB 1865-1917; DLB 17, 54;
MAICYA; MTCW; SATA 8

Sandburg, Charles
See Sandburg, Carl (August)

Sandburg, Charles A.
See Sandburg, Carl (August)

Sanders, (James) Ed(ward) 1939- ... **CLC 53**
See also CA 13-16R; CAAS 21; CANR 13,
44; DLB 16

Sanders, Lawrence 1920-.......... **CLC 41**
See also BEST 89:4; CA 81-84; CANR 33;
MTCW

Sanders, Noah
See Blount, Roy (Alton), Jr.

Sanders, Winston P.
See Anderson, Poul (William)

Sandoz, Mari(e Susette)
1896-1966 .... **CLC 28**
See also CA 1-4R; 25-28R; CANR 17;
DLB 9; MTCW; SATA 5

Saner, Reg(inald Anthony) 1931- .... **CLC 9**
See also CA 65-68

Sannazaro, Jacopo 1456(?)-1530 ...... **LC 8**

Sansom, William 1912-1976....... **CLC 2, 6**
See also CA 5-8R; 65-68; CANR 42;
DLB 139; MTCW

Santayana, George 1863-1952 ..... **TCLC 40**
See also CA 115; DLB 54, 71

Santiago, Danny .... **CLC 33**
See also James, Daniel (Lewis); James,
Daniel (Lewis)
See also DLB 122

Santmyer, Helen Hoover
1895-1986 .... **CLC 33**
See also CA 1-4R; 118; CANR 15, 33;
DLBY 84; MTCW

Santos, Bienvenido N(uqui) 1911-... **CLC 22**
See also CA 101; CANR 19, 46

Sapper .... **TCLC 44**
See also McNeile, Herman Cyril

Sappho fl. 6th cent. B.C.-.... **CMLC 3; PC 5**

Sarduy, Severo 1937-1993 .... **CLC 6**
See also CA 89-92; 142; DLB 113; HW

Sargeson, Frank 1903-1982 .... **CLC 31**
See also CA 25-28R; 106; CANR 38

Sarmiento, Felix Ruben Garcia
See Dario, Ruben

Saroyan, William
1908-1981 ..... **CLC 1, 8, 10, 29, 34, 56;**
                              DA; WLC
See also CA 5-8R; 103; CANR 30; DLB 7,
9, 86; DLBY 81; MTCW; SATA 23;
SATA-Obit 24

Sarraute, Nathalie
1900- .... **CLC 1, 2, 4, 8, 10, 31, 80**
See also CA 9-12R; CANR 23; DLB 83;
MTCW

Sarton, (Eleanor) May
1912- .... **CLC 4, 14, 49**
See also CA 1-4R; CANR 1, 34; DLB 48;
DLBY 81; MTCW; SATA 36

Sartre, Jean-Paul
1905-1980 .... **CLC 1, 4, 7, 9, 13, 18, 24,**
                   44, 50, 52; DA; DC 3; WLC
See also CA 9-12R; 97-100; CANR 21;
DLB 72; MTCW

Sassoon, Siegfried (Lorraine)
1886-1967 .... **CLC 36; PC 12**
See also CA 104; 25-28R; CANR 36;
DLB 20; MTCW

Satterfield, Charles
See Pohl, Frederik

Saul, John (W. III) 1942- .... **CLC 46**
See also AAYA 10; BEST 90:4; CA 81-84;
CANR 16, 40

Saunders, Caleb
See Heinlein, Robert A(nson)

Saura (Atares), Carlos 1932-....... **CLC 20**
See also CA 114; 131; HW

Sauser-Hall, Frederic 1887-1961.... **CLC 18**
See also Cendrars, Blaise
See also CA 102; 93-96; CANR 36; MTCW

Saussure, Ferdinand de
1857-1913 .... **TCLC 49**

Savage, Catharine
See Brosman, Catharine Savage

Savage, Thomas 1915- .... **CLC 40**
See also CA 126; 132; CAAS 15

Savan, Glenn 19(?)- .... **CLC 50**

Sayers, Dorothy L(eigh)
1893-1957 .... **TCLC 2, 15**
See also CA 104; 119; CDBLB 1914-1945;
DLB 10, 36, 77, 100; MTCW

Sayers, Valerie 1952-............. **CLC 50**
See also CA 134

Sayles, John (Thomas)
1950- .... **CLC 7, 10, 14**
See also CA 57-60; CANR 41; DLB 44

Scammell, Michael .... **CLC 34**

Scannell, Vernon 1922- .... **CLC 49**
See also CA 5-8R; CANR 8, 24; DLB 27;
SATA 59

Scarlett, Susan
See Streatfeild, (Mary) Noel

Schaeffer, Susan Fromberg
1941- .... **CLC 6, 11, 22**
See also CA 49-52; CANR 18; DLB 28;
MTCW; SATA 22

Schary, Jill
See Robinson, Jill

Schell, Jonathan 1943-............ **CLC 35**
See also CA 73-76; CANR 12

Schelling, Friedrich Wilhelm Joseph von
1775-1854 .... **NCLC 30**
See also DLB 90

Schendel, Arthur van 1874-1946 ... **TCLC 56**

Scherer, Jean-Marie Maurice 1920-
See Rohmer, Eric
See also CA 110

Schevill, James (Erwin) 1920-....... **CLC 7**
See also CA 5-8R; CAAS 12

Schiller, Friedrich 1759-1805 .... **NCLC 39**
See also DLB 94

Schisgal, Murray (Joseph) 1926-..... **CLC 6**
See also CA 21-24R; CANR 48

Schlee, Ann 1934-................ **CLC 35**
See also CA 101; CANR 29; SATA 44;
SATA-Brief 36

Schlegel, August Wilhelm von
1767-1845 .... **NCLC 15**
See also DLB 94

Schlegel, Friedrich 1772-1829 .... **NCLC 45**
See also DLB 90

Schlegel, Johann Elias (von)
1719(?)-1749 .... **LC 5**

Schlesinger, Arthur M(eier), Jr.
1917- .... **CLC 84**
See also AITN 1; CA 1-4R; CANR 1, 28;
DLB 17; MTCW; SATA 61

Schmidt, Arno (Otto) 1914-1979.... **CLC 56**
See also CA 128; 109; DLB 69

Schmitz, Aron Hector 1861-1928
See Svevo, Italo
See also CA 104; 122; MTCW

Schnackenberg, Gjertrud 1953-..... **CLC 40**
See also CA 116; DLB 120

Schneider, Leonard Alfred 1925-1966
See Bruce, Lenny
See also CA 89-92

Schnitzler, Arthur
1862-1931 .... **TCLC 4; SSC 15**
See also CA 104; DLB 81, 118

Schopenhauer, Arthur
1788-1860 .... **NCLC 51**
See also DLB 90

Schor, Sandra (M.) 1932(?)-1990 ... **CLC 65**
See also CA 132

Schorer, Mark 1908-1977 .... **CLC 9**
See also CA 5-8R; 73-76; CANR 7;
DLB 103

Schrader, Paul (Joseph) 1946-...... **CLC 26**
See also CA 37-40R; CANR 41; DLB 44

Schreiner, Olive (Emilie Albertina)
1855-1920 .... **TCLC 9**
See also CA 105; DLB 18

Schulberg, Budd (Wilson)
1914- .... **CLC 7, 48**
See also CA 25-28R; CANR 19; DLB 6, 26,
28; DLBY 81

Schulz, Bruno
1892-1942 .... **TCLC 5, 51; SSC 13**
See also CA 115; 123

Schulz, Charles M(onroe) 1922- .... **CLC 12**
See also CA 9-12R; CANR 6; SATA 10

Schumacher, E(rnst) F(riedrich)
1911-1977 . . . . **CLC 80**
See also CA 81-84; 73-76; CANR 34

Schuyler, James Marcus
1923-1991 . . . . **CLC 5, 23**
See also CA 101; 134; DLB 5

Schwartz, Delmore (David)
1913-1966 . . . **CLC 2, 4, 10, 45, 87; PC 8**
See also CA 17-18; 25-28R; CANR 35;
CAP 2; DLB 28, 48; MTCW

Schwartz, Ernst
See Ozu, Yasujiro

Schwartz, John Burnham   1965- . . . . **CLC 59**
See also CA 132

Schwartz, Lynne Sharon   1939- . . . . . **CLC 31**
See also CA 103; CANR 44

Schwartz, Muriel A.
See Eliot, T(homas) S(tearns)

Schwarz-Bart, Andre   1928- . . . . **CLC 2, 4**
See also CA 89-92

Schwarz-Bart, Simone   1938- . . . . **CLC 7**
See also BW 2; CA 97-100

Schwob, (Mayer Andre) Marcel
1867-1905 . . . . **TCLC 20**
See also CA 117; DLB 123

Sciascia, Leonardo
1921-1989 . . . . **CLC 8, 9, 41**
See also CA 85-88; 130; CANR 35; MTCW

Scoppettone, Sandra   1936- . . . . **CLC 26**
See also AAYA 11; CA 5-8R; CANR 41;
SATA 9

Scorsese, Martin   1942- . . . . **CLC 20, 89**
See also CA 110; 114; CANR 46

Scotland, Jay
See Jakes, John (William)

Scott, Duncan Campbell
1862-1947 . . . . **TCLC 6**
See also CA 104; DLB 92

Scott, Evelyn   1893-1963 . . . . **CLC 43**
See also CA 104; 112; DLB 9, 48

Scott, F(rancis) R(eginald)
1899-1985 . . . . **CLC 22**
See also CA 101; 114; DLB 88

Scott, Frank
See Scott, F(rancis) R(eginald)

Scott, Joanna   1960- . . . . **CLC 50**
See also CA 126

Scott, Paul (Mark)   1920-1978 . . . . **CLC 9, 60**
See also CA 81-84; 77-80; CANR 33;
DLB 14; MTCW

Scott, Walter
1771-1832 . . . . . . **NCLC 15; DA; PC 12;
                                                    WLC**
See also CDBLB 1789-1832; DLB 93, 107,
116, 144; YABC 2

Scribe, (Augustin) Eugene
1791-1861 . . . . **NCLC 16; DC 5**

Scrum, R.
See Crumb, R(obert)

Scudery, Madeleine de   1607-1701 . . . . . **LC 2**

Scum
See Crumb, R(obert)

Scumbag, Little Bobby
See Crumb, R(obert)

Seabrook, John
See Hubbard, L(afayette) Ron(ald)

Sealy, I. Allan   1951- . . . . **CLC 55**

Search, Alexander
See Pessoa, Fernando (Antonio Nogueira)

Sebastian, Lee
See Silverberg, Robert

Sebastian Owl
See Thompson, Hunter S(tockton)

Sebestyen, Ouida   1924- . . . . **CLC 30**
See also AAYA 8; CA 107; CANR 40;
CLR 17; JRDA; MAICYA; SAAS 10;
SATA 39

Secundus, H. Scriblerus
See Fielding, Henry

Sedges, John
See Buck, Pearl S(ydenstricker)

Sedgwick, Catharine Maria
1789-1867 . . . . **NCLC 19**
See also DLB 1, 74

Seelye, John   1931- . . . . **CLC 7**

Seferiades, Giorgos Stylianou   1900-1971
See Seferis, George
See also CA 5-8R; 33-36R; CANR 5, 36;
MTCW

Seferis, George . . . . **CLC 5, 11**
See also Seferiades, Giorgos Stylianou

Segal, Erich (Wolf)   1937- . . . . **CLC 3, 10**
See also BEST 89:1; CA 25-28R; CANR 20,
36; DLBY 86; MTCW

Seger, Bob   1945- . . . . **CLC 35**

Seghers, Anna . . . . **CLC 7**
See also Radvanyi, Netty
See also DLB 69

Seidel, Frederick (Lewis)   1936- . . . . . **CLC 18**
See also CA 13-16R; CANR 8; DLBY 84

Seifert, Jaroslav   1901-1986 . . . . . **CLC 34, 44**
See also CA 127; MTCW

Sei Shonagon   c. 966-1017(?) . . . . . . **CMLC 6**

Selby, Hubert, Jr.
1928- . . . . **CLC 1, 2, 4, 8; SSC 20**
See also CA 13-16R; CANR 33; DLB 2

Selzer, Richard   1928- . . . . **CLC 74**
See also CA 65-68; CANR 14

Sembene, Ousmane
See Ousmane, Sembene

Senancour, Etienne Pivert de
1770-1846 . . . . **NCLC 16**
See also DLB 119

Sender, Ramon (Jose)
1902-1982 . . . . **CLC 8; HLC**
See also CA 5-8R; 105; CANR 8; HW;
MTCW

Seneca, Lucius Annaeus
4B.C.-65 . . . . **CMLC 6; DC 5**

Senghor, Leopold Sedar
1906- . . . . **CLC 54; BLC**
See also BW 2; CA 116; 125; CANR 47;
MTCW

Serling, (Edward) Rod(man)
1924-1975 . . . . **CLC 30**
See also AAYA 14; AITN 1; CA 65-68;
57-60; DLB 26

Serna, Ramon Gomez de la
See Gomez de la Serna, Ramon

Serpieres
See Guillevic, (Eugene)

Service, Robert
See Service, Robert W(illiam)
See also DLB 92

Service, Robert W(illiam)
1874(?)-1958 . . . . . . **TCLC 15; DA; WLC**
See also Service, Robert
See also CA 115; 140; SATA 20

Seth, Vikram   1952- . . . . **CLC 43**
See also CA 121; 127; DLB 120

Seton, Cynthia Propper
1926-1982 . . . . **CLC 27**
See also CA 5-8R; 108; CANR 7

Seton, Ernest (Evan) Thompson
1860-1946 . . . . **TCLC 31**
See also CA 109; DLB 92; JRDA; SATA 18

Seton-Thompson, Ernest
See Seton, Ernest (Evan) Thompson

Settle, Mary Lee   1918- . . . . **CLC 19, 61**
See also CA 89-92; CAAS 1; CANR 44;
DLB 6

Seuphor, Michel
See Arp, Jean

**Sevigne, Marie (de Rabutin-Chantal) Marquise
de**   1626-1696 . . . . **LC 11**

Sexton, Anne (Harvey)
1928-1974 . . . . **CLC 2, 4, 6, 8, 10, 15, 53;
                                                    DA; PC 2; WLC**
See also CA 1-4R; 53-56; CABS 2;
CANR 3, 36; CDALB 1941-1968; DLB 5;
MTCW; SATA 10

Shaara, Michael (Joseph, Jr.)
1929-1988 . . . . **CLC 15**
See also AITN 1; CA 102; 125; DLBY 83

Shackleton, C. C.
See Aldiss, Brian W(ilson)

Shacochis, Bob . . . . **CLC 39**
See also Shacochis, Robert G.

Shacochis, Robert G.   1951-
See Shacochis, Bob
See also CA 119; 124

Shaffer, Anthony (Joshua)   1926- . . . . **CLC 19**
See also CA 110; 116; DLB 13

Shaffer, Peter (Levin)
1926- . . . . **CLC 5, 14, 18, 37, 60**
See also CA 25-28R; CANR 25, 47;
CDBLB 1960 to Present; DLB 13;
MTCW

Shakey, Bernard
See Young, Neil

Shalamov, Varlam (Tikhonovich)
1907(?)-1982 . . . . **CLC 18**
See also CA 129; 105

Shamlu, Ahmad   1925- . . . . **CLC 10**

Shammas, Anton   1951- . . . . **CLC 55**

Shange, Ntozake
1948- . . . . **CLC 8, 25, 38, 74; BLC; DC 3**
See also AAYA 9; BW 2; CA 85-88;
CABS 3; CANR 27, 48; DLB 38; MTCW

Shanley, John Patrick   1950- . . . . **CLC 75**
See also CA 128; 133

Shapcott, Thomas W(illiam) 1935- .. **CLC 38**
See also CA 69-72; CANR 49

Shapiro, Jane.................... **CLC 76**

Shapiro, Karl (Jay) 1913- .. **CLC 4, 8, 15, 53**
See also CA 1-4R; CAAS 6; CANR 1, 36;
DLB 48; MTCW

Sharp, William 1855-1905 .... **TCLC 39**

Sharpe, Thomas Ridley 1928-
See Sharpe, Tom
See also CA 114; 122

Sharpe, Tom...................... **CLC 36**
See also Sharpe, Thomas Ridley
See also DLB 14

Shaw, Bernard................... **TCLC 45**
See also Shaw, George Bernard
See also BW 1

Shaw, G. Bernard
See Shaw, George Bernard

Shaw, George Bernard
1856-1950 .... **TCLC 3, 9, 21; DA; WLC**
See also CA 104; 128; CDBLB 1914-1945;
DLB 10, 57; MTCW

Shaw, Henry Wheeler
1818-1885 .... **NCLC 15**
See also DLB 11

Shaw, Irwin 1913-1984...... **CLC 7, 23, 34**
See also AITN 1; CA 13-16R; 112;
CANR 21; CDALB 1941-1968; DLB 6,
102; DLBY 84; MTCW

Shaw, Robert 1927-1978 .... **CLC 5**
See also AITN 1; CA 1-4R; 81-84;
CANR 4; DLB 13, 14

Shaw, T. E.
See Lawrence, T(homas) E(dward)

Shawn, Wallace 1943- .... **CLC 41**
See also CA 112

Shea, Lisa 1953-................ **CLC 86**
See also CA 147

Sheed, Wilfrid (John Joseph)
1930- .... **CLC 2, 4, 10, 53**
See also CA 65-68; CANR 30; DLB 6;
MTCW

Sheldon, Alice Hastings Bradley
1915(?)-1987
See Tiptree, James, Jr.
See also CA 108; 122; CANR 34; MTCW

Sheldon, John
See Bloch, Robert (Albert)

Shelley, Mary Wollstonecraft (Godwin)
1797-1851 .... **NCLC 14; DA; WLC**
See also CDBLB 1789-1832; DLB 110, 116;
SATA 29

Shelley, Percy Bysshe
1792-1822 .... **NCLC 18; DA; WLC**
See also CDBLB 1789-1832; DLB 96, 110

Shepard, Jim 1956-................ **CLC 36**
See also CA 137

Shepard, Lucius 1947- .... **CLC 34**
See also CA 128; 141

Shepard, Sam
1943- .... **CLC 4, 6, 17, 34, 41, 44; DC 5**
See also AAYA 1; CA 69-72; CABS 3;
CANR 22; DLB 7; MTCW

Shepherd, Michael
See Ludlum, Robert

Sherburne, Zoa (Morin) 1912-...... **CLC 30**
See also AAYA 13; CA 1-4R; CANR 3, 37;
MAICYA; SAAS 18; SATA 3

Sheridan, Frances 1724-1766........ **LC 7**
See also DLB 39, 84

Sheridan, Richard Brinsley
1751-1816 ... **NCLC 5; DA; DC 1; WLC**
See also CDBLB 1660-1789; DLB 89

Sherman, Jonathan Marc.......... **CLC 55**

Sherman, Martin 1941(?)- .... **CLC 19**
See also CA 116; 123

Sherwin, Judith Johnson 1936-... **CLC 7, 15**
See also CA 25-28R; CANR 34

Sherwood, Frances 1940-.......... **CLC 81**

Sherwood, Robert E(mmet)
1896-1955 .... **TCLC 3**
See also CA 104; DLB 7, 26

Shestov, Lev 1866-1938 .... **TCLC 56**

Shiel, M(atthew) P(hipps)
1865-1947 .... **TCLC 8**
See also CA 106; DLB 153

Shiga, Naoya 1883-1971........... **CLC 33**
See also CA 101; 33-36R

Shih, Su 1036-1101............. **CMLC 15**

Shilts, Randy 1951-1994 .... **CLC 85**
See also CA 115; 127; 144; CANR 45

Shimazaki Haruki 1872-1943
See Shimazaki Toson
See also CA 105; 134

Shimazaki Toson.................. **TCLC 5**
See also Shimazaki Haruki

Sholokhov, Mikhail (Aleksandrovich)
1905-1984 .... **CLC 7, 15**
See also CA 101; 112; MTCW;
SATA-Obit 36

Shone, Patric
See Hanley, James

Shreve, Susan Richards 1939-...... **CLC 23**
See also CA 49-52; CAAS 5; CANR 5, 38;
MAICYA; SATA 46; SATA-Brief 41

Shue, Larry 1946-1985............. **CLC 52**
See also CA 145; 117

Shu-Jen, Chou 1881-1936
See Lu Hsun
See also CA 104

Shulman, Alix Kates 1932- ...... **CLC 2, 10**
See also CA 29-32R; CANR 43; SATA 7

Shuster, Joe 1914- .... **CLC 21**

Shute, Nevil...................... **CLC 30**
See also Norway, Nevil Shute

Shuttle, Penelope (Diane) 1947- ..... **CLC 7**
See also CA 93-96; CANR 39; DLB 14, 40

Sidney, Mary 1561-1621 .... **LC 19**

Sidney, Sir Philip 1554-1586.... **LC 19; DA**
See also CDBLB Before 1660

Siegel, Jerome 1914- .... **CLC 21**
See also CA 116

Siegel, Jerry
See Siegel, Jerome

Sienkiewicz, Henryk (Adam Alexander Pius)
1846-1916 .... **TCLC 3**
See also CA 104; 134

Sierra, Gregorio Martinez
See Martinez Sierra, Gregorio

Sierra, Maria (de la O'LeJarraga) Martinez
See Martinez Sierra, Maria (de la
O'LeJarraga)

Sigal, Clancy 1926-................ **CLC 7**
See also CA 1-4R

Sigourney, Lydia Howard (Huntley)
1791-1865 .... **NCLC 21**
See also DLB 1, 42, 73

Siguenza y Gongora, Carlos de
1645-1700 .... **LC 8**

Sigurjonsson, Johann 1880-1919... **TCLC 27**

Sikelianos, Angelos 1884-1951 .... **TCLC 39**

Silkin, Jon 1930- .... **CLC 2, 6, 43**
See also CA 5-8R; CAAS 5; DLB 27

Silko, Leslie (Marmon)
1948- .... **CLC 23, 74; DA**
See also AAYA 14; CA 115; 122;
CANR 45; DLB 143; NNAL

Sillanpaa, Frans Eemil 1888-1964... **CLC 19**
See also CA 129; 93-96; MTCW

Sillitoe, Alan
1928- .... **CLC 1, 3, 6, 10, 19, 57**
See also AITN 1; CA 9-12R; CAAS 2;
CANR 8, 26; CDBLB 1960 to Present;
DLB 14, 139; MTCW; SATA 61

Silone, Ignazio 1900-1978 .... **CLC 4**
See also CA 25-28; 81-84; CANR 34;
CAP 2; MTCW

Silver, Joan Micklin 1935- .... **CLC 20**
See also CA 114; 121

Silver, Nicholas
See Faust, Frederick (Schiller)

Silverberg, Robert 1935- .... **CLC 7**
See also CA 1-4R; CAAS 3; CANR 1, 20,
36; DLB 8; MAICYA; MTCW; SATA 13

Silverstein, Alvin 1933- .... **CLC 17**
See also CA 49-52; CANR 2; CLR 25;
JRDA; MAICYA; SATA 8, 69

Silverstein, Virginia B(arbara Opshelor)
1937- .... **CLC 17**
See also CA 49-52; CANR 2; CLR 25;
JRDA; MAICYA; SATA 8, 69

Sim, Georges
See Simenon, Georges (Jacques Christian)

Simak, Clifford D(onald)
1904-1988 .... **CLC 1, 55**
See also CA 1-4R; 125; CANR 1, 35;
DLB 8; MTCW; SATA-Obit 56

Simenon, Georges (Jacques Christian)
1903-1989 .... **CLC 1, 2, 3, 8, 18, 47**
See also CA 85-88; 129; CANR 35;
DLB 72; DLBY 89; MTCW

Simic, Charles 1938-... **CLC 6, 9, 22, 49, 68**
See also CA 29-32R; CAAS 4; CANR 12,
33; DLB 105

Simmons, Charles (Paul) 1924-..... **CLC 57**
See also CA 89-92

Simmons, Dan 1948-............... **CLC 44**
See also CA 138

Simmons, James (Stewart Alexander)
1933- . . . . **CLC 43**
See also CA 105; CAAS 21; DLB 40

Simms, William Gilmore
1806-1870 . . . . **NCLC 3**
See also DLB 3, 30, 59, 73

Simon, Carly 1945- . . . . **CLC 26**
See also CA 105

Simon, Claude 1913- . . . . **CLC 4, 9, 15, 39**
See also CA 89-92; CANR 33; DLB 83;
MTCW

Simon, (Marvin) Neil
1927- . . . . **CLC 6, 11, 31, 39, 70**
See also AITN 1; CA 21-24R; CANR 26;
DLB 7; MTCW

Simon, Paul 1942(?)- . . . . **CLC 17**
See also CA 116

Simonon, Paul 1956(?)- . . . . **CLC 30**

Simpson, Harriette
See Arnow, Harriette (Louisa) Simpson

Simpson, Louis (Aston Marantz)
1923- . . . . **CLC 4, 7, 9, 32**
See also CA 1-4R; CAAS 4; CANR 1;
DLB 5; MTCW

Simpson, Mona (Elizabeth) 1957- . . . **CLC 44**
See also CA 122; 135

Simpson, N(orman) F(rederick)
1919- . . . . **CLC 29**
See also CA 13-16R; DLB 13

Sinclair, Andrew (Annandale)
1935- . . . . **CLC 2, 14**
See also CA 9-12R; CAAS 5; CANR 14, 38;
DLB 14; MTCW

Sinclair, Emil
See Hesse, Hermann

Sinclair, Iain 1943- . . . . **CLC 76**
See also CA 132

Sinclair, Iain MacGregor
See Sinclair, Iain

Sinclair, Mary Amelia St. Clair 1865(?)-1946
See Sinclair, May
See also CA 104

Sinclair, May . . . . **TCLC 3, 11**
See also Sinclair, Mary Amelia St. Clair
See also DLB 36, 135

Sinclair, Upton (Beall)
1878-1968 . . . . . . **CLC 1, 11, 15, 63; DA;**
WLC
See also CA 5-8R; 25-28R; CANR 7;
CDALB 1929-1941; DLB 9; MTCW;
SATA 9

Singer, Isaac
See Singer, Isaac Bashevis

Singer, Isaac Bashevis
1904-1991 . . . . **CLC 1, 3, 6, 9, 11, 15, 23,**
38, 69; DA; SSC 3; WLC
See also AITN 1, 2; CA 1-4R; 134;
CANR 1, 39; CDALB 1941-1968; CLR 1;
DLB 6, 28, 52; DLBY 91; JRDA;
MAICYA; MTCW; SATA 3, 27;
SATA-Obit 68

Singer, Israel Joshua 1893-1944 . . . **TCLC 33**

Singh, Khushwant 1915- . . . . **CLC 11**
See also CA 9-12R; CAAS 9; CANR 6

Sinjohn, John
See Galsworthy, John

Sinyavsky, Andrei (Donatevich)
1925- . . . . **CLC 8**
See also CA 85-88

Sirin, V.
See Nabokov, Vladimir (Vladimirovich)

Sissman, L(ouis) E(dward)
1928-1976 . . . . **CLC 9, 18**
See also CA 21-24R; 65-68; CANR 13;
DLB 5

Sisson, C(harles) H(ubert) 1914- . . . . . **CLC 8**
See also CA 1-4R; CAAS 3; CANR 3, 48;
DLB 27

Sitwell, Dame Edith
1887-1964 . . . . **CLC 2, 9, 67; PC 3**
See also CA 9-12R; CANR 35;
CDBLB 1945-1960; DLB 20; MTCW

Sjoewall, Maj 1935- . . . . **CLC 7**
See also CA 65-68

Sjowall, Maj
See Sjoewall, Maj

Skelton, Robin 1925- . . . . **CLC 13**
See also AITN 2; CA 5-8R; CAAS 5;
CANR 28; DLB 27, 53

Skolimowski, Jerzy 1938- . . . . **CLC 20**
See also CA 128

Skram, Amalie (Bertha)
1847-1905 . . . . **TCLC 25**

Skvorecky, Josef (Vaclav)
1924- . . . . **CLC 15, 39, 69**
See also CA 61-64; CAAS 1; CANR 10, 34;
MTCW

Slade, Bernard . . . . **CLC 11, 46**
See also Newbound, Bernard Slade
See also CAAS 9; DLB 53

Slaughter, Carolyn 1946- . . . . **CLC 56**
See also CA 85-88

Slaughter, Frank G(ill) 1908- . . . . . . **CLC 29**
See also AITN 2; CA 5-8R; CANR 5

Slavitt, David R(ytman) 1935- . . . . **CLC 5, 14**
See also CA 21-24R; CAAS 3; CANR 41;
DLB 5, 6

Slesinger, Tess 1905-1945 . . . . **TCLC 10**
See also CA 107; DLB 102

Slessor, Kenneth 1901-1971 . . . . **CLC 14**
See also CA 102; 89-92

Slowacki, Juliusz 1809-1849 . . . . . **NCLC 15**

Smart, Christopher
1722-1771 . . . . **LC 3; PC 12**
See also DLB 109

Smart, Elizabeth 1913-1986 . . . . **CLC 54**
See also CA 81-84; 118; DLB 88

Smiley, Jane (Graves) 1949- . . . . **CLC 53, 76**
See also CA 104; CANR 30

Smith, A(rthur) J(ames) M(arshall)
1902-1980 . . . . **CLC 15**
See also CA 1-4R; 102; CANR 4; DLB 88

Smith, Anna Deavere 1950- . . . . **CLC 86**
See also CA 133

Smith, Betty (Wehner) 1896-1972 . . . **CLC 19**
See also CA 5-8R; 33-36R; DLBY 82;
SATA 6

Smith, Charlotte (Turner)
1749-1806 . . . . **NCLC 23**
See also DLB 39, 109

Smith, Clark Ashton 1893-1961 . . . . **CLC 43**
See also CA 143

Smith, Dave . . . . **CLC 22, 42**
See also Smith, David (Jeddie)
See also CAAS 7; DLB 5

Smith, David (Jeddie) 1942-
See Smith, Dave
See also CA 49-52; CANR 1

Smith, Florence Margaret 1902-1971
See Smith, Stevie
See also CA 17-18; 29-32R; CANR 35;
CAP 2; MTCW

Smith, Iain Crichton 1928- . . . . **CLC 64**
See also CA 21-24R; DLB 40, 139

Smith, John 1580(?)-1631 . . . . **LC 9**

Smith, Johnston
See Crane, Stephen (Townley)

Smith, Lee 1944- . . . . **CLC 25, 73**
See also CA 114; 119; CANR 46; DLB 143;
DLBY 83

Smith, Martin
See Smith, Martin Cruz

Smith, Martin Cruz 1942- . . . . **CLC 25**
See also BEST 89:4; CA 85-88; CANR 6,
23, 43; NNAL

Smith, Mary-Ann Tirone 1944- . . . . . **CLC 39**
See also CA 118; 136

Smith, Patti 1946- . . . . **CLC 12**
See also CA 93-96

Smith, Pauline (Urmson)
1882-1959 . . . . **TCLC 25**

Smith, Rosamond
See Oates, Joyce Carol

Smith, Sheila Kaye
See Kaye-Smith, Sheila

Smith, Stevie . . . . **CLC 3, 8, 25, 44; PC 12**
See also Smith, Florence Margaret
See also DLB 20

Smith, Wilbur (Addison) 1933- . . . . . **CLC 33**
See also CA 13-16R; CANR 7, 46; MTCW

Smith, William Jay 1918- . . . . **CLC 6**
See also CA 5-8R; CANR 44; DLB 5;
MAICYA; SATA 2, 68

Smith, Woodrow Wilson
See Kuttner, Henry

Smolenskin, Peretz 1842-1885 . . . . **NCLC 30**

Smollett, Tobias (George) 1721-1771 . . **LC 2**
See also CDBLB 1660-1789; DLB 39, 104

Snodgrass, W(illiam) D(e Witt)
1926- . . . . **CLC 2, 6, 10, 18, 68**
See also CA 1-4R; CANR 6, 36; DLB 5;
MTCW

Snow, C(harles) P(ercy)
1905-1980 . . . . **CLC 1, 4, 6, 9, 13, 19**
See also CA 5-8R; 101; CANR 28;
CDBLB 1945-1960; DLB 15, 77; MTCW

Snow, Frances Compton
See Adams, Henry (Brooks)

Snyder, Gary (Sherman)
1930- . . . . **CLC 1, 2, 5, 9, 32**
See also CA 17-20R; CANR 30; DLB 5, 16

Snyder, Zilpha Keatley 1927- ...... **CLC 17**
See also CA 9-12R; CANR 38; CLR 31;
JRDA; MAICYA; SAAS 2; SATA 1, 28,
75

Soares, Bernardo
See Pessoa, Fernando (Antonio Nogueira)

Sobh, A.
See Shamlu, Ahmad

Sobol, Joshua .... **CLC 60**

Soderberg, Hjalmar 1869-1941 .... **TCLC 39**

Sodergran, Edith (Irene)
See Soedergran, Edith (Irene)

Soedergran, Edith (Irene)
1892-1923 .... **TCLC 31**

Softly, Edgar
See Lovecraft, H(oward) P(hillips)

Softly, Edward
See Lovecraft, H(oward) P(hillips)

Sokolov, Raymond 1941- .... **CLC 7**
See also CA 85-88

Solo, Jay
See Ellison, Harlan (Jay)

Sologub, Fyodor .... **TCLC 9**
See also Teternikov, Fyodor Kuzmich

Solomons, Ikey Esquir
See Thackeray, William Makepeace

Solomos, Dionysios 1798-1857 ... **NCLC 15**

Solwoska, Mara
See French, Marilyn

Solzhenitsyn, Aleksandr I(sayevich)
1918- ...... **CLC 1, 2, 4, 7, 9, 10, 18, 26,
34, 78; DA; WLC**
See also AITN 1; CA 69-72; CANR 40;
MTCW

Somers, Jane
See Lessing, Doris (May)

Somerville, Edith 1858-1949 ...... **TCLC 51**
See also DLB 135

Somerville & Ross
See Martin, Violet Florence; Somerville,
Edith

Sommer, Scott 1951- .... **CLC 25**
See also CA 106

Sondheim, Stephen (Joshua)
1930- .... **CLC 30, 39**
See also AAYA 11; CA 103; CANR 47

Sontag, Susan 1933- ... **CLC 1, 2, 10, 13, 31**
See also CA 17-20R; CANR 25; DLB 2, 67;
MTCW

Sophocles
496(?)B.C.-406(?)B.C..... **CMLC 2; DA;
DC 1**

Sordello 1189-1269 .... **CMLC 15**

Sorel, Julia
See Drexler, Rosalyn

Sorrentino, Gilbert
1929- .... **CLC 3, 7, 14, 22, 40**
See also CA 77-80; CANR 14, 33; DLB 5;
DLBY 80

Soto, Gary 1952- .... **CLC 32, 80; HLC**
See also AAYA 10; CA 119; 125; CLR 38;
DLB 82; HW; JRDA; SATA 80

Soupault, Philippe 1897-1990 ...... **CLC 68**
See also CA 116; 147; 131

Souster, (Holmes) Raymond
1921- .... **CLC 5, 14**
See also CA 13-16R; CAAS 14; CANR 13,
29; DLB 88; SATA 63

Southern, Terry 1926- .... **CLC 7**
See also CA 1-4R; CANR 1; DLB 2

Southey, Robert 1774-1843 .... **NCLC 8**
See also DLB 93, 107, 142; SATA 54

Southworth, Emma Dorothy Eliza Nevitte
1819-1899 .... **NCLC 26**

Souza, Ernest
See Scott, Evelyn

Soyinka, Wole
1934- .... **CLC 3, 5, 14, 36, 44; BLC;
DA; DC 2; WLC**
See also BW 2; CA 13-16R; CANR 27, 39;
DLB 125; MTCW

Spackman, W(illiam) M(ode)
1905-1990 .... **CLC 46**
See also CA 81-84; 132

Spacks, Barry 1931- .... **CLC 14**
See also CA 29-32R; CANR 33; DLB 105

Spanidou, Irini 1946- .... **CLC 44**

Spark, Muriel (Sarah)
1918- .... **CLC 2, 3, 5, 8, 13, 18, 40;
SSC 10**
See also CA 5-8R; CANR 12, 36;
CDBLB 1945-1960; DLB 15, 139; MTCW

Spaulding, Douglas
See Bradbury, Ray (Douglas)

Spaulding, Leonard
See Bradbury, Ray (Douglas)

Spence, J. A. D.
See Eliot, T(homas) S(tearns)

Spencer, Elizabeth 1921- .... **CLC 22**
See also CA 13-16R; CANR 32; DLB 6;
MTCW; SATA 14

Spencer, Leonard G.
See Silverberg, Robert

Spencer, Scott 1945- .... **CLC 30**
See also CA 113; DLBY 86

Spender, Stephen (Harold)
1909- .... **CLC 1, 2, 5, 10, 41**
See also CA 9-12R; CANR 31;
CDBLB 1945-1960; DLB 20; MTCW

Spengler, Oswald (Arnold Gottfried)
1880-1936 .... **TCLC 25**
See also CA 118

Spenser, Edmund
1552(?)-1599 .... **LC 5; DA; PC 8; WLC**
See also CDBLB Before 1660

Spicer, Jack 1925-1965 ...... **CLC 8, 18, 72**
See also CA 85-88; DLB 5, 16

Spiegelman, Art 1948- .... **CLC 76**
See also AAYA 10; CA 125; CANR 41

Spielberg, Peter 1929- .... **CLC 6**
See also CA 5-8R; CANR 4, 48; DLBY 81

Spielberg, Steven 1947- .... **CLC 20**
See also AAYA 8; CA 77-80; CANR 32;
SATA 32

Spillane, Frank Morrison 1918-
See Spillane, Mickey
See also CA 25-28R; CANR 28; MTCW;
SATA 66

Spillane, Mickey .... **CLC 3, 13**
See also Spillane, Frank Morrison

Spinoza, Benedictus de 1632-1677 .... **LC 9**

Spinrad, Norman (Richard) 1940-... **CLC 46**
See also CA 37-40R; CAAS 19; CANR 20;
DLB 8

Spitteler, Carl (Friedrich Georg)
1845-1924 .... **TCLC 12**
See also CA 109; DLB 129

Spivack, Kathleen (Romola Drucker)
1938- .... **CLC 6**
See also CA 49-52

Spoto, Donald 1941- .... **CLC 39**
See also CA 65-68; CANR 11

Springsteen, Bruce (F.) 1949- ...... **CLC 17**
See also CA 111

Spurling, Hilary 1940- .... **CLC 34**
See also CA 104; CANR 25

Spyker, John Howland
See Elman, Richard

Squires, (James) Radcliffe
1917-1993 .... **CLC 51**
See also CA 1-4R; 140; CANR 6, 21

Srivastava, Dhanpat Rai 1880(?)-1936
See Premchand
See also CA 118

Stacy, Donald
See Pohl, Frederik

Stael, Germaine de
See Stael-Holstein, Anne Louise Germaine
Necker Baronn
See also DLB 119

**Stael-Holstein, Anne Louise Germaine Necker
Baronn** 1766-1817 .... **NCLC 3**
See also Stael, Germaine de

Stafford, Jean 1915-1979 ... **CLC 4, 7, 19, 68**
See also CA 1-4R; 85-88; CANR 3; DLB 2;
MTCW; SATA-Obit 22

Stafford, William (Edgar)
1914-1993 .... **CLC 4, 7, 29**
See also CA 5-8R; 142; CAAS 3; CANR 5,
22; DLB 5

Staines, Trevor
See Brunner, John (Kilian Houston)

Stairs, Gordon
See Austin, Mary (Hunter)

Stannard, Martin 1947- .... **CLC 44**
See also CA 142

Stanton, Maura 1946- .... **CLC 9**
See also CA 89-92; CANR 15; DLB 120

Stanton, Schuyler
See Baum, L(yman) Frank

Stapledon, (William) Olaf
1886-1950 .... **TCLC 22**
See also CA 111; DLB 15

Starbuck, George (Edwin) 1931-.... **CLC 53**
See also CA 21-24R; CANR 23

Stark, Richard
See Westlake, Donald E(dwin)

Staunton, Schuyler
See Baum, L(yman) Frank

Stead, Christina (Ellen)
1902-1983 . . . . **CLC 2, 5, 8, 32, 80**
See also CA 13-16R; 109; CANR 33, 40;
MTCW

Stead, William Thomas
1849-1912 . . . . **TCLC 48**

Steele, Richard 1672-1729 . . . . **LC 18**
See also CDBLB 1660-1789; DLB 84, 101

Steele, Timothy (Reid) 1948- . . . . . . **CLC 45**
See also CA 93-96; CANR 16; DLB 120

Steffens, (Joseph) Lincoln
1866-1936 . . . . **TCLC 20**
See also CA 117

Stegner, Wallace (Earle)
1909-1993 . . . . **CLC 9, 49, 81**
See also AITN 1; BEST 90:3; CA 1-4R;
141; CAAS 9; CANR 1, 21, 46; DLB 9;
DLBY 93; MTCW

Stein, Gertrude
1874-1946 . . . . . . **TCLC 1, 6, 28, 48; DA;**
WLC
See also CA 104; 132; CDALB 1917-1929;
DLB 4, 54, 86; MTCW

Steinbeck, John (Ernst)
1902-1968 . . . . . . **CLC 1, 5, 9, 13, 21, 34,**
45, 75; DA; SSC 11; WLC
See also AAYA 12; CA 1-4R; 25-28R;
CANR 1, 35; CDALB 1929-1941; DLB 7,
9; DLBD 2; MTCW; SATA 9

Steinem, Gloria 1934- . . . . **CLC 63**
See also CA 53-56; CANR 28; MTCW

Steiner, George 1929- . . . . **CLC 24**
See also CA 73-76; CANR 31; DLB 67;
MTCW; SATA 62

Steiner, K. Leslie
See Delany, Samuel R(ay, Jr.)

Steiner, Rudolf 1861-1925 . . . . **TCLC 13**
See also CA 107

Stendhal
1783-1842 . . . . . **NCLC 23, 46; DA; WLC**
See also DLB 119

Stephen, Leslie 1832-1904 . . . . **TCLC 23**
See also CA 123; DLB 57, 144

Stephen, Sir Leslie
See Stephen, Leslie

Stephen, Virginia
See Woolf, (Adeline) Virginia

Stephens, James 1882(?)-1950 . . . . . . **TCLC 4**
See also CA 104; DLB 19, 153

Stephens, Reed
See Donaldson, Stephen R.

Steptoe, Lydia
See Barnes, Djuna

Sterchi, Beat 1949- . . . . **CLC 65**

Sterling, Brett
See Bradbury, Ray (Douglas); Hamilton,
Edmond

Sterling, Bruce 1954- . . . . **CLC 72**
See also CA 119; CANR 44

Sterling, George 1869-1926 . . . . **TCLC 20**
See also CA 117; DLB 54

Stern, Gerald 1925- . . . . **CLC 40**
See also CA 81-84; CANR 28; DLB 105

Stern, Richard (Gustave) 1928- . . . **CLC 4, 39**
See also CA 1-4R; CANR 1, 25; DLBY 87

Sternberg, Josef von 1894-1969 . . . . . **CLC 20**
See also CA 81-84

Sterne, Laurence
1713-1768 . . . . **LC 2; DA; WLC**
See also CDBLB 1660-1789; DLB 39

Sternheim, (William Adolf) Carl
1878-1942 . . . . **TCLC 8**
See also CA 105; DLB 56, 118

Stevens, Mark 1951- . . . . **CLC 34**
See also CA 122

Stevens, Wallace
1879-1955 . . . . **TCLC 3, 12, 45; DA;**
PC 6; WLC
See also CA 104; 124; CDALB 1929-1941;
DLB 54; MTCW

Stevenson, Anne (Katharine)
1933- . . . . **CLC 7, 33**
See also CA 17-20R; CAAS 9; CANR 9, 33;
DLB 40; MTCW

Stevenson, Robert Louis (Balfour)
1850-1894 . . . . **NCLC 5, 14; DA;**
SSC 11; WLC
See also CDBLB 1890-1914; CLR 10, 11;
DLB 18, 57, 141; JRDA; MAICYA;
YABC 2

Stewart, J(ohn) I(nnes) M(ackintosh)
1906-1994 . . . . **CLC 7, 14, 32**
See also CA 85-88; 147; CAAS 3;
CANR 47; MTCW

Stewart, Mary (Florence Elinor)
1916- . . . . **CLC 7, 35**
See also CA 1-4R; CANR 1; SATA 12

Stewart, Mary Rainbow
See Stewart, Mary (Florence Elinor)

Stifle, June
See Campbell, Maria

Stifter, Adalbert 1805-1868 . . . . . . **NCLC 41**
See also DLB 133

Still, James 1906- . . . . **CLC 49**
See also CA 65-68; CAAS 17; CANR 10,
26; DLB 9; SATA 29

Sting
See Sumner, Gordon Matthew

Stirling, Arthur
See Sinclair, Upton (Beall)

Stitt, Milan 1941- . . . . **CLC 29**
See also CA 69-72

Stockton, Francis Richard 1834-1902
See Stockton, Frank R.
See also CA 108; 137; MAICYA; SATA 44

Stockton, Frank R. . . . . **TCLC 47**
See also Stockton, Francis Richard
See also DLB 42, 74; SATA-Brief 32

Stoddard, Charles
See Kuttner, Henry

Stoker, Abraham 1847-1912
See Stoker, Bram
See also CA 105; DA; SATA 29

Stoker, Bram . . . . **TCLC 8; WLC**
See also Stoker, Abraham
See also CDBLB 1890-1914; DLB 36, 70

Stolz, Mary (Slattery) 1920- . . . . **CLC 12**
See also AAYA 8; AITN 1; CA 5-8R;
CANR 13, 41; JRDA; MAICYA;
SAAS 3; SATA 10, 71

Stone, Irving 1903-1989 . . . . **CLC 7**
See also AITN 1; CA 1-4R; 129; CAAS 3;
CANR 1, 23; MTCW; SATA 3;
SATA-Obit 64

Stone, Oliver 1946- . . . . **CLC 73**
See also CA 110

Stone, Robert (Anthony)
1937- . . . . **CLC 5, 23, 42**
See also CA 85-88; CANR 23; DLB 152;
MTCW

Stone, Zachary
See Follett, Ken(neth Martin)

Stoppard, Tom
1937- . . . . . . **CLC 1, 3, 4, 5, 8, 15, 29, 34,**
63; DA; WLC
See also CA 81-84; CANR 39;
CDBLB 1960 to Present; DLB 13;
DLBY 85; MTCW

Storey, David (Malcolm)
1933- . . . . **CLC 2, 4, 5, 8**
See also CA 81-84; CANR 36; DLB 13, 14;
MTCW

Storm, Hyemeyohsts 1935- . . . . **CLC 3**
See also CA 81-84; CANR 45; NNAL

Storm, (Hans) Theodor (Woldsen)
1817-1888 . . . . **NCLC 1**

Storni, Alfonsina
1892-1938 . . . . **TCLC 5; HLC**
See also CA 104; 131; HW

Stout, Rex (Todhunter) 1886-1975 . . . **CLC 3**
See also AITN 2; CA 61-64

Stow, (Julian) Randolph 1935- . . **CLC 23, 48**
See also CA 13-16R; CANR 33; MTCW

Stowe, Harriet (Elizabeth) Beecher
1811-1896 . . . . . . **NCLC 3, 50; DA; WLC**
See also CDALB 1865-1917; DLB 1, 12, 42,
74; JRDA; MAICYA; YABC 1

Strachey, (Giles) Lytton
1880-1932 . . . . **TCLC 12**
See also CA 110; DLB 149; DLBD 10

Strand, Mark 1934- . . . . . . **CLC 6, 18, 41, 71**
See also CA 21-24R; CANR 40; DLB 5;
SATA 41

Straub, Peter (Francis) 1943- . . . . . . **CLC 28**
See also BEST 89:1; CA 85-88; CANR 28;
DLBY 84; MTCW

Strauss, Botho 1944- . . . . **CLC 22**
See also DLB 124

Streatfeild, (Mary) Noel
1895(?)-1986 . . . . **CLC 21**
See also CA 81-84; 120; CANR 31;
CLR 17; MAICYA; SATA 20;
SATA-Obit 48

Stribling, T(homas) S(igismund)
1881-1965 . . . . **CLC 23**
See also CA 107; DLB 9

Strindberg, (Johan) August
1849-1912 . . . . . . **TCLC 1, 8, 21, 47; DA;**
WLC
See also CA 104; 135

Stringer, Arthur 1874-1950 . . . . **TCLC 37**
See also DLB 92

Stringer, David
See Roberts, Keith (John Kingston)

Strugatskii, Arkadii (Natanovich)
1925-1991 . . . . **CLC 27**
See also CA 106; 135

Strugatskii, Boris (Natanovich)
1933- . . . . **CLC 27**
See also CA 106

Strummer, Joe 1953(?)- . . . . **CLC 30**

Stuart, Don A.
See Campbell, John W(ood, Jr.)

Stuart, Ian
See MacLean, Alistair (Stuart)

Stuart, Jesse (Hilton)
1906-1984 . . . . **CLC 1, 8, 11, 14, 34**
See also CA 5-8R; 112; CANR 31; DLB 9,
48, 102; DLBY 84; SATA 2;
SATA-Obit 36

Sturgeon, Theodore (Hamilton)
1918-1985 . . . . **CLC 22, 39**
See also Queen, Ellery
See also CA 81-84; 116; CANR 32; DLB 8;
DLBY 85; MTCW

Sturges, Preston 1898-1959 . . . . . . **TCLC 48**
See also CA 114; DLB 26

Styron, William
1925- . . . . **CLC 1, 3, 5, 11, 15, 60**
See also BEST 90:4; CA 5-8R; CANR 6, 33;
CDALB 1968-1988; DLB 2, 143;
DLBY 80; MTCW

Suarez Lynch, B.
See Bioy Casares, Adolfo; Borges, Jorge
Luis

Su Chien 1884-1918
See Su Man-shu
See also CA 123

Suckow, Ruth 1892-1960
See also CA 113; DLB 9, 102; SSC 18

Sudermann, Hermann 1857-1928 . . **TCLC 15**
See also CA 107; DLB 118

Sue, Eugene 1804-1857 . . . . **NCLC 1**
See also DLB 119

Sueskind, Patrick 1949- . . . . **CLC 44**
See also Suskind, Patrick

Sukenick, Ronald 1932- . . . . . **CLC 3, 4, 6, 48**
See also CA 25-28R; CAAS 8; CANR 32;
DLBY 81

Suknaski, Andrew 1942- . . . . **CLC 19**
See also CA 101; DLB 53

Sullivan, Vernon
See Vian, Boris

Sully Prudhomme 1839-1907 . . . . . . **TCLC 31**

Su Man-shu . . . . **TCLC 24**
See also Su Chien

Summerforest, Ivy B.
See Kirkup, James

Summers, Andrew James 1942- . . . . . **CLC 26**

Summers, Andy
See Summers, Andrew James

Summers, Hollis (Spurgeon, Jr.)
1916- . . . . **CLC 10**
See also CA 5-8R; CANR 3; DLB 6

Summers, (Alphonsus Joseph-Mary Augustus)
Montague 1880-1948 . . . . **TCLC 16**
See also CA 118

Sumner, Gordon Matthew 1951- . . . . **CLC 26**

Surtees, Robert Smith
1803-1864 . . . . **NCLC 14**
See also DLB 21

Susann, Jacqueline 1921-1974 . . . . . . **CLC 3**
See also AITN 1; CA 65-68; 53-56; MTCW

Suskind, Patrick
See Sueskind, Patrick
See also CA 145

Sutcliff, Rosemary 1920-1992 . . . . . . **CLC 26**
See also AAYA 10; CA 5-8R; 139;
CANR 37; CLR 1, 37; JRDA; MAICYA;
SATA 6, 44, 78; SATA-Obit 73

Sutro, Alfred 1863-1933 . . . . **TCLC 6**
See also CA 105; DLB 10

Sutton, Henry
See Slavitt, David R(ytman)

Svevo, Italo . . . . **TCLC 2, 35**
See also Schmitz, Aron Hector

Swados, Elizabeth (A.) 1951- . . . . . . **CLC 12**
See also CA 97-100; CANR 49

Swados, Harvey 1920-1972 . . . . **CLC 5**
See also CA 5-8R; 37-40R; CANR 6;
DLB 2

Swan, Gladys 1934- . . . . **CLC 69**
See also CA 101; CANR 17, 39

Swarthout, Glendon (Fred)
1918-1992 . . . . **CLC 35**
See also CA 1-4R; 139; CANR 1, 47;
SATA 26

Sweet, Sarah C.
See Jewett, (Theodora) Sarah Orne

Swenson, May
1919-1989 . . . . **CLC 4, 14, 61; DA**
See also CA 5-8R; 130; CANR 36; DLB 5;
MTCW; SATA 15

Swift, Augustus
See Lovecraft, H(oward) P(hillips)

Swift, Graham (Colin) 1949- . . . . **CLC 41, 88**
See also CA 117; 122; CANR 46

Swift, Jonathan
1667-1745 . . . . . . **LC 1; DA; PC 9; WLC**
See also CDBLB 1660-1789; DLB 39, 95,
101; SATA 19

Swinburne, Algernon Charles
1837-1909 . . . . . . **TCLC 8, 36; DA; WLC**
See also CA 105; 140; CDBLB 1832-1890;
DLB 35, 57

Swinfen, Ann . . . . **CLC 34**

Swinnerton, Frank Arthur
1884-1982 . . . . **CLC 31**
See also CA 108; DLB 34

Swithen, John
See King, Stephen (Edwin)

Sylvia
See Ashton-Warner, Sylvia (Constance)

Symmes, Robert Edward
See Duncan, Robert (Edward)

Symonds, John Addington
1840-1893 . . . . **NCLC 34**
See also DLB 57, 144

Symons, Arthur 1865-1945 . . . . **TCLC 11**
See also CA 107; DLB 19, 57, 149

Symons, Julian (Gustave)
1912-1994 . . . . **CLC 2, 14, 32**
See also CA 49-52; 147; CAAS 3; CANR 3,
33; DLB 87; DLBY 92; MTCW

Synge, (Edmund) J(ohn) M(illington)
1871-1909 . . . . **TCLC 6, 37; DC 2**
See also CA 104; 141; CDBLB 1890-1914;
DLB 10, 19

Syruc, J.
See Milosz, Czeslaw

Szirtes, George 1948- . . . . **CLC 46**
See also CA 109; CANR 27

Tabori, George 1914- . . . . **CLC 19**
See also CA 49-52; CANR 4

Tagore, Rabindranath
1861-1941 . . . . **TCLC 3, 53; PC 8**
See also CA 104; 120; MTCW

Taine, Hippolyte Adolphe
1828-1893 . . . . **NCLC 15**

Talese, Gay 1932- . . . . **CLC 37**
See also AITN 1; CA 1-4R; CANR 9;
MTCW

Tallent, Elizabeth (Ann) 1954- . . . . . **CLC 45**
See also CA 117; DLB 130

Tally, Ted 1952- . . . . **CLC 42**
See also CA 120; 124

Tamayo y Baus, Manuel
1829-1898 . . . . **NCLC 1**

Tammsaare, A(nton) H(ansen)
1878-1940 . . . . **TCLC 27**

Tan, Amy 1952- . . . . **CLC 59**
See also AAYA 9; BEST 89:3; CA 136;
SATA 75

Tandem, Felix
See Spitteler, Carl (Friedrich Georg)

Tanizaki, Jun'ichiro
1886-1965 . . . . **CLC 8, 14, 28**
See also CA 93-96; 25-28R

Tanner, William
See Amis, Kingsley (William)

Tao Lao
See Storni, Alfonsina

Tarassoff, Lev
See Troyat, Henri

Tarbell, Ida M(inerva)
1857-1944 . . . . **TCLC 40**
See also CA 122; DLB 47

Tarkington, (Newton) Booth
1869-1946 . . . . **TCLC 9**
See also CA 110; 143; DLB 9, 102;
SATA 17

Tarkovsky, Andrei (Arsenyevich)
1932-1986 . . . . **CLC 75**
See also CA 127

Tartt, Donna 1964(?)- . . . . **CLC 76**
See also CA 142

Tasso, Torquato 1544-1595 . . . . **LC 5**

Tate, (John Orley) Allen
1899-1979 . . . . . **CLC 2, 4, 6, 9, 11, 14, 24**
See also CA 5-8R; 85-88; CANR 32;
DLB 4, 45, 63; MTCW

Tate, Ellalice
See Hibbert, Eleanor Alice Burford

Tate, James (Vincent) 1943- ... **CLC 2, 6, 25**
See also CA 21-24R; CANR 29; DLB 5

Tavel, Ronald 1940- .... **CLC 6**
See also CA 21-24R; CANR 33

Taylor, C(ecil) P(hilip) 1929-1981... **CLC 27**
See also CA 25-28R; 105; CANR 47

Taylor, Edward 1642(?)-1729.... **LC 11; DA**
See also DLB 24

Taylor, Eleanor Ross 1920- .... **CLC 5**
See also CA 81-84

Taylor, Elizabeth 1912-1975 ... **CLC 2, 4, 29**
See also CA 13-16R; CANR 9; DLB 139;
MTCW; SATA 13

Taylor, Henry (Splawn) 1942-...... **CLC 44**
See also CA 33-36R; CAAS 7; CANR 31;
DLB 5

Taylor, Kamala (Purnaiya) 1924-
See Markandaya, Kamala
See also CA 77-80

Taylor, Mildred D. .... **CLC 21**
See also AAYA 10; BW 1; CA 85-88;
CANR 25; CLR 9; DLB 52; JRDA;
MAICYA; SAAS 5; SATA 15, 70

Taylor, Peter (Hillsman)
1917-1994 ..... **CLC 1, 4, 18, 37, 44, 50,**
71; SSC 10
See also CA 13-16R; 147; CANR 9;
DLBY 81, 94; MTCW

Taylor, Robert Lewis 1912-........ **CLC 14**
See also CA 1-4R; CANR 3; SATA 10

Tchekhov, Anton
See Chekhov, Anton (Pavlovich)

Teasdale, Sara 1884-1933......... **TCLC 4**
See also CA 104; DLB 45; SATA 32

Tegner, Esaias 1782-1846........ **NCLC 2**

Teilhard de Chardin, (Marie Joseph) Pierre
1881-1955 .... **TCLC 9**
See also CA 105

Temple, Ann
See Mortimer, Penelope (Ruth)

Tennant, Emma (Christina)
1937- .... **CLC 13, 52**
See also CA 65-68; CAAS 9; CANR 10, 38;
DLB 14

Tenneshaw, S. M.
See Silverberg, Robert

Tennyson, Alfred
1809-1892 .. **NCLC 30; DA; PC 6; WLC**
See also CDBLB 1832-1890; DLB 32

Teran, Lisa St. Aubin de .... **CLC 36**
See also St. Aubin de Teran, Lisa

Terence 195(?)B.C.-159B.C...... **CMLC 14**

Teresa de Jesus, St. 1515-1582...... **LC 18**

Terkel, Louis 1912-
See Terkel, Studs
See also CA 57-60; CANR 18, 45; MTCW

Terkel, Studs .... **CLC 38**
See also Terkel, Louis
See also AITN 1

Terry, C. V.
See Slaughter, Frank G(ill)

Terry, Megan 1932-.............. **CLC 19**
See also CA 77-80; CABS 3; CANR 43;
DLB 7

Tertz, Abram
See Sinyavsky, Andrei (Donatevich)

Tesich, Steve 1943(?)-.......... **CLC 40, 69**
See also CA 105; DLBY 83

Teternikov, Fyodor Kuzmich 1863-1927
See Sologub, Fyodor
See also CA 104

Tevis, Walter 1928-1984 .... **CLC 42**
See also CA 113

Tey, Josephine................... **TCLC 14**
See also Mackintosh, Elizabeth
See also DLB 77

Thackeray, William Makepeace
1811-1863 .... **NCLC 5, 14, 22, 43; DA;**
WLC
See also CDBLB 1832-1890; DLB 21, 55;
SATA 23

Thakura, Ravindranatha
See Tagore, Rabindranath

Tharoor, Shashi 1956- .... **CLC 70**
See also CA 141

Thelwell, Michael Miles 1939-..... **CLC 22**
See also BW 2; CA 101

Theobald, Lewis, Jr.
See Lovecraft, H(oward) P(hillips)

Theodorescu, Ion N. 1880-1967
See Arghezi, Tudor
See also CA 116

Theriault, Yves 1915-1983........ **CLC 79**
See also CA 102; DLB 88

Theroux, Alexander (Louis)
1939- .... **CLC 2, 25**
See also CA 85-88; CANR 20

Theroux, Paul (Edward)
1941- .... **CLC 5, 8, 11, 15, 28, 46**
See also BEST 89:4; CA 33-36R; CANR 20,
45; DLB 2; MTCW; SATA 44

Thesen, Sharon 1946-............. **CLC 56**

Thevenin, Denis
See Duhamel, Georges

Thibault, Jacques Anatole Francois
1844-1924
See France, Anatole
See also CA 106; 127; MTCW

Thiele, Colin (Milton) 1920- .... **CLC 17**
See also CA 29-32R; CANR 12, 28;
CLR 27; MAICYA; SAAS 2; SATA 14,
72

Thomas, Audrey (Callahan)
1935- .... **CLC 7, 13, 37; SSC 20**
See also AITN 2; CA 21-24R; CAAS 19;
CANR 36; DLB 60; MTCW

Thomas, D(onald) M(ichael)
1935- .... **CLC 13, 22, 31**
See also CA 61-64; CAAS 11; CANR 17,
45; CDBLB 1960 to Present; DLB 40;
MTCW

Thomas, Dylan (Marlais)
1914-1953 ... **TCLC 1, 8, 45; DA; PC 2;**
SSC 3; WLC
See also CA 104; 120; CDBLB 1945-1960;
DLB 13, 20, 139; MTCW; SATA 60

Thomas, (Philip) Edward
1878-1917 .... **TCLC 10**
See also CA 106; DLB 19

Thomas, Joyce Carol 1938-........ **CLC 35**
See also AAYA 12; BW 2; CA 113; 116;
CANR 48; CLR 19; DLB 33; JRDA;
MAICYA; MTCW; SAAS 7; SATA 40,
78

Thomas, Lewis 1913-1993 .... **CLC 35**
See also CA 85-88; 143; CANR 38; MTCW

Thomas, Paul
See Mann, (Paul) Thomas

Thomas, Piri 1928-.............. **CLC 17**
See also CA 73-76; HW

Thomas, R(onald) S(tuart)
1913- .... **CLC 6, 13, 48**
See also CA 89-92; CAAS 4; CANR 30;
CDBLB 1960 to Present; DLB 27;
MTCW

Thomas, Ross (Elmore) 1926-...... **CLC 39**
See also CA 33-36R; CANR 22

Thompson, Francis Clegg
See Mencken, H(enry) L(ouis)

Thompson, Francis Joseph
1859-1907 .... **TCLC 4**
See also CA 104; CDBLB 1890-1914;
DLB 19

Thompson, Hunter S(tockton)
1939- .... **CLC 9, 17, 40**
See also BEST 89:1; CA 17-20R; CANR 23,
46; MTCW

Thompson, James Myers
See Thompson, Jim (Myers)

Thompson, Jim (Myers)
1906-1977(?) .... **CLC 69**
See also CA 140

Thompson, Judith .... **CLC 39**

Thomson, James 1700-1748...... **LC 16, 29**
See also DLB 95

Thomson, James 1834-1882...... **NCLC 18**
See also DLB 35

Thoreau, Henry David
1817-1862 ......**NCLC 7, 21; DA; WLC**
See also CDALB 1640-1865; DLB 1

Thornton, Hall
See Silverberg, Robert

Thurber, James (Grover)
1894-1961 ... **CLC 5, 11, 25; DA; SSC 1**
See also CA 73-76; CANR 17, 39;
CDALB 1929-1941; DLB 4, 11, 22, 102;
MAICYA; MTCW; SATA 13

Thurman, Wallace (Henry)
1902-1934 .... **TCLC 6; BLC**
See also BW 1; CA 104; 124; DLB 51

Ticheburn, Cheviot
See Ainsworth, William Harrison

Tieck, (Johann) Ludwig
1773-1853 .... **NCLC 5, 46**
See also DLB 90

Tiger, Derry
See Ellison, Harlan (Jay)

Tilghman, Christopher 1948(?)-..... **CLC 65**

Tillinghast, Richard (Williford)
1940- .... **CLC 29**
See also CA 29-32R; CANR 26

Timrod, Henry 1828-1867 . . . . . . NCLC 25
See also DLB 3

Tindall, Gillian 1938- . . . . CLC 7
See also CA 21-24R; CANR 11

Tiptree, James, Jr. . . . . CLC 48, 50
See also Sheldon, Alice Hastings Bradley
See also DLB 8

Titmarsh, Michael Angelo
See Thackeray, William Makepeace

**Tocqueville, Alexis (Charles Henri Maurice
Clerel Comte)** 1805-1859 . . . . . NCLC 7

Tolkien, J(ohn) R(onald) R(euel)
1892-1973 . . . . . . CLC 1, 2, 3, 8, 12, 38;
DA; WLC
See also AAYA 10; AITN 1; CA 17-18;
45-48; CANR 36; CAP 2;
CDBLB 1914-1945; DLB 15; JRDA;
MAICYA; MTCW; SATA 2, 32;
SATA-Obit 24

Toller, Ernst 1893-1939 . . . . TCLC 10
See also CA 107; DLB 124

Tolson, M. B.
See Tolson, Melvin B(eaunorus)

Tolson, Melvin B(eaunorus)
1898(?)-1966 . . . . CLC 36; BLC
See also BW 1; CA 124; 89-92; DLB 48, 76

Tolstoi, Aleksei Nikolaevich
See Tolstoy, Alexey Nikolaevich

Tolstoy, Alexey Nikolaevich
1882-1945 . . . . TCLC 18
See also CA 107

Tolstoy, Count Leo
See Tolstoy, Leo (Nikolaevich)

Tolstoy, Leo (Nikolaevich)
1828-1910 . . . . . . TCLC 4, 11, 17, 28, 44;
DA; SSC 9; WLC
See also CA 104; 123; SATA 26

Tomasi di Lampedusa, Giuseppe 1896-1957
See Lampedusa, Giuseppe (Tomasi) di
See also CA 111

Tomlin, Lily . . . . CLC 17
See also Tomlin, Mary Jean

Tomlin, Mary Jean 1939(?)-
See Tomlin, Lily
See also CA 117

Tomlinson, (Alfred) Charles
1927- . . . . CLC 2, 4, 6, 13, 45
See also CA 5-8R; CANR 33; DLB 40

Tonson, Jacob
See Bennett, (Enoch) Arnold

Toole, John Kennedy
1937-1969 . . . . CLC 19, 64
See also CA 104; DLBY 81

Toomer, Jean
1894-1967 . . . . . . CLC 1, 4, 13, 22; BLC;
PC 7; SSC 1
See also BW 1; CA 85-88;
CDALB 1917-1929; DLB 45, 51; MTCW

Torley, Luke
See Blish, James (Benjamin)

Tornimparte, Alessandra
See Ginzburg, Natalia

Torre, Raoul della
See Mencken, H(enry) L(ouis)

Torrey, E(dwin) Fuller 1937- . . . . CLC 34
See also CA 119

Torsvan, Ben Traven
See Traven, B.

Torsvan, Benno Traven
See Traven, B.

Torsvan, Berick Traven
See Traven, B.

Torsvan, Berwick Traven
See Traven, B.

Torsvan, Bruno Traven
See Traven, B.

Torsvan, Traven
See Traven, B.

Tournier, Michel (Edouard)
1924- . . . . CLC 6, 23, 36
See also CA 49-52; CANR 3, 36; DLB 83;
MTCW; SATA 23

Tournimparte, Alessandra
See Ginzburg, Natalia

Towers, Ivar
See Kornbluth, C(yril) M.

Towne, Robert (Burton) 1936(?)- . . . . CLC 87
See also CA 108; DLB 44

Townsend, Sue 1946- . . . . CLC 61
See also CA 119; 127; MTCW; SATA 55;
SATA-Brief 48

Townshend, Peter (Dennis Blandford)
1945- . . . . CLC 17, 42
See also CA 107

Tozzi, Federigo 1883-1920 . . . . TCLC 31

Traill, Catharine Parr
1802-1899 . . . . NCLC 31
See also DLB 99

Trakl, Georg 1887-1914 . . . . TCLC 5
See also CA 104

Transtroemer, Tomas (Goesta)
1931- . . . . CLC 52, 65
See also CA 117; 129; CAAS 17

Transtromer, Tomas Gosta
See Transtroemer, Tomas (Goesta)

Traven, B. (?)-1969 . . . . CLC 8, 11
See also CA 19-20; 25-28R; CAP 2; DLB 9,
56; MTCW

Treitel, Jonathan 1959- . . . . CLC 70

Tremain, Rose 1943- . . . . CLC 42
See also CA 97-100; CANR 44; DLB 14

Tremblay, Michel 1942- . . . . CLC 29
See also CA 116; 128; DLB 60; MTCW

Trevanian . . . . CLC 29
See also Whitaker, Rod(ney)

Trevor, Glen
See Hilton, James

Trevor, William
1928- . . . . CLC 7, 9, 14, 25, 71
See also Cox, William Trevor
See also DLB 14, 139

Trifonov, Yuri (Valentinovich)
1925-1981 . . . . CLC 45
See also CA 126; 103; MTCW

Trilling, Lionel 1905-1975 . . . . CLC 9, 11, 24
See also CA 9-12R; 61-64; CANR 10;
DLB 28, 63; MTCW

Trimball, W. H.
See Mencken, H(enry) L(ouis)

Tristan
See Gomez de la Serna, Ramon

Tristram
See Housman, A(lfred) E(dward)

Trogdon, William (Lewis) 1939-
See Heat-Moon, William Least
See also CA 115; 119; CANR 47

Trollope, Anthony
1815-1882 . . . . . . NCLC 6, 33; DA; WLC
See also CDBLB 1832-1890; DLB 21, 57;
SATA 22

Trollope, Frances 1779-1863 . . . . . NCLC 30
See also DLB 21

Trotsky, Leon 1879-1940 . . . . TCLC 22
See also CA 118

Trotter (Cockburn), Catharine
1679-1749 . . . . LC 8
See also DLB 84

Trout, Kilgore
See Farmer, Philip Jose

Trow, George W. S. 1943- . . . . CLC 52
See also CA 126

Troyat, Henri 1911- . . . . CLC 23
See also CA 45-48; CANR 2, 33; MTCW

Trudeau, G(arretson) B(eekman) 1948-
See Trudeau, Garry B.
See also CA 81-84; CANR 31; SATA 35

Trudeau, Garry B. . . . . CLC 12
See also Trudeau, G(arretson) B(eekman)
See also AAYA 10; AITN 2

Truffaut, Francois 1932-1984 . . . . CLC 20
See also CA 81-84; 113; CANR 34

Trumbo, Dalton 1905-1976 . . . . CLC 19
See also CA 21-24R; 69-72; CANR 10;
DLB 26

Trumbull, John 1750-1831 . . . . NCLC 30
See also DLB 31

Trundlett, Helen B.
See Eliot, T(homas) S(tearns)

Tryon, Thomas 1926-1991 . . . . CLC 3, 11
See also AITN 1; CA 29-32R; 135;
CANR 32; MTCW

Tryon, Tom
See Tryon, Thomas

Ts'ao Hsueh-ch'in 1715(?)-1763 . . . . LC 1

Tsushima, Shuji 1909-1948
See Dazai, Osamu
See also CA 107

Tsvetacva (Efron), Marina (Ivanovna)
1892-1941 . . . . TCLC 7, 35
See also CA 104; 128; MTCW

Tuck, Lily 1938- . . . . CLC 70
See also CA 139

Tu Fu 712-770 . . . . PC 9

Tunis, John R(oberts) 1889-1975 . . . CLC 12
See also CA 61-64; DLB 22; JRDA;
MAICYA; SATA 37; SATA-Brief 30

Tuohy, Frank . . . . CLC 37
See also Tuohy, John Francis
See also DLB 14, 139

Tuohy, John Francis 1925-
See Tuohy, Frank
See also CA 5-8R; CANR 3, 47

Turco, Lewis (Putnam) 1934- . . . **CLC 11, 63**
See also CA 13-16R; CANR 24; DLBY 84

Turgenev, Ivan
1818-1883 . . . . . . **NCLC 21; DA; SSC 7;**
WLC

Turgot, Anne-Robert-Jacques
1727-1781 . . . . **LC 26**

Turner, Frederick 1943- . . . . **CLC 48**
See also CA 73-76; CAAS 10; CANR 12,
30; DLB 40

Tutu, Desmond M(pilo)
1931- . . . . **CLC 80; BLC**
See also BW 1; CA 125

Tutuola, Amos 1920- . . . **CLC 5, 14, 29; BLC**
See also BW 2; CA 9-12R; CANR 27;
DLB 125; MTCW

Twain, Mark
. . . . . **TCLC 6, 12, 19, 36, 48, 59; SSC 6;**
WLC
See also Clemens, Samuel Langhorne
See also DLB 11, 12, 23, 64, 74

Tyler, Anne
1941- . . . . **CLC 7, 11, 18, 28, 44, 59**
See also BEST 89:1; CA 9-12R; CANR 11,
33; DLB 6, 143; DLBY 82; MTCW;
SATA 7

Tyler, Royall 1757-1826 . . . . **NCLC 3**
See also DLB 37

Tynan, Katharine 1861-1931 . . . . . . **TCLC 3**
See also CA 104; DLB 153

Tyutchev, Fyodor 1803-1873 . . . . . **NCLC 34**

Tzara, Tristan . . . . **CLC 47**
See also Rosenfeld, Samuel

Uhry, Alfred 1936- . . . . **CLC 55**
See also CA 127; 133

Ulf, Haerved
See Strindberg, (Johan) August

Ulf, Harved
See Strindberg, (Johan) August

Ulibarri, Sabine R(eyes) 1919- . . . . . **CLC 83**
See also CA 131; DLB 82; HW

Unamuno (y Jugo), Miguel de
1864-1936 . . . . **TCLC 2, 9; HLC; SSC 11**
See also CA 104; 131; DLB 108; HW;
MTCW

Undercliffe, Errol
See Campbell, (John) Ramsey

Underwood, Miles
See Glassco, John

Undset, Sigrid
1882-1949 . . . . **TCLC 3; DA; WLC**
See also CA 104; 129; MTCW

Ungaretti, Giuseppe
1888-1970 . . . . **CLC 7, 11, 15**
See also CA 19-20; 25-28R; CAP 2;
DLB 114

Unger, Douglas 1952- . . . . **CLC 34**
See also CA 130

Unsworth, Barry (Forster) 1930- . . . . **CLC 76**
See also CA 25-28R; CANR 30

Updike, John (Hoyer)
1932- . . . . . . **CLC 1, 2, 3, 5, 7, 9, 13, 15,**
23, 34, 43, 70; DA; SSC 13; WLC
See also CA 1-4R; CABS 1; CANR 4, 33;
CDALB 1968-1988; DLB 2, 5, 143;
DLBD 3; DLBY 80, 82; MTCW

Upshaw, Margaret Mitchell
See Mitchell, Margaret (Munnerlyn)

Upton, Mark
See Sanders, Lawrence

Urdang, Constance (Henriette)
1922- . . . . **CLC 47**
See also CA 21-24R; CANR 9, 24

Uriel, Henry
See Faust, Frederick (Schiller)

Uris, Leon (Marcus) 1924- . . . . . . **CLC 7, 32**
See also AITN 1, 2; BEST 89:2; CA 1-4R;
CANR 1, 40; MTCW; SATA 49

Urmuz
See Codrescu, Andrei

Ustinov, Peter (Alexander) 1921- . . . . **CLC 1**
See also AITN 1; CA 13-16R; CANR 25;
DLB 13

Vaculik, Ludvik 1926- . . . . **CLC 7**
See also CA 53-56

Valdez, Luis (Miguel)
1940- . . . . **CLC 84; HLC**
See also CA 101; CANR 32; DLB 122; HW

Valenzuela, Luisa 1938- . . . **CLC 31; SSC 14**
See also CA 101; CANR 32; DLB 113; HW

Valera y Alcala-Galiano, Juan
1824-1905 . . . . **TCLC 10**
See also CA 106

Valery, (Ambroise) Paul (Toussaint Jules)
1871-1945 . . . . **TCLC 4, 15; PC 9**
See also CA 104; 122; MTCW

Valle-Inclan, Ramon (Maria) del
1866-1936 . . . . **TCLC 5; HLC**
See also CA 106; DLB 134

Vallejo, Antonio Buero
See Buero Vallejo, Antonio

Vallejo, Cesar (Abraham)
1892-1938 . . . . **TCLC 3, 56; HLC**
See also CA 105; HW

Valle Y Pena, Ramon del
See Valle-Inclan, Ramon (Maria) del

Van Ash, Cay 1918- . . . . **CLC 34**

Vanbrugh, Sir John 1664-1726 . . . . . . **LC 21**
See also DLB 80

Van Campen, Karl
See Campbell, John W(ood, Jr.)

Vance, Gerald
See Silverberg, Robert

Vance, Jack . . . . **CLC 35**
See also Vance, John Holbrook
See also DLB 8

Vance, John Holbrook 1916-
See Queen, Ellery; Vance, Jack
See also CA 29-32R; CANR 17; MTCW

**Van Den Bogarde, Derek Jules Gaspard Ulric
Niven** 1921-
See Bogarde, Dirk
See also CA 77-80

Vandenburgh, Jane . . . . **CLC 59**

Vanderhaeghe, Guy 1951- . . . . **CLC 41**
See also CA 113

van der Post, Laurens (Jan) 1906- . . . **CLC 5**
See also CA 5-8R; CANR 35

van de Wetering, Janwillem 1931- . . **CLC 47**
See also CA 49-52; CANR 4

Van Dine, S. S. . . . . **TCLC 23**
See also Wright, Willard Huntington

Van Doren, Carl (Clinton)
1885-1950 . . . . **TCLC 18**
See also CA 111

Van Doren, Mark 1894-1972 . . . . . **CLC 6, 10**
See also CA 1-4R; 37-40R; CANR 3;
DLB 45; MTCW

Van Druten, John (William)
1901-1957 . . . . **TCLC 2**
See also CA 104; DLB 10

Van Duyn, Mona (Jane)
1921- . . . . **CLC 3, 7, 63**
See also CA 9-12R; CANR 7, 38; DLB 5

Van Dyne, Edith
See Baum, L(yman) Frank

van Itallie, Jean-Claude 1936- . . . . **CLC 3**
See also CA 45-48; CAAS 2; CANR 1, 48;
DLB 7

van Ostaijen, Paul 1896-1928 . . . . . **TCLC 33**

Van Peebles, Melvin 1932- . . . . . . **CLC 2, 20**
See also BW 2; CA 85-88; CANR 27

Vansittart, Peter 1920- . . . . **CLC 42**
See also CA 1-4R; CANR 3, 49

Van Vechten, Carl 1880-1964 . . . . . . **CLC 33**
See also CA 89-92; DLB 4, 9, 51

Van Vogt, A(lfred) E(lton) 1912- . . . . . **CLC 1**
See also CA 21-24R; CANR 28; DLB 8;
SATA 14

Varda, Agnes 1928- . . . . **CLC 16**
See also CA 116; 122

Vargas Llosa, (Jorge) Mario (Pedro)
1936- . . . . **CLC 3, 6, 9, 10, 15, 31, 42, 85;**
DA; HLC
See also CA 73-76; CANR 18, 32, 42;
DLB 145; HW; MTCW

Vasiliu, Gheorghe 1881-1957
See Bacovia, George
See also CA 123

Vassa, Gustavus
See Equiano, Olaudah

Vassilikos, Vassilis 1933- . . . . **CLC 4, 8**
See also CA 81-84

Vaughan, Henry 1621-1695 . . . . **LC 27**
See also DLB 131

Vaughn, Stephanie . . . . **CLC 62**

Vazov, Ivan (Minchov)
1850-1921 . . . . **TCLC 25**
See also CA 121; DLB 147

Veblen, Thorstein (Bunde)
1857-1929 . . . . **TCLC 31**
See also CA 115

Vega, Lope de 1562-1635 . . . . **LC 23**

Venison, Alfred
See Pound, Ezra (Weston Loomis)

Verdi, Marie de
See Mencken, H(enry) L(ouis)

Verdu, Matilde
See Cela, Camilo Jose

Verga, Giovanni (Carmelo)
1840-1922 . . . . TCLC 3
See also CA 104; 123

Vergil
70B.C.-19B.C. . . . . CMLC 9; DA; PC 12

Verhaeren, Emile (Adolphe Gustave)
1855-1916 . . . . TCLC 12
See also CA 109

Verlaine, Paul (Marie)
1844-1896 . . . . NCLC 2, 51; PC 2

Verne, Jules (Gabriel)
1828-1905 . . . . TCLC 6, 52
See also CA 110; 131; DLB 123; JRDA;
MAICYA; SATA 21

Very, Jones 1813-1880 . . . . NCLC 9
See also DLB 1

Vesaas, Tarjei 1897-1970 . . . . CLC 48
See also CA 29-32R

Vialis, Gaston
See Simenon, Georges (Jacques Christian)

Vian, Boris 1920-1959 . . . . TCLC 9
See also CA 106; DLB 72

Viaud, (Louis Marie) Julien 1850-1923
See Loti, Pierre
See also CA 107

Vicar, Henry
See Felsen, Henry Gregor

Vicker, Angus
See Felsen, Henry Gregor

Vidal, Gore
1925- . . . . . CLC 2, 4, 6, 8, 10, 22, 33, 72
See also AITN 1; BEST 90:2; CA 5-8R;
CANR 13, 45; DLB 6, 152; MTCW

Viereck, Peter (Robert Edwin)
1916- . . . . CLC 4
See also CA 1-4R; CANR 1, 47; DLB 5

Vigny, Alfred (Victor) de
1797-1863 . . . . NCLC 7
See also DLB 119

Vilakazi, Benedict Wallet
1906-1947 . . . . TCLC 37

**Villiers de l'Isle Adam, Jean Marie Mathias
Philippe Auguste Comte**
1838-1889 . . . . NCLC 3; SSC 14
See also DLB 123

Villon, Francois 1431-1463(?) . . . . PC 12

Vinci, Leonardo da 1452-1519 . . . . . . LC 12

Vine, Barbara . . . . CLC 50
See also Rendell, Ruth (Barbara)
See also BEST 90:4

Vinge, Joan D(ennison) 1948- . . . . . . CLC 30
See also CA 93-96; SATA 36

Violis, G.
See Simenon, Georges (Jacques Christian)

Visconti, Luchino 1906-1976 . . . . CLC 16
See also CA 81-84; 65-68; CANR 39

Vittorini, Elio 1908-1966 . . . . . . CLC 6, 9, 14
See also CA 133; 25-28R

Vizinczey, Stephen 1933- . . . . CLC 40
See also CA 128

Vliet, R(ussell) G(ordon)
1929-1984 . . . . CLC 22
See also CA 37-40R; 112; CANR 18

Vogau, Boris Andreyevich 1894-1937(?)
See Pilnyak, Boris
See also CA 123

Vogel, Paula A(nne) 1951- . . . . CLC 76
See also CA 108

Voight, Ellen Bryant 1943- . . . . CLC 54
See also CA 69-72; CANR 11, 29; DLB 120

Voigt, Cynthia 1942- . . . . CLC 30
See also AAYA 3; CA 106; CANR 18, 37,
40; CLR 13; JRDA; MAICYA;
SATA 48, 79; SATA-Brief 33

Voinovich, Vladimir (Nikolaevich)
1932- . . . . CLC 10, 49
See also CA 81-84; CAAS 12; CANR 33;
MTCW

Vollmann, William T. 1959- . . . . CLC 89
See also CA 134

Voloshinov, V. N.
See Bakhtin, Mikhail Mikhailovich

Voltaire
1694-1778 . . . LC 14; DA; SSC 12; WLC

von Aue, Hartmann 1170-1210 . . . CMLC 15

von Daeniken, Erich 1935- . . . . CLC 30
See also AITN 1; CA 37-40R; CANR 17,
44

von Daniken, Erich
See von Daeniken, Erich

von Heidenstam, (Carl Gustaf) Verner
See Heidenstam, (Carl Gustaf) Verner von

von Heyse, Paul (Johann Ludwig)
See Heyse, Paul (Johann Ludwig von)

von Hofmannsthal, Hugo
See Hofmannsthal, Hugo von

von Horvath, Odon
See Horvath, Oedoen von

von Horvath, Oedoen
See Horvath, Oedoen von

von Liliencron, (Friedrich Adolf Axel) Detlev
See Liliencron, (Friedrich Adolf Axel)
Detlev von

Vonnegut, Kurt, Jr.
1922- . . . . . . CLC 1, 2, 3, 4, 5, 8, 12, 22,
40, 60; DA; SSC 8; WLC
See also AAYA 6; AITN 1; BEST 90:4;
CA 1-4R; CANR 1, 25, 49;
CDALB 1968-1988; DLB 2, 8, 152;
DLBD 3; DLBY 80; MTCW

Von Rachen, Kurt
See Hubbard, L(afayette) Ron(ald)

von Rezzori (d'Arezzo), Gregor
See Rezzori (d'Arezzo), Gregor von

von Sternberg, Josef
See Sternberg, Josef von

Vorster, Gordon 1924- . . . . CLC 34
See also CA 133

Vosce, Trudie
See Ozick, Cynthia

Voznesensky, Andrei (Andreievich)
1933- . . . . CLC 1, 15, 57
See also CA 89-92; CANR 37; MTCW

Waddington, Miriam 1917- . . . . CLC 28
See also CA 21-24R; CANR 12, 30;
DLB 68

Wagman, Fredrica 1937- . . . . CLC 7
See also CA 97-100

Wagner, Richard 1813-1883. . . . . . NCLC 9
See also DLB 129

Wagner-Martin, Linda 1936- . . . . CLC 50

Wagoner, David (Russell)
1926- . . . . CLC 3, 5, 15
See also CA 1-4R; CAAS 3; CANR 2;
DLB 5; SATA 14

Wah, Fred(erick James) 1939- . . . . . . CLC 44
See also CA 107; 141; DLB 60

Wahloo, Per 1926-1975 . . . . CLC 7
See also CA 61-64

Wahloo, Peter
See Wahloo, Per

Wain, John (Barrington)
1925-1994 . . . . CLC 2, 11, 15, 46
See also CA 5-8R; 145; CAAS 4; CANR 23;
CDBLB 1960 to Present; DLB 15, 27,
139; MTCW

Wajda, Andrzej 1926- . . . . CLC 16
See also CA 102

Wakefield, Dan 1932- . . . . CLC 7
See also CA 21-24R; CAAS 7

Wakoski, Diane
1937- . . . . CLC 2, 4, 7, 9, 11, 40
See also CA 13-16R; CAAS 1; CANR 9;
DLB 5

Wakoski-Sherbell, Diane
See Wakoski, Diane

Walcott, Derek (Alton)
1930- . . . . CLC 2, 4, 9, 14, 25, 42, 67, 76;
BLC
See also BW 2; CA 89-92; CANR 26, 47;
DLB 117; DLBY 81; MTCW

Waldman, Anne 1945- . . . . CLC 7
See also CA 37-40R; CAAS 17; CANR 34;
DLB 16

Waldo, E. Hunter
See Sturgeon, Theodore (Hamilton)

Waldo, Edward Hamilton
See Sturgeon, Theodore (Hamilton)

Walker, Alice (Malsenior)
1944- . . . . CLC 5, 6, 9, 19, 27, 46, 58;
BLC; DA; SSC 5
See also AAYA 3; BEST 89:4; BW 2;
CA 37-40R; CANR 9, 27, 49;
CDALB 1968-1988; DLB 6, 33, 143;
MTCW; SATA 31

Walker, David Harry 1911-1992. . . . CLC 14
See also CA 1-4R; 137; CANR 1; SATA 8;
SATA-Obit 71

Walker, Edward Joseph 1934-
See Walker, Ted
See also CA 21-24R; CANR 12, 28

Walker, George F. 1947- . . . . CLC 44, 61
See also CA 103; CANR 21, 43; DLB 60

Walker, Joseph A. 1935- . . . . CLC 19
See also BW 1; CA 89-92; CANR 26;
DLB 38

Walker, Margaret (Abigail)
1915- . . . . CLC 1, 6; BLC
See also BW 2; CA 73-76; CANR 26;
DLB 76, 152; MTCW

Walker, Ted. . . . . CLC 13
See also Walker, Edward Joseph
See also DLB 40

Wallace, David Foster   1962- . . . . CLC 50
See also CA 132

Wallace, Dexter
See Masters, Edgar Lee

Wallace, (Richard Horatio) Edgar
1875-1932 . . . . TCLC 57
See also CA 115; DLB 70

Wallace, Irving   1916-1990 . . . . CLC 7, 13
See also AITN 1; CA 1-4R; 132; CAAS 1;
CANR 1, 27; MTCW

Wallant, Edward Lewis
1926-1962 . . . . CLC 5, 10
See also CA 1-4R; CANR 22; DLB 2, 28,
143; MTCW

Walpole, Horace   1717-1797. . . . . LC 2
See also DLB 39, 104

Walpole, Hugh (Seymour)
1884-1941 . . . . TCLC 5
See also CA 104; DLB 34

Walser, Martin   1927- . . . . CLC 27
See also CA 57-60; CANR 8, 46; DLB 75,
124

Walser, Robert
1878-1956 . . . . TCLC 18; SSC 20
See also CA 118; DLB 66

Walsh, Jill Paton. . . . . CLC 35
See also Paton Walsh, Gillian
See also AAYA 11; CLR 2; SAAS 3

Walter, Villiam Christian
See Andersen, Hans Christian

Wambaugh, Joseph (Aloysius, Jr.)
1937- . . . . CLC 3, 18
See also AITN 1; BEST 89:3; CA 33-36R;
CANR 42; DLB 6; DLBY 83; MTCW

Ward, Arthur Henry Sarsfield   1883-1959
See Rohmer, Sax
See also CA 108

Ward, Douglas Turner   1930- . . . . CLC 19
See also BW 1; CA 81-84; CANR 27;
DLB 7, 38

Ward, Mary Augusta
See Ward, Mrs. Humphry

Ward, Mrs. Humphry
1851-1920 . . . . TCLC 55
See also DLB 18

Ward, Peter
See Faust, Frederick (Schiller)

Warhol, Andy   1928(?)-1987. . . . . CLC 20
See also AAYA 12; BEST 89:4; CA 89-92;
121; CANR 34

Warner, Francis (Robert le Plastrier)
1937- . . . . CLC 14
See also CA 53-56; CANR 11

Warner, Marina   1946- . . . . CLC 59
See also CA 65-68; CANR 21

Warner, Rex (Ernest)   1905-1986. . . . CLC 45
See also CA 89-92; 119; DLB 15

Warner, Susan (Bogert)
1819-1885 . . . . NCLC 31
See also DLB 3, 42

Warner, Sylvia (Constance) Ashton
See Ashton-Warner, Sylvia (Constance)

Warner, Sylvia Townsend
1893-1978 . . . . CLC 7, 19
See also CA 61-64; 77-80; CANR 16;
DLB 34, 139; MTCW

Warren, Mercy Otis   1728-1814. . . NCLC 13
See also DLB 31

Warren, Robert Penn
1905-1989 . . . . CLC 1, 4, 6, 8, 10, 13, 18,
39, 53, 59; DA; SSC 4; WLC
See also AITN 1; CA 13-16R; 129;
CANR 10, 47; CDALB 1968-1988;
DLB 2, 48, 152; DLBY 80, 89; MTCW;
SATA 46; SATA-Obit 63

Warshofsky, Isaac
See Singer, Isaac Bashevis

Warton, Thomas   1728-1790. . . . . LC 15
See also DLB 104, 109

Waruk, Kona
See Harris, (Theodore) Wilson

Warung, Price   1855-1911. . . . . TCLC 45

Warwick, Jarvis
See Garner, Hugh

Washington, Alex
See Harris, Mark

Washington, Booker T(aliaferro)
1856-1915 . . . . TCLC 10; BLC
See also BW 1; CA 114; 125; SATA 28

Washington, George   1732-1799 . . . . . . LC 25
See also DLB 31

Wassermann, (Karl) Jakob
1873-1934 . . . . TCLC 6
See also CA 104; DLB 66

Wasserstein, Wendy
1950- . . . . CLC 32, 59; DC 4
See also CA 121; 129; CABS 3

Waterhouse, Keith (Spencer)
1929- . . . . CLC 47
See also CA 5-8R; CANR 38; DLB 13, 15;
MTCW

Waters, Frank (Joseph)   1902- . . . . . . CLC 88
See also CA 5-8R; CAAS 13; CANR 3, 18;
DLBY 86

Waters, Roger   1944- . . . . CLC 35

Watkins, Frances Ellen
See Harper, Frances Ellen Watkins

Watkins, Gerrold
See Malzberg, Barry N(athaniel)

Watkins, Paul   1964- . . . . CLC 55
See also CA 132

Watkins, Vernon Phillips
1906-1967 . . . . CLC 43
See also CA 9-10; 25-28R; CAP 1; DLB 20

Watson, Irving S.
See Mencken, H(enry) L(ouis)

Watson, John H.
See Farmer, Philip Jose

Watson, Richard F.
See Silverberg, Robert

Waugh, Auberon (Alexander)   1939- . . CLC 7
See also CA 45-48; CANR 6, 22; DLB 14

Waugh, Evelyn (Arthur St. John)
1903-1966 . . . . . . CLC 1, 3, 8, 13, 19, 27,
44; DA; WLC
See also CA 85-88; 25-28R; CANR 22;
CDBLB 1914-1945; DLB 15; MTCW

Waugh, Harriet   1944- . . . . CLC 6
See also CA 85-88; CANR 22

Ways, C. R.
See Blount, Roy (Alton), Jr.

Waystaff, Simon
See Swift, Jonathan

Webb, (Martha) Beatrice (Potter)
1858-1943 . . . . TCLC 22
See also Potter, Beatrice
See also CA 117

Webb, Charles (Richard)   1939- . . . . . . CLC 7
See also CA 25-28R

Webb, James H(enry), Jr.   1946- . . . . CLC 22
See also CA 81-84

Webb, Mary (Gladys Meredith)
1881-1927 . . . . TCLC 24
See also CA 123; DLB 34

Webb, Mrs. Sidney
See Webb, (Martha) Beatrice (Potter)

Webb, Phyllis   1927- . . . . CLC 18
See also CA 104; CANR 23; DLB 53

Webb, Sidney (James)
1859-1947 . . . . TCLC 22
See also CA 117

Webber, Andrew Lloyd. . . . . CLC 21
See also Lloyd Webber, Andrew

Weber, Lenora Mattingly
1895-1971 . . . . CLC 12
See also CA 19-20; 29-32R; CAP 1;
SATA 2; SATA-Obit 26

Webster, John   1579(?)-1634(?) . . . . DC 2
See also CDBLB Before 1660; DA; DLB 58;
WLC

Webster, Noah   1758-1843 . . . . NCLC 30

Wedekind, (Benjamin) Frank(lin)
1864-1918 . . . . TCLC 7
See also CA 104; DLB 118

Weidman, Jerome   1913- . . . . CLC 7
See also AITN 2; CA 1-4R; CANR 1;
DLB 28

Weil, Simone (Adolphine)
1909-1943 . . . . TCLC 23
See also CA 117

Weinstein, Nathan
See West, Nathanael

Weinstein, Nathan von Wallenstein
See West, Nathanael

Weir, Peter (Lindsay)   1944- . . . . CLC 20
See also CA 113; 123

Weiss, Peter (Ulrich)
1916-1982 . . . . CLC 3, 15, 51
See also CA 45-48; 106; CANR 3; DLB 69,
124

Weiss, Theodore (Russell)
1916- . . . . CLC 3, 8, 14
See also CA 9-12R; CAAS 2; CANR 46;
DLB 5

Welch, (Maurice) Denton
      1915-1948 .... TCLC **22**
      See also CA 121

Welch, James 1940- .... CLC **6, 14, 52**
      See also CA 85-88; CANR 42; NNAL

Weldon, Fay
      1933- .... CLC **6, 9, 11, 19, 36, 59**
      See also CA 21-24R; CANR 16, 46;
      CDBLB 1960 to Present; DLB 14;
      MTCW

Wellek, Rene 1903- .... CLC **28**
      See also CA 5-8R; CAAS 7; CANR 8;
      DLB 63

Weller, Michael 1942- .... CLC **10, 53**
      See also CA 85-88

Weller, Paul 1958- .... CLC **26**

Wellershoff, Dieter 1925-.......... CLC **46**
      See also CA 89-92; CANR 16, 37

Welles, (George) Orson
      1915-1985 .... CLC **20, 80**
      See also CA 93-96; 117

Wellman, Mac 1945- .... CLC **65**

Wellman, Manly Wade 1903-1986 .. CLC **49**
      See also CA 1-4R; 118; CANR 6, 16, 44;
      SATA 6; SATA-Obit 47

Wells, Carolyn 1869(?)-1942 ...... TCLC **35**
      See also CA 113; DLB 11

Wells, H(erbert) G(eorge)
      1866-1946 .... TCLC **6, 12, 19; DA;**
                                      SSC 6; WLC
      See also CA 110; 121; CDBLB 1914-1945;
      DLB 34, 70; MTCW; SATA 20

Wells, Rosemary 1943-............ CLC **12**
      See also AAYA 13; CA 85-88; CANR 48;
      CLR 16; MAICYA; SAAS 1; SATA 18,
      69

Welty, Eudora
      1909- ...... CLC **1, 2, 5, 14, 22, 33; DA;**
                                      SSC 1; WLC
      See also CA 9-12R; CABS 1; CANR 32;
      CDALB 1941-1968; DLB 2, 102, 143;
      DLBD 12; DLBY 87; MTCW

Wen I-to 1899-1946 .... TCLC **28**

Wentworth, Robert
      See Hamilton, Edmond

Werfel, Franz (V.) 1890-1945 ...... TCLC **8**
      See also CA 104; DLB 81, 124

Wergeland, Henrik Arnold
      1808-1845 .... NCLC **5**

Wersba, Barbara 1932-............ CLC **30**
      See also AAYA 2; CA 29-32R; CANR 16,
      38; CLR 3; DLB 52; JRDA; MAICYA;
      SAAS 2; SATA 1, 58

Wertmueller, Lina 1928- .... CLC **16**
      See also CA 97-100; CANR 39

Wescott, Glenway 1901-1987....... CLC **13**
      See also CA 13-16R; 121; CANR 23;
      DLB 4, 9, 102

Wesker, Arnold 1932- .... CLC **3, 5, 42**
      See also CA 1-4R; CAAS 7; CANR 1, 33;
      CDBLB 1960 to Present; DLB 13;
      MTCW

Wesley, Richard (Errol) 1945-....... CLC **7**
      See also BW 1; CA 57-60; CANR 27;
      DLB 38

Wessel, Johan Herman 1742-1785 .... LC **7**

West, Anthony (Panther)
      1914-1987 .... CLC **50**
      See also CA 45-48; 124; CANR 3, 19;
      DLB 15

West, C. P.
      See Wodehouse, P(elham) G(renville)

West, (Mary) Jessamyn
      1902-1984 .... CLC **7, 17**
      See also CA 9-12R; 112; CANR 27; DLB 6;
      DLBY 84; MTCW; SATA-Obit 37

West, Morris L(anglo) 1916-..... CLC **6, 33**
      See also CA 5-8R; CANR 24, 49; MTCW

West, Nathanael
      1903-1940 ..... TCLC **1, 14, 44; SSC 16**
      See also CA 104; 125; CDALB 1929-1941;
      DLB 4, 9, 28; MTCW

West, Owen
      See Koontz, Dean R(ay)

West, Paul 1930- .... CLC **7, 14**
      See also CA 13-16R; CAAS 7; CANR 22;
      DLB 14

West, Rebecca 1892-1983 .. CLC **7, 9, 31, 50**
      See also CA 5-8R; 109; CANR 19; DLB 36;
      DLBY 83; MTCW

Westall, Robert (Atkinson)
      1929-1993 .... CLC **17**
      See also AAYA 12; CA 69-72; 141;
      CANR 18; CLR 13; JRDA; MAICYA;
      SAAS 2; SATA 23, 69; SATA-Obit 75

Westlake, Donald E(dwin)
      1933- .... CLC **7, 33**
      See also CA 17-20R; CAAS 13; CANR 16,
      44

Westmacott, Mary
      See Christie, Agatha (Mary Clarissa)

Weston, Allen
      See Norton, Andre

Wetcheek, J. L.
      See Feuchtwanger, Lion

Wetering, Janwillem van de
      See van de Wetering, Janwillem

Wetherell, Elizabeth
      See Warner, Susan (Bogert)

Whalen, Philip 1923- .... CLC **6, 29**
      See also CA 9-12R; CANR 5, 39; DLB 16

Wharton, Edith (Newbold Jones)
      1862-1937 ...... TCLC **3, 9, 27, 53; DA;**
                                      SSC 6; WLC
      See also CA 104; 132; CDALB 1865-1917;
      DLB 4, 9, 12, 78; MTCW

Wharton, James
      See Mencken, H(enry) L(ouis)

Wharton, William (a pseudonym)
      .... CLC **18, 37**
      See also CA 93-96; DLBY 80

Wheatley (Peters), Phillis
      1754(?)-1784 .... LC **3; BLC; DA; PC 3;**
                                      WLC
      See also CDALB 1640-1865; DLB 31, 50

Wheelock, John Hall 1886-1978.... CLC **14**
      See also CA 13-16R; 77-80; CANR 14;
      DLB 45

White, E(lwyn) B(rooks)
      1899-1985 .... CLC **10, 34, 39**
      See also AITN 2; CA 13-16R; 116;
      CANR 16, 37; CLR 1, 21; DLB 11, 22;
      MAICYA; MTCW; SATA 2, 29;
      SATA-Obit 44

White, Edmund (Valentine III)
      1940- .... CLC **27**
      See also AAYA 7; CA 45-48; CANR 3, 19,
      36; MTCW

White, Patrick (Victor Martindale)
      1912-1990 .. CLC **3, 4, 5, 7, 9, 18, 65, 69**
      See also CA 81-84; 132; CANR 43; MTCW

White, Phyllis Dorothy James 1920-
      See James, P. D.
      See also CA 21-24R; CANR 17, 43; MTCW

White, T(erence) H(anbury)
      1906-1964 .... CLC **30**
      See also CA 73-76; CANR 37; JRDA;
      MAICYA; SATA 12

White, Terence de Vere
      1912-1994 .... CLC **49**
      See also CA 49-52; 145; CANR 3

White, Walter F(rancis)
      1893-1955 .... TCLC **15**
      See also White, Walter
      See also BW 1; CA 115; 124; DLB 51

White, William Hale 1831-1913
      See Rutherford, Mark
      See also CA 121

Whitehead, E(dward) A(nthony)
      1933- .... CLC **5**
      See also CA 65-68

Whitemore, Hugh (John) 1936-..... CLC **37**
      See also CA 132

Whitman, Sarah Helen (Power)
      1803-1878 .... NCLC **19**
      See also DLB 1

Whitman, Walt(er)
      1819-1892 ..... NCLC **4, 31; DA; PC 3;**
                                      WLC
      See also CDALB 1640-1865; DLB 3, 64;
      SATA 20

Whitney, Phyllis A(yame) 1903-.... CLC **42**
      See also AITN 2; BEST 90:3; CA 1-4R;
      CANR 3, 25, 38; JRDA; MAICYA;
      SATA 1, 30

Whittemore, (Edward) Reed (Jr.)
      1919- .... CLC **4**
      See also CA 9-12R; CAAS 8; CANR 4;
      DLB 5

Whittier, John Greenleaf
      1807-1892 .... NCLC **8**
      See also CDALB 1640-1865; DLB 1

Whittlebot, Hernia
      See Coward, Noel (Peirce)

Wicker, Thomas Grey 1926-
      See Wicker, Tom
      See also CA 65-68; CANR 21, 46

Wicker, Tom .... CLC **7**
      See also Wicker, Thomas Grey

Wideman, John Edgar
      1941- .... CLC **5, 34, 36, 67; BLC**
      See also BW 2; CA 85-88; CANR 14, 42;
      DLB 33, 143

Wiebe, Rudy (Henry) 1934-... **CLC 6, 11, 14**
See also CA 37-40R; CANR 42; DLB 60

Wieland, Christoph Martin
1733-1813 .... **NCLC 17**
See also DLB 97

Wiene, Robert 1881-1938........ **TCLC 56**

Wieners, John 1934-............... **CLC 7**
See also CA 13-16R; DLB 16

Wiesel, Elie(zer)
1928- .... **CLC 3, 5, 11, 37; DA**
See also AAYA 7; AITN 1; CA 5-8R;
CAAS 4; CANR 8, 40; DLB 83;
DLBY 87; MTCW; SATA 56

Wiggins, Marianne 1947-......... **CLC 57**
See also BEST 89:3; CA 130

Wight, James Alfred 1916-
See Herriot, James
See also CA 77-80; SATA 55;
SATA-Brief 44

Wilbur, Richard (Purdy)
1921- .... **CLC 3, 6, 9, 14, 53; DA**
See also CA 1-4R; CABS 2; CANR 2, 29;
DLB 5; MTCW; SATA 9

Wild, Peter 1940-............... **CLC 14**
See also CA 37-40R; DLB 5

Wilde, Oscar (Fingal O'Flahertie Wills)
1854(?)-1900 .... **TCLC 1, 8, 23, 41; DA;
SSC 11; WLC**
See also CA 104; 119; CDBLB 1890-1914;
DLB 10, 19, 34, 57, 141; SATA 24

Wilder, Billy .... **CLC 20**
See also Wilder, Samuel
See also DLB 26

Wilder, Samuel 1906-
See Wilder, Billy
See also CA 89-92

Wilder, Thornton (Niven)
1897-1975 ...... **CLC 1, 5, 6, 10, 15, 35,
82; DA; DC 1; WLC**
See also AITN 2; CA 13-16R; 61-64;
CANR 40; DLB 4, 7, 9; MTCW

Wilding, Michael 1942-........... **CLC 73**
See also CA 104; CANR 24, 49

Wiley, Richard 1944-............. **CLC 44**
See also CA 121; 129

Wilhelm, Kate .... **CLC 7**
See also Wilhelm, Katie Gertrude
See also CAAS 5; DLB 8

Wilhelm, Katie Gertrude 1928-
See Wilhelm, Kate
See also CA 37-40R; CANR 17, 36; MTCW

Wilkins, Mary
See Freeman, Mary Eleanor Wilkins

Willard, Nancy 1936-........... **CLC 7, 37**
See also CA 89-92; CANR 10, 39; CLR 5;
DLB 5, 52; MAICYA; MTCW;
SATA 37, 71; SATA-Brief 30

Williams, C(harles) K(enneth)
1936-.................... **CLC 33, 56**
See also CA 37-40R; DLB 5

Williams, Charles
See Collier, James L(incoln)

Williams, Charles (Walter Stansby)
1886-1945 .... **TCLC 1, 11**
See also CA 104; DLB 100, 153

Williams, (George) Emlyn
1905-1987 .... **CLC 15**
See also CA 104; 123; CANR 36; DLB 10,
77; MTCW

Williams, Hugo 1942-............. **CLC 42**
See also CA 17-20R; CANR 45; DLB 40

Williams, J. Walker
See Wodehouse, P(elham) G(renville)

Williams, John A(lfred)
1925-............. **CLC 5, 13; BLC**
See also BW 2; CA 53-56; CAAS 3;
CANR 6, 26; DLB 2, 33

Williams, Jonathan (Chamberlain)
1929-....................... **CLC 13**
See also CA 9-12R; CAAS 12; CANR 8;
DLB 5

Williams, Joy 1944-.............. **CLC 31**
See also CA 41-44R; CANR 22, 48

Williams, Norman 1952- .... **CLC 39**
See also CA 118

Williams, Sherley Anne
1944- .... **CLC 89; BLC**
See also BW 2; CA 73-76; CANR 25;
DLB 41; SATA 78

Williams, Shirley
See Williams, Sherley Anne

Williams, Tennessee
1911-1983 ..... **CLC 1, 2, 5, 7, 8, 11, 15,
19, 30, 39, 45, 71; DA; DC 4; WLC**
See also AITN 1, 2; CA 5-8R; 108;
CABS 3; CANR 31; CDALB 1941-1968;
DLB 7; DLBD 4; DLBY 83; MTCW

Williams, Thomas (Alonzo)
1926-1990 .... **CLC 14**
See also CA 1-4R; 132; CANR 2

Williams, William C.
See Williams, William Carlos

Williams, William Carlos
1883-1963 .... **CLC 1, 2, 5, 9, 13, 22, 42,
67; DA; PC 7**
See also CA 89-92; CANR 34;
CDALB 1917-1929; DLB 4, 16, 54, 86;
MTCW

Williamson, David (Keith) 1942-.... **CLC 56**
See also CA 103; CANR 41

Williamson, Ellen Douglas 1905-1984
See Douglas, Ellen
See also CA 17-20R; 114; CANR 39

Williamson, Jack.................. **CLC 29**
See also Williamson, John Stewart
See also CAAS 8; DLB 8

Williamson, John Stewart 1908-
See Williamson, Jack
See also CA 17-20R; CANR 23

Willie, Frederick
See Lovecraft, H(oward) P(hillips)

Willingham, Calder (Baynard, Jr.)
1922-1995 .... **CLC 5, 51**
See also CA 5-8R; 147; CANR 3; DLB 2,
44; MTCW

Willis, Charles
See Clarke, Arthur C(harles)

Willy
See Colette, (Sidonie-Gabrielle)

Willy, Colette
See Colette, (Sidonie-Gabrielle)

Wilson, A(ndrew) N(orman) 1950- .. **CLC 33**
See also CA 112; 122; DLB 14

Wilson, Angus (Frank Johnstone)
1913-1991 .... **CLC 2, 3, 5, 25, 34**
See also CA 5-8R; 134; CANR 21; DLB 15,
139; MTCW

Wilson, August
1945- .. **CLC 39, 50, 63; BLC; DA; DC 2**
See also BW 2; CA 115; 122; CANR 42;
MTCW

Wilson, Brian 1942-.............. **CLC 12**

Wilson, Colin 1931-............. **CLC 3, 14**
See also CA 1-4R; CAAS 5; CANR 1, 22,
33; DLB 14; MTCW

Wilson, Dirk
See Pohl, Frederik

Wilson, Edmund
1895-1972 .... **CLC 1, 2, 3, 8, 24**
See also CA 1-4R; 37-40R; CANR 1, 46;
DLB 63; MTCW

Wilson, Ethel Davis (Bryant)
1888(?)-1980 .... **CLC 13**
See also CA 102; DLB 68; MTCW

Wilson, John 1785-1854.......... **NCLC 5**

Wilson, John (Anthony) Burgess 1917-1993
See Burgess, Anthony
See also CA 1-4R; 143; CANR 2, 46;
MTCW

Wilson, Lanford 1937-........ **CLC 7, 14, 36**
See also CA 17-20R; CABS 3; CANR 45;
DLB 7

Wilson, Robert M. 1944-......... **CLC 7, 9**
See also CA 49-52; CANR 2, 41; MTCW

Wilson, Robert McLiam 1964-..... **CLC 59**
See also CA 132

Wilson, Sloan 1920-.............. **CLC 32**
See also CA 1-4R; CANR 1, 44

Wilson, Snoo 1948-............... **CLC 33**
See also CA 69-72

Wilson, William S(mith) 1932- ..... **CLC 49**
See also CA 81-84

Winchilsea, Anne (Kingsmill) Finch Counte
1661-1720 .... **LC 3**

Windham, Basil
See Wodehouse, P(elham) G(renville)

Wingrove, David (John) 1954-...... **CLC 68**
See also CA 133

Winters, Janet Lewis .... **CLC 41**
See also Lewis, Janet
See also DLBY 87

Winters, (Arthur) Yvor
1900-1968 .... **CLC 4, 8, 32**
See also CA 11-12; 25-28R; CAP 1;
DLB 48; MTCW

Winterson, Jeanette 1959-......... **CLC 64**
See also CA 136

Wiseman, Frederick 1930-......... **CLC 20**

Wister, Owen 1860-1938 .... **TCLC 21**
See also CA 108; DLB 9, 78; SATA 62

Witkacy
See Witkiewicz, Stanislaw Ignacy

Witkiewicz, Stanislaw Ignacy
    1885-1939 . . . . **TCLC 8**
    See also CA 105

Wittgenstein, Ludwig (Josef Johann)
    1889-1951 . . . . **TCLC 59**
    See also CA 113

Wittig, Monique 1935(?)- . . . . **CLC 22**
    See also CA 116; 135; DLB 83

Wittlin, Jozef 1896-1976 . . . . **CLC 25**
    See also CA 49-52; 65-68; CANR 3

Wodehouse, P(elham) G(renville)
    1881-1975 . . . **CLC 1, 2, 5, 10, 22; SSC 2**
    See also AITN 2; CA 45-48; 57-60;
    CANR 3, 33; CDBLB 1914-1945;
    DLB 34; MTCW; SATA 22

Woiwode, L.
    See Woiwode, Larry (Alfred)

Woiwode, Larry (Alfred) 1941- . . . **CLC 6, 10**
    See also CA 73-76; CANR 16; DLB 6

Wojciechowska, Maia (Teresa)
    1927- . . . . **CLC 26**
    See also AAYA 8; CA 9-12R; CANR 4, 41;
    CLR 1; JRDA; MAICYA; SAAS 1;
    SATA 1, 28

Wolf, Christa 1929- . . . . **CLC 14, 29, 58**
    See also CA 85-88; CANR 45; DLB 75;
    MTCW

Wolfe, Gene (Rodman) 1931- . . . . **CLC 25**
    See also CA 57-60; CAAS 9; CANR 6, 32;
    DLB 8

Wolfe, George C. 1954- . . . . **CLC 49**

Wolfe, Thomas (Clayton)
    1900-1938 . . . **TCLC 4, 13, 29; DA; WLC**
    See also CA 104; 132; CDALB 1929-1941;
    DLB 9, 102; DLBD 2; DLBY 85; MTCW

Wolfe, Thomas Kennerly, Jr. 1931-
    See Wolfe, Tom
    See also CA 13-16R; CANR 9, 33; MTCW

Wolfe, Tom . . . . **CLC 1, 2, 9, 15, 35, 51**
    See also Wolfe, Thomas Kennerly, Jr.
    See also AAYA 8; AITN 2; BEST 89:1;
    DLB 152

Wolff, Geoffrey (Ansell) 1937- . . . . . **CLC 41**
    See also CA 29-32R; CANR 29, 43

Wolff, Sonia
    See Levitin, Sonia (Wolff)

Wolff, Tobias (Jonathan Ansell)
    1945- . . . . **CLC 39, 64**
    See also BEST 90:2; CA 114; 117; DLB 130

Wolfram von Eschenbach
    c. 1170-c. 1220 . . . . **CMLC 5**
    See also DLB 138

Wolitzer, Hilma 1930- . . . . **CLC 17**
    See also CA 65-68; CANR 18, 40; SATA 31

Wollstonecraft, Mary 1759-1797 . . . . . . **LC 5**
    See also CDBLB 1789-1832; DLB 39, 104

Wonder, Stevie . . . . **CLC 12**
    See also Morris, Steveland Judkins

Wong, Jade Snow 1922- . . . . **CLC 17**
    See also CA 109

Woodcott, Keith
    See Brunner, John (Kilian Houston)

Woodruff, Robert W.
    See Mencken, H(enry) L(ouis)

Woolf, (Adeline) Virginia
    1882-1941 . . . . **TCLC 1, 5, 20, 43, 56;
                                      DA; SSC 7; WLC**
    See also CA 104; 130; CDBLB 1914-1945;
    DLB 36, 100; DLBD 10; MTCW

Woollcott, Alexander (Humphreys)
    1887-1943 . . . . **TCLC 5**
    See also CA 105; DLB 29

Woolrich, Cornell 1903-1968 . . . . . . **CLC 77**
    See also Hopley-Woolrich, Cornell George

Wordsworth, Dorothy
    1771-1855 . . . . **NCLC 25**
    See also DLB 107

Wordsworth, William
    1770-1850 . . . . **NCLC 12, 38; DA; PC 4;
                                      WLC**
    See also CDBLB 1789-1832; DLB 93, 107

Wouk, Herman 1915- . . . . **CLC 1, 9, 38**
    See also CA 5-8R; CANR 6, 33; DLBY 82;
    MTCW

Wright, Charles (Penzel, Jr.)
    1935- . . . . **CLC 6, 13, 28**
    See also CA 29-32R; CAAS 7; CANR 23,
    36; DLBY 82; MTCW

Wright, Charles Stevenson
    1932- . . . . **CLC 49; BLC 3**
    See also BW 1; CA 9-12R; CANR 26;
    DLB 33

Wright, Jack R.
    See Harris, Mark

Wright, James (Arlington)
    1927-1980 . . . . **CLC 3, 5, 10, 28**
    See also AITN 2; CA 49-52; 97-100;
    CANR 4, 34; DLB 5; MTCW

Wright, Judith (Arandell)
    1915- . . . . **CLC 11, 53**
    See also CA 13-16R; CANR 31; MTCW;
    SATA 14

Wright, L(aurali) R. 1939- . . . . **CLC 44**
    See also CA 138

Wright, Richard (Nathaniel)
    1908-1960 . . . . **CLC 1, 3, 4, 9, 14, 21, 48,
                                      74; BLC; DA; SSC 2; WLC**
    See also AAYA 5; BW 1; CA 108;
    CDALB 1929-1941; DLB 76, 102;
    DLBD 2; MTCW

Wright, Richard B(ruce) 1937- . . . . . . **CLC 6**
    See also CA 85-88; DLB 53

Wright, Rick 1945- . . . . **CLC 35**

Wright, Rowland
    See Wells, Carolyn

Wright, Stephen Caldwell 1946- . . . . **CLC 33**
    See also BW 2

Wright, Willard Huntington 1888-1939
    See Van Dine, S. S.
    See also CA 115

Wright, William 1930- . . . . **CLC 44**
    See also CA 53-56; CANR 7, 23

Wroth, LadyMary 1587-1653(?) . . . . . **LC 30**
    See also DLB 121

Wu Ch'eng-en 1500(?)-1582(?) . . . . **LC 7**

Wu Ching-tzu 1701-1754 . . . . **LC 2**

Wurlitzer, Rudolph 1938(?)- . . . **CLC 2, 4, 15**
    See also CA 85-88

Wycherley, William 1641-1715 . . . . **LC 8, 21**
    See also CDBLB 1660-1789; DLB 80

Wylie, Elinor (Morton Hoyt)
    1885-1928 . . . . **TCLC 8**
    See also CA 105; DLB 9, 45

Wylie, Philip (Gordon) 1902-1971 . . . **CLC 43**
    See also CA 21-22; 33-36R; CAP 2; DLB 9

Wyndham, John . . . . **CLC 19**
    See also Harris, John (Wyndham Parkes
    Lucas) Beynon

Wyss, Johann David Von
    1743-1818 . . . . **NCLC 10**
    See also JRDA; MAICYA; SATA 29;
    SATA-Brief 27

Yakumo Koizumi
    See Hearn, (Patricio) Lafcadio (Tessima
    Carlos)

Yanez, Jose Donoso
    See Donoso (Yanez), Jose

Yanovsky, Basile S.
    See Yanovsky, V(assily) S(emenovich)

Yanovsky, V(assily) S(emenovich)
    1906-1989 . . . . **CLC 2, 18**
    See also CA 97-100; 129

Yates, Richard 1926-1992 . . . . . **CLC 7, 8, 23**
    See also CA 5-8R; 139; CANR 10, 43;
    DLB 2; DLBY 81, 92

Yeats, W. B.
    See Yeats, William Butler

Yeats, William Butler
    1865-1939 . . . . . **TCLC 1, 11, 18, 31; DA;
                                      WLC**
    See also CA 104; 127; CANR 45;
    CDBLB 1890-1914; DLB 10, 19, 98;
    MTCW

Yehoshua, A(braham) B.
    1936- . . . . **CLC 13, 31**
    See also CA 33-36R; CANR 43

Yep, Laurence Michael 1948- . . . . . . **CLC 35**
    See also AAYA 5; CA 49-52; CANR 1, 46;
    CLR 3, 17; DLB 52; JRDA; MAICYA;
    SATA 7, 69

Yerby, Frank G(arvin)
    1916-1991 . . . . **CLC 1, 7, 22; BLC**
    See also BW 1; CA 9-12R; 136; CANR 16;
    DLB 76; MTCW

Yesenin, Sergei Alexandrovich
    See Esenin, Sergei (Alexandrovich)

Yevtushenko, Yevgeny (Alexandrovich)
    1933- . . . . **CLC 1, 3, 13, 26, 51**
    See also CA 81-84; CANR 33; MTCW

Yezierska, Anzia 1885(?)-1970 . . . . . **CLC 46**
    See also CA 126; 89-92; DLB 28; MTCW

Yglesias, Helen 1915- . . . . **CLC 7, 22**
    See also CA 37-40R; CAAS 20; CANR 15;
    MTCW

Yokomitsu Riichi 1898-1947 . . . . . . **TCLC 47**

Yonge, Charlotte (Mary)
    1823-1901 . . . . **TCLC 48**
    See also CA 109; DLB 18; SATA 17

York, Jeremy
    See Creasey, John

York, Simon
    See Heinlein, Robert A(nson)

Yorke, Henry Vincent 1905-1974 . . . **CLC 13**
See also Green, Henry
See also CA 85-88; 49-52

Yosano Akiko 1878-1942 . . **TCLC 59; PC 11**

Yoshimoto, Banana . . . . **CLC 84**
See also Yoshimoto, Mahoko

Yoshimoto, Mahoko 1964-
See Yoshimoto, Banana
See also CA 144

Young, Al(bert James)
1939- . . . . **CLC 19; BLC**
See also BW 2; CA 29-32R; CANR 26;
DLB 33

Young, Andrew (John) 1885-1971 . . . . **CLC 5**
See also CA 5-8R; CANR 7, 29

Young, Collier
See Bloch, Robert (Albert)

Young, Edward 1683-1765 . . . . **LC 3**
See also DLB 95

Young, Marguerite 1909- . . . . **CLC 82**
See also CA 13-16; CAP 1

Young, Neil 1945- . . . . **CLC 17**
See also CA 110

Yourcenar, Marguerite
1903-1987 . . . . **CLC 19, 38, 50, 87**
See also CA 69-72; CANR 23; DLB 72;
DLBY 88; MTCW

Yurick, Sol 1925- . . . . **CLC 6**
See also CA 13-16R; CANR 25

Zabolotskii, Nikolai Alekseevich
1903-1958 . . . . **TCLC 52**
See also CA 116

Zamiatin, Yevgenii
See Zamyatin, Evgeny Ivanovich

Zamora, Bernice (B. Ortiz)
1938- . . . . **CLC 89; HLC**
See also DLB 82; HW

Zamyatin, Evgeny Ivanovich
1884-1937 . . . . **TCLC 8, 37**
See also CA 105

Zangwill, Israel 1864-1926 . . . . **TCLC 16**
See also CA 109; DLB 10, 135

Zappa, Francis Vincent, Jr. 1940-1993
See Zappa, Frank
See also CA 108; 143

Zappa, Frank . . . . **CLC 17**
See also Zappa, Francis Vincent, Jr.

Zaturenska, Marya 1902-1982 . . . . **CLC 6, 11**
See also CA 13-16R; 105; CANR 22

Zelazny, Roger (Joseph)
1937-1995 . . . . **CLC 21**
See also AAYA 7; CA 21-24R; 148;
CANR 26; DLB 8; MTCW; SATA 57;
SATA-Brief 39

Zhdanov, Andrei A(lexandrovich)
1896-1948 . . . . **TCLC 18**
See also CA 117

Zhukovsky, Vasily 1783-1852 . . . . **NCLC 35**

Ziegenhagen, Eric . . . . **CLC 55**

Zimmer, Jill Schary
See Robinson, Jill

Zimmerman, Robert
See Dylan, Bob

Zindel, Paul 1936- . . . **CLC 6, 26; DA; DC 5**
See also AAYA 2; CA 73-76; CANR 31;
CLR 3; DLB 7, 52; JRDA; MAICYA;
MTCW; SATA 16, 58

Zinov'Ev, A. A.
See Zinoviev, Alexander (Aleksandrovich)

Zinoviev, Alexander (Aleksandrovich)
1922- . . . . **CLC 19**
See also CA 116; 133; CAAS 10

Zoilus
See Lovecraft, H(oward) P(hillips)

Zola, Emile (Edouard Charles Antoine)
1840-1902 . . . . . . **TCLC 1, 6, 21, 41; DA;
WLC**
See also CA 104; 138; DLB 123

Zoline, Pamela 1941- . . . . **CLC 62**

Zorrilla y Moral, Jose 1817-1893 . . **NCLC 6**

Zoshchenko, Mikhail (Mikhailovich)
1895-1958 . . . . **TCLC 15; SSC 15**
See also CA 115

Zuckmayer, Carl 1896-1977 . . . . **CLC 18**
See also CA 69-72; DLB 56, 124

Zuk, Georges
See Skelton, Robin

Zukofsky, Louis
1904-1978 . . . . **CLC 1, 2, 4, 7, 11, 18;
PC 11**
See also CA 9-12R; 77-80; CANR 39;
DLB 5; MTCW

Zweig, Paul 1935-1984 . . . . **CLC 34, 42**
See also CA 85-88; 113

Zweig, Stefan 1881-1942 . . . . **TCLC 17**
See also CA 112; DLB 81, 118

Literary Criticism Series
Cumulative Topic Index

This index lists all topic entries in Gale's *Classical and Medieval Literature Criticism, Contemporary Literary Criticism, Literature Criticism from 1400 to 1800, Nineteenth-Century Literature Criticism,* and *Twentieth-Century Literary Criticism.*

Age of Johnson LC 15: 1-87
Johnson's London, 3-15
aesthetics of neoclassicism, 15-36
"age of prose and reason," 36-45
clubmen and bluestockings, 45-56
printing technology, 56-62
periodicals: "a map of busy life," 62-74
transition, 74-86

AIDS in Literature CLC 81: 365-416

American Abolitionism NCLC 44: 1-73
overviews, 2-26
abolitionist ideals, 26-46
the literature of abolitionism, 46-72

American Black Humor Fiction TCLC 54: 1-85
characteristics of black humor, 2-13
origins and development, 13-38
black humor distinguished from related literary trends, 38-60
black humor and society, 60-75
black humor reconsidered, 75-83

American Civil War in Literature NCLC 32: 1-109
overviews, 2-20
regional perspectives, 20-54
fiction popular during the war, 54-79
the historical novel, 79-108

American Frontier in Literature NCLC 28: 1-103
definitions, 2-12
development, 12-17
nonfiction writing about the frontier, 17-30
frontier fiction, 30-45
frontier protagonists, 45-66
portrayals of Native Americans, 66-86
feminist readings, 86-98
twentieth-century reaction against frontier literature, 98-100

American Popular Song, Golden Age of TCLC 42: 1-49
background and major figures, 2-34

the lyrics of popular songs, 34-47

American Proletarian Literature TCLC 54: 86-175
overviews, 87-95
American proletarian literature and the American Communist Party, 95-111
ideology and literary merit, 111-17
novels, 117-36
Gastonia, 136-48
drama, 148-54
journalism, 154-59
proletarian literature in the United States, 159-74

American Romanticism NCLC 44: 74-138
overviews, 74-84
sociopolitical influences, 84-104
Romanticism and the American frontier, 104-15
thematic concerns, 115-37

American Western Literature TCLC 46: 1-100
definition and development of American Western literature, 2-7
characteristics of the Western novel, 8-23
Westerns as history and fiction, 23-34
critical reception of American Western literature, 34-41
the Western hero, 41-73
women in Western fiction, 73-91
later Western fiction, 91-9

Art and Literature TCLC 54: 176-248
overviews, 176-193
definitions, 193-219
influence of visual arts on literature, 219-31
spatial form in literature, 231-47

Arthurian Literature CMLC 10: 1-127
historical context and literary beginnings, 2-27
development of the legend through Malory, 27-64
development of the legend from Malory

to the Victorian Age, 65-81
themes and motifs, 81-95
principal characters, 95-125

Arthurian Revival NCLC 36: 1-77
overviews, 2-12
Tennyson and his influence, 12-43
other leading figures, 43-73
the Arthurian legend in the visual arts, 73-6

Australian Literature TCLC 50: 1-94
origins and development, 2-21
characteristics of Australian literature, 21-33
historical and critical perspectives, 33-41
poetry, 41-58
fiction, 58-76
drama, 76-82
Aboriginal literature, 82-91

Beat Generation, Literature of the TCLC 42: 50-102
overviews, 51-9
the Beat generation as a social phenomenon, 59-62
development, 62-5
Beat literature, 66-96
influence, 97-100

***Bildungsroman* in Nineteenth-Century Literature** NCLC 20: 92-168
surveys, 93-113
in Germany, 113-40
in England, 140-56
female *Bildungsroman,* 156-67

Bloomsbury Group TCLC 34: 1-73
history and major figures, 2-13
definitions, 13-17
influences, 17-27
thought, 27-40
prose, 40-52
and literary criticism, 52-4
political ideals, 54-61
response to, 61-71

Bly, Robert, *Iron John: A Book about Men and Men's Work* CLC 70: 414-62

The Book of J CLC 65: 289-311

Businessman in American Literature
TCLC 26: 1-48
portrayal of the businessman, 1-32
themes and techniques in business
fiction, 32-47

Celtic Twilight
See **Irish Literary Renaissance**

Civic Critics, Russian NCLC 20: 402-46
principal figures and background, 402-09
and Russian Nihilism, 410-16
aesthetic and critical views, 416-45

**Colonial America: The Intellectual
Background** LC 25: 1-98
overviews, 2-17
philosophy and politics, 17-31
early religious influences in Colonial
America, 31-60
consequences of the Revolution, 60-78
religious influences in post-revolution-
ary America, 78-87
colonial literary genres, 87-97

**Columbus, Christopher, Books on the
Quincentennial of His Arrival in the
New World** CLC 70: 329-60

Connecticut Wits NCLC 48: 1-95
general overviews, 2-40
major works, 40-76
intellectual context, 76-95

Crime in Literature TCLC 54: 249-307
evolution of the criminal figure in
literature, 250-61
crime and society, 261-77
literary perspectives on crime and
punishment, 277-88
writings by criminals, 288-306

**Czechoslovakian Literature of the
Twentieth Century** TCLC 42: 103-96
through World War II, 104-35
de-Stalinization, the Prague Spring, and
contemporary literature, 135-72
Slovak literature, 172-85
Czech science fiction, 185-93

Dadaism TCLC 46: 101-71
background and major figures, 102-16
definitions, 116-26
manifestos and commentary by
Dadaists, 126-40
theater and film, 140-58

nature and characteristics of Dadaist
writing, 158-70

Darwinism and Literature NCLC 32:
110-206
background, 110-31
direct responses to Darwin, 131-71
collateral effects of Darwinism, 171-205

de Man, Paul, Wartime Journalism of
CLC 55: 382-424

Detective Fiction, Nineteenth-Century
NCLC 36: 78-148
origins of the genre, 79-100
history of nineteenth-century detective
fiction, 101-33
significance of nineteenth-century
detective fiction, 133-46

Detective Fiction, Twentieth-Century
TCLC 38: 1-96
genesis and history of the detective
story, 3-22
defining detective fiction, 22-32
evolution and varieties, 32-77
the appeal of detective fiction, 77-90

**The Double in Nineteenth-Century
Literature** NCLC 40: 1-95
genesis and development of the theme,
2-15
the double and Romanticism, 16-27
sociological views, 27-52
psychological interpretations, 52-87
philosophical considerations, 87-95

Dramatic Realism NCLC 44: 139-202
overviews, 140-50
origins and definitions, 150-66
impact and influence, 166-93
realist drama and tragedy, 193-201

**Electronic "Books": Hypertext and
Hyperfiction** CLC 86: 367-404
books vs. CD-ROMS, 367-76
hypertext and hyperfiction, 376-95
implications for publishing, libraries,
and the public, 395-403

Eliot, T. S., Centenary of Birth CLC 55:
345-75

Elizabethan Drama LC 22: 140-240
origins and influences, 142-67
characteristics and conventions, 167-83
theatrical production, 184-200
histories, 200-12
comedy, 213-20
tragedy, 220-30

The Encyclopedists LC 26: 172-253
overviews, 173-210
intellectual background, 210-32
views on esthetics, 232-41
views on women, 241-52

English Caroline Literature LC 13: 221-
307
background, 222-41
evolution and varieties, 241-62
the Cavalier mode, 262-75
court and society, 275-91
politics and religion, 291-306

English Decadent Literature of the 1890s
NCLC 28: 104-200
fin de siècle: the Decadent period, 105-
19
definitions, 120-37
major figures: "the tragic generation,"
137-50
French literature and English literary
Decadence, 150-57
themes, 157-61
poetry, 161-82
periodicals, 182-96

English Essay, Rise of the LC 18: 238-308
definitions and origins, 236-54
influence on the essay, 254-69
historical background, 269-78
the essay in the seventeenth century,
279-93
the essay in the eighteenth century, 293-
307

English Romantic Poetry NCLC 28: 201-
327
overviews and reputation, 202-37
major subjects and themes, 237-67
forms of Romantic poetry, 267-78
politics, society, and Romantic poetry,
278-99
philosophy, religion, and Romantic
poetry, 299-324

Espionage Literature TCLC 50: 95-159
overviews, 96-113
espionage fiction/formula fiction, 113-26
spies in fact and fiction, 126-38
the female spy, 138-44
social and psychological perspectives,
144-58

European Romanticism NCLC 36: 149-
284
definitions, 149-77
origins of the movement, 177-82
Romantic theory, 182-200
themes and techniques, 200-23
Romanticism in Germany, 223-39

Romanticism in France, 240-61
Romanticism in Italy, 261-64
Romanticism in Spain, 264-68
impact and legacy, 268-82

Existentialism and Literature TCLC 42:
197-268
overviews and definitions, 198-209
history and influences, 209-19
Existentialism critiqued and defended,
220-35
philosophical and religious perspectives,
235-41
Existentialist fiction and drama, 241-67

Familiar Essay NCLC 48: 96-211
definitions and origins, 97-130
overview of the genre, 130-45
elements of form and style, 143-59
elements of content, 159-73
the Cockneys: Hazlitt, Lamb, and Hunt,
173-91
status of the genre, 191-210

**Feminism in the 1990s: Commentary on
Works by Naomi Wolf, Susan Faludi, and
Camille Paglia** CLC 76: 377-415

Feminist Criticism in 1990 CLC 65: 312-
60

Fifteenth-Century English Literature
LC 17: 248-334
background, 249-72
poetry, 272-315
drama, 315-23
prose, 323-33

Film and Literature TCLC 38: 97-226
overviews, 97-119
film and theater, 119-34
film and the novel, 134-45
the art of the screenplay, 145-66
genre literature/genre film, 167-79
the writer and the film industry, 179-90
authors on film adaptations of their
works, 190-200
fiction into film: comparative essays,
200-23

French Drama in the Age of Louis XIV
LC 28: 94-185
overview, 95-127
tragedy, 127-46
comedy, 146-66
tragicomedy, 166-84

French Enlightenment LC 14: 81-145
the question of definition, 82-9
Le siècle des lumières, 89-94
women and the salons, 94-105

censorship, 105-15
the philosophy of reason, 115-31
influence and legacy, 131-44

**French Revolution and English Litera-
ture** NCLC 40: 96-195
history and theory, 96-123
romantic poetry, 123-50
the novel, 150-81
drama, 181-92
children's literature, 192-95

Futurism, Italian TCLC 42: 269-354
principles and formative influences, 271-
79
manifestos, 279-88
literature, 288-303
theater, 303-19
art, 320-30
music, 330-36
architecture, 336-39
and politics, 339-46
reputation and significance, 346-51

Gaelic Revival
See **Irish Literary Renaissance**

**Gates, Henry Louis, Jr., and African-
American Literary Criticism** CLC 65:
361-405

Gay and Lesbian Literature CLC 76: 416-
39

German Exile Literature TCLC 30: 1-58
the writer and the Nazi state, 1-10
definition of, 10-14
life in exile, 14-32
surveys, 32-50
Austrian literature in exile, 50-2
German publishing in the United States,
52-7

German Expressionism TCLC 34: 74-160
history and major figures, 76-85
aesthetic theories, 85-109
drama, 109-26
poetry, 126-38
film, 138-42
painting, 142-47
music, 147-53
and politics, 153-58

**Glasnost and Contemporary Soviet
Literature** CLC 59: 355-97

Gothic Novel NCLC 28: 328-402
development and major works, 328-34
definitions, 334-50
themes and techniques, 350-78
in America, 378-85

in Scotland, 385-91
influence and legacy, 391-400

Graphic Narratives CLC 86: 405-32
history and overviews, 406-21
the "Classics Illustrated" series, 421-22
reviews of recent works, 422-32

Harlem Renaissance TCLC 26: 49-125
principal issues and figures, 50-67
the literature and its audience, 67-74
theme and technique in poetry, fiction,
and drama, 74-115
and American society, 115-21
achievement and influence, 121-22

Havel, Václav, Playwright and President
CLC 65: 406-63

Historical Fiction, Nineteenth-Century
NCLC 48: 212-307
definitions and characteristics, 213-36
Victorian historical fiction, 236-65
American historical fiction, 265-88
realism in historical fiction, 288-306

Holocaust Denial Literature TCLC 58: 1-
110
overviews, 1-30
Robert Faurisson and Noam Chomsky,
30-52
Holocaust denial literature in America,
52-71
library access to Holocaust denial
literature, 72-75
the authenticity of Anne Frank's diary,
76-90
David Irving and the "normalization" of
Hitler, 90-109

Holocaust, Literature of the TCLC 42:
355-450
historical overview, 357-61
critical overview, 361-70
diaries and memoirs, 370-95
novels and short stories, 395-425
poetry, 425-41
drama, 441-48

**Hungarian Literature of the Twentieth
Century** TCLC 26: 126-88
surveys of, 126-47
Nyugat and early twentieth-century
literature, 147-56
mid-century literature, 156-68
and politics, 168-78
since the 1956 revolt, 178-87

Indian Literature in English TCLC 54:
308-406
overview, 309-13

Topic Index

origins and major figures, 313-25
the Indo-English novel, 325-55
Indo-English poetry, 355-67
Indo-English drama, 367-72
critical perspectives on Indo-English
　literature, 372-80
modern Indo-English literature, 380-89
Indo-English authors on their work,
　389-404

Irish Literary Renaissance TCLC 46:
172-287
overview, 173-83
development and major figures, 184-202
influence of Irish folklore and mythol-
　ogy, 202-22
Irish poetry, 222-34
Irish drama and the Abbey Theatre,
　234-56
Irish fiction, 256-86

Irish Nationalism and Literature NCLC
44: 203-273
the Celtic element in literature, 203-19
anti-Irish sentiment and the Celtic
　response, 219-34
literary ideals in Ireland, 234-45
literary expressions, 245-73

Italian Futurism
See **Futurism, Italian**

Italian Humanism LC 12: 205-77
origins and early development, 206-18
revival of classical letters, 218-23
humanism and other philosophies, 224-
　39
humanisms and humanists, 239-46
the plastic arts, 246-57
achievement and significance, 258-76

Larkin, Philip, Controversy CLC 81: 417-
64

**Latin American Literature, Twentieth-
Century** TCLC 58: 111-198
historical and critical perspectives, 112-
　36
the novel, 136-45
the short story, 145-49
drama, 149-60
poetry, 160-67
the writer and society, 167-86
Native Americans in Latin American
　literature, 186-97

**Madness in Twentieth-Century Litera-
ture** TCLC 50: 160-225
overviews, 161-71
madness and the creative process, 171-
　86

suicide, 186-91
madness in American literature, 191-207
madness in German literature, 207-13
madness and feminist artists, 213-24

Metaphysical Poets LC 24: 356-439
early definitions, 358-67
surveys and overviews, 367-92
cultural and social influences, 392-406
stylistic and thematic variations, 407-38

Modern Essay, The TCLC 58: 199-273
overview, 200-07
the essay in the early twentieth century,
　207-19
characteristics of the modern essay, 219-
　32
modern essayists, 232-45
the essay as a literary genre, 245-73

**Muckraking Movement in American
Journalism** TCLC 34: 161-242
development, principles, and major
　figures, 162-70
publications, 170-79
social and political ideas, 179-86
targets, 186-208
fiction, 208-19
decline, 219-29
impact and accomplishments, 229-40

**Multiculturalism in Literature and
Education** CLC 70: 361-413

Native American Literature CLC 76: 440-
76

Natural School, Russian NCLC 24: 205-
40
history and characteristics, 205-25
contemporary criticism, 225-40

Naturalism NCLC 36: 285-382
definitions and theories, 286-305
critical debates on Naturalism, 305-16
Naturalism in theater, 316-32
European Naturalism, 332-61
American Naturalism, 361-72
the legacy of Naturalism, 372-81

Negritude TCLC 50: 226-361
origins and evolution, 227-56
definitions, 256-91
Negritude in literature, 291-343
Negritude reconsidered, 343-58

New Criticism TCLC 34: 243-318
development and ideas, 244-70
debate and defense, 270-99
influence and legacy, 299-315

**New York Intellectuals and *Partisan
Review*** TCLC 30: 117-98
development and major figures, 118-28
influence of Judaism, 128-39
Partisan Review, 139-57
literary philosophy and practice, 157-75
political philosophy, 175-87
achievement and significance, 187-97

New Yorker, The TCLC 58: 274-357
overviews, 274-95
major figures, 295-304
New Yorker style, 304-33
fiction, journalism, and humor at *The
　New Yorker,* 333-48
the new *New Yorker,* 348-56

Newgate Novel NCLC 24: 166-204
development of Newgate literature, 166-
　73
Newgate Calendar, 173-77
Newgate fiction, 177-95
Newgate drama, 195-204

**Nigerian Literature of the Twentieth
Century** TCLC 30: 199-265
surveys of, 199-227
English language and African life, 227-45
politics and the Nigerian writer, 245-54
Nigerian writers and society, 255-62

Northern Humanism LC 16: 281-356
background, 282-305
precursor of the Reformation, 305-14
the Brethren of the Common Life, the
　Devotio Moderna, and education,
　314-40
the impact of printing, 340-56

**Nuclear Literature: Writings and
Criticism in the Nuclear Age** TCLC 46:
288-390
overviews, 290-301
fiction, 301-35
poetry, 335-38
nuclear war in Russo-Japanese literature,
　338-55
nuclear war and women writers, 355-67
the nuclear referent and literary
　criticism, 367-88

Occultism in Modern Literature TCLC
50: 362-406
influence of occultism on literature, 363-
　72
occultism, literature, and society, 372-87
fiction, 387-96
drama, 396-405

**Opium and the Nineteenth-Century
Literary Imagination** NCLC 20: 250-301

original sources, 250-62
historical background, 262-71
and literary society, 271-79
and literary creativity, 279-300

Periodicals, Nineteenth-Century British
NCLC 24: 100-65
overviews, 100-30
in the Romantic Age, 130-41
in the Victorian era, 142-54
and the reviewer, 154-64

Plath, Sylvia, and the Nature of Biography CLC 86: 433-62
the nature of biography, 433-52
reviews of *The Silent Woman,* 452-61

Pre-Raphaelite Movement NCLC 20:
302-401
overview, 302-04
genesis, 304-12
Germ and *Oxford and Cambridge
Magazine,* 312-20
Robert Buchanan and the "Fleshly
School of Poetry," 320-31
satires and parodies, 331-34
surveys, 334-51
aesthetics, 351-75
sister arts of poetry and painting, 375-
94
influence, 394-99

Psychoanalysis and Literature TCLC 38:
227-338
overviews, 227-46
Freud on literature, 246-51
psychoanalytic views of the literary
process, 251-61
psychoanalytic theories of response to
literature, 261-88
psychoanalysis and literary criticism,
288-312
psychoanalysis as literature/literature
as psychoanalysis, 313-34

Rap Music CLC 76: 477-50

Renaissance Natural Philosophy LC 27:
201-87
cosmology, 201-28
astrology, 228-54
magic, 254-86

Restoration Drama LC 21: 184-275
general overviews, 185-230
Jeremy Collier stage controversy, 230-
35
other critical interpretations, 240-75

Revising the Literary Canon CLC 81:
465-509

Robin Hood, Legend of LC 19: 205-58
origins and development of the Robin
Hood legend, 206-20
representations of Robin Hood, 220-44
Robin Hood as hero, 244-56

Rushdie, Salman, *Satanic Verses* Controversy CLC 55: 214-63; 59: 404-56

Russian Nihilism NCLC 28: 403-47
definitions and overviews, 404-17
women and Nihilism, 417-27
literature as reform: the Civic Critics,
427-33
Nihilism and the Russian novel:
Turgenev and Dostoevsky, 433-47

Russian Thaw TCLC 26: 189-247
literary history of the period, 190-206
theoretical debate of socialist realism,
206-11
Novy Mir, 211-17
Literary Moscow, 217-24
Pasternak, *Zhivago,* and the Nobel
Prize, 224-27
poetry of liberation, 228-31
Brodsky trial and the end of the Thaw,
231-36
achievement and influence, 236-46

**Salinger, J. D., Controversy Surrounding
*In Search of J. D. Salinger*** CLC 55: 325-
44

Science Fiction, Nineteenth-Century
NCLC 24: 241-306
background, 242-50
definitions of the genre, 251-56
representative works and writers, 256-
75
themes and conventions, 276-305

Scottish Chaucerians LC 20: 363-412

Scottish Poetry, 18th-Century LC29: 95-
167
overviews, 96-144
the Scottish Augustans, 114-28
the Scots Vernacular Revival, 132-63
Scottish poetry after Burns, 163-66

Sherlock Holmes Centenary TCLC 26:
248-310
Doyle's life and the composition of the
Holmes stories, 248-59
life and character of Holmes, 259-78
method, 278-79
Holmes and the Victorian world, 279-92
Sherlockian scholarship, 292-301

Doyle and the development of the
detective story, 301-07
Holmes's continuing popularity, 307-09

Slave Narratives, American NCLC 20: 1-
91
background, 2-9
overviews, 9-24
contemporary responses, 24-7
language, theme, and technique, 27-70
historical authenticity, 70-5
antecedents, 75-83
role in development of Black American
literature, 83-8

Spanish Civil War Literature TCLC 26:
311-85
topics in, 312-33
British and American literature, 333-59
French literature, 359-62
Spanish literature, 362-73
German literature, 373-75
political idealism and war literature, 375-
83

Spanish Golden Age Literature LC 23:
262-332
overviews, 263-81
verse drama, 281-304
prose fiction, 304-19
lyric poetry, 319-31

Spasmodic School of Poetry NCLC 24:
307-52
history and major figures, 307-21
the Spasmodics on poetry, 321-27
Firmilian and critical disfavor, 327-39
theme and technique, 339-47
influence, 347-51

**Steinbeck, John, Fiftieth Anniversary of
*The Grapes of Wrath*** CLC 59: 311-54

Sturm und Drang NCLC 40: 196-276
definitions, 197-238
poetry and poetics, 238-58
drama, 258-75

**Supernatural Fiction in the Nineteenth
Century** NCLC 32: 207-87
major figures and influences, 208-35
the Victorian ghost story, 236-54
the influence of science and occultism,
254-66
supernatural fiction and society, 266-86

Supernatural Fiction, Modern TCLC 30:
59-116
evolution and varieties, 60-74
"decline" of the ghost story, 74-86

as a literary genre, 86-92
technique, 92-101
nature and appeal, 101-15

Surrealism TCLC 30: 334-406
history and formative influences, 335-43
manifestos, 343-54
philosophic, aesthetic, and political
principles, 354-75
poetry, 375-81
novel, 381-86
drama, 386-92
film, 392-98
painting and sculpture, 398-403
achievement, 403-05

Symbolism, Russian TCLC 30: 266-333
doctrines and major figures, 267- 92
theories, 293-98
and French Symbolism, 298-310
themes in poetry, 310-14
theater, 314-20
and the fine arts, 320-32

Symbolist Movement, French NCLC 20: 169-249
background and characteristics, 170-86
principles, 186-91
attacked and defended, 191-97
influences and predecessors, 197-211
and Decadence, 211-16
theater, 216-26
prose, 226-33
decline and influence, 233-47

Theater of the Absurd TCLC 38: 339-415
"The Theater of the Absurd," 340-47
major plays and playwrights, 347-58
and the concept of the absurd, 358-86
theatrical techniques, 386-94
predecessors of, 394-402
influence of, 402-13

Tin Pan Alley
See **American Popular Song, Golden Age of**

Transcendentalism, American NCLC 24: 1-99
overviews, 3-23

contemporary documents, 23-41
theological aspects of, 42-52
and social issues, 52-74
literature of, 74-96

Travel Writing in the Nineteenth Century NCLC 44: 274-392
the European grand tour, 275-303
the Orient, 303-47
North America, 347-91

Travel Writing in the Twentieth Century TCLC 30: 407-56
conventions and traditions, 407-27
and fiction writing, 427-43
comparative essays on travel writers, 443-54

***Ulysses* and the Process of Textual Reconstruction** TCLC 26: 386-416
evaluations of the new *Ulysses,* 386-94
editorial principles and procedures, 394-401
theoretical issues, 401-16

Utopian Literature, Nineteenth-Century NCLC 24: 353-473
definitions, 354-74
overviews, 374-88
theory, 388-408
communities, 409-26
fiction, 426-53
women and fiction, 454-71

Vampire in Literature TCLC 46: 391-454
origins and evolution, 392-412
social and psychological perspectives, 413-44
vampire fiction and science fiction, 445-53

Victorian Autobiography NCLC 40: 277-363
development and major characteristics, 278-88
themes and techniques, 289-313
the autobiographical tendency in Victorian prose and poetry, 313-47
Victorian women's autobiographies, 347-62

Victorian Novel NCLC 32: 288-454
development and major characteristics, 290-310
themes and techniques, 310-58
social criticism in the Victorian novel, 359-97
urban and rural life in the Victorian novel, 397-406
women in the Victorian novel, 406-25
Mudie's Circulating Library, 425-34
the late-Victorian novel, 434-51

Women's Diaries, Nineteenth-Century NCLC 48: 308-54
overview, 308-54
diary as history, 314-25
sociology of diaries, 325-34
diaries as psychological scholarship, 334-43
diary as autobiography, 343-48
diary as literature, 348-53

Women Writers, Seventeenth-Century LC 30: 2-58
overview, 2-15
women and education, 15-19
women and autobiography, 19-31
women's diaries, 31-39
early feminists, 39-58

World War I Literature TCLC 34: 392-486
overview, 393-403
English, 403-27
German, 427-50
American, 450-66
French, 466-74
and modern history, 474-82

Yellow Journalism NCLC 36: 383-456
overviews, 384-96
major figures, 396-413

Young Playwrights Festival
1988–CLC 55: 376: 376-81
1989–CLC 59: 398-403
1990–CLC 65: 444-48

CMLC Cumulative Nationality Index

ARABIC
Alf Layla wa-Layla (The Arabian Nights) **2**
Averroes **7**
Avicenna **16**

BABYLONIAN
Epic of Gilgamesh **3**

CATALAN
Llull, Ramon **12**

CHINESE
Lao Tzu **7**
Li Po **2**
Su Shih **15**

ENGLISH
The Alliterative *Morte Arthure* **10**
Anglo-Saxon Chronicle **4**
Bacon, Roger **14**
Beowulf **1**
Caedmon **7**
The Dream of the Rood **14**
Layamon **10**
Sir Gawain and the Green Knight **2**

FINNISH
Kalevala **6**

FRENCH
Abelard, Peter **11**
La chanson de Roland (The Song of Roland) **1**
Chretien de Troyes **10**
Marie de France **8**
Ordo Representacionis Ade (Mystery of Adam) **4**
Le Roman de la Rose (The Romance of the Rose) **8**

GERMAN
Albert the Great **16**

Gottfried von Strassburg **10**
Hartmann von Aue **15**
Meister Eckhart **9**
Das Nibelungenlied **12**
Wolfram von Eschenbach **5**

GREEK
Aeschylus **11**
Aristophanes **4**
Demosthenes **13**
Hermogenes **6**
Hesiod **5**
Iliad (Homer) **1**
Longus **7**
Menander **9**
Odyssey (Homer) **16**
Pindar **12**
Plato **8**
Sappho **3**
Sophocles **2**

HEBREW
The Book of Job **14**
Josephus, Flavius **13**
Tehillim (The Book of Psalms) **4**

ICELANDIC
Hrafnkels saga Freysgoda (Hrafnkel's Saga) **2**
Njals saga **13**

INDIAN
Bhagavad Gita **12**
Kalidasa **9**
Mahabharata **5**

ITALIAN
Boccaccio, Giovanni **13**
Inferno (Dante) **3**

Polo, Marco **15**
Sordello **15**

JAPANESE
Lady Murasaki (*Genji monogatori* [*The Tale of Genji*]) **1**
Sei Shonagon **6**

PERSIAN
Khayyam, Omar **11**

PROVENCAL
Betran de Born **5**

ROMAN
Aeneid (Vergil) **9**
Apuleius **1**
Augustine, St. **6**
Boethius **15**
Cicero, Marcus Tullius **3**
Juvenal **8**
Livy **11**
Ovid **7**
Seneca, Lucius Annaeus **6**
Terence **14**

RUSSIAN
Slovo o polku Igoreve (The Igor Tale) **1**

SPANISH
Poema de mio Cid (Poem of the Cid) **4**
Razón de amor **16**

TURKISH
Kitab-i-dedem Qorkut (Book of Dede Korkut) **8**

WELSH
Mabinogion **9**

CMLC Cumulative Title Index

Ab urbe condita libri (*The History of Rome from Its Foundation*) (Livy) **11**:310-86
"Abdallah-the-Hunter" **2**:63
"Abdallah-the-Mariner" **2**:42, 63
Abhijñāna-śakuntala (*Śākuntala*) (Kalidasa) **9**:82, 86-7, 89-97, 100-02, 108-13, 127, 130-34, 136-39
"Aboulhusn ed Duraj and the Leper" **2**:40
About Gods (Cicero)
See *De natura deorum*
"Abu Kasem's Slippers" **2**:32-5
Academics (*The Academics; or, A History and Defense of the Beliefs of the New Academy*) (Cicero) **3**:193,202
The Academics; or, A History and Defense of the Beliefs of the New Academy (Cicero)
See *Academics*
Acharnae (*The Acharnians; Akharnes*) (Aristophanes) **4**:44, 62, 69, 76, 87, 94, 97-99, 105-06, 108-10, 113, 123-28, 131-33, 135, 137, 142-43, 149, 151-52, 157, 159-60, 162-63, 165-66
The Acharnians (Aristophanes)
See *Acharnae*
Ad Atticum (*Letters to Atticus*) (Cicero) **3**:186-87, 200
Ad Brutum (Cicero) **3**:200
Ad familiares (*Letters to Friends*) (Cicero) **3**:200
Ad helviam matrem de consolatione (Seneca) **6**:382, 410
Ad Leptinem (Demosthenes)
See *Against Leptines*
Ad Marciam (Seneca) **6**:382
Ad P. Lentulum (*Epistle ad P. Lentulum*) (Cicero) **3**:186
Ad Polybium de consolatione (Seneca) **6**:382
Ad Q. fratrem (Cicero) **3**:200
Ad Simplicium (Augustine) **6**:9

Adam
See *Ordo Representacionis Ade*
Adelphi (*The Brothers*) (Terence) **14**:301, 303-04, 306-07, 309, 313-14, 316, 320-21, 332-37, 339-40, 347-49, 352, 357-60, 362-66, 368, 370-71, 374-77, 381, 383-85, 387, 394, 397
Adelphoi (*Brothers*) (Menander) **9**:270
The Aeneid (Vergil) **9**:294-447
"After Being Separated for a Long Time" (Li Po) **2**:132
Against Androtion (*Androtion*) (Demosthenes) **13**:148-9, 156, 163-4, 169, 171, 184
Against Aphobus (Demosthenes) **13**:163, 184
Against Apion (Josephus)
See *Contra Apionem*
Against Aristocrates (*Prosecution of Aristocrates*) (Demosthenes) **13**:148, 156-8, 164, 169, 189
Against Aristogiton (Demosthenes) **13**:149
Against Callicles (Demosthenes) **13**:168
Against Catilina (Cicero)
See *In Catilinam*
Against Conon (Demosthenes) **13**:144
Against Eratosthenes (Demosthenes) **13**:179
Against Leptines (*Ad Leptinem; Leptinea; Leptines*) (Demosthenes) **13**:137, 148-51, 156, 163-4, 169-71, 197
Against Medias (Demosthenes)
See *Against Midias*
Against Midias (*Against Medias; Midiana*) (Demosthenes) **13**:140, 149, 165, 169
Against Neaera (Demosthenes) **13**:169
Against Onetor (Demosthenes) **13**:163, 168, 184
Against Superstitions (Seneca) **6**:330, 342
Against the Academicians (Augustine)
See *Contra academicos*
Against the Gentiles (Josephus)
See *Contra Apionem*
Against the Greeks (Josephus)

See *Contra Apionem*
Against Timocrates (Demosthenes) **13**:146-8, 156, 163-4, 169
Agamemnon (Aeschylus) **11**:85-6, 101-02, 104-05, 107-08, 110-11, 113, 116-20, 126, 128, 132-34, 136, 138-42, 148, 150-55, 158, 162-63, 165, 167, 171, 175-76, 179-82, 184-85, 187, 190-91, 194-97, 200-07, 217, 220-22
Agamemnon (Seneca) **6**:339, 343, 363, 366-69, 377-81, 389, 407, 409, 414, 417, 431-32, 440, 442, 447
Ahwāl al-Nafs (Avicenna) **16**:166
"Ailas e que'm miey huelh" (Sordello) **15**:367
Aitnaiai (Aeschylus) **11**:217
Akharnes (Aristophanes)
See *Acharnae*
"Alâ Ed-Dîn Abu Esh-Shamât" **2**:43
De Alchimia (Albert the Great)
See *Libellus de Alchimia*
Alcibiades (Plato)
See *Alcibiades I*
Alcibiades I (*Alcibiades; Alcibiades Major*) (Plato) **8**:218, 305-06, 311, 356
Alcibiades II (*Second Alcibiades*) (Plato) **8**:250, 305, 311
Alcibiades Major (Plato)
See *Alcibiades I*
Alf Layla wa-Layla (*The Arabian Nights; The Arabian Nights' Entertainments; The Book of the Thousand Nights and One Night; Hazar Afsana; The Thousand and One Nights*) **2**:1-73
"Ali and the Kurd Sharper" **2**:40
"Ali Baba and the Forty Thieves" **2**:1-2, 23, 45, 49
"Alî Shâr" **2**:43
"Ali Sher and Zumurrud" **2**:114
"Ali the Son of Bakkar and Shems-en-Nahar" **2**:14

al-Ishārāt wa al-Tanbīhāt (Avicenna) 169, 171

Alku Kalevala
See *Kalevala*

"Alladin and the Wonderful Lamp" 2:1-2, 8, 21, 23-24, 72

Allegoria mitologica (Boccaccio) 13:63-4

"Alliterative*Morte Arthure*"
See *Morte Arthure "Alliterative"*

al-Taclīqāt (Avicenna) 16:167

Ameto (*Ninfale d'Ameto*) (Boccaccio) 13:9, 18, 23, 27-8, 30, 32-3, 44-5, 48, 61

De amicitia (*Laelius; Laelius: On Friendship; On Friendship*) (Cicero) 3:193, 195, 202

Amores (*Erotic Adventures; Love-Poems*) (Ovid) 7:292-93, 295-97, 299, 305, 323, 326, 329, 336, 343, 346-49, 353, 355-56, 376-79, 388, 390, 393, 396, 398, 413, 417, 419-21, 423, 426-27, 436, 441, 444

Amorosa visione (Boccaccio) 13:18, 27-8, 32-3, 68, 72, 87

Analysis of the Analects (Shih) 15:407

Ancient History of the Jews (Josephus)
See *Antiquitates Judaicae*

Andria (*The Girl from Andros; The Lady of Andros; The Maid of Andros; The Woman from Andros*) (Terence) 14:302-08, 311-13, 315-17, 331, 333-35, 337-41, 344-45, 347-49, 352, 355-356, 358, 363-65, 369-70, 383-85, 389-90, 392-93

Androtion (Demosthenes)
See *Against Androtion*

Anger (Menander)
See *Orgē*

Anglo-Saxon Chronicle (*Chronicle*) 4:1-33

De anima (Albert the Great) 16:7, 61, 106, 109, 113, 115

De anima (Avicenna) 16:176

De animalibus (*Animals; On Animals*) (Albert the Great) 16:18, 21, 35-7, 61, 64, 82-3, 103, 107, 110

Animals (Albert the Great)
See *De animalibus*

"Answering a Layman's Question" (Li Po) 2:140

Antigonē (Sophocles) 2:289, 296, 299-301, 303-04, 306-09, 311, 314-15, 318-20, 324-25, 327, 331, 334-35, 338-40, 342-43, 345, 349-55, 360, 366, 368, 377-78, 380-83, 393-97, 417-19, 423, 426-28

Antiquitates Judaicae (*Ancient History of the Jews; Antiquities of the Jews; Concerning the Antiquities of the Jews; Jewish Antiquities*) (Josephus) 13:199-207, 211-3, 215-8, 220, 224, 226-35, 239, 242, 247-51, 256-65, 268-71, 286, 291-2, 294-7, 299-300, 302, 305, 308-9, 311-3, 315-20

Antiquities of the Jews (Josephus)
See *Antiquitates Judaicae*

"Aphrodite Ode" (Sappho)
See "Ode to Aphrodite"

Apion Answered (Josephus)
See *Contra Apionem*

Apionem (Josephus)
See *Contra Apionem*

Apocolocyntosis Divi Claudii (Seneca) 6:244, 374, 382-84

Apologia (*Apology; Defense*) (Plato) 8:250, 260, 277, 306, 357

Apologia sive oratoria de magia (*Apology; Pro se de magia liber*) (Apuleius) 1:7-8, 10, 12-13, 20, 23, 26, 33-4

Apology (Apuleius)
See *Apologia sive oratoria de magia*

Apology (Plato)
See *Apologia*

"The Apples of Paradise" 2:40

The Arabian Nights
See *Alf Layla wa-Layla*

The Arabian Nights' Entertainments
See *Alf Layla wa-Layla*

The Arbitrants (Menander)
See *Epitrepontes*

The Arbitration (Menander)
See *Epitrepontes*

Arbor scientiae (*Arbre de Sciencia; Tree of Science*) (Llull) 12:108-11, 115, 125

El arbre de filosofia d'amor (Llull)
See *The Tree of the Philosophy of Love*

Arbre de Sciencia (Llull)
See *Arbor scientiae*

Archias (*Pro Archia*) (Cicero) 3:198-99, 210

Argo (Aeschylus) 11:124

Arithmetic (Boethius)
See *De Arithmetica*

De Arithmetica (*Arithmetic*) (Boethius) 15:63, 69, 86

Der arme Heinrich (Hartmann von Aue) 15:148-54, 164, 191, 194, 205-07, 209, 220, 224, 241-44, 244-49

Ars Amandi (Ovid)
See *Ars amatoria*

Ars amatoria (*Ars Amandi; Art of Love*) (Ovid) 7:281-83, 292-98, 304-06, 309-10, 326, 329, 331, 342-47, 349, 353, 377-79, 386-87, 396-98, 401-02, 404, 412-13, 416-19, 421-23, 426, 430, 435-43, 446

Ars brevis (*Brief Art of Finding Truth*) (Llull) 12:106-07, 109, 133

Ars demonstrativa (*Compendium artis demonstrativae*) (Llull) 12:105-06, 110, 117, 134

Ars generalis (Llull) 12:104, 107-08

Ars generalis ultima (Llull) 12:114-16, 128

Ars inventiva (*Art of Finding Truth*) (Llull) 12:97, 109, 114-15, 120, 128, 132

Ars magna (Llull) 12:93-4, 104, 111, 132

Art of Contemplation (Llull) 12:125, 129

Art of Finding Truth (Llull)
See *Ars inventiva*

Art of Love (Ovid)
See *Ars amatoria*

Art of Rhetoric (Hermogenes) 6:186

"The Ash Tree" (Marie de France)
See "Le Fraisne"

Asinus aureus (*The Bookes of the Golden Asse; The Golden Ass; The Transformation of Lucius Apuleius Madeura*) (Apuleius) 1:6-9, 11-12, 14-18, 20, 22-23, 26, 32, 37-38, 46-50

Aspis (*The Shield*) (Menander) 9:253-58, 260-61, 263, 265, 267-70, 276-77

Assembly of Women (Aristophanes)
See *Ekklesiazousai*

"At Kuo Hsiang-cheng's When I was Drunk I Painted" (Shih) 15:402

Athamas (Aeschylus) 11:122

"Atretan deu ben chantar finamen" (Sordello) 15:362-63, 368

"Autumn Banks Song" (Li Po) 2:161, 164

The Babylonians (Aristophanes) 4:99, 126, 159, 163, 165

Bad Temper (Menander)
See *Orgē*

"Baghach Khan Son of Dirse Khan" 8:104

"Bamsi Beyrek of the Grey Horse"
See "Bamsi-Beyrek"

"Bamsi-Beyrek" ("Bamsi Beyrek of the Grey Horse"; "The Story of Bamsi Beyrek") 8:98, 103, 108-09

The Banqueters (Aristophanes) 4:37, 100, 163

"The Barber's Sixth Brother" 2:21

Batrakhoi (*The Frogs*) (Aristophanes) 4:44-5, 61-3, 69, 79, 86-90, 94, 98, 102, 105-6, 110-11, 120-21, 123-24, 127, 129-30, 133, 135, 137-38, 140, 145-46, 148, 150, 154, 156, 159, 161-63, 165

"The Battle of Brunanburh" ("Brunanburh") 4:4, 7, 9, 13-15, 17-19, 27-30

"The Battle of Maldon" ("Byrhtnoth's Death"; "Maldon"; "Song of Maldon") 4:2-9, 11-15, 25-7, 29-31

"Battle to the South of the City" (Li Po) 2:132

"Beginning of Autumn: A Poem to Send to Tzu-yu" (Shih) 15:414

"Bel m'es ab motz legiers a far" (Sordello) 15:361-62

Bellum Judaicum (*Concerning the Capture; Concerning the Jewish War; History of the Jewish War; Jewish War; War; Wars of the Jews*) (Josephus) 13:201-5, 209, 211-20, 222, 224, 229-30, 232-5, 239, 241-56, 263-73, 275-301, 303-8, 310-2, 314-5, 317-20

"Bending Bamboos of Yun-tang Valley" (Shih) 15:382, 386

Benedictus (Eckhart)
See *Book of Divine Consolation*

Beowulf 1:53-159

Bhagavad Gītā (*Divine Song; Gita; The Lord's Song; Song of the Lord*) 12:1-90

Bhagavadgītā (*Bhagavat Gita; Gītā; Lord's Song; Song of the Lord*) 5:187, 196-99, 216-19, 223, 226, 228, 235-38, 242-43, 246, 248, 250, 269, 272, 275

Bhagavat Gita
See *Bhagavadgītā*

Bhārata
See *Mahābhārata*

Bidāyat al-mujtahid (Averroes) 7:37, 41, 43

The Birds (Aristophanes)
See *Ornithes*

The Birth of Kumara (Kalidasa)
See *Kumārasambhava*

The Birth of the Prince (Kalidasa)
See *Kumārasambhava*

The Birth of the War-God (Kalidasa)
See *Kumārasambhava*

"Bisclavret" ("The Werewolf") (Marie de France) 8:114, 121-23, 131, 134, 147-48, 154, 158, 161-66, 171, 181

"Bitterness on the Stairs of Jade" (Li Po) 2:144, 160

Black Sea Letters (Ovid)
See *Epistulae ex Ponto*

"The Blacksmith Who Could Handle Fire" 2:40

Blanquerna (*Evast and Blanquerna*) (Llull) 12:93-5, 97, 106-07, 112, 122-24, 126, 129, 133

Bone-Collectors (Aeschylus) 11:124

De bono (Albert the Great) 16:44-7, 49-50, 53-4, 65-7, 69, 71-2, 74-7, 79-81

Book of Chaos (*Lay of the Nibelungen; Lay of the Nibelungs; Nibelung Lay; Der Nibelunge Nôt; Nibelungen Lay; Nibelungen Noth; Nibelungen Song; Nibelungen's Need*) (Llull) **12**:129

Book of Contemplation of God (Llull) **12**:95-8, 100-03, 109, 113-14, 120-23, 125-28, 132

Book of Dede Korkut
    See *Kitabi-i Dedem Qorkut*

Book of Divine Consolation (*Benedictus; Book of Godly Comfort*) (Eckhart) **9**:35-6, 40, 42, 56-7, 70-6

Book of Doctrine for Boys (Llull) **12**:97

Book of Godly Comfort (Eckhart)
    See *Book of Divine Consolation*

Book of Grandfather Qorkut
    See *Kitabi-i Dedem Qorkut*

The Book of Job (*Job*) **14**:117-214

The Book of Korkut
    See *Kitabi-i Dedem Qorkut*

The Book of Marco Polo (Polo)
    See *The Travels of Marco Polo the Venetian*

Book of Minerals (Albert the Great)
    See *Liber mineralium*

The Book of My Grandfather Korkut
    See *Kitabi-i Dedem Qorkut*

The Book of Psalms
    See *Tehillim*

The Book of Purgatory (Marie de France)
    See *L'Espurgatoire Saint Patrice*

Book of Tao (Lao Tzu)
    See *Tao te Ching*

Book of the Ascent and Descent of the Mind (Llull)
    See *Liber de ascensu et descensu intellectus*

Book of the Beasts (Llull) **12**:133-34

The Book of the Five Wise Men (Llull) **12**:125

Book of the Friend and the Beloved (Llull)
    See *Book of the Lover and the Beloved*

Book of the Gentile and the Three Wise Men (Llull) **12**:113, 118, 125-26

Book of the Lover and the Beloved (*Book of the Friend and the Beloved; Libre d'amic e Amat*) (Llull) **12**:93-4, 101, 122-23, 125-29, 131-33

Book of the Order of Chivalry (Llull)
    See *Libre del orde de cavalleria*

Book of the Principles and Grades of Medicine (Llull)
    See *Liber principiorum medicinae*

Book of the Tartar and the Christian (Llull) **12**:125

The Book of the Thousand Nights and One Night
    See *Alf Layla wa-Layla*

Book of Wonders (Llull) **12**:134

The Bookes of the Golden Asse (Apuleius)
    See *Asinus aureus*

Brennu-Njáls Saga
    See *Njáls saga*

Brief Art of Finding Truth (Llull)
    See *Ars brevis*

"Bring in the Wine" (Li Po) **2**:159

Brothers (Menander)
    See *Adelphoi*

The Brothers (Terence)
    See *Adelphi*

"Brunanburh"
    See "The Battle of Brunanburh"

Brut (Layamon) **10**:311-21, 326-29, 333, 335-38, 341, 343-50, 353, 355-60, 362, 364, 370-71

Brutus (Cicero)
    See *De claris oratoribus*

Brutus: On Famous Orators (Cicero)
    See *De claris oratoribus*

Brutus; or the illustrious Orators (Cicero)
    See *De claris oratoribus*

"Buying Rice" (Shih) **15**:416

"By the Passes" (Li Po) **2**:160

"Byrhtnoth's Death"
    See "The Battle of Maldon"

Cabiri (Aeschylus) **11**:124

Caccia di Diana (*Diana's Hunt*) (Boccaccio) **13**:62-3, 65, 67-74, 94-102

De caelo et mundo (Albert the Great) **16**:7, 18, 22, 61

"Camaralzaman and Badoura" **2**:36, 42-3, 50

Canon (Avicenna) **16**:171-80

Cant de Ramon (Llull) **12**:122

Cantar de mio Cid
    See *Poema de mio Cid*

De casibus virorum illustrium (Boccaccio) **13**:33, 38, 45-7, 52, 66

De catechizandis rudibus (Augustine) **6**:93

Catilinarians (Cicero)
    See *In Catilinam*

Cato maior (Cicero)
    See *De senectute*

Cato the Elder: On Old Age (Cicero)
    See *De senectute*

De causis elementorum (Albert the Great)
    See *De causis et proprietatibus elementorum et planetarum*

De causis et procreatione un'iversi (Albert the Great) **16**:7

De causis et proprietatibus elementorum et planetarum (*De causis elementorum; On the Causes and Properties of the Elements and of the Planets; Properties of the Elements*) (Albert the Great) **16**:7, 9, 56, 61, 83, 99

De Celestibus (Bacon)
    See *De Coelestibus*

Cent Noms de Déu (Llull)
    See *Hundred Names of God*

Cerberus (Pindar)
    See *Descent of Heracles into the Underworld*

"Le Chaitivel" ("The Four Sorrows"; "Quatre Dols"; "The Unfortunate One"; "The Wretched One") (Marie de France) **8**:120-21, 130-31, 133-34, 138, 143-44, 147, 151-52, 156, 162, 164-65, 169-70, 182, 186-89

La Chanson de Roland (*The Song of Roland*) **1**:160-267

Charioteer (Menander) **9**:214

"Charite and Tlepolemus" (Apuleius) **1**:40

Charmides (Plato) **8**:255, 263-65, 286, 306, 310, 314, 349, 356

Charrette (Chretien de Troyes)
    See *Lancelot*

Cheat Him Twice (Menander)
    See *Dis Exapaton*

Le Chevalier à l'épée (*The Knight with the Sword*) (Chretien de Troyes) **10**:232

Le Chevalier au Lion (Chretien de Troyes)
    See *Yvain*

Le Chevalier de la Charrette (Chretien de Troyes)
    See *Lancelot*

"Chevrefoil" ("Chievrefueil"; "Goat's Leaf"; "The Honeysuckle") (Marie de France) **8**:116, 120-21, 130-31, 133-34, 137, 139, 147-48, 150, 158-59, 161, 163-65, 170, 179, 182-84, 189

"Chievrefueil" (Marie de France)
    See "Chevrefoil"

Choephori (Aeschylus)
    See *Libation Bearers*

Choephoroe (Aeschylus)
    See *Libation Bearers*

"Christ and Satan" (Caedmon) **7**:84, 91-3, 102-03

Christian Theology (*Theologia Christiana; Theology*) (Abelard) **11**:9, 10, 11, 12, 14, 16, 17, 21, 26, 51-3, 64, 65

Chronicle
    See *Anglo-Saxon Chronicle*

Cimone (Boccaccio) **13**:28

Circe (Aeschylus) **11**:124

"The City Mouse and the Country Mouse" (Marie de France) **8**:190

"City of Brass" **2**:2, 23-4, 40, 51-3

"The City of Irem" **2**:40

De civitate Dei (*On the City of God*) (Augustine) **6**:4, 10-11, 21-22, 29, 43, 54, 57-8, 60, 66-8, 83, 90-1, 105-08, 122-23, 142

De claris mulieribus (*Concerning Famous Women*) (Boccaccio) **13**:33, 38, 45-7, 52, 55-8, 66, 97-8

De claris oratoribus (*Brutus; Brutus: On Famous Orators; Brutus; or the illustrious Orators*) (Cicero) **3**:193, 201-02, 206-09, 218, 259, 261, 263, 288

De clementia (*On Clemency; On Mercy*) (Seneca) **6**:344, 374, 381-82, 397, 399, 401-02, 408

De clementia II (Seneca) **6**:399

Cligés (Chretien de Troyes) **10**:133, 138-44, 147, 149, 159-61, 163-64, 166-69, 171-75, 178-79, 183, 190-95, 198, 204-05, 207-08, 210, 215, 218, 222-25, 229-30, 232-39

Clitophon (Plato) **8**:218, 305, 311

The Cloud-Messenger (Kalidasa)
    See *Meghadūta*

The Clouds (Aristophanes)
    See *Nephelai*

De Coelestibus (*De Celestibus*) (Bacon) **14**:47

Collations (Eckhart)
    See *Rede der Unterscheidungen*

Comedia delle ninfe fiorentine (Boccaccio) **13**:63-5, 97

Commentaries on the Sentences (Albert the Great)
    See *Commentary on the Book of the Sentences*

Commentary on Aristotle's De Generatione et de Coruptione (Averroes) **7**:30

Commentary on Aristotle's Nichomachean Ethics (Averroes) **7**:43

Commentary on Artistotle's Meteorology (Albert the Great) **16**:97

Commentary on III de Anima (Averroes) **7**:24

Commentary on Plato's Republic (Averroes) **7**:30, 38, 40-3

Commentary on St Luke (Albert the Great) **16**:29

Commentary on the Book of the Sentences (*Commentaries on the Sentences; Commentary on the Sentences of Peter Lombard; Scripta Super Sententias; Sentences*) (Albert the Great) **16**:6-7, 14, 16, 26, 31, 44, 66, 68, 76, 86, 93-4

Commentary on the Divine Names (Albert the Great) **16**:28-9

Commentary on the Sentences of Peter Lombard (Albert the Great)
See *Commentary on the Book of the Sentences*

The Commonplace Book of Sei Shōnagon (Sei Shonagon)
See *Makura no sōshi*

Communia Mathematica (Bacon) **14**:15, 46, 80

Communium Naturalium (Bacon) **14**:15, 48, 80, 100, 104-05

Compendium artis demonstrativae (Llull)
See *Ars demonstrativa*

Compendium of Philosophy (Bacon)
See *Compendium Studii Philosophiae*

Compendium of the Logic of al-ghazzāli (Llull) **12**:113-14, 116, 126, 128, 132

Compendium of the Study of Philosophy (Bacon)
See *Compendium Studii Philosophiae*

Compendium Studii Philosophiae (*Compendium of Philosophy; Compendium of the Study of Philosophy*) (Bacon) **14**:8-9, 28-31, 36-37, 42, 45, 50, 68-69, 100-01, 105

Compendium Studii Theologiae (Bacon) **14**:9, 15, 22, 25, 42, 45, 50, 64

Compotus naturalium (Bacon) **14**:63

Concerning Famous Women (Boccaccio)
See *De claris mulieribus*

Concerning the Antiquities of the Jews (Josephus)
See *Antiquitates Judaicae*

Concerning the Capture (Josephus)
See *Bellum Judaicum*

Concerning the Jewish War (Josephus)
See *Bellum Judaicum*

Confessions (Augustine) **6**:4, 8, 14, 16, 19, 21-4, 29, 34, 41, 44, 46, 52-6, 60, 63-9, 72, 78, 84, 92, 96-8, 100-04, 110-13, 116-20, 122, 126-29, 131-33, 136-38, 140-42, 146, 149

Connection by Marriage (Menander)
See *Samia*

Consolatio (Boethius)
See *De consolatione philosophiae*

Consolation (Cicero)
See *Consolationes*

The Consolation of Philosophy (Boethius)
See *The Consolation of Philosophy*

De consolatione philosophiae (*Consolatio*) (Boethius) 3, 4, 9, 10-15, 15-23, 24, 31, 33, 37-43, 43-47, 47-53, 53-58, 58-69, 69-79, 87, 88, 88-97, 97-124, 125-26, 128-32, 134-45

Consolationes (*Consolation*) (Cicero) **3**:227

De constantia (Seneca) **6**:382

De consulatu suo (*On His Consulship*) (Cicero) **3**:198

Conte de la Charrette (Chretien de Troyes)
See *Lancelot*

Conte du Graal (Chretien de Troyes)
See *Perceval*

Li Contes del Graal (Chretien de Troyes)
See *Perceval*

Contest for the Arms (Aeschylus) **11**:125

Contra academicos (*Against the Academicians*) (Augustine) **6**:5, 46, 65, 68, 90

Contra Apionem (*Against Apion; Against the Gentiles; Against the Greeks; Apion Answered; Apionem*) (Josephus) **13**:207-8, 211-2, 214, 219-20, 225-39, 247, 250, 253, 256, 259-60, 262-3, 268, 270, 272, 279, 281, 296, 301-2, 306-8, 312-3, 315, 317-20

Contra epistolum Manichaei (Augustine) **6**:9

Contra Eutychen et Nestorium (Boethius) **15**:86, 125-6, 128, 130, 132-3, 135-6, 138

"Conversation in the Mountains" (Li Po) **2**:144

Corbaccio (Boccaccio) **13**:9, 37, 67, 70-1, 73-4, 88-94

De Corona (Cicero) **3**:267

De correptione et gratia (Augustine) **6**:9-10, 89

De Coruna (Demosthenes)
See *On the Crown*

Counsels on Discernment (Eckhart) **9**:69

Cratylus (Plato) **8**:306, 336, 361

Critias (Plato) **8**:232, 259, 261, 306, 311

Crito (Plato) **8**:282

"Crossing at Seven Li Shallows" (Shih) **15**:396-97

"The Crow Instructing His Child" (Marie de France) **8**:194

Crown Speech (Demosthenes)
See *On the Crown*

Cupid and Psyche (Apuleius) **1**:22, 26, 40-2

Daitaleis (Aristophanes) **4**:62

Danaids (*Daughters of Danäus*) (Aeschylus) **11**:88, 119, 158, 160, 167, 179, 183, 192

Danesh Namesh (Avicenna) **16**:150

"Daniel" (Caedmon) **7**:84, 87, 89-90

Daphnephorica (Pindar) **12**:321

Daphnis (Longus)
See *Daphnis and Chloe*

Daphnis and Chloe (*Daphnis; Lesbian Pastorals; The Lesbian Pastorals of Daphnis and Chloe; The Pastorals of Daphnis and Chloe*) (Longus) 7;214-76

Daughters of Danäus (Aeschylus)
See *Danaids*

Daughters of Phorcus (Aeschylus) **11**:124

De beneficiis (*On Giving and Receiving Favours*) (Seneca) **6**:344, 348, 374, 381-83

De brevitate vitae (*On the Shortness of Life*) (Seneca) **6**:344, 382

De clementia I (Seneca) **6**:399

De ira (*On Anger*) (Seneca) **6**:344, 347, 382, 385, 411, 424, 436-37

De otio (Seneca) **6**:382

De providentia (*On Providence*) (Seneca) **6**:374, 381

De vita beata (*On the Happy Life*) (Seneca) **6**:382, 412

"The Death of Edward the Confessor" **4**:13

"The Death of Enkidu" **3**:336

"The Death of Gilgamesh" **3**:333, 336-37, 349

Decameron (Boccaccio) **13**:3-28, 30-8, 42-3, 45, 47-52, 55-7, 59-65, 67, 71-2, 74-5, 82-4, 86, 88-91, 94, 114-8, 122-31

Decisive Treatise (Averroes)
See *Fasl al-maqāl*

Dede Korkut
See *Kitabi-i Dedem Qorkut*

Dede Korkut nameh
See *Kitabi-i Dedem Qorkut*

"The Defence of Walled Towns" (Sordello) **15**:330, 344

Defense (Plato)
See *Apologia*

Descent of Heracles into the Underworld (*Cerberus*) (Pindar) **12**:321

Descent of the Gods (Hesiod)
See *Theogony*

Desconort (Llull) **12**:108, 120, 122

Destructio destructionis philosophorum (Averroes)
See *Tahāfut al-tahāfut*

Destructio Destructionum (Averroes)
See *Tahāfut al-tahāfut*

Destruction of the Destruction (Averroes)
See *Tahāfut al-tahāfut*

"Deus Amanz" (Marie de France)
See "Les Dous Amanz"

"The Devout Prince" **2**:40

Dialectica (Abelard) **11**:62, 64, 66

De dialectica (Augustine) **6**:133-36, 138

Dialogi (*Dialogues*) (Seneca) **6**:374, 381-82, 410, 413

Dialogue between a Christian and a Jew (Abelard)
See *Dialogue between a Philosopher, a Jew and A Christian*

Dialogue between a Philosopher, a Jew and A Christian (*Dialogue between a Christian and a Jew; Dialogue of the Philosopher with a Jew and a Christian*) (Abelard) **11**:4, 11, 21, 24, 51-53, 67

Dialogue of the Philosopher with a Jew and a Christian (Abelard)
See *Dialogue between a Philosopher, a Jew and A Christian*

Dialogue of Trismegistus (Apuleius) **1**:17

Dialogues (Seneca)
See *Dialogi*

Dialogues on the Supreme Good, the End of All Moral Action (Cicero)
See *De finibus*

Diana's Hunt (Boccaccio)
See *Caccia di Diana*

Dictyluci (Aeschylus)
See *Net-Draggers*

"Dido" (Ovid) **7**:312

"Dirge for Blacatz" (Sordello)
See "Planher vuelh en Blacatz"

Dis Exapaton (*Cheat Him Twice; A Double Deceit*) (Menander) **9**:258, 270

"Discourse on Dragon and Tiger (Lead and Mercury)" (Shih) **15**:400

"Discourse on Literature" (Shih) **15**:420

Disputation (Llull) **12**:119

Dithyrambs (Pindar) **12**:320, 355

De diversis quaestionibus (Augustine) **6**:90

De divinatione (*On Divination*) (Cicero) **3**:216, 243, 248

Divine Song
See *Bhagavad Gītā*

Divisions (*On Division*) (Boethius) **15**:27, 29-30

The Divisions of Oratory (Cicero)
See *Partiones oratoriae*

De doctrina Christiana (*On Christian Doctrine*) (Augustine) **6**:69, 81-2, 85, 92-4, 111, 113, 126, 133-36, 138

Doctrina pueril (Llull) **12**:104-05, 107, 121

"The Doe and Her Fawn" (Marie de France) **8**:193-94

De domo (Cicero) **3**:269

"Dompna meillz qu om pot pensar" (Sordello) **15**:361

De dono perseverantiae (Augustine) **6**:10

A Double Deceit (Menander)
See *Dis Exapaton*

The Dour Man (Menander)
See *Dyskolos*

"Les Dous Amanz" ("Deus Amanz"; "Lai des Deuz Amanz"; "The Two Lovers") (Marie de France) **8**:116-17, 121, 131, 133-34, 136-39, 147, 153-54, 156, 162-65, 181, 187
"A Draught of Sesamum" (Shih) **15**:383, 391
Dream (Cicero)
  See *Somnium Scipionis*
Dream of Scipio (Cicero)
  See *Somnium Scipionis*
The Dream of the Rood (Rood) **14**:215-294
"Dreams of the Sky-land" (Li Po) **2**:134
"Drinking Alone by Moonlight" (Li Po) **2**:132, 143, 163
Drunkenness (Menander) **9**:248
"A Dung-Beetle" (Marie de France)
  See "A Wolf and a Dung-Beetle"
Duties (Cicero)
  See *De officiis*
The Dynasty of Raghu (Kalidasa)
  See *Raghuvamśa*
Dyskolos (*The Dour Man*; *Grumpy*; *Old Cantankerous*) (Menander) **9**:231-33, 235-41, 243-52, 257, 260-65, 269-70, 272-77, 279-84, 286-87
"The Ebony Horse" **2**:51
Ecclesiazusae (Aristophanes)
  See *Ekklesiazousai*
Egyptians (Aeschylus) **11**:88, 160, 179
"Eight Sights of Feng-hsiang" (Shih) **15**:410
Eighth Isthmian (Pindar)
  See *Isthmian 8*
Eighth Olympian (Pindar)
  See *Olympian 8*
"Eighty some paces" (Shih) **15**:398
Eirēnē (*Peace*) (Aristophanes) **4**:44-5, 60-2, 78, 87, 93, 108-09, 124-26, 132-33, 138, 142-44, 148-49, 153-54, 160, 162-63. 165-68
Ekklesiazousai (*Assembly of Women*; *Ecclesiazusae*; *Parliament of Women*; *Women in Assembly*; *Women in Parliament*; *The Women's Assembly*) (Aristophanes) **4**:44, 60-62, 65, 68, 78, 87, 94, 110, 124-26, 128-29, 147, 149-50, 152, 155-56, 161-62, 166, 168-77, 179-80
Elegia di Constanza (Boccaccio) **13**:62-4, 73
Elegia di madonna Fiammetta (Boccaccio)
  See *Fiammetta*
Elegies (Ovid)
  See *Tristia*
Elegies of Gloom (Ovid)
  See *Tristia*
Ēlektra (Sophocles) **2**:289, 293, 300, 314-15, 319-22, 324, 326-27, 331, 335, 338-40, 347, 349, 351, 353-54, 357-58, 368, 380, 384-85, 395-96, 417-18, 421
Elementary Exercises (Hermogenes)
  See *Progymnasmata*
Eleusinians (Aeschylus) **11**:192
Eleventh Nemean (Pindar)
  See *Nemean 11*
Eleventh Olympian (Pindar)
  See *Olympian 11*
Eleventh Pythian (Pindar)
  See *Pythian 11*
"Eliduc" ("Guildeluec and Gualadun") (Marie de France) **8**:114, 118, 121, 129-30, 133, 135, 140, 144-45, 147-49, 152, 158, 160-61, 164-66, 170, 182
Embassy (Demosthenes)
  See *On the Misconduct of the Embassy*
"An Emperor and his Ape" (Marie de France) **8**:175

"Emril Son of Beyril" **8**:105
Enarration on Psalm 90 (Augustine) **6**:111
Enarration on Psalm 136 (Augustine) **6**:116
Enarrationes in psalmos (Augustine) **6**:83
Enchiridion ad laurentium (Augustine) **6**:9, 21, 68
Encomia (*Encomium*) (Pindar) **12**:320-21, 357, 363-64
Encomium (Pindar)
  See *Encomia*
Enid (Chretien de Troyes)
  See *Erec et Enide*
Ensegnamen d'Onor (*Instruction in Honor*; *Lesson of Honour, The Teachings of Honor*) (Sordello) **15**:331-32, 354, 256, 270, 376-76
Epic of Gilgamesh (*Gilgamesh*; *Gilgamesh Epic*; *Gilgamish*) **3**:301-75
Epicleros (Menander) **9**:203
Epinicia (Pindar) **12**:320-22
Epinomis (Plato) **8**:248, 305-06, 311
"Episode of Nala"
  See *Nalopakhyāna*
Epistle XLVII (Seneca) **6**:384
Epistle ad P. Lentulum (Cicero)
  See *Ad P. Lentulum*
Epistles (Ovid)
  See *Heroides*
Epistles (Plato) **8**:305, 311
Epistles (Seneca)
  See *Epistulae morales*
Epistolæ Heroidum (Ovid)
  See *Heroides*
Epistola de secretis operibus naturae (Bacon) **14**:64
Epistola fratris Rogerii Baconis de secretis operibus naturae et de nullitate magiae (*Letter on the Secret Works of Art and the Nullity of Magic*) (Bacon) **14**:44
Epistulae ex Ponto (*Black Sea Letters*; *Ex Ponto*; *Letters from the Black Sea*) (Ovid) **7**:323, 343, 344, 347, 378, 398, 423, 426
Epistulae morales (*Epistles*; *Letters*; *Letters to Lucilius*; *Moral Epistles*) (Seneca) **6**:347, 352-53, 374-75, 381-83, 410-11, 417
Epitrepontes (*The Arbitrants*; *The Arbitration*) (Menander) **9**:203, 207-09, 211-13, 215-18, 223-24, 227, 230, 232, 238-44, 246-47, 249-52, 260, 269-71, 278, 281
Eptiaphios (Demosthenes) **13**:166
"Equitan" (Marie de France) **8**:114, 121, 123, 131-32, 134, 136, 143, 147, 149-50, 157, 159, 162-65, 171, 175, 182
"Er encontra'l temps de mai" (Sordello) **15**:363
Erec (Hartmann von Aue) **15**:158, 164-65, 176, 183, 185, 188-96, 196-202, 207-13, 218-23, 228-41, 244
Erec and Enid (Chretien de Troyes)
  See *Erec et Enide*
Erec et Enide (*Enid*; *Erec and Enid*) (Chretien de Troyes) **10**:132-33, 139, 141-43, 146-48, 159-61, 163, 165-67, 169, 171-73, 178, 183-89, 191-93, 195, 197, 200-01, 204-10, 218-19, 223-26, 229-39
Erga (Hesiod)
  See *Works and Days*
Erotic Adventures (Ovid)
  See *Amores*
Esope (Marie de France)
  See *The Fables*
Esposizioni (Boccaccio) **13**:62, 67
Espurgatoire (Marie de France)

See *L'Espurgatoire Saint Patrice*
L'Espurgatoire Saint Patrice (*The Book of Purgatory*; *Espurgatoire*; *Le Livre de l'Espurgatorie*; *Purgatory*; *The Purgatory of St. Patrice*; *St. Patrick's Purgatory*) (Marie de France) **8**:114-15, 128, 146, 159-61, 173-77
Ethica seu Scito te ipsum (Abelard)
  See *Scito Te Ipsum*
Ethics (Abelard)
  See *Scito Te Ipsum*
De Eucharistico Sacramento (Albert the Great) **16**:42
Eumenides (*Furies*; *Kindly Ones*) (Aeschylus) **11**:85-7, 92, 96, 100, 102, 105, 107, 114, 116-17, 119, 132, 134-35, 137-38, 140, 143, 150, 152-53, 155-57, 162, 165-66, 172, 178-79, 180-85, 191-92, 194, 197-98, 204-05, 207, 216, 218, 222, 225
Eunich (Terence)
  See *Eunuchus*
Eunuchus (*Eunich*; *The Sham Eunich*) (Terence) **14**:299, 303-08, 311-15, 317-18, 321, 330-33, 335, 337, 340, 342-43, 345-49, 352-54, 357-58, 364-66, 369-71, 383-84, 387
Euthydemus (Plato) **8**:218, 250, 265-66, 306, 314, 357, 361
Euthyphro (Plato)
  See *Euthyphron*
Euthyphron (*Euthyphro*) (Plato) **8**:263, 286, 306
Evast and Blanquerna (Llull)
  See *Blanquerna*
Ex Ponto (Ovid)
  See *Epistulae ex Ponto*
"Exile's Letter" (Li Po) **2**:140
"Exodus" (Caedmon) **7**:83-4, 87, 89-90, 93, 104
Expositio epistolae ad Galatas (Augustine) **6**:10
Expositio in Epist. ad Romanos (Abelard) **11**:10, 12, 53
An Exposition of the Methods of Argument Concerning the Doctrine of the Faith and a Determination of Doubts and Misleading Innovations Brought into the Faith (Averroes)
  See *Kitāb al-kashf 'an manāhij al-adilla fī 'aqa'id al-milla,wa ta'rīf ma waqa'a fīha bi-hasb at-ta'wīl min ash-shibah al-muzīgha wal-bida 'al-mudilla*
The Fables (*Esope*) (Marie de France) **8**:115, 128, 146, 160-61, 171-75, 179
"Fall of Angels" (Caedmon)
  See "Lament of the Fallen Angels"
De Falsa Legatione (Demosthenes)
  See *On the Misconduct of the Embassy*
Fasl (Averroes)
  See *Fasl al-maqāl*
Fasl al-maqāl (*Decisive Treatise*; *Fasl*) (Averroes) **7**:39, 41-4, 69-72
Fasti (*De Fastis*; *The Roman Calendar*) (Ovid) **7**:284, 286, 292-93, 323-27, 330, 335, 343-46, 362-65, 377, 389, 401-03, 413-19, 424-35, 444
De Fastis (Ovid)
  See *Fasti*
Felix (*Felix or The Book of Marvels*; *Libre de meravelles*) (Llull) **12**:105-07, 109, 123, 125, 133-34
Felix or The Book of Marvels (Llull)
  See *Felix*

"The Ferryman and the Hermit" 2:40

Fiammetta (Elegia di madonna Fiammetta) (Boccaccio) **13**:7, 29-30, 32-3, 63, 67, 88, 97

De fide catholica (On the Catholic Faith) (Boethius) **15**:9, 24, 3, 43, 52, 57, 62, 67

Fifth Isthmian (Pindar)
See *Isthmian 5*

Fifth Nemean (Pindar)
See *Nemean 5*

"Fighting to the South of the City" (Li Po) 2:132

Filocolo (Boccaccio) **13**:23, 32-3, 44-5, 61-5, 102-3, 105, 112, 114-22

Filocopo (Boccaccio) **13**:9, 26-8, 30

Filostrato (Boccaccio) **13**:9, 29, 32-3, 62-3, 65, 87-8, 102-3, 106, 110, 112

De finibus (Dialogues on the Supreme Good, the End of All Moral Action; On the Chief Good and Evil; On the Greatest Degree of Good and Evil) (Cicero) **3**:193, 202, 260, 288

First Isthmian (Pindar)
See *Isthmian 1*

First Nemean (Pindar)
See *Nemean 1*

First Olympian (Pindar)
See *Olympian 1*

First Olynthiac (Demosthenes)
See *Olynthiac I*

First Philippic (Cicero)
See *Philippics*

First Philippic (Demosthenes)
See *Philippic I*

First Pythian (Pindar)
See *Pythian 1*

"The Fisherman and the Genie" 2:45, 53-5, 68

The Fisherman's Art (Ovid)
See *Halieutica*

The Flatterer (Menander)
See *Kolax*

Florida (Apuleius)
See *Floridium*

Floridium (Florida) (Apuleius) **1**:7, 12, 23-4

"Following the Rhymes of Chiang Hui shi" (Shih) **15**:414, 416

For Cluentius (Cicero)
See *Pro Cluentio*

For Marcus Caelius (Cicero)
See *Pro Caelio*

For Megalopolis (For the Megalopolitans; Megalopolis) (Demosthenes) **13**:137, 148, 156-7, 159, 164, 197

For Phormio (Demosthenes) **13**:184

For Quinctius (Cicero)
See *Pro Quinctio*

For the Liberty of the Rhodians (Demosthenes)
See *For the Rhodians*

For the Megalopolitans (Demosthenes)
See *For Megalopolis*

For the Rhodians (For the Liberty of the Rhodians; On the Freedom of Rhodes; On the Rhodians) (Demosthenes) **13**:137, 148, 156-7, 159, 164, 171

The Four Branches of the Mabinogi
See *Pedeir Keinc y Mabinogi*

"The Four Sorrows" (Marie de France)
See "Le Chaitivel"

Fourteenth Olympian (Pindar)
See *Olympian 14*

Fourth Philippic (Demosthenes)
See *Philippic IV*

Fourth Pythian (Pindar)
See *Pythian 4*

"The Fox and the Bear" (Marie de France) **8**:190

"Le Fraisne" ("The Ash Tree"; "Fresne"; "Lay le Freyne") (Marie de France) **8**:114, 116, 121, 131, 133-34, 136, 138, 140, 147, 152-53, 159-60, 162-63, 165-66, 181

Free Choice of the Will (Augustine)
See *De libero arbitrio voluntatis*

Free Will (Augustine)
See *De libero arbitrio voluntatis*

"Fresne" (Marie de France)
See "Le Fraisne"

The Friars (Aristophanes) **4**:100

The Frogs (Aristophanes)
See *Batrakhoi*

Furens (Seneca)
See *Hercules furens*

Furies (Aeschylus)
See *Eumenides*

Furious Hercules (Seneca)
See *Hercules furens*

"Ganem, Son to Abou Ayoub, and Known by the Surname of Love's Slave" 2:14, 36, 38

Gauvain (Chretien de Troyes)
See *Perceval*

Genealogia deorum gentilium (Genealogies of the Gentile Gods; Genealogies of the Pagan Gods; De genealogiis deorum; Genealogy of the Gods) (Boccaccio) **13**:33, 38, 41, 43-4, 52-4, 62, 66, 96, 98, 103

Genealogies of the Gentile Gods (Boccaccio)
See *Genealogia deorum gentilium*

Genealogies of the Pagan Gods (Boccaccio)
See *Genealogia deorum gentilium*

De genealogiis deorum (Boccaccio)
See *Genealogia deorum gentilium*

Genealogy of the Gods (Boccaccio)
See *Genealogia deorum gentilium*

De generatione et corruptione (Albert the Great) **16**:7, 61

De genesi ad litteram (Augustine) **6**:9, 137, 139

De Genesi ad litteram imperfectum (Augustine) **6**:137

De Genesi adversus Manichaeos (Augustine) **6**:137

"Genesis" *(Paraphrase; Paraphrase of Genesis)* (Caedmon) **7**:78-9, 82-9, 91-4, 104

"Genesis A" (Caedmon) **7**:84-90

"Genesis B" (Caedmon) **7**:85-6, 91, 93

Genesis of the Gods (Hesiod)
See *Theogony*

Genji Monogatari (The Tale of Genji) (Murasaki) **1**:413-76

Georgos (Menander) **9**:250

Gertadés (Aristophanes) **4**:102, 105

Gilgamesh
See *Epic of Gilgamesh*

"Gilgamesh and the Agga of Kish" **3**:336

"Gilgamesh and the Bull of Heaven" **3**:337, 349

"Gilgamesh and the Huluppu Tree" ("Gilgamesh, Enkidu and the Nether World") **3**:326, 337, 349, 362

"Gilgamesh and the Land of the Living" **3**:325, 332-33, 336-37, 349

"Gilgamesh, Enkidu and the Nether World"
See "Gilgamesh and the Huluppu Tree"

Gilgamesh Epic
See *Epic of Gilgamesh*

Gilgamish
See *Epic of Gilgamesh*

The Girl from Andros (Terence)
See *Andria*

The Girl from Samos (Menander)
See *Samia*

The Girl Who Gets Her Hair Cut Short (Menander)
See *Perikeiromenē*

The Girl with Shorn Hair (Menander)
See *Perikeiromenē*

Gīta
See *Bhagavadgīta*

Gita
See *Bhagavad Gītā*

Glaucus Potnieus (Aeschylus) **11**:159, 179

"Goat's Leaf" (Marie de France)
See "Chevrefoil"

The Golden Ass (Apuleius)
See *Asinus aureus*

Gorgias (Plato) **8**:217, 233, 235, 239, 247-48, 255, 264, 266-68, 270, 274, 283, 285-87, 306, 322

De gratia et libero arbitrio (On Grace and Free Will) (Augustine) **6**:89, 118, 122

Great Epic
See *Mahābhārata*

Gregorius (Hartmann von Aue) **15**:164, 171-75, 175-83, 194, 207, 213-18, 218

Grumpy (Menander)
See *Dyskolos*

"Guigemar" (Marie de France)
See "Lay of Guigemar"

"Guildeluec and Gualadun" (Marie de France)
See "Eliduc"

Guillaume d'Angleterre (William of England) (Chretien de Troyes) **10**:137, 139, 142-43, 183, 218, 225, 232

"Guingamor" (Marie de France) **8**:122-23, 126-28, 131

"Gulnare of the Sea" 2:14, 23

Halieticon/On Fishing (Ovid)
See *Halieutica*

Halieutica (The Fisherman's Art; Halieticon/On Fishing) (Ovid) **7**:328-29

"Hard Roads to Shu" (Li Po) 2:131-32, 145, 158, 166

"Hardships of Travel" (Li Po) 2:139

The Harpist (Menander) **9**:288

"Harrowing of Hell" (Caedmon) **7**:79, 91-2

Hated (Menander)
See *Misoumenos*

"The Hawk and the Owl" (Marie de France) **8**:192, 194

Hazar Afsana
See *Alf Layla wa-Layla*

He Clips Her Hair (Menander)
See *Perikeiromenē*

Healing (Avicenna)
See *Kitāb al-Shifā*

Heautontimoreumenos (Self-Punishment; The Self-Tormentor) (Terence) **14**:299, 302-04, 306-07, 309, 311, 313-14, 316-18, 332-35, 337-38, 345, 347, 349, 352, 358-59, 363-66, 381, 383-84, 386-87

Heautontimorumenus (The Man Who Punished Himself) (Menander) **9**:243, 269

Hecyra (The Innocent Mother-in-Law; The Mother-in-Law) (Terence) **14**:299, 301-08, 311-13, 317-20, 325, 329, 332-36, 340, 342-44, 347-49, 352-53, 356-58, 364-65, 368, 383-84, 386, 389, 398

Heliades (Aeschylus)   **11**:211
Hell (Dante)
  See *Inferno*
"Heng-chiang Lyrics" (Li Po)   **2**:161
Hercules furens (*Furens; Furious Hercules;*
  Mad Hercules) (Seneca)   **6**:340, 342-43, 363,
  366, 369-70, 372-73, 379-81, 402-03, 405,
  413, 415-17, 422-23, 431-32, 440-41, 446
Hercules oetaeus (*Hercules on Oeta; Oetaeus*)
  (Seneca)   **6**:342-44, 363, 366, 370, 377, 379,
  381, 414, 417-18, 423, 431-32, 446
Hercules on Oeta (Seneca)
  See *Hercules oetaeus*
Hero (Menander)   **9**:207, 211, 217, 246, 252
Heroides (*Epistles; Epistolæ Heroidum;*
  Heroines; Letters; Letters of the Heroines)
  (Ovid)   **7**:291-93, 296-97, 299-301, 303, 310-
  13, 316-19, 321, 329-36, 343-44, 346-47, 355,
  376-83, 388, 417, 419-20, 425, 444
Heroines (Ovid)
  See *Heroides*
Hikayet-i Oguzname-i Kazan Beg ve Gayri
  See *Kitabi-i Dedem Qorkut*
Hiketides (Aeschylus)
  See *Suppliants*
Hipparchus (Plato)   **8**:305, 311
Hippeis (*The Knights*) (Aristophanes)   **4**:38,
  43, 46, 60, 62-3, 65, 74, 94, 98-9, 101, 114-
  15, 126-28, 132, 143, 146, 148, 152, 162-63,
  167
Hippias maior (*Hippias Major*) (Plato)   **8**:270,
  305-06
Hippias Major (Plato)
  See *Hippias maior*
Hippias Minor (*Lesser Hippias*) (Plato)   **8**:306
Historia Calamitatum (*History of My Troubles;*
  Story of Calamities; Story of His Misfortunes)
  (Abelard)   **11**:24, 28, 32, 33, 40, 45, 48, 51,
  52, 55, 57-59, 61, 63-66
History of My Troubles (Abelard)
  See *Historia Calamitatum*
The History of Rome from Its Foundation
  (Livy)
  See *Ab urbe condita libri*
History of the House of Aragon (Sordello)
  See *Los progres e avansaments dei Res*
  d'Aragon
History of the Jewish War (Josephus)
  See *Bellum Judaicum*
"The Honeysuckle" (Marie de France)
  See "Chevrefoil"
Hortensius (Cicero)   **3**:178, 242, 288
"How Basat Killed Goggle-eye" ("The Story
  of Basat Who Killed Depegöz"; "The Story
  of Basat Who Kills the One-Eyed Giant")
  8:103, 108-09
"How Prince Urez Son of Prince Kazan was
  Taken Prisoner"   **8**:103
"How Salur Kazan's House was Pillaged"
  See "The Plunder of the Home of Salur-
  Kazan"
"How the Outer Oghuz Rebelled Against the
  Inner Oghuz and How Beyrek Died"   **8**:103
Hrafnkatla
  See *Hrafnkel's saga Freysgodi*
Hrafnkel's Saga
  See *Hrafnkel's saga Freysgodi*
Hrafnkel's saga Freysgodi (*Hrafnkatla;*
  Hrafnkel's Saga)   **2**:74-129
"Hsiang-yang Song" (Li Po)   **2**:161
Hundred Names of God (*Cent Noms de Déu*)
  (Llull)   **12**:122, 125

"Hundred Pace Rapids" (Shih)   **15**:410
"Hymn" (Caedmon)   **7**:84-5, 93-7, 100-01,
  103-13
Hymn (Pindar)   **12**:355-56
"Hymn to Aphrodite" (Sappho)
  See "Ode to Aphrodite"
Hymn to Zeus (Pindar)   **12**:276-78, 320
Hymns to the Gods (Pindar)   **12**:320
Hypobolimaeus (Menander)   **9**:203
Hyporcemata (*Hyporcheme; Songs for Dancing*)
  (Pindar)   **12**:320-21, 355-57, 364
Hyporcheme (Pindar)
  See *Hyporcemata*
Hyppolytus (Seneca)   **6**:340, 342, 363, 373
Hypsipyle (Aeschylus)   **11**:124
I. 3 (Pindar)
  See *Isthmian 3*
I. 4 (Pindar)
  See *Isthmian 4*
"I have left my post in Hsu-chou" (Shih)
  15:412
"I shâk El-Mausili with the Merchant"   **2**:43
Ibis (Ovid)   **7**:327-28, 444
Ichneutai (*The Trackers*) (Sophocles)   **2**:289,
  338, 388, 408
De ideis (Hermogenes)
  See *On Types of Style*
Iliad (*Iliads; Ilias*) (Homer)   **1**:268-412
Iliads (Homer)
  See *Iliad*
Ilias (Homer)
  See *Iliad*
De immortalitate animae (Augustine)   **6**:68
In Catilinam (*Against Catilina; Catilinarians*)
  (Cicero)   **3**:193, 196, 198, 268, 270
In Collation (Eckhart)
  See *Rede der Unterscheidung*
In enigmatibus (Bacon)   **14**:62
In Pisonem (Cicero)   **3**:269, 284
"In Quest of the Tao in An-Ling, I Met Kai
  Huan Who Fashioned for Me a Register of
  the Realized Ones; (This Poem) Left Behind
  As a Present When About to Depart" (Li
  Po)   **2**:175
In topica Ciceronis (*De Institutione Musica;*
  Music; De Musica; Principles of Music)
  (Boethius)   **15**:7, 26, 54-5, 62, 74, 95
In Vatinium (Cicero)   **3**:223
Inferno (*Hell*) (Dante)   **3**:1-169
'*Ingredientibus*' (Abelard)
  See *Logica 'Ingredientibus'*
The Innocent Mother-in-Law (Terence)
  See *Hecyra*
"Inscription for Six one Spring" (Shih)
  15:399
"Inscription for the Lotus Clepsydra at Hsu-
  chou" (Shih)   **15**:399,409
De Institutione Musica (Boethius)
  See *In topica Ciceronis*
Instruction in Honor (Sordello)
  See *Ensegnamen d'Onor*
The Intellect (Albert the Great)
  See *De intellectu et intelligibili*
De intellectu et intelligibili (*The Intellect*)
  (Albert the Great)   **16**:61, 112, 116, 118
De interpretatione (Abelard)   **11**:63
Introductio (Abelard)   **11**:10
An Introduction to Categorical Syllogisms
  (Boethius)   **15**:27, 29
Invectiva in quedam ignarum dialectices
  (Abelard)   **11**:67

De inventione (*On Invention; Rhetorica*)
  (Cicero)   **3**:182, 193, 201, 206, 216, 218-19,
  244, 258-60, 263
De inventione (Hermogenes)
  See *On Invention*
Ion (Plato)   **8**:305-06, 331
Iphigenia (Aeschylus)   **11**:125
Ishārāt wa al-Tanbīhāt (Avicenna)   **16**:150
Isth. 9 (Pindar)
  See *Isthmian 9*
Isthm. VII (Pindar)
  See *Isthmian 7*
Isthmian 1 (*First Isthmian*) (Pindar)   **12**:271,
  319, 344, 352, 355-56, 365-66, 369, 378, 383-
  84
Isthmian 2 (Pindar)   **12**:312-13, 319, 352-53,
  362-63, 383
Isthmian 3 (*I. 3*) (Pindar)   **12**:295, 306, 313,
  356, 365-66
Isthmian 4 (*I. 4*) (Pindar)   **12**:288, 295, 301,
  312, 353, 356, 365, 367, 371, 376, 378, 380,
  383
Isthmian 5 (*Fifth Isthmian*) (Pindar)   **12**:273,
  278, 288, 306-07, 310, 323, 337, 357-58, 370,
  378
Isthmian 6 (*Sixth Isthmian*) (Pindar)   **12**:319,
  325-26, 354, 357-58, 366, 370, 377-79, 382-
  83
Isthmian 7 (*Isthm. VII; Seventh Isthmian*)
  (Pindar)   **12**:263, 270, 306-07, 326, 356,
  362, 365-67, 383
Isthmian 8 (*Eighth Isthmian*) (Pindar)
  12:271-73, 319, 325, 355-58, 382-83
Isthmian 9 (*Isth. 9*) (Pindar)   **12**:357
Isthmian Odes (Pindar)   **12**:321, 353, 357
De iuventute et senectute (Albert the Great)
  16:90
Iwein (Hartmann von Aue)   **15**:154-63, 164-
  71, 176, 183-96, 202-06, 233, 244-45
Ixion (Broughton)   **11**:122
"Jaefer and the Old Bedouin"   **2**:40
"Jaudar"   **2**:42
Jaya
  See *Mahābhārata*
Jeu d'Adam
  See *Ordo Representacionis Ade*
Jewish Antiquities (Josephus)
  See *Antiquitates Judaicae*
Jewish War (Josephus)
  See *Bellum Judaicum*
Job
  See *The Book of Job*
"Kafour the Eunuch"   **2**:40
Kalevala (*Alku Kalevala; Kalewala; New*
  Kalevala; Old Kalevala; Proto-Kalevala; Uusi
  Kalevala; Vanha Kalevala)   **6**:206-88
Kalewala
  See *Kalevala*
"Kan Turali Son of Kanli Koja" ("The Story
  of Kan Turali")   **8**:103, 108-09
Kedeia (Menander)
  See *Samia*
"Khalifeh the Fisherman"   **2**:14, 40
Kindly Ones (Aeschylus)
  See *Eumenides*
King Mark and Iseut the Fair (*Tristan*)
  (Chretien de Troyes)   **10**:139, 218
King Oedipus (Sophocles)
  See *Oedipous Tyrannos*
Kitāb al-kashf 'an manāhij al-adilla (Averroes)

See *Kitāb al-kashf 'an manāhij al-adilla fī 'aqa'id al-milla,wa ta'rīf ma waqa'a fīha bi-hasb at-ta'wīl min ash-shibah al-muzīgha wal-bida 'al-mudilla*

Kitāb al-kashf 'an manāhij al-adilla fī 'aqa'id al-milla,wa ta'rīf ma waqa'a fīha bi-hasb at-ta'wīl min ash-shibah al-muzīgha wal-bida 'al-mudilla (*An Exposition of the Methods of Argument Concerning the Doctrine of the Faith and a Determination of Doubts and Misleading Innovations Brought into the Faith; Kitāb al-kashf 'an manāhij al-adilla; Manāhij*) (Averroes) 7:37-43, 45, 69-70

Kitāb al-Najāt (Avicenna) 16:147, 150, 162

Kitāb al-Shifā (*Healing*) (Avicenna) 16:136-37, 147, 150, 157-58, 162-64

Kitabi Qorqut
    See *Kitabi-i Dedem Qorkut*

Kitabi-i Dedem Qorkut (*Book of Dede Korkut; Book of Grandfather Qorkut; The Book of Korkut; The Book of My Grandfather Korkut; Dede Korkut; Dede Korkut nameh; Hikayet-i Oguzname-i Kazan Beg ve Gayri; Kitabi Qorqut; The Story of the Oghuzname-- the Oghuz*) 8:95-110

"The Kite and the Jay" (Marie de France) 8:194

The Knight of the Cart (Chretien de Troyes)
    See *Lancelot*

The Knight with the Lion (Chretien de Troyes)
    See *Yvain*

The Knight with the Sword (Chretien de Troyes)
    See *Le Chevalier à l'épée*

The Knights (Aristophanes)
    See *Hippeis*

Know Thyself (Abelard)
    See *Scito Te Ipsum*

Kolax (*The Flatterer*) (Menander) 9:213, 269

Kulliyyāt (Averroes) 7:66

Kumārasambhava (*The Birth of Kumara; The Birth of the Prince; The Birth of the War-God*) (Kalidasa) 9:82-6, 89-90, 95-6, 102, 107, 114-15, 118-19, 125, 128-29

Laberinto d'amore (Boccaccio) 13:16

Laches (Plato) 8:263-65, 286, 306, 356

Ladies Lunching Together (Menander)
    See *Synaristosai*

The Lady of Andros (Terence)
    See *Andria*

"The Lady of the Highest Prime" 2:174

Laelius (Cicero)
    See *De amicitia*

Laelius: On Friendship (Cicero)
    See *De amicitia*

"Lai des Deuz Amanz" (Marie de France)
    See "Les Dous Amanz"

Lais (*Lays*) (Marie de France) 114-15, 130, 141, 146, 150, 157-62, 167, 172-73, 175, 177, 179-81, 184-85, 187-89, 195

Laïus (Aeschylus) 11:122, 124, 159, 174

"The Lamb and the Goat" (Marie de France) 8:192

"Lament for Blacas" (Sordello)
    See "Planher vuelh en Blacatz"

"Lament for Lord Blacatz" (Sordello)
    See "Planher vuelh en Blacatz"

"Lament of the Fallen Angels" ("Fall of Angels") (Caedmon) 7;91, 93

Lancelot (*Charrette; Le Chevalier de la Charrette; Conte de la Charrette; The Knight of the Cart*) (Chretien de Troyes) 10:133-39, 141-44, 147-49, 157, 159-63, 165-67, 169, 171-74, 176, 178-81, 183, 189-90, 195-98, 200, 208-10, 214-16, 218, 222-26, 228-30, 232-40

"Lanval" (Marie de France) 8:122-23, 125, 127-28, 130-31, 133, 140-47, 149, 154, 156, 158, 161-64, 166, 169-70

"Laostic" (Marie de France)
    See "Laüstic"

Lao-tzŭ (Lao Tzu)
    See *Tao te Ching*

"Laüstic" ("Laostic"; "The Nightingale") (Marie de France) 8:114, 120, 129, 131-34, 136-39, 144-45, 147-48, 153, 158-59, 161-66, 170, 181, 188

The Law (Cicero)
    See *De legibus*

Laws (Cicero)
    See *De legibus*

Laws (*Leges*) (Plato) 8:207, 217-18, 147, 249-50, 258-59, 261-62, 265-68, 279, 282-83, 305-06, 311, 318, 325, 328, 345-46, 362-64

"Lay le Freyne" (Marie de France)
    See "Le Fraisne"

"Lay of Guigemar" ("Guigemar") (Marie de France) 8:114-17, 122-23, 125, 127-28, 130-31, 133-35, 140, 145-49, 152-53, 161-67, 170, 172, 177-79, 181, 184, 188-89

Lay of the Nibelungen
    See *Book of Chaos*

Lay of the Nibelungs
    See *Book of Chaos*

Lays (Marie de France)
    See *Lais*

De lege agraria (Cicero) 3:268

Leges (Plato)
    See *Laws*

De legibus (*The Law; Laws; On Laws*) (Cicero) 3:177, 194, 201, 211, 214-15, 221, 249-51, 256-57, 276-77, 296-98

Leptinea (Demosthenes)
    See *Against Leptines*

Leptines (Demosthenes)
    See *Against Leptines*

Lesbian Pastorals (Longus)
    See *Daphnis and Chloe*

The Lesbian Pastorals of Daphnis and Chloe (Longus)
    See *Daphnis and Chloe*

Lesser Hippias (Plato)
    See *Hippias Minor*

Lesson of Honour (Sordello)
    See *Ensegnamen d'Onor*

"Letter in Answer to Hsieh Min-shihn" (Shih) 15:420

Letter on the Secret Works of Art and the Nullity of Magic (Bacon)
    See *Epistola fratris Rogerii Baconis de secretis operibus naturae et de nullitate magiae*

"Letter to Han Ching-chou" (Li Po) 2:169-73

"Letter to the Chief Administrator of Anchou, P'ei" (Li Po) 2:170

"Letter Written on Behalf of Longevity Mountain in Answer to the Proclamation of Meng Shao-fu" (Li Po) 2:172

Letters (Ovid)
    See *Heroides*

Letters (Seneca)

See *Epistulae morales*

Letters from the Black Sea (Ovid)
    See *Epistulae ex Ponto*

Letters of Hloise and Abelard (Abelard) 11:55-6

Letters of the Heroines (Ovid)
    See *Heroides*

Letters to Atticus (Cicero)
    See *Ad Atticum*

Letters to Friends (Cicero)
    See *Ad familiares*

Letters to Lucilius (Seneca)
    See *Epistulae morales*

"Letting the Intellect Go and Experiencing Pure Ignorance" (Eckhart) 9:24

Libation Bearers (*Choephori; Choephoroe; Libation-Pourers*) (Aeschylus) 11:85, 87-8, 102, 104-05, 107, 116, 118-19, 131, 138, 140, 151, 153-54, 159, 162-64, 181, 184-85, 191, 193-95, 202, 205-07, 211, 217, 223

Libation-Pourers (Aeschylus)
    See *Libation Bearers*

Libellus de Alchimia (*De Alchimia*) (Albert the Great) 16:65

Liber contemplationis (Llull) 12:104

Liber de ascensu et descensu intellectus (*Book of the Ascent and Descent of the Mind*) (Llull) 12:107. 111

Liber de lumine (Llull) 12:110

Liber de retardatione accidentium senectutis (Bacon) 14:64

Liber de sancta virginitate (Augustine) 6:38

Liber Hymnorum (Abelard) 11:45

Liber mineralium (*Book of Minerals; Mineralia*) (Albert the Great) 16:55, 62-4, 97, 100-02

Liber Positionum (Eckhart) 9:56

Liber praedicationis contra Iudaeos (Llull) 12:117

Liber principiorum medicinae (*Book of the Principles and Grades of Medicine*) (Llull) 12:107

De libero arbitrio voluntatis (*Free Choice of the Will; Free Will; Liberum arbitrium voluntatis; On Free Will*) (Augustine) 6:5, 9-10, 68, 102, 117-18, 149

Liberum arbitrium voluntatis (Augustine)
    See *De libero arbitrio voluntatis*

Libre d'amic e Amat (Llull)
    See *Book of the Lover and the Beloved*

Libre de meravelles (Llull)
    See *Felix*

Libre del orde de cavalleria (*Book of the Order of Chivalry*) (Llull) 12:104, 107

Life (Josephus)
    See *Vita*

Life of Dante (Boccaccio)
    See *Vita di Dante*

Le Livre de l'Espurgatorie (Marie de France)
    See *L'Espurgatoire Saint Patrice*

Le Livre de Marco Polo (Polo)
    See *The Travels of Marco Polo the Venetian*

Locri (Menander) 9:203

Logica 'Ingredientibus' (*'Ingredientibus'*) (Abelard) 11:63, 64, 66

Logica 'Nostrorum' (*'Nostrorum'*) (Abelard) 11:62, 64, 66

Logical Treatises (Albert the Great) 16:4

"The Lonely Wife" (Li Po) 2:132

Long Commentary on the Metaphysics (Averroes)
    See *Tafsīr mā ba'd al-tabī'ah*

Longer Work (Bacon)
　See *Opus Majus*
Lord's Song
　See *Bhagavadgīta*
The Lord's Song
　See *Bhagavad Gītā*
Love-Poems (Ovid)
　See *Amores*
"The Lovers of the Benou Udreh"　2:40
"A Lu Mountain Song for the Palace Censor
　Empty-Boat Lu" (Li Po)　2:152, 164
Lykourgeia (Aeschylus)　11:192
Lysis (Plato)　8:254, 264-66, 306, 314
Lysistrata (Aristophanes)　4:44, 60-2, 65, 68,
　88, 93-94, 107-10, 113, 123-26, 133, 142,
　144-45, 151, 153-56, 160, 163, 166, 169-75
The Mabinogion
　See *Pedeir Keinc y Mabinogi*
Mad Hercules (Seneca)
　See *Hercules furens*
"The Mad Lover"　2:40
"The Magic Horse"　2:49
De magistro (Augustine)　6:126, 133-36, 138
Mahābhārata (*Bhārata*; *Great Epic*; *Jaya*)
　5:177-287
The Maid of Andros (Terence)
　See *Andria*
Makura no sōshi (*The Commonplace Book of
　Sei Shōnagon*; *Makura Zōshi*; *The Pillow
　Book of Sei Shōnagon*; *Pillow Sketches*; *Sei
　Shōnagon ga Makura-no-Sōshi*; *Sei
　Shōnagon's Pillow Book*) (Sei Shonagon)
　6:291-96, 299-309, 311-26
Makura Zōshi (Sei Shonagon)
　See *Makura no sōshi*
Mālavikā and Agnimitra (Kalidasa)
　See *Mālavikāgnimitra*
Mālavikāgnimitra (*Mālavikā and Agnimitra*)
　(Kalidasa)　9:82, 85, 90, 96-7, 99-102, 126,
　128, 131-33, 137-38
"Maldon"
　See "The Battle of Maldon"
The Man from Sikyon (Menander)
　See *Sikyonios*
"The Man of Yemen and His Six Slave Girls"
　2:40
The Man She Hated (Menander)
　See *Misoumenos*
"The Man Who Never Laughed Again"　2:40
The Man Who Punished Himself (Menander)
　See *Heautontimorumenus*
Manāhij (Averroes)
　See *Kitāb al-kashf 'an manāhij al-adilla fī
　'aqa'id al-milla,wa ta'rīf ma waqa'a fīha
　bi-hasb at-ta'wīl min ash-shibah
　al-muzīgha wal-bida 'al-mudilla*
Manilian (Cicero)
　See *Pro Lege Manilia*
Marco Polo (Polo)
　See *The Travels of Marco Polo the Venetian*
Marco Polo's Travels (Polo)
　See *The Travels of Marco Polo the Venetian*
Mariale (Albert the Great)　16:42
Marius (Cicero)　3:198
Masters of the Frying Pan (Aristophanes)
　4:167
Medea (Ovid)　7:286, 297, 336, 346-47, 376,
　420, 425, 444-45
Medea (Seneca)　6:336, 344-45, 363, 366, 371,
　373, 377-81, 404-10, 413-18, 426-27, 432-33,
　436, 441
Medicamina Faciei (Ovid)　7:346

Megalopolis (Demosthenes)
　See *For Megalopolis*
Meghadūta (*The Cloud-Messenger*) (Kalidasa)
　9:89-90, 92, 95, 102, 107, 113, 115, 125-26,
　129
*Meister Eckhart: The Essential Sermons,
　Commentaries, Treatises, and Defense*
　(Eckhart)　9:67
De memoria et reminiscentia (Albert the Great)
　16:61, 110
"A Memorial of Self-Introduction Written for
　Assistant Director of the Censorate Sung"
　(Li Po)　2:173-74
Menexenus (Plato)　8:305-07
Meno (*Menon*; *Minos*) (Plato)　8:206, 218,
　250, 264, 283-85, 305-07, 311, 320-22, 328,
　356-57, 362
Menon (Plato)
　See *Meno*
Metamorphoses (*The Transformations*)
　(Apuleius)　1:3, 7-8, 12-13, 15, 17-24, 26-27,
　29-37, 39-43, 45
Metamorphoses (*Metamorphosis*; *The
　Transformation/Transformations*) (Ovid)
　7:286, 291-92, 298-99, 304-05, 314-16, 322,
　324-36, 335-44, 346, 349, 357, 361-63, 365,
　368-77, 379, 383-93, 395-96, 398-402, 404,
　412-18, 430-32, 434-35, 438, 443-46
Metamorphosis (Ovid)
　See *Metamorphoses*
Metaphysics (Avicenna)　16:159-60, 164
Meteora (Albert the Great)
　See *De meteoris*
De meteoris (*Meteora*; *Meteororum*) (Albert the
　Great)　16:7, 36, 55, 61
Meteororum (Albert the Great)
　See *De meteoris*
De methodo vehementiae (Hermogenes)
　See *On the Method of Deinotēs*
*Middle Commentary on Porphyry's Isagoge and
　on Aristotle's Categoriae* (Averroes)　7:67
Midiana (Demosthenes)
　See *Against Midias*
"Milun" (Marie de France)　8:121, 128, 131-
　34, 147-50, 159, 162-66, 170, 175, 182, 187
Mineralia (Albert the Great)
　See *Liber mineralium*
De Mineralibus (Albert the Great)　16:18, 35,
　61
Minos (Plato)
　See *Meno*
Misoumenos (*Hated*; *The Man She Hated*)
　(Menander)　9:258, 260, 269-70, 276, 287
"Misty Yangtze" (Shih)　15:397
"Modern Music in the Yen Ho Palace" (Shih)
　15:385
"The Monkey and Her Baby" (Marie de
　France)　8:191
"The Monkey King" (Marie de France)
　8:191
De montibus (Boccaccio)　13:33, 38, 52
Moral Epistles (Seneca)
　See *Epistulae morales*
Morte Arthure "Alliterative"
　("Alliterative*Morte Arthure*")　10:375-436
De morte et vita (Albert the Great)　16:61
The Mother-in-Law (Terence)
　See *Hecyra*
De motibus animalium (Albert the Great)
　16:61
"A Mouse and a Frog" (Marie de France)
　8:174

Movement of Animals (Albert the Great)　5:
"Moving to Lin-kao Pavilion" (Shih)　15:410
La Mule sans frein (*The Unbridled Mule*)
　(Chretien de Troyes)　10:178-79, 232
Multiplication of Species (Bacon)
　See *Tractatus de Mulitiplicatione Specierum*
De Multiplicatione Specierum (Bacon)
　See *Tractatus de Mulitiplicatione Specierum*
De mundo (*On the Universe*) (Apuleius)　1:12,
　24
Murasaki Shikibu nikki (Murasaki)　1:457
Music (Boethius)
　See *In topica Ciceronis*
De musica (Augustine)　6:33, 68, 73, 133-34
De Musica (Boethius)
　See *In topica Ciceronis*
"The Muslim Champion and the Christian
　Damsel"　2:27
"My Trip in a Dream to the Lady of Heaven
　Mountain" (Li Po)　2:150
Myrmidons (Aeschylus)　11:101, 125, 193
Mystère d'Adam
　See *Ordo Representacionis Ade*
Mystery of Adam
　See *Ordo Representacionis Ade*
Mystical Theology (Albert the Great)　16:29,
　119
N. 4 (Pindar)
　See *Nemean 4*
N. 6 (Pindar)
　See *Nemean 6*
N. 7 (Pindar)
　See *Nemean 7*
N. 9 (Pindar)
　See *Nemean 9*
"Nala and Damayantī"
　See *Nalopakhyāna*
Nalopakhyāna ("Episode of Nala"; "Nala and
　Damayantī")　5:188, 206
De natura deorum (*About Gods*; *On the Nature
　of Gods*) (Cicero)　3:182, 202, 243, 248, 255-
　56, 268, 278, 279, 287
De natura et gratia (Augustine)　6:9-10
De natura et origine animae (Albert the Great)
　16:112
De natura locorum (*The Nature of Places*)
　(Albert the Great)　16:7, 22, 61
Natural Questions (Seneca)
　See *Naturales quaestiones*
Naturales quaestiones (*Natural Questions*;
　Quaestiones Naturales) (Seneca)　6:344, 348-
　49, 374, 381, 383, 387, 410-11
The Nature of Places (Albert the Great)
　See *De natura locorum*
Nem. IV (Pindar)
　See *Nemean 4*
Nem. VIII (Pindar)
　See *Nemean 8*
Nemea (Aeschylus)　11:192
Nemean 1 (*First Nemean*) (Pindar)　12:270,
　347-48, 364-65, 378
Nemean 2 (Pindar)　12:313, 359-60, 362, 378
Nemean 3 (*Third Nemean*) (Pindar)　12:264,
　268, 322, 357-58, 365, 369-70, 374, 378, 382-
　84
Nemean 4 (*N. 4*; *Nem. IV*) (Pindar)　12:264,
　271, 299-301, 303, 321, 330, 353-54, 357-58,
　362, 367, 371, 378, 382-83
Nemean V (Pindar)
　See *Nemean 5*

Title Index

Nemean 5 (*Fifth Nemean*; *Nemean V*) (Pindar) **12**:267, 269-70, 272, 304, 307, 309, 311, 325, 357-58, 360, 366, 371, 378-80, 382-84

Nemean 6 (*N. 6*; *Sixth Nemean*) (Pindar) **12**:267, 269, 271, 273, 302, 304-05, 323, 357-60, 365, 368, 370, 378

Nemean 7 (*N. 7*; *Seventh Nemean*) (Pindar) **12**:276, 288, 299-300, 309, 311, 319, 357-59, 361, 365, 367, 376, 378-79, 383

Nemean 8 (*Nem. VIII*) (Pindar) **12**:263, 269, 288, 309, 311, 323, 326, 357-59, 362, 365, 367, 371, 376, 379, 382-83

Nemean 9 (*N. 9*; *Ninth Nemean*) (Pindar) **12**:296, 307, 321, 353, 364-65, 370, 378, 382

Nemean 10 (*Tenth Nemean*) (Pindar) **12**:270, 274, 321, 348, 353, 355, 362, 365, 368-69

Nemean 11 (*Eleventh Nemean*) (Pindar) **12**:272, 315-16, 321, 365-67, 378

Nemean Odes (Pindar) **12**:353

Nephelai (*The Clouds*) (Aristophanes) **4**:37, 42, 44-5, 50, 53-4, 58-9, 61-7, 87, 89, 98, 100, 102, 105-06, 110-11, 124-26, 130-32, 137, 143-44, 146, 148, 150, 152-53, 159-60, 162-63, 165-66, 168

Nereïds (Aeschylus) **11**:125

Net Drawers (Aeschylus)
 See *Net-Draggers*

Net-Draggers (*Dictyluci*; *Net Drawers*) (Aeschylus) **11**:124, 152

New Kalevala
 See *Kalevala*

Nibelung Lay
 See *Book of Chaos*

Der Nibelunge Nôt
 See *Book of Chaos*

Nibelungen Lay
 See *Book of Chaos*

Nibelungen Noth
 See *Book of Chaos*

Nibelungen Song
 See *Book of Chaos*

Das Nibelungenlied **12**:136-255

Nibelungen's Need
 See *Book of Chaos*

"The Nightingale" (Marie de France)
 See "Laüstic"

Ninfale d'Ameto (Boccaccio)
 See *Ameto*

Ninfale fiesolano (Boccaccio) **13**:28, 32, 63

Ninth Nemean (Pindar)
 See *Nemean 9*

Ninth Paean (Pindar)
 See *Paean 9*

Ninth Pythian (Pindar)
 See *Pythian 9*

Niobe (Aeschylus) **11**:167, 193

Niobe (Sophocles) **2**:348

Njála
 See *Njáls saga*

Njáls saga (*Brennu-Njáls Saga*; *Njála*; *The Story of Burnt Njal*) **13**:322-77

"The Nobleman" (Eckhart) **9**:56-7

Nomothetes (Menander) **9**:203

'*Nostrorum*' (Abelard)
 See *Logica 'Nostrorum'*

Notes for Public Speaking (Hermogenes) **6**:158

"Notice of Hall of Thought" (Shih) **15**:399, 403

De notitia caelestium (Bacon) **14**:62

Nourishment (Albert the Great)
 See *De nutrimento et nutribili*

Novelle (Boccaccio) **13**:13, 15-6

Novelliere (Boccaccio) **13**:22

"Nur-Ed-Din and Shems-Ed-Din" **2**:42

De nutrimento et nutribili (*Nourishment*) (Albert the Great) **16**:61

O. 1 (Pindar)
 See *Olympian 1*

O. 7 (Pindar)
 See *Olympian 7*

O. 8 (Pindar)
 See *Olympian 8*

O. 9 (Pindar)
 See *Olympian 9*

O. 14 (Pindar)
 See *Olympian 14*

Octavia (Seneca) **6**:336, 342-43, 366, 374-75, 379-81, 389

"Ode to a Beloved Woman" (Sappho)
 See "Ode to Anactoria"

"Ode to Anactoria" ("Ode to a Beloved Woman"; "On Anactoria"; "Seizure") (Sappho) **3**:380, 386-87, 396, 416, 436

"Ode to Aphrodite" ("Aphrodite Ode"; "Hymn to Aphrodite"; "Ode to Venus") (Sappho) **3**:381, 385-86, 440

"Ode to Venus" (Sappho)
 See "Ode to Aphrodite"

Odysseis (Homer)
 See *Odyssey*

Odysses (Homer)
 See *Odyssey*

Odyssey (*Odysseis*; *Odysses*) (Homer) **1**:287, 293, 310, 312, 315-17, 319-20, 329, 338, 354, 362-63, 369-72, 375, 379, 388, 396-97, 400, 407-08

Oedipous epi Kolōnōi (*Oedipus at Colonos*; *Oedipus Coloneus*; *Oedipus in Colonos*) (Sophocles) **2**:289, 292, 296, 298, 300-01, 303-05, 312, 314-16, 318-19, 321, 325, 330, 335-36, 338-39, 342, 345-46, 349-52, 362-63, 367-70, 377, 388, 392, 398, 416-19, 421, 425-28

Oedipous Tyrannos (*King Oedipus*; *Oedipus*; *Oedipus Rex*; *Oedipus the King*) (Sophocles) **2**:288-89, 292, 296, 300, 304-05, 309-10, 312-16, 319-21, 324-24, 337-40, 343-45,347, 349-51, 353, 355-57, 359-62, 369-78, 382, 384, 387, 389-92, 394, 409-10, 415-21, 423-29

Oedipus (Aeschylus) **11**:122, 124, 138, 159-60

Oedipus (Seneca) **6**:343-44, 366, 369, 373, 379-81, 388-89, 413, 415, 417, 420-22, 428, 432

Oedipus (Sophocles)
 See *Oedipous Tyrannos*

Oedipus at Colonos (Sophocles)
 See *Oedipous epi Kolōnōi*

Oedipus Coloneus (Sophocles)
 See *Oedipous epi Kolōnōi*

Oedipus in Colonos (Sophocles)
 See *Oedipous epi Kolōnōi*

Oedipus Rex (Sophocles)
 See *Oedipous Tyrannos*

Oedipus the King (Sophocles)
 See *Oedipous Tyrannos*

"Oenone" (Ovid) **7**:311

Oetaeus (Seneca)
 See *Hercules oetaeus*

Of Natural and Moral Philosophy (Apuleius) **1**:12-13

Offices (Cicero)
 See *De officiis*

De officiis (*Duties*; *Offices*; *On Duties*) (Cicero) **3**:192-93, 196, 202-03, 214, 221, 228-29, 242, 245, 254-57, 288-89, 296-98

Ol. IX (Pindar)
 See *Olympian 9*

Ol. XI (Pindar)
 See *Olympian 11*

Old Cantankerous (Menander)
 See *Dyskolos*

Old Kalevala
 See *Kalevala*

"Old Love Is Best" (Sappho) **3**:396

"Olden Airs" (Li Po) **2**:178

Olympian 1 (*First Olympian*; *O. 1*; *Olympian Odes 1*) (Pindar) **12**:263, 269, 295, 298-99, 301, 304-05, 307, 309, 319, 322, 334, 349, 354, 363, 367, 371-72, 377-81, 383

Olympian 2 (*Second Olympian*) (Pindar) **12**:264, 271, 293, 298, 304, 319, 321, 351, 358, 363, 365, 367, 379, 383

Olympian 3 (*Third Olympian*) (Pindar) **12**:266, 312, 319, 353, 363, 368-69, 378, 383-84

Olympian 4 (Pindar) **12**:321, 354, 362-63, 365, 378, 380, 383

Olympian 5 (Pindar) **12**:321, 353, 363, 365, 370, 377-79, 382-83

Olympian 6 (*Sixth Olympian*) (Pindar) **12**:264, 267, 313, 353, 355, 364, 369, 378-84

Olympian 7 (*O. 7*; *Olympian VII*) (Pindar) **12**:264, 267, 296, 298, 308-09, 313, 320, 348, 353, 362, 369, 372, 374, 378, 380, 382-83

Olympian VII (Pindar)
 See *Olympian 7*

Olympian 8 (*Eighth Olympian*; *O. 8*) (Pindar) **12**:269, 289, 302, 326, 357, 359, 365, 369, 378-80, 382-83

Olympian 9 (*O. 9*; *Ol. IX*) (Pindar) **12**:289, 300, 352, 355, 365-66, 368, 370, 372, 378, 381-84

Olympian 10 (*Tenth Olympian*) (Pindar) **12**:272, 304, 309, 322, 352-53, 365-67, 378-79

Olympian 11 (*Eleventh Olympian*; *Ol. XI*) (Pindar) **12**:264, 344, 352-53, 380

Olympian 12 (*Twelfth Olympian*) (Pindar) **12**:309, 343

Olympian 13 (*Thirteenth Olympian*) (Pindar) **12**:304, 320, 322, 338, 348, 353, 355-56, 362, 378, 380, 383-84

Olympian 14 (*Fourteenth Olympian*; *O. 14*) (Pindar) **12**:294-95, 297, 301, 323, 325, 348, 352, 378, 383

Olympian Odes 1 (Pindar)
 See *Olympian 1*

Olynthiac I (*First Olynthiac*) (Demosthenes) **13**:145, 148-9, 166, 171, 197

Olynthiac II (*Second Olynthiac*) (Demosthenes) **13**:148, 151, 171, 180, 197

Olynthiac III (*Third Olynthiac*) (Demosthenes) **13**:144, 146, 148-9, 151, 165, 171

Olynthiacs (Demosthenes) **13**:138, 143, 149-51, 165, 169, 183, 189

"On a Picture Screen" (Li Po) **2**:136

"On Anactoria" (Sappho)
 See "Ode to Anactoria"

On Anger (Seneca)
 See *De ira*

On Animals (Albert the Great)
 See *De animalibus*

On Armaments (Demosthenes) **13**:158

On Christian Doctrine (Augustine)

See *De doctrina Christiana*
On Clemency (Seneca)
　See *De clementia*
On Consolation (Seneca)　6:344
On Divination (Cicero)
　See *De divinatione*
On Division (Boethius)
　See *Divisions*
On Duties (Cicero)
　See *De officiis*
On Forms (Hermogenes)
　See *On Types of Style*
On Free Will (Augustine)
　See *De libero arbitrio voluntatis*
On Friendship (Cicero)
　See *De amicitia*
On Gentleness (Seneca)　6:423
On Giving and Receiving Favours (Seneca)
　See *De beneficiis*
On Glory (Cicero)　3:177
On Good Deeds (Seneca)　6:427
On Grace and Free Will (Augustine)
　See *De gratia et libero arbitrio*
On Halonnesus (Demosthenes)　13:165
On His Consulship (Cicero)
　See *De consulatu suo*
On Ideas (Hermogenes)
　See *On Types of Style*
On Invention (Cicero)
　See *De inventione*
On Invention (*De inventione*) (Hermogenes)
　6:170-72, 185-86, 188, 191, 198-202
On Laws (Cicero)
　See *De legibus*
On Mercy (Seneca)
　See *De clementia*
On Method (Hermogenes)
　See *On the Method of Deinotēs*
On Misconduct of Ambassadors (Demosthenes)
　See *On the Misconduct of the Embassy*
"*On Nourishing Life*" (Shih)　15:401
On Old Age (Cicero)
　See *De senectute*
On Order (Augustine)
　See *De ordine*
On Peace of Mind (Seneca)
　See *De tranquillitate animi*
On Providence (Seneca)
　See *De providentia*
On Qualities of Style (Hermogenes)
　See *On Types of Style*
On Sleep and Waking (Albert the Great)
　16:16
On Staseis (Hermogenes)
　See *On Stases*
On Stases (*On Staseis*; *De statibus*)
　(Hermogenes)　6:158, 170-74, 185-86, 191,
　196, 198-202
"*On Taking Leave of Tzu-yu at Ying-chou:
　Two Poems*" (Shih)　15:411
On the Affairs in the Chersonese (Demosthenes)
　See *On the Chersonese*
On the Best Kind of Orators (Cicero)
　See *De optimo genere oratorum*
On the Blessed Life (Cicero)
　See *Tusculan Disputations*
On the Categoric Syllogism (Apuleius)　1:12-13
On the Categorical Syllogism (Boethius)　15:27
On the Catholic Faith (Boethius)
　See *De fide catholica*
*On the Causes and Properties of the Elements
　and of the Planets* (Albert the Great)

See *De causis et proprietatibus elementorum
　et planetarum*
On the Chersonese (*On the Affairs in the
　Chersonese*) (Demosthenes)　13:138, 146,
　148-9, 152, 161, 166, 193, 195
On the Chief Good and Evil (Cicero)
　See *De finibus*
On the Christian Struggle (Augustine)　6:21
On the City of God (Augustine)
　See *De civitate Dei*
On the Crown (*De Coruna*; *Crown Speech*)
　(Demosthenes)　13:139, 143, 145, 147-52,
　162, 166, 172-5, 179, 183-4, 189, 191-5, 197
On the Divine Unity and Trinity (Abelard)
　See *Theologia 'Summi boni'*
On the False Embassy (Demosthenes)
　See *On the Misconduct of the Embassy*
On the Fraudulent Embassy (Demosthenes)
　See *On the Misconduct of the Embassy*
On the Freedom of Rhodes (Demosthenes)
　See *For the Rhodians*
On the God of Socrates (Apuleius)　1:4, 7, 12-
　13, 23, 32
On the Greatest Degree of Good and Evil
　(Cicero)
　See *De finibus*
On the Happy Life (Seneca)
　See *De vita beata*
On the Hypothetical Syllogism (Boethius)
　15:9, 27,
On the Method of Deinotēs (*De methodo
　vehementiae*; *On Method*; *On the Method of
　Force*) (Hermogenes)　6:158, 188, 191, 202
On the Method of Force (Hermogenes)
　See *On the Method of Deinotēs*
On the Misconduct of the Embassy (*Embassy*;
　De Falsa Legatione; *On Misconduct of
　Ambassadors*; *On the False Embassy*; *On the
　Fraudulent Embassy*) (Demosthenes)
　13:138, 147-9, 165, 168, 172, 183-4, 189,
　194-5
On the Nature of Gods (Cicero)
　See *De natura deorum*
On the Nature of Good (Augustine)　6:9
On the Orator (Cicero)
　See *De oratore*
On the Pattern for Rhetorical Effectiveness
　(Hermogenes)　6:170
On the Peace (*The Peace*) (Demosthenes)
　13:138, 148-9, 159-60, 165
"*On the Red Cliff*" (Shih)
　See "*Rhymeprose on the Red Cliff*"
On the Reorganization (Demosthenes)　13:165
"*On the Restoration of the Examination
　System*" (Shih)　15:385
On the Rhodians (Demosthenes)
　See *For the Rhodians*
On the Science of Moral Habits (Avicenna)
　16:164
On the Shortness of Life (Seneca)
　See *De brevitate vitae*
On the Soul (Avicenna)　16:164
On the State (Cicero)
　See *De republica*
On the Symmories (*Symmories*) (Demosthenes)
　13:145, 148, 159, 163-4, 171, 197
On the Treaties with Alexander (Demosthenes)
　13:166
On the Trinity (Augustine)
　See *De Trinitate*
On the Trinity (Boethius)
　See *On the Trinity*

"*On the twelfth night*" (Shih)　15:398
On the Unity of the Intellect: against Averroes
　(Augustine)　16:57
On the Universe (Apuleius)
　See *De mundo*
On the Usefulness of Mathematics (Bacon)
　See *De utilitate mathematicae*
*On the Vices Contracted in the Study of
　Theology* (Bacon)　14:92
On Types of Style (*De ideis*; *On Forms*; *On
　Ideas*; *On Qualities of Style*) (Hermogenes)
　6:158, 170, 185-92, 196, 200-02, 204
Optics (Bacon)　14:20
De Optimo (Cicero)
　See *De optimo genere oratorum*
De optimo genere dicendi (*The Orator*; *Orator
　ad M. Brutum*; *The Orator: To Marcus
　Brutus*) (Cicero)　3:188, 193, 199, 201, 217-
　18, 259-63, 288
De optimo genere oratorum (*On the Best Kind
　of Orators*; *De Optimo*) (Cicero)　3:201, 261
Opus imperfectum contra Julianum (*Unfinished
　Work Against Julian*) (Augustine)　6:149
Opus Maius (Bacon)
　See *Opus Majus*
Opus Majus (*Longer Work*; *Opus Maius*)
　(Bacon)　14:3-5, 7-8, 15, 18, 20, 22-23, 29-
　31, 34-35, 37, 40, 42, 47, 49-50, 53-54, 59,
　61-65, 68-70, 73, 76-77, 80, 82, 84, 86, 92-
　94, 100, 102, 106-15
Opus Minus (Bacon)　14:15, 18-20, 29, 40, 48,
　52, 54, 62-63, 66-68, 80, 100, 102-03
Opus Sermonum (Eckhart)　9:57
Opus Tertium (Bacon)　14:15, 19-21, 29-30,
　40, 47-48, 52, 54, 58-59, 62-63, 65, 67-68,
　80, 83, 86, 100-05, 108
Opus Tripartitum (Eckhart)　9:55
The Orator (Cicero)
　See *De optimo genere dicendi*
Orator ad M. Brutum (Cicero)
　See *De optimo genere dicendi*
The Orator: To Marcus Brutus (Cicero)
　See *De optimo genere dicendi*
De oratore (*On the Orator*) (Cicero)　3:186,
　193, 200-01, 207-11, 217-18, 227, 246, 258-
　59, 261, 263, 270, 288
De ordine (*On Order*) (Augustine)　6:5, 102
Ordo Representacionis Ade (*Adam*; *Jeu
　d'Adam*; *Mystère d'Adam*; *Mystery of Adam*)
　4:182-221
Oresteia (Aeschylus)　11:77, 100-01, 105-06,
　109, 117-19, 123, 128, 130, 132-34, 136-40,
　153-56, 158-59, 160, 162-63, 167-68, 180,
　184, 190-91, 193-95, 197-99, 206, 209, 211,
　217-19, 222-23
Orestes (Aeschylus)　11:134
Orgē (*Anger*; *Bad Temper*) (Menander)　9:244,
　248, 250, 284
Ornithes (*The Birds*) (Aristophanes)　4:44-6,
　58, 62-7, 87, 93-6. 100. 110, 114, 124-26.
　131-33, 135, 142, 144, 146-49, 155, 159-61,
　165-66, 168
P. 1 (Pindar)
　See *Pythian 1*
P. 2 (Pindar)
　See *Pythian 2*
P. 3 (Pindar)
　See *Pythian 3*
P. 4 (Pindar)
　See *Pythian 4*
P. 5 (Pindar)
　See *Pythian 5*

Title Index

P. 6 (Pindar)
See *Pythian 6*

P. 8 (Pindar)
See *Pythian 8*

Paean 1 (Pindar) **12**:355

Paean 2 (*Paean for the Abderites*) (Pindar)
12:321, 351, 360-61

Paean 4 (Pindar) **12**:352, 382

Paean 5 (Pindar) **12**:359

Paean 6 (*Sixth Paean*) (Pindar) **12**:271, 300, 358-59

Paean 8 (Pindar) **12**:

Paean 9 (*Ninth Paean*) (Pindar) **12**:266, 308-09, 356

Paean for Ceos (Pindar) **12**:318

Paean for the Abderites (Pindar)
See *Paean 2*

Paeans (Pindar) **12**:318, 320-21, 352

"The Palace of the Grotto of Mists" (Sordello)
15:391

Paraphrase (Caedmon)
See "Genesis"

Paraphrase of Genesis (Caedmon)
See "Genesis"

A Parasite's Brain to the Rescue (Terence)
See *Phormio*

Parisian Questions and Prologues (Eckhart)
9:69

Parliament of Women (Aristophanes)
See *Ekklesiazousai*

Parmenides (Plato) **8**:232, 234, 240, 258-60, 264, 282, 293, 306, 310, 317, 320, 328, 333-34, 338, 340-41, 361, 364

Partheneia (*Songs for a Chorus of Maidens*)
(Pindar) **12**:320-21, 351, 356

"The Parting" (Li Po) **2**:138

"A Parting Banquet for the Collator Shu-yün at the Hsieh T'iao Lodge in Hsüan-chou"
(Li Po) **2**:163

Partiones oratoriae (*The Divisions of Oratory*;
Partitiones) (Cicero) **3**:201, 218, 259-60, 263

Partitiones (Cicero)
See *Partiones oratoriae*

Parzival (Wolfram von Eschenbach) **5**:293-94, 296-302, 304-05, 307-10, 312, 314-17, 320-23, 325-26, 333-45, 347, 350-54, 357-58, 360, 362, 366, 369-71, 373, 376, 380-83, 385-86, 390-92, 395-96, 400-01, 403-04, 409, 411, 416-17, 419-23, 425, 429-32

"Passing the Huai" (Shih) **15**:413

The Pastorals of Daphnis and Chloe (Longus)
See *Daphnis and Chloe*

"The Pavilion of Flying Cranes" (Shih)
15:382

"The Pavilion to Glad Rain" (Shih) **15**:382

Peace (Aristophanes)
See *Eirēnē*

The Peace (Demosthenes)
See *On the Peace*

"A Peasant and a Dung-Beetle" (Marie de France) **8**:174

"The Peasant Who Saw His Wife with Her Lover" (Marie de France) **8**:190

Pedeir Keinc y Mabinogi (*The Four Branches of the Mabinogi*; *The Mabinogion*) **9**:144-98

Penelope (Aeschylus) **11**:124

Perceval (*Conte du Graal*; *Li Contes del Graal*;
Gauvain; *Perceval le Gallois*; *Percevax le viel*;
The Story of the Grail) (Chretien de Troyes)
10:133, 137, 139, 143, 145-46, 150, 157, 159, 161-66, 169, 178-79, 183, 189-90, 195-96, 199, 206-09, 216-20, 223-26, 228-40

Perceval le Gallois (Chretien de Troyes)
See *Perceval*

Percevax le viel (Chretien de Troyes)
See *Perceval*

Peri hermeneias (Apuleius) **1**:24

Perikeiromenē (*The Girl Who Gets Her Hair Cut Short*; *The Girl with Shorn Hair*; *He Clips Her Hair*; *The Rape of the Locks*;
Shearing of Glycera; *Shorn Lady*; *The Short-Haired Lass*) (Menander) **9**:207, 210-11, 213, 215, 217, 221, 223, 225, 228, 230, 232, 238-39, 246-48, 250-52, 260, 267, 269-71, 276-77, 281, 288

Persae (Aeschylus)
See *Persians*

Persians (*Persae*) (Aeschylus) **11**:77, 85, 88, 96, 102, 112-13, 117-18, 121, 127, 133-35, 139, 151-53, 156, 158-60, 179, 181-84, 191, 193-95, 198, 200, 202-03, 205, 211, 215-20

Perspective (Bacon)
See *De Scientia Perspectiva*

Phaedo (Plato) **8**:204-07, 209, 233, 235-36, 239, 261, 268, 305-07, 312, 320, 322-25, 328, 331, 340-41, 358, 361-62

Phaedra (Seneca) **6**:341, 366, 368-70, 377, 379-81, 389, 403-06, 413-16, 418, 424-26, 432, 448

Phaedrus (Plato) **8**:205, 210, 220, 230, 232-33, 241, 244, 254-55, 259, 262, 264-66, 270, 275, 283, 299, 306-07, 317, 322-25, 331, 334, 355, 359, 362, 364

Philebus (Plato) **8**:248, 260, 264-68, 270, 306, 310, 333, 341, 361, 363-64

Philippic I (*First Philippic*) (Demosthenes)
13:137, 148-9, 152, 165, 171, 183, 190-2, 195, 197

Philippic II (*Second Philippic*) (Demosthenes)
13:138, 148-9, 151, 160, 165, 172

Philippic III (*Third Philippic*) (Demosthenes)
13:138, 143-5, 148, 161, 166, 172, 177, 180, 192-3, 195

Philippic IV (*Fourth Philippic*) (Demosthenes)
13:162, 166

Philippics (*First Philippic*; *Second Philippic*)
(Cicero) **3**:192-93, 196, 198-99, 229-30, 253, 268, 271-73

Philippics (Demosthenes) **13**:139, 142-3, 149-52, 158, 161-2, 172, 174, 180, 183, 189

Philoctetes (Aeschylus) **11**:125, 140

Philoctetes at Troy (Sophocles) **2**:341

Philoktētēs (Sophocles) **2**:289, 294-95, 302-05, 314, 316, 318, 320, 325, 338, 341, 346, 352-54, 357, 367-68, 377, 385-87, 397-408, 415-16, 419, 426

Philomena (Chretien de Troyes) **10**:137

Philosopher (Plato) **8**:259

Phineus (Aeschylus) **11**:159, 174

The Phoenician Women (Seneca)
See *Phoenissae*

Phoenissae (*The Phoenician Women*) (Seneca)
6:363, 366, 379-80, 402, 413, 421, 432, 437

"Phoenix Song" (Li Po) **2**:152

Phormio (*A Parasite's Brain to the Rescue*)
(Terence) **14**:303, 306-07, 311, 313-18, 320, 333, 335, 340, 341, 347-49, 352-53, 356-57, 364, 376-80, 383-85, 389-90

Phychostasia (Aeschylus)
See *Weighing of Souls*

"Phyllis" (Ovid) **7**:311

Physica (*Physics*) (Albert the Great) **16**:4, 36, 61

Physicorum (Albert the Great) **16**:

Physics (Albert the Great)
See *Physica*

The Pillow Book of Sei Shōnagon (Sei Shonagon)
See *Makura no sōshi*

Pillow Sketches (Sei Shonagon)
See *Makura no sōshi*

"Pine Wine of the Middle Mountains" (Shih)
15:382

"The Pious Black Slave" **2**:40

Planctus (Abelard) **11**:55, 68

"Planher vuelh en Blacatz" ("Dirge for Blacatz"; "Lament for Blacas"; "Lament for Lord Blacatz") (Sordello) **15**:332, 337, 343, 365, 375, 377

De Plantis (Albert the Great) **16**:18

Plants (Albert the Great)
See *De vegetabilibus*

De Platone et eius dogmate (Apuleius) **1**:24

Ploutos (*Plutus*; *Wealth*) (Aristophanes) **4**:44, 46, 62, 67, 76, 90, 94, 111, 115, 124-26, 147-48, 153, 161, 165-68, 174-75, 177-80

"The Plunder of the Home of Salur-Kazan"
("How Salur Kazan's House was Pillaged";
"The Story of the House of SalurKazan")
8:97, 103, 109

Plutus (Aristophanes)
See *Ploutos*

Poema de mio Cid (*Cantar de mio Cid*)
4:222-341

"Poignant Grief During a Sunny Spring" (Li Po) **2**:132

Politicus (Plato)
See *Politikos*

Politikos (*Politicus*; *Statesman*) (Plato) **8**:249, 258-60, 282, 306, 310, 333-34, 349, 359, 361

Polydectes (Aeschylus) **11**:124-25, 193

Pontius Glaucus (Cicero) **3**:198

"The Porter and the Ladies" **2**:47

Possessed Woman (Menander) **9**:211

Posteritati (Boccaccio) **13**:66

"Postscript to the Calligraphy of the Six T'ang Masters" (Shih) **15**:421

"Postscript to the Paintings of P'u Yung-sheng" (Shih) **15**:420

Practical Oratory (Hermogenes) **6**:204

De praedestinatione sanctorum (Augustine)
6:89

"The Pregnant Hound" (Marie de France)
8:190

Priestess (Menander) **9**:214

"Prince Ahmed and the Fairy Pari Banou"
2:36, 49

De principiis motus processivi (Albert the Great) **16**:61

Principles of Music (Boethius)
See *In topica Ciceronis*

Pro Archia (Cicero)
See *Archias*

Pro Balbo (Cicero) **3**:271

Pro Caecina (Cicero) **3**:214

Pro Caelio (*For Marcus Caelius*) (Cicero)
3:176, 197-99, 269-70

Pro Cluentio (*For Cluentius*) (Cicero) **3**:197-99, 214, 267-68

Pro Lege Manilia (*Manilian*) (Cicero)   **3**:198-99

Pro Ligario (Cicero)   **3**:272

Pro Marcello (Cicero)   **3**:198-99, 271-72

Pro Milone (Cicero)   **3**:198-99, 270-71

Pro Murena (Cicero)   **3**:198, 203

Pro Plancio (Cicero)   **3**:198

Pro Quinctio (*For Quinctius*) (Cicero)   **3**:264

Pro Roscio Amerino (*Rosciana*) (Cicero)   **3**:198, 265-66

Pro Roscio comoedo (Cicero)   **3**:265

Pro se de magia liber (Apuleius)
  See *Apologia sive oratoria de magia*

Pro Sestio (Cicero)   **3**:198, 269, 298

Processional Hymns (Pindar)
  See *Prosodia*

Los progres e avansaments dei Res d'Aragon (*History of the House of Aragon; The Progress and Power of the Kings of Arragon*) (Sordello)   **15**:330, 338, 344

The Progress and Power of the Kings of Arragon (Sordello)
  See *Los progres e avansaments dei Res d'Aragon*

Progymnasmata (*Elementary Exercises*) (Hermogenes)   **6**:162, 170, 185, 191, 198, 202

Prometheia (Aeschylus)
  See *Prometheus Bound*

Prometheus Bound (*Prometheia; Prometheus Vinctus*) (Aeschylus)   **11**:88, 98-9, 101-02, 105-06, 109-10, 113, 118-19, 123, 128-29, 135-37, 140, 143, 148, 151-55, 157, 166-67, 175, 179, 181, 183, 193-95, 197, 200, 208-09, 217, 219

Prometheus Delivered (Aeschylus)
  See *Prometheus Unbound*

Prometheus the Fire Bringer (Aeschylus)
  See *Prometheus the Firebearer*

Prometheus the Firebearer (*Prometheus the Fire Bringer*) (Aeschylus)   **11**:88, 159, 179

Prometheus the Firekindler (Aeschylus)   **11**:167, 175

Prometheus Unbound (*Prometheus Delivered*) (Aeschylus)   **11**:88, 90, 106, 123, 136, 175, 179

Prometheus Vinctus (Aeschylus)
  See *Prometheus Bound*

Properties of the Elements (Albert the Great)
  See *De causis et proprietatibus elementorum et planetarum*

Prosecution of Aristocrates (Demosthenes)
  See *Against Aristocrates*

Prosodia (*Processional Hymns*) (Pindar)   **12**:320-21

Proteus (Aeschylus)   **11**:162

Protogoras (Plato)   **8**:219, 232, 247-48, 253-54, 266-68, 283-84, 305-07, 310, 347

Proto-Kalevala
  See *Kalevala*

De provinciis consularibus (Cicero)   **3**:215, 271

Psalm 1   **4**:387, 390, 402, 417, 427, 434, 442, 450

Psalm 2   **4**:355, 357, 364-65, 368, 384, 447, 450

Psalm 3   **4**:359, 379, 386, 389, 432-33, 439, 446, 448

Psalm 4   **4**:364, 390, 426, 438, 448

Psalm 5   **4**:359, 383, 389, 390, 406, 438, 448

Psalm 6   **4**:359, 370, 373, 387, 390, 418, 432-33, 438, 448

Psalm 7   **4**:359, 426, 446, 448

Psalm 8   **4**:357, 361, 368, 373, 385, 390, 395-96, 398, 419, 434, 439, 441, 448, 453

Psalm 9   **4**:359, 364, 405, 432, 440, 450

Psalm 10   **4**:359, 364, 379, 450

Psalm 11   **4**:59, 364, 366, 389, 448

Psalm 12   **4**:426, 453, 455

Psalm 13   **4**:359, 432, 434, 448

Psalm 14   **4**:359, 364, 370, 378-79, 416, 426, 434

Psalm 15   **4**:357, 367-68, 377, 383, 450

Psalm 16   **4**:364, 368, 379, 434

Psalm 17   **4**:359, 364, 387, 391, 426, 448

Psalm 18   **4**:359, 364, 372, 382, 384, 388-89, 406, 443, 445-47, 449, 454

Psalm 19   **4**:345, 354, 359, 368, 380, 384, 388, 395, 397, 426, 441-42, 450

Psalm 20   **4**:345, 357, 365, 368, 373, 384, 388

Psalm 21   **4**:357, 359, 368, 384, 440

Psalm 22   **4**:359, 364-66, 368, 373, 382-83, 386-87, 389-90, 392, 419, 427, 434, 448, 450-51

Psalm 23   **4**:356, 377, 386, 389, 392, 417, 427, 434, 448

Psalm 24   **4**:345, 357, 373, 375, 378, 380, 383, 406-07, 450

Psalm 25   **4**:359, 390, 394, 402, 432, 449

Psalm 26   **4**:359, 364, 376, 378, 382, 387, 391, 406, 426, 448

Psalm 27   **4**:359, 373, 376, 378, 382, 389-90, 404-06, 432, 434, 441, 448

Psalm 28   **4**:359, 373, 383, 385, 407, 440

Psalm 29   **4**:345, 357, 368, 379-80, 384, 395, 401, 434, 439, 441

Psalm 30   **4**:359, 377, 394, 434, 455

Psalm 31   **4**:365, 402, 431-33

Psalm 32   **4**:359, 387, 390, 433-34

Psalm 33   **4**:359, 371, 381, 427, 434, 440-41, 446, 449

Psalm 34   **4**:346, 359, 381, 388, 426, 434, 449

Psalm 35   **4**:350, 359, 378, 382, 434

Psalm 36   **4**:359, 368, 427

Psalm 37   **4**:346, 359, 370, 382, 387, 402, 434

Psalm 38   **4**:383, 390, 392, 433, 448

Psalm 39   **4**:359, 433, 455

Psalm 40   **4**:381-82, 386, 389, 393, 433-34, 440, 449-50

Psalm 41   **4**:350, 359, 368, 439

Psalm 42   **4**:347, 368, 377-78, 380, 383, 386, 405, 407, 432, 451

Psalm 43   **4**:368, 377-78, 405, 440

Psalm 44   **4**:359, 381, 385, 387, 394, 413, 432

Psalm 45   **4**:357, 365, 368, 384, 440, 443, 450

Psalm 46   **4**:354, 385, 401

Psalm 47   **4**:345, 357, 381, 389, 405, 434, 438, 440

Psalm 48   **4**:357, 389, 407-08, 453

Psalm 49   **4**:359, 370, 434, 442

Psalm 50   **4**:357, 362, 364, 370, 384, 387, 395, 405, 434, 440

Psalm 51   **4**:364, 373, 375, 383, 385, 387, 406-07, 426-28, 431-32, 434, 446

Psalm 52   **4**:359, 446

Psalm 53   **4**:389

Psalm 54   **4**:446, 448, 450

Psalm 55   **4**:350, 448

Psalm 56   **4**:446, 450

Psalm 57   **4**:372, 405, 433, 441, 446, 448-49

Psalm 59   **4**:359, 446, 450

Psalm 60   **4**:359, 368, 381, 387, 446, 449

Psalm 61   **4**:357, 359, 368, 385, 442

Psalm 62   **4**:354, 359, 401

Psalm 63   **4**:359, 368, 378, 385, 405-06

Psalm 64   **4**:359

Psalm 65   **4**:359, 405, 407, 434

Psalm 66   **4**:359, 381-82, 387, 389, 406, 413, 434, 441, 450

Psalm 67   **4**:357

Psalm 68   **4**:357, 369, 372-73, 377, 395, 404, 406-08, 440-42, 450, 453

Psalm 69   **4**:351, 359, 365, 382, 386, 394, 427, 432-33, 441, 448, 450

Psalm 70   **4**:433, 449

Psalm 71   **4**:359

Psalm 72   **4**:345, 365, 373, 384, 421, 439

Psalm 73   **4**:347, 362, 364, 387, 389, 434

Psalm 74   **4**:381, 385, 432

Psalm 76   **4**:357, 362, 400-01

Psalm 77   **4**:354, 440

Psalm 78   **4**:362, 369, 393, 442, 447

Psalm 79   **4**:381, 385, 432, 434

Psalm 80   **4**:369, 381, 385

Psalm 81   **4**:395, 401, 405, 407, 434, 438, 440, 442

Psalm 82   **4**:370, 385

Psalm 83   **4**:385

Psalm 84   **4**:368, 378, 385, 405-06

Psalm 85   **4**:359, 385, 387, 450

Psalm 86   **4**:359, 389, 406, 434, 440

Psalm 87   **4**:357, 368, 373, 408

Psalm 88   **4**:359, 382-83, 386, 432-34, 437, 440, 443, 454

Psalm 89   **4**:368, 381, 384-85, 401, 447

Psalm 90   **4**:356, 368, 374, 377, 389, 411, 434, 440

Psalm 91   **4**:359, 368, 377, 434, 452

Psalm 92   **4**:377, 379

Psalm 93   **4**:353, 369, 409, 434, 450

Psalm 94   **4**:353, 359, 378-79, 381, 386, 391, 451

Psalm 95   **4**:380, 440, 442, 446

Psalm 96   **4**:357, 381, 389, 421, 434, 445, 449

Psalm 97   **4**:353, 387, 405, 434, 454

Psalm 98   **4**:381, 441

Psalm 99   **4**:357, 441

Psalm 100   **4**:380-81, 383, 434, 442

Psalm 101   **4**:357, 384

Psalm 102   **4**:373-74, 382, 440, 448, 450

Psalm 103   **4**:359, 364, 368, 377-78, 381, 385, 387, 390, 427, 434, 449

Psalm 104   **4**:368, 379, 381, 385, 387, 393, 395, 398, 414-16, 434, 441

Psalm 105   **4**:345, 353, 369, 381, 385, 401, 442, 445, 449

Psalm 106   **4**:345, 369, 383, 390, 401, 439, 445, 449

Psalm 107   **4**:345, 377, 383, 450, 453

Psalm 108   **4**:368, 449-50

Psalm 109   **4**:359, 386, 391, 434

Psalm 110   **4**:357, 365-66, 368, 384

Psalm 111   **4**:357, 449

Psalm 112   **4**:434, 449

Psalm 113   **4**:357, 369, 382, 434, 441

Psalm 114   **4**:345, 353, 357, 368, 427, 434

Psalm 115   **4**:359, 443, 449

Psalm 116   **4**:359, 382, 390, 408

Psalm 117   **4**:434

Psalm 118   **4**:345, 347, 359, 369, 377, 383, 406-08, 413, 439, 442, 450

Psalm 119   **4**:359, 367, 376, 390, 393-94, 428, 434, 442, 449-50

Psalm 120   **4**:350, 357, 368, 450, 455

Psalm 121   **4**:368, 373, 387, 418, 452

Psalm 122   **4**:345, 375, 395, 439, 447

Psalm 123   **4**:386

Psalm 124 4:434
Psalm 125 4:395
Psalm 126 4:345, 358, 379, 385, 387
Psalm 127 4:357, 373
Psalm 128 4:387
Psalm 129 4:353, 357, 382
Psalm 130 4:386, 434, 440
Psalm 131 4:359, 386, 434
Psalm 132 4:359, 368, 373, 384, 386, 406, 447
Psalm 133 4:356, 392, 428, 434
Psalm 134 4:368, 378, 380, 407, 450
Psalm 135 4:434, 439, 449-50
Psalm 136 4:352, 368, 383
Psalm 137 4:358, 393-94, 418, 422, 434, 446
Psalm 138 4:359, 382, 450
Psalm 139 4:359, 364, 366, 378-79, 393, 411, 437
Psalm 140 4:359
Psalm 142 4:359, 446
Psalm 143 4:434, 455
Psalm 144 4:374, 377, 384, 443, 447, 449
Psalm 145 4:359, 434, 449
Psalm 146 4:369, 391, 434
Psalm 147 4:391, 397, 434
Psalm 148 4:398, 434, 441
Psalm 149 4:372, 385, 391, 434, 440
Psalm 150 4:357, 369, 405, 421, 434, 438, 441, 443, 450
Psalm Book
   See *Tehillim*
Psalms
   See *Tehillim*
"*Psalms of David*"
   See *Tehillim*
Psalter
   See *Tehillim*
Psophodes (Menander) 9:203
Psychology (Avicenna) 16:166-68
Purgatory (Marie de France)
   See *L'Espurgatoire Saint Patrice*
The Purgatory of St. Patrick (Marie de France)
   See *L'Espurgatoire Saint Patrice*
Pyth. III (Pindar)
   See *Pythian 3*
Pyth. X (Pindar)
   See *Pythian 10*
Pyth XI (Pindar)
   See *Pythian 11*
Pythian 1 (*First Pythian*; *P. 1*) (Pindar) 12:260, 267, 273, 295-96, 298-99, 304-05, 309, 319, 323, 335, 338, 347, 349, 354, 356-57, 359, 361, 364, 366-67, 376, 378-80, 382-84
Pythian 2 (*P. 2*; *Second Pythian*) (Pindar) 12:269, 274, 298, 302, 306-07, 317, 319, 352, 355, 360, 364, 366, 378-81, 383-84
Pythian 3 (*P. 3*; *Pyth. III*; *Third Pythian*) (Pindar) 12:264, 270, 278, 298-99, 306, 313, 340, 346, 354, 364-65, 367, 369, 376, 378-80, 382-83
Pythian 4 (*Fourth Pythian*; *P. 4*) (Pindar) 12:272, 296, 298-99, 304-05, 312, 320-22, 326, 343, 354, 375-79, 382
Pythian 5 (*P. 5*) (Pindar) 12:271, 296-97, 307, 317, 320, 353, 357, 376-80, 382
Pythian 6 (*P. 6*; *Sixth Pythian*) (Pindar) 12:267, 273, 296, 319, 337, 353-54, 363-64, 377, 379
Pythian 7 (Pindar) 12:317, 325, 353, 359, 361-62, 383

Pythian 8 (*P. 8*) (Pindar) 12:272, 288, 297, 300, 304, 309, 314, 320, 323, 326, 337-38, 349, 356, 359-60, 362, 365, 378-80, 382-84
Pythian 9 (*Ninth Pythian*) (Pindar) 12:264, 283, 313, 320, 322, 356, 366, 368-69, 372
Pythian 10 (*Pyth. X*; *Pythian Odes 10*; *Tenth Pythian*) (Pindar) 12:263, 270, 303, 312-13, 318, 322, 325, 334, 337, 343, 357, 365-66, 371, 377-79, 383-84
Pythian 11 (*Eleventh Pythian*; *Pyth XI*) (Pindar) 12:263, 270, 274, 322, 326, 347, 352-53, 356, 365-66, 379, 382, 384
Pythian XII (Pindar)
   See *Pythian 12*
Pythian 12 (*Pythian XII*; *Twelfth Pythian*) (Pindar) 12:271, 319, 353, 363, 367
Pythian Odes 10 (Pindar)
   See *Pythian 10*
Quaestiones evangeliorum (Augustine) 6:68, 94
Quaestiones Naturales (Seneca)
   See *Naturales quaestiones*
Quaestiones super libros i-vi Physicorum Aristotelis (*Questions on Aristotle*; *Questions on Aristotle's Physics*) (Bacon) 14:49, 66
De quantitate animae (Augustine) 6:68
"*Quatre Dols*" (Marie de France)
   See "*Le Chaitivel*"
Questions on Aristotle (Bacon)
   See *Quaestiones super libros i-vi Physicorum Aristotelis*
Questions on Aristotle's Physics (Bacon)
   See *Quaestiones super libros i-vi Physicorum Aristotelis*
Raghuvaṃśa (*The Dynasty of Raghu*) (Kalidasa) 9:82, 84-5, 89-91, 102, 115, 118-19, 121, 125-26, 138
"*Raising a Cup of Wine to Query the Moon*" (Li Po) 2:166
"*The Rajah's Diamond*" 2:36
Ransom of Hector (Aeschylus) 11:125, 193
The Rape of the Locks (Menander)
   See *Perikeiromenē*
Razón de amor (*Razón de amor con los denuestos del agua y el vino*) 16:336-376
Razón de amor con los denuestos del agua y el vino
   See *Razón de amor*
Rbaiyyat (Khayyam)
   See *Rubáiyát*
"*Ready for a Drink*" (Li Po) 2:166
De Rebus Metallicis (Albert the Great) 16:18
"*The Red Cliff*" (Shih)
   See "*Rhymeprose on the Red Cliff*"
Rede der Unterscheidungen (*Collations*; *In Collation*) (Eckhart) 9:35, 42
Remedia Amoris (*Remedies of Love*) (Ovid) 7:344-46, 353, 377, 379, 398, 429, 440, 444
Remedia studii (Bacon) 14:62
Remedies of Love (Ovid)
   See *Remedia Amoris*
The Republic (Cicero)
   See *De republica*
Republic (Plato) 8:206, 211, 217, 219, 223, 225-28, 232-33, 236, 239, 241, 243-44, 246, 248-50, 252-53, 255, 259-61, 263-68, 270, 276-83, 285, 287, 290-92, 294, 299, 305-06, 308-11, 313, 317, 322, 324-25, 328-29, 331, 339-48, 352, 357-58, 363-64

De republica (*On the State*; *The Republic*; *State*) (Cicero) 3:177-78, 194, 200-01, 211-12, 214, 221, 225-26, 232, 244, 249-51, 254, 256-57, 285, 288, 296-98
De rerum generatione ex elementis (Bacon) 14:62
De Resurrectione (Albert the Great) 16:118, 125
Retractiones (Augustine) 6:9, 32, 116
"*Rhapsody of Remorse*" (Li Po) 2:169
Rhetorica (Cicero)
   See *De inventione*
"*Rhymeprose on the Red Cliff*" ("*On the Red Cliff*"; "*The Red Cliff*") (Shih) 15:382, 385, 398, 419, 421-24
Risālat al-Adwīyyah (Avicenna) 16:147
Rivals (Plato) 8:305, 311
"*Rock of Yen-yu*" (Shih) 15:387
Roman
   See *Le Roman de la Rose*
The Roman Calendar (Ovid)
   See *Fasti*
Le Roman de la Rose (*Roman*; *The Romance*; *The Romance of the Rose*; *Romanz de la Rose*; *Rose*) 8:374-453
The Romance
   See *Le Roman de la Rose*
The Romance of the Rose
   See *Le Roman de la Rose*
Romanz de la Rose
   See *Le Roman de la Rose*
Rood
   See *The Dream of the Rood*
Rosciana (Cicero)
   See *Pro Roscio Amerino*
Rose
   See *Le Roman de la Rose*
"*Rose in Bloom*" 2:23
Rtusaṃhāra (*The Seasons*) (Kalidasa) 9:89-90, 103-05, 107
Ruba'iyat (Khayyam)
   See *Rubáiyát*
Rubáiyát (*Rbaiyyat*; *Ruba'iyat*) (Khayyam) 11:228-309
Sacred Treatises (Boethius)
   See *Theological Tractates*
De Sacrificio Missae (Albert the Great) 16:42
"*Saif El-Mulûk*" 2:43
Sākuntala (Kalidasa)
   See *Abhijñāna-śakuntala*
Samia (*Connection by Marriage*; *The Girl from Samos*; *Kedeia*; *The Samian Woman*; *The Woman from Samos*) (Menander) 9:205-06, 211, 213, 215, 217, 220-21, 224, 238, 246, 249, 252-53, 255, 257-61, 264, 269-72, 275-78, 281, 287-88
The Samian Woman (Menander)
   See *Samia*
"*Satire Against Three Disinherited Lords*" (Sordello) 15:276
Satires (Juvenal) 8:7, 14, 19, 22, 27-8, 59-60, 66, 68-9, 73-8
"*Saying Farewell to the Children at Nanling as I Leave for the Capital*" (Li Po) 2:174
"*The Scavenger and the Noble Lady*" 2:40
Schionatulander (Wolfram von Eschenbach)
   See *Titurel*
De scientia experimentali (Bacon) 14:5, 80
De Scientia Perspectiva (*Perspective*) (Bacon) 14:20, 47
Scipio's Dream (Cicero)
   See *Somnium Scipionis*

Scite Teipsum (Abelard)
  See *Scito Te Ipsum*
Scito Te Ipsum (*Ethica seu Scito te ipsum;
  Ethics; Know Thyself; Scite Teipsum*)
  (Abelard)   **11**:5, 10, 12, 16, 20, 24, 49, 51,
  53, 54, 57, 68
Scripta Super Sententias (Albert the Great)
  See *Commentary on the Book of the
    Sentences*
Scriptum Principale (Bacon)   **14**:15
The Seasons (Kalidasa)
  See *Rtusaṃhāra*
Second Alcibiades (Plato)
  See *Alcibiades II*
Second Olympian (Pindar)
  See *Olympian 2*
Second Olynthiac (Demosthenes)
  See *Olynthiac II*
Second Philippic (Cicero)
  See *Philippics*
Second Philippic (Demosthenes)
  See *Philippic II*
Second Pythian (Pindar)
  See *Pythian 2*
"Seeing off Wei Wan, Recluse of Wang-wu
  Mountain, on His Trip Home" (Li Po)
  2:168
"Segrek Son of Ushun Koja"   **8**:103
Sei Shōnagon ga Makura-no-Sōshi (Sei
  Shonagon)
  See *Makura no sōshi*
Sei Shōnagon's Pillow Book (Sei Shonagon)
  See *Makura no sōshi*
"Seizure" (Sappho)
  See "Ode to Anactoria"
Self-Punishment (Terence)
  See *Heautontimoreumenos*
The Self-Tormentor (Terence)
  See *Heautontimoreumenos*
De senectute (*Cato maior; Cato the Elder: On
  Old Age; On Old Age*) (Cicero)   **3**:193, 195,
  202, 204, 227, 231, 288
"Senh' En Sordel mandamen" (Sordello)
  15:362
De sensu et sensato (Albert the Great)   **16**:61,
  106, 110
Sentences (Albert the Great)
  See *Commentary on the Book of the
    Sentences*
Septem (Aeschylus)
  See *Seven against Thebes*
Sermon on St. John the Baptist (Abelard)
  11:66
Seven against Thebes (*Septem; Seven before
  Thebes*) (Aeschylus)   **11**:77, 83-5, 88, 96,
  102-03, 107, 111, 113, 117, 119, 124, 127,
  133-35, 137-39, 142, 151-54, 156, 159, 167,
  173, 179, 181, 184, 194, 200, 205, 207, 217
Seven before Thebes (Aeschylus)
  See *Seven against Thebes*
Seventh Epistle (Plato)
  See *Seventh Letter*
Seventh Isthmian (Pindar)
  See *Isthmian 7*
Seventh Letter (*Seventh Epistle*) (Plato)   **8**:222,
  305-06, 334, 338-41, 349
Seventh Nemean (Pindar)
  See *Nemean 7*
The Sham Eunich (Terence)
  See *Eunuchus*
Shearing of Glycera (Menander)
  See *Perikeiromenē*

The Shield (Menander)
  See *Aspis*
Shield of Heracles (Hesiod)
  See *Shield of Herakles*
Shield of Herakles (*Shield of Heracles*)
  (Hesiod)   **5**:74, 82-83, 118, 174
Shorn Lady (Menander)
  See *Perikeiromenē*
Short Treatise in Praise of Dante (Boccaccio)
  See *Trattatello in lode di Dante*
The Short-Haired Lass (Menander)
  See *Perikeiromenē*
Shoulder Bite (Chretien de Troyes)   **10**:232
"Si co'l malaus ge no se sap gardar" (Sordello)
  15:363
Sic et Non (*Yes and No*) (Abelard)   **11**:4, 7, 9,
  10, 14, 16, 21, 24, 27, 31, 48, 66
The Sikyonian (Menander)
  See *Sikyonios*
Sikyonios (*The Man from Sikyon; The
  Sikyonian*) (Menander)   **9**:260, 269-70, 278,
  288
"Sinbad the Sailor"   **2**:1-3, 8, 19, 21, 27, 30,
  45, 55-6, 63, 72
De sinderesi (Albert the Great)   **16**:49
Sir Gawain and The Green Knight   **2**:181-287
Sisyphus (Aeschylus)   **11**:123
Sixth Isthmian (Pindar)
  See *Isthmian 6*
Sixth Nemean (Pindar)
  See *Nemean 6*
Sixth Olympian (Pindar)
  See *Olympian 6*
Sixth Paean (Pindar)
  See *Paean 6*
Sixth Pythian (Pindar)
  See *Pythian 6*
"Sleeper Awakened"   **2**:20
Slovo o polku Igoreve (*The Song of Ivor's
  Campaign; The Story of Igor's Campaign;
  The Tale of Igor's Campaign*)   **1**:477-530
Soliloquia (*Soliloquies*) (Augustine)   **6**:53, 62,
  68-9, 90, 126
Soliloquies (Augustine)
  See *Soliloquia*
Soliloquy (Abelard)   **11**:67
Somnium Scipionis (*Dream; Dream of Scipio;
  Scipio's Dream*) (Cicero)   **3**:181, 200, 211,
  289, 293-95
De somno et vigilia (Albert the Great)   **16**:7,
  61, 110
"Song Before Drinking" (Li Po)   **2**:140
"Song of Ch'ang-kan" (Li Po)   **2**:144
The Song of Ivor's Campaign
  See *Slovo o polku Igoreve*
"Song of Lu-shan" (Li Po)   **2**:144
"Song of Maldon"
  See "The Battle of Maldon"
The Song of Roland
  See *La Chanson de Roland*
"Song of the Cranes" (Shih)   **15**:382
"Song of the Heavenly Horse" (Li Po)   **2**:144-
  156
Song of the Lord
  See *Bhagavadgīta*
Song of the Lord
  See *Bhagavad Gītā*
"Song of the Roosting Crows" (Li Po)   **2**:140,
  157-58
"Song of the Stone Drums" (Shih)   **15**:410
Songs for a Chorus of Maidens (Pindar)
  See *Partheneia*

Songs for Dancing (Pindar)
  See *Hyporcemata*
"Songs of the Marches" (Li Po)   **2**:132
Sophist (Plato)   **8**:258-60, 282, 306, 309-10,
  321-22, 333-34, 338, 359, 361
Soul Conductors (Aeschylus)
  See *Spirit-Raisers*
"Sparrow Song" (Li Po)   **2**:138
Sphēkes (*The Wasps*) (Aristophanes)   **4**:44-5,
  62, 65, 67, 93-4, 110, 125-26, 130-31, 134,
  144, 149, 152, 154, 159, 162, 165-66
Sphinx (Aeschylus)   **11**:159
Spirit-Raisers (*Soul Conductors*) (Aeschylus)
  11:124
De Spiritu et Anima (Albert the Great)
  16:128
De spiritu et respiratione (Albert the Great)
  16:61
St. Patrick's Purgatory (Marie de France)
  See *L'Espurgatoire Saint Patrice*
State (Cicero)
  See *De republica*
"Statement of Resolutions after Being Drunk
  on a Spring Day" (Li Po)   **2**:132
Statesman (Plato)
  See *Politikos*
De statibus (Hermogenes)
  See *On Stases*
"The Story of Bamsi Beyrek"
  See "Bamsi-Beyrek"
"The Story of Basat Who Killed Depegöz"
  See "How Basat Killed Goggle-eye"
"The Story of Basat Who Kills the One-Eyed
  Giant"
  See "How Basat Killed Goggle-eye"
The Story of Burnt Njal
  See *Njáls saga*
Story of Calamities (Abelard)
  See *Historia Calamitatum*
"The Story of Deli Dumril"
  See "Wild Dumril Son of Dukha Koja"
"The Story of Emrem"   **8**:108
Story of His Misfortunes (Abelard)
  See *Historia Calamitatum*
The Story of Igor's Campaign
  See *Slovo o polku Igoreve*
"The Story of Kan Turali"
  See "Kan Turali Son of Kanli Koja"
"The Story of Ma'aruf"   **2**:39
"The Story of the Captivity of Salur Kazan"
  8:108
The Story of the Grail (Chretien de Troyes)
  See *Perceval*
"The Story of the House of SalurKazan"
  See "The Plunder of the Home of Salur-
    Kazan"
The Story of the Oghuzname--the Oghuz
  See *Kitabi-i Dedem Qorkut*
Summa de Bono (Albert the Great)   **16**:31
Summa de creaturis (Albert the Great)   **16**:26,
  31, 42, 86, 103, 107-08, 112
Summa de homine (Albert the Great)   **16**:31,
  112-13
"Summa Juris" (Sordello)   **15**:338
Summa Theologiae (Albert the Great)
  See *Summa Theologica*
Summa Theologica (*Summa Theologiae*)
  (Albert the Great)   **16**:7, 14, 16, 26, 28, 30,
  32, 36, 39, 42, 93-4, 104, 108-11, 121
Super Oratione Dominica (Eckhart)   **9**:42
The Superstitious Man (Menander)   **9**:214
Suppliant Maidens (Aeschylus)

See *Suppliants*
Suppliant Women (Aeschylus)
  See *Suppliants*
Suppliants (*Hiketides; Suppliant Maidens; Suppliant Women; Supplices*) (Aeschylus) **11**:88, 101-02, 108, 110-11, 116-18, 123, 127, 133-40, 148, 150, 152-53, 156, 158-60, 175, 178-79, 180-81, 183-84, 190-91, 193-95, 198, 201, 205, 207-09, 211, 216-17
Supplices (Aeschylus)
  See *Suppliants*
"The Swallow and the Other Birds" (Marie de France) **8**:174
Symmories (Demosthenes)
  See *On the Symmories*
Symposium (Plato) **8**:210, 234-35, 254-55, 259, 265-66, 270, 280, 283, 305-07, 310, 317, 330-31, 355-56, 358-59, 361, 363-69
Synaristosai (*Ladies Lunching Together, A Women's Lunch-Party*) (Menander) **9**:270
"The Szechwan Road" (Li Po) **2**:138
Tafsīr mā ba'd al-tabī'ah (*Long Commentary on the Metaphysics*) (Averroes) **7**:64-5, 67
Tahāfut (Averroes)
  See *Tahāfut al-tahāfut*
Tahāfut al-tahāfut (*Destructio destructionis philosophorum; Destructio Destructionum; Destruction of the Destruction; Tahāfut; Tahāfut at-tahāfut*) (Averroes) **7**:16, 21, 24-6, 30, 42, 68, 71
Tahāfut at-tahāfut (Averroes)
  See *Tahāfut al-tahāfut*
The Tale of Genji (Murasaki)
  See *Genji Monogatari*
The Tale of Igor's Campaign
  See *Slovo o polku Igoreve*
Talkhīs (Averroes) **7**:63-5
Talks of Instruction (Eckhart) **9**:56-7
Tao te Ching (*Book of Tao; Lao-tzŭ; Tao-teh ching; The Way and Its Nature*) (Lao Tzu) **7**:116-213
Tao-teh ching (Lao Tzu)
  See *Tao te Ching*
The Teachings of Honor (Sordello)
  See *Ensegnamen d'Onor*
Tehillim (*The Book of Psalms; Psalm Book; Psalms; "Psalms of David"; Psalter*) **4**:342-456
"Temple Inscription for Han Wen-kung at Ch'ao-chou" (Shih) **15**:399
De temporibus meis (Cicero) **3**:198
"The Temptation" (Caedmon) **7**;91
Tenth Nemean (Pindar)
  See *Nemean 10*
Tenth Olympian (Pindar)
  See *Olympian 10*
Tenth Pythian (Pindar)
  See *Pythian 10*
Tereus (Sophocles) **2**:348
De termino Paschali (Bacon) **14**:63
"The Terraced Road of the Two-Edged Sword Mountains" (Li Po) **2**:132
Teseida (Boccaccio) **13**:9, 29, 32-3, 44-5, 62, 65, 87, 102-14
Thais (Menander) **9**:237
Theaetetus (Plato) **8**:221-22, 254-55, 259, 264, 284, 306, 309-10, 321, 361
Theages (Plato) **8**:305, 311
Thebais (Seneca) **6**:339, 342-43

Theogony (*Descent of the Gods; Genesis of the Gods*) (Hesiod) **5**:70-5, 77-9, 83, 86-7, 92-6, 99-100, 102-05, 108-10, 113-18, 121-23, 128-30, 134-35, 137, 140-43, 145-50, 159-68, 170, 173-74
Theologia Christiana (Abelard)
  See *Christian Theology*
Theologia 'Scholiarum' (Abelard) **11**:53, 66
Theologia 'Summi boni' (*On the Divine Unity and Trinity; de Unitate et Trinitate Divina*) (Abelard) **11**:10, 24, 65, 66
Theological Tractates (*Sacred Treatises; Theological Treatises; Tractates*) (Boethius) **15**:24, 31-33
Theological Treatises (Boethius)
  See *Theological Tractates*
Theology (Abelard)
  See *Christian Theology*
"Thesaurus Thesaurum" (Sordello) **15**:329, 338, 377
Thesmophoriazusae (*Women at the Thesmophoria; Women Keeping the Festival of the Thesmophoria*) (Aristophanes) **4**:44, 60-63, 67-68, 94, 105-06, 110, 113, 116, 124-26, 130, 137, 145, 150, 152, 155, 161, 163, 175
Third Nemean (Pindar)
  See *Nemean 3*
Third Olympian (Pindar)
  See *Olympian 3*
Third Olynthiac (Demosthenes)
  See *Olynthiac III*
Third Philippic (Demosthenes)
  See *Philippic III*
Third Pythian (Pindar)
  See *Pythian 3*
Thirteenth Olympian (Pindar)
  See *Olympian 13*
The Thousand and One Nights
  See *Alf Layla wa-Layla*
Thracian Women (Aeschylus) **11**:125
"The Three Calenders, Sons of Kings, and the Five Ladies of Baghdad" **2**:16, 49, 51, 72
Threnoi (Pindar) **12**:320
Thyestes (Seneca) **6**:339-40, 342-43, 366, 368, 377-81, 389-91, 393, 400, 402-04, 406-10, 414-15, 418, 426, 428-29, 431-32, 441, 444-45
"T'ien Mountain Ascended in a Dream" (Li Po) **2**:144, 164, 166
Timaeus (Plato) **8**:209, 211, 222, 232, 241, 244, 255, 259-61, 265, 306, 310-11, 317-18, 320, 323, 325, 328, 332, 341, 349, 351-53, 361-63
Titurel (*Schionatulander*) (Wolfram von Eschenbach) **5**:301-02, 314, 317, 323, 325-26, 335, 359, 386, 390-91, 429-32
"To a Beautiful Woman on the Road" (Li Po) **2**:144
"To Li Yung" (Li Po) **2**:169
"To Wang Lun" (Li Po) **2**:143
"To Wei Liang-tsai, Prefect of Chiang-hsia— Written on My Exile to Yen-Lang by the Grace of the Emperor after the Uprising to Express Thoughts Arising from Memories of Past Travels" (Li Po) **2**:168
Topica (Cicero)
  See *Topica: To Gaius Trebatius*
Topica: To Gaius Trebatius (*Topica*) (Cicero) **3**:201, 259-60, 263
De topicis differentiis (*Topics*) (Boethius) **15**:7, 27, 29, 88, 129, 131, 136

Topics (Boethius)
  See *De topicis differentiis*
"The Tower of Tranquillity" (Shih) **15**:383
The Trachinian Women (Sophocles)
  See *The Trakhiniai*
Trachinians (Sophocles)
  See *The Trakhiniai*
The Trackers (Sophocles)
  See *Ichneutai*
Tractates (Boethius)
  See *Theological Tractates*
Tractatus de astronomia (Llull) **12**:103-10
Tractatus de Mulitiplicatione Specierum (*Multiplication of Species; De Multiplicatione Specierum*) (Bacon) **14**:20, 47, 62-63, 80
Tractatus de natura boni (Albert the Great) **16**:31, 66, 72-3, 75, 80
Tractatus expositorius enigmatus alchemiae (Bacon) **14**:63-64
Tractatus novus de astronomia (Llull) **12**:110
The Trakhiniai (*The Trachinian Women; Trachinians; The Women of Trachis*) (Sophocles) **2**:289, 294, 296, 300, 302, 315, 319-20, 322, 324, 338-39, 343-45, 349-51, 353, 358, 377, 379, 382, 415-16, 418-19, 422-23
De tranquillitate animi (*On Peace of Mind*) (Seneca) **6**:344, 382, 393
The Transformation of Lucius Apuleius Madeura (Apuleius)
  See *Asinus aureus*
The Transformation/Transformations (Ovid)
  See *Metamorphoses*
The Transformations (Apuleius)
  See *Metamorphoses*
Trattatello in lode di Dante (*Short Treatise in Praise of Dante*) (Boccaccio) **13**:51, 101
The Travels of Marco Polo the Venetian (*The Book of Marco Polo; Le Livre de Marco Polo; Marco Polo; Marco Polo's Travels*) (Polo) **15**:251-320
Tree of Science (Llull)
  See *Arbor scientiae*
The Tree of the Philosophy of Love (*El arbre de filosofia d'amor*) (Llull) **12**:122, 131-32
"Le –Tresor" (Sordello) **15**:339
De Trinitate (*On the Trinity*) (Augustine) **6**:21, 27, 62, 68, 70, 77, 85-7, 90-1, 116, 119-21, 138-40
De trinitate (Boethius) **15**:31-2, 43, 56, 59, 79, 86, 95, 125-30, 136, 141
Tristan (Chretien de Troyes)
  See *King Mark and Iseut the Fair*
Tristan and Iseult
  See *Tristan und Isolde*
Tristan and Isolde
  See *Tristan und Isolde*
Tristan und Isolde (*Tristan and Iseult; Tristan and Isolde; Tristan und Isolt*) (Gottfried von Strassburg) **10**:247-48, 250, 254-60, 263-64, 267-68, 274-79, 282-83, 298, 300-01, 303-06
Tristan und Isolt
  See *Tristan und Isolde*
Tristia (*Elegies; Elegies of Gloom; Tristibus*) (Ovid) **7**:291, 293-94, 300, 306, 320-23, 332, 341, 343, 346-47, 349, 376-78, 392, 398, 426, 430, 435, 446
Tristibus (Ovid)
  See *Tristia*
Troades (*Troas; The Trojan Women*) (Seneca) **6**:340, 342-43, 363, 366-70, 375-80, 389, 413, 415, 425, 428-29, 431-32

Troas (Seneca)
  See *Troades*
The Trojan Women (Seneca)
  See *Troades*
Tusculan Disputations (*On the Blessed Life*;
  Tusculans) (Cicero) **3**:177, 183, 193, 196,
  202, 211, 242, 255, 274, 287
Tusculans (Cicero)
  See *Tusculan Disputations*
Twelfth Olympian (Pindar)
  See *Olympian 12*
Twelfth Pythian (Pindar)
  See *Pythian 12*
"The Two Jealous Sisters" **2**:45
"The Two Lovers" (Marie de France)
  See "Les Dous Amanz"
"The Two Wolves" (Marie de France) **8**:192
The Unbridled Mule (Chretien de Troyes)
  See *La Mule sans frein*
Unfinished Work Against Julian (Augustine)
  See *Opus imperfectum contra Julianum*
"The Unfortunate One" (Marie de France)
  See "Le Chaitivel"
de Unitate et Trinitate Divina (Abelard)
  See *Theologia 'Summi boni'*
"Upon His Returning Home to Pei-hai, I
  Respectfully Offer a Farewell Banquet to
  Reverend Master Kao Ju-Kuei, Gentleman
  of the Tao after He Transmitted to Me a
  Register of the Way" (Li Po) **2**:177
Urvaśī Won by Valor (Kalidasa)
  See *Vikramorvaśīya*
De utilitate grammaticae (Bacon) **14**:46, 64
De utilitate mathematicae (*On the Usefulness of
  Mathematics*) (Bacon) **14**:5
Uusi Kalevala
  See *Kalevala*
Valiant Woman (Albert the Great) **16**:29
Vanha Kalevala
  See *Kalevala*
De vegetabilibus (*Plants*) (Albert the Great)
  16:20, 36-7, 61, 64
De vera religione (Augustine) **6**:68
Verrines (Cicero) **3**:196-99, 202, 267, 268, 286
Vikramorvaśīya (*Urvaśī Won by Valor*)
  (Kalidasa) **9**:82, 86-8, 90-1, 96-7, 99-100,
  102, 125, 131-34, 136-39
"Visit to Gold Mountain Temple" (Shih)
  15:410
Vita (*Life*) (Josephus) **13**:217, 220, 222, 235,
  239, 249, 253, 255, 263, 265, 268, 270-2,
  302, 305, 307-8, 311, 316-8
Vita di Dante (*Life of Dante*) (Boccaccio)
  13:53-4
De vulgari eloquentia (Boccaccio) **13**:65
"Waking from Drunkenness on a Spring Day"
  (Li Po) **2**:141
War (Josephus)
  See *Bellum Judaicum*
Wars of the Jews (Josephus)
  See *Bellum Judaicum*
The Wasps (Aristophanes)
  See *Sphēkes*
The Way and Its Nature (Lao Tzu)
  See *Tao te Ching*
Wealth (Aristophanes)
  See *Ploutos*
Weighing of Souls (*Phychostasia*) (Aeschylus)
  11:123-24, 193
"The Werewolf" (Marie de France)
  See "Bisclavret"

"Wild Dumril Son of Dukha Koja" ("The
  Story of Deli Dumril") **8**:104, 108-09
Willehalm (*Willehalm von Oranse*) (Wolfram
  von Eschenbach) **5**:293, 296, 298-302, 309-
  14, 317, 322-23, 326, 335-37, 343, 350-53,
  357-62, 366, 373, 383, 386, 396-97, 399-400,
  420, 429, 431
Willehalm von Oranse (Wolfram von
  Eschenbach)
  See *Willehalm*
William of England (Chretien de Troyes)
  See *Guillaume d'Angleterre*
"Wine Will Be Served" (Li Po) **2**:143
"The Wisdom of Dede Korkut" **8**:103, 107
"A Wolf and a Dung-Beetle" ("A Dung-
  Beetle") (Marie de France) **8**:174-75
"The Wolf and the Kid" (Marie de France)
  8:193
"The Wolf and the Sow" (Marie de France)
  8:190
"A Wolf as King of the Beasts" (Marie de
  France) **8**:175
"A Woman and Her Hen" (Marie de France)
  8:171
The Woman from Andros (Terence)
  See *Andria*
The Woman from Samos (Menander)
  See *Samia*
Woman of Leucas (Menander) **9**:211
Woman of Thessaly (Menander) **9**:214
Women at the Thesmophoria (Aristophanes)
  See *Thesmophoriazusae*
Women in Assembly (Aristophanes)
  See *Ekklesiazousai*
Women in Parliament (Aristophanes)
  See *Ekklesiazousai*
*Women Keeping the Festival of the
  Thesmophoria* (Aristophanes)
  See *Thesmophoriazusae*
Women of Salamis (Aeschylus) **11**:125
The Women of Trachis (Sophocles)
  See *The Trakhiniai*
The Women's Assembly (Aristophanes)
  See *Ekklesiazousai*
A Women's Lunch-Party (Menander)
  See *Synaristosai*
Works (Hesiod)
  See *Works and Days*
Works and Days (*Erga*; *Works*) (Hesiod)
  5:70, 72-4, 75-7, 79-84, 86-101, 103-05, 108,
  110-11, 114-16, 121-27, 129-51, 153, 156,
  160-63, 167-68, 170-74
"The Wretched One" (Marie de France)
  See "Le Chaitivel"
"The Wrong Box" **2**:36
Xantriae (Aeschylus) **11**:124
"Yearning" (Li Po) **2**:159-60
Yes and No (Abelard)
  See *Sic et Non*
"Yigenek Son of Kazilak Koja" **8**:104
"Yonec" (Marie de France) **8**:114, 116-17,
  121-23, 127-28, 131, 134, 139-40, 142, 144-
  45, 147, 149, 154, 161-65, 170, 181
"The Young King of the Black Isles" **2**:72
"The Young Man from Baghdad" **2**:43
Yvain (*Le Chevalier au Lion*; *The Knight with
  the Lion*) (Chretien de Troyes) **10**:131, 133-
  34, 136, 138-39, 141, 143-47, 149, 157, 159-
  69, 171, 173, 182-90, 194-97, 199, 206, 208,
  210, 215-16, 218-21, 223, 225-26, 229-32,
  234-35, 237-39

Title Index

CMLC Cumulative Critic Index

Abe Akio
Sei Shōnagon **6**:299

Abusch, Tzvi
Epic of Gilgamesh **3**:365

Adams, Charles Darwin
Demoshenes **13**:148

Adams, Henry
The Song of Roland **1**:166

Addison, Joseph
Aeneid **9**:310
Iliad **1**:282
Ovid **7**:292
Sappho **3**:379
Sophocles **2**:293

Adler, Mortimer J.
Plato **8**:342

Adlington, William
Apuleius **1**:6

Aiken, Conrad
Murasaki, Lady **1**:423

Albert, S.M.
Albert the Great **16**:33

Alighieri, Dante
Aeneid **9**:297
Bertran de Born **5**:4
Seneca, Lucius Annaeus **6**:331
Sordello **15**:323

Ali-Shah, Omar

Khayyám **11**:288

Allen, Archibald W.
Livy **11**:334

Allen, Richard F.
Njáls saga **13**:358

Allinson, Francis G.
Menander **9**:204

Allison, Rev. William T.
The Book of Psalms **4**:371

Al-Nadīm
Arabian Nights **2**:3

Alphonso-Karkala, John B.
Kalevala **6**:259

Alter, Robert
The Book of Psalms **4**:451

Ambivius, Lucius
Terence **14**:302

Amis, Kingsley
Beowulf **1**:112

Anacker, Robert
Chrétien de Troyes **10**:144

Anderson, George K.
Beowulf **1**:98
The Dream of the Rood **14**:245

Anderson, William S.
Juvenal **8**:59

Andersson, Theodore M.
Hrafnkel's Saga **2**:103

Apuleius, Lucius
Apuleius **1**:3

Aquinas, St. Thomas
Augustine, St. **6**:5
Averroës **7**:3
Plato **8**:217

Arendt, Hannah
Augustine, St. **6**:116

Aristophanes
Aeschylus **11**:73

Aristotle
Aeschylus **11**:73
Hesiod **5**:69
Iliad **1**:273
Plato **8**:202
Sophocles **2**:291

Arnold, E. Vernon
Seneca, Lucius Annaeus **6**:362

Arnold, Edwin
Hesiod **5**:71
Iliad **1**:308
Odyssey **16**:208
Sappho **3**:384

Arnold, Mary
Poem of the Cid **4**:226

Arnold, Matthew
Aeneid **9**:316

Aristophanes **4**:54
Iliad **1**:300
Mabinogion **9**:146
The Song of Roland **1**:162
Sophocles **2**:311

Arnott, Geoffrey
Menander **9**:261

Arnott, W. G.
Menander **9**:253

Arnstein, Adolf
Meister Eckhart **9**:4

Arrowsmith, William
Aristophanes **4**:131

'Arùdì, Nizàmì-i-
Avicenna **16**:147

Ascham, Roger
Cicero, Marcus Tullius **3**:186

Ashe, Geoffrey
Arthurian Legend **10**:2

Asquith, Herbert Henry
Demosthenes **13**:135

Aston, W. G.
Murasaki, Lady **1**:416
Sei Sh nagon **6**:291

Athanasius
The Book of Psalms **4**:344

Atkins, J. W. H.

Aristophanes **4**:104

Atkinson, James C.
Mystery of Adam **4**:207

Auden, W. H.
Iliad **1**:347
Njáls saga **13**:330

Auerbach, Erich
Augustine, St. **6**:79
Inferno **3**:72, 95
Mystery of Adam **4**:193
Odyssey **16**:221
Poem of the Cid **4**:251

Augustine, St.
Apuleius **1**:4
Augustine, St. **6**:4
Cicero, Marcus Tullius **3**:177
Plato **8**:208
Seneca, Lucius Annaeus **6**:330

Aurobindo, Sri
Bhagavad G t **12**:32

Austerlitz, Robert
Kalevala **6**:255

Averroës
Plato **8**:212

Avery, Peter
Khayyám **11**:297

Ayscough, Florence
Li Po **2**:132

Bachofen, J. J.
Aeschylus **11**:92
Sappho **3**:382

Bacon, Francis
Plato **8**:219

Bagley, F. R. C.
Khayyám **11**:283

Baker, Donald C.
Beowulf **1**:154

Baldwin, Charles Sears
Sir Gawain and the Green Knight **2**:186

Banks, Mary Macleod
Morte Arthure **10**:377

Barber, Richard
Sir Gawain and the Green Knight **2**:215

Barbi, Michele
Inferno **3**:87

Barfield, Owen
Bhagavad Gītā **12**:71
The Book of Psalms **4**:392

Bargen, Doris G.
Murasaki, Lady **1**:467

Baricelli, Jean-Pierre

Kalevala **6**:280

Barker, E. Phillips
Seneca, Lucius Annaeus **6**:375

Barney, Stephen A.
Romance of the Rose **8**:435

Barnstone, Willis
Llull, Ramon **12**:126
Sappho **3**:435

Barolini, Teodolinda
Sordello **15**:368

Barr, William
Juvenal **8**:86

Barron, W. R. J.
Layamon **10**:360
Sir Gawain and the Green Knight **2**:261

Barth, John
Arabian Nights **2**:43

Başgöz, Ilhan
Book of Dede Korkut **8**:108

Basore, John W.
Seneca, Lucius Annaeus **6**:374

Bassett, Samuel Eliot
Iliad **1**:329
Odyssey **16**:214

Bates, William Nickerson
Sophocles **2**:336

Batts, Michael S.
Gottfried von Strassburg **10**:293
Hartmann von Aue **15**:183

Bayerschmidt, Carl F.
Njáls saga **13**:326
Wolfram von Eschenbach **5**:311

Beare, W.
Terence **14**:343

Bede
Cædmon **7**:77

Bell, Aubrey F. G.
Poem of the Cid **4**:251

Bennett, James O'Donnell
Arabian Nights **2**:27

Benson, Eugene
Sordello **15**:33

Benson, Larry D.
Morte Arthure **10**:386
Sir Gawain and the Green Knight **2**:227

Bentwich, Norman
Josephus, Flavius **13**:199

Bergin, Thomas G.
Boccaccio, Giovanni **13**:74

Berkeley, George

Plato **8**:221

Berry, Francis
Sir Gawain and the Green Knight **2**:194

Berthoud, J. A.
Inferno **3**:116

Bespaloff, Rachel
Iliad **1**:343

Besserman, Lawrence
Sir Gawain and the Green Knight **2**:280

Bettelheim, Bruno
Arabian Nights **2**:53

Beye, Charles Rowan
Hesiod **5**:131

Bilde, Per
Josephus, Flavius **13**:302

Billson, Charles J.
Kalevala **6**:233

Bittinger, J. B.
The Book of Psalms **4**:363

Bixby, James T.
Kalevala **6**:217
Lao Tzu **7**:118

Blair, Hugh
Iliad **1**:289
Sophocles **2**:296

Blamires, David
Wolfram von Eschenbach **5**:342

Bloch, R. Howard
The Song of Roland **1**:240

Blomfield, Joan
Beowulf **1**:85

Blondel, Maurice
Augustine, St. **6**:28

Bloomfield, Morton W.
Sir Gawain and the Green Knight **2**:214

Blow, Susan E.
Inferno **3**:42

Bluestine, Carolyn
Poem of the Cid **4**:309

Boatner, Janet W.
The Song of Roland **1**:211

Boccaccio, Giovanni
Boccaccio, Giovanni **13**:3, 17
Inferno **3**:4

Bollard, J. K.
Mabinogion **9**:176

Bolton, W. F.
Hrafnkel's Saga **2**:106

Plato **8**:221

Bonjour, Adrien
Beowulf **1**:105

Bonnard, André
Sappho **3**:424

Bonner, Anthony
Llull, Ramon **12**:133

Boren, James L.
Morte Arthure **10**:415

Borges, Jorge Luis
Anglo-Saxon Chronicle **4**:21
Arabian Nights **2**:29, 37, 67
Inferno **3**:141
Layamon **10**:327

Bosley, Keith
Kalevala **6**:283

Bostock, J. Knight
Hartmann von Aue **15**:163

Botta, Anne C. Lynch
Arabian Nights **2**:8
Cicero, Marcus Tullius **3**:192

Bowra, C. M.
Aeneid **9**:358
Aeschylus **11**:178
Aristophanes **4**:140
Epic of Gilgamesh **3**:313
Iliad **1**:321
Pindar **12**:323
Poem of the Cid **4**:259
Sappho **3**:398, 399
Sophocles **2**:342

Bowring, Richard
Murasaki, Lady **1**:457

Braddock, Joseph
Sappho **3**:438

Braden, Gordon
Seneca, Lucius Annaeus **6**:399

Branca, Vittore
Boccaccio, Giovanni **13**:62

Bowra, C.M.
Odyssey **16**:292
Sordello **15**:353

Branch, M. A.
Kalevala **6**:267

Brandes, Georg
The Igor Tale **1**:478
Iliad **1**:317

Brandon, S. G. F.
Epic of Gilgamesh **3**:314

Brault, Gerard J.
The Song of Roland **1**:256

Braun, Richard E.
Juvenal **8**:67

Brennan, Gerald

Poem of the Cid 4:256

Brewer, Derek
Sir Gawain and the Green Knight
2:241, 270

Brewer, J. S.
Bacon, Roger 14:6

Bridges, John Henry
Bacon, Roger 14:14

Briscoe, J.
Livy 11:375

Brodeur, Arthur Gilchrist
Beowulf 1:112

Bromwich, Rachel
Arthurian Legend 10:49
Mabinogion 9:171

Brooke, Christopher
Abelard 11:28

Brooke, Stopford A.
Beowulf 1:63
The Dream of the Rood 14:216

Broshi, Magen
Josephus, Flavius 13:271

Brothers, A. J.
Terence 14:385

Brown, Norman O.
Hesiod 5:109

Brown, Peter
Augustine, St. 6:100

Browning, Robert
Aristophanes 4:55

Bruce, James Douglas
Arthurian Legend 10:120

Brueggemann, Walter
The Book of Psalms 4:434

Bryant, Nigel
Chrétien de Troyes 10:216

Bryant, William Cullen
Iliad 1:306

Brzezinski, Monica
The Dream of the Rood 14:288

Buber, Martin
The Book of Job 14:206
The Book of Psalms 4:401

Buck, Philo M., Jr.
Aristophanes 4:86
Inferno 3:83
Mahābhārata 5:220

Burn, Andrew Robert
Sappho 3:430

Burnett, Anne Pippin
Pindar 12:377

Sappho 3:481

Burrow, J. A.
The Dream of the Rood 14:238
Sir Gawain and the Green Knight
2:235, 277

Burshatin, Israel
Poem of the Cid 4:329

Burton, Richard F.
Arabian Nights 2:13, 15

Bussanich, John
Hesiod 5:163

Butler, Samuel
Iliad 1:311
Odyssey 16:200, 221

Butterworth, Charles E.
Avicenna 16:163

Byron, Lord
Aeneid 9:385

Cadell, Jessie E.
Khayyám 11:243

Caesar, Julius
Terence 14:326

Cairns, Huntington
Cicero, Marcus Tullius 3:237

Calin, William C.
Mystery of Adam 4:200

Calvin, John
The Book of Job 14:118
The Book of Psalms 4:349
Seneca, Lucius Annaeus 6:332

Campbell, Joseph
Arabian Nights 2:39
Epic of Gilgamesh 3:319
Mah bh rata 5:238

Campbell, Lewis
Aeschylus 11:108
Sophocles 2:313

Campbell, Mary B.
Polo, Marco 15:311

Cantarino, Vicente
Averroës 7:47

Canter, H. V.
Livy 11:321

Canuteson, John
The Dream of the Rood 14:276

Carlyle, John A.
Inferno 3:19

Carlyle, Thomas
Inferno 3:12
Nibelungenlied, Das 12:138

Carne-Ross, D. S.
Pindar 12:367

Cassell, Anthony K.
Boccaccio, Giovanni 13:94
Inferno 3:151

Cassirer, Ernst
Augustine, St. 6:52, 77

Cather, Willa
Sappho 3:388

Catullus, Gaius Valerius
Cicero, Marcus Tullius 3:174

Cawley, Frank Stanton
Hrafnkel's Saga 2:83

Caxton, William
Arthurian Legend 10:27

Chadwick, Henry
Boethius 15:53, 58

Chambers, E. K.
Mystery of Adam 4:184

Chambers, R. W.
Beowulf 1:74

Chandler, Richard E.
Poem of the Cid 4:266

Chapman, George
Iliad 1:276
Odyssey 16:184

Charlesworth, Martin Percival
Josephus, Flavius 13:220

Chateaubriand, Viscount de
Augustine, St. 6:11
Inferno 3:7

Chaucer, Geoffrey
Inferno 3:5

Chaytor, H. J.
Bertran de Born 5:21
Sordello 15:332

Chen, Ellen Marie
Lao Tzu 7:176

Chen, Yu-Shih
Su Shih 15:417

Ch'ên Shou-yi
Li Po 2:142

Cherniss, Michael D.
Romance of the Rose 8:431

Chesterton, G. K.
Arabian Nights 2:18
The Book of Job 14:188
The Song of Roland 1:174

Chrétien de Troyes
Chrétien de Troyes 10:131, 141, 160

Christine de Pizan
Romance of the Rose 8:376

Christoph, Siegfried Richard

Wolfram von Eschenbach 5:386,
409

Chuangtse
Lao Tzu 7:117

Cicero
Plato 8:205
Terence 14:305

Čiževskij, Dmitrij
The Igor Tale 1:501

Clark, Cyril Drummond Le Gros
Su Shih 15:381, 15:385

Clark, Donald Lemen
Hermogenes 6:161

Clark, James M.
Meister Eckhart 9:45, 54

Clark, John
Poem of the Cid 4:230

Clark, S. L.
Hartmann von Aue 15:228

Clarke, H. Butler
Poem of the Cid 4:229

Clarke, Howard W.
Odyssey 16:279

Clifton-Everest, J. M.
Hartmann von Aue 15:202

Cline, Ruth Harwood
Chrétien de Troyes 10:195

Closs, August
Gottfried von Strassburg 10:255

Cohen, Shaye J. D.
Josephus, Flavius 13:263, 273

Col, Pierre
Romance of the Rose 8:380

Coleridge, H. N.
Hesiod 5:70

Coleridge, Samuel Taylor
Arabian Nights 2:4
Aristophanes 4:47
Inferno 3:10
Pindar 12:260
Poem of the Cid 4:224

Colish, Marcia L.
Augustine, St. 6:123

Colledge, Edmund
Meister Eckhart 9:68

Collinder, Björn
Kalevala 6:247

Collins, Christopher
Longus 7:251

Colum, Padraic
Arabian Nights 2:26

Critic Index

Mabinogion 9:165

Comfort, W. W.
Chrétien de Troyes 10:137

Comparetti, Domenico
Kalevala 6:219

Conant, Martha Pike
Arabian Nights 2:20

Condren, Edward I.
Hrafnkel's Saga 2:112

Congreve, William
Pindar 12:259

Conybeare, John Josias
Beowulf 1:55

Cook, Albert
Ovid 7:412
Poem of the Cid 4:270
Sophocles 2:404

Cook, Charles W.
Epic of Gilgamesh 3:352

Cook, Robert G.
Chrétien de Troyes 10:183

Cooper, Arthur
Li Po 2:145

Copleston, Frederick C.
Abelard 11:14
Averroës 7:16

Copleston, Reginald S.
Aeschylus 11:95

Copley, Frank O.
Livy 11:363
Terence 14:349

Corcoran, Thomas H.
Seneca, Lucius Annaeus 6:436

Cornford, Francis Macdonald
Aristophanes 4:78
Plato 8:272

Cornwallis, William
Seneca, Lucius Annaeus 6:334

Cosman, Madeleine Pelner
Gottfried von Strassburg 10:292

Costa, C. D. N.
Seneca, Lucius Annaeus 6:413

Courthope, W. J.
Beowulf 1:59

Courtney, W. L.
Sappho 3:394

Cowell, Edward Byles
Khayyám 11:230

Cowley, Abraham
The Book of Psalms 4:351
Pindar 12:258

Crabbe, Anna
Boethius 15:69

Cracroft, Bernard
Arabian Nights 2:9

Craigie, W. A.
Hrafnkel's Saga 2:78

Crawford, John Martin
Kalevala 6:214

Crawford, S. J.
Cædmon 7:92

Creekmore, Hubert
Juvenal 8:64

Croce, Benedetto
Inferno 3:58
Plato 8:269
Terence 14:326

Croiset, Maurice
Aristophanes 4:70

Crombie, A. C.
Bacon, Roger 14:79

Crump, M. Marjorie
Ovid 7:314

Cummings, Hubertis M.
Boccaccio, Giovanni 13:87

Cunliffe, John W.
Seneca, Lucius Annaeus 6:339

Cunningham, Stanley B.
Albert the Great 16:43, 65

Curley III, Thomas F.
Boethius 15:97

Curtius, Ernst Robert
Aeneid 9:345, 376
Augustine, St. 6:56
Hermogenes 6:158
Inferno 3:98

Dahlberg, Charles
Romance of the Rose 8:414

Dall, Caroline H.
Sordello 15:328

D'Alton, Rev. J. F.
Cicero, Marcus Tullius 3:207

Damon, S. Foster
Marie de France 8:120

Dandekar, R. N.
Mahābhārata 5:227

Dane, Joseph A.
Mystery of Adam 4:216

Darrow, Clarence
Khayyám 11:274

Dashti, Ali
Khayyám 11:280

Davenport, Guy
Sappho 3:471

Davenport, W. A.
Sir Gawain and the Green Knight 2:273

David, E.
Aristophanes 4:174

Davidson, A. B.
The Book of Job 14:138

Davidson, Herbert A.
Avicenna 16:147

Davidson, Thomas
Sappho 3:388

Davis, J. Cary
Poem of the Cid 4:260

Davis, Scott
Kalevala 6:278

Dawson, Christopher
Bacon, Roger 14:65

De Boer, T. J.
Averroës 7:7

De Chasca, Edmund
Poem of the Cid 4:295

De la Mare, Walter
Arabian Nights 2:35

De Ley, Margo
Razón de Amor 16:347

De Quincey, Thomas
Arabian Nights 2:8
Iliad 1:294
Odyssey 16:197
Sophocles 2:309

De Sanctis, Francesco
Boccaccio, Giovanni 13:17
Inferno 3:23, 31

De Vere, Aubrey
Poem of the Cid 4:229
The Song of Roland 1:163

De Vericour, Professor
Poem of the Cid 4:225

Dean, Christopher
Arthurian Legend 10:65
Morte Arthure 10:431

Demetillo, Ricaredo
Murasaki, Lady 1:429

Deyermond, A. D.
Poem of the Cid 4:289

Diamond, Robert E.
The Dream of the Rood 14:236

Dill, Samuel
Juvenal 8:26

Seneca, Lucius Annaeus 6:345

Dimler, G. Richard
Wolfram von Eschenbach 5:344

Dinsmore, Charles Allen
Iliad 1:326

Dionysius of Halicarnassus
Sappho 3:379

Disraeli, Issac
Beowulf 1:56

Dobson, J. F.
Demosthenes 13:141

Dodds, E. R.
Augustine, St. 6:21

Donner, Morton
Sir Gawain and the Green Knight 2:224

Donohoe, Joseph I., Jr.
The Song of Roland 1:228

Donovan, Mortimer J.
Marie de France 8:145

Doolittle, Hilda
Sappho 3:432

Dorfman, Eugene
Poem of the Cid 4:271

Dover, K. J.
Aristophanes 4:147, 159
Demosthenes 13:185

Dronke, Peter
Abelard 11:39

Dryden, John
Aeneid 9:300
Apuleius 1:7
Iliad 1:282
Juvenal 8:5
Ovid 7:291
Pindar 12:258

Ducharme, Lèonard
Albert the Great 16:86

Duckett, Eleanor Shipley
Boethius 15:23

Duckworth, George E.
Terence 14:337

Duclow, Donald F.
Meister Eckhart 9:70

Duff, J. Wight
Cicero, Marcus Tullius 3:197
Juvenal 8:34
Livy 11:336
Terence 14:305

Duggan, Joseph J.
Poem of the Cid 4:312

Dumezil, Georges

Mahābhārata 5:254

Dunn, Charles W.
Romance of the Rose 8;417

Dunne, M.A.
Sordello 15:339

Earle, John
Beowulf 1:57

Easton, Stewart C.
Bacon, Roger 14:73

Eaton, John H.
The Book of Psalms 4:438

Ebenstein, William
Cicero, Marcus Tullius 3:251

Echard, Lawrence
Terence 14:297

Eckermann, Johann Peter
Longus 7:217
Sophocles 2:303

Eckhart, Meister
Meister Eckhart 9:24

Edgerton, Franklin
Kālidāsa 9:113

Edgren, A. Hjalmar
Kālidāsa 9:87

Edmonds, J. M.
Longus 7:220

Ehrenberg, Victor
Aristophanes 4:117

Eide, Elling O.
Li Po 2:149

Einarsson, Stefán
Hrafnkel's Saga 2:97

Eliade, Mircea
Bhagavad Gt 12:74
Epic of Gilgamesh 3:341
Mah bh rata 5:235

Eliot, George
Sophocles 2:311

Eliot, T. S.
Aeneid 9:380
Inferno 3:67
Pindar 12:265
Seneca, Lucius Annaeus 6:371

Elwell-Sutton, L. P.
Khayyám 11:304

Elyot, Thomas
Ovid 7:286

Emerson, Oliver Farrar
Beowulf 1:68

Emerson, Ralph Waldo
The Book of Psalms 4:360

Plato 8:235

Engelhardt, George J.
Sir Gawain and the Green Knight
2:204

Enright, D. J.
Murasaki, Lady 1:447
Sei Sh nogan 6:301

Erasmus, Desiderius
Cicero, Marcus Tullius 3:184
Seneca, Lucius Annaeus 6:332

Eusebius
Josephus, Flavius 13:219

Eustathios
Iliad 1:274

Evelyn-White, Hugh G.
Hesiod 5:83

Everett, Dorothy
Layamon 10:329
Morte Arthure 10:378
Sir Gawain and the Green Knight 2:197

Ewert, Alfred
Marie de France 8:129

Fant, Maureen B.
Sappho 3:481

Farnell, Ida
Sordello 15:330

Faris, Wendy B.
Arabian Nights 2:69

Farnell, Ida
Bertran de Born 5:18

Farnham, Willard
Boccaccio, Giovanni 13:62

Fauriel, C. C.
Bertran de Born 5:10

Faust, Diana M.
Marie de France 8:185

Fedotov, George P.
The Igor Tale 1:491

Feldman, Louis H.
Josephus, Flavius 13:256

Felson-Rubin, Nancy
Odyssey 16:321

Feng, Kuan
Lao Tzu 7:155

Fennell, John
The Igor Tale 1:521

Ferguson, John
Juvenal 8:84
Sophocles 2:408

Ferguson, Margaret W.

Augustine, St. 6:109

Fergusson, Francis
Sophocles 2:359

Ferrante, Joan
Marie de France 8:158

Festugière, Andre-Jean
Apuleius 1:24

Ficino, Marsilio
Plato 8:217

Field, P. J. C.
Sir Gawain and the Green Knight
2:258

Fielding, Henry
Aristophanes 4:41

Finlayson, John
Morte Arthure 10:391

Finley, John H., Jr.
Pindar 12:287

Finley, M. I.
Odyssey 16:253

Fiore, Silvestro
Epic of Gilgamesh 3:325

Fitch, George Hamlin
Arabian Nights 2:22

Fite, Warner
Plato 8:280

FitzGerald, Edward
Khayyám 11:233

Flaccus, Statylius
Sophocles 2:292

Fleming, John V.
The Dream of the Rood 14:245

Fletcher, Jefferson Butler
Inferno 3:56

Foley, Helene P.
Aristophanes 4:169

Ford, J. D. M.
Poem of the Cid 4:233

Forehand, Walter E.
Terence 14:381

Forster, E. M.
Arabian Nights 2:26

Foscolo, Ugo
Boccaccio, Giovanni 13:13

Fowles, John
Marie de France 8:157

Fowlie, Wallace
Inferno 3:144

Fox, Denton

Njáls saga 13:339

Frank, Grace
Mystery of Adam 4:191, 197

Frank, Tenney
Cicero, Marcus Tullius 3:211

Fränkel, Hermann
Hesiod 5:99
Ovid 7:319
Sappho 3:418

Frappier, Jean
Chrétien de Troyes 10:160

Freccero, John
Inferno 3:145

Fredericks, S. C.
Juvenal 8:79

Frese, Delores Warwick
Anglo-Saxon Chronicle 4:27

Freud, Sigmund
Sophocles 2:313

Frey, John A.
Marie de France 8:132

Friberg, Eino
Kalevala 6:275, 278

Friedländer, Ludwig
Juvenal 8:20

Friedländer, Paul
Plato 8:355

Friedrich, Paul
Sappho 3:457

Friedrich, Rainer
Odyssey 16:330

Fromm, Erich
The Book of Psalms 4:416

Fronto, Marcus Cornelius
Cicero, Marcus Tullius 3:176

Frye, Northrop
Aristophanes 4:130
The Book of Job 14:189

Fu, Charles Wei-hsun
Lao Tzu 7:167

Gadamer, Hans-Georg
Plato 8:333

Galinsky, G. Karl
Ovid 7:383

Gantz, Jeffrey
Mabinogion 9:159, 186

Garci-Gomez, Miguel
Poem of the Cid 4:335

Gardner, John
Epic of Gilgamesh 3:340

Critic Index

Morte Arthure **10**:399
Sir Gawain and the Green Knight
  2:233

Garner, John Leslie
Khayyám **11**:262

Gaselee, S(tephen)
Apuleius **1**:17

Gassner, John
Terence **14**:339

Gayley, Charles Mills
Mystery of Adam **4**:186

Geddes, J., Jr.
The Song of Roland **1**:169

Gellius, Aulus
Cicero, Marcus Tullius **3**:176

Geoffrey of Monmouth
Arthurian Legend **10**:18

Gerhardt, Mia I.
Arabian Nights **2**:42

Gerow, Edwin
Kālidāsa **9**:130

Ghazoul, Ferial Jabouri
Arabian Nights **2**:61

Gibb, H. A. R.
Arabian Nights **2**:28

Gibbon, Edward
Augustine, St. **6**:10
Boethius **15**:2

Gibbs, J.
Apuleius **1**:13

Gibbs, Marion E.
Wolfram von Eshcenbach **5**:347,
  429

Gifford, William
Juvenal **8**:6

Gilson, Etienne
Abelard **11**:17
Augustine, St. **6**:44
Averroës **7**:18, 26
Bacon, Roger **14**:86
Meister Eckhart **9**:42, 60

Gilula, Dwora
Terence **14**:389

Girard, René
The Book of Job **14**:191
Sophocles **2**:408

Gladstone, W. E.
Iliad **1**:297

Godwin, William
Poem of the Cid **4**:225

Goethe, Johann Wolfgang von
Kālidāsa **9**:130

Longus **7**:217
Menander **9**:227
Sophocles **2**:303

Goldberg, Harriet
Razón de Amor **16**:360

Goldberg, Sander M.
Menander **9**:276
Terence **14**:372

Goldin, Frederick
The Song of Roland **1**:251

Golding, Arthur
Ovid **7**:287

Goldsmith, Margaret E.
Beowulf **1**:134

Gollancz, I.
Sir Gawain and the Green Knight
  2:186

Göller, Karl Heinz
Morte Arthure **10**:418

Gombrowicz, Witold
Inferno **3**:131

Gomme, A. W.
Menander **9**:259

Good, Edwin M.
The Book of Job **14**:206

Goodell, Thomas Dwight
Aeschylus **11**:112

Goodheart, Eugene
The Book of Job **14**:171

Goodrich, Norma Lorre
Arthurian Legend **10**:100, 108

Gordis, Robert
The Book of Job **14**:175

Gordon, E. V.
Hrafnkel's Saga **2**:86

Gosse, Edmund
Beowulf **1**:73

Gottfried von Strassburg
Gottfried von Strassburg **10**:246,
  249, 258
Wolfram von Eschenbach **5**:291

Gradon, Pamela
Beowulf **1**:138

Grahn, Judy
Sappho **3**:494

Grane, Leifu
Abelard **11**:25

Granrud, John E.
Cicero, Marcus Tullius **3**:205

Gransden, Antonia
Anglo-Saxon Chronicle **4**:21

Grant, Michael
Aeschylus **11**:175
Apuleius **1**:26
Cicero, Marcus Tullius **3**:285, 291
Josephus, Flavius **13**:240
Livy **11**:367
Ovid **7**:405

Graves, Robert
Aeneid **9**:394
Apuleius **1**:20
Iliad **1**:361
Menander **9**:236
Terence **14**:341

Gray, Wallace
Iliad **1**:405

Green, D. H.
Hartmann von Aue **15**:206
Wolfram von Eschenbach **5**:391

Green, Peter
Juvenal **8**:68
Ovid **7**:419
Sappho **3**:438

Greenberg, Moshe
The Book of Job **14**:196

Greene, Thomas
Aeneid **9**:399

Greenfield, Stanley B.
Beowulf **1**:119
The Dream of the Rood **14**:243

Greenwood, Thomas
Albert the Great **16**:17

Gregory, Eileen
Sappho **3**:495

Grene, David
Aeschylus **11**:220

Grierson, Herbert J. C.
Beowulf **1**:90

Grieve, Patricia E.
Razón de Amor **16**:364

Griffin, Jasper
Iliad **1**:392
Odyssey **16**:304

Grigson, Geoffrey
Sei Shōnagon **6**:300

Grimm, Charles
Chrétien de Troyes **10**:141

Groden, Suzy Q.
Sappho **3**:436

Groos, Arthur
Wolfram von Eschenbach **5**:423

Grossman, Judith
Arabian Nights **2**:57

Grossvogel, Steven
Boccaccio, Giovanni **13**:114

Grube, G. M. A.
Aristophanes **4**:136
Cicero, Marcus Tullius **3**:258

Gruffydd, W. J.
Mabinogion **9**:159

Grunmann-Gaudet, Minnette
The Song of Roland **1**:248

Guardini, Romano
Augustine, St. **6**:95
The Book of Psalms **4**:414

Guarino, Guido A.
Boccaccio, Giovanni **13**:52

Gudzy, N. K.
The Igor Tale **1**:485

Gunkel, Hermann
The Book of Psalms **4**:379

Gunn, Alan M. F.
Romance of the Rose **8**:402

Guthrie, W. K. C.
Plato **8**:321, 360

Hackett, Jeremiah M. G.
Bacon, Roger **14**:99, 110

Hadas, Moses
Aeschylus **11**:150
Apuleius **1**:23
Aristophanes **4**:121
Hesiod **5**:98
Juvenal **8**:45
Plato **8**:304
Sappho **3**:417
Seneca, Lucius Annaeus **6**:378, 385

Hägg, Tomas
Longus **7**:262

Haight, Elizabeth Hazelton
Apuleius **1**:18

Haines, C. R.
Sappho **3**:397

Haley, Lucille
Ovid **7**:310

Hallam, Henry
Bacon, Roger **14**:16
Poem of the Cid **4**:225

Hallberg, Peter
Hrafnkel's Saga **2**:124
Njáls saga **13**:339

Hallett, Judith P.
Sappho **3**:465

Halleux, Pierre
Hrafnkel's Saga **2**:99, 102

Halverson, John
Beowulf **1**:131

Hamilton, Edith
Aeschylus **11**:128

Aristophanes **4:**109
Sophocles **2:**328
Terence **14:**322

Hamori, Andras
Arabian Nights **2:**51

Handley, E. W.
Menander **9:**243, 276

Hanford, James Holly
Razón de Amor **16:**337

Hanning, Robert
Marie de France **8:**158

Hanson-Smith, Elizabeth
Mabinogion **9:**192

Hardison, O. B., Jr.
Mystery of Adam **4:**203

Hardy, E. G.
Juvenal **8:**17

Hardy, Lucy
Boccaccio, Giovanni **13:**30

Harris, Charles
Kālidāsa **9:**81

Harrison, Ann Tukey
The Song of Roland **1:**261

Harrison, Robert
The Song of Roland **1:**220

Harsh, Philip Whaley
Menander **9:**216

Hart, Henry H.
Polo, Marco **15:**309

Hart, Thomas R.
Poem of the Cid **4:**306

Hartley, L. P.
Murasaki, Lady **1:**422

Hastings, R.
Boccaccio, Giovanni **13:**59

Hatto, A. T.
Gottfried von Strassburg **10:**259
Nibelungenlied, Das **12:**194

Havelock, Eric A.
Hesiod **5:**111, 150
Iliad **1:**382, 386

Hay, John
Khayyám **11:**261

Haymes, Edward R.
Nibelungenlied, Das **12:**244

Headstrom, Birger R.
Boccaccio, Giovanni **13:**35

Hearn, Lafcadio
Khayyám **11:**258

Hegel, G. W. F.

Aristophanes **4:**46
The Book of Job **14:**157
Inferno **3:**12
Plato **8:**225
Sophocles **2:**297

Heidegger, Martin
Plato **8:**295
Sophocles **2:**376

Heidel, Alexander
Epic of Gilgamesh **3:**310

Heine, Heinrich
Bertran de Born **5:**10

Heinemann, Frederik J.
Hrafnkel's Saga **2:**120, 123

Heiserman, Arthur
Apuleius **1:**46
Longus **7:**254

Herder, Johann Gottfried von
The Book of Psalms **4:**355
K lid sa **9:**102

Herington, John
Aeschylus **11:**210

Hermann, Fränkel
Pindar **12:**305

Herodotus
Hesiod **5:**68

Herriott, J. Homer
Polo, Marco **15:**289

Hesse, Hermann
Arabian Nights **2:**28
Boccaccio, Giovanni **13:**32

Hewlett, Maurice
Hesiod **5:**83

Hickes, George
Cædmon **7:**78

Hieatt, Constance
The Song of Roland **1:**209

Highet, Gilbert
Arabian Nights **2:**41
Beowulf **1:**97
Cicero, Marcus Tullius **3:**232, 241
The Dream of the Rood **14:**243
Juvenal **8:**40, 45
Pindar **12:**279
Romance of the Rose **8:**399

Hillebrandt, A.
Kālidāsa **9:**95

Hillgarth, J. N.
Llull, Ramon **12:**112

Hirsch, S. A.
Bacon, Roger **14:**23

Hisamatsu, Sen'ichi
Sei Shōnagon **6:**292

Hobbes, Thomas
Odyssey **16:**189

Hölderlin, Friedrich
Sophocles **2:**297

Hole, Richard
Arabian Nights **2:**4

Hollander, Lee M.
Njáls saga **13:**326

Hollander, Robert
Boccaccio, Giovanni **13:**67, 88

Hollister, C. Warren
Anglo-Saxon Chronicle **4:**19

Holmes, Urban T., Jr.
Chrétien de Troyes **10:**150

Holyday, Barten
Juvenal **8:**4

Homann, Holger
Nibelungenlied, Das **12:**239

Honko, Lauri
Kalevala **6:**271

Hopkins, E. Washburn
Mahābhārata **5:**192

Horowitz, Irving L.
Averroës **7:**28

Hough, Lynn Harold
The Book of Psalms **4:**388

Hourani, George F.
Averroës **7:**36

Housman, Laurence
Khayyám **11:**278

Howard, Donald R.
Sir Gawain and the Green Knight **2:**221

Howes, Robert C.
The Igor Tale **1:**517

Hroswitha, Abess
Terence **14:**349

Hsu, Sung-peng
Lao Tzu **7:**182, 190

Huang Kuo-pin
Li Po **2:**164

Hueffer, Francis
Bertran de Born **5:**12

Hügel, Baron Friedrich von
Meister Eckhart **9:**27

Hugill, William Meredith
Aristophanes **4:**107

Hugo, Victor
Inferno **3:**22

Huizinga, Johan

Abelard **11:**6

Hulbert, James R.
Beowulf **1:**90

Hull, Denison Bingham
Iliad **1:**398

Hume, David
Cicero, Marcus Tullius **3:**188

Humphries, Rolfe
Juvenal **8:**58

Hunt, H. A. K.
Cicero, Marcus Tullius **3:**253

Hunt, J. William
Aeneid **9:**433

Huppé, Bernard F.
Augustine, St. **6:**92
Cædmon **7:**105
The Dream of the Rood **14:**278

Hutson, Arthur E.
Nibelungenlied, Das **12:**162

Hutton, Richard Holt
Khayyám **11:**271

Huxley, Aldous
Bhagavad G t **12:**54
Meister Eckhart **9:**68
Sappho **3:**398

Ing, Paul Tan Chee
Lao Tzu **7:**164

Ingalls, Daniel H. H.
K lid sa **9:**122

Inge, William Ralph
Meister Eckhart **9:**25

Irving, Edward B., Jr.
Beowulf **1:**123
The Dream of the Rood **14:**283

Isenberg, M.
The Igor Tale **1:**515

Isherwood, Christopher
Bhagavad Gītā **12:**54

Isidore of Seville
Plato **8:**211

Ivry, Alfred L.
Averroës **7:**52

Jackson, F. J. Foakes
Josephus, Flavius **13:**226

Jackson, Holbrook
Khayyám **11:**264

Jackson, W. H.
Hartmann von Aue **15:**188

Jackson, W. T. H.
Chrétien de Troyes **10:**218
Gottfried von Strassburg **10:**267,

Critic Index

285, 302

Jacob, Alfred
Razón de Amor **16**:340

Jacobs, Joseph
Longus **7**:217

Jacobsen, Thorkild
Epic of Gilgamesh **3**:342

Jacobson, Howard
Ovid **7**:378

Jaeger, C. Stephen
Gottfried von Strassburg **10**:298, 303

Jaeger, Werner
Aeschylus **11**:133
Aristophanes **4**:96
Demosthenes **13**:152
Hesiod **5**:91
Plato **8**:281
Sappho **3**:413
Sophocles **2**:331
Odyssey **16**:209

Jakobson, Roman
The Igor Tale **1**:499

Janeira, Armando Martins
Sei Sh nogan **6**:302

Jaspers, Karl
Augustine, St. **6**:69
Lao Tzu **7**:139
Plato **8**:312

Jastrow, Morris, Jr.
The Book of Job **14**:150
Epic of Gilgamesh **3**:303

Jebb, Richard C.
Hesiod **5**:77
Sophocles **2**:322

Jenkins, T. Atkinson
The Song of Roland **1**:175

Jenkyns, Richard
Sappho **3**:479

John, Ivor B.
Mabinogion **9**:148

John of Salisbury
Augustine, St. **6**:4
Plato **8**:211

Johnson, Ann S.
Anglo-Saxon Chronicle **4**:17

Johnson, Leslie Peter
Wolfram von Eschenbach **5**:373

Johnson, Samuel
Aeneid **9**:316

Johnson, Sidney M.
Wolfram von Eschenbach **5**:429

Johnson, W. R.

Aeneid **9**:439
Ovid **7**:401
Sappho **3**:476

Jones, George Fenwick
The Song of Roland **1**:194

Jones, Gwyn
Beowulf **1**:144
Hrafnkel's Saga **2**:84
Mabinogion **9**:167, 174
Njáls saga **13**:323

Jones, Martin H.
Wolfram von Eschenbach **5**:354

Jones, Rufus M.
Meister Eckhart **9**:40

Jones, Thomas
Arthurian Legend **10**:18
Mabinogion **9**:167

Jones, W. Lewis
Layamon **10**:319

Jump, John D.
Pindar **12**:327

Jung, C. G.
Meister Eckhart **9**:30

Juvenal
Cicero, Marcus Tullius **3**:175

Kafka, Franz
Odyssey **16**:208

Kant, Immanuel
Plato **8**:223

Kato, Shuichi
Murasaki, Lady **1**:450
Sei Shōnogon **6**:304

Keene, Donald
Murasaki, Lady **1**:432

Keith, A. Berriedale
Kālidāsa **9**:96

Kemp-Welch, Alice
Marie de France **8**:114

Kendall, Willmoore
Cicero, Marcus Tullius **3**:274

Kennedy, Charles W.
Beowulf **1**:89
Cædmon **7**:84
The Dream of the Rood **14**:227

Kennedy, George A.
Demosthenes **13**:167
Hermogenes **6**:184, 194
Ovid **7**:376

Kenney, E. J.
Ovid **7**:345, 443

Ker, W. P.
Anglo-Saxon Chronicle **4**:2
Beowulf **1**:59, 64

Boccaccio, Giovanni **13**:42
Chrétien de Troyes **10**:131
The Dream of the Rood **14**:229
The Song of Roland **1**:164

Kerényi, C.
Kalevala **6**:241

Kibler, William W.
Chrétien de Troyes **10**:231

Kibre, Pearl
Albert the Great **16**:97

Kieckhefer, Richard
Meister Eckhart **9**:66

Kierkegaard, Søren
Aristophanes **4**:48
The Book of Job **14**:125
Plato **8**:232
Sophocles **2**:305

King, K. C.
Hartmann von Aue **15**:171

Kirk, G. S.
Epic of Gilgamesh **3**:331
Iliad **1**:371
Odyssey **16**:273

Kirkby, Helen
Boethius **15**:79

Kirkham, Victoria
Boccaccio, Giovanni **13**:94

Kirkwood, G. M.
Sappho **3**:445
Sophocles **2**:377

Kitto, H. D. F.
Aeschylus **11**:137
Odyssey **16**:287
Sophocles **2**:393

Klaeber, Friederich
Beowulf **1**:69

Klein, Karen Wilk
Bertran de Born **5**:35

Kleiner, Yu. A.
Cædmon **7**:111

Knapp, Charles
Aeneid **9**:341

Knapp, Peggy Ann
Sir Gawain and the Green Knight **2**:268

Knight, W. F. Jackson
Ovid **7**:340

Knoche, Ulrich
Juvenal **8**:56

Knox, Bernard M. W.
Aeschylus **11**:183
Sophocles **2**:371, 397

Koht, Halvdan

Hrafnkel's Saga **2**:82

Konishi, Jin'ichi
Murasaki, Lady **1**:471
Sei Shōnogon **6**:322

Konstan, David
Menander **9**:282
Terence **14**:376

Kott, Jan
Sophocles **2**:410

Koyré, Alexandre
Plato **8**:284

Kraft, Kent T.
Cicero, Marcus Tullius **3**:293

Kratz, Henry
Hrafnkel's Saga **2**:126
Wolfram von Eschenbach **5**:365

Krishnamoorthy, K.
Kālidāsa **9**:114

Kristeller, Paul Oskar
Augustine, St. **6**:64
Plato **8**:326

Krohn, Julius
Kalevala **6**:216

Kroll, Paul W.
Li Po **2**:174

Kupfer, Joseph
Bacon, Roger **14**:95

Kustas, George L.
Hermogenes **6**:175, 178

Laborde, E. D.
Anglo-Saxon Chronicle **4**:7

Lacey, W. K.
Cicero, Marcus Tullius **3**:281

Lactantius, Lucius Caelius Firmianus
Cicero, Marcus Tullius **3**:177

Lacy, Norris J.
Chrétien de Troyes **10**:169

Lagercrantz, Olof
Inferno **3**:134

Laidlaw, W. A.
Cicero, Marcus Tullius **3**:252

Laistner, M. L. W.
Livy **11**:325

Lamberton, Robert
Hesiod **5**:170

Landor, Walter Savage
Seneca, Lucius Annaeus **6**:337

Lang, Andrew
Kalevala **6**:212, 230
Khayyám **11**:266

Layamon 10:317
Odyssey 16:204

Lanham, Richard A.
Ovid 7:395

Latham, Ronald
Polo, Marco 15:298

Lattimore, Richmond
Iliad 1:344

Lau, D. C.
Lao Tzu 7:147

Lawrence, William Witherle
Beowulf 1:75

Lawton, W. C.
Hesiod 5:79

Layamon
Layamon 10:311, 314

Leach, Anna
Arabian Nights 2:16

Leaman, Oliver
Averroës 7:66

Le Bossu, René
Aeneid 9:298
Iliad 1:278
Odyssey 16:187

Lecky, W. E. H.
Bacon, Roger 14:11

Lee, Alvin A.
Beowulf 1:140

Leech, Kenneth
Llull, Ramon 12:124

Leff, Gordon
Abelard 11:22
Augustine, St. 6:88

Lefkowitz, Mary R.
Sappho 3:481

Le Gentil, Pierre
The Song of Roland 1:203

Legouis, Emile
Layamon 10:319

Leibniz, Gottfried Wilhelm
Augustine, St. 6:8
Averroës 7:5
Plato 8:220

Leiter, Louis H.
The Dream of the Rood 14:256

Leon, Harry J.
Cicero, Marcus Tullius 3:218

Lerer, Seth
Boethius 15:124

Lesky, Albin
Aeschylus 11:158, 190

Demosthenes 13:162
Hesiod 5:112
Odyssey 16:304
Pindar 12:317
Sophocles 2:378

Lessing, Gotthold Ephraim
Sophocles 2:294

Lever, Katherine
Aristophanes 4:123
Menander 9:227, 233

Levy, G. R.
Epic of Gilgamesh 3:313

Lewis, C. S.
Aeneid 9:364
Apuleius 1:32
Beowulf 1:87
Boethius 15:43
The Book of Psalms 4:403
Chrétien de Troyes 10:147
Layamon 10:343
Romance of the Rose 8:387
Sir Gawain and the Green Knight 2:221

Levy, Reuben
Avicenna 16:180

Lewis, Geoffrey
Book of Dede Korkut 8:103

Lewis, Rev. Gerrard
Poem of the Cid 4:228

Liebeschuetz, W.
Boethius 15:47
Livy 11:357

Likhachov, Dmitry
The Igor Tale 1:523

Lindberg, David C.
Bacon, Roger 14:106

Lindsay, Jack
Bertran de Born 5:55
Longus 7:229

Lindsay, Thomas B.
Juvenal 8:17

Littell, Robert
Murasaki, Lady 1:419

Liu Wu-chi
Li Po 2:143

Livy
Livy 11:311

Lloyd-Jones, Hugh
Aeschylus 11:168
Menander 9:231
Odyssey 16:321
Pindar 12:342

Lodge, Thomas
Seneca, Lucius Annaeus 6:335

Lofmark, Carl

Wolfram von Eschenbach 5:358

Long, J. Bruce
Mahābhārata 5:270

Longfellow, Henry Wadsworth
Beowulf 1:57
Inferno 3:23

Longinus
Aeschylus 11:83
Cicero, Marcus Tullius 3:174
Odyssey 16:192
Plato 8:206
Sappho 3:379
Sophocles 2:292

Longus
Longus 7:216

Lönnrot, Elias
Kalevala 6:208, 210

Loomis, Roger Sherman
Arthurian Legend 10:57, 90, 110
Layamon 10:341

Lord, Albert B.
Iliad 1:363
Odyssey 16:259

Lowell, Amy
Murasaki, Lady 1:417

Lowth, Robert
The Book of Psalms 4:352

Lucas, F. L.
Epic of Gilgamesh 3:309
Li Po 2:135
Seneca, Lucius Annaeus 6:363

Luck, Georg
Ovid 7:346

Luke, J. Tracy
Epic of Gilgamesh 3:343

Luscombe, D. E.
Abelard 11:48, 61

Lü-shih, Lin
Lao Tzu 7:155

Luther, Martin
The Book of Psalms 4:347
Cicero, Marcus Tullius 3:185

Luttrell, Claude
Chrétien de Troyes 10:195

Macaulay, Thomas Babington
Ovid 7:292

Macdonell, Arthur A.
Mahābhārata 5:185

Mackail, J. W.
Aeneid 9:327
Iliad 1:315
Odyssey 16:243
Sappho 3:389
Seneca, Lucius Annaeus 6:344

Sophocles 2:317
Terence 14:302

MacKay, L. A.
Apuleius 1:32

Macrae-Gibson, O. D.
The Dream of the Rood 14:278

Macrobius, Ambrosius Theodosius
Aeneid 9:294
Apuleius 1:3
Cicero, Marcus Tullius 3:178

Maeterlinck, Maurice
Arabian Nights 2:17

Magnus, Albertus
Albert the Great 16:65

Magnus, Leonard A.
The Igor Tale 1:480

Magnusson, Magnus
Njáls saga 13:332

Magoun, Francis Peabody, Jr.
Cædmon 7:101
Kalevala 6:246

Maier, John
Epic of Gilgamesh 3:354

Mair, Victor H.
Li Po 2:168

Maki, J. M.
Murasaki, Lady 1:426

Makin, Peter
Bertran de Born 5:56
Sordello 15:360

Mallery, Richard D.
Polo, Marco 15:295

Malone, Kemp
Beowulf 1:92
Cædmon 7:109

Malory, Sir Thomas
Arthurian Legend 10:44

Malvern, Marjorie M.
Marie de France 8:171

Mandal, Paresh Chandra
Kālidāsa 9:137

Mandelstam, Osip
Inferno 3:74

Manilius
Menander 9:214

Mann, Cameron
Arabian Nights 2:19

March, Andrew L.
Su Shih 15:395

Margesson, Helen P.
Polo, Marco 15:273

Marie de France
Marie de France **8**:113

Maritain, Jacques
Augustine, St. **6**:24
Inferno **3**:101

Markman, Alan M.
Sir Gawain and the Green Knight
2:209

Marks, Claude
Bertran de Born **5**:48

Marmura, Michael
Avicenna **16**:165

Marotta, Joseph
Wolfram von Eschenbach **5**:396

Marquardt, Patricia
Hesiod **5**:161

Marrou, Henri
Augustine, St. **6**:60

Marsh, George P.
Polo, Marco **15**:269

Martin, Christopher
Ovid **7**:430

Martin, R. H.
Terence **14**:354

Mascaró, Juan
Bhagavad Gītā **12**:57

Mason, Herbert
Epic of Gilgamesh **3**:336

Masters, Edgar Lee
Li Po **2**:137

Matthews, Caitlín
Mabinogion **9**:186

Matthews, William
Morte Arthure **10**:380

Maxwell, Herbert
Bacon, Roger **14**:14

May, Rollo
Inferno **3**:154

Mayer, Frederick
Bacon, Roger **14**:69

Mayer, J. P.
Cicero, Marcus Tullius **3**:220

Maynadier, Howard
Arthurian Legend **10**:115

Mays, James Luther
The Book of Psalms **4**:443

McCallum, J. Ramsay
Abelard **11**:10

McConnell, Winder
Hartmann von Aue **15**:241

McCoy, Patricia
Nibelungenlied, Das **12**:162

McCulloh, William E.
Longus **7**:242

McDonald, William C.
Hartmann von Aue **15**:244

McGregor, James H.
Boccaccio, Giovanni **13**:102

McGuire, Michael D.
Meister Eckhart **9**:60

McKeon, Richard
Cicero, Marcus Tullius **3**:241

McKeown, J. C.
Ovid **7**:424

McNamee, Maurice B., S. J.
Beowulf **1**:116

McNary, Sarah F.
Beowulf **1**:58

Meaney, Audrey L.
Anglo-Saxon Chronicle **4**:31

Mendell, Clarence W.
Seneca, Lucius Annaeus **6**:375

Merchant, Frank Ivan
Seneca, Lucius Annaeus **6**:357

Meredith, George
Aristophanes **4**:56
Menander **9**:243
Terence **14**:303

Mérimée, Ernest
Poem of the Cid **4**:246

Merriman, James Douglas
Arthurian Legend **10**:35

Merton, Thomas
Meister Eckhart **9**:58

Mew, James
Arabian Nights **2**:11

Michael, Ian
Poem of the Cid **4**:291

Michelangelo
Inferno **3**:6

Michener, Richard L.
Chrétien de Troyes **10**:171

Mickel, Emanuel J., Jr.
Marie de France **8**:150

Mill, J. S.
Plato **8**:247

Miller, Barbara Stoler
Bhagavad Gītā **12**:85

Miller, Frank Justus
Seneca, Lucius Annaeus **6**:362

Miller, Norma
Menander **9**:284

Miller, Patrick D., Jr.
The Book of Psalms **4**:430, 448

Milman, Henry Hart
Inferno **3**:22

Milton, John
The Book of Psalms **4**:351

Mirsky, Prince D. S.
The Igor Tale **1**:484

Mitchell, John D.
Kālidāsa **9**:108

Mittelstadt, Michael C.
Longus **7**:238

Mommsen, Theodor
Cicero, Marcus Tullius **3**:189
Terence **14**:304

Monahan, Michael
Sappho **3**:397

Montaigne, Michel de
Cicero, Marcus Tullius **3**:187
Iliad **1**:275
Seneca, Lucius Annaeus **6**:333
Terence **14**:362

Montgomery, Thomas
Poem of the Cid **4**:331

Mookerjee, Arun Kumar
Mahābhārata **5**:276

Moon, Harold
Poem of the Cid **4**:267

Moore, George
Longus **7**:223

Moore, Olin H.
Bertran de Born **5**:29

Moorman, Charles
Iliad **1**:376
Mabinogion **9**:195
Nibelungenlied, Das **12**:223
The Song of Roland **1**:231

Moorman, Frederic W.
Sir Gawain and the Green Knight
2:184

Morgan, Bayard Quincy
Wolfram von Eschenbach **5**:307

Morgan, Wendy
Mystery of Adam **4**:211

Morghen, Raffaello
Inferno **3**:121

Morley, Henry
Layamon **10**:312

Morrall, J. B.
Cicero, Marcus Tullius **3**:295

Morris, George S.
Bacon, Roger **14**:13

Morris, Ivan
Murasaki, Lady **1**:434, 438
Sei Shōnogon **6**:303

Morris, Mark
Sei Shōnogon **6**:307

Morris, Rosemary
Arthurian Legend **10**:95

Morris, William
Arthurian Legend **10**:81

Morrison, Madison
Lao Tzu **7**:203

Mortimer, Raymond
Murasaki, Lady **1**:417, 423

Motto, Anna Lydia
Seneca, Lucius Annaeus **6**:384,
411

Moulton, Carroll
Menander **9**:272

Moulton, Richard G.
Arabian Nights **2**:22
The Book of Psalms **4**:366

Mowatt, D. G.
Nibelungenlied, Das **12**:177, 220

Mowinckel, Sigmund
The Book of Psalms **4**:405

Mudrick, Marvin
Marie de France **8**:166

Mueller, Werner A.
Nibelungenlied, Das **12**:179

Muir, Edwin
Odyssey **16**:287

Muir, Lynette R.
Mystery of Adam **4**:204

Mullally, Evelyn
Chrétien de Troyes **10**:229

Muller, Herbert J.
Aeschylus **11**:152

Murasaki, Lady
Sei Shōnagon **6**:291

Murdoch, Iris
Plato **8**:362

Murnaghan, Sheila
Odyssey **16**:310

Murphy, Mabel Gant
Aeneid **9**:330

Murray, Gilbert
Aeschylus **11**:144
Demosthenes **13**:137
Iliad **1**:312

Ovid 7:303
Pindar 12:303
Sophocles 2:340

Murray, Thomas Chalmers
The Book of Psalms 4:361

Murry, J. Middleton
Beowulf 1:69

Muscatine, Charles
Romance of the Rose 8:407

Musurillo, Herbert
Juvenal 8:61

Myerowitz, Molly
Ovid 7:435

Nabokov, Vladimir
The Igor Tale 1:504

Nadeau, Ray
Hermogenes 6:170

Nakosteen, Mehdi
Khayyám 11:295

Naumann, Hans
Wolfram von Eschenbach 5:304

Needler, George Henry
Nibelungenlied, Das 12:153

Nehamas, Alexander
Plato 8:364

Nelson, Deborah
Chrétien de Troyes 10:199

Nepaulsingh, Colbert I.
Razón de Amor 16:366

Nethercut, William R.
Apuleius 1:38

Newbold, William Romaine
Bacon, Roger 14:37

Newby, P. H.
Arabian Nights 2:38

Newman, John Henry Cardinal
Cicero, Marcus Tullius 3:188,
191

Nichols, James R.
Murasaki, Lady 1:442

Nichols, Stephen G., Jr.
The Song of Roland 1:189

Niebuhr, H. Richard
Augustine, St. 6:56

Nietzsche, Friedrich
Aeschylus 11:98
Aristophanes 4:57
Inferno 3:46
Plato 8:251
Sophocles 2:312

Niles, John D.

Beowulf 1:150

Nisbet, R. G. M.
Cicero, Marcus Tullius 3:263

Nisetich, Frank J.
Pindar 12:335

Nissen, Christopher
Boccaccio, Giovanni 13:122

Noble, Peter S.
Chrétien de Troyes 10:210

Nohrnberg, James
Inferno 3:139

Nordal, Sigurður
Hrafnkel's Saga 2:91

Norinaga, Motoori
Murasaki, Lady 1:415

Northcott, Kenneth J.
Wolfram von Eschenbach 5:403

Norton, Charles Eliot
Khayyám 11:236

Norwood, Frances
Apuleius 1:26

Norwood, Gilbert
Aeschylus 11:116
Aristophanes 4:92
Menander 9:205
Pindar 12:266
Terence 14:309, 315

Nothnagle, John T.
Chrétien de Troyes 10:157

Nutt, Alfred
Wolfram von Eschenbach 5:299

Nyland, Waino
Kalevala 6:238

Obata, Shigeyoshi
Li Po 2:133

Obuchowski, Mary Dejong
Murasaki, Lady 1:444

Odenkirchen, Carl V.
Mystery of Adam 4:205

Ogilvy, J. D. A.
Beowulf 1:154

Oinas, Felix J.
Kalevala 6:254

Oldfather, W. A.
Cicero, Marcus Tullius 3:206

Olschki, Leonardo
Polo, Marco 15:293

Oppenheim, A. Leo
Epic of Gilgamesh 3:321

Ormsby, John

Poem of the Cid 4:226

Osgood, Charles G.
Boccaccio, Giovanni 13:37

Osterud, Svein
Hesiod 5:145

Otis, Brooks
Aeneid 9:429
Ovid 7:356

Otto, Rudolph
Meister Eckhart 9:35

Ovid
Ovid 7:281

Owen, D. D. R.
Chrétien de Troyes 10:173
The Song of Roland 1:191, 236

Owen, S. G.
Juvenal 8:25

Owen, Stephen
Li Po 2:156

Paden, William D., Jr.
Bertran de Born 5:51, 61

Page, Denys
Odyssey 16:300
Sappho 3:430

Pagels, Elaine
Augustine, St. 6:140

Palgrave, Francis T.
Ovid 7:299
Sappho 3:386

Pálsson, Hermann
Hrafnkel's Saga 2:108

Palumbo, Donald
Arabian Nights 2:71

Pancoast, Henry S.
Layamon 10:314

Pandiri, Thalia A.
Longus 7:265

Pandit, R. S.
Kālidāsa 9:103

Papini, Giovanni
Augustine, St. 6:37

Park, Katharine
Albert the Great 16:112

Parker, Douglass
Terence 14:352

Parry, Adam
Aeneid 9:421

Parshall, Linda B.
Wolfram von Eschenbach 5:378

Patch, Howard R.

Boethius 15:15
The Dream of the Rood 14:218

Pater, Walter
Apuleius 1:14
Plato 8:252

Paterson, John
The Book of Psalms 4:395

Paton, Lucy Allen
Layamon 10:315

Patrick, Mary Mills
Sappho 3:393

Patten, Faith H.
The Dream of the Rood 14:268

Patterson, Annabel M.
Hermogenes 6:178

Patton, John H.
Meister Eckhart 9:60

Paul, Herbert
Cicero, Marcus Tullius 3:194

Payne, John
Arabian Nights 2:12

Pearson, C. H.
Juvenal 8:11

Pearson, Karl
Meister Eckhart 9:9

Pearson, Lionel
Demosthenes 13:182

Peck, Russell A.
Morte Arthure 10:406

Peers, E. Allison
Llull, Ramon 12:92, 95

Pei, Mario A.
The Song of Roland 1:178

Pekarik, Andrew
Murasaki, Lady 1:460

Penwill, J. L.
Apuleius 1:42

Penzer, N. M.
Polo, Marco 15:276

Perrier, Joseph Louis
Bertran de Born 5:24

Perry, Ben Edwin
Apuleius 1:34

Perry, Henry Ten Eyck
Menander 9:214
Terence 14:333

Perse, St.-John
Inferno 3:131

Petrarch, Francesco
Augustine, St. 6:7

Critic Index

Boccaccio, Giovanni **13**:4
Cicero, Marcus Tullius **3**:181, 182

Petronio, Giuseppe
Boccaccio, Giovanni **13**:47

Philippides, Marios
Longus **7**:260

Philostratus
Hermogenes **6**:158

Pickering, Charles J.
Khayyám **11**:249
Avicenna **16**:156

Pickering, F. P.
Hartmann von Aue **15**:218

Pidal, Ramón Menéndez
Poem of the Cid **4**:234

Pinkerton, Percy E.
Wolfram von Eschenbach **5**:293

Piramus, Denis
Marie de France **8**:113

Plato
Aristophanes **4**:38
Iliad **1**:270
Plato **8**:200

Plumptre, E. H.
Bacon, Roger **14**:10

Plutarch
Aeschylus **11**:84
Aristophanes **4**:40
Demosthenes **13**:148, 163, 185
Menander **9**:203
Sappho **3**:379

Poag, James F.
Wolfram von Eschenbach **5**:400

Podlecki, Anthony J.
Pindar **12**:351
Sappho **3**:491

Poe, Joe Park
Seneca, Lucius Annaeus **6**:389

Poggioli, Renato
The Igor Tale **1**:507
Inferno **3**:123

Pomeroy, Sarah B.
Aristophanes **4**:155

Pope, Alexander
Aeneid **9**:313, 358
Iliad **1**:284
Odyssey **16**:192

Pope, John C.
Cædmon **7**:110

Pope, Marvin H.
The Book of Job **14**:181

Popper, K. R.
Plato **8**:348

Portalié, Eugène
Augustine, St. **6**:17

Portor, Laura Spencer
Arabian Nights **2**:23

Pöschl, Viktor
Aeneid **9**:377

Post, Chandler Rathfon
Razón de Amor **16**:338

Post, L. A.
Menander **9**:218

Pound, Ezra
Bertran de Born **5**:22
Inferno **3**:99
Odyssey **16**:279
Poem of the Cid **4**:232
The Song of Roland **1**:173
Sordello **15**:347

Powell, F. York
Hrafnkel's Saga **2**:76

Power, Eileen
Polo, Marco **15**:291

Powys, John Cowper
Iliad **1**:358
Inferno **3**:88

Powys, Llewelyn
Khayyám **11**:275

Prabhavananda, Swami
Bhagavad Gītā **12**:54

Pratt, Norman T.
Seneca, Lucius Annaeus **6**:429

Prescott, Henry W.
Aeneid **9**:335

Press, Alan R.
Bertran de Born **5**:48

Price, Arnold H.
Nibelungenlied, Das **12**:164

Priest, George Madison
Wolfram von Eschenbach **5**:301

Pritchett, V. S.
Murasaki, Lady **1**:452
Poem of the Cid **4**:263, 264

Proclus
Plato **8**:209

Prothero, Rowland E.
The Book of Psalms **4**:373

Proust, Marcel
Arabian Nights **2**:25

Prowett, C. G.
Apuleius **1**:13

Pruyser, Paul W.
Epic of Gilgamesh **3**:343

Pseudo-Longinus
Demosthenes **13**:134, 175

Puette, William J.
Murasaki, Lady **1**:463

Purser, Louis C.
Ovid **7**:299

Putnam, Michael C. J.
Aeneid **9**:428

Quasimodo, Salvatore
Inferno **3**:113
Sappho **3**:435

Quennell, Peter
Apuleius **1**:22

Quiller-Couch, Sir Arthur
Beowulf **1**:67

Quinn, Kenneth
Aeneid **9**:408

Quinones, Ricardo J.
Inferno **3**:140

Quintilian
Aeneid **9**:294
Aristophanes **4**:40
Hesiod **5**:69
Menander **9**:203
Ovid **7**:286
Seneca, Lucius Annaeus **6**:403

Radhakrishnan, Sarvepalli
Bhagavad Gītā **12**:14
Mahābhārata **5**:195

Radice, Betty
Abelard **11**:56
Terence **14**:363

Rahman, Fazlur
Avicenna **16**:134

Raleigh, Walter
Boccaccio, Giovanni **13**:32

Ralphs, Sheila
Inferno **3**:135

Rāmānuja
Bhagavad Gītā **12**:3

Ramsay, G. G.
Juvenal **8**:38

Rand, Edward Kennard
Aeneid **9**:350
Boethius **15**:4
Cicero, Marcus Tullius **3**:210, 231

Randall, Dale B. J.
Sir Gawain and the Green Knight **2**:212

Rapin, René
Iliad **1**:276

Rascoe, Burton
Apuleius **1**:17

Boccaccio, Giovanni **13**:42

Rawlinson, Henry
Polo, Marco **15**:267

Reckford, Kenneth J.
Menander **9**:238

Reid, Margaret J. C.
Arthurian Legend **10**:44, 62

Reinhardt, Karl
Sophocles **2**:351

Reiss, Edmund
Boethius **15**:88

Rejak, Tessa
Josephus, Flavius **13**:278

Renan, Ernest
The Book of Job **14**:170
Mabinogion **9**:144

Renoir, Alain
The Song of Roland **1**:199

Rexroth, Kenneth
Abelard **11**:55
Apuleius **1**:37
Beowulf **1**:118
Bhagavad Gt **12**:73
Epic of Gilgamesh **3**:323
Kalevala **6**:252
Mahābhārata **5**:242
Murasaki, Lady **1**:441

Rhys, John
Mabinogion **9**:147

Richards, Herbert
Aristophanes **4**:75

Richey, Margaret Fitzgerald
Gottfried von Strassburg **10**:274
Wolfram von Eschenbach **5**:309, 323

Rickert, Edith
Marie de France **8**:113

Rider, Jeff
Layamon **10**:355

Riha, T.
The Igor Tale **1**:515

Rimmer, J. Thomas
Sei Shōnogon **6**:325

Robinson, David Moore
Sappho **3**:396

Robinson, Fred C.
Beowulf **1**:153

Robinson, H. Wheeler
The Book of Psalms **4**:377

Roche, Paul
Sappho **3**:434

Romilly, Jacqueline de

Aeschylus **11**:192
Hesiod **5**:158

Rose, H. J.
Aristophanes **4**:103
Rosenmeyer, Thomas G.
Aeschylus **11**:196

Ross, E. Denison
Polo, Marco **15**:284

Rossi, Paolo
Llull, Ramon **12**:109

Rostovtzeff, Mikhail
Aristophanes **4**:79

Routh, James
Beowulf **1**:64

Royce, Josiah
The Book of Job **14**:130
Meister Eckhart **9**:14

Ruskin, John
Inferno **3**:14, 19, 21

Russell, Bertrand
Abelard **11**:9
Augustine, St. **6**:53
Averroës **7**:15
Avicenna **16**:171
Bacon, Roger **14**:68
Plato **8**:290

Russell, D. A.
Hermogenes **6**:192

Ryder, Arthur W.
Kālidāsa **9**:87

Ryder, Frank G.
Nibelungenlied, Das **12**:187

Sabra, A. I.
Averroës **7**:62
Avicenna **16**:156

Sacker, Hughes
Hartmann von Aue **15**:154
Nibelungenlied, Das **12**:220
Wolfram von Eschenbach **5**:336

Saint Palaye, Jean Bapstiste de La
Curne de
Bertran de Born **5**:4

Saintsbury, George
Aristophanes **4**:69
Longus **7**:221

Saklatvala, Beram
Arthurian Legend **10**:13

Salinas, Pedro
Poem of the Cid **4**:247

Samuel, Maurice
The Book of Psalms **4**:425

Sandars, N. K.
Epic of Gilgamesh **3**:315

Sandbach, F. H.
Aristophanes **4**:156
Menander **9**:259, 268
Terence **14**:367

Sankovitch, Tilde A.
Bertran de Born **5**:61
Marie de France **8**:177

Sansom, George
Sei Shōnagon **6**:294

Santayana, George
Inferno **3**:54
Plato **8**:257

Sargeant, Winthrop
Bhagavad Gītā **12**:79

Sarna, Nahum A.
The Book of Psalms **4**:421

Sarton, George
Bacon, Roger **14**:61

Sasson, Jack M.
Epic of Gilgamesh **3**:336

Saunders, A. N. W.
Demosthenes **13**:175

Savage, Henry Littleton
Sir Gawain and the Green Knight **2**:206

Sayers, Dorothy L.
The Song of Roland **1**:183

Scartazzini, G. A.
Inferno **3**:39

Schach, Paul
Njáls saga **13**:374

Schein, Seth L.
Iliad **1**:399

Schelling, Friedrich Wilhelm Joseph
von
Inferno **3**:8

Scherer, W.
Gottfried von Strassburg **10**:248
Wolfram von Eschenbach **5**:295

Schirmer, Walter F.
Layamon **10**:336

Schlauch, Margaret
The Dream of the Rood **14**:223

Schlegel, August Wilhelm
Aeschylus **11**:84
Aristophanes **4**:42
Seneca, Lucius Annaeus **6**:336
Sophocles **2**:299

Schlegel, Frederich
Wolfram von Eschenbach **5**:293

Schleiermacher, Friedrich Ernst
Daniel
Plato **8**:228

Schnyder, Hans
Sir Gawain and the Green Knight **2**:217

Schoenberner, Franz
Nibelungenlied, Das **12**:169

Schopenhauer, Arthur
Meister Eckhart **9**:45
Plato **8**:244

Schreckenberg, Heinz
Josephus, Flavius **13**:299

Schücking, Levin L.
Beowulf **1**:78

Schwartz, Kessel
Poem of the Cid **4**:266

Schwertner, Thomas M.
Albert the Great **16**:19

Scodel, Ruth
Sophocles **2**:426

Scragg, D. G.
Anglo-Saxon Chronicle **4**:25

Sealey, Rapha l
Kalevala **6**:245

Sedgefield, Walter John
Anglo-Saxon Chronicle **4**:3

Segal, Charles
Pindar **12**:375
Sappho **3**:442
Seneca, Lucius Annaeus **6**:447
Sophocles **2**:423

Sei Shōnagon
Sei Shōnagon **6**:289

Seidensticker, Edward
Murasaki, Lady **1**:455

Sellar, W. Y.
Aeneid **9**:318
Ovid **7**:293

Seneca, Lucius Annaeus, the Elder
Aeneid **9**:294
Ovid **7**:285

Serafini-Sauli, Judith Powers
Boccaccio, Giovanni **13**:84

Setälä, E. N.
Kalevala **6**:235

Sewall, Richard B.
The Book of Job **14**:165
Sophocles **2**:388

Shaftesbury, Anthony Earl of
Seneca, Lucius Annaeus **6**:335

Shaw, James R.
Albert the Great **16**:81

Shedd, Gordon M.
Sir Gawain and the Green Knight 2:245

Shelley, Percy Bysshe
Aeschylus **11**:89

Shenoy, Anasuya R.
Mahābhārata **5**:247

Shepard, G.
Cædmon **7**:97

Sheppard, J. T.
Aeschylus **11**:126

Shippey, T. A.
Beowulf **1**:146

Shirazi, J. K. M.
Khayyám **11**:268

Shklar, Judith N.
Hesiod **5**:128

Shorey, Paul
Plato **8**:262

Showerman, Grant
Cicero, Marcus Tullius **3**:203

Shumway, Daniel Bussier
Gottfried von Strassburg **10**:250

Shutt, R. J. H.
Josephus, Flavius **13**:235, 267

Sidney, Sir Philip
The Book of Psalms **4**:351

Sighart, Joachim
Albert the Great **16**:3

Sikes, E. E.
Aeneid **9**:329

Simmons, Merle E.
Poem of the Cid **4**:310

Simonides
Sophocles **2**:290

Singer, Carl S.
Nibelungenlied, Das **12**:211

Singleton, Charles S.
Inferno **3**:102

Singleton, Mack
Poem of the Cid **4**:254

Siraisi, Nancy G.
Avicenna **16**:171

Sisam, Kenneth
Beowulf **1**:121

Sismondi, J. C. L. Simonde de
Bertran de Born **5**:8

Skinner, John V.
Meister Eckhart **9**:54

Slater, Anne Saxon
Hrafnkel's Saga **2**:104

Smertenko, Johan J.
Li Po **2:**135

Smiley, Charles N.
Hesiod **5:**85

Smith, Adam
Sophocles **2:**293

Smith, Colin
Poem of the Cid **4:**277, 316

Smith, Huston
Meister Eckhart **9:**66

Smith, J. C.
Beowulf **1:**90

Smith, J. M. Powis
The Book of Psalms **4:**375

Smith, Justin H.
Bertran de Born **5:**18

Smith, Morton
Josephus, Flavius **13:**290

Smyth, Herbert Weir
Aeschylus **11:**120
Sappho **3:**434

Smythe, Barbara
Bertran de Born **5:**23

Snell, Bruno
Aristophanes **4:**120
Pindar **12:**275
Sappho **3:**417

Solomos, Alexis
Aristophanes **4:**153

Sonstroem, David
Khayyám **11:**292

Sørensen, Villy
Seneca, Lucius Annaeus **6:**418

Southern, R. W.
Abelard **11:**33

Spearing, A. C.
Sir Gawain and the Green Knight
2:248

Speirs, John
Sir Gawain and the Green Knight
2:188

Spence, Sarah
Aeneid **9:**442

Spender, Stephen
Sophocles **2:**427

Spenser, Edmund
Arthurian Legend **10:**61

Spiegel, Harriet
Marie de France **8:**189

Sponsler, Lucy A.
Poem of the Cid **4:**293

Springer, Otto
Wolfram von Eschenbach
5:321

Stäblein, Patricia H.
Bertran de Born **5:**61

Staines, David
Chrétien de Troyes **10:**218

Stanford, W. B.
Odyssey **16:**247
Sappho **3:**415

Stapylton, Robert
Juvenal **8:**3

Starkie, Walter
Poem of the Cid **4:**252

Steele, R. B.
Livy **11:**315

Steele, Robert
Bacon, Roger **14:**45

Stehle, Eva
Sappho **3:**469

Steiner, George
Iliad **1:**368

Steiner, Rudolf
Bhagavad Gītā **12:**7

Stendhal
Arabian Nights **2:**6

Steneck, Nicholas H.
Albert the Great **16:**103

Stephens, Anna Cox
Kalevala **6:**228

Stephens, Wade C.
Ovid **7:**337

Stephenson, William E.
Apuleius **1:**29

Stevens, John
Marie de France **8:**137

Stewart, Douglas J.
Hesiod **5:**118, 124

Stone, Brian
Arthurian Legend **10:**85

Stone, Charles J.
Mah bh rata **5:**179

Stone, Edward Noble
Mystery of Adam **4:**190

Strahan, James
The Book of Job **4:**144

Studer, Paul
Mystery of Adam **4:**186

Stump, Eleonore
The Book of Job **14:**138

Suetonius
Terence **14:**339

Suhm, P. A.
Njáls saga **13:**330

Sukthankar, V. S.
Mah bh rata **5:**225

Sümer, Faruk
Book of Dede Korkut **8:**98

Suso, Henry
Meister Eckhart **9:**7, 8

Sutton, Dana Ferrin
Aristophanes **4:**162
Terence **14:**393

Suzuki, Daisetz Teitaro
Meister Eckhart **9:**49

Sveinsson, Einar Ólafur
Njáls saga **13:**347

Swanton, Michael
Layamon **10:**350

Swinburne, Algernon Charles
Aristophanes **4:**57
Sappho **3:**392

Syme, Ronald
Cicero, Marcus Tullius **3:**222

Symonds, John Addington
Aeschylus **11:**99
Aristophanes **4:**58
Boccaccio, Giovanni **13:**26
Hesiod **5:**74
Pindar **12:**261
Sappho **3:**385

Symons, Arthur
Augustine, St. **6:**16

Syrianus
Hermogenes **6:**158

Tagore, Rabindranath
Kālidāsa **9:**92

Taine, H. A.
The Song of Roland **1:**162

Tambling, Jeremy
Inferno **3:**158

Tate, Allen
Inferno **3:**112

Tatlock, John S. P.
Layamon **10:**318, 349

Taylor, Beverly
Arthurian Legend **10:**74

Taylor, Henry Osborn
Bacon, Roger **14:**16
Inferno **3:**55
Wolfram von Eschenbach **5:**302

Taylor, Thomas

Apuleius 1:12

Ten Brink, Bernard
Cædmon **7:**80

Tennyson, Alfred Lord
Aeneid **9:**317
Arabian Nights **2:**6
Arthurian Legend **10:**64, 90

Terrien, Samuel
The Book of Job **14:**162

Thackeray, H. St. John
Josephus, Flavius **13:**206

Thierry, Augustin
Bertran de Born **5:**9

Thomas, Calvin
Gottfried von Strassburg
10:254
Nibelungenlied, Das **12:**160

Thomas, R. George
Hrafnkel's Saga **2:**116

Thompson, Maurice
Sappho **3:**386

Thompson, Raymond H.
Chrétien de Troyes **10:**197

Thoreau, Henry D.
Aeschylus **11:**91
Iliad **1:**296

Thorndike, Lynn
Albert the Great **16:**7
Bacon, Roger **14:**48

Thornley, George
Longus **7:**216

Thorpe, Benjamin
Cædmon **7:**78

Ticknor, George
Poem of the Cid **4:**228

Tigay, Jeffrey H.
Epic of Gilgamesh **3:**349

Tillyard, E. M. W.
Aeneid **9:**384
Beowulf **1:**111
Boccaccio, Giovanni **13:**43
Iliad **1:**348
Odyssey **16:**243

The Song of Roland **1:**180

Tobin, Frank J.
Hartmann von Aue **15:**213, 223

Todorov, Tzvetan
Arabian Nights **2:**44, 48

Tolkien, J. R. R.
Anglo-Saxon Chronicle **4:**11
Beowulf **1:**80
Sir Gawain and the Green Knight
2:201

Tolman, Albert H.
Kalevala **6:**231

Tolstoy, Leo
Odyssey **16:**253

Topsfield, L. T.
Chrétien de Troyes **10:**201

Tornay, Stephen Chak
Averroës **7:**10

Toy, C. H.
The Book of Job **14:**138

Tracy, H. L.
Aeschylus **11:**147

Trapp, Joseph
Terence **14:**385

Trevelyan, G. Otto
Ovid **7:**292

Trever, Albert Augustus
Hesiod **5:**88

Trollope, Anthony
Cicero, Marcus Tullius **3:**192

Trypanis, C. A.
Sappho **3:**474

Tsanoff, Radoslav
Augustine, St. **6:**41

Tu Fu
Li Po **2:**132

Tugwell, Simon
Albert the Great **16:**115

Turbervile, George
Ovid **7:**290

Turner, Eric G.
Menander **9:**257

Turner, Paul
Longus **7:**235

Turunen, Aimo
Kalevala **6:**258

Twomey, Michael W.
Morte Arthure **10:**425

Tyrwhitt, Thomas
Layamon **10:**311

Uhland, Johann
Bertran de Born **5:**10

Uitti, Karl D.
Chrétien de Troyes **10:**190
Romance of the Rose **8:**446
The Song of Roland **1:**243

Urwin, Kenneth
Mystery of Adam **4:**191

Uysal, Ahmet E.
Book of Dede Korkut **8:**98

Vaidya, C. V.
Mahābhārata **5:**189

Van Antwerp, Margaret
Razón de Amor **16:**353

Van Buitenen, J. A. B.
Mahābhārata **5:**267

Van Buskirk, William R.
Lao Tzu **7:**119

Van Doren, Mark
Aeneid **9:**366
The Book of Psalms **4:**425
Iliad **1:**336
Murasaki, Lady **1:**420
Odyssey **16:**231

Van Nooten, Barend A.
Mah bh rata **5:**249

Vance, Eugene
The Song of Roland **1:**214

Vellacott, Philip
Aeschylus **11:**207

Verdenius, W. J.
Plato **8:**296

Vergil
Aeneid **9:**312, 329

Versényi, Laszlo
Hesiod **5:**137
Sappho **3:**455

Very, Jones
Homer **1:**292

Vigfusson, Gudbrand
Hrafnkel's Saga **2:**76

Vinaver, Eugène
Arthurian Legend **10:**81
Chrétien de Troyes **10:**180
The Song of Roland **1:**234

Vivekananda, Swami
Bhagavad G t **12:**5

Voltaire, François-Marie Arouet
Aeneid **9:**314
Aristophanes **4:**41
The Book of Job **14:**123
Iliad **1:**288

Vossler, Karl
Inferno **3:**51

Wa, Kathleen Johnson
Lao Tzu **7:**196

Wailes, Stephen L.
Nibelungenlied, Das **12:**231

Waldock, A. J. A.
Sophocles **2:**368

Waley, Arthur
Lao Tzu **7:**128
Li Po **2:**137

Murasaki, Lady **1:**421

Walhouse, Moreton J.
Sappho **3:**385

Waliszewski, K.
The Igor Tale **1:**479

Walker, Roger M.
Razón de Amor **16:**346

Walker, Warren S.
Book of Dede Korkut **8:**98

Wallace, David
Boccaccio, Giovanni **13:**87, 94

Walpole, Horace
Arabian Nights **2:**3

Walsh, George B.
Hesiod **5:**166

Walsh, P. G.
Livy **11:**342, 350

Walshe, M. O'C.
Gottfried von Strassburg **10:**274
Nibelungenlied, Das **12:**171
Wolfram von Eschenbach **5:**333

Warburton, William
Apuleius **1:**7

Warmington, B. H.
Seneca, Lucius Annaeus **6:**395

Warton, Joseph
Inferno **3:**6

Watling, E. F.
Seneca, Lucius Annaeus **6:**387

Watson, Burton
Si Shih **15:**391

Webbe, Joseph
Terence **14:**296

Webbe, William
Ovid **7:**290

Webber, Ruth H.
Poem of the Cid **4:**286

Weber, Alfred
Bacon, Roger **14:**20

Webster, T. B. L.
Menander **9:**246

Weigand, Hermann J.
Wolfram von Eschenbach **5:**315, 370

Weil, Simone
Iliad **1:**331

Weiler, Royal W.
K lid sa **9:**113

Weinberg, Julius R.
Averroës **7:**44

Bacon, Roger **14:**94

Weinberg, S. C.
Layamon **10:**360

Weiss, Paul
The Book of Job **14:**157

Welch, Holmes
Lao Tzu **7:**141

West, M. L.
Pindar **12:**333

Westcott, John Howell
Livy **11:**312

Westermann, Claus
The Book of Psalms **4:**428

Westlake, John S.
Anglo-Saxon Chronicle **4:**4

Weston, Jessie L.
Arthurian Legend **10:**28
Chrétien de Troyes **10:**133
Gottfried von Strassburg **10:**247
Wolfram von Eschenbach **5:**300

Wetherbee, Winthrop
Romance of the Rose **8:**422

Whewell, William
Bacon, Roger **14:**3

Whibley, Charles
Apuleius **1:**15

Whinfield, E. H.
Khayyám **11:**255

Whitehead, Alfred North
Plato **8:**271

Whitelock, Dorothy
Beowulf **1:**101

Whitman, Cedric H.
Aristophanes **4:**133
Iliad **1:**350
Odyssey **16:**254
Sophocles **2:**362

Wicksteed, Philip H.
Inferno **3:**46

Wiersma, S.
Longus **7:**274

Wilhelm, James J.
Bertran de Born **5:**39

Wilhelmsen, Frederick D.
Cicero, Marcus Tullius **3:**274

Wilkinson, L. P.
Ovid **7:**329

Williams, Harry F.
Chrétien de Troyes **10:**225

Willson, H. B.
Gottfried von Strassburg **10:**278

Critic Index

Hartman **15**:148, 165, 175, 196

Wilson, B. W. J. G.
Cicero, Marcus Tullius **3**:281

Wilson, Edmund
Sophocles **2**:341

Wilson, H. Schütz
Khayyám **11**:238

Wilson, Harry Langford
Juvenal **8**:23

Wilson, R. M.
Layamon **10**:335

Windelband, Wilhelm
Abelard **11**:3
Augustine, St. **6**:11
Averroës **7**:6

Winkler, John J.
Apuleius **1**:47

Winnington-Ingram, R. P.
Aeschylus **11**:206
Sophocles **2**:415

Winternitz, Moriz
Mahābhārata **5**:202

Witte, Karl
Inferno **3**:41

Wittgenstein, Ludwig
Augustine, St. **6**:55

Wolf, Carol Jean
The Dream of the Rood **14**:280

Wolff, Hope Nash
Epic of Gilgamesh **3**:328

Wolfram von Eschenbach
Wolfram von Eschenbach **5**:292,
293

Wolpert, Stanley
Mahābhārata **5**:281

Wood, Anthony à
Bacon, Roger **14**:3

Woodman, A. J.
Livy **11**:382

Woodruff, F. Winthrop
Bacon, Roger **14**:66

Woodruff, Paul
Plato **8**:364

Woolf, Rosemary
The Dream of the Rood **14**:230

Woolf, Virginia
Aeschylus **11**:126
Murasaki, Lady **1**:418
Sappho **3**:395
Sophocles **2**:326

Wooten, Cecil W.

Demosthenes **13**:189
Hermogenes **6**:202

Wordsworth, William
Arabian Nights **2**:5
Sophocles **2**:304

Wrenn, C. L.
Anglo-Saxon Chronicle **4**:13
Beowulf **1**:107
Cædmon **7**:93

Wright, F. A.
Ovid **7**:304
Sappho **3**:396

Wright, Henry Parks
Juvenal **8**:22

Wright, Thomas
Polo, Marco **15**:261

Wyckoff, Dorothy
Albert the Great **16**:54

Wyld, Henry Cecil
Layamon **10**:320

Wyld, M. Alice
Inferno **3**:50

Wynn, Marianne
Wolfram von Eschenbach **5**:326,
416

Yadin, Yigael
Josephus, Flavius **13**:239

Yarmolinsky, Avrahm
The Igor Tale **1**:496

Yates, Frances A.
Cicero, Marcus Tullius **3**:273
Llull, Ramon **12**:103

Yavetz, Zvi
Josephus, Flavius **13**:250

Young, Karl
Mystery of Adam **4**:190

Yourcenar, Marguerite
Murasaki, Lady **1**:455

Yoshikawa, Kojiro
Su Shih **15**:410

Yu-lan, Fung
Lao Tzu **7**:126

Yutang, Lin
Lao Tzu **7**:135

Zaehner, R. C.
Bhagavad Gita **12**:67
Mahābhārata **5**:243

Zedler, Beatrice H.
Averroës **7**:22

Zeydel, Edwin H.
Gottfried von Strassburg **10**:258
Wolfram von Eschenbach **5**:307

Zhirmunsky, Victor
Book of Dede Korkut **8**:96

Zimmer, Heinrich
Arabian Nights **2**:32
Bhagavad Gītā **12**:45
Sir Gawain and the Green Knight
2:187

Zweig, Stefan
Cicero, Marcus Tullius **3**:225